CAREER DEVELOPMENT INTERVENTIONS IN THE 21ST CENTURY

SECOND EDITION

SPENCER G. NILES
Pennsylvania State University

JOANN HARRIS-BOWLSBEY
Loyola College in Maryland

PEARSON

Merrill
Prentice Hall

Upper Saddle River, New Jersey
Columbus, Ohio

Library of Congress Cataloging-in-Publication Data

Niles, Spencer G.
    Career development interventions in the 21st century / Spencer G. Niles, JoAnn
Harris-Bowlsbey.--2nd ed.
        p. cm.
    Includes bibliographical references and index.
    ISBN 0-13-113781-6
        1. Career development. 2. Career development--Case studies. I. Harris-Bowlsbey,
JoAnn. II. Title.

HF5381.N547 2005
650.14--dc22

                                                                    2004052437

Vice President and Executive Publisher: Jeffery W. Johnston
Publisher: Kevin M. Davis
Editorial Assistant: Margaret Bowen
Production Editor: Mary Harlan
Production Coordinator: Jolynn Feller, Carlisle Publishers Services
Design Coordinator: Diane C. Lorenzo
Text Design and Illustrations: Carlisle Publishers Services
Cover Design: Terry Rohrbach
Cover Image: Corbis
Production Manager: Laura Messerly
Director of Marketing: Ann Castel Davis
Marketing Manager: Autumn Purdy
Marketing Coordinator: Tyra Poole

This book was set in Sabon by Carlisle Communications, Ltd. It was printed and bound by
Phoenix Color Book Group. The cover was printed by Phoenix Color Corp.

Pearson Education Ltd.   Pearson Education Australia Pty. Limited
Pearson Education Singapore Pte. Ltd.   Pearson Education North Asia Ltd.
Pearson Education Canada, Ltd.   Pearson Educación de Mexico, S.A. de C.V.
Pearson Education—Japan   Pearson Education Malaysia Pte. Ltd.

10 9 8 7 6 5 4 3 2 1
ISBN: 0-13-113781-6

PREFACE

We have taught career courses to students in numerous universities in the United States, as well as in Canada, Japan, Denmark, Portugal, England, and Spain, to mention just a few. Wherever students are interested in learning about career development theory and practice, we are eager to go! In each instance, however, we not only teach students about career development interventions but students also teach us. The idea for this book began in response to student requests (pleas) for a career development textbook that was readable, useful, and interesting. These are high, but reasonable, expectations. These expectations served as our guiding principles as we composed the chapters of this book.

To make the book more readable, most chapters include case studies. Our goal is to help readers connect chapter content with the lives of people represented in the cases. Although the cases are, for the most part, fictional, they reflect the career concerns of people with whom we have worked as career counselors in schools, in community settings, and in higher education. Thus, we are indebted to our clients, in addition to our students, for teaching us about the career development process. We seek to share these experiences with the readers of this book.

Another goal is to convey to our readers the deep respect and long-term commitment we have for career development theory and practice. We emphasize this goal in Chapter 1. As we note in the book, there are few things more personal than a career choice, and we were cognizant of this fact as we wrote each chapter. Making career decisions involves deciding how we will spend one of the most precious commodities we have—our time on Earth. We realize that these decisions are often very difficult and overwhelming. Thus, we draw upon the work of our colleagues in the field to present readers with state-of-the-art career theory and practice. However, the current situation evolved from the past contributions of many leaders in the field. We acknowledge their important foundational contributions in Chapter 1.

Although we cover a wide variety of theoretical perspectives in the book (especially in Chapters 2 and 3), we emphasize that careers develop over time. A decision point in one's career development is just that, a point in time at which one makes decisions based on previous and current career development experiences. Although knowing how to help people at these important points in their career development is crucial, career practitioners can also intervene proactively in the lives of children, adolescents, and adults in ways that facilitate positive career development prior to career crises occurring. Being able to provide assistance in both instances is critical.

We are especially concerned that career development theory and practice be inclusive. Constructing culturally inclusive career development interventions should be standard practice within the field. Unfortunately, this has not been the case. In part because of their historical context, career theories and practices focused primarily on the career experiences of European American middle-class males. Although we devote a chapter to diverse populations (Chapter 4), throughout the book we also address the need for inclusive career interventions. Our cases also tend to highlight the career experiences of clients from diverse backgrounds. We think both approaches (i.e., having a single chapter devoted to the topic and infusing diversity throughout the book) are needed to begin to more adequately address the career development needs of all people.

The need to provide clients with culturally sensitive career interventions provides an important foundation for discussing career counseling interventions in Chapter 8 and career assessment approaches in Chapter 5. The career counseling process and outcomes information provided here reflects the most recent work within the field. We also provide career information, resources, and Website references (Chapters 6 and 7) that represent important aspects of the career development process. We highlight the essential considerations in designing and implementing career development programs in Chapter 9. Finally, we highlight developmental approaches to providing career assistance in the schools, community settings, and higher education in Chapters 10 through 13.

Of course, the desire to engage in ethical practice is also a standard in the field. However, there are many challenges confronting career practitioners. Web-based services such as career counseling and career assessment, the possibility of dual relationships, and theories with deeply rooted value sets present challenges to practitioners as they engage in ethical practice. Thus, we address many of these current ethical challenges in Chapter 14. This is one of the few career development textbooks with a chapter devoted to ethical practice.

Finally, we emphasize the importance of engaging in the ongoing evaluation of career services. This is important for improving service delivery. However, when resources are limited, as they are in many situations, the need for both accountability and the ability to demonstrate effectiveness is great. We present readers with important topics related to the evaluation of career services in Chapter 15.

To make the book even more useful to readers, we use a framework developed by the National Career Development Association (NCDA). Specifically, we use the NCDA's (2003) career couseling competencies and the 2001 CACREP Standards to guide us in the identification of chapter topics. These competencies and standards appear in the appendices at the end of the book and at the following Website addresses: **http://www.ncda.org/about/polccc.html#career** and **http://www. counseling. org/ cacrep/2001standards700.htm.** Please note that in Appendix E we identify the chapters that are most relevant to each competency category and CACREP standard.

The rationale for using the NCDA competencies and CACREP Standards is that the profession deems these content areas as representing the requisite knowledge and skills for providing career development interventions; therefore, we seek in this book to help readers learn this information and develop these skills. Here again, we also hope that the case studies facilitate the learning process. The Companion Website for the book also contributes to knowledge and skill acquisition, and we hope that readers find this resource to be a valuable tool. The Companion Website will be updated periodically, so we encourage readers to return to it at regular intervals for up-to-date information and Web links.

We hope that we have accomplished the goals that motivated us to write the book. We also hope that we have fulfilled our students' expectations. In teaching our career courses, we consider it high praise when students tell us that they have a new respect and appreciation for career development interventions as a result of the class experience. This is what we hope occurs with this book. We invite readers to send us their feedback via the book's Companion Website. We are committed to improving the book in any way that we can. Your comments will guide us in the revisions that we make. Finally, we wish you the best of luck as you embark on a very exciting adventure within the counseling profession.

ACKNOWLEDGMENTS

I am grateful for and humbled by the support and love I have received from my family members and mentors. My mother taught me at an early age about the importance of Donald Super's life-space theory segment as she balanced work and family demands as a single parent in the 1960s and 1970s. She was a pioneer who has always lived with grace and dignity—despite substantial challenges presented to professional women and single parents.

My wife, Kathy, provides encouragement, challenges statements of self-doubt, and has tolerated my long work hours for more than two decades. My children, Jenny and Jonathan, teach me about love each day and help to make me a better person. Maggie, our golden retriever, has been nearby for every chapter I have contributed to this book.

My professional mentors and cherished friends have guided me through multiple career development tasks. Edwin L. Herr was the first to provide support and guidance, and he has continued to do so for 20 years. He embodies the best of what a mentor should represent. I will forever be indebted to Ed for his personal and professional assistance. Mark L. Savickas and Donald E. Super have also provided guidance, and I am honored that, at various times in my career, they have cared.

Spencer G. Niles

Like Spencer, my life was molded by a mother who was a single parent and who worked incredibly hard to assure that I had a level of education and access that she never enjoyed. She taught me the principles of faith, responsibility, commitment, and service. I want to acknowledge her role in laying the foundation that made my present life and contributions possible.

My most valued professional mentor was Donald E. Super, who was kind enough to share his writings and thoughts with me for 30 years. I have personally enjoyed the fullness of his career rainbow in my life. Nancy Schlossberg and David Tiedeman also contributed mightily to my conception of the process of career development and have enriched the well from which the content of this book flows.

My professional contributions would not be possible without the ongoing support of my husband, Stan. For 30 years he has placed a very high priority on my career and has done all that he could—editing, proofreading, doing home chores—to nourish it, never pressuring for more of my time. And, though my poodle Prissy is considerably smaller than Spencer's Maggie, she has played an important role in the production of this book because she has cuddled beside me through its every page.

JoAnn Harris-Bowlsbey

We both appreciate the dedicated assistance and support provided by Kevin Davis, Autumn Benson, and Mary Harlan at Merrill/Prentice Hall and Jolynn Feller, Carlisle Publishers Services.

We wish to thank those who reviewed the first edition and made suggestions for improvement: Christopher McCarthy, University of Texas at Austin; Ellen McWhirter, University of Oregon; Lee Richmond, Loyola University; and Hector Rios, Rowan University.

RESEARCH NAVIGATOR: RESEARCH MADE SIMPLE!

www.ResearchNavigator.com

Merrill Education is pleased to introduce Research Navigator—a one-stop research solution for students that simplifies and streamlines the entire research process. At www.researchnavigator.com, students will find extensive resources to enhance their understanding of the research process so they can effectively complete research assignments. In addition, Research Navigator has three exclusive databases of credible and reliable source content to help students focus their research efforts and begin the research process.

HOW WILL RESEARCH NAVIGATOR ENHANCE YOUR COURSE?

- Extensive content helps students understand the research process, including writing, Internet research, and citing sources.
- Step-by-step tutorial guides students through the entire research process from selecting a topic to revising a rough draft.
- Research Writing in the Disciplines section details the differences in research across disciplines.
- Three exclusive databases—EBSCO's ContentSelect Academic Journal Database, *The New York Times* Search by Subject Archive, and "Best of the Web" Link Library—allow students to easily find journal articles and sources.

WHAT'S THE COST?

A subscription to Research Navigator is $7.50 but is **free** when ordered in conjunction with this textbook. To obtain free passcodes for your students, simply contact your local Merrill/Prentice Hall sales representative, and your representative will send you the Evaluating Online Resource Guide, which contains the code to access Research Navigator as well as tips on how to use Research Navigator and how to evaluate research. To preview the value of this website to your students, please go to www.educatorlearningcenter.com and use the Login Name "Research" and the password "Demo."

DISCOVER THE COMPANION WEBSITE ACCOMPANYING THIS BOOK

THE PRENTICE HALL COMPANION WEBSITE: A VIRTUAL LEARNING ENVIRONMENT

Technology is a constantly growing and changing aspect of our field that is creating a need for content and resources. To address this emerging need, Prentice Hall has developed an online learning environment for students and professors alike—Companion Websites—to support our textbooks.

In creating a Companion Website, our goal is to build on and enhance what the textbook already offers. For this reason, the content for each user-friendly website is organized by chapter and provides the professor and student with a variety of meaningful resources.

For the Professor—

Every Companion Website integrates **Syllabus Manager**™, an online syllabus creation and management utility.

- **Syllabus Manager**™ provides you, the instructor, with an easy, step-by-step process to create and revise syllabi, with direct links into Companion Website and other online content without having to learn HTML.
- Students may log on to your syllabus during any study session. All they need to know is the web address for the Companion Website and the password you've assigned to your syllabus.
- After you have created a syllabus using **Syllabus Manager**™, students may enter the syllabus for their course section from any point in the Companion Website.
- Clicking on a date, the student is shown the list of activities for the assignment. The activities for each assignment are linked directly to actual content, saving time for students.
- Adding assignments consists of clicking on the desired due date, then filling in the details of the assignment—name of the assignment, instructions, and whether it is a one-time or repeating assignment.

- In addition, links to other activities can be created easily. If the activity is online, a URL can be entered in the space provided, and it will be linked automatically in the final syllabus.
- Your completed syllabus is hosted on our servers, allowing convenient updates from any computer on the Internet. Changes you make to your syllabus are immediately available to your students at their next log on.

For the Student—

Common Companion Website features for students include:

- **Chapter Objectives**—Outline key concepts from the text.
- **Interactive Self-quizzes**—Complete with hints and automatic grading that provide immediate feedback for students. After students submit their answers for the interactive self-quizzes, the Companion Website **Results Reporter** computes a percentage grade, provides a graphic representation of how many questions were answered correctly and incorrectly, and gives a question-by-question analysis of the quiz. Students are given the option to send their quiz to up to four email addresses (professor, teaching assistant, study partner, etc.).
- **Web Destinations**—Links to www sites that relate to chapter content.
- **Message Board**—Virtual bulletin board to post or respond to questions or comments from a national audience.

To take advantage of the many available resources, please visit the *Career Development Interventions in the 21st Century,* Second Edition, Companion Website at

www.prenhall.com/niles

BRIEF CONTENTS

CONTENTS

Note: Every effort has been made to provide accurate and current Internet information in this book. However, the Internet and information posted on it are constantly changing, so it is inevitable that some of the Internet addresses listed in this textbook will change.

CHAPTER 1

INTRODUCTION TO CAREER DEVELOPMENT INTERVENTIONS

Like it or not, work (our job) becomes and remains one of the most omnipresent parts of our lives. In many ways it defines who we are. And lets face it, it's the essential element in which to provide ourselves with the basic needs of day-to-day living, such as food, shelter, transportation. In time, as our careers progress, it can provide more: quality leisure time, a pool in the back yard, investments for our children's education. Everyday we get up and go to work. There's no getting out of it so it's imperative to choose a field of endeavor that enriches our lives. It needs to add a certain quality, not only to our personal worlds, but to the world around us. And not with great bursts of genius, rather with a slow, steady infusion of our knowledge and skills.

Regarding the many complexities of work, I believe one of the most important aspects of any job is the finished product. Whether we are contractors building a house, doctors repairing a heart, or teachers educating a student, from the very onset we need to focus on the finished product and take pride in the process that achieves that finished product. We should never settle for anything less than our best effort, because it matters. It matters to the homeowner, the patient, the student. And it most certainly should matter to us. Pride in our work, our accomplishments and the diligence we put into them can and will make all the difference in the world.

David H.
Contractor

Work is something that I do because I have to. If I won the lottery, I wouldn't work. As a single parent of two young children, I have to be responsible. I do it for them. Can work be "meaningful?" I hope to experience that some day. Right now, it's how my family and I get by—that's the most important thing and most days it's not fun.

Ann D.
Food service worker

My work means everything to me (well, almost everything). As an oncologist, I am dedicated to my work and my patients. I feel a tremendous responsibility to be the best physician that I can be. I also feel a responsibility to be the best I can be as a representative of my family and the African American community. I have dedicated much of my life to this activity. It is what gives me meaning and purpose. I feel fortunate to do the work that I do.

Camille S.
Physician

As Stephanie and her classmates discussed their new lives as master's degree students in counselor education, their attention turned toward their new class in career development. They wondered why they needed to take this course. José confidently declared that he had no interest in providing career counseling and that he was not likely to ever need to know much about the topics they would cover in the career development course. Jonathan agreed and stated that he found the prospect of giving people tests to be rather boring. Beth was clear that she was headed toward private practice as a licensed professional counselor and that she would probably just refer clients with career concerns to other practitioners interested in that sort of work. Chandra felt differently, but her peers seemed so clearly negative about this class that she was reluctant to say so. She had witnessed the influence work had on her family, and she knew it was an important topic to understand. Her father had been laid off from his job as an engineer when the company he worked for moved overseas. Her family had struggled to "make ends meet" as Chandra's father searched for new employment. Her mother struggled to keep her full-time job while also working as the primary caregiver for Chandra and her two younger brothers. When her father was forced to settle for a job providing far less than his previous one in terms of pay, challenge, and satisfaction, she watched as he became more depressed and the tension between her parents increased. Even her brothers were behaving differently and getting into more trouble at school. Chandra worried about the future of her family and she knew that their future was being influenced significantly by her parents' career development. Chandra saw connections between work and life through the experience of her own family, and she hoped that the career development course would help her understand how to help people in similar situations.

Unfortunately, Chandra's experience is not unusual today. Thus, it is no surprise that the need to provide career assistance exists in every setting in which counselors work. Counselors in schools, higher education, and community settings will, to varying degrees and at various times, encounter clients confronting career development issues. For example, the American School Counselors Association identifies career development as one of three key areas essential to the work of school counselors. Survey results examining the concerns expressed by students in higher education consistently identify the need for career planning assistance as the most dominant area of concern that students experience. Employers downsize frequently, making career issues a constant for adult workers.

Despite the prevalence of career issues confronting people in contemporary society, many students in counseling and related educational programs are similar to

José, Jonathan, and Beth in that they react less than enthusiastically to enrolling in the required "career information" course (Heppner, O'Brien, Hinkelman, & Flores, 1996). Perhaps some students imagine course requirements forcing them to memorize sections of occupational information books or spending hours learning how to administer and interpret tests to advise clients as to what occupations they should choose. Perhaps they view career development interventions as separate from more general counseling interventions, with the skills requirements of the former involving information dissemination, advising, and test administration and the skills of the latter involving more "sophisticated" therapeutic techniques. Maybe they envision career development interventions that resemble mechanistic processes in which the counselor acts in directive ways and takes complete responsibility for career intervention outcomes. Or, perhaps, like Beth, they view career development interventions as irrelevant to their future work as a counselor. Whatever the reasons for the lack of enthusiasm, many students feel toward courses related to career development, we challenge such views and assumptions.

We believe (and we think that Chandra would agree!) that competent career practitioners must possess expertise in a broad and challenging array of counseling-related competencies. The knowledge and skills required for providing career assistance effectively encompass and go beyond those required in more general counseling (Blustein & Spengler, 1995; Crites, 1981; Gysbers, Heppner, & Johnston, 2003; Liptak, 2001). For example, the career counseling competencies identified by the National Career Development Association (NCDA) (2003a) indicate that career counselors need knowledge and skills in career development theory; individual and group counseling; individual/group assessment; career information/resources; program promotion, management, and implementation; career coaching/consultation; multicultural counseling; supervision; ethical/legal issues; and using technology effectively in the career intervention process. These skill areas obviously extend far beyond those limited to career advising and test administration!

Moreover, the topics related to career development interventions are exciting and challenging. In many ways, career development interventions connect with recent emphases in psychology on optimal human functioning, maximizing happiness, and fulfilling human potential (Hartung, 2002). Essentially, career practitioners seek to help their clients increase their life satisfaction. At their core, career development interventions focus on helping people consider how they will develop and use their talents as they live their lives. Career development practitioners in the 21st century seek to empower people to construct meaning out of their unique life experiences and then translate that derived meaning into appropriate occupational and other life-role choices. Translating life experiences into career choices requires people to possess a relatively high level of self-awareness (Issacson & Brown, 2000). Accordingly, career practitioners strive to provide interventions that help their clients clarify and articulate their self-concepts. These interventions can include formal, standardized assessments as well as informal, nonstandardized assessment activities that actively and creatively engage clients in the career intervention process (Amundson, 1998). Because sorting through career concerns and engaging in career planning are complex processes, competent career practice requires counselors to be skilled at developing effective working alliances with their clients (Anderson & Niles, 2000; Multon,

Heppner, Gysbers, Zook, & Ellis-Kalton, 2001). Career practitioners meet their clients at the intersection of what has been and what might be in their clients' lives. When career counselors work collaboratively and innovatively with their clients to construct a clear career direction, both the client and the counselor experience the intervention process as exciting and positive (Anderson & Niles).

We also realize that multiple challenges confront career practitioners in the career intervention process. Career decision making is rarely a simple task and, therefore, good career counseling is never mechanistic and routine. When we consider the fact that decisions about work are made within a life context that intertwines with other life roles and responsibilities, the complex, and often stressful, nature of career decision making becomes clear. What might seem on the surface to be a relatively straightforward process of making a decision about work can quickly become overwhelming, frustrating, and complicated when important factors such as family expectations, limited occupational opportunities, financial limitations, and multiple life-role commitments are considered (Vondracek, Lerner, & Schulenberg, 1986). Clearly, Chandra had already learned this fact as a result of her parents' career development experiences.

Given the complexity of career decision making, there should be little surprise that many clients seeking career counseling experience substantial levels of psychological distress (Niles & Anderson, 1993; Multon et al., 2001). Obviously, career counselors must address their clients' distress as they also help their clients clarify their values, skills, life-role salience, interests, and motivation. When clients also experience low self-esteem, weak self-efficacy, and little hope that the future can be more satisfying than the past, the career counselor's task becomes even more challenging (Lent, Brown, & Hackett, 2002). Clients coping with such issues require more assistance in resolving their career dilemmas than a test battery can provide. Given this fact, it is not surprising that career counseling clients describe the support and the experience of an effective therapeutic alliance with their career counselors as one of the most helpful aspects of their career counseling experience (Anderson & Niles, 2000; Multon et al.,). Obviously, skills found to be essential counseling skills (e.g., establishing rapport, reflective listening, expressing empathic understanding) are also essential career counseling skills.

Working collaboratively and effectively with clients also requires career practitioners to possess multicultural competencies at an advanced level (Leong, 1995). For instance, clients operating from a collectivistic orientation engage in the career planning process in important ways that differ from clients operating from an individualistic orientation (Hartung, Speight, & Lewis, 1996). Working with the client's cultural context is essential to providing effective career assistance. For example, Kim, Li, and Liang (2002) found that career counselors focusing on the expression of emotion were perceived as having greater cross-cultural competence than counselors focusing on the expression of cognition when working with Asian American college students with high adherence to Asian values. Leong (2002) found acculturation to be positively related to job satisfaction and negatively related to occupational stress and strain. Gomez and colleagues (2001) found that Latina career development is strongly influenced by sociopolitical, cultural, contextual, and personal variables. Specifically, factors such as socioeconomic status, family, cultural identity, and the existence of a support network all helped to shape the course of career development for the Latinas participating in the Gomez et al. study. The client's constellation of cultural/contextual variables clearly matters in the career intervention process. Thus, similar to general counseling interventions, the career development intervention process is a dynamic, complex, and challenging one that requires career practitioners to draw upon multicultural counseling skills to effectively help their clients move forward in their career development.

Additionally, indications are that the career development process will become more, rather than less, complex in the near future. The current work context requires workers to demonstrate an extensive set of skills, behaviors, and attitudes to manage their careers effectively. Among other things, effective career self-management today requires the ability (a) to continuously learn new skills, (b) to cope with change and tolerate ambiguity, (c) to acquire and use occupational information effectively, (d) to interact competently with diverse coworkers, (e) to adjust quickly to changing work demands, (f) and to use technology effectively. To help people acquire these competencies, career development interventions must be holistic, comprehensive, and systematic. Moreover, because career development is an essential aspect of human development, career practitioners must be skilled at helping their clients cope with their career concerns within a developmental context. Because children, adolescents, and adults are presented with career development tasks, counselors are required to be skilled at providing career interventions and understanding the career development process, regardless of their work setting (Niles & Pate, 1989).

THE MEANING OF WORK ACROSS TIME

Obviously, understanding the career development process and being able to provide holistic, comprehensive, and systematic career development interventions across the life span requires career practitioners to appreciate the role that work plays in the lives of people. In the United States, especially, many people view work as the most important source of their identity. This is not surprising given that the work you choose influences the persons with whom you will associate for a major portion of your daily life, how much vacation you take and when it will occur, the types of continuing education and training that you will engage in, the type of supervision you will have, the degree of autonomy you will experience, and the lifestyle you will enjoy. Thus, it is no surprise that one of the first questions people ask each other when first meeting is, "What do you do?" Such interactions reinforce the contention that in a fluid industrial society occupation is one of the principal determinants of social status (Super, 1976). Such interactions also support Sigmund Freud's statement that "work is the individual's link to reality." For better or worse, our choice of work colors the perceptual lens through which others often view us and through which we often view ourselves. No doubt, we make differing assumptions about people who tell us they are neurosurgeons as compared with those who tell us they are employed at a local fast-food restaurant. Occupational titles tend to be used, correctly or incorrectly, to identify a person more than any other single characteristic.

It is important to note, however, that in some countries, and at different periods of history, one's choice of work was not so closely connected to one's identity as it is today. Other characteristics, such as one's surname or residence, provided a primary means for self-identification. How is it that work has evolved to become such a core component of one's identity? Obviously, in primitive societies work was taken for granted. One worked to survive. In the classical societies, work was viewed as a curse insofar as it involved manual labor as opposed to intellectual labor. (It is interesting to note that the Greek word for "work" has the same root as the word for "sorrow.") The early Christians viewed work as providing the opportunity to help those less fortunate by sharing the fruits of one's labor. The notion that "idleness was akin to sinfulness" also emerged from early Christianity and was maintained through the Middle Ages, with the idea growing that work was appropriate for all people as a means of spiritual purification. The Reformation brought little change to this attitude except for the influence of Martin Luther and John Calvin. Luther viewed work as a form of serving God. Whatever type of work a person engaged in, if it was performed to the best of one's ability, then it had equal spiritual value with all other forms of work.

A more dramatic shift in the meaning of work resulted from the theological perspective espoused by John Calvin and his followers. John Calvin built upon earlier traditions that viewed work as the will of God by adding the idea that the results of work (i.e., profits) should be used to finance new ventures for additional profit and, in turn, for additional investment. Additionally, Calvin's doctrine of predestination (i.e., that one's fate after life is predestined) led his followers to search for visible signs in this life that one was predestined for eternal life. Success in work came to be viewed as a visible sign that one was predestined for eternal life. This view of work resulted in the notion that one was obligated to God to achieve the highest possible, and most rewarding, occupation. As a result, striving for upward mobility became morally justified. This coincided with the belief that God rewards those who devote time and effort to work. Thus, the Reformation brought about a view of work labeled as the "Protestant work ethic." The value attached to hard work, the need for all persons to work, and the justification of profit emerging from Calvinism would eventually form the basis of modern capitalism and industrialism. The values associated with the Protestant work ethic also served as the basis for the 19th-century view of work labeled by Savickas (1993) as the "vocational ethic." This ethic valued independent effort, self-sufficiency, frugality, self-discipline, and humility and was brought to the United States by the Puritans.

The meaning of work continued to evolve as the United States industrialized and increased its reliance on mechanically generated energy. The determination of a person's status became a question not only of how hard one worked, but also a question of the type of work in which one engaged. In essence, *occupation* replaced *work* as a means of determining one's status. Savickas (1993) noted that this shift in the nature of work occurred on the brink of the 20th century because at this point in history individuals turned their vocational efforts to organizing craftspeople into companies and forming large cities built around industries. The rugged individualism reflected in self-employment on farms and in small craft-oriented businesses was replaced for many people with the challenge of working for a company and moving up the corporate ladder. Because people working for companies found little reinforcement for independence, self-sufficiency, and self-management, a new work ethic emerged as the United States entered the 20th century. Maccoby and Terzi (1981) described this new ethic in the nature of work in the 20th century as the "career" ethic. The career ethic could be described as challenging workers to "find their fit and don't quit." That is, successful careers became defined as finding work that led to having long tenures within the same company and successful career paths were those with an upward incline reflecting one's vertical climb through the organizational ranks. Today, it seems clear that this largely male, White, middle- and upper-socioeconomic class model provides, at best, a minimally useful description of the careers most people experience.

Recent developments in the nature of work bring into question the viability of the career ethic (McCortney & Engels, 2003). For example, many of the organizations served by the career ethic are downsizing in unprecedented numbers. Many workers have found computers performing the work tasks they once performed. Many employers view workers as expendable commodities. Those workers who have been downsized are often left feeling betrayed, anxious, and insecure about the future (Savickas, 1993). After working long hours and/or relocating to new communities to maintain their employment, many workers are becoming less willing to sacrifice everything for their employers when their employers are so willing to sacrifice them. Survivors of downsizing realize that their situation is anything but secure and their anxiety manifests itself in working longer hours and experiencing more alienation at home (McCortney & Engels).

Additionally, companies are flattening their organizational structures, resulting in fewer career ladders to climb. The elimination of vertical hierarchies brings into question the definition of a "successful" career. Hall and his associates (1996) argue that recent changes occurring in the structure of employment opportunities portend a future in which "people's careers will increasingly become a succession of 'ministages' of exploration-trial-mastery-exit, as they move in and out of various product areas, technologies, functions, organizations and other work environments" (p. 33). These shifts have led some to suggest that "work has ended" and the "career has died" (Bridges, 1994; Rifkin, 1995). More recently, we are still sorting through the ways in which the tragic events of September 11, 2001 will shape the ways in which people approach work.

Such statements highlight the fact that new ethics are emerging in the 21st century. Maccoby and Terzi (1981) contend that one emerging work ethic is best described as a "self-fulfillment ethic" represented by those who seek personal *and* professional growth. Those adhering to the self-fulfillment ethic seek work that is not so consuming that it denies opportunities for involvement in family, community, leisure, and other life roles. Data exist that indicate that many workers now focus on "working to live" rather than "living to work." For example, in the United States, free time increased from an average of 34 hours per week in 1965 to 40.5 hours per week in 1985 (Robinson, 1990). Robinson and Blair (1995) noted that the hours reported in 1985 were similar to free time hours reported in 1993 studies. Moreover, people spend a substantial percentage of these nonwork hours engaged in leisure activities (Robinson). Supporting the move toward a self-fulfillment ethic, researchers indicate that increased leisure participation is positively correlated with increased opportunities for skill utilization, self-expression, self-actualization, need gratification, and autonomy (Melamed, Meir, & Samson, 1995). However, an important issue to raise within the discussion of an emerging work ethic is whether it is viable to apply a singular work ethic across multiple cultures. McCortney and Engels (2003) agree, noting that "it is essential to consider whether the current concept of the work ethic can be accurately, uniformly applied to all individuals in the 'salad bowl' of the United States today" (p. 135). Thus, the dust has yet to settle regarding the emerging meanings people attach to their work activity.

What is clear is that, collectively, these changes in work ethics highlight the fact that career development occurs within a context of constant economic, social, cultural, technological, political, and historical change. These changes also underscore the fact that career development, like human development, is an evolutionary process. However, unlike biological expressions of development—which are ontogenetic and, therefore, fairly predictable—career development is a process that is dynamic, interactive, contextual, relational, and often unpredictable.

LINKING WORK WITH WORTH

It also seems clear that, despite historical changes in the meaning people attach to work, and whether it is viewed as a blessing or a curse, work continues to play a central role in our lives. The centrality of work in people's lives was evident in a speech made nearly 25 years ago by then-U.S. Secretary of Education Terrence Bell:

> Work in America is the means by which a person is tested as well as identified. It is the way in which a youngster becomes an adult. Work shapes the thoughts and life of the worker. A change in atmosphere and lifestyle can be effected by changing the way one earns a living. For most of us in adult life, being without work is not living. (Riegle 1982, p. 114)

These are strong words. If they were an accurate reflection of the meaning attached to work during the latter half of the past century, it is not likely that the meaning people attach to work has changed dramatically in the past 20 to 30 years. That work maintains its standing as a central role in the lives of many has also been supported empirically (Brief & Nord, 1990; Mannheim, 1993). Moreover, this phenomenon is not limited to the United States—results from cross-national studies suggest that many people in other countries view work to be more important than leisure, community, and even religion. Harpaz (1999) found that in several multinational studies work was second in importance only to family activities. Not only do we continue to place an extremely high value on work, but those in the United States also tend to use psychological definitions of work. For example, Super (1976) defined work as:

> The systematic pursuit of an objective valued by oneself (even if only for survival) and desired by others; directed and consecutive, it requires expenditure of effort. It may be compensated (paid work) or uncompensated (volunteer work or an avocation). The objective may be intrinsic enjoyment of work itself, the structure given to life by the work

role, the economic support which work makes possible, or the type of leisure which it facilitates. (p. 12)

Super's psychologically oriented definition of work places the perceptions and motivations relative to work within the individual's actions and ability to develop one's career. Such definitions reflect the largely American view toward work, which emphasizes individual control in career development (e.g., motivation, discipline, perseverance, goal-directedness) and de-emphasizes the role that sociological variables (e.g., the opportunity structure, the economy, socioeconomic status) play in shaping one's career. Thus, if a person has a "successful career," we tend to make a number of very positive attributions to the person who is a "success" (regardless of whether we actually know the person). The corresponding assumption is that the "unsuccessful" person is inferior. Our denial of the sociological factors influencing the pattern of one's career development, and the centrality of work in our culture, become problematic for many of us because we link work with self-worth (Shanahan & Porfeli, 2002; Subich, 2001). Obviously, if our sense of self-worth is substantially dependent upon how we feel about our work contributions, then our self-esteem can unravel fairly quickly if our work situations go awry (Herr, Cramer, & Niles, 2004). If you have ever felt undecided about your career choice, been fired from a job, worked in a job that was extremely dissatisfying, and/or been unable to find a job, then you probably have a good sense of the negative emotions that often surface in negative work-related situations.

Linking work with self-worth also becomes problematic when we develop unrealistic expectations for work. For example, O'Toole (1981) suggests that "when it is said that work should be meaningful, what is meant is that it should contribute to the self-esteem, to the sense of self-fulfillment, through the mastering of one's self and one's environment, and to the sense that one is valued by society" (p. 15). Although these are clearly desirable experiences, issues such as dehumanizing work conditions, unemployment, prejudicial hiring practices, downsizing, and mismatches between people and their jobs lead to the conclusion that for many people, work is anything but meaningful (Warnath, 1975). Denying contextual factors influencing career situations can lead people to engage in excessive self-blame when work experiences are negative for reasons beyond the worker's control.

Research conducted by O'Toole (1981) indicates that not only do many workers experience negative work situations and job dissatisfaction, but also they do not know how to improve their situations. A poll conducted by the NCDA (1988) revealed that a significant percentage of Americans (39%) did not have a career plan, and an even larger percentage of Americans (69%) did not know how to make informed career choices. Obviously, many adults have information and skill deficits related to career planning and career self-management. Many people have also had limited opportunities to engage in systematic self-exploration for career development, and they are unclear about their training and educational needs. Results from the same poll indicated that almost half of all U.S. workers experience job-related stress and think that their skills are being underutilized in their jobs. If these are the experiences of many, and if we link work with self-worth, then it seems reasonable to suggest that the need for competent career practitioners in contemporary society is substantial and urgent.

Unfortunately, there is a pattern of difficulty in managing career tasks that can be tracked developmentally. For example, Mortimer, Zimmer-Gembeck, Holmes, and Shanahan (2002) provide evidence that many adolescents do not receive assistance in acquiring the skills required for managing their career development effectively. Drawing upon results from 69 interviews (43 women, 26 men) of participants in the Youth Development Project ($n = 1000$), which is a longitudinal study of work through adolescence and early adulthood, these researchers report that study participants experienced few formal mechanisms for helping them locate suitable work as they moved into postsecondary school experiences. The lack of institutional support for young people as they make the school-to-work transition is perplexing given the centrality of work in people's lives. Mortimer and her colleagues contend that "more systematic efforts are needed to provide vocational information to youth in high schools" (p. 463) and that effort should be made to connect students with the schools and occupations in which they express an interest. Having actual experiences with potential occupations is important in differentiating between satisfied and dissatisfied entrants to the labor force, as well as those whose interest and jobs are congruent. "For youth who lack vocational direction, shifting schools and jobs can entail substantial economic, personal, and social costs" (Mortimer et al., p. 463).

Herr (1989) agrees, noting that high levels of career uncertainty and occupational dissatisfaction are positively correlated with high levels of psychological and physical distress. High levels of unemployment have been associated with increased rates of chemical dependency, interpersonal violence, suicide, criminal activity, and admissions to psychiatric facilities (Herr et al., 2004; Kalton, 2001; Liem & Rayman, 1982). Clearly, the ripple effects occurring when career situations go awry are dramatic and tragic. Moreover, all counselors, regardless of their work settings, will encounter these ripple effects either directly (by working with a client experiencing career difficulties) or indirectly (by working with a family member of a person experiencing career difficulties).

PROVIDING SYSTEMATIC CAREER DEVELOPMENT INTERVENTIONS

It is clear that the need for providing systematic assistance to individuals attempting to deal more effectively with the influence of work in their lives is tremendous. The young, the elderly, the unemployed, the underemployed, the displaced homemaker, the displaced worker, and members of diverse racial, ethnic, and socioeconomic groups are each confronted with work-related issues that have significant implications for their lives. How well they are able to cope with these issues may well be the difference between living a life that is meaningful and productive and one that is largely void of meaning and satisfaction.

Counselors provide career assistance to their clients in a number of ways. For example, counselors in high school, postsecondary, and community settings can teach clients the types of skills (e.g., self-assessment, job search, and career information acquisition) that are necessary for effective career planning and career decision making. Counselors in all settings can also help their students/clients to realize that decisions about work influence one's total life. Correspondingly, counselors can help clients develop realistic expectations for what work can provide in terms of personal satisfaction. When work is lacking in personal satisfaction, meaningful participation in other life roles helps offset this lack of satisfaction. Given the extreme emphasis we place on intra-individual variables in career development, a major task confronting counselors involves helping people to realize that self-worth is not defined by one's work situation. Self-worth relates more to how one lives rather than where one works. These are important lessons that counselors in school, postsecondary, and community settings can teach and reinforce in their students/clients.

More specifically, to help people manage their career development effectively in the 21st century, career counselors help their clients or students learn the following:

1. How to use both rational and intuitive approaches in career decision making
2. How to be clear about the importance attached to each life role and the values one seeks to express through participating in the roles of life
3. How to cope with ambiguity, change, and transition
4. How to develop and maintain self-awareness, especially in the areas of interests, values, motivation, and aptitudes
5. How to develop and maintain occupational and career awareness
6. How to develop and keep one's occupationally relevant skills and knowledge current
7. How to access and participate in lifelong learning opportunities
8. How to search for jobs effectively, even when one is not looking for a job
9. How to provide and receive career mentoring
10. How to develop and maintain skills in multicultural awareness and communication

Skills related to each of these learning areas must be placed in a developmental context so that counselors working with children, adolescents, and/or adults can provide appropriate career interventions. When counselors provide systematic career development interventions that help people acquire these skills, they are effectively responding to Labor Secretary Elaine L. Chao's point that "To succeed in the 21st century, our nation must be prepared to adapt to changes in our economy—in how we work, where we work, and how we balance our professional and family lives. We cannot simply react to changes. We must anticipate them, thus helping all workers to have as fulfilling and financially rewarding careers as they aspire to have" (http://www.dol.gov/).

DEFINITION OF TERMS

Career development interventions are shaped, in part, by how we define our terms. A major issue within the area of career development interventions is the misuse of terminology among career practitioners as well as clients. For example, it is not uncommon for professional counselors to use the terms *career* and *work* interchangeably. It is also not unusual to hear professionals talk about "doing career development" as if career development were an intervention rather than the object of an intervention.

Similarly, counselors often confuse the terms *career guidance* and *career counseling*. This lack of precision confuses practitioners, students, and clients and, therefore, is a barrier to advancing the efficacy of career development interventions. When language lacks precision, the implication is that terminology does not matter. However, words have power in that career development practitioners are "engaged in a verbal profession in which words and symbols frequently become the content of the interactions they have with clients" (Herr, 1997, p. 241). Thus, the need exists for greater clarity and specificity with regard to the key terms related to career development interventions. Such specificity enhances the credibility of our profession and provides a common ground for devising, implementing, and evaluating career development interventions. In this book, we define key terms as explained in the following paragraphs.

Career

Rather than limiting the definition of career to work, we advocate viewing *career* as a lifestyle concept. Accordingly, we concur with Super's (1976) view of career as the course of events constituting a life, and Herr et al.'s (2004) notion of career as the total constellation of roles played over the course of a lifetime. These definitions are broader than the one offered by Sears (1982), which defines career as the totality of work one does in a lifetime. Broader definitions highlight the multiple life roles people play and acknowledge differences across people regarding life-role salience generally and the importance of work in people's lives in particular (Richardson, 1993). For example, broad definitions of career apply to those locating work in the life role of homemaker or in volunteer activities.

Career Development

Career development refers to the lifelong psychological and behavioral processes as well as contextual influences shaping one's career over the life span. As such, career development involves the person's creation of a career pattern, decision making style, integration of life roles, values expression, and life-role self-concepts.

Career Development Interventions

Career development interventions, defined broadly, involve any activities that empower people to cope effectively with career development tasks (Spokane, 1991). For example, activities that help people develop self-awareness, develop occupational awareness, learn decision making skills, acquire job-search skills, adjust to occupational choices after they have been implemented, and cope with job stress can each be labeled as career development interventions. Specifically, these activities include individual and group career counseling, career development programs, career education, computer-assisted career development programs, and computer information delivery systems, as well as other forms of delivering career information to clients.

Career Counseling

Career counseling involves a formal relationship in which a professional counselor assists a client, or group of clients, to cope more effectively with career concerns (e.g., making a career choice, coping with career transitions, coping with job-related stress, or job searching). Typically, career counselors seek to establish rapport with their clients, assess their clients' career concerns, establish goals for the career counseling relationship, intervene in ways that help clients cope more effectively with career concerns, evaluate clients' progress, and, depending on clients' progress, either offer additional interventions or terminate career counseling.

Career Education

Career education is the systematic attempt to influence the career development of students and adults through various types of educational strategies, including providing occupational information, infusing career-related concepts into the academic curriculum, offering various worksite-based experiences, and offering career planning courses (Isaacson & Brown, 2000).

Career Development Programs

Career development programs can be defined as "a systematic program of counselor-coordinated information and experiences designed to facilitate individual career development" (Herr & Cramer, 1996, p. 33). These programs typically contain goals, objectives, activities, and methods for evaluating the effectiveness of the activities in achieving the goals.

IMPORTANT EVENTS IN THE HISTORY OF CAREER DEVELOPMENT INTERVENTIONS

The rise of career development interventions accelerated in the late 1800s as the national economy in the United States shifted from one based primarily in agriculture to one that was grounded in the industrial and manufacturing processes. This economic shift brought with it new sets of occupational opportunities. These new occupational opportunities connected to industrial and manufacturing activities created new dilemmas for workers in the United States. Particularly, workers were confronted with the new challenge of identifying and accessing the new jobs emerging in the United States. Moreover, the emerging jobs were often located in urban areas of the country, requiring many workers to move from rural areas to the growing cities. These trends were accompanied by increasing numbers of immigrants seeking new lives and opportunities in the United States (Herr, 2001).

Thus, it is not surprising that in the early part of the 20th century, emphasis was placed on helping people identify appropriate occupational options and make vocational choices. The time frame was limited as career guidance for vocational decision making emphasized the act of making a choice and viewed the decision making process as a single, point-in-time event. In his brief history of career counseling in the United

States, Pope (2000) notes that this early period in the evolution of career development interventions continued until 1920 and was characterized by an emphasis on job-placement services.

The early emphasis on job placement, in part, reflected the prevailing White, lower- and middle-class, male linear model of career development that dominated the field until recent times. Put simply, this view involved choosing an occupation early in one's career (usually upon leaving secondary or postsecondary school) and then staying in one's chosen occupation until retirement. To help people cope with vocational decision making tasks, practitioners used objectivistic methodologies, usually in the form of standardized aptitude and interest tests.

Important advances regarding the development and use of aptitude and interest tests were identified and articulated in books such as *Aptitude Testing,* authored by Clark Hull and published in 1927; *Aptitudes and Aptitude Testing,* authored by Walter Bingham and published in 1937; and *Vocational Interests of Men and Women,* authored by E. K. Strong and published in 1943. For most of the 20th century, the process of matching people to jobs based on the person's characteristics or traits and the requirements of occupations was the dominant approach to helping people identify appropriate occupational options.

FRANK PARSONS

Thus, early approaches to career development interventions reflected an emphasis on testing clients, providing them with occupational information, and advising them as to which occupational choices seemed to offer a reasonable chance for experiencing occupational success. This was the approach articulated by Frank Parsons in the early 1900s. An engineer by training and a social reformer by personal commitment, Parsons merged his training and commitment to outline a systematic process of occupational decision making, which he referred to as "true reasoning." Zytowski (2001) noted that Parsons delivered a lecture in 1906, entitled "The Ideal City," to the Economic Club of Boston. In this lecture, Parsons discussed the need for young people to receive assistance in the choice of a vocation. The lecture generated interest and requests by recent high school graduates for personal meetings with Parsons. From these activities, Parsons generated his systematic approach to vocational guidance. This approach was described in detail in Parsons' book *Choosing a Vocation* (1909). In his book, published one year after his death, Parsons discussed various principles and techniques that he found useful in helping the adolescents with whom he worked, first at the Breadwinners' College at the Civic Service House, a settlement house in Boston, and then at the Boston Vocation Bureau. Specifically, Parsons noted the following principles pertaining to vocational counseling:

1. It is better to choose a vocation than merely to hunt a job.
2. No one should choose a vocation without careful self-analysis, thorough, honest, and under guidance.
3. The youth should have a large survey of the field of vocations, and not simply drop into the convenient or accidental position.

4. Expert advice, or the advice of men who have made a careful study of men [sic] and vocations and of the conditions of success, must be better and safer for a young man than the absence of it.
5. Putting it down on paper seems a simple matter, but it is one of supreme importance in study. (Parsons, 1909, p. viii)

These principles provided the basis for the techniques Parsons relied upon to help young people achieve the goal of "choosing a vocation." Parsons advocated activities such as reading biographies, observing workers in their settings, and reading existing occupational descriptions. These techniques were incorporated into the "Parsonian approach," which consisted of three steps or requirements for helping someone make an occupational choice. These requirements were:

1. Develop a clear understanding of yourself, aptitudes, abilities, interests, resources, limitations, and other qualities.
2. Develop knowledge of the requirements and conditions of success, advantages and disadvantages, compensation, opportunities, and prospects in different lines of work.
3. Use "true reasoning" on the relations of these two groups of facts. (Parsons, 1909, p. 5)

Parsons developed his model against a background of social (e.g., rapid urbanization, child labor, immigration), economic (e.g., the rise of industrialism and the growing division of labor), and scientific (e.g., the emergence of human and behavioral sciences) changes occurring in the United States. These changes resulted in the need to place workers in jobs requiring specific skills and aptitudes, to help young people develop career plans, and to protect young people from child abuse in the labor force. Parsons' approach also fit nicely with the dominant scientific thinking of the 20th century, which emphasized positivism and objective methodology. That is, the Parsonian model encouraged practitioners to objectify interests, values, and abilities through the use of standardized assessment to guide people in identifying where they fit within the occupational structure.

The three requirements of the Parsonian approach formed the basic elements of what is now labeled as the *actuarial* or *trait-and-factor* approach to career development interventions. These elements are essentially self-knowledge, occupational knowledge, and decision making skills.

The basic assumptions of the trait-and-factor approach are:

1. As a result of one's self-characteristics, each worker is best fitted for a specific type of work.
2. Groups of workers in different occupations have different self-characteristics.
3. Occupational choice is a single, point-in-time event.
4. Career development is mostly a cognitive process relying on rational decision making.
5. Occupational adjustment depends on the degree of agreement between worker characteristics and work demands.

The trait-and-factor approach emphasizes the identification of a person's relevant traits or characteristics, usually through the use of standardized tests or inventories. The same approach is used in describing occupational factors or requirements (i.e., occupations are profiled according to the degree to which they require certain traits such as aptitudes). Then the individual's profile of traits is matched with the factors or requirements of specific occupations. The goal of this type of matching is to identify the degree of fit between the person and an occupation.

When conducting trait-and-factor career counseling, Williamson (1939) advocated a six-step process:

1. Analysis
2. Synthesis
3. Diagnosis
4. Prognosis
5. Counseling
6. Follow-up

In this model, the counselor collects clinical (using interview techniques) and statistical (often using standardized assessment) data and then synthesizes these data to draw inferences about the client's strengths and weaknesses. These inferences help to clarify the client's presenting problem and to identify probable causes. For Williamson (1939), the client's presenting problems can be diagnosed as either: (a) no choice, (b) uncertain choice, (c) unwise choice, or (d) a discrepancy between interests and aptitudes. Once the client's problem is diagnosed, the counselor offers a prognosis that includes alternative courses of action or alternative adjustments and the associated degree of success the client is likely to encounter with each alternative. Counseling in Williamson's model involves "helping the client marshal and organize personal and other resources to achieve optimal adjustment either now or in the future" (Isaacson, 1985, p. 82). Finally, the counselor conducts a follow-up by checking later with the client to ascertain the effectiveness of the counseling and whether any further assistance is required.

In classic trait-and-factor approaches, the counselor is active and directive while the client is a relatively passive participant in the process. It is the counselor's responsibility to take the lead in the collection, integration, and organization of client data. Moreover, the counselor uses these data in conjunction with occupational information to help the client identify a plan of action.

The Theory of Work Adjustment (TWA) developed by Rene Dawis and Lloyd Lofquist at the University of Minnesota in the 1960s is an excellent example of more recent theories within the trait-and-factor tradition (Dawis, 1996). TWA addresses the "correspondence between the individual (abilities and needs) and the environment (ability requirements and reinforcer system)" (Dawis, England, & Lofquist, 1964, p. 11). Thus, TWA focuses on person and environment interactions and posits that "the person and environment attempt to maintain correspondence with each other" (Dawis, 1996, p. 81). Both the worker and the work environment have needs and requirements, respectively, that must be satisfied. Adjustment to work is achieved when the person and environment are coresponsive to each other's requirements. Such correspondence is not always achieved, however. The degree to which the worker is willing to tolerate discorrespondence defines the worker's flexibility. Work environments also demonstrate varying degrees of flexibility. The worker's tenure in a specific job is influenced by the worker's satisfactoriness (defined as the work environment's degree of satisfaction with the worker), satisfaction (defined as the degree to which the work environment provides the worker with sufficient and appropriate reinforcers), and the work environment's perseverance (Dawis et al., 1964). Although research results pertaining to TWA constructs have been generally supportive, unfortunately, TWA has failed to generate sufficient research activity and few empirical tests of TWA have been published within the past 15 years (Swanson & Gore, 2000).

Although the level of sophistication regarding the techniques currently used in trait-factor approaches, such as TWA, is much greater than the techniques advocated originally by Parsons, Parsons' contributions to the field remain significant. In his book *History of Vocational Guidance,* John Brewer (1942) listed Parsons' contributions to the field as follows:

1. He paved the way for vocational guidance in the schools and colleges by advocating their role in it and offering methods they could use.
2. He began the training of counselors.
3. He used all of the scientific tools available to him at the time.
4. He developed "steps" to be followed in the vocational progress of the individual.
5. He organized the work of the Vocation Bureau in a way that laid the groundwork for groups to model in schools, colleges, and other agencies.
6. He recognized the importance of his work and secured for it the appropriate publicity, financial support, and endorsements from influential educators, employers, and other public figures.
7. He laid the groundwork leading to the continuance and expansion of the vocational guidance movement by involving friends and associates in it and preparing the manuscript for *Choosing a Vocation.* (p. 27)

However, Parsons was not the only significant contributor to early advances in vocational counseling. For example, the testing movement exemplified through the work of James Cattell, Alfred Binet, and Walter Bingham was also a primary force in the growth of career development interventions and helped to operationalize Parsons' emphasis on self-understanding.

Influential publications, organizations, and legislation also emerged in the early part of the 20th century. For example, *The Vocational Guidance Newsletter* was first published by Boston's Vocation Bureau in 1911 (which opened in 1908 with Parsons as its first director and vocational counselor); the National Vocational Guidance Association (NVGA) was founded in Grand Rapids, Michigan, in 1913; the U.S. Department of Labor was organized in 1913; the *Vocational Guidance Bulletin* was first published in 1915 by NVGA; the Vocational Rehabilitation Act became law in 1918; and Harry D. Kitson of Teachers College authored the book *The Psychology of Adjustment,* published in 1925.

In 1931 the Minnesota Employment Stabilization Research Institute was established. Among the Institute's conclusions from its research studies was the principle that improved guidance services were needed to create a more stable labor force and to foster an economic recovery from the Great Depression. The U.S. Employment

Service was created in 1933 by the Wagner-Peyser Act. In 1939 the U.S. Employment Service published the first edition of the *Dictionary of Occupational Titles,* in which 18,000 occupations were titled, coded, and defined.

In the early 1940s personnel testing and placement activities were greatly expanded as a result of World War II (the G.I. Bill was enacted in 1944). An excellent example of the advances being made in testing at this time is provided in E. K. Strong, Jr.'s publication, *Vocational Interests of Men and Women,* in which he documents nearly 20 years of interest-measurement research. Also during World War II, women entered the workforce in unprecedented numbers, many finding successful employment in manual and technical jobs that were previously held exclusively by men.

At the same time that testing and placement activities were being expanded, Carl Rogers' book *Counseling and Psychotherapy* (1942) was published. In this book, Rogers highlighted the importance of attending to clients' verbalized feelings: "Among the significant developments which resulted were a revamping of the older cognitive concept of the client in vocational guidance to include the dynamics of affective and motivational behavior, the increased emphasis on self-acceptance and self-understanding as goals of vocational counseling" (Borow, 1964, p. 57).

Another significant influence in the evolution of career development interventions occurred in 1951 when Donald E. Super launched the Career Pattern Study, one of the first longitudinal studies of career development. In his excellent historical review, Borow (1964) noted that Super, more than anyone else, helped shift the focus of career development interventions from a "static, single-choice-at-a-point-in-time concept" (p. 60) focused on vocational choice toward a model that conceptualized career development as an ongoing process involving the congruent implementation of the person's self-concept in a compatible occupational role. Super was primarily responsible for changing the definition of vocational guidance from "the process of assisting an individual to choose an occupation, prepare for it, enter upon it, and progress in it" to

> [t]he process of helping a person to develop and accept an integrated and adequate picture of himself [sic] and of his role in the world of work, to test this concept against reality, and to convert it into reality, with satisfaction to himself and to society. (Super, 1951, p. 89)

Additionally, Super's multidisciplinary approach to studying career development incorporated contributions from economics and sociology while placing career behavior in the context of human development.

The 1940s and 1950s also saw the emergence of a number of professional organizations related to career development. In 1947, The American Psychological Association (APA) created organizational divisions resulting in the establishment of Division 17, which from 1947 to 1952 was known as the Division of Counseling and Guidance but was later renamed Counseling Psychology. Since its creation, this division has served as the primary APA division for psychologists interested in career development interventions. More recently, a special interest group within Division 17 has formed to focus more directly on the topic of career development theory and practice.

The merging of the National Vocational Guidance Association, the American College Personnel Association, the National Association of Guidance Supervisors and Counselor Trainers, and the Student Personnel Association for Teacher Education resulted in the formation of the American Personnel and Guidance Association in 1951. The American School Counselor Association formed in 1953, and its primary focus was the provision of career services to young people. Finally, in 1957, the American Personnel and Guidance Association created the American Board on Professional Standards in Vocational Counseling, the functions of which "were to evaluate and certify qualified vocational counseling agencies and to foster the maintenance of high professional standards, including standards of ethical practice" (Borow, 1964, p. 62).

However, the primary organization for professional career counselors has been the NVGA (which changed its name to the National Career Development Association [NCDA] in 1985). From its inception, NCDA has been dedicated to improving the quality of services provided by career development practitioners. As early as 1920, NCDA established a code of principles to guide practitioners in the delivery of career-related services. In 1981 the NVGA Board of Directors approved the first policy statement for the roles and competencies of career counselors. This statement has been updated several times since then (most recently in 2003). The most recent competencies are listed in Figure 1.1. This statement reflects a broad range of general

---

These competency statements are for those professionals interested and trained in the field of career counseling. For the purpose of these statements, career counseling is defined as the process of assisting individuals in the development of a life career with focus on the definition of the worker role and how that role interacts with other life roles.

Professional competency statements provide guidance for the minimum competencies necessary to perform effectively a particular occupation or job within a particular field. Professional career counselors (master's degree or higher) or persons in career development positions must demonstrate the knowledge and skills for a specialty in career counseling that the generalist counselor might not possess. Skills and knowledge are represented by designated competency areas, which have been developed by professional career counselors and counselor educators. The Career Counseling Competency Statements can serve as a guide for career counseling training programs or as a checklist for persons wanting to acquire or enhance their skills in career counseling.

Minimum Competencies

In order to work as a professional engaged in career counseling, the individual must demonstrate minimum competencies in 11 designated areas. These 11 areas are: Career Development Theory, Individual and Group Counseling Skills, Individual/Group Assessment, Information/Resources, Program Management and Implementation, Consultation, Diverse Populations, Supervision, Ethical/Legal Issues, Research/Evaluation, and Technology. These areas and their respective performance indicators are defined as follows:

Career Counseling Competencies and Performance Indicators

Career Development Theory

Theory base and knowledge considered essential for professionals engaging in career counseling and development. Demonstration of knowledge of:

1. Counseling theories and associated techniques
2. Theories and models of career development
3. Individual differences related to gender, sexual orientation, race, ethnicity, and physical and mental capacities

Continued

Figure 1.1

Introduction to career counseling competency statements.

4. Theoretical models for career development and associated counseling and information-delivery techniques and resources
5. Human growth and development throughout the life span
6. Role relationships which facilitate life-work planning
7. Information, techniques, and models related to career planning and placement

Individual and Group Counseling Skills

Individual and group counseling competencies considered essential to effective career counseling. Demonstration of ability to:

1. Establish and maintain productive personal relationships with individuals
2. Establish and maintain a productive group climate
3. Collaborate with clients in identifying personal goals
4. Identify and select techniques appropriate to client or group goals and client needs, psychological states, and developmental tasks
5. Identify and understand clients' personal characteristics related to career
6. Identify and understand social contextual conditions affecting clients' careers
7. Identify and understand familial, subcultural, and cultural structures and functions as they are related to clients' careers
8. Identify and understand clients' career decision-making processes
9. Identify and understand clients' attitudes toward work and workers
10. Identify and understand clients' biases toward work and workers based on gender, race, and cultural stereotypes
11. Challenge and encourage clients to take action to prepare for and initiate role transitions by:
    • locating sources of relevant information and experience
    • obtaining and interpreting information and experiences
    • acquiring skills needed to make role transitions
12. Assist the client to acquire a set of employability and job-search skills
13. Support and challenge clients to examine life-work roles, including the balance of work, leisure, family, and community in their careers

Individual/Group Assessment

Individual/group assessment skills considered essential for professionals engaging in career counseling. Demonstration of ability to:

1. Assess personal characteristics such as aptitude, achievement, interests, values, and personality traits.
2. Assess leisure interests, learning style, life roles, self-concept, career maturity, vocational identity, career indecision, work environment preference (e.g., work satisfaction), and other related lifestyle/development issues
3. Assess conditions of the work environment (such as tasks, expectations, norms, and qualities of the physical and social settings)
4. Evaluate and select valid and reliable instruments appropriate to the client's gender, sexual orientation, race, ethnicity, and physical and mental capacities.
5. Use computer-delivered assessment measures effectively and appropriately
6. Select assessment techniques appropriate for group administration and those appropriate for individual administration
7. Administer, score, and report findings from career assessment instruments appropriately
8. Interpret data from assessment instruments and present the results to clients and to others

Figure 1.1 *Continued*

9. Assist the client and others designated by the client to interpret data from assessment instruments
10. Write an accurate report of assessment results

Information/Resources

Information/resource base and knowledge essential for professionals engaging in career counseling. Demonstration of knowledge of:

1. Education, training, and employment trends; labor market information and resources that provide information about job tasks, functions, salaries, requirements and future outlooks related to broad occupational fields and individual occupations
2. Resources and skills that clients utilize in life-work planning and management
3. Community/professional resources available to assist clients in career planning, including job search
4. Changing roles of women and men and the implications that this has for education, family, and leisure
5. Methods of good use of computer-based career information delivery systems (CIDS) and computer-assisted career guidance systems (CACGS) to assist with career planning

Program Promotion, Management, and Implementation

Knowledge and skills necessary to develop, plan, implement, and manage comprehensive career development programs in a variety of settings. Demonstration of knowledge of:

1. Designs that can be used in the organization of career development programs
2. Needs assessment and evaluation techniques and practices
3. Organizational theories, including diagnosis, behavior, planning, organizational communication, and management useful in implementing and administering career development programs
4. Methods of forecasting, budgeting, planning, costing, policy analysis, resource allocation, and quality control
5. Leadership theories and approaches for evaluation and feedback, organizational change, decision making, and conflict resolution
6. Professional standards and criteria for career development programs
7. Societal trends and state and federal legislation that influence the development and implementation of career development programs

Demonstration of ability to:

8. Implement individual and group programs in career development for specified populations
9. Train others about the appropriate use of computer-based systems for career information and planning
10. Plan, organize, and manage a comprehensive career resource center
11. Implement career development programs in collaboration with others
12. Identify and evaluate staff competencies
13. Mount a marketing and public relations campaign on behalf of career development activities and services

Coaching, Consultation, and Performance Improvement

Knowledge and skills considered essential in relating to individuals and organizations that impact the career counseling and development process. Demonstration of ability to:

1. Use consultation theories, strategies, and models
2. Establish and maintain a productive consultative relationship with people who can influence a client's career
3. Help the general public and legislators to understand the importance of career counseling, career development, and life-work planning

4. Impact public policy as it relates to career development and workforce planning
5. Analyze future organizational needs and current level of employee skills and develop performance improvement training
6. Mentor and coach employees

Diverse Populations

Knowledge and skills considered essential in relating to diverse populations that impact career counseling and development processes. Demonstration of ability to:

1. Identify development models and multicultural counseling competencies
2. Identify development needs unique to various diverse populations, including those of different gender, sexual orientation, ethnic group, race, and physical or mental capacity
3. Define career development programs to accommodate needs unique to various diverse populations
4. Find appropriate methods or resources to communicate with limited-English-proficient individuals
5. Identify alternative approaches to meet career planning needs for individuals of various diverse populations
6. Identify community resources and establish linkages to assist clients with specific needs
7. Assist other staff members, professionals, and community members in understanding the unique needs/characteristics of diverse populations with regard to career exploration, employment expectations, and economic/social issues
8. Advocate for the career development and employment of diverse populations
9. Design and deliver career development programs and materials to hard-to-reach populations

Supervision

Knowledge and skills considered essential in critically evaluating counselor or career development facilitator performance, maintaining and improving professional skills. Demonstration of:

1. Ability to recognize own limitations as a career counselor and to seek supervision or refer clients when appropriate
2. Ability to utilize supervision on a regular basis to maintain and improve counselor skills
3. Ability to consult with supervisors and colleagues regarding client and counseling issues and issues related to one's own professional development as a career counselor
4. Knowledge of supervision models and theories
5. Ability to provide effective supervision to career counselors and career development facilitators at different levels of experience
6. Ability to provide effective supervision to career development facilitators at different levels of experience by:
   - knowledge of their roles, competencies, and ethical standards
   - determining their competence in each of the areas included in their certification
   - further training them in competencies, including interpretation of assessment instruments
   - monitoring and mentoring their activities in support of the professional career counselor and scheduling regular consultations for the purpose of reviewing their activities

Ethical/Legal Issues

Information base and knowledge essential for the ethical and legal practice of career counseling. Demonstration of knowledge of:

1. Adherence to ethical codes and standards relevant to the profession of career counseling (e.g., National Board of Certified Counselors [NBCC], NCDA, and American Counseling Association [ACA])
2. Current ethical and legal issues which affect the practice of career counseling with all populations
3. Current ethical/legal issues with regard to the use of computer-assisted career guidance systems

Figure 1.1 Continued

4. Ethical standards relating to consultation issues
5. State and federal statutes relating to client confidentiality

Research/Evaluation

Knowledge and skills considered essential to understanding and conducting research and evaluation in career counseling and development. Demonstration of ability to:

1. Write a research proposal
2. Use types of research and research designs appropriate to career counseling and development research
3. Convey research findings related to the effectiveness of career counseling programs
4. Design, conduct, and use the results of evaluation programs
5. Design evaluation programs which take into account the need of various diverse populations, including persons of both genders, differing sexual orientations, different ethnic and racial backgrounds, and differing physical and mental capacities
6. Apply appropriate statistical procedures to career development research

Technology

Knowledge and skills considered essential in using technology to assist individuals with career planning. Demonstration of knowledge of:

1. Various computer-based guidance and information systems as well as services available on the Internet
2. Standards by which such systems and services are evaluated
3. Ways in which to use computer-based systems and Internet services to assist individuals with career planning that are consistent with ethical standards
4. Characteristics of clients which make them profit more or less from use of technology-driven systems
5. Methods to evaluate and select a system to meet local needs

---

Figure 1.1 *Continued*

Source: Revised by the NCDA Board of Directors, July, 2003. © 2003 National Career Development Association. Retrieved from http://www.ncda.org

counseling skills and specific career-related competencies. The competencies reflect the belief of NVGA/NCDA that professional career counselors are professionally trained counselors with additional and specialized training related to career development. In addition, the competencies reflect the importance of providing a wide range of career development interventions to meet the needs of diverse client populations. An excellent history of the NVGA/NCDA is presented in *The Career Development Quarterly,* Volume 36, No. 4, 1988.

In the 1960s, the field experienced tremendous growth in the area of theory generation, with behavioral, developmental, and psychoanalytical theories of career development emerging during this time period. At the same time, the number of career assessment instruments also grew dramatically (see Kapes & Whitfield, 2002). Concurrently, the use of computer-assisted career guidance and information-delivery systems in the provision of career services primarily in secondary schools and higher education settings emerged during this time period (Bowlsbey, Dikel, & Sampson, 2002).

During the 1970s, career education emerged as a federal priority, highlighting the importance of providing career development interventions to young people and adults. "The term 'career education' also symbolized the need to address systematically a range of conditions that were changing the relationship between education and work, particularly with regard to preparing students to understand the linkages between educational opportunities and the subsequent implications of these in work choice and work adjustment" (Herr & Cramer, 1996, p. 34). Recent efforts in the 1990s by school-to-work transition proponents focused on imparting the knowledge, skills, and attitudes essential for effective workforce participation closely resemble the ideas of career education efforts initiated in the 1970s (Lent & Worthington, 1999).

Another critically important development in recent years has been the increased attention to addressing the career development needs of diverse client populations (Lee & Richardson, 1991). Research related to career development theory and practice has gone beyond addressing the career development of White, middle-class men. Issues of gender, class, sexual orientation, and cultural bias in career development theories and practices have been exposed, resulting in greater attention to how such variables factor into the career development process and bringing into focus the importance of including the cultural context in career development theories and interventions (Chung, 2001; Leong & Hartung, 2000; Pope, 2000). Models of identity development as they relate to areas such as gender, race, sexual orientation, and disability status are increasingly being integrated into career development theory and practice (Pope). Career treatment outcome studies are also beginning to move beyond the traditional college student samples to examine career intervention effects with more diverse populations (Luzzo, 2000).

Interestingly, acknowledging the multiple ways in which the societal context artificially limits career development for many people has led commentators to remind career theorists and practitioners of the importance of addressing social justice in career development interventions in the 21st century (Herr & Niles, 1998; O'Brien, 2001). Lee (1989) agrees, stating that career counselors must act as "career development advocates for disenfranchised clients by actively challenging long-standing traditions that stand in the way of equity in the workplace" (p. 219). Indeed, striving for social justice through career interventions commenced with the work of Frank Parsons and, therefore, is an important theme throughout the history of the career development field. In this regard, Herr and Niles note:

> ... for most of the last 100 years, whether or not it has been explicit, counseling and, in particular, career counseling and career guidance have become sociopolitical instruments, identified by legislation at the federal level, to deal with emerging social concerns such as equity and excellence in educational and occupational opportunities, unemployment, human capital development, persons with disabilities, child abuse, AIDS, teenage pregnancy, substance abuse, career decision making relative to the preparation for entrance into emerging skilled occupations, and the identification and encouragement of students with high academic potential to enter higher education in science and mathematics. (p. 121)

Recapturing the spirit of social justice by acting as agents of social change to maximize the career development opportunities available to all members of our society is emerging as an essential aspect of career interventions for many career practitioners today.

Conducting career interventions for social action requires counselors to provide multifaceted career interventions and to expand their roles beyond traditional individual career counseling practice. Career counseling for social action begins with career counselors possessing the multicultural competencies (i.e., knowledge, skills, and attitudes) necessary for understanding how the environments their clients occupy interact to influence the interpretations and meanings clients attach to work and occupational opportunities. Multicultural competencies serve as the foundation for identifying social action strategies aimed at facilitating career development.

Career practitioners engaged in social action also use community resources to provide clients access to information and opportunities (e.g., employment offices, "one-stop career shops," support groups). Learning about career resources available in the community facilitates appropriate referrals and increases the probability that clients will receive the services they need. Therefore, career counselors engaging in social action play the role of facilitator by providing information, referrals, and encouragement to clients (Enright, Conyers, & Szymanski, 1996). Playing this role effectively requires career counselors to maintain files of useful resources, including names of potential mentors representing a diversity of backgrounds (e.g., African American, Asian American, individuals with disabilities, gay and lesbian men and women), information on accommodations for disabled individuals with different functional limitations, names of employers willing to provide opportunities for job shadowing and internship experiences, and names of individuals willing to participate in informational interviewing experiences (Enright et al., p. 111).

Having a thorough knowledge of career resources available in the community also allows counselors to identify areas in which services are lacking. In these instances, counselors once again take on a strong advocacy role and seek to rectify service deficiencies in their communities (Lee, 1989).

Advocacy is also important when clients' career concerns are the result of external factors such as large-scale downsizing, wage stagnation, and salary inequities experienced by women, persons of color, and persons with disabilities. More often than many care to acknowledge, workers struggle to earn a living. On average, women must work 66 weeks to earn what men earn in 52 weeks (Armendariz, 1997). The inequities experienced by persons with disabilities are even greater. According to Uchitelle and Kleinfeld (1996), in the past 20 years, nearly 75% of all households in the United States have experienced a job loss either directly or indirectly (i.e., they have a friend or relative who has lost a job). Those in the dwindling minority of persons not experiencing an encounter with job loss are also acutely aware of the tenuous nature of job security and experience high levels of guilt, fear, and anxiety.

In each of these instances, career counselors concerned with social action address not only the career concerns of individual clients, but also the career concerns of the community at-large (Cahill & Martland, 1996). This is accomplished by integrating individual career counseling skills with community counseling skills. Integrating career counseling and community counseling strategies is especially critical in rural communities in which economic restructuring can threaten the very existence of the community. Cahill and Martland argue that community career counseling builds on the strength of individual career counseling and offers assistance to people in their struggle to maintain their communities as they create opportunities for career development. Thus, in addition to individual career counseling skills, career practitioners need skills in facilitating group problem solving, consensus building, and an understanding of social and economic factors that affect careers in contemporary society.

Essentially, career counselors who instill hope in their clients and empower them to manage their careers are multiculturally competent, act as facilitators of information and referrals, advocate for their clients when employment practices and community traditions stand in the way of equity in the workplace, and integrate individual career counseling skills with community counseling skills to assist people in their struggle to maintain their communities and create opportunities for career development. Only time will tell if the recent attention related to addressing social justice issues in career development interventions will blossom into a more common and prominent role for career practitioners.

FUTURE TRENDS IN CAREER DEVELOPMENT INTERVENTIONS

Bingham and Ward (1994) note that "if vocational counseling was born from the changing demographics and economic needs of this century, then clearly career counseling will need to change in response to the changing needs of the coming century" (p. 168). Indeed, the rapid changes occurring in the world-of-work influenced by technological developments, the emergence of an interdependent global economy, and an increasingly diverse workforce bring into question whether career development interventions need to be revised to meet the career development tasks confronting people in the 21st century. The evidence seems clear that people, both young and old, are struggling to cope more effectively with these tasks. Research results also indicate clearly that when an individual's career situations go awry, the effects are far-reaching and often negative, for both the person and society (Herr, 1989).

We are confronted daily with news reports citing statistics about high levels of global unemployment, corporate downsizing, and a jobless economic recovery. These statistics provide examples of the fact that the social contract between employer and employee is gone. Other evidence that the nature of work is changing is found in the number of companies now offering day care and parental leave; increases in the number of families requiring dual earners; and increases in the number of people working at home. These themes reflect the strong intertwining of work and family roles. Thus, career theories, career interventions, and career development professionals must respond to these evolutionary shifts occurring in the nature of work. Moreover, career development interventions must be embedded in assumptions that reflect the shifts we are experiencing in work (e.g., that adults change occupations many times over the course of their lives, that lifelong learning is essential to maintaining one's marketability, that life roles interact, that rapid changes in the world-of-work are a constant, and that everyone must become skilled at interacting with diverse coworkers). Herr (2003) contends that the demand for career assistance will expand due to rising unemployment rates and an increase in part-time work.

How we intervene in the lives of the people we serve is guided by our understanding of how these shifts influence what is required for people to move forward in their careers. The emerging career concerns people experience in contemporary society point to the need for career counselors to continue their historical tradition of responding to current concerns with current interventions. Precious little appears in the professional literature proposing future directions for career counseling. Because the discourse barely exists, the direction remains unclear. Thus, career counseling's identity status resembles that of a client who lacks vocational identity and clearly articulated goals (Niles, 2003).

Savickas (1993) discusses his interpretation of what is required to move the profession forward. Specifically, he notes that in the 21st century, career development professionals will shift from supporting the 20th-century notion of careerism to fostering self-affirmation in their clients. Career counselors, Savickas contends, will teach people to be more critical of authority. People will need to be encouraged to make a commitment to their culture and community as well as learn how to develop and express their values in the real world. Rather than providing clients with predefined services in a sort of "one size fits all" approach, career counselors will collaborate with their clients to help them interpret and shape their career development. Rather than emphasizing a singular truth and objectivity, career counselors will move toward appreciating multiple realities, perspectivity, and relationships in their work with clients (Savickas). In the emerging scenario, it seems clear that a primary task of career practitioners involves clarifying (rather than assuming) how they can be *useful* to their clients. Achieving this basic and essential understanding requires career practitioners to be skilled at providing culturally appropriate career interventions.

In addition to the Savickas (1993) article, a special issue of *The Career Development Quarterly* (September, 2003) stands as one of the few examples in the literature in which future directions for career counseling are identified. Building upon these contributions, we identify several ways in which career development professionals can construct career interventions that respond to clients' career concerns in the 21st century.

VIEW CAREER DECISIONS AS VALUES-BASED DECISIONS

Brown (2002) has presented an emerging career theory that highlights the importance of addressing clients' values in career development interventions. Brown reminds us that career decisions are essentially values-based decisions. Some values will figure prominently in a future scenario and others will be left behind, subordinated, or perhaps even distorted in a career transition. Indeed, career decisions entail determining what is to prevail and what is to be sacrificed (Cochran, 1997). Without the promise of gain and the threat of loss, there is no decision to make. One could just follow a "perfect" possibility that was presumably all positive. Yet, in an ordinary decision, one must evaluate to decide. It can be argued that these evaluations are primarily values-based and that the way one evaluates defines the person one is to become and the life one is to live. Our identity is defined by these fundamental evaluations. Thus, helping clients clarify and articulate their values will become even more important in providing career development interventions in the 21st century. Career practitioners can empower clients to make choices that implement their declared values through serving as a counselor, coach, and advocate for their clients.

MOVE BEYOND OBJECTIVE ASSESSMENT

An increased emphasis on values clarification reflects the fact that today, perhaps more than ever, it should be clear that providing clients with information about themselves and the world-of-work (through objective assessment) is necessary, but not sufficient, for empowering people to manage their careers effectively. To be sure, having information about how one's interests compare with others and where one stands on the normal curve is helpful in the process of identifying viable career options. However, most people do not think of themselves as locations on a normal curve. Rather, they focus on the process of trying to make meaning out of their life experiences. Certain life experiences capture more attention in this regard than others do. Most likely, the experiences that capture the most attention are those that have been the most painful. A painful or negative experience creates a yearning for its opposite, which becomes an ideal toward which to strive (Watkins & Savickas, 1990). In this sense, one's early life preoccupations provide the direction for what later in life can become one's occupation. Our life experiences provide the crucial backdrop against which we sort through our values, interests, and skills and then try to connect them to career options. Career development interventions in the 21st century must be directed toward helping people clarify and articulate the meaning they seek to express in their career activities.

MOVE TO COUNSELING-BASED CAREER ASSISTANCE

Implicit in what we have discussed thus far is that "personal" and "career" concerns are inextricably intertwined. Research by Niles and Anderson (1995) indicates that many adults in career counseling are coping with concerns related to uncertainty, ambiguity, self-efficacy, and personal, as well as occupational, information deficits. Career counseling clients also report valuing the relationship dimension of the career counseling experience, and they often take advantage of the opportunity to discuss general concerns in the career counseling process (Anderson & Niles, 2000). Accordingly, many researchers now conclude that there are few things more personal than a career choice and that the overlap between career and general concerns is substantial (Anderson & Niles, 1995; Krumboltz, 1993; Subich, 1993). Career development practitioners can respond to this overlap by offering counseling-based career assistance.

Career practitioners offering counseling-based career assistance do not view their clients as the problem and the counselor as the solution (Savickas, 1993). Rather, they seek to empower clients to articulate their experiences and construct their own lives. Savickas noted that career counselors operating from this perspective function as collaborators in the career counseling process and pay special attention to the relationship within career counseling (Anderson & Niles, 2000). Functioning in this way also requires career development practitioners to possess multicultural counseling skills.

MOVE TO A STRONGER EMPHASIS ON MULTICULTURAL CAREER DEVELOPMENT THEORIES AND INTERVENTIONS

Concern about meeting the career development needs of culturally diverse clients has been a significant issue in the literature since the early 1980s (Sue et al., 1982). This issue becomes even more critical given the increasing diversity within the workforce (Parmer & Rush, 2003). Career development interventions must address the "effects of social and economic barriers such as economic hardship, immigration disruption, and racial discrimination on the career behavior of ethnic minority individuals" (Leong, 1995, p. 550). Certainly, Leong's list can be expanded to include persons with disabilities and persons who are gay, lesbian, or transgendered. Moreover, career practitioners must be aware of the worldviews embedded in their interventions and offer assistance that is congruent with the client's worldview. Thus, providing multicultural career development interventions requires counselors to be culturally aware, sensitive to their own values, and sensitive to how their cultural assumptions may affect their clients. Pope-Davis and Dings (1995) noted that multiculturally competent counselors must also:

> . . . consider factors such as the impact of the sociopolitical system on people of color in the United States, have knowledge and information about particular cultural groups, and be able to generate a wide range of appropriate verbal/nonverbal responses to client needs. (p. 288)

These statements are in contrast to many career theories and practices that have limited relevance for clients not adhering to Eurocentric worldviews emphasizing individualistic and self-actualizing perspectives regarding career behavior (Leong, 1995). Such statements also reinforce the importance of context in career development. Blustein (1994) defined context as "that group of settings that influence developmental progress, encompassing contemporary and distal familial, social, and economic circumstances" (p. 143). Diversity in clients and client concerns makes it clear that context must be considered in the construction and implementation of career development interventions. To act otherwise is to risk providing "culturally encapsulated" (Wrenn, 1962) career assistance.

MOVE TO FOCUSING ON MULTIPLE LIFE ROLES

Incorporating context into career development interventions also requires career practitioners to acknowledge that the metaphor of the "boxes of life" does not reflect life as many people live it. Life is not lived in compartmentalized life role "silos." Theories and interventions that are not sensitive to this basic fact address a life situation that does not exist. Life roles interact and influence each other so that the same job holds different meanings for two individuals who live in different contexts. Because people seek to express specific values in each of the life roles they play, career development practitioners must encourage their clients to clarify and articulate the values they seek to express in the life roles that are important to them. Once clarified and articulated, clients can be encouraged to identify outlets for values expression within each of their salient life roles (Super, 1980). Career development interventions in the 21st century will need to address the totality of career concerns people experience so that people can be empowered to not only make a good living, but also to live a good life.

SUMMARY

Careers are person-specific and created by the choices we make throughout our lives. Careers emerge from the constant interplay between the person and the environment. They include activities engaged in prior to entering the workforce and after formal activity as a worker has been completed. Careers encompass the total constellation of life roles that we play. Thus, managing our careers effectively also involves integrating the roles of life effectively. In a very real sense, careers are the manifestations of our attempts at making sense out of our life experiences. The career development process is, in essence, a spiritual journey reflecting our choices concerning how we will spend our time on Earth. Professional counselors must be mindful of these facts as they attempt to intervene in the lives of their clients and assist them in their journeys. We hope that if Stephanie and her classmates were to read this book, they would agree.

REFERENCES

Amundson, N. E. (1998). *Active engagement.* Richmond, Canada: Ergon Communications.

Anderson, W. P., & Niles, S. G. (1995). Career and personal concerns expressed by career counseling clients. *Career Development Quarterly, 43,* 240–245.

Anderson, W. P., Jr., & Niles, S. G. (2000). Important events in career counseling: Client and counselor descriptions. *Career Development Quarterly, 48,* 251–263.

Armendariz, Y. (1997, April 11). Today women's pay catches up to men's. *El Paso Times,* p. C1.

Bingham, R. P., & Ward, C. M. (1994). Career counseling with ethnic minority women. In W. B. Walsh & S. H. Osipow (Eds.), *Career counseling for women* (pp. 165–196). Hillsdale, NJ: Erlbaum.

Blustein, D. L. (1994). "Who am I?" The question of self and identity in career development. In M. L. Savickas & R. W. Lent (Eds.), *Convergence in career development theories: Implications for science and practice* (pp. 139–154). Palo Alto, CA: Consulting Psychologists Press.

Blustein, D. L., & Spengler, P. M. (1995). *Personal adjustment: Career counseling and psychotherapy.* In W. B. Walsh and S. H. Osipow (Eds.). *Handbook of vocational psychology: Theory, research, and practice* (2nd ed., pp. 295–330). Mahwah, NJ: Lawrence Erlbaum Associates.

Borow, H. (1964). (Ed.). *Man in a world at work.* Boston, MA: Houghton Mifflin.

Bowlsbey, J. H., Dikel, M. R., & Sampson, J. P. (2002). *The Internet: A tool for career planning* (2nd ed.). Tulsa, OK: National Career Development Association.

Brewer, J. M. (1942). *History of vocational guidance.* New York: Harper.

Bridges, W. (1994). *Jobshift: How to prosper in a workplace without jobs.* Reading, MA: Addison-Wesley.

Brief, A., & Nord, W. (1990). Work and meaning: Definitions and interpretations. In A. Frief & W. Nord (Eds.), *The meaning of occupational work* (pp. 21–45). Lexington, MA: Lexington.

Brown, D. (2002). The role of work values and cultural values in occupational choice, satisfaction, and success: A theoretical statement. In D. Brown & Associates (Eds.), *Career choice and development* (4th ed., pp. 465–509). San Francisco: Jossey-Bass.

Cahill, M., & Martland, S. (1996). Community career counseling for rural transition. *Canadian Journal of Counseling, 30,* 155–164.

Cochran, L. (1997). *Career counseling: A narrative approach.* Thousand Oaks: Sage.

Chung, Y. B. (2001). Work discrimination and coping strategies: Conceptual frameworks for counseling lesbian, gay, and bisexual clients. *The Career Development Quarterly, 50,* 33–44.

Crites, J. O. (1981). *Career counseling: Models, methods, and materials.* New York: McGraw-Hill.

Dawis, R. V. (1996). The theory of work adjustment and person-environment correspondence counseling. In D. Brown, L. Brooks, & Associates (Eds.), *Career choice development* (3rd ed.) (pp. 75–120). San Francisco, CA: Jossey-Bass.

Dawis, R. V., England, G. W., & Lofquist, L. H. (1964). A theory of work adjustment. *Minnesota Studies in Vocational Rehabilitation, No. XV,* 1–27.

Enright, M., Conyers, L., & Szymanski, E. M. (1996). Career and career-related educational concerns of college students with disabilities. *Journal of Counseling & Development, 74,* 103–114.

Gomez, M. J., Fassinger, R. E., Prosser, J., Cooke, K., Mejia, B., & Luna, J. (2001). Voces abriendo caminos (Voices forging paths): A qualitative study of the career development of notable Latinas. *Journal of Counseling Psychology, 48,* 286–300.

Gysbers, N. C., Heppner, M. J., & Johnston, J. A. (2003). *Career counseling: Process, issues, and techniques* (2nd ed.). Boston, MA: Allyn & Bacon.

Hall, D. T. & Associates (1996). *The career is dead—long live the career: A relational approach to careers.* San Francisco, CA: Jossey-Bass.

Harpaz, I. (1999). The transformation of work values. *Israel Monthly Review, 122,* 46–50.

Hartung, P. J. (2002). Development through work and play. *Journal of Vocational Behavior, 61,* 424–438.

Hartung, P. J., Speight, J. D., & Lewis, D. M. (1996). Individualism-collectivism and the vocational behavior of majority culture college students. *The Career Development Quarterly, 45,* 87–96.

Heppner, M. J., O'Brien, K. M., Hinkelman, J. M., & Flores, L. Y. (1996). Training counseling psychologists in career development: Are we our own worst enemies? *The Counseling Psychologist, 24,* 105–125.

Herr, E. L. (1989). Career development and mental health. *Journal of Career Development, 16,* 5–18.

Herr, E. L. (1997). Super's life-span, life-space approach and its outlook for refinement. *The Career Development Quarterly, 45,* 238–246.

Herr, E. L. (2001). Career development and its practice: A historical perspective. *The Career Development Quarterly, 49,* 196–211.

Herr, E. L. (2003). The future of career counseling as an instrument of public policy. *The Career Development Quarterly, 52,* 8–17.

Herr, E. L., & Cramer, S. H. (1996). *Career guidance and counseling through the lifespan: Systemic approaches* (5th ed.). New York: HarperCollins.

Herr, E. L., Cramer, S. H., & Niles, S. G. (2004). *Career guidance and counseling through the lifespan: Systemic approaches* (6th ed.). Boston, MA: Allyn & Bacon.

Herr, E. L., & Niles, S. G. (1998). Career: Social action in behalf of purpose, productivity, and hope. In C. Lee & G. R. Walz (Eds.), *Social action: A mandate for counselors* (pp. 117–156). Alexandria, VA: American Counseling Association.

Isaacson, L. E. (1985). *Basics of career counseling.* Boston, MA: Allyn & Bacon.

Isaacson, L. E., & Brown, D. (2000). *Career information, career counseling, and career development.* Boston, MA: Allyn & Bacon.

Kalton, C. A. (2001). Client psychological distress: An important factor in career counseling. *The Career Development Quarterly, 49,* 324–335.

Kapes, J. T., & Whitfield, E. A. (2002). *A counselor's guide to career assessment instruments* (4th ed.). Alexandria, VA: National Career Development Association.

Kim, B. S. K., Li, L. C., & Liang, C. T. H. (2002). Effects of Asian American client adherence to Asian cultural values, session goal, and counselor emphasis of client expression on career counseling process. *Journal of Counseling Psychology 49,* 3–13.

Krumboltz, J. D. (1993). Integrating career and personal counseling. *The Career Development Quarterly, 42,* 143–148.

Lee, C. C. (1989). Needed: A career development advocate. *The Career Development Quarterly, 37,* 218–220.

Lee, C. C., & Richardson, B. L. (Eds.). (1991). *Multicultural issues in counseling: New approaches to diversity.* Alexandria, VA: American Counseling Association.

Lent, R. W., & Worthington, R. L. (1999). Applying career development theories to the school-to-work transition process. *The Career Development Quarterly, 47,* 291–296.

Lent, R. W., Brown, S. D., & Hackett, G. (2002). Social cognitive career theory. In D. Brown & Associates (Eds.), *Career choice and development* (4th ed., pp. 255–311). San Francisco, CA: Jossey-Bass.

Leong, F. T. L. (1995). *Career development and vocational behavior of racial and ethnic minorities.* Mahwah, NJ: Lawrence Erlbaum Associates.

Leong, F. T. L. (2002). Challenges for career counseling in Asia: Variations in cultural accommodation. *The Career Development Quarterly, 50,* 277–284.

Leong, F. T. L. & Hartung, P. J. (2000). Adapting to the changing multicultural context of career. In A. Collin & R. A. Young (Eds.), *The future of career* (pp. 212–227). Cambridge, England: Cambridge University Press.

Leung, S. A. (1995). Career development and counseling: A multicultural perspective. In J. G. Ponterotto, J. M. Casas, L. A. Suzuki, & C. M. Alexander. *Handbook of multicultural counseling* (pp. 549–566). Thousand Oaks, CA: Sage.

Liem, R., & Rayman, P. (1982). Health and social costs of unemployment. *American Psychologist, 37,* 1116–1123.

Liptak, J. J. (2001). *Treatment planning in career counseling.* Belmont, CA: Brooks/Cole.

Luzzo, D. A. (2000). *Career counseling of college students: An empirical guide to strategies that*

work. Washington, DC: American Psychological Association.

Maccoby, M., & Terzi, K. (1981). What happened to the work ethic? In J. O'Toole, J. L. Scheiber, & L. C. Wood (Eds.), *Working, changes, and choices* (pp. 162–171). New York: Human Sciences Press.

Mannheim, B. (1993). Gender and the effects of demographics status and work values on work centrality. *Work and Occupations, 20,* 3–22.

McCortney, A. L., & Engels, D. W. (2003). Revisiting the work ethic in America. *The Career Development Quarterly, 52,* 132–140.

Melamed, S., Meir, E. I., & Samson, A. (1995). The benefits of personality-leisure congruence: Evidence and implications. *Journal of Leisure Research, 27,* 25–40.

Mortimer, J. T., Zimmer-Gembeck, T., Holmes, M., & Shanahan, M. J. (2002). The process of occupational decision making: Patterns during the transition to adulthood. *Journal of Vocational Behavior, 61,* 439–465.

Multon, K. D., Heppner, M.J., Gysbers, N.C., Zook, C., & Ellis-Katton, C.A. (2001). Client psychological distress: An important factor in career counseling. *The Career Development Quarterly, 49,* 324–335.

National Career Development Association (2003a). *The professional practice of career counseling and consultation: A resource document.* Tulsa, OK: Author.

National Career Development Association (2003b). *Career counseling competencies.* Tulsa, OK: Author.

Niles, S. G. (2003). Career counselors confront critical crossroads: A vision of the future. *The Career Development Quarterly, 52,* 70–77.

Niles, S. G., & Anderson, W. P. (1993). Career development and adjustment: The relation between concerns and stress. *Journal of Employment Counseling, 30,* 79–87.

Niles, S. G., & Anderson, W. P. (1995). A content analysis of career and personal concerns expressed by career counseling clients. *Educational and Vocational Guidance Bulletin, 57,* 59–62.

Niles, S. G., & Pate, P. H., Jr. (1989). Competency and training issues related to the integration of career counseling and mental health counseling. *Journal of Career Development, 16,* 63–71.

O'Brien, K. M. (2001). The legacy of Parsons: Career counselors and vocational psychologists as agents of social change. *The Career Development Quarterly, 50,* 66–76.

O'Toole, J. (1981). Work in America. In J. O'Toole, J. L. Schiber, & L. C. Wood (Eds.), *Working: Changes and choices* (pp. 12–17). New York: Human Sciences Press.

Parmer, T., & Rush, L. C. (2003). The next decade in career counseling: Cocoon maintenance or metamorphosis? *The Career Development Quarterly, 52,* 26–34.

Parsons, F. (1909). *Choosing a vocation.* Boston: Houghton Mifflin.

Pope, M. (2000). A brief history of career counseling in the United States. *The Career Development Quarterly, 48,* 194–211.

Pope-Davis, D. B., & Dings, J. G. (1995). The assessment of multicultural counseling competencies. In J. G. Ponterotto & J. M. Casas (Eds.), *Handbook of multicultural counseling* (pp. 287–311). Thousand Oaks, CA: Sage.

Richardson, M. S. (1994). From agency/empowerment to embodied empowerment. *Theoretical & Philosophical Psychology, 14,* 79–82.

Riegle, D. W., Jr. (1982). Psychological and social effects of unemployment. *American Psychologist, 21,* 113–115.

Rifkin, J. (1995). *The end of work.* New York: Putnam.

Robinson, J. P. (1990). The leisure pie (use of leisure time). *American Demographics, 12,* 39.

Robinson, J. P., & Blair, J. (1995). *The national macroenvironmental activity pattern survey (preliminary report).* Washington, DC: Environmental Protection Agency.

Rogers, C. R. (1942). *Counseling and psychotherapy: Newer concepts in practice.* Boston: Houghton Mifflin.

Savickas, M. L. (1993). Predictive validity criteria for career development measures. *Journal of Career Assessment, 1,* 93–104.

Sears, S. (1982). A definition of career guidance terms. A National Vocational Guidance Association perspective. *The Vocational Guidance Quarterly, 31,* 137–143.

Shanahan, M. J., & Porfeli, E. (2002). Integrating the life course and life-span: Formulating research questions with dual points of entry. *Journal of Vocational Behavior, 61,* 398–406.

Spokane, A. R. (1991). *Career interventions.* Upper Saddle River, NJ: Prentice Hall.

Subich, L. M. (1993). How personal is career counseling? *The Career Development Quarterly, 42,* 129–131.

Subich, L. M. (2001). Introduction: Special section on contextual factors in career services delivery. *The Career Development Quarterly, 50,* 20.

Sue, D. W., Bernier, Y., Durran, A., Feinberg, L., Pedersen, P., Smith, E. J., & Nuttall, E. V. (1982). Position paper: Cross-cultural counseling competencies. *The Counseling Psychologist, 10*(2), 45–52.

Super, D. E. (1951). Vocational adjustment: Implementing a self-concept. *Occupations, 51,* 88–92.

Super, D. E. (1976). *Career education and the meaning of work.* Washington, DC: Office of Education.

Super, D. E. (1980). A life-span, life-space approach to career development. *Journal of Vocational Behavior, 16,* 282–298.

Swanson, J. L., & Gore, P. A., Jr. (2000). Advances in vocational psychology theory and research. In S. D. Brown & R. W. Lent (Eds.), *Handbook of counseling psychology* (3rd. ed., pp. 233–269). New York: Wiley.

Uchitelle, L., & Kleinfield, N. R. (1996, March 3). On the battlefield of business, millions of casualties. *The New York Times,* Section 1, p. 1ff.

Vondracek, F. W., Lerner, R. M., & Schulenberg, J. E. (1986). *Career development: A life-span developmental approach.* Hillsdale: Erlbaum.

Warnath, L. F. (1975). Vocational theories: Directions to nowhere. *Personnel and Guidance Journal, 53,* 422–428.

Watkins, C. E., Jr., & Savickas, M. L. (1990). Psychodynamic career counseling. In W. B. Walsh, & S. H. Osipow (Eds.), *Career counseling: Contemporary topics in vocational psychology* (pp. 79–116). Hillsdale, NJ: Erlbaum.

Williamson, E. G. (1939). *How to counsel students.* New York: McGraw-Hill.

Wrenn, C. G. (1962). The culturally encapsulated counselor. *Harvard Educational Review, 32,* 444–449.

Zytowski, D. G. (2001). Frank Parsons and the progressive movement. *The Career Development Quarterly, 50,* 57–65.

CHAPTER 2

UNDERSTANDING AND APPLYING
THEORIES OF CAREER DEVELOPMENT

Don't Let Theories Boggle Your Mind

    It is easy to be intimated by the word theory. The real world is an extremely complicated place. Human beings and their behavior are so complex that no one understands completely why people think, feel, and act as they do. A theory is just an explanation—an oversimplified explanation of what is going on.

    A theory is like a road map. Suppose you have a road map of California and you want to drive from San Francisco to Los Angeles. You see a red line marked "101" stretching between the two cities on the map. Aha, you think, I'll drive down that red highway 101. But when you get to the highway, you see it is black asphalt. Why does the map show it to be red? The map lies! Why does the map lie? Because the map-marker wants to make it easier for you to see the path. You drive down the highway and see office buildings, gardens, and swimming pools, but none of them are indicated on the map. The map not only distorts reality—it omits zillions of details. Why? Because all those details would make it too complicated to find the best route between two cities.

    In the same way, a theory attempts to explain a complex situation by overemphasizing and distorting the importance of certain variables while ignoring completely other variables that the theory-maker considers irrelevant. Theories are oversimplifications just as road maps are oversimplifications. Yet road maps are very useful for certain purposes—even with all of their faults. Similarly, theories can be useful—even with their faults.

    A theory is just one way of oversimplifying a complex situation so that it is easier for you to see the big picture. That picture is not reality itself—just one theory-maker's version of it.

John D. Krumboltz
Stanford University

Juanita is a 17-year-old Latina student in the 11th grade in a predominantly White, middle-class neighborhood. She is "normal" in intelligence but reports that she dislikes school. She associates with a group of girls that are often in trouble with the police. It is your impression, however, that these friendships are superficial. Recently, some of the girls in her circle of friends have been arrested for drug possession (marijuana). Juanita is not hostile or disrespectful. However, she routinely hands in school work late, if at all. Her parents have asked you to help her "make a good career choice."

In most classes, Juanita is apathetic, but she enjoys art class (especially painting) and being in the school band (she plays the flute). She dislikes math classes. Juanita has two younger sisters, ages 12 and 14. Her mother is employed as a teacher's aide in a local elementary school and her father is employed as a car salesperson in a local dealership. Juanita's current plans are to finish high school but she has not made plans for what she will do beyond that point. She stated that she "might like to be in a rock band." She agrees to meet with you to discuss her career plans.

CAREER DEVELOPMENT THEORIES

Career development theories differ in their coverage of the career development process versus career decision-making content. Savickas (2002) notes that theories emphasize either "individual differences" related to occupations (viewed as describing how people can find their fit within the occupational structure) or "individual development" related to careers (viewed as how people express career behavior across time). For example, developmental theories (e.g., Super, Gottfredson) highlight the expression of career behavior over time. Person-environment theories (e.g., Work Adjustment Theory, Holland) address the essential ingredients (i.e., occupational and self-information) for choosing an occupation. One of the major reasons for studying the various approaches to career theory rather than concentrating on only one emphasis, whatever that emphasis may be, is the fact that no one theory is sufficient to explain the totality of individual or group career behavior. As Super (1992) observed, the question of "which theory is better" is specious because the theories complement each other in addressing various facets of the complexity of career behavior. In this sense, each theory adds to the comprehensiveness of insight about career behavior that now exists.

Some career development experts suggest that career theories are actually converging, becoming more similar in their constructs and thus increasing the probability that they will be brought together into a unified theory (Savickas, 2000; Savickas & Lent, 1994). Osipow (1990), for example, has analyzed how four major sets of career theories—trait and factor, social learning, developmental, and work adjustment—resemble each other in important ways. Hackett, Lent, and Greenhaus (1991) suggest that a focus on integrating career theories is needed to bring together conceptually related constructs (e.g., self-concept, self-efficacy), provide a more complete explanation of outcomes that are common to a number of career theories (e.g., satisfaction, stability), and identify the crucial variables for constructing an overarching theory of career development (p. 28).

Herr, Cramer, and Niles (2004) view the plan of action outlined by Hackett and her colleagues (1991) as both reasonable and valuable, but also not likely to occur in the near future given the magnitude of the task and the constant infusion into the literature of new concepts and research findings. "Theory unification is also a daunting task because of the current lack of coverage of the career behavior of selected subpopulations: persons with disabilities, women, persons of color, immigrants, nonprofessional/nonskilled workers, and persons who are gay, lesbian, bisexual, or transgendered. Research deficits in knowledge about the career behavior of such populations leaves significant voids in the ability to be comprehensive and unified in explanations of career behavior" (Herr et al., p. 165). This knowledge gap has led researchers to point to the need to more fully understand contextual factors influencing career development of individuals from diverse backgrounds (Subich, 2001).

In addressing such issues, Richardson (1993) states that "the theoretical and research literature in vocational psychology-career development is notably oriented toward the White middle class. Moreover, there is almost no acknowledgement that poor and lower class populations, regardless of race or ethnicity, are almost totally absent from the literature" (p. 426). Tinsley (1994) counters that a substantial body of research over the years has not provided support for sex or economic-level differences. Tinsley expresses concern that "there is a tendency to dismiss general models that have applicability to both sexes and all economic class levels as limited in applicability only to White, middle-class men" (p. 109). These varying views, offered by leading scholars in the field, require serious consideration and thoughtful reflection. Thus, we encourage you to consider the following questions as you read the theories presented in Chapters 2 and 3:

1. How well do the theories describe the career development process for members of diverse groups?
2. How well do the theories describe the career development process in general?
3. How well do the theories describe the factors involved in making a career choice?
4. How well do the theories inform the practice of career counseling?
5. To what degree is there empirical support for the theories?
6. What gaps can you identify within the theories presented?

Because no one theory is likely to "do it all," we think it is important to identify each theory's strengths and limitations. Doing so will allow you to draw upon the best the field has to offer. For those interested in career development research, identifying the gaps will also provide useful information for potentially fruitful research pursuits.

There are many ways to present career theories. Often, theories are presented in chronological order, beginning with the work of Frank Parsons and proceeding to the most recent theories. Other times they are grouped by categories (e.g., psychological, developmental, trait-factor; objective vs. subjective). In determining how to organize the career theories, we attempted to present them in a fashion that we thought made sense as practitioners.

The work of Parsons and later trait-factor theorists was discussed in the previous chapter, largely because these models are intimately intertwined with the historical roots of career development interventions. The work of contributors such as Parsons, Williamson, and Dawis and Lofquist highlights the importance of considering the interactions between the person's traits and factors in the work environment in career decision making. Building upon our discussion of Parsons' model and trait-factor approaches (e.g., TWA) presented in Chapter 1, we begin the current chapter with Donald Super's theory for several reasons. First, Super's theory provides a useful framework for conceptualizing career development over the life span. His theory also acknowledges the various personal (e.g., needs, values, abilities) and situational (e.g., peer groups, family, labor market) determinants that influence career development. Super's theory places work within the context of multiple roles played in life. Finally, his theory addresses helping people clarify, articulate, and implement their life-role self-concepts. Thus, Super's theory provides a useful, overarching framework for viewing career development processes.

To expand on the influence of personal and situational influences on career development, we then describe Linda Gottfredson's theory. Gottfredson's theory addresses the fact that men and women tend to differ in their occupational aspirations (Gottfredson, 1996; 2002). Her theory offers a developmental and sociological perspective of career development. The theory is focused primarily on the career development process as it relates to the types of compromises people make in formulating their occupational aspirations.

We then discuss Holland's theory. Holland's theory has generated more research than any other career theory. Arguably, Holland's typology provides the most useful framework for understanding and predicting individual behavior (i.e., job satisfaction, job performance, and occupational stability) within work environments. Through the use of assessment instruments, Holland applies his typology to help individuals clarify and implement their vocational identities (Spokane, Luchetta, & Richwine, 2002).

There are times, however, when "faulty" or irrational thinking impedes individuals in their career development. The cumulative effect of a variety of learning experiences can result in varying degrees of functionality among individuals with regard to their ability to make effective career decisions. For example, when individuals receive adequate support and are exposed to effective role models, they often develop interests and skills leading to satisfying career options. Conversely, when such support is lacking or individuals are misinformed, they often disregard appropriate options because they lack confidence or they adhere to beliefs (e.g., "I must decide now what I will do for the rest of my life") that keep them "stuck" in their career development. In the latter cases, individuals need assistance in developing beliefs that are more useful in making effective career decisions. In these instances, the work of John Krumboltz provides a useful framework for helping practitioners foster career development in their clients. We discuss this theory in the final section of this chapter. In Chapter 3, we focus attention on emerging theories of career development that hold promise for providing effective descriptions of career development processes and practices. Table 2.1 summarizes the theories discussed in Chapters 2 and 3.

Table 2.1
Brief Overview of Career Theories

Theory	Theorists	Orientation	Key Constructs	Research Support	Multicultural Emphasis
Work Adjustment	Rene Dawis Lloyd Lofquist	Trait-factor Career choice/adjustment	Satisfaction Satisfactoriness Person-in-an environment Correspondence	Moderate	Low
Life-Span, Life-Space	Donald Super	Developmental	Life span Career stages Career development tasks Life space Self-concept Career maturity Career adaptability	High	Moderate
Circumscription, Compromise, and Self-Creation	Linda Gottfredson	Developmental/sociological Career choice/development	Circumscription Compromise	Low	High
Vocational Personalities and Work Environments	John Holland	Trait-factor Career choice	Congruence Consistency Differentiation Vocational identity	High	Low
Learning Theory of Career Counseling	John Krumboltz	Social learning Career choice development	Learning experience Self-observation generalizations Worldview generalizations Task approach skills, actions Planned happenstance	Moderate	High

Approach	Authors	Type	Key Concepts		
Social Cognitive Career Theory	Robert Lent, Steven Brown, Gail Hackett	Social cognitive career choice / Development	Self-efficacy / Outcome expectations / Personal goals / Triadic reciprocal model	Moderate	High
Cognitive Information Processing Approach	Gary Peterson, James Sampson Jr., Robert Reardon, Janet Lentz	Cognitive career choice	Pyramid of information processing / CASVE cycle / Executive processing domain / Career thoughts inventory	Moderate	Moderate
Values-Based, Holistic Model of Career and Life-Role Choice and Satisfaction	Duane Brown	Trait-factor / Career choice/adjustment	Life values inventory / Work values / Cultural values	Moderate	High
Integrative Life Planning	L. Sunny Hansen	Contextual career choice/adjustment	Social justice / Social change / Connectedness / Diversity / Spirituality / Integrative life planning inventory	Low	High
Postmodern	Richard Young, Ladislav Valach, Audrey Collin	Action-theory	Context / Joint action / Career project / Interpretation / Functional steps	Low	High
	Vance Peavey	Constructivist	Meaning-making	Low	High
	Larry Cochran	Narrative	Career problem / Life history / Future narrative	Low	High

SUPER'S LIFE-SPAN, LIFE-SPACE THEORY

The leading developmental approach describing how careers develop and proposing developmental career interventions is Donald Super's "life-span, life-space" theory (Super, 1990; Super, Savickas, & Super, 1996). The life-span, life-space theory evolved over a 40-year time period as Super and his colleagues worked to elaborate and refine the various aspects of the theory (Super et al., 1996). Although Super's theory is primarily developmental in nature, he labeled it as a "differential-developmental-social-phenomenological career theory" (Super, 1969). This label communicates Super's efforts at synthesizing and extending extant developmental and career theories. Super understood that describing a process as complex as career development requires synthesizing the work of scholars from various disciplines (e.g., psychology and sociology). For example, Super synthesized work by Buehler (1993), Havighurst (1951), Miller and Form (1951), Rogers (1951), and Kelly (1955) in conceptualizing various aspects of his theory of career development.

Super extended career theories by addressing shortcomings he perceived in the theories proposed by his predecessors and his contemporaries. For example, Super's contemporaries, Ginzberg, Ginsburg, Axelrad, and Herma (1951), proposed a career theory asserting that career choice is a developmental process (rather than a single decision) in which compromises are made between the individual's wishes and occupational possibilities. They viewed the developmental process as spanning three stages: (a) fantasy (birth to age 11), (b) tentative (age 11 to 17), and (c) realistic (age 17 to early twenties). They theorized that four factors (individual values, emotional factors, the amount and kind of education, and the effect of reality through environmental pressures) converged to shape the individual's career decisions.

Super argued that the theory proposed by Ginzberg and his associates was deficient in that it (a) did not take into account research related to the role of interests in career decision making, (b) failed to operationally describe "choice," (c) made a sharp distinction between choice and adjustment, and (d) lacked a clear articulation of the process of compromise as it relates to career choice. Responding to conditions such as these, Super developed his "differential-developmental-social-phenomenological career theory."

Rather than developing a unified theory, however, Super developed his theory segmentally. In fact, Super noted that in one sense "there is no 'Super's theory'; there is just the assemblage of theories that I have sought to synthesize. In another sense, the synthesis is a theory" (1990, p. 199). The result is really a "segmental theory" describing three key aspects of career development: (a) life span, (b) life space, and (c) self-concept. The theory culminates in an intervention model labeled as the Career Development Assessment and Counseling (C-DAC) model (Super, Osborne, Walsh, Brown, & Niles, 1992). The C-DAC model translates the three theory segments into career practice to help persons articulate their career concerns, examine their life-role salience, and clarify their self-concepts.

Life-span, life-space theory builds upon 14 assumptions proposed by Super (1990)[1]:

1. People differ in their abilities, personalities, needs, values, interests, traits, and self-concepts.

2. People are qualified, by virtue of these characteristics, each for a number of occupations.

3. Each occupation requires a characteristic pattern of abilities and personality traits, with tolerance wide enough to allow both some variety of occupations for each individual and some variety of individuals in each occupation.

4. Vocational preferences and competencies, the situations in which people live and work, and, hence, their self-concepts change with time and experience, although self-concepts, as products of social learning, are increasingly stable from late adolescence until later maturity, providing some continuity in choice and adjustment.

5. This process of change may be summed up in a series of life stages (a "maxi-cycle") characterized as a sequence of growth, exploration, establishment, maintenance, and decline, and these stages may in turn be subdivided into (a) the fantasy, tentative, and realistic phases of the exploratory stage and (b) the trial and stable phases of the establishment stage. A small (mini) cycle takes place in transitions from one stage to the next or each time an individual is destabilized by a reduction in force, changes in type of manpower needs, illness or injury, or other socioeconomic or personal events. Such unstable or multiple-trial careers involve new growth, reexplorations, and reestablishment (recycling).

6. The nature of the career pattern—that is, the occupational level attained and the sequence, frequency, and duration of trial and stable jobs—is determined by the individual's parental socioeconomic level, mental ability, education, skills, personality characteristics (needs, values, interests, and self-concepts), and career maturity and by the opportunities to which he or she is exposed.

7. Success in coping with the demands of the environment and of the organism in that context at any given life-career stage depends on the readiness of the individual to cope with these demands (that is, on his or her career maturity). *Career maturity* is a constellation of physical, psychological, and social characteristics; psychologically, it is both cognitive and affective. It includes the degree of success in coping with the demands of earlier stages and substages of career development, especially with the most recent.

8. Career maturity is a hypothetical construct. Its operational definition is perhaps as difficult to formulate as is that of intelligence, but its history is much briefer and its achievements even less definitive. Contrary to the impressions created by some writers, it does not increase monotonically, and it is not a unitary trait.

9. Development through the life stages can be guided, partly by facilitating the maturing of abilities and interests and partly by aiding in reality testing and in the development of self-concepts.

10. The process of career development is essentially that of development and implementing occupational self-concepts. It is a synthesizing and compromising process in which the self-concept is a product of the interaction of inherited aptitudes, physical

makeup, opportunity to observe and play various roles, and evaluations of the extent to which the results of role playing meets with the approval of superiors and fellows (interactive learning).

11. The process of synthesis of or compromise between individual and social factors, between self-concepts and reality, is one of role playing and of learning from feedback, whether the role is played in fantasy, in the counseling interview, or in such real-life activities as classes, clubs, part-time work, and entry jobs.

12. Work satisfactions and life satisfactions depend on the extent to which the individual finds adequate outlets for abilities, needs, values, interests, personality traits, and self-concepts. They depend on establishment in a type of work, a work situation, and a way of life in which one can play the kind of role that growth and exploratory experiences have led one to consider congenial and appropriate.

13. The degree of satisfaction people attain from work is proportional to the degree to which they have been able to implement self-concepts.

14. Work and occupation provide a focus for personality organization for most men and women, although for some persons this focus is peripheral, incidental, or even nonexistent. Then other foci, such as leisure activities and homemaking, may be central. (Social traditions, such as sex-role stereotyping and modeling, racial and ethnic biases, and the opportunity structure, as well as individual differences, are important determinants of preferences for such roles as worker, student, leisurite, homemaker, and citizen.)

These 14 propositions represent an expansion of Super's original list of 10 proposed in 1953. The propositions incorporate statements from diverse theoretical perspectives (e.g., trait-and-factor, developmental, social learning, and psychodynamic), thus supporting Super's contention that his theory is more than a developmental one. Super's propositions also introduce some relatively novel concepts into the career development literature. Specifically, Super expanded career development concepts by encouraging the field to consider the notion that there is intraoccupational variability among workers, that multiple life-role development is important to consider in career development, and that self-concepts evolve over time, making choice and adjustment a continuous process. Thus, when Super's propositions are placed in historical context, they provide the impetus for shifting the paradigm within the field from one that focuses on "vocation" to one that focuses on "career"; from one that focuses exclusively on the content of career choice to one that highlights the process of career development over the life span.

Life Span

Although career development, like physical development, is a lifelong process it is unlike physical development in that career development is not ontogenetic. Rather, careers develop within the context of psychosocial development and societal expectations and against the backdrop of the occupational opportunity structure. Early in life, career development is relatively homogeneous and age related. Most young people are enrolled in educational institutions that require them to make decisions at specific grade levels (e.g., students in eighth grade must select a curriculum of study for high school, students leaving high school must make choices about what they will do when their secondary-school experience ends). Thus, in childhood and adolescence the term *career maturity* is used in relationship to career decision making readiness. Career development in adulthood, however, is heterogeneous and not as directly connected to age. Adult careers develop in response to the challenges presented by changing occupational opportunities and evolving patterns of life-role participation. Thus, adults may re-cycle through various career development stages and tasks, depending on their situations in life. Because career development in adulthood is heterogeneous, the term *career adaptability* (rather than *career maturity*) is used when referring to an adult person's career decision making readiness. The term *career adaptability* reflects the fact that "as adults cope with their changing work and working conditions, adults make an impact on their environments and their environments make an impact on them" (Niles, Anderson, & Goodnough, 1998, p. 273). In this sense, career adaptation parallels Piaget's model of adaptation based on the two processes of assimilation and accommodation. Career adaptability also supports the view that adults are "responsible agents acting within dynamic environmental settings" to find ways to effectively manage their career development (Super & Knasel, 1981, p. 199).

Although Super originally applied "adaptability" to adult career development, it seems reasonable to suggest that the term *career adaptability* can also be applied to children and adolescents. Despite their relative homogeneity in career development when compared with adults, young people experience differences in their readiness to cope with career development tasks. Some young people encounter environmental obstacles (e.g., poverty, racism, sexism) that influence their career development in less than positive ways. Some young people are provided with environmental experiences (e.g., the opportunity to enroll in outstanding schools, opportunities to engage in multiple recreational and co-curricular school activities) that foster career development. Differences in contextual "affordances" (Vondracek, Lerner, & Schulenberg, 1986) have implications for career development. Thus, *career adaptability* seems a more fitting term for young people than does *career maturity*. Savickas (1997) agrees and states that "career adaptability should replace career maturity as the critical construct in the developmental perspective" (p. 247).

In describing the process of career development over the life span, Super drew on the research of Buehler (1933), Miller and Form (1951), and Havighurst (1953). Super conceptualized career as "the life course of a person encountering a series of developmental tasks and attempting to handle them in such a way as to become the kind of person he or she wants to become" (Super, 1990, pp. 225–226). Super identified the series of developmental tasks typically encountered and related these tasks to stages and substages of career development. The stages of career development in their typical sequence are growth (childhood), exploration (adolescence), establishment (early adulthood), maintenance (middle adulthood), and disengagement (late adulthood).

Growth.   Children ages 4 to 13 are confronted with the career development tasks of developing a beginning sense of self and a basic understanding of the world-of-work. In so doing, children progress through the substages of fantasy, interest, and capacity. They progress through these substages by using their innate sense of curiosity, first to engage in occupational fantasies, and then, through exploring their environment (e.g., home, school, parental, and peer relationships). Their curiosity leads them to acquire information about work and about their own interests and capacities. When things go well, children begin to develop a sense of mastery and control over their environment and in their ability to make decisions. Moving through the growth stage, children begin to realize the importance of planning for the future and that their behavior in the present influences their future lives. Moreover, they are increasingly able to use what they have learned about themselves and work to explore the viability of various educational and occupational opportunities.

Exploration.   Using self and occupational information, and their heightened sense of awareness that the present influences the future, adolescents ages 14 to 24 turn to planning for the future. Within the career development domain, future planning involves addressing the tasks of crystallizing and specifying occupational preferences. Once a preference is specified, people turn to implementing an occupational choice. These tasks occur within the substages of tentative, transition, and trial (with little commitment), respectively.

Crystallizing an occupational preference requires people to clarify the type of work they would enjoy. The process of crystallization builds upon the occupational and self-information acquired during the growth stage. Using this information, people focus on acquiring more in-depth occupational information to explore the degree to which specific occupations may allow for self-concept implementation. Thus, accurate self-understanding is essential for identifying appropriate occupational preferences.

The process of specifying occupational preferences requires the ability to make decisions by choosing from among the occupations being considered. The process of implementing varies depending on what choice has been specified. Some choices require further training and education in order to gain entry into an occupation. Other choices provide the opportunity for direct entry into an occupation. Regardless of the choice, implementing requires taking action toward getting started in one's chosen occupational field.

Establishment.   Getting established in a career generally occurs from about age 25 to age 45. The career development tasks associated with this stage are stabilizing, consolidating, and advancing. Stabilizing begins immediately after entering an occupation as one evaluates whether the occupational preference one has implemented provides adequate opportunity for self-concept expression. Specifically, one must assess the organizational culture and determine whether he or she possesses the skills and interests necessary for succeeding in the occupation he or she has entered.

As one becomes more stabilized in an occupation, he or she turns attention away from questioning whether the choice was a good one and begins focusing on becoming a dependable producer and developing a positive reputation in the occupation (i.e., consolidating). Focusing on becoming a dependable producer often leads to moving into a position of higher pay and responsibility (i.e., advancing). The reputation for successful performance one sought to develop is now achieved.

It is important to note, however, that at any time in this process workers may decide that the occupational choice they made is no longer a good one. If this occurs, re-cycling to exploration occurs so that a more appropriate occupational choice can be crystallized, specified, and implemented.

Maintenance. During maintenance (approximately ages 45 to 65), workers encounter the career development tasks of holding, updating, and innovating. Many workers are confronted with the choice of either keeping up with the advancements in their field to maintain or improve their level of performance or opting for changing occupational fields. In the latter instance, workers must re-cycle through exploration- and establishment-stage tasks. In the former (i.e., holding), workers turn their attention to updating their skills and applying new skills in innovative ways within their current occupations. Workers who decide to stay in their current occupations but not to update their skills often become poor performers and stagnate in their work (i.e., they become "stuck" at the holding task). In these instances, career interventions addressing career renewal are required. Workers who update and innovate often become excellent mentors to less experienced workers.

Disengagement. At some point toward the end of the maintenance stage, often as physical capacities begin to decline, interest in work activities begins to wane. Workers become more concerned with planning for retirement living. Thus, the disengagement stage involves the career development tasks of deceleration, retirement planning, and retirement living. As workers begin decelerating from their work activities (currently at about age 65), they begin to become concerned about their lifestyle and activities in retirement. Often, these concerns contain physical, spiritual, and financial considerations.

Life Space

While workers are busy earning a living, they are also busy living a life (Super et al., 1996). The "simultaneous combination of life roles we play constitutes the lifestyle; their sequential combination structures the life space and constitutes the life cycle. The total structure is the career pattern" (Super, 1980, p. 288). Life roles interact so that the same job holds different meaning for two individuals who live in different situations. For example, the meaning and purpose your professor finds in his or her job is influenced by previous roles your professor has played in life (e.g., child, student, worker in previous occupations) as well as the current roles your professor is playing (e.g., partner, parent, child, homemaker, sibling, friend). Because of the life roles each professor plays, your professor's dedication to work, and the way in which your professor defines the work role, may differ from someone else who is also a professor.

The salience people attach to the constellation of life roles they play defines what Super referred to as the "life structure." The life-space segment of Super's theory acknowledges that people differ in the degree of importance they attach to work. Unfortunately, as we mentioned in Chapter 1, many people link work with self-worth in such a way that de-values the various life roles that have so much to contribute to one's sense of self-esteem and self-efficacy (not to mention to society). Many models of career counseling have disregarded the effects of life-role interactions and that effective participation in multiple life roles allows for maximal opportunities for values expression.

Super noted that people tend to play nine major roles throughout their lives. In approximate chronological order these roles are (1) son or daughter, (2) student, (3) leisurite, (4) citizen, (5) worker, (6) spouse (or partner), (7) homemaker, (8) parent, and (9) pensioner. The individual's career comprises the total constellation of life roles engaged in over the course of a lifetime (Super, 1980, p. 284). Life roles are generally played out in specific theaters. These theaters are (1) the home, (2) the school, (3) the workplace, and (4) the community.

Effective life-role participation is very difficult to achieve. Conflicting life-role demands make effective life-role participation feel like a "moving target." At various times, priority must be given to specific life roles. Sometimes deciding which role takes priority is relatively easy (e.g., giving priority to one's job when there are low demands from one's children) and sometimes not (e.g., when the demands from job and family are concurrently high). At times, life roles typically played in one theater spill over into another theater and create conflict (Eagle, Miles, & Icenogle, 1997; Loscocco, 1997). For example, when work spills over from the workplace to the home, the roles of worker, partner, and parent become enmeshed and insufficient attention is paid to each role. Thus, life roles interact in ways that can be extensive or minimal; supportive, supplementary, compensatory, or neutral. Life is best when the life roles we play nurture each other and offer opportunities for us to express our values. Life is stressful when the life roles we play are at odds with each other and provide little opportunity for us to express what we value.

Thus, it is not surprising that many career counseling clients present with concerns related to life-structure issues. That is, many career counseling clients are seeking assistance in coping more effectively with changing life-role demands. For such clients, career interventions that address only one life role—work—are inadequate. Super's theory embraces this fact by focusing on how clients structure the basic roles of work, play, friendship, and family into a life (Super et al., 1996).

Self-Concepts

Super defined self-concept as a "picture of the self in some role, situation, or position, performing some set of functions, or in some web of relationships" (1963, p. 18). Super (1980) uses the Archway Model (Figure 2.1) and the Life-Career Rainbow (Figure 2.2) to depict the various personal (e.g., aptitudes, values, needs) and situational (e.g., the family, the community, the economy, society) determinants that shape the constellation of life roles that individuals play over the course of a life span and that interact to influence the development of the person's self-concepts.

Using the Archway model and Life-Career Rainbow, Super delineates both the longitudinal processes of career development as well as the more situation-specific content of career decision making. Career decisions reflect our attempts at translating our self-understanding (i.e., our self-concepts) into career terms (Super, 1984).

Self-concepts contain both objective and subjective elements. Objectively, we develop self-understanding by comparing ourselves with others (e.g., "I am like accountants in that I am good with numbers" or "I am in the 95th percentile on

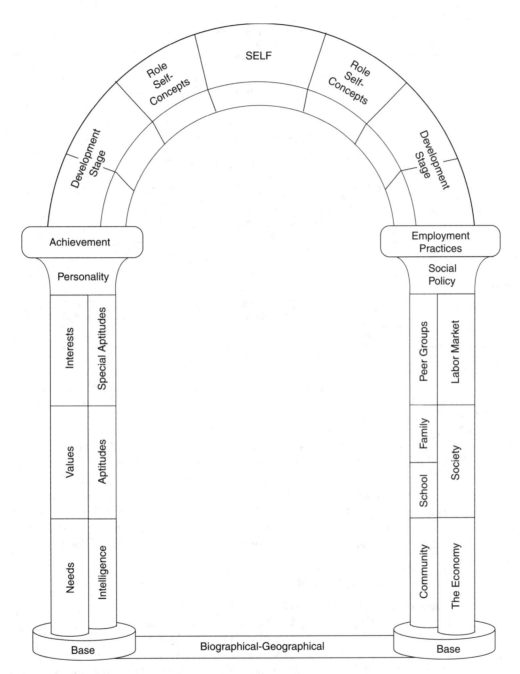

Figure 2.1

The archway of career determinants. From *Career Choice and Development: Applying Contemporary Theories to Practice* (2nd ed.), Duane Brown, Linda Brooks, and Associates. Copyright © 1990, Jossey-Bass Inc. This material is used by permission of Jossey-Bass, Inc., a subsidiary of John Wiley & Sons, Inc.

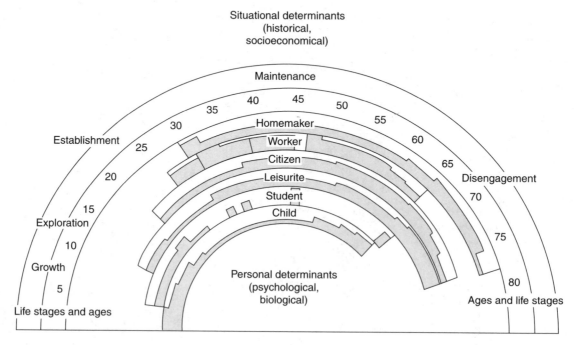

Figure 2.2

The Life-Career Rainbow: Six life roles in schematic life space. From *Career Choice and Development* (2nd ed.), Duane Brown, Linda Brooks, and Associates. Copyright © 1990, Jossey-Bass Inc. This material is used by permission of Jossey-Bass, Inc., a subsidiary of John Wiley & Sons, Inc.

mechanical ability"). Subjectively, we develop understanding through focusing on our uniqueness emerging out of our life stories. Our life stories represent our efforts at constructing meaning from our life experiences. We use our objective and subjective understanding to identify appropriate career goals. Such understanding guides us as we make choices about the degree and the nature of our life-role participation. Because self-concepts continue to develop over time, the need to make choices and the process of adjusting to the choices implemented represent lifelong tasks.

Applying Super's Theory

Toward the end of his career, Super increasingly focused on translating his theory into practice (Super et al., 1992). As noted, Super labeled his approach the Career Development Assessment and Counseling (C-DAC) model. Like other theorists (e.g., Holland, Krumboltz), Super translated his theory into practice, in part, through the systematic application of career assessment instruments emanating from each of his theory segments. Although these assessment instruments are key elements in the C-DAC model, they are not required for addressing the Super's theory segments in career counseling.

The primary emphasis of the C-DAC model (and the traditional focus of career counseling) is on helping clients cope with concerns arising within the exploration stage of the life-span theory segment (Super, 1957; Super et al., 1996). Many people associate exploration only with adolescents who are at the preimplementation stage of career development; however, exploration continues throughout life: "Exploration has come to be expected not only in adults who are changing career direction, but also in adults who are responding to the demands of progressing in the career they have chosen and in which they wish to remain" (Phillips, 1982, p. 130).

Persons encountering the exploration stage for the first time focus on clarifying their values, skills, and interests and connecting these attributes to initial occupational options. However, persons re-cycling through the exploration stage use exploratory behavior to resolve a wide variety of career issues (Niles et al., 1998). For example, some people use exploratory behavior to maintain their current positions while they focus on retirement living. Others use exploration to start over in new occupations, whereas still others use exploratory behavior to become more innovative in their current positions. It is not uncommon for people to experience career concerns across multiple career stages concurrently. It is important to note, therefore, that understanding the full range of a client's career concerns provides important information regarding the career tasks with which the client is attempting to cope. Although exploration always involves learning more about ourselves or our situation, what needs to be learned depends on our developmental status and salient life roles (Super, 1983). Development through the career stages rarely occurs in a linear fashion. Thus, identifying each client's constellation of developmental task concerns is an important first step in constructing appropriate career interventions.

For example, Juanita (presented at the beginning of the chapter) is confronting the career development tasks of crystallizing and specifying occupational preferences for the first time (i.e., she is an "initial career explorer"). To cope effectively with the exploration-stage tasks, Juanita will need to acquire much more self-information (e.g., values, interests, and abilities) and information about the world-of-work. She may also need to learn about the career decision making process (i.e., how good career decisions are made). Then she will need assistance in translating the information she acquires into a career plan. That is, she must be able to make concrete connections between this information and her future career. It is hoped that in the process of developing a career plan, Juanita will also be able to make connections between her school activities and her future, thereby becoming more motivated at school. As Juanita crystallizes her occupational self-concept, she will need to reality test her tentative choices. Activities such as role playing, participating in school clubs, job shadowing, volunteering, and part-time employment will be useful to her in increasing her self-knowledge and occupational information.

To measure concern with life-span career development stages and tasks with adult clients, Super and his colleagues developed the Adult Career Concerns Inventory (ACCI) (Super, Thompson, & Lindeman, 1988). The ACCI measures planfulness or concern for the developmental tasks of the four career stages of exploration, establishment, maintenance, and disengagement posited in life-span, life-space theory (Super et al., 1988). Each career stage includes three tasks, which respondents rate in terms of level of concern using a 5-point Likert-type scale ranging from 1 (*no concern*) to 5 (*great concern*) with the associated task. For example, the exploration stage consists of the tasks of crystallization, specification, and implementation. The tasks for each of the stages are arranged in 5-item substages, resulting in a total of 60 items. Summing each set of three-task substage scores yields a total score for the corresponding career stage.

The ACCI is useful at the onset of career counseling to identify clients' developmental task concerns and for identifying the exploratory resources that may be of most use in helping clients cope effectively with their career concerns. For example, clients concerned with the task of updating can be encouraged to attend meetings and seminars on new methods in their fields, to visit places where they can see new developments in their fields, to conduct information interviews with knowledgeable people, and to take refresher training (items 36 to 40, respectively, on the Updating scale of the ACCI). Counselors can use ACCI scores to identify the client's career development status regarding the constellation of career concerns with which the client is attempting to cope.

Some clients, however, may be unable to make career choices due to the fact that they lack the resources necessary for choosing (e.g., adolescents may be lacking career maturity and adults may be lacking career adaptability). Individuals who are not ready to make good career choices need to (a) develop positive attitudes toward career exploration and planning, (b) learn how to gather information about themselves and occupational options, and (c) learn how to make career decisions.

The Career Development Inventory (CDI) (Thompson, Lindeman, Super, Jordaan, & Myers, 1984) assesses whether high school and college students are ready to make career decisions. Specifically, the CDI assesses career planning, career exploration, world-of-work information, and knowledge of career decision making principles. Scores indicate the client's degree of readiness for career decision making. CDI scores can be used to answer questions such as: Does the respondent know how to make career decisions? Is the respondent aware of the need to make career plans? Does the respondent possess both general information about the world-of-work and specific information about the preferred occupation? Does the respondent know how to make use of exploratory resources for gathering information relevant to the career decision making process?

High scores on the CDI scales indicate affirmative answers to these questions (i.e., that the client has been involved in making career plans, possesses occupational information, has used exploratory resources effectively, and knows how to make decisions). In such instances, clients are often able to proceed with career decision making.

Low scores on CDI scales indicate deficiencies that must be remediated prior to proceeding with career decision making. For example, a low Career Planning score suggests that the client is not aware of the need to make a career choice and is not involved in planning for the future. Low scores related to occupational information indicate the need to become more aware of occupational requirements and tasks. Using the CDI with Juanita will help identify specific areas in which she may need assistance in becoming ready to make career decisions (i.e., in developing career maturity).

The next step in applying the C-DAC model involves determining the priority clients attach to the life roles they play. This step in the C-DAC model distinguishes Super's approach from most other career counseling models because it helps clients understand how they "structure the basic roles of work, play, friendship, and family into a life" (Savickas, 1993, p. 211).

Achieving this understanding involves exploring the importance, or salience, clients attach to their life roles. It also means realizing that the problems clients present in career counseling cannot be precisely categorized as reflecting either "personal" or "career" concerns. Because few issues are more personal than those related to career choice and adjustment, it is not surprising that career and noncareer concerns overlap substantially (Betz & Corning, 1993; Krumboltz, 1993; Subich, 1993; Super, 1993). Research supports this perspective by indicating that clients seeking career counseling often experience high levels of psychological stress and discuss concerns related to non-work roles throughout the duration of the career counseling process (Anderson & Niles, 1995; Lucas, 1993; Niles & Anderson, 1993). Such findings point to the importance of attending to the emotional issues clients encounter as they cope with problems emerging in the context of their unique life structures.

Counselors can encourage clients to examine the personal meaning they attach to the life roles they play by asking questions such as: How do you spend your time during a typical week? How important are the different roles of life to you? What do you like about participating in each of the life roles you play? What life roles do you think will be important to you in the future? What do you hope to accomplish in each of the life roles that will be important to you in the future? What life roles do members of your family play? What do your family members except you to accomplish in each of the life roles? Questions such as these would be important to discuss with Juanita to help her consider what life roles will be important to her in the future and what she can do in the present to begin preparing for those life roles. Asking clients to describe how they spend their time in the course of a typical week and then to consider the values reflected in their weekly activities is also a useful strategy for inviting clients to consider life-structure issues in career counseling. Counselors can also encourage clients to describe how they would like to spend their time at some future point (e.g., 5 years in the future). The counselor can then encourage the client to engage in planning by identifying specific strategies for increasing the probability that the future life-structure scenario will occur. In a similar fashion the counselor and client can use Super's Life-Career Rainbow, Figure 2.2, to fill in the past and present constellation of life roles comprising the client's life structure. The future can then be addressed by inviting the client to create the preferred future life-career rainbow.

Counselors can also use the Salience Inventory (Super & Nevill, 1986) as a starting point for discussing life-role salience. The Salience Inventory measures the relative importance of five life roles (student, worker, citizen, homemaker, and leisurite) on three dimensions, one behavioral and two affective. The behavioral component, Participation, assesses what the individual does or has done recently in each of the life roles. The first affective component, Commitment, requires the inventory-taker to indicate how he or she feels about each of the five life roles. The second affective component, Values Expectations, requires the respondent to indicate the degree to which there will be opportunities now or in the future to express important values in each of the life roles.

Finally, life-role activities can be examined using the "Pie of Life" exercises. In the Pie of Life activity, clients divide a circle into "slices" reflecting the amount of time they spend in various life activities during the course of a typical week. They are then asked to identify the values that they think are reflected in their life pie. After listing the values, the counselor and client then discuss how the client feels about the values exposed in the slices of pie. The counselor focuses on reinforcing the time spent in activities that the client feels good about and explores changes the client can make in pie of life slices that do not reflect the client's value structure. The counselor and client can also discuss what the client would like to accomplish in each of the life roles that are important to the client. They can then focus on what the client needs to do to increase the chances of accomplishing the life-role goals identified.

To further guide the self-concept crystallization process, career counselors can use the Values Scale (VS) (Nevill & Super, 1986). The VS measures 21 intrinsic (e.g., creativity, altruism) and extrinsic (e.g., economic rewards) values individuals hope to express in their life roles. Counselors can use the results of the VS to help clients focus their exploration on life roles and occupational options. Thus, the VS can be a useful supplement to measures of interests and abilities for clients attempting to crystallize work and life goals.

With the information provided by the Salience Inventory and the Values Scale, counselors help clients identify the life roles in which they are currently spending most of their time, those to which they are emotionally committed, the values they hope to express in their life roles, and the life roles they expect to be important to them in the future.

With regard to the latter, counselors can help clients construct strategies for preparing for their salient life roles. For example, if the life role of worker is one that Juanita expects to be salient in her future, she can discuss ways to plan and prepare for that role. She can identify present activities that can help her develop her readiness for the role of worker. Special attention can be given to helping Juanita make connections between her current life role as a student and her future as a worker. Information from the Salience Inventory can also be used to encourage Juanita to think proactively about areas of potential role conflict and discuss strategies for coping with excessive demands from multiple life roles.

Contextual Factors Influencing Life-Role Salience

Super's Archway model suggests that life-role self-concepts are shaped by our contexts (i.e., personal and situational determinants). However, many individuals lack an awareness of the ways in which contextual factors (e.g., the dominant culture, culture of origin) interact with identity development to shape life-role salience (Blustein, 1994).

Dominant Culture.   Often persons simply "inherit" patterns of life-role salience that are passed on from the dominant or popular culture. Such inheritances can be problematic when they are embedded in beliefs based on gender and racial stereotypes. For example, researchers have consistently found gender bias in life-role salience and occupational sex-role stereotyping in portrayals of workers in the popular culture. With regard to the former, Niles and Goodnough (1996) reported in a literature review that researchers have consistently found gender differences in role salience that coincide with traditional sex-role expectations (e.g., women participating more in home and family and expecting more from this life role than men). Women who have high salience for the worker role are placed at an obvious disadvantage in the workforce by such traditional expectations. Also, men limit their opportunities for participating in the home and family when they adhere to traditional expectations for life-role salience. Concerning sex-role stereotyping, Coltrane and Adams (1997) found that women are typically portrayed in popular culture as unemployed or employed in service or clerical occupations, thus perpetuating gender inequality in the workplace. Raising client awareness regarding the influence of the dominant culture on patterns of life-role salience helps clients minimize the influence of racist beliefs and sexist attitudes on their career decision making.

Culture of Origin.   Discussions related to the influence of the dominant culture on life-role salience can also lead to discussions focusing on how clients' cultural backgrounds influence their career development. Counselors and clients can explore how cultures of origin influence the values expressed in life roles (e.g., seeking to express self-actualization in work for the individual from a Eurocentric cultural background or seeking to express cultural identity in work for the individual from an Asian background). When these discussions occur in small groups, they stimulate increased awareness of, and sensitivity to, cultural diversity in life-role salience.

This type of exploration can also lead to exploring the various cultural prescriptions (e.g., Eurocentric men are expected to be "good providers" and upwardly mobile in their occupations) that are generally assigned to specific life roles. In these discussions, counselors can encourage clients to identify how they perceive and interpret the role expectations emanating from their cultures of origin and how these expectations influence their decisions as to whether a particular life role is important. Special attention can be paid to exploring how these expectations influence the client's understanding of the behaviors required for effective role performance (e.g., men who define their parenting role primarily as being a good provider can consider whether this behavior is sufficient for good parenting).

One specific activity for discussing these topics is suggested by Borodovsky and Ponterotto (1994). Borodovsky and Ponterotto have found the family genogram to be a useful tool for exploring the interaction between family background, cultural prescriptions, and career planning. The genogram provides a tool for tracking career decisions across generations and identifying sources of important career beliefs and life themes that people have acquired.

This technique can be expanded to address the same topics for other life roles. That is, by using the genogram, counselors can encourage clients to identify the beliefs and life themes pertaining to specific life roles (e.g., parent, and citizen) that they have acquired from members of their immediate and extended families. Counselors can also use the information provided by clients to contrast the influences on life-role salience emanating from group-oriented cultures with influences from more individualistic cultures. Terms such as "cultural assimilation" and "cultural accommodation" can be introduced in these discussions. The effects of sex-role stereotyping on life-role salience can also be examined in these discussions. The goal of these interventions is to increase client awareness as to the factors influencing their beliefs about the primary roles of life so they can make informed decisions about their future life-role participation.

Although examining life-role participation more holistically is very important, the central concern in career development interventions continues to be helping clients clarify their occupational self-concepts. In the C-DAC model, clients use their understanding of life-role salience as a foundation to build upon as they move forward with clarifying and articulating their vocational identities.

Vocational identities are clarified using two methods: the actuarial method (Super, 1954; 1957) and the developmental method (Super, 1954; 1961). The actuarial method relates to the trait-and-factor approach of using test scores to predict future occupational performance and satisfaction. For instance, Juanita might be given an interest inventory, such as the Strong Interest Inventory (SII) (Harmon, Hansen, Borgen, & Hammer, 1994), to compare her interests with those of people already employed in various occupations. Using the actuarial method, the counselor "acts like an actuary, consults tables, graphs, and formulas seeking the optimal prediction, in probability terms, based on the observed correlations with similar performances of other people" (Jepsen, 1994, p. 45). Juanita's pattern of interests would be related to the patterns of workers within a variety of occupations. The counselor would focus on similar patterns (as starting points for further exploration) and dissimilar patterns (to identify types of occupations Juanita is not likely to find satisfying). Ability tests could be used in the same way. Juanita's abilities can be compared with the abilities required for successful performance in specific occupations. Occupations for which her interests and abilities merge to predict satisfying and successful performance can be identified and focused on for further consideration.

Values inventory results or values card sorts can then be used to guide further exploration. Some occupations might be appropriate for a client's interests and abilities, but they may not provide sufficient opportunities for values expression. For clients like Juanita who are attempting to crystallize occupational preferences, values inventories or values card sorts may be especially helpful supplements to results from measures of interests and abilities (Super et al., 1996).

Using the developmental method (which Super also described as the Thematic-Extrapolation Method), counselors act more like historians (rather than actuaries) by inviting clients to construct autobiographical stories of development. Specifically, clients construct chronologies of what they did in the past. These life histories are then examined for recurrent themes or "threads of continuity" that are used to "make sense of the past, explain the present, and draw a blueprint for the future" (Super et al., 1996, p. 157). Whereas the actuarial method is based on traits (e.g., How do my traits compare with the traits of others? In what occupations do my traits predict success?), the developmental method is based on life patterns (e.g., What patterns are revealed in my life history? Which of these patterns and themes are important to incorporate in my future planning?). Jepsen (1994) has noted that the developmental or thematic-extrapolation method contains three distinct steps:

1. Analyze past behavior and development for recurring themes and underlying trends.
2. Summarize each theme and trend, taking into account the other themes and trends.
3. Project the modified themes and trends into the future by extrapolation. (p. 45)

Encouraging the client to consider his or her life as if it were a book and then asking the client to identify the "chapters of his or her life" is a strategy for identifying recurring life themes and underlying trends. The future can then be described as "chapters that must be lived for the client to feel as if his or her life is complete" and the focus can shift toward identifying future goals and aspirations.

The actuarial and developmental methods can be incorporated into career counseling by using Super's (1957) cyclical model of nondirective and directive methods. Super noted that: "Since vocational development consists of implementing a self-concept, and since self-concepts often need modification before they can be implemented, it is important that the student, client, or patient put his [sic] self-concept into words early in the counseling process. The client needs to do this for himself, to clarify his actual role and his role aspirations; he needs to do it for the counselor, so that the counselor may understand the nature of the vocational problem confronting him" (p. 308). Specifically, Super (1957) described the cycles of career counseling as follows:

1. Nondirective problem exploration and self-concept portrayal (i.e., the client tells his or her story)
2. Directive topic setting, for further exploring (i.e., the counselor and client clarify the career concerns and identify which concerns will be the initial focus of career counseling)
3. Nondirective reflection and clarification of feeling for self-acceptance and insight (i.e., the career counselor uses empathic responding and basic counseling skills to help the client clarify his or her situation, feelings, and thoughts)
4. Directive exploration for factual data from tests, occupational pamphlets, extracurricular experiences, grades, and so forth, for reality testing (i.e., the counselor and client collect relevant information regarding the client's characteristics and potential occupational options; they also identify options for reality testing or "trying out" potential options via job shadowing, occupational information interviewing, volunteering, and externships)
5. Nondirective exploration and working through of attitudes and feelings aroused by reality testing (i.e., the client tries out potential options and then reflects upon the experiences with the counselor, focusing on the client's thoughts and feelings and how the experience may inform the client in terms of next steps)
6. Nondirective consideration of possible actions, for help in decision making (i.e., the client identifies what she or he will do next to move forward in her or his career development). (p. 308)

Essentially, the career counseling model articulated by Super emphasizes helping clients clarify and articulate their self-concepts and then move toward implementing their self-concepts in appropriate life-role activity. Specific career counseling interventions, such as the C-DAC model and the thematic extrapolation method, can be incorporated into Super's cyclical model (most likely at steps 3–6).

Evaluating Super's Theory

Super's theory continues to stimulate career development research. For example, Lewis, Savickas, and Jones (1996) used the Career Development Inventory (Super, Thompson, Lindeman, Jordaan, & Myers, 1981) to predict success in medical school. Their results supported Super's (1981) contention that having a future orientation and being planful are important ingredients for achieving career maturity and career adaptability.

Reviewing literature pertaining to Super's Work Importance Study led Niles and Goodnough (1996) to three conclusions. First, life-role salience and values must be viewed within specific developmental and cultural contexts. Second, in diverse settings, and with different groups, there are sex differences related to the relative importance of life roles and values. And, third, in order to facilitate their clients' career development, counselors must attend to life-role salience and values issues in career counseling (see also Parasuraman, Purhoit, Godshalk, & Beutell, 1996).

Salomone (1996) provided a historical perspective by tracing the evolution of three key segments of Super's theory over a 40-year period: (a) theoretical propositions, (b) conceptualization of the career stages, and (c) definition of career. Salomone's review led him to several conclusions. First, Super's theoretical propositions have not changed substantially in 40 years. Second, there is the need for more research related to Super's propositions and career stage model. Finally, Salomone noted that Super's contributions represent an unparalleled legacy in developmental career theory. Additionally, Super's theory segments provide a useful framework for helping clients clarify their life-role identities and the values they seek to express in their life roles. Moreover, Super's theory provides a useful framework for researchers investigating the process of life-role identity development.

A number of journal articles provide examples of the systematic application of the C-DAC assessment instrument. For example, articles by Nevill and Kruse (1996) (Values Scale), Nevill and Calvert (1996) (Salience Inventory), Savickas and Hartung (1996) (Career Development Inventory), and Cairo, Kritis, and Myers (1996) (Adult Career Concerns Inventory) provide useful literature reviews, test descriptions, and information concerning the practical application of each assessment in career counseling practice. Hartung et al. (1998) describe strategies for appraising the client's cultural identity in the initial stages of the C-DAC model and offer techniques for considering cultural factors throughout the C-DAC process, thereby making the model more applicable to clients representing diverse contexts.

Commenting on Super's theory and the research it has generated, Osipow and Fitzgerald (1996) noted that Super's theory "has the virtue of building upon aspects of the mainstream of developmental psychology and personality theory and has considerable utility for practice and research" (p. 143). They also noted that "most of the research reported on Super's theory generally supports his model" (p. 143). Borgen (1991) noted that Super's theory "has splendidly stood the test of time" (p. 278). Brown (1996) pointed out that Super's theory "will forever be the segmental legacy of a brilliant thinker" (p. 522). The development of the C-DAC model should provide stronger links between Super's theory and career development intervention research.

LINDA GOTTFREDSON'S THEORY OF CIRCUMSCRIPTION, COMPROMISE, AND SELF-CREATION

One theory that describes the process leading to the formulation of occupational aspirations in childhood and adolescence is Gottfredson's theory of circumscription, compromise, and self-creation (Gottfredson, 2002). Gottfredson developed her theory, in part, to address the following question: "Why do children seem to re-create the social inequalities of their elders long before they themselves experience any barriers to pursuing their dreams?" (Gottfredson, 2002, p. 85). Gottfredson addresses the compromises that people make in their career aspirations, particularly as these compromises relate to sex-typed learning and experiences. Specifically, compromise involves the process of modifying career choices due to limiting factors, such as prestige, sex type, and field of interest (Gottfredson, 1981). Gottfredson's theory emphasizes the view that "career choice is an attempt to place oneself in the broader social order" (1996, p. 181). Thus, Gottfredson offers a developmental and sociological perspective of career development.

Gottfredson (2002) notes that people distinguish occupations according to the dimensions of: "masculinity-femininity, occupational prestige, and field of work" (p. 88). Gottfredson further suggests that occupational prestige is positively correlated with the degree of intellectual capacity required for job performance. The person's self-concept interacts with the person's occupational stereotypes when making decisions about the perceived compatibility of different occupations. Compatibility, or the suitability of any occupation, is determined when the individual considers factors such as the perceived gender appropriateness (most important), prestige (second in importance), and, finally, the degree to which the occupation will fulfill the person's preferences and personality needs (last in importance within the compromise process). The "zone of acceptable occupational alternatives" or "social space" (2002, p. 91) represents the person's conclusions as to his or her fit in society. Gottfredson contends that people compromise in their search process because they typically search for an occupational choice that is "good enough," but not necessarily the best possible choice. This is because the best possible choice requires substantially more intensive information gathering related to factors such as values clarification and determining the accessibility of various occupational alternatives than what is required for a choice that is "good enough." People become indecisive when they perceive the options within their social space as undesirable. Occupational satisfaction hinges on the degree to which "the compromise allows one to implement a desired social self, either through the work itself or the lifestyle it allows self and family" (2002, p. 107).

[Circumscription involves the process of eliminating unacceptable occupational alternatives based primarily on gender and prestige.]Circumscription highlights the fact that young people begin eliminating occupational options from consideration "as soon as they are able to perceive essential distinctions among people and lives" (Gottfredson, 2002, p. 131). The circumscription process is guided by five principles (2002, pp. 94–95). The first principle notes that circumscription is guided by the growing capacity of children to understand and organize complex information about themselves and the world. Children move from magical to abstract thinking as they develop. The second principle reflects the belief that because occupational aspirations are inextricably linked with one's sense of self, occupational preferences reflect attempts to both implement and enhance one's self-concept. The third principle underlying the circumscription process is that children begin to grapple with more complex distinctions among people (e.g., perceptions related to prestige) while they are still in the process of integrating more concrete phenomena (e.g., sex roles) into their self-conceptions. The fourth circumscription principle emphasizes the belief that children progressively eliminate occupational options as their self-conceptions increase in complexity and clarity. At the same time, Gottfredson notes that "people reconsider options they have ruled out as unacceptable in sextype and prestige only when they are prompted to do so by some formative new experience or some notable change in their social environment" (2002, p. 95). Finally, the circumscription process is gradual and typically not immediately obvious despite its strong effect on the individual. These principles operate throughout the stages of cognitive development Gottfredson (1996) delineated to describe the circumscription process.

Stage One: Orientation to Size and Power

The first stage occurs between the ages of 3 and 5 and reflects the onset of object constancy in cognitive development. At this stage, children classify people in simple terms, such as big versus little. Thus, children orient themselves to the size difference between themselves and adults.

Stage Two: Orientation to Sex Roles

This stage occurs between the ages of 6 and 8. During this stage, children become aware of different sex roles between men and women. They think dichotomously (e.g., good-bad, rich-poor) and interpret sex role stereotypes as behavioral imperatives. Their occupational aspirations also reflect this concern for behaving in ways that are appropriate for one's sex (e.g., certain jobs are for boys and certain jobs are for girls). Thus, it is during this stage that children develop their "tolerable-sextype boundary" (Gottfredson, 1996).

Stage Three: Orientation to Social Valuation

During this stage, which occurs between the ages of 9 and 13, children become aware of social class and prestige. Occupations that are not in line with their perceived ability levels and that do not meet with the approval of their social reference group are no longer considered. The elements of social class and ability determine the "tolerable-level boundary," which represents the lower limit of occupations children in this stage are willing to consider (i.e., which occupations are "beneath" them and, therefore, not worthy of their consideration). Children also establish a "tolerable-effort level" based on the upper limit of effort children are willing to exert and the risks children are willing to take in pursuing occupational options (i.e., those occupational goals that are not beyond their ability to achieve). Together, these levels determine the zone of occupations children consider as acceptable (Gottfredson, 1996).

Stage Four: Orientation to the Internal, Unique Self

This stage occurs from age 14 to beyond. During this stage, adolescents become more introspective and self-aware. Now able to engage in more abstract thinking than in previous stages, adolescents begin identifying internally generated goals and self-concepts.

Adolescents engage in exploring occupational options that are congruent with their emerging sense of self. Thus, this stage represents a shift from the previous stages in that the emphasis turns from eliminating unacceptable options to identifying options that are most preferred and acceptable. It is also during this stage that the process of compromise is introduced. Specifically, compromise occurs as preferred occupational options are eliminated from further consideration due to factors such as the perceived accessibility of any occupational option. Compromise can be anticipatory (i.e., prior to actual encounters with external barriers) or experiential (i.e., after encountering an external barrier to a preferred option).

Applying Gottfredson's Theory to Practice

Gottfredson (1996) noted that, traditionally, career development interventions occur during stage four when people are attempting to crystallize and clarify their self-concepts. However, Gottfredson's theory highlights the importance of providing career development interventions, often in the form of career education programs, to young people in earlier stages of development. Accordingly, career education programs should focus on exploring the full range of occupational options to promote systematic exploration in career choice (Gottfredson, 1996). Clearly, interventions that address occupational sex-role stereotypes and that expose children to options across occupational levels should be cornerstones of such programs. Specifically, Gottfredson (1996) identified four principles to guide the design of career education programs:

1. Programs should be sensitive to the mental capabilities of the age group. Younger students will not be able to handle abstractions about self and occupations that older ones will.
2. Programs should introduce students to the full breadth of options but in a manageable way.
3. Programs should display for youngsters their circumscription of alternatives so that its rationale can be explored.
4. Programs should be sensitive to the dimensions of self and occupations along which circumscription and compromise take place (sex type, social class, ability, vocational interests) so that their role, positive or not, can be explored where appropriate. (p. 221)

From Gottfredson's perspective, a major concern to address in individual career counseling is the degree to which clients have engaged in the unnecessary restriction of occupational options. "The problem in compromise is the failure to come to grips with reality, either by ignoring it or failing to deal with it effectively" (Gottfredson, 1996, p. 217). Gottfredson identified the following five criteria to guide counselors attempting to clarify the degree to which their clients may have engaged in the unnecessary restriction of options[2]:

1. The counselee is able to name one or more occupational options.
2. The counselee's interests and abilities are adequate for the occupation(s) chosen.

---

[2]From *Career Choice and Development* (3rd ed.), by Duane Brown, Linda Brooks, and Associates. Copyright © 1996, Jossey-Bass Inc. This material is used by permission of Jossey-Bass, Inc., a subsidiary of John Wiley & Sons, Inc.

3. The counselee is satisfied with the alternatives he or she has identified.
4. The counselee has not unnecessarily restricted his or her alternatives.
5. The counselee is aware of opportunities and realistic about obstacles for implementing the chosen occupation. (p. 218)

In examining these criteria with clients, career counselors can explore their clients' tolerable level and effort boundaries, perceptions of barriers, and the contextual factors influencing clients' perceptions of acceptable career options. For example, in Juanita's case it is important that the counselor explore with her what occupational options she has considered thus far (in addition to being in a band). It would also be important to build upon Juanita's strengths and interests. Understanding her interests in artistic endeavors might be a good starting point. In discussing these interests, the counselor can assess whether Juanita has unnecessarily restricted her options. Her counselor can also address questions such as: Is her ability sufficient for a performance career? Is Juanita aware of the obstacles likely to be encountered in pursuing this option? Has Juanita considered additional opportunities for expressing her values, interests, and abilities? What has caused her to eliminate other occupational options from further consideration? The counselor can support and challenge Juanita as she becomes increasingly aware of her emerging sense of self and attempts to identify congruent options.

Evaluating Gottfredson's Theory

Research related to Gottfredson's theory has not been extensive. Moreover, research activity related to the theory seems to be in decline and existing research results have been equivocal. Much of the research has focused on circumscription related to social class, gender, and intelligence. For example, using a sample of Canadian 12th-grade students, Hannah and Kahn (1989) found that students from higher social classes held higher aspirations than students from lower social classes. Helwig (2001) conducted two studies testing the applicability of Gottfredson's theory to the career development of children. This longitudinal research followed students from 2nd to 12th grades. In the first study, Helwig examined the occupational aspirations of children and found support for Gottfredson's theory of circumscription and compromise. Support for Gottfredson's theory was found in the second study as well; Helwig reported that students abandoned fantasy occupational ideals in favour of more realistic occupational aspirations toward the end of their high school education. Other researchers applaud Gottfredson's theoretical emphasis on career development in childhood and gender differences, nothing that the theory fills an important gap in the career literature (McLennan & Arthur, 1999).

Empirical results from a study focusing on New Zealand students between the ages of 5 and 14 and conducted by Henderson, Hesketh, and Tuffin (1988) did not support the importance of gender in Gottfredson's stage two (Orientation to Sex Roles). Their findings were supportive of the importance of social class in stage three (Orientation to Social Valuation). A study conducted by Hesketh, Elmslie, and Kaldor (1990) suggested an alternative model of compromise in which interests were more important in career choices than either sex type or prestige, because interests incorporate the latter. Leung and Plake (1990) found that women, more often than men, opted for cross-sex work rather than same-sex work if the former provided them with higher prestige. Blanchard and Lichtenberg (2003) studied Gottfredson's compromise process and found that study participants who were engaged in a moderate or high degree of compromise placed an equal amount of importance on prestige and sex-type, thus differing from what the theory purports. The same study participants did, however, place a greater importance on prestige and sex-type than they did on interests as they considered factors influencing the compromise process.

In evaluating Gottfredson's theory, Brown (1996) noted "the propositions relating to the factors that lead to circumscription and compromise are too general. The result is that we are left with questions about what actually occurs in the career choice and selection process" (p. 523). Nonetheless, Gottfredson's theory provides many interesting concepts describing boundaries and motivational dimensions related to the formation of occupational aspirations (Herr et al., 2004). Her theory also addresses important gaps within the career-related literature (i.e., career development in childhood and gender differences). Research studies testing Gottfredson's theory using a longitudinal and cross-sectional design would be particularly useful.

JOHN HOLLAND'S THEORY OF TYPES AND PERSON-ENVIRONMENT INTERACTIONS

Holland's (1966, 1973, 1985, 1997) theory belongs to a long tradition of theoretical perspectives seeking to describe individual differences in personality types (e.g., Murray, 1938; Spranger, 1928). Holland's theory has been described as structural-interactive "because it provides an explicit link between various personality characteristics and corresponding job titles and because it organizes the massive data about people and jobs" (Weinrach, 1984, p. 63). The theory is based on four basic assumptions:

1. In our culture, most persons can be categorized as one of six types: realistic, investigative, artistic, social, enterprising, or conventional.
2. There are six kinds of environments: realistic, investigative, artistic, social, enterprising, and conventional.
3. People search for environments that will let them exercise their skills and abilities, express their attitudes and values, and take on agreeable problems and roles.
4. A person's behavior is determined by an interaction between personality and the characteristics of the environment. (Holland, 1973, pp. 2–4)

From these assumptions it is clear that a key to understanding and using Holland's theory is in understanding his typology. A good starting point for this is to consider how personality types develop. To a large degree, "types produces types" (Holland, 1973, p. 11). That is, personality types are both genetically and environmentally based:

A child's special heredity and experience first lead to preferences for some kinds of activities and aversions to others. Later, these preferences become well-defined interests from which the person gains self-satisfaction as well as reward from others. Still later, the pursuit of these interests leads to the development of more specialized competencies as well as to the neglect of other potential competencies. At the same time, a person's differentiation of interests with age is accompanied by a crystallization of correlated values. These events—an increasing differentiation of preferred activities, interests, competencies, and values—create a characteristic disposition or personality type that is predisposed to exhibit characteristic behavior and to develop characteristic personality traits. (Holland, 1973, p. 12)

Holland contends that, to a large degree, career interests are an expression of the individual's personality (Holland, 1959, 1966, 1973, 1985, 1992). As Spokane (1996) elaborated, "Interests, however, are complex measures that reflect personality as well as preferences, values, self-efficacy and so on. Types, then, are complex theoretical groupings based upon personality and interests" (p. 40). Personality traits are identified by preferences for leisure activities, school subjects, avocational interests, and work. To varying degrees, each individual resembles one of six basic personality types. The more one resembles any particular personality type, the more likely it is that the person will manifest the behaviors and traits associated with that type (Weinrach, 1984). Following is a discussion of each of the six personality types defined by Holland (1973, pp. 14–18; 1994, pp. 2–3).

The Realistic Type

The realistic personality type prefers activities that entail the explicit, ordered, or systematic manipulation of objects, tools, machines, and animals and has an aversion to educational or therapeutic activities. The realistic person has mechanical abilities but may lack social skills. Realistic types prefer jobs such as automobile mechanic, aircraft controller, surveyor, farmer, or electrician. Realistic types are often described as:

conforming, humble, normal, frank, materialistic,

persistent, genuine, modest, practical, hardheaded, natural,

shy, honest, and thrifty

The Investigative Type

The investigative personality type prefers activities that entail the observational, symbolic, systematic, and creative investigation of physical, biological, and cultural phenomena in order to understand and control such phenomena. Investigative types have an aversion to persuasive, social, and repetitive activities. These tendencies lead to an acquisition of scientific and mathematical competencies and to a deficit in leadership ability. Investigative types prefer jobs such as biologist, chemist, physicist, anthropologist, geologist, or medical technologist. Investigative persons are often described as:

analytical, independent, modest, cautious, intellectual,

pessimistic, complex, introverted, precise, critical,

methodical, rational, curious, and reserved

The Artistic Type

The artistic personality type prefers ambiguous, free, unsystematized activities that entail the manipulation of physical, verbal, or human materials to create art forms or products. Artistic persons have an aversion to explicit systematic and ordered activities. These tendencies lead to an acquisition of artistic competencies in language, art, music, drama, and writing and to a deficit in clerical- or business-system competencies. Artistic types like jobs such as composer, musician, stage director, writer, interior decorator, or actor/actress. Artistic persons are often described as:

> complicated, imaginative, introspective, disorderly,
>
> impractical, intuitive, emotional, impulsive, nonconforming,
>
> expressive, independent, open, idealistic, original

The Social Type

The social personality type prefers activities that entail the manipulation of others to inform, train, develop, cure, or enlighten. They have an aversion to explicit, ordered, and systematic activities involving materials, tools, or machines. These tendencies lead to an acquisition of human relations competencies such as interpersonal and educational competencies and to a deficit in mechanical and scientific ability. Social types like jobs such as teacher, religious worker, counselor, clinical psychologist, psychiatric case worker, or speech therapist. Social persons are often described as:

> convincing, idealistic, social, cooperative, kind,
>
> sympathetic, friendly, patient, tactful, generous,
>
> responsible, understanding, helpful, and warm

The Enterprising Type

The enterprising personality type prefers activities that entail the manipulation of others to attain organizational or economic gain. They have an aversion to observational, symbolic, and systematic activities. These tendencies lead to an acquisition of leadership, interpersonal, and persuasive competencies and to a deficit in scientific ability. Enterprising types like jobs such as salesperson, manager, business executive, television producer, sports promoter, or buyer. Enterprising persons are often described as:

> acquisitive, domineering, optimistic, adventurous,
>
> energetic, pleasure-seeking, agreeable, extroverted,
>
> attention-getting, ambitious, impulsive, self-confident,
>
> sociable, and popular

The Conventional Type

The conventional personality type prefers activities that entail the explicit, ordered, and systematic manipulation of data, such as keeping records, filing materials, reproducing materials, organizing written and numerical data according to a prescribed plan, and operating computers to attain organizational or economic goals. Conventional types have an aversion to ambiguous, free, exploratory, or unsystematized activities. These tendencies lead to an acquisition of clerical, computational, and business system competencies and to a deficit in artistic competencies. Conventional types like jobs such as bookkeeper, stenographer, financial analyst, banker, cost estimator, or tax expert. Conventional persons are often described as:

conforming, inhibited, persistent, conscientious, obedient,

practical, careful, orderly, thrifty, efficient, and

unimaginative

Holland (1973) used the same six types to describe occupational environments (pp. 29–33). For example, the realistic environment requires the explicit, ordered, or systematic manipulation of objects, tools, machines, and animals. It encourages people to view themselves as having mechanical ability. It rewards people for displaying conventional values and encourages them to see the world in simple, tangible, and traditional terms.

The investigative environment requires the symbolic, systematic, and creative investigation of physical, biological, or cultural phenomena. It encourages scientific competencies and achievements and seeing the world in complex and unconventional ways. It rewards people for displaying scientific values. The artistic environment requires participation in ambiguous, free, and unsystematized activities to create art forms or products. It encourages people to view themselves as having artistic abilities and to see themselves as expressive, nonconforming, independent, and intuitive. It rewards people for the display of artistic values.

The social environment requires participation in activities that inform, train, develop, cure or enlighten others. It requires people to see themselves as liking to help others, as being understanding of others, and as seeing the world in flexible ways. It rewards people for the display of social values.

The enterprising environment requires participation in activities that involve the manipulation of others to attain organizational and self-interest goals. It requires people to view themselves as aggressive, popular, self-confident, sociable, and as possessing leadership and speaking ability. It encourages people to view the world in terms of power and status and in stereotyped and simple terms. It rewards people for displaying enterprising goals and values.

The conventional environment requires participation in activities that involve the explicit, ordered, or systematic manipulation of data, such as record keeping, filing materials, and organizing written and numerical data according to a prescribed plan. It requires people to view themselves as conforming, orderly, nonartistic, and as having clerical competencies. It rewards people for viewing the world in stereotyped and conventional ways.

Congruence

The key construct in Holland's theory is that of congruence. Congruence describes the degree of fit between an individual's personality type and current or prospective work

You e ENVIRON

environment. A person is in a congruent work environment when the person's personality type matches the occupational environment (e.g., a social type working as a counselor). Conversely, incongruence occurs when individuals are in environments that do not match their personality type (e.g., a social type working as an auto mechanic). Individuals tend to be more satisfied and perform better in environments that match (or are congruent with) their personality types. Thus, congruence is based on the assumption that "birds of a feather flock together" and that "different types require different environments" (Holland, 1973, p. 4). Also, "environments are characterized by the people who occupy them" (Weinrach, 1984, pp. 63–64). To distinguish "congruence" from Holland's other constructs, students often find it helpful to view the "u" and "e" in "congruence" as representing the fact that congruence refers to the relationship between "you" and the "environment."

Holland uses a hexagonal model to represent the relationships within and between types (Figure 2.3). Concerning the latter, the highest level of congruence exists when there is a direct correspondence between workers' personality types and their work environments (e.g., an investigative personality types in an investigative work environment). The next highest level of congruence exists when individuals are in work environments that are adjacent to their type on the hexagon (e.g., a realistic personality type in an investigative work environment). The lowest level of congruence exists when individuals are in work environments that are opposite to their personality type on the hexagonal model (e.g., a social type in a realistic work environment). The primary goal of career counseling is helping clients identify and connect with congruent work environments.

Differentiation

To describe people and their work environments, Holland focuses on the three types the person or environment most closely resembles. However, some people and environments are more clearly defined, or differentiated, than others. For example, a person may more predominantly resemble one Holland type and have little resemblance to other types, or a single type may dominate an environment. Other persons or environments may resemble multiple types equally and, therefore, be relatively undifferentiated or poorly defined. Holland referred to the degree of crystallization of among types as "differentiation." Because people who are undifferentiated can have difficulty making career decisions, career interventions are often directed toward helping clients achieve greater differentiation among Holland types.

Consistency

The degree of relatedness within types is referred to as *consistency*. The hexagonal model is useful in illustrating the similarities across types. For example, types located next to each other on the hexagon (e.g., realistic and investigative) have more in common than types that are farther apart (e.g., realistic and social). Higher degrees of consistency within personality types suggest more integration regarding traits, interests, values, and perceptions than lower degrees of consistency. Holland assumes

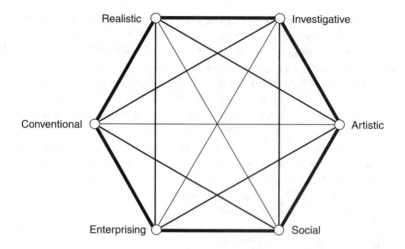

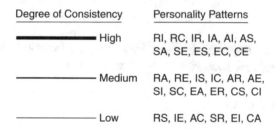

Figure 2.3

The relationships among Holland types. Adapted from *Holland's Hexagon, ACT Research Report No. 29*, by J. L. Holland, D. R. Whitney, N. S. Cole, and J. M. Richards, Jr., 1969, Iowa City: The American College Testing Program. Copyright © 1969 The American College Testing Program. Reprinted by permission.

that consistent persons are more predictable in their behavior and more likely to be higher achievers in their careers than persons who are not consistent. It is important to note, however, that it is not a goal of career counseling to make clients more consistent. Rather, the primary use of consistency in career counseling relates to client awareness. Specifically, it is important for clients with low consistency (e.g., a realistic-social personality type) to be aware of the fact that it may be difficult for them to find an occupational environment that will allow them to express the diverse aspects of their personality. In such cases it is often necessary for clients to identify avocational activities that provide opportunities for expressing personality types that are not expressed in work. For example, a realistic-social personality type working as a social worker may choose to spend her leisure time in woodworking activities.

Vocational Identity

Vocational identity is defined as the "possession of a clear and stable picture of one's goals, interests, and talent" (Holland, 1985, p. 5). Vocational identity is an important goal of many career development interventions and is dependent upon acquiring sufficient occupational and self-information.

Applying Holland's Theory

Congruence, differentiation, consistency, and vocational identity are the key theoretical constructs used to link Holland's theory to practice. "All things being equal, an individual with high identity who is congruent, consistent, and differentiated should be more predictable and better adjusted than one who is incongruent, inconsistent, and undifferentiated" (Spokane et al., 2002, p. 385). Assessment instruments developed by Holland and his associates are typically used to measure these constructs and the results from these measures provide the stimuli for career counseling content.

For example, the Self-Directed Search (SDS) (Holland, 1994) and the Vocational Preference Inventory (VPI) (Holland, 1985) are used to translate individuals' self-estimates of interests and competencies into Holland types. The SDS consists of an assessment booklet (used to identify the individual's Holland type), an Occupations Finder (two versions are available, each contain a listing of 1334 occupations classified according to either three-letter Holland codes or presented in alphabetical order), and an interpretive guide entitled *You and Your Career*. The latter provides individuals with additional information, activities, and readings related to using Holland's theory in career decision making. The SDS, which is the most widely used interest inventory, is available in different versions based on reading level (SDS Form E), setting (SDS CP, Corporate Version), and language spoken.

The SDS provides a useful starting point and straightforward approach for focusing Juanita's career exploration and information gathering. First, Juanita can use the assessment booklet to identify her three-letter summary code. (Because researchers have found a high error rate in summary code calculations [e.g., Miller, 1997], it is important that counselors take precautions to minimize such errors.) Then Juanita and the career counselor can review her summary code ("ASI" with low differentiation) to explore how her abilities and interests relate to the characteristics of the types her summary code comprises.

It is especially important to discuss with the client his or her summary code when the code lacks consistency. A client with a code of RSA, for example, may have difficulty finding occupations that resemble this code exactly (few jobs require workers to have strong mechanical abilities and strong social skills). Clients who do not understand this fact can experience a sort of "pendulum shifting" in their career choices. That is, a person may opt for a realistic, or R, occupation and find that, for a time, it is satisfactory in that it offers the opportunity for engaging in R tasks and rewards R competencies. Over time, however, the person may begin noticing the absence of social, or S, opportunities in his or her R work. The absence of S opportunities may lead to a growing sense that the R occupation needs to be replaced with one that in the S environment. If this occupational change occurs, it may provide satisfaction initially, but, over time, the person may experience that the occupation is too S and not enough R and the pendulum may shift back toward desiring an R occupation.

Helping the client who is low in consistency to become aware of the possible "pendulum shifting" that can occur in occupational decision making is important because if a congruent occupational environment is not possible, appropriate avocational activities may provide the solution (rather than an ongoing shifting from occupations in one Holland environment to another). In these instances, counselors may use the Leisure Activities Finder (Holmberg, Rosen, & Holland, 1990) to help clients identify opportunities to express important dimensions of their personalities that they may not be able to express in work. For example, the person with an RSA code may choose to emphasize working with things (R) at work (perhaps as a cook), but spend leisure time in activities emphasizing the social (S) theme (e.g., as youth group leader for a church). As noted, it is important for career counselors to understand that consistency is not a goal of career counseling. Rather, consistency is a construct that helps clients understand who they are and then use this understanding to make effective career decisions.

Clients with codes that lack differentiation (determined by comparing either the client's highest score minus the lowest score among the six types or by examining the numerical difference among the client's three-letter code) often experience a lack of focus in their career direction for a number of reasons. Persons may lack differentiation because: (a) they lack exposure to activities across Holland environments, (b) they have difficulty in decision making, (c) they have multipotentiality, or (d) they are depressed.

Clients lacking in exposure to Holland environments (e.g., young people with little or no work experience, homemakers returning to the labor market after an extended departure) may need help increasing their self-understanding related to interests, abilities, and values. In such instances, counselors may use activities such as values inventories, values card sorts, or skills checklists to foster client understanding of these career decision making variables. Those persons returning to the labor market after an extended departure may find it particularly useful to engage in an "accomplishments exercise" in which the counselor invites the client to list activities, or accomplishments, about which the client feels especially proud. As the client describes the activity, the counselor encourages the client to list the skills embedded in the successful performance of the activity. After engaging in this discussion for several activities, the counselor and client will have generated a long list of skills the client demonstrated in the successful completion of each activity he or she described. These skills can then be categorized according to Holland type and the counselor and client can review which skills they enjoy using most to identify the Holland type that reflects the client's dominant type. Undifferentiated clients with limited work experiences may also need to take steps such as information interviewing, volunteering, and job shadowing to increase their self-understanding and become more differentiated.

Clients with decision making difficulties can be taught decision making skills and then encouraged to retake the SDS and/or to discuss their perceptions as to which Holland types they most closely resemble. As an alternative to retaking the SDS in these instances, the client can engage in a Holland card sort activity in which the client sorts through activities according to the degree to which they like, dislike, or feel neutral toward each activity. Each group of cards can then be reviewed in light of the Holland types they reflect. During this activity, the counselor can observe how difficult it is for the client to make decisions. After having been taught decision making skills and after engaging in self-assessment activities and reviewing occupational information, some clients may remain undecided. Indecisive clients may have concerns that result in a "fear of deciding." Clients may be fearful of making choices for a variety of factors. For example, a client may have excessive fears related to failing, succeeding, or disappointing significant others. In these instances, the counselor and client will need to engage in a counseling or therapy-like process to help the client understand his or her fears.

COULD BE POSSIBLY MORE THAN ONE

Scores on the SDS that are elevated and undifferentiated may also reflect the fact that, rather than being indecisive or lacking experience, the client is multipotentialed in interests and competencies. This is, in fact, the case for Holland himself, who has elevated and undifferentiated scores across almost all Holland types (Weinrach, 1996)! For clients with elevated and undifferentiated SDS scores, the counselor may find it useful to focus on the client's values as a guide for making occupational decisions. Finally, counselors also need to determine whether clients with low scores for all Holland types are having difficulty with depression or low self-esteem. Given Juanita's difficulties in school and her young age, all of the aforementioned possibilities should be explored in relationship to the low differentiation in her summary code.

With a general understanding of the Holland typology and a specific understanding of their own Holland summary codes, clients are ready to examine the Occupations Finder to locate occupations that resemble their summary codes. Each client focuses on occupations resembling all combinations of his or her summary code (e.g., Juanita would explore occupations in the categories of ASI, SIA, AIS, SAI, IAS, and ISA). Clients then identify specific occupations within these categories that are of interest to them.

Next, counselors encourage clients to take some sort of action (e.g., information interviewing, reading about occupational requirements, job shadowing) to increase their understanding of occupations of interest. Clients can then discuss with their counselors the information they acquire from these activities and narrow their list of occupational options. In these discussions, counselors encourage clients to take additional steps (e.g., volunteering, taking courses related to a particular occupation, job searching) toward implementing tentative occupational choices. In discussing the information the client obtains, the counselor and client also review how each specific option provides opportunities for expressing the types comprising the client's summary code. The overarching goals in this process are to clarify the client's vocational identity and help the client make a congruent career decision.

In addition to the SDS, counselors can use the VPI in helping clients identify their Holland type and connect their summary codes to congruent occupational environments. The VPI (1985) contains 160 occupational titles, the six type scales, and five supplemental scales (self-control, masculinity, status, infrequency, and acquiescence). To assess vocational identity, counselors can use the instrument entitled *My Vocational Situation* (MVS) (Holland, Gottfredson, & Power, 1980). Specifically, the MVS measures vocational identity and perceived career development barriers.

The Vocational Identity scale measures awareness of and the ability to specify one's interests, personality characteristics, strengths, and goals as they relate to career choices. The Occupational Information (OI) scale of the MVS measures the respondent's need for occupational information.

Gottfredson and Holland (1996) have also created an inventory (the Position Classification Inventory; PCI) for classifying specific work environments using the Holland typology. Prior to the PCI, which uses the workers' judgments to classify the work environment, researchers and counselors relied on conducting an actual census of workers to classify a specific work environment according to the Holland types. Because variability exists across same-type occupations in different work environments, the PCI may be particularly useful in helping clients understand their degree of congruence in a specific job. Miller and Bass (2003) have found the PCI to be useful in classifying work environments in a paper manufacturing plant. Other inventories also use the Holland typology in reporting assessment results. For example, the Strong Interest Inventory (SII) (Harmon et al., 1994), the Career Assessment Inventory (CAI) (Johannson, 1986), and the Armed Services Vocational Aptitude Battery (ASVAB) (U.S. Department of Defense, 1993) each use Holland's types in reporting assessment results.

Evaluating Holland's Theory

Research emanating from Holland's theory is extensive. Gottfredson and Richards (1999) note that a major advantage of Holland's theory is that it provides a parallel way of describing people and environments. In 1996, Holland summarized research findings supporting the use of his typology to explain career certainty, career change, and career satisfaction. From Holland's review it is evident that his theory continues to stimulate much research activity. Generally this activity focuses on (a) the relations between congruence and important career outcomes, (b) methods for calculating constructs such as congruence, and (c) the application of Holland's theory to diverse populations.

Spokane et al. (2002) summarized the congruence-related research, noting that although research results are somewhat mixed, there is a "modest relationship between person-environment fit and job satisfaction" (p. 400). Spokane, Fouad, and Swanson (2001) argued that most of the congruence-related research, especially in the early years, was correlational in nature and, therefore, does not reflect the complexity inherent in person-environment interactions. Longitudinal, cross-sectional, and experimental studies are needed to more accurately represent person-environment interactions and to understand the validity of the congruence construct.

Though there are data to support the importance of congruence in vocational satisfaction, research support for the relationship between consistency and differentiation to vocational outcomes has been weak. Perhaps to an even greater degree than what is true for the congruence research, research methodologies employed in these studies have not been sufficiently sophisticated to examine the complex processes related to consistency, differentiation, and relevant occupational outcomes (e.g., satisfaction, stability).

IT IS VALID?

FOUND HOLLANDS ASSUMPTIONS TO BE TRUE ABOUT JOB CHANGE

Nonetheless, some interesting studies provide intriguing data related to the validity of Holland's theory. For example, Miller (2002) investigated the degree of change in a male client's three-letter Holland code over a 10-year time span. The client initially took the SDS when he was 16 years old. The client's Holland code remained stable across the 10-year period, thus supporting Holland's contention that personality types measured by the SDS remain stable over time.

Oleski and Subich (1996) provided an example of the first type of research in their investigation of adults in the process of changing careers. Studying 42 nontraditional students (mean age 34.4) pursuing a career change, Oleski and Subich found support for Holland's (1985) basic assumption that people change careers to achieve greater congruence.

Lent and Lopez (1996) investigated the relationship between congruence indices and job satisfaction among adult workers. Although they found partial overlap among methods for calculating congruence in their study, Lent and Lopez noted the need for more research to understand the relations among indices of congruence, methods for coding work environments, and the antecedents to congruence.

Of course, achieving congruence is, in part, dependent upon the availability of occupations allowing for the expression of one's personality. Downes and Kroeck (1996) hypothesized that there is an overall discrepancy between normative occupational interests and the number of existing positions in the United States. Using normative interest data from the Self-Directed Search and data extracted from the *Monthly Labor Review*, Downes and Kroeck found support for their hypothesis. Specifically, they found a lack of interest for Conventional and Enterprising jobs relative to the number of existing positions. They found the opposite with regard to the remaining Holland categories. For instance, there was excess interest among high school students for Social, Artistic, and Investigative jobs relative to the number of existing positions. Investigative and Realistic jobs represented high-interest areas for the adults in the study. Based on their findings, Downes and Kroeck called for a concerted effort to reshape the interests and skills of the U.S. labor force in order to meet the labor needs of corporations and educational institutions.

Ryan, Tracey, and Rounds (1996) and Rounds and Tracey (1996) studied the generalizability of Holland's (1985) model of vocational interests across ethnicity, gender, and socioeconomic status (SES). Ryan, Tracey, and Rounds found similar interest structures in the Caucasian and the African American high school students in their study. Ryan and her colleagues also found no differences in the structure of interests between low- and high-SES groups. A similar result was obtained when comparing low- and high-SES Caucasian groups. However, the low-SES African American group was better fit by Holland's model than the high-SES African American group. Both male and female students fit Holland's model. Thus, Ryan and her colleagues concluded that Holland's model is generalizable across ethnicity, gender, and socioeconomic status as defined in their study.

Finally, Mihalik (1996) examined whether clients' types predicted reactions to counselor intentions. Using a sample of undergraduate college students, Mihalik found that clients' vocational interests as measured by the Self-Directed Search (Holland, 1987) were predictive of client reactions to counselor interventions. For example, participants with high Enterprising scores responded positively to feeling challenged in counseling and participants with high Social scores responded positively to being supported by the counselor.

This very brief sample of research provides an indication of the fact that Holland's theory has generated more research than any other model of career choice. Much of this research supports the theory (Holland, 1996; Spokane, 1985; Spokane et al., 2002). Also, the theory provides a clear link to practice: "The combination of empirical support and practical application accounts for the theory's popularity among the public as well as among professionals" (Spokane, 1996, p. 62). More studies investigating the validity of Holland's method across cultural contexts are needed.

JOHN KRUMBOLTZ'S LEARNING THEORY OF CAREER COUNSELING

Krumboltz and his colleagues (especially Mitchell and Jones) developed a learning theory of career counseling comprising two distinct parts. The first part focuses on explaining the origins of career choice and is labeled as the "social learning theory of career decision making" (SLTCDM) (Mitchell & Krumboltz, 1996). The second part focuses on career counseling and is labeled the "learning theory of career counseling" (LTCC) (Krumboltz & Henderson, 2002; Mitchell & Krumboltz, 1996). Because the SLTCDM identifies the factors influencing the career decisions people make (and is, therefore, subsumed under the LTCC part of the theory) and because the LTCC explains what career counselors can do to help clients make effective career decisions, Mitchell and Krumboltz labeled the entire theory as the LTCC.

LTCC is based on the application of Bandura's (1977, 1986) social learning theory to career decision making. Bandura's theory emphasizes the influence of reinforcement theory, cognitive information processing, and classical behaviorism on human behavior. Social learning theory "assumes that people's personalities and behavioral repertoires can be explained most usefully on the basis of their unique learning experiences while still acknowledging the role played by innate and developmental processes" (Mitchell & Krumboltz, 1996, p. 234). Social learning theory also assumes that "humans are intelligent, problem-solving individuals who strive at all times to understand the reinforcement that surrounds them and who in turn control their environments to suit their own purposes and needs" (Mitchell & Krumboltz, 1984, p. 236). Bandura (1986) described the interaction of environment, self-referent thought, and behavior as the "triadic reciprocal interaction system."

Krumboltz and his colleagues drew upon these theoretical assumptions in developing LTCC. As noted earlier, SLTCDM describes the factors influencing individuals' career decisions and LTCC describes what career counselors can do to help their clients make effective career choices.

SLTCDM

The SLTCDM identifies four factors that influence our career decision making:

1. **Genetic endowment and special abilities.** Genetic endowments are inherited qualities, such as sex, race, and physical appearance. Special abilities such as intelligence, athletic ability, and musical and artistic talents result from the interaction of genetic factors and exposure to selected environmental events.

2. Environmental conditions and events. Factors in this category are generally outside our control and can involve a wide variety of cultural, social, political, and economic forces. For example, government-sponsored job-training programs, such as the Comprehensive Employment Training Act and the Job Training Partnership Act, can provide opportunities for learning new skills and increasing employability. Technological developments (e.g., computer technologies) create new job opportunities and make others obsolete. Legislation related to welfare, labor laws, and union policies influences job availability and facilitates or restricts job entry. Natural disasters can dramatically influence career opportunities and career paths. Family traditions, as well as neighborhood and community resources, can also significantly affect individuals' career decision making. Job entry requirements can persuade or deter us from considering specific occupational opportunities. Our geographical location can also play a prominent feature in influencing our career choices and the availability of job opportunities (e.g., climatic differences between Maine and Florida result in differences in the availability of some job opportunities; the availability of counseling jobs is greater in the United States than in other countries in which counseling concerns are resolved by spiritual leaders).

3. Instrumental and associative learning experiences. Instrumental learning experiences involve antecedents, behaviors, and consequences (Figure 2.4). According to Mitchell and Krumboltz (1996):

> Antecedents include the genetic endowments, special abilities, and environmental conditions and events previously discussed as well as the characteristics of a particular task or problem. Behavioral responses include cognitive and emotional responses as well as overt behavior. Consequences include immediate and delayed effects produced by the behavior as well as "self-talk" about those consequences. (p. 238)

To illustrate, consider Jennifer, a master's degree student in counselor education. She is very competent interpersonally (genetic endowment, special abilities, and skills) but feels anxious about enrolling in the required research course. Statistics and research design especially intimidate her. Because the research course is a program requirement, she must take this course (planned environmental condition). The professor in this course, however, is well acquainted with counselor education students and knows that many feel anxious about the program requirement in research. Hence, in teaching the course the professor works hard at praising students for their successes and supporting them when they struggle with course content. In this situation, Jennifer decides to apply herself and work as hard as she can to master the course content (covert and overt action). On her first exam, Jennifer earns a B grade—far better than she ever had imagined (consequences). As a result, she begins to think that, rather than being frightening, research is fun and that she might be able to become a competent researcher (convert reactions to consequences). As the semester goes on, Jennifer begins to tutor her peers who are struggling with this course. In her second year, she serves as a graduate assistant in the research course and enjoys helping students who feel anxious about being able to succeed in the course (impact on significant others).

Associative learning experiences occur when a neutral stimulus is paired with a positive and/or negative stimulus or consequences. For example, Juanita's school counselor encourages her to attend a job fair at her high school because Juanita is undecided

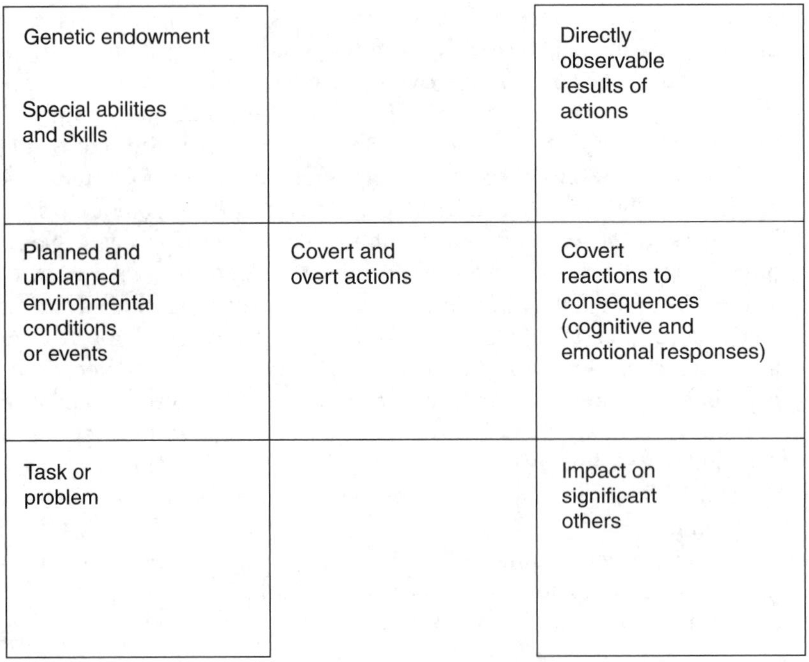

Genetic endowment Special abilities and skills		Directly observable results of actions
Planned and unplanned environmental conditions or events	Covert and overt actions	Covert reactions to consequences (cognitive and emotional responses)
Task or problem		Impact on significant others

Figure 2.4

Instrumental learning experience, general model. From *Career Choice and Development* (3rd ed.), by Duane Brown, Linda Brooks, and Associates. Copyright © 1996, Jossey-Bass Inc. This material is used by permission of Jossey-Bass, Inc., a subsidiary of John Wiley & Sons, Inc.

about her career options. Juanita agrees to attend the fair. She has no real career options in mind but decides she will "browse" to see what options seem interesting. At the job fair, Juanita encounters a news anchor, who also happens to be Latina, for the local television station. Juanita had never given much thought to jobs in TV journalism (neutral stimulus), but thoroughly enjoys her meeting with the local anchor (positive stimulus). Juanita is even invited to take a tour of the studio and sit in on a live broadcast. After taking the tour and observing the broadcast, Juanita decides to enroll in a formal externship program the high school has established with the television station (positive consequences).

4. Task approach skills. Juanita will need to use many skills in determining whether journalism is a good career choice for her. For example, Juanita will need to be able to clarify her interests, values, and skills; to gather occupational information; and to know how to integrate this information in her decision making. In this process, Juanita will need to consider her genetic characteristics, special abilities, and environmental influences (e.g., family support, training opportunities, financial resources, and occupational opportunities). These behaviors are examples of task approach skills that Juanita must use in making a career choice. Task approach skills also include the individual's work habits, mental set, emotional responses, cognitive processes, and problem-solving skills. Additionally, if Juanita decides to pursue a career as a television journalist, she will need to develop a wide range of journalistic skills in order to achieve her goal. Thus, task approach skills influence outcomes and are themselves outcomes.

These four factors influence our beliefs about ourselves (e.g., what we are good at, what our interests are, what we value) and our beliefs about the world (e.g., "hard work always pays off," "all accountants are stuffy," "all counselors value altruism over economic rewards"). Although the interactions of these four factors influence people differently, there are generally four ways in which they can influence our career decision making.

1. **Self-observation generalizations.** Overt or covert statements evaluating our actual or vicarious performance or self-assessments of our interests and values are defined as self-observation generalizations (Mitchell & Krumboltz, 1996, p. 244). Learning experiences lead us to draw conclusions about ourselves. We compare our performance with the performance of others and to our own performance expectations. We use these comparisons to draw conclusions about our performance capabilities. Conclusions about our interests and values also result from learning experiences. In SLTCDM, interests link learning experiences with specific actions (as when doing well in a research course leads to the decision to participate in research projects and teach others about research). Self-observations about values are, in essence, statements about the desirability of specific outcomes, behaviors, or events (Mitchell & Krumboltz, 1996). For example, the statement that "it is important that my job provides ample time for me to be with my family" is a values-related self-observation generalization about desirable outcomes resulting from previous learning experiences.

2. **Worldview generalizations.** Likewise, generalizations about the nature and functioning of the world (e.g., "It's not what you know, it's who you know," "It is better to try and fail than to not try at all") are formed from learning experiences. The accuracy of worldview generalizations is dependent on the learning experiences shaping such generalizations.

3. **Task approach skills.** Mitchell and Krumboltz (1996) define these outcomes as "cognitive and performance abilities and emotional predispositions for coping with the environment, interpreting it in relation to self-observation generalizations, and making covert and overt predictions about future events" (p. 246). As noted earlier, task approach skills both influence career decision making and are outcomes of learning experiences that shape individuals' career development. Task approach skills critical to career development are those involved in decision making, problem solving, goal setting, information gathering, and values clarifying.

4. **Actions.** Learning experiences eventually lead individuals to take actions related to entering a career. These actions can include applying for a job, entering a training program, applying to college, changing jobs, or taking other overt steps to make progress in one's career.

The SLTCDM suggests that career decision making is "influenced by complex environmental (e.g., economic) factors, many of which are beyond the control of any single individual" (Krumboltz, Mitchell, & Gelatt, 1976, p. 75). The theory also underscores "the interaction between innate predispositions and learning experiences within the intra-individual, family, social, educational and cultural context"

(Krumboltz & Henderson, 2002, p. 43). Also, based on SLTCDM, Krumboltz (1994) noted that people will prefer an occupation if:

1. They have succeeded at tasks they believe are like tasks performed by members of that occupation.
2. They have observed a valued model being reinforced for activities like those performed by members of that occupation.
3. A valued friend or relative stressed its advantages to them and/or they observed positive words and images being associated with it. (p. 19)

Conversely, Krumboltz noted that people will avoid an occupation if:

1. They have failed at tasks they believe are similar to tasks performed by people in that occupation.
2. They have observed a valued model being punished or ignored for performing activities like those performed by members of that occupation.
3. A valued friend or relative stressed its disadvantages to them and/or they have observed negative words and images being associated with it. (p. 19)

The Learning Theory of Career Counseling

The strength of SLTCDM is that it provides a description of factors influencing career decision making and identifies outcomes resulting from those influential factors. As such, it is a useful theory for understanding career paths retrospectively. The understanding acquired from such a perspective is helpful in making current career decisions and in formulating future career goals.

When career concerns arise, they typically involve one or more of the following: (a) the absence of a goal, or career indecision (Juanita's presenting concern), (b) expressed feeling of concern about high aspirations, or unrealism, and (c) a conflict between equally appropriate alternatives, or multipotentiality (Krumboltz & Thoresen, 1969). Krumboltz developed the learning theory of career counseling (LTCC) to guide counselors in constructing career development interventions to help clients cope more effectively with these career concerns. Specifically, counselors using LTCC help clients: (a) acquire more accurate self-observation generalizations, (b) acquire more accurate worldview generalizations, (c) learn new task approach skills, and (d) take appropriate career-related actions. LTCC assumes that counselors must be prepared to help their clients cope with four current career-related trends identified by Mitchell and Krumboltz (1996, pp. 250–252).

1. People need to expand their capabilities and interests, not base decisions on existing characteristics only. Interest inventories assess what we know and what we have experienced. To maximize a client's career choice options, counselors must encourage that client to explore new activities, develop new interests, and consider new options based on newly formed interests and capabilities.
2. People need to prepare for changing work tasks, not assume that occupations will remain stable. Because change is constant, career counselors must help their

clients identify new skills to learn and develop strategies for coping with the stress inherent in an ever-changing world of work.

3. People need to be empowered to take action, not merely to be given a diagnosis. For some clients, implementing a career choice is more challenging than making the choice. Many clients need ongoing assistance from their career counselors as they attempt to adjust to the career choice made and implemented.

4. Career counselors need to play a major role in dealing with all career problems, not just career selection. Career-related concerns exist beyond this concern of identifying a career choice. Many clients struggle with the burnout, underemployment, relationships with coworkers, family members' reactions to career choices, and low self-efficacy.

These four trends suggest the importance of providing clients with learning experiences to (a) correct faulty assumptions, (b) learn new skills and interests, (c) identify effective strategies for addressing issues emanating from interactions between work and other life-role activities and concerns, and (d) learn skills for coping with changing work tasks. Career counselors can use assessments to help clients identify what characteristics (e.g., beliefs, skills, values, interests, personality) they have learned and to identify opportunities for learning new characteristics. Thus, the task of the career counselor is to promote client learning and the goal of career counseling is to enhance the ability of clients to create satisfying lives for themselves (Krumboltz, 1996).

Applying LTCC

Krumboltz (1996) divides career development interventions into two categories: (a) developmental/preventive and (b) targeted/remedial. The former includes career education programs, school-to-work initiatives, job club programs, study materials, and simulations. These career development interventions facilitate the acquisition of accurate and occupational self-information and the use of this information in the career decision making process. Learning through active on-the-job participation (e.g., job shadowing, internships, and worksite observation) is emphasized. It is important to note that although many clients, such as Juanita, could certainly benefit from participating in many of these activities, they must first receive more targeted and remedial career development interventions.

Targeted and remedial career development interventions include goal clarification, cognitive restructuring, cognitive rehearsal, narrative analysis, role playing, desensitization, paradoxical intention, and humor (Krumboltz, 1996, pp. 66–72). LTCC also emphasizes the importance of teaching decision making skills to clients. Learning how to make career decisions helps clients resolve current career concerns and equips clients with an important task approach skill for coping with changing work and personal conditions in the future (Krumboltz, 1976). For example, once Juanita has clarified her goals and learns how to make good decisions, she will then be ready to participate in more focused on-the-job activities (e.g., job shadowing, volunteering).

To help counselors identify problematic client beliefs related to each of the career problem categories (i.e., indecision, unrealism, and multipotentiality), Krumboltz (1988) developed the Career Beliefs Inventory (CBI). The CBI is based on the rationale that people make career decisions according to what they believe about themselves and the world-of-work. As Krumboltz wrote in 1994, "If their beliefs are accurate and constructive, they will act in ways that are likely to help them achieve their goals. If their beliefs are inaccurate and self-defeating, they will act in a way that makes sense to them but may not help them achieve their goals" (p. 424). The CBI helps counselors understand their clients' career beliefs and assumptions. Thus, the instrument is most useful when administered at the beginning of career counseling. The CBI contains 25 scales organized into the following five categories: My Current Career Situation, What Seems Necessary for My Happiness, Factors That Influence My Decisions, Changes I Am Willing to Make, and Efforts I Am Willing to Initiate. These categories are related to mental barriers blocking clients from taking action. As Krumboltz and Henderson (2002) remind us, meaningful journeys, including our career journey, contain obstacles that must be confronted. Some clients allow discouragement and other problematic beliefs to dominate their thinking and thwart efforts to take positive actions. Self-defeating beliefs such as those measured by the CBI must be addressed if the client is to move forward. Counseling strategies such as cognitive restructuring and reframing are useful in helping the client to address these issues.

Related to the notion of career beliefs is the fact that often in career counseling, clients refer to significant events in ways that suggest the client had little to do with the experience. For example, a client may say "I just got lucky" or "I just happened to be in the right place at the right time." Krumboltz and his associates (Mitchell, Levin, & Krumboltz, 1999) recognize that career counseling often involves helping clients understand and take advantage of the chance events they encounter in daily living. In fact, they note that "unplanned events are not only inevitable, they are desirable" (p. 118) and refer to this phenomenon as "planned happenstance." Planned happenstance can be incorporated into career counseling by teaching clients "to generate, recognize, and incorporate chance events into the process of their career development" (Krumboltz & Henderson, 2002, p. 49). Specifically, career counselors can ask their clients questions such as: "How have unplanned events influenced your career in the past? How did you enable each event to influence your career development? How do you feel about encountering unplanned events in your future?" (2002, p. 50). Counselor and client interactions that intentionally address the role of chance in career development help to normalize such occurrences, help clients see their thematic influence upon their career development, and help clients be increasingly open to noticing and acting upon unplanned events in the future. In essence, an internal locus of control and increased sense of personal self-efficacy are fostered.

Mitchell et al. (1999) focus on the skills clients need to develop to take advantage of unplanned events in their career development. They note that developing a sense of curiosity, being persistent, being flexible, maintaining a sense of optimism, and being willing to take risks represent a set of skills that increase the individual's ability to take advantage of unplanned events.

Evaluating Career Development Interventions

Typically, counselors evaluate the success of career development interventions by standards determining whether clients experience a reduction in career indecision. Krumboltz recommends that career counselors consider revising these criteria. For example, counselors using LTCC view indecision as a desirable quality for motivating clients to engage in new learning activities. Hence, Krumboltz recommends reframing "indecision" to "open-mindedness."

Krumboltz also suggests that the goal of achieving congruence between individuals and their work environments is unnecessarily restricting because "birds of a feather" do not always flock together (i.e., there is intraoccupational variability among people). Two very different people can be successful in the same occupation. Krumboltz (1996) also argues that the congruence criterion is less useful today because it is based on stagnant definitions of occupational environments, thereby overlooking changes in work environments: "Heterogeneity, not homogeneity, within occupations is now more highly valued" (p. 73).

In place of these two traditional outcome criteria, Krumboltz recommends focusing on measuring changes in client characteristics such as skills, values, beliefs, interests, and work habits. Counselors can ask themselves whether their career development interventions have stimulated their clients to engage in new learning activities. Process measures can focus on assessing the degree to which clients have made efforts to create more satisfying lives (e.g., Have they engaged in career exploratory or information-seeking behaviors?).

Evaluating LTCC

LTCC is new and relatively untested by research. There is, however, extensive research supporting the general social learning theory (Hackett et al., 1991). Additionally, Krumboltz (1996) cites several studies supporting SLTCDM hypotheses related to the development of educational and occupational preferences, task approach skills, and action.

A strength of LTCC is that it addresses both environmental and intra-individual variables affecting career development. As such, LTCC is very compatible with Super's Archway model of career development, with LTCC offering a bit more in terms of specific ways in which environmental and personal variables influence career decision making. LTCC also can be used as a framework for understanding the development of interests leading to one's personal modal orientation as described by Holland's theory. Finally, the development of the CBI, and subsequent application of strategies such as cognitive restructuring and reframing, provide useful and important applications of the theory to career development interventions.

SUMMARY

The theories discussed in this chapter form the foundation for how the leading theorists and practitioners have conceptualized the career development process for more than 50 years. There are ways in which these theories converge, but there are many ways in which they do not. They each contribute important perspectives for conceptualizing how careers develop and how career choices are made. Thus, there is no one theory that sufficiently addresses all possible factors influencing career development and all client career concerns. This is not surprising given the highly complex nature of career development. However, these theories do provide a solid foundation upon which to expand our thinking about the career development process and career development interventions. Particular areas ripe for expansion include describing how careers develop for a wider range of people. Most of the early theories of career development were based on the career experience of White males and may lack applicability to women and members of diverse racial, ethnic, socioeconomic, and religious groups. Another area ripe for theory expansion is the process and content of career counseling. Most early theories of career development emphasize the career development process rather than career development interventions. More treatment-outcome studies directed toward determining which interventions are appropriate for which clients with what career concerns are needed.

Nonetheless, the theories discussed in this chapter provide an important stimulus in the evolutionary process of theory development. As these theories continue to evolve and as new theories emerge, it is hoped that theorists will continue the process of providing fuller, more detailed, and more comprehensive descriptions of the career development process that can be used to provide effective career development interventions to a wide range of people. The emerging theories discussed in the next chapter provide evidence of such progress.

REFERENCES

Anderson, W. P., & Niles, S. G. (1995). Career and personal concerns expressed by career counseling clients. *The Career Development Quarterly, 43,* 240–245.

Bandura, A. (1977). *Social learning theory.* Upper Saddle River, NJ: Prentice Hall.

Bandura, A. (1986). *Social foundations of thought and action: A social-cognitive theory.* Upper Saddle River, NJ: Prentice Hall.

Betz, N. E., & Corning, A. F. (1993). The inseparability of "career" and "personal" counseling. *The Career Development Quarterly, 42,* 137–148.

Blanchard, C. A., & Lichtenberg, J. W. (2003). Compromise in career decision making: A test of Gottfredson's theory. *Journal of Vocational Behavior, 62,* 250–271.

Blustein, D. L. (1994). "Who am I?" The question of self and identity in career development. In M. L. Savickas & R. W. Lent (Eds.), *Convergence in career development theories: Implications for science and practice* (pp. 139–154). Palo Alto, CA: Consulting Psychologists Press.

Borgen, F. H. (1991). Megatrends and milestones in vocational behavior: A 20-year counseling psychology perspective. *Journal of Vocational Behavior, 39,* 263–290.

Borodovsky, L., & Ponterotto, J. (1994). A family-based approach to multicultural career development. In P. Pedersen & J. Carey (Eds.), *Multicultural counseling in schools* (pp. 195–206). Boston: Allyn & Bacon.

Brown, D. (1996). Brown's values-based, holistic model of career and life-role choices and satisfaction. In D. Brown, L. Brooks, & Associates (Eds.), *Career choice and development* (3rd ed., pp. 337–372). San Francisco: Jossey-Bass.

Buehler, C. (1933). *Der menschliche lebenslauf als psychologisches problem.* Leipzig: Hirzel.

Cairo, P. C., Kritis, K. J., & Myers, R. M. (1996). Career assessment and the Adult Career Concerns Inventory. *Journal of Career Assessment, 4,* 189–204.

Coltrane, S., & Adams, M. (1997). Work-family imagery and gender stereotypes: Television and the reproduction of difference. *Journal of Vocational Behavior, 50,* 323–347.

Downes, M., & Kroeck, K. G. (1996). Discrepancies between existing jobs and individual interests:

An empirical investigation of Holland's model. *Journal of Vocational Behavior, 48*, 107–117.

Eagle, B. W., Miles, E. W., & Icenogle, M. L. (1997). Interrole conflicts and the permeability of work and family domains: Are there gender differences? *Journal of Vocational Behavior, 50*, 168–184.

Ginzberg, E., Ginsburg, S. W., Axelrad, S., & Herma, J. (1951). *Occupational choice: An approach to a general theory.* New York: Columbia University Press.

Gottfredson, L. S. (1981). Circumscription and compromise: A developmental theory of occupational aspirations. *Journal of Counseling Psychology, 28*, 545–579.

Gottfredson, L. S. (1996). A theory of circumscription and compromise. In D. Brown, L. Brooks, & Associates (Eds.), *Career choice and development* (3rd ed., pp. 179–281). San Francisco: Jossey-Bass.

Gottfredson, L. S. (2002). Gottfredson's theory of circumscription, compromise, and self-creation. In D. Brown & Associates (Eds.), *Career choice and development* (4th ed., pp. 85–148). San Francisco: Jossey-Bass.

Gottfredson, L. S., & Holland, J. L. (1996). *Position classification inventory.* Odessa, FL: PAR.

Gottfredson, L. S., & Richards J. M. (1999). The meaning and measurement of environments in Holland's theory. *Journal of Vocational Behavior, 42*, 200–211.

Hackett, G., Lent, R., & Greenhaus, J. (1991). Advances in vocational theory and research: A 20-year retrospective. *Journal of Vocational Behavior, 38*, 3–38.

Hannah, J., & Kahn, S. (1989). The relationship of socioeconomic status and gender to the occupational choices of Grade 12 students. *Journal of Vocational Behavior, 34*, 161–178.

Harmon, L. W., Hansen, J. C., Borgen, F. H., & Hammer, A. L. (1994). *Strong Interest Inventory applications and technical guide.* Stanford, CA: Stanford University Press.

Hartung, P. J., Vandiver, B. J., Leong, F. T. L., Pope, M., Niles, S. G., & Farrow, B. (1998). Appraising cultural identity in career development assessment and counseling. *The Career Development Quarterly, 46*, 276–293.

Havighurst, R. J. (1951). Validity of the Chicago Attitude Inventory as a measure of personal adjustment in old age. *Journal of Abnormal and Social Psychology, 46*, 24–29.

Havighurst, R. J. (1953). *Human development and education.* New York: Longmans Green.

Helwig, A. A. (2001). A test of Gottfredson's theory using a ten-year longitudinal study. *Journal of Career Development, 28*, 77–95.

Henderson, S., Hesketh, B., & Tuffin, A. (1988). A test of Gottfredson's theory of circumscription. *Journal of Vocational Behavior, 32*, 37–48.

Herr, E. L., & Cramer, S. H. (1996). *Career guidance and counseling through the lifespan* (5th ed.). New York: HarperCollins.

Herr, E. L., Cramer, S. H., & Niles, S. G. (2004). *Career guidance and counseling through the lifespan: Systematic approaches* (6th ed.). Boston, MA: Allyn & Bacon.

Hesketh, B., Elmslie, S., & Kaldor, W. (1990). Career compromise: An alternative account to Gottfredson's theory. *Journal of Counseling Psychology, 37*, 49–56.

Holland, J. L. (1959). A theory of vocational choice. *The Journal of Counseling Psychology, 6*, 35–45.

Holland, J. L. (1966). *The psychology of vocational choice.* Waltham, MA: Blaisdell.

Holland, J. L. (1973). *Making vocational choices: A theory of careers.* Upper Saddle River, NJ: Prentice Hall.

Holland, J. L. (1985). *Making vocational choices: A theory of vocational personalities and work environments* (2nd ed.). Upper Saddle River, NJ: Prentice Hall.

Holland, J. L. (1987). Current status of Holland's theory of careers: Another perspective. *The Career Development Quarterly, 36*, 31–44.

Holland, J. L. (1992). *Making vocational choices* (2nd ed.). Odessa, FL: Psychological Assessment Resources.

Holland, J. L. (1994). Separate but unequal is better. In M. L. Savickas & R. W. Lent (Eds.), *Convergence in career development theories: Implications for science and practice* (pp. 45–51). Palo Alto, CA: CPP Books.

Holland, J. L. (1996). Integrating career theory and practice: The current situation and some potential remedies. In M. L. Savickas & W. B. Walsh (Eds.), *Handbook of career counseling theory and practice* (pp. 1–12). Palo Alto, CA: Davies-Black.

Holland, J. L., Gottfredson, G., & Power, P. (1980). Some diagnostic scales for research in decision-making and personality: Identity, information, and barriers. *Journal of Personality and Social Psychology, 39*, 1191–1200.

Holmberg, K., Rosen, D., & Holland, J. L. (1990). *Leisure activities finder*. Odessa, FL: Psychological Assessment Resources.

Jepsen, D. A. (1994). The thematic-extrapolation method: Incorporating career patterns into career counseling. *The Career Development Quarterly, 43*, 43–53.

Johannson, C. B. (1986). *The Career Assessment Inventory*. Minneapolis, MN: NCS Assessments.

Kelly, G. A. (1955). *The psychology of personal constructs*. New York: Norton.

Krumboltz, J. D. (1976). A social learning theory of career choice. *Counseling Psychologist, 6*, 71–80.

Krumboltz, J. D. (1993). Integrating career and personal counseling. *The Career Development Quarterly, 42*, 143–148.

Krumboltz, J. D. (1994). The Career Beliefs Inventory. *Journal of Counseling and Development, 72*, 424–428.

Krumboltz, J. D. (1996). A learning theory of career counseling. In M. Savickas & B. Walsh (Eds.), *Integrating career theory and practice* (pp. 233–280). Palo Alto, CA: CPP Books.

Krumboltz, J. D. (1988). *Career beliefs inventory*. Palo Alto, CA: Consulting Psychologists Press.

Krumboltz, J. D., & Henderson, S. J. (2002). A learning theory for career counselors. In S. Niles (Ed.), *Adult career development: Concepts, issues, and practices* (pp. 39–56). Tulsa, OK: National Career Development Association.

Krumboltz, J. D., Mitchell, A., & Gelatt, H. G. (1976). Applications of social learning theory of career selection. *Focus on Guidance, 8*, 1–16.

Krumboltz, J. D., & Thoresen, C. E. (1969). *Behavioral Counseling: Cases and Techniques*. New York: Holt, Rinehart and Winston.

Lent, E. B., & Lopez, F. G. (1996). Congruence from many angles: Relations of multiple congruence indices to job satisfaction among adult workers. *Journal of Vocational Behavior, 49*, 24–37.

Leung, S. A., & Plake, T. S. (1990). A choice dilemma approach for examining the relative importance of sex type and prestige preferences in the process of career choice compromise. *Journal of Counseling Psychology, 37*, 399–406.

Lewis, D. M., Savickas, M. L., & Jones, B. J. (1996). Career development predicts medical schools success. *Journal of Vocational Behavior, 49*, 86–98.

Loscocco, K. A. (1997). Reactions to blue-collar work: A comparison of men and women. *Work and Occupations, 17*, 152–177.

Lucas, M. S. (1993). A validation of types of career indecision at a counseling center. *Journal of Counseling Psychology, 40*, 440–446.

McLennan, N. A., & Arthur, N. (1999). Applying the cognitive information processing approach to career problem solving and decision making to women's career development. *Journal of Employment Counseling, 36*, 82–96.

Mihalik, J. R. (1996). Client vocational interests as predictors of client reactions to counselor intentions, *Journal of Counseling and Development, 74*, 416–421.

Miller, D. C., & Form, W. H. (1951). *Industrial sociology*. New York: Harper.

Miller, M. J. (1997). Error rates on two forms on the Self Directed Search and satisfaction with results. *Journal of Employment Counseling, 34*, 98–103.

Miller, M. J. (2002). A longitudinal examination of a three-letter Holland code. *Journal of Employment Counseling, 39*, 43–48.

Miller, M. J., & Bass, C. (2003). Application of Holland's theory to a nonprofessional occupation. *Journal of Employment Counseling, 40*, 17–23.

Mitchell, L. K., & Krumboltz, J. D. (1996). Krumboltz's theory of career choice and counseling. In D. Brown, L. Brooks, & Associates (Eds.), *Career choice development* (3rd ed., pp. 233–280). San Francisco, CA: Jossey-Bass.

Mitchell, A., Levin, A., & Krumboltz, J. D. (1999). Planned happenstance: Constructing unexpected career opportunities. *Journal of Counseling and Development, 77*, 115–124.

Murray, H. (1938). *Explorations in personality*. New York: Oxford University Press.

Nevill, D. D., & Calvert, P. D. (1996). Career assessment and the Salience Inventory. *Journal of Career Assessment, 4*, 399–412.

Nevill, D. D., & Kruse, S. J. (1996). Career assessment and the Values Scale. *Journal of Career Assessment, 4*, 383–397.

Nevill, D. D., & Super, D. E. (1986). *The Values Scale: Theory, application, and research manual* (research ed.). Palo Alto, CA: Consulting Psychologists Press.

Niles, S. G., & Anderson, W. P. (1993). Career development and adjustment: The relation between concerns and stress. *Journal of Employment Counseling, 30*, 79–87.

Niles, S. G., Anderson, W. P., & Goodnough, G. (1998). Exploration to foster career development. *The Career Development Quarterly, 46*, 262–275.

Niles, S. G., & Goodnough, G. E. (1996). Life-role salience and values: A review of recent research. *The Career Development Quarterly, 45,* 65–86.

Oleski, D., & Subich, L. M. (1996). Congruence and career change in employed adults. *Journal of Vocational Behavior, 49,* 221–229.

Osipow, S. H. (1990). Convergence in theories of career choice and development: Review and prospect. *Journal of Vocational Behavior, 36,* 122–131.

Osipow, S. H., & Fitzgerald, L. F. (1996). *Theories of career development* (4th ed.). Needham, MA: Allyn & Bacon.

Parasuraman, S., Purhoit, Y. S., Godshalk, V. M., & Beutell, N. J. (1996). Work and family variables, entrepreneurial career success, and psychological well-being. *Journal of Vocational Behavior, 48,* 275–300.

Phillips, S. D. (1982). Career exploration in adulthood. *Journal of Vocational Behavior, 20,* 129–140.

Richardson, M. S. (1993). Work in people's lives: A location for counseling psychologists. *Journal of Counseling Psychology, 40,* 425–433.

Rogers, C. R. (1951). *Client-centered therapy, its current practice, implications, and theory.* Boston: Houghton Mifflin.

Rounds, J., & Tracey, T. J. G. (1996). Cross-cultural structural equivalence of RIASEC models and measures. *Journal of Counseling Psychology, 43,* 310–329.

Ryan, J. M., Tracey, T. J. G., & Rounds, J. (1996). Generalizability of Holland's structure of vocational behavior interest across ethnicity, gender, and socioeconomic status. *Journal of Counseling Psychology, 43,* 330–337.

Salomone, P. R. (1996). Tracing Super's theory of vocational development: A 40-year retrospective. *Journal of Career Development, 22,* 167–184.

Savickas, M. L. (1993). Predictive validity criteria for career development measures. *Journal of Career Assessment, 1,* 93–104.

Savickas, M. L. (1997). Career adaptability: An integrative concept for life-span, life-space theory. *The Career Development Quarterly, 45,* 247–259.

Savickas, M. L. (2000). Career development and public policy: The role of values, theory, and research. In B. Hiebert & L. Bezanson (Eds.), *Making waves: Career development and public policy* (pp. 52–68). Ottawa, Canada: Human Resources Development Canada/Canadian Career Development Foundation.

Savickas, M. L. (2002). Career construction: A developmental theory of vocational behavior. In D. Brown & Associates (Eds.), *Career choice and development* (4th ed., pp. 149–205). San Francisco: Jossey-Bass.

Savickas, M. L., & Hartung, P. J. (1996). The Career Development Inventory in review: Psychometric and research findings. *Journal of Career Assessment, 4,* 171–188.

Savickas, M. L., & Lent, R. W. (Eds.). (1994). *Convergence in career development theories: Implications for science and practice.* Palo Alto, CA: CPP Books.

Spokane, A. (1985). A review of research on person-environment congruence in Holland's theory of careers. *Journal of Vocational Behavior, 26,* 306–343.

Spokane, A. (1996). *Holland's theory* in D. Brown, L. Brook, & Associates (Eds.), *Career choice and development* (3rd ed., pp. 33–74). San Francisco, CA: Jossey-Bass.

Spokane, A. R., Fouad, N., & Swanson, J. (2001). (S. *Culture-centered career intervention. Paper presented at a symposium on career intervention.* (S. Whiston, Chair). San Francisco: American Psychological Association.

Spokane, A., Luchetta, E., & Richwine, M. (2002). Holland's theory of personalities. In D. Brown & Associates (Eds.), *Career choice and development* (4th ed., pp. 373–426). San Francisco, CA: Jossey-Bass.

Spranger, E. (1928). *Types of men: The psychology and ethics of personality* (Paul J. W. Pigors, Trans.). Halle, Germany: Max Niemeyer Verlag.

Subich, L. M. (1993). How personal is career counseling? *The Career Development Quarterly, 42,* 129–131.

Subich, L. M. (2001). Introduction: Special section on contextual factors in career services delivery. *The Career Development Quarterly, 50,* 20.

Super, D. E. (1954). Career patterns as a basis for vocational counseling. *Journal of Counseling Psychology, 1,* 12–20.

Super, D. E. (1957). *The psychology of careers.* New York: Harper & Row.

Super, D. E. (1961). The self concept in vocational development. *Journal of Vocational and Educational Guidance, 8,* 13–29.

Super, D. E. (1963). Self-concepts in vocational development. In D. E. Super, R. Starishevsky, N. Matlin, & J. P. Jordaan, (Eds.), *Career development: Self-concept theory* (pp. 17–32). New York: College Entrance Examination Board.

Super, D. E. (1969). Vocational development theory: Persons, positions, processes. *The Counseling Psychologist, 1,* 2–9.

Super, D. E. (1980). A life-span, life-space approach to career development. *Journal of Vocational Behavior, 16,* 282–298.

Super, D. E. (1981). Approaches to occupational choice and career development. In A. G. Watts, D. E. Super, & J. M. Kidd (Eds.), *Career development in Britain* (pp. 28–42). Cambridge, England: Hobsons Press.

Super, D. E. (1983). Assessment in career guidance: Toward truly developmental counseling. *Personnel and Guidance Journal, 61,* 555–562.

Super, D. E. (1984). Leisure: What it is and might be. *Journal of Career Development, 11,* 71–80.

Super, D. E. (1990). A life-span, life-space approach to career development. In D. Brown, L. Brook, & Associates (Eds.), *Career choice and development: Applying contemporary theories to practice* (2nd ed., pp. 197–261). San Francisco, CA: Jossey-Bass.

Super, D. E. (1992). Toward a comprehensive theory of career development. In D. Montross & C. Shinkman (Eds.), *Career development: Theory and practice* (pp. 35–64). Springfield, IL: Charles C. Thomas.

Super, D. E. (1993). The two faces of counseling: Or is it three? *The Career Development Quarterly, 42,* 132–136.

Super, D. E., & Knasel, E. G. (1981). Career development in adulthood: Some theoretical problems and a possible solution. *British Journal of Guidance and Counselling, 9,* 194–201.

Super, D. E., & Nevill, D. D. (1986). *The Salience Inventory.* Palo Alto, CA: Consulting Psychologists Press.

Super, D. E., Osborne, W. L., Walsh, D. J., Brown, S. D., & Niles, S. G. (1992). Developmental assessment and counseling: The C-DAC model,

Journal of Counseling and Development, 71, 74–80.

Super, D. E., Savickas, M. L., & Super, C. (1996). A life-span, life-space approach to career development. In D. Brown, L. Brook, & Associates (Eds.), *Career choice and development* (3rd ed., pp. 121–128). San Francisco, CA: Jossey-Bass.

Super, D. E., Thompson, A. S., & Lindeman, R. H. (1988). *Adult Career Concerns Inventory: Manual for research and exploratory usage in counseling.* Palo Alto, CA: Consulting Psychologists Press.

Super, D. E., Thompson, A. S., Lindeman, R. H., Jordaan, J. P., & Myers, R. A. (1981). *Career Development Inventory.* Palo Alto, CA: Consulting Psychologists Press.

Thompson, A. S., Lindeman, R. H., Super, D. E., Jordaan, J. P., & Myers, R. A. (1984). *Career Development Inventory: Technical manual.* Palo Alto, CA: Consulting Psychologists Press.

Tinsley, H. E. A. (1994). Construct your reality and show us its benefits: Comment on Richardson, *Journal of Counseling Psychology, 40,* 108–111.

U. S. Department of Defense. (1993). *Technical supplement to the counselor's manual for the Armed Services Vocational Aptitude Battery.* North Chicago, IL: U. S. Military Entrance Processing Command.

Vondracek, F. W., Lerner, R. W., & Schulenberg, J. E. (1986). *Career development: A life-span developmental approach.* Hillsdale, NJ: Erlbaum.

Weinrach, G. (1984). Determinants of vocational choice: Holland's theory. In D. Brown, L. Brooks, & Associates (Eds.), *Career choice and development: Applying contemporary theories to practice* (3rd ed., pp. 61–93). San Francisco, CA: Jossey-Bass.

Weinrach, S. G. (1996). The psychological and vocational interest patterns of Donald Super and John Holland. *Journal of Counseling & Development, 75,* 5–16.

CHAPTER 3

UNDERSTANDING AND APPLYING EMERGING THEORIES OF CAREER DEVELOPMENT

Career theory provides a framework through which to view the career situations of individuals. Theory serves as a "road map" to help us understand individuals' career journeys, what factors along the way may have shaped their career development, what barriers and obstacles they may face now and in the future, and how to plot a course for the future. Like a prism, career theory enables us to view careers from many different angles. The constructs and concepts that comprise various theoretical approaches can serve as guides in helping us learn more about the unique characteristics of individuals. Theories can sensitize us to factors that may have negatively impacted a person's career development and strategies for moving forward in a positive direction. Some career theories help us learn about and see the connection between persons and their options, including work, education, and leisure. Career theories also help us understand how work interacts with the other life roles an individual may pursue. Finally, career theories provide models to further our insight into the career decision-making and problem-solving process. Theories come alive when they move beyond the written page and further inform our work with individuals who are making career choices and exploring career transitions.

Janet G. Lenz, Ph.D., MCC, NCC
President, National Career Development Association (2004–2005)
Associate Director
Career Center,
Florida State University

Ronald, a 20-year-old African American male, presents for career counseling during the second semester of his sophomore year in college. In his initial appointment he states that he has not given much serious consideration to "life after college" and that he feels "confused" about his career goals. As the starting quarterback for the university's football team, Ronald had always thought he would play professional football. However, an injury and lackluster performance in the past season have left him feeling less confident about his ability to achieve this goal. He reports feeling "overwhelmed" and "doubtful" that he will be able to identify a suitable occupational alternative to professional football.

Ronald has a high grade-point average (3.6 out of 4.0) and has taken a wide variety of courses without declaring a college major. He is very personable and reports interests in math, literature, and music (he has played the piano since elementary school). He is also very involved in community service and is a mentor for two junior high school students. From his comments, it is clear that Ronald has high expectations for himself. He now feels very anxious because he is not sure what he wants to do. Both of Ronald's parents are educators. His mother is employed as a high school math teacher, and his father is employed as a high school principal.

EMERGING THEORIES

Several very promising career theories have recently emerged onto the scene. The social cognitive career theory developed by Lent, Brown, and Hackett (1996; 2002), the cognitive information processing theory developed by Peterson, Sampson, Reardon, and Lenz (1996) and Peterson, Sampson, Lenz and Reardon (2002), the values-based model of career choice developed by Brown (1995; 2002), and the integrative life-planning model developed by Hansen (1997) are each excellent examples of such theories. Additionally, a group of theories described as "postmodern" approaches to career development interventions have been developed to address the client's "subjective" experiences of career development (Cochran, 1997; Young, Valach, & Collin, 1996). Approaches emphasizing the subjective career highlight the ways in which meaning is made out of life experiences and then translated into a career choice (Carlsen, 1988; Cochran, 1990, 1997; Savickas, 1995).

For the most part, each of these emerging theories draws upon a solid foundation of research support. Emerging career theories strive to address the career development experiences of diverse client populations. Emerging career theories also reflect two major trends within career theory and practice. One trend is the rising prominence of cognitive theories within the career domain. The second trend is the growing realization that career interventions must fit the client (rather than the other way around) and that clients are active agents in the career construction process. Finally, each of the emerging theories discussed in this chapter are particularly useful in advancing career development practice.

LENT, BROWN, AND HACKETT'S SOCIAL COGNITIVE CAREER THEORY

The social cognitive career theory (SCCT) (Brown & Lent, 1996; Lent & Brown, 2002; Lent et al., 1996, 2002) provides a conceptual framework for understanding how people develop career-related interests, make occupational choices, and achieve career success and stability. SCCT builds upon the assumption that cognitive factors play an important role in career development and career decision making. SCCT is closely linked to Krumboltz's learning theory of career counseling, or LTCC (Mitchell & Krumboltz, 1996). Lent et al. (1996) noted, however, that SCCT differs from Krumboltz's theory in several ways. For example, in comparison to LTCC, SCCT "is more concerned with the specific cognitive mediators through which learning experiences guide career behavior; with the manner in which variables such as interests, abilities, and values interrelate; and with the specific paths by which person and contextual factors influence career outcomes. It also emphasizes the means by which individuals emphasize personal agency" (p. 377).

SCCT also draws heavily from Albert Bandura's (1986) social cognitive theory. Specifically, SCCT incorporates Bandura's triadic reciprocal model of causality, which assumes that personal attributes, the environment, and overt behaviors "operate as interlocking mechanisms that affect one another bidirectionally" (Lent et al., 1996, p. 379). Within this triadic reciprocal model, SCCT highlights self-efficacy beliefs, outcome expectations, and personal goals (Figure 3.1). Thus, SCCT also incorporates research, applying self-efficacy theory to the career domain (Hackett & Betz, 1981; Lent & Brown, 2002; Lent & Hackett, 1987).

Bandura defines self-efficacy beliefs as "people's judgments of their capabilities to organize and execute courses of action required to attain designated types of performances" (1986, p. 391). Self-efficacy beliefs are dynamic self-beliefs and are domain specific. Self-efficacy beliefs provide answers to questions pertaining to whether we can perform specific tasks (e.g., Can I make this presentation? Can I pass the statistics exam? Can I learn person-centered counseling skills?). Our beliefs about our abilities play a central role in the career decision making process. We move toward those occupations requiring capabilities we think we either have or can develop. We move away from those occupations requiring capabilities we think we do not possess or that we cannot develop.

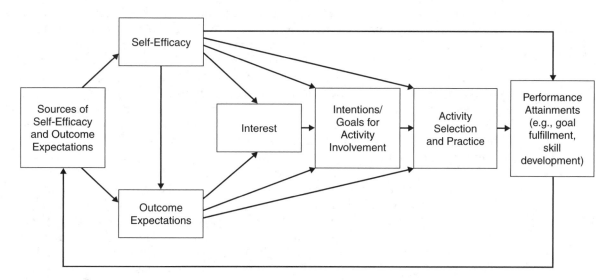

Figure 3.1

The development of basic career interests over time. From Toward a Unifying Social Cognitive Theory of Career and Academic Interest, Choice, and Performance, by R. W. Lent, S. D. Brown, and G. Hackett, 1994, *Journal of Vocational Behavior, 45,* 79–122. Copyright 1993 by R. W. Lent, S. D. Brown, and G. Hackett. Reprinted by permission.

Four sources shape self-efficacy beliefs: (a) personal performance accomplishments, (b) vicarious learning, (c) social persuasion, and (d) physiological states and reactions (Bandura, 1986). The most influential of these sources is the first (personal performance accomplishments). Successful accomplishments result in more positive or stronger domain-specific self-efficacy beliefs and failures lead to more negative or weaker domain-specific beliefs.

Outcome expectations are beliefs about the outcomes of performing specific behaviors (e.g., What is likely to happen if I apply for an internship at the university counseling center? What job opportunities am I likely to have if I earn a doctoral degree in counseling?). Outcome expectations include our beliefs about "extrinsic reinforcement (receiving tangible rewards for successful performance), self-directed consequences (such as pride in oneself for mastering a challenging task), and outcomes derived from the process of performing a given activity (for instance, absorption in the task itself)" (Lent et al., 1996, p. 381). Outcome expectations influence behavior to a lesser degree than self-efficacy beliefs (e.g., even though I might like to have more job options, I am not likely to enroll in a doctoral program in counseling if I think there is a low probability that I will be successful in this program of study). Thus, outcome expectations are what we imagine will happen if we perform specific behaviors.

Personal goals also influence career behaviors in important ways. Personal goals relate to our determination to engage in certain activities to produce a particular outcome (Bandura, 1986). Goals help to organize and guide our behavior over long periods of time (e.g., I will persist in my research course because it is an important step along the way toward earning my master's degree in counseling and obtaining a job as a counselor).

The relationship among goals, self-efficacy, and outcome expectations is complex and occurs within the framework of Bandura's (1986) triadic reciprocal model of causality (i.e., personal attributes, external environmental factors, and overt behavior). In essence, this model describes how *person inputs* (e.g., predisposition, gender, and race) interact with contextual factors (e.g., culture, geography, family, gender-role socialization) and learning experiences to influence our self-efficacy beliefs and outcome expectations. Self-efficacy beliefs and outcome expectations in turn shape our interests, goals, actions, and eventually our attainments. However, these are also influenced by contextual factors (e.g., job opportunities, access to training opportunities, financial resources).

For example, our client Ronald stated that, as a young child, he was athletically gifted and large for his age (person inputs). Because he lived in the United States and because his father had been an outstanding football player (contextual factors), Ronald was encouraged to play football at an early age (persuasion). His physical size and talents led to success as a football player (positive reinforcement). He came to believe he was good at this sport (self-efficacy beliefs) and that if he continued playing it, he would continue to do well (outcome expectations). His interest in this activity led him to develop the goal of playing football in college at a major university (personal goal). To achieve this goal, Ronald continued to practice hard and develop his skills as a football player (actions). His family could financially afford to send him to the best football camps where Ronald was able to further develop his skills and be exposed to football coaches from the best university football programs (proximal contextual factors). Eventually, Ronald was awarded a football scholarship to a major university (performance attainment).

Obviously, Ronald's path may have been very different if he had possessed different person inputs (e.g., lacked athletic ability, been born as a girl), had different contextual influences (e.g., been born in Europe), and experienced different learning experiences (e.g., received no support for participating in athletics, performed poorly as a football player). No doubt these differences would have resulted in different efficacy beliefs, outcome expectations, interests, goals, actions, and performance attainments.

Applying SCCT

SCCT is particularly useful in addressing two areas of career concern: performance attainment and persistence at overcoming obstacles. Performance is influenced by ability, self-efficacy, outcome expectations, and goals. Ability affects performance both directly and indirectly through influencing self-efficacy beliefs and outcome expectations. According to Lent and Brown (1996), "Higher self-efficacy and anticipated positive outcomes promote higher goals, which help to mobilize and sustain performance behavior" (p. 318). Problems in career development emerge when individuals prematurely foreclose on occupational options due to inaccurate self-efficacy beliefs, outcome expectations, or both, and when individuals forego further consideration of occupational options due to barriers they perceive as insurmountable (Brown & Lent, 1996).

For example, given Ronald's early and intense commitment to becoming a professional football player, it is possible that he did not fully explore a wide range of occupational possibilities prior to selecting professional football. His recent difficulties as a football player have caused him to realize that he has not explored other career options. In fact, Ronald reports feeling overwhelmed by the prospect of engaging in career exploration. He even questions whether there are occupations that will allow him to experience success and satisfaction. Thus, career development interventions in SCCT are often directed toward self-efficacy beliefs and outcome expectations.

To examine premature foreclosure on occupational options, Brown and Lent (1996) recommend that counselors encourage their clients to discuss those options that they have eliminated from further consideration. Specifically, in discussing occupations of low interest, counselors should analyze the experiences and beliefs upon which their clients' lack of interest is based. Here counselors focus on identifying any inaccuracies in their clients' self-efficacy beliefs and occupational information. Brown and Lent also state, "The basic processes for facilitating interest exploration are, therefore, fairly straightforward and include assessing discrepancies between self-efficacy and demonstrated skill and between outcome expectations and occupational information" (p. 357).

One approach used by Brown and Lent for facilitating interest exploration involves the use of a card sort exercise. In this exercise, clients sort occupations according to (a) those they would choose, (b) those they would not choose, and (c) those they question. Clients are then instructed to focus on the latter two categories by identifying occupations in these categories that they might choose if they thought they had the skills (self-efficacy beliefs), those they might choose if they thought the occupation offered them things they value (outcome expectations), and those they definitely would not choose under any circumstances. Occupations placed in the first two categories (relating to self-efficacy beliefs and outcome expectations) are then examined for accuracy in skill and outcome perceptions.

To analyze obstacles or barriers to their clients' career development, Brown and Lent (1996) recommend adapting Janis and Mann's (1977) decisional balance sheet procedure. Their adaptation of this procedure involves asking clients to first list their preferred career option(s) and then to identify the negative consequences they imagine will occur in pursuing any specific option. Negative consequences are explored as possible career-choice-implementation barriers by asking clients (a) to consider the probability of encountering each barrier and (b) to develop strategies for preventing or managing the barriers clients are most likely to encounter.

For example, in career counseling, Ronald noted that he would be interested in becoming a math teacher but was reluctant to do so because teachers have to deal with a lot of "grief from students and parents." He also stated that teachers do not make a salary that is sufficient for raising a family. The counselor suggested to Ronald that much of the "grief" encountered from students represented opportunities to help them deal with difficulties in their lives (Ronald placed a high value on helping others). It was also suggested that teachers can receive skill training to learn how to respond effectively to many student and parent concerns. To explore the issue of salary, the counselor encouraged Ronald to conduct information interviews with teachers in several local school districts (his parents were employed in a district that was known for having below-average teaching salaries). When he learned that there can be significant salary differences between school districts, Ronald began to think that it might be possible to earn a decent wage as a schoolteacher. Ronald also began to identify ways he could eventually increase his salary (e.g., coaching, moving into administration) if he were to become a teacher.

Clients can be helped to modify their self-efficacy beliefs in several ways. When ability is sufficient, but self-efficacy beliefs are low due to factors such as racism and sex-role stereotyping, clients can be exposed to personally relevant vicarious learning opportunities. For example, a woman who is African American and who possesses ability sufficient for a career in engineering, but has low self-efficacy beliefs, can be exposed to engineers who are also African American and female (Hackett & Byars, 1996). Clients with sufficient ability but low self-efficacy beliefs can also be encouraged to gather ability-related data from friends, teachers, and others to counteract faulty self-efficacy beliefs. Counselors can also work collaboratively with these clients to construct success experiences (e.g., taking specific academic courses, participating in volunteer experiences) to strengthen weak self-efficacy beliefs. In processing these success experiences, counselors can challenge clients when they identify external attributions for their successes and disregard internal, stable causes (i.e., ability) for their successes.

Evaluating SCCT

Most research related to SCCT focuses on self-efficacy. In summarizing this litera-ture, Lent et al. (1996) noted support for the following theory-related conclusions: (1) domain-specific measures of self-efficacy are predictive of career-related inter-ests, choice, achievement, persistence, indecision, and career exploratory behavior; (2) intervention, experimental, and path-analytic studies have supported certain hy-pothesized causal relations between measures of self-efficacy, performance, and in-terests; and (3) gender differences in academic and career self-efficacy frequently help explain male-female differences in occupational consideration (p. 397).

Additionally, research findings indicate some support for SCCT's theorized rela-tionships among self-efficacy beliefs, outcome expectations, goals, and interests (Lent, Brown, & Hackett, 1994). For example, Lent et al. (2001) investigated the applicability of SCCT to educational choices made by college students. In this study they found that contextual barriers and supports indirectly affect educational choic-es through their influence on self-efficacy and the individual's willingness to convert interests into educational choices. Nauta, Kahn, Angell, and Cantarelli (2002) inves-tigated the SCCT assumption that changes in self-efficacy precede changes in inter-ests. Using a cross-lagged panel research design and structural equation modeling, they found a reciprocal relationship between self-efficacy and interests but no clear pattern of temporal precedence. Flores and O'Brien (2002) conducted path analyses on data acquired from a sample of 364 Mexican American adolescent women to as-sess SCCT's propositions related to the influence of contextual and social cognitive variables on career aspiration, career choice prestige, and traditionality of career choice. These researchers found partial support for SCCT as nontraditional career self-efficacy, parental support, barriers, acculturation, and feminist attitudes pre-dicted career choice prestige. Additionally, acculturation, feminist attitudes, and nontraditional career self-efficacy predicted career choice traditionality. Finally, feminist attitudes and parental support predicted career aspiration. Gainor and Lent (1998) examined the relations among SCCT, racial identity, math-related interests, and choice of major within a sample of 164 African American first-year university students. They found that self-efficacy and outcome expectations predicted inter-ests, and interests predicted choice intentions across racial identity attitude levels. Diegelman and Subich (2001) found that raising outcome expectations among col-lege students considering pursuing a degree in psychology resulted in an increased interest in pursuing this degree option for their study participants.

Although more treatment outcome research is needed, several additional studies have demonstrated positive outcomes for SCCT-based interventions used with di-verse client groups (e.g., Chartrand & Rose, 1996; Chung, 2002; Hackett & Byars, 1996). An additional strength of SCCT is that it addresses both intra-individual and contextual variables in career development. Incorporating these two dimensions in-creases the applicability of the theory for diverse career development issues and pop-ulations. (It is interesting to note that the earliest research extending social cognitive theory to the career domain was conducted by Hackett and Betz [1981] to demon-strate how self-efficacy might be used to explain specific aspects of women's career development.) Finally, Brown (1996) noted that SCCT is a carefully developed theory that deserves high marks for translating theory into practice.

THE COGNITIVE INFORMATION PROCESSING APPROACH

The cognitive information processing (CIP) approach (Peterson et al., 1996; Peterson et al., 2002) is rooted in the three-factor Parsonian model for making career choices (i.e., self-understanding, occupational knowledge, and bringing self-understanding and occupational knowledge together to make a choice). The CIP approach extends the Parsonian model, however, by incorporating more recent developments related to how people engage in cognitive information processing. Peterson and his associates apply what is known about cognitive information processing to career counseling.

There are four assumptions underlying the theory. The first assumption is that career decision making involves the interaction between cognitive and affective process. Second, the capacity for career problem solving depends on the availability of cognitive operations and knowledge. Third, career development is ongoing and knowledge structures continually evolve. And fourth, enhancing information processing skills is the goal of career counseling (Peterson et al., 2002).

The CIP approach to career intervention includes several dimensions: (1) the pyramid of information processing, (2) CASVE cycle of decision making skills, and (3) the executive processing domain. First, the approach uses an information processing pyramid to describe the important domains of cognition involved in a career choice (Figure 3.2). The first three of these domains are those traditionally included in career theories: self-knowledge (values, interests, skills), occupational knowledge (understanding specific occupations and educational/training opportunities), and decision making skills (understanding how one typically makes decisions). The fourth

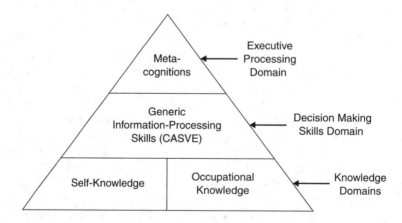

Figure 3.2

Pyramid of information-processing domains in career decision making. From *Career Development and Services: A Cognitive Approach*, by G. W. Peterson, J. P. Sampson, Jr., and R. C. Reardon. Copyright © 1991. Reprinted with permission of Wadsworth, an imprint of the Wadsworth Group, a division of Thomson Learning. Fax 800 730–2215.

domain is metacognitions and includes self-talk, self-awareness, and the monitoring and control of cognitions (Sampson, Peterson, Lenz, & Reardon, 1992). Knowledge of self and occupations forms the foundation of the pyramid, and then decision making skills and metacognitions build upon this foundation.

The second dimension of the CIP approach is labeled the CASVE cycle of career decision making skills (Figure 3.3). The CASVE cycle represents a generic model of information-processing skills related to solving career problems and making career decisions. These skills are (a) communication, (b) analysis, (c) synthesis, (d) valuing, and (e) execution (CASVE).

The use of these skills is cyclical, beginning with the realization that a gap exists between a real state and an ideal state (e.g., an existing state of career indecision and a more desired state of career decidedness). Becoming aware of such gaps can occur internally through the existence of ego-dystonic emotional states (e.g., depression, anxiety); the occurrence of behaviors such as excessive tardiness, absenteeism, or drug use; or the existence of somatic symptoms (e.g., headaches, loss of appetite).

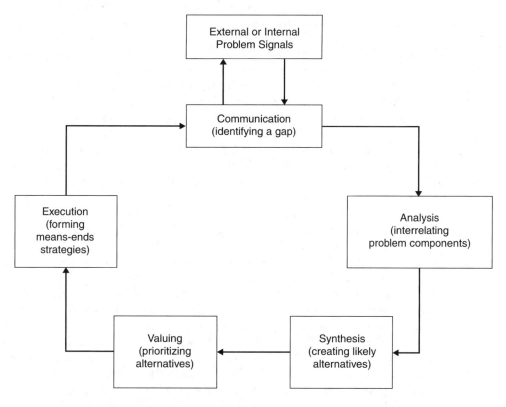

Figure 3.3

The five stages of the CASVE cycle of information-processing skills used in career decision making. From *Career Development and Services: A Cognitive Approach*, by G. W. Peterson, J. P. Sampson, Jr., and R. C. Reardon. Copyright © 1991. Reprinted with permission of Wadsworth, an imprint of the Wadsworth Group, a division of Thomson Learning. Fax 800 730–2215.

Or, we can become aware of such gaps through external demands (e.g., the need to select a curriculum of study in high school or college, the need to make a decision to accept or reject a job offer). Career problems, therefore, involve cognitive, affective, behavioral, and physiological components. Interpreting these internal and external cues involves *communication*. Specifically, clients must ask themselves two questions: (a) "What am I thinking and feeling about my career choice at this moment?" and (b) "What do I hope to attain as a result of career counseling?" (Peterson et al., 1996, p. 436).

Once we recognize that a gap or career problem exists, we must *analyze* what is required for problem resolution. For example, do we need more information about ourselves (e.g. values, interests) and/or the situation (e.g., my supervisor's expectations, job requirements)? What must we do to acquire the information or resources necessary to cope more effectively with the career problem (e.g., take an interest inventory, conduct an occupational information interview, seek counseling to understand our feelings related to our job situation)?

Synthesis involves two phases: (1) elaboration and (2) crystallization. During elaboration, clients seek to identify as many potential solutions to their career problems as possible (as in brainstorming, the focus is on quantity rather than quality solutions). During crystallization, clients identify those solutions that are consistent with their abilities, interests, or values. The outcome of these two phases that synthesis comprises is a manageable list of alternatives that are acceptable to the client.

Valuing involves first examining and prioritizing each of the alternatives generated in light of one's value system, the benefits to be gained and the costs incurred with each alternative, each alternative's impact on significant others and society, and the probability that the alternative will result in a successful outcome (i.e., removing the gap). Once the alternatives have been prioritized, the optimal alternative is identified. The primary question for clients engaged in the process of valuing is "Which alternative is the best course of action for me, my significant others, and society?" (Peterson et al., 1996, p. 437).

The *execution* phase involves converting the optimal alternative into action. A plan of action is developed to implement the alternative and achieve its goal (e.g., I will enroll in psychology courses, study 3 hours per day, and take a course to improve my Graduate Record Examination scores in order to achieve my goal of gaining entry into a highly selective counselor education program). Thus, the execution phase requires clients to identify the specific steps necessary to operationalize the solution chosen in the valuing phase. The primary question in execution is "How can I transform my choice into an action plan?" (Peterson et al., 1996, p. 437).

Once the plan has been enacted, clients return to the communication phase to determine whether the alternative was successful in resolving the career problem. Once again, cognitive, affective, behavioral, and physiological states are assessed in evaluating the success of the alternative (e.g., Do I feel less anxious? Am I more content with my career situation? Has my class attendance improved?). If the evaluation is positive, then clients move on, but if the evaluation is negative, then clients recycle through the CASVE phases with the new information acquired from enacting the first alternative.

A third dimension of the CIP approach is the *executive processing domain*. The function of the executive processing domain is to initiate, coordinate, and monitor the storage of and retrieval of information (Peterson, Sampson, & Reardon, 1991). This domain involves metacognitive skills (Meichenbaum, 1977), such as self-talk, self-awareness, and control. Positive self-talk (e.g., "I am capable of making a good career choice") is required for effective career problem solving. Negative self-talk ("I can't make a good decision") leads to career indecisiveness. Self-awareness is necessary in monitoring and controlling internal and external influences on career decisions. Effective problem solvers and decision makers are aware of their values, beliefs, biases, and feelings. They use this awareness in generating and selecting problem solutions. Control and monitoring are essential for deciphering the information needed to resolve a career problem and for knowing when one is ready to move to the next phase in the CASVE cycle. The "control and monitoring of lower-order functions ensures that an optimal balance is met between impulsivity and compulsivity" (Peterson et al., 1991, p. 39), thereby providing a "quality control mechanism to ensure a complete, orderly, and timely progression through the CASVE cycle" (Peterson et al., 1996, p. 439).

Applying the CIP Approach

The pyramid model can be used as a framework for providing career development interventions. For example, the self-knowledge domain can be addressed through standardized and nonstandardized assessments. The occupational knowledge domain can be addressed by engaging in job-shadowing exercises and by reading about occupational biographies (as when Ronald was encouraged to conduct occupational information interviews). The five steps of the CASVE cycle can be used to teach decision making skills, and the executing processing domain provides a framework for exploring and challenging clients' dysfunctional metacognitions.

Peterson et al. (1991) have outlined a seven-step sequence for delivering individual, group, and classroom career development interventions. Step one involves conducting an initial interview with the client. During this step, the counselor attempts to understand the context and nature of the client's career problem. The counselor develops an effective working relationship with the client by responding empathically to client statements and by using basic counseling skills (e.g., clarification, summarization, reflection of affect, immediacy, self-disclosure).

Counselors introduce clients to the pyramid model and the CASVE cycle to clarify client concerns and to provide clients with a model for understanding the career decision making and problem-solving processes (Sampson et al., 1992). During this step, counselors focus on questions such as "What are the client's perceptions of the extent of development in each of the domains? How does the client typically make career decisions? Which metacognitions, if any, are dysfunctional and need changing? At which phase is the client currently focused?" (Sampson et al., 1992, p. 73).

In Ronald's case, he was feeling stuck because he was not clear about the process typically used in making career decisions. He was also stuck because he believed that there were no occupational options that would be suitable for him (although he had not really engaged in any systematic exploration of occupational options). Moreover, he doubted his ability to make an effective occupational choice. Using the pyramid model to explain the decision process could provide Ronald with a sense of control and structure, thereby lessening his feeling of being "overwhelmed." Establishing an effective working relationship with Ronald and offering him a sense of hope that he could learn the skills necessary for managing his career could also help Ronald feel more confident and reassured that he could cope effectively with these career development tasks.

Step two involves conducting a preliminary assessment to determine the client's readiness for career decision making. The CIP approach uses the Career Thoughts Inventory (CTI) (Sampson, Peterson, Lenz, Reardon, & Saunders, 1996) to identify clients with dysfunctional career thoughts and, thereby, provide an indication of career development interventions that may be required to address the client's executive processing domain. For example, Ronald may be adhering to beliefs such as "I must be absolutely certain an occupation will be satisfying to me before I can take action," "All teachers are paid poor salaries," or "I must decide now what I want to do for the rest of my life." Adherence to such beliefs will be problematic for Ronald as he engages in career planning. Thus, these beliefs need to be challenged and restructured for him to move forward (Lewis & Gilhousen, 1981).

In step three, counselors and clients work collaboratively to define the career problem(s) and to analyze potential causes of the problem. Here, counselors communicate nonjudgmentally their perceptions of clients' gaps between a real state of career indecision and the desired or ideal state of career decidedness (Cochran, 1997). Clients respond by agreeing with counselors' perceptions or by clarifying and restating the gap they are experiencing.

In step four, counselors and clients continue collaborating by formulating achievable career problem-solving and decision making goals. The formulation of goals leads to developing an individual learning plan in step five. Individual learning plans provide clients with a guide concerning what activities they need to engage in and what resources they need to use to achieve their goals. Although individual learning plans provide a mechanism for monitoring and evaluating client progress, they may also be revised as clients acquire more information about themselves and their career concerns.

Step six in the CIP approach requires clients to execute their individual learning plans. Counselors can provide support, feedback, and assistance to clients as they complete their individual learning plans. Counselors can challenge clients with dysfunctional career thoughts to revise their thinking and then take action to complete their individual learning plans. Finally, during step seven, counselors and clients conduct a summative review of client progress and then generalize new learning to other current and future career problems.

Evaluating CIP

Although research investigating CIP theory is not extensive, the number of studies based on CIP theory is growing. The development of the CTI should serve as a catalyst for CIP researchers investigating theoretical propositions related to the executive processing domain. The workbook accompanying the CTI, entitled *Improving Your Career Thoughts: A Workbook for the Career Thoughts Inventory* (Sampson et al., 1996), is an excellent example of translating theory into practice. This more recent extension of the CIP approach builds upon what one reviewer noted as the major contribution of the theory—the executive processing domain (Helwig, 1992). Brown (1996) noted that the description of the decision making process outlined in Peterson et al. (1996) "is perhaps the clearest description of the variables involved in this process yet to emerge" (p. 521).

A recent study conducted by Reed, Reardon, Lenz, and Leier (2001) examined the effectiveness of a career planning course based on the CIP approach. Using the CTI, results of this study indicated a significant decrease in negative career thoughts from pretest to posttest. Saunders, Peterson, Sampson, and Reardon (2000) used the CTI to investigate depression and dysfunctional career thinking as components of the state of career indecision among a sample of 215 undergraduate university students. They found a significant positive correlation between dysfunctional career thoughts as measured by the CTI and career indecision and, thus, recommend using the CTI in career counseling to help identify appropriate treatment strategies for clients experiencing career indecision.

Osborn, Peterson, Sampson, and Reardon (2003) used CIP as the theoretical framework for investigating client anticipations prior to using a computer-assisted career guidance system. Clients' most frequent anticipations for computer use included increased career options, enhanced self-knowledge, and strengthened occupational knowledge. Reardon and Wright (1999) describe how the CIP approach can be used in conjunction with Holland's theory to help a 19-year-old college student become aware of negative thought patterns serving as obstacles to choosing a college major. Similarly, McLennan and Arthur (1999) decribe how CIP is useful for helping women cope effectively with structural and individual barriers in their career development.

The fact that the CIP research team (i.e., Peterson, Reardon, Lenz, and Sampson) built their theory upon a solid foundation of research in cognitive psychology, have developed clear definitions of the different dimensions of the theory, and are committed to translating theory into practice suggests a bright future for the CIP approach to career development interventions. Plus, the CIP approach appears to be robust enough to address a wide array of client concerns and client populations.

BROWN'S VALUES-BASED, HOLISTIC MODEL OF CAREER AND LIFE-ROLE CHOICES AND SATISFACTION

D. Brown (1995, 1996, 2002) has formulated a model of career development based on the importance of values in career decision making. Brown contends that his model addresses the neglect of cultural issues reflected in many career development theories. His values-based model draws upon the work of Rokeach (1973), Super (1953, 1990), and Beck (1987). For example, in defining values Brown used Rokeach's (1973) notion that values are beliefs containing cognitive, affective, and behavioral dimensions. Additionally, Brown (1996, 2002) pointed out that values serve as standards by which people evaluate their own actions and the actions of others. For example, working 80 hours a week for 50 weeks out of the year to earn a significant salary makes sense to the person who values materialism but is hard to understand for the person who values spending time with family. Thus, values direct our behavior in specific directions and toward particular goals. Values systems include cultural and work values. Cultural values include beliefs about human nature, one's orientation to time, one's orientation to the group (i.e., collectivism) and the individual (i.e., individualism), and one's mode of self-expression (Brown, 2002). Values help explain why some people experience occupational dissatisfaction even when their occupational performance is satisfactory. Specifically, when occupational activities do not coincide with one's value structure, then it is likely that a person will experience occupational dissatisfaction.

Brown (1996, 2002) theorized that values are shaped by genetics and environment. Environmental factors influencing values development include family, media, community, school, and culture. As values emerge, they "influence all aspects of function, including processing of data, and thus what may be clear to one person who holds one value may be unclear or irrational to a person who does not hold that value" (Brown, 1996, p. 341). As a result of genetic and environmental influences, specific values become more important than others. As values become crystallized and prioritized, people use them to guide and explain their behavior. For example, a graduate student with excellent grades and high entrance exam scores could probably enroll in a variety of graduate school programs but will probably choose a particular type of program over another (e.g., a counselor education program rather than a graduate-level business school) due to the values she has crystallized and prioritized (e.g., helping others is more important than economic rewards). Thus, "values orient individuals to those aspects of their environment that may provide desired outcomes" (Brown & Crace, 1996, p. 216).

The values-based model of career choice is based on seven propositions as stated by Brown and Crace (1996):

1. Values with high priorities are the most important determinants of choices made, providing that the individuals have more than one alternative available that will satisfy their values.
2. The values included in the values system are acquired from society, and each person develops a small number of values.
3. Culture, sex, and socioeconomic status influence opportunities and social interaction, and thus considerable variation in the values of subgroups in U.S. society can be expected.
4. Making choices that coincide with values is essential to satisfaction.
5. The result of role interaction is life satisfaction, which differs from the sum of the marital, job, leisure, and other role satisfaction indices taken separately.
6. High-functioning people have well-developed and prioritized values.
7. Success in any role depends on the abilities and the aptitudes required to perform the functions of that role. (pp. 212–220)

For each proposition, Brown and Crace (1996) identified research findings supporting their assumptions and noted that these assumptions reflect a synthesis of other theories and their own speculations (in addition to values-related research).

Applying the Values-Based Approach

The application of the values-based approach is based on a number of assumptions with varying degrees of research support (Brown, 2002). For example, the values-based approach assumes that because life roles interact, these interactions need to be incorporated into the career counseling process; that mood-related problems should be dealt with prior to career-related concerns; that career counselors need to be able to translate various types of psychological data (e.g., interests) into values-based terms; and that because understanding one's values is key to making effective career decisions, counselors must be skilled at helping clients clarify and understand their values.

The values-based approach classifies clients into one of two categories: those clients who are making planned decisions and those who are making unplanned decisions (Brown, 1996). Some career development interventions are provided to all clients. For example, developing an effective therapeutic alliance is crucial in all career counseling relationships. For all clients, counselors must assess whether (a) there are intrapersonal values conflicts, (b) mood problems exist, (c) values have been crystallized and prioritized, (d) the client is able to use the values-based information already acquired, and (e) the client understands how potential career choices may impact other life roles.

When working with clients making planned career changes, counselors assess (a) how issues related to intrarole and interrole conflict may be contributing to client career dissatisfaction and (b) how client flexibility relates to geographic location, training opportunities, and qualifications. Clients making unplanned career changes are assessed (a) for the existence of mood problems, (b) for financial concerns, (c) as to whether existing career opportunities can satisfy values, and, when this is not possible, (d) what changes clients can make to increase the satisfaction they derive from their other life roles.

Values assessment can be accomplished through qualitative or quantitative methods. Qualitative methods include card sorts, checklists, and guided fantasies (Brown, 1996; Brown & Brooks, 1991). Quantitative methods include the use of inventories such as Rokeach's Values Survey (1973), the Values Scale (Super & Nevill, 1986), and the Life Values Inventory (Crace & Brown, 1996).

When clients have crystallized and prioritized their values, they then focus on career decision making. When this is not the case, Brown uses Rokeach's (1973) suggestion that values can be clarified and changed by the processes of contemplation and conflict. The former process can be incorporated into career counseling through the use of qualitative exercises (e.g., values clarification activities, analysis of daydreams, and discussion of reasons clients admire specific individuals) or through the use of more quantitative activities using values inventory assessments (Brown & Crace, 1996).

Conflict involves self-confrontation of various values. This type of conflict can be incorporated into career counseling through the use of guided imagery and role-playing exercises. In these exercises counselors can introduce scenarios in which conflicts among life roles must be confronted and choices between specific values can be juxtaposed. Brown (1996) also recommends using the "Why" technique as a means for helping clients crystallize and prioritize their values. The "Why" technique involves continuously challenging clients by asking why they are making specific statements.

To help Ronald clarify and prioritize his values, it might be useful to start by using a values sorting exercise. To begin this activity, Ronald is given a list of values as follows:

Values List

_____ Good family relationships	_____ Associating with people I like
_____ Financial security	_____ Success
_____ Job security	_____ Freedom to live where I choose
_____ A world that is free of discrimination	_____ Leisure time
_____ Creativity	_____ Fame
_____ Having a set routine	_____ Strong religious faith
_____ Time by myself	_____ Adventure
_____ Community activities	_____ World peace
_____ Physical activities	_____ Helping others
_____ An attractive physical appearance	_____ Having children
_____ Variety	_____ Good health
_____ Power	_____ A beautiful home
_____ Recognition	_____ Autonomy
_____ Prestige	_____ Other
_____ Freedom from stress	

Ronald is then asked to identify his top 10 values from this list by putting an X next to the values that are most important to him (the values chosen are not ranked at this point).

After discussing his experience of conducting this initial values sort, Ronald is provided with five slips of paper and asked to identify his top 5 values from the list of his top 10 and to write one value on each slip of paper (again, these values are not ranked). The counselor then informs Ronald that she will be taking a value from him, one at a time. Thus, he must now decide which of his top five values he is willing to part with first. Immediately after giving a value to the counselor, she instructs Ronald to record and define what that value means to him (e.g., "financial rewards: having an income of more than $45,000 a year with good health and retirement benefits"). This process is continued for each of the remaining values. At the conclusion of the exercise, Ronald will have a list of his top five values, with definitions, in descending order. For example,

Values Definitions

5. Financial rewards: having an income of more than $45,000 a year with good health and retirement benefits.
4. Helping others: working with young people to help them overcome their problems and achieve their potential.

3. Associating with people I like: being able to be friends with my coworkers and to do things together outside of work.
2. Good health: eating right and exercising regularly.
1. Strong religious faith: going to church on a regular basis and volunteering as a mentor for troubled youth.

After completing the exercise, the counselor can explain to Ronald how the activity relates to career decision making. The counselor can explain that in every decision there is the promise of gain and the threat of loss (otherwise, one could simply choose the "perfect" option in every instance) and that the risk involved in decision making is lessened when the options selected are based on the individual's key values.

Ronald can also be encouraged to consider how he spends his time in the course of a typical week and if he spends time in activities reflecting the top values he identified. If he does not, then Ronald can be encouraged to identify strategies for increasing his participation in activities reflecting his values (e.g., agreeing to a moderate exercise program, identifying opportunities for volunteering). This activity represents an example of ways to incorporate contemplation and conflict (self-confrontation) related to values clarification into the career counseling process.

Evaluating the Values-Based Approach

Brown's values-based approach fills a gap in the literature related to an important dimension of career development—values. Moreover, Brown does an excellent job of incorporating values-related research in formulating theoretical propositions for the approach. Brown also addresses the ways in which contextual factors (e.g., the person's cultural values) influence career decisions. Additional research is needed to increase understanding related to ways in which cultural values interact with work values to influence career decisions.

In some respects, the values-based approach is a useful supplement to other theories (e.g., Super's theory) that identify values as important but does not offer extensive explanations for how values develop and influence career decision making. Another strength of the values-based approach is the use of the Life Values Inventory (LVI) (Crace & Brown, 1996) for translating theory into practice. The LVI helps clients examine their values in ranked fashion as well as how they relate to their primary life roles (e.g., career, relationships, leisure/personal). As with all emerging theories, more research is needed examining the theoretical assumptions of the values-based approach, especially those pertaining to career counseling. Also, more extensive information (i.e., theory explication and research) is needed related to cultural influences on values development and how those cultural influences impact the career counseling process within the values-based approach.

HANSEN'S INTEGRATIVE LIFE PLANNING

Of all the theories discussed in Chapters 1 and 2, Hansen's integrative life planning model (ILP) (Hansen, 1997) is unique in that rather than offering a theory that can be translated into individual counseling, Hansen contends that ILP is a new worldview for addressing career development. As such, ILP centrally addresses diversity issues related to ethnicity, race, gender, socioeconomic status, and spirituality. The "integrative" aspect of ILP relates to the emphasis on integrating the mind, body, and spirit. The "life planning" concept acknowledges, in a fashion similar to Super's (1980) life-space theory, that multiple aspects of life are interrelated. "Planning" is included in the title because, despite recent discussions about the value of planning in a time of uncertainty, it connotes a sense of personal agency in the career development process (Hansen, 2002). The ILP framework also draws upon psychology, sociology, economics, multiculturalism, and constructivism and takes a holistic approach by encouraging people to connect various aspects of life. Rather than a life-span model, ILP focuses on adult career development and is based on the following assumptions (Hansen, 2002):

1. Changes in the nature of knowledge support the addition of new ways of knowing to career development theory, research, and practice.
2. Career professionals need to help students, clients, and employees develop skills of integrative thinking—seeing connections in their lives and in their local and global communities.
3. Broader kinds of self-knowledge (beyond interests, abilities, and values) and societal knowledge (beyond occupational and educational information) are critical to an expanded view of career, including multiple roles, identities, and critical life tasks in diverse cultures.
4. Career counseling needs to focus on career professionals as change agents, helping clients to achieve more holistic lives and become advocates and agents for positive societal change through the choices and decisions they make.

Hansen (1997) uses these four broad assumptions to identify six career development tasks confronting adults today. The six tasks reflect Hansen's emphasis on social justice, social change, connectedness, diversity, and spirituality. For example, the first task is labeled as "finding work that needs doing in changing global contexts." Here Hansen suggests that adults consider focusing on work that will result in a more socially just world (e.g., preserving the environment, understanding and celebrating diversity, advocating for human rights, and exploring spirituality). Similar to early notions of "bad" work and "good" work, Hansen encourages people to identify what they can do to contribute to positive change for social and environmental justice.

The second task Hansen identifies is "weaving our lives into a meaningful whole." This task emphasizes the point that few things are more personal than a career choice (Niles & Pate, 1989). Occupational choices are intertwined with other life-role choices and must be considered holistically and within the greater context of one's life. This task also suggests that persons must draw upon their subjective experiences in clarifying and articulating their career choices.

Hansen's third task is an extension of the second. Labeled as "connecting family and work," it emphasizes life-role integration and the importance of negotiating roles and relationships (Hansen, 2002). This task also highlights the need to examine gender-role expectations and stereotypes. ILP envisions men and women as partners in the home and in the workplace. Hansen also advocates for valuing self-sufficiency and connectedness within men and women. Although not stated in ILP, one would expect that the same notions of equity in work and home activities would also be applied to same-sex couples.

"Valuing pluralism and inclusivity" represents the fourth task confronting adults. Hansen notes the importance of celebrating diversity and developing multicultural competencies as critical for work and nonwork activities. Valuing pluralism recognizes the importance of difference and establishes a foundation for celebrating diversity.

Hansen's fifth task relates to "managing personal transitions and organizational change." Given the constancy of change in everyday experience, developing skills to cope effectively with transition is an essential task of adult development. In fact, Hansen (2002) suggests that transition counseling may be one of the most needed skills in career counseling. Tolerating ambiguity, developing personal flexibility, and being able to draw upon a reservoir of self-awareness and social support all help to negotiate life changes successfully. Finally, incorporating both rational and logical decision making skills with intuitive orientations that value "positive uncertainty" (Gelatt, 1989) and "planned happenstance" (Mitchell, Levin, & Krumboltz, 1999) is also important for coping effectively with transitions in a time of change, instability, and ambiguity in career development.

The sixth task in ILP is that of "exploring spirituality and life purpose." Spirituality may or may not be defined as religion. Spirituality embraces purpose, meaning, connectedness, and a sense of community. Career choices are, at their best, spiritual in that they are expressions of one's gifts and talents. Career practitioners help their clients consider spiritual issues in career decision making when they explore questions such as: "What does work mean in and for my life?" and "What do I want to mean to others through my work?" People engage in spiritually based career decision making when they examine the degree to which career options foster positive treatment of others, the environment, and themselves. The ILP approach joins Miller-Tiedeman's (1997) Lifecareer Theory and the work of Bloch and Richmond (1998) as a small but growing body of career development literature addressing the important topic of spirituality in career development. Collectively, spiritual approaches to career development emphasize common themes that can be summarized as follows:

1. Career development intertwines with human development. Life cannot be compartmentalized into "silos" of activity; thus, careers should be viewed holistically.
2. Clients should be encouraged to embrace and celebrate their life journeys, rather than judging past experiences negatively. All life experiences provide opportunities for learning and growth.
3. Maintaining an attitude of flexibility and openness fosters development as well as the opportunity to identify new opportunities for growth and learning.
4. Change should be celebrated and embraced rather than feared and avoided.
5. Career development interventions that actively and collaboratively engage the client in career counseling, incorporate intuition as well as reason in decision making, and draw upon subjective assessment activities, imagery, meditation, and positive self-affirmations also engage the spirit in the career development process.

Applying ILP

ILP suggests that career counselors should help their clients understand these six tasks, help clients see the interrelatedness of the various tasks, and help clients prioritize the tasks according to their needs. The specifics of how ILPM is applied in career counseling are still being developed. Hansen, Hage, and Kachgal (1999) developed the Integrative Life Planning Inventory to help clients identify where they are in relation to integrative thinking and planning. The assumptions and tasks of ILPM also form the basis for career development programs aimed at teaching participants holistic career planning. Currently, ILPM seems most useful as a framework for teaching an approach to life planning that emphasizes connectedness, wholeness, and community.

Evaluating ILP

ILP offers a creative approach to life planning. It appears to be a very useful framework from which counselors can encourage clients to consider important life issues in their career decisions. It is one of the few models to include spirituality as an important aspect of the career development process. The topic of spirituality is growing in interest as evidenced by the fact that it was the theme of the National Career Development Association's 2004 conference ("Celebrating the Spirit in Career Development"), and ILP is at the forefront of addressing this important topic. Similar to many recent models, ILP acknowledges the importance of context in career development. Moreover, it embraces social action by encouraging clients to consider the impact of their career choices on others and the environment. More research of ILP is needed, both in terms of the model's concepts as well as the ways in which the model can be applied effectively in career development interventions. It is also interesting to note that ILP has much in common with the emerging postmodern approaches to career development interventions and, in many ways, could be placed in this category.

POSTMODERN APPROACHES

Recently, attention has been given to career development theories and interventions "that depart from the positivistic scientific tradition that has dominated social and behavioral science research, in general, and most of the normative career development research, in particular" (Vondracek & Kawasaki, 1995, p. 115). The label of *postmodern* can be used to refer to those approaches (e.g., narrative, contextual, constructivist) that emphasize the importance of understanding our careers as they are lived or, to put it another way, our subjective experience of career development. Postmodernism embraces multicultural perspectives and emphasizes the belief that there is no one fixed truth but, rather, we each construct our own realities and truths. In this way, postmodern views include constructivist assumptions. Postmodern approaches also emphasize personal agency in the career construction process. For example, Cochran's (1994) narrative approach contends that career development theories should "provide systematic accounts of how persons become active agents rather than patients or victims of circumstances regarding career. The aim of career counseling is to enhance agency regarding career" (p. 209).

Creating Narratives

The narrative approach represents an example of a postmodern approach that highlights personal agency in career development. Specifically, career counseling from the narrative approach emphasizes understanding and articulating the main character to be lived out in a specific career plot (Cochran, 1997). This type of articulation uses the process of composing a narrative as the primary vehicle for defining the character and plot. Howard (1989) noted that "people tell themselves stories that infuse certain parts of their lives and actions with great meaning and de-emphasize other aspects. But had any of them chosen to tell himself or herself a somewhat different story, the resulting pattern of more-meaningful and less-meaningful aspects of his or her life would have been quite different" (p. 168). By constructing personal career narratives, we can come to see our movement through life more clearly and understand our specific decisions within a greater life context that has meaning and coherence.

Cochran (1997, pp. 5–9) identified several ways in which narratives help persons make meaning out of their life experiences:

1. **A narrative provides a temporal organization, integrating a beginning, middle, and end into a whole.** Such temporal organization offers the possibility of establishing personal continuity over a lifetime (e.g., the end provides a future goal and purpose, the middle concerns activity in the present that is directed toward the goal, and the beginning contains the past that informs the present, which, in turn, guides us to the future).
2. **A story is a synthetic structure that configures an indefinite expansion of elements and spheres of elements into a whole.** As Bateson (1979) stated, "Any A is relevant to any B if both A and B are parts or components of the same story" (p. 13). As long as something has a bearing on moving a plot along or expanding the meaning of that movement, it belongs in the story. Thus, narrative is a "meaning structure that organizes events and human actions into a whole, thereby attributing significance to individual actions and events according to their effect on the whole" (Polkinghorne, 1988, p. 18).
3. **The plot of a narrative carries a point.** It is not a meaningless rambling toward an end, but an integration of implicit convictions about the kind of person one is, the way other people are, the way the world is, and how things work or something gets accomplished. The structure of a narrative communicates a problem to be overcome (beginning), attempts at resolving the problem (middle), and an ending that, if positive, represents a solution to the problem, or, if negative, represents a resignation to the problem. In either case, the overall pattern of the story reveals a moral that influences behavior (e.g., if I work hard and succeed, I learn that hard work pays off and am likely to continue working hard to succeed).

Career counseling from a narrative approach begins with the identification of a career problem. Career problems are defined as gaps between one's current career situation and a desired career future (Cochran, 1985, p. 145). In the narrative sense, the career problem represents the beginning, and the middle relates to the way one is to move from the beginning to an end (Cochran, 1997, p. 36). The career counseling process involves a number of "episodes" that are incorporated into counseling depending on each client's career concerns. Cochran (1997) identified episodes of career counseling and their related techniques:

1. **Elaborating a career problem (pp. 35–51).** Techniques include using a vocational card sort (Gysbers & Moore, 1987), a laddering technique (Kelly, 1955), drawing (Dail, 1989), and testing.
2. **Composing a life history (pp. 55–78).** Techniques for composing a life history include constructing a life line (Goldman, 1992), the life chapters exercise (Carlsen, 1988), the accomplishments interview (Bolles, 1998), identifying early life-role models (Watkins & Savickas, 1990), and identifying early life recollections (Watkins & Savickas, 1990).
3. **Founding a future narrative (pp. 85–90).** Techniques include constructing a life line, using the life chapters exercise, using guidance material such as the Self-Directed Search (Holland, 1985), using the accomplishments interview, and using guided fantasy.
4. **Constructing reality (pp. 106–108).** Techniques include job shadowing, volunteering, internships, externships, occupational information interviews, and part-time employment.
5. **Changing a life structure (pp. 108–112).** Cochran recommends techniques discussed by Dunst, Trivette, and Deal (1988). These techniques involve first identifying needs and establishing priorities. Next, strengths in the way an individual and family function to get things done are identified. Third, the formal (e.g., a community agency) and informal (e.g., friends) sources of support that might be useful in solving a problem or moving the client forward are identified. Finally, the counselor attempts to align the client's needs, strengths, support resources, and resources available to meet the client's needs.
6. **Enacting a role (pp. 112–114).** Participating in meaningful and enjoyable activities provides clients with opportunities to actualize their ideals. Thus, enacting a role involves treating the present as an end in itself. Previous accomplishments, role models, and early life recollections provide indications as to what activities might be most significant. As roles are enacted, we refine our choices by considering the positive and negative aspects of the activities in which we engage. We use this new information to inform our subsequent decisions about which activities might be most enjoyable and meaningful. Cochran noted that this process is similar to a creativity cycle of striving and resting, participating and reflecting, as described by Ghiselin (1955).
7. **Crystallizing a decision (pp. 122–128).** Making a choice translates potentialities into actualities. To facilitate this process, clients can examine their values in light of specific career options via a career grid activity (Neimeyer, 1989), guided fantasy exercises, and identifying life themes (Watkins & Savickas, 1990). As

clients crystallize a decision, they may encounter internal and external barriers or obstructions (e.g., Will I succeed? Will the option be satisfying? What will my family think?). They may also need assistance in identifying activities that provide opportunities to connect with their "new stories" constructed earlier in the career counseling process. Opportunities for making connections with new stories are labeled as *actualizations* by Cochran (1997, p. 127).

Narrative approaches to describing career development and for providing career development interventions highlight the notion that "we are the stories that we live." Career counseling from this perspective provides clients with opportunities to reconstruct a coherent life story. As Peavy (1992) writes, "Stories of self and career can be used by counselor and client to consolidate present self-knowledge and to help guide forward movement into anticipated futures" (p. 219).

The life chapters exercise mentioned earlier is very useful in helping clients construct narratives and sensitizing them to the subjective experience of career (Cochran, 1997). In this exercise, clients are encouraged to consider their lives as if they were a book by dividing their lives into chapters. Clients are asked to give titles to the chapters of their lives. They are also invited to identify three important lessons they learned by living each chapter of their life. Then, clients are asked to look ahead at the rest of their lives and create chapter titles that go from the present on through to death. They are asked to identify the chapters they expect to happen and the chapters they want to make sure happen if their lives are to be complete. In processing this activity, positive chapters are restored and negative chapters are reversed in the future.

Contextualizing Career Development

Evident in our discussion thus far is the fact that postmodern approaches to career development interventions are sensitive to the immediate (e.g., family, cultural heritage, level of acculturation) and distal (e.g., economics, environmental opportunities) contextual factors influencing the meaning-making process for individuals (Blustein, 1994; Vondracek, Lerner, & Schulenberg, 1986; Young, Valach, & Collin, 1996, 2002). Postmodern approaches to career development interventions that identify ways in which contextual factors can be incorporated into the career counseling process are labeled as contextual career theories. Young, Valach, and Collin (1996) noted several assumptions pertaining to contextual career theories:

1. Acts are viewed as purposive and as being directed toward specific goals.
2. Acts are embedded in their context.
3. Change has a prominent role in career development. Because events take shape as people engage in practical action with a particular purpose, analysis and interpretation are always practical. Researchers look at action for a particular purpose.
4. Contextualism rejects a theory of truth based on the correspondence between mental representations and objective reality. (p. 480)

In their contextual theory, Young and his associates view career development as an action system that achieves social meaning through an interaction between individual intention and social context (Young & Collin, 1992). In their view, people construct their careers through action. Action can be organized according to hierarchical, sequential, and parallel dimensions (Young et al., 1996, 2002). Hierarchy relates to the prioritization of career goals into superordinate and subordinate construct categories. Sequence pertains to the sequencing or ordering of actions, and actions can be parallel in that "different actions for different goals can coexist" (1996, p. 484).

Thus, career and action are related constructs through which people make sense out of their lives and through which events in people's lives acquire meaning (Young & Valach, 1996). Of special importance are goal-directed actions people take in the career construction process. Such actions can be viewed from three perspectives: manifest behavior (i.e., the explicit career-related behavior taken), internal processes (i.e., thoughts and feelings related to the behavior being manifested), and social meaning (i.e., the meaning of the action to self and others). These three perspectives provide a framework both for explaining career development and for explaining career development interventions. Concerning the latter, we can view client–counselor interactions as manifest behaviors; client–counselor thoughts and feelings represent internal processes concerning the behaviors being manifested; and both clients and counselors are embedded in contexts from which they make social meaning concerning the career counseling experience. Thus, career counseling represents a project involving joint action between the counselor and client. Career and action emerge as the counselor and client engage in the career counseling process (Young et al., 2002).

The perspective of manifest behavior, internal processes, and social meaning also provides a framework for the ongoing assessment process within career counseling. For example, clients can participate in career-related actions (e.g., discuss post-high school plans with parents) and identify the thoughts, feelings, and social meaning associated with the career-related action (Young et al., 2002).

Social meaning also figures prominently in the interpretive process associated with career counseling. In discussing interpretation in career counseling, Young and Valach (1996, p. 367) note several assumptions. First, "people interpret their own and others' behavior as actions." Behavior is viewed as intentional and directed toward particular goals. Second, "people interpret ongoing action as part of some superordinate process such as career." Third, "people reinterpret their present action, and possibly career, thus establishing the relevance of career and similar constructs." Finally, "people not only interpret but also plan their behavior in terms of social meaning." Language and narrative also play an important role in interpretation. As noted earlier, language and narrative help people make sense out of their life events. They are the means by which people construct coherence and continuity out of their past, present, and goal-directed actions. Thus, Young, Valach, and Collin (2002) advise counselors to identify three important elements within a client's story: coherence, continuity, and causality. Coherent stories make sense chronologically. Continuity is revealed in goal-directed behavior. Explaining how events occurred reveals the causality within the client's story. Focusing on these three dimensions within a client's story place the client in the role of active agent in the career construction process.

To help place the client's actions in context, Young and his associates propose three constructs that relate and extend the notion of action: (1) joint action, (2) project, and (3) career (Young et al., 2002). *Joint actions* are any actions that people take together (e.g., having a conversation, engaging in career counseling) and they include manifest behavior, internal processes, and social meaning. A *project* is a superordinate construct that represents goal-oriented actions (e.g., making plans to attend graduate school to pursue a master's degree in counselor education). The *project* is comprised of multiple actions necessary to achieve the goal (e.g., researching various counselor education programs, deciding which counselor education program to apply to, getting the application materials, completing and submitting the application). *Career* is also a superordinate construct that extends over a longer period of time than a project and allows people to construct connections among actions. All actions are comprised of elements (verbal and physical behaviors), functional steps (a series of contiguous behaviors), and goals (the person's general intention). Constructing narratives represents attempts at interpreting meaning in people's actions. To bring important contextual information into the career counseling process, Young and his associates recommend that career counselors use narratives to help clients reconfigure their pasts and futures to make meaningful actions possible.

Constructivist Career Counseling

A theme connecting the narrative approach of Cochran and the contextual theory of Young and his associates is that people are active organizers of their own experiences. People construct meaning through the decisions they make and the actions they take. This theme forms the basic assumption upon which Kelly (1955) developed his theory of personal constructs. Constructs represent personal theories we develop regarding people and events. Constructs are our perceptions of events and include the judgments and evaluations we make about ourselves, others, and the world. We use our theories, or personal constructs, to predict future events (e.g., because I value helping others and counseling provides the opportunity to help others, if I become a counselor, then I am likely to experience occupational satisfaction). Constructs with greater predictive validity tend to be more stable than those that are not as useful in predicting events. Our constructs become refined over time, and we revise our perceptions based on life experience.

Peavy (1992) draws upon Kelly's theory in identifying four questions that are important for career counselors to consider in what he labels as "constructivist career counseling":

1. How can I form a cooperative alliance with this client? (Relationship factor)
2. How can I encourage the self-helpfulness of this client? (Agency factor)
3. How can I help this client to elaborate and evaluate his or her constructions and meanings germane to this decision? (Meaning-making factor)
4. How can I help this client to reconstruct and negotiate personally meaningful and socially supportable realities? (Negotiation factor) (p. 221)

Herr and Cramer (1996) note that the questions posed by Peavy connect with Cochran's view that "agency in career, the willingness to act, to bring something about, to achieve life goals, should be the prime topic in career theory" (p. 191). This view, in turn, is consistent with Kelly's (1955) personal construct theory. Particularly useful here is Kelly's (1955) notion that personal constructs cohere to form a matrix of meaning or a system of hierarchically organized dimensions that can be adjusted to a range of events (Neimeyer, 1992, p. 164). Personal constructs evolve across time. Life transitions (e.g., marriage, divorce, having children, children leaving home) often stimulate changes in our personal constructs. These assumptions led to the development of several career counseling interventions aimed at exploring and reconstructing the client's unique matrix of meaning.

One such technique is the laddering technique (Hinkle, 1965; Neimeyer, 1992). Neimeyer described the laddering technique as a strategy for helping clients identify their more important (superordinate) and less important (subordinate) constructs. The laddering technique can be initiated in a more open fashion or it can be based on a specific dilemma confronting the client. For example, we could begin the laddering technique by asking our client, Ronald, to identify three occupations he is currently considering. Let's imagine that Ronald identified the occupations of engineer, social worker, and school administrator. We could then ask Ronald to identify any way in which two of the occupations he selected are alike, but different from, the third. Ronald might note that social workers and school administrators help people and that engineers might be helpful but only indirectly. We could then ask Ronald which he would prefer, helping people directly or indirectly. If Ronald noted that his preference was for working directly with people in a helping way, we would then ask Ronald why he preferred helping directly as opposed to indirectly. Ronald might state that it is important to him to see whether he is actually making a difference in people's lives as opposed to not knowing whether he has made a positive impact. The laddering technique would be continued with our asking Ronald why he would prefer each contrast. Laddering is completed when the elicited construct is so obvious that justification is evident and unnecessary.

A more elaborate technique for identifying personal constructs is called the *vocational reptest*. Based on Kelly's (1955) Role Construct Repertory Test, the reptest requires clients to systematically compare and contrast a set of career-related elements (e.g., occupations). This technique can be initiated in a fashion similar to the laddering technique just discussed. By considering several occupations at a time, clients identify ways in which two are similar to, but different from, the third. For example, construction worker and landscape architect are similar in that they involve working outdoors and this makes them different from the work of an accountant, which involves working indoors. Another group of three occupations is then presented to the client and the client identifies how two of the occupations are similar to each other and different from the third. The ways in which the client identifies occupations as being similar and different represent the client's personal constructs. The client's personal constructs are used to help the client evaluate occupational options. Once 7 to 10 personal constructs (e.g., working indoors versus working outdoors) are identified, the client provides ratings for each of the occupations along each of the constructs he or she identified (e.g., using a scale of 1, *strongly dislike*, to 10, *strongly prefer*). Neimeyer (1992) noted that "when completed, the vocational reptest provides a useful window into the unique considerations that each person brings to bear in career decision making, as well as the interrelationship among those considerations" (p. 166).

Vocational card sorts can also be used within constructivist career counseling. For example, the career counselor can provide the client with a stack of cards, each containing an occupational title. The client can be instructed to sort the cards according to occupations they would consider, those that they would not consider, and those that they are uncertain about. Each occupation in the "would consider" and "would not consider" stacks can then be discussed with regard to reasons why the client would or would not consider the occupation. As each reason is discussed, the counselor listens for, and helps the client identify, important constructs the client uses in making decisions about occupational options (e.g., being able to engage in creative self-expression, having autonomy in work, having an occupation that provides job security). The constructs can then be reviewed and summarized.

From the constructivist perspective, career counseling outcomes are considered in terms of their "fruitfulness." Fruitfulness refers to the assumption that counseling should result in a changed outlook or new perspective on some aspect of life (Peavy, 1992). Career development interventions are framed as "experiments" conducted both in-session and out-of-session that are directed toward helping clients think, feel, and act more productively in relation to their career concerns. Peavy noted that experiments can be conducted in the imagination of the client (e.g., guided fantasy), by engaging the client in critical self-reflection (e.g., laddering technique), by engaging the client in simulation or vicarious experiences (e.g., role playing or skill learning), and by engaging the client in real-world experiences (e.g., job shadowing, job interviewing).

SUMMARY

Strengths in Emerging Theories

The emerging career development theories discussed in this chapter reflect the vitality existent within the field. Emergent theories maintain vitality within the career field by advancing new notions for career development theory and practice. Moreover, the theories discussed in this chapter fill numerous gaps in the literature. Strengths inherent in the emerging theories include (a) the theoretical propositions espoused are often applicable to diverse client populations, (b) most emerging theories have clear links with practice, and (c) many of the emerging theories incorporate and extend the theory and research base of preexisting theories (e.g., Bandura, 1986; Kelly, 1955; Rokeach, 1973).

Need for More Attention to the Career Experiences of Diverse Populations

Despite increased attention on constructing career theories that are applicable to diverse populations, there is much more work to be done in this regard. Not surprisingly, there is the need for more extensive research testing the theoretical propositions and the practical applications of emerging career theories. Although the emerging theories generally incorporate a stronger emphasis on culture and context in career development, the need for more research investigating the applicability of the emerging models for diverse population remains. A series of articles published in *The Career Development Quarterly* (September, 2001) emphasized the need for career theorists and practitioners to pay greater attention to ways in which contextual factors (culture, gender, sexual orientation, sociopolitical events, etc.) shape career development.

Historically, career theories and practices in North America have de-emphasized the person's context. This is a serious limitation as it restricts our ability to understand a person's career development. Context provides essential data to help us understand the dynamic interactions between the person and the environment that shape a person's career. Without context all we can hope for is to describe a career (e.g., she worked as a physician specializing in oncology; he pursued a major in electrical engineering and secured a position with Florida Power and Light Company upon graduation from college; he moved from job to job with no apparent direction or focus).

Although some career theorists (most often, those in the trait-factor category) seem to ignore the influence of discrimination in career development, other theories (many in the developmental and emerging theories categories) acknowledge the fact that there is not equal access to a full range of occupational opportunities. Understanding the dynamic interaction between the individual and various levels of environments (e.g., family, school, community) in which individual development and career behavior are embedded will deepen our capacity to understand career decisions and pathways.

Clearly, placing a greater emphasis on culture and context in career theory, research, and practice will increase our sensitivity to how factors such as racism, sexism, ageism, classism, and discriminatory behavior towards persons who are gay, lesbian, transgendered, and disabled influence career development by artificially constraining the opportunity structure for millions of people. Increased understanding of these processes should lead to increased effectiveness at counteracting negative effects of environmental influences in career development. This is a goal toward which all within the profession should strive.

Theory Integration

Although some (e.g., Patton & McMahon, 1999) contend that we are moving toward career theory convergence, others view it differently (e.g. Brown, 2002). It is clear, as Brown also points out, that we are experiencing the emergence of paradigm shift from theories based in logical positivism (e.g., trait-factor) to postmodern perspectives emphasizing subjectivity, perspectivity, and counselor–client collaboration in career development interventions. It also is clear that although no one theory is superior, the field is stronger because of the multiple perspectives currently espoused. For example, Super's theory provides an overarching framework for understanding career development processes; Holland's theory offers a useful vocabulary to help the counselor and client engage in the complex activity of career decision making; Gottfredson reminds us that careers develop from an early age and societal influences shape our thinking about future possibilities (often in negative ways); Krumboltz, Lent, Brown, and Hackett highlight how interactions between the person and the environment create self-beliefs that affect our career decisions; Peterson, Sampson, Lenz, and Reardon offer important descriptions as to how we make career decisions;

Brown points out that career decisions must be guided by what we value; Hansen calls us to consider a greater context that includes spirituality and cultural influences; and the postmodern theorists remind us to never lose sight of the ways in which the person's unique life experiences provide meaning and purpose in career behavior. Each of the theories we have discussed in Chapters 2 and 3 are part of the rich tapestry that career practitioners can draw upon systematically to guide their conceptualizations of their client's career concerns and to inform their decisions regarding appropriate career interventions. Finally, we hope that future research results in even more clearly defined theoretical statements that are applicable to diverse populations and have strong connections with career development interventions.

Thus, the stage has been set for a future that looks bright. Although learning about multiple theoretical perspectives can seem overwhelming at times, it is important to remember that these multiple perspectives also indicate the vitality that exists within the career development field. We encourage you to not only become more familiar with the theories that we have discussed but to also engage in the task of constructing your own career development theory. Draw upon extant theory and reflect upon how you think careers develop. Incorporate career development research results into your reflection process. Such personal reflections will be useful to you as a counselor and may even be useful to you in your own career development!

REFERENCES

Bandura, A. (1986). *Social foundations of thought and action: A social cognitive theory*. Upper Saddle River, NJ: Prentice Hall.

Bateson, G. (1979). *Mind and nature*. New York: E. P. Dutton.

Beck, A. T. (1987). *Beck Depression Inventory*. New York: Guilford Press.

Bloch, D. P., & Richmond, L. J. (1998). *Soul work: Finding the work you love, loving the work you have*. Palo Alto, CA: Davies-Black.

Blustein, D. (1994). "Who am I?" The question of self and identity in career development. In M. L. Savickas & R. W. Lent (Eds.), *Convergence in career development theories: Implications for science and practice* (pp. 139–154). Palo Alto, CA: Consulting Psychologists Press.

Bolles, R. N. (1998). *What color is your parachute?* Berkeley, CA: Ten Speed Press.

Brown, D. (1995). A values-based model for facilitating career transitions. *Career Development Quarterly, 44,* 4–11.

Brown, D. (1996). Brown's values-based, holistic model of career and life-role choices and satisfaction. In D. Brown, L. Brooks, & Associates (Eds.), *Career choice and development* (3rd ed., pp. 337–372). San Francisco: Jossey-Bass.

Brown, D. (2002). The role of work values and cultural values in occupational choice, satisfaction, and success: A theoretical statement. In D. Brown & Associates (Eds.), *Career choice and development* (4th ed., pp. 465–509). San Francisco: Jossey-Bass.

Brown, D., & Brooks, L. (1991). *Career counseling techniques*. Needham Heights, MA: Allyn & Bacon.

Brown, D., & Crace, R. K. (1996). Values in life role choices and outcomes: A conceptual model. *The Career Development Quarterly, 44,* 211–223.

Brown, S. D., & Lent, R. W. (1996). A social cognitive framework for career choice counseling. *The Career Development Quarterly, 44,* 354–366.

Carlsen, M. B. (1988). *Making meaning: Therapeutic processes in adult development*. New York: W. W. Norton.

Chartrand, J. M., & Rose, M. L. (1996). Career interventions for at-risk populations: Incorporating social cognitive influences. *The Career Development Quarterly, 44,* 341–353.

Chung, Y. B. (2002). Career decision-making self-efficacy and career commitment: Gender and ethnic differences among college students. *Journal of Career Development, 28,* 277–284.

Cochran, L. (1985). *Position and nature of personhood*. Westport, CT: Greenwood.

Cochran, L. (1994). What is a career problem? *The Career Development Quarterly, 42*, 204–215.

Cochran, L. (1997). *Career counseling: A narrative approach*. Thousand Oaks: Sage.

Cochran, L. R. (1990). Narrative as a paradigm for career research. In K. A. Young & W. E. Borgen (Eds.), *Methodological approaches to the study of careers* (pp. 71–86). New York: Praeger.

Crace, R. K., & Brown, D. (1996). *Life Values Inventory*. Minneapolis, MN: National Computer Systems.

Dail, H. (1989). *The lotus and the pool*. Boston: Shambala.

Diegelman, N. M., & Subich, L. M. (2001). Academic and vocational interests as a function of outcome expectancies in social cognitive career theory. *Journal of Vocational Behavior, 59*, 394–405.

Dunst, C., Trivette, C., & Deal, A. (1988). *Enabling and empowering families*. Cambridge, MA: Brookline Books.

Flores, L. Y., & O'Brien, K. M. (2002). The career development of Mexican American adolescent women: A test of social cognitive career theory. *Journal of Counseling Psychology, 49*, 14–27.

Gainor, K. A., & Lent, R. W. (1998). Social cognitive expectations and racial identity attitudes in predicting the math choice intentions of Black college students. *Journal of Counseling Psychology, 45*, 403–413.

Gelatt, H. B. (1989). Positive uncertainty: A new decision-making framework for counseling. *Journal of Counseling Psychology, 36*, 252–256.

Ghiselin, B. (1955). *The creative process*. New York: Mentor.

Goldman, L. (1992). Qualitative assessment: An approach for counselors. *Journal of Counseling and Development, 70*, 616–621.

Gysbers, N. C., & Moore, E. J. (1987). *Career counseling: Skills and techniques for practitioners*. Upper Saddle River, NJ: Prentice Hall.

Hackett, G., & Betz, N. (1981). A self-efficacy approach to the career development of women. *Journal of Vocational Behavior, 18*, 326–329.

Hackett, G., & Byars, A. (1996). Social cognitive theory and the career development of African American women. *The Career Development Quarterly, 44*, 322–340.

Hansen, L. S. (1997). *Integrative life planning—Critical tasks for career development and changing life patterns*. San Francisco, CA: Jossey-Bass.

Hansen, L. S. (2002). *Integrative life planning: A holistic theory for career counseling with adults*. In S. G. Niles (Ed.), *Adult career development: concepts, issues, and practices* (3rd ed., pp. 59–76). Tulsa, OK: National Career Development Association.

Hansen, L. S., Hage, S., & Kachgal, M. (1999). *Integrative life planning inventory*. University of Minnesota, MN: Integrative Life Planning, Counseling and Student Personnel Psychology.

Helwig, A. A. (1992). Book review of career development and services. *Journal of Employment Counseling, 29*, 77–78.

Herr, E. L., & Cramer, S. H. (1996). *Career guidance and counseling through the lifespan* (5th ed.). New York: HarperCollins.

Hinkle, D. (1965). *The change of personal constructs from the viewpoint of a theory of implications*. Unpublished doctoral dissertation, Ohio State University, Columbus, Ohio.

Holland, J. L. (1985). *Making vocational choices: A theory of vocational personalities and work environments* (2nd ed.). Upper Saddle River, NJ: Prentice Hall.

Howard, G. S. (1989). *A tale of two stories: Excursions into a narrative approach to psychology*. Notre Dame, IN: Academic.

Janis, I. L., & Mann, L. (1977). *Decision-making: A psychological analysis of conflict, choice, and commitment*. New York: Free Press.

Kelly, G. A. (1955). *A theory of personality: The psychology of personal constructs*. New York: Norton.

Lent, R. W., & Brown, S. D. (1996). Social cognitive approach to career development: An overview. *The Career Development Quarterly, 44*, 310–321.

Lent, R. W., & Brown, S. D. (2002). Social cognitive career theory and adult career development. In S. Niles (Ed.), *Adult career development: Concepts, models, and practices* (3rd ed., pp. 77–98). Tulsa, OK: National Career Development Association.

Lent, R. W., Brown, S. D., Brenner, B., Chopra, S. B., Davis, T., Talleyrand, R., & Suthakaran, V. (2001). The role of contextual supports and barriers in the choice of math/science educational options: A test of social cognitive hypotheses. *Journal of Counseling Psychology, 48,* 474–483.

Lent, R. W., Brown, S. D., & Hackett, G. (1994). Toward a unifying social cognitive theory of career and academic interests, choice, and performance. *Journal of Vocational Behavior, 45,* 79–122.

Lent, R. W., Brown, S. D., & Hackett, G.(1996). Career development from a social cognitive perspective. In D. Brown, L. Brooks, & Associates (Eds.), *Career choice and development* (3rd ed., pp. 373–416). San Francisco, CA: Jossey-Bass.

Lent, R. W., Brown, S. D., & Hackett, G. (2002). Social cognitive career theory. In D. Brown & Associates (Eds.), *Career choice and development* (4th ed., pp. 255–311). San Francisco, CA: Jossey-Bass.

Lent, R. W., & Hackett, G. (1987). Career self-efficacy: Empirical status and future directions. *Journal of Vocational Behavior, 30,* 347–382.

Lewis, R. A., & Gilhousen, M. R. (1981). Myths of career development: A cognitive approach to vocational counseling. *The Personnel and Guidance Journal, 5,* 296–299.

McLennan, N. A., & Arthur, N. (1999). Applying the cognitive information processing approach to career problem solving and decision making to women's career development. *Journal of Employment Counseling, 36,* 82–96.

Meichenbaum, D. (1977). *Cognitive behavior modification.* New York: Plenum.

Miller-Tiedeman, A. L. (1997). The Lifecareer process theory: A healthier choice. In D. P. Bloch & L. J. Richmond (Eds.), *Connection between spirit and work in career development* (pp. 87–114). Palo Alto, CA: Davies-Black.

Mitchell, L. K., & Krumboltz, J. D. (1996). Krumboltz's learning theory of career choice counseling. In D. Brown, L. Brooks, & Associates (Eds.), *Career choice and development* (3rd ed., pp. 233–276). San Francisco, CA: Jossey-Bass.

Mitchell, L. K., Levin, A. S., & Krumboltz, J. D. (1999). Planned happenstance: Constructing unexpected career opportunities. *Journal of Counseling & Development, 77,* 115–124.

Nauta, M. M., Kahn, J. H., Angell, J. W., & Cantarelli, E. A. (2002). Identifying the antecedent in the relation between career interests and self-efficacy: Is it one, the other, or both? *Journal of Counseling Psychology, 49,* 290–301.

Neimeyer, G. J. (1989). Personal constructs systems in vocational development and information processing. *Journal of Career Development, 16,* 83–96.

Neimeyer, G. J. (1992). Personal construct and vocational structure: A critique of poor status. In R. A. Neimeyer & G. J. Neimeyer (Eds.), *Advances in personal construct psychology* (pp. 91–120). Greenwich, CT: Jai Press.

Niles, S. G., & Anderson, W. P. (1995). A content analysis of career and personal concerns expressed by career counseling clients. *Educational and Vocational Guidance Bulletin, 57,* 59–62.

Niles, S. G., & Pate, R. H. (1989). Competency and training issues related to the integration of career counseling and mental health counseling. *Journal of Career Development, 16,* 63–71.

Osborn, D. S., Peterson, G. W., Sampson, J. P., Jr., & Reardon, R. C. (2003). Client anticipations about computer-assisted career guidance system outcomes. *The Career Development Quarterly, 51,* 356–367.

Patton, W., & McMahon, M. (1999). *Career development and systems theory: A new relationship.* Pacific Grove, CA: Brooks/Cole.

Peavy, R. V. (1992). A constructivist model of training for career counselors. *Journal of Career Development, 18,* 215–228.

Peterson, G. W., Lumdsden, J. A., Sampson, J. P., Reardon, R. C., & Lenz, J. G. (2002). Using a cognitive information processing approach in career counseling with adults. In S. Niles (Ed.), *Adult career development: Concepts, models, and practices* (3rd ed., pp. 99–120). Tulsa, OK: National Career Development Association.

Peterson, G. W., Sampson, J. P., Jr., & Reardon, R. C. (1991). *Career development and services: A cognitive approach.* Pacific Grove, CA: Brooks/Cole.

Peterson, G. W., Sampson, J. P., Reardon, R. C., & Lenz, J. G. (1996). A cognitive information processing approach. In D. Brown, L. Brooks, & Associates (Eds.), *Career choice and development* (3rd ed., pp. 423–476). San Francisco, CA: Jossey-Bass.

Peterson, G. W., Sampson, J. P., Jr., Lenz, J. G., & Reardon, R. C.(2002). A cognitive information processing approach to career problem solving and decision making. In D. Brown & Associates (Eds.), *Career choice and development* (4th ed., pp. 312–372). San Francisco, CA: Jossey-Bass.

Polkinghorne, D. E. (1988). *Narrative knowing and the human sciences*. Albany, NY: State University of New York Press.

Reardon, R. C., & Wright, L. K. (1999). The case of Mandy: Applying Holland's theory and cognitive informational processing theory. *The Career Development Quarterly, 47,* 195–203.

Reed, C. A., Reardon, R. C., Lenz, J. G., & Leierer, S. J. (2001). A cognitive career course: From theory to practice. *The Career Development Quarterly, 50,* 158–167.

Rokeach, M. (1973). *The nature of human values.* New York: Free Press.

Sampson, J. P., Jr., Peterson, G. W., Lenz, J. G., & Reardon, R. C. (1992). A cognitive approach to career services: Translating concepts into practice. *The Career Development Quarterly, 41,* 67–74.

Sampson, J. P., Peterson, G. W., Lenz, J. G., Reardon, R. C., & Saunders, D. E. (1996). *The Career Thoughts Inventory (CTI).* Odessa, FL: Psychological Assessment Resources.

Saunders, D. E., Peterson, G. W., Sampson, J. P., Jr., & Reardon, R. C. (2000). Relation of depression and dysfunctional career thinking to career indecision. *Journal of Vocational Behavior, 56,* 288–298.

Savickas, M. L. (1995). Constructivist counseling for career indecision. *The Career Development Quarterly, 43.* 363–373.

Super, D. E. (1953). A theory of vocational development. *American Psychologist, 30,* 88–92.

Super, D. E. (1980). A life-span, life-space approach to career development. *Journal of Vocational Behavior, 16,* 282–298.

Super, D. E. (1990). A life-span, life-space approach to career development. In D. Brown, L. Brooks, & Associates (Eds.), *Career choice and development: Applying contemporary theories to prac-*

tice (2nd ed., pp. 197–261), San Francisco, CA: Jossey-Bass.

Super, D. E., & Nevill, D. D. (1986). *Salience Inventory.* Palo Alto, CA: Consulting Psychologists Press.

Vondracek, F. W., & Kawasaki, T. (1995). Toward a comprehensive framework for adult career development theory and intervention. In B. W. Walsh & S. H. Osipow (Eds.), *Handbook of vocational psychology: Theory, research, and practice* (2nd ed., pp. 111–141). Mahwah, NJ: Erlbaum.

Vondracek, F. W., Lerner, R. M., & Schulenberg, S. E. (1986). *Career development: A life-span developmental approach.* Hillsdale, NJ: Erlbaum.

Watkins, C. E., Jr., & Savickas, M. L. (1990). Psychodynamic career counseling. In W. B. Walsh & S. H. Osipow (Eds.), *Career counseling: Contemporary topics in vocational psychology* (pp. 79–116). Hillsdale, NJ: Erlbaum.

Young, R. A., & Collin, A. (Eds.). (1992). *Interpreting career: Hermeneutical studies of lives in context.* Westport, CT: Praeger.

Young, R. A., & Valach, L. (1996). Interpretation and action in career counseling. In M. L. Savickas & W. B. Walsh (Eds.), *Handbook of career counseling theory and practice.* Palo Alto, CA: Davies-Black Consulting Psychologist Press.

Young, R. A., Valach, L., & Collin, A. (1996). A contextual explanation of career. In D. Brown, L. Brooks, & Associates (Eds.), *Career choice and development* (3rd ed., pp. 477–508). San Francisco, CA: Jossey-Bass.

Young, R. A., Valach, L., & Collin, A. (2002). A contextualist explanation of career. In D. Brown & Associates (Eds.), *Career choice and development.* (4th ed., pp. 206–254). San Francisco, CA: Jossey-Bass.

CHAPTER 4

CAREER DEVELOPMENT AND DIVERSE POPULATIONS

Though the U.S. population and workforce have become increasingly diverse in culture, in addition to the globalization of economy and business trades, it is essential for career counselors and career development professionals to be multiculturally sensitive and competent. The recent multicultural counseling movement has matured from an exclusive focus on race/ethnicity to the inclusion of all cultural dimensions such as gender, gender identity, sexual orientation, disability, spirituality, religion, age, and social class. We all have multiple identities and our personalities are built on many cultural identities. To become a multiculturally competent counselor requires a lifelong commitment to self-reflection and growth. It is also important to help all people and workers become multiculturally sensitive. Such sensitivity benefits not only oppressed group members, but all people—only when everybody feels respected as a human and cultural being are we able to be free.

Y. Barry Chung
Associate Professor
Georgia State University

Ju-Shin, a 28-year-old first-generation Asian American (her parents were from Taiwan), presented for career counseling expressing concern about her current career choice. She was nearing completion of her doctoral degree in counselor education. Initially, she planned on becoming a counselor educator. Recently, she was having second thoughts. Ju-Shin reported that lately, her interest in counseling was fading. She also confided that she had enjoyed her research and statistics courses very much. One of her friends was enrolled in a doctoral program in educational research and Ju-Shin was now wondering if this might be a better choice for her. As she spoke, the counselor noticed that she was very anxious. As the session continued, Ju-Shin expressed a substantial amount of concern over how her parents would react if she were to switch degree programs. In fact, she seemed convinced that her parents would not approve of such a change. The more Ju-Shin discussed her concern, the more reluctant she seemed to consider changing her program of study. Yet, she also continued to note how much she seemed to enjoy her research-oriented courses.

A counselor operating from a traditional trait-factor approach and an individualistic approach to career decision making may be inclined to provide Ju-Shin with a test battery that would provide her with more self-information concerning her degree of fit for research-oriented programs of studies and related occupations versus becoming a counselor educator. Once Ju-Shin had relevant information about traits such as interests, skills, and so on, the counselor would encourage her to consider how well her traits fit with the factors required for success in the occupations Ju-Shin was considering.

Although acquiring such information would undoubtedly be useful to Ju-Shin, there are other issues surrounding her career dilemma. Ju-Shin's cultural background is based in a group-oriented approach to career decision making. Ju-Shin is not alone in her decision making. Her career decisions play out within the context of her family. It would be critical for Ju-Shin's counselor to explore this contextual factor in career counseling. Ju-Shin's counselor will need to understand how familial expectations interact with other factors (e.g., her interest in research) influencing Ju-Shin's career exploration. It would also be important for the counselor to understand the degree to which cultural stereotypes and discriminatory behavior influence Ju-Shin's views as to what might be possible for her to achieve in her career. Such interactions exist for all clients, and counselors must develop the requisite multicultural knowledge, skills, and awareness for conducting culturally appropriate career counseling.

Ju-Shin demonstrates the fact that cultural variables rest at the core of the career intervention process. To construct culturally appropriate career interventions, counselors need to embrace this fact. Counselors need to be sensitive to the tremendous cultural shifts occurring in society. During the past four decades the United States has been awash in cultural pluralism (Axelson, 1985). According to Lee and Richardson (1991), "The concept of cultural pluralism has received its impetus not only from the great economic, legislative, and civil rights struggles of the 1960s, but, more recently, from changing population demographics." Throughout the 21st century, people of color will experience significant growth in numbers while the White population will decline significantly. The influx of new immigrants into the United States will also continue in large numbers (Spencer, 1989). The Census Bureau predicts that 820,000 to 1.2 million immigrants per year will enter the United States between 1996 and 2006. From 1980 to 1990, while the White population grew about 5%, the African American population increased by approximately 10%, Hispanics by almost 55%, Asian Americans by almost 110%, and Native Americans by about 38%. Hispanics are expected to surpass African Americans to become the largest minority group in the United States sometime within the next two decades (Herr, Cramer, & Niles, 2004).

Lee and Richardson (1991) noted that changing population demographics provided the impetus for the development of multicultural counseling. Axelson (1985) defined *multicultural counseling* as a helping process that places the emphasis for counseling theory and practice equally on the cultural impression of both the counselor and client. Lee and Richardson suggested that:

Within this context, counseling professionals must consider differences in language, social class, and, most importantly, culture between helper and client. These factors may be potential impediments to effective intervention, and counselors need to work to overcome the barriers such variables might produce in the helping process. (p. 3)

Changing demographics, multiple worldviews, and cultural plurality also influence the career development intervention process. Whereas the workforce was once dominated by White males, it now more closely reflects the cultural pluralism existing within society. Many projections concerning the labor force made by Johnston and Packer in 1987 have proven accurate.

Specifically, Johnston and Packer predicted that:

1. The average age of the workforce will rise, and the pool of young workers entering the labor market will shrink. (The average age of the workforce increased from 36 in the late 1980s to 39 in the year 2000.)
2. More women will enter the workforce. (Two-thirds of the new entrants in the workforce between the late 1980s and the year 2000 were women.)
3. Minorities will be a larger share of new entrants into the labor force. (Non-Whites represented 29% of the new entrants in the labor force from the late 1980s to the year 2000.)
4. Immigrants will represent the largest share of the increase in the population and the workforce since the first World War. (Approximately 600,000 legal and illegal immigrants entered the United States annually in the last two decades of the 20th century. It is estimated that two-thirds or more of those immigrants of working age join the labor force.)

Thus, non-Whites, women, and immigrants represented more than five-sixths of the net additions to the workforce in the last 15 years of the 20th century (Johnston & Packer, 1987, pp. 23–25).

Despite these developments, there is also ample evidence to suggest that women, people of color, persons with disabilities, gay men, lesbian women, and transgendered persons continue to encounter tremendous obstacles in their career development. For example, more than 50% of young, urban African American men were unemployed, worked part-time jobs involuntarily, or earned poverty-level wages in the 1980s (Lichter, 1988). The unemployment rate for African Americans has been above 11% each year since 1978 and has run about 2.5 times the rate for Whites in the last decades of the 20th century (Swinton, 1992). Swinton also noted that only 36.9% of African American men are employed as executives, administrators, salespersons, and managers as compared with 61.8% of White men. Hispanic Americans are also concentrated in lower-paid, lesser-skilled occupations. According to Herr and Cramer (1996), "more than half of the employed Hispanic women are either clerical workers or nontransport operatives (dress-makers, assemblers, machine operators, and so on)" (p. 277). Herr, Cramer, and Niles (2004) also noted that "no other minority group in the United States has experienced deeper prejudice or is in a less-advantaged posture than Native Americans" (p. 267). The poverty rate of Native American families is twice the rate (23.7%) of the general population in the United States (U.S. Bureau of Census, 1992). The 1980 U.S. Census report indicated that only 56% of Native Americans over the age of 25 had completed 4 or more years of high school (as compared with 66.5% of the general U.S. population). The unemployment rate for Native Americans living on reservations is 45%, and 14% of those living on reservations have incomes of less than $2500 per year (Herring, 1991). Moreover, occupational desegregation rates tend to be highest in occupations in which men are paid less and in which the number of workers are declining. Men are still 18.7 times more likely than women to be in higher-prestige occupations in science, math, or technology (Farmer, Rotella, Anderson, & Wardrop, 1998).

Despite legislation aimed at protecting their rights (e.g., Public Law 93-112, the Rehabilitation Act of 1973; Public Law 94-142, the Education for All Handicapped Children Act of 1975; Public Law 95-602, the Rehabilitation, Comprehensive Services, and Developmental Disabilities Amendment of 1978; Public Law 101-476, the Education of the Handicapped Amendments of 1990; Public Law 101-336, the Americans with Disabilities Act of 1990), Americans with disabilities have fared no better. As Isaacson and Brown (1997) write, "Of the 13 million people considered to have a work disability, 33.6% are in the labor force and 15.6% are unemployed; thus nearly half of those with a work disability are outside the work structure" (p. 313). Gay, lesbian, and bisexual individuals also experience discriminatory treatment in the labor force. Goleman (1990) suggested that the negative bias toward this group is often more intense than that directed toward any other group. Herr and Cramer (1996, p. 292) noted that gay, lesbian, and bisexual persons are essentially barred from certain occupations and find vertical mobility blocked simply because of their sexual orientation. Despite this obvious discrimination, career development theorists and practitioners have been slow to respond (Chung, 2003; Pope & Barret, 2002).

These statistics suggest that many women, people of color, persons with disabilities, and gay/lesbian/bisexual/transgendered individuals regularly experience discriminatory practices in hiring and promoting, insufficient financial resources, and a lack of role models and mentors. Thus, it may be that traditional approaches may not be appropriate for assisting members of diverse groups in their career development (Sue, Arrendondo, & McDavis, 1992). If so, then career development interventions in the 21st century must be reconceptualized to more adequately meet the career development needs of the members of an increasingly diverse society (Arbona, 1990; Leong, 1986).

TRADITIONAL ASSUMPTIONS OF CAREER THEORIES IN THE UNITED STATES

Historically, career development theories and interventions, especially in the United States, have emphasized a psychological perspective highlighting the role that intra-individual variables (e.g., motivation, internal locus of control, perseverance, ability) play in shaping one's career. Comparing career development theories in the United States with those in the United Kingdom, Watts, Super, and Kidd (1981) noted that career development theories in the United States have focused

> on the actions of individuals, while in Britain indigenous theoretical work has been more preoccupied with the constraints of social structures. ... Thus, in the United States a dominant career-related belief is that the individual controls his or her own career destiny.

Although individual control clearly plays a vital role, control is exerted within a context that varies relative to the degree to which it provides support for a person's career aspirations. Clearly, factors such as racism, sexism, socioeconomic status, ageism, and heterosexism constrain access to occupational opportunities for many people. Although theories in the United Kingdom may overemphasize social structures, theories in the United States have generally underemphasized the contextual influences shaping career development. (p. 3)

Gysbers, Heppner, and Johnston (2003) pointed out that career development interventions in the United States, having arisen out of a specific context, tend to favor five tenets reflecting a European-American perspective: (a) individualism and autonomy, (b) affluence, (c) structure of opportunity open to all, (d) the centrality of work in people's lives, and (e) the linearity, progressiveness, and rationality of the career development process. These tenets reflect specific assumptions that do not represent the contextual experiences many people encounter. Accordingly, Herr and Cramer (1996) remind us that "decision making, the development of self-identity, and life changes . . . occur within political, economic, and social conditions that influence the achievement images and belief systems on which individuals base their actions" (p. 203).

Although many early theories of career development acknowledged the influence of such person-environment interactions in shaping careers, descriptions of these interactions were not developed fully. Despite these theoretical inadequacies, Leong and Brown (1995) suggest that it is premature to regard these theories as inapplicable to diverse populations, as some have concluded (e.g., Cheatham, 1990). Such a conclusion ignores that "at least some concepts drawn from extant theories have found demonstrable empirical support when applied to some diverse populations" (Leong & Brown, p. 147). However, it is clear that a more diversified career counseling clientele and a heightened awareness of the important role that culture plays in career choice and career counseling highlight the need for theorists and practitioners to integrate multicultural perspectives into their theory descriptions and career interventions (Swanson, 1993).

UNIVERSAL VERSUS CULTURE-SPECIFIC MODELS

Many statements pertaining to multicultural career development interventions reflect the tension between *etic* (i.e., universal) and *emic* (i.e., culturally specific) approaches to counseling. Etic perspectives maintain that career development interventions for members of minority groups should be the same as the career development interventions used for those representing the majority. As such, proponents of etic perspectives contend that current career theories and techniques are robust enough to have universal applicability.

Emic perspectives, on the other hand, highlight the importance of designing career development interventions that are specific to the client's culture. Wohl (1995) suggests that "culturally specific approaches are psychotherapeutic methods designed to be congruent with the cultural characteristics of a particular ethnic clientele, or for problems believed to be especially prominent in a particular ethnic group" (p. 76). By extension, then, culture-specific career development theories are required to provide more comprehensive and accurate descriptions of the career development process for diverse groups.

Several authors resolve the tension between etic versus emic approaches by incorporating useful elements of both perspectives into multicultural career development theory and practice (Fischer, Jome, & Atkinson, 1998; Leong, 1993). For example, Leong focuses on similarities and differences in the career counseling process for majority and minority clients by adapting Kluckhorn and Murray's (1950) tripartite personality theory to the career counseling process. Kluckhorn and Murray contended that personality consists of universal (individuals are like all others in certain ways), group (individuals are like some others in certain ways), and individual (individuals are unique in certain ways) dimensions. Career counselors act in culturally encapsulated ways (Wrenn, 1962) when they attend to only the universal levels of their clients and ignore clients' important group, cultural, and individual dimensions. Leong (1995) argues that "effective cross-cultural counseling would consist of the appropriate shifting between dimensions as the counseling relationship develops" (p. 195).

Fischer et al. (1998) contend that researchers have focused a significant amount of attention on culturally specific (emic) counseling interventions, perhaps "at the expense of attention to common factors in multicultural counseling and research" (p. 528). Proposing a common factors perspective in multicultural counseling, Fischer and her associates suggest that "the curative properties of a given psychotherapy lie not in its theoretically unique components (e.g., insight for psychoanalytic approaches, modification of cognitions for cognitive approaches) but in components common to all psychotherapies" (pp. 529–530). Thus, Fischer and her associates identify four factors that appear to be "the universal elements of healing in all cultures" (p. 532). These factors are (1) the therapeutic relationship, (2) shared worldview, (3) client expectations, and (4) ritual or intervention. A cornerstone of the therapeutic relationship is the establishment of trust and rapport between the counselor and client. Fischer et al. cite the strong research support indicating that the establishment of an effective therapeutic relationship is a significant predictor of therapeutic outcome.

A key aspect in establishing the therapeutic relationship is a shared worldview between the counselor and client. This common factor reflects Rogers' notion of empathic understanding, which he defined as "trying to experience the client's world as if it were your own without losing the 'as if' quality" (1957, p. 97). Fischer et al. (1998) suggest that understanding each other's worlds enables the client and counselor to establish the therapeutic relationship and sets the stage for positive expectations regarding counseling outcomes. Empathic understanding also minimizes the probability that counselors will operate on the myth of cultural uniformity, "which assumes that all individuals regardless of race, ethnicity, sex, age, and social class" have values and goals that are similar to the counselors' values and goals (Leong, 1993, p. 32). Thus, achieving this type of understanding is critical for providing effective multicultural career development interventions and requires the counselor to have adequate knowledge, skills, and awareness of the client's culture. Obviously, counselors must also be aware of their own cultural biases and assumptions within this process.

The third common factor identified by Fischer and her colleagues is client expectations: "Counselors and healers raise client expectations and gain credibility through the setting in which they conduct therapy, the training and degrees they possess, working within a shared worldview with the client, and developing a therapeutic relationship with the client" (Fischer et al., 1998, p. 538). When clients have positive expectations for their counseling experience, there is a greater likelihood that positive outcomes will occur (Torrey, 1986).

The first three common factors set the stage and are preconditions for the fourth common factor, which is ritual or intervention. Fischer et al. (1998) point out that "an intervention that is relevant and effective for one client may not be as relevant for another client, depending on the degree of relationship, shared worldview, and positive expectation" (p. 540). All of these factors are relevant to the career development intervention process, regardless of the career practitioner's theoretical orientation. Providing appropriate interventions requires career counselors to be aware of several important additional issues: ethnocentrism, acculturation, and identity development.

ETHNOCENTRISM

When counselors assume that one value system (their own) is superior and preferable to another, they engage in ethnocentric behavior that is insensitive to their clients' worldviews. Ethnocentrism can easily occur in career development interventions when counselors assume that individualistic and self-sufficient actions are preferable to collectivistic actions reflecting interdependence and group loyalty. Individualists use individual attitudes, private interests, and personal goals to guide their behavior, whereas collectivists rely on shared interests, group norms, and common goals to inform their decision making (Hartung, Speight, & Lewis, 1996). For many people the emphasis on individualism found within numerous theories of career development generated in the United States does not mesh with worldviews in which the family or group is the principal arbiter of appropriate occupational choices.

Clearly, Ju-Shin, the client presented at the beginning of the chapter, is in the process of making a career decision from a collectivistic perspective. Another illustration of this point is provided by the career counseling case of "Munier." Having recently relocated to the United States from Iraq, Munier came to the career services office during his first year in college with the concern of whether poor performance in his physics and math courses would prevent him from being able to major in chemical engineering. In the course of meeting with Munier, it became obvious that although his concerns were projected toward a college major in engineering, his interests and abilities pointed toward a program of study in a nonscience area. In fact, he had failed physics in high school and just barely passed a math course in his first semester of college. He thoroughly enjoyed literature and had performed well in classes related to this area in both high school and college. When asked to discuss his tentative decision to pursue a major in engineering, it quickly became apparent that this decision was based in a collectivistic worldview. His father had made his career plans for him.

When asked about the appropriateness of this goal, given his prior academic performance and his interests, it was clear that Munier was not going to enlarge the range of options under consideration. In this case, a counselor blindly adhering to the need for students to develop traditional Western career development values of individual action and an internal locus of control may decide to use a counseling strategy that would challenge Munier's tendency to adhere to the wishes of others (his father in this case) rather than to make decisions based on his own sense of what was right for him. The projected treatment plan may even include assertiveness training with the goal of having Munier confront his father about his career development goals. Unfortunately, this type of counseling strategy is not sensitive to Munier's culture of origin, in which it is not uncommon for fathers to dominate the career decision making of their sons. In fact, it is a responsibility that the father takes seriously and a duty about which the child feels strongly. Any attempts at influencing the career direction of Munier would need to be sensitive to this very important cultural dynamic. Culturally diverse students such as Munier must be provided with opportunities to sort through the implications of these cultural differences for their own career development and to learn coping strategies for dealing with differences in cultural expectations. Often, as in the case of Munier, this sorting process must occur within the context of the family.

Such value conflicts illustrate the point that decision making, the development of self-identity, and life choices do not occur in a vacuum. They occur within political, economic, and social conditions that influence the achievement images and belief systems on which individuals base their actions. There are numerous instruments available that can be used to assess the worldview construct. For example, the "Scale to Assess World View" (Ibrahim & Kahn, 1987; Ibrahim & Owens, 1992) and "The Person-in-Culture Interview" (Berg-Cross & Zoppetti, 1991) are examples of useful assessments for exploring the worldview construct.

ACCULTURATION

Although knowing that specific cultures are oriented toward individualism (e.g., European Americans) or collectivism (e.g., Asian Americans) is useful, it is also inappropriate to apply this knowledge to clients in a stereotypical fashion (e.g., "all European Americans are individualistic," "all Asian Americans are collectivistic"). Thus, another important variable to assess in understanding the client's worldview is that of acculturation. Acculturation can be defined as "the process of adopting the cultural traits or social patterns of another group" (Stein, 1975, p. 10). Results of acculturation research conducted in the United States have indicated that English language proficiency is one of the best measures of acculturation (Fouad, 1993). However, acculturation is a complex and multifaceted process.

Early models of acculturation (e.g., Park & Burgess, 1921) were based on assumptions that reflected an "either/or" perspective toward acculturation (e.g., one either accepted the "new" culture and rejected the "old," or one rejected the "new" and maintained acceptance of the "old" culture). Inherent in such models is the notion of the *marginal person* (Park, 1928). The marginal person is someone who is psychologically "caught" between two cultures. Marginal persons hold negative views toward both their own culture and the host culture, such as when a Chinese American woman is unwilling to give unquestioned obedience to the traditional values of her Chinese parents, but also finds it difficult to accept many of the values inherent in a European American culture associated with racist attitudes and behaviors (Leong & Brown, 1995). Such instances often result in the experience of an identity crisis characterized by chronic restlessness, self-consciousness, and feelings of inferiority (Atkinson, Morten, & Sue, 1993).

More recent models of acculturation, however, reflect a bicultural perspective toward acculturation. Such models embrace the notion that individuals can be highly acculturated to multiple cultures—a sort of "both/and" approach versus the earlier "either/or" models. Atkinson et al. (1993) note that the bicultural person and the marginal person respond differently to their socialization in two cultures. The marginal person "feels caught between the conflicting values of two cultures and consequently feels little commitment to either" (Atkinson et al., p. 23). In contrast, the bicultural person "feels committed to both cultures and selectively embraces the positive aspects of each culture" (Atkinson et al., p. 23). Thus, the client's level of acculturation is an important within-group variable that must be addressed to provide appropriate career interventions.

It is important that counselors do not assume that the client's level of acculturation is at the same level as the client's family. Differences in this regard are important to address in the career development intervention process—especially for young people attempting to crystallize initial occupational preferences. Grieger and Ponterotto (1995) noted that it is not uncommon for first-generation U.S. college students to experience cultural or bicultural strain, and consequently conflict, when their families' level of acculturation is at variance with their own. This could have been the case with Munier had he been oriented to more Western notions concerning the career decision making process rather than the values inherent in his culture of origin.

Numerous factors contribute to the degree to which individuals experience acculturative change. For example, Padilla (1980) noted that language familiarity and usage, cultural heritage, ethnicity, ethnic pride and identity, interethnic interactions, and interethnic distance influence acculturative change. Each of these factors clearly influences persons differently, in both degree and kind. Sue and Sue (1990) pointed out that even small variations in the influence of these variables can have powerful effects on the career development intervention process. Such variability reinforces the important notion that general statements about cultural groups must not be applied uniformly (cultural uniformity myth). These general statements (e.g., White Americans tend to be individualistic, Asian Americans tend to be collectivistic) must be tempered by understanding how factors such as those identified by Padilla influence the individual's goals, career behavior, and career decision making.

IDENTITY DEVELOPMENT MODELS

The factors discussed by Padilla (1980) influence the client's level of identity development. Understanding the client's stage of identity development is essential for providing appropriate career development interventions.

Racial Identity Models

Models of racial identity help us understand that the status of racial identity (for both counselors and clients) can influence the career development intervention process at several levels. For example, Atkinson, Morten, and Sue (1989, 1993) describe five stages of racial identity development, each with corresponding counseling implications: (a) conformity, (b) dissonance, (c) resistance and immersion, (d) introspection, and (e) synergistic.

Individuals in the *conformity* stage adhere to the dominant culture's value system, including its perception of racial/ethnic minorities. Their self-perceptions, as well as their perceptions of others, are viewed through the lens of the dominant culture. They tend to deny the existence of racism and discriminatory treatment on the part of the dominant culture and have a strong desire to "assimilate and acculturate" (Atkinson et al., 1993, p. 29). Moreover, their attitudes toward members of their own group may be very negative. In other words, individuals in the conformity stage may experience feelings of racial self-hatred as a result of cultural racism. Because of their strong identification with the dominant culture, individuals in the conformity stage may express a preference for a career counselor from the dominant culture. In the career development intervention process, they may display a high level of compliance and a need to please the counselor. Atkinson et al. (1993) suggest that these clients are likely to present career concerns that are most amenable to career development interventions focused on problem-solving approaches.

Individuals often move gradually into the *dissonance* stage, but the occurrence of significant events can serve as catalysts for propelling a person into the dissonance stage. In either scenario, the process of movement into the dissonance stage typically occurs when the individual in the conformist stage encounters a person or situation that runs counter to conformist-stage beliefs (for example, when an Asian American in the conformist stage, and thus adhering to negative stereotypes regarding the Asian culture, encounters a person who expresses pride in her Asian heritage, or when an African American in the conformist stage experiences racism on a personal level). In such instances, information is acquired that suggests alternative views toward the culture of origin (e.g., that there are positive aspects in cultural traditions, values, and customs) and the dominant culture (e.g., certain behaviors and practices in the dominant culture are discriminatory). Such information causes denial to break down and opens a window to further identity development. Specifically, individuals moving from conformity to dissonance may increasingly engage in self-exploration regarding self-concepts, identity, self-esteem, and group affiliation (Atkinson et al., 1989). Career development practitioners working with individuals in the dissonance stage need to have a thorough understanding of the individual's culture-of-origin.

Individuals adhering to beliefs and attitudes reflecting Atkinson et al.'s (1989) third stage of racial identity development, *resistance and immersion*, tend to reject the views and values of the dominant culture. They express a complete endorsement of the views and values of their culture-of-origin. Additionally, their resolution of the confusion experienced in the dissonance stage often leads to intense anger as they become more aware of racism and how it has impacted their lives. Sue and Sue

(1990) note that as individuals begin to question their feelings of cultural shame, they often experience guilt and anger for having "sold out in the past and contributed to his/her own group's oppression, and anger at having been oppressed and 'brainwashed' by the forces in the dominant society" (cited in Atkinson et al., 1993, p. 31). Individuals in this stage often view oppression as the primary source of their career development concerns. Atkinson et al. suggest that individuals in this stage tend not to seek counseling, but if they do it is likely to be with an ethnically similar counselor and for more crisis-like concerns. Individuals in the resistance and immersion stage may also prefer group career counseling that is action-oriented and directed toward challenging racism. Sue and Sue point out that counselors, regardless of their degree of similarity to their clients, will be challenged concerning their own racism and role in society by clients in the resistance and immersion stage.

As individuals begin to experience discomfort with the rigidly held beliefs characterizing the resistance and immersion stage (e.g., "all Whites are bad") they begin to focus on greater individual autonomy. That is, as they move into the *introspection* stage, they begin to entertain the notion that perhaps not everything in the dominant culture is negative. Rather than blind adherence to positive or negative views toward cultural systems, there is a greater need to examine the merits of any particular cultural system on a more personal level. This notion emerges as a greater sense of security is experienced with one's own racial identity. As the individual becomes more autonomous, a more personal value system is developed. Atkinson et al. suggest that the emerging need for personal freedom in the face of a preponderant identification with their culture-of-origin often leads individuals to seek counseling to sort through the growing tension created by these conflicting dynamics. In such instances, career counselors who are similar to clients in race and ethnicity are often preferred; however, counselors from other cultures may be accepted if they share an appreciation for the client's cultural dilemma. Atkinson et al. suggest an approach that emphasizes self-exploration and decision making when working with clients in the introspection stage.

The final stage of the Atkinson et al. (1989) model is labeled as *synergistic articulation and awareness*. Individuals in this stage objectively examine the cultural values of their own group as well as those espoused by the dominant group. They accept or reject cultural values based on their experiences in earlier stages of identity development. They experience a genuine desire to eliminate all forms of oppression in society. Consequently, individuals in the synergistic stage tend to experience a sense of self-fulfillment regarding their cultural identity. Atkinson and his colleagues suggest that because clients in this stage have developed "the internal skills and knowledge necessary to exercise a desired level of personal freedom . . . attitudinal similarity between the client and counselor becomes a more important determinant of counseling success than membership-group similarity" (1989, p. 36).

The model developed by Atkinson and his colleagues has similarities with Nigrescence theory of Black identity development first articulated by Cross in the early 1970s and then revised in 1995. Cross notes that Nigrescence theory essentially describes a resocializing experience that Cross (1995) describes as "the transformation of a preexisting identity (a non-Afrocentric identity) into one that is Afrocentric" (p. 97). The first stage in the Cross model is labeled as the *pre-encounter* stage. In this stage, persons often place values in things other than their Blackness (e.g., religious beliefs, occupation). Some individuals, however, adhere to anti-Black attitudes reflected in hatred for other Blacks. Persons in the pre-encounter stage often favor Eurocentric cultural perspectives.

The *encounter* stage is the second stage in the Cross model. Cross (1995) notes that the encounter stage in the Nigrescence process "pinpoints circumstance and events that are likely to induce identity metamorphosis" (p. 104). Rather than a single event, the encounter stage more often involves a series of episodes that move the person toward Nigrescence over time. These episodes create dissonance as the person discovers that there is another level of "Blackness" to which he or she should aspire. This realization tends to be accompanied by powerful emotional experiences (e.g., guilt, intense anger toward Whites). These experiences often create the opportunity for a more Afrocentrically oriented person to emerge.

The third stage in the Cross model is a transition stage labeled as *immersion-emersion*. Immersion reflects the process of immersing oneself in the "world of Blackness" (Cross, 1995, p. 107). The strong emotions emerging during the encounter stage provide the driving force for this intense immersion experience. Eventually, the person emerges from the emotionality of the immersion period and experiences a leveling off and greater control of his or her emotions. The new identity begins to be internalized.

The fourth stage in the Cross model is *internalization*. In this stage, the person ascribes high salience to his or her Blackness. Cross suggests:

> The internalized identity seems to perform three dynamic functions in the everyday life of a person: (a) to defend and protect a person from psychological insults that stem from having to live in a racist society, (b) to provide a sense of belonging and social anchorage, and (c) to provide a foundation or point of departure for carrying out transactions with people, cultures, and human situations beyond the world of Blackness. (p. 113)

The final stage is labeled as *internalization-commitment*. The main difference between Blacks in the internalization or internalization-commitment stages is that in the latter there is a commitment to Black affairs that is expressed over an extended period of time. Future research in the Cross model will focus on fostering a more differentiated understanding of the internalization-commitment stage.

Gender Identity Models

Gender relates to differences in masculinity and femininity. Individual and societal expectations for men and women differ across cultures. We are all influenced by gender and gender expectations. Understanding the influence of gender in career development is critical to providing appropriate career development interventions. Sex-role socialization exerts a powerful influence on girls and boys early in life (Gottfredson, 1981, 2002; Hageman & Gladding, 1983).

Stereotypically, this influence reinforces competition and skill mastery in boys and relationships and connectedness in girls (Gilligan, 1982). As men and women enter the workforce, sex-role socialization continues as women are often confronted with discrimination in selection and promotion practices. Such practices not only limit the opportunity for women to advance in the workplace, but also limit opportunities for receiving mentoring because women are excluded from the informal social networks often used by men to advance in their occupations.

The influence of socialization is not felt only by women, however. Men are expected to achieve and to be ambitious in their occupational pursuits. Many consider those men who are striving to achieve a balance in their life roles as lacking in ambition and the desire to work hard to achieve success. Moreover, men employed in occupations typically populated by women (e.g., men working as day care providers, nurses, or clerical workers) are often viewed as overly feminine. Many men who place a high value on family involvement and career achievement experience increased rates of depression as they struggle to fulfill roles in both of these life domains (Lease, 2003).

Differential socialization of the sexes has led to their unequal representation within occupations. As Herr and Cramer (1996) have written, "The fact that many occupations are sex-traditional simply perpetuates sex-role stereotypes, sustaining the division of labor as a self-fulfilling prophecy" (p. 260). Such sex-role stereotyping occurs beyond the life role of worker. In a review of recent research related to life-role salience, Niles and Goodnough (1996) noted the significant influence of societal expectations on life-role participation. For example, it is a consistent finding that women place greater importance on the home and family than do men. It is also evident that those women who place importance both on work and on home and family are at risk for experiencing role conflict. For male-female couples, this conflict is exacerbated by the fact that men consistently report lower participation in the home and family role when compared with women. In this regard, it is important that men identify ways in which they can participate in activities within the home and family role that will allow them to express important values in this life role. Given the centrality of work in male identity, the exploration of fears and resistance to committing more time to home and family must often be addressed within the career development intervention process. Cook (1994) noted that in terms of life-role participation, "behaving differently may seem to be a practical option but it may feel like a gender role violation, or alternatively, a personal affirmation that had not been considered because of its novelty" (p. 90). To be clear, we are not suggesting that increased participation in home and family on the part of men will eliminate work-home role conflict; rather, a more likely outcome may be that this burden will be more equally shared.

It is also apparent from the research reviewed by Niles and Goodnough (1996) that women tend to rely on work to provide them with an important network for social support. It is important, therefore, that career counselors examine the degree to which their female clients experience a lack of social support when their participation in work is reduced. When social support is lacking, strategies for maintaining a network of support can be identified. Thus, it is evident that the construct of gender must be thoroughly integrated into the career development intervention process.

To help achieve the goal of integrating gender in the career development intervention process, Gysbers et al. (2003) recommend using gender-related identity development models. For example, they cite a feminist identity development model proposed by Downing and Roush (1985). This model consists of five stages: (a) Stage 1: passive acceptance, (b) Stage 2: revelation, (c) Stage 3: embeddedness-emancipation, (d) Stage 4: synthesis, and (e) Stage 5: active commitment.

Stage 1 involves the passive acceptance of sexism and discrimination. There is an implicit, if not explicit, acceptance of sex-traditional gender roles. Stage 2 occurs when a life event exposes oppression of women in a way that is not able to be denied (e.g., a woman may directly experience discrimination in job hiring or promotion). Stage 3 is characterized by the perception that men possess only negative traits (e.g., men are not trustworthy, all men treat women unfairly) and women possess only positive traits. There is a strong desire to separate from men and bond only with other women. All men are viewed as oppressors and all women are viewed as victims. In Stage 4, women view men as individuals rather than automatically considering all men as being members of an oppressive group. Women are also evaluated on an individual basis. The influence of internal and external factors is recognized in the behavior of both sexes. Finally, individuals in Stage 5 become actively involved in managing their career development and in changing oppressive environmental influences.

Oppressive environmental influences restricting the career development of women occur in the home, school, community, and workplace. Stereotypes are perpetuated pervasively in books, movies, television shows, and magazines. These stereotypes often result in women encountering issues such as the "glass ceiling" (i.e., the barring of women from upper levels of administration and leadership), a lack of available mentors, discrimination in hiring, sexual harassment, unavailable adequate and affordable child-care options, and a general lack of support for women aspiring to nontraditional occupations. Gysbers, Heppner, and Johnston (2003) contend that "understanding feminist identity development may help us learn a great deal more about our clients' reactions to the gendered environment. For example, a woman whose attitudes and beliefs are at Stage 1 may either be unaware of, or actually accepting of, sex bias, whereas a client in the middle stages may prefer a female counselor and may benefit from processing the anger she feels about sexism" (p. 95).

To address inadequacies in career theories as they relate to the career development of women, Cook, Heppner, and O'Brien (2002) propose using an ecological perspective to help illuminate the dynamic interaction between the person and the environment. Cook and her associates suggest that an ecological perspective is particularly useful in addressing the White, male, Western experiences and worldviews implicit in career counseling models. They note that an ecological perspective encourages greater sensitivity to ways in which environmental factors do not support the career development of women. Specifically, Cook et al. note the need for career counselors to address the following assumptions that are implicit in career development models: (a) the separation of work and family roles in people's lives, (b) the emphasis on individualism and autonomy, (c) the view that work is the central activity in people's lives, (d) the notion that career development is a linear and rational process, and (e) the White, male bias existing in the occupational opportunity structure. Additionally, Cook and her colleagues emphasize the need for career counselors to address ways in which female clients experience the macrosystem imperatives concerning caring for others (i.e., how the client assigns importance to the needs of significant others and family members in her career development); how women might be able to influence their microsystems (e.g., the workplace) through learning or refining negotiation skills to enable them to ask for what they need (e.g., more flexible work hours, salary increases); how to identify and access quality child care; empowering women to handle sexual harassment in the workplace, and, therefore, lessen the likelihood of victimization; and helping women to access mentors. Of course, each of these issues provides opportunities for macrosystem (e.g., advocating for equitable workplace policies and treatment) and microsystem (e.g., within the career counseling relationship) interventions.

Integrating gender into the career development intervention process is important in working with men as well. Men are socialized to value power, competition, action, strength, logic, and achievement (O'Neil, 1982). They are taught to avoid emotional intimacy and to fear femininity (Skovholt, 1990). O'Neil contended that this type of socialization process results in men being restricted in self-disclosure and experiencing various physical and emotional problems. The push toward achievement and success leads many men to overemphasize work activity and minimize their activity in the home and family (Niles & Goodnough, 1996). Many men realize too late in life that they have too frequently missed opportunities to connect more meaningfully with their partners and/or children. Providing men with opportunities (via individual and/or group career counseling) to explore how the socialization process influences their career behavior, learn how to express their feelings, learn how to manage and reduce stress, and identify strategies for participating more fully in life roles beyond work are important components of career development interventions for this population.

Understanding the identity development status of men can help career development practitioners provide appropriate career development interventions. In this respect, it can be argued that a model of identity development similar to the one offered by Downing and Roush (1985) could also be applied to men. For example, a man whose attitudes and beliefs are at Stage 1 (i.e., passive acceptance) may be unaware of his acceptance of sex bias in his career behavior, whereas a client in the middle stages may prefer a male counselor and may benefit from processing the anger he feels about pressure to compete, achieve, and succeed at work. Men at Stage 5 (active commitment) may find male support groups helpful in maintaining behaviors that do not coincide with sex-role stereotyping (e.g., spending more time in nurturing activities related to the home and family role). Helping men understand the importance of actively engaging in life roles beyond work and supporting them in these involvements (e.g., by offering support groups) may empower men to move toward a less constricted range of life-role involvements. This outcome benefits men, women, and children.

Gay/Lesbian/Bisexual Identity Models

There is little research investigating the career development of gay, lesbian, and bisexual people (GLB). Because each of these groups experience oppression, Morgan and Brown (1991) suggested using minority career development theories to describe the career development of experiences of persons who are GLB. Although there is undoubtedly significant overlap due to oppressive environmental conditions, this suggestion offers, at best, a temporary solution to the lack of theory and research pertaining to these populations. However, as with racial and gender identity, assessing identity development levels of GLB clients represents a crucial element in the career counseling process (Chung, 2003; Morgan & Brown, 1991; Pope, 1995). When working with GLB clients, Orzek (1992) noted that counselors must understand the meaning that their clients attach to their sexual identity to construct career development interventions that mesh with their clients' stages of identity development.

According to Cass (1979), gay men and lesbian women encounter six stages of identity development: (a) confusion, (b) comparison, (c) tolerance, (d) acceptance, (e) pride, and (f) synthesis. The stages in the Cass model parallel those in racial identity models. The Cass model proposes that, as progression is made through the six stages, GLB persons experience an enhanced sense of self-acceptance and self-esteem; become increasingly empowered to form a stronger community with other gay, lesbian, and bisexual individuals; feel more comfortable in disclosing their sexual orientation; and experience more congruence between their feelings and behaviors. Sophie (1986) proposed a four-stage model of lesbian identity development. The four stages consisted of:

1. Self-awareness of GLB feelings without disclosing those feelings to others.
2. Testing and exploration of emerging GLB identity with limited disclosure to straight persons.
3. Identity acceptance and preference for gay social interactions.
4. Identity integration with movement from a dichotomous worldview (GLB, straight) to a more integrated worldview.

Chapman and Brannock (1987) developed a five-stage model of lesbian identity development. Fassinger (1995, p. 151) described this model as follows:

1. Same-sex orientation, characterized by feeling different about other girls and women, but lacking a name for those feelings.
2. Incongruence, social isolation, and confusion about heterosexual dating.
3. Self-questioning and exploration, involving strong bonds with or attraction to other girls and women, and possible exploration of homosexuality.
4. Identification, characterized by thinking or feeling "I am a lesbian."
5. Choice of lifestyle, characterized by a decision to seek women as long-term mates, or maintaining a lesbian orientation without choosing women as long-term mates.

More recently, Chung (2003) conducted a SWOT (strengths, weaknesses, opportunities, and threats) analysis of the literature related to career counseling with GLB persons. He identified several strengths within the existing literature. For example, Chung noted that recently numerous researchers have engaged in studying the career behavior of GLB persons through the application of existing career theories [e.g., Holland, Super, and social cognitive career theory (SCCT)]. Chung also noted the important contributions of researchers, such as Fassinger (1995) and Prince (1995), who have applied lesbian identity development and gay male identity development models, respectively, to career behavior. A third recent and important development within the literature noted by Chung has been the more focused attention given to career issues experienced by GLB persons (e.g., sexual identity disclosure and management, work discrimination, and discrimination coping strategies). Future research is needed that integrates the latter body of research into theoretical models. In addition to the need for more theory-based research in this area, Chung also calls for researchers to engage in more programmatic research efforts to advance understanding of the career development of GLB persons. Finally, Chung highlights the fact that research related to the career development of lesbian and bisexual persons lags behind research efforts focused on gay men; thus, there is the important need for additional research in these areas in particular.

Pope and Barret (2002) also note the need for more research related to the career development experiences of persons who are gay, lesbian, bisexual or transgendered. Using the extant literature, Pope and Barret identify several intervention strategies for career counselors working with gay and lesbian clients. For example, as a first step for career counselors, Pope and Barret stress the importance of counselors taking a personal inventory of ways in which subtle or unconscious biases may influence career counseling (e.g., when a heterosexually oriented career counselor attempts to move a young man toward becoming more masculine in his behaviors). Pope and Barret also stress the importance of becoming more familiar with gay and lesbian culture (e.g., by attending workshops, reading relevant literature, participating in lesbian/gay culture). They note the ethical requirement that career counselors who cannot be gay/lesbian affirmative must refer clients to a career counselor who has experience with sexual minorities and can work with clients in a more affirming manner. With regard to "client-focused" career interventions, Pope and Barret highlight helping clients cope effectively with issues such as "coming out," dealing with workplace discrimination, negotiating dual-career couples' concerns (e.g., benefits issues, relocation issues), and the selection/use of assessment instruments. In addition to client-focused interventions, Pope and Barret discuss program-focused interventions. Recommended interventions in this category include: sharing information on existing gay/lesbian community resources, offering special programming such as talks by gay/lesbian professionals, arranging career shadowing opportunities with gay/lesbian workers, maintaining a list of "out" gay/lesbian individuals who are available for information interviews, facilitating experiential opportunities (e.g., internships, externships) with gay/lesbian owned or operated businesses, and establishing mentoring programs with gay/lesbian mentors. Finally, Pope and Barret stress the importance of career counselors engaging in advocacy or social action interventions. For example, positive advocacy for gay and lesbian clients could include lobbying for the inclusion of sexual orientation in nondiscrimination policies of local employers. While providing effective career counseling services for our lesbian and gay clients is not easy due to social issues, internalized homophobia, employment discrimination, and so on, we view it as critically important for career counselors to develop the awareness, knowledge, and skills necessary to competently assist sexual minorities.

Persons with Disabilities

Persons with disabilities represent another group that commonly experiences discrimination in career development. "Individuals with disabilities lag behind those without disabilities in virtually every indicator of economic activity" (Ettinger,

1996, p. 239). For example, only 31% of persons with disabilities who were also college graduates were employed in 1998 (compared with 85% of those who were not disabled and possessed only high school degrees) (Hitchings et al., 2000). Despite these facts, career development researchers pay little attention to the career experiences of persons with disabilities. For example, in a recent issue of *The Career Development Quarterly* (September, 2003) devoted to advancing career interventions in the next decade, there was barely a mention of the need for career development theory and practice to pay greater attention to persons with disabilities. Even scholars who call on the profession to engage in more advocacy often fail to identify the near silence that exists on behalf of persons with disabilities. This is perplexing given that 18.7% of Americans between the ages of 15 and 64 have a disability (U.S. Department of Education). Clearly, this is an embarrassing, and inexcusable, gap in the career development literature.

Herr et al. (2004) define a person with disabilities as "one who is usually considered to be different from a normal person—physically, physiologically, neurologically, or psychologically—because of accident, disease, birth, or developmental problems" (p. 280). The Americans with Disabilities Act of 1990 (ADA) identifies a person with disabilities as:

> A person who has physical or mental impairment that substantially limits one or more "major life activities," or has a record of such an impairment, or is regarded as having such an impairment. Examples of physical or mental impairments are contagious and noncontagious diseases and conditions such as orthopedic, visual, speech, and hearing impairments, cerebral palsy, epilepsy, muscular dystrophy, multiple sclerosis, cancer, heart disease, diabetes, mental retardation, emotional illness, specific learning disabilities, HIV disease, tuberculosis, drug addiction, and alcoholism. "Major life activities" include functions such as caring for oneself, performing manual tasks, walking, seeing, hearing, speaking, breathing, learning, and working. (U.S. Department of Justice, 1991, pp. 3–4)

The ADA stipulates that employers can consider only essential job functions when hiring or promoting employees. Employers may require prospective employees to demonstrate how they will perform specific job-related functions. Although employers can make employment decisions based on job-related qualifications, they cannot make employment decisions based on reasons that are related to the person's disability.

Additionally, employers must provide reasonable accommodations to qualified individuals with disabilities to enable them to do the essential functions of a job, unless the change imposes undue hardship on the employers. Those desiring more information about the ADA can write to the Office of the Americans with Disabilities Act, Civil Rights Division, U.S. Department of Justice, Box 66118, Washington, D.C. 20035–6118. (See Figure 4.1.)

Zunker (1998, pp. 458–461) identifies several career development issues that typically confront persons with disabilities. Specifically, he notes that issues related to adjusting to disabilities (as when people experience physical trauma and then have difficulty adjusting to and accepting their disability) include confronting attitudinal barriers, based on misinformation and discriminatory beliefs; overcoming generalizations formed as a result of being labeled disabled or handicapped; having a

General

- *Public accommodations such as restaurants, hotels, theaters, doctors' offices, pharmacies, retail stores, museums, libraries, parks, private schools, and day-care centers may not discriminate on the basis of disability. Private clubs and religious organizations are exempt.*
- Reasonable changes in policies, practices, and procedures must be made to avoid discrimination.

Auxiliary aids

- Auxiliary aids and services must be provided to individuals with vision or hearing impairments or other individuals with disabilities, unless an undue burden would result.

Physical barriers

- Physical barriers in existing facilities must be removed, if removal is readily achievable. If not, alternative methods of providing the services must be offered, if they are readily achievable.
- All new construction in public accommodations, as well as in "commercial facilities" such as office buildings, must be accessible. Elevators are generally not required in buildings under three stories or with fewer than 3000 square feet per floor, unless the building is a shopping center, mall, or a professional office of a health care provider.
- Alterations must be accessible. When alterations to primary function areas are made, an accessible path of travel to the altered area (and the bathrooms, telephones, and drinking fountains serving that area) must be provided to the extent that the added accessibility costs are not disproportionate to the overall cost of the alterations. Elevators are required as previously described.

Employment

- Employers may not discriminate against an individual with a disability in hiring or promotion if the person is otherwise qualified for the job.
- Employers can ask about one's ability to perform a job, but cannot inquire if someone has a disability or subject a person to tests that tend to screen out people with disabilities.
- Employers will need to provide "reasonable accommodation" to individuals with disabilities. This includes steps such as job restructuring and modification of equipment.
- Employers do not need to provide accommodations that impose an "undue hardship" on business operations.

Who needs to comply

- All employers with 25 or more employees must comply, effective July 26, 1992.
- All employers with 15–24 employees must comply, effective July 26, 1994.

Transportation

- New public transit buses ordered after August 26, 1990, must be accessible to individuals with disabilities.
- Transit authorities must provide comparable paratransit or other special transportation services to individuals with disabilities who cannot use fixed route bus services, unless an undue burden would result.
- Existing rail systems must have one accessible car per train by July 26, 1995.
- New rail cars ordered after August 26, 1990, must be accessible.
- New bus and train stations must be accessible.
- Key stations in rapid, light, and commuter rail systems must be made accessible by July 26, 1993, with extensions up to 20 years for commuter rail (30 years for rapid and light rail).
- All existing Amtrak stations must be accessible by July 26, 2010.

Figure 4.1

Americans with Disabilities Act requirements specified in the Public Accommodations Fact Sheet. *Source:* From *Americans with Disabilities Act Handbook* (Coordination and Review Section), U.S. Department of Justice, Civil Rights Division, 1991, Washington, DC: U.S. Department of Justice.

lack of role models and norm groups; coping with issues associated with the age of onset of disability; developing social/interpersonal skills; developing a positive self-concept; and developing skills for independent living. These issues each require specific career development interventions to facilitate the career development of persons with disabilities.

For those lacking role models, exposure to employed individuals with similar disabilities can serve as an important source of self-efficacy enhancement (Bandura, 1986). Cook (1981) noted that those having difficulty adjusting to their disability due to physical trauma might need assistance in coping with grief associated with losing their prior level of functioning. Zunker (1998) notes that those experiencing a disability at an early age may require assistance in developing assertiveness and independence and those experiencing the onset of a disability in adulthood may need to be reintroduced to the overall career development process. Supported employment (e.g., sheltered workshops) opportunities may help persons with disabilities gain exposure to role models, experience enhanced self-esteem through work-related accomplishments, and develop important interpersonal skills.

Zunker (1998) and Levinson (1994) provide thorough descriptions of the assessment process for people with disabilities. For example, Levinson describes a comprehensive vocational assessment for persons with disabilities as including psychological, social, educational-academic, physical-medical, and vocational functioning assessments. Zunker suggests that vocational evaluations for persons with disabilities could include (in ascending order): gathering biographical data, conducting an evaluation interview, conducting psychological testing, providing opportunities to acquire occupational information and engage in career exploration, completing work samples, completing situational or workshop tasks, conducting informal conferences with other staff members, offering job tryouts, holding formal staff conferences, and providing vocational counseling for career decision making, implementation, and adjustment to the career choice implemented (p. 151).

Cummings, Maddux, and Casey (2000) note that much of the career literature related to persons with disabilities focuses on persons with physical disabilities and little attention is directed toward those with learning disabilities. Persons with learning disabilities often experience challenges that negatively influence their career development. Some common challenges include: a failure to understand how personal characteristics relate to career choice, low self-esteem, an inability to engage in self-advocacy, difficulties in establishing routines, difficulties in accurately observing and effectively imitating the work habits of role models, challenges related to information processing, and a tendency toward passive learning styles. Cummings and her associates identify several strategies that career practitioners can use to more effectively address the concerns of persons with learning disabilities. First, and foremost, they note the need for career practitioners to help secondary school students with learning disabilities engage in more systematic transition planning as they move from high school to postsecondary experiences. To achieve this goal, counselors must work to improve the coordination between high schools and postsecondary education and community agencies. Although IDEA requires that each student's transition plan include information regarding postsecondary services (e.g., vocational rehabilitation, independent living options), linkages to these services are often not identified for students with learning disabilities. Because college students with learning disabilities often experience lower career decision making self-efficacy and a more pessimistic attributional style for career decision making than their peers without disabilities (Luzzo, Hitchings, Retish, & Shoemaker, 1999), the need also exists to provide more systematic and adequate transition planning to students with learning disabilities who are moving from high school to postsecondary education. Finally, Cummings and her colleagues advocate for taking a K–12 approach to transition planning. In this regard, Levinson (1998) argues for a three-level transition assessment program for students with learning disabilities. Specifically, Levinson suggests a Level 1 assessment during the elementary school years that focuses on identifying the student's needs, values, abilities, interests, interpersonal skills, and decision-making skills. Assessment outcomes at this level should be connected to transition goals/objectives that focus on career exploration and self-awareness. Level 2 assessments should occur during the middle school years and involve formal and informal measures related to interests, aptitudes, work habits, and career maturity. Assessment outcomes should be linked to additional career exploration moving toward a narrowing of tentative career options and goals. Level 3 assessment should include work samples and situational assessments and additional emphasis on identifying the student's skills, interests, and career goals. Empowering persons with learning disabilities to engage in effective self-advocacy is also essential.

The challenges experiences by persons with disabilities require career practitioners to work on multiple fronts to provide effective career assistance (Levinson, 1998). For example, because empirically supported career theories for persons with disabilities are lacking, career practitioners must consider how extant theories can be applied to foster understanding of the intra-individual and contextual factors that influence the career development of persons with disabilities. Hypotheses generated in this regard should be subjected to empirical validation to advance general understanding of career development processes for persons with disabilities. To generate sound hypotheses, career practitioners will need to possess specific knowledge that extends beyond a general familiarity with career theories. Specifically, career practitioners will need to have knowledge pertaining to the following:

1. Federal and state legislation, guidelines, and policies applicable to persons with disabilities
2. Types of disability classifications, diagnostic tools or processes and their limitations
3. Informal assessment procedures for assessing interests, values, goals
4. Characteristics of different types of disabilities, their causes, and their likely effects upon work behavior
5. Opportunities available in the local labor market for persons with different types of skills and different types of challenges
6. The meaning of functional limitation and its use in counseling
7. The effects of social stigma, labeling, and stereotyping on the self-concept of persons with disabilities
8. Essential employability skills, the availability of training programs as well as occupational and educational opportunities

9. Ways to work effectively with other specialists to facilitate a comprehensive approach to career exploration, career preparation, and career placement of persons with disabilities
10. Examples of job redesign that employers use to accommodate the capabilities and/or functional limitations for persons with various types of disability
11. Methods of developing individual employment plans and individualized educational plans
12. Fears, concerns, and needs of parents or partners of persons with disabilities and ways to work systemically to foster the career development of persons with disabilities
13. Models of developing daily living, mobility, job search, and work skills
14. Strategies for teaching self-advocacy skills related to accessing disability-related services

Persons with disabilities encounter specific obstacles in their career development that are often due to a lack of awareness and sensitivity on the part of employers, educational institutions, and the general public. Many employers adhere to the false (and stereotypical) beliefs that persons with disabilities will be absent more often, less productive, and less invested in their career development than their nondisabled peers. Providing effective career development interventions requires practitioners to possess the requisite knowledge, skills, and awareness for adequately addressing the career concerns of persons with disabilities. Many times, this requires career development professionals to play an advocacy role with prospective employers and coworkers to dispel discriminatory myths.

ASSESSMENT

Our discussion of career development interventions for persons with disabilities leads into some important points to consider in conducting career assessments with diverse client populations. Walsh and Betz (1990) defined assessment as "a process of understanding and helping people cope with problems" (p. 12). Often assessment involves using a test as a "method of acquiring a sample of behavior under controlled conditions" (p. 21). However, as we discussed previously, assessment can also involve activities such as observing client behaviors as they engage in specific work-related tasks, participating in job simulation activities, and engaging the client in a counseling interview to gather important current information pertaining to the client's career concerns as well as relevant client biographical data.

Numerous career assessment models exist. For example, Zunker (1998) describes an assessment process that is cyclical and continuous. He proposes that counselors begin by working collaboratively with clients to analyze a client's needs, determining specific purpose(s) for testing, determining the measuring instruments that are most appropriate for achieving the purpose of testing, and then utilizing the results to make a decision concerning work or additional training. Walsh and Betz (1990) describe a four-part assessment model that includes clarifying the problem, gathering the information, understanding the problem, and coping with the problem.

Regardless of the assessment model used, Fouad (1993) notes that career counselors must be mindful of the fact that the client's culture plays a significant role throughout all phases of the assessment process. For example, analyzing the client's needs requires counselors to understand a client's worldview. Empathizing with the client from the client's perspective requires counselors to be aware of their own cultural background and how the client's culture may influence the assessment process. When encouraging clients to discuss their understanding of the assessment results, career counselors must be sure that the client's cultural context is factored into the review process. For example, because the history of Native American identity is typically maintained through oral tradition, a Native American client is likely to define words as powerful and value-laden. Thus, the tendency to use words casually might be avoided at all costs (Sage, 1991) and silence may predominate in sessions. Such silences should be allowed to occur naturally and should not necessarily be determined as client resistance. In this regard, many of the points raised by Fischer et al. (1998) concerning multicultural counseling also pertain to conducting culturally appropriate career assessments.

When selecting a test, career counselors must ensure that the instrument is valid, reliable, and appropriate for the client's cultural and linguistic context. Fouad (1993) identified several important issues that need to be considered in conducting career assessments across cultures. Specifically, Fouad noted that career counselors must determine whether a test is functionally and conceptually equivalent for the client's culture. Functional equivalence relates to "the role or function that behavior plays in different cultures" (Fouad, p. 8). Conceptual equivalence "refers to the similarity in meaning attached to behavior or concepts" (Fouad, p. 8). Fouad also identified metric equivalence (i.e., whether the scales of a test measure the same constructs across cultures) and linguistic equivalence (i.e., whether the translation of items results in equivalent language across cultures) as important areas to address in test selection.

Fouad (1993) also cautions career counselors to consider whether systematic bias exists in any test being considered for use in career counseling. For example, content bias exists when test items are more familiar to members of one group than they are for another group. Lack of familiarity with item content obviously places a test taker at a significant disadvantage and leads to spurious test results. Internal structure bias exists when the relationships among items is not consistent across cultural contexts. Finally, selection bias occurs when a test has differential predictive validity across groups.

As with any career development intervention, selecting tests properly requires career counselors to be aware of their own worldviews, a client's worldview, and the psychometric concerns identified by Fouad. Too many times, counselors have disregarded these factors when using tests in career counseling. In such instances, career counselors do a disservice to the client and the profession. When used properly, assessments can provide clients with vital information for resolving their career concerns.

Ponterotto, Rivera, and Sueyoshi (2000) use a culturally sensitive semistructured protocol during career counseling intake sessions. Their "career-in-culture" (CiCl) interview incorporates recent theoretical advancements in multicultural counseling and social cognitive career theory (Lent, Brown, & Hackett, 2002). The CiCl interview focuses on understanding the client from five spheres of career development influence: cuture; family and religion; community and larger society; self-view and self-efficacy; barriers and oppression; and narrative and relationship. Questions from each sphere foster a collaborative career counseling relationship and move from a focus on individual-based questions to those more broadly focused on family, religion, culture, and community. For example, the career counselor encourages the client to consider the following:

1. Is there anything you would like to know about me and my role as a career counselor?
2. Tell me about yourself.
3. Tell me about your career concerns and career goals.
4. What are some things that are important to you (and unimportant to you) in a career?
5. What type of occupations were you aware of growing up?
6. Name three things you are good at, and why.
7. Name three things you are not good at, and why.
8. Do you believe you can accomplish whatever goals you set for yourself? Why or why not?
9. Tell me about your cultural and ethnic background.
10. Tell me about your religious background.
11. How has your family influenced your career goals?
12. How do your career goals match with your family's expectations?
13. Draw a family genogram and tell me about the lives and work experiences of the family members identified.
14. What are some organizations in your community that have influenced you?
15. Who are some of the people in your community who have influenced you?
16. As a _____ (race/ethnicity, female/male, older/younger, gay/lesbian/bixsexual/transgendered/straight, abled/disabled) person, what do you see as your greatest challenges to pursuing your career goals?

The CiCl draws upon SCCT and multicultural counseling to directly address essential spheres of influence in living and makes clear from the start that these topics are important in considering career concerns.

Scholl (1999) devised the "Career Path Tournament" as group intervention for middle school through university levels to help students consider the effects of sociological influences on career development. The tournament uses a round-by-round elimination format to achieve the following goals: (a) to stimulate awareness of sociological barriers to career advancement; (b) to increase participants' awareness of feelings (e.g., anger, anxiety, confusion); (c) to gain a better understanding of the career development process as it is reflected in education practices, professional training, and employment practices; and (d) to increase awareness of the need to intentionally cope with discriminatory practices. Herring (2002) provides excellent suggestions for additional group and classroom activities that engage students in the consideration of cultural and sociological influences in career development.

Degges-White and Shoffner (2002) describe how the Theory of Work Adjustment can be used effectively to provide career counseling with lesbian clients. Casella (in press) describes how Super's theory can also be used to help lesbian clients advance in their career development. Additional interventions such as those from postmodern theoretical perspectives (e.g., career laddering, "my life as a book," life-role salience questions that incorporate family and societal expectations) can also be used to acknowledge the central role of culture in shaping identity and career development.

SUMMARY

The tremendous changes occurring in the population demographics within American society have given rise to many important developments related to career development interventions. Many existing career development theories have been expanded to be more inclusive. New theories with a greater sensitivity toward describing the career development process for diverse populations are emerging. Career development practitioners are becoming increasingly sensitive to the fact that treating all clients in the same way is, in fact, discriminatory treatment because such an approach ignores the contextual factors shaping the client's career behavior.

Despite these advances, much more needs to be done. For example, research is needed to more fully understand the career development process for members of diverse groups. Career development interventions still need to be expanded to address both intra-individual and extra-individual variables influencing career behavior. Greater understanding is needed regarding how differences between the career counselor and the client regarding language, social class, and, most importantly, culture influence the career counseling process. In this regard, Trusty (2002, pp. 204–207) offers several cautions to those engaged in research to advance our understanding of multicultural infuences in career development processes:

1. Comparison studies have limited usefulness.
2. Many studies are piecemeal.
3. Researchers often ignore the possibility of interactions or other curvilinear relationships.
4. Too little attention is paid to external validity, transferability of findings.
5. Research and theory from areas other than multicultural and career counseling are often ignored.
6. There is a double standard regarding cause in correlational studies.
7. We need more studies that focus on the effectiveness of interventions.
8. More research is needed on developmental processes.

In addition to these suggestions that emphasize quantitative research methods, Trusty also views recent advances in qualitative research as very useful for helping to broaden our understanding of factors that are influential in career development processes for diverse populations. For example, Hernandez and Morales (1999) conducted a qualitative study to increase understanding related to Latinas working in higher education. Hernandez and Morales revealed strong images of an inhospitable and nonsupportive work environment for Latinas. The qualitative data from this study supported important career development interventions for addressing individual and environmental factors influencing the career experiences of Latinas and other members of underrepresented groups.

Beyond increasing the rigor and amount of research (quantitative and qualitative) related to multicultural career development, counselor preparation programs need to infuse multiculturalism into the curriculum, especially as it pertains to career development intervention courses (Swanson, 1993; Swanson & O' Brien, 2002). Encouraging students to consider how career theories are not and/or are relevant for diverse groups and to identify culturally appropriate career interventions should be the rule within counselor training.

In short, our pluralistic society has provided an excellent catalyst to making career development theories and interventions more inclusive, for providing opportunities for the profession to grow, and for more effectively serving the needs of greater numbers of people. Toward this end, we offer the following suggestions to career counselors:

1. Career counselors should, above all, possess essential counseling knowledge, skills, and understanding that reflect multicultural competencies.

2. Career counselors should be aware of their own attitudes and values generally, but they should also understand how their own attitudes and values may interact with their client's attitudes and values; career counselors should work to ensure that their internal frames of reference do not form roadblocks to successful counseling.

3. Career counselors should be aware of their client's cultural context, but they should also understand that we are each first and foremost individuals and only secondarily representatives of our specific immediate and distal cultural contexts.

4. Career counselors should empower clients who experience discrimination to "reject the rejection" within discriminatory attitudes and behavior.

5. Career counselors must be sure that they understand how experiences with racist, sexist, homophobic, classist, ageist, and discriminatory practices toward persons who are disabled influence their clients' career development.

6. Career counselors should engage in proactive programming to provide experiential opportunities, information resources, mentoring opportunities, and psychoeducational activities that are relevant to persons from diverse groups.

7. Career counselors must engage in social action and advocacy to address systemic discrimination.

8. Career counselors should engage in programmatic research efforts to develop and advance theories of career development that apply to diverse groups.

REFERENCES

Arbona, C. (1990). Career counseling research and Hispanics: A review of the literature. *The Counseling Psychologist, 18*, 300–323.

Atkinson, D. R., Morten, G., & Sue, D. W. (1989). A minority identity development model. In D. R. Atkinson, G. Morten, & D. W. Sue (Eds.), *Counseling American minorities* (pp. 35–52). Dubuque, IA: William C. Brown.

Atkinson, D. R., Morten, G., & Sue, D. W. (Eds.). (1993). *Counseling American minorities* (4th ed.). Madison, WI: Brown & Benchmark.

Axelson, J. A. (1985). *Counseling and development in a multicultural society.* Pacific Grove, CA: Brooks/Cole.

Bandura, A. (1986). *Social foundations of thought and action: A social cognitive theory.* Englewood Cliffs, NJ: Prentice-Hall.

Berg-Cross, L., & Zoppetti, L. (1991). Person-In-Culture interview: Understanding culturally different students. *Journal of College Student Psychotherapy, 5*(4), 5–21.

Casella, C. (in press). Using Super's theory in career counselilng with lesbian clients. *The Career Development Quarterly.*

Cass, V. C. (1979). Homosexual identity formation: A theoretical model. *Journal of Homosexuality, 7*, 219–235.

Chapman, B. E., & Brannock, J. C. (1987). Proposed model of lesbian identity development: An empirical examination. *Journal of Homosexuality, 14*, 69–80.

Cheatham, H. E. (1990). Africentricity and career development of African-Americans. *The Career Development Quarterly, 38*, 334–336.

Chung, Y. B. (2003). Career counseling with lesbian, gay, bisexual, and transgendered persons: The next decade. *The Career Development Quarterly, 52*, 78–86.

Cook, D. W. (1981). Impact of disability on the individual. In R. M. Parker & C. E. Hansen (Eds.), *Rehabilitation counseling*. Boston: Allyn & Bacon.

Cook, E. (1994). Role salience and multiple roles: A gender perspective. *The Career Development Quarterly, 43,* 85–95.

Cook, E., Heppner, M. J., & O'Brien, K. M. (2002). Feminism and women's career development: An ecological perspective. In S. Niles (Ed.), *Adult career development: Concepts, models, and practices* (3rd ed., pp. 169–190). Tulsa, OK: National Career Development Association.

Cross, W. E. (1971). The Negro-to-Black conversion experience: Toward a psychology of Black liberation. *Black World, 20,* 13–27.

Cross, W. E. (1995). The psychology of Nigrescence: Revising the Cross model. In J. G. Ponterotto, J. M. Casas, L. A. Suzuki, & C. M. Alexander (Eds.), *Handbook of multicultural counseling* (pp. 93–122). Thousand Oaks, CA: Sage.

Cummings, R., Maddux, C. D., & Casey, J. (2000). Individualized transition planning for students with learning disabilities. *The Career Development Quarterly, 49,* 60–72.

Degges-White, S., & Shoffner, M. (2002). Career counseling with lesbian clients: Using the theory of work adjustment as a framework. *The Career Development Quarterly, 51,* 87–96.

Downing, N. E., & Roush, K. L. (1985). From passive acceptance to active commitment: A model of feminist identity development for women. *The Counseling Psychologist, 13,* 195–209.

Ettinger, J. (1996). Meeting the career development needs of individuals with disabilities. In R. Feller & G. Walz (Eds.), *Career transitions in turbulent times: Exploring work, learning and careers* (pp. 239–244). Greensboro, NC: Educational Resources Information Center, Counseling and Student Services Clearinghouse.

Farmer, H., Rotella, S., Anderson, C., & Wardrop, J. (1998). Gender differences in science, math and technology careers: Prestige level and Holland interest type. *Journal of Vocational Behavior, 53,* 73–96.

Fassinger, R. E. (1995). From invisibility to integration: Lesbian identity in the workplace. *The Career Development Quarterly, 44,* 148–167.

Fischer, A. R., Jome, L. M., & Atkinson, D. R. (1998). Reconceptualizing multicultural counseling:

Universal healing conditions in a culturally specific context. *Counseling Psychologist, 26,* 525–588.

Fouad, N. A. (1993). Cross-cultural vocational assessment. *The Career Development Quarterly, 42,* 4–13.

Gilligan, C. (1982). *In a different voice.* Cambridge, MA: Harvard University Press.

Goleman, D. (1990, July 10). Homophobia: Scientists find clues to its roots. *The New York Times,* pp. C1, C11.

Gottfredson, L. S. (1981). Circumscription and compromise: A developmental theory of occupational aspirations. *Journal of Counseling Psychology, 28,* 545–579.

Gottfredson, L. S. (2002). Gottfredson's theory of circumscription, compromise, and self-creation. In D. Brown & Associates (Eds.), *Career choice and development* (4th ed., pp. 85–148). San Francisco: Jossey-Bass.

Grieger, I., & Ponterotto, J. G. (1995). A framework for assessment in multicultural counseling. In J. G. Ponterotto, J. M. Casas, L. A. Suzuki, & C. M. Alexander (Eds.), *Handbook of multicultural counseling* (pp. 357–374). Thousand Oaks, CA: Sage.

Gysbers, N. C., Heppner, M. J., & Johnston, J. A. (2003). *Career counseling: Process, issues, and techniques* (2nd ed.). Boston, MA: Allyn & Bacon.

Hageman, M. B., & Gladding, S. T. (1983). The art of career exploration: Occupational sex-role stereotyping among elementary school children. *Elementary School Guidance and Counseling, 17,* 280–287.

Hartung, P. J., Speight, J. D., & Lewis, D. M. (1996). Individualism-collectivism and the vocational behavior of majority culture college students. *The Career Development Quarterly, 45,* 87–96.

Hernandez, T. J., & Morales, N. E. (1999). Career, culture, and compromise: Career development experiences of Latinas working in higher education. *The Career Development Quarterly, 48,* 45–58.

Herr, E. L., & Cramer, S. H. (1996). *Career guidance and counseling through the lifespan* (5th ed.). New York: HarperCollins.

Herr, E. L., Cramer, S. H., & Niles, S. G. (2004). *Career guidance and counseling through the lifespan: Systemic approaches* (6th ed.). Boston, MA: Allyn & Bacon.

Herring, R. D. (1991). Counseling Native American youth. In C. C. Lee & B. L. Richardson (Eds.), *Multicultural issues in counseling: New approaches to diversity* (pp. 37–47). Alexandria, VA: American Counseling Association.

Herring, R. D. (2002). Multicultural counseling for career development. In J. Trusty, E. J. Looby, & D. S. Sandhu (Eds.), *Multicultural counseling: Context, theory and practice, and competence* (pp. 219–246). Huntington, NY: Nova Science.

Hitchings, W. E., Luzzo, D. A., Retish, P., Horvath, M., Ristow, R., & Tanners, A. (2000). Identifying the needs of college students with disabilities. *Journal of College Student Development, 39,* 23–32.

Ibrahim, F. A., & Kahn, H. (1987). Assessment of world views. *Psychological Reports, 60,* 163–176.

Ibrahim, F. A., & Owens, S. V. (1992, August). *Factor analytic structure of the scale to assess world view.* Paper presented at the annual meeting of the American Psychological Association, Washington, DC.

Isaacson, L. E., & Brown, D. (1997). *Career information, career counseling, and career development* (6th ed.). Needham Heights, MA: Allyn & Bacon.

Johnston, W. B., & Packer, A. H. (1987). *Workforce 2000: Work and workers for the twenty-first century.* Indianapolis, IN: Hudson Institute.

Kluckhohn, C., & Murray, H. A. (1950). Personality formation: The determinants. In C. Kluckhorn & H. A. Murray (Eds.), *Personality in nature, society, and culture* (pp. 35–48). New York: Knopf.

Lease, S. H. (2003). Testing a model of men's nontraditional occupational choices. *The Career Development Quarterly, 51,* 244–258.

Lee, C. C., & Richardson, B. L. (Eds.). (1991). *Multicultural issues in counseling: New approaches to diversity.* Alexandria, VA: American Counseling Association.

Lent, R. W., Brown, S. D., & Hackett, G. (2002). Social cognitive career theory. In D. Brown & Associates (Eds.), *Career choice and development* (4th ed., pp. 255–311). San Francisco, CA: Jossey-Bass.

Leong, F. T. L. (1986). Counseling and psychotherapy with Asian-Americans: Review of the literature. *Journal of Counseling Psychology, 33,* 196–206.

Leong, F. T. L. (1993). The career counseling process with racial-ethnic minorities: The case of Asian Americans. *The Career Development Quarterly, 42,* 26–40.

Leong, F. T. L., & Brown, M. T. (1995). Theoretical issues in cross-cultural career development: Cultural validity and cultural specificity. In W. B. Walsh & S. H. Osipow (Eds.), *Handbook of vocational psychology: Theory, research, and practice* (2nd ed., pp. 143–180). Mahwah, NJ: Erlbaum.

Levinson, E. M. (1998). *Transition: Facilitating the post-school adjustment of students with disabilities.* Boulder, CO: Westview Press.

Levinson, H. (1994). Why the behemoths fell: Psychological roots of corporate failure. *American Psychologist, 49,* 428–436.

Lichter, D. (1998). Race, employment hardship and inequality in American non-metropolitan South. *American Sociological Review, 54,* 436–446.

Luzzo, D. A., Hitchings, W. E., Retish, P., & Shoemaker, A. (1999). Evaluating differences in college students' career decision making on the basis of disability status. *The Career Development Quarterly, 46,* 142–156.

Morgan, K. S., & Brown, L. S. (1991). Lesbian career development, work behavior, and vocational counseling. *Counseling Psychologist, 19,* 273–291.

Niles, S. G., & Goodnough, G. (1996). Life-role salience and values: A review of recent research. *The Career Development Quarterly, 45,* 65–86.

O' Neil, W. M. (1982). Gender role conflict and strain in men's lives: Implications for psychiatrists, psychologists, and other human-service providers. In K. Solomon & N. B. Levy (Eds.), *Men in transition.* New York: Plenum.

Orzek, A. M. (1992). Career counseling for the gay and lesbian community. In S. H. Dworkin & F. J. Guitierrez (Eds.), *Counseling gay men and lesbians: Journey to the end of the rainbow* (pp. 23–24). Alexandria, VA: American Association for Counseling and Development.

Padilla, A. M. (1980). The role of cultural awareness and ethnic loyalty in acculturation. In A. M. Padilla (Ed.), *Acculturation: Theory, models, and some new findings* (pp. 47–84). Boulder, CO: Westview.

Park, R. E. (1928). Human migration and the marginal man. *American Journal of Sociology, 33,* 881–893.

Park, R. E., & Burgess, E. W. (1921). *Introduction to the science of sociology.* Chicago: The University of Chicago Press.

Ponterotto, J. G., Rivera, L., & Sueyoshi, L. A. (2000). The career-in-culture interview: A semi-structured protocol for the cross-cultural intake interview. *The Career Development Quarterly, 49,* 85–95.

Pope, M. (1995). Gay and lesbian career development: Introduction to the special section. *The Career Development Quarterly, 44,* 146–147.

Pope, M., & Barret, R. (2002). Providing career counseling services to gay and lesbian clients. In S. Niles (Ed.), *Adult career development: Concepts, models, and practices* (3rd ed., pp. 215–232). Tulsa, OK: National Career Development Association.

Prince, J. P. (1995). Career assessment with lesbian, gay, and bisexual individuals. *Journal of Career Assessment, 5,* 168–177.

Rogers, C. R. (1957). The necessary and sufficient conditions of therapeutic personality change. *Journal of Consulting Psychology, 21,* 95–103.

Sage, G. P. (1991). Counseling American Indian adults. In C. C. Lee & B. L. Richardson (Eds.), *Multicultural issues in counseling: Approaches to diversity* (pp. 23–36). Alexandria, VA: American Association for Counseling and Development.

Scholl, M. B. (1999). The career path tournament: Developing awareness of sociological barriers to career advancement. *The Career Development Quarterly, 47,* 230–242.

Skovholt, T. M. (1990). Career themes in counseling and psychotherapy with men. In D. Moore & F. Leafgren (Eds.), *Problem solving strategies and interventions for men in conflict* (pp. 39–53). Alexandria, VA: American Association for Counseling and Development.

Sophie, J. (1986). A critical examination of stage theories of lesbian identity development. *Journal of Homosexuality, 12*(3), 39–51.

Spencer, G. (1989). *Projections of the population of the United States by age, sex, and race: 1998–2080.* (Current Population Reports. Population estimates and projections. Series P-25, No. 1018). Washington, DC: Bureau of the Census.

Stein, J. (1975). *The Random House college dictionary* (rev. ed.). New York: Random House.

Sue, D. W., Arrendondo, P., & McDavis, R. J. (1992). Multicultural counseling competencies/standards: A call to the profession. *Journal of Counseling and Development, 70,* 477–486.

Sue, D. W., & Sue, D. (1990). *Counseling the culturally different: Theory and practice* (2nd ed.). New York: Wiley.

Swanson, J. L. (1993). Integrating a multicultural perspective into training for career counseling: Programmatic and individual interventions. *The Career Development Quarterly, 42,* 41–49.

Swanson, J. L., & O' Brien, K. M. (2002). Training career counselors: Meeting the challenges of clients in the 21st century. In S. Niles (Ed.), *Adult career development: Concepts, issues, and practices* (3rd ed., pp. 354–369). Tulsa, OK: National Career Development Association.

Swinton, D. H. (1992). The economic status of African Americans: Limited ownership and persistent in equality. In B. J. Tidwell (Ed.), *The state of Black America 1992* (pp. 61–117). New York: Urban League.

Torrey, E. F. (1986). *Witchdoctors and psychiatrists: The common root of psychotherapy and its future.* New York: Harper and Row.

Trusty, J. (2002). Counseling for career development with people of color. In S. Niles (Ed.), *Adult career development: Concepts, models, and practices* (3rd ed., pp. 191–214). Tulsa, OK: National Career Development Association.

U. S. Bureau of Census. (1992). *Population projections of the United States, by age, sex, race, and Hispanic origin: 1992 to 2050.* (Current Population Reports, P25-10920). Washington, DC: U.S. Government Printing Office.

U.S. Department of Justice. (1991). *Americans with disabilities handbook.* Washington, DC: U.S. Government Printing Office.

Walsh, W. B., & Betz, N. E. (1990). *Tests and assessment* (3rd ed.). Englewood Cliffs, NJ: Prentice Hall.

Watts, A. G., Super, D. E., & Kidd, J. M. (1981). *Career development in Britain.* Cambridge, England: Hobson's Press.

Wohl, J. (1995). Traditional individual psychotherapy and ethnic minorities. In J. F. Aponte, R. Y. Rivers, & R. Young (Eds.), *Psychological interventions and cultural diversity* (pp. 74–91). Boston, MA: Allyn & Bacon.

Wrenn, C. G. (1962). The culturally encapsulated Counselor. *Harvard Educational Review, 32,* 444–449.

Zunker, V. G. (1998). *Career counseling: Applied concepts of life planning* (5th ed.). Pacific Grove, CA: Brooks/Cole.

CHAPTER 5

ASSESSMENT AND CAREER PLANNING

Assessment is a process by which you learn about your abilities, likes or in-terests, personality, and values or those qualities that give you personal sat-isfaction. I prefer using self-assessment procedures because they directly involve the person in a self-discovery process. I have found that most indi-viduals like knowing more about themselves, creating self-motivation for the process. Another assessment process is the use of tests that some profes-sionals believe are more scientific procedures than self-assessments. In this process professionals learn information about the person and then filter the data back to that person. Tests rely on creating knowledge about a person in comparison with others. Depending on the situation, the comparability of the validity of either approach is equivalent.

I have been professionally associated with using ability, interest, per-sonality, and value information to identify career goals. I like to remind peo-ple that this same information, however, is equally important for several other purposes. Abilities and personalities are involved in the development of self-concepts—critical dimensions of a person and his or her functioning. Also, consider the value self-knowledge plays in relationships. Awareness of similarities and differences, identifying commonalities of interests and val-ues, and being sensitive to personal preference styles all contribute to the dy-namics of developing relationships.

In sum, self-knowledge is a critical human development requirement. Assessment is a valuable skill that facilitates this goal.

Thomas Harrington, Ph.D.
Professor Emeritus
Northeastern University

Melissa, a college sophomore, encouraged by her parents and academic advisor to choose a major, sought help from the career planning and placement center in mak-ing a career choice and selecting a related major. The counselor began by administering an interest inventory that summarizes interests related to the six ACT-Holland clusters. Melissa's profile of interests was low and flat; that is, there was very little difference among the scores for the six occupational clusters, and all were below the 25th percentile related to those of a norm group of college students. The counselor appropriately concluded that Melissa was not ready to make a selection of possible occupations or majors and developed a plan for additional assessment and counseling sessions before moving on with the specific goal stated by Melissa.

The context for making career choices in the 21st century is decidedly different from that of the 20th century. The tasks of occupations are constantly changing. Some occupations are rapidly becoming obsolete while others are emerging. Some experts and agencies even predict that the concept of *occupation* will disappear altogether and that we will think of ourselves as possessing a set of skills that can be applied to work tasks in many different settings, producing a variety of products and services. Work is done in a different way in this century, using a constantly expanding array of electronic equipment that has led to a variety of new settings, including working from home, working with team members electronically, and sending work to distant countries because it can be done less expensively there and can easily be sent electronically to a central source.

Not only are jobs different in the 21st century, but so are the people who perform the jobs. They face many more transitions in their work than their 20th-century counterparts. They need a broader base of general skills, a higher level of knowledge of technology, and a commitment to lifelong learning to upgrade and update their skills. They need to have a better knowledge of the career choice and planning process because they need to use it more often. They have to assume personal responsibility for their careers and financial security because the 20th-century model of the paternalistic corporation has disappeared. They increasingly view career development as an ongoing, lifelong process, one which needs to integrate the various life roles related to work, family, leisure, and community.

These changes in the context and core of career choice and development require a change in the purpose and use of assessment. The first model of career guidance is attributed to Frank Parsons (Miller, 1961), who founded the Boston Vocation Bureau. Parsons (1909) advocated a three-step process that became the basis for what is called the *trait-and-factor* approach of the 20th century. The steps include gaining knowledge of self, gaining knowledge of the world-of-work, and applying decision-making skill to making an occupational choice.

The development of many different kinds of tests in the 20th century, partly encouraged by two world wars during which it was important to identify specific levels of intelligence and ability, provided an array of instruments that persons could use to gain knowledge of self. Similarly, it was easy in the 20th century to gain knowledge about the world-of-work. The tasks involved in occupations changed more slowly, and many individuals could assume that they would remain in the same occupation, even with the same organization, for a lifetime, while moving through the stages described by Super (1957) in his early theory. Typically, at least until the 1980s, education for life was attained between the traditional ages of 14 and 22 because the tools and tasks of work remained stable. For these reasons, accomplishing the second step of Parsons' formula for career guidance—gaining knowledge of the world-of-work—was feasible.

So it was that the trait-and-factor approach dominated the 20th century in helping individuals with career choice. The movement was led by giants in the field such as Thorndike, Hagen, Binet, Terman, Kitson, Strong, Kuder, Paterson, Super, and Williamson. Test development was promoted through funding from government agencies, such as the U.S. Employment Service, and by a myriad of for-profit and not-for-profit organizations.

Assessment—defined here as the use of any formal or informal technique or instrument to collect data about a client—should still be valued in the 21st century as a tool used by counselors or by clients themselves to gather data useful in the career planning process. Its most important use is to assist individuals at a given point in time to identify their current interests and skills in order to identify the next educational or vocational choice in the sequence that makes up career development. There is a danger in the use of assessment of leading the client to believe that the process of career planning and choice is simplistic.

Given the changes noted in both the context in which career planning occurs and in the experience of individuals, it is clear that the characteristics of the use of assessment should be markedly different in the 21st century in the following ways:

- The results of assessment tools (such as tests and inventories) should be viewed as *one* piece of data that the client and the counselor use as the client considers career options. Many other sources of data should also be used, including the client's self-knowledge and intentionality, past educational and vocational experience, and the best predictions possible about work demands of the future.
- Assessment should be used less for prediction of valid options, as the future will be different from the present, and more for identifying new concepts of self, needed areas for growth, and new possibilities for exploration.
- The client should be more involved in making a decision about whether to engage in assessment, and for what purposes, and should be viewed as an equal participant in the assessment process, rather than as the receiver of knowledge to which a counselor has some special access and ability to decode.

THE RELATIONSHIP OF ASSESSMENT TO THE CAREER PLANNING PROCESS

The process of career development is complex and continuous, comprising multiple cycles of decision making. Each time a person faces a new career choice in the process, that choice, if informed, is likely to include the steps illustrated in Figure 5.1.

Step 1: Become Aware of the Need to Make Career Decisions

At first glance, this step may appear unnecessary. Psychologists tell us that we are not motivated to take new actions until and unless we are aware that we need to do so. Depending upon the work setting, clients may always come to counselors voluntarily as Melissa did. In that case, they do have some awareness of a need to make decisions, or they would not have initiated the contact. In other settings, such as in middle schools or high schools, students may be required to attend a career class or go to a counselor for help with career planning but may, in fact, have no awareness that they need such help or how it may affect their futures. There are some assessment instruments, described later in this chapter, that counselors may administer at

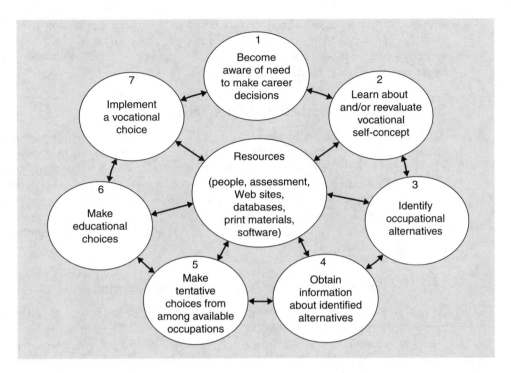

Figure 5.1
The career planning process. *Source*: From *The Internet: A Tool for Career Planning*, 2nd Edition, by JoAnn Harris-Bowlsbey, Margaret Riley Dikel, and James Sampson, p. 2, published by the National Career Development Association (2002). Used by permission.

this step of the individual's career planning process to provide some information about the degree of awareness that clients have and also about their specific needs as they enter the process.

Step 2: Learn About or Reevaluate Vocational Self-Concept

We know from the theories of Parsons, Holland, and Super that work is satisfying when people are doing what they like to do (using their interests), have the needed skills to do their work (using their abilities), and believe their work is important to do (attaining their values). Thus, it is essential to focus on the client, who must focus on self during this step of the process.

In addition to what the counselor learns or helps the client to learn through interviewing, it may also be beneficial to use formal or informal assessment to expand this knowledge or confirm it. Either purpose is very valuable. With informal assessment, the client might be asked to use a checklist, a card sort, or a fantasy. These may be especially effective with clients who have difficulty talking freely in an interview. If formal assessment is used, the counselor might choose inventories or tests of interests, skills, abilities, values, and/or personality characteristics. In the case of

Melissa, formal assessment of interests failed to reveal any pattern of defined interests and gave no indication of why this was true. The counselor might help Melissa identify some possible occupational goals by administering an assessment of skills, abilities, values, or personality characteristics.

Step 3: Identify Occupational Alternatives

At this stage counselor and client are identifying occupations or jobs in which the client can implement his or her vocational self-concept (Super, Starishevsky, Matlin, & Jordaan, 1963). The profile that Melissa had on the interest inventory seemed to reveal that she had no defined picture of her vocational self-concept related to interests. When assessment is administered in print form, typically there are accompanying manuals that link the client's results to titles of occupations. When assessment is administered by a computer, a customized list of related occupations can be provided as part of the score report.

Step 4: Obtain Information About Identified Alternatives

At this step of the career planning process, clients are encouraged to gather extensive information about possible occupations through reading print materials, using computer databases and Web sites, job shadowing, and information interviewing. Assessment is not typically used at this step of the process.

Step 5: Make Tentative Choices from Among Available Occupations

At this step the client, with the counselor's assistance, is comparing alternatives and attempting to discard some while placing others in priority order. One type of assessment that may be helpful at this stage is formal or informal assessment related to work values. Though occupational alternatives may be identified on the basis of interests, abilities, and/or personality type, values serve as a filter to determine which of many options have highest priority. At this stage a counselor might use a values card sort, checklist, or inventory. Follow-through would include the client's investigation to determine the potential of each occupation under consideration to satisfy the work values selected as most important.

Step 6: Make Educational Choices

Educational choices—high school courses, college major, and type and place of postsecondary education—should flow from selection of high-priority occupations. At this stage in the process, a publication such as *The Educational Opportunities Finder* (Rosen, Holmberg, & Holland, 1999) might be used to assist the client in identifying possible majors or training specialties. Further, instruments such as the *ACT Assessment Program* (ACT, 2001) or the College Entrance Examination Board's *Scholastic Aptitude Test* (College Entrance Examination Board, 2001) are used for placement (in the case of the ACT) and/or for determining eligibility for entrance to specific schools. The *Armed Services Vocational Aptitude*

Battery (U.S. Department of Defense, 1995) is an instrument to provide guidance in selecting training programs in the branches of the military, using both interests and abilities as guidelines.

Step 7: Implement a Vocational Choice

At this step, clients enter the job market. Many organizations have their own instruments for screening applicants for jobs. Others use an instrument such as *WorkKeys* (ACT, 1995), which profiles a person's skills in 11 areas, comparing them to the level of skills needed in those same areas for specific jobs within an organization.

As indicated by the arrows between the steps of the model in Figure 5.1, the career planning process is cyclical and iterative. Note, for example, that a person may hold a job (Step 7) for a period of time and then move on to Step 1 again because of dissatisfaction with the job or a decision by the employer to reduce the number of employees. Also, note that career deciders may deal with the tasks of one step—such as identifying occupational alternatives (Step 3)—and then return to do more in-depth introspection (Step 2).

PURPOSES OF ASSESSMENT

Assessment should not be used unless there is a specific reason for doing so, a reason that both the client and counselor understand. Often, the findings identified through formal or informal assessment could be learned through an interview, a type of informal assessment. Choosing to substitute interviewing for more formal assessment depends on whether the counselor possesses knowledge comprehensive enough to sample the domains (such as areas of career maturity, interests, skills, and values) typically covered by assessment and has sufficient time to devote to comprehensive interviewing. Given the demands of time and knowledge in multiple domains, counselors typically rely on assessment for data gathering, both to alleviate these time and knowledge demands and to take advantage of the considerable benefits that scientific rigor adds to assessment.

What are the reasons that counselors ask their clients to spend time and perhaps money to engage in assessment? They can be summarized in three main categories: (1) learning more about the needs of an individual or group of individuals, (2) learning more about the characteristics of individuals and helping them learn more about themselves, and (3) determining the progress of a person or group of persons in areas related to career development. We will consider each of these in detail.

Learning More About the Needs of the Student or Client

School counselors are charged with helping all students with the career planning process through stages of career exploration (at the elementary and middle school levels), career preparation (at the high school level), and career decision making (at the high school and postsecondary levels). They typically accomplish this through a systematic set of services offered to or required by all, though there is great variability in the needs of subgroups of the population.

In other settings in which more attention is given on a one-to-one basis, it is typical for counselors to ask clients to state the reasons for entering a counseling relationship. Many clients have sufficient awareness to be able to state their needs with considerable accuracy. Others are able to state the conditions they are experiencing without understanding the underlying reasons for these conditions (for example, "I can't seem to make up my mind about a major" or "My boss and I are very different, and I can't seem to learn how to get along with him"). Still others are unable to state the specific problems they need to deal with at all.

A counselor may administer certain assessments, to be described fully later in this chapter, in order to define the needs of the student or client more precisely. Melissa appears to be a case in which using assessment for further exploration of her needs is warranted. Here are two additional examples:

A high school counselor who was responsible for 500 students in all areas of school guidance wanted to devise a program of career planning services that would optimally meet the varying needs of all sophomores. He administered the *Career Decision Scale* (Osipow, Carney, Winer, Yanico, & Koschier, 1997). This 19-item inventory measures the degree of an individual's certainty or indecision related to career choice. In this case, the counselor was less interested in students' individual scores (and indeed did not reveal them to students) than in forming groups of students with similar needs so that these needs could be addressed in the most cost-effective ways. Using the results of the *Career Decision Scale,* he formed three groups of students according to their level of career decidedness and designed programs of services with different components for each of the three groups.

Iantha came to a career counselor stating that she needed help to identify some possible occupations so that she could declare a college major. Using a common interest inventory, the counselor helped her to identify some possible occupations. After spending considerable time researching most of these, Iantha was still as undecided as she was when she came in several sessions earlier. The counselor began to suspect that there were reasons for this continued undecidedness and administered *The Career Thoughts Inventory* (Sampson, Peterson, Lenz, Reardon, & Saunders, 1996). This 48-item inventory is designed to measure a person's dysfunctional thinking that may affect the career decision-making process. These items provide scores related to three scales: Decision-Making Confusion, Commitment Anxiety, and External Conflict. By looking at the scores on these scales and at the client's response to specific items, the counselor was able to identify and deal with some specific barriers in the client's thought processes before attempting to provide further assistance with selection of a college major.

Learning More About Clients and Helping Them Learn More About Themselves

Since the initial theory of Frank Parsons, supported by preeminent theorists in the field such as Donald Super (Super et al., 1963) and John Holland (1997), self-knowledge has been hailed as an absolute requirement for exploration and choice of occupations, majors, and jobs. The self-attributes most often proposed by theorists are interests, abilities, skills, values, and personality characteristics. An abundance of instruments exist to measure these characteristics. Sample instruments will be described later in this chapter.

Knowledge of all of these characteristics can be helpful both to the client and the counselor in synthesizing a self-image that can be matched to an environment (using Holland's terminology) or implemented in an occupation (using Super's terminology). Counselors may ask clients to take only one instrument, take an instrument that measures two or three of these characteristics, or take several instruments whose combined results provide a more comprehensive picture. Here are two examples:

Roberto, a high school junior, came to his counselor for assistance in identifying some possible occupations. He stated that he wanted to go to work immediately after high school. The counselor decided to ask him to take the *Campbell Interest and Skill Survey* (Campbell, 1992), which measures both interests and skills related to the six Holland-like clusters. The results showed high skill in the Technical cluster and high interest in both the Technical (called Producing) and Science (called Analyzing) clusters. From these results the counselor was able to help Roberto find occupations he could enter immediately after high school with some changes in his planned courses for the next three semesters. He was also able to help him learn about many additional occupations that he could consider if he would attend a 2- or 4-year college.

Mary Sue, a 35-year-old woman reentering the workforce after 10 years of child rearing, sought the assistance of a career counselor in determining possible jobs she could pursue. She stated that she did not have time to engage in further training or education but needed to find a job that could use her present skills. The counselor decided to administer *WorkKeys* (ACT, 1995), which measures an individual's current skills in 11 areas, including Reading for Information, Applied Mathematics, Listening, Writing, Locating Information, Applied Technology, Teamwork, Motivation, Learning, Observing, and Speaking. The counselor recommended that Mary Sue apply for jobs at three specific local companies that use the same instrument to profile the requirements of their positions. By talking with the human resource development personnel at these three companies, Mary Sue can identify jobs requiring her current level of skills and others which could be attainable in the future if she is willing to pursue additional training.

In both of these cases a counselor used the results of formal assessment to assist individuals to gain self-information that they had not been fully able to state or organize, as well as to gain information to guide their exploration.

Determining the Change or Progress of an Individual or Group

Some assessment instruments are designed to measure academic achievement, interests, or specific conditions, such as career maturity or career decidedness, over time, allowing the setting of benchmarks at specific points in a person's development. By comparing progress, change, or stability over time, it is possible to get a picture of a person's development. Following are two examples:

A middle school used the National Career Development Guidelines (see Chapter 13) as a framework for integrating career development concepts and activities into its curriculum. The superintendent required that the program include an evaluation component that would measure the degree to which the competencies stated in the guidelines had been reached. A customized version of the *Iowa Career Learning Assessment* (National Career Assessment Services, 1998) instrument was administered before delivery of the services and repeated afterward. There was a significant increase in scores in specific content areas after delivery of the program, providing objective data that the program was effective in building the desired competencies.

All of the students in a large, suburban school district took a series of tests called *EXPLORE* (8th grade), *PLAN* (10th grade), and the *ACT Assessment Program* (11th or 12th grade), all developed and published by ACT, Inc. (ACT, 2000a, 2000b, 2001). Each of these three batteries of tests measures academic achievement in Language Usage, Mathematics, Social Studies, and Science as well as current interests by means of a 90-item interest inventory called *UNIACT*. By looking at the results of this group of tests at three different grade levels, a counselor in a university counseling center was able to reflect to a student that each of three times he took the interest inventory he had made steady and good growth in the four academic areas and that his most predominant area of interest was in the Social Service cluster. Based on these longitudinal results, the counselor felt secure in acquainting the student with the entire list of available university majors that relate to the Social Service cluster.

RESPONSIBILITIES AND COMPETENCIES OF THE COUNSELOR

Assessment and its interpretation can be harmful to clients if counselors are not adequately trained to deal with them. Counselors have responsibilities that are detailed specifically in the ethical guidelines that exist in the profession. Ethical guidelines, called the Code of Fair Testing Practices (Joint Committee on Testing Practices, 1999), have been developed by the American Education Research Association, the American Psychological Association, and the National Council on Measurement in Education. These are posted on the Web at http://ericae.net/code.txt and may be summarized into four areas: (1) developing and selecting tests, (2) interpreting scores, (3) striving for fairness, and (4) informing test takers. The Code of Professional Responsibilities in Educational Measurement (National Council on Measurement in Education, 1995), a document that covers the responsibilities of a wider audience—those who develop, market, select, administer, score, and interpret tests—is posted at http://www.natd.org/Code_of_Professional_Responsibilities.html.

Possess a General Knowledge About Assessment

Agencies that govern the accreditation of counselor education programs and the licensing of individuals require counselors to take a course in tests and measurements. According to the standards included in *A Counselor's Guide to Career Assessment Instruments* (Kapes et al., 2002) published by the National Career Development Association (NCDA), counselors should possess the knowledge and competencies related to assessment shown in Figure 5.2. Students who have already taken the

Basic Concepts

Concepts important to the informal *use* of tests are listed below. Persons with final responsibility for *evaluating* and *selecting* assessment instruments will require knowledge beyond these basic concepts.

Use the following key in responding to the statements:

3 = I am able to apply the concept and explain it to others.

2 = I have some knowledge but little experience in applying the concept.

1 = I have little or no knowledge of this concept.

Enter the appropriate number in the blank at the left of each statement.

1. Statistics used in testing and test manuals

_____ a. Measures of central tendency (mean, median, mode)

_____ b. Measures of variability (range, variance, standard deviation)

_____ c. Distributions (frequency, normal)

_____ d. Scales of measurement (nominal, ordinal, interval, ratio)

_____ e. Correlation coefficients (Pearson product-moment, point biserial)

2. Types of instruments

_____ a. Measures of maximum performance

_____ b. Measures of typical performance

_____ c. Similarities and differences among measures of intelligence, aptitude, ability, and achievement

_____ d. Similarities and differences among self-reports, self-ratings, inventories, and tests

3. Score reporting procedures

_____ a. Percentile ranks

_____ b. Standard scores (including stanines)

_____ c. Grade placement (equivalent) scores

_____ d. Score profiles and profile analysis

_____ e. Group similarity indices

_____ f. Expectancy (experience) tables

_____ g. Estimates of probability of success and/or level of success; standard error of estimate

4. Standardization and norms

_____ a. Standardized administration and scoring

_____ b. Limitations of raw scores

_____ c. Types of norms (e.g., local, national, gender, grade); their applications and limitations

_____ d. Norm-based versus criterion-referenced interpretation

Continued

Figure 5.2

Assessment knowledge and competencies.

5. Reliability

    _____ a. Meaning of test reliability

    _____ b. Sources of measurement error

    _____ c. Types of test reliability (test-retest, parallel forms, internal consistency, including split-half, inter-rater)

    _____ d. Standard error of measurement and error bands

6. Validity

    _____ a. Meaning of test validity

    _____ b. Implications of test use for validation procedures

    _____ c. Types of test validity (content, criterion-related, construct)

    _____ d. Factors affecting test validity

    _____ e. Differential validity of test batteries for diverse criteria

    _____ f. Potential sources of bias affecting validity

Figure 5.2 *Continued*

Source: From *A Counselor's Guide to Career Assessment Instruments* (pp. 42–43), by J.T. Kapes, and E.A. Whitfield. Published by the National Career Development Association (2002). Used by permission.

required course on assessment may want to use this form as a checklist for their own competencies.

Have a Detailed Knowledge About the Instruments Used

Besides the general knowledge of testing just summarized, counselors need to have very detailed knowledge about the assessments they select for use. This knowledge can be gained in a variety of ways. It is likely that counselors will initially consider an instrument because they have identified it through a search on a Web site, from reading about it on the Web site of its publisher, from publications such as *A Counselor's Guide to Career Assessment Instruments* (NCDA, 2002), or because it was displayed at a conference. The first task, then, is to determine whether it has the characteristics—such as purpose, reading level, reliability, validity, and gender fairness—that it needs in order to qualify. These characteristics should be described in the technical manual that accompanies the instrument. The manual should report such important facts as the kind of research the instrument has undergone, what it is designed to measure, the norm groups that have been used in testing its properties, and its reading level. If there is no technical manual, the counselor must be wary about the amount of research that has been applied to the instrument.

It is also useful to read the critiques that others have written about the instrument. Such critiques are found in *A Counselor's Guide to Career Assessment Instruments* (Kapes & Whitfield, 2002), the *Mental Measurement Yearbook* (Impara & Plake, 1998), and on the Web site of the Buros Institute (http://www.unl.edu/buros). Also, talks with other counselors who have used the instrument can provide their views of its strengths and weaknesses.

If the instrument passes this quality-control review, counselors may continue their exploration by taking the instrument themselves and getting a score report. This action will yield a firsthand knowledge of the kinds of items it has, the kind of score report it provides, and a sense of the accuracy of the instrument in measuring some characteristics about themselves. Next, the counselor may want to administer the instrument to a friend or to one or two individuals in order to become more familiar with it.

Prepare Students or Clients Adequately

Assuming that instruments have been selected, the counselor's next responsibility is to prepare those who will take the instrument for that experience. Such preparation consists of (1) explaining why they should take an assessment instrument, in other words, what they should expect to get from it; (2) getting agreement that they believe that its results will be helpful; (3) explaining what the items of the instrument are like and how long it will likely take to complete it; (4) telling them when the results will be available; (5) explaining what the score report will be like, perhaps by showing a mock score report; and (6) indicating what will happen to the results of the assessment—who will see them and where they will be stored.

Administer Instruments Properly

The manual provided with each formal assessment gives detailed instructions about the administration of the instrument. Some instruments, such as self-help interest inventories, can be given to an individual to take home. They are not timed, no supervision is needed, and there are no "right" or "wrong" answers. Other tests, such as college entrance examinations, are very high-stake tests and must be administered under the strictest conditions. These conditions include security of the test items prior to the testing session, identification of the examinee, room setup, lighting, silence, and exact timing. There are many other instruments that specify the conditions of administration somewhere between these two extremes. The point is to know, by reading the instructions provided with the instrument, what the appropriate conditions for administration are and then meet those conditions.

Interpret Instruments Properly

Correct interpretation of any instrument relates to three different considerations: (1) an overall understanding of the relevance of assessment to the process of career planning and choice, (2) the reason the individual has taken the instrument, and (3) the guidelines provided by the publisher for use of the instrument and/or the instrument' technical manual.

This chapter began with discussion of how the context of career planning and choice has changed in the 21st century. The discussion indicated that, concomitant with that changed context, the old model of the trait-and-factor approach (often called the "test-'em and tell-'em" approach) should be replaced with a view of assessment that has the following characteristics:

- Assessment is *one* of several tools that are used to assist the client with career choices; others may include interviewing, use of computer-based systems and Web sites, group work, and completion of specific assignments (such as informational interviewing, job shadowing, internships, and coursework). Any plans that may emerge from use of these approaches should take into account the learning that occurs from all of these approaches.

- Assessment should be administered with the person's full understanding of its purpose and with agreement that the activity may provide some helpful information that can be used to guide exploration.

- The counselor has the responsibility to prepare the client well, administer the instrument correctly, treat the results in a confidential manner, and interpret the results in a knowledgeable way. The counselor also has the responsibility to interpret the instrument flexibly; in other words, its results are not used as if they offer superior knowledge, but rather as data that may be used to stimulate further exploration of alternatives, growth or change, or confirmation of information already possessed. Clients have the responsibility to evaluate the results of the assessment and determine whether they are appropriate representations of the self-attributes the instrument is designed to measure and how, if at all, to use the results as a part of the data that guide personal decision making.

The reason why the counselor has asked the client to take the assessment also guides the appropriate interpretation of the instrument. For example, a counselor may suggest that a client take the *Strong Interest Inventory* (Strong, 1994) in order to confirm a tentative occupational choice he or she has made, in accordance with a scale on the *Strong Interest Inventory*. The counselor will have also suggested that the client engage in other activities—such as taking related coursework, having informational interviews with people in the occupation, and participating in job shadowing or an internship—that will contribute to this confirmation or lack of it. In this case, however, the counselor would provide a general interpretation of the inventory, but also focus on the client's scores as they relate to the profile of the norm group for the specific occupation of the client's choice.

A second example: if the purpose for suggesting that a client take the *Myers-Briggs Type Indicator* (Myers & Briggs, 1998) was to help the client understand why she is having difficulty in relating to a supervisor, the counselor would not only interpret the instrument in general, but would also ask the client how she would assess the supervisor on each of the four pairs of personality dimensions covered by the instrument. Where there were contrasts, the counselor would interpret the client's results in a way that would help her to get a clearer picture of why the supervisor's style and expectations are different from her own.

Finally, it is imperative that counselors interpret instruments within the confines of the research and intentions of the authors and publishers of the instrument. Some publishers offer—even require—thorough training on their instruments by means of a nationwide series of workshops. These publishers are demonstrably concerned about having their instruments interpreted correctly. Other publishers require that those who want to purchase their instruments have training related to the instrument before allowing them to make purchases.

If, however, counselors are using assessment without these requirements, they have the ethical responsibility to train themselves to have competence: reading the manuals that the publisher provides with the instrument, attending workshops or sessions offered at professional conferences, and/or acquiring training through a graduate course that focuses on career planning instruments.

Follow Through with Clients

Assessment is a waste of time and money if its results are not used to inform decision making. Counselors have an ethical responsibility to move beyond interpretation to assisting the client or student to use the results in the clarification of self-concept and/or the making of informed career choices. This is the most difficult step in the process because it involves making a leap from presentation of objective data to making inferences about the meaning of those data. Such inferences must be made within the context of all that a counselor knows about a student or client, not from test data alone. Thus, there are no prescriptive answers, but here are some suggestions:

- Think about the characteristics (such as liking to work with people face-to-face and using verbal skills) that are measured by the instrument and then assist the individual to think broadly about how that combination of characteristics may relate to a broad array of occupations, not only to the specific titles provided in the publisher's materials.
- Assist the individual to think about the implications for education, training, and/or certification of the occupational options provided by the assessment; and discuss these.
- Assist the individual to think about the lifestyle implications of the occupational options identified by an instrument, including work hours, time to be with family, requirement for travel, income, and capability to merge dual careers.
- Prescribe near-to-reality ways for individuals to explore occupational options once they are identified. Such ways include related coursework, videos, job shadowing, internships, part-time jobs, informational interviewing, and mentoring.
- After individuals pursue one or more of these ways to do reality testing, follow through with an interview to help them evaluate what they have learned and to make a choice about keeping specific occupations on a short list of options or discarding them.

INFORMAL ASSESSMENTS

Assessment instruments and techniques are commonly divided into two broad categories: *informal* and *formal*. Checklists, games, fantasies, forced-choice activities, card sorts, and structured interviews are examples of informal assessments.

A *checklist* is a series of items that may relate to an individual's preferred work setting, job characteristics, work tasks, work values, or skills. Such a checklist may be developed by the counselor, or the counselor can borrow—with permission—one that someone else has developed, or purchase one. As an illustration, assume that you are working with a group of women who are planning to return to the workforce after some years of child-rearing. Such women often have the perception that they have few or no work skills that employers would value. As a means of helping them change this perception, the counselor may give them a checklist containing the following items and ask them to check those that they believe they possess to a moderate or high degree:

_____ Manage multiple tasks at the same time

_____ Decide which of competing tasks has priority

_____ Manage time

_____ Budget and manage money

_____ Teach or train others

_____ Resolve conflicts between and among individuals

_____ Create and maintain an attractive environment

_____ Manage people

A *game* may be used with small or large groups to make individuals aware of realities related to career choice and planning. As a part of such a game, an individual may be asked to play a specific role in a simulated environment or become subject to a variety of opportunities and setbacks represented on the game board. One good example of this kind of informal assessment is the *Real Game Series* (Real Game, 2000), available in six versions for different age populations, ranging from grade 3 through adults. Information about these games is available at http://www.realgame.com; it is also possible to play a round on-line.

A *career fantasy* is an activity in which a counselor asks one or more individuals to relax, close their eyes, and imagine an ideal day that includes time at a worksite. Individuals' fantasies can be stimulated by using instructions such as the following:

I'd like you to relax, close your eyes if you wish, and put out of your mind any concerns that you may be dealing with. I want you to imagine that this is an ideal day of work. During this activity, you can have any job you want, and you have the skills and education to perform it.

Imagine that you have completed breakfast and that you are now leaving your home to go to work. What kinds of clothes are you wearing—informal clothes, some kind of uniform, a business suit? How are you getting to work—on the metro, in your car, on a train, on an airplane, or are you working from home? How long does it take to get to work? What does your place of work look like? How many other people work directly with you? What is your relationship to these people?

What are your work tasks today? Do you have any flexibility in how you perform them, or does someone supervise you closely? What kinds of tools or equipment do you work with? How much responsibility do you have for what you do? Is your pace frenetic, leisurely, or something in between?

This is a brief illustration. This fantasy can be embellished and expanded not only to include work activities but also to relate work to lifestyle, such as the kind of home, neighborhood, car, and leisure activities the person fantasizes. Discussion of this activity with individuals or small groups can help identify many characteristics that they desire in a job or lifestyle that the income from a job may impact. This technique might work with Melissa, because the counselor could identify key components in the ideal work day she describes that express interests and values.

A *forced-choice activity* is one in which an individual is asked to make a choice between two options that are quite different from each other or to rank-order three or more activities. This kind of assessment may be applied to work values, job characteristics, and work settings, for example. Following are three illustrations of the kind of items that may be used for these three purposes:

Work values: Through your life's work, would you rather

_____ make a lot of money   or   _____ make a contribution to society?

Job characteristics: In your ideal job, would you rather

_____ tell someone else what to do   or   _____ have someone tell you what to do?

Work setting: In your ideal job, would you rather

_____ work outside   or   _____ work inside?

This technique might be used with Melissa. Since it forces some choice, and therefore does not allow a series of responses such as "indifferent," it will reveal some interests.

A *card sort,* another informal assessment tool that might be helpful with Melissa, is an activity in which an individual or a group is given a deck of cards. Each card represents something related to career choice, such as a work value, a skill, a work task, or a characteristic of a work setting. Typically, the card would contain the name of the characteristic (such as Variety, Managing People, or Making or Repairing Things) and a definition of it.

If the number of cards in the deck is relatively few (up to 15), clients may be asked to rank-order the cards, placing the one that is most important in first position, followed by all of the others in priority order. If the number of cards in the deck is large, clients are typically asked to sort them into three different stacks: those that are very important or essential, those that are somewhat important, and those that are not important. Such a card sort may be made by the counselor or may be purchased from those who have specialized in the development of such instruments. If self-made, it is important to cover the full range of possible values, skills, work tasks, or characteristics that clients might choose—a process that will require review of the literature.

Finally, in a *structured interview* a counselor asks questions that are related to some theoretical base. For example, during an intake interview, a counselor might ask a student to provide information about coursework, past jobs, or extracurricular or volunteer activities and prompt or organize the responses around Holland's or ACT's six clusters of occupations. With sufficient knowledge about the characteristics of these six work environments, the counselor can formulate questions and analyze responses in skillful ways that yield an accurate assessment of a person's Holland code (see Chapter 2 for information about Holland's theory and codes) as well as acquire a great deal of information about the client. This approach would be a very helpful one with Melissa and others who have undifferentiated profiles of interest. Similarly, with sufficient knowledge of Jungian types (Jung, 1959), a skillful counselor might estimate a person's Jungian type without administering one of the instruments that measures personality type in these terms.

Informal assessment instruments have characteristics quite different from those of formal assessments, which we will examine next. Some of the characteristics of informal assessments are as follows:

- They have not been subjected to scientific rigor, nor do they have known *properties,* such as reliability and validity.
- They are not supported by any data that allows a person to compare his or her results with those of other people.
- Though inferences can be made by the client and the counselor, there are no documents that facilitate a connection between the choices made by the client and specific occupations.
- There is no standard way to interpret the results of these activities, leaving such interpretation totally to the competence of the counselor.

Advantages of informal assessments include the following: (1) they are low-cost or free of charge, (2) they may not require the ordering of materials in advance, (3) they may not require as much time to administer as formal assessments, and (4) they may be less anxiety-producing for the client.

FORMAL ASSESSMENTS

Assessments labeled *formal* may be timed standardized tests or non-timed standardized inventories. It is common to call an instrument an *inventory* if it is assessing content areas in which there are no right or wrong answers and to call it a *test* if the items do have right or wrong answers. Thus, an instrument measuring a person's interests is an inventory, whereas an instrument measuring a person's achievement in mathematics is a test.

The hallmark of formal assessments is that they have been subjected to scientific rigor; that is, authors and publishers have invested professional expertise, time, and money in order to develop a quality product. They have performed research on the instrument in an effort to assure quality and to be able to know the *properties* that the instrument possesses. Some of the most important properties that counselors need to know when selecting instruments include the following:

- *Validity.* There are several types of validity, and it is beyond the scope of this book to define them. An instrument is said to have *validity* if it measures what it is supposed to measure. For example, if the instrument purports to measure interests, does it do so, as opposed to measuring skills or work values? An ethical counselor will need to read the technical manual provided by the publisher in order to learn what procedures have been taken to assure that it measures what its marketing literature says that it does.
- *Reliability, often called test-retest reliability.* The construct of reliability deals with whether an instrument will measure what it is purported to measure reliably

over time. In other words, if a client takes an interest inventory today and then takes it again 3 weeks from now, will the results be the same or approximately the same? Intervals of time used for testing reliability typically range from 2 weeks to several months. Obviously, some factors related to career choice, such as interests, skills, and work values, can and do change over time. Thus, the challenge with measuring reliability is to have a sufficient period of time between the first administration and a subsequent one so that the client is unlikely to remember the items or previous responses to them. On the other hand, if the period of time is too long, change in the way the client responds may be at least partially the result of normal development.

Test-retest reliability is measured as a *correlation coefficient,* defined as the correlation between two measurements obtained in the same manner. A test-retest correlation coefficient of .8 is considered good and acceptable for selection of an instrument. Data about reliability should be provided in the technical manual as well as a description of how it was established, including the size and characteristics of the group used for this purpose.

- *Fairness related to diversity.* Increasingly in the 21st century, counselors will deal with clients who represent a wide range of diversity—in gender, sexual orientation, ethnic background, race, age, and types of disability. It is important to know about the populations used to test and norm the instrument. The groups used for such testing need to be large enough to include a wide range of diversity, or the author and publisher need to state that the instrument has been tested only with selected populations. The former approach allows us to assume that the characteristics of clients are similar to those in the populations used for testing. This statement has profound implications for the use of instruments with members of diverse populations.

- *Comparison.* This property refers to whether or not the results that clients receive compare them to other people or rank-order characteristics related only to themselves. For example, some interest inventories are *norm-referenced;* an individual's scores are compared with those of one or more "norm" groups. For some inventories the score report will indicate that the examinee's responses place him or her at the 85th *percentile* compared with a norm group of persons of a similar age. This group of persons, or *norm group,* may be small or large, representative in various demographic ways of the population in general or only of a subset, national in scope or relatively local, or comprise both genders or one gender. In contrast, a different inventory may provide *raw scores;* that is, the total number of responses related to some category (right or wrong, or assigned to some scale) is reported. Such data does not provide a picture of how examinees compare with others but does allow them to rank-order their own interests, values, abilities, or whatever is being measured. Further, if norms are being used, the individual's standing related to them may be expressed in a variety of ways, including percentiles, stanines, and standard scores, to be explained later in this chapter.

Types of Formal Assessments

Earlier in this chapter three different purposes for assessment were described: to identify clients' needs, to help clients and the counselor know more about the self, and to measure progress or change. This section of the chapter describes more specifically the types of instruments, providing a sample list of the most common ones, that can be organized into each of these three categories.

Identifying the needs of clients.   Instruments that fall into this category may be administered to a single client or may be administered to a target group of clients. In the first case, the counselor is attempting to identify the needs of a specific client and may, therefore, interpret the results to that client as a part of the career counseling process. For example, if a counselor finds that the usual techniques of assessing interests, identifying some occupations, and learning about those occupations does not seem to be helping a client to deal with career concerns, he or she may want to determine if this client has barriers, such as irrational beliefs, that prevent moving forward. Under these circumstances the counselor might choose *The Career Beliefs Inventory* (Krumboltz, 1991) and suggest that the client take it. If that inventory reveals that the client is invested in a belief that he or she cannot enter a specific occupational field because the opportunities are too limited, the counselor may suggest that the basis for this belief be investigated through some occupational research before further work is done to consider other possible career choices.

On the other hand, a counselor may be seeking to identify different levels of need for career services in the target population. He or she might administer *My Vocational Situation* (Holland, Daiger, & Power, 1987) to the entire group and then make some informed assumptions about the needs of those whose scores placed them in the top 25% of the distribution, those in the middle 50%, and those in the lower 25%. In this case, it is unlikely that the counselor would interpret individual scores for members of the group because that was not the designated purpose for the assessment.

Some examples of this type of instrument, with a brief description and information about the publisher, are listed next. However, new instruments emerge with frequency, and some cease to be published. When selecting an instrument, counselors should consult the latest versions of reference books that summarize what is currently available and consult the Web sites of major publishers (provided at the end of this chapter).

Career Attitudes and Strategies Inventory (CASI), Holland and Gottfredson (1994). A self-scored instrument designed to identify the attitudes, feelings, and obstacles that affect the careers of adults. The scales are Job Stability, Family Commitment, Risk-Taking Style, Geographical Barriers, Job Satisfaction, Work Involvement, Skill Development, Dominant Style Career Worries, and Interpersonal Abuse.

Career Beliefs Inventory (CBI), Krumboltz, 1991. For persons over 13 years of age, designed to identify career beliefs that may be preventing them from reaching career goals. There are 25 scales organized under five categories: My Current Career Situation, What Seems Necessary for My Happiness, Factors That Influence My Decisions, Changes I Am Willing to Make, and Effort I Am Willing to Initiate.

Career Factors Inventory (CFI), Chartrand, Robbins, and Morrill, 1997. For persons over age 13, designed to identify persons' difficulties in the career planning and decision making process. The scales are Need for Information, Need for Self-Knowledge, Career Choice Anxiety, and Generalized Indecisiveness.

Career Maturity Inventory (CMI), Crites and Savickas, 1995. Designed to measure how ready a student is to make a career decision. For students in grades 6–12. Published by Crites Career Consultants, Boulder, CO.

Career Thoughts Inventory (CTI), Sampson et al., 1996. Designed to identify irrational thoughts that the client may have that could affect the career decision making process. For use with students and clients from the high school level through adulthood. Published by Psychological Assessment Resources, Odessa, FL.

Career Development Inventory (CDI), Super, Thompson, Lindeman, Jordaan, and Myers, 1984. Designed to measure career development and career maturity. For use with high school and college students. Published by Consulting Psychologists Press, Palo Alto, CA.

Career Decision Scale (CDS), Osipow et al., 1997. Designed to measure the reasons for career indecision and inability to make a vocational choice. For use with high school and college students. Published by Psychological Assessment Resources, Odessa, FL.

Career Decision Profile (CDP), Jones, 1986. Designed to measure level of decidedness about career choice, self-knowledge, and knowledge about occupations and training. Published by Lawrence K. Jones, Department of Counselor Education, North Carolina State University, Raleigh, NC.

My Vocational Situation (MVS), Holland et al., 1987. Designed to measure the degree to which lack of vocational identity, lack of information or training, and barriers may affect a person's ability to make a career choice. For use with students in grade 9 through adult years. Published by Consulting Psychologists Press, Palo Alto, CA.

Most of the instruments just listed are designed for use with high school students and adults. This is the case because they measure constructs (such as career maturity, career beliefs, and decision making skill) that are developmental in nature and should not be measured prior to the life stage in which their development is expected.

Learning More About Clients.   In this category is a rich array of inventories of interests, skills, abilities, work values, personality types, and combinations of these. In each case, the purpose is to allow the client and the counselor to explore characteristics that may help identify occupations or jobs for consideration. Following the theoretical work of Holland and Super and of trait-and-factor theory in general, the purpose of these instruments is to identify personal characteristics that can be related to those of occupations or jobs in order to focus exploration of options. The lists and short summaries provided next divide the most common instruments into those measuring interests, abilities, skills, work values, personality types, and combinations of any of these.

Interest inventories.   *Campbell Interest and Skill Survey,* Campbell, 1992. An integrated measure of self-assessed interests and skills that offers 7 orientation scales, 29 basic interest scales, and 58 occupational scales, with additional occupations and majors in the companion booklet called *The CISS Career Planner.*

Career Assessment Inventory (CAI), Johannson, 1986. Designed to measure interests in Holland's six personality types, 23 basic interest scales, and 111 occupations. Can be used with high school students, college students, and adults. Published by NCS Assessments, Minnetonka, MN.

Career Occupational Preference Survey (COPS), Knapp and Knapp, 1992. Designed to measure interest in eight career clusters, five of which are divided into professional and skilled levels. Can be used with students in grades 7–12, college students, and adults. Published by Edits, San Diego, CA.

Career Quest, Chronicle Guidance Publications, 1991 and 2001. Two self-scored versions—middle and high school and adult—that measure interests related to the U.S. Office of Education 12-cluster system.

Harrington-O'Shea Career Decision Making System (CDMS), Harrington and O'Shea, 2000. Designed to measure interest in Holland's six personality types, though names of scales have been changed. Different versions allow use from grade 7 to adulthood. Published by American Guidance Service, Circle Pines, MN.

Interest Determination, Exploration, and Assessment System (IDEAS), Johansson, 1996 and 2000. Two self-scored inventories—one for middle and high schools and one for adults—that measure interest in 16 areas.

Interest Explorer, Riverside Publishing, 1998. For use with middle school students, high school students, and adults, the inventory measures interest in 14 career areas that are linked to the *Guide for Occupational Exploration, Occupational Outlook Handbook,* and O∗Net.

Jackson Vocational Interest Survey (JVIS), Jackson, 1999. Designed to measure interests on 34 basic interest scales. For use with high school students, college students, and adults. Published by Sigma Assessment Systems, Port Huron, MI.

Kuder Career Search with Person Match™, Zytowski and Kuder, 1999. Designed to measure interests in 10 categories of activities and six occupational clusters; also compares the profile of the inventory-taker with those of 1500 real people in a database and identifies and describes the specific jobs of the top matches. For use with high school students, college students, and adults. Available on the Internet. Published by National Career Assessment Services, Inc., Adel, IA.

O∗Net Interest Profiler, United States Employment Service, 2001. Self-scored instrument designed to measure interests by Holland's six personality types for persons in middle school through adult. May be printed out, copied, and distributed along with the score report and an interpretive booklet from http://www.onetcenter.org. Executable code may also be downloaded from this site onto a compact disc.

Self-Directed Search (SDS), Holland, 1994. Designed to measure personality type and interest in six different occupational groups. There are multiple forms for different age ranges, languages, and reading levels. Can be used with high school students, college students, and adults. Published by Psychological Assessment Resources, Odessa, FL.

The Strong Interest Inventory (SII), Strong, 1994. Measures interests in eight different areas—occupations, school subjects, activities, leisure activities, types of people preferred as coworkers, preference between two activities, personal characteristics, and preference in the world-of-work. Provides a Holland code, scores on 25 basic interest scales, four personal style themes, and similarity of examinee's profile to the profile of workers in 211 occupations. Available in English, French, and Italian. Appropriate for use with high school juniors and seniors, college students, and adults. Published by Consulting Psychologists Press, Palo Alto, CA.

Unisex Edition of the ACT Interest Inventory (UNIACT), Swaney, 1995. Measures interests in the six Holland types and uses the Holland code to suggest job families on the World-of-Work Map for exploration. Due to different sets of items and norms, it is appropriate for use with high school students, college students, and adults. Included in DISCOVER (a computer-based system) and the *Career Planning Survey* and as a part of ACT's tests called *EXPLORE, PLAN,* and the *ACT Assessment.* Published by ACT, Inc., Iowa City, IA.

Vocational Interest Intentory, Lunneborg, 1993. Measures interests in Roe's eight occupational areas (Service, Business Contact, Organization, Technical, Outdoor, Science, General Cultural, Arts and Entertainment). It has the unusual feature of comparing the scores of high school students with those of other high school students who have gone on to specific college majors.

Skills inventories.   *SkillScan,* Beckhusen and Gazzano, 1987. Provides opportunity for users to sort a large number of skills by areas of competence, preference, and need for development and to identify skills with a combination of high competence and preference. Appropriate for use with high school students, college students, and adults. Published by SkillScan Professional Pack, Orinda, CA.

WorkKeys, ACT, 1995. Measures skills in 11 areas: Reading for Information, Applied Mathematics, Listening, Writing, Locating Information, Applied Technology, Teamwork, Motivation, Learning, Observing, and Speaking. Specific jobs can be profiled on the same skills, allowing the relationship of an individual's skills with the level required by specific occupations and jobs. Can be used with high school students and adults. Published by ACT, Inc., Iowa City, IA.

Combination of interests and skills.   *Campbell Interest and Skill Survey (CISS),* Campbell, 1992. Measures interests and self-reported skills in seven areas that are roughly parallel to the Holland six types and contains 29 basic scales and 60 occupational scales. Can be used with high school students, college students, and adults. Published by NCS Assessments, Minneapolis, MN.

Passion Revealer Assessment Package, Borchard, 1998. Measures interests and skills related to six areas called Analytics, Creators, Organizers, Inspirers, Technicals, and Performers. Appropriate for use with adults. Published by author. Tests of abilities combined with interest inventories.

The Armed Services Vocational Aptitude Battery (ASVAB), U.S. Department of Defense, 1995. Measures abilities in 10 content areas and includes measurement of interests by Holland typology and personal preferences (values). Designed for high school seniors and adults. Used for admission to various specialties in the armed forces but is also provided to high school seniors in general. Published by the U.S. Department of Defense.

The Career Planning Survey (CPS), ACT, 1997. Measures abilities in three areas and interests in the six Holland personality types, linking these to the World-of-Work Map. Can be used with high school students, college students, and adults. Published by ACT, Inc., Iowa City, IA.

O*Net Ability Profiler, United States Employment Service, 2003. This instrument is a career exploration tool that helps clients plan their work lives. The O*Net Ability Profiler uses a paper and pencil format with optional apparatus parts and computerized scoring. Individuals can use O*Net Ability Profiler results to identify their strengths and areas for which they might want to receive more training and education, or to identify occupations that fit their strengths.

The O＊Net Ability Profiler measures nine job-relevant abilities: Verbal Ability, Arithmetic Reasoning, Computation, Spatial Ability, Form Perception, Clerical Perception, Motor Coordination, Finger Dexterity, and Manual Dexterity. This instrument can be downloaded without charge from the O＊Net Web site at http://www.onetcenter.org/AP.html.

Inventories of personality type.   *The Myers-Briggs Type Indicator (MBTI),* Consulting Psychologists Press, 1998. Measures the psychological types described by Jung, yielding a four-letter code that can be related to typical profiles of groups of people who work in specific occupations or that can be used to develop teams or understand the interactions among members of a team. Can be used with high school students, college students, and adults. Published by Consulting Psychologists Press, Palo Alto, CA.

Note that as with the previous group of assessment instruments, these are targeted primarily to individuals in the high school, college, and adult years. This is the case because interests are not crystallized until the adolescent years, and the development of abilities and skills to support them typically occurs in the high school and college years.

Inventories measuring work values.   *O＊Net Work Importance Profiler,* United States Employment Service, 2002. The *Work Importance Profiler* measures the importance of six work values—achievement, independence, recognition, relationships, support, and working conditions. Individuals who take the instrument begin by rank-ordering 21 work need statements by comparing them with one another. The results are linked to occupational titles. The instrument can be downloaded without charge either as a print document or as executable code from http://www.onet.center.org.

Super's Work Values Inventory—revised, Zytowski, 2002. Measures importance of 12 of Super's work values and provides percentile scores of level of importance. For use by high school students and adults. Available only in Web-based form at http://www.kuder.com.

Measuring Progress or Change.   In the third category of reasons to use assessment, instruments are used to measure some kind of change that is considered desirable in an individual or a group of individuals. For example, it is common to use a pretest and a posttest to measure change that should occur because of some kind of treatment—such as a career guidance curriculum, a series of workshops, or use of a computer-based system. In this case, the purpose of the assessment is to note the difference in an individual's or group's scores before the treatment and after the treatment. The same instruments listed under category one (finding out the needs of clients) can be used to measure this progress or change.

WAYS IN WHICH ASSESSMENT INSTRUMENTS MAY BE ADMINISTERED

Traditionally, assessment instruments have been provided in print form. They are administered either by licensed or certified professional counselors or, more recently, by trained career development facilitators. In this mode, instructions are read by the administrator, and the examinee responds to the items of the instrument on a worksheet or optical scan form. The results may then be calculated by the examinee, by the test administrator, by computer software that has been acquired for that purpose, or by computer scoring at some central place. These different options for scoring also determine how soon the results will be available for interpretation to the client.

In recent years, the widespread availability of computers and access to the Internet have introduced additional ways in which administration and interpretation take place. Beginning in the late 1960s with the advent of computer-based career planning systems, some types of instruments—such as inventories of interests, skills, abilities, and values—became a part of such systems, described more fully in Chapter 6. In keeping with ethical standards, developers of computer-based systems engaged in research to assure that instruments delivered in this way yielded the same results as if they were administered in print form. In this mode, it was possible for an inventory to be scored immediately and for the computer to provide a very standard report, though customized for the individual examinee, that could be viewed on the screen and/or printed. The report was typically also made available to a counselor who could follow through with the client for more in-depth interpretation and application of this to the client's specific needs.

Subsequent to their inclusion in computer-based career planning systems, many assessment instruments became available from their publishers in software form. In this mode, a site can purchase a computer disk that contains the instrument and the computer code required to administer and interpret it. This software may be installed on machines at the user site and is typically limited according to how much has been paid for it or for how many individual uses the site has been authorized.

The advent of the Internet and its ever-increasing use have introduced yet another venue for administration and interpretation of assessment. It has also made it more difficult to determine the quality of available assessments, especially those offered by sites that do not charge a fee and cannot provide a manual that describes the research and development work invested in the instrument. As trends are unfolding in these areas, three different observations can be made: (1) many instruments and their results are available to the general public without charge and without opportunity to learn about the quality of the instrument; (2) well-known and researched instruments are being offered via the Internet for a fee, and their results are available immediately to the examinee; and (3) well-known and researched instruments are being offered via the Internet, and their results are electronically sent to a counselor specified by the examinee; the results are interpreted either face-to-face or via electronic exchange with the counselor.

Numerous inventories are available on the Internet—some without fees and others on a fee basis. Examples of formal and informal no-fee assessment Web sites are as follows:

- University of Waterloo Career Services: http://www.careerservices.uwaterloo.ca_docs_self-assess.html—A collection of six assessment tools that can be printed out and completed, covering personality and attitude, skills and achievements, knowledge and learning style, values, interests (based on Holland's types), and entrepreneurism.
- The Career Key: http://www.ncsu.edu_careerkey—An interest inventory for middle school students, high school students, or adults that yields a Holland code.

- University of Missouri Career Center Career Interests Game: http:career. missouri.edu_holland—An informal assessment in which the six Holland types are described and users self-select a Holland code.
- Motivational Assessment of Personal Potential: http://www.assessment.com— Offers an interest inventory that measures one's interest in working with people or things and other job characteristics, suggests occupations linked to their O*Net descriptions.

Often there is little or no information about the developers of these instruments and sites. Counselors have the ethical responsibility to become knowledgeable about the quality of an instrument before recommending that students or clients take it.

Some of the inventories described earlier are available on the Internet as well as in print or off-line electronic form. These for-fee sites include the following:

- The Kuder Career Planning System: http://www.kuder.com—Offers the *Kuder Career Search with Person Match* (an interest inventory), the *Kuder Skills Assessment,* and the revised *Super Work Values Inventory*. The first two inventories provide a rank-order percentile score based on the six Holland personality types by different titles. Also provides an interactive score report with linkage to occupational information and postsecondary school search. Includes a lifetime electronic portfolio.
- The Self-Directed Search: http://www.self-directed-search.com—Offers Holland's interest inventory and provides an extensive interpretive report.

The availability of an expanding plethora of instruments and their interpretation via the Internet poses a significant professional challenge. Counselors who prescribe the use of such instruments have an ethical responsibility to find out about and be professionally satisfied with the quality of the instrument before prescribing it.

Another trend of the 21st century is to administer many kinds of tests—such as tests that govern entrance to colleges, graduate schools, or licensure or certification for a given occupation—through secure test sites in addition to (or instead of) through the traditional paper and pencil approach. Because tests of this nature are used to make decisions that appreciably affect people's lives, their items must be kept secure; and it must be assured that examinees do not use materials that will help them identify the correct responses. They must be administered in secure environments. That means that specific places are designated to which examinees must travel. These places have computer equipment that provides good service and response time. Monitors at these locations assure that the persons taking the tests are those who registered to take them and that the test items themselves are sent to work stations from central computers where security is guarded. This method of administration also has the capability to immediately score the tests, electronically send the results to persons or organizations authorized to receive them, and use adaptive tests. *Adaptive tests* are those that include a large number of items that measure a specific content field. These items are arranged in hierarchical order related to their level of difficulty. Using formulas developed with scientific rigor, the computer software begins by presenting a few items that are easy. If the examinee answers these correctly, the software displays items of greater difficulty. This pattern continues until the general level of the examinee's knowledge is determined. Then, a greater number of items is presented from this category of items. The characteristics of this type of testing are (1) shorter testing time in general, (2) variable testing time for each examinee, (3) immediate scoring and feedback to authorized persons, and (4) potential capability to do a more thorough testing at the specific competency level of the examinee.

TYPES OF REPORTS

Reports of the result of a test or inventory typically come to a client in print form. If the instrument has been taken on a computer or from a Web site, the report may also appear on the screen, but it is typically sent to a printer device. Counselors may receive reports in print form, on a computer disk from which they can be printed, or by electronic transfer via the Internet.

The results provided in the report may be idiosyncratic—that is, related only to the individual for whom the report was prepared—or may compare that person with one or more norm groups. If the report is idiosyncratic, the results are typically provided as raw scores and may also be represented in some graphic form. The following two examples illustrate both approaches.

Raw Scores on Sample Copy of *Self-Directed Search*™

	R	I	A	S	E	C
Activities	10	1	0	3	6	4
Competencies	3	0	2	2	1	3
Occupations	1	0	0	1	2	2
Self-Estimates	1	1	1	2	1	2
	2	1	1	3	2	5
Total Scores	17	3	4	11	12	16

If the results are *norm-referenced,* they will be presented in some combination of standard scores, stanines, and/or percentiles, each of which relates the user to the distribution of scores of the norm group(s).

Profile on the *Kuder Career Search*™

Scale	Score	Profile
Business Operations	91	xxxxxxxxxxxxxxxx
Sales & Management	88	xxxxxxxxxxxxxxx
Social & Personal Services	84	xxxxxxxxxxxxxx
Outdoor & Mechanical	51	xxxxxxxxxx
Arts & Communications	47	xxxxxxxxx
Science & Technical	28	xxxxxx

A *percentile score* such as those just reported, indicates a point or range on a normal distribution where the examinee's score falls compared with the scores of those in the norm group. A percentile score indicates the percent of the norm group that scored lower than the examinee and, by subtraction of the score from 100, provides the percent of the norm group that scored higher. Norm groups can vary widely, and the score reports of some instruments will report the examinee's position related to more than one norm group. Depending on the specific instrument, a norm group may be a large national sample representative of those for whom the instrument is suggested, including both genders, a variety of ages, racial-ethnic diversity, and a variety of educational levels. Other norm groups may be one gender; specific grade level; local school district, state, or national representation; or with some interest and abilities measures, by occupational group membership.

Further, scores for some instruments will be reported as a single-point score on a continuum or as a range, typically called a *band of confidence*. Reporting a band of confidence is an indication by a publisher that the examinee's score falls somewhere within that range, though an exact point is uncertain. Instruments have a property called a *standard error of measurement*, and the band of confidence shows what the range of this error of measurement may be.

Percentile scores are always on a range of 1 to 99. Another way of expressing a similar concept, but with less precision, is to report a *stanine*. By definition, a stanine is a prescribed range of percentile points, and that range is the same for all instruments and all populations to which they are administered. The nine stanines have the following definitions:

Stanine 1 = the lowest 4% of a distribution

Stanine 2 = the next 7%, percentile values 5 to 11

Stanine 3 = the next 12%, percentile values 12 to 25

Stanine 4 = the next 17%, percentile values 26 to 40

Stanine 5 = the next 20%, percentile values 41 to 60

Stanine 6 = the next 17%, percentile values 61 to 77

Stanine 7 = the next 12%, percentile values 78 to 89

Stanine 8 = the next 7%, percentile values 90 to 96

Stanine 9 = the top 4%, percentile values 97 to 100

In summary, stanines 1 through 3 represent the lowest quarter (called a *quartile*) of any distribution; stanines 4 through 6, the middle 50%; and stanines 7 through 9, the top quarter (*quartile*).

A third way of describing how an individual's score relates to that of a norm group is the concept of a *standard score* (also called a *T-score*). This term is related to the term *standard deviation*, which is a way of measuring how far an individual's score is from the middle (that is, the 50th percentile) of the distribution. *Standard T-scores* range from 20 to 80, with 50 at the mean (50%), and each standard deviation counted as 10 percentile points. Thus, an individual's score may be said to be

2 standard deviations (12) above the mean (that is, at the 70th percentile), or 2.5 standard deviations (22.5) below the mean (that is, at the 25th percentile).

SELECTION OF INSTRUMENTS

In summary, there is a wide variety of types and purposes for assessment, and the results emanating from assessment can take many forms. Instruments represent a wide variety of quality related to their psychometric properties and may be based on a wide range of theory or on none at all. Further, these instruments can be administered to individuals or groups and in multiple modes. Counselors may choose to administer only one assessment, a variety of different assessments, or a "package" of instruments placed together so that they can measure different but complementary attributes. These facts combined with the ethical standards that are cited in this chapter make the task of selecting instruments complex. When selecting an assessment instrument, counselors must be mindful of these guidelines:

- Determine the specific purpose(s) for assessment. Then, begin by identifying instruments that fit that purpose.
- Consider the characteristics of the person or group for whom the instrument is being selected. Determine if gender, racial or ethnic background, reading ability, intelligence level, or disability signal an alert to take special care in selection.
- Review the data about the groups used for testing and norming the instrument. Determine whether these groups are representative of those to whom the instrument will be administered or at least contain a reasonable number of persons similar to the population to be tested.
- For instruments that still qualify, search their technical manuals for data about reliability (.80 or above) and evidence of their validity.
- Read critical reviews of the instruments in reference books and/or Web sites. Talk with at least three other counselors who use the instrument.
- Purchase a sample copy of the instrument and take it. Study the score report, and consider whether its results seem appropriate. Read the manual to understand how the publisher suggests that the instrument be interpreted.
- Before adopting the instrument for wide use, administer it to a few individuals, and practice preparing them for taking it and providing an interpretation.
- If the instrument still qualifies, find out how much it costs, its various modes of administration and scoring, and adopt it.

SUMMARY

Assessment, in its many and varied forms, has been presented as one tool among many that counselors can use with students and clients for three specific purposes: to identify their needs, help them learn more about themselves, and monitor their progress. The responsibilities of the counselor were listed. A plea was made for using assessment in combination with many other tools and techniques, in harmony with where a client is in the career development process. Cautions were stated related to not over-interpreting the meaning of scores, and counselors were admonished to use the data from career planning instruments for exploration, guidance, and confirmation rather than for prediction. In this process the client is proposed as an active agent and is encouraged not to position the counselor in a role of superior knowledge.

The types, purposes, and characteristics of assessment instruments and their reports were reviewed. Some of the most common instruments were named and briefly described, and the counselor was encouraged to explore beyond this list. Finally, guidelines for selecting instruments for individuals or groups of clients were listed.

REFERENCES

ACT, Inc. (1995). *WorkKeys*. Iowa City, IA: Author.

ACT, Inc. (1997). *Career Planning Survey*. Iowa City, IA: Author.

ACT, Inc. (2000a). *EXPLORE*. Iowa City, IA: Author.

ACT, Inc. (2000b). *PLAN*. Iowa City, IA: Author.

ACT, Inc. (2001). *ACT Assessment Program*. Iowa City, IA: Author.

Beckhusen, L., & Gazzano, L. (1987). *SkillScan*. Orinda, CA: SkillScan Professional Pack.

Borchard, D. (1998). *Passion Revealer Assessment Package*. Washington, DC: Author.

Campbell, D. (1992). *Campbell Interest and Skill Survey*. Minnetonka, MN: National Computer Systems.

Chartrand, J. M., Robbins, S. B., & Morrill, W. H. (1997). *The Career Factors Inventory*. Palo Alto, CA: Consulting Psychologists Press.

Chronicle Guidance Publications (1991). *Career Quest* (Middle School Version). Moravia, NY: Author.

Chronicle Guidance Publications. (2000). *Career Quest* (High School and Adult Version). Moravia, NY: Author.

College Entrance Examination Board. (2001). *Scholastic Aptitude Test (SAT)*. New York: Author.

Crites, J., & Savickas, M. (1995). *Career Maturity Inventory*. Boulder, CO: Crites Career Consultants.

Harrington, T., & O'Shea, A. (1992). *Harrington-O'Shea Career Decision Making System*. Circle Pines, MN: American Guidance Service.

Harris-Bowlsbey, J., Riley-Dikel, M., & Sampson, J. P., Jr. (2002). *The Internet: A Tool for Career Planning* (2nd ed.). Tulsa, OK: National Career Development Association.

Holland, J. L. (1994). *Self-Directed Search.*™ Odessa, FL: Psychological Assessment Resources.

Holland, J. L. (1997). *Making vocational choices: A theory of vocational personalities and work environments* (3rd ed.). Odessa, FL: Psychological Assessment Resources.

Holland, J. L., Daiger, D. C., & Power, P. G. (1987). *My Vocational Situation*. Palo Alto, CA: Consulting Psychologists Press.

Holland, J. L., & Gottfredson, G. D. (1994). *Career Attitudes and Strategies Inventory*. Lutz, FL: Psychological Assessment Resources.

Impara, J. C., & Plake, B. S. (Eds.). (1998). *The thirteenth mental measurements yearbook*. Lincoln, NE: Buros Institute.

Jackson, D. N. (1999). *Jackson Vocational Interest Survey*. Port Huron: MI: Sigma Assessment Systems.

Johansson, C. B. (1986). *Career Assessment Inventory*. Minnetonka, MN: NCS Assessments.

Johansson, C. B. (1996, 2000). *Interest Determination, Exploration, and Assessment System (IDEAS)*. Minneapolis, MN: NCS Assessments.

Joint Committee on Testing Practices. (1999). *Code of fair testing practices*. Washington, DC: Author.

Jones, L. K. (1986). *Career Decision Profile*. Raleigh, NC: Author.

Jung, C. G. (1959). The archetypes and the collective unconscious. In C. G. Jung, *Collected works* (vol. 9, part I). Princeton: Princeton University Press.

Kapes, J. T., & Whitfield, E. A. (2002). *A counselor's guide to career assessment instruments*. Tulsa, OK: National Career Development Association.

Knapp, R. R., & Knapp, L. (1992). *Career Occupational Preference Survey*. San Diego, CA: EDITS.

Krumboltz, J. D. (1991). *The Career Beliefs Inventory*. Palo Alto, CA: Consulting Psychologists Press.

Lunneborg, P. W. (1993). Vocational Interest Inventory, Revised. Los Angeles, CA: Western Psychological Services.

Miller, C. H. (1961). *Foundations of guidance*. New York: Harper & Row.

Myers, I., & Briggs, K. (1998). *The Myers-Briggs Type Indicator.*® Palo Alto, CA: Consulting Psychologists Press.

National Career Assessment Services, Inc. (1998). *Iowa Career Learning Assessment.*™ Adel, IA: Author.

National Council on Measurement in Education. (1995). *The code of professional responsibilities in educational measurement.* Washington, DC: Author.

Osipow, S. H., Carney, C. G., Winer, J., Yanico, B., & Koschier, M. (1997). *Career Decision Scale.* Odessa, FL: Psychological Assessment Resources.

Parsons, F. (1909). *Choosing a vocation.* Boston: Houghton Mifflin.

Real Game. (2000). *The real game series.* Retrieved June 10, 2004 from http://www.realgame.com.

Riverside Publishing. (1998). Interest Explorer. Itasca, IL: Riverside Publishing.

Rosen, D., Holmberg, K., & Holland, J. L. (1999). *The educational opportunities finder.* Odessa, FL: Psychological Assessment Resources.

Sampson, J. P., Peterson, G. W., Lenz, J. G., Reardon, R. C., & Saunders, D. E. (1996). *Career Thoughts Inventory.* Odessa, FL: Psychological Assessment Resources.

Strong, E. K. (1994). *The Strong Interest Inventory.* Palo Alto, CA: Consulting Psychologists Press.

Super, D. E. (1957). *The psychology of careers.* New York: Harper.

Super, D. E., Starishevsky, R., Matlin, N., & Jordaan, J. P. (1963). *Career development: Self-concept theory* (Research Monograph No. 4). New York: College Entrance Examination Board.

Super, D. E., Thompson, A. S., Lindeman, R. H., Jordaan, J. P., & Myers, R. A. (1984). *Career Development Inventory.* Palo Alto, CA: Consulting Psychologists Press.

Swaney, K. B. (1995). *Technical manual: Revised unisex edition of the ACT Interest Inventory (UNIACT).* Iowa City, IA: ACT, Inc.

United States Employment Service. (2001). *O*Net Interest Profiler.* Washington, DC: Author.

United States Employment Service. (2003). *O*Net Ability Profiler.* Washington, DC: Author.

United States Employment Service. (2002). *O*Net Work Importance Profiler.* Washington, DC: Author.

U.S. Department of Defense. (1995). *Armed Services Vocational Aptitude Battery.* Monterey, CA: Author.

Zytowski, D. G., & Kuder, F. (1999). *Kuder Career Search with Person Match.*™ Adel, IA: National Career Assessment Services, Inc.

Zytowski, D. G. (2002). Super's Work Values Inventory, revised. Adel, IA: National Career Assessment Services, Inc.

PUBLISHERS

ACT, Inc.
P.O. Box 168
Iowa City, IA 52240
URL: http://www.act.org

American Guidance Service
4201 Woodland Road
Circle Pines, MN 55014
URL: http://www.agsnet.com

Consulting Psychologists Press
P.O. Box 10096
Palo Alto, CA 94303
URL: http://www.cpp-db.com

EDITS
P.O. Box 7234
San Diego, CA

National Career Assessment Systems, Inc.
P.O. Box 277
Adel, IA 50003
URL: http://www.ncasi.com

NCS Assessments
5605 Green Circle Drive
Minnetonka, MN 55343

Psychological Assessment Resources (PAR)
P.O. Box 998
Odessa, FL 33556–9908
URL: http://www.parinc.com

CHAPTER 6

CAREER INFORMATION AND RESOURCES

Career information can be a dry topic to learn and teach. Labor market information (LMI) can appear cold and "unsexy" to counselors-in-training. The daily accountability of counselor educators may create gaps between understanding the changing school and workplace and providing current career information resources. Though entering counselor training to enjoy nurturing relationships, some counselors give little attention to the systems clients face as they move through career transitions. Moving immediately into "trait-factor" matching mode to provide just the right occupational or education information to gain the client's respect is also a common trap. Knowing how to integrate LMI into the career development intervention process is an essential skill for helping others move forward in their career development.

Dr. Rich Feller
Professor, Colorado State University

Clarice is a 28-year-old single parent of three children who lives in a modest apartment and receives support from public aid. Recent legislation mandates that she go to work within a year and provides access to funding for some training. She dropped out of high school in her sophomore year after her first child was born. She has held part-time jobs at various fast-food restaurants since that time. Clarice goes to a no-fee community agency for assistance in determining what she can do to meet the requirements of the legislation.

Chapter 5 addressed assessment as a tool that counselors can use to help an individual make informed choices in the career planning process. Similarly, what is commonly called *career information* needs to be placed within this same context. As with assessment, counselors often make the mistake of viewing career information as an end in and of itself. Actually, it is another tool that the counselor can use to assist clients to make informed choices.

As suggested by the title of this chapter and its introductory paragraph, the common term for what will be presented is career *information*. The authors, however, prefer career *data*, meaning a collection of facts about occupational and educational opportunities. Borrowing from Tiedeman and O'Hara (1963), the authors endorse the perspective that students and clients, often with the assistance of counselors and technology, collect *data*. These data become *information* only when they are understood by clients and used to *inform* decision making, that is, to assist them to choose one alternative over another.

For the sake of making the linkage between data and an individual's career planning process, please review Figure 5.1. Notice the centrality of the oval labeled Resources. This is a pool of data that needs to be available to a person who is in the process of career planning. Notice that at each of Steps 2 through 7, the person making a career choice needs to access data. These data may be contained in the results of assessment instruments, in print materials, in curriculum, or in computer databases resident in computer-based career planning systems or on Web sites. At Step 2, data gained from instruments measuring interests, skills, abilities, personality type, and/or values may be very useful.

At each step of the career planning process, the type, quantity, and depth of data needed may be different. This difference relates to the age of the persons going through the process. Middle school students may learn about themselves through informal assessment techniques, learn only about clusters of occupations (rather than individual occupations), and learn about possible ways of getting training and the importance of getting and maintaining satisfying jobs. Adults, on the other hand, may take formal assessment inventories and tests, seek the assistance of professional counselors in gaining self-information, read highly specific occupational and educational information, and need detailed information about companies and specific jobs. In other words, the process is common whereas the level of specificity of the data required at each step changes with age and population.

At Step 3 search strategies that help students and clients find the titles of occupations that have or relate to the characteristics they have selected are most helpful. At Step 4, clients need to access databases or print materials that contain detailed descriptions of these identified occupations—including their work tasks, requirements for training, employment outlook, benefits and limitations, typical salary range, and sources for further information. At Step 5, which requires eliminating some of the identified occupations and keeping others, even more detailed data are needed about each. At this step students and clients may seek data by talking with individuals who have experienced these occupations or seeking some direct contact with the worksite as well as by reading and viewing slides and videos.

At Step 6, students and clients need data about different ways (that is, apprenticeship, 2-year college, 4-year college, vocational-technical school, etc.) to get training for occupations of their tentative choice and about options within the category they have chosen. At Step 7, students and clients need data about specific job openings and the companies or organizations that offer them.

THE COUNSELOR'S ROLE IN PROVIDING DATA

Counselors have three specific responsibilities related to career data. First, they have the responsibility to select high-quality print materials, computer-based systems, and Web sites—the most common sources of career data—that conform to the guidelines provided by professional associations. The most comprehensive set of guidelines is provided by the National Career Development Association (NCDA), and these are available in their entirety at http://www.ncda.org under the section titled "NCDA Policy Statements." (These are also available in the NCDA's publication, *Guidelines for the Preparation and Evaluation of Career and Occupational Information Literature* [1991].) Counselors choosing resources should become familiar with this entire document.

Following are some of the salient points[1]:

- The source of the data should be clearly stated.
- Data should be updated on a regular schedule, and the date of last update should be displayed clearly.
- The material should be accurate and free from distortion caused by self-serving bias, sex stereotyping, or dated resources. Whenever possible, resources more than 5 years old should be avoided. Occupational descriptions should be written or at least reviewed by persons knowledgeable about each occupation.
- The data should be conveyed in a clear, concise, and interesting manner. A standard style and format for grammar should be adopted and used throughout the documents.
- The vocabulary used should be appropriate for those who will be reading the material. Technical terminology or jargon should be fully explained or avoided, and use of nonsexist language is essential.
- Care should be taken to eliminate bias and stereotyping against persons with a disability, or based on gender, race, social status, ethnicity, age, or religion.
- If graphics or pictures are used, these should be current, accurately depict the environment, and represent without stereotype persons of both sexes and of different races, ages, and physical abilities.
- If the data source deals with occupations, it should describe clearly the duties and nature of the work, work settings and conditions, preparation required for entry, special requirements or considerations, methods of entry, earnings and other benefits, usual advancement possibilities, employment outlook, opportunities for experience and exploration, related occupations, and sources of additional information.

A second responsibility of counselors is to make the availability of these high-quality resources known to students and clients and to make them as user-friendly as possible. A later section of this chapter will describe a *career center*, the usual repository for these resources, and methods of organizing it. Counselors have the responsibility to acquaint students and clients with the resources, how they can be accessed, and even more importantly, to refer them to the specific ones that may be most helpful at a given point in their decision making process. This statement underscores the fact that counselors must know these resources in detail in order to refer clients to them and to be able to discuss their content. For example, students'

---

[1]NCDA Policy Statements on Career Information. Copyrighted by the National Career Development Association. Reprinted with permission from NCDA.

and clients' use of a computer-based career planning system or of a Web site will be far less effective if counselors simply direct them to the system or site as opposed to providing a marked flowchart or site map accompanied with a statement such as "I'd like you to use *CareerInfoNet*, selecting the option titled General Outlook on the opening screen."

A third and more difficult responsibility of the counselor is to assist the client to process, or make meaningful use of, the data acquired. The goal is to turn the *data* into *information*—in other words, for the client to absorb and understand the data so that the client can provide practical assistance in placing some alternatives in high priority while discarding others. This is the most important of the counselor's roles. The counselor should have the following concerns:

- Is this client ready to receive data and deal with it effectively?
- What barriers does the client potentially have to using data effectively?
- What kinds of data, and how much, will be most helpful?
- What methods of receiving data—print material, computers and Web sites, personal contact—will be most effective?
- What kind of decision style does the client use, and how will that affect his or her ability to use data effectively?

Barriers and Decision Styles

Students and clients may experience a variety of different kinds of barriers as they search and use data. Some of these barriers may be physical, such as sight or hearing disabilities. Others may be intellectual, such as poor reading skill, poor comprehension skill, or low intelligence. Others may be cognitive, such as possession of irrational beliefs (Krumboltz, 1991) or negative thoughts (Sampson, Peterson, Lenz, Reardon, & Saunders, 1996). Another barrier may be the lack of a strong self-concept or vocational identity, what some call a sense of self-efficacy. Sampson and his colleagues describe a condition of cognitive inability to understand or follow a logical information-processing model.

Dinklage (1968) studied the way in which different individuals face the decision making process. Little is known about how persons acquire a specific decision making style, but it is clear from the definitions of the eight types of "deciders" identified by Dinklage that the role of data, and therefore the work of the counselor, is different for each style. The eight types of deciders are as follows:

- *Planful.* One who approaches decision making in a systematic, step-by-step manner. Steps include setting a goal, identifying alternatives that will help reach the goal, collecting information about those alternatives, identifying one that is most likely to reach the goal, and taking action steps to implement that alternative.
- *Agonizing.* One who attempts to engage in decision making in a systematic, step-by-step manner but becomes so engrossed in finding alternatives, collecting information about them, and trying to choose one over others that he or she is never able to actually reach a decision.

- *Impulsive.* One who does not know how to follow a systematic process or does not value it; rather, this type of decider selects an alternative quickly and does not spend the time to identify alternatives or collect information about them.
- *Intuitive.* One who seems to be able to select one alternative over another, with good outcomes, without having to go through the steps of the planful process. This type of decider seems to be able to determine what his or her personal goals are quite quickly and then substitute experience and good judgment for extensive data collection.
- *Compliant.* One who, either due to personal style or societal norms, allows others to make decisions for him or her.
- *Delaying.* One who recognizes that a decision needs to be made but continues to delay making it out of fear, lack of data, or lack of motivation.
- *Fatalistic.* One who believes that he or she does not have control over the events of life, but rather that they are largely determined by external forces.
- *Paralytic.* One who recognizes the need to make a decision but is not able to move forward in the process because the process or the possible outcomes are very frightening.

So students and clients present a variety of decision making styles and levels of belief about their self-worth and self-efficacy. Yet using a planful decision making process increases the probability of making an informed decision, affecting significantly the *outcomes* or *consequences*.

THE CLIENT'S ROLE IN RECEIVING DATA

Though the counselor has a significant role in the data-gathering process, students and clients also have responsibilities: (a) to complete the assignments or suggestions provided by the counselor; (b) to work committedly with the counselor to process the data, that is, to use it in ways that inform personal decision making; and (c) to assume responsibility for their own decision making.

The first responsibility of students and clients is to complete the data-gathering assignments that counselors give them. Unfortunately, many students and clients want quick and easy answers to their questions about career choice or change. Some expect a computer-based career planning system, a Web site, or a test to provide those answers. Others want counselors to advise what to do and would like to shift the responsibility for decision making to them. The fact is, though, that the process of career choice and development is difficult and time consuming. It requires that one commit time and energy to it and develop skill at data processing. Students and clients should be informed early in the counseling relationship about the need to spend considerable time doing the data-gathering homework that is assigned.

A second primary responsibility of students and clients is to engage in activities with the counselor that will help with the processing—that is, analyzing and making personal application—of the data that have been gathered. A student or client may, for example, read and print out the descriptions of 20 occupations identified by an interest inventory. The time required to complete that work may be wasted if the counselor and the client do not move from there to answer the question "so what?". Interests, abilities, and personality traits are very useful constructs to help students and clients identify possible occupations. Their use usually results in the identification of far more options than can be followed. The data-processing function occurs, then, when the counselor assists the client to identify and apply criteria that can be used to rank-order alternatives.

Criteria that guide decisions are typically called *values* or *characteristics*. Thus a counselor might use interviewing, a values inventory, or a card sort to help the client select several values and characteristics that can be used to eliminate and rank-order alternatives. Values are broader and deeper than characteristics. Examples of values are independence, altruism, high income, prestige, and authority. Examples of characteristics, applied to occupations, are working outside, being able to avoid overtime and night work, having longer-than-average vacations, and being able to enter the occupation without a college degree. Once preferred values and characteristics have been identified, it is possible to examine each identified alternative, using the data collected, for its potential to satisfy these. Doing so will provide a framework for eliminating some alternatives and rank-ordering the remainder, resulting in a short list of good alternatives.

A third responsibility of students and clients is to assume responsibility for their decisions. Some types of deciders—such as those described as compliant, paralytic, and agonizing—may attempt to relinquish to the counselor their right and responsibility to make decisions. Early in the career planning process it is wise to structure the expectations of the client by reviewing the roles of the counselor and the client. There are times when counselors have to confront students and clients with the fact that they are not carrying out their responsibilities in the relationship.

TYPES OF DATA NEEDED BY CLIENTS

Career planning is defined as the sequential process of making educational and vocational choices based on knowledge of self and of the environment. Using this definition, it follows that, in addition to developing information about the self, students and clients need to learn about programs of study, occupations, schools and other types of training, financial aid opportunities, military service, and organizations offering jobs. Each of these databases will be considered separately.

Programs of Study

The term *programs of study* is used to describe sequences of high school courses; specialties in vocational-technical schools, apprenticeships, and the military; and majors in colleges and universities. Though it is highly desirable for individuals to have a broad base of knowledge in the liberal arts and a set of work skills like those described in the SCANS Report (U.S. Department of Labor, 1992), it is also highly desirable that individuals have coursework and training directed to the specific skills needed in the occupations of their choice. For that reason, it is very helpful to organize the courses in the high school curriculum, specialties in on-the-job training opportunities, and majors in college by the same organizational system used for occupations when these are presented to students. Further, the assessment used to identify interests, abilities, and/or values would also ideally be linked to the same organizational system.

Holland's typology has been applied to people through assessment instruments such as *The Self-Directed Search*™ (Holland, 1994b), *The Career Assessment Inventory* (Johansson, 1984), *The Career Decision-Making System* (Harrington & O'Shea, 2000), the *UNIACT Interest Inventory* (ACT, 1989b), the *Kuder Career Search* (Kuder & Zytowski, 1999), the *Inventory of Work-Relevant Abilities* (ACT, 1989a), and the *Campbell Interest and Skill Survey* (Campbell, 1992). The same system has been applied to occupations in *The Occupations Finder* (Holland, 1994a), *The Dictionary of Holland Occupational Codes* (Gottfredson & Holland, 1996), and the *O*Net* (1998a, 1998b) database. It has been applied to vocational-technical and college majors in *The Educational Opportunities Finder* (Rosen, Holmberg, & Holland, 1999), and to leisure activities in *The Leisure Activities Finder* (Holmberg, Rosen, & Holland, 1999); it could be applied to job openings and company positions. Given this fact, one way to help students and clients process data that they collect about themselves, occupations, and educational opportunities is to organize all of this information—as well as school course offerings, career days, and data in the career center—within the same structural framework. Thus, a listing of courses offered at the high school level or majors/specialties offered at the postsecondary level, organized by the Holland typology, would be very useful in decision making.

Another system, described later in this chapter, that can be used to organize all of these pieces is ACT's World-of-Work Map (Prediger, 1981), based on the Holland typology. In this organizational scheme, ACT's assessment instruments (such as *The Career Planning Survey* in print form and parts of *DISCOVER* in computer-based form) would be used, along with ACT's *Career Area Charts* or *DISCOVER* databases.

The most comprehensive source of general information about postsecondary majors and programs of study is the *Classification of Instructional Programs* (Morgan, Hunt, & Carpenter, 1990), published by the U.S. Government Printing Office. Another valuable source, focusing on postsecondary 1- and 2-year programs of study is the *Counseling for High Skills* (ACT, 1997b) database. As suggested earlier, high schools and colleges could easily provide a listing and descriptions of their courses and majors by Holland or World-of-Work Map categories, thus creating a local, organized database of descriptions of majors. Data about programs of study and how they relate to occupations are most relevant at Step 6 of the career planning process.

Representative print resources:

- *College Admission Index of Majors and Sports* (Mac Donald-Murray, 2001)
- *Major Decisions: A Guide to College Majors* (Wintergreen-Orchard House, 1998a)

Extensive data about military programs of study are offered in *America's Top Military Careers: The Official Guide to Occupations in the Armed Forces* (U.S. Department of Defense, 2000), also available through recruiting offices and on a Web site (http://www.militarycareers.com). This publication provides a description of almost 200 military occupations, most of which have civilian counterparts, including typical work tasks, eligibility for entry, and the code numbers and titles assigned to the relevant military training program in each of the branches. In addition to this comprehensive database, which covers the offerings of all branches of the armed forces, each branch also has its own Web site:

- U.S. Army: http://www.armedforcescareers.com
- U.S. Navy: http://www.navy.com
- U.S. Air Force: http://www.af.mil
- U.S. Marine Corps: http://www.usmc.mil
- U.S. Coast Guard: http://www.uscg.mil/jobs

Data about military training programs are particularly relevant at Step 6 of the decision making model as it may be possible in the military to get the training needed for a chosen civilian occupation. If not, serving in the military may provide the educational benefits needed to take coursework while serving or to continue education after leaving.

Data about apprenticeship programs in general and about programs offered in a given state are available from the Federal Bureau of Apprenticeship and Training (http://www.doleta.gov/atels_bat) and from state apprenticeship offices. Such programs allow high school graduates to receive 144 hours of classroom instruction, typically provided without charge at the local community college, and the practical experience of learning a trade from an experienced worker while receiving a salary.

For college students, an internship program offers a valuable opportunity to learn about an occupation by experiencing it. These work-study programs allow students to work in a given occupation under supervision, receive pay for doing so, and typically earn college credit simultaneously. Data about apprenticeships and internships are relevant at Step 6 of the career planning process.

Print resources:

- *America's Top Internships* (Oldman & Hamadeh, 2000)
- *Cooperative Apprenticeships: A School-to-Work Handbook* (Cantor, 1997)
- *The Back Door Guide to Short Term Job Adventures: Internships, Extraordinary Experiences, Seasonal Jobs, Volunteering, Work Abroad* (Landes, 2002)
- *2000 Internships: The Largest Source of Internships Available* (Peterson's Publishing, 2000)

Web site for apprenticeships:

- Bureau of Apprenticeship and Training: http://www.doleta.gov/atels_bat

Web site for internships:

- Snagajob: http://snagajob.com
- Internship Programs. com: http://internships.wetfeet.com

Occupations

The guidelines for occupational information provided by the NCDA (1991) indicate that occupational descriptions should provide content in the following 11 areas: duties and nature of the work, work setting and conditions, preparation required, special requirements or considerations, methods of entry, earnings and other benefits, usual advancement possibilities, employment outlook, opportunities for experience and exploration, related occupations, and sources of additional information. The single most important source for data about occupations is the U.S. Department of Labor. In addition to providing descriptions of work tasks, work settings, entry methods and requirements, related occupations, and sources of additional information, the Department of Labor also conducts surveys about the *labor market* in general and its needs. The term *labor market* refers, on the one hand, to the supply of individuals who want and are able to work and, on the other hand, to the demand for workers from public and private employers. Surveys conducted at the state and federal level yield salaries for hundreds of occupations at the entry, median, and upper levels of experience. They also provide data about the expected growth or decline in the number of workers needed at both federal and state level for hundreds of occupations. These figures are based upon estimates of the number of persons in an occupational group who will retire, of students preparing for entry into the occupation, and of openings expected due to growth. Labor market forecasts for different occupations are provided by the Department of Labor in the following standard categories:

Phrase used:	Meaning:
Grow much faster than the average	Increase 41% or more
Grow faster than the average	Increase 27–40%
Grow about as fast as average	Increase 14–26%
Little change or grow more slowly than average	Increase 0–13%
Decline	Decrease 1% or more

Counselors need to remember that there is a great variance in the number of people in the hundreds of occupations about which the Department of Labor makes projections. Thus, the percentage of growth is meaningful only in combination with the number of people in the occupation. For example, growth of 14% to 26% in an occupation that has 130,000 incumbents represents more potential job openings than growth of 27% to 40% in an occupation that has 39,000 incumbents.

In the past, the most definitive source of occupational information was *The Dictionary of Occupational Titles*, 4th edition (U.S. Department of Labor, 1991), which contains descriptions of almost 13,000 occupations. This two-volume publication has been replaced by *O∗Net*, a database available in print form, within the prominent computer-based career information systems, and on a Web site at http://www.onetcenter.org. This database describes 1122 occupations by 483 characteristics. This organization allows students and clients to relate information about themselves in many different ways, focusing on single characteristics or a combination of characteristics. It also provides a skills inventory; completion of this inventory identifies occupations in the database. Further, the site allows the download of three assessment instruments—the *O∗Net Interest Profiler*, the

*O *Net Ability Profiler*, and the *O *Net Work Importance Profiler*—either in print form or as executable code.

A second publication of the U.S. Department of Labor is *The Occupational Outlook Handbook (OOH)* (2002a), available both in print form and on a Web site (http://www.bls.gov/oco). This book, updated every 2 years, provides extensive data about approximately 250 occupations, covering about 104 million jobs. Lengthy descriptions include all of the topics included in the NCDA's guidelines. The content of this book is updated and expanded on a quarterly basis in *The Occupational Outlook Quarterly (OOQ)*, a publication available by subscription and at http://www.bls.gov/opub/ooq/ooqhome.html.

The Guide for Occupational Exploration (GOE) (Farr, 2001), a publication developed by the U.S. Employment Service, relates interests, skills, aptitudes, values, school courses, and activities to the requirements of occupations. Occupations are divided into 12 interest areas, 66 work groups, and 348 subgroups. The 12 interest areas are the following (the Holland groups that relate to each are in parentheses):

Artistic (A)	Business Detail (C)
Scientific (I, R)	Selling (E)
Plants and Animals (I, R)	Accommodating (S, E, R)
Protective (S, R)	Humanitarian (S)
Mechanical (I, R)	Leading/Influencing (E)
Industrial (R)	Physical Performing (A)

Occupations are listed under each work group. Their titles include a statement of the industry or industries in which this occupation and related ones are found, the amount of physical strength needed to perform the occupation, the amount of math and language knowledge needed, and length of training for entry.

A recent important thrust of the U.S. Department of Labor is the ongoing development and maintenance of three significant Web sites, which together make up what is called *America's Career Kit*. They are *America's Job Bank*, *America's Talent Bank* (combined at http://www.ajb.dni.us), and *CareerInfoNet* (http://www.acinet.org). The latter provides a keyword-search capability for hundreds of occupations as well as extensive descriptions of them, including detailed data about their employment outlook and salary range as a national average and by each state. There are also videos about the work tasks of most of the occupations. The site also provides a listing and data about the fastest-growing occupations, those with the largest employment, those that are declining, and those that pay the highest salaries. The Resources section of the site offers linkages to a wide array of Web sites that provide assessment, occupational information, and general career planning support.

In addition to the publications, Web sites, and databases developed by the federal government, many private publishers offer high-quality material. Examples of these are listed next. Searches for relevant occupational titles and detailed descriptions of them are most useful at Steps 3, 4, and 5 of the career planning process model.

Representative print resources include:

- *Career Discovery Encyclopedia* (8 vols.) (J. G. Ferguson Publishing, 2003)
- *Encyclopedia of Career and Vocational Guidance* (Morkes, 2003)
- *Enhanced Guide for Occupational Exploration* (Maze & Mayall, 1995)
- *Four-Year College Level Careers, Occupational Briefs* (Chronicle Guidance Publications, 1998a)
- *Guide for Occupational Exploration System* (Farr, 2001)
- *The Occupational Outlook Handbook* (U.S. Department of Labor, 2002a)
- *O*Net Dictionary of Occupational Titles* (JIST, 1998a; Chronicle Guidance Publications, 1998)
- *Two-Year College Level Careers, Occupational Briefs* (Chronicle Guidance Publications, 1998b)
- *Vocational-School Level Careers, Occupational Briefs* (Chronicle Guidance Publications, 1998c)
- *Young Person's Occupational Outlook Handbook* (U.S. Department of Labor, 2002b)

Representative software:

- State career information delivery systems (CIDS)
- *Career Futures for Middle Schools* (Bridges, 2000b)
- *Chronicle Perspectives Plus* (Chronicle Guidance Publications, 2000a)
- *CHOICES* (Bridges, 2000a)
- *COIN* (COIN Educational Products, 2000)
- *DISCOVER* (ACT, 2000a)
- *Paws in Jobland* (Bridges, 2000c)

Representative Web sites:

- U.S. Department of Labor: http://www.acinet.org (*CareerInfoNet*), http://www.onetcenter.org (*O*Net*), and http://www.bls.gov/oco (*Occupational Outlook Handbook*)
- *Wall Street Journal*: http://collegejournal.com
- *U.S. News and World Report*: http://usnews.com
- JobSmart/JobStar: http://www.jobstar.org
- State of Indiana: http://icpac.indiana.edu
- State of Minnesota: http://www.mnworkforcecenter.org
- State of Michigan: http://www.talentfreeway.com

Schools

Prior to seeking data about individual schools, students and clients need to understand the various types of schools, training, and degrees or certifications. These types include the following:

   1. Private (often called *proprietary*) vocational-technical schools. These are for-profit schools that typically provide training for specific vocational fields within a 3-month to 2-year time frame. Though some offer an associate degree, most offer certificates that document the fact that students have successfully completed a program of study. There is a wide variation in the quality of these schools.

Representative print data sources:

- *Guide to Technical, Trade, and Business Schools* (Wintergreen-Orchard House, 1998b)

Representative Web site:

- Yahoo, Career and Vocational Education: http://www.yahoo.com/education/careerandvocational

2. Public community colleges. These schools offer two categories of majors: transfer and career-related. Students who enter the transfer program plan to continue at a 4-year institution after 2 years at the community college. They typically receive an associate degree. Students in the career-related program expect to end formal education after completion of a career-technology program in fields such as electronics, information sciences, auto body repair, X-ray technology, and many more. These students receive either a certificate (in a program of less than 2 years' length) or an associate degree. Community colleges offer training in the same fields as private vocational-technical schools, often with much lower tuition fees and higher quality teaching.

Representative print resources:

- *Black American Colleges and Universities: Profiles of Two-Year, Four-Year, and Professional Schools* (Hill & Wilson, 1994)
- *Guide to Technical, Trade, and Business Schools* (Wintergreen-Orchard House, 1998b)
- *Lovejoy's Two-Year College Guide* (Straughn, 1997b)
- *Peterson's Two-Year Colleges* (Peterson's Publishing, 2003b)

Representative software:

- State career information delivery systems (CIDS)
- *CHOICES* (Bridges, 2000a)
- *DISCOVER* (ACT, 2000a)

3. Four-year colleges and universities. These come in many sizes and types. They may be funded by private or public funds, may be liberal arts colleges or universities, may be church-related or not, and may have a wide range of admission standards. They also have a wide variety of majors, and different schools have outstanding programs in specific areas.

Representative print resources:

- *Black American Colleges and Universities: Profiles of Two-Year, Four-Year, and Professional Schools* (Hill & Wilson, 1994)
- *Chronicle Four-Year College Databook: A Directory of Accredited Four-Year Colleges 2001–2002* (Chronicle Guidance Publications, 2001)
- *College Admissions Data Handbook* (French, 2001)
- *College Planning and Search Handbook* (ACT, 1999)
- *Guide to the Most Competitive Colleges* (Barron's Educational Publications, 2003)
- *Lovejoy's Four-Year College Guide* (Straughn, 1997a)
- *Peterson's Four-Year Colleges 2003* (Peterson's Publishing, 2003a)

Representative software:

- State career information delivery systems (CIDS)
- *CHOICES* (Bridges, 2000a)
- *COIN* (COIN Educational Products, 2000)
- *DISCOVER* (ACT, 2000a)

Representative Web sites:

- CollegeNET: http://collegenet.com
- COOL: College Opportunities Online:http://nces.ed.gov/ipeds/cool
- Go College: http://www.gocollege.com
- Peterson's Education Center: http://www.petersons.com
- Yahoo, HigherEducation: http://www.yahoo.com/education/higher_education
- *U.S. News and World Report:* http://www.usnews.com.

4. Graduate schools. These include universities offering master's degrees, certificates of advanced study, and doctorates, as well as schools of medicine, dentistry, veterinary science, and pharmacy.

Representative print resources:

- *Barron's Guide to Medical and Dental Schools* (Wischnitzer & Wischnitzer, 1997)
- *Insider's Guide to Graduate Programs in Clinical and Counseling Psychology* (Mayne, Norcross, & Sayette, 2002)
- *Official American Bar Association Guide to Approved Law Schools* (Margolis, 2002)
- *The Best Distance Learning Graduate Schools: Earning Your Degree Without Leaving Home* (Phillips & Yager, 1998)
- *The Best Medical Schools* (Stoll & Bilstein, 2000)
- *The Best 80 Business Schools* (Gilbert, 2000)
- *The Best Graduate Business Schools* (Bachhuber, 1999)
- *The Best Graduate Programs: Engineering* (Kolberg, 1998)

Representative software:

- State career information delivery systems (CIDS)
- *CHOICES* (Bridges, 2000a)
- *COIN* (COIN Educational Products, 2000)
- *DISCOVER* (ACT, 2000a)

Representative Web sites:

- Peterson's Education Center: http://www.petersons.com
- *U.S. News and World Report*: http://www.usnews.com

Financial Aid

Many students need financial aid in order to pursue the type of education they would like to have. Most schools use a federally established formula for determining whether a family or independent student needs financial assistance. This formula is embodied in the *Free Application for Federal Student Aid (FAFSA)*, a form that students and parents complete and submit for processing. It is available in print form from high school counselors or college financial aid officers and on the Internet at http://www.ed.gov/prog_info/SFA/StudentGuide. Completing the form results in a number, called the *expected family contribution*, which reveals the dollar figure that a family (or an independent student not supported by family) is considered capable of contributing toward a year of college. The formula used in FAFSA can be summarized as follows:

Total cost of one year at college minus Expected Family Contribution for one year equals Unmet need.

Using this general formula, note these two examples:

$25,000 (expensive college)	$12,000 (less expensive college)
$14,600 (parent contribution)	$14,600 (parent contribution)
$10,400 (unmet need)	$0 (unmet need)

The college financial aid officer at the expensive college would try to provide financial assistance to the student who filed this application in the amount of the *unmet need*, that is, $10,400. This amount may be awarded from three kinds of resources: private, state, or federal grants funds; federal loan funds; and/or part-time work on campus. Money allocated from the first source would not have to be repaid. Loans, however, would have to be repaid. Typically, repayment starts after graduation and entry into a job, and the rate of interest is reasonable.

High school counselors and college financial aid officers know about many hidden sources of financial aid information. These may be grants from community organizations, professional associations, companies, and individuals who have set up trust funds for this purpose. Further, many types of financial aid are provided by the state and federal government. In addition to learning about private sources on the job, counselors find the following resources to be valuable.

Representative print resources:

- *Barron's Complete College Financing Guide* (Dennis, 1997)
- *College Board Scholarship Handbook* (College Entrance Examination Board, 1997)
- *College Financial Aid for Dummies* (Davis & Kennedy, 1999)
- *Paying for College Without Going Broke* (Chaney and Martz, 2003)
- *The Big Book of Minority Opportunities* (Oakes, 1997)

Representative software:

- State career information delivery systems (CIDS)
- *CHOICES* (Bridges, 2000a)
- *COIN* (COIN Educational Products, 2000)
- *DISCOVER* (ACT, 2000a)
- *Financial Aid Search* (Chronicle Guidance Publications, 2000b)

Representative Web sites:

- *U.S. News and World Report*: http://www.usnews.com
- United States Department of Education: http://www.ed.gov
- National Association of Financial Aid Administrators: http://www.finaid.org

Information about financial aid is relevant at Step 6 of the career planning process.

Jobs

In many settings counselors assist students and clients to write resumes, learn job-interviewing skills, and identify job openings, activities related to Step 7 of the career planning process. Many good books and Web sites exist to assist with this step.

The U.S. Employment Service Web site is so important that it is singled out for description. This extensive site combines the databases of the state Job Service offices of all 50 states, merging and updating them each night. Two sites, merged into one, are called *America's Job Bank* and *America's Talent Bank*, available at http://www.ajb.dni.us. The jobs listed in America's Job Bank are entered on-line by employers on a daily basis. The people listed in America's Talent Bank are individuals who register, without charge, on this site. Job seekers may search the database describing hundreds of thousands of jobs by type of work, geographic location, keywords, occupational codes, or military specialty (for those leaving military service). They may also post their resumés by entering data on an on-line resume form. If users release an e-mail address, they automatically receive an e-mail notification when a new job matching their specifications is placed in the database. Data about job openings are not published in print form because there is constant change. Thus, the best sources in this category are the state Employment Service offices (also called Job Service offices, or one-stop centers), private employment agencies, and Web sites.

Representative software:

- ALEX, a system available in the local Employment Service (Job Service) offices in each state. Consult the telephone directory to find nearby offices.

Representative Web sites:

- America's Job Bank: http://www.ajb.dni.us
- CareerBuilder: http://www.careerbuilder.com
- NationJob: http://www.nationjob.com
- MonsterBoard: http://www.monsterboard.com
- Richard Bolles's site: http://www.jobhuntersbible.com
- The Riley Guide: http://www.dbm.com/jobguide

OTHER METHODS OF COLLECTING DATA

The previous section focused on collecting data to inform the decision making process through reading books or computer databases. Reading the resources listed in this chapter will be very helpful to support Steps 3 (identify occupational alternatives), 4 (collect data), 5 (make tentative choices), 6 (make educational choices), and 7 (implement a vocational choice). However, it will be even more helpful at Step 5 (make tentative choices) to collect data from additional sources, including career days, job shadowing, part-time jobs, and internships.

Career days, commonly offered in high schools, expose students to a wide variety of occupations through direct contact with people who work in those occupations. Speakers may be brought into the school, or students may be taken to workplaces. In either case the experience will have greater meaning if (a) the occupations are categorized in some meaningful way and (b) there has been some prior activity that suggests specific occupations for exploration. The occupations represented in the career fair may be organized by the six Holland or ACT clusters. Assessment may have been administered to identify two of the students' preferred clusters. Students are then scheduled to hear speakers or visit sites that represent those clusters.

In job shadowing, arrangements are made for students to spend a day with a person in an occupation they are considering. This firsthand experience allows students to view day-to-day activities of the occupation, experience a typical worksite, and ask questions of a person in the occupation. Part-time jobs, carefully chosen, can offer the same kind of experience for a longer period of time. At the college level, students may apply for an internship in an occupation of their choice. An internship allows students to take coursework and work part-time simultaneously. Students receive pay for the work and may also receive college credit.

These methods of providing on-site exploration of occupations can be very valuable when well supported. First, they need to be well planned and organized so that students with specific interests are matched with people and sites that represent those interests. Second, students should be prepared for the experience in advance. Such preparation would include explaining the purpose of the experience and providing worksheets or guidelines for what the student should learn. It is as valuable to find out that interest in the occupation is not confirmed as it is to find out that there is interest in that occupation. Finally, as with all kinds of data collection, there should be a follow-through activity, either individual or group, that helps students analyze what they have learned and what the learning means for personal decision making or further exploration.

ORGANIZING OCCUPATIONS

As mentioned earlier, nearly 13,000 occupations are described in the *Dictionary of Occupational Titles* (U.S. Department of Labor, 1991) and 1122 groups of occupations are detailed in the *Dictionary's* replacement, called O*Net. This vast difference in number of occupations exists because *The Dictionary of Occupational Titles (DOT)* breaks occupations into finer divisions; for example, the DOT describes multiple types of cooks (fast-food cook, pastry cook, pizza cook, etc.), whereas O*Net provides a general description of cook.

Even with the smaller number of 1122 occupations, it is necessary to present these to career planners in some organized way. It is impossible to learn about all occupations individually, and providing information about groups of occupations allows students and clients to narrow their search to specific groups prior to getting into great detail. There are five common organizational systems used in schools and agencies: Holland's system (Holland, 1997), ACT's classification system (Prediger, 1981), the Department of Labor system used in the *Guide to Occupational Exploration*, the Department of Labor O*Net system, and the U.S. Department of Education career clusters. Each is briefly described.

The Holland System

Holland's theory (1997) proposes that work environments can be described as combinations of six different types: Realistic, Investigative, Artistic, Social, Enterprising, and Conventional. Definitions of these six types are provided in Chapter 2. Based on more than 30 years of research, Holland and his collaborators have provided three-letter Holland codes for most occupations. *The Occupations Finder* (Holland, 1994a) provides codes for hundreds of occupations; the *Dictionary of Holland Occupational Codes* (Gottfredson & Holland, 1996) provides codes for thousands of occupations. As reviewed in Chapter 5, taking one of several inventories of interests and/or skills will provide a personal Holland code for a student or client. Use of such assessment will make it easy for counselors to recommend, or students to choose, speakers or sites that are most likely to be of interest to them.

The World-of-Work Map

Based on the research done by Holland while employed by ACT, the original hexagonal model was expanded to a circle called the World-of-Work Map (Figure 6.1). In addition to changing the hexagon to a circle, the six Holland personality types describing characteristics of people were changed to titles for six groups of occupations that provide work tasks and environments that the persons of a given Holland type would be likely to enjoy. Further, the concept of primary work tasks—that is, working with People, Data, Things, and/or Ideas—was added based on further research (Prediger, 1981). Thus, the Holland types have the following equivalents on the World-of-Work Map:

Holland type	ACT occupational cluster	Primary work tasks
Social	Social Service	Work with People
Enterprising	Administration/Sales	Work with People and Data
Conventional	Business Organization	Work with Data and Things
Realistic	Technical	Work with Things
Investigative	Science and Technology	Work with Things and Ideas
Artistic	Arts	Work with Ideas and People

Finally, ACT's research identified 26 families of occupations called *career areas,* groups of homogenous occupations, based on their work tasks. These 26 families were plotted on the Map based on the degree to which the occupations in the family require work with data, people, things, or ideas. On a horizontal continuum through the Map, those families that require relatively more contact with people are placed to the left of center, and those requiring more work with things/equipment are plotted to the right of center. On a vertical continuum through the Map, those families that require relatively more work with data are plotted above the center line of the Map, and those requiring relatively more work with ideas are plotted below the center line of the Map.

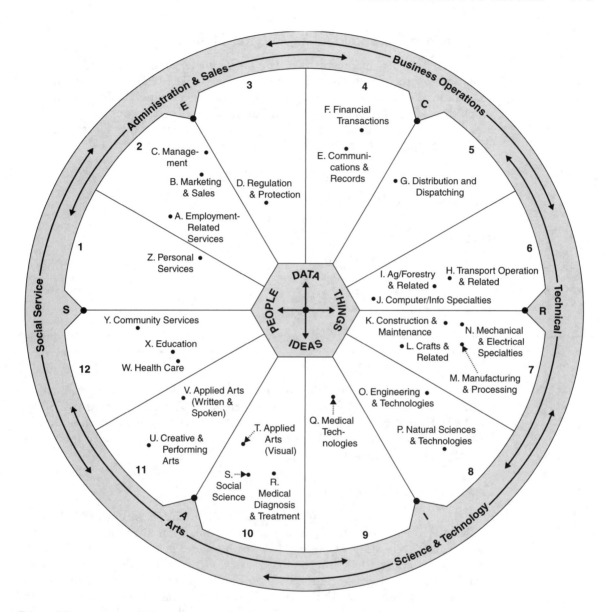

Figure 6.1

World-of-work map. *Source:* Copyright © 2001 by ACT, Inc. All rights reserved. Used by permission.

Using *Career Area Charts* (ACT, 2000b), it is possible to find out where more than 500 common occupations are plotted on the Map. Using *DISCOVER* (ACT, 2000a), it is possible to determine where almost 300 majors are plotted on the Map. Using ACT's career planning assessment or *DISCOVER*, it is possible to plot individuals on the Map based on their interests, and/or self-estimated abilities, and/or values. High schools, vocational-technical schools, and colleges can relate their majors to the 26 career areas, and thus, to occupations.

The Guide to Occupational Exploration Clusters

As indicated earlier in this chapter, *The Guide to Occupational Exploration* is a publication of the U.S. Employment Service (USES). The *Guide* organizes and lists occupations in 12 clusters (see page 9 of the *Guide*). Further, it lists industries in which these occupations can be found. Besides the 12 broad groups into which occupations are categorized, each of those groups has subgroups, as illustrated in the following example for Group 7, Business Detail:

07	Business Detail
07.01	Administrative Detail
07.02	Mathematical Detail
07.03	Financial Detail
07.04	Oral Communications
07.05	Records Processing
07.06	Clerical Machine Operation
07.07	Clerical Handling

This system represents a third system that could be used for organizing occupational files, career days, and job-shadowing experiences. The U.S. Employment Service has the USES Interest Inventory, which measures interests related to each of these 12 broad groups. Clearly, this would be the interest assessment of choice if this organizational scheme were used.

O*Net Classification System

O∗Net is still relatively new, a pilot version having been released in 1997. This system has potential to become a prominent system due to the richness of the database that is being developed. As mentioned earlier, it offers a description of 1122 occupations related to the content and context of work. Occupations are described by more than 300 characteristics, including worker requirements, knowledge areas needed, basic and cross-functional skills needed, education requirements, experience, and training. A skills search allows individuals to assess their own skills and to relate them to occupations in the database.

U.S. Department of Education Career Clusters

The U.S. Department of Education has established 16 broad career clusters. Each cluster consists of entry-level through professional-level occupations in a broad industry area. The cluster also includes the academic and technical skills and knowledge needed for further education and work in the occupations contained in the cluster. Descriptions of these clusters are available at http://www.careerclusters.org.

THE CAREER CENTER

The resources cited in this chapter and many others—including videos, journals, books, assessment instruments, and a variety of software programs—need to be housed in some physical place, typically called a *career center*. This physical place should be of sufficient size to handle the collection, be an attractive place to read or use computers, be centrally located within the larger facility, and be well organized. Especially given the growing importance of Web sites as providers of career data, the center needs to contain computers both for the use of locally resident software and for linkage to the Internet. It also needs to contain equipment for viewing videos and taking assessment instruments.

There are various methods of organizing materials in a career center: (1) by type (print, video, software locally used, Internet access); (2) by content (self-information, occupational information, school information, financial aid information, etc.); (3) by step of the career planning process (see model on p. 149); or (4) by life role (student, worker, parent, leisurite, citizen, etc.).

Career centers should be staffed with one or more trained persons who have extensive content knowledge of all of their resources. In recognition of the need for trained personnel to work in career centers in support of counselors and clients, the National Occupational Information Coordinating Committee (NOICC) funded the development of a curriculum in the early 1990s for training paraprofessionals. This new occupation has been titled career development facilitator (CDF). The curriculum addresses 12 basic competencies that these paraprofessionals need, including basic helping skills, knowledge of labor market and occupational information, job-seeking skills, and ability to navigate computer-based systems and Web sites. Upon successful completion of this curriculum and application to the Center for Credentialing and Education (CCE), individuals can be certified. Trained CDFs can help students and clients acquire data to assist with career planning. Counselors need to assume responsibility for assisting students and clients in processing and making effective use of those data for personal decision making.

Virtual career centers are increasingly being developed on the Internet. Typically, these contain a combination of on-line assessments, locally developed databases (such as descriptions of majors available at a given institution), linkages to a selected and organized list of Web sites, and support from a counselor via the Internet. Such support may be by synchronous (both persons at the computer at the same time) or asynchronous (persons not at the machine at the same time) e-mail or video conferencing. With the rapidly expanding technology that allows images to be transmitted in real time, it has become feasible for counselors and clients to have real-time, face-to-face conversation via the Internet, removing the barrier of distance.

HELPING CLIENTS TURN DATA INTO INFORMATION

The most difficult and also most essential role of the counselor is to assist students and clients to make sense out of what can be an overload of data about occupations, schools and other training opportunities, financial aid, and so on. The goal is to use the data to make it clear which of the various alternatives (about occupational choice, type of training or school, scholarships available, and/or jobs to apply for) should be further explored and which should be removed from consideration. This section of the chapter illustrates how counselors can perform this essential work and offers two case studies.

Chris is a high school junior who feels pressured both by his counselor and his parents to state an occupational goal and an educational plan. As a part of some special career guidance activities the counselors are doing in English classes, he spent 2 hours in the school's career center. While there he took an interest inventory included in a computer-based career planning system, which provided a printout with the titles of 48 occupations. At the direction of the paraprofessional in the center, he found many facts about 12 of these occupations through reading reference books, using the computer system's database, and linking to some sites on the Internet. As a result, he has 34 pages of printout and feels more confused about his possible choice of occupation than he did when he came into the center. Fortunately, he is going to have an interview with his counselor; he hopes that she can help him out of his confusion.

In this typical case, what can a counselor do to provide helpful assistance that will cut through this pile of paper and help the student move to some certainty about next career planning steps? Here are some suggestions:

- If the student has taken the interest inventory only in the computer-based system, the counselor should consider what other kind(s) of assessment, if any, might be helpful in this specific case. Since Chris is a high school junior, an assessment of values might be premature. A simple checklist of job characteristics, from which Chris is asked to select 5 to 10 items that are most important, would be one good approach.
- The counselor may ask Chris to tell about some of the most interesting courses, experiences, or leisure activities he has had and ask why he found these interesting, relating these reasons to characteristics of occupations.
- A review of Chris's high school record may help him identify some courses and abilities that surpass others. The counselor may also ask him about his plans or aspirations for education after high school.
- Chris may be asked to list occupations about which he has daydreamed in the past and tell what was attractive to him about these, even though he may not know the details of the work tasks or training. From this activity and previous ones, he can make a list of characteristics (such as having a lot of independence, making more than the average amount of money, not having to travel long distances as a requirement of work, or not working with numbers and mathematics) of importance to him.
- Chris could share the list of occupations identified by the interest inventory he took on the computer, relating which, if any, of these occupational titles were attractive to him, and why. He could state which, if any, of these he would not consider and why, and compare the characteristics of occupations on the list with the personal list he has just developed.

- Using the list from the computer and any others that may have been added during interviews, Chris might be asked to place the titles in three columns: those he would definitely not pursue, those that hold some promise, and those that he is favoring most.

- Chris should be given assignments designed to help him learn more about the list of occupations he is favoring most. This may initially include further research in the career center, using books, software, or Internet sites, depending on whether Chris has already adequately researched the favored occupations in this way. Additional activities may be designed to put Chris directly in touch with people who work in this occupation. This may be a job-shadowing assignment or an information interview with one or more persons who work in each of these occupations. He should be given a worksheet as a part of the assignment to assure that he collects the data that he needs. This worksheet should include questions that he suggests as well as the ordinary ones, such as benefits and limitations of the job, training required, opportunities for promotion, degree of independence, and what the person wishes he or she had known before entering the occupation.

- Following this assignment, Chris should be scheduled for another interview to discuss what he has learned from these assignments. He may analyze each of the occupations he has researched further by the list of important characteristics developed in the previous session and write down his current list of preferred occupations in priority order. He should be aware that he will make numerous career changes during his lifetime and that he should consider and be prepared for more than one occupation.

- With a short list of occupations in mind, Chris and his counselor should review the amount and type of education needed for these jobs and determine whether they all require the same level of education, such as community college or 4-year college, or whether some could be entered through apprenticeship. Based on this review, Chris may be able to select a postsecondary educational goal. This might be an ideal time to include his parents in the discussion of his goals.

- Dependent upon the postsecondary plans, Chris may be directed to other resources (computer searches, Web sites, books) that will assist with the selection of schools in which the needed training can be acquired. The counselor can provide a worksheet that lists the characteristics (such as geographic location, size of school, level of admission selectivity, type of school, cost range, student activities, etc.) that he and his parents can consider. He also needs to determine how various selections (such as how large the school is or how far away from home it is) will affect him and his parents.

- The counselor may help Chris select the most relevant courses for his senior year and to make a timetable for coming back to talk about school selection, taking entrance tests, and filing applications for entry and financial aid.

This suggested approach combines good use of technology for acquiring data with counselor support for processing the data in a way that helps Chris and his parents make informed decisions.

As indicated at the beginning of this chapter, Clarice is a 28-year-old single parent of three children who lives in a modest apartment and receives support from public aid. Recent legislation, however, has mandated that she go to work within a year and provides access to funding for some training. She dropped out of high school in her sophomore year after her first child was born. She has held part-time jobs at various fast-food restaurants since that time. Clarice goes to a no-fee community agency for assistance in determining what she can do to meet the requirements of the legislation.

What can a counselor do? Here are some suggestions:

- An extensive intake interview is a needed first step. During this interview, the counselor can learn about high school courses taken, expressed interests, motivational level, skills, details of part-time jobs, family situation, support system (network of friends and family), barriers (such as physical handicaps, need for child care, and lack of transportation), and goals.
- The counselor might decide to administer some assessment, such as an interest inventory (to broaden the options that the client may have expressed). From the list of occupations suggested by this inventory and the intake interview, the counselor and client can develop a list of reasonable (in terms of the amount of training needed) options. Clarice and the counselor make a list of five characteristics that are most important for the occupation to be selected: (1) does not require more than 2 years of training beyond high school completion, (2) does not require work during the evening or on weekends, (3) offers an opportunity to work directly with people and with equipment, (4) offers an opportunity for career growth when additional education can be attained when children are older, and (5) offers a beginning salary of at least $25,000 per year.
- The counselor asks Clarice to go to the local library and access *The Occupational Outlook Handbook* and *CareerInfoNet* to learn details about the identified occupations. Clarice has not used the Internet before, so the counselor provides a worksheet with step-by-step instructions about how to access each of these sites and how to find the assigned information. Further, the counselor instructs the client to go to a specific person at the library to receive some general instruction about how to use the equipment and how to obtain assistance that may be needed in completing the assignment. The counselor asks Clarice to bring the printout to the next session or good, detailed notes if the library charges for printed pages and the cost of this is not feasible for the client.
- Clarice completes the assignment and comes back the next week with printouts, descriptions of several occupations that require high school completion and training beyond that. The counselor helps Clarice evaluate each of the occupations in relation to the five criteria developed during the intake interview. Three occupations pass that review: radiation therapist, dental assistant, and dental hygienist. According to *CareerInfoNet*, there is a high demand for workers in all three of these occupations in Clarice's state of residence, and beginning salaries for all three are above $25,000.
- The counselor suggests that Clarice complete two homework assignments before the next session: (1) have an informational interview with a person in each of these

three occupations and (2) investigate sources of getting a high school diploma by taking the General Educational Development (GED) exam. The counselor explains what an information interview is and gives Clarice a list of suggested questions to which she can add others. The counselor makes some phone calls and sets up these three interviews at times when Clarice's mother will care for the youngest child. The counselor also gives Clarice the URL address of the Web site of the state labor department. One section of this site provides a list of opportunities for completing the GED exam.

- Clarice returns after completion of these assignments with enthusiasm about the opportunity to prepare for taking the GED exam through a course offered by the local community college. Her mother has agreed to stay with the children one night per week so that she can attend this course. Further, she indicates that, based on the visits she has made, she would like to pursue training to become an X-ray technician.

- The counselor works with Clarice, using a specific form, to develop an action plan and a time schedule designed to accomplish two primary goals: (1) getting a high school diploma by preparing to take the GED exam and (2) seeking entry into the X-ray technician program at the community college. The plan includes funding by the agency for the GED preparation course and coursework in the X-ray technician program at the community college. The plan also includes child care during class times and transportation to the community college. The counselor invites Clarice to call her at any time and indicates that she should call each month to make an appointment so that they can review progress in completion of the action plan.

SUMMARY

This chapter has described various types of resources available in print and electronic form that are critical sources of data as individuals engage in the career planning process. The responsibilities of counselors in selecting and using these resources wisely are reviewed. Similarly, the responsibilities of students and clients to spend the time and effort needed to acquire data are reviewed. Great emphasis is placed upon the fact that providing good data to students and clients is not in and of itself sufficient to ensure that career decision making will be informed. The counselor's responsibility and role to help students and clients sort through a mass of data and transform elements of it into meaningful information is stressed. Finally, two cases have been presented with suggestions about how a counselor might deal with them.

REFERENCES

ACT, Inc. (1989a). *Inventory of Work-Relevant Abilities*. Iowa City, IA: Author.

ACT, Inc. (1989b). *UNIACT Interest Inventory*. Iowa City, IA: Author.

ACT, Inc. (1997a). *The Career Planning Survey*. Iowa City, IA: Author.

ACT, Inc. (1997b). *Counseling for high skills* [Computer software]. Iowa City, IA: Author.

ACT, Inc. (1999). *The college planning and search handbook*. Iowa City, IA: Author.

ACT, Inc. (2000a). *DISCOVER* [Computer software]. Iowa City, IA: Author.

ACT, Inc. (2000b). *Career area charts*. Iowa City, IA: Author.

Bachhuber, T. (1999). *The best graduate business schools*. Lawrenceville, NJ: Arco.

Barron's Educational Publications. (2003). *Guide to the most competitive colleges*. Hauppauge, NY: Author.

Bridges, Inc. (2000a). *CHOICES* [Computer software]. Kelowna, British Columbia: Author.

Bridges, Inc. (2000b). *Career futures for middle schools*. Kelowna, British Columbia: Author.

Bridges, Inc. (2000c). *Paws in jobland*. Kelowna, British Columbia: Author.

Campbell, D. (1992). *Campbell Interest and Skill survey*. Minneapolis, MN: NCS Assessments.

Cantor, J. A. (1997). *Cooperative apprenticeships: A school-to-work handbook*. Kent, England: Scarecrow Press.

Chaney, K. A., & Martz, G. (2003). *Paying for college without going broke*. New York: Princeton Review.

Chronicle Guidance Publications. (1998a). *Four-year college level careers, occupational briefs*. Moravia, NY: Author.

Chronicle Guidance Publications. (1998b). *Two-year college level careers, occupational briefs*. Moravia, NY: Author.

Chronicle Guidance Publications. (1998c). *Vocational-school level careers, occupational briefs*. Moravia, NY: Author.

Chronicle Guidance Publications. (2000a). *Chronicle perspectives plus*. Moravia, NY: Author.

Chronicle Guidance Publications. (2000b). *Financial aid search* [Computer software]. Moravia, NY: Author.

Chronicle Guidance Publications. (2001). *Chronicle four-year college databook: A directory of accredited four-year colleges*. Moravia, NY: Author.

COIN Educational Products. (2000). *COIN* [Computer software]. Toledo, OH: Author.

College Entrance Examination Board. (1997). *College board scholarship handbook*. New York: Author.

Davis, H., & Kennedy, J. L. (1999). *College financial aid for dummies*. New York: Hungry Minds, Inc.

Dennis, M. J. (1997). *Barron's complete college financing guide*. Hauppauge, NY: Barron's Educational Publications.

Dinklage, L. B. (1968). *Decision strategies of adolescents*. Unpublished doctoral dissertation, Harvard University, Cambridge, MA.

Farr, M. J. (Ed.). (2001). *Guide for occupational exploration system*. Indianapolis, IN: JIST Works.

French, K. I. (Ed). (2001). *College admissions data handbook*. Itasca, IL: Wintergreen-Orchard House.

Gilbert, N. (2000). *The best 80 business schools*. New York: Princeton Review.

Gottfredson, G. D., & Holland, J. L. (1996). *The dictionary of Holland occupational codes*. Odessa, FL: Psychological Assessment Resources.

Harrington, T., & O' Shea, A. J. (2000). *Career decision-making system*. Circle Pines, MN: American Guidance Service.

Hill, L., & Wilson, R. (Eds.). (1994). *Black American colleges and universities: Profiles of two-year, four-year, and professional schools*. Farmington Hills, MI: Gale Group.

Holland, J. L. (1994a). *The occupations finder*. Odessa, FL: Psychological Assessment Resources.

Holland, J. L. (1994b). *The Self-Directed Search*™. Odessa, FL: Psychological Assessment Resources.

Holland, J. L. (1997). *Making vocational choices: A theory of vocational personalities and work environments* (3rd ed.). Odessa, FL: Psychological Assessment Resources.

Holmberg, K., Rosen, D., & Holland, J. L. (1999). *The leisure activities finder*. Odessa, FL: Psychological Assessment Resources.

J. G. Ferguson Publishing. (2003). *Career discovery encyclopedia* (8 vols). Chicago, IL: Author.

Johansson, C. B. (1984). *Career Assessment Inventory*. Minneapolis, MN: NCS Assessments.

Kolberg, S. (1998). *The best graduate programs: Engineering*. New York: Princeton Review.

Krumboltz, J. D. (1991). *The Career Beliefs Inventory*. Palo Alto, CA: Consulting Psychologists Press.

Kuder, F., & Zytowski, D. (1999). *The Kuder career search*. Adel, IA: National Career Assessment Services, Inc.

Landes, M. (2002). *The back door guide to short-term job adventures: Internships, extraordinary experiences, seasonal jobs, volunteering, work abroad*. Berkeley, CA: Ten Speed Press.

MacDonald-Murray, M. (2001). *College admission index of majors and sports*. Itasca, IL: Wintergreen-Orchard House.

Margolis, W. (Ed.). (2002). *Official American Bar Association guide to approved law schools*. Lawrenceville, NJ: Arco.

Mayne, T. J., Norcross, J. G., & Sayette, M. A. (2002). *Insider's guide to graduate programs in clinical and counseling psychology*. New York: Guilford Press.

Maze, M., & Mayall, D. (Eds.). (1995). *Enhanced guide for occupational exploration*. Indianapolis, IN: JIST Publishing.

Morgan, R. E., Hunt, S., & Carpenter, J. M. (1990). *Classification of instructional programs*. Washington, DC: U.S. Government Printing Office.

Morkes, A. (Ed.). (2003). *Encyclopedia of career and vocational guidance*. Chicago, IL: J. G. Ferguson.

National Career Development Association. (1991). *Guidelines for the preparation and evaluation of career and occupational information literature*. Alexandria, VA: Author.

*O*Net dictionary of occupational titles*. (1998a). Indianapolis, IN: JIST Publishers.

*O*Net dictionary of occupational titles*. (1998b). Moravia, NY: Chronicle Guidance Publications.

Oakes, E. (Ed.). (1997). *The big book of minority opportunities*. Chicago, IL: J. G. Ferguson.

Oldman, M., & Hamadeh, S. (2000). *America's top internships*. New York: Princeton Review.

Peterson's Publishing. (2000). *2000 internships: The largest source of internships available*. Lawrenceville, NJ: Author.

Peterson's Publishing. (2003a). *Peterson's four-year colleges 2003*. Lawrenceville, NJ: Author.

Peterson's Publishing. (2003b). *Peterson's two-year colleges 2003*. Lawrenceville, NJ: Author.

Phillips, V., & Yager, C. (1998). *The best distance learning graduate schools: Earning your degree without leaving home*. New York: Princeton Review.

Prediger, D. P. (1981). Aid for mapping occupations and interests: A graphic for vocational guidance and research. *Vocational Guidance Quarterly, 30*, 21–36.

Rosen, D., Holmberg, K., & Holland, J. L. (1999). *The educational opportunities finder*. Odessa, FL: Psychological Assessment Resources.

Sampson, J. P., Peterson, G., Lenz, J., Reardon, R., & Saunders, D. (1996). Negative thinking and career choice. In R. Feller & G. Walz (Eds.), *Career transitions in turbulent times* (pp. 323–330). Greensboro, NC: ERIC/CASS Publications.

Stoll, M., & Bilstein, P. (2000). *The best medical schools*. New York: Princeton Review.

Straughn, C. T. (1997a). *Lovejoy's four-year college guide* (24th ed.). New York: Hungry Minds.

Straughn, C. T. (1997b). *Lovejoy's two-year college guide* (24th ed.). New York: Hungry Minds.

Tiedeman, D., & O'Hara, R. (1963). *Career development: Choice and adjustment*. New York: College Entrance Examination Board.

U.S. Department of Defense. (2000). *America's top military careers: The official guide to occupations in the armed forces*. Washington, DC: U.S. Government Printing Office.

U.S. Department of Labor. (1991). *The Dictionary of occupational titles*. Washington, DC: U.S. Government Printing Office.

U.S. Department of Labor. (1992). *What work requires of schools*. SCANS Report. Washington, DC: U.S. Government Printing Office.

U.S. Department of Labor. (2002a). *The occupational outlook handbook*. Washington, DC: U.S. Government Printing Office.

U.S. Department of Labor. (2002b). *Young person's occupational outlook handbook*. Washington, DC: Author.

U.S. Department of Labor. *Occupational outlook quarterly*. Washington, DC: U.S. Government Printing Office.

Wintergreen-Orchard House. (1998a). *Major decisions: A guide to college majors*. Itasca, IL: Author.

Wintergreen-Orchard House. (1998b). *Guide to technical, trade, and business schools*. Itasca, IL: Author.

Wischnitzer, S., & Wischnitzer, E. (1997). *Barron's guide to medical and dental schools*. Hauppauge, NY: Barron's Educational Publishers.

CHAPTER 7

Using Technology to Support Career Counseling and Planning

Technology changes lives. For some, the changes are better; for others the changes are perceived as negative. In many ways, career counselors have been at the forefront of changes in society and mental health. They have been among the first to use new tools and techniques in their work. Nowhere has this been truer than in the use of technology. The use of computers and, more recently, the Internet have changed the ways in which career counselors assist their clients. Though career counselors are, first and foremost, counselors, they are also providers of information. The provision of information when assisting clients with resumé writing, interview coaching, networking, and choosing education and training venues has been made better, faster, and more comprehensive through the Internet. Career counselors are now able to devote more time to counseling and coaching their clients while being able to quickly and easily locate information that supports their work. Popular Web sites have come and gone. But in the 10 years since the Internet became mainstream, it has significantly changed the way career counselors do their work. Now there is no going back. We must learn to use technology in order to be effective and in order to provide our clients with the service they need and expect.

David M. Reile, Ph.D., NCCC
Career Development Leadership Alliance

In Chapter 2 you learned about Juanita, a 17-year-old Hispanic student in the 11th grade who appears to be struggling with poor self-concept, low motivation, low career maturity, lack of role models, and other factors related to making an informed vocational choice. Using one or more theoretical models presented earlier in the text, Juanita's counselor dealt with these factors through one-to-one and small-group interventions. After noting positive change in self-concept, motivation, and career maturity, the high school counselor decided to give Juanita some specific assignments related to the computer-based career planning system that the school has as well as use of several Web sites. You will note those assignments as you read this chapter.

The purposes of this chapter are to define and describe the primary technologies that have an impact on the delivery of career planning services in the 21st century and to propose how they can best be used to enhance the delivery of career planning services. It is an understandable tendency to confine our perception of technology to that provided by the computer or the Internet. Actually, the field of career planning has been impacted by technologies other than the computer—the test-scoring machine, the video camera, and the telephone, for example. Computers, however, have exerted the most powerful impact on the field because of their capabilities to administer, score, and interpret tests and inventories; teach skills and concepts; facilitate interactive dialogue; store, search, and interrelate huge databases; store a record of the user's interaction; and prompt and monitor a user's interaction with the system.

These computer capabilities have been progressively developed and applied to the field of career counseling and support since the late 1960s. This chapter reviews that historical sequence, resulting in descriptions of three different kinds of systems: (1) career planning and information systems on stand-alone and networked computers, (2) career planning and information sites on the Internet, and (3) supportive cybercounseling and assistance offered via the Internet. This progression of the use of computer-based technology can be viewed in the light of two different contexts. The first context relates to the ever-growing capability of computers progressing from early, stand-alone mainframe computers to networked mini- and personal computers to the World Wide Web of computers, with each of these progressive steps offering the opportunity to serve an increased number of individuals.

The second context is the growing awareness and body of research that informs counselors and their managers about the effectiveness of computer-delivered services for different populations and for different purposes. This chapter attempts to show the progression within both of these contexts in describing more than 35 years of development in this field and making some predictions about a possible future.

COMPUTER-ASSISTED CAREER GUIDANCE SYSTEMS

A computer-assisted career guidance system (often called a CACGS) is a group of activities, delivered by computer, designed to help with one or more steps of the career planning process. A less comprehensive system may, for example, administer an interest inventory, interpret it, and suggest a list of occupations. A very comprehensive system includes content and activities related to all or most steps of the career planning process, including assessment, search strategies for occupations, occupational information, search strategies for majors and training opportunities, and educational information. It may also include instruction about how occupations can be organized, how to make career decisions, and/or about job-seeking skills. Of course there are systems that fit somewhere between these two examples.

Computer-assisted career guidance systems had their genesis in the late 1960s. The IBM Corporation released the first cathode ray tube in the mid-1960s, moving computers from batch-processing work to the capability of simulating an interactive dialogue between the machine and a user at a terminal device, which, at that time, could be as far as 1000 feet away. This invention prompted several early developers—JoAnn Harris, Joseph Impelleteri, Martin Katz, Donald Super, and David Tiedeman (Super, 1970)—to design systems that could simulate the kind of career counseling interview that a counselor might have with a student or client.

The theorists in the early development group—Katz, Super, and Tiedeman—viewed the computer as a tool that could be used to teach their theories directly to users and hoped that those users would be able to internalize the processes learned. Katz (1963) developed the *System for Interactive Guidance Information (SIGI)* and designed it to teach 10 specific work values (such as prestige, high income, early entry, leisure, leadership, helping others, variety, and security) that he had identified through extensive research; SIGI then assisted the user in assigning each value a level of importance. These weighted values were used to identify occupations from the computer's database that could help the user attain the selected values. Next, test scores measuring the user's abilities were used to estimate the latter's probability of being able to complete the education needed for each of the identified occupations. By multiplying the value of the occupation times the probability of successfully completing the required education, a numerical score could be assigned to each occupation under consideration, ranking them in order of desirability. This early system became the basis for later versions, including the current *SIGI Plus* (Educational Testing Service, 1997) described later in this chapter.

Working as a consultant to the IBM Corporation, Super developed the *Education and Career Exploration System (ECES)*. This system operationalized some parts of Super's theoretical work, specifically the capability to use the results of assessment to identify occupations for exploration and the capability to engage in exploratory behavior by accessing microfilm files of occupational descriptions that included black-and-white pictures of work settings and tasks as well as text. Though this system was a significant one in its theoretical base, it was not taken to market by IBM; instead, it was given to Genessee County, Michigan, the site of its field trial.

David Tiedeman, who had a large grant at Harvard University from the U.S. Office of Education, developed the *Information System for Vocational Decisions (ISVD)*. His goal was to have the computer monitor the user's path through an extensive system and teach his seven-step decision making paradigm (Tiedeman & O'Hara, 1963). In addition to engineering its elegant content design, Tiedeman included two features that were many years ahead of their time: multimedia and natural language capability. The multimedia consisted of the mainframe computer triggering the display of slides by a carousel projector that showed pictures of colleges and occupations. The natural language capability offered the user the opportunity to type in any question or request and have the computer "understand" the meaning sufficiently to provide a logical answer. Due to the great sophistication of this system before technology could support it, it never became operational outside of its developmental setting.

Other developers—practitioners in orientation—developed less elegant systems. At Pennsylvania State University, Impelleteri (1970) developed the *Computer Occupational Information System (COIS)*, which allowed students to explore a variety of vocational-technical programs of study and occupations and make a selection. His untimely death in the early 1970s resulted in the demise of this system. Harris (1970), director of guidance at Willowbrook High School in Illinois, developed the *Computerized Vocational Information System (CVIS)* with funding provided by the Illinois State Board of Vocational Education. This system gave students the opportunity to explore and get information about occupations, colleges, military programs, and apprenticeships. The occupational database was organized by Roe's (1956) classification system, which divides occupations into six educational levels and eight interest fields. Choice of interest field was guided by the results of the Kuder (Science Research Associates, 1968) interest inventory, and selection of educational level was determined by the student. This system also included a variety of on-line capabilities for counselors, including the changing of student schedules and review of student records. CVIS was a precursor to *DISCOVER* (ACT, 2000), a more elegant system described later in this chapter.

In summary, the earliest computer-based systems had several things in common, as follows:

- They were comprehensive career planning systems, offering a planned sequence of activities for the user.
- They were based, at least in part, on the career development theory available at the time—that of Super, Tiedeman, Katz, and Roe.
- They stored a user record so that a summary of a person's use was kept in order to be accessed by a counselor for follow-through work and to allow the user to continue sequentially from past use.
- They implicitly or explicitly taught a decision making process considered by the developer to be the most appropriate for career planning.
- They were supported by external sources of public or private funding.
- They operated on large mainframe computers and, each in its own way, pushed the limit of capabilities of the host machine.

Following these early systems came the era of less-comprehensive information systems. These systems were not based on a theoretical model, did not intend to support the entire career planning process, and focused on databases and search strategies. Bruce McKinlay led the development in this arena with the *Career Information System (CIS)* (University of Oregon, 1997). Coming from the labor market information perspective rather than the career development perspective, *CIS* and other systems that followed it had the occupational database and strategies to search it as their hallmark. In these systems, there was very high concern for the quality and currency of the occupational information. As development continued, these systems were expanded to include multiple databases, including searches for vocational-technical schools, 2-year and 4-year colleges, and financial aid opportunities.

In 1976 a federal organization called the National Occupational Information Coordinating Committee (NOICC) was formed. One of the many initiatives that this organization championed was the development of state *career information delivery systems (CIDS),* computer-based delivery systems that provide occupational and educational information, typically customized for students and adults in a specific state. *CIS* was used, and still is used, as a basis for these systems in many states. Most states have a state career information delivery system that uses *CIS* or various other systems listed later as their base. These systems are supported by a combination of federal funding, state funding, and user fees. These state systems collaborate through a professional association called the Association of Computer-Based Systems for Career Information (ACSCI), which has set standards for their quality and promotes their continual expansion and improvement. Similarly, the National Career Development Association (NCDA) has developed standards (NCDA, 1991) for the quality of computer-assisted systems. These standards are available at these organizations' Web sites—http://www.acsci.org and http://ncda.org.

Characteristics of systems that focus on information are as follows:

- They typically offer multiple databases (occupations, schools, financial aids, etc.), and great care is given to the quality and timeliness of the data.
- They typically provide labor market information (that is, employment outlook and salary) for specific states and regions within the state.
- They typically do not store a user record.
- They do not attempt to provide support to all components (i.e., assessment, instruction, etc.) of the career planning process.
- They are not theory-based, nor do they attempt to teach a planful decision making process.

COMPUTER CAPABILITIES

The sequence of development and use of computer-assisted systems from the late 1960s to the present—spanning the generations of the mainframe, minicomputer, and microcomputer—has identified and confirmed the strengths of computer technology related to assisting people in the career planning process. Those strengths are as follows:

- *Test and inventory administration and interpretation.* Computers can consistently administer inventories of interests, abilities, skills, experiences, personality, values, and so on, and score them, providing a comprehensive printed report. In the multimedia age, they can also enhance items by displaying slides or graphics that help to communicate the meaning of an item.
- *Database searches.* Computers can search large databases of occupations, majors, schools, financial aid opportunities, and military programs quickly, using many different search characteristics in combination. Further, they can display data and provide multimedia treatment (slides, audio, video, graphics) about the options identified in the search. These databases can be updated quickly at periodic intervals—even daily, if the system is connected to an Internet site that maintains them continually.
- *Crosswalking.* Computers are capable of crosswalking, that is, relating one database to another with ease. For example, when users are learning about a specific occupation and its list of related school majors, they might crosswalk to a database of majors to read the descriptions of those related to a given occupation. From the database of majors, the user might select one and crosswalk to the financial aid database to determine if there are scholarship programs for those who pursue this major. Similarly, the user might crosswalk from the database of majors to schools that offer a specific major.
- *Standard delivery.* Computers are uniquely capable of delivering the same service to users at any time from any location that has appropriate technology. The

content is provided in a standard way, though if a record is kept in the computer for each user, this standard content can be customized for each individual based on the results of assessment, past use, identified need, and/or age range. For example, the computer may select different interest inventory items for persons of different age ranges, use different norms tables to score inventories, or display information at different reading levels.

- *Monitoring progress of the user through the career planning process.* By use of a computer-stored record that retains information about users, the computer can monitor a user's progress through the system and report it to those who need to know it, providing an opportunity to link human support services with computer support services.

- *Delivering instruction.* Providing interactive instruction is a computer strength. Examples of instructional topics related to career planning include how to make decisions, how occupations can be organized, how to write an effective resumé, or how to conduct a job interview. The instruction may include the use of graphics, audio, video, interactive activities, and quizzes.

- *Linking resources.* It is possible to expand the user's resources by linking from the career planning software to Web sites or individuals that can provide further information. For example, an occupational description stored within the system may be expanded by a linkage to the description on the U.S. Department of Labor's site called *CareerInfoNet* (http://www.acinet.org). Similarly, a student who is interested in learning more about a particular occupation may be connected by e-mail to alumni or community members who work in that occupation.

ADDING HIGH TOUCH TO HIGH TECH

The list of capabilities just provided is impressive. At first glance, it might appear that computer-assisted systems could provide career planning services without counselor support. There are at least three reasons why this is not the case. First, when students or clients say that they need help with career planning, this statement may be one that masks a variety of other needs and concerns. As a counselor talks with a student or client, these other needs become apparent, if they exist. Obviously, a computer does not have this power of discernment. Second, not all individuals with a primary need for career planning can profit optimally from receiving these services by computer, because everyone has a different learning style and personality type. Further, some clients are not ready to receive information because of a lack of readiness to process it effectively. Third, research (Taber & Luzzo, 1999) designed to determine the best way to deliver career planning services has consistently indicated that the optimal treatment for students/clients is the combination of human support services and computer services. Invaluable responsibilities of counselors include the following:

- Determining the readiness of the person to receive information from a computer and apply it effectively
- Expanding on the interpretation of tests and inventories so that they are more likely to inform the client's decision making appropriately

- Assisting the client to identify the personal values that will guide the reduction of options provided by the computer
- Providing motivation and emotional support for continued work related to career planning
- Suggesting creative alternatives that the computer doesn't "know"

THE INTERNET AS THE DELIVERER OF COMPUTER-ASSISTED SYSTEMS

Most of the computer-assisted systems described next offer a parallel version on the Internet or are in the process of developing one. The Internet as a delivery tool—in contrast to a stand-alone or networked computer—has the following advantages:

- The system is available from home, the library, and many other places on a 24/7 basis.
- There is a potential to serve an incredibly larger audience.
- Databases can be updated more frequently because they are developed and updated from one central source to which all end-user stations are connected.
- Linkage to the resources of the Internet and to e-mail communication can be more seamlessly included in the system.
- Technology now makes it possible for a counselor to communicate with system users, also via the Internet, while they are on-line.

At this time there are also the following disadvantages to using the Internet for delivery of computer-assisted services:

- Access and operation can be slow, depending upon the user's hardware configuration and the traffic on the Web site providing service.
- Bandwidth and other technical concerns make the use of audio and video unwise at this time, though slides, graphics, and very short audio or video clips are feasible.
- The Internet is not a secure environment; thus, user data may not be confidential.

Just as early developers struggled with similar problems in the early years with stand-alone computers until the technology could support development needs, current Internet-delivered systems face these obstacles, which will be solved as the capabilities of the Internet expand.

TYPES OF COMPUTER-ASSISTED SYSTEMS

Computer-assisted systems, whether delivered from a local computer or via the Internet, can be categorized in three types: assessment only, career information systems, and career planning systems. Over time, systems move from one category to another as features are added, and systems may not neatly fit into a category. They are described next, however, as a means of helping the reader make distinctions and recognize differences.

Assessment Systems

These systems administer one or more tests or inventories that measure interests, abilities or skills, personality characteristics, and/or work values and interpret them. Examples include:

- *Kuder Career Search with Person Match*™ (Kuder & Zytowski, 1999), administered from the publisher's Web site (http://www.kuder.com)
- *The Self-Directed Search*™ (Holland, 1994), administered on either a stand-alone or networked computer or from the publisher's Web site (http://www.self-directed-search.com)
- *Campbell Interest and Skill Survey*™ (Campbell, 1992), administered from http://www.profiler.com/ciss
- *SkillScan* (Beckhusen & Gazzano, 1987), administered from http://www.skillscan.net
- *The Strong Interest Inventory* (Strong, 1994), administered from the publisher's Web site at http://www.cpp-com/products/strong/index.html or from that of private practitioners who have arrangements with the publisher
- *The Myers-Briggs Type Indicator*® (Myers & Briggs, 1993), administered on a stand-alone or networked computer or from Web sites of private practitioners who have arrangements with the publisher
- *The Keirsey Character Sorter* (Keirsey, 1999) at http://www.keirsey.com

Career Information Systems

Career information systems or Web sites specialize in databases and searches. The databases may be comprehensive, including occupations, majors, all types of schools, scholarships, apprenticeships, and jobs. Their search strategies typically give the user great flexibility in adding or deleting items used for searching (called *search variables*). It may be possible to enter the results of inventories taken on paper as one method of searching. There are two types of systems:

- *State career information delivery systems (CIDS)*. See the Web site of the Association of Computer-Based Systems for Career Information (http://www.acsci.org) for a complete listing and other information.
- *Commerically available systems*. For descriptions of these systems, use the following Web sites:
  Bridges, http://usa.cx.bridges.com
  Career Information System (CIS), http://oregoncis.uoregon.edu
  Career and College Quest, http://www.petersons.com
  CHOICES, http://www.careerware.com
  Career Perspectives and C_Lect, 101565.1244@compuserv.com (e-mail)
  COIN, http://www.coin3.com
  Focus II, http://www.focuscareer.com

Career Planning Systems

Career planning systems typically include on-line assessment, entry of results of an assessment completed on paper, extensive databases, instruction, interactive activities, and searches. Their hallmark, however, is the monitoring of the career planning process that takes place within the system. Because of that unique feature, these systems are typically based on career theory, keep a record of the details of each person's ongoing use, and provide reports to counselors. The two systems in this category are owned by nonprofit organizations—ACT, Inc., and Educational Testing Service, respectively:

- *DISCOVER* (various versions, including an Internet-delivered version), http://www.act.org
- *SIGI-PLUS* (including an Internet-based version), http://www.ets.org/sigi/

For additional information about Web sites that can be used for career planning, see the NCDA publication *The Internet: A Tool for Career Planning* (Harris-Bowlsbey, Riley-Dikel, & Sampson, 2002). For more detailed information about computer-based systems, see the Web site of the Florida State University Center for the Study of Technology in Counseling and Career Development at http://www.career.fsu.edu/techcenter/. This site offers a comparative study of all computer-assisted career information and planning systems.

CHOOSING A COMPUTER-ASSISTED CAREER GUIDANCE SYSTEM

Counselors are typically included as part of a team to decide which of the systems should be selected for use at their site or if the one presently being used should be replaced by another. In this event, it is necessary to gain in-depth knowledge of each system under consideration. Though presentations made by marketing representatives are helpful, the best ways to gain truly in-depth knowledge are to acquire and read the system's professional manual and then, or simultaneously, to use the entire system as a student would. The topics listed next are critical ones to use as benchmarks while making an evaluation.

- *Theoretical base of the system.* Some systems, such as those that focus on file searches and data displays, are atheoretical; that is, they do not propose any process for career decision making, nor do they offer any content that is related to the work of any specific theorist. Other systems do both; they propose and offer a specific process for career decision making and use the theoretical work of one or more of the theorists included in this text as the basis for that process and/or other content. Clients need to follow a logical process. Counselors need to decide whether the computer will be the presenter and monitor of that process or whether the counselor will play a more active role, using the computer as a support system at points in the process.

- *Presence of on-line inventories and/or the capability to enter the results of assessment taken in print form.* For most clients and students, assessment of interests and skills/abilities—and perhaps also work values—is important. This being the case, counselors need to determine how such assessment will be administered. There are three possibilities, each of which can be used exclusively or combined with another. First, assessment can be administered, scored, and interpreted on-line as a part of a computer-assisted career planning system, an Internet Web site, or by software licensed from a test publisher and resident on a local computer. Second, assessment may be administered in print form and either self-scored (possible for some types of inventories) or sent elsewhere for scoring. In the latter case, the computer-assisted career guidance system may allow individual users to enter their own scores or clerical support persons may enter the results for multiple individuals into the system so that they can be used to assist with their search for occupations. Results of tests and inventories may be provided in electronic form by their publishers, and these data may be accepted and used by the computer-assisted system.

- *Quality and comprehensiveness of databases.* Databases are an essential part of computer-assisted career guidance systems and their quality is critical to the quality of the system. Such quality includes accuracy of descriptions of items in the databases (occupations, schools, financial aids, etc.), sources of data, and currency and frequency of update. Some systems contain only two databases—usually, occupations and schools. The school database may comprise 4-year colleges only or may also include vocational-technical schools, 2-year colleges, and graduate schools. These files may be only for the state of installation, for a geographic region, or for the entire nation. Some systems offer data about 200 to 300 occupations, whereas others include thousands. Some have many databases in addition to occupations and schools, including financial aid, apprenticeships, internships, military occupations, and majors. Some vendors make maximum use of databases developed by reliable government sources, such as the departments of labor, education, and defense; others do not. Some vendors of systems update their files once annually; others send a quarterly or biannual update. Some update files by sending diskettes or compact discs; others download the update from the Internet. Another factor to consider is the style of writing used for the databases. Some systems use a factual, documentary writing style, whereas others describe an occupation in an informal, "what I do on the job everyday" kind of format.

- *Ease of searches.* Being able to search databases by specific characteristics is a core function of computer-based systems. Searches can be intuitive and user-friendly, or they can be awkward. Upon review of a system, note how easy or difficult it is to remove an already selected search characteristic, to add one, or to go back to the results of your last search and change only one or two variables.

- *Content of system.* The first item in this list addressed the matter of theoretical base, and the second dealt with assessment, both of which are elements of content. However, there can be other vast differences in content. Some systems contain instructional material, such as how occupations can be organized, how to write a resumé, how to participate in a job interview, and how to find possible job openings through networking. At least one system provides content related to the planning of multiple life roles, using Super's definition of *career,* and offers assistance with making transitions, using Schlossberg's (Schlossberg, 1989) theory and model. The content you desire in a system obviously relates both to the needs of the people served and to the elements of content provided in other ways.

- *User-friendliness and appeal.* The appearance of a computer-assisted system is determined by its graphics and icons, color scheme, the availability of multimedia (video, slides, audio), the simplicity and attractiveness of screen layout, and the readability and attractiveness of the fonts used for text. Items that relate to user-friendliness include having a consistent way of navigating throughout the system, ease of moving from one part to another, and integration of all materials needed within the system rather than having to rely on two or more media.

- *Multimedia capabilities.* Users of computer-based systems find them more appealing and are more motivated to use them if they have multimedia assets such as slide images, video, and audio. The positive aspect of having multimedia is its motivational appeal and capability to give much more information to a user about occupations or schools, for example, than text alone. The challenging side of multimedia is the software and hardware requirements. Use of sound, video, and full-screen images demands a large storage capability if the files are resident on the machine used by students or clients. If the service is Internet-delivered, use of these features requires not only specific software but also high-speed communication lines.

- *Relationship to the Internet.* The Internet may be used in at least three ways. First, the software may be run from a computer resident at a worksite and may have no linkage to the Internet, but it may include Internet addresses that may be printed and used from a different machine. Second, the computer may have phone-line access to the Internet and a browser, in which case the software may offer the capability to launch to the Internet for certain services (such as searching *America's Job Bank* or linking to the Web site of a college that has been identified) and then return to the software on the local computer. Third, some systems are delivered in an interactive mode from a Web site. Thus all transactions are between the local computer and the Web site with nothing permanently resident on the local computer.

- *Quality and track record of vendor.* Some career planning systems and Web sites have been developed on a low budget by individuals who are not known in the career development field. Further, the support capabilities they offer related to training and technical support are sparse. Other systems are developed and maintained by large organizations that have a long history of high-quality support and product development. These organizations are able to invest a large portion of their revenue in system enhancements, training, and keeping up with the next technological trend.

The NCDA has a document titled *Software Review Guidelines,* which is available on its Web site at http://ncda.org. It lists 67 items that should be reviewed, and the worksheet allows the system reviewer to rate each item on a scale of 1 to 5, 1 being unsatisfactory and 5 being outstanding.

THE COUNSELOR AND THE COMPUTER

As indicated earlier in this chapter, a sequence of studies (Taber & Luzzo, 1999) provides data indicating that the most effective means of providing career planning assistance to students or clients is by a combination of computer and counselor. The same studies indicate that receiving assistance from a computer-delivered system provides better outcomes than no assistance at all, but significantly greater gains are achieved when counselors can lend specific competencies to the picture. Pyle (2001) has identified the following list of needed counselor competencies:

- *Knowledge of computer-assisted software and Web sites.* Good content knowledge of valid and reliable computer-assisted guidance systems and Internet sites
- *Capability to diagnose.* Ability to diagnose a client's needs effectively in order to determine whether use of a computer-assisted intervention is appropriate
- *Capability to motivate.* Ability to explain the value of computer-assisted systems or Web sites in a way that will motivate the client to invest time in using them
- *Capability to help the client process data.* Ability to assist a client to turn data into personally meaningful information
- *Capability to move the client to an action plan.* Ability to assist a client to develop an action plan and then move forward on it

These competencies may be applied in combination with different models of service delivery combining technology and counselor support, of which there are at least four: one-to-one counseling plus use of technology, group guidance plus use of technology, group counseling plus use of technology, and counselor support via the Internet plus use of Web sites.

In one-to-one counseling plus use of technology, the counselor gives the student or client specific assignments to use a computer-assisted system or Web sites between sessions. It is important that the assignments be specific instead of referring individuals to a comprehensive CACGS or Web site without direction about which specific part(s) to use. For example, Juanita's counselor determined that she would profit from taking *The Self-Directed Search* (Holland, 1994). The counselor asked Juanita to take the instrument from its Web site, to print out and read the extensive report, and to return the next week. At the second session, the counselor expanded on the interpretation of the instrument and helped Juanita develop some guidelines for determining which of the many occupations suggested by the instrument to explore. Together, they developed a short list. The counselor asked Juanita to gather information about this list of occupations by using the *Occupational Outlook Handbook* (http://www.bls.gov/oco) and *CareerInfoNet* (http://www.acinet.org) on-line. At the third session, the counselor and Juanita discussed the information collected, and Juanita decided to learn more about training opportunities for Web designers. The counselor suggested that she search for such opportunities by using the National Center for Educational Statistics site (http://www.nces.ed.gov/ipeds/cool) and to bring a printed list of these, with information about each, to the next session. This example illustrates how counselors can use either a CACGS or Web sites as a valuable resource to help the client identify options and gain information about them.

The group guidance or classroom-plus-technology model is highly similar, though it may serve a group of 15 to 30 simultaneously. For example, a community college may offer a two-credit course in career planning, and its enrollment may be as many as 30 students. During class sessions, the instructor teaches basic concepts of career planning, using a curriculum such as *Take Hold of Your Future* (Harris-Bowlsbey & Lisansky, 2002) and leads the group in activities designed to apply those concepts to personal decision making. Further, the instructor may give specific assignments to use parts of *DISCOVER* (ACT, 2000), available via the campus network, between class sessions to take inventories on-line, identify occupations, get occupational descriptions, select a major, identify schools, and learn job-seeking skills. This approach not only makes wise use of technology, but gives the instructor class time to offer additional activities.

The group-counseling-plus-technology model is similar but serves students in groups not larger than eight and features counseling as opposed to guidance. Pyle (2001) has developed a model that requires three 1½-hour group sessions and use of a computer-based system or Web sites between the first and second and the second and third sessions. The sequence of activities is as follows:

Session 1: Encounter and Exploration Stage

- Introduction of persons in group, including statement of a career fantasy when in fifth or sixth grade
- Establishment of group rules and goals
- Exploration of values—The Million Dollar Exercise (each member of the group is given one million dollars in fake money and must decide how to spend it)
- Review of past work-related experiences and evaluation of each as positive or negative
- Discussion of decision making strategies
- Assignment to use a computer-based system or Web sites to identify occupations related to interests, abilities, or values

Session 2: Working Stage

- Discussion of homework assignment, asking participants to list five occupations in which they might be interested and two they definitely do not want to pursue
- Discussion of sex-role stereotyping

- Cool Seat activity, in which participants suggest occupations for each person in the group and give their reasons for the suggestions
- Assignment to use a computer-based system or Web site to collect detailed information about possible occupations

Session 3: Action Stage

- Discussion of the occupational information that participants have gathered

- Discussion of three different styles of decision making (dependent, objective, intuitive) in the context of recent decisions made

- Activity to prioritize identified occupations related to their fit with values and interests

- Strength bombardment activity (each person individually becomes the focus of attention while other members describe the strengths they see in this person)

- Development of next action steps

The age of cybercounseling is upon us. *Cybercounseling* is the provision of counseling support to a client by a qualified professional via the Internet. Hardware and software exist to make such service possible, and indeed there are a few Web sites offering it; however, experience and ethical guidelines are insufficient at this time to allow an evaluation of its effectiveness. In such service delivery, a cybercounselor and a cyberclient may be physically located anywhere where there is an Internet connection, and they can communicate with each other synchronously (that is, at the same time) via interactive e-mail or video conferencing (being able to see each other because both have digital cameras and appropriate software on their machines). Though likely less effective, the interaction could take place asynchronously (that is, the two are not at the machine at the same time). In such a relationship, the counselor and client may discuss any topics for which the Internet is a secure-enough platform, and the counselor may or may not assign the use of Web sites appropriate to those topics. Ethical guidelines for cybercounseling have been developed by the NCDA (http://www. ncda.org), the National Board for Certified Counselors (NBCC) (http://www.nbcc. org), and the American Counseling Association (ACA) (http://www.counseling. org) and are posted on their respective Web sites. These guidelines are summarized in Table 7.1.

ISSUES RELATED TO CYBERCOUNSELING

Though the hope of providing good counseling service at a reasonable rate to a much larger audience through the Internet is bright, there are also issues and concerns that the profession must wrestle and research. The most critical of these are counseling environment, content topics, client characteristics, security and confidentiality, counselor qualities and qualifications, and supporting services. Each of these will be addressed briefly.

Table 7.1

Comparison of Three Sets of Ethical Guidelines for Use of the Internet

	ACA	NBCC	NCDA
Responsibilities of Counselors	Develop procedures to maintain client communication as securely as possible	Reveal self-information but limit disclosure of personal information	Develop Web sites with content input from professional counselors
	Provide background information about all counselors related to site		State, on site, the credentials of those who developed both content and site design
	Indicate who will see client data, if it will be saved, and how it may be transferred	Identify and state topics for which Web-counseling may not be appropriate	Determine if content is appropriate for Internet and state appropriate topics on site
	Assure that liability insurance covers on-line counseling	Assure that liability insurance covers; also, check state and national certifying bodies, and licensing boards	
	Must practice within scope of training and practice	Must identify a specific counselor-on-call and crisis intervention numbers	
			Must be aware of free public access points so that service can be available for all who desire it in this mode
Selection of Clients	Counselor cannot provide service in states in which professional counselors are not licensed.		
	Clients must be above minority age and able to enter counseling relationship with informed consent (or have signed permission of authorized representative).	Clients must be above minority age; counselor must verify identity of client; suggests use of code words, numbers, or graphics	Counselors must do appropriate screening by phone to determine if client can profit.
	Counselor must verify client identity and have alternate ways of contacting client in case of emergency.		Counselor must monitor the client's progress to assure that he or she is profiting from service in this mode.
Client Responsibilities	Sign waiver statement acknowledging limitations and potential lack of security of Internet		
			Assessment must meet same criteria on-line as in print format (or client must be informed).
			Instruments must be validated for self-help or have appropriate client preparation and interpretation.
Content			Databases must be of high quality and updated often (date listed on site).
	Counselor can only transfer information to third parties if both sites are secure.	Includes similar statement, but less specific.	

216

	ACA	NBCC	NCDA
Security of Information	Site must be secure through various methods (including encryption, firewalls, etc.) it one-on-one counseling is provided. Clients must be informed about levels of security and limitations of confidentiality.	Includes similar statement; also, must be informed about how long records will be kept.	
Links to Other Sites	Counselor is responsible for doing a quality check of Web sites to which his or her site is linked.	Counselors should provide links to all appropriate certification bodies and licensure boards for the purpose of consumer protection.	Web sites to which site is linked must also meet NCDA guidelines.
Online Relationship	Counselor must have specified intake procedures to assure that client can profit from online counseling.		Counselor should have a specific contract with client that includes counselor's credentials, client goals, cost of service, how client can report unethical behavior, security of the Internet, and what data will be stored and how long.
	Counselor must develop with client individual counseling plans related to client needs and Internet limitations.		
	Counselor must cease to provide services if it is evident that client cannot profit from cybercounseling. Must suggest alternate means of help, including other counselors and/or contact by phone, fax, and so on.	Counselor must explain how to cope with potential misunderstandings arising from lack of visual cues.	Counselor must identify appropriate counselor in client's geographic area if face-to-face is needed and make the referral.
		Must instruct client what to do if there is a problem with technology, such as calling collect. Also, must inform client about differences in time zones, possible delays in e-mail transmission, and how often e-mail messages will be checked.	

Source: American Counseling Association (October, 1999); National Board for Certified Counselors (December, 1997); and the National Career Development Association (October, 1997).

Counselors have been traditionally trained to create a nonpressured, accepting environment and to use specific relationship-building skills, including eye contact, attending behavior, immediate feedback through reflection, and intuitive questioning. Despite the use of digital cameras on workstations (or counseling stations), achieving a psychologically warm environment and good facilitative skills in the medium of the Internet is challenging and currently at a primitive stage. Responsiveness may be seriously impacted by the limitations of phone-line speed and computer hardware or simply by the lack of synchronicity in the communication.

A second concern relates to the selection of presenting problems for attention via the Internet. Clients typically begin a counseling relationship by discussing topics that they believe will be acceptable ones, such as making a career choice or dealing with stress. However, it is typical that other concerns surface as the counseling relationship builds. The current guidelines indicate that counselors should state on their Web sites the topics that they believe to be appropriate for cybercounseling. This raises a concern as to whether the Internet should be used for counseling or only for the provision of guidance and information. It also raises the question of whether it is possible to stack presenting problems in hierarchical order and to divide them into the categories of "appropriate" and "inappropriate" for cybercounseling.

A third concern relates to determining which clients can profit from service via cybercounseling. The guidelines indicate that it is the responsibility of a counselor to determine whether a given client has the capability to maintain a relationship via the Internet and to profit from it. Yet, as a profession we have neither researched nor defined what the client characteristics are that would enhance their capability to profit from service in this mode or how a counselor may identify them, especially without a face-to-face interview.

A fourth concern relates to the fact that the Internet is an insecure environment. The counseling profession has always placed very high priority on the necessity to keep client communication and records secure and confidential. Encryption and other methods are being used to minimize the risk of having counselor case notes, client communication, and client records accessed by unauthorized persons; yet, these methods are not ironclad. The current guidelines indicate that counselors have the responsibility to inform their clients that the Internet is an insecure environment, but this may not be an adequate way to absolve counselors of this responsibility.

A fifth concern is how to identify and train counselors to work in this new mode. It is likely that counselors who are effective in delivering service via the Internet have characteristics that are different from those of their colleagues who work in a direct, face-to-face service mode. It is also very likely that counselors need to be trained differently for effective cybercounseling than for traditional counseling. Research is needed to understand what those counselor personality and skill differences are so that appropriate people can be selected and be taught appropriate skills.

Finally, it would be very helpful to understand what kinds of supportive services cyberclients need and how to determine when they need them. The current guidelines suggest that on-line services might be supplemented by support by phone, fax, linkage to other Web sites, and referral to qualified face-to-face counselors. The issue here is how to know when service in other modes would be critical or beneficial and how best to provide those additional services.

SUMMARY

The computer has been used as a powerful tool in the delivery of career planning information and service since the late 1960s, when such systems had their genesis. Delivered initially by stand-alone mainframe computers, these services have migrated to networked computers of all sizes and, more recently, to the Internet. Though far more effective than no service at all, their function is optimally enhanced by the support of counselors in one-on-one counseling, group guidance, group counseling, or cybercounseling. The latter is in a primitive stage at this writing but will likely become an important delivery mode as technology, ethical standards, and cybercounseling training progress. In this chapter, three sets of ethical guidelines are summarized and compared, and six specific issues related to cybercounseling are defined.

REFERENCES

ACT, Inc. (2000). *DISCOVER* [Computer software]. Iowa City, IA: Author.

American Counseling Association. (1999). *Ethical standards for Internet on-line counseling.* Alexandria, VA: Author.

Beckhusen, L., & Gazzano, L. (1987). *SkillScan.* Orinda, CA: Skillscan Professional Pack.

Campbell, D. P. (1992). *Campbell Interest and Skill Survey.* Minneapolis, MN: National Computer Systems.

Educational Testing Service. (1997). *SIGI Plus.* Princeton, NJ: Author.

Harris, J. (1970). The computerization of vocational information. In Super, D. E. (Ed.), *Computer-assisted counseling* (pp. 46–59). New York: Teachers College, Columbia University.

Harris-Bowlsbey, J., & Lisansky, R. (2002). *Take hold of your future.* Finksburg, MD: CareerGuide.

Harris-Bowlsbey, J., Riley-Dikel, M., & Sampson, J. P., Jr. (2002). *The Internet: A tool for career planning.* Tulsa, OK: National Career Development Association.

Holland, J. L. (1994). *The Self-Directed Search™.* Odessa, FL: Psychological Assessment Resources.

Impelleteri, J. (1970). A computerized occupational information system. In Super, D. E. (Ed.), *Computer-assisted counseling* (pp. 60–63). New York: Teachers College, Columbia University.

Katz, M. (1963). *Decisions and values.* New York: College Entrance Examination Board.

Keirsey, D. (1999). *The Keirsey Character Sorter.* Costa Mesa, CA: Matrix Books.

Kuder, F., & Zytowski, D. (1999). *The Kuder Career Search with Person Match™.* Adel, IA: National Career Assessment Services, Inc.

Myers, I., & Briggs, K. (1993). *The Myers-Briggs Type Indicator®.* Palo Alto, CA: Consulting Psychologists Press.

National Board for Certified Counselors. (1997). *Standards for the ethical practice of Webcounseling.* Greensboro, NC: Author.

National Career Development Association. (1991). *Software review criteria.* Columbus, OH: Author.

National Career Development Association. (1997). *NCDA guidelines for the use of the Internet for provision of career information and planning services*. Columbus, OH: Author.

Pyle, K. R. (2001). Career counseling in an information age. *The career planning and adult development journal* (Vol. 16n3). San Jose, CA: Career Research and Testing.

Roe, A. (1956). *The psychology of occupations*. New York: Wiley.

Schlossberg, N. K. (1989). *Overwhelmed: Coping with life's ups and downs*. New York, NY: Lexington Books.

Science Research Associates. (1968). *Kuder Preference Record*. Chicago, IL: Author.

Strong, E. K. (1994). *The Strong Interest Inventory*. Palo Alto, CA: Consulting Psychologists Press.

Super, D. E. (Ed.). (1970). *Computer-assisted counseling*. New York: Teachers College, Columbia University.

Taber, B. J., & Luzzo, D. A. (1999). *ACT Research Report 99–3: A comprehensive review of research evaluating the effectiveness of DISCOVER in promoting career development*. Iowa City, IA: ACT, Inc.

Tiedeman, D. V., & O'Hara, R. (1963). *Career development: Choice and adjustment*. New York: College Entrance Examination Board.

University of Oregon. (1997). *Career information system* [Computer software]. Portland, OR: Author.

CHAPTER 8

CAREER COUNSELING STRATEGIES AND TECHNIQUES FOR THE 21ST CENTURY

Because we're human beings, career counselors can fall into the understandable trap of hearing and interpreting clients' stories from our own frame of reference. Developing the discipline to thoughtfully apply a range of theories in our work with clients enables us to push beyond our own perspectives in conceptualizing salient issues and interventions. By challenging ourselves to consider clients' career and life choices from different theoretical frameworks, we can view their worlds through a variety of lenses, each bringing a distinct focus to the work. Sometimes, when mulling over a first session with a client and reasoning through the presenting information, I push myself a bit by asking, "How would Super—or Holland or Krumboltz or Schlossberg—view this client's situation; and what would each of them focus on in helping this client?" For me, the application of theory is a powerful tool that improves with frequent sharpening. It's a means for considering a series of possibilities and thus, for keeping the work fresh and honoring the uniqueness of each client.

Barbara Hilton Suddarth, PhD, NCCC
Kensington Consulting

Maggie, a 28-year-old, single, European American woman, presented for career counseling. Maggie desperately wanted out of her current work situation. Her current retail sales position was simply not working out for her. However, Maggie had no clear sense of her career options. She also possessed very limited information about the career development process. At the first session, she was clearly distressed and anxious. She wondered whether there was any hope for her future and she wanted to move onto something else as soon as possible. This was her first experience in career counseling.

Career development interventions provide the historical foundation for the counseling profession (Dorn, 1992). Herr, Cramer, and Niles (2004) point out that the counseling field emerged from three distinct movements: (1) vocational/career guidance, (2) psychological measurement, and (3) personality development. Despite the substantial influence of career development interventions on the counseling field and recent advances in career development theory, we know relatively little about the career counseling process (Anderson & Niles, 2000; Swanson, 1995; Whiston, 2003). Career counselors rarely study how career counseling actually "works" (Swanson). Rather, many career development researchers focus their efforts on career counseling outcomes (e.g., studying whether a career counseling intervention leads to less career indecision). Although career outcome research is obviously important, we also need to learn more about what happens within the career counseling process.

The results of a small group of empirical studies account for much of what we know about the career counseling process. It is noteworthy that as we take a closer look at what happens in career counseling, the more we realize that career counseling and general counseling have much in common (Multon, Heppner, Gysbers, Zook, & Ellis-Kalton, 2001). For example, Holland, Magoon, and Spokane (1981) reported that positive career counseling outcomes were related to techniques and strategies that included cognitive rehearsals of clients' career aspirations, providing clients with occupational information and social support, and cognitive structuring of clients' dysfunctional career beliefs. Heppner, Multon, Gysbers, Ellis, and Zook (1998) reported a positive relationship between career counselor confidence in establishing therapeutic relationships and client confidence in coping with career transitions. Heppner and Hendricks (1995) reported that both a career-indecisive client and a career-undecided client attached substantial importance to the development of a therapeutic relationship with their career counselor. Anderson and Niles (1995) reported that clients devoted considerable attention to noncareer concerns in career counseling sessions and often discussed family of origin and relationship concerns with their career counselors. Anderson and Niles (2000) reported that career counseling participants (i.e., counselors and clients) most frequently identified aspects of self-exploration, support, and educating as the most important and helpful career counseling interventions. One result from this small group of studies is the support for a close relationship between the processes of psychotherapy and career counseling. It is particularly evident that an effective working alliance is critical to positive outcomes in career counseling. Thus, many of the counseling skills used to establish rapport with clients (e.g., reflective listening, paraphrasing, demonstrating positive regard) also apply to effective career counseling.

Career counseling outcome research indicates that career counseling is moderately to highly effective in helping clients resolve their career concerns (Oliver & Spokane, 1988). Whiston (2002) also notes that there is convincing evidence that career interventions that do not include counseling are not as effective as career interventions that include a counseling component. Brown, Ryan, and Krane (2000) note that career counseling is most effective when it contains individualized interpretation and feedback, occupational information, modeling opportunities, attention to building support for the client's choices within the client's social network, and written exercises. Despite more general evidence that career counseling is effective, we know less about the effectiveness of specific career counseling models (Whiston, 2003). This lack of information becomes more glaring when considering the question of which career counseling models work with which clients under what conditions. These issues expose the rather substantial gap that exists between career counseling research and practice. We agree with Whiston's (2003) call for a "surge in research that focuses on the process and outcome of career counseling" (p. 40).

EXPANDING THE LIMITED VIEW OF CAREER COUNSELING

Despite the need for more career counseling process and outcome research, it is possible to offer some summary statements regarding needed changes within career counseling practice. For example, over the past 10 to 15 years, researchers have noted the close relationship that exists between the processes of psychotherapy and career counseling (Subich, 1993). Despite this relationship, many people still conceptualize the career counseling process as limited to measuring individual characteristics to identify congruent matches between people and prospective occupational environments. It is not surprising that this perception persists given the close connection between the development of interest inventories and aptitude tests during the early part of the last century and the use of these measures to help young people and veterans of the armed forces identify occupational preferences. Generations of people were exposed to this approach and, thus, the predominant perception that this is the only approach to career counseling is pervasive and long-standing. Although this emphasis on finding the "best occupational fit" was crucial to the evolution of career development interventions and is an essential aspect of many current career counseling strategies, it does not describe the totality of career counseling interventions.

Clearly, there is a substantial body of evidence providing empirical support for career counseling strategies focused on person-environment fit; however, this limited view of career counseling is often accompanied by some less than desirable outcomes. For example, the widespread use of standardized tests in career counseling has led many clients to make the following request when presenting for career counseling: "I want to take a test that will tell me what I should do." Although no such test exists, many practitioners have been eager to comply with these requests, usually for a fairly steep financial fee.

The notion that career counseling is a process limited to test administration and interpretation also contributes to less than enthusiastic attitudes toward career counseling on the part of students in counselor training programs (Heppner, O'Brien, Hinkelman, & Flores, 1996). Students often conclude that career counseling is a rather mechanical process with a sequence of interventions that resembles the following:

Step 1 The client presents for career counseling.
Step 2 The counselor gathers client information and administers a test battery.
Step 3 The counselor interprets the tests and identifies a few appropriate occupational options for the client.

In this approach, the counselor is in charge of the process. The counselor is directive and authoritative. Clients are passive recipients of a predetermined test battery. In this scenario the career counseling "process" is described as "test'em and tell'em" and "three interviews and a cloud of dust." Because some counselors use the same test battery over and over, regardless of the client's background and context, career counseling in these instances becomes something that is done to clients rather than something the counselor and client participate in collaboratively.

Many mental health practitioners also lack enthusiasm for the practice of career counseling (Spokane, 1991). Perhaps this is because practitioners also conceptualize career counseling as a process of administering tests and providing occupational information. Such views freeze career counseling at the middle of the last century and do not acknowledge the increased use of a variety of creative counseling strategies within career counseling (Amundson, Harris-Bowlsbey, & Niles, 2005).

Increasingly, career counselors infuse career counseling with general counseling strategies (Multon et al., 2001). There is a growing recognition on the part of practitioners that the dichotomy between career and personal counseling does not reflect life as most people live it. There is growing recognition that work and mental health are interwoven (Herr, 1989). Niles and Pate (1989) observe that:

> Given the relationship between work and mental health, it is perplexing that there has been an artificial distinction between career counseling and mental health counseling on the part of many clients and counselors. Career counseling and personal counseling are often referred to as if they were completely separate entities. In fact, there are few things more personal than a career choice. (p. 64)

Moreover, clients present with career concerns in virtually every setting in which counselors work. Accordingly, Niles and Pate (1989) argue for counselors to be systematically trained in both the career and noncareer intervention domains. Blustein and Spengler (1995) agree that a systematic and comprehensive integration of training experiences across career and noncareer domains is necessary to prepare competent counselors in the 21st century.

Although Brown and Brooks (1985) acknowledge that not all counselors can be skilled career counselors, they also encourage all counselors to at least become competent at recognizing situations in which career counseling is an appropriate intervention that warrants referral. To address the goals identified by career development scholars such as Brown and Brooks, we will now identify strategies for effective career counseling in the 21st century and offer a framework for conceptualizing the career counseling process.

CAREER COUNSELING IN THE 21ST CENTURY

Career counseling has evolved as both a counseling specialty and a core element of the general practice of counseling (Council for the Accreditation of Counseling and Related Educational Programs, 2001). Thus, career counselors are professional counselors or psychologists with specialized training in the delivery of career development interventions. Career counselors possess the competencies required to provide general individual and group counseling interventions to their clients while also possessing knowledge, skills, and awareness particular to the career domain (e.g., career development theories, career counseling theories and techniques, occupational information resources, career concerns of diverse populations, career assessment, consultation, program management, and ethical issues related to career service delivery).

Career counseling can be classified within the general category of counseling because of the overlap in skills required to conduct general and career counseling (Sampson, Vacc, & Loesch, 1998). In this regard, Crites (1981) suggests that "career counseling often embraces personal counseling but it goes beyond this to explore and replicate the client's role in the main area of life—the world of work" (p. 11). Crites further contends that:

1. The need for career counseling is greater than the need for psychotherapy.
2. Career counseling can be therapeutic.
3. Career counseling should follow psychotherapy.
4. Career counseling is more effective than psychotherapy.
5. Career counseling is more difficult than psychotherapy. (pp. 14–15)

Brown and Brooks (1991) take a similar view and define career counseling as "an interpersonal process designed to assist individuals with career development problems" (p. 5). Career indecision, work performance, stress and adjustment, unsatisfactory integration of life roles, and person-environment fit concerns are some of the issues Brown and Brooks include within the career counseling domain.

Brown and Brooks (1991) also suggest that career counseling clients must possess *cognitive clarity* to be able to benefit from career counseling. They define cognitive clarity as "the ability to objectively assess one's own strengths and weaknesses and relate the assessment to environmental situations" (p. 5). Brown and Brooks suggest that when counselors determine that their clients do not possess cognitive clarity, they should postpone addressing the client's career concerns until cognitive clarity is attained. Although on the surface this notion seems reasonable, and probably is very applicable for clients with more severe psychological disorders, there is little empirical evidence to support this view for clients with normal developmental concerns. In fact, it is typical that career and general counseling concerns are so intertwined within career counseling that compartmentalizing them is not realistic for most clients (Kirschner, Hoffman, & Hill, 1994; Subich, 1993). For example, Niles and Anderson (1995) examined the content of more than 250 career counseling sessions and investigated when clients discussed career and noncareer concerns within career counseling. They found no pattern for the presentation of career and noncareer concerns in the career counseling process. Thus, it may be more appropriate to view career counseling as a type of psychological intervention that, at times throughout the course of career counseling, may require the counselor and client to focus on noncareer concerns.

Rounds and Tinsley (1984) support this view, stating "we believe that a conceptual shift in which career interventions are understood as psychological interventions (and career counseling as psychotherapy) would foster advances in the understanding of vocational behavior change and processes" (p. 139). In some instances, students and clients may simply need minimal self and/or occupational information to be able to cope with their career concerns. In other instances, more therapeutic interventions may be required to help students and clients move forward in their career development.

DESIGNING CAREER COUNSELING STRATEGIES FOR THE 21ST CENTURY

Such notions pertaining to career counseling reflect the widely recognized belief that career issues are contextual and that the context of the 21st century is not the same as the context of the early 20th century. Savickas (1993) argued for career counselors to respond to societal changes occurring in the new millennium by stating that "counseling for career development must keep pace with our society's movement to a postmodern era. Thus, counselors must innovate their career interventions to fit the new *zeitgeist*" (p. 205).

It should also be evident that the career counseling interventions used by professional counselors and psychologists must be guided by an understanding of how the current *zeitgeist* shapes the career tasks presented to students and workers. For instance, as we noted in Chapter 1, career counselors must be cognizant of the fact that the hierarchical organizational pyramids, which once fostered the notion that career success is represented by climbing up the corporate career ladder, have been flattened. Career patterns now resemble roller coasters rather than gradual inclines, thereby requiring workers to redefine notions of what it means to be a "success" in one's career. Many adults present for career counseling with concerns that reflect unsuccessful attempts at coping with such changes. Adolescents worry about what they will experience in their careers as they watch their parents struggle to manage their career development.

To respond to these issues effectively, we contend that professional counselors and psychologists must provide counseling-based career assistance and support to their students and clients (although these may at first glance appear to be obvious recommendations, we have too often observed career counselors who seem to blatantly disregard them in their work with clients). We view these recommendations as essential to providing career counseling that is sensitive to the career concerns young people and adults experience in the 21st century.

Providing Counseling-Based Career Assistance

Career counselors offering counseling-based career assistance do not view their clients as the problem and the counselor as the solution. Rather, they seek to empower clients to articulate their experiences, clarify their self-concepts, and construct their own lives. Accordingly, career counselors function as collaborators in this process and pay special attention to the therapeutic relationship. As we have noted, providing counseling-based career assistance requires counselors to possess multicultural competencies. These skills are essential in the career counseling process and every counseling relationship is cross-cultural (Leong, 1993). It is essential, therefore, that counselors understand how contextual factors such as gender, socioeconomic status, racial/ethnic identity, sexual orientation, and disability status influence each client's worldview, identity, and career goals.

To help counselors consider these factors in the career counseling process, Ward and Bingham (1993) devised a multicultural career counseling checklist that can be used to help counselors identify issues of race/ethnicity that may need to be addressed in career counseling. When necessary, counselors help their clients develop strategies for overcoming prejudice and discrimination in employment and training practices. Interventions such as cognitive-behavioral counseling techniques, mentoring, and advocacy are especially useful in this regard (Herr & Niles, 1998). Additional strategies for culturally appropriate career counseling (e.g., the Career-in-Culture

Interview) were discussed in Chapter 4 and serve as foundational skills for effective career counseling.

Providing counseling-based career assistance to clients also requires using basic skills such as summarizing client statements, reflecting clients' feelings, paraphrasing, using indirect and/or open questions, expressing positive regard for the client, and empathic responding. These skills are essential for creating an effective working alliance with clients regardless of the theoretical perspective used by the counselor (Brammer, 1993).

Establishing an effective working alliance with clients is fairly straightforward when clients are eager career counseling participants who are motivated to make changes. However, not all career counseling clients are eager and motivated. Some secondary school students, for example, present for career counseling because their parents have pressured them to make career choices and these students do not yet see the importance of career planning in their lives. School systems expect all students to make curricular choices, which are essentially prevocational choices, at specific points in the educational process. Some students do not possess the readiness for making these choices and are not motivated to develop readiness. Some adolescents may be reluctant to identify career goals that run counter to their parents' plans for them. Adults who are victims of outplacement may experience resentment and bitterness toward their former employers. They may feel that what happens in their careers is out of their control and that it is useless to engage in career counseling. Other clients may be more comfortable dreaming about options than implementing them. Fears that they may fail or that the new options will not live up to the expectations they have for them may keep some clients "stuck." Expressing the need to make a career change is much easier for most people than taking actions to implement a career change. Clients in each of these situations can be described as *resistant clients*. Although they recognize at some level that their career concerns need to be addressed, they are fearful of making changes in their lives.

Resistance represents a particularly interesting paradox in general counseling, and career counseling is no exception. People present for career counseling out of a desire to make changes in their career situations, yet, due to fear of changing, people resist making career changes. Because resistance exists, at some level, within all clients, career counselors must be competent at recognizing and dealing with resistance when it occurs. A starting point for working effectively with resistance involves understanding the different forms in which clients can express their resistance. To this end, Otani (1989) offers a taxonomy for classifying various forms of client resistance. Her taxonomy includes four categories: (a) response-quantity resistance (e.g., silence, minimum talk, verbosity), (b) response-content resistance (e.g., intellectualizing, symptom preoccupation, small talk, future/past preoccupation), (c) response-style resistance (e.g., discounting, thought censoring, second-guessing, last-minute disclosing, externalizing, forgetting, false promising), and (d) logistic management resistance (e.g., poor appointment keeping, personal favor asking). Otani notes that for client behaviors to be appropriately labeled as resistant, they need to occur repeatedly over several sessions. Thus, occasional silence, for example, may simply reflect the fact that the client is pondering a particular point rather than being resistant to change.

Being alert to resistant behaviors can help counselors identify client concerns that may be important to explore within career counseling. Understanding the various ways in which clients can express their fear of changing, or resistance, also helps counselors to manage their countertransference when they encounter client expressions of resistance. Clearly, understanding the client's motivation for resistance (i.e., the affective experience the client hopes to avoid encountering) is critical to working effectively with resistant clients.

Spokane (1991) suggests guidelines that career counselors can use to cope with client resistance. (Spokane adapted these guidelines to career counseling from suggestions Meichenbaum and Turk [1987] offered to encourage compliance in therapy.)

1. Anticipate resistance.
2. Consider the career counseling process from the client's perspective.
3. Foster a collaborative relationship with the client.
4. Be client oriented.
5. Customize interventions to meet the client's needs.
6. Enlist family support.
7. Provide interventions that are continuous and accessible (e.g., as in job-search groups).
8. Use other career personnel and community resources to increase the range of social support to which the client has access.
9. Manage your countertransference and don't give up. (pp. 45–47)

These strategies obviously require career counselors to use general counseling techniques in the career counseling process. Providing counseling-based career assistance helps clients engage in career exploration and cope effectively with the career-change process.

Providing Support in Career Counseling

Given the career development challenges confronting people today, professional counselors recognize that offering support to clients is essential to effective career counseling (Brehm, 1987; Holland et al., 1981; Kirschner, 1988). Counselor-initiated supportive acts engender feelings of hope, confidence, and purpose within clients (Highlen & Hill, 1984; Kalton (2001)). As Brammer (1993) notes, support "helps to counter feelings of 'falling apart,' 'being at loose ends,' or 'pulled in many directions at once' " (pp. 105–106). When clients acknowledge that they are unsure about their current and/or future career goals, it is common for them to experience feelings such as hopelessness, anxiety, confusion, and/or depression. Career counselors offering supportive acts help their clients to begin the process of coping more effectively with their career dilemmas.

Career counselors offer support to clients in a variety of ways. As noted, establishing an effective relationship between the counselor and the client is an essential first step in the career counseling process. However, the type of support clients need depends on the stage of career counseling and the specific career concerns being addressed. For example, Amundson (1995) discussed the importance of support in helping clients cope with unemployment. Specifically, he advocated connecting cognitive reframing interventions with the client's time perspective by focusing on the client's past (e.g., normalizing reactions to unemployment, recalling accomplish-ments, and identifying transferable skills), present (e.g., affirming the client's capac-ity to cope, externalizing the problem, limiting negative thinking), and future (e.g., identifying new cycles of activity, creating focused goal statements).

Support is also useful for highly self-conscious clients who are having difficulty making career decisions (Leong & Chervinko, 1996). Adolescents who have little work experience and limited self-knowledge to draw upon in their career planning may be tentative and insecure decision makers. Leong and Chervinko found that in-dividuals who fear making a commitment and who internalize high standards from parents and significant others (i.e., socially prescribed perfectionism) also tend to have career decision making difficulties. Counselors can help these clients by en-couraging them to examine the beliefs that stop them from making commitments and moving forward with their career decision making. In this regard, it may be use-ful to have clients first identify barriers to their career development and then focus on what clients have done in the past to overcome similar barriers (Luzzo, 1996). Counselors may need to take a more educative role in helping clients who have lim-ited experience in coping with the barriers they are encountering (Krumboltz, 1996).

By offering support, career counselors help clients cope with the challenges they encounter as they attempt to manage their career development more effectively. Supportive acts in career counseling include all counselor-initiated interactions that involve one or more of the following key elements: affect, affirmation, and aid (Kahn & Antonucci, 1980). Supportive acts can be used to extend emotional sup-port, informational support, and assessment support to clients (House, 1981).

Emotional support involves providing caring, trust, and empathy to clients. Informational support involves providing clients with information they can use in resolving their career concerns. Assessment support involves providing clients with information that is useful in making accurate self-evaluations (e.g., interest invento-ries, card sorts, measures related to career thoughts and beliefs). Although it is pos-sible to make distinctions among the types of support counselors provide to clients, the three types of support we have identified are not mutually exclusive (e.g., pro-viding clients with assessment support can be an emotionally supportive act as well). Informational and assessment support, however, focus on the transmission of infor-mation rather than the affect involved in emotional support (House, 1981).

Emotional Support in Career Counseling.   The need to provide emotional support to clients is a basic presupposition of most forms of career counseling (Amundson, 1995; Crites, 1976; Salomone, 1982; Super, 1957). Communicating caring and empathy are the essential supportive acts involved in extending emotional sup-port to clients. These acts of emotional support are important throughout career counseling, but they are especially critical in the early phase of career counseling when an effective working alliance is being established (Amundson, 1995; Kirschner, 1988).

Offering emotional support requires career counselors to understand their clients' multiple perspectives and subjective experiences. Emotionally supportive acts, therefore, are grounded in multicultural counseling competencies (Pope-Davis & Dings, 1995; Sue et al., 1982). Although this seems to be a statement of the obvious, career counselors often act otherwise. That is, some career counselors demonstrate insufficient understanding of clients' multiple perspectives as evidenced by the inappropriate use of assessment instruments (Fouad, 1993), the application of culturally inappropriate career counseling processes (Leong, 1993), and the lack of attention given to career concerns beyond the exploration stage of career development (Niles & Anderson, 1995).

To provide culturally appropriate career counseling assistance, Savickas (1993) recommends that career counselors move from acting as experts to acting as "cultural workers," from focusing on occupational choice to focusing on life design, and from focusing on test scores to focusing on clients' stories (pp. 210–214). Ignoring clients' perspectives and subjective experiences (at best) minimizes opportunities for providing effective emotional support to career counseling clients. The absence of an emotionally supportive relationship in career counseling increases the risk of poor goal clarification and the use of inappropriate career interventions (Leong, 1993).

Providing emotional support to clients in career counseling essentially helps clients feel as though they "matter" (Schlossberg, 1984). Schlossberg refers to this as *mattering,* which she defines as the "beliefs people have, whether right or wrong, that they matter to someone else, that they are the object of someone else's attention, and that others care about them and appreciate them." Amundson et al. (p. 45, 2005) note that helping clients feel as though they matter requires skilled actions as well as good intentions on the part of career counselors. Amundson and his associates recommend that career counselors use the acronym PLEASE as an aid for expressing mattering to their clients.

> *P—protecting.* Providing a secure and safe haven for exploratory efforts. Ensuring that clients receive all of the benefits to which they are entitled.
> *L—listening.* Taking the time to hear all aspects of a person's story. Paying attention to underlying feelings in the telling of the story.
> *E—enquiring.* Expressing interest in the story through questions and requests for clarification. Being naturally curious and asking about events in the person's life.
> *A—acknowledging.* Noticing the other person and expressing greetings both verbally and nonverbally.
> *S—supporting.* Expressing encouragement and praise. Identifying positive attitudes and behaviors and providing specific feedback.
> *E—exchanging.* Sharing information about oneself. This self-disclosure should be genuine and appropriate to the situation. (p. 40)

Helping clients feel that they matter is clearly an effective way to extend emotional support and establishes a firm foundation for career counseling interventions. Although emotional support is a necessary condition for effective career counseling, it is usually not sufficient for supporting clients as they develop their careers.

Informational Support in Career Counseling.   Informational support is an additional form of support that aids clients in their career development. Essentially, informational support empowers clients to help themselves. There are numerous examples of supportive acts that career counselors can use to extend informational support to their clients. Among these are teaching clients job-search strategies, providing clients with access to lists of job openings, teaching decision making strategies, examining clients' dysfunctional career beliefs, and providing clients with lists of reading materials that are relevant to their career concerns.

Informational support can also be provided to clients in the early phase of career counseling. Specifically, supportive acts can be used to provide information about the structure of career counseling. Because so many clients enter career counseling expecting counselors to use tests, it is important that career counselors discuss the career development process as well as the career counseling process with their clients. For instance, clients can be informed that career counseling is a collaborative process in which counselors offer feedback, affirmation, and support as clients interpret their needs and shape their lives. This information helps counteract clients who expect to be tested by an expert who will then identify appropriate career options. Clarifying roles and responsibilities for career counseling helps clients understand that career counseling is a shared experience in which they are active participants. Informing a client that most people make career changes multiple times during their lives and that career change is often a very adaptive response to personal changes and/or changes in work helps normalize the client's career concerns.

Thus, extending informational support in the early phase of career counseling allows clients to take full advantage of the career counseling experience. Providing clients with emotional support and informational support in the early phase of career counseling helps establish an effective working alliance and sets the stage for the incorporation of assessment support in the career counseling process.

Assessment Support in Career Counseling.   Assessment support provides clients with opportunities to acquire information that is useful in making accurate self-evaluations (see Chapter 5). Assessment information can be used in the early phase of career counseling to support clients as they clarify their career concerns and identify their career counseling goals. Here again, exploring clients' multiple perspectives is an important step in providing culturally sensitive assessment support (Ibrahim, Ohnishi, & Wilson, 1994). Exploring the multiple perspectives of clients is important because clients' patterns of career concerns are influenced by various personal and situational determinants that shape their life-role self-concepts (Super, 1980). Some individuals view work as the central role in life, whereas others see it as on the periphery. Some view a career choice as the expression of personal fulfillment and others view it as the fulfillment of familial expectations. Thus, understanding the client's worldview, cultural identity, gender identity, sexual orientation, and disability status is a prerequisite for engaging in effective assessment activities.

Given the uncertainty related to career paths today, it should be clear that providing clients with information about themselves and the world-of-work through objective, standardized assessments is necessary, but often not sufficient, for empowering people to manage their careers effectively. To be sure, having information about how one's interests compare with others is helpful in the process of identifying viable career options. But, an overreliance on objective assessment ignores that "what exists for individuals is purpose, not positions on a normal curve" (Savickas, 1993, p. 213). Thus, two people with similar aptitude test and interest inventory results may select different occupations due to other factors influencing their decision making and sense of self. Our unique life experiences provide the clay out of which we sculpt our career decisions. To help people make meaning out of life experiences, career counselors pay attention to each client's subjective career (Carlsen, 1988). Most likely, the experiences that capture the most attention are those that have been the most painful (Adlerians call it "actively mastering what we at one time passively suffered" [Watkins & Savickas, 1990, p. 104]). Counselors can help clients sift through these experiences by augmenting traditional standardized assessment strategies with interventions that help clients translate their subjective experiences into purposeful career activities.

Savickas (1989) offers the career-style assessment model as a strategy for helping clients identify subjective themes that guide their career development. In this approach, Savickas queries clients as to their early role models; early life recollections; their favorite books, movies, and magazines; and their life mottoes. Answers to these questions contain themes clients use to guide their decisions as they work to turn their problems into opportunities. For example, one of our career counseling clients (Verneda) noted that her role model in early life was her high school principal because she "helped others overcome obstacles in their lives." Verneda, an African American woman, had experienced early life tragedies, serious chronic illness, and numerous instances of discriminatory treatment. Through using the career-style assessment, Verneda become aware of her life theme—"overcoming obstacles"—and decided to become a counselor to "help others overcome obstacles." She actively mastered what she had passively suffered early in her life and turned her preoccupation (overcoming obstacles) into an occupation (helping others overcome obstacles) through her work as a counselor. Savickas' approach focuses on working collaboratively with clients to translate their life themes into career goals. The use of projective techniques, autobiographies, laddering techniques, and card sorts are also useful, subjectively oriented strategies for incorporating life experiences into the career counseling process (Neimeyer, 1992; Peavy, 1994).

Watkins and Savickas (1990) note that four types of clients tend to benefit the most from incorporating subjective assessment strategies into career counseling: (a) indecisive clients, (b) "difficult cases" or clients who have received career counseling but have yet to resolve their career concerns, (c) mid-career changers, and (d) culturally diverse clients who may not be served adequately by objective-only interventions. To be of most use to clients, Savickas (1993) contends that counselors should augment, rather than replace, objective and standardized assessments focusing on congruence, developmental tasks, vocational identity, and career adaptability with subjective-oriented assessment strategies. Thus, career counselors must understand the purposes, strengths, and limitations of subjective and objective assessments. Specifically, subjective assessment strategies can be used to help clients address the following questions:

1. How do my life experiences connect to my career development?
2. What gives me meaning?
3. What sort of life do I want to construct?
4. What do I want to be able to express through my work?
5. Which work options will allow me to come the closest to expressing who I am?

Objective assessment strategies help clients address questions such as:

1. How do my interests compare with others?
2. How much aptitude do I possess in specific areas?
3. How strong are my values?
4. What is my readiness for career decision making?

Of course, each approach has its own strengths and limitations that guide career counselors in decisions about which might be more useful to a client. Strengths of subjective assessments include:

1. They help clients understand themselves on a deep level
2. They help clients consider the relevance of their life experiences to their career development
3. They help clients attach a sense of purpose to their activities
4. They are often inexpensive to use
5. They actively engage clients in the career counseling process
6. The assessment results are clearly connected to client responses to assessment questions

Limitations of the subjective approach to assessment include:

1. A lack of psychometric evidence related to the assessment activities
2. They require substantial career counselor time within the career counseling process
3. They typically have no clear interpretation guidelines for career counselors to follow
4. They typically require more work on the part of the client than do objective assessments

Strengths of objective assessments include:

1. They allow the client to make comparisons with others
2. They are outcome oriented
3. They do not require as much in-session career counselor time as subjective assessments
4. They often provide a useful starting point for subsequent consideration of career options

Limitations of objective assessments include:

1. The results are not easily connected to specific responses
2. They are counselor controlled
3. They can be expensive
4. Clients often have inappropriate expectations for what can be accomplished through the use of an objective assessment
5. Measures do not always fit the client's context

Career counselors need to adapt their assessment strategies to their client's career concerns. Being skilled in incorporating objective and subjective assessments in career counseling helps counselors to more effectively serve their clients.

A FRAMEWORK FOR CAREER COUNSELING

Numerous frameworks exist for conducting career counseling. For example, Isaacson (1985) suggests that over the course of career counseling, counselors typically address six issues: (1) getting started, (2) helping clients deal with change, (3) helping clients engage in self-assessment activities, (4) helping clients learn about the world of work, (5) helping clients expand or narrow choices, and (6) helping clients make plans.

Gysbers, Heppner, and Johnston (2003) view the career counseling process as typically progressing through several phases: (a) an opening phase in which the working alliance is established, (b) a gathering information phase in which the counselor and client gather data about the client's career situation, (c) a working phase in which the counselor and client use the information gathered to develop career goals and action plans, and (d) a final phase in which the counselor and client bring closure to career counseling.

Spokane (1991) proposes that career counseling consists of three overlapping and sequential phases labeled as a beginning phase, an activation phase, and a completion phase. During the beginning phase, career counselors provide clients with (a) structure concerning the career counseling process, (b) opportunities to rehearse their career aspirations either to themselves or to others, and (c) opportunities to uncover or identify conflicts engendered by their aspirations. During the activation phase, counselors provide support to clients as they process self-assessment data, test hypotheses about their career aspirations based on the new data they acquire, and begin formulating a commitment to a particular career option. During the completion phase, the career counselor helps the client implement and sustain a commitment to a career choice while also focusing on termination of the career counseling process.

Crites (1981) integrates multiple career counseling theories in his comprehensive model of career counseling and offers a generic framework for considering the career counseling process. In his model, Crites suggests that career counseling typically proceeds from an initial focus on diagnosis, in which the client and counselor work collaboratively to understand the client's career concerns, to a focus on process, which encompasses the implementation of career counseling interventions to address the client's career concerns. It then proceeds to an examination of the outcomes in which the career counselor and client reexamine the status of the client's concerns and determine whether additional career counseling is needed or if termination is appropriate.

Regardless of the framework used to conceptualize the career counseling process, most experts agree that career counseling typically involves a beginning or initial phase, a middle or working phase, and an ending or termination phase.

The Beginning or Initial Phase of Career Counseling

During the initial phase of career counseling, an effective career counseling relationship is developed, the counselor begins the process of gathering information about the client, and preliminary goals for career counseling are identified. Many career counselors begin sessions with their clients by asking them how they can be useful to the client. To clarify concerns, counselors encourage clients to identify individual and contextual factors contributing to their career dilemmas. Career counselors invite clients to discuss the strategies they have tried thus far to resolve their career dilemmas. Career counselors also seek to gather preliminary data concerning the clients' values, interests, and skills. Perhaps most importantly, career counselors work to establish rapport with their clients (Anderson & Niles, 2000).

The initial phase of career counseling involves counselors providing clients with structure concerning the career counseling process. Career counselors work to clarify their clients' preferences and expectations for career counseling. Because clients seem clearer about what they prefer in career counseling than what they anticipate occurring, it is essential that counselors discuss with clients what they can expect to experience during the course of career counseling (Galassi, Crace, Martin, James, & Wallace, 1992; Swanson, 1995). For example, Spokane (1991) recommends that counselors distribute to clients a brief handout describing the career counseling process and what is likely to occur in career counseling sessions. Informing clients about what they can anticipate occurring within the career counseling process helps clients clarify the type of concerns that are appropriate to discuss in sessions. Additional structuring topics include the payment of fees, the length of sessions, confidentiality, counselor-client roles and responsibilities, and the career counselor's theoretical framework.

Theoretical frameworks help to organize the data counselors collect from clients. For example, using Holland's theory, a career counselor could focus on collecting data to organize the counselor's understanding of the client's Holland types. This information helps counselors make initial assessments concerning the client's degree of congruence (What is the goodness of fit between the person's characteristics and the expectations of the person's current and/or most recent occupational environments?), consistency (How diverse or focused are the client's interests and competencies?), and aspirations (To which environments does the client aspire?).

A counselor relying on Super's (1990) life-span, life-space theory would be concerned with understanding the constellation of career development tasks confronting the client (e.g., Is the client an adolescent engaged in exploration stage tasks for the first time or an adult re-cycling through exploration stage tasks while also coping with tasks of other career stages?) and the client's life-role salience (e.g., What does the client hope to accomplish in each salient life role? To what degree is the client able to express important values in salient life roles?). Collecting this information in the initial phase of career counseling helps the counselor understand the client's life-role self-concepts (Super, 1990).

A career counselor operating from Krumboltz's (1996) learning theory of career counseling might organize the information collected from the client to understand the client's self-observation generalizations (How does the client describe himself or herself?), career beliefs (What does the client believe about the career development process? Are the client's beliefs functional or dysfunctional?), and which learning experiences have been most influential in the client's career development.

In these ways, career counseling theories provide the organizing structures used by career counselors to understand the information presented by their clients. Theories help shape the content of career counseling and provide a structure for conceptualizing client's career concerns. Theories also provide a vocabulary the counselor and client can use to discuss the client's experiences.

Regardless of the theoretical perspectives used by career counselors, the following topics are addressed in the initial phase of career counseling:

1. The client's view of self; self-characteristics, worldview, racial/ethnic identity, view of the future; the client's health and physical status; the client's previous experiences in counseling (if any); and the client's presenting concerns and goals.

2. The client's family (e.g., Who are they? What has been their influence? What type of relationship does the client have with family members? What goals and aspirations do the family members have for the client? What is the client's attitude toward the family members?); the client's educational background (What type and level of education does the client have? Is the client open to considering additional education? What is the likelihood that the client could pursue additional education if desired?); and cultural influences (e.g., What cultural factors influence the client's attitudes, behavior, goals?).

3. The client's significant work and life experiences (e.g., How have these experiences influenced the client's attitudes, behavior, and goals? How has the client coped with difficulties in the past?); and significant individuals in the client's life (e.g., What role models does the client have? In what ways have the client's role models influenced the client's attitudes, behavior, and goals? What sources of support does the client have?).

Isaacson (1985) recommends using a checklist to estimate clients' attributes for career counseling. Figure 8.1 provides a checklist adapted from Isaacson. Career counselors can review the checklist during or after initial sessions with their clients. Responses can be used by the counselor to formulate impressions of the client's concerns and resources. This information is also useful in helping clients articulate and clarify their goals for career counseling.

Goals for career counseling must achieve several criteria. Goals should be specific, observable, time-specific, and achievable. Sometimes, goal identification can be facilitated by helping clients clarify the questions they are asking when they present for career counseling. For example, Maggie (the client introduced at the beginning of the chapter) presented for career counseling and declared in the first 10 minutes of her first session that her goal was "to get out of my miserable work situation" (she worked as a sales associate in a department store at the local mall). The counselor responded supportively to Maggie by reflecting her feelings of frustration and anger. This encouraged Maggie to tell more details about her work situation. When asked what occupations she had in mind, Maggie expressed in frustration that she didn't know but that "anything has to be better than what I am doing now." These statements provided the career counselor with a clear sense that Maggie wanted things to change and that she was not happy in her current job; however, it did little to provide the counselor and client with an indication as to what Maggie wanted to move toward in her career. Thus, the counselor clarified with Maggie that she already knew that she wanted to stop doing what she was currently doing but that she did not know what she wanted to do next. The counselor provided Maggie with informational support by explaining the career development and career counseling process to her. The counselor was sure to emphasize the necessity of clarifying important self-information before attempting and acquiring relevant occupational information prior to making career decisions. To help Maggie clarify important self-information, the counselor asked Maggie for more information:

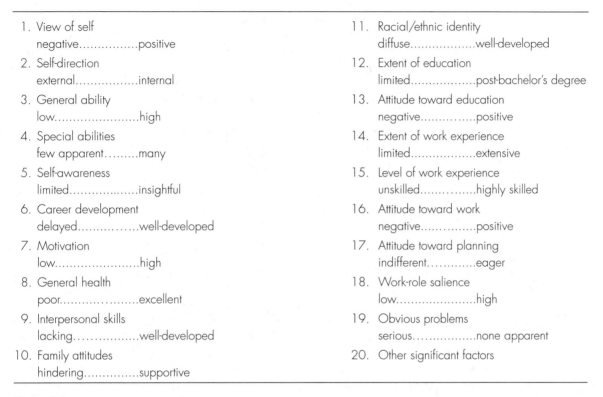

1. View of self
   negative...............positive

2. Self-direction
   external................internal

3. General ability
   low.......................high

4. Special abilities
   few apparent.........many

5. Self-awareness
   limited..................insightful

6. Career development
   delayed................well-developed

7. Motivation
   low.......................high

8. General health
   poor.....................excellent

9. Interpersonal skills
   lacking.................well-developed

10. Family attitudes
    hindering...............supportive

11. Racial/ethnic identity
    diffuse..................well-developed

12. Extent of education
    limited.................post-bachelor's degree

13. Attitude toward education
    negative...............positive

14. Extent of work experience
    limited..................extensive

15. Level of work experience
    unskilled...............highly skilled

16. Attitude toward work
    negative...............positive

17. Attitude toward planning
    indifferent.............eager

18. Work-role salience
    low......................high

19. Obvious problems
    serious.................none apparent

20. Other significant factors

Figure 8.1

Checklist for estimating client attributes for career counseling. *Source:* From *Basics of Career Counseling,* by Lee E. Isaacson, 1985. Copyright © 1985 by Allyn & Bacon. Reprinted/adapted by permission.

> *Counselor:* Maggie, can you tell me some more about what you don't like about your current job?
>
> *Maggie:* I work for a sexist creep who takes credit for my work and never has anything positive to say about what I do. I have no opportunities for advancement and the pay stinks.

After discussing with Maggie what specifically was wrong in her current situation and what she would like more of in her next situation, Maggie began to crystallize more specific, observable, time-specific, and achievable goals for career counseling. By clarifying the questions she was asking about her career situation, Maggie was able to state that her initial goal for career counseling was to identify occupational options that would allow her to engage in activities she enjoyed, use the skills she prized most, and express her important values. Maggie also felt that she was currently underemployed and hoped to get a job that would allow her to use her bachelor's degree in business administration. Thus, Maggie quickly acknowledged that her statement that "anything would be better than what she was doing now" was not exactly accurate and did not reflect the questions she was asking about her career. There were certain things she wanted in a job and certain things she did not want to be part of her work.

To help Maggie answer the question as to what job she would like to pursue next, Maggie felt that focusing on clarifying her interests and values would be especially useful. After additional discussion of Maggie's interests, values, and skills, Maggie stated that "In the next few career counseling sessions, I would like to learn more about my interests and values. After we do that, I would like to identify some jobs that make sense for me." Articulating and clarifying goals provides the opportunity for the counselor and client to identify an initial plan of action for career counseling.

The initial phase of career counseling culminates in the establishment of an effective counselor-client relationship, a mutual understanding of the structure of the career counseling experience (e.g., roles, responsibilities, limits), and a shared understanding of the client's presenting issues and initial goals for career counseling. Providing emotional and informational support to clients also helps establish an effective working alliance in career counseling.

The Middle or Working Phase of Career Counseling

The middle or working phase of career counseling is the time when a client's concerns and goals are explored in depth and a specific plan of action for career counseling is more fully developed and implemented. Career counseling goals are often revised and/or refined in the middle phase of career counseling. For example, to help Maggie clarify her interests and values, she and her career counselor decided to use an interest inventory and values card sort exercise. Thus, assessment support became an important component of the middle phase of career counseling with Maggie. As Maggie proceeded to clarify important self-information, she was able to clarify a plan of action by stating that "In 6 months I would like to have a job that allows me to have more opportunities to use my verbal and computer skills. I want to work more independently and have more control over my success. I also want a job with more income potential and that offers opportunities for advancement into higher levels of management."

Maggie and her counselor then began the process of identifying prospective occupational options related to her interests, values, and skills. Based on this exploration, Maggie came to the tentative conclusion that a career in computer sales offered her the opportunity to express her most important characteristics. To gather more information about computer sales positions, Maggie and her counselor decided that information interviewing would be useful. Maggie had never engaged in information interviewing, so she and her counselor decided that learning how to conduct an information interview would be a good first step in gathering additional occupational information. As they reviewed the steps involved in information interviewing, it became evident to the counselor that Maggie lacked assertiveness skills. Thus, the counselor and Maggie decided that it would be helpful to focus on developing assertiveness skills because these skills are essential for effective interviewing for occupational information (and interviewing for jobs). Maggie and her counselor engaged in assertiveness training.

Soon, Maggie was ready to begin information interviewing. A family friend actually worked in computer sales and Maggie thought that this person would provide a good starting point for her information interviewing. They met for a 30-minute interview during which Maggie received answers to many of her questions pertaining to work as a computer salesperson. At the end of the interview, Maggie asked for names of other computer salespeople with whom she could meet. Before she could schedule her second information interview, however, her interviewee learned of a vacancy in his company. He recommended Maggie for the position and she was offered an interview that resulted in her being hired as a computer salesperson.

Career counseling theories provide guideposts to direct the career counseling process. For example, interventions with Maggie focused on her information and skill deficits. Such interventions reflect a behavioral or social learning theory approach to career counseling. A developmental counselor working with Maggie might have encouraged her to clarify her life-role salience by constructing current and ideal life-career rainbows (Super, Savickas, & Super, 1996). This information would be useful in helping Maggie sort through occupational options (e.g., she could evaluate each option in light of the opportunity each option provided for participating in life roles that were important to her).

A counselor oriented toward using Holland's theory might have decided to teach Maggie Holland's typology. Learning the Holland types would provide a structure and vocabulary that Maggie could use to increase her self-understanding and sort through prospective occupational options. A counselor oriented toward Krumboltz's (1996) learning theory of career counseling might have encouraged Maggie to identify her career beliefs. The counselor may have administered the Career Beliefs Inventory (Krumboltz, 1988). Results from the Career Beliefs Inventory might have been used to highlight the specific beliefs causing Maggie difficulty and could have provided a starting point for forming more functional beliefs about the career development process.

Of course, how career counselors intervene depends not only on the counselor's theoretical framework but also on the type of decisional difficulty clients are experiencing. Decision making difficulties occurring at the *beginning* of the decision making process may be due to a lack of self- and/or occupational information, dysfunctional career beliefs, a lack of motivation, or more general indecisiveness within the client (Gati, Krausz, & Osipow, 1996). Decisional difficulties occurring *during* the career decision making process could be due to insufficient information, conflicts related to personal characteristics and occupational options (e.g., skill levels insufficient for the occupation desired), and conflicts due to the influence of significant others (Gati et al.). Difficulties arising after decisions have been implemented may be the result of a poor choice of occupation, problems within the occupational environment, or the inability of the client to adjust to a particular work or educational situation.

When clients have made a poor occupational choice, they will need to re-cycle through Super's (1990) exploration-stage tasks. Maggie re-cycled through exploration-stage tasks as a more informed career explorer. She used information from her first sales position to help crystallize more appropriate occupational options.

Clients experiencing problems within the occupational environment may need to consider other jobs within the same occupation or may focus on strategies they can use to change their current work environment (e.g., clarifying with a supervisor one's roles and responsibilities, confronting a coworker). Maggie's situation was very limited in this regard. Her boss was not likely to change his attitudes and behaviors.

Clients having difficulty adjusting to their work environments may need to focus on developing important effective work competencies, such as developing interpersonal skills, assertiveness, and reliability. For example, an unassertive client experiencing ambiguity regarding work responsibilities may need assertiveness training to approach a supervisor to ask for more clarity concerning work tasks. Maggie decided that approaching her boss concerning his sexist attitudes was not as important to her as developing assertiveness skills to engage in information interviewing. These skills were essential to her in learning more about her new occupation and in succeeding in her job search.

It is interesting to note that career counseling research typically focuses on issues related to helping clients make and implement career choices. However, as implied by the previous discussion, career concerns continue after choices have been implemented (Carson, Carson, Phillips, & Roe, 1996). Indeed, many individuals have difficulty adjusting to the work they have chosen. Hershenson (1996) offers a systems model for career counselors to use in addressing work adjustment issues. Hershenson's system for work adjustment highlights the relationships among the subsystems of the person (work personality, work competencies, and work goals), the elements of the work setting (behavioral expectations, skill requirements, and rewards/opportunities), and the components of work adjustment (work-role behavior, task performance, and worker satisfaction). The formative influences of culture, family, school, and peer/reference group are also addressed in Hershenson's model of work adjustment. Thus, career counseling for work adjustment focuses on the relationship between the worker and the work environment.

Career counseling for work adjustment begins by assessing whether the problem is related to work-role behavior, task performance, worker satisfaction, or some combination of these three factors. If it is the former, then interventions focus on work personality. For issues of task performance, work competencies are addressed. Issues related to worker satisfaction require addressing work goals. Contextual factors (e.g., family, culture, and economics) are considered in all cases.

Thus, career counseling interventions are theory based and emerge from information gathered during the initial and middle phases of career counseling. When selecting interventions, the counselor provides the client with an explanation as to how the proposed intervention relates to the client's career concern and how the intervention might be useful to the client. The counselor and client discuss collaboratively whether the intervention seems appropriate. When it does, then there is a clear sense as to how career counseling will proceed. When the intervention does not make sense to the client, then there may be the need for counselors to clarify their understanding of the client's concern. Perhaps the counselor has missed important elements of the client's situation. For example, a client who is dissatisfied in his current job may be reluctant to engage in broad career exploration with the goal of entering a new and potentially more satisfying occupation when he has significant financial obligations that restrict his ability to experience substantial periods of time without a paycheck. Although finding a more satisfying occupation may be an ideal goal from the counselor's perspective, in this instance it may not be realistic from the client's perspective.

When counselors discuss their understanding of the client's career concerns and propose interventions for addressing the client's concerns, they have the opportunity to receive important formative feedback from the client. Establishing an effective working alliance allows clients to feel comfortable discussing their perceptions of the career counseling process thus far. Working collaboratively in this fashion provides the opportunity for the client to take ownership of the career counseling process and outcome because the client has been actively involved in the entire career counseling experience.

Moreover, during the middle phase of career counseling, clients may become aware of important aspects of their career concerns that they were not aware of in the initial phase of career counseling. This new information may influence the client's goals for career counseling and result in the identification of alternative interventions that may be more appropriate for addressing the client's revised goals and concerns. In fact, Niles, Anderson, and Cover (2000) suggest that clients typically revise their concerns and goals during the course of career counseling and counselors need to be alert to this phenomenon. Therefore, counselors need to maintain flexibility in responding to clients' concerns as they emerge during the course of career counseling and, when necessary, invite clients to consider revising their goals for career counseling.

Maggie and her counselor began by focusing on helping her clarify the questions she was asking about her career. Maggie was also encouraged to learn more about her important self-characteristics. As she learned more about herself, especially her interests and values, she began to crystallize a career preference. As career counseling progressed, it became clear that Maggie would need to learn new skills to move forward in her career development. Thus, the counselor and Maggie revised their goals for career counseling to include training in information interviewing and assertiveness.

The Ending or Termination Phase of Career Counseling

In the ending or termination phase career counselors connect the work done in the beginning and middle phases of career counseling by assessing the client's current status and relating that status to the client's goals for career counseling. If the client's goals for career counseling have been achieved, then termination becomes the focus. Steps are taken to prepare for ending the career counseling relationship. The counselor and client review the progress the client has made; discuss what the client has learned as a result of career counseling; consider how the learning the client has experienced can be generalized into future scenarios; and review what the client can do if difficulties are encountered in the future.

In reflecting on where the client was initially and where the client is now in his or her career development, differences in cognitions, affect, and behavior can be highlighted. For example, when Maggie presented for career counseling she was confused, angry, and ready to quit her job for any job that she could get. As career counseling progressed, she became more focused on the specific questions she was asking. She became more focused on what she needed to do to move forward in her career. She systematically acquired new information and skills she needed to help her cope more effectively with her career concerns. As Maggie did this, she began to crystallize new options that connected more closely with important self-characteristics.

Additionally, Maggie became an active participant in her career planning. As she became more active (e.g., participating in information interviews), Maggie developed important skills for helping her acquire a job she wanted. The ultimate reward was that Maggie eventually acquired a more satisfying job. This process would be important for Maggie and her counselor to review. By reviewing her progress, Maggie's counselor can take opportunities to reinforce important learning experiences in Maggie's career counseling:

Maggie: When I think about how I felt when I first came to see you, I remember feeling anxious, frustrated, and even somewhat hopeless.

Counselor: How does that compare to how you feel now?

Maggie: I've come 180 degrees. I now feel more in control, confident, and satisfied.

Counselor: What do you think has helped you to feel so good?

Maggie: Obviously, having my new job helps! But, I think that I learned to approach my career more systematically. I never really thought that much about my interests and values. Career counseling helped me organize that information and connect it with career options. I think I am much more in control of my career now. I also know how good career decisions are made. I don't think I really understood that before.

Maggie and her counselor continued to discuss what Maggie learned in her career counseling. The counselor was careful to point out the many strengths that Maggie exhibited in her career counseling (e.g., she took control of her situation, she was willing to learn new skills, she was able to put her new skills to use in effective ways, she was able to communicate clearly to the counselor and others, she followed through on assignments the counselor gave to her). They also considered how Maggie could put her new learning to use in the future. However, the counselor invited Maggie to return for career counseling in the future if she felt the need. Finally, Maggie and her counselor discussed what was most useful to Maggie in her career counseling as well as what Maggie thought was not as useful to her. Acquiring this information from the client's perspective provides important evaluative data that the counselor can use to improve his or her career counseling skills. To help structure the feedback Maggie provided, she was given an evaluation form (see Figure 8.2) to complete. Finally, Maggie was encouraged to consider whether there were any things that she would like to say to the counselor before terminating. As a result of her career counseling, not only did Maggie feel more satisfied with her new job, she also felt more confident about her ability to manage the career concerns she would encounter in the future.

Not all termination experiences are as positive as Maggie's, however. Termination can also occur when the client decides that now is not the time to take action. This decision can occur for a variety of reasons. For example, it may be that the client has decided to attend college but cannot do so at this time due to financial constraints. Or the client may decide that the current situation is simply preferable to a change and, therefore, may lack motivation for changing. In these instances, the counselor can discuss the steps the client can take if, in the future, making a change seems more reasonable.

CAREER COUNSELING EVALUATION

This evaluation of the Counseling Center's career counseling services will help us improve the quality of assistance to the students.

Use the rating scale below to indicate your response to each statement. Write the number that corresponds to your response in the blank.

0	1	2	3	4
Not Applicable	Strongly Disagree	Disagree	Agree	Strongly Agree

_____ 1. The counselor understood what my noncareer concerns were.

_____ 2. The counselor understood what my career concerns were.

_____ 3. The counselor has helped me to identify effective ways to cope with my noncareer concerns.

_____ 4. The counselor has helped me to identify effective ways to cope with my career concerns.

_____ 5. The time and activities spent learning about my interests, skills, and values were helpful.

_____ 6. The time and activities spent in learning about my different occupational and/or educational choices were helpful.

_____ 7. The time and activities spent in learning about the career planning and decision making process were helpful.

_____ 8. Career counseling is helping me to achieve personal and career goals.

_____ 9. Career counseling is helping me to function more effectively as a student, worker, and as a human being.

_____ 10. Overall, my career counseling experience has been helpful to me.

Please describe below the most helpful activities and moments in career counseling.

Please describe below the least helpful activities and moments in career counseling.

Your social security number will allow us to connect your responses to demographic data to help understand our effectiveness with various populations. It will also identify you to your counselor and help them better understand your evaluation so your counselor can improve his/her effectiveness. Your reply, as well as all other information you provide to the Center, will be kept confidential. If you would prefer to respond anonymously, leave the social security number blank.

Social Security Number: _____   Date: _____

Counselor name: _____

Approximate number of counseling sessions: _____

Thank you for your assistance.

Figure 8.2
Sample career counseling evaluation.

There are also instances of "premature closure" that occur when clients end counseling before the counselor thinks the client is ready. Brown and Brooks (1991) suggest four possibilities as to why premature closure occurs: (1) clients believe that they have achieved their goal, (2) the career counseling experience does not meet clients' expectations, (3) clients fear what may be uncovered in career counseling, and (4) clients lack commitment to career counseling. When premature closure happens, it is essential that the career counselor try to understand the reasons for it occurring. In such instances supervision or consulting with a colleague can be very useful. For example, if the client terminated because the career counseling experience did not meet the client's expectations, the counselor and supervisor can explore what factors might have contributed to the client drawing this conclusion. Was the counselor sensitive to the client's concerns? Did the counselor establish an effective working relationship with the client? Were their factors associated with the client's background or concerns that were difficult for the counselor and therefore limited the counselor's effectiveness with this particular client?

Gysbers et al. (2003) note that when a client terminates prematurely by unexpectedly dropping out of career counseling, then the counselor must make a decision as to how this will be handled. What the counselor decides to do in these instances is based on the counselor's beliefs about how much responsibility he or she should take in encouraging a client to return to career counseling. Gysbers and his colleagues suggest that placing a phone call to the client has several advantages:[1]

1. It allows for the expression of caring and concern for the client.
2. It gives the counselor a chance to collect information about the client's reasons for terminating.
3. It provides the counselor with the opportunity to make a referral that is appropriate.
4. It provides the counselor with the opportunity to "leave the door open" for counseling in the future. (p. 363)

Although it is not a pleasant experience, premature closure provides opportunities for counselors to learn about themselves and the career counseling process. Career counselors should take full advantage of these opportunities by consulting with other professionals and, when possible, communicating with clients.

Clearly, termination is an important phase of career counseling. It provides an opportunity for the career counselor and client to review the important work they have done together. It provides important feedback to the counselor and helps the client to consider what he or she can do to cope with future career concerns. Given the importance of termination, it clearly should be a career counseling phase for which the counselor and client prepare ahead of time. The counselor must alert the client to the fact that termination is approaching. The counselor can help the client prepare for termination by encouraging the client to consider what has been learned in the time they have spent together and how the client feels about termination. The counselor also needs to be in touch with his or her feelings about termination. Because career counseling is an interactive experience, counselors often learn a great deal about themselves as a result of any career counseling relationship.

[1]From Norman Gysbers, Mary Heppner, and Joseph Johnston *Career Counseling: Process, Issues, and Techniques* (2nd ed.). Published by Allyn & Bacon, Boston, MA. Copyright © 2003 by Pearson Education. Reprinted/adapted by permission of the publisher.

It is important that the counselor reflect on what has been learned as a result of working with each client.

To assess whether termination has been handled thoroughly, Gysbers et al. (2003) offer a seven-point checklist and recommend that the counselor ask:[2]

1. Did I review the content of what happened in counseling?
2. Did I review the process of what happened in counseling?
3. Did I reemphasize the client's strengths that were evident in counseling?
4. Did I evaluate what went well and what went poorly?
5. Did I explore things unsaid in counseling?
6. Did I discuss feelings related to the ending of the counseling relationship?
7. Did I provide clear and direct structure for the client's next steps? (p. 363)

Taking a planful approach to termination contributes to a positive career counseling experience and helps the client, and counselor, take full advantage of the career counseling process.

CAREER COUNSELING GROUPS

Group counseling offers a mode of service delivery that can be used instead of, or in addition to, individual career counseling. Hansen and Cramer (1971) describe group counseling as an intervention for 5 to 15 members, with 5 to 8 members optimal. Structured career counseling groups address a specific issue that is a common concern to the group members (e.g., job search, outplacement, choosing a college major, career decision making, career planning). Activities in structured career counseling groups tend to resemble group career-guidance activities. Because structured groups focus on specific career development topics, there is often a teaching component provided by the group leader. Thus, structured groups tend to be more information oriented and didactic than less structured groups. Structured career counseling groups typically meet for three to seven sessions.

Teaching students and clients about job-search strategies represents an excellent topic for a structured group experience. For example, in session one the career counselor can provide an overview of job-search strategies. Active and passive job-search techniques could be described, resumé styles reviewed, job interview techniques highlighted, and strategies for managing a job search could be discussed.

Session two could address active versus passive job-search strategies in depth. Specifically, the career counselor could teach group participants about the importance of engaging in an active job-search campaign, noting that many people rely solely on a passive approach to job searching—they compose a general resumé and send it to employers who have placed advertisements for a specific job opening. This approach has a low probability of succeeding for a variety of reasons. First, because it is a common approach it is likely to result in a large number of applications being submitted for the same position. Secondly, employers favor hiring "known commodities." That is, they are more comfortable employing a person with whom they

[2]From Norman Gysbers, Mary Heppner, and Joseph Johnston *Career Counseling: Process, Issues, and Techniques* (2nd ed.). Published by Allyn & Bacon, Boston, MA. Copyright © 2003 by Pearson Education. Reprinted/adapted by permission of the publisher.

have had previous contact or who has been highly recommended by a trusted associate. When employers have multiple applicants for a position, persons having had positive previous contacts with the employer have a decided edge over those without such contacts. Finally, when all a job searcher knows about a vacancy is what is listed in the job vacancy announcement, it is rather difficult to compose a cover letter and resumé that connects closely with the specific opening. Resumés composed in a general way are almost always poor resumés. When employers read resumés they look for connections with the skills required for being successful in the position for which they are hiring. A general, or "shotgun," approach to composing a resumé is likely to miss its target. Those candidates using a focused (rather than general) resumé that clearly connects with the responsibilities related to the job for which one is applying are the candidates most likely to be invited for an interview. Thus, describing relevant accomplishments in action-oriented terms (e.g., *managed, led, organized, developed, coordinated*) is key to an effective resumé.

Active job searchers do not rely on employers to announce job vacancies. Rather, they actively engage in meeting with those who may be most likely to employ people to do what it is that the job searcher wants to do. Active job searchers work diligently to activate and develop a *network* of persons who fit this description. They attend professional meetings and explore employment possibilities with friends, acquaintances, and relatives. They query others as to whether they know persons who work in a job in which they are interested and/or whether they know people who hire people to work in a job in which they are interested. They rely upon information interviewing to gather data about specific jobs and work environments as well as to expand their network of personal contacts within their field of interest. They activate a system of contacts that eventually helps them to connect with prospective employers in a personal way. After discussing the importance of networking, the career counselor could conclude session two by demonstrating effective information-interviewing skills and then have the group members engage in a role play using these skills (e.g., by asking questions related to what the person likes about his/her job, what sort of training is required, what the challenges of the job are, what a typical day is like, and whether the interviewee would be willing to provide a name of another person likely to be an information interview candidate).

Session three could address the different styles of resumés job searchers use and the pros and cons of each. For example, most people use (and employers tend to prefer) a chronological resumé. Chronological resumés contain important information related to the job searcher's educational and work experiences, listed in reverse chronological order. A useful strategy for composing a chronological resumé is to first itemize the essential skills required to succeed in the job in which the person is interested. Then, the job searcher should consider ways in which his or her experience can be described to match the requisite skills. As much as possible these skills should be described as achievements within each listing on the chronological resumé. Determining whether particular information should be included on the resumé is based upon whether the information is relevant to the job for which the person is applying. Although employers prefer a one-page resumé, workers with extensive experience may opt for a two-page resumé. In all cases, the resumé should be neat, professional in appearance, and error-free. Many job searchers find it helpful to review many sample resumés as they seek to identify a resumé format that they will use.

When job searchers do not have experiences that connect directly with the skills required for success in the job they are seeking, they often resort to using functional resumés. Functional resumés rely on the use of functional skill categories (e.g., managerial skills, organizational skills, communication skills, computer skills) that are relevant to the job. The job searcher first identifies the essential skills for the job being pursued and then lists accomplishments/experiences within each of the functional skills categories. The most relevant and highest priority skills areas should be listed first on the resumé. Functional resumés become useful when a job searcher has developed relevant skill sets via activities such as volunteering and independent learning. A final option for job searchers is a hybrid or chronological/functional resumé. Hybrid resumés can be used when a job searcher has some relevant employment experiences but also has developed relevant skills in nontraditional ways. In all cases a resumé should convince prospective employers that the job searcher could do the job for which the employer is seeking to hire someone. If the resumé does not connect to the job the searcher is pursuing, then the resumé will be viewed as weak and not accomplish the goal of gaining an interview. At the conclusion of session three the career counselor could assign participants the task of developing a resumé. The career counselor could meet with the participants individually to provide ongoing feedback pertaining to the resumé being developed.

After reviewing resumés with group participants, the career counselor could explore the essentials of job interview skills in session four. For example, the counselor could explain that all job interviews involve getting responses to three questions: Can you do the job? Will you do the job? Will you fit in? These are the essential questions employers have in mind when meeting with job candidates. A goal of the interviewee should be to address these three questions (whether the interviewer asks them or not). If the job searcher has engaged in a thorough process of self-assessment to decide which job(s) she or he wants to pursue, then the answers to these three questions should be apparent. That is, the job searcher should be clear about the relevant interests, skills, values, and other self-characteristics that predict a high probability for success in the job. Moreover, by identifying the requisite skills for success in the job when composing a resumé, the job searcher has already taken an important step in preparing for the job interview.

During the interview, the job searcher offers specific examples of relevant accomplishments that provide important data to the employer (the best predictor of success in the future is having been successful at a similar task in the past). For example, group participants can be told that rather than simply stating that you are confident in your organizational skills, you can also provide specific examples in which you successfully demonstrated organizational ability.

The question pertaining to whether the job searcher will "fit in" represents a key concern in the interview process. Perhaps more than anything else, employers want to know if a job candidate will demonstrate the sort of behaviors that contribute positively to the work climate. Skills such as getting along well with others, having effective communication skills, being reliable, being dependable, being stable in one's behavior, and staying on task represent the sort of self-management skills that employers strongly desire in their employees. Job interviewees must communicate that they possess these skills. This can be demonstrated in multiple ways (e.g., being on time for the interview, demonstrating effective interpersonal skills in the interview, dressing appropriately for the interview, discussing the fact that the job searcher possesses these skills—"I tend to be the sort of person who gets along well with others and works hard to contribute positively to my work environment, for example, . . . "). Finally, the career counselor can demonstrate effective (and not-so-effective interview skills) in the group session and then have group members discuss the demonstration before practicing effective job interview role plays.

The final group session can address the activities required for managing a job search effectively (e.g., keeping records of all contacts, setting goals to make a particular number of contacts each week, the importance of engaging in good self-care and positive self-talk, connecting with others who can be supportive, joining a job-search group). Last, but not least, the final session should involve collecting evaluative data to inform the career counselor about ways in which the experience can be improved in the future.

Typically, structured groups like the one we have just described blend didactic information with experiential information as career counselors seek to help their clients acquire pertinent knowledge, awareness, and skills connected to the purpose of the group. The career counselor should identify specific goals, objectives, and outcomes for each group session.

Career counseling groups can also be more process oriented and less structured. Less-structured groups tend to focus on the intrapersonal and interpersonal concerns clients experience in their career development. They also tend to be more affective oriented than structured group experiences. Spokane (1991) contends that less-structured career counseling groups will increase in popularity as career development interventions and general counseling interventions become more interwoven. Less-structured career counseling groups tend to meet over a longer period of time than structured groups. Pyle (2000) contends that less-structured groups are often useful for clients struggling with career choice or direction. Job searchers who are fully engaged in the job search process (i.e., they have already learned the skills described in the structured group) can also benefit from a process-oriented group experience. Riordan and Kahnweiler (1996) provide an excellent description of ways in which job-search support groups can be beneficial to job seekers.

The skills required for group career counseling are the same as those required in any group counseling experience; however, the counselor also needs to possess the requisite career knowledge pertaining to career development theory and practice. Pyle (2000, pp. 122–127) identifies four stages in group career counseling:

1. **Opening Stage:** The group members meet, the counselor provides an overview of the content of the group program, and goals are established. The counselor uses basic counseling skills, such as attending, concreteness, and genuineness.

2. **Investigation Stage:** Members focus on discussing the issues and topics pertinent to the group's purpose. For example, they may explore self-information (e.g., values, skills, interests), barriers to career development, or understanding the world-of-work. The counselor uses skills such as facilitative responses, self-disclosure, and personalizing to encourage group discussion.

3. **Working Stage:** Members process, synthesize, and identify actions they can take to advance their career development. The counselor uses skills such as accurate empathy, confrontation, providing feedback, and information processing to help clients during this stage.

4. **Decision/Operational Stage:** Members take action and provide support to each other regarding their action steps. The counselor uses skills such as drawing conclusions, helping members articulate their action plans, and bringing closure to the group experience.

There is mixed research evidence related to the effectiveness of career counseling groups. However, most of this evidence focuses on the effectiveness of structured group experiences. Most experts agree that there are several advantages to group career counseling experiences. For example, group career counseling is an efficient mode of service delivery. It maximizes the use of the counselor's time. This is especially important in school settings in which counselors often have very high caseloads and cannot offer individual counseling to every student for which they are responsible.

Kivlighan (1990) notes that career groups also provide opportunities for group members to (a) learn new information about themselves and others, (b) receive social and emotional support from other group members, and (c) learn from peers who are in similar situations. Group interventions also offer the opportunity for group members to share resources and ideas with each other, thereby maximizing opportunities for learning new strategies for coping with their career concerns. For example, Sullivan and Mahalik (2000) found that encouraging group members to focus on performance accomplishments, emotional arousal, vicarious experiences, and verbal persuasion was effective in helping group members increase career self-efficacy. Mawson and Kahn (1993) found that information-sharing aspects of the group process were helpful to group members in identifying stable career goals.

Group career counseling experiences are enhanced when the counselor is able to create a cooperative and inclusive group environment in which the members focus on commonly accepted goals. Hansen and Cramer (1971) note six additional criteria that contribute to successful groups:

1. Members of the group are in interaction with one another (i.e., there is open communication among group members).
2. Members of the group share a common goal.
3. The group members set norms that direct and guide their activities.
4. The group members develop a set of roles to play within the group.
5. The group members develop a network of interpersonal attraction (i.e., they develop likes and dislikes for each other).
6. The group works toward the satisfaction of individual needs of the group members.

CAREER COUNSELING PROFESSIONAL DESIGNATIONS AND RELATED SERVICE PROVIDERS

Regardless of whether a career counselor provides individual and/or group career assistance, we encourage counselors to develop a professional disclosure statement describing their training, experience, services offered, and approach to service delivery. This is important for a variety of reasons. As we have noted, many clients have clear expectations for career counseling (i.e., that they will be tested and informed as to which occupations are appropriate for them), and these expectations often do not mesh with current approaches to career counseling. Moreover, career services providers differ substantially in their training and areas of expertise, thus making the process of selecting a service provider an overwhelming one for consumers. For example, a popular movement today is the emergence of career coaching (Chung & Gfroerer, 2003). Career coaches can range from persons with professional counseling degrees and expertise in career development interventions to persons who are essentially paraprofessionals attempting to practice career counseling without the proper training and credentials. Generally, career coaches aspire to help persons identify their skills, make better career choices, and become more productive and satisfied workers. Career coaches seek to help their clients identify strategies for accomplishing their goals in their work lives. We take the view that (because few things are more personal than a career choice) it is difficult to engage in career coaching without delving into issues/concerns that require professional training as a counselor or psychologist. We agree with the NCDA's view that career coaching is an essential role for career counselors as exemplified by its being one of the core career counseling competencies identified by the NCDA (NCDA, 1997).

Unfortunately, when career coaches lack proper training and credentials, then they can easily tread into domains in which they engage in what professional counselors and psychologists label as *unethical practice*. Chung and Gfroerer (2003) recently highlighted the practice, training, professional, and ethical issues existing within the practice of career coaching. Chung and Gfroerer point out the lack of training, the absence of enforceable ethical standards, weak professional credentials, and the paucity of research investigating the efficacy of career coaching practices as areas that pose substantial difficulties for those engaging in career coaching without professional counselor training. When career counselors provide a clear description of their training and credentials to prospective clients, they help consumers understand the difference between professionals who provide career coaching as part of their career counseling practice and others who lack appropriate credentials and expertise.

One important designation for career counselors is the Master Career Counselor (MCC) designation offered by the NCDA. A MCC has at least 3 years of post-master's experience in career counseling and is also a nationally certified counselor, licensed professional counselor, and/or licensed psychologist. MCCs must have successfully completed at least three credits of coursework in each of the six NCDA career counseling competency areas and have completed a supervised career counseling practicum or 2 years of supervised career counseling work experience under a certified supervisor or licensed counseling professional. MCCs are skilled in administering and interpreting career assessments and provide the highest quality of career counseling services.

SUMMARY

Career development interventions are the cornerstone of the counseling profession (Dorn, 1992). However, we know relatively little about the career counseling process. Many view career counseling from a perspective that is frozen in the past. Rounds and Tinsley (1984) suggest that conceptualizing career counseling as psychotherapy "would foster advances in the understanding of vocational behavior change and processes" (p. 139). Such notions pertaining to career counseling reflect the widely recognized belief that career issues are contextual and that the context of the 21st century is not the same as the context of the early 20th century. Savickas (1993) encourages career counselors to respond to the societal changes occurring in the new millennium by stating that "counselors must innovate their career interventions to fit the new *zeitgeist*" (p. 205).

It should also be evident that the career counseling interventions used by professional counselors and psychologists must be guided by an understanding of how the current *zeitgeist* shapes the career tasks presented to students and workers. To help clients address career tasks in contemporary society, career practitioners should provide counseling-based career assistance and support to their students and clients. By expanding their career interventions in these ways, career counselors provide assistance that is sensitive to the career concerns students and clients experience in the 21st century.

REFERENCES

Amundson, N. E. (1995). An interactive model of career decision making. *Journal of Employment Counseling, 32,* 11–21.

Amundson, N. E., Harris-Bowlsbey, J., & Niles, S. G. (2005). *Essential elements of career counseling.* Upper Saddle River, NJ: Merrill/ Prentice Hall.

Anderson, W. P., & Niles, S. G. (1995). Career and personal concerns expressed by career counseling clients. *The Career Development Quarterly, 43,* 240–245.

Anderson, W. P., & Niles, S. G. (2000). Important events in career counseling: Client and counselor descriptions. *The Career Development Quarterly, 48,* 251–263.

Blustein, D. L., & Spengler, P. M. (1995). Personal adjustment: Career counseling and psychotherapy. In W. B. Walsh & S. H. Osipow (Eds.), *Handbook of vocational psychology* (2nd ed., pp. 295–329). Hillsdale, NJ: Erlbaum.

Brammer, L. M. (1993). *The helping relationship: Process and skills* (5th ed.). Boston: Allyn & Bacon.

Brehm, S. S. (1987). Social support and clinical practice. In J. Maddux, C. Stoltenberg, &

R. Rosenwein (Eds.), *Social processes in clinical and counseling psychology* (pp. 26–38). New York: Springer-Verlag.

Brown, D., & Brooks, L. (1985). Career counseling as a mental health intervention. *Professional Psychology: Research and Practice, 16,* 860–867.

Brown, D., & Brooks, L. (1991). *Career counseling techniques.* Needham Heights, MA: Allyn & Bacon.

Brown, S. D., Ryan, J. M., & Krane, N. E. (2000). Four (or five) sessions and a cloud of dust: Old assumptions and new observations about career counseling. In S. D. Brown & R. W. Lent (Eds.), *Handbook of counseling psychology* (3rd. ed., pp. 740–766). New York: Wiley.

Carlsen, M. B. (1988). *Making meaning: Therapeutic processes in adult development.* New York: W. W. Norton.

Carson, K. D., Carson, P. P., Phillips, J. S., & Roe, C. W. (1996). A career retrenchment model: Theoretical development and empirical outcomes. *Journal of Career Development, 22,* 273–286.

Chung, Y. B., & Gfroerer, M. C. A. (2003). Career coaching: Practice, training, professional, and ethical issues. *The Career Development Quarterly, 52,* 141–152.

Council for the Accreditation of Counseling and Related Educational Programs. (2001). *Standards.* Alexandria, VA: American Counseling Association.

Crites, J. O. (1976). A comprehensive model of career development in early adulthood. *Journal of Vocational Behavior, 9,* 105–118.

Crites, J. O. (1981). *Career counseling: Models, methods, and materials.* New York: McGraw-Hill.

Dorn, F. J. (1992). Occupational wellness: The integration of career identity and personal identity. *Journal of Counseling and Development, 71,* 176–178.

Fouad, N. A. (1993). Cross-cultural vocational assessment. *The Career, Development Quarterly, 42,* 4–13.

Galassi, J. P., Crace, R. K., Martin, G. A., James, R. M., & Wallace, R. L. (1992). Client preferences and anticipations in career counseling: A preliminary investigation. *Journal of Counseling Psychology, 39,* 46–55.

Gati, I., Krausz, M., & Osipow, S. H. (1996). A taxonomy of difficulties in career decision making. *Journal of Counseling Psychology, 43,* 510–526.

Gysbers, N. C., Heppner, M. J., & Johnston, J. A. (2003). *Career counseling: Process, issues, and techniques.* Boston, MA: Allyn & Bacon.

Hansen, J. C., & Cramer, S. H. (Eds.). (1971). *Group guidance and counseling in the schools.* New York: Appleton-Century-Crofts.

Heppner, M. J., & Hendricks, F. (1995). A process and outcome study examining career indecision and indecisiveness. *Journal of Counseling and Development, 73,* 426–437.

Heppner, M. J., Multon, K. D., Gysbers, N. C., Ellis, C. A., & Zook, C. E. (1998). The relationship of trainee self-efficacy to the process and outcome of career counseling. *Journal of Counseling Psychology, 45,* 393–402.

Heppner, M. J., O'Brien, K. M., Hinkelman, J. M., & Flores, L. Y. (1996). Training counseling psychologists in career development: Are we our own worst enemies? *The Counseling Psychologist, 24,* 105–125.

Herr, E. L. (1989). Career development and mental health. *Journal of Career Development, 16,* 5–18.

Herr, E. L., Cramer, S. H., & Niles, S. G. (2004). *Career guidance and counseling through the lifespan: Systemic approaches* (6th ed.). Boston, MA: Allyn & Bacon.

Herr, E. L., & Niles, S. G. (1998). Career: Social action in behalf of purpose, productivity, and hope. In C. Lee & G. Walz (Eds.), *Social action: A mandate for counselors* (pp. 117–136). Alexandria, VA: American Counseling Association.

Hershenson, D. B. (1996). Work adjustment: A neglected area in career counseling. *Journal of Counseling & Development, 74,* 442–446.

Highlen, P. S., & Hill, C. E. (1984). Factors affecting client change in individual counseling: Current status and theoretical speculations. In S. Brown & R. Lent (Eds.), *Handbook of counseling psychology* (pp. 334–396). New York: Wiley.

Holland, J. L., Magoon, T. M., & Spokane, A. R. (1981). Counseling psychology: Career interventions, research, and theory. *Annual Review of Psychology, 32,* 279–300.

House, J. S. (1981). *Work stress and social support.* Reading, MA: Addison-Wesley.

Ibrahim, F. A., Ohnishi, H., & Wilson, R. P. (1994). Career assessment in a culturally diverse society. *Journal of Career Assessment, 2,* 276–288.

Isaacson, L. E. (1985). *Basics of career counseling.* Boston, MA: Allyn & Bacon.

Kahn, R. L., & Antonucci, T. (1980). Convoys over the life course: Attachment, roles, and social support. In P. B. Baltes and O. Brim (Eds.), *Lifespan development and behavior* (vol. 3). Boston, MA: Lexington Press.

Kalton, C. A. (2001). Client psychological distress: An important factor in career counseling. *The Career Development Quarterly, 49,* 324–335.

Kirschner, T. (1988). *Process and outcome of career counseling.* Unpublished doctoral dissertation, University of Maryland, College Park.

Kirschner, T., Hoffman, M. A., & Hill, C. E. (1994). Case study of the process and outcome of career counseling. *Journal of Counseling Psychology, 35,* 216–226.

Kivlighan, D. M. (1990). Career group therapy. *The Counseling Psychologist, 18,* 64–80.

Krumboltz, J. D. (1988). *Career Beliefs Inventory.* Palo Alto, CA: Consulting Psychologists Press.

Krumboltz, J. D. (1996). *A social learning theory of career counseling.* Stanford, CA: Stanford University.

Leong, F. T. L. (1993). The career counseling process with racial-ethnic minorities: The case of Asian

Americans. *The Career Development Quarterly, 42*, 26–40.

Leong, F. T. L., & Chervinko, S. (1996). Construct validity of career indecision: Negative personality traits as predictors of career indecision. *Journal of Career Assessment, 4*, 315–329.

Luzzo, D. A. (1996). Exploring the relationship between the perception of occupational barriers and career development. *Journal of Career Development, 22*, 239–248.

Mawson D. L., & Kahn, S. E. (1993). Group process in a women's career intervention. *The Career Development Quarterly, 41*, 238–245.

Meichenbaum, D., & Turk, D. C. (1987). *Facilitating treatment adherence: A practitioner's guidebook.* New York: Plenum Press.

Multon, K. D., Heppner, M. J., Gysbers, N. C., Zook, C., & Ellis-Kalton, C. A. (2001). Client psychological distress: An important factor in career counseling. *The Career Development Quarterly, 49*, 324–325.

Neimeyer, G. J. (1992). Personal constructs in career counseling and development. *Journal of Career Development, 18*, 163–174.

Niles, S. G., & Anderson, W. P. (1995). A content analysis of career and personal concerns expressed by career counseling clients. *Educational and Vocational Guidance Bulletin, 57*, 59–62.

Niles, S. G., Anderson, W. P., Jr., & Cover, S. (2000). Comparing intake concerns and goals with career counseling concerns. *The Career Development Quarterly, 49*, 135–145.

Niles, S. G., & Pate, R. H. (1989). Competency and training issues related to the integration of career counseling and mental health counseling. *Journal of Career Development, 16*, 63–71.

Oliver, L. W., & Spokane, A. R. (1988). Career-intervention outcome: What contributes to client gain? *Journal of Counseling Psychology, 35*, 447–462.

Otani, A. (1989). Client resistance in counseling: Its theoretical rationale and taxonomic classification. *Journal of Counseling and Development, 67*, 458–461.

Peavy, R. V. (1994). A constructivist perspective for counseling. *Educational and Vocational Guidance Bulletin, 55*, 31.

Pope-Davis, D. B., & Dings, J. G. (1995). The assessment of multicultural counseling competencies. In J. G. Ponterotto, J. M. Casas, L. A.

Suzuki, & C. M. Alexander (Eds.), *Handbook of multicultural counseling* (pp. 287–311). Thousand Oaks, CA: Sage.

Pyle, K. R. (2000). A group approach to career decision-making. In N. Peterson & R. C. Gonzalez (Eds.), *Career counseling models for diverse populations: Hands-on applications for practitioners* (pp. 121–136). Belmont, CA: Wadsworth/Thompson Learning.

Riordan, R. J., & Kahnweiler, W. (1996). Job support groups: Three configurations. *Journal of Counseling & Development, 74*, 517–520.

Rounds, J. B., & Tinsley, H. E. A. (1984). Diagnosis and treatment of vocational problems. In S. Brown & R. Lent (Eds.), *Handbook of counseling psychology* (pp. 137–177). New York: Wiley.

Salomone, P. R. (1982). Difficult cases in career counseling: II. The indecisive client. *The Personnel and Guidance Journal, 60*, 496–500.

Sampson, J. P., Vacc, N. A., & Loesch, L. C. (1998). The practice of career counseling by specialists and counselors in general practice. *The Career Development Quarterly, 46*, 404–415.

Savickas, M. L. (1989). Annual review: Practice and research in career counseling and development, 1988. *The Career Development Quarterly, 38*, 100–134.

Savickas, M. L. (1993). Career counseling in the postmodern era. *Journal of Cognitive Psychotherapy: An International Quarterly, 7*, 205–215.

Schlossberg, N. K. (1984). *Counseling adults in transition, linking practice with theory.* New York: Springer.

Spokane, A. R. (1991). *Evaluating career interventions.* Upper Saddle River, NJ: Prentice Hall.

Subich, L. M. (1993). How personal is career counseling? *The Career Development Quarterly, 42*, 129–131.

Sue, D. W., Bernier, J. E., Durran, A., Feinberg, L., Peterson, P., Smith, E. J., & Vasquez-Nutall, E. (1982). Position paper: Cross-cultural counseling competencies. *The Counseling Psychologist, 10*(2), 45–52.

Sullivan, K. R., & Mahalik, J. R. (2000). Increasing career self-efficacy for women: Evaluating a group intervention. *Journal of Counseling & Development, 78*, 54–62.

Super, D. E. (1957). *The psychology of careers.* New York: Harper & Row.

Super, D. E. (1980). A life-span, life-space approach to career development. *Journal of Vocational Behavior, 16,* 282–298.

Super, D. E. (1990). A life-span, life-space approach to career development. In D. Brown, L. Brooks & Associates (Eds.), *Career choice and development: Applying contemporary theories to practice* (2nd ed., pp. 197–261). San Francisco: Jossey-Bass.

Super, D. E., Savickas, M. L., & Super, C. (1996). A life-span, life-space approach to career development. In D. Brown, L. Brooks, & Associates (Eds.), *Career choice and development* (3rd ed.). San Francisco, CA: Jossey-Bass.

Swanson, J. L. (1995). The process and outcome of career counseling. In W. B. Walsh & S. H. Osipow (Eds.), *Handbook of vocational psychology: Theory, research, and practice* (pp. 217–259). Hillsdale, NJ: Erlbaum.

Ward, C. M., & Bingham, R. P. (1993). Career assessment of ethnic minority women. *Journal of Career Assessment, 1,* 246–257.

Watkins, C. E., Jr., & Savickas, M. L. (1990). Psychodynamic career counseling. In W. B. Walsh & S. H. Osipow (Eds.), *Career counseling: Contemporary topics in vocational psychology* (pp. 79–116). Hillsdale, NJ: Erlbaum.

Whiston, S. C. (2002). Applications of the principles: Career counseling and interventions. *The Counseling Psychologist, 30,* 218–237.

Whiston, S. C. (2003). Career counseling: 90 years old yet still healthy and vital. *The Career Development Quarterly, 52,* 35–42.

CHAPTER 9

DESIGNING AND IMPLEMENTING CAREER DEVELOPMENT PROGRAMS AND SERVICES

It is evident that career counseling embraces career/life-planning concerns. What is not as obvious is that providing career services demands structures that encompass business principles.

Those principles address such issues as strategic planning, program design, financial and marketing concerns, evaluation and review processes. Being exposed to the development of successful programs that deliver effective services strengthens the foundation of all we learn in our graduate programs.

As a private practitioner for the past 17 years I have found that my own career has benefited from knowing about the systems involved in the work we do. It is my belief that we approach this study from two perspectives. One is for our own career success. Whether the original goal is counseling, teaching, private practice, consulting, training or any of the options open to us, we will ultimately work within systems. Career Development asks us to explore the world of work. Career programs and service delivery systems are our world of work.

Secondly, we prepare ourselves for the multiple roles we will be expected to fulfill in our work settings. We will undoubtedly be called upon to be part of a program design team, to determine criteria to evaluate the success of a program, or to market the program so that funding is available to provide services.

We prepare ourselves to take an active role in the success of a program. We expand our options. We add another dimension to our suitcase of transferable skills.

Martha Russell, M. S. NCC
Career Services
Board of Directors
NCDA

Previous chapters, especially Chapters 4 through 8, have provided a great deal of information about the content of career planning services. This chapter focuses on the process of designing these programs and then delivering them to the students or clients for whom they are developed. The step-by-step process of design, development, and delivery is described, and five sample programs are presented as examples.

There are important reasons for engaging in program design. The first is that it is impossible for counselors in any setting other than private practice to provide all of the assistance needed by the students or clients they serve on a one-to-one basis. Schools typically have counselor-student ratios ranging from 1:300 to 1:1000, and among the mix of services provided by school counselors, attention to career concerns is low. Thus, without having a systematic program of career planning services that can be offered to groups of students, only a very small percentage of students would receive assistance.

Even if these services could be provided on a one-to-one basis, this would be a cost-ineffective way to provide them to all. The goal of career guidance services should be to provide the maximum benefit to students and clients at the lowest per-person cost. Clearly, given the workload and time restraints of counselors in schools and other settings, the goal should be to save one-on-one time for persons that need such specialized service while providing service to most students through a variety of methods, including classroom instruction, group guidance, group counseling, computer-based career planning systems, and Internet Web sites.

A second rationale for careful program planning is to require that career services be carefully thought out before their delivery. Such thought, following a process detailed later in this chapter, results in much higher program quality. It also provides the basis for determining program content, methods of delivery, evaluation, and a clear description of the program for administrators, parents, and recipients of the program.

Counselors may play a variety of roles related to the design and implementation of career development programs and services in their work settings. These roles may include advocacy, coordination, participation, designing, and managing. Let's look at each of those roles separately.

In the role of advocacy, counselors use their skills and influence to work with the various stakeholders, which may include faculty, administrators and managers, and, in some settings, parents, to achieve improved career planning services. This role may include serving on advisory boards or committees, making presentations, or exerting influence in a variety of other ways.

In the role of coordination, counselors collaborate with internal staff (such as other counselors, teachers, and managers) and external entities (such as employers, advisory board members, agencies, community organizations, and parents) to deliver parts of the program of services. They may work with teachers to develop curriculum that includes career planning concepts, with managers to develop workshops, with community organizations to serve as mentors for students, with parents to raise money for some parts of the program, or with employers to offer job-shadowing experiences or internships.

In the role of participation, counselors personally deliver all or part of the program of service. They may do this through a combination of group work, one-to-one counseling, instruction, assessment, and support of use of computer-based systems and Web sites.

Counselors may be the only persons in schools or other organizations who are trained in career development theory and practice. Thus they are likely to be the persons who are called upon as designers and developers of services for students or clients. For example, a counselor may be employed by a middle school, high school, or university that wishes to provide career development services for all of its students. Or, a counselor may work in a corporation as a personnel worker and be called upon to develop services that meet immediate needs caused by corporate restructuring, downsizing, or other kinds of change. A company undergoing such changes would likely ask a counselor to develop ways to help employees make these upsetting transitions with less stress and with a better image of the company.

If the school, university, or company has hundreds or thousands of students or employees who need to benefit from career planning services, it is impossible to meet this need exclusively by dealing with everyone on a face-to-face, interview basis. It is essential to design a program and then to deliver it in ways that will reach the largest number of people and will do so cost-effectively. A process for accomplishing this is presented in 10 steps, each explained in detail.

STEPS FOR DESIGNING AND IMPLEMENTING A CAREER DEVELOPMENT PROGRAM

Step 1: Define the Target Population and Its Characteristics

The purpose of this step of the program design process is to get a clear picture of the people the program will serve. It is necessary to describe the population with some clarity as indicated in the following illustrations. This description might contain demographic data such as racial-ethnic background, mean and range of scores on achievement or aptitude tests, gender, age range, and types of diversity.

High School. Midtown High School has 673 students, who are fairly evenly divided over the 4 years (freshman, sophmore, junior, senior). They come from families in a small city and areas as far as 10 miles from the city. Sixty-one percent of the students are male and 39% are female. Seventy percent are Caucasian, 14% African American, and 16% Hispanic. Most students come from middle-income families in which wage-earners work in the area's tourist industry, are retail merchants, or work as assembly workers in the local factories. In the past, no attention has been given to teaching students about planning for future jobs.

College/University. Upstate University, located in a rural area of the state, has approximately 14,000 full-time undergraduate students, 900 full-time graduate students, 1700 part-time undergraduate students, and 2500 part-time graduate students. It draws students from all over the state as well as 12% from other states and 5% from other countries. The mean age of undergraduate students is 19.4 years; of graduate students, 29.4 years. Twenty percent of undergraduate students continue on to graduate school; the remainder seek jobs immediately after graduation, most of them within the state. Job placement for those who complete the university's undergraduate and graduate programs has traditionally been very high, approaching 95% within 3 months after completion. Within the past 3 years, however, this figure has declined to approximately 90%, likely because major corporations in the state are reducing the number of new employees in order to be able to retain as many of their current employees as possible. In the past, no services have been provided to students to help them know how to seek employment or plan their careers.

Corporation.   The Royal Corporation, located about 40 miles south of a large urban area, has almost 12,000 employees, ranging in age from 18 to 65. The corporation makes audio and video boards for computers. It offers positions in management, sales, advertising, and light factory-assembly work in which manual dexterity and accuracy are critical to the quality of its products. The turnover rate of employees is 26% each year. In this company no assistance has ever been provided with topics such as how to make transitions, how to conduct a successful job search, or how to analyze one's skills so that they can be transferred to another position.

Job Service Office.   This office serves the northeast area of the city. Typical clients include adults in the age range of 35 to 65 who have been laid off, or are displaced homemakers, veterans, ex-offenders from the local state prison, or persons on public aid. Most clients have very low skill levels in reading, mathematics, and language usage and have no or little past work experience. Further, they have a mean educational level of sixth grade and have not acquired marketable job skills.

There are at least two ways to gather the information that will provide a description of a target population in some detail. One way that may yield sufficient detail is to review the records that already exist in a school, agency, or company. The second way is to develop a questionnaire to administer to all potential students or clients, or at least to a group that has been selected as a random sample. A random sample is a small group taken from the whole group by using a computer program or by drawing specific numbers (which may be student- or employee-identification numbers) from a book of random numbers. Before using this approach, one should consult someone who knows research and sampling techniques or read a chapter on this topic in a relevant book.

It is important to understand the nature of a target population before beginning to design a program of services. This information provides insight about the topics, reading level, methods, tools, time available, and level of sophistication for the material to be presented in the career planning program.

Step 2: Determine the Needs of the Target Population

Obviously, it is impossible for counselors to develop a program of services to meet student, client, or employee needs if they do not know in considerable detail what those needs are. If the target population consists of high school students, it is possible to infer from their age and stage in career planning that they have certain needs, such as deciding whether to attend a vocational-technical school, attend a university, or go directly to work. It is also safe to assume that they need assistance in selecting the occupation(s) they plan to enter. But, there may be other needs that cannot be identified by age or life stage alone—such as a need to have more information about the community colleges in the area—if needs are not assessed in a more formal way.

If the target population is in a college or university, it can be assumed, because of the age of these students and their stage in career planning, that they need to (1) understand the relationship between majors and specific occupations, (2) select one or more occupations, and (3) learn how to find job openings and get a job effectively. It cannot be known, however, without a needs assessment, if a large percentage of the students do not know how changes in the job market may affect their career planning significantly.

If the target population consists of employees in a corporation, less is known from theory about their needs. One may surmise that those who will be laid off need to learn how to write a resumé and engage in job interviews, but program designers might not assume that a significant percentage would like to leave the corporation voluntarily because of job dissatisfaction without administering a questionnaire or working with focus groups.

There are at least four ways to identify the needs of any group. First, there may be some information already available from past questionnaires that can be used to identify some needs. Second, a short questionnaire can be made and administered in written form to everyone in the target group, potentially via the organization's intranet or in several, small focus groups. A focus group is a group of 10 to 15 people who are selected for a specific purpose (in this case, to help identify needs) and are believed to be representative of the total population. Use of a focus group allows not only the completion of a questionnaire, but also the opportunity to discuss the answers given by people in the group, thus gaining more in-depth information. Third, consultants may be hired to make recommendations based upon thier knowledge of normal developmental needs or of the needs of others in similar settings.

Finally, there are often needs in schools (such as a high percentage of drop-outs) or corporations (such as unmotivated employees) that are related to poor or inadequate career planning. Thus in some settings it would be wise and helpful to ask administrators and managers to identify problems that need solutions. Then, services can be devised that address those particular problems. If solutions are found, it is likely that there will be support from management for the delivery of the career planning service. Following are examples of the kinds of needs that might be identified for different settings.

Middle School. According to theory, these are the years for broad-based exploration of occupations and gaining awareness of the work world through becoming acquainted with clusters of occupations. It is also the time to motivate awareness on the part of the students that career choices need to be made in the future and that there is a relationship between current schoolwork and future plans.

High School. Almost no students realize that there have been many changes in the past few years that will make their approach to career planning quite different from that of their parents. Students have no knowledge of how occupations are organized or how their work tasks vary. Almost no students can describe their interests or their best abilities, and those who can do not know how these may relate to their future work. Many students do not understand that different jobs require different amounts of education, and they cannot define the different paths of education (i.e., vocational-technical school, 2-year college, university, apprenticeship, military service, etc.) that lead to work.

College/University. As with the high school students, few realize that there have been many changes in the past few years that should make their approach to career planning different from that of their parents. Further, they do not realize that they are likely to change occupations several times during their lifetime and that this will become the accepted pattern. Students on the whole do not understand how the world-of-work is organized, nor how specific subject-matter specialties relate to this organization and to jobs that they will be seeking. Many cannot state their personal interests, their best skills or abilities, nor the values that they would hope to attain through work. Many have had no instruction about how to decide what kinds of jobs they might like, how to find openings in these jobs, how to have successful job interviews, or how to evaluate one job over another in accordance with personal preferences.

Corporation.   Many employees still believe that the corporation should be responsible for them for the remainder of their working lives. Based on a survey administered to all employees, most (91%) indicate that they have no knowledge about how to plan for a career change, leaving this company and going to another or to self-employment. About half (52%) report that they are dissatisfied with their current position and would like to have an opportunity to move elsewhere in the company. Some (15%) indicate that they would leave the company and pursue different employment if they had any idea how to do that.

Step 3: Write Measurable Objectives to Meet Needs

A measurable objective is the clear statement of a goal, including how to determine whether or not the goal has been reached. There are at least two reasons for writing objectives for the career planning services. First, having to follow the discipline of writing objectives will require a counselor to think carefully about what he or she is trying to achieve and how to know if it has been achieved. Second, the objectives will become the basis for the content and evaluation of the services. It is almost universally true that management will not support a program, either psychologically or financially, that is not explained adequately and does not show evidence of being effective. So, in order to get and retain support for career planning services, it is necessary to define them clearly (via the objectives) and also measure the outcomes of providing them (via evaluation).

The identified needs of the target population become the basis for writing measurable objectives. If, for some reason, the time and money required to do a needs analysis is not available, it may be necessary to use broad statements of goals at the various age levels provided by such documents as the Career Development Guidelines published by the National Occupational Information Coordinating Committee (NOICC) (NOICC, 1996), presented in Chapters 10 and 11, or similar documents developed by state or local entities. Measurable objectives should always begin with the statement, "At the end of this (workshop, program of services, school year, course), students (employees, clients) will be able to .... " The statement of the objective, described in some way that makes it possible to measure its accomplishment, should follow this general statement. Some sample measurable objectives are listed next.

High School.   By the end of the second year of high school, students will be able to

1. Describe changes in the American workplace that will affect their own career planning.

2. State at least two areas of interest, using either Holland (1997) clusters or job families on the World-of-Work Map (ACT, 2000) for future work.
3. Describe the courses or curricula available in their high school to help prepare them for these areas of work.
4. Describe different paths of education or training that they might pursue after high school related to these areas of work.

By the end of the third year of high school, students will be able to

1. State one or more tentative occupational choices.
2. List specific schools or ways in which they can get the postsecondary training needed for these occupations.
3. Complete an action plan that lists the steps needed to move from these choices through the education needed to enter the occupation.
4. Demonstrate job-seeking skills such as completing a job application and engaging effectively in mock job interviews (for those not planning to seek further education).

College/University.   By the end of the first year, students will be able to

1. State at least two areas of their highest interest, using either Holland (1997) clusters or job families on the World-of-Work Map (ACT, 2000).
2. Describe in detail at least three occupations in each of these two areas, based on research through use of reference books, computer software, Web sites, and informational interviews.
3. Tentatively select an occupation or group of occupations.
4. Select a major that is related to the occupational choice.

By the end of the third year, students will be able to

1. List at least three companies in the geographic area where they offer positions like those desired.
2. Describe each of these companies in terms of its products, number of employees, recent history related to reducing its workforce and/or restructuring, and potential for employees' further growth or training.
3. Write a high-quality resumé in electronic and one other format.
4. Exhibit skill, through participation in mock interviews, in the job-interviewing process.
5. State five personal criteria for identifying jobs or for selecting one job offer over another.

Corporation.   At the end of this series of workshops, employees will be able to

1. State how recent changes in the American workplace are affecting their personal careers.
2. Describe the career planning process that they may need to use either because they choose to make career changes or because the company needs to make adjustments.
3. List their top-10 transferable skills, usable should they need to make a career change.

4. Write a high-quality resumé, in electronic and one other format, that describes their education, work skills, and employment history.
5. State the type and length of training that would expand or update some of their job skills, making them more productive for the company or more marketable should they decide to leave the company.

Agency Serving Low-Income Adults.   At the end of these three sessions, participants will be able to

1. Identify skills learned in home management and state how to describe them in a resumé.
2. Identify jobs in which these identified skills can be used.
3. Write an attractive resumé that capitalizes on these skills.

As indicated, these objectives become the basis for the content of career planning services as well as the methods of evaluating them.

Step 4: Determine How to Deliver the Career Planning Services

In this step the goal is to provide as rich an array of services to as many people as possible in the most cost-effective way. Providing service via one-to-one interviews is the most expensive and the most time-consuming way to deliver service. For this reason, it is desirable to do as much as possible through other methods that are effective but demand less time. Methods other than one-to-one interviewing include the following (of course, any of these could be combined with one-to-one interviewing).

- Offering special courses or units within existing courses about career planning topics (middle school, high school, and perhaps college/university) in face-to-face and/or Web-based delivery
- Offering workshops that serve 8 to 15 people (university and corporation)
- Using software that addresses career planning topics
- Developing or using Web sites that provide career planning content
- Providing self-help materials that may include assessment inventories and a companion workbook

The methods chosen to provide the career planning services will relate to available time, staff, budget, and resources (such as assessment inventories or self-help books) that fit the population's needs and objectives; the amount of time people have to spend on career planning needs at the school or worksite; and available technical resources (for use of computer software or Internet Web sites).

Middle School and High School.   Much of the content could be provided in the classroom by training teachers to include some of the topics in their curriculum or through a well-planned and staffed career center. Alternatively, a career planning course may be offered to students during designated class periods or through homeroom or advisement periods. This curriculum may be developed locally, or the site might use a curricular package such as Develop Your Future I and II (Harris-Bowlsbey & Perry, 2003a, 2003b). Individual interviews with counselors could be offered to students who need individualized help.

College/University.   The content could be provided through a series of workshops, offered by a career counselor or certified career development facilitator, as a part of the services of a well-equipped physical career center, through a virtual career center (i.e., a Web site), and/or through individual interviews with students who need them. Another viable method is offering a for-credit, one-semester career planning course. This course may be developed at the local level or may utilize an already-developed course such as Take Hold of Your Future (Harris-Bowlsbey & Lisansky, 2002).

Corporation.   The content could be provided through a series of workshops provided by a career counselor or a certified career development facilitator, through workshops and individual interviews provided by a trained manager, or via the corporation's intranet or Web site. Many corporations have a career management center that provides a wealth of printed information, access to computer software and Web sites, and one-to-one counseling provided by a certified, professional counselor.

Community Agencies.   The content may be provided through a series of workshops or through one-to-one interviews. Web sites may also be used for assessment, career information, and job searching. Individual counseling may also be available.

Step 5: Determine the Content of the Program

The content of the program is determined by its objectives, so it is necessary to look at each objective and imagine different ways it could be addressed. Here is one example for each of the populations.

High School.   Objective: Describe changes in the American workplace that affect personal career planning.

Methods of meeting objective: Ask representatives from companies or government organizations to describe these changes in a scheduled meeting; ask students to read a book, use Web sites, or read several articles on this topic. Have a group discussion after use of any of these methods of providing the basic information.

College/University.   Objective: State at least two areas of their highest interest, using either job families on the World-of-Work Map or Holland clusters.

Method of meeting objective: Administer one or a combination of several instruments that measure interests, skills/abilities, and/or values by Holland typology. Provide score reports to students, and interpret the results for them.

Corporation.   Objective: Describe the career planning process that they may need to use either because they choose to make career changes or because the company needs to make adjustments.

Methods of meeting objective: Provide a workshop in which the career planning process is described; prepare a brochure for all employees; train managers in this process, and ask them, in turn, to provide this information and instruction in meetings that they have with employees; place this information on the corporate intranet or Web site.

Step 6: Determine the Cost of the Program

It is rare indeed that any project will be approved without knowledge of its cost. In order to calculate cost accurately, it is necessary that the objectives be defined, that the method(s) of meeting each objective be detailed, and that the content proposed for each objective be solidified. At that point, it should be possible to calculate a budget that includes all of the following components:

- Staff time for designing, developing, and evaluating the products and services
- Staff time needed either to deliver or train others to deliver the program
- Software that may be needed
- Equipment and materials needed, such as computers, reference books, or copies of assessment inventories
- Printing costs, if any
- Technical costs (if computer software or Internet material is being developed)
- Cost for using facilities, if any
- Cost of refreshments for participants, if any

A manager would want to know how much of the total cost requires spending additional money and how much represents the use of staff, equipment, and materials that already exist. In some settings, it may also be necessary to project expected gains from having delivered the program of services. For example, if offered in a university setting and the expectation is that the services will reduce the loss of enrolled students, the strategy of comparing the cost of delivering the service to one current student with that of recruiting and orienting one new student may be effective. If in a corporate setting the goal of a program of services is to improve the satisfaction of employees, resulting in higher productivity, cost may be justified by comparing the cost of delivering the service to one employee to the value of the increased productivity of that employee.

Because managers are always very busy, the budget should be presented in a very succinct way, summarizing the services, the benefits that are expected from the services, and the total or per-client cost of delivering them.

Step 7: Begin to Promote and Explain Your Services

In any environment there are always some who are willing to support career planning services and others who are ready to criticize them. It is important to build an understanding and supportive environment for introducing any new program. There are several ways to accomplish this:

- Early in the design process, invite or appoint a committee of people to help design the program, or at least to provide feedback about preliminary plans. It is important to choose people who are respected by others and are influential. When others see that the proposed program is being supported by these people, they will be more likely to do so as well.
- As soon as preliminary ideas are formed, begin to explain them to managers and ask for their input, either in individual meetings or through the circulation of a document to which they are invited to add their comments.

- Start with a small pilot test. Try to get some respected and visible students or employees to participate in the pilot test. Not only will a pilot test help to expand and refine ideas and procedures, but it will also begin to provide publicity by word of mouth. Capitalize on that by having short articles in the school or corporate newsletter in which someone talks about the new program and how it has benefited him or her.
- If the school or company is facing challenges or problems that might be alleviated by some part of the proposed career planning program, begin with that part. Ideally, the career planning assistance will help solve those problems and will thus be viewed positively when it is time for expansion.

Step 8: Start Promoting and Delivering the Full-Blown Program of Services

It is important to notice that seven time-consuming planning steps have occurred before starting to deliver the services that have been designed and planned. Though this seems tedious, the time and energy spent in the long planning cycle will result in a higher-quality end product.

No matter how good a product or service is, it does not meet its objectives if people do not avail themselves of it. It is very important, at the same time the content is being designed, to plan how the program will be promoted. Thus plans for promotion should be ready to implement prior to the time the service itself is implemented.

Just as the first impression in a job interview is extremely critical, so is the impression that is created the first time new services are offered. Make sure that everything is ready for launching the program before beginning and that its first round of delivery is of very high quality. Thereby, the program will gain an image of quality and usefulness from the outset.

Step 9: Evaluate the Program

There are at least three reasons why career planning services need to be evaluated. First and foremost, it is essential to know if the program is helping people achieve the objectives that were set at Step 3. Those objectives were written in order to meet the needs identified in the target population. If the program does not help people achieve those objectives, then it is not meeting their needs.

Second, it is necessary to evaluate the program so that it can be improved. No matter how well the design and development stages have been accomplished, implementation of a new program will always identify additional needs, different possible approaches, and good ideas for enhancement. Program development and delivery is a cyclical process, so new ideas should be included in the program at next delivery.

Third, but certainly not least, is the need to provide ongoing information to managers about the success of the program. Success, in the minds of managers, relates both to how many people are availing themselves of the program and to the effectiveness of the program in meeting the identified needs. Therefore, two kinds of data are needed: quantitative data (How many people did the program serve?) and qualitative data (What did the people think of it? Did it achieve the objectives laid out for it?). It is quite easy to collect quantitative data by having people sign in if they come for one-to-one career assistance or attend a workshop, or to have the computer count them if they are using software or accessing Web sites. It is more difficult to collect qualitative data. Following are some ways to do so:

- Develop a questionnaire that individuals complete at the end of one or more of a series of interviews, workshops, or class sessions (depending upon how the services were delivered). Do not ask individuals to put their names on the questionnaire. Make sure that the questions target the objectives determined at Step 3.
- Instead of, or in addition to, having everyone complete a questionnaire, conduct an exit interview with a representative sample (that is, include people from various categories of the target population in proportion to their numbers in the population). Get the answers to the same questions through direct conversation. This approach requires more time and gets more details. With some objectives, it is helpful to administer what is called a pre-post questionnaire. Let us say, for example, that an objective for students at the high school level is "At the end of this course, students will be able to list five occupations in which they are interested." Evaluating this objective may be as simple as asking students, before the career planning course begins, to list the names of occupations that interest them but that they had not previously considered. Then at the end of the course, have them complete the same question. We might expect that, as a result of the program, students would be able to list more occupations in which they are interested at the end than at the beginning. Further, it could be expected that these might be more realistic options for them related to their interests and skills.
- With some objectives (such as "By the end of this series of curriculum units, students will show a significant increase in career decidedness."), evaluation may be accomplished by use of one of the instruments described in Chapter 5 under the category of "Determining the Change or Progress of a Client or Group of Clients." In the best research conditions, it would be possible to have two randomly selected groups—an experimental group that will receive the new service and a control group that will not receive it—during the time of the study. In that event, both groups can take the instrument selected to measure career decidedness after all units of the curriculum have been delivered. Because, by the theory of random assignment, it is believed that the two groups are equal at the beginning of the study, any difference in career decidedness in the experimental group from that of the control group would be deemed attributable to the curriculum (called *the treatment*). In many situations, however, it is not possible to randomly select subjects; therefore, another version of this kind of evaluation is pre-post testing. In other words, the group receiving the curriculum takes the measure of career decidedness before the course begins and again at the end of the course. Any change in individual scores or the mean scores of the group are considered to be the result of the treatment.

It is likely that, as a result of program evaluation, good ideas will emerge about how to improve the program. For this reason it is important to summarize these ideas in writing so that they are readily available for the next step.

Step 10: Revise the Program as Needed

In this step of the process, developers use the results of evaluation of the previous delivery of the program, feedback from managers, and additional creative ideas in order to revise the program and prepare for its next delivery.

Some sample programs

A wealth of information about career development theory and practice has been covered in this book. The purpose of this content, of course, is to enable counselors to create programs to serve different kinds of clients in a variety of settings, using curricular, group, and one-to-one approaches, all enhanced by the use of computer software and/or Web sites. This section of the chapter provides examples of the program design process in five different settings. These are merely illustrations provided for the purpose of providing further clarity about the development process.

Example 1: A Middle School

You have been a teacher in a middle school (grades 6 to 8) of approximately 400 students. You recently completed a master's degree in counseling, and your principal has asked you to work with a task force of teachers to figure out how to incorporate career guidance objectives and content into the curriculum. Your team used the NOICC guidelines for the middle school years (see Chapter 11) as the basis for this work. Though individual teachers have provided some content and activities related to occupational choice, there has been no integrated plan for providing career exploration for the students. For that reason, under your leadership, the task force begins by writing a document for the principal, briefly describing your proposal.

Executive Summary.   Career development is a lifelong process. Within the context of this process, students at the middle school level should be encouraged to engage in career exploration, that is, to become aware of their personal characteristics (self-awareness), occupations and their similarities and differences (occupational exploration), and career preparation (curricular choices). The NOICC, a federal agency, in collaboration with appropriate professional organizations, has developed detailed guidelines. The committee has used the middle school guidelines as the basis for its own development of specific objectives for our school.

Needs.   The needs of middle school students are well defined by the NOICC guidelines. The specific objectives included are drawn both from theory (especially that of Donald E. Super) and from the demands of their transition to high school. Thus, the needs are to develop a strong base of self- and occupational knowledge during these years and to accomplish the objectives provided below.

Specific Objectives.   By the time students transition to high school, they will be able to

1. Describe the world-of-work as six clusters of occupations and differentiate the work tasks, work settings, skills, and educational levels unique to each cluster.
2. Select one or two clusters of highest interest.

3. Develop a tentative 4-year high school plan that would prepare them for work in or further educational preparation for work in the selected cluster(s).

4. Describe work as one significant role among others that make up one's personal career.

Proposed Plan.

1. It is proposed that the World-of-Work Map (ACT, 2000) be taught in social studies classes at the sixth-grade level as a way to help students understand how occupations are organized and the different roles that workers play in our society in order to make it function economically with sufficient production of goods and services. Also, Super's (1980) definition of career as a combination of life roles being played at any point in life will be used and explained.

2. At the seventh grade level, a concerted effort would be made to provide information to students about the work tasks, work setting, and academic preparation needed for work in each of these six clusters. In order to facilitate this, school subjects would be assigned to each of the six clusters, and teachers of those subjects would be provided with a list of occupations (at various educational entry levels) that belong to the cluster to which their subject matter is related. Teachers would be asked to make linkages as often as possible between subject matter being taught and tasks of occupations in the cluster. They would also be encouraged to invite speakers into the class to talk about occupations in the cluster and how the subject matter being taught relates to their work. Further, the school counselor will coordinate a career day that is organized by the six clusters, inviting representatives of many occupations to the school so that students can talk with them. The counselor will also increase the resources of the career center and organize all occupational information by the same six clusters.

3. The counselor will work with the high school to organize the high school curriculum by the same six clusters. During the eighth grade the counselor will work with students and their parents in groups to draft a 4-year high school plan related to each student's selected cluster(s) and future educational plans.

Resources Needed.

1. Purchase of posters from ACT that provide a graphic representation of the World-of-Work Map and copies of the Job Family Charts that list occupations

2. One to 2 hours of time in department or faculty meetings during which the counselor can explain these materials to teachers and suggest ways in which they may be used as a part of their course

3. A budget of $500 to be used for expenses related to planning for, advertising, and sponsoring the career day

4. Time allocated to the counselor to organize and be in charge of the career day

5. Time allocated to the counselor to meet with members of the high school guidance department to plan and complete the work related to organizing the high school courses by the World-of-Work Map organizational system

Expected Outcomes.

1. Students will be able to make meaningful relationships between schoolwork and later work.
2. Students will gain broad awareness of the meaning of career and of how the world-of-work is organized.
3. Students will make informed occupational choices and take high school courses that will validate and/or prepare them for those choices.

Methods of Evaluation.

1. Students will have a quiz after instruction on the World-of-Work Map. They will be asked to place occupational titles (which include short descriptions) into the six clusters.
2. Students will be asked to select one or two clusters of their preference and to list at least five occupations in each of these clusters in which they might have interest.
3. Students will develop a 4-year high school plan related to the cluster(s) they have selected.

Example 2: A High School

Suppose that you have just been hired as a counselor in a local high school that has approximately 1500 students. The first thing you did was to request space and funds for a career center that would house many of the resources described in Chapter 6. This request was granted, and the materials have been ordered.

In the past there has been no service of any kind for helping students plan for future occupational choices. Some time can be made available during the school day for sophomores, so you decide to begin your program at this level. Further, you decide to develop a program that provides service to all sophomores in a cost-effective manner, though you are willing to see those with special needs individually. The school principal asks you to provide a short document that describes what you have in mind and what your needs are. Your document might look like the one that follows.

Executive Summary. This brief document describes the needs, objectives, content, expected outcomes, and requested resources for a career guidance program proposed for all sophomores. The needs listed can be assumed from our knowledge of career development theory and of the context in which the young people of the United States find themselves. Based on these needs, several specific objectives for the program are listed and content and activities are proposed. Finally, the document summarizes expected outcomes, resources needed, and methods of evaluation.

Needs. Given the age of these students and the contextual changes occurring in the United States, sophomore students have the following needs:

1. To understand the changes in the workplace and how these changes will affect their personal career planning

2. To learn the process of career planning that they can apply now and will need to apply again and again throughout their lives
3. To identify their personal interests and abilities
4. To relate these interests and abilities to possible occupations
5. To learn about these occupations
6. To select courses in high school that will lay the academic basis for further education and entry into one or more of these occupations

Specific Objectives.   At the end of the proposed program, at least 80% of the students who complete the program will be able to

1. Describe in detail three significant trends in the United States that are changing employers and jobs and the implications of these for personal career planning.
2. Describe the steps of a planful process for making career decisions.
3. State three to five groups (families) of occupations that relate to their personal interests and abilities.
4. Make a list of occupational titles from those groups.
5. Describe in detail at least five occupations from that list.
6. Select at least three occupations of highest interest.
7. State the educational implications of preparing for those three occupations.

Summary of Plan.   It is proposed that the following sessions be held with sophomores:
Session 1: Learn about changes that are occurring in the workplace.

Three speakers will be invited from three different companies. Each will talk about changes that have occurred in the past 5 years and what the projected changes are for the future, including what these may mean for young people entering the job market.

All sophomores will be assembled in the auditorium. A one-page worksheet will be given to each student on which he or she can record the main points of each speaker as well as a summary that includes at least three implications of what speakers said for personal career planning.

Projected time: $1\frac{1}{2}$ hours

Session 2: Learn a process for making personal career decisions.

The career planning process (copy of a graphic enclosed for your information) will be described by the counselor to sophomores in groups of 40 using a PowerPoint presentation. Students will receive a short handout that provides a graphic of the career decision making process and an explanation of each of its steps.

An interest inventory (copy enclosed for your information) will be administered to each group of 40 students. Answer sheets will be scored and results printed, using the computer program licensed with the instrument.

Proposed time: 2 hours—1 hour for presentation of the career planning model, including answering student questions, and 1 hour for describing the purpose and administering the interest inventory. Because there are 400 students in the sophomore class, this will require 20 hours of counselor time plus another 3 hours for preparation of visual materials and handout.

Session 3: Interpret the results of the interest inventory to students in groups of 40.

Give each student his or her score report. Describe the score report by use of a sample (for some fictitious student) score report projected on the screen, and explain each section of the report. Then ask the students to look at their own reports. Answer as many questions as possible in the group sessions. If students have additional questions, invite them to make an appointment for an interview. Ask students to circle the names of three job families that interest them on the material provided with the score report.

Projected time: 1 hour for each of 10 groups of students, requiring 10 hours of counselor time for presentations, an additional 2 hours for preparation, and an estimated 10 hours for individual interviews requested by students or invited by the counselor because of the pattern of results.

Session 4: Assist students to identify occupations that belong in the three job families they have selected and to get information about those occupations.

Schedule students in groups of 20 to come to the career center. Provide brief instruction about the materials in the center that contain occupational descriptions, including two specific Web sites. Also, explain what an information interview is and how students can find people who are willing to talk with them. Provide students with a worksheet that will guide their use of materials so that they can record the titles of occupations and information gained about each. Assign an information interview for each of three occupations, and provide a worksheet for students' use in summarizing their learning.

Projected time: 2 hours each for 20 groups of students—a total of 40 hours of counselor time.

Session 5: Offer opportunities for students to discuss their learning from the research in the career center and from informational interviews, and give students time to complete a personal Career Action Plan.

Students will come to the center in groups of 20. Students will be asked to share with the group some of the things they learned by doing the research and by interviewing individuals who work in occupations that interest them. Ask students to complete a one-page career action plan which lists three occupations of highest interest at this time, indicates the level and kind of education needed for entering each occupation, and lists next steps. These steps may include taking courses that are needed in high school, doing more research on the occupation, or requesting an interview with the counselor.

Projected time: 40 hours of counselor time for the group sessions plus an estimated 10 additional hours for individual interviews.

Resources Needed.

1. Use of the auditorium and audiovisual equipment for Session 1
2. 400 copies of the interest inventory
3. Permission to duplicate handouts for students that will total about 20 pages per student

Expected Outcomes.

1. High student motivation because of school's concern for their future planning
2. Improved student choice of curriculum while in high school

3. Learning of decision making and research skills that will be needed many times later in life
4. Support and involvement of parents

Methods of Evaluation.

1. Review of work forms completed by students to assure that they have been able to complete assigned tasks
2. Questionnaire that each student completes at the end of the five sessions
3. Interview with 20 randomly selected students to ask them how they rate the effectiveness of the program and to capture ideas they have for improvement

Another idea related to this program is to have an evening meeting with parents prior to beginning the program. If this is not feasible, then it may be possible to send a letter from the principal to each home. Either of these approaches would explain the purpose of these meetings with students, describe the general content, and offer parents a chance to talk with a counselor if they have questions.

Example 3: A University

Imagine that you have just been hired as a career counselor at a major university. Other than the assistance that faculty mentors may give to students, there has previously been no staff or program to assist students with the selection of majors, occupations, or jobs. One of the conditions you stated when you considered the job was that the university would invest in the facilities and resources needed to establish a career center for students and alumni. This request was granted, and you are in the process of drawing a layout for the center and of ordering the furnishings and resource material. You are anxious to get permission for a program of services for students, but because this is a new idea, your dean asks you to provide a short proposal, which you do, as follows.

Executive Summary.   This document describes a voluntary program of services for seniors at the university that will assist them to prepare the documents needed for searching for jobs and will provide them with skills to identify job openings, secure job interviews, conduct themselves effectively in job interviews, and select a good place of employment.

Needs.   The needs stated here have been identified both by a review of the career development literature and by a random survey of alumni who graduated from the university last year. Based on these sources, graduates of this university have the following needs:

1. To understand how the workplace they are about to enter has changed
2. To learn a process for career decision making that they can use now and in the future
3. To develop an effective resumé for today's job market
4. To know how to find or create job openings
5. To know how to identify personal skills and relate them to job openings
6. To know how to participate in an effective interview

Objectives.   Based on these identified needs, students who participate in the program of services described next will be able to

1. Describe at least three trends in the United States today that affect their personal careers and what they should expect of their future employers.
2. Describe a process for making career choices.
3. Show a personal resumé, in at least two formats (e.g., electronic format), that can be used for a job search.
4. In mock interviews, demonstrate an ability to participate effectively in job interviews, including relating personal skills to a job opening.

Content.   The content described next will be presented in a series of three 2-hour workshops to be presented four times throughout the academic year.

Session 1 (2 hours): A presentation by the counselor, using audiovisual aids, about the systemic changes in the workplace, how these will affect personal careers, and how individuals will need to take responsibility for their own career choices; presentation (with handout) of a career decision making model.

Session 2 (2 hours): Presentation about the purpose of a resumé and of three different formats for preparing one, including an electronic format. Via a handout, show good examples of sample resumés, and provide worksheets that each student can use to write his or her own resumé in the three different formats. Ask students to prepare these sample resumés by the next session. Invite students who wish to come for an individual interview to do so. Offer to review and make suggestions about their resumés.

Session 3 (2 hours): Presentation about the characteristics and stages of an effective interview, with handout. Following that, do a mock interview with one student. Then hand out descriptions of a job opening and an applicant; ask students to form triads, with one playing the role of an employer; one the role of an applicant; and the third the role of an observer who is noting whether the characteristics of a successful interview are present. Videotape the job interviews, and use these videos as a basis for discussion of effective and ineffective interview behaviors.

Expected Outcomes.

1. Students will learn about changes in the U.S. job market that affect their careers and what their expectations of employers should be in the future.
2. Students will learn a decision making model that they can use to assume personal responsibility for their own career decisions again and again.
3. Students will be able to prepare effective resumés, including an electronic one.
4. Students will be more comfortable and more effective in job interviews.
5. The percentage of students who are able to find satisfying jobs will increase by 60%.

Resources Needed.

1. Capability to advertise these workshops in all university media
2. Permission to duplicate handouts to support these workshops

3. Use of a larger facility if the number of students who wish to attend exceeds the capacity of the career center
4. Postage and time for follow-up study

Methods of Evaluation.

1. Ask students who attended all three workshops to complete a questionnaire at the end of the sequence.
2. Tally the number of students who attend each workshop and the number who attend all three.
3. Do a follow-up survey by mail of 100 students 1 year after the workshop series to determine what percentage have jobs, their degree of satisfaction with these jobs, and how they believe the workshops helped them to find and acquire employment.

Example 4: A Corporation

Imagine that you have just been hired as a career counselor by a large corporation that needs to reduce the size of its workforce. It is doing this by offering older employees an early-retirement financial package and terminating 456 middle managers. When you were hired, you were told that your services were desperately needed to help these two specific target populations. You asked for the physical space and the funds to set up a career management center, and these requests were granted. You are asked to provide a proposal for serving one of these two target populations as soon as possible. You decide to initiate a program for the 456 mid-level managers first, because their needs are more immediate than those of the early retirees who have 6 more months of employment left. You submit the following proposal.

Executive Summary. This document describes a program of services that will be initiated with 456 middle managers who are to be terminated in 2 weeks. The program focuses on assisting them to learn and practice job-search skills so that they can find another job quickly.

Needs. These employees are understandably in a state of shock, anger, and denial. They need an opportunity to talk about the present situation, with the hope that they will be able to get through the anger and denial stages and move quickly to being able to formulate an action plan for reemployment. Also, because these employees are in the age range of 42 to 50 and most have worked for this company for many years, it is assumed that they need to review the latest job-search techniques and to practice these until they are comfortable.

Objectives. At the end of this series of workshops, employees who are going to be terminated will be able to

1. Recognize that the situation they are facing is a result of economic conditions and resultant corporate decisions and that it has no relationship to their work performance.

2. Accept that, though the situation is unfortunate and stressful, it is not catastrophic and that they can find a way to make a successful transition.
3. Write an effective resumé in multiple formats that adequately expresses their skills and experience.
4. Participate effectively in mock job interviews.
5. Describe three effective ways of finding job openings.
6. Using Schlossberg's model, develop a plan for coping successfully with this transition.

Content.   Employees will be allowed to use normal working hours to attend a series of workshops, have individual interviews with the counselor, and use the Career Management Center. There will be a series of four 2-hour workshops, which these employees will be encouraged to attend. Because 30 people would be a maximum number for each workshop, multiple sequences of these workshops will be scheduled.

Workshop 1 (2 hours): This workshop will be less structured than the remaining three. Because employees are unlikely to be able to focus on action planning until they have been able to express their anger and grief about job loss, this session will allow individuals to talk about their feelings. Several people from top management will be invited to attend, and when appropriate, they may answer questions or provide information about the events that led the corporation to make the decision about termination of these employees.

Workshop 2 (2 hours): This session will focus on the preparation of a good resumé, in at least two formats, that expresses the skills and experience of each employee. A presentation will be made about how to develop such a resumé, and good examples will be provided as handouts. Individuals will spend the remaining time preparing a first draft of their own resumés. They will be invited to make individual interviews with the counselor, if they wish, and/or to leave their resumés in the counselor's office for review and feedback.

Workshop 3 (2 hours): This session will focus on a review of good interviewing skills. The various stages of the job interview will be described. Particular emphasis will be placed on teaching individuals how to research companies via the Internet and other means so that when they have interviews, they are able to relate their skills and experience to the particular job for which they are applying. Two good interviews will be role-played for the group. A checklist will be provided that outlines the characteristics of a good interview. Then, members of the group will be asked to divide into triads. One will play the role of interviewer; one the role of job-seeker; and the third the role of observer, evaluating the interview using the checklist of characteristics.

Workshop 4 (2 hours): This session will focus on how to find job openings (including use of placement agencies, the Internet, and direct application to companies) and on learning how to network with others to identify job openings that are never publicly listed. Schlossberg's model for coping with transition will be described, and a worksheet will be provided on which individuals in the group can list ways they will cope with the transition, planning specific action steps. Members of the group will share these plans with others in the group.

Expected Outcomes.

1. Terminated employees will be able to get rid of some of their anger and frustration and may leave the company with a more positive attitude.
2. Terminated employees will have improved chances of finding another job within a reasonable time because of instruction on job-seeking skills.

Resources Needed.

1. Permission to invite people to come to the workshops on company time
2. Cooperation from division heads to help publicize and promote the workshops through newsletters and other communications
3. A budget for refreshments
4. Use of audiovisual equipment and printing facilities
5. Postage for follow-up study

Methods of Evaluation.

1. Questionnaire completed by participants at the end of the four sessions
2. Follow-up of a random sample of participants 90 days after completion of the workshop to determine if they have found a job and if the content of the workshop helped them to do so

Example 5: A Community Agency

Imagine that you have accepted a position as a counselor in a one-stop center. Your manager asks you to develop a service to assist community adults who, for whatever reason, want to pursue a different occupation from the one in which they are currently engaged.

Executive Summary.   This document describes a proposed program of service for adult men and women who come to the agency seeking assistance with making a new career choice. Given the restraints of time, these individuals will be offered three group sessions with the requirement of an intake interview prior to the first session and an opportunity for a counseling interview following the three group sessions. The content of these sessions has determined by the counselors' past experience with similar clients as well as through work with a randomly selected focus group of members of the target population. The intake interview, workshop sessions, and potential content of the counseling interview are described. Further, a summary of needed resources and the plan for evaluation are provided.

Needs.

1. To understand the implications of career change
2. To assess the resources and barriers related to making the change
3. To consider possible choices and to define one
4. To draft a realistic action plan for making the change

Objectives.   By the end of the sequence of activities, clients will be able to

1. Describe realistically the transition they have chosen to make.
2. Identify forces for and forces against accomplishing the change.
3. State a definite career goal and how they plan to reach it.

Content.   Each client who expresses a desire to make a career change (that is, select and pursue a different occupation) will be asked to participate in an intake interview. The format of intake interviews will be the same for all clients. Questions asked by the interviewer will address the following topics:

- Past work history
- Client's view of his or her best skills and greatest work-related accomplishments
- Client's reasons for desiring to make an occupational change
- Ideas the client has about what this change might be
- How much the client knows about the occupation or field he or she now wants to enter
- Resources that support the client's ability to make a change (such as financial situation, persons who will be supportive, children grown and independent, etc.)
- Barriers the client will need to surmount (such as lack of support from some important persons, need for retraining, etc.)
- Willingness to make a commitment to the three group sessions and the follow-up counseling session

The three group sessions will be scheduled for 2 hours on the same night in 3 consecutive weeks. Their content will be as follows:

Session 1: Sharing within the group in regard to the kinds of changes they are seeking to make and the supports and barriers they confront for the transition. Following this, individuals will take three assessment inventories: an interest inventory, a skills inventory, and a values inventory. They will leave the completed instruments with the counselor so that a composite summary of results can be made prior to the second session.

Session 2: The counselor will return the composite assessment results to the clients and then provide a group interpretation, using a fictitious composite score report and a PowerPoint presentation. Group members will have an opportunity to ask questions in general or about their own report. Members of the group will then share their specific occupational goals or dreams and indicate whether or not the results of the assessment support those ideas. The counselor will facilitate discussion. Note: If individuals in the group need individual assistance in identifying possible occupational alternatives, they may make an appointment with the counselor for an individual interview before Session 3.

Session 3: Using worksheets based on the Schlossberg model for transition, clients will draft a plan to pursue a goal they have set for themselves. In this process they will identify specific steps they need to take (such as getting some training or having an information interview), assign a feasible timeline for completion of each step, and identify barriers and methods of dealing with these.

Following the three sessions, each participant will have an individual interview with the counselor. The purpose is to review the action plan together so that the counselor may be able to provide further information or suggest strategies for following the plan.

Expected Outcomes.   As a result of this sequence of activities, it is expected that clients will

1. Have a specific plan for making a career change.
2. Have a realistic career goal in keeping with self-information that has been gained.
3. Experience the support of the counselor and the group for moving forward with this plan.

Resources Needed.

1. A pleasant meeting room that will hold 15 people for 2 hours on one evening on each of three consecutive weeks
2. Fifteen copies of an interest inventory, a skills inventory, and a values inventory and the companion booklets that provide lists of occupations related to different patterns
3. Fifteen copies of the Schlossberg model worksheet
4. Use of the Center's career development facilitator to conduct the intake interviews
5. Counselor time for reviewing assessment results, developing a composite score report for each client, preparing a PowerPoint interpretation, facilitating the three workshop sessions, and conducting individual counseling sessions

Methods of Evaluation.

1. Each client will be asked to complete a questionnaire at the end of the entire sequence.
2. Participants will be contacted by phone or e-mail 3 months after the sequence of activities to assess the degree to which they have followed, or are following, the action plan they developed.

SUMMARY

After building a rationale for program development and defining the roles counselors may play in it, this chapter has described a 10-step process for developing a program of career planning services for a specific target population. This process begins with understanding the characteristics of the target population, assessing its needs, and writing clear, measurable objectives focused on meeting those needs. It then includes developing program content, determining a combination of ways in which the program will be delivered, determining how to promote and evaluate the program, and finally using the information gained from that evaluation to improve the program for its next delivery.

In order to make this process more practical, five sample programs for different target populations are described in some detail. They are proposed only as examples of the many different approaches to providing career planning service.

References

ACT, Inc. (2000). *World-of-Work Map, 2000 revision*. Iowa City, IA: Author.

Harris-Bowlsbey, J., & Lisansky, R. (2002). *Take hold of your future*. Finksburg, MD: CareerGuide.

Harris-Bowlsbey, J., & Perry, N. (2003a). *Develop your future I*. Adel, IA: National Career Assessment Services.

Harris-Bowlsbey, J., & Perry, N. (2003b). *Develop your future II*. Adel, IA: National Career Assessment Services.

Holland, J. L. (1997). *Making vocational choices: A theory of vocational personalities and work environments* (3rd ed.). Odessa, FL: Psychological Assessment Resources.

National Occupational Information Coordinating Committee. (1996). *National career development guidelines, K–adult handbook*. Washington, DC: Author.

Super, D. E. (1980). A life-span, life-space approach to career development. *Journal of Vocational Behavior, 16*, 282–298.

CHAPTER 10

CAREER DEVELOPMENT INTERVENTIONS IN THE ELEMENTARY SCHOOLS

Providing career development interventions in my work as an elementary school counselor is important because it allows children to gain an awareness of careers in their community. It helps children to identify their own skills, abilities, and interests related to the world of work. Students gain an understanding of what makes them special and unique. Most importantly, career development activities allow students to connect school to their hopes and dreams about what they want to be when they grow up.

Colleen Yeager
Professional School Counselor
North Graham Elementary School
Graham, NC

Rosita was only 5 years old but she had already experienced many difficult situations in her life. Her father, Enrique, left home before she was born. Her mother, Rosa, struggled with substance abuse problems. Rosa's lack of education (she never completed high school) severely limited her employment opportunities. She was able to find occasional employment as a waitress; however, she had a pattern of absenteeism and tardiness. These behaviors typically resulted in her termination from work. During her periods of unemployment, Rosa often turned to drugs to numb the pain. Rosa loved Rosita, but did not know how to extricate herself from this self-defeating behavioral pattern. Fortunately, Rosa's mother lived nearby and provided much-needed emotional support to her daughter and granddaughter. Despite this support, Rosita struggled with her father's absence and her mother's frequent bouts with substance abuse and unemployment. Today, however, Rosita had other thoughts. It was her first day of school. She felt scared and anxious as she wondered what school would be like. She took comfort in the fact that her best friend, Melissa, was also starting kindergarten today.

OVERVIEW OF CAREER DEVELOPMENT INTERVENTIONS IN THE SCHOOLS

Throughout their history, professional school counselors have been engaged in helping students, such as Rosita, advance in their career and educational planning. The

National Standards for School Counseling Programs (Campbell & Dahir, 1997) and the American School Counselor Association (ASCA) National Model for School Counseling (ASCA, 2003) reinforce this fact by identifying career development as an essential element in effective school counseling programs. The National Standards consist of four levels. There are three general domains (academic, career, and personal/social development), under which there are nine standards (three per domain) that, in turn, are each connected to student competencies linked to specific knowledge and skills students will develop as outcomes of their exposure to school counseling programs. Specifically, the career development domain in the National Standards contains the following standards, competencies, and indicators:

Standard A: Students will acquire the skills to investigate the world of work in relation to knowledge of self and to make informed career decisions.

C:A1 Develop Career Awareness

C:A1.1	Develop skills to locate, evaluate, and interpret career information
C:A1.2	Learn about the variety of traditional and nontraditional occupations
C:A1.3	Develop an awareness of personal abilities, skills, interests, and motivations
C:A1.4	Learn how to interact and work cooperatively in teams
C:A1.5	Learn to make decisions
C:A1.6	Learn how to set goals
C:A1.7	Understand the importance of planning
C:A1.8	Pursue and develop competency in areas of interest
C:A1.9	Develop hobbies and vocational interests
C:A1.10	Balance between work and leisure time

C:A2 Develop Employment Readiness

C:A2.1	Acquire employability skills such as working on a team, problem-solving, and organizational skills
C:A2.2	Apply job readiness skills to seek employment opportunities
C:A2.3	Demonstrate knowledge about the changing workplace
C:A2.4	Learn about the rights and responsibilities of employers and employees
C:A2.5	Learn to respect individual uniqueness in the workplace
C:A2.6	Learn how to write a resumé
C:A2.7	Develop a positive attitude toward work and learning
C:A2.8	Understand the importance of responsibility, dependability, punctuality, integrity, and effort in the workplace
C:A2.9	Utilize time- and task-management skills

Standard B: Students will employ strategies to achieve future career goals with success and satisfaction.

C:B1 Acquire Career Information

C:B1.1	Apply decision making skills to career planning, course selection, and career transition

C:B1.2   Identify personal skills, interests, and abilities and relate them to current career choice

C:B1.3   Demonstrate knowledge of the career planning process

C:B1.4   Know the various ways in which occupations can be classified

C:B1.5   Use research and information resources to obtain career information

C:B1.6   Learn to use Internet to access career planning information

C:B1.7   Describe traditional and nontraditional career choices and how they relate to career choice

C:B1.8   Understand how changing economic and societal needs influence employment trends and future training

C:B2 Identify Career Goals

C:B2.1   Demonstrate awareness of the education and training needed to achieve career goals

C:B2.2   Assess and modify their educational plan to support career goals

C:B2.3   Use employability and job-readiness skills in internship, mentoring, shadowing, and/or other work experience

C:B2.4   Select coursework that is related to career interests

C:B2.5   Maintain a career planning portfolio

Standard C: Students will understand the relationship between personal qualities, education, training, and the world of work.

C:C1 Acquire Knowledge to Achieve Career Goals

C:C1.1   Understand the relationship between educational achievement and career success

C:C1.2   Explain how work can help to achieve personal success and satisfaction

C:C1.3   Identify personal preferences and interests influencing career choice and success

C:C1.4   Understand that the changing workplace requires lifelong learning and acquiring new skills

C:C1.5   Describe the effect of work on lifestyle

C:C1.6   Understand the importance of equity and access in career choice

C:C1.7   Understand that work is an important and satisfying means of personal expression

C:C2 Apply Skills to Achieve Career Goals

C:C2.1   Demonstrate how interests, abilities, and achievement relate to achieving personal, social, educational, and career goals

C:C2.2   Learn how to use conflict management skills with peers and adults

C:C2.3   Learn to work cooperatively with others as a team member

C:C2.4   Apply academic and employment readiness skills in work-based learning situations such as internships, shadowing, and/or mentoring experiences (ASCA, 2003, pp. 79–80)

Clearly, the National Standards represent a comprehensive and holistic view of career development. By themselves, however, the standards could seem overwhelming to the novice professional school counselor seeking to use the standards as a developmental framework from which specific career development programs can be designed and implemented. Fortunately, the ASCA National Model for School Counseling Programs provides crosswalks to link the standards with other national standards such as the National Career Development Guidelines (National Occupational Information Coordinating Committee [NOICC], 1992). We contend that these two national models present an outstanding structure that professional school counselors can use to construct career development interventions. When constructing career interventions, we think it is especially important for professional school counselors to be cognizant of the ways in which environmental constraints (e.g., sexism, racism, heterosexism, discrimination experienced by students with disabilities) negatively affect students' career development. Clearly, career development interventions must be designed to address these experiences (Jackson & Grant, 2004).

Several authors (e.g., Gysbers & Henderson, 2001; Schmidt, 2003) advocate for making career development programs an integral part of the school curriculum, rather than an ancillary service. Niles, Trusty, and Mitchell (2004) take a systems perspective to designing career development interventions and emphasize that professional school counselors must communicate effectively with important subsystems (students, teachers, administrators, parents and families) regarding the goals and objectives of the career development program. Effective communication with students includes conducting a needs assessment to guide professional school counselors in the construction of career development programs and to serve as a basis for evaluation of program effectiveness. Effective communication with parents and families includes helping parents understand how they can positively influence their children's career development. Teachers need assistance connecting academic content to career and educational planning. Providing and/or delivering classroom career guidance activities assists teachers in making such connections. Professional school counselors can also help teachers become aware of research data that indicate the positive correlation between career planning and school success (Herr, Cramer, & Niles, 2004). Educating administrators regarding these data also helps increase the probability that the career development program will be an integral part of the school curriculum. The critical point here is that, in a very real sense, professional school counselors operate within a political context that does not always understand and support the need for career services. Therefore, professional school counselors must work as advocates for career development as they deliver systematic and coordinated career services to students (Perusse & Goodnough, 2004).

Those questioning the usefulness of career development interventions assume that career-related activities take students away from time spent focusing on core academic subjects. Additionally, career education critics assume that career education programs pressure students to pursue work immediately after high school rather than pursuing a college education. Many people who are unfamiliar with how careers develop do not understand why career development interventions are important at the elementary and secondary school levels. The fact that career education initiatives were funded with monies external to school districts and that, in many instances, career education proponents had not generated local support for career education were also factors contributing to negative attitudes toward the career education movement (Isaacson & Brown, 1997, p. 228). Thus, career education initiatives often become entangled in the political issues common to education today (e.g., the "back-to-basics" movement, the push to eliminate teaching of values in education, and the misconception that career education is the same as vocational education).

Those questioning the usefulness of career interventions in the schools are often even more adamant about their opinion that career interventions are not necessary for elementary school students. Those arguing against career interventions for elementary school students often view career decision making as events that occur at particular points during the course of secondary school education (e.g., when students must select a curriculum of study, when they leave high school). Such perspectives lack an appreciation of the precursors to effective career decision making.

Another issue related to the implementation of career education programs relates to the fact that many school districts do not provide career development programs in a systematic and coordinated fashion (Herr et al., 2004; Walz & Benjamin, 1984). The piecemeal implementation of career development interventions obviously limits the degree to which such interventions can positively influence students. Moreover, such an approach often creates confusion as to the meaning and purpose of career development programs by those not directly involved in their creation and implementation. Thus, it is essential that school counselors at the elementary and secondary school level engage in systematic and coordinated planning prior to implementing career development programs (Gysbers & Henderson, 1998; Myrick, 1993).

SYSTEMATIC AND COORDINATED PLANNING FOR CAREER DEVELOPMENT PROGRAMS IN THE SCHOOLS

Herr et al. (2004) recommend using a five-stage planning model for facilitating the implementation of systematic career development intervention programs. The stages are:

Stage 1: Develop a program rationale and philosophy

Stage 2: State program goals and behavioral objectives

Stage 3: Select program processes

Stage 4: Develop an evaluation design

Stage 5: Identify program milestones

An important component of Stage 1 involves conducting a needs assessment to determine appropriate program rationales, goals, and interventions (Niles et al., 2004). As we have noted, the needs assessment provides benchmarks against which program outcomes can be assessed. Herr et al. (2004) emphasize the importance of incorporating teachers, students, parents, and community participants in the needs assessment to increase understanding of, and involvement in, career development programs. Clearly, a properly conducted needs assessment provides a firm foundation upon which effective career development intervention programs can be constructed.

Walz and Benjamin (1984) also provide important recommendations for developing systematic career development intervention programs. Their recommendations include the following:

1. Involve a team of knowledgeable professionals, parents, and representatives from the community in all phases of program planning.
2. Use developmentally appropriate interventions.
3. Be sure that the program goals and objectives are clearly communicated to all involved in the program.
4. Make sure the program is based on student needs.
5. Have an evaluation component to determine the degree to which the program goals and objectives have been achieved.
6. Make sure that those involved in program delivery are highly competent.

Once again, the implicit theme in both sets of recommendations just mentioned is that professional school counselors need to be sensitive to the political climate in which they operate. For example, in some locations, not clearly connecting career development interventions to student academic achievement will significantly decrease the chances of program success. Also, not adequately communicating successful program outcomes will result in the program resources being vulnerable to funding cuts. If school personnel view the program as an additional burden to their already heavy workloads, then there is little chance that the program will succeed. Thus, the "marketing" of the program to all stakeholders becomes an important aspect of program development and implementation. Having clearly defined behavioral objectives that address the specific needs of program participants will be useful in marketing the program and providing outcome data demonstrating program benefits.

Similar to the systems approach advocated by Niles et al. (2004), these recommendations highlight the importance of taking a team approach to service delivery. Although there is no one prescription for how the roles and responsibilities for delivering career development interventions should be distributed, it is logical that counselors take the lead (not the sole) role in developing and implementing career development programs. Counselors are often the only professionals in the school system with specific training in career development. Therefore, counselors possess the knowledge of career development theory and practice necessary for formulating appropriate career development program interventions. Moreover, the processes typically used in program delivery relate to counselors' primary areas of expertise. These processes are counseling, assessment, career information services, placement services, consultation procedures, and referrals. Professional school counselors can use their knowledge and skills related to career development to empower teachers and parents/guardians to function as collaborators in career services delivery.

Developing a systematic and coordinated career development program across grades K–12 requires understanding the developmental tasks confronting students as they progress through school. Understanding the tasks students deal with at all levels of schooling prepares school personnel to work collaboratively in program development and implementation. A comprehensive understanding of the career development process also sets the stage for developing program interventions that are sequential and cohesive. Thus, the following sections of this chapter (and the primary topics of the following chapter) focus on career development tasks, program goals, and recommended interventions for elementary, middle/junior high school, and high school students, respectively.

CAREER DEVELOPMENT IN THE ELEMENTARY SCHOOLS

Careers unfold and develop throughout the life course. To ignore the process of career development occurring in childhood is similar to a gardener disregarding the quality of the soil in which a garden will be planted. For children and adolescents, their school and leisure activities represent their work. These activities provide essential learning experiences that shape self-perceptions and understandings of the world-of-work. They form the seedbed from which children begin to identify their preferences and connect themselves to their futures as workers.

Prior to entering elementary school, children have moved through the first two of Erikson's (1963) eight stages of development. Those who have coped successfully with these stages have developed a sense of trust and autonomy. Thus, children ideally enter school believing they can trust the adults in their world and that they will be able to cope successfully with challenges they will encounter. Children operating from a perspective of trust and self-sufficiency are likely to approach school tasks with a positive and enthusiastic attitude. Children who have not been as successful in developing trust and autonomy will operate from a different attitudinal stance. These children will be more likely to question whether they can trust others. They may also lack confidence concerning their ability to master the tasks they confront. Erikson notes that when trust and autonomy are not achieved, children experience the emotional consequences of mistrust, doubt, and shame. To overcome these negative consequences, it is critical that children experience success and support.

Havighurst (1972) notes that during infancy and early childhood (ages 0 to 5), children encounter a series of critical developmental tasks. For example, during this developmental stage children:

1. Learn to walk
2. Learn to eat solid foods
3. Learn to talk
4. Learn to control elimination of body wastes
5. Learn sex differences and modesty
6. Learn to relate emotionally to family members
7. Prepare to read
8. Learn to identify the difference between right and wrong

Havighurst notes that to progress to subsequent stages of development, children must be successful in coping with these tasks. Failure to cope with these tasks successfully "leads to unhappiness in the individual, disapproval of society, and difficulty with later tasks" (p. 2).

Rosita, introduced earlier in the chapter, had experienced events in her life that did not foster the acquisition of many of the skills identified by Havighurst (1972). Her father's absence and her mother's drug-induced emotional absences also made it difficult for Rosita to believe that she could count on adults being there for her. She also wondered about her own self-worth and capabilities. She hoped that she would do okay at school, but deep down she was convinced that she would not do well. What she needed most as she entered school was to encounter adults who consistently supported her. She would also need remedial assistance to enhance her interpersonal and academic skills, especially in the area of reading.

During the elementary school years, children begin formulating a sense of identity through greater interaction with the world beyond their immediate families. Interactions with peers, teachers, parents, and community members shape the child's self-perceptions. Through exposure to adult life patterns via observations in schools, community activities, home, and the media, children draw conclusions about their lives. The conclusions children draw include assumptions about their current and future place in the world.

Erikson (1963) proposes that during elementary school, children encounter developmental stages related to developing initiative (ages 4 to 6) and industry (ages 6 to 12). These qualities are essential to the career development process. If they are not developed, then children experience guilt and inferiority. These negative consequences do not foster the sort of active and broad-based exploration that is necessary for children to advance in their career development. When a sense of initiative and industry are achieved, then children use their curiosity as a stimulus for exploring and gathering information about themselves and their worlds. Moreover, children experience feelings of personal effectiveness when they begin to do things on their own and experience positive outcomes associated with their self-initiated activities.

Havighurst (1972) suggests that during middle childhood (ages 6 to 11), children encounter an array of developmental tasks related to motor coordination, emotional development, and attitudinal perspectives related to self and others. Specifically, he notes that children during this stage must:

1. Develop physical skills for participating in games
2. Build positive attitudes toward themselves
3. Develop interpersonal skills
4. Become more tolerant
5. Learn appropriate gender social roles
6. Develop academic skills in reading, writing, and mathematics
7. Achieve a greater sense of independence
8. Develop attitudes toward groups and institutions

Applying these tasks to Rosita, it is clear that to advance in her career development Rosita would need continued support and assistance. Positive reinforcement for her accomplishments, encouragement to engage in new activities of interest to her, and guidance in helping her identify tasks and chores that would foster a sense of industry are all important developmental interventions for Rosita. Although some interventions would require Rosita to work independently, it would also be important for her to engage in some group-oriented activities. Group activities would provide Rosita with opportunities to develop her interpersonal skills while also increasing her circle of friends. Thus, Rosita provides an excellent example of how general statements of developmental tasks must be contextualized for the individual student.

GOALS OF CAREER DEVELOPMENT INTERVENTIONS AT THE ELEMENTARY SCHOOL LEVEL

Obviously, there is tremendous variability in the quality of the life patterns to which children are exposed. Television, for example, often provides children with examples of men and women in gender-stereotyped roles and occupations (e.g., only women working as nurses, only men working as auto mechanics, women taking the primary or sole responsibility for homemaking and parenting). Children use this information to draw conclusions about the life patterns that are appropriate for them. As children are increasingly exposed to stereotypical behaviors and expectations, they begin to eliminate nontraditional life patterns and occupations from further consideration. Gottfredson (2002) contends that this gender-based elimination process begins as early as age 6. Gottfredson also suggests that between the ages of 9 and 13 children begin to eliminate those occupations from further consideration that they perceive to be less prestigious for their social class. Such variables as sex-typing and prestige rankings interact with self-perceptions of abilities and interests, as well as family and community expectations, to shape the decisions young people make about potential occupational options. Geography also factors into this equation because children in rural areas tend to be exposed to different (and often fewer) occupational options than children in more urban locations (Lee, 1984). Because elementary school children have not yet had the opportunity to fully explore their options and potentialities, an important goal of career development interventions in elementary school is to counteract environmental factors that pressure students to prematurely commit to educational and occupational options (Marcia, 1966). The use of nontraditional role models (e.g., male nurses, male secretaries, female physicians, female engineers) and exposure to a broad range of occupational environments in career development interventions is encouraged during the elementary school years.

Rosita could benefit from being exposed to women working in a wide variety of occupational environments. Because the women in her immediate and extended families have worked in traditional occupations, it would be useful for Rosita to learn about women working in nontraditional occupations. Having the opportunity to be mentored by a woman in an occupation of interest to her might also help Rosita develop a sense of trust, autonomy, initiative, and industry.

Another goal of career development interventions with elementary school children is to provide an environment in which each student's natural sense of curiosity can flourish (Super, 1990). Curiosity provides the foundation for exploring. Children naturally express curiosity through fantasy and play. For example, children often engage intensely in fantasy-based play related to occupations such as physician, firefighter, teacher, professional athlete, and nurse. Curiosity can be guided to help students learn accurate information about themselves and their environments. For example, field trips to occupational environments related to a child's fantasy-based occupational interests reinforce the child's sense of curiosity and stimulate further exploring and the gradual crystallization of interests (Super, 1957).

It would obviously be useful for Rosita if her counselor would encourage her to identify and explore activities of high interest and then work with Rosita to help her process what she learns about herself as a result of participating in exploratory activities. Fostering a sense of curiosity related to herself and the world of work will help to increase Rosita's sense of what might be possible and counteract environmental limitations she may be experiencing. In other words, it is a way to begin empowering Rosita.

Encouraging students to participate in activities relating to their interests nurtures a sense of autonomy, the anticipation of future opportunities for exploring, and the beginning of planful behaviors (Watts, Super, & Kidd, 1981). When interests connect with skills and capacities, a positive self-concept emerges which, in turn, provides the foundation for coping with the career development tasks of adolescence (Super, 1994). As children move toward adolescence, they must accomplish four major career development tasks. Specifically, they must (a) become concerned about the future, (b) increase personal control over their lives, (c) convince themselves to achieve in school and at work, and (d) develop competent work habits and attitudes (Super, Savickas, & Super, 1996, p. 131).

Unfortunately, when these four tasks are compared with data from the National Assessment of Educational Progress's Career and Occupational Development Project (a survey of approximately 28,000 9-year-old children), one might conclude that elementary school students have been only marginally successful in accomplishing these tasks. Results from this survey indicate that children have limited self-knowledge and limited occupational information and take limited responsibility for their behavior and future career decision making (Miller, 1977). Clearly, these results provide cause for concern because children who are not able to accomplish the career development tasks they encounter in the elementary school are at risk for even more difficulty when they encounter the career development tasks presented to them during their secondary school experience. Thus, there is the need to consider how career development interventions might be provided to elementary school students in a more systematic and effective fashion.

CAREER DEVELOPMENT GUIDELINES FOR ELEMENTARY SCHOOL STUDENTS

The NOICC developed National Career Development Guidelines to help counselors identify developmentally appropriate career development goals and interventions across the life span (NOICC, 1992). The specific career development competencies identified as appropriate for elementary school children are:

1. Self-Knowledge
    a. Knowledge of the importance of self-concept
    b. Skills to interact with others
    c. Awareness of the importance of growth and change
2. Educational and Occupational Exploration
    a. Awareness of the benefits of educational achievement
    b. Awareness of the relationship between work and learning
    c. Skills to understand and use career information
    d. Awareness of the importance of personal responsibility and good work habits
    e. Awareness of how work relates to the needs and functions of society
3. Career Planning
    a. Understanding how to make decisions
    b. Awareness of the interrelationship of life roles

    c. Awareness of different occupations and changing male/female roles

    d. Awareness of the career planning process

CAREER DEVELOPMENT INTERVENTIONS IN THE ELEMENTARY SCHOOLS

These guidelines provide a framework for establishing career development goals and interventions. Because self-awareness provides the foundation for processing career information, career development interventions in the primary grades can focus first on helping students develop more sophisticated self-knowledge. For example, in grades K and 1, students can increase their self-knowledge by describing themselves through drawings, writing sentences describing the things they like and the things that are important to them, and bringing some of their favorite things to school to show to their classmates. Sharing their self-descriptions with others helps students to clarify their self-concepts. Each of these activities can also emphasize the importance of appreciating the similarities and differences that exist among students in the classroom. Differences among students can be described as valuable contributions to the learning process because we often learn more from students who are different from us than those who are like us in our interests, skills, or backgrounds. Activities that encourage students to focus on clarifying their global self-concepts can be emphasized and can be easily infused into the curriculum during the first years of school. Differences in cultural traditions among students can be highlighted and celebrated.

In clarifying her self-concept, it is likely that Rosita would benefit from understanding that her family situation is not something that she caused. Emphasizing her positive relationship with her grandmother may be useful as well. In processing the contextual differences among students, it would be important for Rosita's teacher to discuss the different ways to define "family." This may help Rosita focus on what she has rather than what she has lost regarding her family structure.

Activities that help students learn more about themselves can be supplemented with activities that focus on educational and occupational exploration as children progress through the primary and intermediate grades. For example, in the primary grades students can identify the occupations of their family members (e.g., parents, grandparents, aunts, and uncles) as well as the level and type of education each family member attained. As students share this information, the relationship between education and work can be stressed (e.g., some jobs require a college education and others may require a different type of training such as trade school or an apprenticeship). Differences in family members' occupations can be discussed as strengths (e.g., it takes people working in a wide variety of occupations to make our society function effectively). To counteract occupational sex-typing, men and women working in nontraditional occupations can be invited to school to discuss their work. (To expand Rosita's awareness of occupational options, it would be useful for Rosita to be exposed to Latinas working in professional occupations.)

Beale and Williams (2000) discuss the "anatomy of a school-wide career day" in an elementary school setting. Specifically, they point out that much planning goes into making the career day successful. They note that successful career days provide opportunities to break down occupational stereotypes, involve parents/guardians as well community and business representatives in the school counseling curriculum, and help students begin making positive connections between themselves and their futures.

To prepare for the career day, Beale and Williams (2000) suggest that a planning committee (involving the counselor, teachers, administrators, community representatives, and parents) be established. The first step of the planning committee is to establish goals and objectives (e.g., expand students' awareness of the school-work connection, increase students' understanding of workers in the community, increase students' understanding of the interrelatedness of workers, increase students' awareness of traditional and nontraditional careers) for the career day.

Next, the planning committee should identify a timeline for completing specific tasks (writing and mailing letters informing parents and teachers of the date, time, place, goals, and objectives of the career day). Concerning the timing of the career day, counselors may want to connect the career day to the NCDA's Career Development Month (usually in November). The NCDA sponsors a poetry and picture contest during National Career Development Month and offers resources that counselors can use to prepare for activities such as a schoolwide career day. Clearly, the planning committee must systematically select speakers for career day. Using Holland's occupational categories (i.e., Realistic, Investigative, Artistic, Social, Enterprising, and Conventional) as a guide for identifying representative occupations may be useful. Surveying teachers and parents, contacting the local chamber of commerce, and soliciting suggestions from the planning committee members are ways to identify potential career day speakers. When inviting potential speakers to participate, it helps to identify the time and place of the event, the purpose of the career day, the specific topics to be discussed, and the format (e.g., "show and tell" versus lecture) for discussing the work-related topics. Once workers agree to participate, Beale and Williams (2000) recommend sending speakers a confirmation letter containing the vital information for their participation. As the day approaches, school announcements reminding students and school personnel of the event should be made.

Additional issues to be addressed by the planning committee include deciding on the format to be used during the career day (e.g., whether a central location will be used, whether students will rotate from classroom to classroom to meet with speakers, or whether speakers will rotate from classroom to classroom). Once the plans for the career day are finalized, counselors should construct a detailed schedule to distribute to all participants.

Student preparation for the career day can include creating a mural of all workers in the school, having students interview their parents/guardians to gain information about their work, having students create poster presentations of workers using pictures in magazines and newspapers, and having students generate a list of possible interview questions to be used during the career day.

On career day, volunteers should be assigned to meet speakers when they arrive and help them to get oriented to the day. Speakers should also be asked to complete an evaluation of their experience that can be turned in at the end of the day. Evaluating the effectiveness of the day is important for improving future career days. Thank you notes should be sent to all involved. After the career day, counselors can engage in classroom guidance activities to help students assimilate the information they learned, discuss their perceptions of the jobs they learned about, and identify next steps to take to learn more about the world of work.

Students in grades K and 1 can begin the process of learning about work by focusing on occupations with which they have the most immediate relationship (e.g., occupations of family members, occupations in the school setting, occupations in their neighborhoods). Then, elementary school students can gradually learn about occupations that are more remote (e.g., occupations in the community, occupations in the state, occupations in the nation, and occupations throughout the world) as they progress from grades 2 to 5. Using a proximity-distance scheme to guide students in the acquisition of occupational information helps students understand the relevance of work in their lives and the ways in which various workers contribute to society. At each level of proximity, the relationship between work and the educational requirements for performing specific occupations can be highlighted. Students can also discuss what is required to perform occupations successfully. Job-content skills (the specific skill requirements for each occupation), functional skills (the skills that are transferable across occupations), and self-management skills (e.g., being reliable, getting along with coworkers, being trustworthy, completing assignments on time) can be integrated into these discussions as well.

Beale (2000) provides an excellent example as to how a well-conceived field trip can enhance career awareness in elementary school students. Using a field trip to a hospital as an illustrative example, Beale notes that for this sort of activity to be useful, it must be carefully planned and implemented. For example, in planning for a career awareness field trip, counselors need to involve teachers, students, workplace personnel, and parents. In addition to identifying specific objectives of the trip, securing consent from administrators, parents, and teachers, counselors should also engage in a "dry run" through the worksite prior to the trip. During the preliminary worksite visit, the counselor should meet with worksite representatives (e.g., administrators and workers with whom the students will interact) to clarify the purpose and duration of the visit and what opportunities will be made available to the students. Copies of any interview questions the students will be asking should be provided to all relevant employees. Eliminating surprises during the visit and helping employees to be prepared will help to maximize the effectiveness of the trip.

It is important to note, however, that students also need to be well prepared for the field trip. Strengthening the pre-visit interest and motivation of students will increase the chances of the trip being successful. Ways to accomplish this involve engaging students in pre-trip classroom career activities. For example, in preparing bulletin boards related to the field trip, students can bring in pictures of workers and services provided in the worksite. Students can engage in classroom discussions related to what to look for during the field trip. Preparing sample questions (e.g., How long have you been doing this kind of work? What do you like best/least about your job? How long did you have to go to school to do what you do?) that students can ask of workers helps guide student learning for the field trip. (It is also important to let students know that questions such as "How much money do you make?" are inappropriate.) Having workers come to the classroom (in their work clothes) can also raise student interest and motivation for the field trip. Here, counselors should keep in mind the importance of providing examples of nonstereotypical workers (e.g., a female physician, a male nurse, an African American CEO). Additional preparatory activities can include drawing pictures of the worksite, looking in the Yellow Pages and identifying the number of related worksites in the area, and talking about whether they have ever visited a similar worksite.

Beale (2000) also recommends that counselors use the time en route to the worksite as an opportunity for preparing students. For example, giving each student a list of specific occupations to look for in the worksite and providing students with scrambled work sheets, hidden word puzzles, or crossword puzzles using words related to the different occupations, work materials, and equipment that they will see on the tour are ways to focus student thinking en route to the worksite.

After the visit, Beale (2000) recommends activities that reinforce student learning and career awareness. For example, class discussions related to student reactions to the visit that focus on listing the occupations observed, identifying school subjects related to the occupations the students observed, and discussing the interrelationship of various occupations (e.g., "What would happen if there were no nurses, custodians, receptionists, orderlies, etc.?") represent useful follow-up activities. Having students prepare a scrapbook containing information related to the field trip, and/or developing a slide presentation of the visit (in which students compose and narrate the script) also represent important activities that can be connected to the curriculum. Conducting an evaluation of the activity (e.g., asking students to identify whether they learned more about work in the worksite visited and whether they enjoyed the activities before, during, and after the visit) is an important final step in the process.

Educational and occupational exploration activities can be infused into the curriculum in a variety of additional ways. For example, assignments highlighting the various types of work required in different geographical locations can be integrated into the social studies curriculum. Language arts assignments (e.g., short story writing) can also be constructed to help students learn more about what workers do in different occupations and to express their important self-characteristics (e.g., writing an autobiography). The art curriculum can include drawing, painting, and photographing workers in various occupations.

Activities to help students learn about the career planning and decision making process could include having students read biographies and then discuss the important career decisions people made in the biographies they read. Students can be encouraged to consider what constitutes a "good" rather than "bad" career decision as they discuss the biographies they read. Additionally, students can use a timeline to chart the important events that influenced the decisions that the people they read about made in their lives.

Encouraging students to read stories about people working in nontraditional occupations can contribute to counteracting the effects of occupational sex-typing. Discussions can include the ways in which culture, gender, and social class may have influenced the career development of the person in the biography.

Another key focus in providing career development interventions at the elementary school level is that of increasing students' awareness. Interventions that increase students' self-awareness, occupational awareness, awareness of the relationship between work and education, and awareness of how career decisions are made are all important topics to address with elementary school students. Students should be encouraged to engage in activities that foster broad self- and career exploration to arouse interest in the future. A sense of internal control (e.g., "I can influence my direction"); the belief that it is important to be concerned about the future (e.g., "what happens to me is important to me"), and an attitude of personal competence or self-efficacy (e.g., "I am able to do what I am expected to do") should also be outcomes of career development interventions at the elementary school level (Super et al., 1996). Armed with these beliefs, students are prepared to cope with the career development tasks they will confront at the middle/junior high school level.

Magnuson and Starr (2000) offer the following thoughts to guide the planning of career development interventions:

1. Become a constant observer of children:
   Notice how children approach tasks.
   Notice the activities in which children choose to participate.
   Observe and encourage the child's initiative-taking.
   Notice the thematic patterns emerging in each child's activities.

2. Consider the processing of an activity as important as the activity itself.
   To help children develop a sense of industry rather than inferiority, focus feedback on the specifics of children's efforts.

   Accompany career awareness and career exploration activities with opportunities for students to express their beliefs about themselves in relation to various occupations. (p. 100)

PARENTAL INVOLVEMENT

Parents have substantial influence over the career development of their children. Basow and Howe (1979) examined the career development of 300 college students and found that parents had the greatest influence in the career development of the students participating in their study. This finding is not surprising. Parents provide the greatest amount of indirect and direct exposure to work for their children. Most adults can recount numerous instances in which they recall their parents conveying positive and negative expressions of their work experiences. These expressions influence children vicariously as they formulate their understanding of an area of life they have yet to encounter directly. Thus, children rely upon adults and peers for information. As has been noted, children use the information they receive to make preliminary decisions about the appropriateness of the occupational options of which they are aware.

Young (1994) suggests that the influence parents exert on the career development process is most effective when it is planned, intentional, and goal-oriented. However, many parents possess minimal knowledge regarding career development theory and how environmental factors influence the career development process of children. Thus, it is important that counselors help parents learn ways to contribute positively to the career development of their children. Counselors can begin by providing parents with information about the career development process (e.g., during elementary school, children are encouraged to expand their awareness related to self and the world-of-work). Counselors can also explain to parents how the environment affects options children are willing to consider. For example, the influence of occupational stereotyping within the media and gender-role stereotyping can be discussed with parents. Finally, counselors can help parents identify specific strategies they can use to facilitate career development in their children. Engaging in conversations in which parents provide accurate occupational information and challenge occupational stereotyping represents an obvious, yet important, way that parents can foster positive career development in their children. Parent-child career conversations regarding career development should foster a sense of curiosity, openness to possibilities, awareness of options, and a positive attitude toward the world of work.

Herr and Cramer (1996) identify eight ways parents can help children advance in their careers. These strategies include:

1. Parents can encourage children to analyze important self-characteristics (e.g., interests, capacities, and values).
2. When parents are familiar with specific work requirements for jobs, they can communicate these to their children.
3. Parents can discuss the importance of work values in work behavior.
4. Parents can explain the relationship between work, pay, and the economic condition of the family.
5. Parents can connect children with informational resources (e.g., other workers, books, films) for acquiring accurate career information.
6. Parents can be careful to avoid stereotyping occupational alternatives and workers.
7. Parents can provide children with opportunities for work in the home and community.
8. Parents can provide children with opportunities to learn and practice decision making skills. (p. 364)

Helping parents become aware of their own attitudes toward work and occupations, exposing children to work opportunities in the home and community, and providing support to children as they engage in career decision making tasks are all ways to help children cope effectively with the career development process. By empowering parents with knowledge and information that can be used to help their children cope effectively with career development tasks, counselors make an important contribution to the career development of the students with whom they work.

Both Rosita and her mother could benefit from learning more about the career development process. Helping Rosa understand how careers develop would give her information that she could use to manage her own career development more effectively. Coaching Rosa as to the ways she could help Rosita with her career development would not only help Rosita but would also help Rosa feel more effective as a parent. Strengthening the bond between Rosa and Rosita would help Rosita develop the trust and autonomy she needs to move forward in her development.

SUMMARY

New parents often wonder which occupations their children will select later in life. What many parents do not realize is that children begin charting courses toward specific occupations early in life. Occupational selection represents the confluence of genetic and environmental influences that shape the career course. Like any developmental task, the career development process can be approached systematically and intentionally, or, it can be approached haphazardly and passively. Most parents would prefer that their children receive systematic career development assistance oriented toward providing children with the competencies required for managing their careers effectively. For elementary school children, the task is to learn more about themselves and the educational/occupational options that are available. By providing support and helping children acquire accurate information about themselves and the world of work, counselors provide children with the foundation for effective career planning and decision making.

REFERENCES

American School Counselor Association (ASCA). (2003). *The ASCA National Model: A framework for school counseling programs.* Alexandria, VA: American School Counselor Association.

Basow, S. A., & Howe, K. G. (1979). Model influences on career choices of college students. *Vocational Guidance Quarterly, 27,* 239–243.

Beale, A. V. (2000). Elementary school career awareness: A visit to a hospital. *Journal of Career Development, 26,* 65–72.

Beale, A. V., & Williams, C. J. (2000). The anatomy of an elementary school career day. *Journal of Career Development, 26,* 205–213.

Campbell, C. A., & Dahir, C. A. (1997). *The national standards for school counseling programs.* Alexandria, VA: American School Counselor Association.

Erikson, E. H. (1963). Childhood and society. New York: W. W. Norton.

Gottfredson, L. S. (2002). Gottfredson's theory of circumscription, compromise, and self-creation. In D. Brown & Associates (Eds.), *Career choice and development* (4th ed., pp. 85–148). San Francisco: Jossey-Bass.

Gysbers, N. C., & Henderson, P. (1998). *Developing and managing your school guidance program.* Alexandria, VA: American Counselors Association.

Gysbers, N. C., & Henderson, P. (2001). Comprehensive guidance and counseling programs: A rich history and a bright future. *Professional School Counseling, 4,* 246–256.

Havighurst, R. J. (1972). *Developmental tasks and education* (3rd ed.). New York: D. McKay.

Herr, E. L., & Cramer, S. H. (1996). *Career guidance and counseling through the lifespan* (5th ed.). New York: HarperCollins.

Herr, E. L., Cramer, S. H., & Niles, S. G. (2004). *Career guidance and counseling through the lifespan: Systematic approaches* (6th ed.). Boston: Allyn & Bacon.

Jackson, M., & Grant, D. (2004). Fostering positive career development in children and adolescents. In R. Perusse & G. Goodnough (Eds.), *Leadership, advocacy, and direct service strategies for professional school counselors* (pp. 125–154). Belmont, CA: Brooks/Cole.

Isaacson, L. E., & Brown, D. (1997). *Career information, career counseling, and career development.* Boston, MA: Allyn and Bacon.

Lee, C. C. (1984). Predicting the career choice attitudes of rural Black, White, and Native American high school students. *Vocational Guidance Quarterly, 32,* 177–184.

Magnuson, C. S., & Starr, M. F. (2000). How early is too early to begin life career planning? The importance of the elementary school years. *Journal of Career Development, 27,* 89–101.

Marcia, J. E. (1966). Development and validation of ego-identity status. *Journal of Personality and Social Psychology, 3,* 551–558.

Miller, J. (1977). *Career development needs of nine-year-olds: How to improve career development programs.* Washington, DC: National Advisory Council for Career Education.

Myrick, R. (1993). *Developmental guidance and counseling: A practical approach* (2nd ed.). Minneapolis, MN: Educational Media.

National Occupational Information Coordinating Committee (NOICC). (1992). *The National Career Development Guidelines Project.* Washington, DC: U.S. Government Printing Office.

Niles, S. G., Trusty, J., & Mitchell, N. (2004). Fostering positive career development in children and adolescents. In R. Perusse & G. Goodnough (Eds.), *Leadership, advocacy, and direct service strategies for professional school counselors* (pp. 102–124). Belmont, CA: Brooks/Cole.

Perusse, R., & Goodnough, G. (2004). *Leadership, advocacy, and direct service strategies for professional school counselors.* Belmont, CA: Brooks/Cole.

Schmidt, J. J. (2003). *Counseling in schools: Essential services and comprehensive programs* (4th ed.). Boston, MA: Allyn & Bacon.

Super, D. E. (1957). *A psychology of careers.* New York: Harper & Row.

Super, D. E. (1990). Career and life development. In D. Brown & L. Brooks (Eds.), *Career choice and development: Applying contemporary theories to practice* (2nd ed., pp. 197–261). San Francisco: Jossey-Bass.

Super, D. E. (1994). A life-span, life space perspective on convergence. In M. L. Savickas & R. W. Lent (Eds.), *Convergence in career development theories: Implications for science and practice* (pp. 63–74). Palo Alto, CA: CPP Books.

Super, D. E., Savickas, M. L., & Super, C. M. (1996). The life-span, life-space approach to careers. In D. Brown & L. Brooks (Eds.), *Career choice and development: Applying contemporary theories to practice* (3rd ed., pp. 121–178). San Francisco: Jossey-Bass.

Walz, G. R., & Benjamin, L. (1984). A systems approach to career guidance. *Vocational Guidance Quarterly, 33,* 26–34.

Watts, A. G., Super, D. E., & Kidd, J. M. (1981). *Career development in Britain.* Cambridge, England: Hobson's Press.

Young, R. A. (1994). Helping adolescents with career development: The active role of parents. *The Career Development Quarterly, 42,* 195–203.

Sample Career Development Activities for Elementary School Students

Interesting Activities

NOICC CAREER DEVELOPMENT GUIDELINES: Self-Knowledge

ASCA STANDARDS: Standard A—Students will acquire the skills to investigate the world of work in relation to knowledge of self and to make informed career decisions.

PURPOSE: To discuss interests related to various activities.

OBJECTIVE: Students will learn to connect interests to activities.

MATERIALS: Magazines and scissors

INTRODUCTION: Discuss the importance of participating in activities that we find enjoyable. All activities, including work, can be fun when we participate in activities that we enjoy. The opposite is also true, however. When we participate in activities, including work, that we do not enjoy, we experience different reactions. Ask students to discuss how they feel when they participate in activities they like versus activities they do not like.

ACTIVITIES: Have each student cut out pictures from magazines demonstrating people engaged in activities that the student enjoys. Students will share the pictures with the class and tell what the activity is and what they like about it using the following phrase: "What I find interesting about this activity is...."

DISCUSSION: Discuss the different activities and interests revealed. Ask students if any of them liked the activities that were shared by any of the other students. Have the students identify which activities they like and say what they find interesting about that activity. Ask students if they disliked any of the activities shared. Have the students identify which activities they do not like and what they do not like about that activity.

CLOSURE: Emphasize that there is no "right or wrong" associated with the likes and dislikes expressed by students. What really matters is that the students are clear about what they find interesting. Discuss how students' interests can be linked to vocational and avocational activities. Emphasize the importance of both types of activities for providing outlets for expressing interests.

TIME: 45 minutes

EVALUATION/ASSIGNMENT: Have students construct a list of the activities they find interesting and the activities that they do not find interesting.

Skills I Have

NOICC CAREER DEVELOPMENT GUIDELINES: Self-Knowledge

ASCA STANDARDS: Standard A—Students will acquire the skills to investigate the world of work in relation to knowledge of self and to make informed career decisions.

PURPOSE: To discuss the skills students have developed.

OBJECTIVE: Students will be able to identify the skills they possess.

MATERIALS: Skills list handout, paper, and pencils

INTRODUCTION: Discuss the fact that all people have many skills. Some skills are learned in school, some are learned at home or in play, and others seem to be "natural" skills. Distribute a list of skills to the students. Review the list to be sure that the students understand the skills listed.

ACTIVITIES: Have students list three activities they participate in that they enjoy. Divide students into groups of four. Assign each student one of the following roles: interviewer (2 students), interviewee, and recorder. The interviewee must identify one activity that he or she enjoys. The interviewers must try to identify as many skills as possible that the interviewee uses when participating in the activity. The interviewee must say either yes or no to the skills the interviewers identify. The recorder lists the skills that the interviewee uses in the activity. After 10 minutes, the leader should stop the activity and ask students to rotate their roles. At the conclusion of each interview, the recorder's list is given to the interviewee.

DISCUSSION: Discuss the importance of recognizing the skills we possess. Identify why it is useful to identify the skills we use when we participate in activities that we enjoy. Review how identifying these skills can be useful in career planning.

CLOSURE: Repeat the activity until the students have a skills list for all three activities (it is recommended that

this activity take place over multiple sessions, e.g., three 30-minute sessions). Have students review their skills lists. Ask them to circle the skills that appear on more than one list. Discuss the importance of focusing on these skills in career exploration.

TIME: 60–90 minutes

EVALUATION/ASSIGNMENT: Ask students to identify occupations relating to the skills appearing on more than one list.

Feelings

NOICC CAREER DEVELOPMENT GUIDELINES: Self-Knowledge

ASCA STANDARDS: Standard A—Students will acquire the skills to investigate the world of work in relation to knowledge of self and to make informed career decisions.

PURPOSE: To discuss the importance of understanding the feelings of others.

OBJECTIVE: Students will identify feelings from nonverbal cues and identify ways to respond to the feelings of others.

MATERIALS: Pictures of persons expressing various emotions, chalkboard, and chalk

INTRODUCTION: Explain the importance of being sensitive to the feelings of others. Talk with students about how they feel when others are insensitive to their feelings. Contrast these situations with those in which others are sensitive to students' feelings. Begin by brainstorming feelings. List the feelings students identify on the board.

ACTIVITIES: Brainstorm feelings and list them on the board. Then show students pictures of persons expressing

various emotions. Have students guess the feelings being expressed. List the feelings on the board.

DISCUSSION: Discuss with students how they could respond to each of the feelings listed. Role play various responses (noneffective responses and effective responses). Have students react to each response by identifying how they might feel if someone responded to them in that way.

CLOSURE: Emphasize that being able to recognize and respond to the feelings of others is very important in effective interpersonal communication.

TIME: 45 minutes

EVALUATION/ASSIGNMENT: Give students three statements, each of which expresses different feelings (e.g., happiness, sadness, anger). For example, "It hurt my feelings when the teacher yelled at me for something I did not do." Instruct the students to write how they would respond to each statement if it were expressed by one of their friends (e.g., "You sound sad that the teacher yelled at you.").

What Is a Friend?

NOICC CAREER DEVELOPMENT GUIDELINES: Self-Knowledge

ASCA STANDARDS: Standard A—Students will acquire the skills to investigate the world of work in relation to

knowledge of self and to make informed career decisions.

PURPOSE: To identify what is valued in friendships with others.

Objective: To enhance self-awareness and the awareness of others; to determine valued attributes in a friend.

Materials: Paper, pencils, posterboard or chalkboard

Introduction: Ask students the questions, "What is a friend?"

Activities: Students will answer individually or divide into groups to answer the question, "What is a friend?" The leader will write on the chalkboard or posterboard words that describe a friend. Students may then draw an illustration of "what a friend is."

Discussion: Discuss students' definitions of what a friend is; prioritize these definitions (e.g., number them from 1 to 10); ask students if they have followed their own guidelines of "friendship" and why or why not; ask: is it important and why? Focus on how friends can provide a source of support that helps one achieve goals or they can influence a person in ways that are counterproductive to goal achievement.

Closure: Discuss how true friends help each other to achieve their goals.

Time: 30–45 minutes

Evaluation/Assignment: Have students list five characteristics they want in a friend.

The "Problem Bucket"

NOICC Career Development Guidelines: Self-Knowledge

ASCA Standards: Standard A—Students will acquire the skills to investigate the world of work in relation to knowledge of self and to make informed career decisions.

Purpose: To discuss a range of problems that individuals are experiencing and possible solutions.

Objective: Students will assist one another in thinking about problems that each is experiencing and possible solutions.

Materials: Pencils, container ("bucket"), and note cards

Introduction: Explain to students the purpose of the "problem bucket": Individuals anonymously contribute, into the bucket, problems facing them. The problems will then be discussed and solutions explored.

Activities: Ask students to write down on note cards problems they are experiencing. Put these note cards into the bucket. Move students into small groups to discuss the problems and possible solutions. Ask students to handle information seriously and confidentially and to respect the anonymity of contributors.

Discussion: Allow small groups to present problems they were discussing, as well as any solutions they developed, to the larger group. Encourage other groups to offer solutions as well.

Closure: Discuss how many students share similar problems. Focus additional discussion on how it feels to talk with others about problems and how almost all problems have solutions.

Time: 30–45 minutes

Evaluation/Assignment: Ask students to write a response to the following question: As a result of this activity, what did you learn about "problems" and how to solve them? Answers should focus on the topics discussed in the activity, especially the closure segment of the activity.

Comic Strips

NOICC Career Development Guidelines: Self-Knowledge; Educational and Occupational Exploration

ASCA Standards: Standard A—Students will acquire the skills to investigate the world of work in relation to knowledge of self and to make informed career decisions; Standard C—Students will understand the relationship between personal qualities, education, training, and the world of work.

Purpose: To explore the ways in which comic strips reflect human behavior, personality, lifestyle, and so on.

Objective: Students will be able to identify and discuss the ways in which comic strips reflect real people and society.

MATERIALS: A newspaper comic strip, comic books, books with collections of comic strips, etc.; pencil; paper; chalk; and a blackboard

INTRODUCTION: Students will be asked to look through the newspaper comic section or comic books to find the ways in which comics reflect truth about life.

ACTIVITIES: Ask students to list the ways in which characters in the comics reflect human behavior and personality. Ask students to find examples in the comics of a family crisis, a conflict, a human value, a social problem, a prejudice, stereotypes (particularly about work-related issues, if desired), and a problem at work. Then ask students to draw their own comic strip about a particular aspect of their own lives, such as school, a sport they play, or their choice of occupations.

DISCUSSION: Ask students how these comics reflect or fail to reflect real life in our culture. Discuss what about the comics is humorous and why students think others laugh at the situations in comics. Ask students to choose a comic character whom they would like to be and why. Ask students if they feel comics are purposeful, or if the influence of comics is somehow negative (e.g., violence in a comic might be seen as a negative influence on children).

CLOSURE: Comics tell us about both common experiences in our culture and culture-specific problems people encounter. They often reveal how culture influences our response to the problems we encounter. Finally, the main theme of comics is the importance of keeping perspective in dealing with problems and maintaining a sense of humor. By developing effective coping strategies, one can manage all problem situations more effectively and the situations are less stressful.

TIME: 1 hour, but this activity can also be used over multiple meetings, especially if students are assigned to draw their own comic strip.

EVALUATION/ASSIGNMENT: Students can respond to the following question: "How does humor help you handle the problems you encounter?"

Workers I Know

NOICC CAREER DEVELOPMENT GUIDELINES: Educational and Occupational Exploration

ASCA STANDARDS: Standard A—Students will acquire the skills to investigate the world of work in relation to knowledge of self and to make informed career decisions; Standard B—Students will employ strategies to investigate the world of work in relation to knowledge of self and to make informed career decisions.

PURPOSE: To introduce students to occupations that they encounter each day.

OBJECTIVE: Students will identify the workers that they see every day in their lives.

MATERIALS: Chalkboard, chalk

INTRODUCTION: Discuss the fact that there are many types of workers that students encounter each day. Emphasize the point that each of these workers plays an important role in keeping our society functioning.

ACTIVITIES: List the workers that students see each day. Identify the role that each worker plays in helping the community function.

DISCUSSION: Discuss the importance of each occupation listed, the training required for each occupation, and the benefits associated with each occupation. Be sure to address gender stereotyping with each occupational selection (i.e., challenge students who assume that only members of one gender can perform a particular occupation).

CLOSURE: Reinforce the importance of learning more about occupations. Encourage students to continue listing occupations that they observe for the next 2 days.

TIME: 30–45 minutes

EVALUATION/ASSIGNMENT: Ask students to list the workers and their occupations that they observe in their school and community for the next 2 days.

Women and Men at Work

NOICC CAREER DEVELOPMENT GUIDELINES: Self-Knowledge; Educational and Occupational Exploration

ASCA STANDARDS: Standard A—Students will acquire the skills to investigate the world of work in relation to knowledge of self and to make informed career decisions; Standard C—Students will understand the relationship between personal qualities, education, training, and the world of work.

PURPOSE: To discuss gender-role stereotyping in work.

OBJECTIVE: Students will recognize that occupational selection does not have to be gender based.

MATERIALS: Two flip charts, markers

INTRODUCTION: Ask students to think about the workers that they see each day.

ACTIVITIES: Ask students to list on a sheet of paper at their desks the workers they see each day and whether they are male or female (e.g., principal—female; custodian—male; bus driver—female). Then, using two flip charts, label one "women" and the other one "men." Have students call out occupations that they have noticed. List the occupation under either "women" or "men," depending on the gender of the worker in the occupation the student noticed.

DISCUSSION: Discuss the overlap of occupations on the "women" and the "men" charts. Ask students what conclusions they draw from the overlap. For occupations listed only on one chart, ask students to discuss whether they think a person of the opposite sex could perform those jobs. challenge gender-based assumptions expressed by students.

CLOSURE: Emphasize the importance of not assuming that an occupation is for "women only" or "men only," just because a particular occupation may be more populated by members of one gender than another.

TIME: 30–45 minutes

EVALUATION/ASSIGNMENT: Ask students to identify two people who are opposite in gender from the workers they listed originally. For example, if on the original list students noted a principal who was female, instruct them to identify a male who is a principal. If they cannot identify someone in their immediate environment, they can ask their family members if they know anyone who works in a particular occupation and is opposite in gender from the person on the original list.

Future Skills

NOICC CAREER DEVELOPMENT GUIDELINES: Self-Knowledge; Educational and Occupational Exploration; Career Planning

ASCA STANDARDS: Standard A—Students will acquire the skills to investigate the world of work in relation to knowledge of self and to make informed career decisions; Standard B—Students will employ strategies to achieve future career goals with success and satisfaction; Standard C—Students will understand the relationship between personal qualities, education, training, and the world of work.

PURPOSE: To discuss the future and the impact of technology on our daily lives.

OBJECTIVE: Students will become aware of the impact of technology on their future lives.

MATERIALS: Chalkboard and chalk

INTRODUCTION: Discuss how many of the things we do today are influenced by technology. For example, communication via e-mail, satellite television, microwave ovens, computers in cars, facsimile machines, and car phones all allow us to do things in ways that are very different than when our parents were growing up. Discuss the jobs that exist now because of technology. Compare how things are accomplished today with how things were done 100 years ago.

ACTIVITIES: Divide students into groups. Have each group work collaboratively on creating posters in which they make drawings of "life in the future."

DISCUSSION: Have students share their drawings and discuss the pictures they drew. Discuss what the pictures suggest regarding jobs in the future. Discuss what jobs might not exist in the future due to technology.

CLOSURE: Emphasize the implications of life in the future for career planning. For example, students can discuss the skills that will be needed to work in the future.

TIME: 45 minutes

EVALUATION/ASSIGNMENT: Have students write a short report identifying what they think will be fun about work in the future and what they think will be scary about work in the future.

Picture This!

NOICC CAREER DEVELOPMENT GUIDELINES: Self-Knowledge; Educational and Occupational Exploration; Career Planning

ASCA STANDARDS: Standard B—Students will employ strategies to achieve future career goals with success and satisfaction; Standard C—Students will understand the relationship between personal qualities, education, training, and the world of work.

PURPOSE: To discuss assumptions students make about workers based on race/ethnicity and gender.

OBJECTIVE: Students will recognize that race/ethnicity and gender are not occupational requirements.

MATERIALS: Magazines and scissors

INTRODUCTION: Explain to students that many people draw conclusions about occupational requirements based on false assumptions and factors that have nothing to do with the tasks of the job.

ACTIVITIES: Show students pictures of persons employed in different occupations (be sure to use a diverse sample of persons at work). Ask students to guess each person's occupation.

DISCUSSION: Discuss the assumptions students made in guessing each person's occupation. Discuss why it is not appropriate to relate demographic information to occupations. Discuss ways in which students' assumptions may be counterproductive in their own career development (e.g., because it can lead to eliminating occupations that might be very appropriate for the student).

CLOSURE: Encourage students to identify reasons that they might eliminate nontraditional occupations from consideration in their own career planning. Discuss whether these reasons are a good basis for career decision making.

TIME: 45 minutes

EVALUATION/ASSIGNMENT: Have students interview one person employed in a nontraditional occupation and ask the person to respond to questions such as:

1. What do you like about your occupation?
2. Was it difficult to choose a nontraditional occupation?
3. What are the challenges you face working in a nontraditional occupation?
4. Would you encourage others to consider working in a nontraditional occupation?

ABC List of Occupations

NOICC CAREER DEVELOPMENT GUIDELINES: Educational and Occupational Exploration

ASCA STANDARDS: Standard B—Students will employ strategies to achieve future career goals with success and satisfaction; Standard C—Students will understand the relationship between personal qualities, education, training, and the world of work.

PURPOSE: To have students list as many occupations as they can think of alphabetically and determine which require the most work from the worker.

OBJECTIVE: To identify occupations and consider which students think would require the most energy to perform.

MATERIALS: Chalkboard, pencils, and paper

INTRODUCTION: Ask students to construct an ABC list of occupations so that you have one job listed for each letter of the alphabet. Ask students which three jobs they think require the most work from the worker and why (be sure to have them discuss the criteria they used for defining the "most work"—manual labor, hours worked per day, etc.).

A variation of this activity is to divide the group into two and have each group compete against each other in constructing an alphabetical list of occupations within a prespecified amount of time (e.g., 2 minutes). The leader can time the activity.

ACTIVITIES: Students will list occupations on the board or on paper.

DISCUSSION: Discuss the definition of work and the energy required in performing specific occupations are perceived by the students. Discuss whether the jobs with the least or the most energy requirements are the least or most desirable to the students and why. Ask students which jobs they feel earn the most money. Do they feel energy expended always leads to higher pay?

CLOSURE: Discuss the importance of knowing about jobs and job requirements. Emphasizing how our personal preferences influence our opinions about jobs is also an important part of this activity. The latter point also reinforces the notion that there is no one way to list preferred jobs. Each person will have his or her own list and reasons for preferring certain jobs and particular types of jobs.

TIME: 30–45 minutes

EVALUATION/ASSIGNMENT: Ask each student to write responses to the following questions:

What type of "work" do I prefer? After this activity, I think I know (choose 1): (a) a lot about jobs, (b) an average amount about jobs, or (c) a little about jobs. Then ask students to identify three jobs they would like to learn more about based on this activity.

School and Work

NOICC CAREER DEVELOPMENT GUIDELINES: Career Planning; Self-Knowledge; Educational and Occupational Exploration

ASCA STANDARDS: Standard B—Students will employ strategies to achieve future career goals with success and satisfaction; Standard C—Students will understand the relationship between personal qualities; education, training, and the world of work.

PURPOSE: To discuss the relationship between school and work.

OBJECTIVE: Students will identify occupations that relate to specific school subjects.

MATERIALS: Chalkboard, chalk, pencils, and paper

INTRODUCTION: Begin by discussing the relationship between school and work.

ACTIVITIES: List school subjects (e.g., math, science, language arts, music, and physical education) on the chalkboard. Divide students into small groups. Ask students to list occupations under each school subject that require the use of that subject (e.g., math—accounting, bank teller, cashier). Have each group write its list on the board.

DISCUSSION: Review the list from each group. Have students identify how they think the subject matter is used in each occupation. Discuss what would happen if a person in each occupation didn't have a background in a relevant subject matter.

CLOSURE: Reinforce the connection between school subjects and work.

TIME: 30–45 minutes

EVALUATION/ASSIGNMENT: Have students interview their family members to identify the subject areas that are important for performing their jobs.

Leaders and Followers

NOICC CAREER DEVELOPMENT GUIDELINES: Self-Knowledge; Educational and Occupational Exploration

ASCA STANDARDS: Standard A—Students will acquire the skills to investigate the world of work in relation to knowledge of self and to make informed career decisions; Standard B—Students will employ strategies to achieve future career goals with success and satisfaction; Standard C—Students will understand the relationship between personal qualities, education, training, and the world of work.

PURPOSE: To discuss the attributes of individuals considered to be "leaders."

OBJECTIVE: Students will be able to identify characteristics of a "leader" and compare them with the characteristics of a "hero."

MATERIALS: Chalkboard, pencils, and paper

INTRODUCTION: Begin by brainstorming the words that come to their minds when students think of the words *leader* and *follower*. List the words on the chalkboard under each term.

ACTIVITIES: Students should make a list of persons they consider to be great leaders, including artists, athletes, politicians, scientists, writers, pioneers, businesspersons, and entertainers. Write down the major achievements of these leaders and five common traits these individuals share (e.g., hard worker,

natural talent, etc.). Ask students to name someone they know that has these leadership qualities (from home, school, etc.). Discuss the difference between a leader and a follower. What are the positive traits of both?

DISCUSSION: Review the characteristics of a leader. Ask if being a leader is always a good thing, and why or why not. Ask students to discuss if they prefer being a leader or a follower and to identify reasons for their preferences. Note that they may have preferences for leading in certain situations. When this latter situation occurs, ask students to discuss why they may prefer leading in certain situations but not others. They should focus on the activities they are engaged in, how they feel about their abilities to complete these particular activities, and so on. Finally, discuss how people become leaders (e.g., Are they "born leaders" or can these skills be developed?). The same discussion can take place for "followers."

CLOSURE: Discussion should focus on the importance of leaders and followers in the workplace. Emphasize the importance of both. What would happen if everyone wanted to be a leader? What would happen if everyone wanted to be a follower?

TIME: 30–45 minutes

EVALUATION/ASSIGNMENT: Have students write down what skills they need to develop to become better leaders and better followers.

School: The Good and The Bad

NOICC CAREER DEVELOPMENT GUIDELINES: Self-Knowledge; Educational and Occupational Exploration

ASCA STANDARDS: Standard A—Students will acquire the skills to investigate the world of work in relation to knowledge of self and to make informed career decisions; Standard C—Students will understand the relationship between personal qualities, education, training, and the world of work.

PURPOSE: To have students explore their feelings about school in general.

OBJECTIVE: Students will think about what they like about school as well as their complaints about school.

MATERIALS: Chalkboard, chalk

INTRODUCTION: Make two lists on the board with headings "good" and "bad."

ACTIVITIES: Ask students to take turns writing something under a list of good or bad things about school. If the first student writes under the "bad" list, the next student must write under the "good" list, and vice versa. Examples might be, "I get to see my friends" or "I hate the school lunches."

DISCUSSION: Have students discuss the items on the lists. Encourage them to think of the ways school enhances their lives. Students will then brainstorm ideas for turning "bad" items into "good" items. For example, if a bad item is "homework," then participants can discuss what might be useful about homework. Students could also share strategies they use for making homework better or more enjoyable. Students can also talk about how and when they do their homework. Different strategies can be discussed. The same

approach can be used for other "bad" items. Note that it is likely that all "bad" items may not be converted into "good" items. The leader will need to select which items to focus on in this exercise.

CLOSURE: Center the discussion on whether anything in life is all good. Emphasize the importance of turning "bad" into "good."

TIME: 30–45 minutes

EVALUATION/ASSIGNMENT: Students can list three items in their "bad" category that they could change into "good." Strategies for converting these items from bad to good should be identified.

Changes

NOICC CAREER DEVELOPMENT GUIDELINES: Self-Knowledge; Educational and Occupational Exploration; Career Planning

ASCA STANDARDS: Standard A—Students will acquire the skills to investigate the world of work in relation to knowledge of self and to make informed career decisions; Standard C—Students will understand the relationship between personal qualities, education, training, and the world of work.

PURPOSE: To explore the ways people change.

OBJECTIVE: Students will be able to discuss ways in which they have experienced change as individuals and changes that may likely occur in the future.

MATERIALS: Pencils, paper

INTRODUCTION: Ask students to list or name something about themselves that has changed.

ACTIVITIES: The activity leader will ask students to name something about themselves that has changed: in the past 24 hours (such as clothes); in the past week (something new learned in school); in the past year (joined a sports team, changed grades); since birth. Students will

then be asked to predict changes that are likely to occur in the future (next year, in 5 years, in 10 years, etc.).

DISCUSSION: Discuss the changes that each student has experienced and whether he or she considers these changes positive or negative. Discuss which changes students feel have had the greatest impact on who they are today. Discuss fears about changes likely to occur in the future and how individuals successfully deal with change in their lives. Ask what students might like to change about themselves or their environment and what impedes these changes from occurring.

CLOSURE: Review the discussion and ask students to write down things they notice about themselves that are changing in the next week or month. Request that each student choose something they would like to work to change in the next few weeks, and ask that they keep a journal of their progress regarding this change (e.g., get homework done on time, get up 10 minutes earlier, help with household chores, change looks somehow, etc.).

TIME: 45 minutes to 1 hour

EVALUATION/ASSIGNMENT: Share the journal with the leader.

CHAPTER 11

CAREER DEVELOPMENT INTERVENTIONS IN MIDDLE AND HIGH SCHOOLS

Providing career development interventions in my work as a middle school counselor is important because students need to learn how to explore their interests and strengths. By offering career guidance at this level, counselors can help middle school students build the foundation necessary to understand possibilities and expectations in the world of work.

Many of the work habits that students develop at this level are carried over to high school and beyond. It is crucial that educators provide the assistance students need to form healthy habits and make informed decisions. The earlier students learn about careers and occupations, the better prepared they are to explore the pathways leading toward their own future goals.

Through interest inventories, career fairs, mock job interviews, visits from community business members, and numerous other middle school activities, students are introduced to career development. Teachers from all disciplines combine to provide a full-circle approach to educating students on the importance of career exploration.

Self-awareness is critical at the middle school level. These activities provide a realistic view of potential career paths and opportunities for students to match them with their likes and abilities. Our middle school also offers numerous clubs and activities so students can try out new ideas and experiences to further define their future aspirations.

Overall, the more we encourage our students to pursue interests and new experiences, the more we help them to form good work habits and positive life skills. These skills highlight the importance of using sound judgment when exploring careers and planning for the future.

Michael J. Brannigan
Professional School Counselor
Queensbury Middle School
Queensbury, NY

Career development interventions in my work as high school counselor are important because high school counselors are preparing students to go directly into the working world. At the high school level, career development involves teaching students how to plan and prepare for the workforce. Many teenagers have no idea what direction they want to head into and need help sorting through their interests and abilities. This can dictate everything from how they choose their postsecondary education to what jobs they search for while in school. As such, they need to know how to create resumés, fill out applications, and prepare for interviews. Counselors must also teach students life management skills and how career choice can affect your ability to support yourself and others. An additional aspect of career development for counselors can be job placement, more unique to the high school level. Students of all levels are looking for various types of employment. Some students need help finding part-time positions to help pay for expenses or save for college. Other students need training and basic skills for full-time employment that will begin as soon as they graduate. High school counselors must be in contact with community resources and businesses to find out what positions are available to students and sometimes to monitor a student's on-the-job performance. These contacts not only may employ students, but also provide opportunities for apprenticeships or internships, job shadowing experiences, and coming into the schools for presentations or recruitment. Career development for counselors in high schools serves to bring students and the workforce together to find the best fit.

Megan Martin, M.Ed.
Professional School Counselor
Orange County High School
Hillsboro, NC

Antonio was new to the school. He and his parents had recently moved from Los Angeles to rural Pennsylvania. As a seventh grader in L.A., Antonio had lots of friends, knew most of his teachers, and was one of the star players on the soccer team. In Belltoona, Pennsylvania, Antonio was new, disoriented, and unsure of himself. He was angry about moving, felt alone, and was depressed. Antonio's parents noticed that he had become apathetic and uninvolved in many of the activities that once gave him a sense of satisfaction and pride.

MIDDLE/JUNIOR HIGH SCHOOL

Students at the middle/junior high school level are confronted with a more sophisticated set of developmental tasks than they experienced during their elementary school years. Erikson (1963) notes that between the ages of 12 and 18 adolescents must clarify their identities. If identity clarification is not achieved, then adolescents will experience confusion as they attempt to negotiate the tasks presented to them.

Specifically, Havighurst (1972) suggests that adolescents must accomplish the following developmental tasks:

1. Achieve new and more sophisticated relations with peers
2. Achieve emotional independence from parents and other adults
3. Set vocational goals
4. Prepare for marriage and family life
5. Develop skills for civic competence
6. Acquire a set of values and an ethical system as a guide to behavior
7. Set realistic goals and make plans for achieving these goals.

These tasks present a daunting challenge to young people as they move from childhood to adolescence and early adulthood. The often stormy experience of transitioning from childhood to adolescence not only presents a challenge to the young person experiencing this transition but also to those who are part of the young person's social network. Physiological and social development encourage the preadolescent to take strides toward independence. Strides toward independence, however, are often accompanied by feelings of insecurity, conflict, fear, and anxiety; as Vernon (1993) states, "Dramatic changes in cognition and the intensification of affect contribute to a fluctuating sense of self" (p. 10). Bireley and Genshaft (1991) describe early adolescence as the process of "struggling toward maturity" (p. 1). As a result of their advancing development, middle/junior high school students are preoccupied with belonging and are influenced significantly by their same-sex peers. Thus, counselors providing career interventions for middle school students need to challenge students to become active agents in the career development process while at the same time offering supportive assistance as students acquire additional self- and career information.

Antonio's parents asked his school counselor to meet with Antonio. They wanted Antonio to become more connected with the school and to begin working harder at making new friends. During their meeting, Antonio's counselor convinced him to join a school activity. Together, they explored the wide range of activities available at Antonio's school. The school counselor also encouraged Antonio to explore the various options with his parents. After these discussions, Antonio reluctantly agreed to join a community service group at the school. The counselor also asked the captain of the middle school's soccer team to "mentor" Antonio and help him to become more familiar with the school and other students. Antonio met with his counselor on a regular basis for the first half of the school year and was clearly becoming more connected with the school and making new friends. Antonio and his counselor discussed a variety of topics, including Antonio's experience in the community service group. These discussions also focused on other areas of interest for Antonio. A seemingly natural leader, Antonio's counselor encouraged him to assume a leadership role within the community service group. Antonio liked "being in charge" and at the next election of group officers was voted in as the president. Because Antonio had not thought much about life after high school, his counselor suggested that they spend some time discussing his career plans. Soon, Antonio and his counselor began to explore how his interests related to various occupational options.

Understanding the career development status of middle school students is crucial for developing goals for career development interventions. As at the elementary school level, counselors in secondary school settings also view providing career assistance to students as central to their work (Campbell & Dahir, 1997). Here again, data from the National Assessment of Educational Progress's Project on Career and Occupational Development provide useful information for understanding the career development status of middle/junior high school students. For example, survey results from a national sample of 38,000 13-year-olds indicate that young people at this age have made progress in crystallizing their self-concepts, as exemplified by the fact that they tend to be able to identify their strengths and weaknesses. Students at this age also evidence a growing understanding of the world-of-work. Often this progress is the result of students participating in school activities, hobbies, and/or part-time work. Boys and girls at age 13 tend to be equally knowledgeable about highly visible occupations and can link at least one school subject to a job. Most students at this age indicate that they have at least started the process of thinking about a future job. Interestingly, their choices for future jobs tend to be occupations requiring college degrees or lengthy training periods beyond high school, rather than jobs now held by the majority of the workforce (i.e., those not requiring a college degree). Of most concern in the data provided by the National Assessment of Educational Progress's Project on Career and Occupational Development is the fact that racial minority students and students living in poverty tend to lag behind other students in their career development. Thus, the effectiveness of current career development interventions provided to middle/junior high school students is variable.

This variability points to the importance of being clear about the societal expectations placed upon students in the middle/junior high school. As these students transition between Super's growth and exploration stages, they encounter the task of crystallizing occupational preferences. They are expected by teachers, counselors, and designers of the school curriculum to develop a realistic self-concept and to acquire additional information about more opportunities (Super, 1984). Specifically, middle/junior high school students are required to learn about themselves and the world-of-work and then translate this learning into an educational plan for the remainder of their secondary school education. Super, Savickas, and Super (1996) refer to the crystallization process by noting that "when habits of industriousness, achievement, and foresight coalesce, individuals turn to daydreaming about possible selves they may construct. Eventually, these occupational daydreams crystallize into a publicly recognized vocational identity with corresponding preferences for a group of occupations at a particular ability level" (p. 132). Thus, to establish an appropriate course of action for high school and beyond, career development interventions during middle/junior high school must be directed toward helping students cope successfully with the tasks of crystallizing and specifying occupational preferences (Super et al., 1996).

The ASCA National Standards (Campbell & Dahir, 1997) also provide direction for professional school counselors as they construct career development interventions for middle school students. Specifically, the standards indicate that middle school students should: "(a) acquire the skills to investigate the world of work in relation to knowledge of self and to make informal career decisions, (b) employ strategies to achieve future success and satisfaction, and (c) understand the relationship between personal qualities, education and training, and the world of work" (p. 17).

During his meetings with his counselor, Antonio discussed how working in the community service group helped him feel less lonely and better about himself in general. Antonio enjoyed planning and organizing the group's service activities. He had quickly become a leader in this group and enjoyed this role as well. Antonio confided to his counselor that he had often dreamed about being a CEO for a company that does something to help others. He stated that "being in charge" and "helping others" were two things that were fun and important to him. Antonio's counselor carefully listened to Antonio's important self-referent statements. The counselor helped underscore for Antonio how this self-knowledge could be used to direct Antonio's further exploration of career options. Specifically, Antonio's counselor suggested that he use the computer information delivery system available at the school to find out which occupations would provide him with opportunities to "be in charge" and "help others." After generating a list from the computer, Antonio met with his counselor to discuss the options on the list and determine where he could get more information about the options that interested him the most.

Career Development Guidelines for Middle/ Junior High School Students

The NOICC developed National Career Development Guidelines (NOICC, 1992) for middle/junior high school students to provide information concerning the specific knowledge, skills, and awareness that students need to acquire in the domains of self-knowledge, educational and occupational exploration, and career planning.

1. Self-Knowledge
   a. Knowledge of the influence of a positive self-concept
   b. Skills to interact with others
   c. Knowledge of the importance of growth and change
2. Educational and Occupational Exploration
   a. Knowledge of the benefits of educational achievement to career opportunities
   b. Understanding the relationship between work and learning
   c. Skills to locate, understand, and use career information
   d. Knowledge of skills necessary to seek and obtain jobs
   e. Understanding how work relates to the needs and functions of the economy and society
3. Career Planning
   a. Skills to make decisions
   b. Knowledge of the interrelationship of life roles
   c. Knowledge of different occupations and changing male/female roles
   d. Understanding the process of career planning

As with the elementary school guidelines, a variety of career development interventions can be constructed systematically by using the middle/junior high level guidelines. Prior to discussing possible interventions, however, it is useful to examine the career planning considerations offered by Herr and Cramer (1996):

1. Because middle school is a transitional experience from the structured and general education of the elementary school to the less structured but more specialized education of the secondary school, students must be provided with a broad opportunity to explore their personal characteristics as well as those of the educational options from which they must choose. Opportunities to relate curricular options to the possible and subsequent educational and occupational outcomes seem highly desirable.

2. Because wide ranges in career maturity, interests, values, and abilities characterize middle school students, a wide variety of methods are needed to accommodate the range of individual differences. Students whose parents have not completed high school frequently have not had the developmental experience or occupational knowledge enjoyed by students from homes in which the parents are well educated.

3. Although students in middle school are capable of verbal and abstract behavior, exploration will be enhanced if they are given concrete, hands-on, direct experiences as well.

4. Fundamental to the rapid changes that students experience in middle school is a search for personal identity. Therefore, career guidance programs must encourage students to explore feelings, needs, and uncertainties as a base for evaluating educational and vocational options. Values clarification and other similar processes are helpful in this regard (p. 392).

In addition to these important considerations, professional school counselors need to remain cognizant of the ways in which gender and racial stereotyping related to occupational options can artificially constrict the range of options students are considering. Clearly, counselors must deliver career development interventions that aggressively attack these discriminatory influences.

Career Development Interventions in Middle/Junior High Schools

Thematic consideration of middle/junior high school-level career development competencies reveals the importance of students acquiring the necessary knowledge, skills, and understanding to advance in their career development. Interventions that combine psychoeducational activities and experiential tasks are useful in helping students cope with the career development tasks confronting them. Examples of the former include teaching students about the relationship between education and work, the importance and interaction of life roles, the importance of understanding issues related to equity and access in career choice, the career development tasks they will confront now and in the future, and the ways in which they can access and evaluate occupational information. These interventions can easily occur in group and/or classroom guidance activities. The ASCA National Model (ASCA, 2003) provides an excellent guide for identifying topics to incorporate in psychoeducational activities with students. Examples of experiential tasks include job shadowing; attending career fairs; conducting occupational information interviews; and engaging in activities to clarify interests, values, and skills. Both psychoeducational and experiential activities help students acquire the knowledge, skills, and understanding needed to develop the attitudes and skills of readiness for educational and career decision making (Super, 1990).

With the help of his counselor, Antonio decided that it would be helpful to him to speak with a local hospital administrator, the executive director of a local social service agency, and the minister of his church. The purpose of the meetings was to learn more about each of these occupations (e.g., what each person liked and did not like about his or her occupation, training required for each of the occupations, and the academic subjects that were more important for doing the work well). After conducting these occupational information interviews, Antonio expressed an interest in job shadowing with the hospital administrator. He also stated that after he finished high school, it would be important for him to attend college.

It is also important at this developmental level that career interventions continue to stimulate curiosity in students. Students who are curious about their emerging self-concepts (e.g., their avocational and vocational interests, skills, and values) are more likely to engage in exploratory behavior to acquire the information they need for self-concept clarification (Super, 1981). Helping students identify and connect with role models can also facilitate a sense of internal control and future time perspective, which can, in turn, lead to planful behaviors and the development of effective problem-solving skills (Super, 1990).

To help guide students in their exploration, counselors can administer career assessments. In selecting career assessments, it is important that the reading level, language, and normative samples are appropriate for the school population with which the assessments will be used. Interest inventory results can foster more systematic thinking about the activities in which students enjoy participating. Aptitude tests can also help students acquire accurate estimates of their abilities. Interest and aptitude assessments are often administered to students during the middle/junior high school grades. Combining interest inventory results with aptitude test results provides a useful foundation for the exploration process. Students will find it useful to explore occupational areas for which they have high interest and high aptitude. When the results of an interest inventory suggest that a student has no area of above average or high interest, it may be that the student needs exposure to activities across several interest areas to determine if any will interest the student. Thus, a key to making assessments, especially interest inventories, useful is that students must have the experiential base to draw upon to respond to assessment items. Students with limited exposure to a variety of activities will be forced to guess at appropriate responses to questions requiring them to identify their likes and dislikes. (One counselor related that he attempted to administer an interest inventory to his daughter when she was in sixth grade. Her reading level at that time far exceeded the reading level of the inventory, but her experiential base was such that she did not understand many of the items presented to her on the inventory. It very quickly became evident that the inventory results would not serve to foster her career development!) When school systems have a systematic career development intervention program in place for all grades, it is safer to assume that middle/junior high school students have been exposed to activities that have fostered their self- and career exploration. When no such programs exist, counselors must be especially cognizant of the possibility that many students will need more remedial career development interventions prior to being administered career assessments.

Providing middle school students with exposure to work facilitates the acquisition of knowledge, skills, and awareness related to the career development domains within NOICC's National Career Development Guidelines of (a) educational and occupational exploration and (b) career planning. These activities also connect to Standards C:A1 (Develop Career Awareness) and C:B1 (Acquire Career Information) of the ASCA's National Standards. Teaching students how families of occupations can be clustered according to factors such as skill requirements, interests, and/or training helps students organize the world-of-work and connect their characteristics to occupational options (NOICC's Self-Knowledge, Educational and Occupational Exploration, and Career Planning domains; ASCA's Develop Career Awareness and Identify Career Goals standards). For example, Holland's classification system uses the six personality types described in Chapter 3 to group occupations. *Realistic* occupations include skilled trades and technical occupations. *Investigative* occupations include scientific and technical occupations. *Artistic* occupations include creative occupations in the expressive arts. *Social* occupations include the helping professions. *Enterprising* occupations involve managerial and sales occupations. Lastly, *conventional* occupations include office and clerical occupations. Occupations are classified according to the degree to which the activities of the occupation draw upon the Holland types. The three most dominant types reflected in the occupation are used to classify each occupation.

Antonio was administered The Self-Directed Search and obtained the Holland code of enterprising, social, and artistic. He met with other students and the counselor to discuss the inventory results. They talked about their Holland codes and whether they thought the codes were accurate. With the counselor's assistance, they also brainstormed a list of occupations for each Holland type. Antonio decided that it made sense for him to continue exploring the occupations of hospital administrator and social service director.

The U.S. Office of Education (USOE) clusters occupations according to whether they involve producing goods or providing services. The two broad categories are then subdivided into 15 occupational clusters as follows:

1. Business and office
2. Marketing and distribution
3. Communications and media
4. Construction
5. Manufacturing
6. Transportation
7. Agribusiness and natural resources
8. Marine science
9. Environment
10. Public services
11. Health
12. Recreation and hospitality
13. Personal services
14. Fine arts and humanities
15. Consumer and homemaking education

Within each cluster, there is a hierarchy of occupations ranging from professional to unskilled.

Clustering systems such as the USOE's and Holland's can be used to guide career exploration by using the types to organize career information resources, career fairs, curricula experiences (e.g., students can be assigned the task of writing an essay about occupations that fall within their dominant Holland type), job-shadowing experiences, participation in extracurricular activities, avocational pursuits, college exploration, and part-time employment experiences.

To develop effective interpersonal skills related to the work environment (ASCA's Develop Employment Readiness competency, C:A2), students can be provided with difficult interpersonal interactions (e.g., a coworker who interacts angrily for no apparent reason, an angry boss who places unreasonable demands on workers); and students can brainstorm ways of coping with the situation. Students can then role play solutions to handling difficult interpersonal interactions at work.

To increase students' thinking about the interrelationship of life roles (ASCA's Acquire Knowledge to Achieve Career Goals competency, C:C1, and NOICC's Career Planning domain), counselors can use a group guidance format to help middle/junior high school students examine their current life-role salience by responding to such questions as: How do you spend your time during a typical week? How important are the different roles of life to you? What do you like about participating in each of the life roles? What life roles do you think will be important to you in the future? What do you hope to accomplish in each of the life roles that will be important to you in the future? What life roles do members of your family play? What do your family members expect you to accomplish in each of the life roles?

Obviously, patterns of life-role salience are significantly influenced by immediate (e.g., family, cultural heritage, level of acculturation) and distal (e.g., economics, environmental opportunities for life-role participation) contextual factors (Blustein, 1994). Contextual factors, therefore, contribute to patterns of life-role salience. However, many middle/junior high school students lack an awareness of the ways in which contextual factors (such as the dominant culture and the student's culture of origin) interact with identity development to shape life-role salience (Blustein). Group discussions pertaining to these topics can help middle/junior high school students develop their sense of which life roles are important to them now, which life roles will be important to them in the future, and how life roles interact to influence life satisfaction.

An effective tool for helping middle/junior high school students engage in purposeful planning, exploring, information gathering, decision making, and reality testing related to two prominent life roles (i.e., student and worker) is an educational and career planning portfolio. Educational and career planning portfolios are typically used to help students chart their academic and career decision making. This charting process can begin in middle/junior high school and continue until the student leaves high school. By making at least annual entries into the portfolio, the student and counselor can track the student's career development progress. They can also make systematic educational and career plans that build upon the growing base of self- and occupational knowledge the student is developing. In essence, the portfolio provides a vehicle for the student and counselor to discuss what the student has done and what the student will do next to advance his or her career development. There are several very useful portfolios available (e.g., "Get a Life" developed by the

American School Counselors Association), and portfolios are fairly easy to develop locally (see the portfolio developed by Niles for the Virginia Department of Education in Appendix C).

To help students focus on the interrelationship of life roles and to engage in planning related to their salient life roles, the educational and career planning portfolio can be expanded to a *life-role portfolio* by addressing students' readiness for life roles beyond those of student and worker. Students can be encouraged to plan, explore, and gather information for each of the major roles of life. For example, students who anticipate one day being a parent can plan for this role by considering how parenting interacts with other roles. Students can explore different styles of parenting by interviewing parents about their parenting practices and philosophies. Students can also gather information about the skills required for effective parenting (perhaps by taking a class). Through these activities students can learn about the factors that are important to consider in making decisions about parenting. Finally, students can reality-test their interest through participating in child-care activities. Thus, the life-role portfolio serves as a stimulus for counselor and student meetings focused on planning, exploring, information gathering, decision making, and reality-testing vis-á-vis the major life roles. When the portfolio is used over successive years, it also provides developmental documentation of activities and decisions related to major life roles.

This expanded use of the planning portfolio is an example of a counseling activity that is intended to help students cope with the developmental task of identity formation within the context of developing life-role readiness. It also provides additional opportunities for discussing contextual influences on life-role salience. Regardless of the life role, it is important that counselors are sensitive to cultural diversity in life-role salience and life-role behaviors among their students.

HIGH SCHOOL

As students transition to high school, they focus more directly on the tasks of identifying occupational preferences and clarifying career/lifestyle choices (these tasks build upon all of the ASCA competencies within the Career Development domain as well as all of the NOICC tasks within the National Career Development Guidelines). According to Super (1957), the tasks of crystallizing, specifying, and implementing tentative career choices occur during early (ages 12 to 15), middle (ages 16 to 18), and late (ages 18 to 24) adolescence. Super et al. (1996) described the process of coping with these career development tasks of crystallizing and specifying as follows:

> When habits of industriousness, achievement, and foresight coalesce, individuals turn to daydreaming about possible selves they may construct. Eventually, these occupational daydreams crystallize into a publicly recognized vocational identity with corresponding preferences for a group of occupations at a particular ability level. Through broad exploration of the occupations in this group, individuals eventually complete the task of specifying an occupational choice by translating the privately experienced occupational self-concept into educational/vocational choices. (p. 132)

Antonio acquired other experiences through volunteering in the local hospital and a local social service agency. These experiences helped him learn more about himself and the world of work. The more he learned, the more he liked the idea of becoming a hospital administrator. He decided that this would be his tentative career goal. He used this information to guide his exploration of postsecondary educational opportunities.

When adolescents complete the relevant training/preparatory experiences, they then implement their occupational choices by acquiring positions in their specified occupations. Implementation is followed by a period of adjustment to the occupational requirements and workplace expectations of the implemented choice (Tiedeman, 1961). Thus, the key elements to a successful school-to-work and school-to-school transition involve being able to implement and adjust to career choice.

In this regard, it is important to note that a substantial portion of secondary school students in the United States enter work immediately upon leaving high school or prior to completing a college degree (Marshall & Tucker, 1992). Regarding the latter, although 84% of high school seniors plan to get a 2- or 4-year college degree, only 41% of high school graduates age 30 to 34 actually have college degrees (Rosenbaum & Person, 2003). Feller (2003) reports that over 70% of high school seniors expect to hold professional jobs (i.e., those requiring a college degree). Many school counselors, Feller notes, hesitate to confront this "silent dream" of obtaining a college degree.

This trend toward "college for all" aspirations emerged from three revolutionary changes (Rosenbaum & Person, 2003, p. 252). First, the labor market dramatically increased its skill demands and augmented the earnings advantages for college graduates. Second, college enrollment became dramatically more accessible in recent decades. Third, community colleges instituted an open admissions policy. Although there has been a popular concern about school counselors being too restrictive by encouraging some students not to attend college, now the opposite situation may be true. The point here is that school counselors need to do a better job informing students, parents, and school personnel that jobs leading to rewarding careers exist in a wide variety of fields including technical specialties, financial services, construction, and trades. Unfortunately, too little is known about jobs in these areas. Moreover, because 31% of college entrants (52% of whom are students with high school grades of C or lower) actually earn no college credits (Rosenbaum, 2001), these students are in reality work-bound and they do not benefit from the "college for all" approach. Thus, we advocate that professional school counselors help students make choices from a full range of options including those occupations not requiring a college degree. Rosenbaum and Person recommend that professional school counselors also help others become aware of the following new rules regarding the labor market and college:

- All students can attend college, but low-achieving students should be cautioned about the need to take remedial courses once they enter college.
- Even if high school students have college plans, they must prepare for work.
- College plans require substantial effort and good academic planning in middle/high school.
- Many good jobs do not require a college degree.

- High school students improve their chances for obtaining good jobs by having better academic achievement, taking vocational courses, getting job placement assistance from teachers, and developing "soft skills" such as interpersonal competence and good work habits.

These points highlight the importance of developing workforce readiness to cope successfully with the school-to-work transition. The definition of *workforce readiness* changes with the times. Until recently this term may have focused solely on helping adolescents acquire training for a specific job, but now employers are more concerned with "finding youth who can read and write, have a good attitude, are motivated, are dependable, follow directions, and can be good team members" (Krumboltz & Worthington, 1999, p. 316). Academic skills, interpersonal skills, and engaging in lifelong learning have emerged as important skills for youth to acquire if they are to be successful workers. In this regard, Hansen (1999) argues for expanding school-to-work career development interventions to include student development in addition to the more traditional emphasis on workforce development. Hansen points to curricula such as the Missouri Life Career Development System, the Minnesota Career Development Curriculum, and a model development by the Florida Department of Education titled "A Framework for Developing Comprehensive Guidance and Counseling Programs for a School-to-Work System" as excellent examples of comprehensive career development interventions to help youth prepare for the transition from secondary school to work.

Baker (2000) emphasizes the importance of school counselors providing "transition enhancement" assistance to secondary school students as they progress toward further education, training, or employment. Because such transitions are a regular part of high school students' development, Baker recommends that counselors view transitions as a process rather than as events or a sequence of events. The basic needs of students coping with the transition process can be classified into the categories of support, awareness, and skills.

Students need emotional support to lessen the anticipatory anxiety they may experience as they consider the transitions they will encounter. Moving from the familiar to the unknown creates anxiety in all people. However, it is reasonable to expect this anxiety to be fairly high among adolescents who have lived their lives primarily in the arenas of home and school. Postsecondary work, training, and education present new challenges and experiences. Although some of these challenges may seem somewhat intimidating, counselors can remind students that the competencies they have developed thus far in their lives will also be helpful to them as they negotiate the postsecondary transition experience. Reassuring students that it is "normal" to feel a bit anxious during a transition also provides emotional support to students as they move forward in their career development. In many respects, school counselors are the human development specialists in the schools. Educating stakeholders about the developmental process students will experience as they move through school helps students, teachers, administrators, and parents develop the awareness to think proactively about the tasks students will encounter. Thus, infusing the academic and school counseling curriculum with developmental concepts helps students acquire the awareness that fosters a planful approach to coping with career development tasks.

When conceptualized as a process, the skills required for coping with the school-to-work and school-to-school transition are linked to the elementary and middle school career development competencies discussed previously. That is, transition skills build upon the self-awareness, occupational awareness, and decision making skills students have developed throughout their educational experience. Transition skills also build upon the basic educational competencies related to reading, writing, and arithmetic (Baker, 2000). For example, composing a resumé and cover letter requires writing skills. Performing effectively in a job or college interview requires skills in oral communication and interpersonal communication. Acquiring information about jobs, colleges, and training programs requires research, technology, and reading skills. Transition skills can also be expanded to include skills related to stress and anxiety management. The ASCA (1985) takes the position that counselors in the schools must assume the primary (but not the sole) responsibility for fostering these skills in students: "The school counselor's role covers many areas within the school setting and career guidance is one of the most important contributions to a student's lifelong development" (p. 165). Thus, proactively bolstering students' readiness to cope with the career development tasks they are likely to encounter is a primary component of the school counselor's role. Likewise, counselors must be competent in strategies to help students who encounter difficulty in coping with career development tasks.

Much of Super's research focused on understanding how adolescents can develop their readiness to cope effectively with the various career development tasks confronting them. The term initially used by Super (1955) to describe career readiness in adolescence was *career maturity*. Because the career development tasks confronting adolescents emerge from expectations inherent in academic curricula and society (e.g., family, teachers), the career development process during this life stage is more homogeneous than in adulthood. The school system expects students to make career decisions at specific points in the curriculum (e.g., eighth graders choosing an academic program that they will study in high school). Because the timing of these career development tasks can be predicted, career development practitioners can provide a systematic set of interventions to foster adolescent career development. Super et al. (1996) reinforced this point in stating that adolescent career development can be guided "partly by facilitating the maturing of abilities, interests, and coping resources and partly by aiding in reality testing and in the development of self-concepts" (p. 125).

Other researchers such as Marcia (1966) have also identified important variables for adolescent career development. Specifically, Marcia focuses on two variables—crisis/exploration and commitment—as central to the career development process during adolescence. Crisis/exploration refers to the process of sorting through identity issues; questioning parentally defined goals, values, and beliefs; and identifying personally appropriate alternatives regarding career options, goals, values, and beliefs. Commitment refers to the extent that the individual is personally involved in, and expresses allegiance to, self-chosen aspirations, goals, values, beliefs, and career options (Muuss, 1998). The degree to which adolescents resolve the tasks associated with crisis/exploration and commitment provides the conceptual structure for Marcia's taxonomy of adolescent identity (Marcia, 1980). This taxonomy comprises four identity statuses: identity diffused (or identity confused), foreclosed, moratorium, and identity achieved.

1. The *identity-diffused* person has yet to experience an identity crisis or exploration and has not made any personal commitment to an occupation, much less to a set of goals, values, and beliefs.

2. The *foreclosed* person has yet to experience an identity crisis or exploration but has committed to an occupation and to a set of goals, values, and beliefs (usually due to indoctrination or social pressure by parents and/or significant others). This type of foreclosure is premature because it has occurred without exploring and struggling with the basic existential questions related to identifying one's values, beliefs, goals, and so on.

3. The *moratorium* person is engaged in an active struggle to clarify personally meaningful values, goals, and beliefs. Committing to a particular set of values, goals, and beliefs has been placed "on hold" until the process of identity clarification is more complete.

4. The *identity-achieved* person has sorted through the process of identity clarification and resolved these issues in a personally meaningful way. Moreover, as a result of exploring and resolving identity issues, the identity-achieved person commits to an occupation and a personal value system.

Rather than being a singular process of exploring and committing to a set of values, goals, and beliefs, identity formation occurs across several domains, such as occupation, religion, politics, and sexuality. In many respects, these domains parallel Super's (1980) notion of life-role self-concepts (e.g., worker, leisurite, student, and homemaker) and reinforce Hansen's (1999) call for holistic career development interventions in the schools. Additionally, the individual's identity status within each domain is not static but rather an ongoing process involving back-and-forth movement across stages (Muuss, 1996). Marcia (1980) notes that although any of the identity statuses can become terminal, the foreclosed person experiences the greatest risk of closed development. Thus, career development interventions for preadolescents and adolescents (who by definition enter into these life stages with a relatively diffused identity) should be carefully designed to foster exploration and identity development related to the career domain.

Career Development Guidelines for High School Students

The National Career Development Guidelines (NOICC, 1992) and the extensive body of literature related to adolescent career development help counselors identify appropriate career development goals and interventions for high school students. The specific career development competencies identified as being appropriate for high school students are:

1. Self-Knowledge
   a. Understanding the influence of a positive self-concept
   b. Skills to interact positively with others
   c. Understanding the impact of growth and development

2. Educational and Occupational Exploration
   a. Understanding the relationship between educational achievement and career planning
   b. Understanding the need for positive attitudes toward work and learning
   c. Skills to locate, evaluate, and interpret career information
   d. Skills to prepare to seek, obtain, maintain, and change jobs
   e. Understanding how societal needs and functions influence the nature and structure of work
3. Career Planning
   a. Skills to make decisions
   b. Understanding the interrelationship of life roles
   c. Understanding the continuous changes in male/female roles
   d. Skills in career planning

In constructing interventions to foster the development of these competencies, Herr and Cramer (1996) recommend attending to several potential issues confronting high school students. These include:[1]

1. Because many students complete their formal schooling with high school, there is the need to help all students develop and implement a career plan.
2. Career development interventions at the high school level must take into account the fact that career development interventions are often not implemented in a systematic way across all grade levels and there are individual differences in the degree to which previous interventions have been effective. Thus, interventions at the high school level will need to address heterogeneity in adolescent career development.
3. Career development interventions should address the internal and environmental pressure many students experience in making career decisions.
4. Career development interventions at the high school level should foster the examination of the advantages and disadvantages related to the various postsecondary school options students may be considering.

Career Development Interventions in High Schools

The emphasis on knowledge, skills, and understanding that emerged in the middle/junior high school level competencies is continued in the high school competencies. The high school competencies, however, challenge students to become more focused on making career plans by translating their self- and career information into career goals. Savickas (1999) proposed career development interventions that foster the sort of self-knowledge, educational and occupational exploration, and career planning described in the high school competencies. Specifically, these interventions focus on (a) orienting students' comprehension of careers, (b) developing students' competence at planning and exploring, (c) coaching students to develop effective career

[1]From *Career Guidance and Counseling Through the Life Span*, by E. C. Herr and S. H. Cramer. Copyright © 1996 by Allyn & Bacon. Reprinted/adapted by permission.

management techniques, and (d) guiding students in behavioral rehearsals to become prepared for coping with job problems (pp. 331–333). Interventions that focus on these areas address the ASCA standards in the Career Development domain.

To orient ninth-grade students to the planning tasks they will encounter as they move through high school, Savickas (1999) recommends using a group guidance format to discuss items on career development inventories such as the Career Maturity Inventory (Crites, 1978) or the Adult Career Concerns Inventory (Super, Thompson, Lindeman, Jordaan, & Myers, 1988). Using inventory items to orient students to the tasks they need to address to manage their career development effectively helps provide a stimulus for planning and exploring behaviors (Savickas, 1990). For example, the Adult Career Concerns Inventory (ACCI) (Super et al. 1988) measures developmental task concern for the career stages of Exploration, Establishment, Maintenance, and Disengagement. Reviewing the career stages and tasks within the ACCI teaches high school students about the general process of career development. Using ACCI items, adolescents can identify those career development tasks they are likely to encounter in the near future. Strategies for coping with current and near-future career development tasks can be identified. In this way, high school students' understanding of time perspective or "planfulness" can be enhanced (Savickas, Stilling, & Schwartz, 1984). These activities connect with Standards A, B, and C in the Career Development domain of the National Standards for School Counseling.

Antonio's counselor used a group guidance format to discuss students' scores on Holland's Self-Directed Search. They brainstormed occupational options for each type and then discussed what sort of education would be required to enter each occupation. The group members also discussed which school subjects they thought would be most important for each occupation.

Sharing this information with parents and guardians helps foster parental awareness of the career development tasks confronting their children. To this end, evening informational sessions and newsletters provide opportunities to orient parents and guardians to the career development tasks they can expect their children to encounter. These activities also provide opportunities to advise parents as to how they can help their children manage these career development tasks more effectively (Turner & Lapan, 2002).

Antonio's counselor sent materials home that described the Holland types and the Self-Directed Search. The counselor invited parents to an evening meeting in which they were given an informal assessment of their Holland types. In a fashion similar to what the counselor had done with the students, parents were then encouraged to brainstorm occupations for each type, identify educational requirements for each occupation, and then list the academic subjects they thought were most important for each occupation. After this activity, the counselor identified ways in which the parents could help their children use the information they had acquired in their career planning.

To help increase self-knowledge and to encourage educational and occupational exploration (ASCA Standards A and C in the Career Development domain), counselors can facilitate student participation in informational interviews. To prepare for these experiences, counselors and teachers guide students in composing interview questions that relate to the high school-level career development competencies. For example, questions pertaining to the importance of interpersonal communication, positive work attitudes, and the relationship between educational achievement and career planning can be identified.

Results from interest and abilities measures administered at the end of middle school or at the beginning of high school provide direction as to which occupational environments offer the best potential for fruitful exploration. As noted previously, the range of career assessment possibilities that can be used systematically with youth is substantial. To measure interests, counselors can use instruments that provide information related to students' Holland types, such as the Self-Directed Search (Holland, 1985) and the Career Assessment Inventory (Johansson, 1986). Ability measures include the Differential Aptitude Test (Bennett, Seashore, & Wesman, 1992), the Ability Explorer (Harrington, 1996), and assessments of functional skills from school transcripts or educational and career planning portfolios. Areas of high interest and ability can be matched to occupational clusters and students can identify specific occupations for in-depth exploration (C:B2 in the National Standards).

Although interest and ability assessment results provide important data pertaining to career choice content (i.e., relating students' abilities and interests to occupational options), these data fail to address whether students have developed readiness for career decision making (Super, 1983). Approaches to career assessment must attend to both content and process variables in order to adequately address the needs of youth (Savickas, 1993). Specifically, interests and abilities can be considered as career-choice content data that must be viewed in light of career-choice process data such as readiness for career decision making, life-role salience, and values—which can be labeled as moderator variables (Super, Osborne, Walsh, Brown, & Niles, 1992). To be ready to effectively choose, and adapt to, an occupation, it is important for high school students to "see themselves as coping with certain developmental tasks, at a stage in life at which they are expected, and may expect themselves to make certain decisions and acquire certain competencies" (Super, 1983, p. 559). Students who have not successfully accomplished the career development tasks presented to them at previous educational levels will need remedial interventions (e.g., additional opportunities for self-concept clarification, training in acquiring occupational information) prior to focusing on career decision making.

From this perspective, addressing career choice readiness (Super, 1990) becomes a necessary precursor to the effective use of ability- and interest-assessment data. According to Super, career choice readiness involves five dimensions: (a) having a planful attitude toward coping with career stages and tasks, (b) gathering information about educational and occupational opportunities, (c) exploring the world-of-work, (d) knowing how to make good career decisions, and (e) being able to make realistic judgments about potential occupations (p. 231). These dimensions (which relate to Standards A–C in the National Standards) are important because if an adolescent knows little about the world of work, his or her interest inventories that use occupational titles or activities may produce misleading scores and the student may make poor choices (Super et al., 1996). Likewise, when adolescents do not engage in appropriate career planning, they often encounter career tasks for which they are not prepared (Herr & Cramer. 1996). Thus, assessing high school students' resources for choosing, and adapting to, an occupation requires conducting appraisals of career choice content (e.g., abilities, interests, values) and process (e.g., life-role salience, career choice readiness) variables. When a student is lacking in any of the five dimensions that make up career choice readiness, then the counselor should focus interventions to help the student progress in that particular domain prior to focusing on career choice content.

It is important to note that traditional assessment approaches focusing only on career-choice content variables assume that all individuals place a high value on work and that all individuals view work as the prime means of values realization. It can be argued that this is a Western, middle-class, male view of career development and, thus, is a culturally encapsulated view of life-role salience. Different patterns of life-role salience exist and they must be considered in helping high school students clarify and articulate their career goals (Niles & Goodnough, 1996). For example, when salience for the work role is high, youths view work as providing meaningful opportunities for self-expression. In such cases, high school students are often motivated to develop the career maturity necessary (e.g., to be planful, to explore opportunities, to gather information) for making good career decisions. When work-role salience is low, however, adolescents often lack motivation and career maturity. In the latter instances, counselors need to begin the career development intervention process by arousing the individual's sense of importance for the worker role (Super, 1990). Disputing irrational beliefs, exposing young people to effective role models, and providing mentors are examples of activities that foster career arousal (Krumboltz & Worthington, 1999).

To help young people further clarify their life-role self-concepts, counselors can encourage high school students to revisit life-role salience questions posed during the middle/junior high school years (e.g., How do I spend my time during the course of a typical week?, What changes would I like to make in how I spend my time?, How important is each life role to me?, How important is each life role to my family?, What do I like about participating in each life role?, What do I hope to accomplish in each life role?, What does my family expect me to accomplish in each life role?, What life roles do I think will be important to me in the future?, and What must I do to become more prepared for the life roles that will be important to me in the future?). Discussing these questions helps high school students clarify and articulate their life-role self-concepts. Specifically, by discussing these questions during the first years of high school, adolescents can become clearer as to the values they seek to express in each life role. This information is vital not only for guiding high school students in the selection and pursuit of appropriate educational and occupational options, but also in developing appropriate expectations for values satisfaction within the respective life roles.

These discussion questions also provide opportunities for exploring the individual's level of acculturation, cultural identity, and worldview. For example, high school students can discuss family expectations and other cultural factors influencing their life-role participation. Finally, discussing these questions helps counselors become aware of potential barriers, as well as potential sources of support, for students as they move closer to negotiating the school-to-work or school-to-school transition. These discussions also foster the acquisition of the high school-level career development competencies related to understanding the interrelationship of life roles and understanding the changing nature of male/female roles. This information also helps high school students identify those roles in which they spend most of their time, those to which they are emotionally committed, and those that they expect to be important to them in the future. By clarifying information concerning life-role salience (and the cultural factors influencing role salience), high school students establish the foundation for making accurate self-evaluations and developing career choice readiness.

An important task in acquiring adequate self-knowledge for effective educational and occupational exploration is clarifying values. Clarifying values is important because values are indications of the qualities people desire and seek in "the activities in which they engage, in the situations in which they live, and in the objects which they make or acquire" (Super, 1970, p. 4). Because values reflect the individual's goals, they provide a sense of purpose and direction in the career planning process (Savickas et al., 1996). However, though many agree that values clarification is critical to choosing an occupation, relatively few put forth the effort to examine their values in a systematic way (Harrington, 1996). Values card sorts (e.g., Career Values Card Sort Kit, Nonsexist Vocational Card Sort) and instruments such as the Career Orientation Placement and Evaluation Survey (COPES) are instruments that are useful in values clarification. Interest inventory results can also be used to identify work-related activities that provide opportunities for values expression.

Regarding parental involvement in the career intervention process, Amundson and Penner (1998) recommend that professional school counselors consider involving parents/guardians directly in the career counseling experience. To this end, Amundson and Penner devised an innovative parent-involved career exploration process (PICE) that includes five steps. In step one (Introduction), two students and at least one parent, or guardian, for each student are invited to participate in an innovative career exploration activity. The participants' roles are explained (it is the student's career counseling session and parents are invited as observers) and the participants are introduced. The next step is labeled as the Pattern Identification Exercise (PIE) activity and requires the students to each identify a leisure activity and specify an instance when their participation in the activity went very well and an instance when it was less than positive. The counselor works with each student to elaborate regarding the people involved in both instances and the student's feelings, thoughts, challenges, successes, and motivation. The purpose of this discussion is to elucidate each student's strengths and weaknesses. Once a full description is outlined, each student is asked to consider the types of patterns suggested in the information presented. Specifically, students are asked to consider the various goals, values, aptitudes, personality traits, and interests revealed in the information. The final step in the PIE activity links the identified patterns to the career choices the student is facing. Then, the counselor invites input from the students' parents. Parents can confirm what has been discussed and add their perspectives. The next step in PICE is to examine the academic experience. Specifically, students discuss what courses they are taking, how they are performing in each of their courses, and what their feelings are about each of the courses. As before, parents are then asked to provide their perspective of the information the student has shared. Next, students discuss the options under consideration in light of the current labor market situation (e.g., current labor market trends, the need for flexibility, information interviewing, anxiety about the future, admissions to postsecondary opportunities, etc.). Parents are also asked to contribute to this discussion and offer their perspectives about labor market trends and strategies for coping with the current nature of work. The final step in PICE involves action planning. Students and parents are provided with information about school and community career resources. Students are asked to identify what step(s) they will take next in their career planning.

These interventions represent examples of ways in which high school counselors can help students prepare for a successful school-to-work or school-to-school transition. When counselors at all grade levels work collaboratively to develop systematic career development interventions, then there is the likelihood that high school students will be prepared for the career development tasks they will encounter as they move through secondary school. Two more recent publications provide additional examples of effective strategies for fostering career development in students. Specifically, Perusse and Goodnough (2004) and Erford (2003) are excellent resources for professional school counselors. Both publications contain chapters that address career development with recommended activities, which, in the case of Perusse and Goodnough, are connected to the National Standards.

SUMMARY

Today, perhaps more than ever, systematic career development interventions are needed to help young people advance in their career development. The nature of work is changing dramatically, requiring new skills sets (e.g., transition skills, stress management, the ability to engage in lifelong learning, personal flexibility, computer skills) that suggest that change, rather than constancy, will be the norm. Workers in the 21st century will experience multiple career changes that will bring associated levels of stress that must be managed effectively. It is naive to expect parents, many of whom are struggling to manage their own careers effectively, to provide children and adolescents with the competencies they need to advance in their careers. Career development interventions help students prepare for the tasks they will encounter as adults. Moreover, career development interventions help students connect current school activities with their futures. This connection is key to increasing school involvement and school success. Clearly, "when professional school counselors provide career and educational guidance to their students, they influence the future by helping clarify developmental decisions that often last a lifetime" (Erford, 2003, p. 153).

REFERENCES

American School Counselor Association. (2003). *The ASCA National Model: A framework for school counseling programs.* Alexandria, VA: American School Counselor Association.

American School Counselors Association (ASCA). (1985). The role of the school counselor in career guidance: Expectations and responsibilities. *The School Counselor, 29,* 164–168.

Amundson, N. E., & Penner, K. (1998). Parent involved career exploration. *The Career Development Quarterly, 47,* 135–144.

Baker, S. (2000). *School counseling for the 21st century* (3rd ed.). Upper Saddle River, NJ: Merrill/Prentice Hall.

Bennett, G. K., Seashore, H. G., & Wesman, A. G. (1992). *Technical manual: Differential Aptitude Tests* (5th ed.). San Antonio, TX: The Psychological Corporation.

Bireley, M., & Genshaft, J. (1991). Adolescence and giftedness: A look at the issues. In M. Bireley & J. Genshaft (Eds.), *Understanding the gifted adolescent: Educational, developmental, and multicultural issues. Education and psychology of the gifted series* (pp. 1–17). New York: Teachers College Press.

Blustein, D. (1994). "Who am I?" The question of self and identity in career development. In M. L. Savickas & R. W. Lent (Eds.), *Convergence in career development theories* (pp. 139–154). Palo Alto: Consulting Psychologists Press.

Campbell, C. A., & Dahir, C. A. (1997). *The National Standards for school counseling programs.* Alexandria, VA: American School Counselor Association.

Crites, J. O. (1978). *Theory and research handbook for the Career Maturity Inventory.* Monterey, CA: CTB, McGraw Hill.

Erford, B. T. (2003). *Transforming the school counseling profession.* Upper Saddle River, NJ: Merrill/Prentice Hall.

Erikson, E. H. (1963). *Childhood and society.* New York: W. W. Norton.

Feller, R. W. (2003). Aligning school counseling, the changing workplace, and career development assumptions. *Professional School Counseling, 6,* 262–271.

Hansen, L. S. (1999). Beyond school-to-work: Continuing contributions of theory and practice to career development of youth. *The Career Development Quarterly, 47,* 353–358.

Harrington, T. (1996). *Ability Explorer.* Itasca, IL: Riverside Publishing.

Havighurst, R. J. (1972). *Developmental tasks and education* (3rd ed.). New York: D. McKay.

Herr, E. L., & Cramer, S. H. (1996). *Career guidance and counseling through the lifespan* (5th ed.). New York, NY: HarperCollins.

Holland, J. L. (1985). *Making vocational choices: A theory of vocational personalities and work environments* (2nd ed.). Upper Saddle River, NJ: Prentice Hall.

Johansson, C. B. (1986). *Career Assessment Inventory.* Minneapolis, MN: NCS Assessments.

Krumboltz, J. D., & Worthington, R. (1999). The school-to-work transition from a learning theory perspective. *The Career Development Quarterly, 47,* 312–325.

Marcia, J. E. (1966). Development and validation of ego-identity status. *Journal of Personality and Social Psychology, 3,* 551–558.

Marcia, J. E. (1980). Identity in adolescence. In J. Adelson (Ed.), *Handbook of adolescent psychology* (pp. 159–187). New York: Wiley.

Marshall, R., & Tucker, M. (1992, November 9–15). The best imports from Japan and Germany. *Washington Post National Weekly Edition,* p. 24.

Muuss, R. L. (1998). Marcia's expansion of Erikson's theory of identity formation. In R. Muuss, H. Porton, and Associates (Eds.), *Adolescent behavior and society: A book of readings* (5th ed., pp. 260–270). New York: McGraw-Hill.

National Occupational Information Coordinating Committee (NOICC). (1992). *The National Career Development Guidelines, Local Handbook.* Washington, DC: Author.

Niles, S. G., & Goodnough, G. E. (1996). Life-role salience and values: A review of recent research. *The Career Development Quarterly, 45,* 65–86.

Perusse, R., & Goodnough, G. (2004). *Leadership, advocacy, and direct service strategies for professional school counselors.* Belmont, CA: Brooks/Cole.

Rosenbaum, J. E. (2001). *Beyond college for all.* New York: Russell Sage.

Rosenbaum, J. E., & Person, A. E. (2003). Beyond college for all: Policies and practices to improve transitions into college and jobs. *Professional School Counseling, 6*, 252–261.

Savickas, M. L. (1990). The career decision-making course: Description and field test. *The Career Development Quarterly, 38*, 275–284.

Savickas, M. L. (1993). Predictive validity criteria for career development measures. *Journal of Career Assessment, 1*, 93–104.

Savickas, M. L. (1999). The transition from school to work: A developmental perspective. *The Career Development Quarterly, 47*, 326–336.

Savickas, M. L. Stilling, S. M., & Schwartz, S. (1984). Time perspective in vocational maturity and career decision making. *Journal of Vocational Behavior, 25*, 258–269.

Super, D. E. (1955). Transition: From vocational guidance to counseling psychology. *Journal of Counseling Psychology, 2*, 3–9.

Super, D. E. (1957). *A psychology of careers*. New York: Harper & Row.

Super, D. E. (1970). *The Work Values Inventory*. Boston: Houghton Mifflin.

Super, D. E. (1980). A life-span, life-space approach to career development. *Journal of Vocational Behavior, 16*, 282–298.

Super, D. E. (1981). Approaches to occupational choice and career development. In A. G. Watts, D. E. Super, & J. M. Kidd (Eds.), *Career development in Britain*. Cambridge, England: Hobson's Press.

Super, D. E. (1983). Assessment in career guidance: Toward truly developmental counseling. *Personnel and Guidance Journal, 61*, 555–562.

Super, D. E. (1984). Leisure: What it is and might be. *Journal of Career Development, 11*, 71–80.

Super, D. E. (1990). Career and life development. In D. Brown & L. Brooks (Eds.), *Career choice and development: Applying contemporary theories to practice* (2nd ed., pp. 197–261). San Francisco: Jossey-Bass.

Super, D. E., Osborne, W. L., Walsh, D. J., Brown, S. D., & Niles, S. G. (1992). Developmental assessment and counseling: The C-DAC model. *Journal of Counseling and Development, 71*, 74–80.

Super, D. E., Savickas, M. L., & Super, C. M. (1996). The life-span, life-space approach to careers. In D. Brown & L. Brooks (Eds.), *Career choice and development: Applying contemporary theories to practice* (3rd ed., pp. 121–178). San Francisco: Jossey-Bass.

Super, D. E., Thompson, A. S., Lindeman, R. H., Jordaan, J. P., & Myers, R. M. (1988). *Adult Career Concerns Inventory: Manual for research and exploratory use in counseling*. Palo Alto, CA: Consulting Psychologists Press.

Tiedeman, D. V. (1961). Decision and vocational development: A paradigm and its implications. *Personnel and Guidance Journal, 40*, 15–20.

Turner, S., & Lapan, R. T. (2002). Career self-efficacy and perceptions of parent support in career development. *The Career Development Quarterly, 51*, 44–55.

Vernon, A. (1993). *Developmental assessment and intervention with children and adolescents*. Alexandria, VA: American Counseling Association.

Sample Career Development Activities for Middle/Junior and High School Students

An Interesting Journal

NOICC CAREER DEVELOPMENT GUIDELINES: Self-Knowledge; Career Planning

ASCA STANDARDS: Standard A—Students will acquire the skills to investigate the world of work in relation to knowledge of self and to make informed career decisions; Standard C—students will understand the relationship between personal qualities, education, training, and the world of work.

PURPOSE: This activity encourages students to identify their interests and to consider how their interests can inform their career decisions.

OBJECTIVE: To help students identify their interests and connect their interests to career possibilities.

MATERIALS: Notebook or journal

INTRODUCTION: Discuss how our interests should guide career plans: "Do what you enjoy and you will never work a day in your life." By focusing on the things that we find most enjoyable, we can begin to clarify those activities that we should incorporate into our career plans.

ACTIVITIES: Instruct students to keep a log of how they spend their out-of-school time over the course of

1 week. As they enter the activity in their journals, they should give the activity a rating from 1 ("hated it") to 5 ("loved it"). The time frame can be lengthened to get a better sense of the activities students liked and disliked.

DISCUSSION: Students can discuss the activities they liked and did not like. They can also identify reasons for their reactions to their activities.

CLOSURE: The leader can help students understand how they can use their interests to guide their career exploration. For example, if a student enjoys working with animals, then the group can brainstorm additional activities that can provide that student with the opportunity to work with animals. The group can also brainstorm career opportunities that provide people with the opportunity to work with animals. As each student discusses his or her likes, the group can brainstorm in a similar fashion.

TIME: 45–60 minutes

EVALUATION/ASSIGNMENT: At the end of the activity, each student should identify two activities in which they are interested and two things they can do to gain additional exposure to their interests.

Values Sorting

NOICC CAREER DEVELOPMENT GUIDELINES: Self-Knowledge; Educational and Occupational Exploration

ASCA STANDARDS: Standard A—Students will acquire the skills to investigate the world of work in relation to knowledge of self and to make informed career decisions.

PURPOSE: Good career decisions are values-based. However, few career options provide individuals with the opportunity to express all of their important values. Thus, we must prioritize values and identify those that are most important to us. We must be clear as to which values we are willing to part with, if necessary. Each decision we make requires us to sort our values and make choices accordingly. Being able to

select career options that provide us with maximal opportunities for values expression requires us to subjectively define our important values. For example, although many people value "financial rewards," this value is defined somewhat definitely across individuals. Understanding how we define the most important values in our lives helps us to determine which options fit best. Finally, it is important to understand how values are connected to our participation in the life roles we play.

OBJECTIVES: As a result of participating in this activity, participants will (a) learn the importance of values clarification, (b) become aware of their most important values, and (c) understand the importance of considering values in career decision making and career planning.

MATERIALS: Handouts of the values list and five slips of paper per participant

INTRODUCTION: Introduce this activity as an exercise that helps participants identify and define important values in their lives.

ACTIVITY: To start this activity, give participants a list of values such as this one:

VALUES LIST

_____ Financial security

_____ Job security

_____ Good family relationships

_____ A world that is free of discrimination

_____ Creativity

_____ Having a set routine

_____ Time by myself

_____ Community activities

_____ Physical activities

_____ An attractive physical appearance

_____ Variety

_____ Power

_____ Recognition

_____ Prestige

_____ Freedom from stress

_____ Associating with people I like

_____ Success

_____ Freedom to live where I choose

_____ Leisure time

_____ Fame

_____ Strong religious faith

_____ Adventure

_____ World peace

_____ Helping others

_____ Having children

_____ Good health

_____ A beautiful home

_____ Autonomy

_____ Other

_____ Other

Instruct students to identify their top-10 values from this list by putting an X next to the values that are most important to them (the values chosen are not ranked at this point). Then, after discussing their experience of conducting this initial values sort, provide participants with five slips of paper. Ask them to identify their top-5 values from the list of their top-10 and to write one value on each slip of paper (again these values are not ranked). Participants are then informed that the activity leader will be taking a value from them, one at a time. Thus, participants must now decide which of their top-5 values they are willing to part with first. At this point, the activity leader actually goes around the room taking a value from each participant.

Immediately after students give a value to the leader, instruct the participants to record and define what that value means to them (e.g., "financial rewards: having an income of more than $45,000/year with good health and retirement benefits"). Continue this process for each of the remaining values. At the conclusion of the exercise, participants have a list of their top-5 values, with definitions, in descending order. For example, here are five value definitions:

5. Financial rewards: having an income of more than $45,000/year with good health and retirement benefits
4. Autonomy: being able to make my own decisions as to how to best accomplish my job duties, but having a colleague who can give me advice when I need it
3. Associating with people I like: being friends with my coworkers and doing things together outside of work
2. Good health: eating right and exercising three times per week
1. Strong religious faith: going to church on a regular basis and volunteering at a soup kitchen

DISCUSSION: After completing the exercise, explain how the activity relates to career decision making. Explain that in every decision there is the promise of gain and the threat of loss (otherwise, one could simply choose the "perfect" option in every instance). The risk involved in decision making is lessened when options are selected based on the individual's key values.

CLOSURE: Encourage participants to consider how they spend their time in the course of a typical week and if they spend time in activities reflecting their top values. If the answer is no, then encourage participants to identify strategies for increasing their participation in activities reflecting their values (e.g., agreeing to a moderate exercise program, identifying opportunities for volunteering).

The Pie of Life

NOICC CAREER DEVELOPMENT GUIDELINES: Self-Knowledge; Educational and Occupational Exploration; Career Planning

ASCA STANDARDS: Standard A—Students will acquire the skills to investigate the world of work in relation to knowledge of self and to make informed career decisions; Standard B—Students will employ strategies to achieve future career goals with success and satisfaction; Standard C—Students will understand the relationship between personal qualities, education, training, and the world of work

PURPOSE: To focus on how students spend their time now and how they hope to spend their time in the future.

OBJECTIVE: To enhance self-awareness regarding values and life-role participation.

MATERIALS: Paper, pencils

INTRODUCTION: Encourage students to consider a typical week in their lives and ask them how they spend their time. Emphasize with students the importance of spending time in activities that reflect their interests and values.

ACTIVITIES: Ask each student to draw a circle on a piece of paper. Encourage students to consider the circle as if it were a "pie of life." Instruct them to consider how they spend their time over the course of a typical week (24 hours a day, 7 days a week). Tell them to divide the circle or pie into "slices" according to how much of their time is spent in each activity over the

course of a week. Once they have divided their pies into slices, ask students to write answers to the following question: "What conclusions could someone draw from your 'pie of life' about what you like to do and what you value?"

DISCUSSION: Divide students into small groups. Encourage them to share their "pies of life" with each other. Then encourage students to share with the entire class any reactions they had to dividing their "pies of life" into slices as well as any reactions they had to hearing how their peers divided their pies.

CLOSURE: Emphasize the importance of having a "pie of life" that reflects your interests and values as much as possible. If students do not have a pie that reflects their interests and values, then encourage them to consider what changes they can make to increase the degree to which their "pies of life" reflect their values and interests.

TIME: 45 minutes

EVALUATION/ASSIGNMENT: Have students draw a second circle that reflects their lives as an adult (choose a specific age, such as 35 years old). Instruct them to divide their "pies of life" into slices according to how they hope to spend their time in the future. Ask them to identify how their slices relate to their interests and values. Ask them to identify the life roles reflected in their future slices of life. Finally, ask students to identify five things they can do between now and when they turn age 35 to increase the chances that their future "pies of life" will come true.

TIME: Approximately 30 minutes

EVALUATION/ASSIGNMENT: Students will list their five most important values and identify three jobs in which they could express these values.

Time Capsule

NOICC CAREER DEVELOPMENT GUIDELINES: Self-Knowledge; Career Planning

ASCA STANDARDS: Standard A—Students will acquire the skills to investigate the world of work in relation to knowledge of self and to make informed career decisions; Standard B—Students will employ strategies to

achieve future career goals with success and satisfaction; Standard C—Students will understand the relationship between personal qualities, education, training, and the world of work.

PURPOSE: To explore what possessions are valuable to students and why.

OBJECTIVE: Students will learn about themselves and others by examining a valued possession; students will explore what they would like future generations of people to know about them. Students will also discuss how the possessions they value are influenced by the culture in which they live.

MATERIALS: Ask students to bring a valued object from home, something that tells something about them that they might leave behind in an imaginary time capsule for future generations of middle school students.

INTRODUCTION: Ask students to bring an item from home to show other participants; students should be prepared to explain what the item is and why it is important to them.

ACTIVITIES: Each student will describe the possession, explain why it is important to him or her, how it reflects something about the student, and what he or she would like to communicate to future middle school students by placing this item in an imaginary time capsule.

DISCUSSION: Students may discuss the items, any common concerns/messages for future generations, what they would like others to know about them, what is valued and why, and so on. Students will also discuss the group similarities and differences in the items they chose as valuable. Students can discuss how these items might be different if they lived in another country.

CLOSURE: Students can discuss the fact that the things we value are reflected in the things that are valuable to us. They are, in essence, symbolic representations of things that are important to us due to a variety of reasons (e.g., what the objects represent, because a person who is important to us gave us the object). The uniqueness of the objects selected tells us something important about ourselves.

TIME: 45 minutes to 1 hour

EVALUATION/ASSIGNMENT: Students will complete the following sentences: "Three things that are important to me are ____." and "These objects are important to me because ____.".

Becoming a Member of Another Culture: A Fantasy

NOICC CAREER DEVELOPMENT GUIDELINES: Self-Knowledge; Educational and Occupational Exploration; Career Planning

ASCA STANDARDS: Standard A—Students will acquire the skills to investigate the world of work in relation to knowledge of self and to make informed career decisions; Standard B—Students will employ strategies to achieve future career goals with success and satisfaction; Standard C—Students will understand the relationship between personal qualities, education, training, and the world of work.

PURPOSE: For students to learn what it would be like to suddenly find themselves as members of another culture.

OBJECTIVES:

1. For students to think about what privileges go along with certain cultures.
2. For students to recognize how they perceive their culture and others' cultures.

MATERIALS: None

INTRODUCTION: Say to students, "I am going to need everyone to relax and close his or her eyes. We are going to use our imaginations in this exercise to think about what it would be like to be a member of another culture."

ACTIVITY: (Read aloud) "You're feeling relaxed now; you're very calm; it's the middle of the week, just prior to bedtime. You find yourself sitting in your comfortable chair, very relaxed. Your eyes are closed. . . You are tired, very tired, and decide to go to bed. You enter a very restful sleep, very restful sleep. (Pause 10 seconds.) Now, visualize yourself awakening the next morning. You see yourself entering your bathroom. Take a careful look in the mirror; you see there's been a rather startling transformation during the night. . . .You woke up as a member of another culture with physical characteristics typical of those from that culture. . . You went to bed a member of one culture and you woke up a member of another! (Pause.) How does it feel? (Pause.) Now you find yourself walking outside and meeting your best friend. How does your friend react? (Pause.) Now, visualize yourself walking across the campus. How do people react to you? You meet your favorite teacher—what happens? How do you feel? What is the overall reaction toward you? (Pause.) Okay. Open your eyes now."

DISCUSSION: Place students in small groups to take turns sharing their fantasies. Ask members to ask each other open-ended questions about what they share (what, how, when, or where). Request that they do not "interpret" another's fantasy.

Who Am I?

NOICC CAREER DEVELOPMENT GUIDELINES: Self-Knowledge; Educational and Occupational Exploration; Career Planning

ASCA STANDARDS: Standard A—Students will acquire the skills to investigate the world of work in relation to knowledge of self and to make informed career decisions; Standard B—Students will employ strategies to achieve future career goals with success and satisfaction; Standard C—Students will understand the relationship between personal qualities, education, training, and the world of work.

PURPOSE: To help members learn more about themselves and each other in the group.

OBJECTIVE: Students will have an increased level of understanding among students about what makes each of them uniquely different and also what are some of their similarities.

MATERIALS: Pins, 4 × 6 cards for each student

INTRODUCTION: Tell students: "We will be learning a lot about who we are. It is important to understand yourself and what has influenced who you are today. The activity we will be starting with is a great way to remind us about what things are unique to each of us and help us to recognize the differences in others."

ACTIVITIES: Give each student a 4 × 6 card and read aloud the following instructions.

A. Print your first name in the center of the index card. Write large enough so other people can read it.
B. In the upper left-hand corner, write or put a symbol for
   1. Where you were born
   2. A favorite place you would like to visit on a vacation

CLOSURE: Discuss some of the themes in the students' fantasies and their specific reactions to suddenly being a member of a different culture.

TIME: 20–30 minutes

EVALUATION/ASSIGNMENT: Ask students to write two paragraphs describing how it felt to be a member of a culture different from their own.

C. In the upper right-hand corner, put a symbol or write words that depict something you like to do to have fun.
D. In the lower left-hand corner, write three words your best friend might use to describe you if you were not present.
E. In the lower right-hand corner, describe one characteristic about the specific culture to which you belong (Anglo, African American, etc.) that you value and appreciate.
F. Finally, somewhere on your card put another symbol that tells something you are really looking forward to doing in the future.

After they have completed their "Who Am I" card, have students fasten the cards to the fronts of their shirts or blouses. Then ask them to find an individual they do not know very well, preferably of a different culture or gender, someone with whom they can pair up. Each pair should interview one another concerning the data on the cards for 10 minutes.

DISCUSSION: Next, form a large circle with pairs standing together. Each pair should in turn step forward and introduce one another to the group. Afterward, have students share something they have learned regarding a student and what they would like to know more about.

CLOSURE: Ask the participants to wear their name tags to subsequent sessions until everyone knows everyone else.

TIME: 1 hour

EVALUATION/ASSIGNMENT: Have students follow through on the activity by instructing them to learn more about one person in the group.

Responding to Labels

NOICC CAREER DEVELOPMENT GUIDELINES:
Self-Knowledge; Educational and Occupational Exploration; Career Planning

ASCA STANDARDS: Standard A—Students will acquire the skills to investigate the world of work in relation to knowledge of self and to make informed career decisions; Standard B—Students will employ strategies to achieve future career goals with success and satisfaction; Standard C—Students will understand the relationship between personal qualities, education, training, and the world of work.

PURPOSE: For students to think about some of the ways society labels people and how one can sometimes use some of the conflict resolution techniques when they feel like they are possibly being labeled.

OBJECTIVE:

1. Let the students experience what it is like when society labels certain individuals.
2. Help students to decide how to handle labeling, such as peer-group labels.

MATERIALS: Sheets of paper, tape, and a marker

INTRODUCTION: Place labels on certain individuals' backs. People in the room will respond to these individuals according to the labels they have on their backs. The individuals with labels will not know what they are and should pay close attention to how others in the room are treating them. While doing this activity, think about other labels that society gives people. For example, there are probably labels that your peers give to people in school.

ACTIVITIES: Write one of the following labels on separate sheets of paper and tape them on a few of the students' backs. Have the students without the labels walk around and react to the students as if they actually were what they are labeled.

- Famous movie star
- Person with HIV
- Mental patient
- Deaf person
- Criminal
- Drug addict
- Famous athlete

DISCUSSION:

1. Have the students who had labels talk about what it felt like to wear the labels. Have each guess what they think his or her label might be.
2. Next, have the students who did not have labels talk about how it felt to treat people according to their labels.

Ask the students if they think this happens in our society. What are some of the labels people attach to others? Have students consider how damaging these labels can be to the individuals assigned the labels by society.

Ask the students what they can do to deal with labeling. Have them refer back to some of the skills they learned in the conflict resolution activities. List their answers on the board.

CLOSURE: Ask students to think about how knowledge gained from this activity can make us more aware of labeling in our society and ways of handling situations in which someone is being labeled.

TIME: 30 minutes

EVALUATION/ASSIGNMENT: Ask students to list ways in which they encounter labeling each day (e.g., television, music, newspapers, family, and friends).

Educational and Occupational Exploration

Informational Interviewing

NOICC CAREER DEVELOPMENT GUIDELINES: Educational and Occupational Exploration; Career Planning

ASCA STANDARDS: Standard A—Students will acquire the skills to investigate the world of work in relation to knowledge of self and to make informed career decisions; Standard B—Students will employ strategies to achieve future career goals with success and satisfaction; Standard C—Students will understand the relationship between personal qualities, education, training, and the world of work.

PURPOSE: To provide students with information concerning their possible career goals.

OBJECTIVE: Students will learn about specific occupations. Students will gather information pertaining to occupational requirements, training requirements, occupational conditions, and so on for occupations that interest them.

MATERIALS: Writing materials and interview guide

INTRODUCTION: Tell students: "To get real-life information about jobs, it is useful to interview people working in a job in which you are interested. Workers can provide important information concerning what they like about their work and what they do not like. They can also tell you about the training requirements involved in preparing for the job."

ACTIVITIES: Students will interview workers who enjoy doing their jobs and are good at them. In other words, the interviewees will need to be screened to ensure that they meet these two requirements (the first requirement being more important than the second). Students will conduct a structured interview asking the following questions:

1. What do you like most about your job?
2. How did you decide that this job was a good choice for you?

3. What type of training is required for this job?
4. What types of benefits are provided in a job like this?
5. How many hours do you usually work each week?
6. How much vacation time do you have each year?
7. What are the most important things for doing this job well?
8. What things do you not like about your job?
9. What is the most important piece of advice you would give to someone interested in doing this job?
10. Is there anything else you think I should know?

DISCUSSION: Have students review the responses to these questions and share them with the group. Have them respond (in writing and/or verbally) to the following question: "This job would or would not (select one) be a good match for me because ____."

CLOSURE: Encourage students to compare the information they learned about the job with the information they have learned about themselves (e.g., their interests, values, skills, etc.). Students can eliminate jobs that do not seem like a good fit from further consideration. Students can identify next steps for additional exploration of jobs that seem like a good fit, such as participating in job shadowing and engaging in additional research to learn more about the job.

TIME: Varies depending on the number of interviews; each interview should take 20–30 minutes

EVALUATION/ASSIGNMENT: Students will complete the question listed in the Discussion section.

Work Lessons

NOICC CAREER DEVELOPMENT GUIDELINES: Self-Knowledge; Educational and Occupational Exploration; Career Planning

ASCA STANDARDS: Standard A—Students will acquire the skills to investigate the world of work in relation to knowledge of self and to make informed career decisions; Standard B—Students will employ strategies to achieve future career goals with success and satisfaction; Standard C—Students will understand the relationship between personal qualities, education, training, and the world of work.

PURPOSE: To provide students with information concerning the jobs their family members have held.

OBJECTIVE: Students will link their family's history with the world of work.

MATERIALS: Interview guide

INTRODUCTION: Remind students that we learn a lot about work from our family members. Often, family members pass on to their children and grandchildren the lessons they have learned from their work experiences.

ACTIVITIES: Students will interview immediate and extended family members concerning their work experiences. Students will conduct a structure interview asking the following questions:

1. What jobs have you held in your life?
2. How did you choose each of these jobs?
3. Which job did you like the most and why?
4. What type of training is required to do the job you liked most?
5. What are the most important skills and interests for doing this job well?
6. What did you learn about working as a result of doing this job?
7. Would you recommend this job to me? Why or why not?
8. What job did you like least and why?
9. What did you learn about working as a result of doing this job?
10. What is the most important piece of advice you could give to me about making a career choice?

DISCUSSION: Students can review the responses to these questions and share them with the group. They can also respond (in writing and/or verbally) to the following question: "The job that one of my family members has held that is most interesting to me is ____. This job is interesting to me because ____."

CLOSURE: Encourage students to discuss what they learned about work as a result of interviewing their family members. Encourage students to talk about what they like or dislike about what they learned. Finally, encourage students to discuss how they can use what they learned in their own career planning.

TIME: Varies depending on the number of interviews; each interview should take 20–30 minutes

EVALUATION/ASSIGNMENT:

1. Students will complete the question listed in the Discussion section.
2. Students can gather information about the job that they liked most.

Family Meeting Role Play

NOICC CAREER DEVELOPMENT GUIDELINES: Self-Knowledge; Career Planning

ASCA STANDARDS: Standard A—Students will acquire the skills to investigate the world of work in relation to knowledge of self and to make informed career decisions; Standard B—Students will employ strategies to achieve future career goals with success and satisfaction; Standard C—Students will understand the relationship between personal qualities, education, training, and the world of work.

PURPOSE: To explore the pros and cons, and concerns about, college attendance from the points of view of a range of family members.

OBJECTIVE: To clarify values and identify obstacles to going to college (real, imagined, attitudes, etc.).

MATERIALS: Students may role play family members and/or bring in family members for this activity; use hats or costumes if desired.

INTRODUCTION: Explain to students the role-play task: Each student must role play a family member other than himself or herself. Then students switch roles to see different points of view or concerns of all family members. Encourage real family members to participate when possible. Identify questions to ponder, such as "Where will the money for college come from?", "Will a parent/sibling be okay when the college student leaves home?", "Why do you want to go to college when there are jobs here at home you can do?"

ACTIVITIES: Conduct the role plays and follow-up questions. Monitor group discussions and identify a note-taker that lists barriers, concerns, and general attitudes.

DISCUSSION: Review concerns and barriers, discuss solutions, and identify feelings that arise and the impact of those feelings upon college decisions.

CLOSURE: Focus on sorting out which concerns are real and which are imagined. Identify solutions (via brainstorming) to the real concerns. Encourage students to "let go" of the imagined concerns.

TIME: 30 minutes to 1 hour

EVALUATION/ASSIGNMENT: Have students complete a table with two columns in which they list the real concerns about attending college in one column and the imagined concerns about attending college in the other column.

What Can I Buy? Comparing Incomes: College or No College

NOICC CAREER DEVELOPMENT GUIDELINES: Educational and Occupational Exploration; Career Planning

ASCA STANDARDS: Standard A—Students will acquire the skills to investigate the world of work in relation to knowledge of self and to make informed career decisions; Standard B—Students will employ strategies to achieve future career goals with success and satisfaction; Standard C—Students will understand the relationship between personal qualities, education, training, and the world of work.

PURPOSE: To compare an average college graduate's income with the income of a high school graduate, and give examples of what extra income might be used for in a given period of time.

OBJECTIVE: Students will be able to visually compare the purchasing power a college-degree income has over that of a high school degree.

MATERIALS: Store catalogs with pictures, car brochures, newspaper photos (e.g., houses for sale), etc.

INTRODUCTION: Ask students if they would rather earn more money or less money in their lives. Then tell students that there is a way to increase significantly the probability that they will be able to achieve their goal of earning more money. Use the chart that follows to explain to students that a man or woman with a college degree may earn from 82% to 96% more than a person with a high school diploma. Show examples of annual differences in income, 5-year differences, and 10-year differences on the blackboard.

	H.S. Grad.	College Grad.	Difference
In 1 year	$10,000	$19,000 (90% more)	$9,000
In 5 years	$50,000	$95,000	$45,000
In 10 years	$100,000	$190,000	$90,000

ACTIVITIES: Have students draw, cut out pictures, or describe verbally what the differences in incomes could purchase for an individual with a college degree (e.g., first year—number of pairs of sneakers, basketballs, a small car; fifth year—two medium-sized cars; tenth year—a home). Ask students to construct a weekly budget based on a high school degree versus a college degree.

DISCUSSION: Review income differences and examples of the purchasing power of college versus no college incomes. Ask students, "Is this important? Why?"

CLOSURE: Discuss how extra effort (e.g., staying in school 4 years longer) can make a significant difference in one's life. Emphasize that the decisions we make, especially about education, have real and long-term effects in our lives.

TIME: 30–40 minutes

EVALUATION/ASSIGNMENT: Have students respond to the following question: "What is meant by the phrase 'the more you learn, the more you earn'?"

The Value of Work

NOICC CAREER DEVELOPMENT GUIDELINES: Self-Knowledge; Educational and Occupational Exploration; Career Planning

ASCA STANDARDS: Standard A—Students will acquire the skills to investigate the world of work in relation to knowledge of self and to make informed career decisions; Standard B—Students will employ strategies to achieve future career goals with success and satisfaction; Standard C—Students will understand the relationship between personal qualities, education, training, and the world of work.

PURPOSE: To learn that the compensation for work is not always equal to the value of a particular service provided by workers.

OBJECTIVE: Students will be able to state which occupations they feel are the most valuable and/or which they feel should be compensated at a higher rate for the work performed.

MATERIALS: Pencils, paper, and a blackboard and chalk

INTRODUCTION: Give students a list of jobs and services, including teacher, police officer, garbage collector, professional athlete, firefighter, secretary, computer programmer, doctor, writer, bus or cab driver, rock musician.

ACTIVITIES: Have students rank the jobs according to the amount they feel they should be paid, from lowest to highest salary.

DISCUSSION: Have students compare their lists and discuss the reasons for ranking each as they did.

People and Things

NOICC CAREER DEVELOPMENT GUIDELINES: Self-Knowledge; Educational and Occupational Exploration; Career Planning

ASCA STANDARDS: Standard A—students will acquire the skills to investigate the world of work in relation to knowledge of self and to make informed career decisions; Standard B—students will employ strategies to achieve future career goals with success and satisfaction; Standard C—students will understand the relationship between personal qualities, education, training, and the world of work.

PURPOSE: To explore tasks that require interpersonal skills and those that do not.

OBJECTIVE: Students will be able to identify activities that require interpersonal skills and differentiate between tasks that do or do not require interpersonal skills.

MATERIALS: Paper; pencils; lists of activities, such as hobbies, pet care, sports, clubs, going to school, and so on

INTRODUCTION: Ask students to list activities that they or others might do in any given day.

CLOSURE: Discuss with the students the difference between the economic value of a job (i.e., the salary of a job determined by the economic principles of supply and demand) and the social value of a job (i.e., the degree to which the job contributes to society and others).

TIME: 30 minutes

EVALUATION/ASSIGNMENT: Each participant will be able to list three jobs with high economic value (i.e., those that pay well but do not necessarily contribute to society, such as athlete and performer). Each participant will be able to list three jobs with high social value (i.e., those that contribute to the betterment of society).

ACTIVITIES: Ask students to differentiate between the activities requiring interpersonal skills and those that do not. Write these lists on the blackboard.

DISCUSSION: Review and compare the lists of activities. Ask students to determine which of these activities are their favorites, which they'd like to avoid, which are particularly difficult due to the need for compromise with others, and so on.

CULTURE: Emphasize the importance of focusing on the category of activities (those relying on a high level of interpersonal skills vs. those that do not) to which students seem most drawn in their career planning. Encourage students to identify occupations within each category.

TIME: 30–45 minutes

EVALUATION/ASSIGNMENT: Ask students to list occupations that fall within two categories: (a) those that rely heavily on interpersonal skills and (b) those that do not rely heavily on interpersonal skills.

Career Planning

Map of My Life

NOICC CAREER DEVELOPMENT GUIDELINES: Self-Knowledge; Career Planning

ASCA STANDARDS: Standard A—Students will acquire the skills to investigate the world of work in relation to knowledge of self and to make informed career decisions; Standard C—Students will understand the relationship between personal qualities, education, training, and the world of work.

PURPOSE: Students will recognize how different events and people have changed their lives.

OBJECTIVE: Each student will construct a personal road map with dates, his or her birthplace, family, schools, friends, significant influences, accomplishments, setbacks, interests, and short- and long-term goals.

MATERIALS: Large piece of art paper and colored markers

INTRODUCTION: Tell students: "You will be making a map of your life on a large piece of art paper. To learn more about ourselves and events and people who have influenced who we are today, we are going to make a personal road map."

ACTIVITIES: Have students complete their maps using words and illustrations and then pair off to discuss their maps.

DISCUSSION: Ask the class to discuss these questions: "Did anyone learn something new about themselves?" "Was it difficult to think of future goals?" and "Were some people surprised by how much they had on their maps?"

CLOSURE: Tell students: "I hope this activity helped you understand some of the things that have influenced you. It is important to have self-understanding before making decisions. We will be looking at our goals in some later activities."

TIME: 35 minutes

EVALUATION/ASSIGNMENT: Have students identify one long-term goal and three things they can do to achieve that goal.

My Roles in Life

NOICC CAREER DEVELOPMENT GUIDELINES: Self-Knowledge; Career Planning

ASCA STANDARDS: Standard A—Students will acquire the skills to investigate the world of work in relation to knowledge of self and to make informed career decisions; Standard B—Students will employ strategies to achieve future career goals with success and satisfaction; Standard C—Students will understand the relationship between personal qualities, education, training, and the world of work.

PURPOSE: To provide students with the opportunity to consider life roles that are and will be important to them.

OBJECTIVE: Students will engage in life-role planning.

MATERIALS: Writing materials, chalk, and a chalkboard

INTRODUCTION: Tell students: "While busy making livings, people are busy living their lives. All the things we do can contribute to our life satisfaction. We can describe our activities in life in terms of 'life roles.' For example, one life role most adults play is the role of 'worker.' Many adults are also parents. All young people play the life role of 'student.'" Discuss additional life-role possibilities for young people and adults. Write them on the chalkboard under either the heading of "young people" and/or "adults," according to which category or categories are most appropriate. Emphasize that participating effectively in the life roles we play (e.g., being a good worker, being a good parent, being a good student) has much to do with our life satisfaction, and we need to give serious consideration to what life roles we want to play and how we want to play them.

ACTIVITIES: Have students respond to the following questions:

1. What life roles are important to me now?
2. What life roles will be important to me when I am an adult?
3. What can I do to prepare for the life roles that will be important to me in the future?

DISCUSSION: Divide students into small groups. Encourage students to share their responses to the first two questions listed in the Activities section. Then have the students brainstorm responses to the third question for each student.

CLOSURE: Discuss the importance of planning for future life-role participation. Ask each student to list the life roles they plan to participate in when they are adults. Have them list two things they can do between now and then to prepare for participating in that life role.

TIME: 45–60 minutes

EVALUATION/ASSIGNMENT: Have students discuss with their parents/guardians the following questions:

1. What life roles do you play?
2. What do you like about each life role you play?
3. What life roles do you expect me to play when I am an adult?
4. What do you expect me to accomplish in the life roles I will play as an adult?

Have students discuss in small groups the results of the interviews with their parents/guardians. Encourage them to consider how the results of their interviews may influence their career planning.

My Life as a Book

NOICC CAREER DEVELOPMENT GUIDELINES: Self-Knowledge; Career Planning

ASCA STANDARDS: Standard A—Students will acquire the skills to investigate the world of work in relation to knowledge of self and to make informed career decisions; Standard B—Students will employ strategies to achieve future career goals with success and satisfaction; Standard C—Students will understand the relationship between personal qualities, education, training, and the world of work

PURPOSE: To help students see the themes or patterns in their lives and to encourage students to consider their future "stories."

OBJECTIVE: Students will identify activities that they find meaningful and discuss ways to gain additional exposure to these activities. Students will identify goals toward which they would like to strive.

MATERIALS: Writing materials

INTRODUCTION: Explain to the student that a person's career is like a story. Each story has a beginning, middle, and end. Each person can take an active role in writing his or her own story or autobiography. Students should consider their lives as if they were a book. Just like there are happy stories and sad stories, we can work hard to write the type of story about our life that we would like. By understanding our story or life as we have lived it thus far, we can decide if we want to continue in the same direction or make changes. By considering the direction we would like our lives to take, we can establish goals for our future.

ACTIVITIES: Ask students to consider their lives as if they were books. They should give a title to their book or life as they have lived it thus far (e.g., "The Baseball Player," "The Dancer," "The Next Bill Gates"). Then ask students to divide the life they have lived thus far into chapters. Their chapters may reflect developmental stages (e.g., infancy, preschool, primary grades, intermediate grades) and/or they may reflect important life events (moving from home, parents divorcing, having a new sibling). Encourage the students to give titles to their life chapters. Next, have the students consider their futures. What do they want these chapters to be like? What goals can they identify in their future chapters?

DISCUSSION: Students can discuss their lives thus far and share the titles of their books. They can also discuss what future chapters they would like to live. In discussing future chapters, students can identify goals they would like to achieve and the group can help each student brainstorm strategies for achieving their goals.

CLOSURE: Tell students that each can take an active role in writing his or her own destiny. Our pasts can help us to make decisions about what we would like to achieve in the future. By identifying what we would like our futures to look like, we can identify goals toward which to strive. We can also then begin to develop a plan for achieving our goals.

TIME: 60–90 minutes

EVALUATION/ASSIGNMENT: At the conclusion of the activity, students should be able to identify two or three goals they would like to achieve in their lives and strategies that they can use to help them achieve their goals.

The Rocket Kid's Story

NOICC CAREER DEVELOPMENT GUIDELINES: Self-Knowledge; Educational and Occupational Exploration; Career Planning

ASCA STANDARDS: Standard A—Students will acquire the skills to investigate the world of work in relation to knowledge of self and to make informed career decisions; Standard C—Students will understand the relationship between personal qualities, education, training, and the world of work.

PURPOSE: To learn about the life of a real scientist and explore the manner in which a boy achieved his career goal despite numerous obstacles.

OBJECTIVE: Students will be able to identify the goals of the movie characters in the film they are about to watch. They will also be able to identify the risks taken to achieve those goals and the role of teamwork in achieving goals.

MATERIALS: The movie "October Sky," paper, pencils, a blackboard and chalk, rocket-making kit (if desired)

INTRODUCTION: Develop a list of questions for students to respond to, such as "Do you know anyone like the movie characters?"; "How did teamwork play a role in the success of the 'rocket boys'?"; "What was the father's attitude toward college and the son's career interests?"; "What was the family's attitude toward sports, and what role did sports play in the lives of the young people?"; "What was Homer's original destiny, and how and why did that change?"; "What risks did Homer take to implement his career goal?"

ACTIVITIES:

1. Ask students to watch the video "October Sky" or, if preferred, to read the book *Rocket Boys* by Homer Hickam. (Note: Parents may need to give permission to see this movie, as its rating is PG-13, and there is some language that may be offensive to some individuals.) After watching the movie, students will respond to the questions in the Introduction section or others you develop. Follow this by actually building and/or setting off a rocket (kits to simplify the building can be purchased at toy and crafts stores), if circumstances allow.

2. Students can then list their "dream" jobs or "occupational fantasies."

3. To provide examples of people who have overcome obstacles and achieved their goals, invite past program participants to the session. The past participants could share their stories and discuss what obstacles they overcame to achieve their goals. If it is not possible to have past participants, consider videotaping interviews from past participants. In the interviews the past participants could share their stories and identify the obstacles they overcame to achieve their goals.

DISCUSSION: Review the questions in the Introduction section and others that arise as students watch the movie. Ask students to take notes or write down a list of questions that arise as they watch this video. Emphasize the risks taken by the characters in the story and the role of teamwork in creating success in one's career. Students should list the obstacles the movie characters overcame to achieve their goals. Feelings may also be discussed, such as "Do you feel as if success similar to that of the movie characters is within your reach?" Share stories of past students who have achieved their goals (e.g., being admitted to college, graduating from college, attaining a job with a college degree).

CLOSURE: Discuss the fact that everyone must overcome obstacles to achieve their goals in life. Obstacles can be viewed as opportunities rather than reasons not to pursue a goal.

TIME: 2–3 hours

EVALUATION: Students can list the obstacles they have already overcome in their lives.

Resources for Information on Colleges

NOICC CAREER DEVELOPMENT GUIDELINES: Self-Knowledge; Educational and Occupational Exploration; Career Planning

ASCA STANDARDS: Standard A—students will acquire the skills to investigate the world of work in relation to knowledge of self and to make informed career decisions; Standard B—students will employ strategies to achieve future career goals with success and satisfaction; Standard C—students will understand the relationship between personal qualities, education, training, and the world of work.

PURPOSE: To provide students with information about colleges.

INTRODUCTION: Say to students: "There are many college resources available to you. Here are some ideas to get you started. Your school counselor should be your most valuable resource in your college search. Your counselor can provide you with help on testing, college requirements, choosing colleges to apply to, academic programs, the application process, and financial aid. You should visit your counselor as soon as possible to discuss your plans for after high school."

THE INTERNET

General College Sites

College Board On-line: http://www.collegeboard.org
Connects to a tremendous range of college materials. Use the Fundfinder to search for scholarships, grants, internships, and loans. Use ExPan to get in-depth information about colleges, careers, and financial aid from 3,000 colleges. To custom-fit your search, create a program of your ideal college. ExPan will list colleges that match only your interests.

Minority Information: http://web.fie.com/web/mol
Molis (Minority On-Line Information Service) offers data on historically Black colleges and universities, Hispanic- and Tribal-serving institutions, and on financial aid for minorities.

Adventures in Education: http://www.tgslc.org
Includes a wide array of college and career information to help students and parents.

CollegeNET: http://collegenet.com
CollegeNET lets students search for institutions by geography, tuition, enrollment, and college major. Provides separate databases for 4-year colleges and community, technical, and junior colleges; lists colleges by category; and links to sources of financial aid information.

Internet College Exchange: http://www.usmall.com
Provides assistance in identifying potential colleges, finding financial aid, and completing college applications.

Peterson's Education Center: http://www.petersons.com
Peterson's Education Center includes information about educational programs at all levels and provides searchable databases of colleges and academic programs. All college/university sites provide basic information and many provide extensive descriptive material, on-line viewbooks, and applications.

Financial Aid Sites

FastWEB: http://www.fastweb.com
Includes a database of 375,000 scholarships; plug in your name for a free scholarship search.

FinAid: http://www.finaid.org
The Internet's most complete financial aid site, with links to other key college sites. It also includes a "Scholarship Scam Alert" with information about scams and how to avoid them.

The Federal Government's Sites

http://www.ed.gov/prog_info/SFA/FYE
Offers information about the U.S. Department of Education's federal student financial aid programs.

http://www.fafsa.ed.gov/
Provides an on-line form you must complete in order to receive federal student aid. You can submit it by regular mail or at this site over the Internet.

College Loan Sites

http://mapping-your-future.org
Sponsored by agencies that take part in the Federal Family Education Loan Program (FFELP).

http://www.salliemae.com/home/index_d.html

A financial services corporation that funds education.

College and University Home Pages

At individual college Web sites, you can read catalogs and admission requirements, check activities, and learn more about the school.

University Pages: http://www.isi-garnet.uah.edu/Universities

Courtesy of the University of Alabama at Huntsville, this site provides easy access (by state) to college and university home pages.

Yahoo: http://www.Yahoo.com/Regional/Countries/United States/Educational/Colleges and Universities.

This site contains brief descriptions of U.S. colleges and universities.

CHAPTER 12

CAREER DEVELOPMENT INTERVENTIONS IN HIGHER EDUCATION

It is now fairly universally acknowledged that career development is a complex, lifelong process—a process that many college students are ill-prepared to negotiate effectively and that many find supremely challenging. It is further acknowledged that the career development needs of our increasingly heterogeneous, multicultural society do not lend themselves to one-size-fits-all, recipe-driven career interventions or service delivery models. In response to these acknowledged conditions and the recent societal trend away from institutional/corporate responsibility for career development and toward greater individual responsibility, institutions of higher education are struggling to implement career services, programs, and interventions that meet the ever-changing needs of today's college student. In an era of unprecedented accountability, college and university career services professionals must choose from a complex array of career interventions and career service-delivery models. This chapter provides the reader with exposure to the career development needs of higher education students; a discussion of the evolution of career development interventions in higher education; and some models, services, and standards for career development interventions in higher education. It is a "must read" for those charged with setting the future course for the delivery of career services in our nation's institutions of higher learning.

Jack Rayman, Ph.D.
Director of Career Services
Affiliate Professor, Counseling Psychology and Education
Penn State University

Presently, almost all colleges and universities provide a variety of career interventions. Career guidance services have roots in counseling and testing centers established in the early 20th century to assist college students in clarifying career goals. Also, colleges routinely established placement offices to assist graduates in securing employment. During the later portion of the 20th century, many higher education institutions merged the missions for career guidance and employment and established career development and placement offices. These offices evolved to 21st-century career centers that hold the university-wide mission for career guidance, experiential education, and employer relations. Typically, comprehensive career centers today offer a variety of services ranging from career counseling, assessment, and programming through employment recruitment.

Technological innovations to career services have exploded during recent years to include many Web-based applications. Today's career centers continue to offer personal and group-based career interventions in addition to technologically driven services. Career services have gained considerable respect by higher education administrators and are viewed as important offices that support recruitment, retention, and fundraising efforts in facilitating the career preparation of graduates. As a result, career centers are often located in centralized, highly visible campus locations. Career development interventions are at the heart of the counseling profession. Today's comprehensive career centers boast services assisting thousands of clients annually, including college recruits, freshmen, seniors, graduate students, as well as alumni representing all career fields ranging from the liberal arts to business and engineering. This chapter reflects the dynamic and exciting nature as well as the significance of higher education career development interventions in the 21st century.

Joff W. Garis, Ph.D,
Career Center Director
Florida State University

Robert had experienced substantial success in his career since graduating with an associate degree in business from the local community college. Over the past 15 years, he had worked his way up to a middle management position with a medium-sized manufacturing firm. His success has come at a price, however. He has consistently worked long hours and weekends. He was growing increasingly uneasy with the time he was spending on the job. His two children were both in middle school and he realized that he had already missed important moments in their lives due to his involvement at work. Moreover, he had come to feel that his work was "not contributing anything positive to the world." A series of layoffs within his company heightened his sense that it was time to make a change. His precarious employment situation, combined with his desire to spend more time with his family and engage in work that he felt was meaningful, led him to decide to explore his career and educational options. After several sessions with a career counselor in the community, Robert decided he would like to return to college to earn a 4-year degree. However, he was anxious about returning to school. Among other things, he wondered if he would be "smart enough" to finish his degree, if he would be able to cover the tuition costs, if his family would support his decision, and if, at age 35, he would be the "old man" in his classes. Because his desire to make a change was stronger than his anxieties about changing, he decided to meet with a career counselor at the local college. He hoped this person would help him sort through his educational and career options in a way that would turn his desire for change into a concrete plan.

A substantial portion of people in the United States view postsecondary educational experiences as essential to their career development. In 2001 slightly more than 15 million students were enrolled in 3885 higher education institutions (Herr, Cramer, & Niles, 2004). Many of these students emerge from high school experiences in which they received minimal career development assistance. For those students, who may also have diffuse vocational identities, negotiating the tasks of selecting a college major and identifying potential occupations is daunting at best. Statistics support this contention, only 50% of students who enter colleges and universities graduate in 6 years, if ever (Gray & Herr, 2000). Survey results from the American Council on Education (1999) indicate that most first-year college students (77%) indicate that they chose to attend college to "get a better job" and 75% report that they chose to attend college "to make more money." Obviously, many students view higher education as a means for advancing their careers. Helping students crystallize and implement their career identities is a critical role of career services professionals in higher education. It is important to note, however, that students enrolled in higher education today represent a vast array of cultural and ethnic backgrounds. Many students are, like Robert, returning adult students. Other students have disabilities that require accommodations. Still others represent the first generation in their families to attend higher education. Thus, in this chapter we discuss the career needs of those enrolled in higher education today; the evolution of career services in higher education; the competencies students in higher education must develop to cope effectively with career development in adulthood; models, services, and standards for career services; and issues that must be considered in managing career services.

THE CAREER NEEDS OF HIGHER EDUCATION STUDENTS

Although a large number of students enroll in higher education immediately following their high school graduation, increasingly, students enrolled in postsecondary education do not fit the traditional stereotype of the American college student (i.e., age 18 to 22, enrolled full time, and living on campus). In fact, fewer than one in six students in higher education fit this traditional stereotype (Colozzi, 2000). More than ever in the history of higher education, today's students represent a diverse mix in terms of their backgrounds, characteristics, developmental levels, and career development needs.

For example, Herr et al. (2004) note that there are approximately 6 million adults (i.e., those over the age of 25) attending college each year. The majority of adults returning to higher education do so primarily to enhance their career opportunities

(Luzzo, 2000). However, many adult students must balance their pursuit of higher education with child rearing and other life-role responsibilities. Moreover, many adult students experience insecurity over their decision to return to school, are uncertain about their ability to succeed academically, and are anxious about whether they will be able to convert their academic experience into new career opportunities (Marron & Rayman, 2002).

International students also represent a substantial percentage of those enrolled in higher education within the United States. For instance, Herr et al. (2004) report that approximately 500,000 international students were enrolled in higher education in 2001. Historically, international students have not received sufficient assistance with their career development. Specifically, international students tend to receive inadequate information concerning employment opportunities in their home countries, often receive inadequate academic advising from advisors who are not sensitive to concerns of international students, and frequently experience difficulty in self-expression in an unfamiliar culture. Since September 11, 2001 many international students from the Middle East experience undeserved hostility. These experiences do not foster career development and they reflect special needs that career practitioners must address to provide comprehensive career services to international students.

Within the past two decades, higher education institutions have also experienced a surge in enrollment of people with disabilities (Conyers & Szymanski, 1998). For example, more than 130,000 students with learning disabilities currently attend college in the United States (Ohler, Levinson, & Barker, 1996). Two federal laws have opened the doors to higher education for many Americans with disabilities. Specifically, section 504 of the Rehabilitation Act of 1973 and the Americans with Disabilities Act of 1990 created an environment of increased access to higher education for persons with disabilities. Despite increased access to higher education, people with disabilities have not fared well in the labor market (Hitchings & Retish, 2000). Thus, students with disabilities need assistance during their higher education experience to increase their chances of being successful in their careers following graduation. For example, Ohler and her colleagues report that students with learning disabilities who require many accommodations demonstrate lower levels of career maturity when compared with students with learning disabilities. Despite the need for career assistance, Friehe, Aune, and Leuenberger (1996) report that college students with disabilities use career services at a significantly lower rate than nondisabled students. Clearly, career practitioners in higher education must do a better job of meeting the career development needs of students with disabilities.

Although students in the early centuries of higher education were predominantly European American men, women now constitute the majority (57.5%) of students enrolled in higher education. Fassinger and O'Brien (2000) contend that the career development needs of female students are considerably different than those of college males. Specifically, Fassinger and O'Brien note that two themes characterize the differences between female and male college students' career development: (a) women experience a pervasive and persistent underutilization of their abilities and talents resulting in occupationally segregating women into jobs that are typically lower in pay and status than jobs held by the majority of men, and (b) women experience a higher level of participation in family roles than men. This results in a higher frequency of role overload issues being experienced by women as their career aspirations are juxtaposed with family responsibilities. Career practitioners must address these themes to foster the career development of women enrolled in higher education.

The percentage of students enrolled in higher education who are members of racial/ethnic minority groups has also increased in recent years. Herr et al. (2004) point out that the total enrollment for racial/ethnic minorities represented 22.5% of all students in higher education in 1999. Despite this level of enrollment within higher education, Herring (1998) points out that ethnic minorities are still less likely than European Americans to attend college, complete college degrees, and enter professional training programs. Dunn and Veltman (1989) suggest that occupational stereotyping by high school counselors, lack of role models, and few perceived opportunities may lead to restricted career-choice patterns among ethnic minority students. Luzzo (1992) hypothesizes that a lack of positive work experiences, low expectations for success, and restricted occupational aspirations may impede the career development of some racial/ethnic minorities. The discriminatory treatment experienced by students of color presents a wide range of issues that must be addressed in the career development process.

Lesbian, gay, and bisexual students also encounter numerous contextual barriers in their career development. Unfortunately, the career development needs of lesbian and gay students have long been ignored by career services in higher education. Pope, Prince, and Mitchell (2000) urge career professionals to work to change this by providing a safe and welcoming environment on college campuses for gay and lesbian students. One way to contribute to creating an environment that is more responsive to the needs of lesbian and gay students is to offer career services that more thoroughly address their career development needs. Pope and his colleagues note that lesbian and gay students are likely to have encountered biased career information, may be reluctant to consider certain career options because of concerns about discrimination or negative stereotyping, and may need help considering the advantages and disadvantages of coming out in the workplace. Career services can be provided to help lesbian and gay students cope with these and other career concerns related to their sexual orientation. For example, providing students with information on employment antidiscrimination laws and policies and lists of gay and lesbian resources and community agencies, encouraging gay and lesbian students to attend workshops addressing complex career/relationship issues, providing names of gay and lesbian alumni who are willing to provide mentoring and networking opportunities, and making sure that career development interventions are appropriate/relevant to lesbian and gay students are some of the ways in which career services can be made more responsive to this substantial population of students in higher education (Pope et al., 2000).

This sampling of the career concerns of students enrolled in higher education clearly paints a landscape that is very different than that of previous centuries. What was once an environment populated by European American men of privileged socioeconomic status is now characterized by heterogeneity at all levels. This increased diversity suggests that career development interventions in higher education must be comprehensive and planned systematically to meet the myriad career development needs of students today. The current scenario is very different from the one out of which career services in higher education emerged early in the last century.

THE EVOLUTION OF CAREER DEVELOPMENT INTERVENTIONS IN HIGHER EDUCATION

Career development interventions have a long history in higher education. Comprehensive career services ranging from helping students select a major to helping students find a job are relatively recent in higher education. Current approaches to career services were preceded by a "system" of service delivery that primarily depended upon the efforts of professors who provided mentoring and placement assistance to selected students. Herr, Rayman, and Garis (1993) note that

> "career services" were essentially confined to how a professor or a don advocated for or mentored a student prodigy as part of his induction into a profession. This was a male-dominated activity, an "old boy's network" by which a faculty member would speak in behalf of a student to persons of importance who might employ him as a favor to, or out of respect for, the professor. (p. 1)

Job placement was the focus of this sort of career assistance. The rate of success for this placement activity depended on the professor's contacts and stature within the field as well as the professor's degree of regard for a particular student. In other words, this system probably worked well for some students, but not as well for other students.

In the early 1800s commercial employment agencies offered placement services to graduates from teacher training programs. By the late 1800s there were nearly 200 employment agencies in the United States (Herr et al., 1993). As enrollments in higher education increased and student services emerged in university settings, placement offices were created to provide all students with placement assistance. For example, Yale University established a placement office in 1919 to provide vocational guidance to students and to match them with employment positions during the academic year, the summer months, and after graduation (Herr et al., 1993).

From prototypical efforts such as those initiated at Yale, the influence of the emerging vocational guidance movement being pioneered by the concepts of Frank Parsons in the early 1900s, and the growing interest of students and employers for placement assistance, employment offices or placement bureaus were instituted on campuses throughout the United States. Often these offices were combined with efforts of faculty, other college and university student personnel officials, and alumni who sought to identify employment opportunities and match students to them.

The focus on placement services resulted in the separation of placement offices from other student affairs functions that were more focused on student development. Rather than training in areas such as counseling and psychology, career placement "officers" tended to have a variety of backgrounds, many times linked to business. Placement was a process by which the students were matched to the requirements of commerce, industry, and the professions based on the careers they had developed through their college experiences (Herr et al., 1993). Services provided by placement officials emphasized job-search skills (e.g., interviewing and résumé writing). Typically, these services tended to be in more demand as students approached graduation. In contrast, counseling centers were more likely to be concerned with student development (e.g., the remediation of emotional or academic distress) and services were provided at any time during the student's collegiate experience.

A shift occurred in career services in higher education beginning in the late 1950s and early 1960s. Career planning activities that had been a part of many counseling centers were relocated to placement offices and combined with placement services: "In essence, in many colleges and universities, an organizational entity frequently known as the career planning and placement office or the career development and placement center or service was formed" (Herr et al., 1993, p. 4). This shift reflected an expanded perspective of career services that moved beyond a singular focus on placement to a developmental perspective of career planning. The developmental perspective included the use of interventions to help students engage in systematic career planning. Placement was now viewed as the culminating activity, rather than the only activity, in the career development of students enrolled in higher education.

Herr et al. (1993) note that currently "there is no single type of counseling center or career development and placement center. Each of these evolves from different institutional histories. In some cases, college and university counseling centers embrace the full range of career services; in others, they have essentially none" (p. 3). Survey results from 963 institutions participating in a study conducted by Whiteley, Mahaffey, and Geer (1987) provide evidence of the variety of approaches used for delivering career services in higher education today. Specifically, these researchers identified five major approaches used in higher education for delivering career services:

1. **Macrocenter:** broad range of services, including career and personal counseling, testing, and special functions such as training and consultation with some advising services offered
2. **Counseling orientation:** similar to macrocenters except with fewer career services
3. **General-level service:** broader functions, including some "dean of students"-type functions, more services to more students than a conventional counseling center
4. **Career planning and placement:** career-oriented services with minimal counseling and other functions
5. **Minimal service:** characterized by providing minimal services in all areas

It is unfortunate that some institutions of higher education are unwilling or unable to provide a full range of career services to students. For example, had Robert (the returning student mentioned at the beginning of this chapter) presented for assistance at a career services office focused exclusively on placement, he would have received limited assistance. The career placement officer may have provided him with placement statistics and information on job openings and job search strategies. But Robert was clearly at a place in his career development where he needed other assistance. He needed help clarifying his vocational identity and learning about the options available to him. He also needed information about financial aid. Finally, it would have been very useful for him to speak with someone who is knowledgeable about the concerns confronting returning students. In many ways, Robert's career situation reflects the variety of contextual and intrapersonal challenges students confront in their career development. Given this complexity, it is not surprising that most major surveys examining the needs of students enrolled in higher education reveal the fact that students express a strong desire for help with a variety of career-related concerns (Healy & Reilly, 1989; Weissburg, Berenstein, Cote,

Cravey, & Health, 1982). For example, Healy and Reilly report that students in their study of 1540 women and 1386 men enrolled in 10 community colleges in California desired assistance in:

1. Knowing more about themselves
2. Identifying career goals
3. Becoming more certain of their career plans
4. Exploring career options
5. Educational planning
6. Learning job-search skills

Such survey results provide evidence that students enrolled in higher education, regardless of their backgrounds and characteristics, are very concerned about their ability to make and implement career choices. It seems reasonable to expect institutions of higher education to provide assistance to students as they attempt to translate their life and academic experiences into career choices. Providing career assistance effectively requires, in part, understanding the career development tasks students confront while they are enrolled in higher education and as they move forward in their career development beyond higher education.

CAREER DEVELOPMENT COMPETENCIES IN ADULTHOOD

The National Career Development Guidelines developed by the NOICC (NOICC, 1992) describe the competencies adults need to manage their careers effectively. These guidelines provide the target skills toward which comprehensive and systematic career services in higher education must be directed. Like the NOICC competencies identified for students in grades K–12, the adult-level competencies are categorized within three domains: (a) self-knowledge, (b) educational and occupational exploration, and (c) career planning.

Self-Knowledge

Self-knowledge competencies involve:

1. The skills to maintain a positive self-concept
2. The skills to maintain effective behaviors
3. Understanding developmental changes and transitions

Adults need to develop a positive self-concept that encompasses an accurate understanding of their strengths, interests, abilities, and values. Moreover, adults need to understand how these important self-characteristics influence their career decisions. A holistic understanding of one's self-concepts across life roles provides the foundation for educational and career exploration. Skills related to interpersonal communication, stress management (e.g., engaging in positive self-care activities, identifying resources for social support, and overcoming self-defeating behaviors), and an understanding of life-span development are essential for helping adults manage their career development (NOICC, 1992).

Most often, career services providers help students in higher education develop an accurate understanding of their self-characteristics through the use of self-assessment activities. Assessment results can be reviewed in individual career counseling or small-group counseling sessions. Career counselors provide a variety of standardized assessments, such as interest inventories, personality measures, and career maturity measures. Career counselors in higher education also expose students to computer-assisted career guidance systems that provide opportunities for engaging in self-exploration. To develop an understanding of life-span development and to enhance skills in areas such as stress management, practitioners encourage students to enroll in career planning courses. In these courses students receive career development assistance in large- and small-group interactions. Thus, skills in interpersonal communication are also enhanced. Students also learn about various approaches to career decision making (Niles, Erford, Hunt, & Watts, 1997). Reed, Reardon, Lenz, and Leierer (2001) describe a career planning course based on the cognitive information processing theory. Reed and her colleagues divide their course into three units. Unit I covers career concepts and applications focusing on self-knowledge, knowledge of options, and decision making. Unit II addresses social conditions affecting career development, focusing on current social, economic, family, and organizational changes affecting the career planning process. Finally, Unit III focuses on employability skills and strategies for implementing academic and career plans. To gain a fuller understanding of the range of material typically covered in career planning courses, we refer readers to the career planning course syllabus presented at the end of this chapter.

Education and Occupational Exploration

Competencies within the educational and occupational exploration domain involve:

1. The skills to enter and participate in education and training
2. The skills to participate in work and lifelong learning
3. The skills to locate, evaluate, and interpret career information
4. The skills to prepare to seek, obtain, maintain, and change jobs
5. An understanding of how the needs and functions of society influence the nature and structure of work

Self-concepts evolve over time, making career choice and adjustment a continuous process (Super, 1984). Thus, adults must know how to access and use the information they gather in their educational and occupational exploration. Using self-knowledge and career information effectively requires the ability to identify short- and long-range career goals. Goals emerge from connecting self-knowledge with accurate career information. Making this connection requires the ability to locate relevant career information, identify job opportunities, understand training requirements related to jobs, and demonstrate a general understanding of the nature of work in a global economy (NOICC, 1992).

Inevitably, adults will need to develop strategies for overcoming obstacles in their career paths (e.g., finding adequate child care, obtaining financial resources to cover educational costs). Because engaging in lifelong learning is a common requirement for most career options, adults need to possess the requisite skills for experiencing academic success (e.g., skills related to taking tests, studying, and taking lecture notes). Successful career management also involves being able to seek, obtain, maintain, and change jobs (e.g., using effective job-search skills and demonstrating effective work attitudes and behaviors).

Career practitioners in higher education use a variety of interventions to help students develop knowledge, skills, and awareness in educational and occupational exploration. Career planning courses contain units to help students learn goal-setting skills. Instructors encourage students to identify short- and long-range career plans based on the occupational and self-information they have acquired. Career services centers in higher education contain resources related to educational and occupational information. Career information libraries provide students with printed materials describing educational programs, occupational options, and prospective employers. Career information delivery systems offer students state-specific information describing various educational and occupational opportunities. To access information online, career services centers provide students with listings of Web sites that provide useful occupational information. Career planning courses, workshops, and small groups give students opportunities to learn about the process of locating, evaluating, and interpreting career information. Externships provide students with opportunities to acquire hands-on exposure to specific occupational environments. Students are assigned to job shadow a person employed in an occupation that is of interest to the student. Typically, these assignments last from 3 to 5 days and provide students with important information they can use in their educational and career planning.

Career Planning

Career planning competencies include:

1. The skills to make decisions
2. Understanding the impact of work on individual and family life
3. Understanding the continuing changes in male/female roles
4. The skills required to make career transitions

Like the competencies involved in the two previous domains, effective career planning in adulthood involves a variety of skill sets. For example, adults need to possess suffiicient self-understanding for making decisions about training, education, and work. Such understanding encompasses intra-individual characteristics (e.g., skills, values, interests, personality traits) and extra-individual factors (e.g., demands from nonwork life roles, accessibility of training opportunities, financial resources, family support). Because choosing and adjusting to choices are continual processes in career development, skills to manage transitions from one circumstance to another are also essential to effective career planning (NOICC, 1992). Skills in stress management and interpersonal communication and engaging in positive self-talk all contribute to coping with transitions. Because work activity occurs amidst demands from other nonwork life roles, being able to balance demands from multiple life roles is imperative for reducing the stress associated with making transitions.

Thus, career planning involves not ony planning for work but also planning for the sort of life one hopes to live. Because we live within a social system, planning is often a collective activity encompassing the needs and hopes of the individual and other prominent people in the individual's social network (e.g., partner, children, and parents).

Career practitioners help students in higher education develop career planning skills via individual and/or small-group counseling, workshops, and career planning courses. To develop decision making skills, researchers suggest that it is important for students to understand multiple approaches that can be used for making decisions. For example, Johnson (1978) identified systematic, spontaneous, internal, and external decision making styles. Individuals using the systematic decision making style approach decisions in a rational and logical fashion. They actively seek all relevant information and accept personal responsibility for their decision making. Spontaneous decision makers make decisions holistically and quickly. Internal decision makers process information privately and quietly. External deciders think out loud and talk to others about decisions. Niles et al. (1997) found that students who rely upon a systematic/internal decision making style tend to be less advanced in their career development and less confident in their ability to complete career development tasks than students who rely upon a systematic/external style. Moreover, the students in the Niles et al. study who had the highest career decision making self-efficacy and the lowest career indecision were those who preferred a systematic/external decision making style, had clarified their values, and had acquired occupational information. The students with the lowest career decision making self-efficacy preferred a systematic/internal style of decision making and were not clear about how to make career decisions. Thus, it seems important to provide career assistance that is sensitive to students' preferences for gathering and analyzing data in the decision making process. For example, students who prefer to analyze data internally may benefit from maintaining career decision making journals and writing career autobiographies. Additionally, to analyze data effectively, internalizers need accurate information about how career decisions are made. Students who prefer to analyze data externally are likely to find participating in career counseling groups and career planning classes to be useful forms of career assistance.

The goals of interventions directed toward helping students develop career planning skills include:

1. Helping students learn to identify and transfer career interests to a plan of action
2. Helping students to relate interests and goals to opportunities
3. Helping students to relate their career plans to life goals and opportunities
4. Helping students learn how to evaluate their progress toward career goals through academic preparation

Career planning courses contain content to help students understand life-structure issues and to help students formulate plans that provide opportunities for participating in their most salient life roles (Halasz & Kempton, 2000). Computer-assisted career guidance systems such as *DISCOVER* (ACT, 1995) provide students with opportunities to clarify their salient life roles and consider which roles they think will be important to them in their future. Standardized and nonstandardized assessment opportunities can be provided to help students consider the impact of work on individual and family life. Group discussions in career planning courses can focus on the continuing changes in male/female roles. By incorporating activities directed toward enhancing stress-management skills, counselors help students acquire skills that are essential to managing career transitions effectively.

Clearly, this list of competencies required for successful career management in adulthood is daunting. Moreover, one could analyze the competencies identified by NOICC at microlevel and expand the list of knowledge, skills, and behaviors exponentially. Expecting students to develop all of these skills while they are enrolled in higher education is an unrealistic expectation. However, career service practitioners in higher education can strive to help sensitize students to the challenges they are likely to encounter as their careers develop. Career practitioners in higher education can also foster students' career development by providing comprehensive and systematic interventions directed toward developing basic competencies in the three domains of self-knowledge, educational/career exploration, and career planning. Although our returning student, Robert, probably needs assistance across all three domains, he first needs help enhancing his self-knowledge, his understanding of the transition process, and bolstering his self-esteem.

MODELS, SERVICES, AND STANDARDS FOR CAREER DEVELOPMENT INTERVENTIONS IN HIGHER EDUCATION

Models

Delivering career services systematically and comprehensively requires practitioners to operate from models of service delivery that are also systematic and comprehensive. There are a variety of models for career services that can be used to address the competencies identified by NOICC as being essential for managing effectively one's career in adulthood (e.g., Colozzi, 2000; Crites, 1981; Reardon, Lenz, Sampson, & Peterson, 2000). For example, Crites suggests that as students progress through higher education, they need assistance in narrowing the range of occupational options under consideration. Typically, students begin the career development process in higher education by: (a) exploring a variety of options, (b) then crystallizing a narrow range of specific options, (c) at which point the student makes a commitment to a particular choice and specifies a college major, (d) which leads to implementing the option selected. Crites recommends that career development professionals help students progress through this process by first assessing each student's career development needs and then offering group and individual career development interventions based on the needs identified for each student. (Interventions with Robert need to begin with a comprehensive assessment of his needs; however, it seems clear he will need to begin at the beginning of the Crites model, i.e., exploring.) To further assess students' development, Crites recommends readministering the needs assessment to students at the end of their first year of study. Data from the second assessment can be used to identify further interventions needed to foster each student's career development.

Powell and Kirts (1980) propose a systems approach to career services in higher education. Their approach focuses on providing awareness programming to new students. Awareness programming involves giving all new students an overview of career services. In large-group meetings, career services staff members and upper-level students describe the career development process and the services available to help students advance in their careers. Voluntary small-group meetings of fewer than 30 students then follow these large-group meetings. In the small-group meetings career counselors and student peer counselors describe in greater detail the career services available and respond to students' specific questions and concerns. Students needing additional assistance are then referred to the appropriate career service (e.g., individual career counseling, career planning courses).

The second component in the Powell and Kirts (1980) model involves self-assessment activities. Powell and Kirts recommend offering small groups in which students first view a videotape of upper-class students who discuss the ways in which various career services have been useful to them. Students use information provided via the videotape to identify resources that they think might help them learn more about themselves (e.g., workshops, individual counseling, and groups).

The next phase in the Powell and Kirts model focuses on exposure as students engage actively in career exploration. Career exploration activities are offered to help students integrate self-assessment information and occupational information. Powell and Kirts note that, in this phase of their model, career counseling and traditional placement functions merge. They recommend using career courses in which alumni and local business leaders link educational and career information (i.e., they identify how academic subjects are relevant for various occupations). Alumni and local business leaders can also serve as resources for creating externship and internship opportunities to expose students to career opportunities.

The final phase of the Powell and Kirts model (1980) is training, which involves providing students who are approaching graduation with training in job-search skills. This phase of the model involves an approach similar to the one used in the awareness phase. Specifically, career services staff members provide students in their last year of study with a large-group (convocation-like) overview of placement services. Students are then invited to participate in small-group sessions according to their academic majors. These sessions focus on the specifics of job searching using videotapes of recent graduates discussing the requisite skills and attitudes for effective job searching. Subsequent group meetings focus on resumé writing, mock interviewing, accessing information about job opportunities, and so on.

Awareness programming would be especially useful to Robert. As a returning student, Robert needs to learn about the range of services available to him. Including returning students in the videotapes focused on how students have found career services useful would be very important to Robert. Because Robert is experiencing many of the fears typically experienced by returning students, it would be beneficial for him to hear other returning students express similar concerns and discuss how they coped with them. As he moves through career exploration and placement activities, career counselors will need to be sensitive to Robert's life situation as a returning student with family responsibilities and, most likely, limited geographical mobility.

Reardon (1996) also describes a comprehensive career services model in use at Florida State Universtiy. The Florida State model is a curricular career information service (CCIS) model with five modules. In the CCIS model career services focus on providing students with an introduction to the service, orienting students to the career decision making process, helping students engage in self-assessment, helping students locate career information, and helping students match majors and jobs. A unique aspect of the CCIS model is that it is self-help oriented and uses paraprofessionals, instructional models, and multimedia resources in service delivery. The CCIS model is a comprehensive and efficient approach to career services. It also allows students to direct their learning about career planning and manage their own career development.

Models for service delivery such as the ones discussed reflect not only the expanded and developmental perspective within career services but also expanded modes of service delivery. They clearly demonstrate the variety of ways in which career services in higher education have gone beyond their initial focus on placement to help students develop the knowledge, skills, and awareness required to manage their career development effectively.

For example, results from a survey from the National Association of Colleges and Employers (NACE) indicate that roughly four out of every five career centers provided group-oriented career counseling interventions and workshops (Collins, 1998). Fifty-two percent of the institutions participating in the NACE survey offered career planning courses. Hardesty (1991) conducted a meta-analysis focusing on the effectiveness of career planning courses and found that students completing career courses were "40% more capable of making career decisions than students who did not complete these courses" (p. 185). For students completing career planning courses, Hardesty found that they were 48% more certain about their career choices at completion of the course than they were at the beginning. A recent meta-analysis conducted by Whiston, Sexton, and Lasoff (1998) compared the effectiveness of workshops, career planning courses, computer programs, and individual counseling and found that individual career counseling was the most effective. However, when one considers the range of needs that must be addressed by career centers and the number of career counselors available, it becomes readily apparent that providing individual career counseling to all students is not possible. Moreover, some students may benefit from the peer support often experienced in group-oriented career interventions. Rayman (1996) contends that though individual career counseling is at the core of the profession, comprehensive career centers should use a wide range of approaches for delivering career services to students.

Services

The models discussed also reflect the fact that career services are delivered to students by a variety of people in a variety of venues. Herr and Cramer (1996) identify four major approaches used for delivering career services to students in higher education: (1) courses, workshops, and seminars that offer structured group experiences in topics such as career decision making, career planning, and job-search skills; (2) group counseling activities directed toward students experiencing such issues as career indecision, career indecisiveness, and job-search anxiety; (3) individual career counseling;

and (4) placement programs such as on-campus and/or online job interviewing. Obviously, the use of computer-assisted career guidance and computer information delivery systems offer vehicles for service delivery that range from career decision making to placement. Computer-assisted career guidance systems have existed for some time; more recent placement-oriented computer services include virtual job fairs, online resumés, and chat rooms for job seekers (Miller & McDaniels, 2001).

Davidson (2001) stresses that as career services professionals increase their reliance on technology in career services delivery, they also need to address the wide range of ethical issues associated with increased use of technology. For example, researchers suggest that it is important to balance "high-tech" with "high-touch." Students need access to humans as well as computer-based services. One does not replace the other. Computer-based services are not yet effective at providing empathy, addressing individual student needs, and responding to subtle, nonverbal expressions in client statements. Moreover, many online services have not been constructed according to the ethical and professional standards to which career services professionals adhere.

These multiple approaches for service delivery provide the means by which students receive a wide array of career-related services. For example, Reardon, Zunker, and Dyal (1979) identify 31 categories of career services delivered by 302 institutions of higher education. These services include, but are not limited to, providing occupational information via computerized and printed resources, job-search skills training, educational information, standardized and nonstandardized assessment opportunities, referrals to campus and community resources, self-help materials, training in decision making, assertiveness training, communications skills training, career planning courses, externships, internships, on-campus and off-campus job interview opportunities, and job interview training via videotaped role-play practice.

Hale (1974) has proposed some useful descriptions of the types of career services that should be available on campus. In his view, services should include career advising, career counseling, and career planning. The first, career advising, is academic advisement by a faculty member who helps students translate career choices into educational goals and programs and helps them relate academic majors to career opportunities. Career counseling includes psychological procedures used to assist students with self-evaluation as well as assessment and understanding of their capabilities and interests. Career planning is the process of helping students relate the outcomes of self-evaluation to information currently available about the world-of-work. Emphases here would involve decision making about specific occupations or corporations in which to seek employment and might include the acquisition of skills pertinent to job seeking, resumé preparation, and interviewing behavior.

Hale (1974) also contends that career interventions should be delivered within an integrated, coordinated system of comprehensive career services. Hale identifies five components that should be part of an integrated and coordinated system of career services:

1. A structured and comprehensive university-wide program of career education
2. A center offering career information, career counseling, and career planning and placement in a one-stop service for students
3. Specially trained academic advisers selected from faculty across a wide range of academic disciplines

4. A central administrator in academic affairs who can devote full time to the supervision and coordination of the career services, including academic advising
5. A commission on academic advising and career services

Herr (1989) observes that, in addition to individual career counseling of students, there are at least nine categories of career services in higher education. These categories affirm the comprehensiveness of career services and include approaches such as:

1. Infusing academic subject matter systematically with information pertinent to career development
2. Providing courses for academic credit that focus on career development
3. Using external resources (e.g., speakers, externships, and internships) to provide direct communication of career-related information
4. Integrating placement and transfer processes in support of career planning
5. Offering opportunities for work-study/cooperative education
6. Providing decentralized counseling using academic departments as the location for counselors who, among other responsibilities, coordinate the career and academic advisement of students
7. Providing seminars in residence halls, student unions, and so on, that focus on college life and educational and career planning
8. Providing group counseling focused on self-awareness and career planning
9. Providing interactive, computer-based career guidance and information systems

From the perspective of the broad goals to be met in career services in higher education, Herr et al. (2004) contend that services such as these are offered to achieve the following goals:

1. Provide students with assistance in the selection of a major field of study
2. Provide students with assistance in self-assessment and self-analysis
3. Provide students with assistance in understanding the world of work
4. Provide students with assistance in decision making
5. Provide assistance that addresses the unique needs of various subpopulations of students
6. Provide students with assistance with access to the world of work

As Robert progressed through career counseling, he increased his career and self-awareness through self-assessment exercises. He also participated in a career planning group consisting of returning students focused on crystallizing their career choices after being employed in the labor force for substantial periods of time. These activities helped Robert decide to pursue a career in education. Specifically, he decided to become a social studies teacher at the secondary school level. He thought this career option would provide him with opportunities to help others in meaningful ways while also spending more time with his family than he had in his previous jobs.

Standards

Because various models and approaches to career development interventions in higher education exist, there is the need for the professional community to identify the essential components of career services programs. Standards provide useful guides for delivering career development interventions in higher education. The comprehensive career models and services discussed thus far are similar to the perspectives advocated by the Council for the Advancement of Standards for Student Services/Development Programs (CAS) (CAS, Miller, 1997). The Council is a consortium of 21 professional associations in higher education that collectively devised and published *Standards and Guidelines*, a document that recommends criteria for student services in colleges and universities. One of these student services is career planning and placement. In the CAS Standards, the mission for career services centers is described as follows:

> Career planning is a developmental process that must be fostered during the entire period of a student's involvement with the institution. The primary purpose of career planning and placement must be to aid students in developing, evaluating, and effectively initiating and implementing career plans. (p. 46)

The CAS Standards also identify the specific services that, in essence, serve to operationalize the mission statement for career services in higher education. These services include career counseling focused on helping students engage in self-assessment, gather and process occupational information, learn decision making skills, and establish short-term and long-term educational and occupational goals.

Other services identified in the CAS Standards focus on placement services. Specifically, these services address the need to help students locate employment-related opportunities as they are enrolled in higher education (e.g., part-time work opportunities during the academic year, summer employment opportunities, and experiential education programs). These services are also important as students negotiate the transition from education to work (e.g., job-search skills training, on-campus and off-campus employment interviewing, and gaining entry to additional educational programs such as graduate school). Collectively, the career services described in the CAS Standards provide a useful framework for addressing the three NOICC competency domains of self-knowledge, educational/career exploration, and career planning.

The CAS Standards (Miller, 1997) also address topics that are essential for the day-to-day operation of career services in higher education. These topics include:

- Leadership (e.g., leaders of career services programs must have appropriate training; be able to articulate a clear vision for career services; set goals and objectives: prescribe and practice ethical behavior; and manage, plan, budget, and evaluate services/personnel)
- Organization and Management (e.g., policies and procedures must be current and accessible, there must be written performance expectations for all staff members, and processes for resolving grievances must be clearly stated)
- Human Resources (e.g., there must be adequate staffing, selection training and staffing procedures must be established, support staff must be adequate, affirmative action policies must be followed, and professional development opportunities must be encouraged and supported)
- Financial Resources (e.g., career services must have adequate funding)
- Facilities, Technology, and Equipment (e.g., facilities and equipment must be adequate and suitably located; facilities, technology, and equipment must comply with federal, state, and local requirements for access and safety)

- Legal Responsibilities (e.g., staff members must be knowledgeable about laws and regulations pertaining to service delivery)
- Equal Opportunity, Access, and Affirmative Action (e.g., staff members and services must not discriminate on the basis of age, color, disability, gender, national origin, race, religious creed, sexual orientation, and/or veteran status)
- Campus and Community Relations (e.g., career services programs establish, maintain, and promote effective relations with relevant campus offices and external agencies)
- Diversity (e.g., career services staff members and programs must nurture environments in which similarities and differences among people are recognized and honored)
- Ethics (e.g., relevant ethical standards must be adhered to in all career services practices)
- Assessment and Evaluation (e.g., regular and systematic quantitative and qualitative evaluations must occur to determine program quality)

The CAS Standards reflect the fact that career services in higher education extend throughout the campus and beyond. Comprehensive career services interact with other student services units (e.g., counseling, residential life), academic units, and community resources. The Standards also provide career practitioners with a useful list of topics and issues that must be addressed in the overall operation of career services in higher education. In these ways, the Standards can be used as benchmarks against which quality and effectiveness of career services can be assessed.

MANAGING CAREER SERVICES IN HIGHER EDUCATION

The CAS Standards highlight important topics for the management of career services in higher education. Although a full discussion of topics pertaining to managing career services in higher education is beyond the scope of this chapter, there are a few topics that are important to review. For example, the organizational structure of the career services operation is important to consider because it substantially influences the planning and delivery of career services.

A prominent issue influencing the delivery of career services in higher education is whether career services should be centralized or decentralized. A centralized structure is the most common structure for organizing career services in higher education (Powell & Kirts, 1980). Centralized services have clear advantages. Because services are located primarily in one place, it is clear to faculty, students, and employers where career services are provided on campus. Herr et al. (1993) note additional advantages of a centralized, rather than decentralized, career services structure:

1. Centralized services are more likely to achieve a critical mass in terms of professional staff.
2. There are substantial efficiencies and economies of scale that occur in terms of interview room use, career information resources, and support staff.
3. Because a centralized career services structure draws a very heterogeneous student population, it creates a more vibrant, challenging, and interesting environment for students and staff. (p. 57)

Herr et al. (1993) are quick to point out, however, that there are also advantages to decentralized career services (e.g., the service may be viewed as more personalized and the services are likely to be more accessible because they are located closer to where students spend a substantial portion of their time). Some institutions provide a combination of centralized and decentralized career services. For example, career counseling services can be decentralized and placement services can be centralized. There is some logic to this approach due to the fact that in decentralized structures, career counselors often have more direct contact with students and, thereby, find it easier to establish relationships with the students with whom they work. Providing centralized placement services is likely to be less confusing to employers as it is clear to everyone where this activity occurs on campus.

Another issue pertaining to managing career services in higher education relates to the place of career services within the institutional structure. Career service units in higher education typically report to the chief administrator responsible for student services or the chief academic administrator. The results of a survey conducted by the College Placement Council (1991) indicate that nearly three-fourths of career services offices report to the vice president of student services. Reporting to the vice president of student services has several advantages. For example, in this administrative structure career services are likely to be viewed as an integral aspect of student services. Because in this structure career services personnel meet regularly with professionals representing other student services units, communication among career services staff members and other student services providers (e.g., counselors, residence life directors) will probably be enhanced. This facilitates service delivery in various ways (e.g., referrals, programming, collaboration among student services professionals). There is a strong possibility that the vice president of student services will have a good understanding of, and appreciation for, the complete range of career services provided by the unit. When career services offices report to the chief academic administrator, they are better aligned with the primary enterprise of the institution. This also provides benefits to career services, such as facilitating relationships with faculty.

The ways in which these administrative issues are resolved in specific institutions will most likely depend on the structure of the overall student services operation and the university itself. Although Herr et al. (1993) view this issue as important for career services delivery, they are careful not to overstate the case, noting that "clearly, the structure of career services must be compatible with the institution in which it operates. Our experience has been that excellent career services often exist despite, rather than because of, a particular organizational structure" (pp. 106–107).

Rayman (1999) identified 10 imperatives for career services in higher education for the next millenium. These imperatives provide college and university career practitioners with useful guidelines as they plan and evaluate the career assistance they provide to students.

- *Imperative 1*: We must acknowledge the lifelong nature of career development and initiate programs and services that enable and encourage students to take responsibility for their own career destiny.

- *Imperative 2*: We must accept and embrace technology as our ally and shape its use to free staff time for those tasks that require human sensitivity.
- *Imperative 3*: We must continue to refine and strengthen our professional identity and that of career services within the academy.
- *Imperative 4*: We must acknowledge and accept that individual career counseling is at the core of our profession and endeavor to maintain and enhance the centrality of individual career counseling in the career development process.
- *Imperative 5*: We must forge cooperative relationships with faculty, advising professionals, other student affairs professionals, administrators, parents, and student groups to take advantage of the "multiplier effect" that such collaborative relationships can have in furthering our goal of enhanced student career development.
- *Imperative 6*: We must redouble our efforts to meet the changing career development needs of an increasingly diverse student body.
- *Imperative 7*: We must accept our position as the most obvious and continuing link between corporate America and the academy, but we also must maintain our focus on career development and not allow ourselves to be seduced into institutional fundraising at the expense of quality career services.
- *Imperative 8*: We must acknowledge and accept that on-campus recruiting as we have known it is a thing of the past and develop alternative means of facilitating the transition from college to work.
- *Imperative 9*: We must resolve the ambiguities that exist about our role in delivering alumni career services and solicit from our alumni associations the resource support necessary to provide these services.
- *Imperative 10*: We must advocate more effectively for resources to maintain and increase our role in facilitating student career development within the academy, and we must become more efficient and innovative in our use of existing resources.

Rayman's imperatives reveal both the challenges and opportunities for career practitioners in higher education in the 21st century. Clearly, the challenges focus on dwindling resources within the context of a growing need to help students in higher education move forward in their career development. The growing need for career services represents a tremendous opportunity to equip students with the knowledge, awareness, and skills to manage their careers effectively in the emerging workplace.

SUMMARY

Career services in higher education have a long and venerable history. In many ways, the evolution of these services reflects the evolution of the field in general as services evolved from an orientation toward job placement to a full range of career planning services being offered to meet the needs of diverse student populations. Increasingly, career services providers in higher education enlist a broad range of resources to deliver comprehensive career assistance to students. Alumni, faculty, peers, and community and business representatives are among those participating in the delivery of career services in higher education. Coordinating and providing comprehensive services requires careful and systematic planning, a familiarity with the career development competencies toward which services must be directed, knowledge of current standards for service delivery, awareness of the current literature identifying efficacious career development interventions, and skills in conducting formative and summative evaluations of career services. It is our hope that comprehensive career services, staffed by an adequate cadre of career professionals committed to meeting the career development needs of diverse student populations, will become the norm in higher education. Given survey results in which students identify career planning as their greatest concern, it would seem difficult, at best, for higher education institutions to justify anything less.

REFERENCES

ACT, Inc. (1995). DISCOVER for colleges and adults [Computer software]. Iowa City, IA: Author.

American Council on Education. (1999). *The American freshman national norms for fall 1998*. Washington, DC: Author.

College Placement Council. (1991, July). *1991 Career Planning and Placement Survey. Special report. Spotlight*. Bethlehem, PA: Author.

Collins, M. (1998). Snapshot of the profession. *Journal of Career Planning and Employment, 41*, 51–55.

Colozzi, E. A. (2000). Toward the development of systemic career guidance. In D. A. Luzzo (Ed.), *Career counseling of college students* (pp. 285–310). Washington, DC: American Psychological Association.

Conyers, L. M., & Szymanski, E. M. (1998). The effectiveness of an integrated career intervention for college students with and without disabilities. *Journal of Postsecondary Education and Disability, 13*, 23–34.

Crites, J. O. (1981). *Career counseling: Models, methods, and materials*. New York: McGraw-Hill.

Davidson, M. M. (2001). The computerization of career services: Critical issues to consider. *Journal of Career Development, 27*, 217–228.

Dunn, C. W., & Veltman, G. C. (1989). Addressing the restrictive career maturity patterns of minority youth: A program evaluation. *Journal of Multicultural Counseling and Development, 17*, 156–164.

Fassinger, R. E., & O'Brien, K. M. (2000). Career counseling with college women: A scientist-practitioner-advocate model of intervention. In

D. A. Luzzo (Ed.), *Career counseling of college students* (pp. 253–265). Washington, DC: American Psychological Association.

Friehe, M., Aune, B., & Leuenberger, J. (1996). Career service needs of college students with disabilities. *The Career Development Quarterly, 44*, 289–300.

Grey, K. C., & Herr, E. L. (2000). *Other ways to win: Creating alternatives for high school graduates* (2nd ed.). Thousand Oaks: CA: Corwin Press.

Halasz, T., & Kempton, C. B. (2000). Career planning workshops and courses. In D. A. Luzzo (Ed.), *Career counseling of college students* (pp. 157–169). Washington, DC: American Psychological Association.

Hale, L. L. (1974). A bold new blueprint for career planning and placement: Part 1. *Journal of College Placement, 35*, 34–40.

Hardesty, P. H. (1991). Undergraduate career courses for credit: A review and meta-analysis. *Journal of College Student Development, 32*, 184–185.

Healy, C. C., & Reilly, K. C. (1989). Career needs of community college students: Implications for services and theory. *Journal of College Student Personnel, 30*, 541–545.

Herr, E. L. (1989). Career development and mental health. *Journal of Career Development, 16*, 5–18.

Herr, E. L., & Cramer, S. H. (1996). *Career guidance and counseling through the lifespan* (5th ed.). New York: HarperCollins.

Herr, E. L., Cramer, S. H., & Niles, S. G. (2004). *Career guidance and counseling through the lifespan: Systematic approaches* (6th ed.). Boston: Allyn & Bacon.

Herr, E. L., Rayman, J., & Garis, J. W. (1993). *Handbook for the college and university career center.* Westport, CT: Greenwood Press.

Herring, R. D. (1998). *Career counseling in schools: Multicultural and developmental perspectives.* Alexandria, VA: American Counseling Association.

Hitchings, W. E., & Retish, P. (2000). The career development needs of students with learning disabilities. In D. A. Luzzo (Ed.), *Career counseling of college students* (pp. 253–265). Washington, DC: American Psychological Association.

Johnson, R. H. (1978). Individual styles of decision-making: A theoretical model for counseling. *Personnel and Guidance Journal, 56,* 531–536.

Luzzo, D. A. (1992). Ethnic group and social class differences in college students' career development. *The Career Development Quarterly, 41,* 161–173.

Luzzo, D. A. (2000). Career development of returning-adult and graduate students. In D. A. Luzzo (Ed.), *Career counseling of college students* (pp. 191–200). Washington, DC: American Psychological Association.

Marron, D., & Rayman, J. R. (2002). Addressing the career development needs of adult students in research university settings. In S. Niles (Ed.), *Adult career development: Concepts, models, and practices* (3rd ed., pp. 319–334). Tulsa: OK: National Career Development Association.

Miller, K. L., & McDaniels, R. M. (2001). Cyberspace, the new frontier. *Journal of Career Development, 27,* 199–206.

Miller, T. K. (1997). *The book of professional standards for higher education.* Washington, DC: Council for the Advancement of Standards in Higher Education.

National Occupational Information Coordinating Committee (NOICC), U.S. Department of Labor. (1992). The National Career Development Guidelines Project. Washington, DC: U.S. Department of Labor.

Niles, S. G., Erford, B. T., Hunt, B., & Watts, R. H. (1997). Decision-making styles and career development of college students. *Journal of College Student Development, 38,* 479–488.

Ohler, D. L., Levinson, E. M., & Barker, W. F. (1996). Career maturity in college students with learning disabilities. *The Career Development Quarterly, 44,* 278–288.

Pope, M. S., Prince, J. P., & Mitchell, K. (2000). Responsible career counseling with lesbian and gay students. In D. A. Luzzo (Ed.), *Career counseling of college students* (pp. 267–281). Washington, DC: American Psychological Association.

Powell, R., & Kirts, D. K. (1980). *Career services today: A dynamic college profession.* Bethlehem, PA: The College Placement Council.

Rayman, J. R. (1996). Apples and oranges in the career center: Reaction to R. Reardon. *Journal of Counseling and Development, 74,* 286–287.

Rayman, J. R. (1999). Career services imperative for the next millenium. *The Career Development Quarterly, 48,* 175–184.

Reardon, R. C. (1996). A program and cost analysis of a self-directed career decision-making program in a university career center. *Journal of Counseling and Development, 74,* 280–285.

Reardon, R. C., Lenz, J. G., Sampson, J. P., Jr., & Peterson, G. W. (2000a). *Career development and planning: A comprehensive approach.* Pacific Grove, CA: Brooks/Cole.

Reardon, R. C., Zunker, V., & Dyal, M. A. (1979). The status of career planning programs and career centers in colleges and universities. *Vocational Guidance Quarterly, 28,* 154–159.

Reed, C. A., Reardon, R. C., Lenz, J. G., & Leirer, S. J. (2001). A cognitive career course: From theory to practice. *The Career Development Quarterly, 50,* 158–167.

Super, D. E. (1984). Leisure: What it is and might be. *Journal of Career Development, 11,* 71–80.

Weissberg, M., Berenstein, M., Cote, A., Cravey, B., & Heath, K. (1982). An assessment of the personal, career, and academic needs of undergraduate students. *Journal of College Student Personnel, 23,* 415–422.

Whiston, S. C., Sexton, T. L., & Lasoff, D. L. (1998). Career-intervention outcome: A replication and extension of Oliver and Spokane (1998). *Journal of Counseling Psychology, 45,* 150–165.

Whiteley, S. M., Mahaffey, P. J., & Geer, C. A. (1987). The campus counseling center: A profile of staffing patterns and services. *Journal of College Student Personnel, 28,* 71–81.

COURSE SYLLABUS FOR COUNSELOR EDUCATION CLASS

Effective Career Decision Making
Fall 2003
Tuesday and Thursday 11:15 AM–12:30 PM
202 Rackley

Office: Career Services
Office Hours: 2:00–3:00 P.M. Tuesday and Wednesday, and by appointment

Text: Sukiennik, Bendat, & Raufman
The Career Fitness Program: Exercising Your Options (6th ed.)

Handout packet provided by the instructor

PURPOSE

Counselor Ed. 297A is designed for students who are undecided about their major and career selection. Counselor Ed. 297A is not appropriate for students who have already chosen a major and developed career goals. It does not cover topics such as job-search strategies, resumé writing, cover letters, and interviewing skills. One of the other career courses offered by Career Services would be more appropriate for these students than Counselor Ed. 297A.

COURSE OBJECTIVES

1. Engage in a variety of activities and experiences useful in building knowledge about yourself, careers, academic majors, and the world-of-work.
2. Know the core concepts and applications of basic career theories.
3. Identification and integration of personal history, interests, values, skills, and abilities.
4. Understand how career assessments (e.g., the Self-Directed Search and the Myers-Briggs Type Indicator) are used to facilitate career decision making.
5. Gain information and support through the use of the University's academic advising and career resources.
6. Learn how to use workplace trends to enhance current and future career decisions.

Students with disabilities who require accommodations should consult with the instructor within the first 2 weeks of class to address modifications that are needed to complete course requirements. Consistent with University policy, any student requesting an accommodation must provide documentation from the Office for Disability Services.

ATTENDANCE POLICY AND PARTICIPATION

Attendance and participation are extremely crucial for success in this class. Class attendance points are given for both attending and participating. Students are expected to not only attend class but to actively participate in discussion and group activities.

Students can miss up to two classes without penalty but are responsible for any missed material that is covered. After two unexcused absences, students will lose three points per missed class.

Excused Absences

Absences are excused only if there is a death, personal trauma, formal religious reason, or uncontrollable emergency. In order for an excused absence to be approved by the instructor, written documentation must be provided in advance if possible, but by the next class session in which the student is in attendance. Assignments are still due on the designated date and can be given to a friend to drop off, dropped off prior to class at the Career Services office, or turned in in advance.

Unexcused Absences

After four unexcused absences (including the two "free" absences), the student will drop a full final letter grade.

Lateness

Class will begin on time. Important announcements will be given at the beginning of each class period. Students arriving to class late will run the risk of missing important information.

GRADING SCALE

A = 279–300	C+ = 231–239	Miscellaneous 15%
A– = 270–278	C = 210–230	Lifeline and Brief Paper 5%
B+ = 261–269	D = 180–209	Occupation Information
B = 249–260	F = Below 180	Interview Paper 20%
B– = 240–248		Career Autobiography Paper 20%
		Exams 20%
		Group Presentation 10%
		Attendance and Participation 10%

LATE ASSIGNMENT POLICY

Assignments: Lose one point per late class period. Career Autobiography Paper and Occupation Interview Paper: lose five points per late class period.

If you will be absent on a day the assignment is due, you are expected to turn the assignment in prior to your absence if possible.

STANDARDS OF CONDUCT

Students are expected to adhere to the academic standards of conduct described in the Student Guide to University Policies and Rules (http://www.sa.psu.edu/ja/discipline.html). These policies address academic dishonesty, plagiarism, harassment, making false statements, and behaviors that endanger the health and safety of others.

Date	Class Topic	Reading	Assignment Due
Tues., August 22	Introduction. Review of course syllabus and requirements. Discussion of student and instructor expectations. (Introduce Introductory Assessments.)		
Thurs., August 24	Effective career decision making. Career planning issues. Orientation to career services.		Introductory Assessments
Tues., August 29	Career development theories. (Introduce Lifeline assignment.)		
Thurs., August 31	Career development theories continued. (Hand out semester packets.)	Chapter 1 "Taking Stock"	
Tues., September 5	Career assessment strategies. The career counseling process. Orientation to academic majors. (Assign DISCOVER.) (Receive group assignments.) (Sign up for tour of Career Information Center.)		
Thurs., September 7	Small Group Workshop 1— Sharing and discussion of Lifelines		
Tues., September 12	Personal and career decision making strategies. (Administer the Myers-Briggs Type Indicator.)	Chapter 8 "Making Decisions"	Exercises 8.1 and 8.15
Thurs., September 14	Values decisions in career and life planning. Values and work satisfaction. Lifeline Brief "Values Paper"	Chapter 3 "Values Clarification"	Lifeline Brief Paper Exercises 3.1 and 3.2
Tues., September 19	Interests. Holland's typology of personality and career interests. (Assign Self-Directed Search.)	"Focusing on You: Personality and Interests"	Interest Checklist for Worker Trait Groups pages 65–69

Date	Class Topic	Reading	Assignment Due
Thurs., September 21	Interpretation of the Self-Directed Search.		Self-Directed Search
Tues., September 26	Personality characteristics and workplace preferences. Interpretation of the Myers-Briggs Type Indicator.		
Thurs., September 28	Abilities and their role in academic and career planning. Synthesis—integration of internal information. (Introduce Career Autobiography.)	Chapter 5 "Skills Assessment"	Assessing Your Skills, pages 85–86 and Exercise 5.8
Tues., October 3	Exam 1		
Thurs., October 5	Small Group Workshop 2—Review of assessment results. Bring results from Self-Directed Search, Myers-Briggs Type Indicator, Values and Skills exercises, Majors Checklist, Discover, and Self-Assessment Summary.		Majors Checklist and Self-Assessment Summary
Tues., October 10	FALL BREAK		
Thurs., October 12	World-of-work work sectors; relationship between basic work tasks, academic majors, and career choice. (Assign Advising Interviews.)	Chapter 7 "Information Integration" Review pages 72–73.	Discover Reaction Paper
Tues., October 17 or Wed., October 18	Career information resources at Career Services. Class meets in room 410 Boucke at 5:00 P.M.		
Thurs., October 19	Small Group Workshop 3—Planning for group presentation. Decision making style and personal issues effect on major/career decision making.		Career Autobiography Paper

(Continued)

(Continued)

Date	Class Topic	Reading	Assignment Due
Tues., October 24	Interviewing for occupational information. (Introduce Occupation Informational Interview paper.)		
Thurs., October 26	Experiential Learning: Internships, externships, summer jobs, education abroad, activities, and volunteer work. Collegiate and community involvement and its role in career development.		Exercise 7.6
Tues., October 31	Guest speakers.		
Thurs., November 2	Discuss academic advising interviews.		Summaries of Advising Interview Experiences
Tues., November 7	Cultural Diversity: personal and career issues related to gender, race/ethnicity, and disability status	Chapter 6 "The World and You"	
Thurs., November 9	Small Group Workshop 4—Cultural Diversity. Discuss the impact of the culturally diverse workplace on career decisions.		Multicultural Me
Tues., November 14	Group Presentations.		
Thurs., November 16	Group Presentations.		
Tues., November 21	Workplace trends and issues.		Article from popular literature about a current workplace trend or issue for group discussion
Thurs., November 23	Thanksgiving		
Tues., November 28	Discuss Informational Interviews.		Occupation Informational Interview Paper
Thurs., November 30	Exam 2. Continue discussion of Informational Interviews.		

Date	Class Topic	Reading	Assignment Due
Tues., December 5	Course wrap-up and evaluations.		
Thurs., December 7	Small Group Workshop 5—Putting it all together. Discussion of course learning as it applies to personal career situations. Next steps for career planning.		Putting It All Together

Assignment descriptions

Assessments

You will be required to take three formal assessments: the Self-Directed Search, the Myers-Briggs Type Indicator, and DISCOVER.

Myers-Briggs Type Indicator (to be completed in class on September 12)

Self-Directed Search   Due: September 21

The Myers-Briggs and the Self-Directed Search are popular assessment tools that measure personality and interests, respectively. As we will discuss in class, personality preferences and tendencies and personal interests are important contributors to the career development process. The instruments will be administered in class. It is your responsibility to attend class and complete the assessments as instructed.

DISCOVER   Reaction Paper Due: October 12

DISCOVER is a computer-assisted career guidance system (CACGS) housed in Career Services, 410 Boucke, which can assist you with making career decisions. You will need to schedule a 1-hour appointment between September 6 and October 11. Appointments can be scheduled by going to 412 Boucke between the hours of 8:00 AM and 5:00 PM. More details on this assignment will be provided in class on September 5.

Lifeline and Paper   Lifeline Due: September 7
                                                          Paper Due: September 14

The lifeline is a collection of important events in your personal development. There are two parts to this assignment. First, you will create the lifeline in any format you choose and present your project to your small-group members. Second, you will prepare a 2-page written statement about your lifeline.

1. The lifeline can be presented in any format you choose. Previous lifelines have included:
   - Drawn, painted, or cartooned pictures of scenes throughout a lifetime
   - A poem describing feelings and/or major events (If you choose this format, make sure the content is substantial.)
   - A physical object representing a person's life, attitude, or an event (Include a written explanation.)
   - A recording of various relevant songs
   - Clip art, sculptures, collages, or creative writing

Although there are no formal requirements for length or content, grades will be determined by the amount of work, thought, or creativity evident through the presentation and the ability to express important events in a person's life.

You will present your lifeline at the first small-group session on September 7. Please be aware that you will have about 10 minutes to share your lifeline, so plan accordingly! If you have more to say, you can write about it in your summary.

Your project is to be turned in to your group leader.

2. A two-page summary of your lifeline should include your reactions to the presentations, thoughts that were triggered, the benefits of the assignment, and so on. Consider the following questions for group discussion and your paper:

Who are/were some of the significant people in your life?

Who has influenced you the most in terms of your educational and/or career planning?

What were some of the highs and lows or significant events in your life?

What accomplishments are you proudest of?

How did you decide to attend college and why did you choose Penn State?

What major(s)/career(s) were you considering when you first decided to attend Penn State?

Are you completely unsure of what you want to major in or what occupation you might enjoy?

How does it feel to be uncertain?

First Paper: Career Autobiography   Due: October 19

The Career Autobiography is meant to help you synthesize and process the information you have gained about yourself from class through various assessments, exercises, and discussions. The paper must be typed, approximately 5 to 7 pages long, and should include the following:

- A discussion of your background and significant life events. Include family background, careers you thought about as a child, how and why you decided to attend Penn State, and so on.

- Consideration of how your experiences to date, including work experience and extracurricular activities, have influenced your past or present educational and career plans.
- A review of the relationship between your life/career plans and information from the course. Discuss how well your assessment results from the SDS and Myers-Briggs "fit" you. Do you agree with your results? Why or why not? What did you learn about yourself from the values and abilities exercises? What is your decision making style and how does it affect your choice of major? Which career theories apply to you? How? Be sure to cite some content from lectures, class discussion, assignments, and/or the text.
- A brief review of your present situation concerning your academic and career plans. Also, review possible future directions, including possible majors.

Please include a cover page. (Your cover page should include your name, course title, title of your paper, and the date.)

The following criteria will be used in grading your paper:

1. Integration of course concepts   20 pts.
2. Effect of your life experience on
   educational and career decisions   15 pts.
3. Present and future career issues   10 pts.
4. Overall presentation organization,
   grammar, and spelling   15 pts.
   _____
   Total 60 pts.

Second Paper: Occupation Informational Interview   Due: November 28

Researching a career is essential to the career decision making process.

The paper must be typed, double-spaced, approximately 5 to 7 pages in length, and should include the following:

- A review and discussion of an informational interview conducted with someone employed in a career area that may be of interest to you. Preferably, the person will not be a relative and will be employed outside of Penn State. (Relatives and Penn State employees must be approved by the instructor before the interview.) Include the reason you chose to interview somebody in this particular field. Consider:
  - The nature of the work (duties, responsibilities)
  - Qualifications necessary (education and/or experience)
  - Typical lines of advancement in this field
  - Typical hiring organizations for this kind of job
- A summary of the nature of the organization in which the professional is employed. Consider:
  - The organization's structure
  - Profits or funding sources
  - Services or products
  - Work environment
  - Types of entry-level positions for college graduates

- If available, any handout information such as an annual report or organizational brochure. This would be included in an appendix.
- A review of your reaction to your interview with the professional.
  - How similar or different was the information you obtained compared with your previous knowledge of the career field?
  - What effect has this information had on your interest in the field and your decision to pursue it?
  - What information do you still need about this career?
  - What are your next steps or plans of action?
  - A cover sheet with the name of the person you interviewed, name of the organization, date of the interview, and the interviewee's full mailing address and telephone number.

You will also be required to make a brief presentation about your informational interview on the day that it is due. You will not be graded on your presentation. The purpose is to share information about occupations to your fellow classmates.

Refer to the handout on "Occupational Information Interviewing" in your packet for ideas on questions to ask.

The following criteria will be used in grading your paper:

1. Information about the interviewee   15 pts.
2. Information about the organization   10 pts.
3. Your reaction and thoughts   20 pts.
4. Overall presentation organization,
   grammar, and spelling   15 pts.
   _____
                                    Total   60 pts.

Group Report and Presentation   Due: November 14 and 16

Each discussion group will select a major and related occupation (or occupations) to research. It may not be possible to find a major and career that all group members would personally consider pursuing, so try to choose one that most members are curious to learn about. The group should review the following information for the selected major:

1. General nature of the program
2. Course and program requirements
3. Entrance requirements
4. Type and ranges of occupations associated with the major as well as opportunities for graduate/professional school
5. Sources of information and relevant student organizations

Information regarding the selected occupation(s) related to the major should include:

1. Nature of the work and typical responsibilities
2. Appropriate academic preparation and training; identify a range of undergraduate majors that could lead to the occupation(s)
3. Types and range of organizations/settings in which the occupation is performed
4. Job outlook and earnings
5. Sources of information and relevant student organizations

This presentation should be fun and informative for you and your classmates! Small skits, television shows, take-offs on movies, game show-style presentations, and other creative ideas are encouraged! Your group will have a time range of 15 to 20 minutes.

The purpose of this assignment is to become familiar with the kinds of information necessary to make informed career choices and ways to research this information.

A few suggested resources: Academic Advising Centers, Student Organization Directory, Career Information Center, Pattee Library, and the Internet.

Each group will turn in a 1-page, typed summary or outline of their presentation on or before the day of the presentation.

ASSIGNMENT DUE DATES AND COURSE GRADING CRITERIA

August 24	Introductory Assessments	3 pts.
September 7	Lifeline	15 pts.
September 12	Myers-Briggs Type Indicator	2 pts.
September 12	Decision Making Exercises 8.1 & 8.15	2 pts.
September 14	Values Exercises 3.1 & 3.2	2 pts.
September 14	Brief Paper	
September 19	Interest Exercise, pages 65–69	2 pts.
September 21	Self-Directed Search	3 pts.
September 28	Skills Exercise, pages 85–86 and Exercise 5.8	2 pts.
October 3	Exam 1	30 pts.
October 5	Majors Checklist	3 pts.
	Self-Assessment Summary	3 pts.
October 12	Discover Reaction Paper	5 pts.
October 19	Career Autobiography Paper	60 pts.
October 26	Gathering the Facts, Exercise 7.6	6 pts.
November 2	Academic Advising Summaries	6 pts.
November 9	Multicultural Me	2 pts.
November 14 & 16	Group Presentation	30 pts.
November 21	Work Trend Article	2 pts.
November 28	Occupation Info. Interview Paper	60 pts.
November 30	Exam 2	30 pts.
December 7	Putting It All Together	2 pts.
	Class Attendance & Participation	30 pts.
	Total	300 pts.

CHAPTER 13

CAREER DEVELOPMENT INTERVENTIONS IN COMMUNITY SETTINGS

So much

"To continue its good work in the next decade, the career counseling profession must intensify efforts to serve a diverse clientele in new settings, . . . construct new tools that exploit the potential of informational technology, . . . and assist counselors worldwide who seek to internationalize the profession of career counseling" ("Special Issue: Career Counseling in the Next Decade,"). These lofty aspirations for 2000–2010 suggest that never before has a profession expected so much *of itself.*

So many

A recent Gallup Organization survey conducted for the NCDA reported that a significant number of adult workers seek assistance from professionals in the careers field. The broadening list of presenting issues includes career dissatisfaction, work-life imbalance, job-loss grief, as well as the traditional job-search training. Will the dawn of the next decade witness increased public demand for professional career services? If so, then it may well be true that never before has so much been owed by so many *individuals and their families.*

So few

Some employers and professional organizations bemoan that there are so few *highly trained professionals providing preventative (i.e., primary, secondary, and tertiary) career services. Small but growing is the demand for evidence-based career interventions that are deliverable in multiple formats (i.e., individual, couple/family, and group services), with returns on investment (ROI) that are measurable, sustainable, and replicable.*

A retrospective at decade's-end may prove whether the words of Prime Minister Winston Churchill during WWII's Battle of Britain characterize the

21st-century workforce: "Never in the field of human conflict was so much owed by so many to so few" (http://www.bartleby.com/59/10/Churchill.win.html).

Michael E. Hall, Ph.D., LPC, C.M.F.
Principal of a solo career-, marital-, and
leadership-development practice in Charlotte, North Carolina

Alexa is a 30-year-old woman with a bachelor's degree in accounting. She has been working as an accountant for 7 years and is greatly dissatisfied with her choice of occupation, one strongly suggested by her father. Not knowing how to get assistance in developing other occupational alternatives, she went to the local Job Service office. The counselor there was very helpful in teaching her how to use America's Job Bank to identify many jobs available in her state and how to use other Web sites developed by the Department of Labor. She was, however, confused by the amount of information on these Web sites and realized that she needed extensive assistance in determining what her interests and values are related to work before being immersed in information and job possibilities. She called her former high school counselor, who was able to refer her to a local certified career counselor in private practice.

Though the profession of counseling had its genesis in 1908 in Frank Parsons' Vocation Bureau in Boston, which was a community-based setting, this specialty of career counseling has experienced a long struggle for recognition. Counseling was first recognized as a necessary function in public high schools; and the National Defense Education Act of 1958, which provided government funds for the training of counselors for placement in high schools, had a tremendous impact on institutionalizing high school counselors. Chapters 10 and 11 of this textbook describe the role and function of counselors in school settings, including elementary, middle, and high schools. Counseling in postsecondary educational settings, as described in Chapter 12, has become a recognized and essential component of the student services provided by 2- and 4-year colleges.

In addition, the need for providing career counseling to adult populations has been recognized. Responding to a need to have a professional organization for all counseling specialties, the American Personnel and Guidance Association (APGA), now the American Counseling Association (ACA), was formed in 1952 by the four professional associations—for career counselors, school counselors, college student personnel, and counselor educators and supervisors—then in existence. Since its founding, ACA has recognized the following specialties in counseling, which have become divisions within the main body of ACA:

- Association for Assessment in Counseling (AAC)
- Association for Adult Development and Aging (AADA)
- American College Counseling Association (ACCA)
- Association for Counselors and Educators in Government (ACEG)
- Association for Counselor Education and Supervision (ACES)
- Association for Gay, Lesbian and Bisexual Issues in Counseling (AGLBIC)

- Association for Multicultural Counseling and Development (AMCD)
- American Mental Health Counselors Association (AMHCA)
- American Rehabilitation Counseling Association (ARCA)
- American School Counselor Association (ASCA)
- Association for Spiritual, Ethical, and Religious Values in Counseling (ASERVIC)
- Association for Specialists in Group Work (ASGW)
- Counseling Association for Humanistic Education and Development (C-AHEAD)
- International Association of Addictions and Offender Counselors (IAAOC)
- International Association of Marriage and Family Counselors (IAMFC)
- National Career Development Association (NCDA)
- National Employment Counseling Association (NECA)

Note that the names of these divisions vary in that some focus on the setting in which the counseling takes place (such as the American School Counselor Association); some, the population (Adult Development and Aging); and some, the primary concern of the counseling (such as the National Career Development Association). However, none of these specifically recognize the community as a setting for providing counseling and career development services. Further, though the members of the NCDA might have the highest degree of interest in providing career counseling and development services, the fact is that counselors who work in all of the specialties and settings represented by other divisions also inevitably work with clients who have major concerns with career choice and development. In addition to membership in these divisions of ACA, counselors specializing in career planning services in any setting might belong to a division of the American Psychological Association (APA), namely Division 17, comprised of members who specialize in vocational psychology.

TRAINING, CERTIFICATION, AND LICENSURE

The basic training for counselors in all specialties is a master's degree in a counseling curriculum that includes training in 12 critical competencies and a supervised practicum. This training may be acquired in a graduate institution that is approved by the Council for Accreditation of Counseling and Related Educational Programs (CACREP) or one that is not. CACREP-approved programs now require 48 hours of graduate work in the field and two academic terms of supervised field experience. CACREP standards recognize a career counseling specialty, but, unfortunately, there are only five institutions that meet those requirements at this time.

The standards referred to in the previous paragraph are standards for graduate school programs; doubtless, these standards result in better preparation of those who attend schools that meet these standards. Other standards, notably those of the National Board for the Certification of Counselors (NBCC) and of state licensure boards, apply more directly to the qualifications of individual counselors. NBCC offers certification to counselors who meet its requirements (48 semester hours of coursework, two academic terms of supervised field experience, and 2 years of post-master's counseling experience); persons who qualify for certification may use the title National Certified Counselor (NCC). In addition to voluntarily applying for and maintaining certification, counselors in 49 of the 50 states must meet the requirements for licensure as defined in their own state's law. In addition to all of this, many career counselors (especially those who want to practice in higher education or in private practice) earn a Certificate of Advanced Study (CAS) or doctoral degree (Ed.D. or Ph.D.) with a specialty in career development theory and practice.

COMPETENCIES

It is easy to view community-based counseling as that which occurs in any setting other than education. This definition appears to be insufficient. A recent definition (Hershenson, Power, & Waldo, 1996) of community-based counseling is "the application of counseling principles and practices in agency, organizational, or individual practice settings that are located in and interact with their surrounding community" (p. 26). Further, these authors have depicted the specialty with the model shown in Figure 13.1. This difference in approach implies that additional competencies (beyond counseling, educating, and programming, which are also used by counselors in educational settings), are needed for those who do career counseling in community settings. These include coordinating, consulting, advocacy, and case management.

Coordination

Coordinating is the process whereby a counselor brings together the needs of a client and the resources of the community. A first step in being able to coordinate is to assess thoroughly the client's strengths and barriers and to investigate and become knowledgeable of the resources that the community has. A client's strengths and barriers are typically identified through informal and formal assessment techniques. The most common informal assessment technique is the interview. The first of such

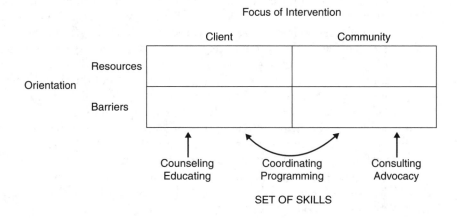

Figure 13.1

Competencies model. *Source:* From D. B. Hershenson, P. W. Power, and M. Waldo, *Community Counseling: Contemporary Theory and Practice.* Published by Allyn & Bacon, Boston, MA. Copyright © 1996 by Pearson Education. Reprinted by permission of the publisher.

interviews is called an intake interview. It is a structured interview in which the counselor uses some predetermined questions to collect the information needed to understand the client's strengths and barriers. One model used for this process is based on Schlossberg's transition theory.

Schlossberg (1989) defines a transition as an event or nonevent that results in change that is significant enough to cause disruption in one's usual roles, relationships, and/or routines. Many of the concerns that send clients to community-based career counselors fit this definition.

Schlossberg proposes that the severity of such transitions can be controlled by use of a four-step process:

- Define the *situation* clearly. This step includes finding out how the client perceives the situation or problem, what its timing is, how long the client has had to absorb it, and how much control the client believes he or she can exert to resolve or manage the situation.
- Learn about the *self* or inner resources the client has. This step includes learning about how the client has dealt with past transitions; what his or her dominant goals, interests, and skills are; and what emotional and spiritual strengths lie in the personal reservoir.
- Learn about the *support system* that does or does not surround the client in this transition. This system includes the support of family, friends, agencies, and material goods that can assist with the transition.
- From the knowledge gained in these three areas, the counselor and the client can develop a *strategy* for coping with the present need or transition.

If a counselor were, for example, using this kind of theoretical base as a guide for asking open-ended questions (those that cannot be answered with a single word), this could be a valuable informal assessment technique for the identification of the client's strengths, barriers, and coping mechanisms.

The other side of the equation is the identification of resources in the community that can meet the identified needs of the client or assist in removing barriers. In this process the career counselor spends significant time finding and cataloging community resources related to specific categories of need—such as job placement, shelter, vocational training, clothing, legal assistance, and so on. Because resources of this kind come and go, there is a need for an ongoing scan of the environment to identify new resources and resources that may no longer be available.

Identification of services is only the first step. The second step is to become knowledgeable about them: visiting the organization that provides the service; establishing and maintaining a personal contact; and getting detailed information about services provided, criteria for those who can access the services, length and cost of services provided, and the best way to access the services.

The third step is to make an informed linkage between the client and available services. One method is to organize client needs by the same descriptors as services provided by organizations. Given that client profiles and resource profiles are entered into a database, a counselor could easily relate the two by a simple computer search. Lacking this capability, counselors may maintain up-to-date print files or notebooks that describe community referral resources.

So, the process of coordination involves the steps of (1) identifying client needs, (2) matching client needs with community resources, (3) introducing the client to these resources through personal contact, (4) referring the client to the resource, and (5) following through with both the client and the resource to determine the effectiveness of the referral and what the next steps should be.

As an example of the task of coordinating, suppose that a counselor working in a prison setting identified vocational training as one of the primary needs of a client. The client is particularly interested in learning to cook, and The Salvation Army has a training program for cooks. The counselor follows all of the steps previously listed, including making a personal contact with The Salvation Army and setting an appointment for his client. The client presents himself effectively in the interview and is accepted in the culinary training program.

Consultation

Consultation is a second important competency for community-based career counselors (Dougherty, 1990). Consultation should not be confused with supervision, which implies that one person has the responsibility for directing the activities of another and for corrective action if performance does not meet expectations. Consultation, on the other hand, is the work of one professional with another in an attempt to find ways to reach compromises that will address the needs of a third party (the client).

As an example, suppose that a 45-year-old, single mother who comes to a community mental health center for career counseling has a heart condition that is potentially significant enough to affect the kind of work that she can do. As the counselor discusses the possible ways that she could afford additional training, he learns that she has always had a goal to attend college but does not believe it is possible considering her age and financial condition. The counselor describes the services of the Division of Vocational Rehabilitation and explains that there may be an opportunity for her to receive funds through this agency to attend the local community college or a state-supported university.

With the client's enthusiastic permission, the counselor makes an appointment with a staff member at the local office of the Division of Vocational Rehabilitation (DVR). During that meeting, the counselor describes his client and her needs. The DVR staff member and counselor compare the client's characteristics with the current policies of DVR and jointly conclude that the client is eligible for a service that would pay for tuition at a publicly supported institution of higher education. The counselor formally refers the client to the contact person at DVR, who proceeds to work with her to develop a formal application for services.

Many clients who receive services from community-based counselors lack skills that are needed to overcome the barriers they face and reach the goals they seek. These skills may be social, academic, or psychological. In other words, there may be deficits in ability to communicate effectively with others, in specific skills needed to perform in a job, or in personal coping skills such as decision making or goal setting. As the counselor identifies these needs, he or she may seek ways to meet these deficits through consultation with persons in community agencies.

Advocacy

A third competency that Hershenson et al. (1996) attribute to community-based counselors is advocacy. This term describes a role that counselors may play to exert pressure on some aspect of the community in order to improve the resources available for clients. Advocacy may be exercised through representation on boards of referral agencies, pressing for specific legislation, writing newspaper columns, joining protests of various kinds, writing to legislators, exerting individual influence, or making presentations to groups that can have influence.

Suppose that you worked as a career counselor in a rehabilitation agency. A local community college offers an excellent program in desktop publishing, and five of your disabled clients are enrolled in it. However, it is very difficult for your clients to get a job, no matter how well they do in this program, because of the prejudice against persons with disabilities. You identify four major employers of persons trained in desktop publishing and make an appointment with the director of human resources in each of the four sites. When you visit, you take a copy of the performance-based curriculum that the community college offers. You also take some work samples and letters written by employers of past graduates of the program. Finally, you show pictures of your five clients and ask the director of human resources to grant an interview to these clients for the next desktop publishing job available. You commit to careful follow-through with your clients who become employees to increase the probability that they will be productive employees. Advocacy includes performance of all of the kinds of activities included in this example.

More than those in any other counseling specialty, community counselors must orchestrate a variety of people, resources, and services in order to meet the needs of their clients. This process of orchestration is called *case management*. In large agencies, the persons involved in case management may be different from those who provide counseling. More typically, however, the community counselor plays a multifaceted role that includes both counselor and case manager. This dual role demands diverse skills, ranging from the facilitative skills of a good counselor to the coordinating, consulting, and advocacy skills just described.

Case Management

The goal of case management is to assure that clients receive the sequence of services they need in a timely and coordinated fashion. Thus, one of the most critical roles of a community-based counselor is to develop a comprehensive case plan, which might be called an action plan, and then to continually monitor it. For some clients, services may be provided by the counselor and the agency that he or she represents with only one external service provider. For other clients, whose needs are complex and include needs outside the scope of the agency such as physical problems, housing needs, financial needs, and job needs, there may be several service providers external to the counselor's home site.

The role of case manager demands skill in assessment (to determine needs), coordination with referral resources, evaluation of services provided, advocacy for the client, and continual follow-through with the client and the external service providers.

Case management requires the development of a sound plan at the outset, establishment and maintenance of excellent relationships with specific persons within referral agencies, tact in communication and evaluation, ongoing instructional and emotional support to the client and perhaps the client's family, and wisdom about when to make a change in service provider or to terminate service to the client. The types of resources that may be included in a case plan are as varied as the needs of clients for whom plans are developed.

It is common for community-based centers to have differentiated staffing. A counselor addressing career concerns may be on a team with psychologists, social workers, nurses, medical doctors, and perhaps career development facilitators (CDFs). A career development facilitator is a paraprofessional trained to work under the supervision of a professional counselor to assist with a number of duties most directly related to career planning and job placement.

SIMILARITIES AND DIFFERENCES IN COMMUNITY-BASED SETTINGS

Career counseling provided to individuals or groups in community-based settings is both similar to and different from career counseling provided in other settings. It is similar to work in educational settings in that it draws upon the same counseling and career development theories for many of its tools and techniques and requires the same facilitative skills when working with clients. In addition, its clients may be dealing with career choice and development problems that in many ways parallel those of students.

Conversely, providing career development services in community-based settings differs from doing so in educational settings in the following ways:

- Clients who seek career counseling in community-based settings are typically adults who have major responsibilities in several life roles—such as spouse, parent, and citizen in addition to worker. They are typically facing one of the following areas of concern: (1) reentry into the workforce after child rearing or loss of job; (2) dealing with being plateaued and wanting to find greater job satisfaction through job change, upward mobility, or job enrichment; or (3) dissatisfaction with an occupation or job and wanting to make a significant change in occupation that may require retraining.
- The options they have for career choice or change are intimately tied to availability of resources and/or dilution of barriers in the community. *Community* is defined as all of that which surrounds the individual: that is, community may be the family, the neighborhood, and/or the organization in which one is imbedded.
- Based on this assumption, the counselor may spend as much time and effort in working with the community to make resources available as with the individual client.
- Work with the community may take the forms of finding training opportunities to augment the individual's current skills, advocating for additional or modified resources, removing barriers to those resources, consulting with appropriate persons or agencies, and/or coordinating between and among the client and community resources.

- The skills of coordination, consultation, advocacy, and case management—though also necessary in educational settings—may be needed and used more often in community-based settings than in school settings.
- These counselors work in the community in settings such as private practice, government agencies, mental health centers, drug and abuse centers, and corporations. They may also work in the global community by delivering services via the Internet.

SETTINGS FOR COMMUNITY-BASED CAREER COUNSELORS

There is an increasingly wide variety of settings in which community-based counselors work—some devoting full time to career-related concerns and others dealing with such concerns in the context of a much broader array. The most common of these community-based settings and the typical tasks of counselors who work in them are summarized next.

Private Practice

The term *private practice* implies that a trained counselor, who may have taken additional coursework related to career development, has chosen to form a company, market career development services, and identify clients who can and are willing to pay for services. Such a person would likely rent facilities or work from home and acquire clients through such approaches as newspaper ads, a Web site, listing in the Yellow Pages, referrals, and word of mouth. Alexa, for example, found out about the services of a career counselor in private practice from her high school counselor.

Because this professional focuses his or her services on career concerns, clients are likely to state a career problem as the reason for seeking assistance. It may be stated as a need to find a different job (because of recent loss of a job or dissatisfaction with a current one), as a desire to get additional training in order to have new skills to use in a different kind of job, or as desire to analyze the reasons why a recent potential for promotion has not been realized. It is rare, however, that the presenting problem is the only problem that needs to be addressed in the counseling sessions because a career choice or change issue is likely to affect other life roles, such as spouse and parent. Further, the career problem presented may be affected by other problems, such as drug abuse, alcoholism, inability to sustain relationships, or poor self-concept. Thus, it is impossible to speak of "career counseling" with adults in community settings as purely related to career choices; presenting problems are almost inevitably entwined with a host of others.

At Alexa's first visit to a career counselor in private practice, she indicated that she was bored with her work as an accountant and was seeking assistance in identifying a different occupation, one in which she could work with people instead of numbers. As her story unfolded, however, she revealed that her father was a prominent figure in her life and that he had continually encouraged her to become an accountant despite her lack of interest in detail. He thought that it was a high-paying occupation for a woman, one without significant emotional or physical stress. Through interviewing and assessment, the counselor helped Alexa to become aware of her interests and values related to working with people in some way. She also assisted Alexa to delve deeply into her relationship with her father and the reasons she was still letting his influence affect major decisions in her life.

Alexa decided that she did not want to spend significant time in retraining because she had purchased a home and established a lifestyle that required continuation of her present level of income. Further, she realized that it would be very difficult for her to go against her father's wishes and advice about her occupational choice. Thus, the counselor suggested that Alexa explore other occupations related to accounting that would give her more opportunity to work with people on a face-to-face basis. After using print resources and Web sites to gather information about such specialties, Alexa had several information interviews with accountants who worked in entirely different settings—helping people with financial planning, providing service to professionals about retirement plans and options, and teaching accounting in a community college. This experience gave her perspectives on how she could use her accounting background in ways she had never thought of before, and she terminated her relationship with the counselor with a 1-year action plan.

Career counselors in private practice typically work with their clients on a one-to-one basis through a sequence of interviews. As in other one-to-one settings, the counselor is likely to begin the sequence by assessing the client's needs and barriers, establishing goals with the client for the counseling relationship, working with the client to reach those goals, and ultimately terminating when the two agree that goals have been reached or that further work together will not be beneficial.

As in other settings, private practitioners, in addition to skilled interviewing, use the tools of assessment, technology (computer-based systems and Web sites), career information, referral, and advocacy to assist their clients to meet established goals. Their services may be short term, as would be the case if the goals are to write an effective resumé, practice job interviewing, identify desirable job openings, and get a job. Conversely, the services may be long term, as would be the case if there are underlying problems of dysfunctional career beliefs, poor self-concept, drug abuse, or role conflict.

Counselors who work as private practitioners should have at least a master's degree in counseling with additional coursework in career development theory and practice. Many have doctorates and, through this additional study, have been able to acquire more background in career development theory than a master's degree counselor would have. They may and should be National Certified Counselors (NCCs) and preferably National Certified Career Counselors (NCCC). Unfortunately, the latter certification has been discontinued. However, the NCDA has established categories of membership that can be helpful to the consumer; those who qualify by educational background and experience to hold NCDA membership as a Master Career Counselor are likely to have the theoretical underpinnings and experience to work as private practitioners. In addition to these academic and experiential qualifications, counselors in private practice need business skills in order to market their services and do the financial accounting required of small businesses. Further, as suggested in an earlier section, they may need additional skills in coordination, consultation, advocacy, and case management.

The World Wide Web: Cybercounseling

The year 2000 signaled the beginning of counseling services via the Internet. To date, these services are being offered by certified counselors who are working from their homes or offices. Their clients are self-selected on the Internet, and provision of service is brokered through a Web site that has the appropriate infrastructure to handle synchronous (both the client and the counselor are at a computer at the same time) text-based or video-based communication, appointment scheduling, and billing. Though initial sets of ethical guidelines have been developed by professional associations (described in Chapter 7), there are many unknowns about this form of counseling at this time. These relate to lack of knowledge about the types of clients and issues that may be addressed in this way, how to know when to refer clients for face-to-face counseling, and what counselor characteristics may predict counselor satisfaction and effectiveness in this mode of intervention. It appears, however, that cybercounseling may become a specialized version of private practice in the 21st century.

Mental Health Centers

Funded by both public and private funds, community mental health centers assist citizens, regardless of their ability to pay, with concerns that may affect the quality of their lives and the community. These concerns include career-related problems. A major goal of mental health centers is early intervention in an attempt to alleviate problems before they have greater impact on the individual and the community. Services for clients include individual counseling, assessment, referral, career information, skill-building, and perhaps job placement. Counselors use the techniques of group and individual counseling, instruction, consultation, referral, and advocacy.

The problems encountered and approaches used do not vary significantly from those encountered and used by a career counselor in private practice. A counselor in this setting may have a larger caseload than in private practice; spend less time per client; have the advantages of a wider network for consultation and referral; and have reduced responsibility related to promotion, marketing, and management.

Substance Abuse Centers

Counselors in substance abuse center settings work with clients who have come voluntarily or have been referred by other organizations, including the courts. The centers may be located in hospitals, in a community mental health center, or in a separate organization. Typical services include individual and group counseling, support groups, educational programs about substance abuse, career counseling and assessment, referral for acquisition of job skills, and perhaps job placement. There may also be follow-through with employers for a period of time for the purpose of assisting substance abuse offenders to develop job-keeping skills.

Rehabilitation Settings

Rehabilitation counselors deal with a variety of client concerns, including career counseling and job placement. They have specialized training and certification because of the additional knowledge and competency they need in addition to those of counselors in all settings.

The Division of Vocational Rehabilitation (DVR) is a government agency whose mission is to remove the barriers to satisfying and productive work that exist for persons with disabilities. Any person with a physical or mental disability that could affect employability may be eligible for the services of DVR. These services include counseling, vocational assessment, vocational training, on-the-job training, work adjustment training, funding for postsecondary education, job site modification, and purchase of equipment or technological devices that will assist the disabled person to perform work duties and maintain employment. Many rehabilitation counselors are employed in the nationwide network of offices of the DVR. Others are employed by private rehabilitation facilities.

Counselors who work with disabled persons use the same techniques and tools as other career counselors—including interviewing, assessment, career information, and technology—in assisting their clients. Because of their disabilities, clients are likely to have a restricted number of career options, need a high level of support in accomplishing action plans, and need counseling in areas such as self-concept and self-efficacy as well as career counseling. Further, counselors working with this population will use coordinating, consulting, advocacy, and case-management skills at a high level in helping their clients with job readiness and placement.

Corrections and Probation

The pendulum swings from time to time with regard to public opinion about the services that offenders and ex-offenders should receive. Currently, given the known relationship between getting and keeping a job upon release and recidivism, there is emphasis from the federal level on providing career planning and job-placement services to offenders. These services are designed to contribute to offenders' capability to select, be trained for, and enter jobs in keeping with their interests and/or skills and to know how to retain those jobs.

The range of services available to offenders and the resources available to deliver them are limited. Work tasks in this setting include one-to-one interviewing, group instruction about career-related concerns, assessment, provision of career information, and job placement. This is a particularly difficult setting in which to work because the nature of the helping relationship, as traditionally defined by counselors, has to be substantially modified and, further, counselors can feel a continual pull between the client's needs and the needs of the prison and the larger society. Goals for career services in correctional facilities are also limited. They focus on acquiring some type of job training, getting a job, and being able to keep the job.

Military Settings

Civilian counselors are common on military bases, and they work both with military personnel and members of their families. Counselors may engage in assessment, educational advisement, individual counseling related to career and personal issues, and referrals. In recent years, because of the significant downsizing of the military, counselors in this setting have focused on assisting military personnel with the transition from military to civilian occupations for which they have transferable skills and on the use of funding available to them to acquire additional education.

Job Service Offices and One-Stop Centers

The U.S. Employment Service has offices in communities and cities nationwide. The purpose of these publicly funded agencies is to serve both employers and clients. The Job Service offices cultivate and maintain a positive relationship with employers so that job openings can be made available to clients. They offer services to individuals to assist them with career choice and placement in jobs. Thus, counselors in Job Service offices are instrumental in the labor market exchange, that is, helping employers to find the workers they need and helping workers to find the employers they desire. Under the Clinton administration, the one-stop center was conceptualized and implemented. These centers combine the usual services of a job-service office with other government services, such as application for and receipt of unemployment insurance, so that there can be better integration between these government functions.

Counselors in these settings provide assessment for clients, hold individual interviews to assist them with career or job choice, communicate with employers about job openings and their requirements, and work with a variety of referral agencies. Because databases of job openings have been developed by each state and integrated as a national data bank (called America's Job Bank), counselors in these settings are likely to be involved in encouraging and assisting employers to enter job openings into this database and in helping clients know how to search it and follow through with job interviews. They also contact employers to set up job interviews with clients. They may teach clients the skills needed to find, acquire, and hold a job—such as what employers expect of employees, job-seeking skills, resumé writing, and job interviewing. Because of the accountability required of such offices, they are likely to spend time in case management and reporting functions.

Corporations and Other Organizations

Many organizations—such as the World Bank and the Federal Deposit Insurance Corporation—as well as private corporations, hire career counselors. They are typically housed in a facility that includes a well-furnished career center. Typical centers include the opportunity for individual career counseling, assessment, use of the Internet or software, and group instruction.

Career counselors working in such settings deal with concerns related to career mobility within the organization or plans to move out of the organization in the case of downsizing. They may offer workshops on topics such as keeping one's resumé updated, how to facilitate one's promotion, or how to profit from mentoring. They may also deal with plans for upgrading skills or acquiring new skills and with issues related to conflicts between supervisors and employees or between employees. Their job descriptions may also include the provision of counseling services that are unrelated to career progression.

In these diverse settings, fees for service may be nonexistent to clients, shared by clients in proportion to their ability to pay, or may be at full rate per session. For some clients in some settings (such as mental health agencies and private practice), the counselor may receive third-party payment, the counselor's services having been approved for coverage under an insurance plan.

SUMMARY

This chapter has addressed the specialty of community-based career counseling that is practiced in a variety of noneducational settings. Not only is the setting for this career counseling specialty different from that of others, but the client characteristics, reasons for intervention, and the roles and functions of the counselor may also be different. Clients are typically adults who face career choice problems as a part of a much larger complex of issues and thus do not have as many options available to them as students do.

Intervention may be the free choice of individuals or may be forced due to lay-offs, legislation, or some life event. Counselor functions extend beyond counseling to coordination, consultation, advocacy, and case management. Further, the counselor providing career assistance may work as part of a team that includes psychologists, social workers, medical specialists, and career development facilitators.

REFERENCES

Dougherty, A. M. (1990). *Consultation: Practice and perspectives*. Pacific Grove, CA: Brooks/Cole.

Hershenson, D. B., Power, P. W., & Waldo, M. (1996). *Community counseling: Contemporary theory and practice*. Boston: Allyn & Bacon.

Schlossberg, N. K. (1989). *Overwhelmed: Coping with life's ups and downs*. Lexington, KY: Lexington Press.

Special Issue: Career Counseling in the Next Decade, *The Career Development Quarterly, 52*(1), 89. Retrieved May 11, 2004 from http://www.bartlyeby.com/59/10/churchill.win.html.

CHAPTER 14

ETHICAL ISSUES IN CAREER DEVELOPMENT INTERVENTIONS

Though not always evident and at the ready point of recognition, ethics is a constant of our daily lives. Frequently unconscious or professionally intuitive, some aspects of ethical decision making are readily evident and require careful attention and deliberation by all people. Vigilant adherence and commitment to ethics, ethical standards, and ethical principles are hallmarks of all professions, and all professionals are ethically accountable and liable. It may surprise many counselors and counselor educators to see the universality of many ethical principles manifest in ethical standards for professions as varied as computer associations, multinational corporations, and the U.S. military. Ethical principles common to the ethical standards of many professions center on respect for human beings; respect for privacy, accountability, responsibility, and truth; and crediting one's sources, among other principles.

Typically in counselor preparation and practice, ethics and ethical standards and principles are considered along with legal principles and practices, yet ethics is different from law in terms of the origins of ethics in philosophy and in terms of legality being far more explicitly definitive than ethics. In law, there is close attention to legal precedent and nuance refining principles of justice in guiding legal behavior and adjudication of perceived illegalities. In ethics, there is attention to more general ethical standards and principles guiding ethical practice and adjudication. In the history of mental health professions, ethical principles and standards frequently are at risk of being lost in attention to the negative reinforcers of law and legal rules for practice. In fact, there is healthy room for attention and adherence to law and ethics, and this chapter does both with some enlightening points of view and examples.

Probably the most vital aspect of ethics in counselor preparation is close and deliberate attention to, and discussion of, ethics, ethical issues, and ethical standards within the quiet calm of a noncrisis classroom environment. Though one might typically think of legal and ethical standards as negative reinforcers highlighting what to avoid, a closer look at ethical standards and principles might help one see the fuller context of ethics as inspiring and empowering. One might sense this uplifting aspect of ethics in the preamble to the American Counseling Association's Ethical Standards, noting counselors' dedication to human worth, dignity, uniqueness, and potential and similar perspectives at points in the Ethical Standards of the American Psychological Association. Finally, as one notes that standards are minimal, the least one must do, counselors and aspiring counselors can begin to ponder and commit to maxima, to aspirational standards focused on the most one can ethically do for one's client.

With these thoughts in mind, welcome to a chapter of considerable breadth and depth and welcome to what may be new perspectives in professional growth for readers of this text. Readers should find much to ponder and much potential for growth. Read, learn, ponder, and enjoy.

Dennis Engels, Ph.D., LPC, NCC, NCCC
Regents Professor
Counseling Program
University of North Texas

The authors of this text, like others who teach and work in the area of career counseling, often deal with questions or statements that suggest that career counseling is not "real" counseling and question whether professional concepts such as ethical standards apply to those who are involved in career development interventions. We believe that all professional counselors are subject to ethical standards. Likewise, those who work for or who are employed or supervised by professional counselors in providing career services must be aware of and in most instances adhere to the same standards. As you know by now, we also view career counseling as "real" counseling that is quite central to a person's life. This chapter is our attempt to provide an orientation to the ethical standards of the counseling profession with emphasis and examples relevant for those who are involved in career interventions. Ethical, professional behavior requires adherence to applicable laws and regulations and in some instances we will suggest that those faced with certain dilemmas seek not only ethical consultation from a supervisor or respected colleague but also seek legal advice. Before we begin our exploration of ethical issues, however, we would like you to meet a counselee, José.

José, a 16-year-old student in the ninth grade, was asked to come into the school counselor's office to review his interest inventory results (the inventory had been administered to all ninth-grade students). José's academic record throughout his school years has been mixed. He had been held back twice in elementary school and was often absent from school. His absences were mostly the result of José working with his father in the fields during harvest season. Lately, he had shown some interest in developing his career plans. A frequent computer user, José had gone online at the local library to explore career options in the computer field. He found a Web site that offered free "vocational aptitude testing." He took the test and was excited that the results seemed to suggest that he had the aptitude necessary for working as a computer programmer. He was eager to receive the information about becoming a computer programmer that the Web site

---

This chapter was co-authored by Robert H. Pate, Jr.

offered to send everyone who took the online test. José was not sure what a computer programmer's job involved, but he knew that he loved playing computer games.

José's father was "dead set against" this type of work. A blue-collar worker all his life with no computer experience and only a ninth-grade education, José's father felt strongly that José should acquire training in a more traditional trade, such as carpentry. José's grandfather had been a carpenter in his home country, Guatemala. When the family relocated to the southeastern United States, the only work José's father could acquire was in agriculture. He thought that he had not been given serious consideration for a number of jobs for which he was qualified due to being Guatemalan. His father thought that becoming a carpenter would be in line with the family tradition and would provide an income that would be sufficient for raising a family (something that was a constant struggle for José's father). José told his counselor that his father wanted to speak with the counselor about José attending vocational school. His father was also interested in exploring options that José might have in the military. In fact, he wanted José to meet with military recruiters when they visited José's school. José had no interest in becoming a carpenter and was not enthusiastic about the prospect of military service.

The counselor had several concerns about José's situation. For example, the counselor was concerned about the quality of the online test José had taken. The counselor was also uneasy about "bursting José's bubble" and deflating the interest José had shown in making career plans. However, the results of the interest inventory administered at school gave no indication that José had high interest in computer-related occupations. His interests were more focused on artistic and helping occupations. The counselor was also anxious about the strong, clear vision José's father had for what occupation and career path José would choose. The counselor wondered whether José's father's encounter with discriminatory hiring practices influenced the career goals he had identified for his son. Finally, the counselor was reluctant to encourage José to meet with the military recruiters but was not sure how to communicate this reluctance to José's father.

You may remember that when we introduced José, his counselor was introduced as a school counselor and not a career counselor. Yet his presenting concern was certainly career related if not career counseling per se. A number of ethical issues and concerns are apparent in the brief scenario. A positive outcome of an increased awareness of ethical and legal concerns that affect counseling practice is that professional counselors have become increasingly concerned with ethical issues in interventions. For example, José presents a variety of ethical issues that would probably never have been identified as ethical concerns 20 years ago. Counselors today would be concerned about some of the ethical questions embedded in José's case: the quality of the assessment he took online and even whether the assessment instrument the counselor administered to José was appropriate for a person from José's background, the ethics of the online service suggesting a specific career option as if it were the result of career counseling rather than a blatant marketing ploy, the ethical dilemma confronting the school counselor regarding José's father's wishes and José's wishes, and the always-present ethical issue of the counselor's competence in dealing with the concerns and issues presented by José.

These are complex issues. To help career practitioners practice ethically, professional columns, publications, and workshops on ethics abound. Despite the increased attention to ethical practice in career services delivery, there are no clear answers to many career practitioners' most difficult questions about proper practice. Given the frequency of litigation in the helping professions, it is perplexing that career development textbooks, at best, pay minimal attention to ethical issues confronting career practitioners. Thus, in this chapter we hope to heighten the awareness of career counselors to ethical issues and provide guidance for career development practitioners as they consider ethical issues. Because readers will have varied backgrounds in the ethical concepts that affect career counselors, we offer a primer on basic principles.

A good starting point for addressing ethical issues in career development interventions is to consider the following question: How can it be that career practitioners have multiple ethics codes to guide their practice and yet ethical violations continue? Even when practitioners are well trained and conscientious, situations can arise in which determining proper practice is a complex task. The following chart provides a useful framework for examining behaviors within the career counseling relationship.[1] This matrix can be used to classify career practitioners' behaviors into one of four categories.

Ethical and Legal	Unethical and Legal
Ethical and Illegal	Unethical and Illegal

The obvious goal for career practitioners is to function ethically and legally and to avoid any activity that would be acknowledged as illegal and/or unethical. Although this goal seems straightforward, there are instances in which achieving this goal is not so simple. A career client might disclose his or her frustration with an unsuccessful job search by saying, "I was so upset over my layoff that when my daughter asked me a question I snapped and hit her. I have never done anything like that before." Some career counselors would suggest an ethical (and legal) obligation to report the possible child abuse. Others might cite the circumstances of one episode without evidence of harm and the primacy of client confidentiality as a reason to oppose reporting. Some career counselors would consider including in the initial discussion of counseling expectations a counselor's "Miranda warning" about the limits of confidentiality and required disclosures as part of informed consent—off-putting at best and demeaning to clients at worst. However, without such an orientation to the limits of confidentiality, the counselor who received the information might be reluctant to even consider reporting it.

Ethical issues can arise in which practices common outside the professional career counseling relationship deviate from what is ethically appropriate in career counseling. For example, a business relationship between a career counselor and a client is considered unethical because it constitutes a dual relationship that could

---

[1]Because we have seen this chart attributed to various authors, and thus its origin is somewhat ambiguous, we simply acknowledge that the concept of this 2×2 matrix is not ours.

impair the counselor's objectivity. A career counselor helping a friend, relative, or the child of a friend may have objectivity strained just as would occur for any other professional, yet the recognition is not so apparent to the person who asks for "a small personal favor." For example, if in the earlier scenario José's father and José's counselor were friends, then how should the counselor proceed to help José in this instance? The situation could become even more complicated if José's counselor were the only counselor in José's high school.

Career practitioners are also likely to face dilemmas that could be labeled as "business ethics." Examples of such dilemmas are when clients ask career counselors questions concerning how much to tell potential employers about other job options they have or how to deal with multiple offers. Likewise, potential employers can ask the career counselors about their clients. Counselors who work in settings that have a placement function often deal with inquiries from potential employers of their clients. The career counselor, in ways not so common in other types of counseling, is often asked to assist clients in dealing with workplace issues such as unethical behavior on the part of supervisors, sexual harassment, and unfair hiring and promotion practices. Career counselors might have access to nonpublic information that might be used unethically. For example, should a placement counselor tell a client that they overheard a recruiter say the client was the top choice for a position? What about information that might lead to a financial gain to the counselor, such as information about the plans of a business that might have implications for noncounseling-related investments of the counselor? Career counselors often need guidance in dealing with ethical situations that are not covered in current ethical codes.

Chapters and sections of chapters throughout this text recognize the role of school counselors in developmental career interventions for both individuals and groups. There is one area of ethical concern that troubles many secondary school counselors that we believe deserves special mention. That is the role of the secondary school counselor in assisting students with determining appropriate educational and/or training plans and the role of the same counselor as a provider of recommendations for their counselees to the institutions at which they might pursue postsecondary education. Many colleges have a specific expectation that secondary school counselors provide a recommendation for applicants. The simultaneous role of helping the students determine an appropriate institution and providing a recommendation to the institution could be considered a dual relationship. These issues are complicated by the role of parents who, in addition to sometimes expecting counselors to help them realize their hopes and dreams for their children's' educational and career plans, often want to review recommendations written for college admission. There are complex ethical and legal issues involved in such activities and we advise school counselors to become well versed in their school system's policies pertaining to student records and recommendations, and to become familiar with the provisions of the Family Educational Rights and Privacy Act (1974). The National Association for College Admissions Counseling (NACAC) has produced a *Statement of Principles of Good Practice* (2001). We suggest that secondary school counselors who provide required recommendations for their students study the statement and consult with supervisors, and when necessary with the legal advisor for their school, when questions and issues arise.

Though studying the ACA's 1995 *Code of Ethics and Standards of Practice* and the NCDA's 2003 *Ethical Standards* is important and effective for the career counselor, more is needed. That "more" is an understanding of the bases and intention of the standards. It is not possible for an ethical code or standard to provide an unambiguous answer to every potential ethical question. There will inevitably be occasions when career counselors will need the assistance of trusted professional colleagues to provide an assessment of the proper action in response to an ethical dilemma. Thus, a useful rule of thumb for career practitioners is to consult with professional colleagues who understand career interventions whenever they are unsure about the proper action to take to resolve an ethical dilemma.

ETHICAL DILEMMAS VERSUS MORAL TEMPTATIONS

Clearly, resolving ethical dilemmas can be a complex task for career counselors. It is important to note, however, that not all issues involving ethics or proper behaviors deserve the title "dilemma." Kidder (1995) contends that an ethical dilemma occurs only in instances in which there are competing "rights" or there is a struggle to determine the "least bad" course of action. Instead of dilemmas, Kidder labels situations in which the struggle is between right and wrong as *moral temptations*. Unfortunately, some career counselors struggle with moral temptations and may take actions that most peers would categorize as unethical.

For example, a career counselor might become interested in a noncounseling business or personal relationship with a client and be tempted to prematurely end a formal career counseling relationship to start the "clock" or deny that a relationship was counseling. The involved counselor might not be the best judge of whether the relationship meets the ethical standards to change from a career counseling to a personal relationship. Attempting to judge the propriety of one's own actions might be the ultimate dual relationship.

Sometimes the career practitioner faces choices between actions that may help the client but have some risk to the counselor. For example, both the ACA (1995) and American Psychological Association (APA) (1992) ethics statements address the topic of bartering (as a means of paying for services) as a specific of dual relationships and discourage the practice. Many bartering relationships begin innocently, and bartering may even be based on the career counselor's desire to provide a way for a client to invest in counseling and be motivated by clinical, rather than financial, reasons. However, if problems develop in either the counseling or the bartering aspect of the relationship, the potential for the client to raise ethical issues *ex post facto* exists.

To guide career development practitioners in resolving ethical dilemmas, we will review the principles on which ethical codes are based. We will then examine the basic ethical concepts included in all counseling ethical codes. It is important to again note, however, that no ethics code and certainly no book chapter can provide answers to all the questions that will arise in the delivery of career services. The following excerpt from the "Purpose" section National Association of Social Workers (NASW) Code of Ethics (1999) reinforces this point:

> A code of ethics cannot guarantee ethical behavior. Moreover, a code of ethics cannot resolve all ethical issues or disputes, or capture the richness and complexity involved in striving to make responsible choices within a moral community. Rather a code of ethics sets forth values, ethical principles, and ethical standards to which professionals aspire and by which their actions can be judged. (p. 2)

The ethical codes require all career counselors who believe an ethical violation has occurred to take action, and the NCDA *Ethical Standards* (2003) cite the *ACA Code of Ethics and Standards of Practice* (1995) as a source of guidance. We hope that your exploration of the topic will heighten your awareness of potential ethical problems and the multiple considerations involved in addressing those problems.

USING PRINCIPLES TO RESOLVE ETHICAL DECISIONS

VanHoose (1986) observed that "ethical principles provide a more solid framework for decision making than do ethical codes or statutes" (p. 168). VanHoose recommended that counselors use the five principles, listed next, upon which the ACA *Code of Ethics and Standards of Practice* (1995) is based, to guide their professional practice.

1. *Autonomy* is the principle that requires counselors to promote client independence and self-determination. Under this principle, counselors respect the freedom of clients to choose their own directions, make their own choices, and control their own lives. Counselors have an ethical obligation to decrease client dependency and foster independent decision making. Counselors refrain from imposing goals, avoid being judgmental, and are accepting of different values.
2. *Nonmaleficence* requires that counselors do no harm. Counselors must take care that their actions do not risk hurting clients, even inadvertently. Counselors have a responsibility to avoid engaging in practices that cause harm or have the potential to result in harm.
3. *Beneficence* requires counselors to promote good, or mental health and wellness. This principle mandates that counselors actively promote the growth and welfare of those they serve.
4. *Justice* is the foundation of counselors' commitment to fairness in professional relationships. The principle of justice includes consideration of such factors as quality of services, allocation of time and resources, establishment of fees, and access to counseling services. This principle also refers to the fair treatment of an individual when his or her interests need to be considered in the context of the rights and interests of others. Many view this principle as the most difficult to consistently apply.
5. *Fidelity* means counselors make honest promises and honor their commitments to clients, students, and supervisees. This principle involves creating a trusting and therapeutic climate in which people can search for their own solutions and taking care not to deceive or exploit clients. (Herlihy & Corey, 1996, pp. 4–5)

The ACA principles are similar to those suggested by Beauchamp and Childress (2001) in their classic text on medical ethics. They identified the following additional principles as relevant for professional-patient relationships:

1. *Veracity:* Tell the truth and do not lie or deceive others.
2. *Privacy:* Allow individuals to limit access to information about themselves.
3. *Confidentiality:* Allow individuals to control access to information they have shared.

Collectively, the ACA principles and those offered by Beauchamp and Childress (2001), including their suggestions for professional-patient relationships, provide guidelines for ethical behavior in career services. When questions arise pertaining to proper practice, these principles can be used to help career development practitioners identify appropriate behaviors. Career counselors should feel especially comfortable with the principles of autonomy and beneficence because they represent the hallmarks of career counseling at its best. Finally, it is worth noting that despite the various purposes and audiences to which ethical codes and principles are addressed, ethical codes and statements for psychologically based helping professions are remarkably similar. However, some ethical questions and decisions related to career interventions cannot be easily resolved by reference to ethical codes that were written to address interventions that were likely to be therapeutic in nature. Some of those issues in career interventions have their basis in values.

THE ROLE OF VALUES IN DEFINING CAREER DEVELOPMENT INTERVENTIONS

Values assumptions underlie all questions (and answers) related to ethical behavior in career development interventions. Values assumptions are particularly relevant regarding the counselor's and client's understanding, and definition, of the career counseling relationship. Bergin (1985) suggests, "values are orienting beliefs about what is good for the clients and how that good should be achieved" (p. 99). As such, value issues permeate the career development intervention process. Any intervention in the lifespace or lifestyle of people carries with it values implications (London, 1964). The need for practitioners to clearly understand their own values represents an essential starting point for career service delivery and is an ethical issue within career services. Because value-free career interventions do not exist, career practitioners must be cognizant of how their personal values influence their work with clients.

Tjeltveit (1986, pp. 515–537) suggests the following strategies for minimizing the likelihood of counselors behaving in ways that are insensitive to clients' values:

1. Become informed about the variety of values held in society.
2. Be aware of your own values.
3. Present value options to clients in an unbiased manner.
4. Be committed to client's freedom of choice.
5. Respect clients with values that differ from your own.
6. Consult with others when necessary.
7. Consider referring clients to another counselor when substantial moral, religious, or political value differences exist.

When career practitioners incorporate Tjeltveit's strategies into their daily practice, they go a long way toward ensuring that their interventions will be ethical. Career counselors must constantly monitor their own values and how those values affect their career interventions.

Tjeltveit's suggestions to consult with professional colleagues and to refer clients to more appropriate service providers when necessary also apply to instances in which the client's concerns extend beyond the traditional issues of clarifying, specifying, and implementing a career choice. For example, it is increasingly evident that adults in career transition experience ego dystonic emotions that must be addressed within the career counseling process (Anderson & Niles, 1995; Subich, 1993). When clients' concerns include depressive feelings, low self-esteem, low self-efficacy, and so on, career practitioners need to evaluate whether they are competent to address such issues. In this regard, Niles and Pate (1989) argue that a career practitioner must, at the minimum, be able to identify mental health issues presented by a client. Once such issues are identified, the career practitioner must determine whether it is appropriate to refer the client to a mental health practitioner (if the career practitioner does not feel competent to deal with these issues a referral is the ethical decision) or address the client's mental health issues within the context of career counseling.

The ACA *Ethical Code and Standards of Practice* (1995) requires that counseling including career development interventions also requires counselors to be aware of the client's values and the values embedded in career development intervention models. Each of these value sets (i.e., the counselor's, the client's, and the values embedded in interventions) interacts. Personal values influence such dynamics as the client behaviors the practitioner attends to in the career counseling process and the intervention strategies selected by the practitioner. Career practitioners communicate personal values through nonverbal and verbal behavior. Thus, the counselor's values can inadvertently influence the client's behavior. For example, if a client seeks to earn the counselor's approval, the client may opt for career options that the client perceives will please the counselor and disregard other factors in the career decision making process. In such instances, career practitioners can unknowingly convert clients to the counselor's values.

Herr and Niles (1988) point out that beyond being sensitive to personal values, the client's values, and the values embedded within career interventions models, counselors need to be cognizant of the values being propagated at the national level. For example, in comparing the evolution of career development theories in Britain and the United States, Watts, Super, and Kidd (1981) observed the following:

> It is intriguing that theories of career development in the USA have been so heavily dominated by psychologists. . . . The dominant focus in the USA has been on the actions of individuals, while in Britain, indigenous theoretical work has been more preoccupied with the constraints of social structures. . . . From the beginning of its independent existence, the USA has been formally committed to the proposition that all people are created equal. As a result, there is the belief that the individual controls his or her own destiny; that with appropriate abilities and with the appropriate development of the appropriate abilities, one's fate lies in one's own hands. (p. 3)

Referring to counseling and psychotherapy, Herr and Niles (1988) noted that:

> Western therapies have a particular way of looking at and processing human behavior; Eastern therapies have a different way of defining such behavior and planning interventions. One is not a substitute for the other because value sets, assumptions, and cultural artifacts make some forms of counseling and psychotherapy unacceptable or ineffective in cultures different from those in which such interventions were invented. (p. 14)

Career intervention models based on European American values emphasizing individualism do not mesh with family expectations or traditions found in societies in which group decisions are the norm and the family is the principle arbiter of appropriate occupational choices. Thus, a career practitioner adhering to European American career intervention models steeped in individual action runs the risk of violating clients' values when those values reflect a collectivistic orientation. An illustration of this point is provided by the career counseling case of Kenji.

Having recently relocated to the United States from China, Kenji came to the guidance office during his senior year in high school with the concern of whether poor performance in his physics and math courses would prevent him from being able to major in engineering in college. In the course of meeting with Kenji, it became obvious to the counselor that although his concerns were projected toward a college major in engineering, his interests and abilities pointed toward a program of study in a nonscience area. In fact, he had failed physics and just barely passed several math courses. He thoroughly enjoyed the social sciences and had performed well in classes related to this area. When asked to discuss his tentative decision to pursue a college major in engineering, it quickly became apparent that his decision was based on the plans his father had made for him. When asked about the appropriateness of this goal, given his prior academic performance and his interests, it was clear that Kenji was not about to enlarge the range of options under consideration.

A counselor who believes Kenji should adhere to the need for students to develop traditional European American career development values of individual action and an internal locus of control may decide to use a counseling strategy that would challenge Kenji's tendency to adhere to the wishes of others (his father in this case) in his career decision making. The projected treatment plan may even include assertiveness training with the goal of having Kenji confront his father about his career development goals. Unfortunately, this type of career counseling strategy is not sensitive to Kenji's culture of origin in which it is not uncommon for fathers to dominate the career decision making of their sons. Any attempts at influencing the career direction of Kenji would need to be sensitive to this very important cultural dynamic. (Interestingly, after the case of Kenji was developed from a composite of the authors' experiences, one of the authors discovered a novel with a plot strikingly similar in many ways to the case [Lee, 1994]. We believe the case of Kenji is based on experiences that are, unfortunately, too common.)

The case of José, presented at the beginning of this chapter, also illustrates the potential for value conflicts between the counselor, José's family, and José. If José has become acculturated into European American values of individualistic action, but his father maintains a collectivistic orientation toward José's career development, then, as with Kenji, the counselor will need to be sensitive to these culturally based values interactions. Such value conflicts illustrate that career development practitioners must be sensitive to the interaction between their personal values, the values prized by the client, and the value sets embedded within specific career counseling models. The latter often reflect the values propagated at the national level.

Because career development interventions promote specific values, national governments vary in their support and expectations of career interventions. Super (1983) notes that countries that are relatively prosperous and free from the threat of outside interventions tend to view career development interventions as vehicles for fostering the individual's abilities, personal values, and interests. Conversely, countries experiencing economic hardships or the possible threat of outside intervention tend to view career development interventions as vehicles for channeling people into occupations deemed as being crucial for national survival. In the United States, *Sputnik* provides an example of the latter. Feeling threatened by the apparent superiority of Soviet space technology in the late 1950s, the U.S. government focused funding and legislative efforts on directing young people into science-related occupations. More recently, the shifting winds of the political climate in the United States have resulted in funding support at the national level moving from school-to-work initiatives to welfare-to-work programs. Often, career development programs, initiatives, and interventions "follow the money" or the financial support that government provides for such initiatives.

In summary, avoiding unethical practice in career development interventions requires career development practitioners to be sensitive to the assumptions underlying their personal values, their clients' values, career interventions models, and the values being propagated at the national level at any point in time (Herr & Niles, 1988). Practicing only within one's area of training and competence is an additional requirement for ethical practice in the career development intervention process. Again, we offer the suggestion of consultation with professional colleagues because counselors may need to help to objectively judge their competence. When career practitioners possess value awareness, use ethical principles in their professional decision making, and adhere to the relevant ethical codes, they increase the likelihood that they will function ethically in providing career development interventions to their clients.

Using ethical codes

Many believe that there are too many ethical codes and that we should move toward a unified ethics code for the counseling profession (Herlihy & Remley, 1995). Most readers of this chapter are, or will be, subject to the ethical codes of the American Counseling Association (1995), the National Career Development Association (2003), the American Psychological Association (1992), the International Association of Educational and Vocational Guidance (1996), and/or the National Board for Certified Counselors (1997a, 1997b).

We agree with the position that too many ethical codes exist and hope that at some future time the counseling profession will move toward a model of a single ethics code with annotations or appendices for special situations and areas of practice. However, we doubt that the multiple codes themselves are the source of ethics violations. There are many situations that are unique to specialized areas of counseling practice such as career counseling. There are three areas for which we find current ethical codes inadequate to provide direction for career counselors: the definition of a career counseling relationship, given the fact that not all career interventions constitute therapy; ethical standards for the appropriate and proper role of those who provide career services but are not professionally trained counselors; and the ethical use of the Internet to provide or enhance services. These three areas demand greater attention in professional training and workshops. They also raise important questions that must be addressed by the profession.

Ethical Challenges Facing Career Counselors

This section explores three issues facing career counselors. The issues are: whether all career interventions are counseling relationships; the proper role of those with training and experience in career interventions but who do not have the training, education, and experience accepted as essential for one to be a professional counselor; and the proper use of Internet technology in career interventions. We have acknowledged that we consider current ethical codes lacking in adequate guidance for career counselors in these areas and offer suggestions about needed clarifications.

Are All Individual Career Interventions Counseling?

Another area of continuing ethical concern is personal relationships with clients. Confidentiality, counseling relationships, professional responsibility, and relationships with other professionals consistently rank at the top of the list of inquiries received by the American Counseling Association (ACA) Ethics Committee (Williams & Freeman, 2002). Some ethical requirements are clear and unambiguous. For example, sexual relationships between career counselors and their clients are unethical. The ethical requirement is clear and unambiguous. However, situations exist in which the expected ethical behavior is not so clearly defined. For example, the psychologically based helping professions are not uniform in their view of how much time must elapse before a "helper" might make a case that an intimate relationship with a former client was not exploitative. The ethical issues for career counselors are sometimes complicated by ethical codes that are written based on an assumption that all career counselors' work is counseling involving a therapeutic relationship that might involve transference and countertransference. The authors of this chapter believe that career counselors are professional counselors with specialized education and experience in career interventions (Niles & Pate, 1989). However, many questions can and do arise about the nature of helping relationships that focus on career issues. Career counselors in and outside educational settings provide services that are typically not considered therapy. For example, consider the case of a counselor in a university career center who reviews a resumé for a student of the same age. Some weeks later they meet at a social event and begin a social relationship. Is that relationship subject to the same ethical scrutiny as a relationship that involved multiple sessions of counseling in a university counseling center and complex career issues? Reasonable professionals might offer different answers.

Additional complications in determining proper action can arise because the specific requirements of many laws governing counselor behavior are far from clear, and the standards of practice incorporated in the regulations of many states are inconsistent with the ethical codes they resemble. For example, the regulations of the Commonwealth of Virginia Board of Counselors and Marriage and Family Therapists (2000) contain a standards of practice section. Included in that section is a statement about sexual relationships, which states:

> Engaging in sexual intimacies with current clients or residents (i.e., counselors under licensure supervision) is strictly prohibited. For at least five years after cessation or termination of professional services, licensees shall not engage in sexual intimacies with a therapy [emphasis added] client or those included in collateral therapeutic services. Since sexual or romantic relationships are potentially exploitative, licensees shall bear the burden of demonstrating that there has been no exploitation. A patient's consent to, initiation of, or participation in sexual behavior or involvement with a practitioner does not change the nature of the conduct nor lift the regulatory prohibition. (p. 16)

The ACA *Code of Ethics and Standards of Practice* (1995) address sexual relationships between counselors and clients without the therapy modifier:

> A.7. Sexual Intimacies with Clients.
> a. Current Clients. Counselors do not have any type of sexual intimacies with clients and do not counsel persons with whom they have had a sexual relationship.
> b. Former Clients. Counselors do not engage in sexual intimacies with former clients within a minimum of 2 years after terminating the counseling relationship. Counselors who engage in such relationship after 2 years following termination have the responsibility to examine and document thoroughly that such relations did not have an exploitative nature, based on factors such as duration of counseling, amount of time since counseling, termination circumstances, client's personal history and mental status, adverse impact on the client, and actions by the counselor suggesting a plan to initiate a sexual relationship with the client. (p. 3)

Thus, a career counselor might believe that engaging in an intimate personal relationship with a former client was permissible because, as in the previous resumé critique example, the professional service was not counseling and certainly not therapy, or was permissible after 2 years so long as that relationship did not have an exploitative nature. However, the same career counselor (who would be required to be licensed if he or she practiced privately in Virginia and called himself or herself a counselor) might be judged to have behaved unethically by those with different interpretations of the ethical requirements.

We want to state clearly our belief that any dual relationship that has the potential to exploit client trust and vulnerability is unethical. Such potentially exploitative dual relationships are not appropriate whether the career professional is teaching a career exploration course, critiquing a resumé, or counseling. We do question whether a "one contact" standard is appropriate for all possible career assistance relationships (e.g., when a person uses a career information center and there has been no formal session with the career practitioner).

Should Those Without Traditional Training and Credentials Provide Career Services?

The issue of the proper role of those providing career services (e.g., providing career information, career advising) without the conventional credentials for counseling relates to managed care and third-party payers because many counselors depend on those sources for their livelihood. These counselors are understandably concerned about anything that would make the competence of those delivering counseling services subject to question. However, many consider the practice of prohibiting persons with appropriate talents and skills from providing services as unethical. Still others contend that having any person other than a fully qualified counselor provide any career services is a threat to client welfare and the reputation of the counseling profession. These are contentious issues within the profession. Regardless of one's opinion, the reality is that many individuals engage in providing career services with little or no formal training in career development theory and practice. Moreover, many of these individuals have no training in the helping professions. Counselor and psychology licensure laws typically do not prohibit unlicensed individuals from providing training in job-search skills, resumé writing, and so on.

After prolonged consideration, the NCDA reached a position on this issue that is reflected in the availability of Career Development Facilitator (CDF) training and credentials. A CDF, who cannot practice independent of a qualified career counselor, is thoroughly trained to provide certain career intervention services. This seems to be a reasonable approach and one that is preferable to individuals offering career services independently by adopting titles for their services that allow the person to practice without a license. As Niles and Pate (1989) suggest in an earlier exploration of the issue, the scope of client issues and concerns is not always discernible from the presenting problem; thus, it is our contention that professionally trained career counselors must always be involved at some level (if even on the periphery) in career service delivery. But, we also recognize that a CDF can provide useful and competent career interventions not requiring the expertise of a career counselor (e.g., providing assistance in using career information resources). We do not support the provision of career services by those without training.

How Should the Internet Be Used in Career Development Interventions?

The dimensions of the Internet counseling controversy are in many ways similar to the issues in endorsing career interventions by the untrained or undertrained professional counselor. Most counselors acknowledge the potential of the Internet as a source of information that can be accessed by people who might not have access to other sources of the information. They also recognize the superiority, breadth, depth, and currency of the information available through the Internet. Although there are some copyright issues about information and assessment provided through the Internet, ethical issues most often arise when the services are considered to be counseling. Many counselors define counseling as face-to-face contact and that ends the consideration. Others allow the possibility that some career counseling services (e.g., resumé critiques) might be provided through the Internet but wonder about regulation. How can service providers potentially thousands of miles from the person helped be accountable? The questions are many and the answers are not yet determined. The ACA, NBCC, and NCDA have struggled with the issues, and the NCDA has developed guidelines for the use of the Internet for providing career information and planning services (NCDA, 1997). In addition, the NCDA published a guide to using the Internet in career planning (Harris-Bowlsbey, Dikel, & Sampson, 1998). These guidelines acknowledge that the Internet can be used in four ways for the purpose of providing career services to clients:

1. To deliver occupational information
2. To provide online searches of occupational databases for the purpose of identifying occupational options
3. To deliver interactive career counseling and career planning services
4. To provide online job searches

These four purposes are subject to guidelines that address a variety of ethical issues. For example, the qualifications of the Web site developer or provider must be clearly stated on the site. Clients have the right to be informed about the expertise and experience of the counselor. Moreover, the counselor must not use a false e-mail identity when interacting with clients. The provider must clearly state the appropriate uses (and limitations) of the Web site. The counselor must appropriately screen clients to determine whether the client can benefit from using the online services provided. The counselor must also provide adequate support for the client via periodic telephone contact or videoconferencing.

Providing career services to clients in other geographical locations presents a variety of challenges to the service provider. For instance, the counselor has the obligation to be aware of local conditions, cultures, and events that may have an impact on the client using the online services. The counselor must also be able to refer clients to local practitioners when the client is in need of additional services.

Internet providers of career services must also ensure that the content of the Web site is current and appropriate for use in electronic form. Current online information is especially critical when the service includes online job searching. The costs of all services provided must be clearly stated. When the services include assessment instruments, only assessments with adequate psychometric evidence of their reliability and validity may be used. The issues of confidentiality and storage of client data must be clearly addressed on the Web site.

The use of the Internet to provide career services increases each day. With its increased use, career practitioners are consistently presented with new ethical issues in service delivery. Adhering to guidelines offered by the NCDA, consulting with others, and having external consultants evaluate online services are some strategies career practitioners can use to ensure that their online services are ethical. Clearly, this mode of service delivery will continue to present practitioners with ethical dilemmas as its use increases in the future.

THE ETHICAL STANDARDS OF THE NCDA

Last, but certainly not least important, we focus directly on the ethical standards of NCDA and offer what we hope will be a primer on counseling ethics for readers who have not yet studied counseling ethics and a review for those whose study of ethics may need to be refreshed.

The NCDA Ethical Standards were last reviewed by the NCDA Board of Trustees in 2003. Because the focus of this book is career development interventions, the NCDA standards provide the framework for our consideration of ethical codes. There are six sections in the NCDA Ethical Standards: General, Counseling Relationship, Measurement and Evaluation, Research and Publication, Consulting, and Private Practice. We hope our analysis of the updated NCDA code sections will motivate careful reading of the ACA and NCDA ethical standards, and will provide a structure for that reading.

Section A: General

The general section of the NCDA Standards is likely so labeled because the ethical behaviors could, for most of the 13 statements, be required of any professional who serves people directly. This section could be labeled as aspirational in nature. That is, it sets professional goals that a career counselor should aspire to follow without providing behavioral specifics. It is the career counselor's responsibility to aspire to follow the critical themes in the general section to ensure that clients receive competent and appropriate professional services in an atmosphere of respect and dignity. Counselors must know and abide by their limits of competence and not accept inappropriate behavior by other counselors.

Section B: The Counseling Relationship

The ACA acknowledges confidentiality as the foundation of a counseling relationship and the NCDA Standards reflect the centrality of confidentiality in counseling. Confidentiality issues are consistently reported as the most troubling for counselors and the topic of most questions. The NCDA Standards, like the codes of other psychologically based helping professions, recognize that the counselor has both a legal and ethical obligation to violate confidentiality to prevent harm to the client or to others. Many of the admonitions about counselors working within the bounds of their professional competence and respecting clients are repeated from the General Section with more specific focus.

The ethical requirement for counselors to protect clients and others from harm became a legal requirement with the case of *Tarasoff vs. the Regents of the University of California at Berkeley* (1976). All counselors are faced with the ethical issue of maintaining confidence when the client is a minor (Ledyard, 1998).

Section C: Measurement and Evaluation

This section of the NCDA Ethical Standards requires career counselors to use assessment devices only when the professional guidelines established for the use of such devices are followed. This section is a good illustration of ethical requirements that necessitate a career counselor to be a competent counselor. For example, statement 12 in this section states, "NCDA members must proceed with caution when attempting to evaluate and interpret performances of minority group members or other persons who are not represented in the norm group on which the instrument was standardized" (p. 30).

Clients of career counselors often expect that "tests" will provide answers to their career questions and concerns. Despite years of attempting to change the image of a career counselor providing test data that tells the client what he or she should do occupationally, the myth persists. Due to that idea in the minds of many who seek career counseling, and the fact that some assessments can be helpful for some clients and not for others, the career counselor must be knowledgeable about assessments. That knowledge must extend to the ability to talk to clients about career assessments in terms they can understand. It also requires career counselors to ensure that their clients understand the limitations of assessment instruments (e.g., that there is no test available that can "tell people what occupation they should choose").

Section D: Research and Publication

This section deals with career counselors' responsibility to research subjects and to their research colleagues and readers. It deals with proper behavior, but the section is not intended to address the clients of career counselors. However, career counselors might be asked to provide information about their clients for legitimate research purposes and may want to receive advice about what is proper.

Those in research settings will have the benefit of the federally required Institutional Review Board that is established to protect human subjects. All career counselors engaged in research must constantly remind themselves of the need to obtain informed consent from research participants, to protect research participants' privacy, and to shield all research subjects from harm or embarrassment.

Section E: Consulting

Like the preceding section, this section addresses proper career counselor behavior when dealing with others that may be called clients but are not clients in the conventional sense. The ambiguous nature of the consulting relationship is demonstrated by statement 5, "NCDA members conscientiously adhere to the NCDA Ethical Standards when announcing consultant availability for services." Consulting is usually a business as well as a professional relationship, but the professional career counselor has an obligation to those for whom the consulting services are provided and to the profession that will be judged by the consultant's behavior.

Section F: Private Practice

This section addresses issues related to securing clients for private practice and managing the counselor's private practice as a small business that is based on concern for the welfare of customers who are clients. A private practice in career counseling is a small business subject to the laws of the jurisdiction in which it operates. For example, licenses and insurance are required. The reported problems surrounding business issues of fees, missed appointments, and expected insurance participation provide ample evidence of the necessity for a complete and thoroughly reviewed professional disclosure statement that is provided to all private career counseling clients.

If you have not read the NCDA Ethical Standards (1991), please stop now and read the code in Appendix B before you proceed. Even better, read both the NCDA Ethical Standards and the ACA *Code of Ethics and Standards of Practice* (1995) presented in Appendix A. As you read these standards, it is important to be aware of the fact that ethical statements contain both mandatory and aspirational standards. The author's reading of the NCDA, ACA, and other ethical statements suggests variation primarily among the aspirational standards (i.e., standards that reflect the philosophy of the profession but are not easily enforceable). There is, in our interpretation, more consistency across ethical codes regarding the mandatory standards.

Based on our interpretation of multiple ethical codes, we offer six standards that are central to ethical standards and ethical practice. These six standards are each based on an overriding principle of concern for the welfare of the client. Maintaining an overriding concern for client welfare means that career counselors must constantly test all potential actions they take against the principles of promoting client autonomy, promoting client good and removing harm, never acting to harm a client, promoting equal treatment of those similarly situated and unequal treatment of those in different situations, and keeping promises to clients. We offer the following as critical ethical concepts for career counselors:

1. Career counselors offer only services they are competent to offer. Competence includes training, supervised experience, and some external validation of that competence. This includes all counseling techniques and strategies, assessment devices, and technology-assisted counseling.

2. Career counselors respect and value individual differences among clients and potential clients. Respecting and valuing require that counselors study ways to serve diverse populations.

3. Career counselors treat information received from and about clients as owned by the client and held in trust by the counselor. Such information is revealed only with the consent of the client, when required by law, or to protect the client or others from harm. The basis of career counselors' relationships with clients is the assumption that their communications will be respected as confidential.

4. The career counselor does not engage in any professional relationship in which the counselor's objectivity and ability to work solely for the welfare of the client might be impaired. This includes but is not limited to intimate emotional and physical relationships. Counselors must anticipate how potential dual relationships could possibly lead to future ethical conflicts and take action to avoid future problems.

5. Career counselors assume professional responsibility for clients, and if they are unable to assist, they help the client to obtain alternative services. This requirement extends to assisting clients who cannot, or do not, pay for services as agreed and for providing services when the career counselor is not available.

6. Career counselors recognize that they have obligations to other members of the profession and to society to act in responsible ways and to consider the effects of their behavior on others. This requirement extends to research and publication, to online services, and to business relationships so that counselors do not use their profession for inappropriate financial gain (e.g., diverting clients from a provided service to a private practice).

SUMMARY

The need for career development practitioners to be vigilant in providing interventions that are ethical is, perhaps, an obvious statement. Unfortunately, determining ethical practice is not always obvious. Career development practitioners and, most importantly, their clients will be best served when practitioners use multiple strategies to guide their ethical decision making. Using ethical principles, possessing values awareness, and adhering to the relevant ethical codes (e.g., those published by the NCDA, ACA, APA, and IAEVG) are strategies that career practitioners can use to increase the probability that they will engage in proper practice. We recommend using the strategies for ethical practice recommended in this chapter. Whenever possible, we also encourage readers to discuss their questions and concerns with trusted and respected consultants. Discussion of these issues will provide multiple perspectives related to each issue presented.

REFERENCES

American Counseling Association. (1995). *Code of ethics and standards of practice*. Alexandria, VA: Author.

American Counseling Association. (1999). *Ethical standards for Internet on-line counseling*. Alexandria, VA: Author.

American Psychological Association. (1992). *Ethical principles of psychologists and code of conduct*. Washington, DC: Author.

Anderson, W. P., Jr., & Niles, S. G. (1995). Career and personal concerns expressed by career counseling clients. *The Career Development Quarterly, 43*, 240–245.

Beauchamp, T. L., & Childress, J. F. (2001). *Principles of biomedical ethics* (5th ed.). New York: Oxford University Press.

Bergin, A. E. (1985). Proposed values for guiding and evaluating counseling and psychotherapy. *Counseling and Values, 29*, 99–115.

Commonwealth of Virginia Board of Professional Counselors and Marriage and Family Therapists. (2000). *Regulations governing the practice of professional counseling*. (18 VAC 115-20-10 et seq.)

Family Educational Rights and Privacy Act of 1974, 20 U. S. C. § 1232g; 34 CFR Part 99.

Harris-Bowlsbey, J., Dikel, M. R., & Sampson, J. P. (1998). *The Internet: A tool for career planning*. Columbus, OH: National Career Development Association.

Herlihy, B., & Corey, G. (1996). *ACA ethical standards casebook* (5th ed.). Alexandria, VA: American Counseling Association.

Herlihy, B., & Remley, T. P. (1995). Unified ethical standards: A challenge for professionalism. *Journal of Counseling and Development, 74*, 130–133.

Herr, E. L., & Niles, S. G. (1988). The values of counseling: Three domains. *Counseling and Values, 33*, 4–17.

International Association for Educational and Vocational Guidance. (1996). *IAEVG ethical standards*. Berlin: Author.

Kidder, R. M. (1995). *How good people make tough choices: Resolving the dilemmas of ethical living*. New York: Fireside.

Ledyard, P. (1998). Counseling minors: Ethical and legal issues. *Counseling and Values, 3*, 171–177.

Lee, G. (1994). *Honor and duty.* New York: Knopf.

London, P. (1964). *The modes and morals of psychotherapy.* New York: Holt, Rinehart, and Winston.

National Association for College Admissions Counseling. (2001). *Statement of principles of good practice.* Alexandria, VA: Author.

National Association of Social Workers. (1999). *Code of ethics of the National Association of Social Workers.* Retrieved March 10, 2004 from http://www.socialworkers.org/pubs/code/default.asp

National Board for Certified Counselors. (1997a). *Code of ethics.* Greensboro, NC: Author.

National Board for Certified Counselors. (1997b). *Standards for the ethical practice of Web counseling.* Greensboro, NC: Author.

National Career Development Association. (1997). *NCDA guidelines for the use of the Internet for provision of career information and planning services.* Columbus, OH: Author.

National Career Development Association. (2003). *Ethical standards.* Columbus, OH: Author.

Niles, S. G., & Pate, R. H. (1989). Competency and training issues related to the integration of career counseling and mental health counseling. *Journal of Career Development, 16,* 63–71.

Subich, L. M. (1993). How personal is career counseling? *The Career Development Quarterly, 42,* 129–131.

Super, D. E. (1983). Assessment in career guidance: Toward truly developmental counseling. *Personnel and Guidance Journal, 61,* 555–562.

Tarasoff vs. Regents of the University of California at Berkeley, 551 P.2d 334, (Cal. 1976).

Tjelveit, A. C. (1986). The ethics of value conversion in psychotherapy: Appropriate and inappropriate therapist influence on client values. *Clinical Psychology Review, 6,* 515–537.

VanHoose, W. H. (1986). Ethical principles in counseling. *Journal of Counseling and Development, 65,* 168–169.

Watts, A. G., Super, D. E., & Kidd, J. M. (1981). *Career development in Britain.* Cambridge, England: Hobson's Press.

Williams, C. B., & Freeman, L. T. (2002). Report of the ACA Ethics Committee: 2000–2001. *Journal of Counseling & Development, 80,* 251–254.

CHAPTER 15

EVALUATION OF CAREER PLANNING SERVICES

It has been reported that the majority of Americans who purchase a new car now consult one of several services that evaluate the quality of different cars being offered. The popularity of these services is attributable to the often-stated view of car purchasers that a new car purchase is too important a decision to base on the unevaluated claims of the manufacturers.

If the choice of a new car is important enough for people to want a source that provides reliable evaluations of the cars offered, it only seems reasonable that career planning services that deal with potentially life-enhancing or life-damaging career advice and information should also be the object of responsible evaluation.

The operative word here is "responsible." All manner of helping services regularly issue claims as to how effective their services are. However, in most situations, too little information is provided to determine if the claims are justified, or the individual lacks the knowledge to determine if the evaluation presented is creditable.

This chapter admirably addresses this problem by both stressing the importance of evaluation in career services, and going a highly important step further of instructing you in how to conduct and use evaluations.

Careful reading of this chapter will enable you to design and plan your own evaluations. Additionally, you will be able to assess if the evaluations undertaken by other services are adequate; a handy thing to know if you wish to refer people to quality programs and services. Specifically, you should be able to determine if the evaluation is formative (useful for improving an ongoing program) or summative (judging the overall worth of the program) or some of both. A useful skill to have, wouldn't you say?

Garry R. Walz, PhD, NCC
Counseling Outfitters, CEO
University of Michigan, Professor Emeritus
(Past President of the American Counseling Association and
the National Career Development Association)

Chapter 8 described the process of providing career counseling and career development services to individuals and groups. Chapter 9 defined the process of developing a program of services for a specific population. This chapter focuses on ways in which these kinds of services can be evaluated.

Because evaluation is a time-consuming and expensive process, let us consider four reasons why evaluation is important. One predominant reason is to determine if the program is helping people achieve the objectives that were defined for it. Those objectives were written in order to meet the needs identified in the target population. If the program does not help people achieve those objectives, it is not meeting needs.

Second, it is necessary to evaluate the services so that they can be improved. No matter how well the design and development stages have been accomplished, implementation of a new program will always identify additional needs, different possible approaches, and good ideas for enhancement. Program development and delivery is a cyclical process; new ideas should be included in the program at next delivery.

Third, evaluation provides ongoing information to supervisors and other stakeholders about the results of the program, meeting the requirement of accountability. Administrators typically want to know how many people are availing themselves of the program and about the effectiveness of the program in meeting identified needs.

Fourth, evaluation is sometimes done in order to determine whether the outcomes of delivering services are worth the money and other resources being invested. The focus of such evaluation is to make a decision to retain, expand, or discontinue services.

Evaluation is typically categorized as being *formative, summative,* or both. According to the Joint Committee on Standards for Educational Evaluation (1994), formative evaluation is done for the purpose of improving an ongoing program, whereas summative evaluation has the goal of drawing conclusions about the overall worth of a program in order to determine whether to retain it. Thus, the first three reasons just given for evaluation fall into the category of formative, whereas the fourth reason fits the category of summative. Evaluation can, of course, be designed to meet all four purposes.

STEPS IN PLANNING EVALUATION

In planning evaluation it is necessary to follow several standard steps that will provide the structure for the implementation of the evaluation plan. The first step is to determine whether the evaluation is formative, summative, or both. The kinds of data collected depend on the answer to this question. For example, in formative evaluation, there will be questions about how the content of the program can be improved and about how the participants valued it. For summative evaluation, it is likely that there will be measurement of outcomes and cost, begging the question of whether or not the outcomes were worth the expenditure of funds to accomplish them. This planning step may also include decision making about who will receive the data.

A second step is to determine what specific knowledge, skills, attitudes, or behaviors are to be evaluated. These may include global constructs, such as change in career maturity, decision making skill, or self-concept; skills, such as job interviewing; or knowledge, such as how to research occupations. Longer-term behaviors, such as consistently getting to work on time or maintaining a job for a long period of time, may be measured. What is measured should relate directly to the statement of objectives for the program.

A third step is to determine what the source(s) of the evaluation data will be. In formative evaluation it is likely that the data will be sought from clients, program participants, or trained observers. In summative evaluation the data may be collected from records, budgets, and follow-up studies. For example, if a correctional system is doing a summative evaluation of a new program of vocational training and counseling services to offenders, the offenders themselves may never evaluate the program. Rather, data collection will focus on calculating the per-offender cost of providing the service and comparing it to the change in job placement rate and, in turn, the effect on recidivism.

A fourth step is to determine how the data will be collected. There is a wide range of formal and informal methods from which to choose. Formal methods include the administration of standardized instruments, structured observation, and follow-up studies. Informal methods include group feedback, questionnaires, and interviews. This planning step will include review and selection of instruments (if these are to be used), development of questionnaires or observer checklists, and/or the design of follow-up studies. This step should also include decisions about who will administer these data-collection instruments and how the data will be collected, tallied or entered, and prepared for analysis.

Related to this step is the question of when the data will be collected. For formative evaluation, administrating a questionnaire or holding exit interviews may be sufficient to provide the feedback needed for program improvement. A higher level of evaluation may involve assessing—through instruments, observation, or changed behaviors—whether a specific knowledge or skill has been acquired. Such evaluation is likely to be done immediately after delivery of the program or treatment. If the focus of evaluation is to determine how skills, attitudes, or knowledge has changed as a result of the program, data may be collected both before and after the treatment.

A fifth step is to determine how the data will be analyzed. This step includes decisions about whether data will simply be tallied, providing the number of respondents and a breakdown of their responses, or whether specific statistical tests will be applied to it. Such tests would likely be selected to compare differences between experimental and control group results, or pretreatment and posttreatment results, and determine their significance.

STAKEHOLDERS

Depending upon the evaluation purpose, data may be sought from sources in addition to the persons who received the services. For example, when evaluating services provided to elementary students, a counselor would likely seek input from parents and school administrators, as well as from the students themselves. At the middle school level, evaluation might be sought from students, parents, teachers, and administrators. At the high school level, these same audiences could be supplemented by colleges and employers who receive graduates. At the college level, evaluative input might be sought from students, administrators, and employers. At the community agency level, clients, employers, and organizations that fund the services could evaluate services.

Before designing evaluation, then, it is necessary to consider who the stakeholders are—that is, who is receiving the services and who cares about them, profits from them, needs to be informed, and provides the approval and funding for their continuation. Ideally, representatives of all of these stakeholders would serve on a committee that drafts the evaluation plan.

TYPES OF DATA COLLECTED

The term *evaluation* implies the collection of data. These data may either be *quantitative* or *qualitative*. Quantitative data reports numbers, and these numbers would answer questions, such as the following, that are often posed by administrators:

- How many elementary school children received help with career awareness through the classroom units taught by the counselor?
- How many sixth graders participated in the career fair?
- Of the seventh graders who participated in the fair, what percentage made a tentative selection of a career cluster?
- How many eighth graders brought their parents for an interview to develop a 4-year plan related to a selected career cluster?
- How many 10th graders were served by the special series of homeroom programs about career planning?
- What percentage of seniors who went to full-time employment after graduation entered an occupation listed in their career portfolio or a highly related one?
- What percentage of college-bound seniors entered one of the majors selected in their career plan?
- What percentage of these were still pursuing that major in the sophomore year?
- How many students at each high school grade level were interviewed by counselors specifically for career planning?
- What percentage of students who attended the job-seeking workshops found a job that was desirable to them within 60 days of graduation?
- How much does it cost each time a counselor spends an hour with a student?
- How many clients have been served this calendar year in the one-stop center?
- What is the breakdown of clients by problem presented?
- Of those seeking jobs, what percentage found them within 60 days after receiving service?

Qualitative data provides information about the perceived value of the services provided and the extent to which predefined program outcomes were achieved. The indicators to measure quality may be different for different stakeholders. Let us imagine that a full-blown career guidance program was approved and funded for a large, urban high school. Different stakeholders may be interested in different outcomes of the intervention. Their different hoped-for outcomes might be as follows:

- Students—that they can decide upon a major (those going on to postsecondary education) and an occupation
- Counselor delivering the program—that the students will experience growth in career maturity, including decision making
- Principal—that the school dropout rate will be reduced because students become aware of the relationship between school and work
- Parents—that students will be directed to occupations and postsecondary education that are "good" for them so that money will not be wasted on further education
- Employers—that students will learn job-seeking skills, especially job-retention skills
- Teachers—that the program is worth the class time that they and the students give up

This list illustrates why individuals representing a range of stakeholders need to be involved in evaluation design.

BENCHMARKS FOR EVALUATION

The word *evaluation* implies that outcomes will be compared with a desired standard. Thus, evaluation is impossible unless a standard has been set for desirable outcomes. Because there are different types of career planning services, each with different expected outcomes and stakeholders, the standard used for evaluation may be different for each.

One primary mode of delivering career services is through one-on-one, face-to-face interviewing. It is customary in such a relationship for clients, assisted by counselors, to set goals for the relationship. Examples of such goals are as follows:

- To identify and discard the irrational beliefs that the client holds that are preventing him or her from being able to formulate career goals and move ahead with them
- To develop a clearer and more positive self-concept
- To identify skills learned from past work experience and determine how to transfer them to at least three occupations that are different from the ones already pursued
- To learn how to market oneself in a job interview

In the case of individual counseling, then, the standard for evaluation for the counselor and the client is whether or *to what extent the relationship results in accomplishment of the client's goal(s).* It is likely that such accomplishment can be measured only by two people—the client and the counselor. Qualitative evaluation of accomplishment with this mode of service delivery may be as simple as these three steps:

- Early in the counseling relationship, specific goals are set by the client and the counselor, and these are placed in writing.

- At the end of the counseling relationship, the client and the counselor separately rate, on a scale of 1 to 5, the degree to which each goal has been accomplished.
- These ratings are shared and discussed.

An administrator in this setting is likely to want to know the number of individual clients served in a year by counselors, the mean number of sessions per client, and the hourly cost of counseling service. Data to answer these questions may be collected by requiring that counselors keep log sheets on paper or electronically or by setting up a system by which a clerical support person logs these data for everyone in the counseling or career planning center.

In group counseling, group guidance, or a career planning class, the goals are typically set for the participants by the facilitator or instructor. As described in Chapter 9, these goals are stated in the form of *measurable objectives,* a second kind of benchmark for program evaluation, which begin with the phrase "At the end of this series of _____ , participants will be able to. . . " Examples for different age levels are as follows:

- Describe activities in which people work with other people, with equipment, with data (facts, numbers), or with ideas (elementary school)
- State the titles of six distinct groups of occupations and correctly sort occupational titles into these groups (middle school)
- Identify specific families of occupations for further exploration (high school)
- Describe in detail three occupations being seriously considered (high school)
- State one or more majors available at the university that are likely to prepare them for occupations they have selected (college)
- Describe three companies in detail that hire people in the occupations they have chosen (community Job Service office)

Accomplishment of these types of objectives can typically be measured by a questionnaire developed by the counselor or program administrator. Such a questionnaire could provide both quantitative and qualitative data. The following illustrate statements that include both qualitative and quantitative data:

After completion of the program,

- 87% of elementary students who participated in it were able to match appropriate work tasks with the four dimensions of the World-of-Work Map—People, Data, Things, and Ideas
- 92% of middle school students were able to sort a list of 30 occupations into the correct Holland clusters
- 96% of high school students were able to list two or three job families by name in which they have interest, including the titles of specific occupations in those families

Administrators may value additional data, including:

- The number of students, clients, or employees served by the program (quantitative)
- The per-person cost of providing the service (quantitative)
- Participant satisfaction with the program measured by a questionnaire in which participants are asked to rate the quality or value of the program (qualitative)
- Feedback from parents about the program (qualitative)

Parent evaluation could be assessed by a questionnaire sent to homes, including questions similar to the following:

- Did your child talk about the career exploration program at home? If so, what kinds of things did he or she say?
- Did this program trigger any conversations at home about your child's career planning? If so, what were the topics of those conversations?
- To what extent, if any, do you think that this program helped your son or daughter to determine either what he or she wants to do in work or does not want to do?

A third benchmark for evaluation of individuals' progress related to career planning is *national* or *local guidelines* that have been adopted. The National Career Development Guidelines (NOICC, 1996) were developed by the National Occupational Information Coordinating Committee in collaboration with several professional organizations. They address desired competencies and behaviors in three areas—self-knowledge, educational and occupational exploration, and career planning—and at four levels—elementary school, middle/junior high, high school, and adult. These have been adopted by many school districts across the nation. Following are a few sample behavioral indicators from the high school version of these guidelines, accompanied by an example of how the existence of the indicator might be assessed.

Indicator	One Way to Assess
Identify and appreciate personal interests, abilities, and skills.	After appropriate interventions, ask students to list three fields/clusters of primary interest and the abilities they believe they have to support these interests.
Demonstrate the ability to use peer feedback.	After completion of a skills bombardment activity, during which all members of a group are asked to tell each person what his or her primary strengths are, ask students to indicate what they have learned from the activity and how their view of self has been modified.
Demonstrate an understanding of environmental influences on one's behaviors.	Ask students to write a short essay about the influence that family members and others have had on their career preferences, as well as events in their lives that have had an influence.
Describe the relationship of academic and occupational skills to achieve personal goals.	Using the results of a recent interest inventory, ask students to write a plan that includes the courses for each remaining year of high school and for postsecondary education related to those interests.
Identify how employment trends relate to education and training.	Using the CareerInfoNet Web site, ask students to list 10 occupations that are growing rapidly. For each, ask them to indicate what courses and further education would be necessary if they decided to enter that growing occupation.

Local school districts or state educational systems often develop their own guidelines for career interventions, modeled after career development theories or this national set of guidelines. When schools adopt or develop guidelines, these should become the basis for both program content and evaluation.

A fourth kind of standard for evaluation is *theory*. Think, for example, about the first three of Super's (1957) five developmental tasks, listed next. These could be used as the basis for both program content development and evaluation at the secondary level.

Super's Developmental Tasks	Possible Methods of Evaluation
Crystallization: shortening a list of occupations to a small number that have the highest potential to implement the self-concept.	After having offered interventions that assist students to develop a list of preferred occupations, ask them to circle three to five that they are considering most seriously. Ask students to write or talk about why they have kept these on the list while discarding others.
Specification: one occupation is selected from the short list of occupations.	Ask students to indicate the occupation that they will plan to enter, what training they will need to complete in high school and thereafter, what the typical duties of this occupation are, what the future employment outlook is, what the beginning salary range will be, which other occupations are closely related (using the same or a similar set of skills), and how they will learn more about this occupation and test it out in reality before further commitment.
Implementation: engaging in the coursework that is desirable or required for the occupation.	Ask students to make a 4-year plan, listing courses available at their high school that will best prepare them for the occupation. Also ask them to describe the post-high school training needed, where it is available, and how they plan to take advantage of it.

METHODS OF EVALUATION

As indicated at the beginning of this chapter, the primary purposes of evaluation are to determine whether specified outcomes are being achieved, to improve services, to provide data to supervisors and other stakeholders, and to make decisions about continuation of services related to cost-effectiveness. Evaluation is possible only through collection and organization of data. The data collected must be directly relevant to answering the evaluation questions, and evaluation questions are possible only when clear objectives for services have been identified. Thus, the evaluation cycle is as follows:

- Determine the specific measurable objectives (desired outcomes) of the program or service.
- Determine the *indicators* or *behaviors* that will be tell-tale signs of having reached the stated objectives.

- Identify the best way(s) to observe or measure these indicators or behaviors.
- Collect data using these methods.
- Organize the data in ways that will answer the specific evaluative questions posed by different stakeholders.
- Deliver the data to these stakeholders.
- Use relevant data for the various purposes of evaluation: to determine whether the program achieved its objectives, to improve the services for future delivery, to serve public relations purposes, or to make decisions about program retention.

There are several common ways of collecting the data needed for evaluation. One common way is through a carefully planned *questionnaire* or *interview*. In either case the same standard questions would be asked, either in written form or in a face-to-face interview process. Examples of such questionnaire items have been provided throughout this chapter. Following are general guidelines for writing items (which may either be questions or statements, such as "List the three best sources of information about job openings"):

- Make sure that the items relate directly to the indicators, behaviors, or outcomes you are trying to evaluate.
- Avoid questions that can be answered with *yes* or *no*.
- Make sure that the items are written clearly, without ambiguity.
- Make sure that the items are at an appropriate reading level for their audience.
- Make sure that the items cover all of the indicators or topics you need to cover in the evaluation.
- Modify the items as needed for different stakeholders.
- Make the questionnaire or interview as short and succinct as possible while still getting the core data that you need.

In most cases, questionnaires are administered to all persons who received a service (the subjects) immediately or in a relatively short time (1 week to 1 month) after its completion. Sometimes, for the sake of documenting change, the same questionnaire is administered prior to receiving the service (called the *treatment*) and again after receiving the service. This type of evaluation allows a comparison of data before and after, leading to evaluative statements such as "Before the career planning unit was taught to all sophomores, 85% of them indicated that they had no idea about their future vocational choice. After the completion of the unit, only 24% indicated that they had no idea."

A second method of evaluation is the *administration of more formal instruments* developed by test publishers, some of which are described in Chapter 5. Such instruments measure global constructs (career maturity, decision making skill, career decidedness, career concerns, and career beliefs) rather than the accomplishment of specific objectives. If the goal of offering a specific service was to increase or modify one or more of these global constructs, use of such instruments could be helpful. These are listed and described in detail in *A Counselor's Guide to Career Assessments* (Kapes & Whitfield, 2001), published by the NCDA and updated periodically.

As with questionnaires, these instruments may be administered to the same group or individual, both before and after the career planning service has been provided, or only after. Typically, the before-after administration is used when the study is nonscientific; that is, when there is no *control group* considered equivalent to the *experimental group* that was denied the service at the time of the evaluation. The use of randomly selected groups is typically required in *research studies*. However, in *evaluation studies* this design is not typically used because it is very difficult to achieve in day-to-day operational settings.

Another common method of collecting data is the *follow-up study*. In such a study, those who have participated in some form of treatment are contacted by phone, e-mail, regular mail, or in person at one or more intervals of time after completion of the program. The purpose of this contact, of course, is to determine whether specific predefined outcomes have been or are being experienced as a result of the treatment. As an example, suppose that an instructional unit was provided to high school seniors who are not planning to enter any kind of postsecondary education. The unit provides extensive instruction about job-seeking skills. A primary objective was stated as follows: "Upon completion of this unit and graduation from high school, at least 85% of students will get a job within a month after graduation." In this case, a counselor might conduct a follow-up study by either sending a questionnaire to graduates or placing a phone call, both of which would be designed to find out if the graduate had found a job and begun work. Thus, it would be easy to determine whether the objective set for the instructional unit had been met.

USING THE RESULTS OF EVALUATION

At the beginning of the chapter, four reasons were given for evaluating career planning services: to determine to what extent they met their objectives, to improve those services, to provide data that helps promote and sustain the services, and to determine whether outcomes justify expenses. These same reasons are used to describe how the results of evaluation can be used.

First, imagine that evaluative results—both qualitative and quantitative—have been collected for the delivery of a unit of career planning instruction to middle school students. Briefly stated, the results are as follows:

From *administrators* (based on receipt of a content outline of the program): This program looks exceptionally good, and its content is needed by all students. Be careful not to take too much class time for the program, however, especially from the core subjects.

From *parents* (based on a short questionnaire included with report cards for students who participated in the program):

- 99% indicated that their students need this instruction
- 76% indicated that their child talked about the program at home
- 32% indicated that their child formed a tentative career goal as a result of the instruction
- 45% indicated that their child would use what was learned in the instructional unit to help with the development of a 4-year plan
- 90% indicated that they thought the school should continue the program

From the *students* (based on an end-of-unit questionnaire):

- 88% of students, when given a list of 30 occupational titles with short descriptions, could place each title in the correct Holland cluster
- 95% of students selected one of the six Holland clusters as a "first-choice" cluster
- The same 95% of students drafted a mock 4-year plan for selection of high school courses related to the cluster of their first choice.

When asked what they learned during the unit,

- 81% indicated that they learned how occupations can be organized
- 92% indicated that they learned more about their own interests
- 73% indicated that they learned about the relationship between school subjects and work

When asked what they liked best about the unit (listing the five top choices),

- 97% selected the field trips
- 94% selected the use of the University of Missouri Web site, which explains the six clusters and gives titles and descriptions of occupations
- 85% selected the guest speakers
- 76% selected the videos about the six clusters
- 74% selected the use of a computer-based system that provides titles and occupational descriptions by cluster

When asked what they liked least about the instructional unit,

- 94% selected the requirement to write a short paper about the cluster of occupations they liked best
- 90% selected the requirement to interview someone who works in the cluster selected as favorite
- 85% selected having to complete a 4-year high school plan for the cluster selected
- 61% selected having to memorize a definition of each of the six clusters
- 25% selected having to miss English class for 3 days

From *classroom teachers who gave their classrooms and class time to make the unit possible* (based on a short interview with each):

- The counselor should have made arrangements for this unit no later than September 15 so that lessons and assignments for the English class could have been modified earlier.
- Students seemed to have more freedom while the counselor was teaching this unit. As a result, the room was more disorderly than usual.
- The bus that took students on the field trip returned to school late, resulting in a need for the teacher to write a late pass for every student before he or she went to the next class period.
- In casual conversation, students showed a lot of enthusiasm for the unit.
- Students need to know this content, but it would be good if it could take less time away from the English class.

Assuming this evaluative feedback, how will the counselor use it to improve the unit the next time it is delivered? These conclusions could be drawn from the data:

- The basic methods of presenting the content (field trip, speakers, videos, Web sites) are well received by the students.
- Specific assignments, though disliked by the students, should be kept because of their value.
- Based on administrator, teacher, and student feedback, the length of the program should be cut without losing its valuable outcomes.
- Great care should be taken to work with English teachers very early in the semester, or even at the end of the previous semester, so that their lesson plans can be modified both to reflect the content being taught in this special guidance unit and to accommodate for the time loss it causes.
- The schedule for field trips must be very carefully monitored so that students never return to the school building late.

How could a counselor use the same results to determine whether program objectives have been met? Though not revealed here, let us imagine that the counselor had several clearly written and measurable objectives for this program and that data listed at the beginning of the previous list indicated that the objectives had been met at an even higher level than indicated in the objectives. Such data would confirm that program objectives had been met.

How would a counselor use these results to promote and explain the program as well as to ensure that it continues? Here are some ideas in that regard:

- A short executive summary of the results could be sent to the administrator, along with a memo that thanks him or her for continued support for the program and indicates that its length, now 6 hours, has been reduced to 4 hours for the next year in order to ensure that the amount of time taken away from English classes is not excessive. The report might contain not only the basic data, but also several positive quotes from parents, teachers, and/or students. The cover memo might also include a summary of the plans for the next semester or year.
- A short summary of the results could be included in the school newsletter to parents, along with some student quotes. Further details might be presented at a PTA meeting.
- An article about the program could be written and sent to the local newspaper. A cover letter might state when the program will be offered again and invite a reporter to cover one or more of the main events (such as the field trip to show the different kinds of work tasks included in the six clusters of occupations) next time.
- A report about the success of the program could be sent, along with a thank-you letter, to the English teachers who gave up class time for the program and to their department chair. The letter might include a paragraph that indicates that some time has been cut from the program in order to use as little English class time as possible and that greater care will be taken in the future about the condition of classrooms and the prompt arrival of buses from field trips.

How might an administrator use the data to determine whether to retain the program of services or to discontinue it? An analysis of the number of hours spent by the counselor and the number of students served reveals that the cost of delivery was $2.45 per student. Based on the strong parent and student feedback, the principal decides to retain the program in spite of some faculty resistance about the fact that class time is taken for its delivery.

ROADBLOCKS TO EVALUATION

It is not easy to find the time or the motivation to do evaluation of career counseling and career planning services. Most counselors work in settings in which there are many conflicting demands on their time and priority. The crisis situations—such as dealing with violence, drugs, excessive absence, and a variety of behavioral problems— receive first priority. In high school settings, planning and changing course schedules often demands second priority; making or finding time to provide career planning services receives, at best, third priority; and designing or evaluating any of these services falls near the bottom of the priority list. Patrick and Niles (1988) identified three additional roadblocks, as follows:

- Because evaluation is designed to reveal the quality of services as perceived by those who receive them, the potential for negative results is threatening. If evaluation did result in negative findings, funding, staff, and program approval could be in jeopardy.
- Unless the services of a guidance or student affairs office have been designed in the way described in Chapter 9, its offerings may be so nonsystematic—that is, without defined objectives—that it is difficult or impossible to evaluate them.
- Many counselors believe that the kind of work they do cannot be objectively evaluated because it is not quantifiable or definable. Thus, they resist any method of evaluation.

In addition to these roadblocks, counselors may not have the financial resources to purchase instruments that would be helpful in evaluation or conduct a follow-up study. Further, they may not have the time or expertise to develop questionnaires, observer checklists, or exit interviews to be used. In cases in which better data would be acquired if there could be an experimental-control group design, the realities of the work setting may not support such a design.

SUMMARY

This chapter describes the purpose of evaluation of career planning services—individual or group counseling, group guidance, career education instruction, workshops— and how data from such evaluation can be used to gain knowledge about accomplishment of predetermined objectives, program improvement, promotion and maintenance, and cost-effectiveness. The steps of the program evaluation process are described. Potential stakeholders in career planning services are identified, including how these different audiences may evaluate the program. Possible benchmarks and methods of evaluation are defined. Finally, methods that may be used to collect data for program evaluation, the nature of reports provided to the different stakeholders, and potential roadblocks to evaluation are described.

REFERENCES

Joint Committee on Standards for Educational Evaluation. (1994). *The program evaluation* (2nd ed.). Thousand Oaks, CA: Sage.

Kapes, J. T., & Whitfield, E. A. (2001). *A counselor's guide to career assessment instruments.* Tulsa, OK: National Career Development Association.

National Occupational Information Coordinating Committee. (1996). *National career development guidelines K–adult handbook.* Washington, DC: Author.

Patrick, J., & Niles, S. G. (1988). Establishing accountability and evaluation procedures in student affairs offices. *NASPA Journal, 25*(4), 291–296.

Super, D. E. (1957). *The psychology of careers.* New York: Harper.

APPENDIX A

AMERICAN COUNSELING ASSOCIATION CODE OF ETHICS AND STANDARDS OF PRACTICE

PREAMBLE

The American Counseling Association is an educational, scientific, and professional organization whose members are dedicated to the enhancement of human development throughout the life span. Association members recognize diversity in our society and embrace a cross-cultural approach in support of the worth, dignity, potential, and uniqueness of each individual. The specification of a code of ethics enables the association to clarify to current and future members, and to those served by members, the nature of the ethical responsibilities held in common by its members. As the code of ethics of the association, this document establishes principles that define the ethical behavior of association members. All members of the American Counseling Association are required to adhere to the Code of Ethics and the Standards of Practice. The Code of Ethics will serve as the basis for processing ethical complaints initiated against members of the association.

SECTION A: THE COUNSELING RELATIONSHIP

A.1. Client Welfare

a. *Primary Responsibility.* The primary responsibility of counselors is to respect the dignity and to promote the welfare of clients.

b. *Positive Growth and Development.* Counselors encourage client growth and development in ways that foster clients' interest and welfare; counselors avoid fostering dependent counseling relationships.

c. *Counseling Plans.* Counselors and their clients work jointly in devising integrated, individual counseling plans that offer reasonable promise of success and are consistent with abilities and circumstances of clients. Counselors and clients regularly review counseling plans to ensure their continued viability and effectiveness, respecting clients' freedom of choice. (See A.3.b.)

d. *Family Involvement.* Counselors recognize that families are usually important in clients' lives and strive to enlist family understanding and involvement as a positive resource, when appropriate.

e. *Career and Employment Needs.* Counselors work with their clients in considering employment in jobs and circumstances that are consistent with the clients' overall abilities, vocational limitations, physical restrictions, general temperament, interest and aptitude patterns, social skills, education, general qualifications, and other relevant characteristics and needs. Counselors neither place nor participate in placing clients in positions that will result in damaging the interest and the welfare of clients, employers, or the public.

A.2. Respecting Diversity

a. *Nondiscrimination.* Counselors do not condone or engage in discrimination based on age, color, culture, disability, ethnic group, gender, race, religion, sexual orientation, marital status, or socioeconomic status. (See C.5.a., C.5.b., and D.1.i.)

b. *Respecting Differences.* Counselors will actively attempt to understand the diverse cultural backgrounds of the clients with whom they work. This includes, but is not limited to, learning how the counselor's own cultural/ethnic/racial identity impacts her/his values and beliefs about the counseling process. (See E.8. and F.2.i.)

A.3. Client Rights

a. *Disclosure to Clients.* When counseling is initiated, and throughout the counseling process as necessary, counselors inform clients of the purposes, goals, techniques, procedures, limitations, potential risks and benefits of services to be performed, and other pertinent information. Counselors take steps to ensure that clients understand the implications of diagnosis, the intended use of tests and reports, fees, and billing arrangements. Clients have the right to expect confidentiality and to be provided with an explanation of its limitations, including supervision and/or treatment of team professionals; to obtain clear information about their case records; to participate in the ongoing counseling plans; and to refuse any recommended services and be advised of the consequences of such refusal. (See E.5.a. and G.2.)

b. *Freedom of Choice.* Counselors offer clients the freedom to choose whether to enter into a counseling relationship and to determine which professional(s) will provide counseling. Restrictions that limit choices of clients are fully explained. (See A.1.c.)

c. *Inability to Give Consent.* When counseling minors or persons unable to give voluntary informed consent, counselors act in these clients' best interests. (See B.3.)

A.4. Clients Served by Others
If a client is receiving services from another mental health professional, counselors, with client consent, inform the professional persons already involved and develop clear agreements to avoid confusion and conflict for the client. (See C.6.c.)

A.5. Personal Needs and Values
a. *Personal Needs.* In the counseling relationship, counselors are aware of the intimacy and responsibilities inherent in the counseling relationship, maintain respect for clients, and avoid actions that seek to meet their personal needs at the expense of clients.

b. *Personal Values.* Counselors are aware of their own values, attitudes, beliefs, and behaviors and how these apply in a diverse society, and avoid imposing their values on clients. (See C.5.a.)

A.6. Dual Relationships
a. *Avoid When Possible.* Counselors are aware of their influential positions with respect to clients, and they avoid exploiting the trust and dependency of clients. Counselors make every effort to avoid dual relationships with clients that could impair professional judgment or increase the risk of harm to clients. (Examples of such relationships include, but are not limited to, familial, social, financial, business, or close personal relationships with clients.) When a dual relationship cannot be avoided, counselors take appropriate professional precautions such as informed consent, consultation, supervision, and documentation to ensure that judgment is not impaired and no exploitation occurs. (See F.1.b.)

b. *Superior/Subordinate Relationships.* Counselors do not accept as clients superiors or subordinates with whom they have administrative, supervisory, or evaluative relationships.

A.7. Sexual Intimacies with Clients
a. *Current Clients.* Counselors do not have any type of sexual intimacies with clients and do not counsel persons with whom they have had a sexual relationship.

b. *Former Clients.* Counselors do not engage in sexual intimacies with former clients within a minimum of two years after terminating the counseling relationship. Counselors who engage in such a relationship after two years following termination have the responsibility to thoroughly examine and document that such relations did not have an exploitative nature, based on factors such as duration of counseling, amount of time since counseling, termination circumstances, client's personal history and mental status, adverse impact on the client, and actions by the counselor suggesting a plan to initiate a sexual relationship with the client after termination.

A.8. Multiple Clients
When counselors agree to provide counseling services to two or more persons who have a relationship (such as husband and wife, or parents and children), counselors clarify at the outset which person or persons are clients and the nature of the relationships they will have with each involved person. If it becomes apparent that counselors may be called upon to perform potentially conflicting roles, they clarify, adjust, or withdraw from roles appropriately. (See B.2.b. and B.4.d.)

A.9. Group Work
a. *Screening.* Counselors screen prospective group counseling/therapy participants. To the extent possible, counselors select members whose needs and goals are compatible with goals of the group, who will not impede the group process, and whose well-being will not be jeopardized by the group experience.

b. *Protecting Clients.* In a group setting, counselors take reasonable precautions to protect clients from physical or psychological trauma.

A.10. Fees and Bartering (See D.3.a. and D.3.b.)
a. *Advance Understanding.* Counselors clearly explain to clients, prior to entering the counseling relationship, all financial arrangements related to professional services including the use of collection agencies or legal measures for nonpayment. (See A.11.c.)

b. *Establishing Fees.* In establishing fees for professional counseling services, counselors consider the financial status of clients and locality. In the event that the established fee structure is inappropriate for a client, assistance is provided in attempting to find comparable services of acceptable cost. (See A.10.d., D.3.a., and D.3.b.)

c. *Bartering Discouraged.* Counselors ordinarily refrain from accepting goods or services from clients in return for counseling services because such arrangements create inherent potential for conflicts, exploitation, and distortion of the professional relationship. Counselors may participate in bartering only if the relationship is not exploitive, if the client requests it, if a clear written contract is established, and if such arrangements are an accepted practice among professionals in the community. (See A.6.a.)

d. *Pro Bono Service.* Counselors contribute to society by devoting a portion of their professional activity to services for which there is little or no financial return (pro bono).

A.11. Termination and Referral

a. *Abandonment Prohibited.* Counselors do not abandon or neglect clients in counseling. Counselors assist in making appropriate arrangements for the continuation of treatment, when necessary, during interruptions such as vacations, and following termination.

b. *Inability to Assist Clients.* If counselors determine an inability to be of professional assistance to clients, they avoid entering or immediately terminate a counseling relationship. Counselors are knowledgeable about referral resources and suggest appropriate alternatives. If clients decline the suggested referral, counselors should discontinue the relationship.

c. *Appropriate Termination.* Counselors terminate a counseling relationship, securing client agreement when possible, when it is reasonably clear that the client is no longer benefiting, when services are no longer required, when counseling no longer serves the client's needs or interests, when clients do not pay fees charged, or when agency or institution limits do not allow provision of further counseling services. (See A.10.b. and C.2.g.)

A.12. Computer Technology

a. *Use of Computers.* When computer applications are used in counseling services, counselors ensure that: (1) the client is intellectually, emotionally, and physically capable of using the computer application; (2) the computer application is appropriate for the needs of the client; (3) the client understands the purpose and operation of the computer applications; and (4) a follow-up of client use of a computer application is provided to correct possible misconceptions, discover inappropriate use, and assess subsequent needs.

b. *Explanation of Limitations.* Counselors ensure that clients are provided information as a part of the counseling relationship that adequately explains the limitations of computer technology.

c. *Access to Computer Applications.* Counselors provide for equal access to computer applications in counseling services. (See A.2.a.)

SECTION B: CONFIDENTIALITY

B.1. Right to Privacy

a. *Respect for Privacy.* Counselors respect their clients' right to privacy and avoid illegal and unwarranted disclosures of confidential information. (See A.3.a. and B.6.a.)

b. *Client Waiver.* The right to privacy may be waived by the client or their legally recognized representative.

c. *Exceptions.* The general requirement that counselors keep information confidential does not apply when disclosure is required to prevent clear and imminent danger to the client or others or when legal requirements demand that confidential information be revealed. Counselors consult with other professionals when in doubt as to the validity of an exception.

d. *Contagious, Fatal Diseases.* A counselor who receives information confirming that a client has a disease commonly known to be both communicable and fatal is justified in disclosing information to an identifiable third party, who by his or her relationship with the client is at a high risk of contracting the disease. Prior to making a disclosure the counselor should ascertain that the client has not already informed the third party about his or her disease and that the client is not intending to inform the third party in the immediate future. (See B.1.c and B.1.f)

e. *Court Ordered Disclosure.* When a court is ordered to release confidential information without a client's permission, counselors request to the court that the disclosure not be required due to potential harm to the client or counseling relationship. (See B.1.c.)

f. *Minimal Disclosure.* When circumstances require the disclosure of confidential information, only essential information is revealed. To the extent possible, clients are informed before confidential information is disclosed.

g. *Explanation of Limitations.* When counseling is initiated and throughout the counseling process as necessary, counselors inform clients of the limitations of confidentiality and identify foreseeable situations in which confidentiality must be breached. (See G.2.a.)

h. *Subordinates.* Counselors make every effort to ensure that privacy and confidentiality of clients are maintained by subordinates including employees, supervisees, clerical assistants, and volunteers. (See B.1.a.)

i. *Treatment Teams.* If client treatment will involve a continued review by a treatment team, the client will be informed of the team's existence and composition.

B.2. Groups and Families

a. *Group Work.* In group work, counselors clearly define confidentiality and the parameters for the specific group being entered, explain its importance, and discuss the difficulties related to confidentiality involved in group work. The fact that confidentiality cannot be guaranteed is clearly communicated to group members.

b. *Family Counseling.* In family counseling, information about one family member cannot be disclosed to another member without permission. Counselors protect the privacy rights of each family member. (See A.8., B.3., and B.4.d.)

B.3. Minor or Incompetent Clients

When counseling clients who are minors or individuals who are unable to give voluntary, informed consent, parents or guardians may be included in the counseling process as appropriate. Counselors act in the best interests of clients and take measures to safeguard confidentiality. (See A.3.c.)

B.4. Records

a. *Requirement of Records.* Counselors maintain records necessary for rendering professional services to their clients and as required by laws, regulations, or agency or institution procedures.

b. *Confidentiality of Records.* Counselors are responsible for securing the safety and confidentiality of any counseling records they create, maintain, transfer, or destroy whether the records are written, taped, computerized, or stored in any other medium. (See B.1.a.)

c. *Permission to Record or Observe.* Counselors obtain permission from clients prior to electronically recording or observing sessions. (See A.3.a.)

d. *Client Access.* Counselors recognize that counseling records are kept for the benefit of clients, and therefore provide access to records and copies of records when requested by competent clients, unless the records contain information that may be misleading and detrimental to the client. In situations involving multiple clients, access to records is limited to those parts of records that do not include confidential information related to another client. (See A.8., B.1.a., and B.2.b.)

e. *Disclosure or Transfer.* Counselors obtain written permission from clients to disclose or transfer records to legitimate third parties unless exceptions to confidentiality exist as listed in Section B.1. Steps are taken to ensure that receivers of counseling records are sensitive to their confidential nature.

B.5. Research and Training

a. *Data Disguise Required.* Use of data derived from counseling relationships for purposes of training, research, or publication is confined to content that is disguised to ensure the anonymity of the individuals involved. (See B.1.g. and G.3.d.)

b. *Agreement for Identification.* Identification of a client in a presentation or publication is permissible only when the client has reviewed the material and has agreed to its presentation or publication. (See G.3.d.)

B.6. Consultation

a. *Respect for Privacy.* Information obtained in a consulting relationship is discussed for professional purposes only with persons clearly concerned with the case. Written and oral reports present data germane to the purposes of the consultation, and every

effort is made to protect client identity and avoid undue invasion of privacy.

b. *Cooperating Agencies.* Before sharing information, counselors make efforts to ensure that there are defined policies in other agencies serving the counselor's clients that effectively protect the confidentiality of information.

Section C: Professional Responsibility

C.1. Standards Knowledge

Counselors have a responsibility to read, understand, and follow the Code of Ethics and the Standards of Practice.

C.2. Professional Competence

a. *Boundaries of Competence.* Counselors practice only within the boundaries of their competence, based on their education, training, supervised experience, state and national professional credentials, and appropriate professional experience. Counselors will demonstrate a commitment to gain knowledge, personal awareness, sensitivity, and skills pertinent to working with a diverse client population.

b. *New Specialty Areas of Practice.* Counselors practice in specialty areas new to them only after appropriate education, training, and supervised experience. While developing skills in new specialty areas, counselors take steps to ensure the competence of their work and to protect others from possible harm.

c. *Qualified for Employment.* Counselors accept employment only for positions for which they are qualified by education, training, supervised experience, state and national professional credentials, and appropriate professional experience. Counselors hire for professional counseling positions only individuals who are qualified and competent.

d. *Monitor Effectiveness.* Counselors continually monitor their effectiveness as professionals and take steps to improve when necessary. Counselors in private practice take reasonable steps to seek out peer supervision to evaluate their efficacy as counselors.

e. *Ethical Issues Consultation.* Counselors take reasonable steps to consult with other counselors or related professionals when they have questions regarding their ethical obligations or professional practice. (See H.1)

f. *Continuing Education.* Counselors recognize the need for continuing education to maintain a reasonable level of awareness of current scientific and professional information in their fields of activity. They take steps to maintain competence in the skills they use, are open to new procedures, and keep current with the diverse and/or special populations with whom they work.

g. *Impairment.* Counselors refrain from offering or accepting professional services when their physical, mental, or emotional problems are likely to harm a client or others. They are alert to the signs of impairment, seek assistance for problems, and, if necessary, limit, suspend, or terminate their professional responsibilities. (See A.11.c.)

C.3. Advertising and Soliciting Clients

a. *Accurate Advertising.* There are no restrictions on advertising by counselors except those that can be specifically justified to protect the public from deceptive practices. Counselors advertise or represent their services to the public by identifying their credentials in an accurate manner that is not false, misleading, deceptive, or fraudulent. Counselors may only advertise the highest degree earned which is in counseling or a closely related field from a college or university that was accredited when the degree was awarded by one of the regional accrediting bodies recognized by the Council on Postsecondary Accreditation.

b. *Testimonials.* Counselors who use testimonials do not solicit them from clients or other persons who, because of their particular circumstances, may be vulnerable to undue influence.

c. *Statements by Others.* Counselors make reasonable efforts to ensure that statements made by others about them or the profession of counseling are accurate.

d. *Recruiting Through Employment.* Counselors do not use their places of employment or institutional affiliation to recruit or gain clients, supervisees, or consultees for their private practices. (See C.5.e.)

e. *Products and Training Advertisements.* Counselors who develop products related to their profession or conduct workshops or training events ensure that the advertisements concerning these products or events are accurate and disclose adequate information for consumers to make informed choices.

f. *Promoting to Those Served.* Counselors do not use counseling, teaching, training, or supervisory relationships to promote their products or training events in a manner that is deceptive or would exert undue influence on individuals who may be vulnerable. Counselors may adopt textbooks they have authored for instruction purposes.

g. *Professional Association Involvement.* Counselors actively participate in local, state, and national associations that foster the development and improvement of counseling.

C.4. Credentials

a. *Credentials Claimed.* Counselors claim or imply only professional credentials possessed and are responsible for correcting any known misrepresentations of their credentials by others. Professional credentials include graduate degrees in counseling or closely related mental health fields, accreditation of graduate programs, national voluntary certifications, government-issued certifications or licenses, ACA professional membership, or any other credential that might indicate to the public specialized knowledge or expertise in counseling.

b. *ACA Professional Membership.* ACA professional members may announce to the public their membership status. Regular members may not announce their ACA membership in a manner that might imply they are credentialed counselors.

c. *Credential Guidelines.* Counselors follow the guidelines for use of credentials that have been established by the entities that issue the credentials.

d. *Misrepresentation of Credentials.* Counselors do not attribute more to their credentials than the credentials represent, and do not imply that other counselors are not qualified because they do not possess certain credentials.

e. *Doctoral Degrees from Other Fields.* Counselors who hold a master's degree in counseling or a closely related mental health field, but hold a doctoral degree from other than counseling or a closely related field do not use the title "Dr." in their practices and do not announce to the public in relation to their practice or status as a counselor that they hold a doctorate.

C.5. Public Responsibility

a. *Nondiscrimination.* Counselors do not discriminate against clients, students, or supervisees in a manner that has a negative impact based on their age, color, culture, disability, ethnic group, gender, race, religion, sexual orientation, or socioeconomic status, or for any other reason. (See A.2.a.)

b. *Sexual Harassment.* Counselors do not engage in sexual harassment. Sexual harassment is defined as sexual solicitation, physical advances, or verbal or nonverbal conduct that is sexual in nature, that occurs in connection with professional activities or roles, and that either: (1) is unwelcome, is offensive, or creates a hostile workplace environment, and counselors know or are told this; or (2) is sufficiently severe or intense to be perceived as harassment to a reasonable person in the context. Sexual harassment can consist of a single intense or severe act or multiple persistent or pervasive acts.

c. *Reports to Third Parties.* Counselors are accurate, honest, and unbiased in reporting their professional activities and judgments to appropriate third parties including courts, health insurance companies, those who are the recipients of evaluation reports, and others. (See B.1.g.)

d. *Media Presentations.* When counselors provide advice or comment by means of public lectures, demonstrations, radio or television programs, prerecorded tapes, printed articles, mailed material, or other media, they take reasonable precautions to ensure that

(1) the statements are based on appropriate professional counseling literature and practice; (2) the statements are otherwise consistent with the Code of Ethics and the Standards of Practice; and (3) the recipients of the information are not encouraged to infer that a professional counseling relationship has been established. (See C.6.b.)

e. *Unjustified Gains.* Counselors do not use their professional positions to seek or receive unjustified personal gains, sexual favors, unfair advantage, or unearned goods or services. (See C.3.d.)

C.6. Responsibility to Other Professionals

a. *Different Approaches.* Counselors are respectful of approaches to professional counseling that differ from their own. Counselors know and take into account the traditions and practices of other professional groups with which they work.

b. *Personal Public Statements.* When making personal statements in a public context, counselors clarify that they are speaking from their personal perspectives and that they are not speaking on behalf of all counselors or the profession. (See C.5.d.)

c. *Clients Served by Others.* When counselors learn that their clients are in a professional relationship with another mental health professional, they request release from clients to inform the other professionals and strive to establish positive and collaborative professional relationships. (See A.4.)

SECTION D: RELATIONSHIPS WITH OTHER PROFESSIONALS

D.1. Relationships with Employers and Employees

a. *Role Definition.* Counselors define and describe for their employers and employees the parameters and levels of their professional roles.

b. *Agreements.* Counselors establish working agreements with supervisors, colleagues, and subordinates regarding counseling or clinical relationships, confidentiality, adherence to professional standards, distinction between public and private material, maintenance and dissemination of recorded information, workload, and accountability. Working agreements in each instance are specified and made known to those concerned.

c. *Negative Conditions.* Counselors alert their employers to conditions that may be potentially disruptive or damaging to the counselor's professional responsibilities or that may limit their effectiveness.

d. *Evaluation.* Counselors submit regularly to professional review and evaluation by their supervisor or the appropriate representative of the employer.

e. *In-Service.* Counselors are responsible for in-service development of self and staff.

f. *Goals.* Counselors inform their staff of goals and programs.

g. *Practices.* Counselors provide personnel and agency practices that respect and enhance the rights and welfare of each employee and recipient of agency services. Counselors strive to maintain the highest levels of professional services.

h. *Personnel Selection and Assignment.* Counselors select competent staff and assign responsibilities compatible with their skills and experiences.

i. *Discrimination.* Counselors, as either employers or employees, do not engage in or condone practices that are inhumane, illegal, or unjustifiable (such as considerations based on age, color, culture, disability, ethnic group, gender, race, religion, sexual orientation, or socioeconomic status) in hiring, promotion, or training. (See A.2.a. and C.5.b.)

j. *Professional Conduct.* Counselors have a responsibility both to clients and to the agency or institution within which services are performed to maintain high standards of professional conduct.

k. *Exploitive Relationships.* Counselors do not engage in exploitive relationships with individuals over whom they have supervisory, evaluative, or instructional control or authority.

l. *Employer Policies.* The acceptance of employment in an agency or institution implies that counselors are in agreement with its general policies and principles. Counselors strive to reach agreement with employers as to acceptable standards of conduct that allow for changes in institutional policy conducive to the growth and development of clients.

D.2. Consultation (See B.6.)

a. *Consultation as an Option.* Counselors may choose to consult with any other professionally competent persons about their clients. In choosing consultants, counselors avoid placing the consultant in a conflict of interest situation that would preclude the consultant being a proper party to the counselor's efforts to help the client. Should counselors be engaged in a work setting that compromises this consultation standard, they consult with other professionals whenever possible to consider justifiable alternatives.

b. *Consultant Competency.* Counselors are reasonably certain that they have or the organization represented has the necessary competencies and resources for giving the kind of consulting services needed and that appropriate referral resources are available.

c. *Understanding with Clients.* When providing consultation, counselors attempt to develop with their clients a clear understanding of problem definition, goals for change, and predicted consequences of interventions selected.

d. *Consultant Goals.* The consulting relationship is one in which client adaptability and growth toward self-direction are consistently encouraged and cultivated. (See A.1.b.)

D.3. Fees for Referral

a. *Accepting Fees from Agency Clients.* Counselors refuse a private fee or other remuneration for rendering services to persons who are entitled to such services through the counselor's employing agency or institution. The policies of a particular agency may make explicit provisions for agency clients to receive counseling services from members of its staff in private practice. In such instances, the clients must be informed of other options open to them should they seek private counseling services. (See A.10.a, A.11.b., and C.3.d.)

b. *Referral Fees.* Counselors do not accept a referral fee from other professionals.

D.4. Subcontractor Arrangements

When counselors work as subcontractors for counseling services for a third party, they have a duty to inform clients of the limitations of confidentiality that the organization may place on counselors in providing counseling services to clients. The limits of such confidentiality ordinarily are discussed as part of the intake session. (See B.1.e. and B.1.f.)

SECTION E: EVALUATION, ASSESSMENT, AND INTERPRETATION

E.1. General

a. *Appraisal Techniques.* The primary purpose of educational and psychological assessment is to provide measures that are objective and interpretable in either comparative or absolute terms. Counselors recognize the need to interpret the statements in this section as applying to the whole range of appraisal techniques, including test and nontest data.

b. *Client Welfare.* Counselors promote the welfare and best interests of the client in the development, publication, and utilization of educational and psychological assessment techniques. They do not misuse assessment results and interpretations and take reasonable steps to prevent others from misusing the information these techniques provide. They respect the client's right to know the results, the interpretations made, and the bases for their conclusions and recommendations.

E.2. Competence to Use and Interpret Tests

a. *Limits of Competence.* Counselors recognize the limits of their competence and perform only those testing and assessment services for which they have been trained. They are familiar with reliability, validity, related standardization, error of measurement, and proper application of any technique utilized. Counselors using computer-based test interpretations are trained in the construct being measured and the specific instrument being used prior to using this type of computer application. Counselors take reasonable measures to ensure the proper use of psychological assessment techniques by persons under their supervision.

b. *Appropriate Use.* Counselors are responsible for the appropriate application, scoring, interpretation, and use of assessment instruments, whether they score and interpret such tests themselves or use computerized or other services.

c. *Decisions Based on Results.* Counselors responsible for decisions involving individuals or policies that are based on assessment results have a thorough understanding of educational and psychological measurement, including validation criteria, test research, and guidelines for test development and use.

d. *Accurate Information.* Counselors provide accurate information and avoid false claims or misconceptions when making statements about assessment instruments or techniques. Special efforts are made to avoid unwarranted connotations of such terms as IQ and grade equivalent scores. (See C.5.c.)

E.3. Informed Consent

a. *Explanation to Clients.* Prior to assessment, counselors explain the nature and purposes of assessment and the specific use of results in language the client (or other legally authorized person on behalf of the client) can understand, unless an explicit exception to this right has been agreed upon in advance. Regardless of whether scoring and interpretation are completed by counselors, by assistants, or by computer or other outside services, counselors take reasonable steps to ensure that appropriate explanations are given to the client.

b. *Recipients of Results.* The examinee's welfare, explicit understanding, and prior agreement determine the recipients of test results. Counselors include accurate and appropriate interpretations with any release of individual or group test results. (See B.1.a. and C.5.c.)

E.4. Release of Information to Competent Professionals

a. *Misuse of Results.* Counselors do not misuse assessment results, including test results, and interpretations, and take reasonable steps to prevent the misuse of such by others. (See C.5.c.)

b. *Release of Raw Data.* Counselors ordinarily release data (e.g. protocols, counseling or interview notes, or questionnaires) in which the client is identified only with the consent of the client or the client's legal representative. Such data are usually released only to persons recognized by counselors as competent to interpret the data. (See B.1.a.)

E.5. Proper Diagnosis of Mental Disorders

a. *Proper Diagnosis.* Counselors take special care to provide proper diagnosis of mental disorders. Assessment techniques (including personal interview) used to determine client care (e.g., locus of treatment, type of treatment, or recommended follow-up) are carefully selected and appropriately used. (See A.3.a. and C.5.c.)

b. *Cultural Sensitivity.* Counselors recognize that culture affects the manner in which clients' problems are defined. Clients' socioeconomic and cultural experience is considered when diagnosing mental disorders.

E.6. Test Selection

a. *Appropriateness of Instruments.* Counselors carefully consider the validity, reliability, psychometric limitations, and appropriateness of instruments when selecting tests for use in a given situation or with a particular client.

b. *Culturally Diverse Populations.* Counselors are cautious when selecting tests for culturally diverse populations to avoid inappropriateness of testing that may be outside of socialized behavioral or cognitive patterns.

E.7. Conditions of Test Administration

a. *Administration Conditions.* Counselors administer tests under the same conditions that were established in their standardization. When tests are not administered under standard conditions or when unusual behavior or irregularities occur during the testing session, those conditions are noted in interpretation, and the results may be designated as invalid or of questionable validity.

b. *Computer Administration.* Counselors are responsible for ensuring that administration programs function properly to provide clients with accurate results when a computer or other electronic methods are used for test administration. (See A.12.b.)

c. *Unsupervised Test-Taking.* Counselors do not permit unsupervised or inadequately supervised use of tests or assessments unless the tests or assessments are designed, intended, and validated for self-administration and/or scoring.

d. *Disclosure of Favorable Conditions.* Prior to test administration, conditions that produce most favorable test results are made known to the examinee.

E.8. Diversity in Testing

Counselors are cautious in using assessment techniques, making evaluations, and interpreting the performance of populations not represented in the norm group on which an instrument was standardized. They recognize the effects of age, color, culture, disability, ethnic group, gender, race, religion, sexual orientation, and socioeconomic status on test administration and interpretation and place test results in proper perspective with other relevant factors. (See A.2.a.)

E.9. Test Scoring and Interpretation

a. *Reporting Reservations.* In reporting assessment results, counselors indicate any reservations that exist regarding validity or reliability because of the circumstances of the assessment or the inappropriateness of the norms for the person tested.

b. *Research Instruments.* Counselors exercise caution when interpreting the results of research instruments possessing insufficient technical data to support respondent results. The specific purposes for the use of such instruments are stated explicitly to the examinee.

c. *Testing Services.* Counselors who provide test scoring and test interpretation services to support the assessment process confirm the validity of such interpretations. They accurately describe the purpose, norms, validity, reliability, and applications of the procedures and any special qualifications applicable to their use. The public offering of an automated test interpretations service is considered a professional-to-professional consultation. The formal responsibility of the consultant is to the consultee, but the ultimate and overriding responsibility is to the client.

E.10. Test Security

Counselors maintain the integrity and security of tests and other assessment techniques consistent with legal and contractual obligations. Counselors do not appropriate, reproduce, or modify published tests or parts thereof without acknowledgment and permission from the publisher.

E.11. Obsolete Tests and Outdated Test Results

Counselors do not use data or test results that are obsolete or outdated for the current purpose. Counselors make every effort to prevent the misuse of obsolete measures and test data by others.

E.12. Test Construction

Counselors use established scientific procedures, relevant standards, and current professional knowledge for test design in the development, publication, and utilization of educational and psychological assessment techniques.

SECTION F: TEACHING, TRAINING, AND SUPERVISION

F.1. Counselor Educators and Trainers

a. *Educators as Teachers and Practitioners.* Counselors who are responsible for developing, implementing, and supervising educational programs are skilled as teachers and practitioners. They are knowledgeable regarding the ethical, legal, and regulatory aspects of the profession, are skilled in applying that knowledge, and make students and supervisees aware of their responsibilities. Counselors conduct counselor education and training programs in an ethical manner and serve as role models for professional behavior. Counselor educators should make an effort to infuse material related to human diversity into all courses and/or workshops that are designed to promote the development of professional counselors.

b. *Relationship Boundaries with Students and Supervisees.* Counselors clearly define and maintain ethical, professional, and social relationship boundaries with their students and supervisees. They are aware of the differential in power that exists and the student's or supervisee's possible incomprehension of that power differential. Counselors explain to students and supervisees the potential for the relationship to become exploitive.

c. *Sexual Relationships.* Counselors do not engage in sexual relationships with students or supervisees and do not subject them to sexual harassment. (See A.6. and C.5.b)

d. *Contributions to Research.* Counselors give credit to students or supervisees for their contributions to research and scholarly projects. Credit is given through coauthorship, acknowledgment, footnote statement, or other appropriate means, in accordance with such contributions. (See G.4.b. and G.4.c.)

e. *Close Relatives.* Counselors do not accept close relatives as students or supervisees.

f. *Supervision Preparation.* Counselors who offer clinical supervision services are adequately prepared in supervision methods and techniques. Counselors who are doctoral students serving as practicum or internship supervisors to master's level students are adequately prepared and supervised by the training program.

g. *Responsibility for Services to Clients.* Counselors who supervise the counseling services of others take reasonable measures to ensure that counseling services provided to clients are professional.

h. *Endorsement.* Counselors do not endorse students or supervisees for certification, licensure, employment, or completion of an academic or training program if they believe students or supervisees are not qualified for the endorsement. Counselors take reasonable steps to assist students or supervisees who are not qualified for endorsement to become qualified.

F.2. Counselor Education and Training Programs

a. *Orientation.* Prior to admission, counselors orient prospective students to the counselor education or training program's expectations, including but not limited to the following: (1) the type and level of skill acquisition required for successful completion of the training, (2) subject matter to be covered, (3) basis for evaluation, (4) training components that encourage self-growth or self-disclosure as part of the training process, (5) the type of supervision settings and requirements of the sites for required clinical field experiences, (6) student and supervisee evaluation and dismissal policies and procedures, and (7) up-to-date employment prospects for graduates.

b. *Integration of Study and Practice.* Counselors establish counselor education and training programs that integrate academic study and supervised practice.

c. *Evaluation.* Counselors clearly state to students and supervisees, in advance of training, the levels of competency expected, appraisal methods, and timing of evaluations for both didactic and experiential components. Counselors provide students and supervisees with periodic performance appraisal and evaluation feedback throughout the training program.

d. *Teaching Ethics.* Counselors make students and supervisees aware of the ethical responsibilities and standards of the profession and the students' and supervisees' ethical responsibilities to the profession. (See C.1. and F.3.e.)

e. *Peer Relationships.* When students or supervisees are assigned to lead counseling groups or provide clinical supervision for their peers, counselors take steps to ensure that students and supervisees placed in these roles do not have personal or adverse relationships with peers and that they understand they have the same ethical obligations as counselor educators, trainers, and supervisors. Counselors make every effort to ensure that the rights of peers are not compromised when students or supervisees are assigned to lead counseling groups or provide clinical supervision.

f. *Varied Theoretical Positions.* Counselors present varied theoretical positions so that students and supervisees may make comparisons and have opportunities to develop their own positions. Counselors provide information concerning the scientific bases of professional practice. (See C.6.a.)

g. *Field Placements.* Counselors develop clear policies within their training program regarding field placement and other clinical experiences. Counselors provide clearly stated roles and responsibilities for the student or supervisee, the site supervisor, and the program supervisor. They confirm that site supervisors are qualified to provide supervision and are informed of their professional and ethical responsibilities in this role.

h. *Dual Relationships as Supervisors.* Counselors avoid dual relationships such as performing the role of site supervisor and training program supervisor in the student's or supervisee's training program. Counselors do not accept any form of professional services, fees, commissions, reimbursement, or remuneration from a site for student or supervisee placement.

i. *Diversity in Programs.* Counselors are responsive to their institution's and program's recruitment and retention needs for training program administrators, faculty, and students with diverse backgrounds and special needs. (See A.2.a.)

F.3. Students and Supervisees

a. *Limitations.* Counselors, through ongoing evaluation and appraisal, are aware of the academic and personal limitations of students and supervisees that might impede performance. Counselors assist students and supervisees in securing remedial assistance when needed, and dismiss from the training program supervisees who are unable to provide competent service due to academic or personal limitations. Counselors seek professional consultation and document their decision to dismiss or refer students or supervisees for assistance. Counselors assure that students and supervisees have recourse to address decisions made, to require them to seek assistance, or to dismiss them.

b. *Self-Growth Experiences.* Counselors use professional judgment when designing training experiences conducted by the counselors themselves that require student and supervisee self-growth or self-disclosure. Safeguards are provided so that students and supervisees are aware of the ramifications their self-disclosure may have, on counselors whose primary role as teacher, trainer, or supervisor requires acting on ethical obligations to the profession. Evaluative components of experiential training experiences explicitly delineate predetermined academic standards that are separate and not dependent on the student's level of self-disclosure. (See A.6.)

c. *Counseling for Students and Supervisees.* If students or supervisees request counseling, supervisors or counselor educators provide them with acceptable referrals. Supervisors or counselor educators do not serve as counselor to students or supervisees over whom they hold administrative, teaching, or evaluative roles unless this is a brief role associated with a training experience. (See A.6.b.)

d. *Clients of Students and Supervisees.* Counselors make every effort to ensure that the clients at field placements are aware of the services rendered and the qualifications of the students and supervisees rendering those services. Clients receive professional disclosure information and are informed of the limits of confidentiality. Client permission is obtained in order for the students and supervisees to use any information concerning the counseling relationship in the training process. (See B.1.e.)

e. *Standards for Students and Supervisees.* Students and supervisees preparing to become counselors adhere to the Code of Ethics and the Standards of Practice. Students and supervisees have the same obligations to clients as those required of counselors. (See H.1.)

SECTION G: RESEARCH AND PUBLICATION

G.1. Research Responsibilities

a. *Use of Human Subjects.* Counselors plan, design, conduct, and report research in a manner consistent with pertinent ethical principles, federal and state laws, host institutional regulations, and scientific standards governing research with human subjects. Counselors design and conduct research that reflects cultural sensitivity appropriateness.

b. *Deviation from Standard Practices.* Counselors seek consultation and observe stringent safeguards to protect the rights of research participants when a research problem suggests a deviation from standard acceptable practices. (See B.6.)

c. *Precautions to Avoid Injury.* Counselors who conduct research with human subjects are responsible for the subjects' welfare throughout the experiment and take reasonable precautions to avoid causing injurious psychological, physical, or social effects to their subjects.

d. *Principal Researcher Responsibility.* The ultimate responsibility for ethical research practice lies with the principal researcher. All others involved in the research activities share ethical obligations and full responsibility for their own actions.

e. *Minimal Interference.* Counselors take reasonable precautions to avoid causing disruptions in subjects' lives due to participation in research.

f. *Diversity.* Counselors are sensitive to diversity and research issues with special populations. They seek consultation when appropriate. (See A.2.a. and B.6.)

G.2. Informed Consent

a. *Topics Disclosed.* In obtaining informed consent for research, counselors use language that is understandable to research participants and that: (1) accurately explains the purpose and procedures to be followed; (2) identifies any procedures that are experimental or relatively untried; (3) describes the attendant discomforts and risks; (4) describes the benefits or changes in individuals or organizations that might be reasonably expected; (5) discloses appropriate alternative procedures that would be advantageous for subjects; (6) offers to answer any inquiries concerning the procedures; (7) describes any limitations on confidentiality; and (8) instructs that subjects are free to withdraw their consent and to discontinue participation in the project at any time. (See B.1.f.)

b. *Deception.* Counselors do not conduct research involving deception unless alternative procedures are not feasible and the prospective value of the research justifies the deception. When the methodological requirements of a study necessitate concealment or deception, the investigator is required to explain clearly the reasons for this action as soon as possible.

c. *Voluntary Participation.* Participation in research is typically voluntary and without any penalty for refusal to participate. Involuntary participation is appropriate only when it can be demonstrated that participation will have no harmful effects on subjects and is essential to the investigation.

d. *Confidentiality of Information.* Information obtained about research participants during the course of an investigation is confidential. When the possibility exists that others may obtain access to such information, ethical research practice requires that the possibility, together with the plans for protecting confidentiality, be explained to participants as a part of the procedure for obtaining informed consent. (See B.1.e.)

e. *Persons Incapable of Giving Informed Consent.* When a person is incapable of giving informed consent, counselors provide an appropriate explanation, obtain agreement for participation, and obtain appropriate consent from a legally authorized person.

f. *Commitments to Participants.* Counselors take reasonable measures to honor all commitments to research participants.

g. *Explanations After Data Collection.* After data are collected, counselors provide participants with full clarification of the nature of the study to remove any misconceptions. Where scientific or human values justify delaying or withholding information, counselors take reasonable measures to avoid causing harm.

h. *Agreements to Cooperate.* Counselors who agree to cooperate with another individual in research or publication incur an obligation to cooperate as promised in terms of punctuality of performance and with regard to the completeness and accuracy of the information required.

i. *Informed Consent for Sponsors.* In the pursuit of research, counselors give sponsors, institutions, and publication channels the same respect and opportunity for giving informed consent that they accord to individual research participants. Counselors are aware of their obligation to future research workers and ensure that host institutions are given feedback information and proper acknowledgment.

G.3. Reporting Results

a. *Information Affecting Outcome.* When reporting research results, counselors explicitly mention all variables and conditions known to the investigator that may have affected the outcome of a study or the interpretation of data.

b. *Accurate Results.* Counselors plan, conduct, and report research accurately and in a manner that minimizes the possibility that results will be misleading. They provide thorough discussions of the limitations of their data and alternative hypotheses. Counselors

do not engage in fraudulent research, distort data, misrepresent data, or deliberately bias their results.

c. *Obligation to Report Unfavorable Results.* Counselors communicate to other counselors the results of any research judged to be of professional value. Results that reflect unfavorably on institutions, programs, services, prevailing opinions, or vested interests are not withheld.

d. *Identity of Subjects.* Counselors who supply data, aid in the research of another person, report research results, or make original data available take due care to disguise the identity of respective subjects in the absence of specific authorization from the subjects to do otherwise. (See B.1.g. and B.5.a.)

e. *Replication Studies.* Counselors are obligated to make available sufficient original research data to qualified professionals who may wish to replicate the study.

G.4. Publication

a. *Recognition of Others.* When conducting and reporting research, counselors are familiar with and give recognition to previous work on the topic, observe copyright laws, and give full credit to those to whom credit is due. (See F.1.d. and G.4.c.)

b. *Contributors.* Counselors give credit through joint authorship, acknowledgment, footnote statements, or other appropriate means to those who have contributed significantly to research or concept development in accordance with such contributions. The principal contributor is listed first and minor technical or professional contributions are acknowledged in notes or introductory statements.

c. *Student Research.* For an article that is substantially based on a student's dissertation or thesis, the student is listed as the principal author. (See F.1.d. and G.4.a.)

d. *Duplicate Submission.* Counselors submit manuscripts for consideration to only one journal at a time. Manuscripts that are published in whole or in substantial part in another journal or published work are not submitted for publication without acknowledgment and permission from the previous publication.

e. *Professional Review.* Counselors who review material submitted for publication, research, or other scholarly purposes respect the confidentiality and proprietary rights of those who submitted it.

SECTION H: RESOLVING ETHICAL ISSUES
H.1. Knowledge of Standards

Counselors are familiar with the Code of Ethics and the Standards of Practice and other applicable ethics codes from other professional organizations of which they are members, or from certification and licensure bodies. Lack of knowledge or misunderstanding of an ethical responsibility is not a defense against a charge of unethical conduct. (See F.3.e.)

H.2. Suspected Violations

a. *Ethical Behavior Expected.* Counselors expect professional associates to adhere to Code of Ethics. When counselors possess reasonable cause that raises doubts as to whether a counselor is acting in an ethical manner, they take appropriate action. (See H.2.d. and H.2.e.)

b. *Consultation.* When uncertain as to whether a particular situation or course of action may be in violation of Code of Ethics, counselors consult with other counselors who are knowledgeable about ethics, with colleagues, or with appropriate authorities.

c. *Organization Conflicts.* If the demands of an organization with which counselors are affiliated pose a conflict with Code of Ethics, counselors specify the nature of such conflicts and express to their supervisors or other responsible officials their commitment to Code of Ethics. When possible, counselors work toward change within the organization to allow full adherence to Code of Ethics.

d. *Informal Resolution.* When counselors have reasonable cause to believe that another counselor is violating an ethical standard, they attempt to first resolve the issue informally with the other counselor if feasible, providing that such action does not violate confidentiality rights that may be involved.

e. *Reporting Suspected Violations.* When an informal resolution is not appropriate or feasible, counselors, upon reasonable cause, take action such as reporting the suspected ethical violation to state or national ethics committees, unless this action conflicts with confidentiality rights that cannot be resolved.

f. *Unwarranted Complaints.* Counselors do not initiate, participate in, or encourage the filing of ethics complaints that are unwarranted or intend to harm a counselor rather than to protect clients or the public.

H.3. Cooperation with Ethics Committees

Counselors assist in the process of enforcing Code of Ethics. Counselors cooperate with investigations, proceedings, and requirements of the ACA Ethics Committee or ethics committees of other duly constituted associations or boards having jurisdiction over those charged with a violation. Counselors are familiar with the ACA Policies and Procedures and use it as a reference in assisting the enforcement of the Code of Ethics.

Standards of Practice

All members of the American Counseling Association (ACA) are required to adhere to the Standards of Practice and the Code of Ethics. The Standards of Practice represent minimal behavioral statements of the Code of Ethics. Members should refer to the applicable section of the Code of Ethics for further interpretation and amplification of the applicable Standard of Practice.

SECTION A: THE COUNSELING RELATIONSHIP

Standard of Practice One (SP-1) Nondiscrimination

Counselors respect diversity and must not discriminate against clients because of age, color, culture, disability, ethnic group, gender, race, religion, sexual orientation, marital status, or socioeconomic status. (See A.2.a.)

Standard of Practice Two (SP-2) Disclosure to Clients

Counselors must adequately inform clients, preferably in writing, regarding the counseling process and counseling relationship at or before the time it begins and throughout the relationship. (See A.3.a.)

Standard of Practice Three (SP-3) Dual Relationships

Counselors must make every effort to avoid dual relationships with clients that could impair their professional judgment or increase the risk of harm to clients. When a dual relationship cannot be avoided, counselors must take appropriate steps to ensure that judgment is not impaired and that no exploitation occurs. (See A.6.a. and A.6.b.)

Standard of Practice Four (SP-4) Sexual Intimacies with Clients

Counselors must not engage in any type of sexual intimacies with current clients and must not engage in sexual intimacies with former clients within a minimum of two years after terminating the counseling relationship. Counselors who engage in such relationships after two years following termination have the responsibility to thoroughly examine and document that such relations did not have an exploitative nature.

Standard of Practice Five (SP-5) Protecting Clients During Group Work

Counselors must take steps to protect clients from physical or psychological trauma resulting from interactions during group work. (See A.9.b.)

Standard of Practice Six (SP-6) Advance Understanding of Fees

Counselors must explain to clients, prior to their entering the counseling relationship, financial arrangements related to professional services. (See A.10. a.–d. and A.11.c.)

Standard of Practice Seven (SP-7) Termination

Counselors must assist in making appropriate arrangements for the continuation of treatment of clients, when necessary, following termination of counseling relationships. (See A.11.a.)

Standard of Practice Eight (SP-8) Inability to Assist Clients

Counselors must avoid entering or immediately terminate a counseling relationship if it is determined that they are unable to be of professional assistance to a client. The counselor may assist in making an appropriate referral for the client. (See A.11.b.)

SECTION B: CONFIDENTIALITY

Standard of Practice Nine (SP-9) Confidentiality Requirement

Counselors must keep information related to counseling services confidential unless disclosure is in the best interest of clients, is required for the welfare of others, or is required by law. When disclosure is required, only information that is essential is revealed and the client is informed of such disclosure. (See B.1. a.–f.)

Standard of Practice Ten (SP-10) Confidentiality Requirements for Subordinates

Counselors must take measures to ensure that privacy and confidentiality of clients are maintained by subordinates. (See B.1.h.)

Standard of Practice Eleven (SP-11) Confidentiality in Group Work

Counselors must clearly communicate to group members that confidentiality cannot be guaranteed in group work. (See B.2.a.)

Standard of Practice Twelve (SP-12) Confidentiality in Family Counseling

Counselors must not disclose information about one family member in counseling to another family member without prior consent. (See B.2.b.)

Standard of Practice Thirteen (SP-13) Confidentiality of Records

Counselors must maintain appropriate confidentiality in creating, storing, accessing, transferring, and disposing of counseling records. (See B.4.b.)

Standard of Practice Fourteen (SP-14) Permission to Record or Observe

Counselors must obtain prior consent from clients in order to electronically record or observe sessions. (See B.4.c.)

Standard of Practice Fifteen (SP-15) Disclosure or Transfer of Records

Counselors must obtain client consent to disclose or transfer records to third parties, unless exceptions listed in SP-9 exist. (See B.4.e.)

Standard of Practice Sixteen (SP-16) Data Disguise Required

Counselors must disguise the identity of the client when using data for training, research, or publication. (See B.5.a.)

SECTION C: PROFESSIONAL RESPONSIBILITY

Standard of Practice Seventeen (SP-17) Boundaries of Competence

Counselors must practice only within the boundaries of their competence. (See C.2.a.)

Standard of Practice Eighteen (SP-18) Continuing Education

Counselors must engage in continuing education to maintain their professional competence. (See C.2.f.)

Standard of Practice Nineteen (SP-19) Impairment of Professionals

Counselors must refrain from offering professional services when their personal problems or conflicts may cause harm to a client or others. (See C.2.g.)

Standard of Practice Twenty (SP-20) Accurate Advertising

Counselors must accurately represent their credentials and services when advertising. (See C.3.a.)

Standard of Practice Twenty-One (SP-21) Recruiting Through Employment

Counselors must not use their place of employment or institutional affiliation to recruit clients for their private practices. (See C.3.d.)

Standard of Practice Twenty-Two (SP-22) Credentials Claimed

Counselors must claim or imply only professional credentials possessed and must correct any known misrepresentations of their credentials by others. (See C.4.a.)

Standard of Practice Twenty-Three (SP-23) Sexual Harassment

Counselors must not engage in sexual harassment. (See C.5.b.)

Standard of Practice Twenty-Four (SP-24) Unjustified Gains

Counselors must not use their professional positions to seek or receive unjustified personal gains, sexual favors, unfair advantage, or unearned goods or services. (See C.5.e.)

Standard of Practice Twenty-Five (SP-25) Clients Served by Others

With the consent of the client, counselors must inform other mental health professionals serving the same client that a counseling relationship between the counselor and client exists. (See C.6.c.)

Standard of Practice Twenty-Six (SP-26) Negative Employment Conditions

Counselors must alert their employers to institutional policy or conditions that may be potentially disruptive or damaging to the counselor's professional responsibilities, or that may limit their effectiveness or deny clients' rights. (See D.1.c.)

Standard of Practice Twenty-Seven (SP-27)
Personnel Selection and Assignment
Counselors must select competent staff and must assign responsibilities compatible with staff skills and experiences. (See D.1.h.)

Standard of Practice Twenty-Eight (SP-28)
Exploitive Relationships with Subordinates
Counselors must not engage in exploitive relationships with individuals over whom they have supervisory, evaluative, or instructional control or authority. (See D.1.k.)

SECTION D: RELATIONSHIP WITH OTHER PROFESSIONALS

Standard of Practice Twenty-Nine (SP-29) Accepting Fees from Agency Clients
Counselors must not accept fees or other remuneration for consultation with persons entitled to such services through the counselor's employing agency or institution. (See D.3.a.)

Standard of Practice Thirty (SP-30) Referral Fees
Counselors must not accept referral fees. (See D.3.b.)

SECTION E: EVALUATION, ASSESSMENT, AND INTERPRETATION

Standard of Practice Thirty-One (SP-31)
Limits of Competence
Counselors must perform only testing and assessment services for which they are competent. Counselors must not allow the use of psychological assessment techniques by unqualified persons under their supervision. (See E.2.a.)

Standard of Practice Thirty-Two (SP-32)
Appropriate Use of Assessment Instruments
Counselors must use assessment instruments in the manner for which they were intended. (See E.2.b.)

Standard of Practice Thirty-Three (SP-33)
Assessment Explanations to Clients
Counselors must provide explanations to clients prior to assessment about the nature and purposes of assessment and the specific uses of results. (See E.3.a.)

Standard of Practice Thirty-Four (SP-34)
Recipients of Test Results
Counselors must ensure that accurate and appropriate interpretations accompany any release of testing and assessment information. (See E.3.b.)

Standard of Practice Thirty-Five (SP-35) Obsolete Tests and Outdated Test Results
Counselors must not base their assessment or intervention decisions or recommendations on data or test results that are obsolete or outdated for the current purpose. (See E.11.)

SECTION F: TEACHING, TRAINING, AND SUPERVISION

Standard of Practice Thirty-Six (SP-36) Sexual Relationships with Students or Supervisees
Counselors must not engage in sexual relationships with their students and supervisees. (See F.1.c.)

Standard of Practice Thirty-Seven (SP-37)
Credit for Contributions to Research
Counselors must give credit to students or supervisees for their contributions to research and scholarly projects. (See F.1.d.)

Standard of Practice Thirty-Eight (SP-38)
Supervision Preparation
Counselors who offer clinical supervision services must be trained and prepared in supervision methods and techniques. (See F.1.f.)

Standard of Practice Thirty-Nine (SP-39) Evaluation Information
Counselors must clearly state to students and supervisees in advance of training, the levels of competency expected, appraisal methods, and timing of evaluations. Counselors must provide students and supervisees with periodic performance appraisal and evaluation feedback throughout the training program. (See F.2.c.)

Standard of Practice Forty (SP-40) Peer Relationships in Training
Counselors must make every effort to ensure that the rights of peers are not violated when students and supervisees are assigned to lead counseling groups or provide clinical supervision. (See F.2.e.)

Standard of Practice Forty-One (SP-41)
Limitations of Students and Supervisees
Counselors must assist students and supervisees in securing remedial assistance, when needed, and must dismiss from the training program students and supervisees who are unable to provide competent service due to academic or personal limitations. (See F.3.a.)

Standard of Practice Forty-Two (SP-42)
Self-Growth Experiences
Counselors who conduct experiences for students or supervisees that include self-growth or self-disclosure must inform participants of counselors' ethical obligations to the profession and must not grade participants based on their nonacademic performance. (See F.3.b.)

Standard of Practice Forty-Three (SP-43)
Standards for Students and Supervisees
Students and supervisees preparing to become counselors must adhere to the Code of Ethics and the Standards of Practice of counselors. (See F.3.e.)

SECTION G: RESEARCH AND PUBLICATION

Standard of Practice Forty-Four (SP-44)

Precautions to Avoid Injury in Research

Counselors must avoid causing physical, social, or psychological harm or injury to subjects in research. (See G.1.c.)

Standard of Practice Forty-Five (SP-45)

Confidentiality of Research Information

Counselors must keep confidential information obtained about research participants. (See G.2.d.)

Standard of Practice Forty-Six (SP-46)

Information Affecting Research Outcome

Counselors must report all variables and conditions known to the investigator that may have research data or outcomes. (See G.3.a.)

Standard of Practice Forty-Seven (SP-47)

Accurate Research Results

Counselors must not distort or misrepresent research data, nor fabricate or intentionally bias research results. (See G.3.b.)

Standard of Practice Forty-Eight (SP-48)

Publication Contributors

Counselors must give appropriate credit to those who have contributed to research. (See G.4.a. and G.4.b.)

SECTION H: RESOLVING ETHICAL ISSUES

Standard of Practice Forty-Nine (SP-49)

Ethical Behavior Expected

Counselors must take appropriate action when they possess reasonable cause that raises doubts as to whether counselors or other mental health professionals are acting in an ethical manner. (See H.2.a.)

Standard of Practice Fifty (SP-50)

Unwarranted Complaints

Counselors must not initiate, participate in, or encourage the filing of ethics complaints that are unwarranted or intended to harm a mental health professional rather than to protect clients or the public. (See H.2.f.)

Standard of Practice Fifty-One (SP-51) Cooperation with Ethics Committees

Counselors must cooperate with investigations, proceedings, and requirements of the ACA Ethics Committee or ethics committees of other duly constituted associations or boards having jurisdiction over those charged with a violation. (See H.3.)

REFERENCES

The following documents are available to counselors as resources to guide them in their practices. These resources are not a part of the Code of Ethics and the Standards of Practice.

American Association for Counseling and Development/Association for Measurement and Evaluation in Counseling and Development. (1989). *The responsibilities of users of standardized tests* (revised). Washington, DC: Author.

American Counseling Association. (1988). *American Counseling Association Ethical Standards*. Alexandria, VA: Author.

American Psychological Association. (1985). *Standards for educational and psychological testing* (revised). Washington, DC: Author.

American Rehabilitation Counseling Association, Commission on Rehabilitation Counselor Certification, and National Rehabilitation Counseling Association. (1995). *Code of professional ethics for rehabilitation counselors*. Chicago, IL: Author.

American School Counselor Association. (1992). *Ethical standards for school counselors*. Alexandria, VA: Author.

Joint Committee on Testing Practices. (1988). *Code of fair testing practices in education*. Washington, DC: Author.

National Board for Certified Counselors. (1989). *National Board for Certified Counselors Code of Ethics*. Alexandria, VA: Author.

Prediger, D. J. (Ed.). (1993, March). *Multicultural assessment standards*. Alexandria, VA: Association for Assessment in Counseling.

Policies and Procedures for Responding to Members' Requests for Interpretations of the Ethical Standards*

SECTION A: APPROPRIATE REQUESTS

1. ACA members may request that the Committee issue formal interpretations of the ACA Code of Ethics for the purpose of guiding the member's own professional behavior.

2. Requests for interpretations will not be considered in the following situations:

a. The individual requesting the interpretation is not an ACA member, or

b. The request is intended to determine whether the behavior of another mental health professional is unethical. In the event an ACA member believes the behavior of another mental health professional is unethical, the ACA member should resolve the issue

*Revised by Governing Council April 1994, effective July 1, 1994.

directly with the professional, if possible, and should file an ethical complaint if appropriate.

SECTION B: PROCEDURES

1. Members must send written requests for interpretations to the Committee at ACA Headquarters.
2. Questions should be submitted in the following format: "Does (counselor behavior) violate Sections ____ or any other sections of the ACA Ethical Standards?" Questions should avoid unique details, be general in nature to the extent possible, and be brief.
3. The Committee staff liaison will revise the question, if necessary, and submit it to the Committee Co-Chair for approval.

4. The question will be sent to Committee members who will be asked to respond individually.
5. The Committee Co-Chair will develop a consensus interpretation on behalf of the Committee.
6. The consensus interpretation will be sent to members of the Committee for final approval.
7. The formal interpretation will be sent to the member who submitted the inquiry.
8. The question and the formal interpretation will be published in the ACA newsletter, but the identity of the member requesting the interpretation will not be disclosed.

Policies and Procedures for Processing Complaints of Ethical Violations

SECTION A: GENERAL

1. The American Counseling Association, hereafter referred to as the "Association" or "ACA", is dedicated to enhancing human development throughout the life span and promoting the counseling profession.
2. The Association, in furthering its objectives, administers the Code of Ethics that have been developed and approved by the ACA Governing Council.
3. The purpose of this document is to facilitate the work of the ACA Ethics Committee ("Committee") by specifying the procedures for processing cases of alleged violations of the ACA Code of Ethics, codifying options for sanctioning members, and stating appeals procedures. The intent of the Association is to monitor the professional conduct of its members to promote sound ethical practices. ACA does not, however, warrant the performance of any individual.

SECTION B: ETHICS COMMITTEE MEMBERS

1. The Ethics Committee is a standing committee of the Association. The Committee consists of six (6) appointed members, including two (2) Co-Chairs whose terms overlap. Two members are appointed annually for three (3) year terms by the President-Elect; appointments are subject to confirmation by the ACA Governing Council. Any vacancy occurring on the Committee will be filled by the President in the same manner, and the person appointed shall serve the unexpired term of the member whose place he or she took. Committee members may be reappointed to not more than one (1) additional consecutive term.
2. One (1) of the Committee co-chairs is appointed annually by the President-Elect from among the Committee members who have two (2) years of service remaining and serves as co-chair for two (2) years, subject to confirmation by the ACA Governing Council.

SECTION C: ROLE AND FUNCTION

1. The Ethics Committee is responsible for:
a. Educating the membership as to the Association's Code of Ethics;
b. Periodically reviewing and recommending changes in the Code of Ethics of the Association as well as the Policies and Procedures for Processing Complaints of Ethical Violations;
c. Receiving and processing complaints of alleged violations of the Code of Ethics of the Association; and,
d. Receiving and processing questions.
2. The Committee shall meet in person or by telephone conference a minimum of three (3) times per year for processing complaints.
3. In processing complaints about alleged ethical misconduct, the Committee will compile an objective, factual account of the dispute in question and make the best possible recommendation for the resolution of the case. The Committee, in taking any action, shall do so only for cause, shall only take the degree of disciplinary action that is reasonable, shall utilize these procedures with objectivity and fairness, and in general shall act only to further the interests and objectives of the Association and its membership.
4. Of the six (6) voting members of the Committee, a vote of four (4) is necessary to conduct business. In the event a Co-Chair or any other member of the Committee has a personal interest in the case, he or she shall withdraw from reviewing the case.
5. In the event Committee members recuse themselves from a complaint and insufficient voting members are available to conduct business, the President shall appoint former ACA Committee members to decide the complaint.

SECTION D: RESPONSIBILITIES OF THE COMMITTEE

1. The Committee members have an obligation to act in an unbiased manner, to work expeditiously, to

safeguard the confidentiality of the Committee's activities, and to follow procedures established to protect the rights of all individuals involved.

Section E: Responsibilities of the Co-Chairs Administering the Complaint

1. In the event that one of the Co-Chairs Administering the Complaint has a conflict of interest in a particular case, the other Co-Chair shall administer the complaint. The Co-Chair administering the complaint shall not have a vote in the decision.

2. In addition to the above guidelines for members of the Committee, the Co-Chairs, in conjunction with the Headquarters staff liaison, have the responsibilities of:

a. Receiving, via ACA Headquarters, complaints that have been certified for membership status of the accused;

b. Determining whether the alleged behavior(s), if true, would violate ACA's Code of Ethics and whether the Committee should review the complaint under these rules;

c. Notifying the complainant and the accused member of receipt of the case by certified mail return receipt requested;

d. Notifying the members of the Committee of the case;

e. Requesting additional information from complainants, accused members and others;

f. Presiding over the meetings of the Committee;

g. Preparing and sending, by certified mail, communications to the complainant and accused member on the recommendations and decisions of the Committee; and

h. Arranging for legal advice with assistance and financial approval of the ACA Executive Director.

Section F: Jurisdiction

1. The Committee will consider whether individuals have violated the ACA Code of Ethics if those individuals:

a. Are current members of the American Counseling Association; or

b. Were ACA members when the alleged violations occurred.

2. Ethics committees of divisions, branches, corporate affiliates, or other ACA entities must refer all ethical complaints involving ACA members to the Committee.

Section G: Eligibility to File Complaints

1. The Committee will receive complaints that ACA members have violated one or more sections of the ACA Code of Ethics from the following individuals:

a. Members of the general public who have reason to believe that ACA members have violated the ACA Code of Ethics.

b. ACA members, or members of other helping professions, who have reason to believe that other ACA members have violated the ACA Code of Ethics.

c. The Co-Chair of the Committee on behalf of the ACA membership when the Co-Chair has reason to believe through information received by the Committee that ACA members have violated the ACA Code of Ethics.

2. If possible, individuals should attempt to resolve complaints directly with accused members before filing ethical complaints.

Section H: Time Lines

1. The time lines set forth in these standards are guidelines only and have been established to provide a reasonable time framework for processing complaints.

2. Complainants or accused members may request extensions of deadlines when appropriate. Extensions of deadlines will be granted by the Committee only when justified by unusual circumstance.

Section I: Nature of Communication

1. Only written communications regarding ethical complaints against members will be acceptable. If telephone inquiries from individuals are received regarding the filing of complaints, responding to complaints, or providing information regarding complaints, the individuals calling will be informed of the written communication requirement and asked to comply.

2. All correspondence related to an ethical complaint must be addressed to the Ethics Committee, ACA Headquarters, 5999 Stevenson Avenue, Alexandria, VA 22304, and must be marked "confidential." This process is necessary to protect the confidentiality of the complainant and the accused member.

Section J: Filing Complaints

1. Only written complaints, signed by complainants, will be considered.

2. Individuals eligible to file complaints will send a letter outlining the nature of the complaint to the Committee at the ACA Headquarters.

3. The ACA staff liaison to the Committee will communicate in writing with complainants. Receipt of complaints and confirmation of membership status of accused members as defined in Section F.1, above, will be acknowledged to the complainant. Proposed formal complaints will be sent to complainants after receipt of complaints have been acknowledged.

4. If the complaint does not involve a member as defined in Section F.1, above, the staff liaison shall inform the complainant.

5. The Committee Co-Chair administering a complaint will determine whether the complaint, if true, would violate one or more sections of the ethical standards or if the complaint could be properly decided if accepted. If not, the complaint will not be accepted and the complainant shall be notified.

6. If the Committee Co-Chair administering the complaint determines that there is insufficient information to make a fair determination of whether the behavior alleged in the complaint would be cause for action by the Committee, the ACA staff liaison to the Committee may request further information from the complainant or others.

7. When complaints are accepted, complainants will be informed that copies of the formal complaints plus evidence and documents submitted in support of the complaint will be provided to the accused member and that the complainant must authorize release of such information to the accused member before the complaint process may proceed.

8. The ACA staff liaison, after receiving approval of the Committee Co-Chair administering a complaint, will formulate a formal complaint, which will be presented to the complainants for their signature.

a. The correspondence from complainants will be received and the staff liaison and Committee Co-Chair administering the complaint will identify all ACA Code of Ethics that might have been violated if the accusations are true.

b. The formal complaint will be sent to complainants with a copy of these Policies and Procedures, a copy of the ACA Code of Ethics, a verification affidavit form, and an authorization and release of information form. Complainants will be asked to sign and return the completed complaint, verification affidavit, and authorization and release of information forms. It will be explained to complainants that sections of the codes that might have been violated may be added or deleted by the complainant before signing the formal statement.

c. If complainants elect to add or delete sections of the ethical standards in the formal complaint, the unsigned formal complaint shall be returned to ACA Headquarters with changes noted and a revised formal complaint will be sent to the complainants for their signature.

9. When the completed formal complaint, verification affidavit form, and authorization and release of information form are presented to complainants for their signature, they will be asked to submit all evidence and documents they wish to be considered by the Committee in reviewing the complaint.

SECTION K: NOTIFICATION OF ACCUSED MEMBERS

1. Once signed formal complaints have been received, accused members will be sent a copy of the formal complaint and copies of all evidence and documents submitted in support of the complaint.

2. Accused members will be asked to respond to the complaint against them. They will be asked to address each section of the ACA Code of Ethics they have been accused of having violated. They will be informed that if they wish to respond they must do so in writing within sixty (60) working days.

3. Accused members will be informed that they must submit all evidence and documents they wish to be considered by the Committee in reviewing the complaint within sixty (60) working days.

4. After accused members have received notification that a complaint has been brought against them, they will be given sixty (60) working days to notify the Committee Co-Chair (via ACA Headquarters) in writing, by certified mail, if they wish to request a formal face-to-face hearing before the Committee. Accused members may waive their right to a formal hearing before the Committee. (See Section P: Hearings).

5. If the Committee Co-Chair determines that there is insufficient information to make a fair determination of whether the behavior alleged in the complaint would be cause for action by the Committee, the ACA staff liaison to the Committee may request further information from the accused member or others. The accused member shall be given thirty (30) working days from receipt of the request to respond.

6. All requests for additional information from others will be accompanied by a verification affidavit form which the information provider will be asked to complete and return.

7. The Committee may, in its discretion, delay or postpone its review of the case with good cause, including if the Committee wishes to obtain additional information. The accused member may request that the Committee delay or postpone its review of the case for good cause if done so in writing.

SECTION L: DISPOSITION OF COMPLAINTS

1. After Receiving the responses of accused members, Committee members will be provided copies of: (a) the complaint, (b) supporting evidence and documents sent to accused members, (c) the response, and (d) supporting evidence and documents provided by accused members and others.

2. Decisions will be rendered based on the evidence and documents provided by the complainant and accused member or others.

3. The Committee Co-Chair administering a complaint will not participate in deliberations or decisions regarding that particular complaint.

4. At the next meeting of the Committee held no sooner than fifteen (15) working days after members received copies of documents related to a complaint, the Committee will discuss the complaint, response, and supporting documentation, if any, and determine the outcome of the complaint.

5. The Committee will determine whether each Code of Ethics the member has been accused of having violated was violated based on the information provided.

6. After deliberations, the Committee may decide to dismiss the complaint or to dismiss charges within the complaint.

7. In the event it is determined that any of the ACA Code of Ethics have been violated, the Committee will impose for the entire complaint one or a combination of the possible sanctions allowed.

SECTION M: WITHDRAWAL OF COMPLAINTS

1. If the Complainant and accused member both agree to discontinue the complaint process, the Committee may, at its discretion, complete the adjudication process if available evidence indicates that this is warranted. The Co-Chair of the Committee, on behalf of the ACA membership, shall act as complainant.

SECTION N: POSSIBLE SANCTIONS

1. Replanted remedial requirements may be stipulated by the Committee.

2. Probation for a specified period of time subject to Committee review of compliance. Remedial requirements may be imposed to be completed within a specified period of time.

3. Suspension from ACA membership for a specified period of time subject to Committee review of compliance. Remedial requirements may be imposed to be completed within a specified period of time.

4. Permanent expulsion from ACA membership. This sanction requires a unanimous vote of those voting.

5. The penalty for failing to fulfill in a satisfactory manner a remedial requirement imposed by the Committee as a result of a probation sanction will be automatic suspension until the requirement is met, unless the Committee determines that the remedial requirement should be modified based on good cause shown prior to the end of the probationary period.

6. The penalty for failing to fulfill in a satisfactory manner a remedial requirement imposed by the Committee as a result of a suspension sanction will be automatic permanent expulsion unless the Committee determines that the remedial requirement should be modified based on good cause shown prior to the end of the suspension period.

7. Other corrective action.

SECTION O: NOTIFICATION OF RESULTS

1. Accused members shall be notified of committee decisions regarding complaints against them.

2. Complainants will be notified of Committee decisions after the deadline for accused members to file appeals or, in the event an appeal is filed, after a filed appeal decision has been rendered.

3. After complainants are notified of the results of their complaints as provided in Section O., Paragraph 2 above, if a violation has been found and accused members have been suspended or expelled, counselor licensure, certification, or registry boards, other mental health licensure, certification, or registry boards, voluntary national certification boards, and appropriate professional associations will also be notified of the results. In addition, ACA divisions, state branches, the ACA Insurance Trust, and other ACA-related entities will also be notified of the results.

4. After complainants have been notified of the results of their complaint as provided in Section O., Paragraph 2, above, if a violation has been found and accused members have been suspended or expelled, a notice of the Committee action that includes the sections of the ACA ethical standards that were found to have been violated and the sanctions imposed will be published in the ACA newsletter.

SECTION P: HEARINGS

1. At the discretion of the Committee, a hearing may be conducted when the results of the Committee's preliminary determination indicate that additional information is needed.

2. When accused members, within sixty (60) working days of notification of the complaint, request a formal face-to-face or telephone conference hearing before the Committee a hearing shall be conducted. (See Section K.6.)

3. The accused shall bear all their expenses associated with attendance at hearings requested by the accused.

4. The Committee Co-Chair shall schedule a formal hearing on the case at the next scheduled Committee meeting and notify both the complainant and the accused member of their right to attend the hearing in person or by telephone conference call.

5. The hearing will be held before a panel made up of the Committee and if the accused member chooses, a representative of the accused member's primary Division. This representative will be identified by the Division President and will have voting privileges.

SECTION Q: HEARING PROCEDURES

1. Purpose.

a. A hearing will be conducted to determine whether a breach of the ethical standards has occurred and, if so, to determine appropriate disciplinary action.

b. The Committee will be guided in its deliberations by principles of basic fairness and professionalism, and will keep its deliberations as confidential as possible, except as provided herein.

2. Notice.

a. The accused members shall be advised in writing by the Co-Chair administering the complaint of the time and place of the hearing and the charges involved at least forty-five (45) working days before the hearing. Notice shall include a formal statement of the complaints lodged against the accused member and supporting evidence.

b. The accused member is under no duty to respond to the notice, but the Committee will not be obligated to delay or postpone its hearing unless the accused so requests in writing, with good cause reviewed at least fifteen (15) working days in advance. In the absence of such 15 day advance notice and postponement by the Committee, if the accused fails to appear at the hearing, the Committee shall decide the complaint on record. Failure of the accused member to appear at the hearing shall not be viewed by the Committee as sufficient grounds alone for taking disciplinary action.

3. Conduct of the Hearing.

a. Accommodations. The location of the hearing shall be determined at the discretion of the Committee. The Committee shall provide a private room to conduct the hearing and no observers or recording devices other than a recording device used by the Committee shall be permitted.

b. Presiding Officer. The Co-Chair in charge of the case shall preside over the hearing and deliberations of the Committee. At the conclusion of the hearing and deliberations of the Committee, the Co-Chair shall promptly notify the accused member and complainant of the Committee's decision in writing as provided in Section O., Paragraphs 1 and 2, above.

c. Record. A record of the hearing shall be made and preserved, together with any documents presented in evidence, at ACA Headquarters for a period of three (3) years. The record shall consist of a summary of testimony received or a verbatim transcript, at the discretion of the Committee.

d. Right to Counsel. The accused member shall be entitled to have legal counsel present to advise and represent them throughout the hearing. Legal counsel for ACA shall also be present at the hearing to advise the Committee and shall have the privilege of the floor.

e. Witnesses. Either party shall have the right to call witnesses to substantiate his or her version of the case.

f. The Committee shall have the right to call witnesses it believes may provide further insight into the matter. ACA shall, in its sole discretion, determine the number and identity of witnesses to be heard.

g. Witnesses shall not be present during the hearing except when they are called upon to testify and shall be excused upon completion of their testimony and any cross-examination.

h. The Co-Chair administering the complaint shall allow questions to be asked of any witness by the opposition or members of the Committee if such questions and testimony are relevant to the issues in the case.

i. The Co-Chair administering the complaint will determine what questions and testimony are relevant to the case. Should the hearing be disturbed by irrelevant testimony, the Co-Chair administering the complaint may call a brief recess until order can be restored.

j. All expenses associated with counsel on behalf of the parties shall be borne by the respective parties. All expenses associated with witnesses on behalf of the accused shall be borne by the accused when the accused requests a hearing. If the Committee requests the hearing, all expenses associated with witnesses shall be borne by ACA.

4. Presentation of Evidence.

a. The staff liaison, or the Co-Chair administering the complaint shall be called upon first to present the charge(s) made against the accused and to briefly describe the evidence supporting the charge. The person presenting the charges shall also be responsible for examining and cross-examining witnesses on behalf of the complainant and for otherwise presenting the matter during the hearing.

b. The complainant or a member of the Committee shall then be called upon to present the case against the accused. Witnesses who can substantiate the case may be called upon to testify and answer questions of the accused and the Committee.

c. If the accused has exercised the right to be present at the hearing, he or she shall be called upon last to present any evidence which refutes the charges against him or her. This includes witnesses as in Subsection (3) above.

d. The accused will not be found guilty simply for refusing to testify. Once the accused member chooses to testify, however, he or she may be cross-examined by the complainant and members of the Committee.

e. The Committee will endeavor to conclude the hearing within a period of approximately three (3) hours. The parties will be requested to be considerate of this time frame in planning their testimony.

f. Testimony that is merely cumulative or repetitious may, at the discretion of the Co-Chair administering the complaint, be excluded.

5. Relevancy of Evidence

a. The Hearing Committee is not a court of law and is not required to observe formal rules of evidence. Evidence that would be inadmissible in a court of law may be admissible in the hearing before the Committee, if it is relevant to the case. That is, if the evidence offered tends to explain, clarify, or refute any of the important facts of the case, it should generally be considered.

b. The Committee will not consider evidence or testimony for the purpose of supporting any charge that was not set forth in the notice of the hearing or that is not relevant to the issues of the case.

6. Burden of Proof

a. The burden of proving a violation of the ethical standards is on the complainant and/or the Committee. It is not up to the accused to prove his or her innocence of any wrong-doing.

b. Although the charge(s) need not be proved "beyond a reasonable doubt," the Committee will not find the accused guilty in the absence of substantial, objective, and believable evidence to sustain the charge(s).

7. Deliberation of the Committee

a. After the hearing is completed, the Committee shall meet in a closed session to review the evidence presented and reach a conclusion. ACA legal counsel may attend the closed session to advise the Committee if the Committee so desires.

b. The Committee shall be the sole trier of the facts and shall weight the evidence presented and assess the credibility of the witnesses. The act of a majority of the members of the Committee present shall be the decision of the Committee. A unanimous vote of those voting is required for permanent expulsion from ACA membership.

c. Only members of the Committee who were present throughout the entire hearing shall be eligible to vote.

8. Decision of the Committee

a. The Committee will first resolve the issue of the guilt or innocence of the accused on each charge. Applying the burden of proof in subsection (5), above, the Committee will vote by secret ballot, unless the members of the Committee consent to an oral vote.

b. In the event a majority of the members of the Committee do not find the accused guilty, the charges shall be dismissed. If the Committee finds the accused member has violated the Code of Ethics, it must then determine what sanctions, in accordance with Section N: Possible Sanctions, shall be imposed.

c. As provided in Section O., above, the Co-Chair administering the complaint shall notify the accused member and complainant of the Committee's decision in writing.

Section R: Appeals

1. Decisions of the ACA Ethics Committee that members have violated the ACA Code of Ethics may be appealed by the member found to have been in violation based on one or both of the following grounds:

a. The Committee violated its policies and procedures for processing complaints of ethical violations; and/or

b. The decision of the Committee was arbitrary and capricious and was not supported by the materials provided by the complainant and accused member.

2. After members have received notification that they have been found in violation of one or more ACA

Code of Ethics, they will be given thirty (30) working days to notify the Committee in writing by certified mail that they are appealing the decision.

3. An appeal may consist only of a letter stating one or both of the grounds of appeal listed in subsection 1 above and the reasons for the appeal.

4. Appealing members will be asked to identify the primary ACA division to which he or she belongs. The ACA President will appoint a three (3) person appeals panel consisting of two (2) former ACA Ethics Committee Chairs and the President of the identified division. The ACA attorney shall serve as legal advisor and have the privilege of the floor.

5. The three (3) member appeals panel will be given copies of the materials available to the Committee when it made its decision, a copy of the hearing transcript if a hearing was held, plus a copy of the letter filed by the appealing member.

6. The appeals panel generally will render its decision regarding an appeal which must receive a majority vote within sixty (60) working days of their receipt of the above materials.

7. The decision of the appeals panel may include one of the following:

a. The decision of the Committee is upheld.

b. The decision of the Committee is reversed and remanded with guidance to the Committee for a new decision. The reason for this decision will be given to the Committee in detail in writing.

8. When a Committee decision is reversed and remanded, the complainant and accused member will be informed in writing and additional information may be requested first from the complainant and then from the accused member. The Committee will than render another decision without a hearing.

9. Decisions of the appeals panel to uphold the Committee decision are final.

Section S: Substantial New Evidence

1. In the Event substantial new evidence is presented in a case in which an appeal was not filed, or in a case which a final decision has been rendered, the case may be reopened by the Committee.

2. The Committee will consider substantial new evidence and if it is found to be substantiated and capable of exonerating a member who was expelled, the Committee will reopen the case and go through the entire complaint process again.

Section T: Records

1. The records of the Committee regarding complaints are confidential except as provided herein.

2. Original copies of complaint records will be maintained in locked files at ACA Headquarters or at an off-site location chosen by ACA.

3. Members of the Committee will keep copies of complaint records confidential and will destroy copies of records after a case has been closed or when they are no longer a member of the Committee.

SECTION U: LEGAL ACTIONS RELATED TO COMPLAINTS

1. Complaints and accused members are required to notify the Committee if they learn of any type of legal action (civil or criminal) being filed related to the complaint.

2. In the event any type of legal action is filed regarding an accepted complaint, all actions related to the complaint will be stayed until the legal action has been concluded. The Committee will consult with legal counsel concerning whether the processing of the complaint will be stayed if the legal action does not involve the same complainant and the same facts complained of.

3. If actions on a complaint are stayed, the complainant and accused member will be notified.

4. When actions on a complaint are continued after a legal action has been concluded, the complainant and accused member will be notified.

APPENDIX B

NATIONAL CAREER DEVELOPMENT ASSOCIATION ETHICAL STANDARDS

These Ethical Standards were developed by the National Board for Certified Counselors (NBCC), an independent, voluntary, not-for-profit organization incorporated in 1982. Titled "Code of Ethics" by NBCC and last amended in February 1987, the Ethical Standards were adopted by the National Career Development Association (NCDA) Board of Directors in 1987 and revised in 1991, with minor changes in wording (e.g., the addition of specific references to NCDA members).

PREAMBLE

NCDA is an educational, scientific, and professional organization dedicated to the enhancement of the worth, dignity, potential, and uniqueness of each individual and, thus, to the service of society. This code of ethics enables the NCDA to clarify the nature of ethical responsibilities for present and future professional career counselors.

SECTION A: GENERAL

1. NCDA members influence the development of the profession by continuous efforts to improve professional practices, services, and research. Professional growth is continuous through the career counselor's career and is exemplified by the development of a philosophy that explains why and how a career counselor functions in the helping relationship. Career counselors must gather data on their effectiveness and be guided by their findings.

2. NCDA members have a responsibility to the clients they are serving and to the institutions within which the services are being performed. Career counselors also strive to assist the respective agency, organization, or institution in providing the highest caliber of professional services. The acceptance of employment in an institution implies that the career counselor is in agreement with the general policies and principles of the institution. Therefore, the professional activities of the career counselor are in accord with the objectives of the institution. If, despite concerted efforts, the career counselor cannot reach agreement with the employer as to acceptable standards of conduct that allow for changes in institutional policy that are conductive to the positive growth and development of clients, then terminating the affiliation should be seriously considered.

3. Ethical behavior among professional associates (e.g., career counselors) must be expected at all times. When accessible information raises doubt as to the ethical behavior of professional colleagues, the NCDA member must take action to attempt to rectify this condition. Such action uses the respective institution's channels first and then uses procedures established by the American Counseling Association, of which NCDA is a division.

4. NCDA members neither claim nor imply professional qualifications which exceed those possessed, and are responsible for correcting any misrepresentations of these qualifications by others.

5. NCDA members must refuse a private fee or other remuneration for consultation or counseling with persons who are entitled to their services through the career counselor's employing institution or agency. The policies of some agencies may make explicit provisions for staff members to engage in private practice with agency clients. However, should agency clients desire private counseling or consulting services, they must be apprised of other options available to them. Career counselors must

From "Ethical Standards of the National Career Development Association" (Revised 1991), Tulsa, OK.

not divert to their private practices, legitimate clients in their primary agencies or of the institutions with which they are affiliated.

6. In establishing fees for professional counseling services, NCDA members must consider the financial status of clients and the respective locality. In the event that the established fee status is inappropriate for the client, assistance must be provided in finding comparable services of acceptable cost.

7. NCDA members seek only those positions in the delivery of professional services for which they are professionally qualified.

8. NCDA members recognize their limitations and provide services or only use techniques for which they are qualified by training and/or experience. Career counselors recognize the need, and seek continuing education, to assure competent services.

9. NCDA members are aware of the intimacy in the counseling relationship, maintain respect for the client, and avoid engaging in activities that seek to meet their personal needs at the expense of the client.

10. NCDA members do not condone or engage in sexual harassment, which is defined as deliberate or repeated comments, gestures, or physical contacts of a sexual nature.

11. NCDA members avoid bringing their personal or professional issues into the counseling relationship. Through an awareness of the impact of stereotyping and discrimination (e.g., biases based on age, disability, ethnicity, gender, race, religion, or sexual preference), career counselors guard the individual rights and personal dignity of the client in the counseling relationship.

12. NCDA members are accountable at all times for their behavior. They must be aware that all actions and behaviors of a counselor reflect on professional integrity and, when inappropriate, can damage the public trust in the counseling profession. To protect public confidence in the counseling profession, career counselors avoid public behavior that is clearly in violation of accepted moral and legal standards.

13. NCDA members have a social responsibility because their recommendations and professional actions may alter the lives of others. Career counselors remain fully cognizant of their impact and are alert to personal, social, organizational, financial, or political situations or pressures which might lead to misuse of their influence.

14. Products or services provided by NCDA members by means of classroom instruction, public lectures, demonstrations, written articles, radio or television programs, or other types of media must meet the criteria cited in Sections A through F of these Ethical Standards.

SECTION B: COUNSELING RELATIONSHIP

1. The primary obligation of NCDA members is to respect the integrity and promote the welfare of the client, regardless of whether the client is assisted individually or in a group relationship. In a group setting, the career counselor is also responsible for taking reasonable precautions to protect individuals from physical and/or psychological trauma resulting from interaction within the group.

2. The counseling relationship and information resulting from it remains confidential, consistent with the legal obligations of the NCDA member. In a group counseling setting, the career counselor sets a norm of confidentiality regarding all group participants' disclosures.

3. NCDA members know and take into account the traditions and practices of other professional groups with whom they work, and they cooperate fully with such groups. If a person is receiving similar services from another professional, career counselors do not offer their own services directly to such a person. If a career counselor is contacted by a person who is already receiving similar services from another professional, the career counselor carefully considers that professional relationship and proceeds with caution and sensitivity to the therapeutic issues as well as the client's welfare. Career counselors discuss these issues with clients so as to minimize the risk of confusion and conflict.

4. When a client's condition indicates that there is a clear and imminent danger to the client or others, the NCDA member must take reasonable personal action or inform responsible authorities. Consultation with other professionals must be used where possible. The assumption of responsibility for the client's behavior must be taken only after careful deliberation, and the client must be involved in the resumption of responsibility as quickly as possible.

5. Records of the counseling relationship, including interview notes, test data, correspondence, audio or visual tape recordings, electronic data storage, and other documents are to be considered professional information for use in counseling. They should not be considered a part of the records of the institution or agency in which the NCDA member is employed unless specified by state statute or regulation. Revelation to others of counseling material must occur only upon the expressed consent of the client; career counselors must make provisions for maintaining confidentiality in the storage and disposal of records. Career counselors providing information to the public or to subordinates, peers, or supervisors have a responsibility to ensure that the content is general; unidentified client information should be

accurate and unbiased, and should consist of objective, factual data.

6. NCDA members must ensure that data maintained in electronic storage are secure. The data must be limited to information that is appropriate and necessary for the services being provided and accessible only to appropriate staff members involved in the provision of services by using the best computer security methods available. Career counselors must also ensure that electronically stored data are destroyed when the information is no longer of value in providing services.

7. Data derived from a counseling relationship for use in counselor training or research shall be confined to content that can be disguised to ensure full protection of the identity of the subject/client and shall be obtained with informed consent.

8. NCDA members must inform clients, before or at the time the counseling relationship commences, of the purposes, goals, techniques, rules and procedures, and limitations that may affect the relationship.

9. All methods of treatment by NCDA members must be clearly indicated to prospective recipients and safety precautions must be taken in their use.

10. NCDA members who have an administrative, supervisory, and/or evaluative relationship with individuals seeking counseling services must not serve as the counselor and should refer the individuals to other professionals. Exceptions are made only in instances where an individual's situation warrants counseling intervention and another alternative is unavailable. Dual relationships with clients that might impair the career counselor's objectivity and professional judgment must be avoided and/or the counseling relationship terminated through referral to another competent professional.

11. When NCDA members determine an inability to be of professional assistance to a potential or existing client, they must, respectively, not initiate the counseling relationship or immediately terminate the relationship. In either event, the career counselor must suggest appropriate alternatives. Career counselors must be knowledgeable about referral resources so that a satisfactory referral can be initiated. In the event that the client declines a suggested referral, the career counselor is not obligated to continue the relationship.

12. NCDA members may choose to consult with any other professionally competent person about a client and must notify clients of this right. Career counselors must avoid placing a consultant in a conflict-of-interest situation that would preclude the consultant's being a proper party to the career counselor's efforts to help the client.

13. NCDA members who counsel clients from cultures different from their own must gain knowledge, personal awareness, and sensitivity pertinent to the client populations served and must incorporate culturally relevant techniques into their practice.

14. When NCDA members engage in intensive counseling with a client, the client's counseling needs should be assessed. When needs exist outside the counselor's expertise, appropriate referrals should be made.

15. NCDA members must screen prospective group counseling participants, especially when the emphasis is on self-understanding and growth through self-disclosure. Career counselors must maintain an awareness of each group participant's welfare throughout the group process.

16. When electronic data and systems are used as a component of counseling services, NCDA members must ensure that the computer application, and any information it contains, is appropriate for the respective needs of clients and is nondiscriminatory. Career counselors must ensure that they themselves have acquired a facilitation level of knowledge with any system they use including hands-on application, search experience, and understanding of the uses of all aspects of the computer-based system. In selecting and/or maintaining computer-based systems that contain career information, career counselors must ensure that the systems provide current, accurate, and locally relevant information. Career counselors must also ensure that clients are intellectually, emotionally, and physically compatible with the use of the computer application and understand its purpose and operation. Client use of a computer application must be evaluated to correct possible problems and assess subsequent needs.

17. NCDA members who develop self-help, stand-alone computer software for use by the general public must first ensure that it is initially designed to function in a stand-alone manner, as opposed to modifying software that was originally designed to require support from a counselor. Secondly, the software must include program statements that provide the user with intended outcomes, suggestions for using the software, descriptions of inappropriately used applications, and descriptions of when and how counseling services might be beneficial. Finally, the manual must include the qualifications of the developer, the development process, validation data, and operating procedures.

Section C: Measurement and Evaluation

1. NCDA members must provide specific orientation or information to an examinee prior to and following the administration of assessment instruments or techniques so that the results may be placed in proper perspective with other relevant factors. The

purpose of testing and the explicit use of the results must be made known to an examinee prior to testing.

2. In selecting assessment instruments or techniques for use in a given situation or with a particular client, NCDA members must evaluate carefully the instrument's specific theoretical bases and characteristics, validity, reliability, and appropriateness. Career counselors are professionally responsible for using unvalidated information with special care.

3. When making statements to the public about assessment instruments or techniques, NCDA members must provide accurate information and avoid false claims or misconceptions concerning the meaning of psychometric terms. Special efforts are often required to avoid unwarranted connotations of terms such as IQ and grade-equivalent scores.

4. Because many types of assessment techniques exist, NCDA members must recognize the limits of their competence and perform only those functions for which they have received appropriate training.

5. NCDA members must note when tests are not administered under standard conditions or when unusual behavior or irregularities occur during a testing session and the results must be designated as invalid or of questionable validity. Unsupervised or inadequately supervised assessments, such as mail-in tests, are considered unethical. However, the use of standardized instruments that are designed to be self-administered and self-scored, such as interest inventories, is appropriate.

6. Because prior coaching or dissemination of test materials can invalidate test results, NCDA members are professionally obligated to maintain test security. In addition, conditions that produce most favorable test results must be made known to an examinee (e.g., penalty for guessing).

7. NCDA members must consider psychometric limitations when selecting and using an instrument, and must be cognizant of the limitations when interpreting the results. When tests are used to classify clients, career counselors must ensure that periodic review and/or retesting are conducted to prevent client stereotyping.

8. An examinee's welfare, explicit prior understanding, and agreement are the factors used when determining who receives the test results. NCDA members must see that appropriate interpretation accompanies any release of individual or group test data (e.g., limitations of instrument and norms).

9. NCDA members must ensure that computer-generated assessment administration and scoring programs function properly, thereby providing clients with accurate assessment results.

10. NCDA members who are responsible for making decisions based on assessment results must have appropriate training and skills in educational and psychological measurement including validation criteria, test research, and guidelines for test development and use.

11. NCDA members must be cautious when interpreting the results of instruments that possess insufficient technical data, and must explicitly state to examinees the specific purposes for the use of such instruments.

12. NCDA members must proceed with caution when attempting to evaluate and interpret performances of minority group members or other persons who are not represented in the norm group on which the instrument was standardized.

13. NCDA members who develop computer-based interpretations to support the assessment process must ensure that the validity of the interpretations is established prior to the commercial distribution of the computer application.

14. NCDA members recognize that test results may become obsolete, and avoid the misuse of obsolete data.

15. NCDA members must avoid the appropriation, reproduction, or modification of published tests or parts thereof without acknowledgment and permission from the publisher.

SECTION D: RESEARCH AND PUBLICATION

1. NCDA members will adhere to relevant guidelines on research with human subjects. These include:

a. Code of Federal Regulations, Title 45, Subtitle A, Part 46, as currently issued.

b. American Psychological Association. (1982). *Ethical principles in the conduct of research with human participants*. Washington, DC: Author.

c. American Psychological Association. (1981). Research with human participants. *American Psychologist, 36*, 633–638.

d. Family Educational Rights and Privacy Act. (Buckley Amendment to P. L. 93–380 of the Laws of 1974).

e. Current federal regulations and various state privacy acts.

2. In planning research activities involving human subjects, NCDA members must be aware of and responsive to all pertinent ethical principles and ensure that the research problem, design, and execution, are in full compliance with the principles.

3. The ultimate responsibility for ethical research lies with the principal researcher, although others involved in research activities are ethically obligated and responsible for their own actions.

4. NCDA members who conduct research with human subjects are responsible for the subjects' welfare throughout the experiment and must take all reasonable precautions to avoid causing injurious psychological, physical, or social effects on their subjects.

5. NCDA members who conduct research must abide by the following basic elements of informed consent:

a. a fair explanation of the procedures to be followed, including an identification of those which are experimental.

b. a description of the attendant discomforts and risks.

c. a description of the benefits to be expected.

d. a disclosure of appropriate alternative procedures that would be advantageous for subjects.

e. an offer to answer any inquiries concerning the procedures.

f. an instruction that subjects are free to withdraw their consent and to discontinue participation in the project or activity at any time.

6. When reporting research results, explicit mention must be made of all the variables and conditions known to the NCDA member that may have affected the outcome of the study or the interpretation of the data.

7. NCDA members who conduct and report research investigations must do so in a manner that minimizes the possibility that the results will be misleading.

8. NCDA members are obligated to make available sufficient original research data to qualified others who may wish to replicate the study.

9. NCDA members who supply data, aid in the research of another person, report research results, or make original data available must take due care to disguise the identity of respective subjects in the absence of specific authorization from the subject to do otherwise.

10. When conducting and reporting research, NCDA members must be familiar with, and give recognition to, previous work on the topic, must observe all copyright laws, and must follow the principles of giving full credit to those to whom credit is due.

11. NCDA members must give due credit through joint authorship, acknowledgment, footnote statements, or other appropriate means to those who have contributed significantly to the research and/or publication, in accordance with such contributions.

12. NCDA members should communicate to others the results of any research judged to be of professional value. Results that reflect unfavorably on institutions, programs, services, or vested interests must not be withheld.

13. NCDA members who agree to cooperate with another individual in research and/or publication incur an obligation to cooperate as promised in terms of punctuality of performance and with full regard to the completeness and accuracy of the information required.

14. NCDA members must not submit the same manuscript, or one essentially similar in content, for simultaneous publication consideration by two or more journals. In addition, manuscripts that are published in whole or substantial part in another journal or published work should not be submitted for publication without acknowledgment and permission from the previous publication.

Section E: Consulting

Consultation refers to a voluntary relationship between a professional helper and help-needing individual, group, or social unit in which the consultant is providing help to the client (s) in defining and solving a work-related problem or potential work-related problem with a client or client system.

1. NCDA members acting as consultants must have a high degree of self-awareness of their own values, knowledge, skills, limitations, and needs in entering a helping relationship that involves human and/or organizational change. The focus of the consulting relationship must be on the issues to be resolved and not on the person(s) presenting the problem.

2. In the consulting relationship, the NCDA member and client must understand and agree upon the problem definition, subsequent goals, and predicted consequences of interventions selected.

3. NCDA members must be reasonably certain that they, or the organization represented, have the necessary competencies and resources for giving the kind of help that is needed or that may develop later, and that appropriate referral resources are available to the consultant.

4. NCDA members in a consulting relationship must encourage and cultivate client adaptability and growth toward self-direction. NCDA members must maintain this role consistently and not become decision makers for clients or create a future dependency.

5. NCDA members conscientiously adhere to the NCDA Ethical Standards when announcing consultant availability for services.

Section F: Private Practice

1. NCDA members should assist the profession by facilitating the availability of counseling services in private as well as public settings.

2. In advertising services as private practitioners, NCDA members must advertise in a manner that accurately informs the public of the professional services, expertise, and counseling techniques available.

3. NCDA members who assume an executive leadership role in a private practice organization do not permit their names to be used in professional notices during periods of time when they are not actively engaged in the private practice of counseling.

4. NCDA members may list their highest relevant degree, type, and level of certification and/or license, address, telephone number, office hours, type and/or description of services, and other relevant information. Listed information must not contain false, inaccurate misleading, partial, out-of-context, or otherwise deceptive material or statements.

5. NCDA members who are involved in partnership or corporation with other professionals must, in compliance with the regulations of the locality, clearly specify the separate specialties of each member of the partnership or corporation.

6. NCDA members have an obligation to withdraw from a private-practice counseling relationship if it violates the NCDA Ethical Standards, if the mental or physical condition of the NCDA member renders it difficult to carry out an effective professional relationship, or if the counseling relationship is no longer productive for the client.

PROCEDURES FOR PROCESSING ETHICAL COMPLAINTS

As a division of the American Counseling Association (ACA) the National Career Development Association (NCDA) adheres to the guidelines and procedures for processing ethical complaints and the disciplinary sanctions adopted by ACA. A complaint against an NCDA member may be filed by any individual or group of individuals ("complainant"), whether or not the complainant is a member of NCDA. Action will not be taken on anonymous complaints. For specifics on how to file ethical complaints and a description of the guidelines and procedures for processing complaints, contact:

ACA Ethics Committee
c/o Executive Director
American Counseling Association
5999 Stevenson Avenue
Alexandria, VA 22304
(800) 347–6647

APPENDIX C

EDUCATIONAL AND CAREER PLANNING PORTFOLIO

Name _____ (Last) _____ (First) _____ (Middle) _____

Name of School/Division _____ Predominant Language Used at Home _____

Dates Contacts Made, Name, and Relationship to Student

Date of Contact	Name	Relationship to Student	Date of Contact	Name	Relationship to Student
_____	_____	_____	_____	_____	_____
_____	_____	_____	_____	_____	_____
_____	_____	_____	_____	_____	_____
_____	_____	_____	_____	_____	_____
_____	_____	_____	_____	_____	_____
_____	_____	_____	_____	_____	_____
_____	_____	_____	_____	_____	_____
_____	_____	_____	_____	_____	_____
_____	_____	_____	_____	_____	_____
_____	_____	_____	_____	_____	_____
_____	_____	_____	_____	_____	_____

Curriculum Emphasis:

- ☐ Apprenticeship
- ☐ Technical Education
- ☐ College Preparatory
- ☐ Youth Work-Study
- ☐ Tech Prep
- ☐ Cooperative Education
- ☐ Occupational & Technical Education
- ☐ Other (Please Specify) _____

Required and Elective Courses

(If this information is available elsewhere, please place a copy of the student's record of required and elective courses in the portfolio.)

School Year: _____

Required Courses	Grade	Credit
_____	____	____
_____	____	____
_____	____	____
_____	____	____

Elective Courses
| _____ | ____ | ____ |
| _____ | ____ | ____ |

School Year: _____

Required Courses	Grade	Credit
_____	____	____
_____	____	____
_____	____	____
_____	____	____

Elective Courses
| _____ | ____ | ____ |
| _____ | ____ | ____ |

School Year: _____

Required Courses	Grade	Credit
_____	____	____
_____	____	____
_____	____	____
_____	____	____

Elective Courses
| _____ | ____ | ____ |
| _____ | ____ | ____ |

School Year: _____

Required Courses	Grade	Credit
_____	____	____
_____	____	____
_____	____	____
_____	____	____

Elective Courses
| _____ | ____ | ____ |
| _____ | ____ | ____ |

Planning Future Assessments/Examinations

(Circle if needed and indicate anticipated dates of examinations)

Literacy Passport Test _____
ACT _____
ASVAB _____
Achievement _____
Aptitude _____

Interest Inventory _____
PSAT _____
SAT _____
Vocational Assessment _____
Virginia VIEW _____

Other _____

Counselor/Student Review of Assessment/Examinations

(Circle when completed and indicate date of review)

Literacy Passport Test _____
ACT _____
ASVAB _____
Achievement _____
Aptitude _____

Interest Inventory _____
PSAT _____
SAT _____
Vocational Assessment _____
Virginia VIEW _____

Other _____

453

Extracurricular or Cocurricular Activities

School Year: _____

Activity _____   Student's Role or Responsibility

_____

_____

School Year: _____

Activity _____   Student's Role or Responsibility

_____

_____

School Year: _____

Activity _____   Student's Role or Responsibility

_____

_____

School Year: _____

Activity _____   Student's Role or Responsibility

_____

_____

School Year: _____

Activity _____   Student's Role or Responsibility

_____

_____

School Year: _____

Activity _____   Student's Role or Responsibility

_____

_____

Career Exploration Activities

School Year: _____

Activity: (e.g., volunteering, job shadowing, work-study, cooperative education, other)   Career(s) Explored

_____

_____

School Year: _____

Activity: (e.g., volunteering, job shadowing, work-study, cooperative education, other)   Career(s) Explored

_____

_____

School Year: _____

Activity: (e.g., volunteering, job shadowing, work-study, cooperative education, other)   Career(s) Explored

_____

_____

School Year: _____

Activity: (e.g., volunteering, job shadowing, work-study, cooperative education, other)   Career(s) Explored

_____

_____

School Year: _____

Activity: (e.g., volunteering, job shadowing, work-study, cooperative education, other)   Career(s) Explored

_____

_____

School Year: _____

Activity: (e.g., volunteering, job shadowing, work-study, cooperative education, other)   Career(s) Explored

_____

_____

Special Prizes, Honors, Offices, and Recognition

School Year: _____

School Year: _____

School Year: _____

School Year: _____

School Year: _____

School Year: _____

Transition Plan (Complete as appropriate)

Services Provided	Activity Completed	Date Completed
Vocational Assessment		
Career Counseling		
Employability Skills		
Work-Based Learning		
Social Skills		
Continuing Ed. Support		
Postsecondary Transition Plan		
Vocational Rehab.		
Employment Services		
Job Placement		
Ongoing Job Support		
Financial Aid Info		
Reference Letters		
Other		

PART II

INDIVIDUAL CAREER PLAN (ICP)–ADOLESCENT EDUCATION

SCHOOL YEAR _____

(ICP to be completed annually)

NAME _____

SCHOOL _____

    Last   First   Middle

1. My interests are:

   _____

   _____

   _____

2. My abilities are:

   _____

   _____

   _____

3. My hobby and recreational/leisure activities are as follows:

   _____

   _____

   _____

4. I do best in these school subjects:

   _____

   _____

   _____

5. I have explored the following careers:

   _____

   _____

   _____

6. I have worked part-time or had some experience with the following jobs or works tasks:

   _____

   _____

   _____

7. My tentative career goal(s) is (are) the following:

   _____

   _____

   _____

8. In order to achieve my career goal(s):

a. I need to develop the following habits or behaviors: (Check the item when it has been successfully accomplished).

_____

_____

b. I plan to develop the following knowledge, skills or attitudes: (Check the item when it has been accomplished successfully).

_____

_____

c. I plan to participate in the following home, school, and community activities to help me develop the knowledge, skills, and attitudes I want: (Check the item when accomplished successfully).

_____

_____

d. I plan to pursue further education beyond high school in the following programs, schools, colleges, or military services:

_____

_____

_____

e. I plan to obtain work after high school in one of the following jobs

_____

_____

_____

Signature _____ (Date) _____ (Date) _____ (Date)

Student   Parent   Counselor

457

APPENDIX D

CAREER COUNSELING COMPETENCIES OF THE NATIONAL CAREER DEVELOPMENT ASSOCIATION (NCDA)

INTRODUCTION TO CAREER COUNSELING COMPETENCY STATEMENTS

These competency statements are for those professionals interested and trained in the field of career counseling. For the purpose of these statements, career counseling is defined as the process of assisting individuals in the development of a life career with focus on the definition of the worker role and how that role interacts with other life roles.

NCDA's Career Counseling Competencies are intended to represent minimum competencies for those professionals at or above the master's degree level of education. These competencies are reviewed on an ongoing basis by the NCDA Professional Standards Committee, the NCDA Board, and other relevant associations. Professional competency statements provide guidance for the minimum competencies necessary to perform effectively a particular occupation or job within a particular field. Professional career counselors (master's degree or higher) or persons in career development positions must demonstrate the knowledge and skills for a specialty in career counseling that the generalist counselor might not possess. Skills and knowledge are represented by designated competency areas, which have been developed by professional career counselors and counselor educators. The Career Counseling Competency Statements can serve as a guide for career counseling training programs or as a checklist for persons wanting to acquire or to enhance their skills in career counseling.

CAREER DEVELOPMENT THEORY

(Chapters 1, 2, and 3)
Theory base and knowledge considered essential for professionals engaging in career counseling and development. Demonstration of knowledge of:

1. Counseling theories and associated techniques
2. Theories and models of career development
3. Individual differences related to gender, sexual orientation, race, ethnicity, and physical and mental capacities
4. Theoretical models for career development and associated counseling and information-delivery techniques and resources
5. Human growth and development throughout the life span
6. Role relationships that facilitate life-work planning
7. Information, techniques, and models related to career planning and placement

INDIVIDUAL AND GROUP COUNSELING SKILLS

(Chapter 8)
Individual and group counseling competencies considered essential to effective career counseling. Demonstration of ability to:

1. Establish and maintain productive personal relationships with individuals
2. Establish and maintain a productive group climate
3. Collaborate with clients in identifying personal goals

From National Career Development Association, 1997, *Career Counseling Competencies*, Tulsa:
http://www.ncda.org/pdf/counselingcompetencies.pdf

458

4. Identify and select techniques appropriate to client or group goals and client needs, psychological states, and developmental tasks

5. Identify and understand clients' personal characteristics related to career

6. Identify and understand social contextual conditions affecting clients' careers

7. Identify and understand familial, subcultural, and cultural structures and functions as they are related to clients' careers

8. Identify and understand clients' career decision-making processes

9. Identify and understand clients' attitudes toward work and workers

10. Identify and understand clients' biases toward work and workers based on gender, race, and cultural stereotypes

11. Challenge and encourage clients to take action to prepare for and initiate role transitions by locating sources of relevant information and experience, obtaining and interpreting information and experiences, and acquiring skills needed to make role transitions

12. Assist the client to acquire a set of employability and job search skills

13. Support and challenge clients to examine life-work roles, including the balance of work, leisure, family, and community in their careers

INDIVIDUAL/GROUP ASSESSMENT

(Chapter 5)

Individual/group assessment skills considered essential for professionals engaging in career counseling. Demonstration of ability to:

1. Assess personal characteristics such as aptitude, achievement, interests, values, and personality traits

2. Assess leisure interests, learning style, life roles, self-concept, career maturity, vocational identity, career indecision, work environment preference (e.g., work satisfaction), and other related life style/development issues

3. Assess conditions of the work environment (such as tasks, expectations, norms, and qualities of the physical and social settings)

4. Evaluate and select valid and reliable instruments appropriate to the client's gender, sexual orientation, race, ethnicity, and physical and mental capacities

5. Use computer-delivered assessment measures effectively and appropriately

6. Select assessment techniques appropriate for group administration and those appropriate for individual administration

7. Administer, score, and report findings from career assessment instruments appropriately

8. Interpret data from assessment instruments and present the results to clients and to others

9. Assist the client and others designated by the client to interpret data from assessment instruments

10. Write an accurate report of assessment results

INFORMATION/RESOURCES

(Chapter 6)

Information/resource base and knowledge essential for professionals engaging in career counseling. Demonstration of knowledge of:

1. Education, training, and employment trends; labor market information and resources that provide information about job tasks, functions, salaries, requirements, and future outlooks related to broad occupational fields and individual occupations

2. Resources and skills that clients utilize in life-work planning and management

3. Community/professional resources available to assist clients in career planning, including job search

4. Changing roles of women and men and the implications that this has for education, family, and leisure

5. Methods of good use of computer-based career information delivery systems (CIDS) and computer-assisted career guidance systems (CACGS) to assist with career planning

PROGRAM PROMOTION, MANAGEMENT, AND IMPLEMENTATION

(Chapters 9, 10, 11, 12, and 13)

Knowledge and skills necessary to develop, plan, implement, and manage comprehensive career development programs in a variety of settings. Demonstration of knowledge of:

1. Designs that can be used in the organization of career development programs

2. Needs assessment and evaluation techniques and practices

3. Organizational theories, including diagnosis, behavior, planning, organizational communication, and management useful in implementing and administering career development programs

4. Methods of forecasting, budgeting, planning, costing, policy analysis, resource allocation, and quality control

5. Leadership theories and approaches for evaluation and feedback, organizational change, decision making, and conflict resolution

6. Professional standards and criteria for career development programs

7. Societal trends and state and federal legislation that influence the development and implementation of career development programs

8. Implement individual and group programs in career development for specified populations

9. Train others about the appropriate use of computer-based systems for career information and planning

10. Plan, organize, and manage a comprehensive career resource center

11. Implement career development programs in collaboration with others

12. Identify and evaluate staff competencies

13. Mount a marketing and public relations campaign in behalf of career development activities and services

COACHING, CONSULTATION, AND PERFORMANCE IMPROVEMENT
(Chapters 9 and 15)
Knowledge and skills considered essential in relating to individuals and organizations that impact the career counseling and development process. Demonstration of ability to:

1. Use consultation theories, strategies, and models

2. Establish and maintain a productive consultative relationship with people who can influence a client's career

3. Help the general public and legislators to understand the importance of career counseling, career development, and life-work planning

4. Impact public policy as it relates to career development and workforce planning

5. Analyze future organizational needs and current level of employee skills and develop performance improvement training

6. Mentor and coach employees

DIVERSE POPULATIONS
(Chapter 4)
Knowledge and skills considered essential in relating to diverse populations that impact career counseling and development processes. Demonstration of ability to:

1. Identify development models and multicultural counseling competencies

2. Identify developmental needs unique to various diverse populations, including those of different gender, sexual orientation, ethnic group, race, and physical or mental capacity

3. Define career development programs to accommodate needs unique to various diverse populations

4. Find appropriate methods or resources to communicate with individuals who have a limited proficiency in English

5. Identify alternative approaches to meet career planning needs for individuals of various diverse populations

6. Identify community resources and establish linkages to assist clients with specific needs

7. Assist other staff members, professionals, and community members in understanding the unique needs/characteristics of diverse populations with regard to career exploration, employment expectations, and economic/social issues

8. Advocate for the career development and employment of diverse populations

9. Design and deliver career development programs and materials to hard-to-reach populations

SUPERVISION
(Chapter 9)
Knowledge and skills considered essential in critically evaluating counselor or career development facilitator performance, maintaining and improving professional skills. Demonstration of:

1. Ability to recognize own limitations as a career counselor and to seek supervision or refer clients when appropriate

2. Ability to utilize supervision on a regular basis to maintain and improve counselor skills

3. Ability to consult with supervisors and colleagues regarding client and counseling issues and related to one's own professional development as a career counselor

4. Knowledge of supervision models and theories

5. Ability to provide effective supervision to career counselors and career development facilitators at different levels of experience

6. Ability to provide effective supervision to career development facilitators at different levels of experience by knowledge of their roles, competencies, and ethical standards; determining their competence in each of the areas included in their certification; further training them in competencies, including interpretation of assessment instruments; monitoring and mentoring their activities in support of the professional career counselor; and scheduling regular consultations for the purpose of reviewing their activities

ETHICAL/LEGAL ISSUES
(Chapter 14)
Information base and knowledge essential for the ethical and legal practice of career counseling. Demonstration of knowledge of:

1. Adherence to ethical codes and standards relevant to the profession of career counseling (e.g., PUNE, NBCC, NCDA, and ACA)

2. Current ethical and legal issues which affect the practice of career counseling with all populations

3. Current ethical/legal issues with regard to the use of computer-assisted career guidance systems

4. Ethical standards relating to consultation issues
5. State and federal statutes relating to client confidentiality

RESEARCH/EVALUATION
(Chapter 15)
Knowledge and skills considered essential in understanding and conducting research and evaluation in career counseling and development. Demonstration of ability to:

1. Write a research proposal
2. Use types of research and research designs appropriate to career counseling and development research
3. Convey research findings related to the effectiveness of career counseling programs
4. Design, conduct, and use the results of evaluation programs
5. Design evaluation programs which take into account the need of various diverse populations, including persons of both genders, differing sexual orientations, different ethnic and racial backgrounds, and differing physical and mental capacities
6. Apply appropriate statistical procedures to career development research

TECHNOLOGY
(Chapter 7)
Knowledge and skills considered essential in using technology to assist individuals with career planning. Demonstration of knowledge of:

1. Various computer-based guidance and information systems as well as services available on the Internet
2. Standards by which such systems and services are evaluated (e.g., NCDA and ACSCI)
3. Ways in which to use computer-based systems and Internet services to assist individuals with career planning that are consistent with ethical standards
4. Characteristics of clients that make them profit more or less from use of technology-driven systems
5. Methods to evaluate and select a system to meet local needs

REFERENCES
National Career Development Association Professional Standards Committee. (1997). *Career counseling competencies.* Alexandria, VA: National Career Development Association.

2001 CACREP Standards Related to Career Development

Career Development—studies that provide an understanding of career development and related life factors, including all of the following:

Book Chapter	CACREP Standard
2, 3	a. career development theories and decision-making models;
6, 7	b. career, avocational, educational, occupational and labor market information resources, visual and print media, computer-based career information systems, and other electronic career information systems;
9, 15	c. career development program planning, organization, implementation, administration, and evaluation;
1, 4	d. interrelationships among and between work, family, and other life roles and factors including the role of diversity and gender in career development;
8, 15	e. career and educational planning, placement, follow-up, and evaluation;
5	f. assessment instruments and techniques that are relevant to career planning and decision making;
7	g. technology-based career development applications and strategies, including computer-assisted career guidance and information systems and appropriate World Wide Web sites;
4, 8, 10–13	h. career counseling processes, techniques, and resources, including those applicable to specific populations; and
14	i. ethical and legal considerations.

From The 2001 CACREP Standards retrieved June 27, 2007. From http://www.cacrep.org/2001standards.html

INDEX

CARROT AND RADISH BUNDLES, MIXED GREENS WITH MA_____NS

AND SUNFLOWER SEEDS, *spring green soup,* BONED LEG OF

LAMB STUFFED WITH TAPENADE, HOISIN-ROASTED GAME HENS, ASPARAGUS AND

SHIITAKE STIR-FRY, BEET, CABBAGE, AND CARROT SLAW WITH CARAWAY SEEDS,

COLCANNON, GRATIN DAUPHINOISE, *parsleyed potatoes,*

GRILLED RATATOUILLE NIÇOISE, POTATO GALETTES, ROSTI POTATOES, SHAVED

fennel salad WITH ALMONDS, ALMOND-ORANGE FINANCIER, BANANA

AND COCONUT CASHEW-CREAM TART, FRESH PEAR AND BERRY COMPOTE IN RED

WINE, *ginger rice pudding,* BABA GHANOUSH, COUSCOUS SALAD,

LAMB KOFTE, CURRIED EGGS, TOMATOES A LA GRECQUE, PUREED SPINACH-POTATO

SOUP, STRACCIATELLA, BROILED *flank-steak sandwiches,*

EGG, PROSCIUTTO, AND ASPARAGUS PIZZA, GRILLED TUNA WITH CHERRY-TOMATO

SALAD AND HERBED BULGHUR, PASTA WITH FENNEL, SARDINES, AND PINE NUTS,

slow-roasted salmon WITH CAPER-AND-HERB RELISH, SMOKED

MACKEREL, CUCUMBER, AND POTATO SALAD WITH MUSTARD DRESSING, WARM

SPRING SALAD WITH POACHED EGGS, CHOCOLATE COOKIES, ELKE WOOD'S LEMON

SQUARES, *lemon poppy-seed lady cake,* LEMON, BLACK-

BERRY, AND MERINGUE PARFAIT, LEMON SPONGE PUDDING, LEMON-BLUEBERRY

PETITS FOURS, LEMON MADELEINES, LEMON PINE-NUT TART, MEYER LEMON

GELATO, PASTIERA WITH STRAWBERRY SAUCE, *rose-water sherbet,*

SUGAR COOKIES, CANDIED LEMON RIND, EMPANADAS, BUTTERMILK VICHYSSOISE

WITH WATERCRESS, CELERY ROOT REMOULADE, HAM-AND-CHEESE TARTINES

ENDIVE WITH PEARS, WALNUTS, AND ROQUEFORT, MUSHROOM CROSTINI,

ricotta cheese torta, FRISEE WITH LARDONS AND POACHED

EGGS, WARM GOAT-CHEESE SALAD, GRILLED PORK PAILLARDS, GRILLED MUSH-

ROOM BURGER WITH WHITE-BEAN PUREE, *vegetable biryani,*

LENTIL SALAD, BEET SALAD, PASTA VERDE, WARM BEAN, SNAP PEA, AND TOMATO

SALAD, LEEKS WITH MUSTARD VINAIGRETTE, HARICOTS VERTS WITH GRAINY

MUSTARD VINAIGRETTE, WHOLE-WHEAT PASTA WITH LENTILS, SPINACH, AND

LEEKS, *angel food cake,* CHERRY ICE, STRAWBERRY TARTLETS,

HONEY LACE COOKIES, EARL GREY POTS DE CREME, CROSTINI WITH SALT-COD

BRANDADE, *sweet-and-sour cucumber salad,*

STUFFED QUAHOGS, SAVORY APRICOT LUNCHEON TARTLETS WITH CORNMEAL

CRUST, CHICKEN AND APRICOT STEW WITH COUSCOUS, GRILLED PROSCIUTTO-

WRAPPED COD AND ONIONS, BLUEFISH WITH HERB STUFFING, GRILLED CHICKEN

TOSTADAS, *black beans with poblano,* MIXED RICE SALAD,

GRILLED TOMATOES, CHEESECAKE WITH POACHED APRICOT HALVES, APRICOT

SHERBET, APRICOT-AND-WALNUT ROLL CAKE, *buttermilk pie,*

HUMMINGBIRD CAKE, BROILED APRICOTS WITH STIRRED CUSTARD, APRICOT

CHERRY BAKE, *margarita cheesecake freezes,* VANILLA

PANNA COTTA WITH POACHED APRICOT HALVES, JOEY GALLAGHER'S APRICOT

HAND PIES, FATHER'S DAY BARBECUE SAUCE, FENNEL, ROASTED TOMATO, AND

BASIL RELISH, *spicy pineapple and mint salsa,*

CILANTRO SALSA WITH COCONUT AND LIME, CORN RELISH, STRAWBERRY JAM,

MARTHA STEWART LIVING

Annual Recipes

2004

MARTHA STEWART LIVING

Annual Recipes

2004

from the editors of **MARTHA STEWART LIVING**

Originally published in book form by Martha Stewart Living Omnimedia, Inc. in 2003.
Published simultaneously by Oxmoor House, Inc.
These recipes were previously published by Martha Stewart Living Omnimedia, Inc.

Printed in the United States of America.

Library of Congress Control Number: 2003112958

ISBN 0-8487-2745-2
ISSN 1541-9541

Acknowledgments

It takes the collaboration of many individuals to publish a collection of more than five hundred inspired recipes every year. Thank you to our food department's deputy editors, Lori Powell and Susan Sugarman, for leading a team of wonderful, inventive cooks, and to senior recipe editor Evelyn Battaglia, recipe editor Miranda Van Gelder, and assistant recipe editor Liesel Davis for their diligence in making sure every recipe is written just so. Thank you to books editor Ellen Morrissey and associate editor Christine Moller for overseeing the creation of this book from start to finish, and to Robert Bowe, Natalie Ermann, and Debra Puchalla for their keen attention to detail. Thanks to Mary Jane Callister, James Dunlinson, and Amber Blakesley, for art directing and designing the pages of this book, and to the production team of Duane Stapp and Denise Clappi. A very special thank you to the food department for their tireless development of wonderful recipes, notably Jennifer Aaronson, Tara Bench, Frances Boswell, Heidi Johannsen, Anna Kovel, Judith Lockhart, Melissa Perry, Elizabeth Pilar, Susan Spungen, Laura Trace, and for the support of Caroline Cleary, Elizabeth Durels, Aida Ibarra, Lillian Kang, and Gertrude Porter. And thanks to everyone who contributed their time and energy to the creation of this book, among them Roger Astudillo, Dora Braschi Cardinale, Douglas Brenner, Elizabeth Brownfield, Peter Colen, Jay Cooper, Stephanie Garcia, Amanda Genge, Eric Hutton, Jennifer Jarett, Johanna Kletter, Matthew Landfield, Stacie McCormick, Jim McKeever, Elizabeth Parson, Meg Peterson, Eric A. Pike, George D. Planding, Ben Rice, Margaret Roach, Lauren Podlach Stanich, Gael Towey, Beverly Utt, and Alison Vanek, and to everyone at Oxmoor House, AGT.seven, and R.R. Donnelley and Sons. Finally, thank you, Martha, for encouraging us to create the most delicious, creative, and easy-to-follow recipes for our readers.

Contents

Introduction

This volume marks the third in our Annual Recipes series, and we are once again delighted to offer a year's worth of recipes from the pages of MARTHA STEWART LIVING. As we put together this collection, we are always pleased to rediscover dishes that seem as if they were created a lifetime ago—we work many months ahead for each issue and tend to be entrenched in new material by the time the book is published. You'll be glad to find so many favorites in one convenient place, too.

Those of us who work in the test kitchen are frequently asked how we come up with new recipes and food stories. The answer is not always straightforward. Oftentimes, it's a vacation or meal that leaves a lasting memory—of a particular dish or well-crafted menu or spectacular setting. A visit to a wonderful Greek restaurant on Long Island, for example, inspired a refreshing look at the celebrated flavors of Greece (see the July recipes). A wedding in Wine Country, with long tables set beautifully among the vineyards, led us to wonder what it might be like to celebrate our most cherished meal—Thanksgiving—in such a compelling environment, and to seek out a family who does just that (see the November recipes).

Other times, one of us gets excited, as most of us at MARTHA STEWART LIVING do, by something from nature. Memories of walks in the wintry woods prompted the creation of this year's holiday dessert story: A pair of Bûches de Noël brings to mind fallen logs; meringue "mushrooms" sprout from a snowy blanket of icing atop a round cake; marshmallow "snowflakes" float in mugs of hot chocolate; and perhaps most whimsical of all, sliced almonds and chocolate curls are carefully arranged on miniature cakes to resemble prickly little pinecones (see the December recipes). These delightful desserts are examples of how the familiar world becomes fantastic—first in our hands, then in yours.

—THE FOOD EDITORS OF
MARTHA STEWART LIVING

Winter

THE CHILL OF WINTER CALLS FOR HEARTY FARE—roasts, stews, casseroles, and the like. All are somehow comforting, but nothing embodies the season quite like the roast's starchy sidekick, the potato. Among the recipes that follow are several variations on this versatile vegetable, including some that are diced and sautéed; sliced, layered, and baked; and boiled and mashed.

January

lemony hummus dip

MAKES 1¾ CUPS

1 can (15½ ounces) chickpeas, rinsed and drained
1 large or 2 small garlic cloves, coarsely chopped
   Pinch of ground cumin
   Pinch of ground nutmeg
5 tablespoons extra-virgin olive oil
2 tablespoons tahini
3 tablespoons freshly squeezed lemon juice (1 lemon)
¾ teaspoon coarse salt

Combine all ingredients in a food processor; add 1 tablespoon water, and pulse until smooth and creamy, adding more water if needed. Transfer to a serving dish with a cover or air-tight container, and place in the refrigerator until ready to serve, up to 5 days. Serve chilled or at room temperature.

from Food, Fun, and Games

potato skins with pancetta and mixed herbs

SERVES 10 TO 12

Assembled wedges can be stored in the refrigerator, covered with plastic wrap, until ready to bake, up to one day.

8 russet potatoes
1 tablespoon olive oil
½ pound pancetta or bacon, finely chopped
4 tablespoons unsalted butter
3 tablespoons finely chopped mixed fresh herbs, such as rosemary, sage, and thyme
16 ounces white and/or yellow sharp cheddar cheese, grated (about 2 cups)
8 ounces fontina cheese, grated (about 1 cup)

1 Preheat oven to 400°F. Place potatoes on a baking sheet, and rub with oil. Bake potatoes until tender when pierced with the tip of a paring knife, 55 to 60 minutes. Remove from oven, and let stand until cool enough to handle. Reduce oven temperature to 350°F.

2 Cut each potato in half lengthwise, and use a small spoon to scoop out flesh, leaving about ¼-inch border all around. Reserve flesh for another use. Slice each potato shell in half again lengthwise for a total of 32 wedges.

3 In a medium skillet, cook pancetta over medium heat, stirring frequently, until just starting to turn brown and crisp, 9 to 10 minutes. Remove from heat; use a slotted spoon to transfer pancetta to paper towels to drain. Set aside.

4 Melt the butter in a small saucepan. Brush inside of each potato wedge with butter; sprinkle with herb mixture. Cover each wedge with about 1 tablespoon cheddar cheese. Sprinkle ½ teaspoon pancetta and a little more herb mixture over each wedge. Sprinkle remaining cheddar and the fontina cheese over the tops.

5 Bake until cheese is melted and potatoes are heated through, 8 to 10 minutes. Remove from oven; serve hot.

from Food, Fun, and Games

roasted eggplant dip

SERVES 4 | **PHOTO ON PAGE 67**

Serve this chunky dip with crusty French bread that has been thinly sliced, brushed with olive oil, sprinkled with salt and pepper, and toasted until golden brown in a 450 degree oven.

1 large eggplant (about 1½ pounds)
8 ounces crème fraîche or sour cream
   Juice of 1 lemon
   Coarse salt and freshly ground pepper

1 Heat broiler. Pierce eggplant several times with a fork; place on a baking sheet. Broil, turning every 5 minutes, until skin is blackened all over and flesh is very soft, about 20 minutes. Remove from oven; let stand until cool enough to handle.

2 Peel off and discard blackened skin. Place eggplant in a food processor; purée until chunky. Transfer to a serving bowl. Stir in crème fraîche and lemon juice; season with salt and pepper. Serve warm or at room temperature.

from What's for Dinner?

sesame crunch sticks

MAKES ABOUT 4½ DOZEN

Toast sesame seeds in a dry skillet over medium heat, shaking frequently, until golden and fragrant, about five minutes. We serve these breadsticks with Hummus Dip (page 15).

- 3 cups all-purpose flour, plus more for work surface
- 2 teaspoons baking powder
- 2 teaspoons salt
- ½ cup (1 stick) chilled unsalted butter, cut into small pieces
- 1 cup buttermilk
- 1¼ cups sesame seeds, toasted
- 1 large egg
- 1 tablespoon sugar
- 1 tablespoon soy sauce

1 In a food processor, pulse flour, baking powder, and salt until combined. Add butter; pulse until mixture resembles coarse meal. Transfer to a medium bowl; stir in buttermilk and 1 cup sesame seeds until mixture forms a dough. Divide into quarters; wrap each in plastic. Chill 20 minutes.

2 Preheat oven to 350°F. In a small bowl, whisk together egg, sugar, and soy sauce. Transfer one piece of dough to a lightly floured work surface; roll out into a rectangle about ⅛ inch thick and 10 inches long. Use a sharp knife or pizza wheel to cut into strips, about ⅜ inch wide. Brush strips with egg mixture; sprinkle with remaining ¼ cup sesame seeds.

3 Arrange strips ½ inch apart on a parchment-lined baking sheet. Bake until just golden, 15 to 20 minutes. Transfer to a wire rack to cool. Repeat with remaining dough.

from Food, Fun, and Games

chicken and kale soup with white beans

SERVES 10 | **PHOTO ON PAGE 67**

This soup can be refrigerated for up to three days in airtight containers or frozen for up to three months.

- 3 tablespoons unsalted butter
- 1 tablespoon olive oil
- 1 large onion, cut into ¼-inch pieces
- 1 medium shallot, finely chopped
- ¼ cup all-purpose flour
- 2½ quarts Basic Chicken Stock (recipe follows) or low-sodium canned chicken broth
- 2 russet potatoes, peeled and cut into ½-inch pieces (about 2 cups)
- 2 parsnips, cut into ½-inch pieces (about 2 cups)
- 1 large turnip, cut into ½-inch pieces (about 2 cups)
- 1 dried bay leaf
- 1 whole chicken breast, skin removed
- 1 bunch fresh kale, stems discarded, leaves cut into 1-inch pieces
- 2 teaspoons finely chopped fresh oregano or 1 teaspoon dried
- 1 can (15½ ounces) white beans, rinsed and drained
- 2 cups low-fat (1 percent) milk
- Coarse salt and freshly ground pepper

1 In a large high-sided skillet or Dutch oven, heat butter and oil over medium heat. Add onion and shallot; cook until translucent, about 8 minutes. Stir in flour, and continue stirring until thoroughly combined, about 1 minute.

2 Stir in chicken stock, and add potatoes, parsnips, turnip, bay leaf, and chicken breast. Cover, and bring to a boil over medium-high heat. Reduce heat, and simmer until chicken is cooked through, about 30 minutes.

3 Transfer chicken to a cutting board. Let stand until cool enough to handle. Pull meat from bones; cut into ½-inch pieces. Return meat to skillet; add kale and oregano. Cook over medium heat until kale is tender, about 20 minutes.

4 Add beans to skillet, and cook 10 minutes. Stir in milk; cook until just heated through, about 5 minutes more. Do not let soup come to a boil or milk may curdle. Remove from heat, and discard bay leaf; season with salt and pepper. Serve.

from Wonderful Winter Soups

basic chicken stock

MAKES ABOUT 5 QUARTS

Toast fennel seeds in a dry skillet over medium heat, shaking frequently, until golden and fragrant, about five minutes. We added canned broth to fortify the stock's flavor, but you can use water if you prefer. Refrigerate stock in airtight containers for up to three days or freeze for up to six months.

3 carrots, each cut into thirds

2 stalks celery, each cut into thirds

1 bulb fennel, trimmed and cut into large chunks

3 tablespoons fennel seeds, toasted

1 teaspoon whole black peppercorns

1 whole chicken (4 to 6 pounds)

2 pounds assorted chicken wings, necks, and backs

3 quarts low-sodium canned chicken broth (two 48-ounce cans)

1 In a large stockpot, combine all ingredients with 2 quarts water. Cover, and bring to a boil over medium-high heat; reduce heat to a very gentle simmer. Cook, uncovered, 1 hour, checking occasionally to make sure liquid is barely bubbling and skimming surface with a large metal spoon as needed.

2 Transfer chicken to a cutting board. Let stand until cool enough to handle. Pull meat from bones. (Reserve meat for another use; refrigerate up to 3 days in an airtight container.)

3 Return bones to pot. Place a smaller pot lid on surface of stock to keep ingredients submerged. Simmer until bones fall apart when poked, 2½ to 4 hours. Skim surface as needed.

4 Prepare a large ice bath. Strain stock through a fine sieve into a large heatproof bowl, discarding solids. Set bowl in ice bath; let stock cool to room temperature, stirring frequently.

5 Transfer stock to airtight containers; refrigerate at least 6 hours or overnight. With a large metal spoon, skim off and discard layer of fat that has collected on surface. If storing, leave layer of fat intact (it helps to seal in flavor).

French lentil soup

SERVES 8 TO 10

This recipe can be doubled. Refrigerate leftovers in airtight containers for up to three days or freeze for up to three months.

2 tablespoons olive oil

1 small onion, finely chopped

2 carrots, finely chopped

1 stalk celery, finely chopped

1 small red bell pepper, seeds and ribs removed, finely chopped

1 teaspoon dried oregano

½ cup French green lentils, picked over and rinsed

3 tablespoons bulghur wheat

1½ quarts Wild Mushroom Stock (recipe follows)
Coarse salt and freshly ground black pepper

1 Place a large saucepan over medium heat, and add oil. Add onion, and cook until translucent, about 5 minutes, stirring occasionally. Stir in carrots, celery, bell pepper, and oregano until combined. Stir in lentils and bulghur wheat.

2 Add stock to saucepan; cover, and simmer over low heat until lentils are just tender, about 45 minutes. Remove from heat; season with salt and pepper. Serve hot.

from Wonderful Winter Soups

wild mushroom stock

MAKES 3 QUARTS

Refrigerate stock in airtight containers for up to three days, or freeze for up to six months.

4 ounces dried porcini mushrooms

2 tablespoons unsalted butter

2 tablespoons olive oil

1 large onion, coarsely chopped

2 large carrots, coarsely chopped

2 parsnips, coarsely chopped

2 stalks celery, coarsely chopped

1 bunch (about 1½ pounds) red or green Swiss chard, cut into 1-inch pieces

1 dried bay leaf
Several sprigs thyme
Several sprigs flat-leaf parsley

1 Bring 4 cups water to a boil. Place dried mushrooms in a medium heatproof bowl; pour boiling water over mushrooms. Let stand until softened, about 20 minutes. Strain through a fine sieve into another bowl, reserving liquid and mushrooms separately. Set aside.

2 In a medium stockpot, heat butter and oil over medium heat. Add onion, and cook until caramelized, stirring occasionally, about 20 minutes. Add reserved mushrooms along with carrots, parsnips, and celery; cook, stirring often, until vegetables are softened and fragrant, about 20 minutes.

3 Stir chard into vegetable mixture in pot. Add 3½ quarts cold water, reserved mushroom liquid (being careful to leave behind any sediment), bay leaf, thyme, and parsley. Cover, and bring to a boil. Reduce heat; simmer, uncovered, 1 hour.

4 Remove pot from heat, and strain mixture through a fine sieve into a large heatproof bowl, pressing down on vegetables with the back of a wooden spoon to extract as much liquid as possible. Discard solids. Let cool, then transfer stock to airtight containers.

hearty beef stew

SERVES 10 | **PHOTO ON PAGE 65**

To peel pearl onions, blanch in boiling water one to two minutes, then plunge into an ice bath. The skins should slip off easily. Serve over egg noodles or rice. Once completely cooled, the stew may be refrigerated for up to three days in airtight containers. Add the peas just before serving.

**Basic Beef Stock (recipe follows), plus
reserved beef and tomatoes**
1 **pound pearl onions, peeled**
5 **carrots, cut into matchsticks**
½ **small bunch fresh dill, coarsely chopped**
Coarse salt and freshly ground pepper
1 **package (10 ounces) frozen green peas, thawed**

1 In a medium stockpot, combine stock and reserved beef and tomatoes. Cover; bring to a simmer over medium heat. Add onions, carrots, and dill. Cook, uncovered, until onions are soft, about 30 minutes. Season with salt and pepper.

2 Add peas, and cook just until tender and heated through, about 3 minutes. Serve hot.

from Wonderful Winter Soups

basic beef stock

MAKES 3½ QUARTS

Reserve the shredded beef and tomato pieces to make Hearty Beef Stew (recipe above). Refrigerate stock in airtight containers for up to three days, or freeze for up to six months.

6 **pounds beef short ribs, trimmed of excess fat**
Coarse salt and freshly ground pepper
1 **can (28 ounces) peeled whole tomatoes,
coarsely chopped, juice reserved**
2 **dried bay leaves**
10 **whole black peppercorns**
½ **small bunch fresh dill, coarsely chopped**

1 Preheat oven to 450°F. Arrange ribs in a large roasting pan; sprinkle generously with salt and pepper. Roast 1½ hours, turning ribs halfway through.

2 Combine 3 quarts water with tomatoes and their juice in a medium stockpot. Bundle bay leaves, peppercorns, and dill in a piece of cheesecloth; tie with kitchen twine, and add to pot.

3 Transfer roasted ribs to pot. Pour off and discard fat from roasting pan. Pour 1 cup water into pan; place over medium-high heat. Bring to a boil, stirring with a wooden spoon to scrape up any browned bits from the bottom, until liquid is reduced by half. Transfer liquid and bits to stockpot.

4 Cover pot; bring mixture to a simmer over medium-high heat, but do not boil. Reduce heat to a gentle simmer, and place a smaller pot lid directly on surface of stock to keep ingredients submerged. Simmer until meat is very tender and pulls away from the bone, about 1½ hours. Skim surface with a spoon as needed.

5 Prepare a large ice bath. Remove herb bundle from pot, squeezing liquid into pot; discard. Strain stock through a fine sieve into a large heatproof bowl. Set bowl in ice bath; let stock cool to room temperature, stirring frequently.

6 Transfer ribs and tomatoes to another bowl. When cool enough to handle, pull rib meat from bones, and shred with your fingers. Discard bones. Store meat and tomatoes in an airtight container in the refrigerator, up to 3 days.

7 Transfer stock to airtight containers; refrigerate at least 6 hours or overnight. With a large metal spoon, skim off and discard layer of fat that has collected on surface. If storing, leave layer of fat intact (it helps to seal in flavor).

shredded chicken and soba noodle soup

SERVES 10 | **PHOTO ON PAGE 68**

Look for soba noodles in specialty markets or the Asian section of most grocery stores.

2½ quarts Basic Chicken Stock (page 17) or low-sodium canned chicken broth

2 whole skinless chicken breasts, halved

Coarse salt

½ pound soba noodles

1 pound firm or extra-firm tofu, cubed

Freshly ground pepper

2 small carrots, julienned

2 red radishes, julienned

½ bunch watercress, tough stems trimmed, for garnish

1 In a medium stockpot, bring stock to a boil over medium heat. Add chicken breasts, and return to a boil. Reduce heat; simmer until chicken is cooked through, about 20 minutes. Using tongs, transfer chicken to a plate; set aside until cool enough to handle. Cover stock, and keep at a low simmer.

2 Meanwhile, bring a medium saucepan of water to a boil over high heat. Add salt, and stir in soba noodles. Cook until al dente according to package instructions. Drain; set aside.

3 Pull chicken from bones, and shred meat into bite-size pieces; set aside. Add tofu to simmering stock just until heated through. Season with salt and pepper.

4 To serve, ladle stock and tofu into soup bowls. Add shredded chicken to each bowl, and mound soba noodles in center. Sprinkle with carrots and radishes; garnish with watercress.

from Wonderful Winter Soups

spicy sweet-potato soup

SERVES 10

Once cooled, this soup can be refrigerated in airtight containers for up to three days or frozen for up to three months.

1¼ teaspoons ground cardamom

1 teaspoon ground turmeric

¾ teaspoon ground cinnamon

⅓ teaspoon chili powder

1 tablespoon unsalted butter

1 tablespoon olive oil

2 leeks, white and pale-green parts only, coarsely chopped and washed well (1 cup)

1 large onion, cut into ¼-inch dice

4 sweet potatoes, cut into ½-inch dice

1 butternut squash (about 1½ pounds), peeled and cut into ½-inch dice

2 carrots, cut into ½-inch dice

3 quarts Basic Chicken Stock (page 17) or low-sodium canned chicken broth

Coarse salt and freshly ground pepper

Radish sprouts, for garnish (optional)

1 Combine cardamom, turmeric, cinnamon, and chili powder in a small bowl; set aside. In a medium saucepan, heat butter and oil over medium heat. Add leeks and onion; cook, stirring occasionally, until translucent, about 8 minutes. Sprinkle leek mixture with spices; add potatoes, squash, and carrots. Stir well to combine.

2 Add stock to saucepan. Bring to a simmer; cook over low heat, partially covered, until vegetables are tender, about 40 minutes. Season with salt and pepper. Remove from heat.

3 Transfer half the soup to a blender, working in batches, if necessary, so as not to fill jar more than halfway; process until smooth. Return purée to saucepan; place over low heat until just heated through. Divide among soup bowls; garnish each bowl with a handful of radish sprouts, if using. Serve.

from Wonderful Winter Soups

tortellini soup

SERVES 10

2 quarts Wild Mushroom Stock (page 17)
Coarse salt and freshly ground pepper
1 pound fresh or frozen tortellini (cheese or sausage)

In a large saucepan, bring stock to a boil over medium heat. Season with salt and pepper, and stir in pasta. Cook until pasta is al dente according to package instructions (tortellini should float). Remove from heat. Serve hot.

from Wonderful Winter Soups

turkey meatball soup

SERVES 10 | **PHOTO ON PAGE 68**

Uncooked meatballs can be frozen for up to two months. Store individual servings in resealable plastic bags or airtight containers; allow for four or five meatballs per serving.

1 package ground turkey (about 1½ pounds)
1 small onion, finely chopped
¼ cup plain breadcrumbs, preferably homemade
1 large egg, lightly beaten
1 tablespoon Worcestershire sauce
2 tablespoons chopped fresh flat-leaf parsley
1 tablespoon chopped fresh thyme leaves
   or 1 teaspoon dried
2 teaspoons chopped fresh oregano leaves
   or ½ teaspoon dried
Coarse salt and freshly ground pepper
1 tablespoon olive oil
2½ quarts Basic Chicken Stock (page 17) or low-sodium canned chicken broth

1 In a medium bowl, combine turkey, onion, breadcrumbs, egg, Worcestershire, parsley, thyme, and oregano; season with salt and pepper. Gently mix together with your hands.

2 Pinch off about 1 tablespoon of the turkey mixture, and shape into a 1-inch ball. Repeat with remaining turkey mixture, placing the meatballs on a rimmed baking sheet. Cover with plastic wrap; freeze until firm, about 2½ hours.

3 When ready to cook, remove meatballs from freezer, and let stand at room temperature until slightly soft on the outside, about 20 minutes. In a large skillet, heat oil over medium heat; add meatballs, working in batches if necessary, to avoid crowding skillet. Cook, stirring occasionally, until well browned on the outside and almost cooked through. Transfer meatballs to a paper-towel–lined plate to drain.

4 Place stock in a large, deep skillet; bring to a boil over medium-high heat. Season with salt and pepper. Add meatballs. Reduce heat; simmer until meatballs are cooked through, about 10 minutes. To serve, spoon four or five meatballs into each soup bowl, and ladle stock over the top. Serve.

from Wonderful Winter Soups

MAIN COURSES

chili with chicken and beans

SERVES 6 | **PHOTO ON PAGE 72**

If you like, spice up this robust chili by adding chopped fresh hot chile peppers. You can also replace the canned beans with cooked dried beans; if you do so, substitute the bean cooking liquid for half of the chicken stock.

1 tablespoon olive oil
3 teaspoons whole cumin seeds
2 onions, finely chopped (about 3 cups)
5 garlic cloves, coarsely chopped
1 green bell pepper, seeds and ribs removed, finely chopped
2 boneless and skinless chicken breasts (about 1¾ pounds), cut into 1-inch cubes
2 teaspoons chili powder
1 teaspoon dried oregano
1 dried bay leaf
1 can (28 ounces) chopped tomatoes with juice
1 can (4 ounces) green chiles, finely chopped
2½ cups Basic Chicken Stock (page 17) or low-sodium canned chicken broth, skimmed of fat
½ teaspoon coarse salt
4 cups canned kidney beans, drained and rinsed
Freshly ground black pepper
2 ounces (¼ cup) low-fat sour cream, for garnish (optional)
Fresh cilantro leaves, for garnish (optional)

1 In a large, heavy-bottom pot or Dutch oven, place the oil and cumin seeds over medium heat, stirring, until the cumin is lightly toasted and aromatic, about 1 minute. Add onions, garlic, and bell pepper; reduce heat to medium-low. Cook, stirring occasionally, until vegetables are lightly golden, about 10 minutes.

2 Raise heat to medium, and stir in chicken, chili powder, oregano, and bay leaf. Cook, stirring frequently, until chicken is seared on the outside and coated thoroughly with spices, about 10 minutes. Add tomatoes and green chiles, and stir to combine. Cook 5 minutes. Add stock, salt, and beans; season with black pepper, and stir to combine.

3 Cover pot, and bring to a simmer. Stir contents, then replace lid to partially cover pot. Reduce heat to medium-low, and cook, stirring occasionally, until chili is thickened and chicken is tender, about 1½ hours.

4 Divide chili among six bowls; garnish with sour cream and cilantro leaves, if desired. Serve immediately.

PER SERVING: 466 CALORIES, 13 G FAT, 127 MG CHOLESTEROL, 32 G CARBOHYDRATE, 884 MG SODIUM, 55 G PROTEIN, 10 G FIBER

from Fit to Eat: Comfort Food

make-your-own-sandwich buffet

SERVES 10 TO 12 | **PHOTO ON PAGE 72**

This recipe is intended as a guide; add or substitute your own favorite fillings and condiments.

1½ pounds (18 to 20 slices) bacon, cooked

2¾ pounds assorted sandwich meats, such as roast beef, pastrami, turkey, Black Forest ham, salami, and prosciutto

8 ounces assorted thinly sliced cheeses, such as Brie, provolone, Swiss, and fresh mozzarella

Assorted lettuces, such as Bibb, Boston, romaine, and arugula

3 large tomatoes, thinly sliced

1 jar (14 ounces) roasted red peppers, sliced

1 jar (7½ ounces) sun-dried tomatoes, packed in oil

1 jar (6 ounces) marinated artichoke hearts, drained and sliced

1 jar (8 ounces) mayonnaise

1 jar (8 ounces) Dijon mustard

1 jar (about 7 ounces) tapenade

2 ripe avocados, peeled, pitted, and thinly sliced

Assorted breads, such as sandwich bread, rolls, baguettes, and focaccia

Place the ingredients on serving dishes; cover with plastic wrap, and chill until ready to serve, up to several hours. Slice bread just before setting on the table.

from Food, Fun, and Games

sautéed shrimp

SERVES 4 | **PHOTO ON PAGE 69**

2 tablespoons extra-virgin olive oil

4 garlic cloves, minced

1½ pounds large shrimp, peeled and deveined, tails left on

2 tablespoons chopped fresh flat-leaf parsley

2 tablespoons chopped fresh oregano

Pinch of crushed red-pepper flakes

½ cup dry white wine

Coarse salt and freshly ground black pepper

Lemon wedges, for serving

1 Heat oil in a large, heavy skillet over medium heat. Add garlic, and cook, stirring, until soft but not browned, 1 to 2 minutes. Add shrimp, parsley, oregano, and red-pepper flakes; cook, stirring frequently, until shrimp are bright pink and opaque, about 2 minutes.

2 Carefully add wine. Raise heat to medium-high, and simmer until most of the liquid has evaporated. Remove from heat; season with salt and pepper. Serve hot, with lemon wedges on the side.

from What's for Dinner?

spaghetti with radicchio and ricotta

SERVES 4

2 tablespoons extra-virgin olive oil

3 garlic cloves, minced

½ cup finely chopped fresh flat-leaf parsley

½ cup plain breadcrumbs, preferably homemade

Coarse salt

1 pound spaghetti

8 ounces fresh ricotta cheese

1 head radicchio, quartered, cored, and thinly sliced crosswise

Freshly ground pepper

1 Heat 1 tablespoon oil in a medium skillet over medium heat. Add garlic, and cook, stirring, until soft but not browned, 1 to 2 minutes. Add parsley and breadcrumbs; cook, stirring frequently, until breadcrumbs are golden, about 3 minutes. Transfer to a bowl, and set aside.

2 Bring a large pot of water to a boil, and add salt. Add pasta, and cook until al dente according to package instructions. Drain, reserving 1 cup cooking liquid. Return pasta and reserved cooking liquid to pot, and add ricotta and remaining tablespoon oil. Toss to combine. Add radicchio and half the reserved breadcrumb mixture; toss evenly. Season with salt and pepper. Serve immediately, sprinkled with remaining breadcrumb mixture.

from What's for Dinner?

turkey meatloaf

SERVES 6 | PHOTO ON PAGE 72

4 slices white bread, trimmed of crusts and torn into pieces

8 small fresh sage leaves

1½ pounds lean ground turkey

1 large yellow onion, cut into eighths

1 stalk celery, cut into 2-inch pieces

½ teaspoon dried thyme

1 large whole egg, lightly beaten

2 tablespoons tomato paste

4 teaspoons Dijon mustard

1¼ teaspoons Worcestershire sauce

¾ teaspoon coarse salt

Freshly ground black pepper

1 large egg white

Garlic Mashed Potatoes, for serving (recipe follows)

Cheater's Gravy, for serving (recipe follows)

1 Preheat oven to 400°F with rack in center. Place bread and sage leaves in a food processor; pulse to form fine crumbs. Transfer to a medium bowl, and add ground turkey.

2 Place onion and celery in food processor; pulse until finely chopped. Add to turkey mixture, using your hands to combine. Add thyme, whole egg, 1 tablespoon tomato paste, mustard, 1 teaspoon Worcestershire, and salt; season with pepper; mix to combine. Pat into a 9-by-5-by-2½-inch nonstick loaf pan.

3 In a small bowl, combine egg white with the remaining tablespoon tomato paste and ¼ teaspoon Worcestershire, whisking with a fork until smooth. Spoon mixture over meatloaf, and spread to coat top evenly.

4 Transfer pan to oven; place a baking sheet on lower rack to catch drippings. Cook until a meat thermometer inserted in center of meatloaf registers 180°F, about 1¼ hours. Remove from oven; let rest 15 minutes covered loosely with foil.

5 To serve, cut meatloaf into 12 slices, and divide evenly among six serving plates. Serve immediately with mashed potatoes and hot gravy.

PER SERVING: 200 CALORIES, 3 G FAT, 86 MG CHOLESTEROL, 13 G CARBOHYDRATE, 451 MG SODIUM, 31 G PROTEIN, 1 G FIBER

from Fit to Eat: Comfort Food

garlic mashed potatoes

SERVES 6 | PHOTO ON PAGE 72

1 pound red potatoes, peeled and cut into eighths

1 pound russet potatoes, peeled and cut into 1½-inch pieces

5 garlic cloves

¾ cup nonfat milk

2 tablespoons unsalted butter

¾ teaspoon coarse salt

Freshly ground pepper

1 In a medium saucepan, combine potatoes and garlic; add enough cold water to cover by about 2 inches. Bring to a boil over high heat. Reduce heat to a simmer, and cook until potatoes are easily pierced with a fork, about 15 minutes. Drain potatoes and garlic, and set aside in a warm place.

2 In the same saucepan, combine milk, butter, and salt; season with pepper. Place over low heat until butter has melted and milk is warm to the touch. Pass potatoes and garlic through a potato ricer or food mill into saucepan, and stir gently to combine with milk mixture. Serve immediately.

PER SERVING: 178 CALORIES, 4 G FAT, 11 MG CHOLESTEROL, 33 G CARBOHYDRATE, 259 MG SODIUM, 4 G PROTEIN, 3 G FIBER

from Fit to Eat: Comfort Food

cheater's gravy

MAKES ABOUT 1 CUP; SERVES 6

We serve this flavorful gravy over meatloaf and mashed potatoes, but it is equally good with other classic comfort foods, such as ham and biscuits.

1 cup Basic Chicken Stock (page 17) or low-sodium canned chicken broth, skimmed of fat
1 teaspoon cornstarch
1 tablespoon chopped fresh flat-leaf parsley

1 In a small saucepan, bring chicken stock to a boil over high heat. Reduce heat to medium, and simmer until stock is reduced by half, about 10 minutes.

2 Meanwhile, in a small bowl, whisk together cornstarch and 1 tablespoon cold water with a fork until smooth; whisk into simmering stock. Raise heat; bring to a full boil. Boil 30 seconds. Remove from heat, and stir in parsley. Serve hot.

PER SERVING: 5 CALORIES, 0 G FAT, 0 MG CHOLESTEROL, 1 G CARBOHYDRATE, 80 MG SODIUM, 0 G PROTEIN, 0 G FIBER

SIDE DISHES

cabbage and chive slaw

SERVES 10 TO 12

For a colorful slaw, use both purple and Savoy cabbages.

1 cup sour cream
2 tablespoons rice-wine vinegar
  Coarse salt and freshly ground pepper
1 pound (1 small head) cabbage
1 bunch chives, cut into 1½-inch lengths
1 ripe but firm pear

1 Prepare dressing: In a small bowl, whisk together sour cream and vinegar, and season with salt and pepper.

2 Using a sharp knife or mandoline, thinly slice cabbage; place in a medium bowl with the chives. Peel and core pear; cut into matchsticks. Add pear to bowl; drizzle with dressing, and toss gently to coat evenly. Serve immediately.

from Food, Fun, and Games

macaroni and cheese with butternut squash

SERVES 6

1 small butternut squash (about 1 pound), peeled, seeded, and cut into 1-inch cubes (about 3 cups)
1 cup Basic Chicken Stock (page 17) or low-sodium canned chicken broth, skimmed of fat
1½ cups nonfat milk
  Pinch of freshly grated nutmeg
  Pinch of cayenne pepper
¾ teaspoon coarse salt
  Freshly ground black pepper
1 pound elbow macaroni
1 cup finely grated extra-sharp cheddar cheese (4 ounces)
½ cup part-skim ricotta cheese
4 tablespoons finely grated Parmesan cheese (1 ounce)
2 tablespoons fine breadcrumbs
1 teaspoon olive oil
  Olive-oil cooking spray

1 Preheat oven to 375°F. Combine squash, stock, and milk in a medium saucepan; bring to a boil over medium-high heat. Reduce heat to medium; simmer until squash is tender when pierced with a fork, about 20 minutes. Remove from heat. Mash contents of saucepan; stir in nutmeg, cayenne, and salt, and season with black pepper. Stir to combine.

2 Meanwhile, bring a large pot of water to a boil. Add pasta; cook until al dente according to package instructions, about 8 minutes. Drain, and transfer to a large bowl; stir in squash mixture, cheddar, ricotta, and 2 tablespoons Parmesan.

3 Lightly coat a 9-inch square baking dish (at least 4 inches deep) with cooking spray. Transfer pasta mixture to dish, spreading evenly. In a small bowl, combine breadcrumbs, remaining 2 tablespoons Parmesan, and the oil; sprinkle evenly over pasta mixture.

4 Cover dish with foil, and bake 20 minutes. Remove foil, and continue baking until lightly browned and crisp on top, 30 to 40 minutes more. Serve hot.

PER SERVING: 350 CALORIES, 6 G FAT, 18 MG CHOLESTEROL, 57 G CARBOHYDRATE, 505 MG SODIUM, 16 G PROTEIN, 2 G FIBER

from Fit to Eat: Comfort Food

twice-baked potatoes with scallions

SERVES 4 | **PHOTO ON PAGE 75**

4 russet potatoes, scrubbed
¾ cup part-skim ricotta cheese
½ cup plain nonfat yogurt
4 scallions, finely chopped
   Pinch of coarse salt
   Freshly ground pepper

1 Preheat oven to 375°F. Place potatoes on a baking sheet. Prick top of each potato a few times with a fork, and bake until easily pierced with a paring knife, about 45 minutes. Remove from oven; let cool slightly, about 10 minutes.

2 Using a serrated knife, cut off top one-quarter of each potato, slicing lengthwise. Use a spoon to scoop flesh into a medium bowl, leaving a ¼-inch border all around. Set shells aside. Mash flesh with a fork until smooth. Add remaining ingredients, and stir until combined.

3 Refill shells with potato mixture. Cook until potato is soft and filling is lightly browned on top, 35 to 40 minutes. Remove from oven; serve immediately.

PER SERVING: 257 CALORIES, 3 G FAT, 11 MG CHOLESTEROL, 49 G CARBOHYDRATE, 377 MG SODIUM, 9 G PROTEIN, 5 G FIBER

from Fit to Eat: Comfort Food

....

DESSERTS

....

brown-butter toffee blondies

MAKES ABOUT 1 DOZEN

We used card-suit cookie cutters to shape the blondies into hearts, clubs, diamonds, and spades—perfect treats for serving at family game nights.

1¼ cups (2½ sticks) unsalted butter, plus more at room temperature for pan
2¼ cups all-purpose flour, plus more for pan
1½ teaspoons baking powder
1½ teaspoons salt
2 cups packed light-brown sugar
½ cup granulated sugar
3 large eggs
2½ teaspoons pure vanilla extract
1 cup chopped walnuts (about 4 ounces)
1 cup toffee bits, such as Skor
   Confectioners' sugar, for dusting (optional)

1 Preheat oven to 350°F. Butter a 9-by-13-inch baking pan. Line bottom of pan with parchment; butter parchment. Sprinkle with flour, and tap out excess; set aside.

2 In a small saucepan over medium heat, cook the butter until it turns dark brown; remove from heat, and let cool. In a medium bowl, whisk together flour, baking powder, and salt.

3 In the bowl of an electric mixer, stir together browned butter and both sugars with a wooden spoon until combined. Add eggs; using the paddle attachment, cream on medium-high speed until light and fluffy, about 3 minutes. Add the vanilla, and beat to combine. Add the flour mixture, walnuts, and toffee bits. Mix until thoroughly combined, and spread into prepared pan, smoothing top.

4 Bake until a cake tester inserted in center comes out clean, 35 to 40 minutes, being careful not to overbake. Transfer to a wire rack to cool completely before turning out of pan onto a cutting board. Peel off parchment paper; cut blondies into suit shapes with 1½- to 2-inch cookie cutters. Just before serving, dust half with confectioners' sugar, if desired. Store in an airtight container at room temperature up to 3 days.

from Food, Fun, and Games

chocolate macadamia tartlets

MAKES 4 TWO-BY-FOUR-INCH TARTLETS

We spread chocolate ganache over some of the tarts and garnished others with chocolate shavings. To make shavings, spread leftover chocolate from step five on a baking sheet; chill until firm, then scrape with a knife or a dough scraper.

   Chocolate Tart Dough (recipe follows)
½ cup macadamia nuts (about 2¼ ounces), halved
1 cup sugar
2 tablespoons light corn syrup
1 cup heavy cream
4 tablespoons unsalted butter, cut into tablespoons
1 tablespoon crème fraîche
½ teaspoon pure vanilla extract
   Pinch of coarse or sea salt
8 ounces bittersweet chocolate, finely chopped

1 Preheat oven to 375°F. Place dough on a piece of parchment; roll out ⅛ inch thick. Transfer to a baking sheet; chill 10 minutes. Remove from refrigerator; cut dough into four 3¾-by-5½-inch rectangles. Fit dough into four 2-by-4-inch tart pans with removable bottoms, pressing into corners. Prick bottom of tarts all over with a fork. Chill at least 15 minutes.

2 Meanwhile, spread nuts in a single layer on a rimmed baking sheet; toast in oven until golden and fragrant, about 10 minutes. Remove from oven; set aside.

3 Remove shells from refrigerator; line with parchment, pressing into edges. Fill shells with dried beans or pie weights. Place on a baking sheet; bake 20 minutes. Remove paper and beans; continue baking until crusts are firm, 5 to 7 minutes. Transfer to a wire rack to cool completely.

4 Make caramel: In a small saucepan, bring sugar, corn syrup, and 2 tablespoons water to a boil over medium-high heat; wash down sides of pan with a pastry brush dipped in water to prevent crystals from forming. Reduce heat to low; cook, swirling pan to color evenly, until caramel is a rich amber color. Remove from heat; carefully add ¼ cup cream (it will spatter), butter, crème fraîche, vanilla, and salt. Stir until smooth. Let cool slightly; stir in nuts.

5 Melt 5 ounces chocolate in a heatproof bowl set over a pan of simmering water, stirring until smooth. Pour 1½ tablespoons chocolate into each shell; spread to coat bottom and sides evenly. Chill until set, about 10 minutes. Remove from refrigerator; pour caramel into shells. Set aside.

6 Make ganache: Place remaining 3 ounces chocolate in a heatproof bowl. Bring remaining ¾ cup cream to a boil in a small saucepan. Pour over chocolate; whisk until smooth. Let cool until slightly thickened, about 10 minutes. Pour 2½ tablespoons ganache over caramel in each shell, and smooth with an offset spatula. Store tartlets at room temperature, in an airtight container, up to 1 day.

from Dessert of the Month

chocolate tart dough

MAKES 4 TWO-BY-FOUR-INCH SHELLS

1½ cups all-purpose flour

¼ cup unsweetened cocoa powder

½ cup sugar

½ teaspoon salt

1 cup (2 sticks) chilled unsalted butter, cut into small pieces

2 large egg yolks

2 tablespoons heavy cream, chilled

½ teaspoon pure vanilla extract

1 Place flour, cocoa, sugar, and salt in a food processor; pulse to combine. Add butter, and pulse until mixture resembles coarse meal, about 10 seconds. Add yolks, cream, and vanilla; process until mixture comes together.

2 Turn out dough onto a piece of plastic; flatten into a disk. Wrap well; refrigerate at least 30 minutes and up to 2 days.

chocolate pudding

MAKES 6 SIX-OUNCE SERVINGS

To make chocolate shavings, use a sharp paring knife or vegetable peeler to scrape a four-ounce bar of semisweet or bittersweet chocolate into paper-thin strips.

⅓ cup plus 1 tablespoon unsweetened cocoa powder

2 tablespoons cornstarch

⅛ teaspoon salt

1 cup sugar

4 large egg yolks

2½ cups milk

½ cup heavy cream

½ teaspoon pure vanilla extract

4 ounces semisweet chocolate, finely chopped

Whipped cream, for garnish (optional)

Chocolate shavings, for garnish (optional)

1 Into a medium bowl, sift together cocoa, cornstarch, and salt. Stir in sugar. Add egg yolks, and pour in ½ cup milk; whisk until well combined.

2 In a medium saucepan, heat remaining 2 cups milk and the heavy cream over medium heat until mixture just comes to a boil. Slowly whisk milk mixture into cocoa mixture.

3 Rinse out saucepan but do not dry (to help prevent scorching). Return custard mixture to saucepan, and place over medium-low heat. Stir in vanilla. While stirring constantly with a wooden spoon, cook until custard has thickened slightly and is the consistency of mayonnaise, about 10 minutes (do not let it boil). Don't worry if lumps form.

4 Pour custard through a fine sieve into a clean bowl, discarding any solids. Add chopped chocolate to custard in two batches, stirring until chocolate is thoroughly melted and combined after each addition.

5 Divide pudding among six serving dishes, cover with plastic wrap, and chill at least 4 hours or up to overnight. Garnish with whipped cream and chocolate shavings, if desired.

from Chocolate Pudding 101

tiramisù sundaes

SERVES 4 | PHOTO ON PAGE 84

We garnished these easy-to-make, sophisticated desserts with chocolate shavings. To shave chocolate, use a sharp paring knife or vegetable peeler to scrape a four-ounce bar of semisweet or bittersweet chocolate into paper-thin strips.

    1 cup heavy cream
1½ cups strong espresso, cooled
    3 tablespoons brandy (optional)
    8 store-bought ladyfingers (about 4 ounces)
    1 pint coffee ice cream or gelato
       Chocolate shavings (optional)

1 Whisk cream in a medium bowl until stiff peaks form. Cover with plastic wrap; place in refrigerator until ready to serve.

2 Combine espresso and brandy, if using, in a medium bowl. Break 4 ladyfingers in half; dip into espresso mixture until soaked but not falling apart, 2 to 3 seconds. Arrange two halves at the bottom of each of four parfait glasses. Top with a scoop of ice cream. Repeat with another layer of soaked ladyfingers, and top with a scoop of ice cream.

3 Garnish each glass with a dollop of whipped cream and a sprinkling of chocolate shavings, if desired. Serve immediately.

from What's for Dinner?

word-game and checkers cookies

MAKES 52 WORD-GAME SQUARES AND
ABOUT 3 DOZEN CHECKERS

We created these letter-tile and round black-and-white cookies to look like word-game and checker pieces, perfect for serving during family game nights. For the word-game pieces, we cut out fifty-two squares from plain cookie dough and two of each letter from chocolate dough. For checkers, we cut both doughs into rounds.

    1 cup (2 sticks) unsalted butter, room temperature
    2 cups sugar
    2 large eggs
    2 teaspoons pure vanilla extract
    4 cups sifted all-purpose flour, plus more
       for work surface and cookie cutters
    1 teaspoon baking powder
½ teaspoon salt
¼ cup unsweetened cocoa powder

1 In the bowl of an electric mixer fitted with the paddle attachment, cream butter and sugar until light and fluffy, about 2 minutes. Add eggs and vanilla; beat until thoroughly combined. Beat in 2 cups flour, baking powder, and salt.

2 Divide dough in half; transfer one half to another bowl. To the remaining half in mixer bowl, add 1¼ cups flour; beat until combined. Transfer to a piece of plastic wrap. Return other dough half to mixer bowl; add cocoa powder and remaining ¾ cup flour. Beat until combined. Transfer to another piece of plastic wrap. Flatten both pieces into disks, and wrap well. Chill at least 30 minutes or overnight.

3 Turn out plain dough onto a lightly floured surface, and divide in half. Roll out one half about ⅛ inch thick. Using a paring knife or cookie cutter, cut dough into 1½-inch squares; arrange on parchment-lined baking sheets. Roll out other dough half to ⅛ inch thick; cut enough additional squares to total 52. Transfer baking sheets to the refrigerator, and chill until firm, at least 20 minutes.

4 Using a 1¼-inch cookie cutter, cut out rounds from remaining plain dough; place on a parchment-lined baking sheet, and chill until firm, at least 20 minutes.

5 Remove chocolate dough from refrigerator, and divide in half. Roll out one half about ⅛ inch thick. Using letter-shape cookie cutters, cut out 2 of each letter (for a total of 52 letters), and place on a parchment-lined baking sheet; dip cookie cutters in flour before each cut, then gently tap side of cutter against counter or your hand to loosen the letter. Transfer baking sheet to the refrigerator, and chill until firm.

6 Roll out remaining chocolate dough to ⅛ inch thick. Using the round cookie cutter, cut out rounds; place on baking sheet with plain rounds. Chill until firm.

7 Preheat oven to 350°F with racks in upper and lower thirds. Remove squares and letters from refrigerator. Using a pastry brush or your fingertip, dampen the top of each square with water; center a letter on top of each. Bake until just starting to brown, 9 to 10 minutes, rotating baking sheets halfway through. Transfer to wire racks to cool completely.

8 Remove rounds from refrigerator, and bake until just starting to brown and turn crisp, 9 to 10 minutes, rotating baking sheet halfway through. Transfer cookies to wire racks to cool. Cookies can be stored in airtight containers at room temperature up to 5 days.

from Food, Fun, and Games

coffee with Cognac and cardamom

SERVES 4 | **PHOTO ON PAGE 81**

This drink has a delectable creaminess similar to Irish coffee. For best results, use strong coffee.

⅔ cup turbinado sugar

6 cardamom pods, lightly crushed

1½ cups heavy cream

⅔ cup Cognac or other brandy

2 cups plus 2 tablespoons freshly brewed coffee

1 In a medium saucepan over medium heat, bring ⅔ cup water, sugar, and cardamom to a simmer, stirring to dissolve sugar; turn off heat. (Syrup mixture can be refrigerated in an airtight container up to 1 week. Before using, gently reheat.)

2 When ready to serve, whip cream to soft peaks. Add Cognac and hot coffee to saucepan with syrup mixture, and stir to combine. Divide among four glasses, and top each with a generous dollop of whipped cream. Serve immediately.

from Hot Drinks

hot buttered rum with ginger and cinnamon

SERVES 4

4 tablespoons Ginger Simple Syrup (recipe follows)

1 cup dark rum

4 whole cinnamon sticks

4 cups boiling water

½ recipe Ginger Butter (recipe follows)

Divide simple syrup among four glasses or mugs, and add ¼ cup rum, 1 cinnamon stick, and 1 cup boiling water to each. Stir well to combine. Top each serving with a round of ginger butter. Serve immediately.

from Hot Drinks

ginger simple syrup

MAKES ¾ CUP

4 ounces fresh ginger, thinly sliced

½ cup granulated sugar

In a small saucepan, bring ginger, sugar, and ½ cup water to a boil over medium heat. Cook 2 minutes. Strain mixture through a fine sieve, discarding ginger. Store syrup in an airtight container in the refrigerator up to 1 week.

ginger butter

MAKES 8 TABLESPOONS

3 pieces crystallized ginger, finely chopped (about 2 tablespoons)

½ teaspoon ground cinnamon

Pinch of ground cloves

Pinch of freshly grated nutmeg

½ cup (1 stick) unsalted butter, room temperature

In a small bowl, stir all ingredients with a fork until combined. Shape into a log by rolling in parchment paper or plastic wrap. Chill until firm, about 1 hour, before slicing into eight rounds.

hot date

SERVES 4

1 quart milk

7 teaspoons unsulfured molasses

¼ teaspoon freshly grated nutmeg

½ teaspoon ground cinnamon

Pinch of ground ginger

¼ teaspoon ground allspice

Pinch of coarse salt

14 dates, pitted

1 In a medium saucepan, heat milk, molasses, spices, and salt over medium heat 5 minutes. Remove from heat.

2 Chop dates in a blender as finely as possible. Add about 1 cup milk mixture; blend, scraping down sides with a rubber spatula to be sure all dates have been puréed.

3 Strain date purée through a fine sieve back into milk mixture in pan; whisk over medium heat until well combined. Divide among four cups, and serve immediately.

from Hot Drinks

hot honey lemonade with ginger

SERVES 4 | PHOTO ON PAGE 80

If you prefer, you can sweeten this drink with extra honey instead of the honey-drop candies.

½ cup Ginger Simple Syrup (page 27)
4 tablespoons freshly squeezed lemon juice
4 teaspoons honey
3 cups boiling water
12 whole cloves
½ lemon, cut into 4 wedges
12 honey-drop candies

1 Pour 2 tablespoons simple syrup in each of four heatproof glasses. Add 1 tablespoon lemon juice, 1 teaspoon honey, and ¾ cup boiling water to each; stir until honey dissolves.

2 Stick 3 cloves into each lemon wedge; drop a wedge and 3 candies into each drink. Serve immediately.

from Hot Drinks

malted hot chocolate

SERVES 4 | PHOTO ON PAGE 85

4 cups milk
1 teaspoon pure vanilla extract
4 ounces semisweet chocolate, coarsely chopped
¾ cup malted-milk powder

1 In a medium saucepan, heat milk and vanilla over medium heat until milk just begins to steam, 5 to 6 minutes. Add chopped chocolate; whisk until melted and combined.

2 Pour malt powder into a warmed serving pitcher or another saucepan. Add hot chocolate mixture, whisking until powder dissolves. Divide among four mugs; serve immediately.

from Hot Drinks

spicy hot-chocolate with cinnamon

SERVES 4 | PHOTO ON PAGE 81

An ancho chile lends a touch of mild heat to this drink.

4 cups milk
1 ancho chile, cut into 4 pieces, seeds removed
2 whole cinnamon sticks, plus 4 for garnish
4 ounces semisweet chocolate, coarsely chopped

1 In a medium saucepan over medium heat, combine milk, ancho chile, and cinnamon sticks; heat until milk just begins to steam, 5 to 6 minutes. Remove from heat, and let steep, covered, about 10 minutes.

2 Place chocolate in a medium bowl; strain milk mixture into bowl, whisking to combine thoroughly. Discard cinnamon sticks. Return mixture to saucepan; continue whisking over low heat until chocolate has melted completely. Divide among four mugs, and serve immediately, garnished with 4 remaining cinnamon sticks.

from Hot Drinks

toasted-almond milk with honey

SERVES 4

8 ounces sliced or slivered almonds
4 cups milk
4½ tablespoons honey
4 shots amaretto (optional)

1 Preheat oven to 350°F. Spread almonds in a single layer on a rimmed baking sheet; toast, stirring occasionally, until golden and fragrant, about 10 minutes. Remove from oven; let cool slightly, and coarsely chop.

2 Place almonds and milk in a medium saucepan; cook over medium heat until milk just begins to steam, 5 to 6 minutes. Remove from heat; let steep, covered, about 30 minutes.

3 Strain milk mixture through a fine sieve into a warmed pitcher or another saucepan; stir in honey until combined. Divide among four coffee cups; add a shot of amaretto, if desired, to each. Serve immediately.

from Hot Drinks

white hot chocolate

SERVES 4 | PHOTO ON PAGE 85

4 cups milk
½ teaspoon pure vanilla extract
4 ounces best-quality white chocolate, finely chopped

In a medium saucepan, heat milk and vanilla over medium heat until milk just begins to steam, 5 to 6 minutes. Remove from heat; add white chocolate, and whisk until melted and combined. Divide among four mugs; serve immediately.

from Hot Drinks

snack crackers

MAKES ABOUT 3 DOZEN

The dough can be frozen for up to two months; slice off what you need, returning the unused portion to the freezer.

1½ cups all-purpose flour, plus more for work surface
2   tablespoons toasted wheat germ
2   tablespoons flax seed
¼   cup rolled oats
¼   cup packed light-brown sugar
½   teaspoon coarse salt
6   tablespoons chilled unsalted butter, cut into small pieces
½   cup smooth peanut butter
¼   cup milk
    Rosemary and Sun-Dried-Tomato Oil, for serving (optional; recipe follows)

1   Place flour, wheat germ, flax seed, oats, sugar, and salt in a food processor. Pulse a few times to combine. Add butter, and pulse just until mixture is crumbly. Add peanut butter, and pulse a few more times. Add milk, and pulse until combined and mixture holds together.

2   Turn out dough onto a lightly floured surface; divide in half. Roll each piece into a 1½-by-6-inch log. Wrap logs tightly in plastic; freeze until firm, at least 45 minutes. If not baking immediately, remove logs from freezer; wrap parchment or waxed paper over plastic. Return to freezer until ready to bake.

3   Preheat oven to 350°F. Remove logs from freezer; let stand until slightly softened, about 5 minutes, depending on how long they have been frozen. Using a serrated knife, slice logs into ¼-inch-thick rounds. Place rounds on baking sheets.

4   Bake until crackers just start to brown, turning once and rotating baking sheets halfway through, about 12 minutes per side. Transfer to wire racks to cool. Store crackers in an airtight container at room temperature up to 7 days. Serve with flavored oil, if desired.

from Wonderful Winter Soups

rosemary and sun-dried-tomato oil

MAKES ABOUT 1 QUART

1   cup sun-dried tomatoes (not oil-packed)
1   bunch fresh rosemary leaves (about 1 cup)
1   quart extra-virgin olive oil

1   In a food processor, combine tomatoes and rosemary, pulsing until finely chopped but not completely puréed. Add oil, and pulse until combined, about 5 seconds.

2   Transfer mixture to an airtight container. Refrigerate at least 2 days to let flavors develop. At this point, oil can be stored up to 10 days in the refrigerator. To store longer than 10 days, strain mixture through a double layer of moistened cheesecloth into another airtight container, discarding solids. Before serving, bring to room temperature.

toasted snack mix

SERVES 10 TO 12

4   cups small cheese crackers (about 8 ounces)
4   cups oyster crackers (about 8 ounces)
4   cups thin pretzel sticks (about 8 ounces)
1   pound mixed nuts (about 4 cups)
½   cup (1 stick) unsalted butter
2   garlic cloves, lightly crushed
1½ tablespoons Worcestershire sauce
1½ teaspoons seasoned salt, such as Lawry's
½   teaspoon dry mustard
½   teaspoon hot-pepper sauce, such as Tabasco

1   Preheat oven to 275°F. In a shallow bowl, combine cheese and oyster crackers, pretzels, and nuts; set aside. In a small saucepan over medium-low heat, cook butter and garlic until butter starts to bubble, about 4 minutes.

2   Add Worcestershire, salt, mustard, and hot sauce to pan; stir to combine. Bring to a simmer, and cook about 2 minutes. Remove from heat. Remove garlic, and discard. Drizzle butter mixture over cracker mixture, tossing to coat.

3   Spread mixture evenly in two rimmed baking sheets. Bake until toasted and fragrant, stirring once or twice to cook evenly, about 30 minutes. Serve warm or at room temperature.

from Food, Fun, and Games

yogurt-nut oat bread

MAKES 1 EIGHT-BY-FOUR-INCH LOAF

To store, wrap loaf tightly in plastic and refrigerate for up to
one week, or freeze for up to two months.

2 cups all-purpose flour

¾ cup whole-wheat flour

1½ teaspoons coarse salt

1 teaspoon cream of tartar

1 teaspoon baking soda

1 teaspoon baking powder

¾ cup walnuts, toasted and chopped

½ cup steel-cut oats

½ cup oat or rice bran

¾ cup plus 3 tablespoons hulled sunflower seeds, toasted

1¼ cups low-fat (1 percent) milk

1 cup low-fat plain yogurt

Vegetable oil cooking spray

White Bean and Roasted Red-Pepper Spread,
for serving (recipe follows)

1   Preheat oven to 350°F. Coat an 8-by-4-inch loaf pan with
cooking spray. Into a large bowl, sift together flours, salt,
cream of tartar, baking soda, and baking powder. Stir in the
nuts, oats, bran, and ¾ cup sunflower seeds. In a separate
bowl, whisk together milk and yogurt, then stir into flour
mixture until just combined.

2   Spoon batter into prepared pan, and smooth the top with
the back of the spoon. Sprinkle remaining 3 tablespoons sunflower seeds evenly over top.

3   Bake bread until golden on top and pulling away from pan,
about 1 hour 10 minutes. Remove from oven; immediately
invert loaf onto a wire rack. Reinvert; let cool completely before
slicing or storing. Serve with bean spread.

from Wonderful Winter Soups

white bean and roasted red-pepper spread

MAKES 1½ CUPS

Serve this spread on Yogurt-Nut Oat Bread or toasted pita.

1 large red bell pepper

1 can (15½ ounces) small white beans, drained and rinsed

¼ teaspoon ground ginger

Pinch of chili powder

1 teaspoon red-wine or balsamic vinegar

Coarse salt and freshly ground black pepper

1   Roast pepper directly over a gas burner until charred,
turning as each side blackens. (Alternatively, roast on a baking sheet under the broiler.) Transfer to a bowl, and cover
with plastic wrap; let steam about 15 minutes. Use a paper
towel to rub off charred skins. Remove and discard ribs
and seeds. Roughly chop pepper, reserving collected juices.

2   In a food processor, combine roasted pepper and juices
with the beans, ginger, chili powder, and vinegar. Process mixture until smooth, about 2 minutes, scraping down sides
with a rubber spatula as needed. Season with salt and black
pepper. Refrigerate in an airtight container up to 1 week.
Serve chilled or at room temperature.

February

baked oysters

SERVES 2

This recipe can easily be doubled.

3 cups coarse salt or gros sel de mer
6 fresh oysters, top shells discarded
2 tablespoons fine breadcrumbs, preferably homemade
½ teaspoon Dijon mustard
1 teaspoon finely chopped fresh flat-leaf parsley
1 tablespoon unsalted butter, melted
  Freshly ground pepper
2 slices bacon, cooked and diced
  Lemon wedges, for serving

Preheat oven to 450°F. Spread salt in a shallow baking dish. Nestle oysters in their bottom shells in the salt. In a bowl, combine breadcrumbs, mustard, parsley, and butter; season with pepper. Sprinkle 1 teaspoon mixture on each oyster, and top with bacon pieces. Bake until edges of oysters begin to curl and topping browns, 10 to 12 minutes. Serve oysters immediately with lemon wedges.

from Good Things

guacamole con frutas

MAKES 3 CUPS

3 ripe avocados (about 1¾ pounds)
  Juice of 2 limes (about 5 tablespoons)
1 ripe peach, pitted, peeled, and cut into ¼-inch dice
¼ pound seedless green grapes, quartered
1 teaspoon finely diced serrano chile
  Coarse salt
  Tortilla chips, for serving

Halve avocados; remove and discard pits. Peel, and cut into ½-inch dice. In a bowl, toss avocados with lime juice. Add diced peach, half the grapes, and serrano; mash with a fork until chunky. Season with salt. Garnish with remaining grapes; serve immediately with chips.

from A Mexican Feast

seviche verde

SERVES 12

When making seviche, it is important to buy the freshest fish available from a reliable source.

2 pounds firm white fish fillets (about ½ inch thick), such as red snapper or halibut, skin and bones removed
1 cup freshly squeezed lime juice (about 10 limes)
2½ teaspoons coarse salt
  Pinch of dried oregano, preferably Mexican
1½ cups lightly packed fresh basil leaves
1½ cups lightly packed fresh flat-leaf parsley leaves
¼ cup lightly packed fresh mint leaves
1 small garlic clove
1 serrano chile, cut into pieces
¼ cup extra-virgin olive oil
¼ cup chopped green olives
½ cup finely diced white onion

1 Cut fish into ½-inch dice, and place in a nonreactive container. Pour lime juice over fish, and sprinkle with 1 teaspoon salt and the oregano; toss to combine. Refrigerate, covered, 6 to 8 hours, tossing occasionally.

2 Purée basil, parsley, mint, garlic, and serrano with ¼ cup water in a blender until smooth but quite thick. With the motor running, add oil in a slow, steady stream until emulsified. Season with remaining 1½ teaspoons salt.

3 Drain marinade from fish; discard. Pour herb sauce over fish; toss to combine. Garnish with olives and onion; serve.

from A Mexican Feast

coconut fish chowder

SERVES 6 | **PHOTO ON PAGE 68**

- 1 tablespoon unsalted butter
- 1 small onion, cut into very thin wedges
- 2 garlic cloves, finely chopped
- 4 fresh or frozen kaffir lime leaves
- 2 cups homemade or frozen fish stock
- 6 ounces baby potatoes, cut into ½-inch chunks
- 2 stalks celery, thinly sliced on the bias
- ¼ pound green beans, stem ends trimmed, cut into 1½-inch lengths
- 1 piece (1 inch) fresh ginger, finely julienned (about 2 tablespoons)
- 3 cups unsweetened coconut milk
- 1 pound cod fillets, cut into large chunks
- Coarse salt and freshly ground pepper
- ½ bunch fresh chives, cut into 1½-inch lengths, for garnish
- 6 tablespoons freshly grated or desiccated coconut, for garnish

1   Heat butter in a large saucepan or small stockpot over medium heat. Add onion; cook, stirring occasionally, until translucent, 3 to 4 minutes. Add garlic and lime leaves; cook 1 minute. Add stock, potatoes, celery, beans, and ginger. Bring to a simmer over medium heat; cook 7 to 9 minutes more.

2   Reduce heat to low. Add coconut milk, and bring almost to a simmer. Add fish; without stirring, simmer until fish is opaque and vegetables are tender, about 5 minutes. Season with salt and pepper. Ladle soup into bowls; garnish with chives and coconut. Serve immediately.

from Coconut

sopa fría de chayote

MAKES 2½ QUARTS; SERVES 12

This chilled soup is made with chayote, a mild-flavored squash native to Central America.

- 2 tablespoons unsalted butter
- 2 leeks, white parts only, thinly sliced, washed well and drained
- 1 white onion, diced (1 cup)
- 1 garlic clove, finely chopped
- 1 small jalapeño chile, finely diced
- 10 chayote squash (about 6 pounds), cored, peeled, and cut into ½-inch dice
- ½ bunch cilantro, tied into a bundle
- Coarse salt
- ¾ cup heavy cream
- 2 Golden Delicious apples

1   Melt butter in a stockpot over medium heat. Add leeks and onion; cook, stirring occasionally, until translucent, about 2 minutes. Add garlic and jalapeño; cook 2 minutes more. Add chayote, cilantro, and enough water to cover (about 8 cups); bring to a boil over medium-high heat. Reduce heat, and simmer until squash is soft, about 25 minutes. Discard cilantro.

2   Prepare an ice bath. Purée mixture in a blender, working in batches so as not to fill more than halfway. Pass through a fine sieve into a large bowl set in ice bath. Season with salt; let cool completely, stirring frequently. Stir in cream.

3   Just before serving, core apples and cut into ¼-inch dice; stir half into soup. Garnish servings with remaining apple.

from A Mexican Feast

spiced red lentil soup with crispy fried ginger

SERVES 6 | **PHOTO ON PAGE 66**

After it has finished cooking, this soup will continue to thicken; thin it with hot chicken stock or water, if desired.

- 1 tablespoon olive oil
- 1 Spanish onion, cut into ½-inch dice
- 4 garlic cloves, minced
- 1 three-inch piece fresh ginger, minced (3 tablespoons), plus 1 five-inch piece, sliced into very thin strips (about ⅛ by 2 inches)
- 1 teaspoon ground cumin
- ½ teaspoon curry powder
- 2 plum tomatoes, cut into ½-inch dice
- 2 cups red lentils, picked over and rinsed
- 4 cups Basic Chicken Stock (page 17) or low-sodium canned chicken broth
- 1 dried bay leaf
- 1 teaspoon coarse salt
  Freshly ground pepper
- 2 teaspoons canola or peanut oil
- ½ cup low-fat plain yogurt, for serving

1   In a large heavy-bottom pot, heat olive oil over medium-high heat. Add onion, garlic, minced ginger, cumin, and curry powder; cook, scraping up any browned bits from the bottom of pot with a wooden spoon, until onion is soft and light golden, about 10 minutes. Reduce heat to medium, and add tomatoes. Cook until soft, about 5 minutes.

2   Stir lentils, chicken stock, 4 cups water, and bay leaf into pot; raise heat to medium-high, and bring to a simmer. Reduce heat to low; cook, stirring occasionally, until lentils are tender, about 30 minutes. Add salt; season with pepper. Remove from heat. Let stand about 10 minutes.

3   Meanwhile, make fried ginger: In a medium sauté pan, heat canola oil over medium heat. Add sliced ginger in a single layer; cook, stirring constantly, until strips begin to turn crisp and deep golden, about 4 minutes. Transfer to paper towels to drain. Keep warm until ready to serve.

4   Remove bay leaf from pot, and discard. Using an immersion or regular blender (working in batches so as not to fill more than halfway), purée soup until completely smooth. Return soup to low heat until warmed through. Divide soup among six serving bowls; top each bowl with about 1 tablespoon yogurt. Garnish with fried ginger, and serve.

PER SERVING: 312 CALORIES, 6 G FAT, 2 MG CHOLESTEROL, 47 G CARBOHYDRATE, 665 MG SODIUM, 18 G PROTEIN, 8 G FIBER

from Fit to Eat: Ginger

udon noodles with shiitake mushrooms in ginger broth

SERVES 4 | **PHOTO ON PAGE 67**

To serve noodles as a main course, add a few cups of diced firm tofu or cooked chicken breast to the broth in step three.

- 8 ounces Japanese udon or soba noodles
- 2 teaspoons sesame oil
- 2 teaspoons vegetable oil
- 1½ tablespoons minced fresh ginger (1½-inch piece)
- 2 shallots, very thinly sliced
- ¼ pound shiitake mushrooms (about 12), stemmed, caps wiped clean and quartered
- 2 cups Basic Chicken Stock (page 17) or low-sodium canned chicken broth
- 1 teaspoon rice-wine vinegar
- 2 teaspoons low-sodium soy sauce
- 3 ounces spinach, tough stems discarded, washed well, drained, and cut into 2-inch-wide strips (3 cups)
- 4 scallions, thinly sliced diagonally into 2-inch pieces

1   Bring a large pot of water to a boil. Add noodles, and cook until al dente according to package instructions. Drain in a colander; toss with sesame oil, and return to pot. Keep warm.

2   Meanwhile, in a medium sauté pan, heat the vegetable oil over medium heat. Add ginger, shallots, and mushrooms; cook, stirring constantly, until the mixture begins to soften and turn golden brown, about 2 minutes.

3   Stir chicken stock, vinegar, and soy sauce into pan, and bring to a simmer. Cook until mushrooms are very tender, about 5 minutes. Add spinach and scallions; stir to combine.

4   To serve, divide noodles among four shallow bowls; ladle soup over noodles.

PER SERVING: 272 CALORIES, 5 G FAT, 0 MG CHOLESTEROL, 48 G CARBOHYDRATE, 832 MG SODIUM, 11 G PROTEIN, 2 G FIBER

from Fit to Eat: Ginger

boeuf bourguignon

SERVES 8; MAKES 2½ QUARTS | **PHOTO ON PAGE 68**

This stew can be prepared a day in advance, refrigerated, and then warmed over medium heat before serving.

- 1 large onion, coarsely chopped
- 2 carrots, coarsely chopped
- 1 head garlic, cloves separated and lightly crushed (unpeeled)
- 10 sprigs flat-leaf parsley, cut in half, plus 3 tablespoons chopped for garnish
- 6 sprigs thyme
- 4 sprigs rosemary
- 2 dried bay leaves
- ½ teaspoon whole black peppercorns
- 2 tablespoons olive oil
- 6 ounces salt pork, trimmed of rind and cut into ¼-by-1-inch pieces
- 3 pounds beef chuck, cut into 1½- to 2-inch cubes
  Coarse salt and freshly ground pepper
- 3 tablespoons all-purpose flour
- 3 cups Basic Beef Stock (page 18) or low-sodium canned beef broth
- 1 750-ml bottle red wine, preferably Burgundy or another Pinot Noir
- 1 teaspoon tomato paste
- 1 pound frozen pearl onions
- 1 tablespoon unsalted butter
- 1 tablespoon sugar
- 10 ounces large white mushrooms, trimmed and quartered

1 Cut two 12-by-22-inch pieces of cheesecloth; lay them on a clean work surface, overlapping them perpendicularly in the center to form a cross. Pile the chopped onion, carrots, garlic cloves, parsley sprigs, thyme, rosemary, bay leaves, and peppercorns in the center.

2 Gather the ends together to enclose the contents completely, and tie the top with kitchen twine. Place bundle in an 8-quart Dutch oven, and set aside.

3 Preheat oven to 300°F. Heat oil in a large skillet over medium heat. Add salt pork, and sauté until brown and crisp, about 7 minutes. Using a slotted spoon, transfer pork to Dutch oven, leaving rendered fat in skillet.

4 Season beef cubes with salt and pepper. Working in three batches, place beef in skillet in a single layer; sear until dark brown on all sides, about 6 minutes total. Using tongs, transfer beef to Dutch oven, reserving fat in skillet.

5 Whisk the flour into reserved fat in skillet. Slowly whisk in beef stock, and bring to a simmer over medium heat, stirring frequently until thickened.

6 Pour mixture into Dutch oven around cheesecloth bundle. Add wine and tomato paste, and season with salt and pepper; stir to combine. Bring to a boil over high heat. Cover; transfer to oven. Cook until beef is very tender, about 2½ hours.

7 Remove pot from oven, and transfer cheesecloth bundle to a large sieve set over a bowl. With a wooden spoon, press down on bundle to release as much liquid as possible. Discard bundle, and pour accumulated juices into Dutch oven.

8 Remove beef and pork from Dutch oven; reserve. Bring liquid to a boil over high heat; reduce to 4 cups, about 10 minutes, skimming surface as needed with a large metal spoon. Reduce heat to low, and return beef and pork to Dutch oven.

9 While sauce is reducing, set skillet over high heat. Add pearl onions, ½ cup water, butter, sugar, and a pinch of salt. Bring to a boil, and reduce heat to medium; simmer until almost all liquid has evaporated, 5 to 8 minutes. Raise heat to medium-high; add mushrooms. Cook, stirring occasionally, until vegetables are browned and glazed, about 5 minutes.

10 Transfer vegetables to Dutch oven, and simmer over medium heat until heated through. Season with more salt and pepper as desired, and serve immediately. Garnish each serving with chopped parsley.

from Boeuf Bourguignon 101

mole de zarzamoras

SERVES 12 AS PART OF A BUFFET | **PHOTO ON PAGE 71**

Blackberries (*zarzamoras* in Spanish) add subtle tartness to a traditional Mexican mole. Mole can be made up to two days ahead; refrigerate in an airtight container.

6 half-pints fresh blackberries, picked over and rinsed

3 tablespoons sugar

4 cups Basic Chicken Stock (page 17) or low-sodium canned chicken broth

2 ancho chiles

2 mulato or poblano chiles

3 pasilla chiles

¼ cup plus 5 tablespoons safflower oil

15 whole shelled almonds

2 tablespoons unsalted peanuts

2 tablespoons pepitas (pumpkin seeds)

2 tablespoons pecan pieces

¼ small white onion, cut into 1-inch pieces

2 garlic cloves

3 tablespoons sesame seeds

⅛ teaspoon anise seeds

⅛ teaspoon coriander seeds

1 whole cinnamon stick, preferably Mexican, broken into pieces

1 whole clove

⅛ teaspoon cumin seeds

Pinch of oregano

1 corn tortilla (6 inches)

Coarse salt

8 chicken legs, cut into serving pieces

Freshly ground pepper

Several sprigs oregano, for garnish

1 Purée 4 half-pints blackberries, sugar, and 1 cup stock in a blender until smooth. Pass through a fine sieve into a large bowl, discarding solids. Set purée aside.

2 Wipe chiles with a damp paper towel. Cut off stems and discard; slit open chiles lengthwise. Remove ribs and seeds, reserving seeds. Set chiles aside.

3 Place a small skillet over medium heat; add 3 tablespoons oil. When oil is hot, add almonds and peanuts; cook, stirring, until lightly golden, about 1 minute. Use a slotted spoon to transfer nuts to a medium bowl.

4 Add pepitas to skillet. Cover, and shake skillet until seeds stop popping, about 30 seconds. Transfer to bowl with nuts. Cook pecans in skillet, stirring, until lightly toasted, about 45 seconds. Transfer to bowl. Reduce heat to medium-low. Cook reserved chiles until color darkens slightly, about 20 seconds per side. Transfer to bowl. Cook onion and garlic until lightly caramelized, 3 to 5 minutes; transfer to bowl.

5 In a small dish, combine sesame seeds, anise seeds, coriander seeds, cinnamon, and 1 tablespoon reserved chile seeds; pour mixture into skillet. Cook until sesame seeds are lightly toasted, stirring constantly; transfer to bowl. Add clove, cumin seeds, and oregano to skillet; cook, stirring, 2 minutes, and transfer to bowl.

6 Toast tortilla over a gas burner or under the broiler, turning frequently with tongs. Remove from heat; crumble tortilla into same bowl. Transfer contents of bowl to a blender, and purée with remaining 3 cups chicken stock until smooth.

7 Heat 2 tablespoons oil in a large saucepan over medium heat. Add puréed nut mixture, and reduce heat to medium-low. Cook, stirring, 5 minutes. Stir in reserved blackberry purée; simmer 30 minutes, or until little pools of oil form around bubbles. Season with salt. Remove from heat.

8 Season chicken well with salt and pepper. Heat remaining ¼ cup oil in a large sauté pan over medium-high heat. Working in batches, cook chicken until browned on all sides.

9 Place mole in a large saucepan, and bring to a simmer over medium heat, stirring occasionally. Add chicken, and simmer until cooked through and well coated with sauce. Keep warm until ready to serve. Garnish with remaining 2 half-pints blackberries and oregano.

from A Mexican Feast

pancetta-wrapped pork roast

SERVES 4 | **PHOTO ON PAGE 70**

1 pork loin (1½ pounds)

Coarse salt and freshly ground pepper

1 tablespoon extra-virgin olive oil

2 tablespoons finely chopped fresh rosemary, plus several sprigs

¼ pound thinly sliced pancetta or bacon

8 to 10 cipollini or small white onions (unpeeled)

1 teaspoon unsalted butter, room temperature

1 teaspoon all-purpose flour

1 cup Basic Chicken Stock (page 17) or low-sodium canned chicken broth

1 Preheat oven to 375°F. Season pork generously with salt and pepper. Heat oil in a large cast-iron or heavy-bottom skillet over medium heat. Sear pork on all sides until browned, about 10 minutes total. Remove from heat.

2 Rub pork with chopped rosemary; wrap with pancetta, overlapping strips slightly. Lay a rosemary sprig on top; tie pork with kitchen twine. Scatter onions and remaining rosemary sprigs around pork. Roast in oven, basting occasionally with cooking juices, until internal temperature registers 145°F on an instant-read thermometer, 35 to 40 minutes. Remove from oven. Transfer pork and onions to a platter; cover with foil.

3 Make pan sauce: In a small bowl, whisk together butter and flour. Pour off fat from skillet; place skillet over medium heat. Add stock, scraping up any browned bits from bottom of skillet with a wooden spoon. Bring to a boil; reduce liquid slightly, about 2 minutes. Whisk in butter mixture, about 1 teaspoon at a time, and cook until just thickened. Season with salt and pepper. Serve hot with pork and onions.

from What's for Dinner?

pescado tikin xik

SERVES 12 AS PART OF A BUFFET | **PHOTO ON PAGE 71**

We serve this baked red snapper over steamed rice.

3½ ounces achiote paste

2 allspice berries

¼ teaspoon cumin seeds

¼ teaspoon whole peppercorns

¼ teaspoon dried oregano, preferably Mexican

2 garlic cloves

2 tablespoons freshly squeezed lime juice

2 tablespoons freshly squeezed orange juice

¼ cup white vinegar

1 teaspoon coarse salt

4 skinless red snapper fillets (about 3 pounds)

Vegetable oil, for brushing

Lemon wedges, for serving

Cebollas Encurtidas, for serving (recipe follows)

Salsa Roja, for serving (recipe follows)

1 Purée all ingredients except fish, oil, and lemon in a blender until smooth. Place fish in a nonreactive container, and pour marinade over top; turn to coat evenly. Cover, and let marinate in the refrigerator up to 1 hour.

2 Preheat oven to 400°F. Brush a baking sheet with oil. Remove fish, letting excess marinade drip off, and arrange in a single layer on sheet; brush top of fish with oil. Bake until fish is firm and cooked through, about 15 minutes. Serve hot, with lemon wedges, marinated onions, and salsa on the side.

from A Mexican Feast

cebollas encurtidas

MAKES 2 CUPS

These marinated onions are a traditional Oaxacan condiment.

2 red onions, very thinly sliced

1 teaspoon whole peppercorns, lightly crushed

1 teaspoon allspice berries, lightly crushed

1 teaspoon dried oregano

1 teaspoon coarse salt

¼ cup white vinegar

¼ cup freshly squeezed lime juice (about 2 limes)

In a large bowl, toss together all ingredients. Refrigerate overnight, covered with plastic wrap, before serving.

salsa roja

MAKES 1 CUP

If you have a *molcajete*, a traditional Mexican mortar and pestle, you can grind the ingredients by hand.

8 plum tomatoes
1 serrano or small jalapeño chile
1 small garlic clove
½ teaspoon coarse salt, plus more for seasoning

1 Heat a small skillet over medium heat. Add tomatoes, and roast until softened and charred, about 12 minutes, turning frequently. Transfer to a plate; set aside. In the same skillet, roast serrano until charred, about 8 minutes. Transfer to a bowl; cover with plastic wrap, and let stand 10 minutes.

2 Use paper towels to rub off skins from tomatoes and pepper. Roughly chop tomatoes; place in a small bowl. Mound chile, garlic, and salt on a cutting board; chop to form a rough paste. Stir into tomatoes, and season with more salt, as desired.

zarapes de pato

SERVES 12 AS PART OF A BUFFET

Zarapes de Pato are soft tacos filled with shredded duck (*pato*). If you like, you can reserve some of the rendered duck fat from this recipe to use in the Refried Beans.

1 duck (about 3 pounds), neck and gizzards removed, rinsed and patted dry
  Coarse salt
3 tablespoons olive oil
1 white onion, finely diced (about 1 cup)
2 garlic cloves, minced (about 2 tablespoons)
1½ pounds plum tomatoes, seeded and chopped (about 5 cups)
2 bay leaves, preferably Mexican
2 tablespoons chipotle purée
1 tablespoon safflower oil, plus more as needed
24 corn tortillas (6 to 8 inches)
2 cups Refried Beans (page 40)
  Poblano Sauce (page 40)

1 Preheat oven to 450°F. Generously season duck inside and out with salt. Prick holes all over skin with a fork. Place duck on a wire rack set in a roasting pan. Roast until skin is browned, about 40 minutes.

2 Reduce oven temperature to 325°F. Continue roasting duck until an instant-read thermometer inserted into the thickest part of the leg (avoiding the bone) registers 165°F, 50 to 60 minutes; the legs should rotate easily in their joints. Remove from oven; let cool. Remove the skin from duck, and reserve. Shred meat with a fork; set aside.

3 Heat olive oil in a large sauté pan over medium heat. Add onion; cook, stirring, until translucent, about 2 minutes. Add garlic, and cook 1 minute. Add tomatoes, bay leaves, and chipotle; season with salt. Stir to combine. Reduce heat to low, and simmer 20 minutes, stirring occasionally. Add the reserved shredded meat, and cook until heated through. Remove from heat; set filling aside, covered, until ready to use.

4 Thinly slice reserved duck skin. Heat 1 tablespoon safflower oil in a medium skillet over medium-low heat. Cook duck skin, stirring occasionally, until golden and crisp. Transfer to a paper-towel–lined plate to drain.

5 Heat about 1 teaspoon safflower oil in a small skillet over medium heat. Lightly fry tortillas, one at a time, just until softened, turning once, 10 to 20 seconds. Transfer to a plate; cover with foil to keep warm. Add more oil to pan as needed.

6 Spread about 1 tablespoon beans on each tortilla, and top with 2 tablespoons duck filling. Roll up to enclose, and place on a serving platter, seam sides down. Pour poblano sauce over tacos, and top with crisped duck skin. Serve remaining sauce on the side.

from A Mexican Feast

refried beans

MAKES ABOUT 2 CUPS

One tablespoon chopped fresh cilantro can be used in place of the epazote.

1 **cup dried black beans, picked over**
½ **teaspoon dried epazote**
1 **garlic clove**
1 **teaspoon coarse salt**
2 **tablespoons vegetable oil or rendered duck fat**

1 Bring beans and 4 cups water to a boil in a medium saucepan over medium-high heat. Reduce heat, and simmer until tender, about 1 hour. Add epazote, garlic, and salt; cook until beans are very soft, about 15 minutes. Remove from heat; let cool in liquid. Drain mixture, reserving cooking liquid.

2 Working in batches, purée mixture in a food processor to form a fairly smooth paste, adding reserved cooking liquid as needed. Heat oil in a large sauté pan over medium-high heat. Add bean purée, and cook, stirring, until oil is incorporated, about 5 minutes. Serve hot.

poblano sauce

MAKES ABOUT 2 CUPS

5 **poblano peppers**
1 **bunch spinach, trimmed and washed well**
¾ **cup Basic Chicken Stock (page 17) or low-sodium canned chicken broth**
1 **cup loosely packed fresh cilantro leaves**
1 **cup heavy cream**
2 **teaspoons coarse salt**

1 Roast peppers directly over a gas burner until charred, turning as each side blackens. (Alternatively, roast on a baking sheet under the broiler.) Transfer to a medium bowl, and cover with plastic wrap; let steam about 15 minutes. Use a paper towel to rub off charred skins. Remove and discard stems, seeds, and ribs. Roughly chop peppers, and set aside.

2 Prepare an ice bath; set aside. Bring a medium pot of water to a boil; blanch spinach until bright green and wilted, about 30 seconds. Using tongs or a slotted spoon, transfer spinach to ice bath to stop the cooking. Drain, and wring spinach to remove as much liquid as possible; roughly chop.

3 Purée the reserved peppers, spinach, stock, and cilantro in a blender. Transfer to a medium saucepan, and bring to a boil. Stir in cream and salt; cook until sauce returns just to a boil. Remove from heat. Sauce can be refrigerated in an airtight container up to 3 days; let cool before storing. Reheat gently over low heat, being careful not to boil.

SIDE DISHES

cauliflower purée

SERVES 4 | **PHOTO ON PAGE 75**

For a garnish, sauté a few thinly sliced cauliflower florets in a bit of butter until tender and lightly golden.

1 **head cauliflower (about 1¾ pounds), stem and tough stalks trimmed, florets coarsely chopped**
1 **cup Basic Chicken Stock (page 17) or low-sodium canned chicken broth**
2 **tablespoons sour cream**
1 **tablespoon unsalted butter, room temperature**
Coarse salt and freshly ground pepper

1 Combine cauliflower and stock in a medium saucepan, and bring to a boil over high heat. Reduce heat to a simmer, and cook until cauliflower is very tender, about 10 minutes.

2 Using a slotted spoon, transfer cauliflower to a food processor. Process until smooth, adding 1 to 2 tablespoons cooking liquid as needed, 15 to 20 seconds. Add sour cream and butter, and process until incorporated, 5 to 10 seconds more. Season with salt and pepper. Serve hot.

from What's for Dinner?

chiles anchos rellenos

SERVES 12 AS PART OF A BUFFET | **PHOTO ON PAGE 71**

Piloncillo, which is also sold as panela, is unrefined dark-brown sugar; you can use regular dark-brown sugar instead.

- 12 ancho chiles
- ⅔ cup cider vinegar
- 4 ounces piloncillo, grated
- 1 whole cinnamon stick, preferably Mexican, broken into pieces
- 1 teaspoon coarse salt
  Picadillo De Pollo Filling (recipe follows)
- 2 cups Mexican crema or crème fraîche
- 1 cup finely diced white onion
- ½ cup finely chopped fresh cilantro

1 Preheat oven to 350°F. Slit an opening in each ancho from stem to tip, being careful not to tear the skin; carefully remove seeds and ribs, and discard.

2 Combine 4 cups water, vinegar, piloncillo, cinnamon, and salt in a medium saucepan; bring to a boil over high heat. Reduce heat to low, and simmer 5 minutes. Remove from heat. Add anchos; cover, and let stand 8 to 10 minutes. Transfer anchos to a paper-towel–lined plate to drain.

3 Spoon filling into each chile, and arrange in a single layer in a baking dish. Bake chiles until heated through, about 15 minutes. Meanwhile, bring crema and onion to a boil in a small saucepan over medium-high heat. Reduce heat, and simmer 8 minutes. Pass through a fine sieve into a bowl; stir in cilantro. Pour sauce over anchos, and serve.

from A Mexican Feast

picadillo de pollo filling

MAKES 7 CUPS

- 4 tablespoons olive oil
- 2 pounds ground chicken
- 1 white onion, diced (about 1¼ cup)
- 1 garlic clove, minced (about 1 tablespoon)
- 1¾ pounds plum tomatoes, seeded and diced (about 4 cups)
- 2 bay leaves, preferably Mexican
- ½ cup raisins
- ½ cup chopped green olives
- 2 tablespoons capers, drained and rinsed
- ½ cup chopped fresh cilantro
- ½ cup chopped fresh flat-leaf parsley
- ½ cup slivered almonds
- ¼ cup chopped fresh mint
- 1 tablespoon coarse salt

1 Heat 2 tablespoons oil in a large skillet over medium-high heat until almost smoking. Add the chicken, and cook, stirring constantly, until lightly browned and cooked through. Transfer to a bowl; set aside.

2 Heat remaining 2 tablespoons oil in skillet. Cook onion until translucent, stirring, about 2 minutes. Add garlic; cook 1 minute. Add tomatoes and bay leaves; reduce heat to medium-low. Simmer until tomatoes are soft, about 15 minutes.

3 Stir raisins, olives, and capers into skillet; cook 3 minutes. Add reserved chicken, and cook 5 minutes. Stir in the remaining ingredients, and remove from heat. Let cool. Filling may be refrigerated up to 1 day in an airtight container. Before using, bring to room temperature; discard bay leaves.

coconut almond rice

SERVES 6 | **PHOTO ON PAGE 73**

We like to serve this creamy rice dish with grilled shrimp and Spicy Lime Dipping Sauce (page 52).

¼ cup slivered almonds

1 stalk fresh lemongrass, outer leaves peeled, 3-inch-long piece cut from root end and sliced in half lengthwise

2 cups unsweetened coconut milk

2 to 4 fresh or frozen kaffir lime leaves

2 teaspoons coarse salt

1½ cups long-grain rice

½ cup lightly packed fresh cilantro leaves, coarsely chopped, plus several sprigs for garnish

Freshly ground pepper

1 Preheat oven to 350°F. Spread almonds in a single layer in a rimmed baking sheet; toast in oven until golden and fragrant, tossing occasionally, about 7 minutes. Remove from oven.

2 In a medium saucepan, combine the lemongrass, 1¾ cups coconut milk, 1 cup water, kaffir lime leaves, and salt. Heat over medium-high heat until milk just begins to simmer. Stir in rice, and return to a simmer. Cover, and cook over low heat until rice is tender, 20 to 25 minutes. Discard lemongrass.

3 Stir toasted nuts, cilantro, and remaining ¼ cup coconut milk into rice; season with pepper. Serve immediately, garnished with cilantro sprigs.

from Coconut

jícama salad

SERVES 12 AS PART OF A BUFFET

½ cup unsalted peanuts

3 jícama (about 2 pounds), peeled

3 beets, trimmed and peeled

3 large carrots, cut into 3-inch lengths

5 navel oranges

⅓ cup freshly squeezed lime juice (3 limes)

5 tablespoons extra-virgin olive oil

Coarse salt and freshly ground pepper

1 Preheat oven to 350°F. Spread peanuts in a single layer on a rimmed baking sheet, and toast in oven until golden and fragrant, tossing occasionally, about 7 minutes. Let cool, then coarsely chop nuts.

2 Using a mandoline or very sharp knife, cut jícama, beets, and carrots into a fine julienne. Toss in a large bowl.

3 Cut off ends of oranges; using a paring knife, remove peel, pith, and outer membranes, following the curve of the fruit. Working over a bowl to catch the juices, cut between sections to remove whole segments; add segments to vegetables. Squeeze juice from membranes into a bowl; measure out ½ cup juice.

4 In a small bowl, whisk together orange juice, lime juice, and oil. Pour over vegetable mixture; toss to coat. Sprinkle with nuts; season with salt and pepper. Serve immediately.

from A Mexican Feast

quick pear chutney

SERVES 4

¼ cup walnuts

1 teaspoon extra-virgin olive oil

1 shallot, minced

2 ripe but firm pears, cored and cut into ¼-inch dice

6 tablespoons cider vinegar

3 tablespoons honey

4 whole cloves

¼ cup golden raisins

1 Preheat oven to 350°F. Spread walnuts in a single layer on a rimmed baking sheet; toast, tossing occasionally, until fragrant and browned, 7 to 9 minutes. Remove from oven; let cool, and roughly chop. Set aside.

2 Heat oil in a small saucepan over medium heat. Add shallot, and sauté until softened, about 2 minutes. Add pears, vinegar, honey, and cloves. Bring to a boil, reduce heat, and cook, stirring occasionally, until pears are tender, 4 to 5 minutes. Discard cloves, and stir in raisins and reserved walnuts. Remove from heat. Serve warm or at room temperature.

from What's for Dinner?

almond flan

MAKES 1 EIGHT-INCH FLAN | **PHOTO ON PAGE 87**

6 ounces blanched whole almonds (about ¾ cup)

½ cup plus ⅔ cup sugar

1 quart half-and-half

Pinch of salt

3 large whole eggs

6 large egg yolks

3 tablespoons amaretto

1 Preheat oven to 350°F. Spread almonds in a single layer on a rimmed baking sheet; toast in oven until golden and fragrant, tossing occasionally, about 10 minutes. Remove from oven; let cool. Transfer almonds to a food processor; process until finely ground. Set aside.

2 Reduce oven heat to 325°F. In a small saucepan over medium heat, stir ½ cup sugar and 2 tablespoons water until sugar has dissolved. Without stirring, cook until syrup is dark amber, about 8 minutes; brush down sides of pan with a wet pastry brush to prevent crystals from forming. Pour syrup into an 8-by-2-inch round tart pan, swirling to coat bottom evenly. Set pan aside.

3 In a medium saucepan over medium-high heat, bring half-and-half and ground almonds just to a boil; remove from heat. Let steep, covered, 20 minutes. Strain mixture through a fine sieve into a clean saucepan, pressing with a rubber spatula to extract the liquid; discard solids.

4 Whisk remaining ⅔ cup sugar and salt into mixture in saucepan; bring to a simmer over medium-high heat. Whisk together eggs and yolks in a medium bowl. Whisking constantly, gradually add half-and-half mixture. Stir in the amaretto. Pour mixture through a fine sieve into prepared tart pan; place in a roasting pan.

5 Cover the flan with foil; poke several holes in foil. Place roasting pan in oven; fill it with boiling water to reach halfway up sides of tart pan. Bake until just set, 50 to 55 minutes. Transfer to a wire rack to cool completely. Cover with plastic wrap, and chill overnight. To serve, run a thin knife around edge of flan, and invert onto a serving plate.

from A Mexican Feast

almond-polenta pound cake

MAKES 1 EIGHT-BY-FOUR-INCH LOAF | **PHOTO ON PAGE 78**

If you plan to serve this cake topped with apples and caramel, sprinkle with toasted hazelnuts just before serving.

½ cup (1 stick) unsalted butter, room temperature, plus more for pan

1 cup cake flour (not self-rising), plus more for pan

⅓ cup almond paste (3¼ ounces)

⅔ cup plus 1½ tablespoons sugar

⅓ teaspoon pure vanilla extract

⅓ teaspoon pure almond extract

⅔ cup heavy cream

4 large eggs, room temperature, separated

½ cup polenta

1 teaspoon baking powder

¼ teaspoon salt

Sautéed Apples or Macerated Citrus (page 44)

Caramel Sauce (optional; page 44)

1 Preheat oven to 350°F, with rack in lower third. Butter an 8-by-4-inch loaf pan; dust with flour, and tap out excess. In the bowl of an electric mixer, cut almond paste into ⅔ cup sugar with two forks until it resembles coarse meal. Add the butter; using the paddle attachment, beat until mixture is light and fluffy, about 4 minutes.

2 In a medium bowl, whisk together extracts, cream, and egg yolks. With mixer on medium, gradually add cream mixture to butter mixture. In a small bowl, stir together flour, polenta, baking powder, and salt. Working in two batches, sift the flour mixture over butter mixture, and fold to combine.

3 In a clean mixing bowl, whisk the egg whites and remaining 1½ tablespoons sugar on medium speed until stiff peaks form, 2 to 3 minutes. Fold into batter.

4 Pour batter into prepared pan; spread evenly with a rubber spatula. Bake until a cake tester inserted in the center comes out clean, about 1 hour. If top begins to brown too much, cover loosely with foil. Let cool in pan about 10 minutes, then invert onto a wire rack. Reinvert, and let cool completely. Top with apples and caramel sauce, or citrus.

from Dessert Party

sautéed apples

SERVES 8 | **PHOTOS ON PAGES 78 AND 79**

Apples can be prepared up to eight hours ahead; keep at room temperature, then reheat in a 450 degree oven.

5 ripe but firm apples (about 2 pounds)
1 tablespoon freshly squeezed lemon juice
3 tablespoons unsalted butter
1 whole cinnamon stick, broken in half
4 tablespoons sugar

1 Peel, core, and slice apples into ½-inch-thick wedges. As you work, toss apples with lemon juice to prevent discoloration.

2 Melt half the butter in a 10-inch skillet over medium-high heat. Add half the apples and cinnamon. Sprinkle with 2 tablespoons sugar, and toss to coat. Sauté until apples are browned, about 5 minutes, tossing often. Transfer to a gratin dish. Repeat process with remaining ingredients; serve warm.

macerated citrus

SERVES 8 | **PHOTO ON PAGE 79**

4 navel oranges
2 ruby red grapefruits
2 white grapefruits
⅓ cup Grand Marnier or orange juice
¼ cup sugar
¼ cup dried cranberries

1 Using a sharp paring knife, cut off ends of all citrus; remove peel and pith, following the curve of the fruit. Cut between the membranes to remove whole segments.

2 In a large bowl, toss fruit with liqueur and sugar; cover and let macerate in the refrigerator at least 1 hour or overnight. Just before serving, sprinkle in cranberries.

caramel sauce

MAKES 2 CUPS | **PHOTO ON PAGE 78**

Sauce can be refrigerated in an airtight container up to one week. Before serving, let it come to room temperature or gently warm over low heat.

2 cups sugar
1 cup heavy cream
½ vanilla bean, split lengthwise and scraped
1 teaspoon freshly squeezed lemon juice
2 tablespoons unsalted butter

1 In a 2-quart saucepan over medium heat, stir sugar and ½ cup water until sugar has dissolved. Without stirring, cook until dark amber, about 20 minutes; wash down sides of pan with a wet pastry brush to prevent crystals from forming.

2 Reduce heat to low. Carefully add cream in a steady stream (it will spatter); stir with a wooden spoon when bubbling subsides. Add vanilla scrapings; stir in lemon juice and butter. Remove from heat; serve warm or at room temperature.

chocolate and hazelnut meringue cake

MAKES 1 NINE-INCH CAKE | **PHOTO ON PAGE 83**

For a version without the meringue topping, bake the chocolate layer until it is slightly firm, forty to forty-five minutes.

10 tablespoons (1¼ sticks) unsalted butter, plus more for pan
All-purpose flour, for pan
1 cup hazelnuts (about 4 ounces)
¾ cup firmly packed light-brown sugar
6 large whole eggs, separated, plus 4 large egg whites
12 ounces bittersweet chocolate, melted and cooled, plus 4 ounces coarsely chopped (1 cup)
1 tablespoon pure vanilla extract
1 tablespoon rum (optional)
Pinch of salt
1 tablespoon cornstarch
¼ teaspoon cream of tartar
1 cup superfine sugar

1 Preheat oven to 350°F. Butter a 9-by-3-inch springform pan. Line bottom with parchment paper. Butter parchment, and sprinkle with flour; tap out excess. Set aside.

2 Spread hazelnuts in a single layer on a rimmed baking sheet. Toast in oven until fragrant and skins start to crack, tossing halfway through, 10 to 15 minutes. Remove from oven;

while still hot, rub vigorously with a clean kitchen towel to remove skins. Let nuts cool; coarsely chop.

3 Make cake batter: In the bowl of an electric mixer fitted with the paddle attachment, cream butter and brown sugar until pale and smooth. Add egg yolks one at a time, beating well after each addition, until mixture is light and fluffy; scrape down sides of bowl as needed. Add melted chocolate, vanilla, and rum, if using; beat until combined. Set aside.

4 In a clean mixing bowl, combine 6 egg whites and salt; using the whisk attachment, beat on high speed until soft peaks form, about 2 minutes. Fold one-third of the egg whites into cake batter. Fold in remaining beaten egg whites until just combined. Pour batter into prepared pan; bake 25 minutes.

5 Meanwhile, make meringue: Combine hazelnuts, chopped chocolate, and cornstarch in a small bowl, and set aside. Place remaining 4 egg whites and cream of tartar in a clean mixer bowl; using a clean whisk attachment, beat on high speed until frothy. With mixer running, add superfine sugar 1 tablespoon at a time; continue beating until stiff peaks form, about 8 minutes. Fold in hazelnut mixture.

6 Remove cake from oven. Using an offset spatula, spread meringue mixture on top of cake, and return to oven. Bake until meringue is lightly browned and crisp, 25 to 30 minutes. Transfer pan to a wire rack; let stand 10 minutes. Run a knife around the edge of the cake to loosen, and release sides of pan. Let cool, about 30 minutes, before slicing and serving.

from Dessert of the Month

coconut-cream–filled macaroons

MAKES ABOUT 2 DOZEN | **PHOTO ON PAGE 82**

You can substitute an equal amount of unsweetened shredded coconut for the desiccated coconut.

3 **cups desiccated coconut**
¾ **cup sugar**
2 **large egg whites**
1 **teaspoon pure coconut extract**
⅛ **teaspoon salt**
   Creamy Coconut Filling (recipe follows)

1 In a large bowl, mix together all ingredients except filling with your hands. Refrigerate, covered with plastic wrap, until well chilled, at least 1 hour or overnight.

2 Preheat oven to 325°F. Line a large baking sheet with parchment paper. Shape heaping teaspoons of dough into balls, and place on the prepared baking sheet, about 1½ inches apart. Gently flatten balls to about 1½ inches wide. Bake until edges start to turn golden, 9 to 10 minutes. Transfer cookies to a wire rack to cool completely.

3 Turn half the cookies flat side up; place 1 heaping teaspoon filling on center of each. Top with remaining cookies; gently press together. Place cookies on a serving tray; cover with plastic wrap. Refrigerate until filling is firm, about 30 minutes. Let stand at room temperature about 10 minutes before serving.

from Coconut

creamy coconut filling

MAKES ENOUGH FOR 2 DOZEN COOKIES

To get creamed coconut—the thick layer of canned coconut milk that rises to the top—open a can without shaking, and skim off cream with a spoon. If you prefer, you can double the amount of butter and omit the creamed coconut.

2 **tablespoons unsalted butter, room temperature**
2 **tablespoons creamed coconut**
¼ **cup solid vegetable shortening**
¾ **cup confectioners' sugar**
1 **teaspoon pure coconut extract**

Combine butter, creamed coconut, and shortening in the bowl of an electric mixer fitted with the paddle attachment; beat until smooth and combined, about 1 minute. Add sugar and coconut extract, and beat until mixture is light and fluffy, about 2 minutes. Use immediately.

coconut cream pie

MAKES 1 NINE-INCH PIE | **PHOTO ON PAGE 77**

 3 large egg yolks
 2 cups unsweetened coconut milk
½ cup sugar
 3 tablespoons cornstarch
    Pinch of salt
⅔ cup freshly grated or desiccated coconut
 1 tablespoon pure coconut extract
    Chocolate Macaroon Crust (recipe follows)
 1 cup heavy cream, whipped
¼ cup toasted shaved coconut, for garnish (optional)

1 In a medium bowl, lightly whisk egg yolks just until frothy; set aside. In a medium saucepan, whisk together coconut milk, sugar, cornstarch, and salt. Bring almost to a boil over medium heat, whisking constantly, 3 to 4 minutes.

2 Whisk one-fourth of the hot milk mixture into reserved egg yolks; return the mixture to saucepan. Whisking constantly, cook until bubbles appear around the edges, about 1 minute. Stir in grated coconut and coconut extract. Transfer to a large bowl; let cool 15 minutes.

3 Pour filling into prepared crust. Refrigerate until set, at least 4 hours or overnight. Spread whipped cream on top; garnish with toasted coconut, if using.

from Coconut

chocolate macaroon crust

MAKES 1 NINE-INCH CRUST

 2 ounces semisweet chocolate, melted
 2 tablespoons unsalted butter, room temperature
 6 tablespoons sugar
1½ cups desiccated coconut
    Pinch of salt
    Nonstick cooking spray

1 Preheat oven to 325°F. Lightly coat a 9-inch glass pie plate with cooking spray; set aside. Place remaining ingredients in a medium bowl; use your hands to mix until combined.

2 Press mixture into bottom and all the way up sides of prepared pie plate. Bake until firm but not yet browning, about 20 minutes. Remove from oven; transfer to a wire rack to cool completely. Crust can be made up to 2 days ahead and refrigerated, covered with plastic wrap.

coconut crêpes

MAKES 12; SERVES 6 | **PHOTO ON PAGE 86**

1¾ cups unsweetened coconut milk
 3 large eggs
 2 teaspoons pure coconut extract
 3 tablespoons superfine sugar, plus ¼ cup for sprinkling
¾ teaspoon ground cardamom
⅛ teaspoon salt
¾ cup all-purpose flour
½ cup plus 2 tablespoons freshly grated or desiccated coconut
 9 tablespoons unsalted butter, room temperature
    Confectioners' sugar, for dusting
 2 fresh mangoes, pitted, peeled, and sliced into thin wedges, for serving

1 Preheat oven to 200°F. Line a baking sheet with several layers of paper towels, and set aside. In a large bowl, whisk together the coconut milk, eggs, coconut extract, 3 tablespoons superfine sugar, cardamom, and salt until well combined. Whisk in flour and coconut.

2 Heat a 10-inch nonstick skillet or crêpe pan over medium heat. Using a paper towel, rub inside of pan with a thin coating of butter. Pour about ¼ cup batter into center of pan, tilting and swirling to evenly coat bottom with a thin layer; pour any excess batter back into bowl.

3 Cook until crêpe is golden on the bottom and the top is almost dry, 1 to 2 minutes. Flip crêpe with a thin spatula, and continue cooking until golden, about 30 seconds more. Slide crêpe onto prepared baking sheet, and keep warm in oven. Repeat with remaining batter, rubbing pan with more butter before making each crêpe.

4 Brush remaining butter over tops of crêpes, and sprinkle with remaining ¼ cup superfine sugar. Fold each crêpe into quarters, and place on a serving platter. Dust with confectioners' sugar. Serve with mango slices.

from Coconut

coconut ice milk

MAKES 1½ QUARTS | **PHOTO ON PAGE 76**

 2 cups unsweetened coconut milk
 2 cups half-and-half
 1 cup sugar

In a large bowl, whisk together ingredients. Freeze in an ice-cream maker according to manufacturer's instructions. Transfer to airtight containers; store in freezer up to 10 days.

from Coconut

coconut macadamia shortbread

MAKES ABOUT 4 DOZEN 2-INCH COOKIES | **PHOTO ON PAGE 82**

To get creamed coconut—the thick layer of canned coconut milk that rises to the top—open a can without shaking, and skim off cream with a spoon. If you prefer, you can replace the coconut with an equal amount of unsalted butter.

1 cup macadamia nuts (3 ounces), toasted

¾ cup plus 2 tablespoons sugar

1 cup sweetened shredded coconut, plus ½ cup for topping

¾ cup (1½ sticks) plus 1 tablespoon unsalted butter, room temperature

¼ cup creamed coconut

2 teaspoons pure coconut extract

2 cups all-purpose flour, plus more for parchment

½ teaspoon coarse salt

1 large egg white, lightly beaten

1 Line two baking sheets with parchment paper, and set aside. In a food processor, finely grind nuts with 2 tablespoons sugar; transfer to a small bowl. Coarsely grind 1 cup coconut, and set aside.

2 In the bowl of an electric mixer fitted with the paddle attachment, beat butter, creamed coconut, and remaining ¾ cup sugar until light and fluffy, about 2 minutes. Beat in extract; beat in flour, salt, and ground nuts and coconut.

3 Divide dough in half. Place each half on plastic wrap, and flatten into disks. Wrap well; chill until firm, at least 1 hour. (Dough can be refrigerated up to 4 days or frozen up to 1 month. Let soften at room temperature before rolling.)

4 Preheat oven to 325°F. Lightly dust a 12-by-15-inch piece of parchment with flour; roll out 1 dough disk to about ¼ inch thick. Repeat with remaining dough. Stack parchment with dough on a baking sheet. Cover with plastic, and chill until firm, about 30 minutes.

5 Remove dough from refrigerator; cut into desired shapes. Arrange on prepared baking sheets, about 1 inch apart. Lightly brush tops with egg white; sprinkle with remaining ½ cup coconut. Bake until golden, 20 to 25 minutes. Transfer cookies to wire racks to cool completely. Store in airtight containers at room temperature up to 1 week.

from Coconut

coconut pecan cake

MAKES 1 NINE-INCH LAYER CAKE

For a Valentine's Day dessert, bake the cake layers in two nine-inch heart-shape cake pans. If you prefer, replace the creamed coconut with an equal amount of unsalted butter.

¾ cup pecan halves (3 ounces)

¾ cup (1½ sticks) unsalted butter, room temperature, plus more for pans

2¼ cups all-purpose flour, plus more for pans

1 cup firmly packed sweetened shredded coconut

2 cups sugar

1 tablespoon baking powder

¾ teaspoon salt

¼ cup creamed coconut

4 large eggs

1 tablespoon pure coconut extract

1 cup plus 2 tablespoons unsweetened coconut milk

Coconut Cake Filling (page 48)

Milk Chocolate Ganache (page 48)

2 cups toasted shaved coconut, for garnish (optional)

1 Preheat oven to 350°F. Spread pecans in a single layer in a rimmed baking sheet; toast in oven until fragrant, tossing occasionally, about 10 minutes. Remove from oven; set aside.

2 Butter two 9-inch round cake pans. Line bottoms with parchment. Butter parchment, and dust with flour; tap out excess, and set aside.

3 In a food processor, finely grind coconut; transfer to a bowl. Finely grind pecans with 2 tablespoons sugar, and set aside. Into a large bowl, sift together flour, baking powder, and salt; stir in ground coconut and pecans. Set aside.

4 In the bowl of an electric mixer fitted with the paddle attachment, beat butter, creamed coconut, and remaining sugar on medium-high speed until light and fluffy, about 4 minutes. Beat in eggs and coconut extract. Beat in flour mixture in three batches, alternating with the coconut milk, and starting and ending with the flour.

5 Divide batter between prepared pans; smooth tops with an offset spatula. Bake until golden and a cake tester inserted in centers comes out clean, about 35 minutes. If tops begin to get too dark, cover loosely with foil. Let cool in pans 30 minutes. Run a knife around edges of cakes, and invert onto a wire rack. Reinvert; let cool completely.

6 Line two rimmed baking sheets with plastic wrap; fit one with a wire rack. Use a serrated knife to trim tops of cake layers, if desired. Transfer one layer to baking sheet with rack; spread with filling. Place remaining cake layer on top.

7 Using an offset spatula, spread 1 cup chilled ganache on sides of cake; smooth with a bench scraper. Pour remaining ganache over cake, coating completely. Transfer cake and rack to second baking sheet; chill until set, about 5 minutes. Scrape up excess ganache from baking sheet; pass through a sieve back into bowl.

8 Coat the cake again with ganache. Chill until set, about 5 minutes. Press toasted coconut on sides of cake, if desired. Keep at room temperature until ready to serve.

from Coconut

coconut cake filling

MAKES ENOUGH FOR 1 NINE-INCH CAKE

1 cup sweetened shredded coconut
¾ cup sweetened condensed milk
4 tablespoons unsalted butter, room temperature
1 tablespoon creamed coconut or unsalted butter
2 large egg yolks, lightly beaten
1 tablespoon pure coconut extract

1 In a food processor, coarsely grind coconut; set aside. Combine milk, butter, and creamed coconut in a small saucepan over medium-low heat; cook, stirring, 3 to 4 minutes. Whisk one-third of the hot milk mixture into egg yolks. Return mixture to saucepan; cook, stirring constantly, until it is the consistency of pudding, about 5 minutes.

2 Remove pan from heat. Stir in coconut extract and reserved coconut. Let cool completely. Refrigerate filling in an airtight container up to 3 days; let stand at room temperature until soft enough to spread.

milk chocolate ganache

MAKES ENOUGH FOR 1 NINE-INCH CAKE

1½ pounds best-quality milk chocolate, finely chopped
2 cups plus 2 tablespoons heavy cream
1 teaspoon light corn syrup

1 Prepare an ice bath; set aside. Place chocolate in a medium heatproof bowl; set aside. Bring cream to a boil in a small saucepan; pour over chocolate, swirling to cover completely. Let stand until chocolate has melted, about 5 minutes. Add corn syrup, and whisk until smooth.

2 Pour 1 cup ganache into a bowl set in ice bath; stir until thick and spreadable. Keep remaining ganache at room temperature, stirring occasionally, until thick enough to coat back of spoon, 12 to 15 minutes. Use immediately.

gelatina de anise con frutas

MAKES 2 DOZEN | **PHOTO ON PAGE 87**

We used three-ounce baba-au-rhum molds to make these fruit-filled gelatin desserts; small ramekins or nonstick muffin tins would work just as well.

4 envelopes unflavored gelatin (¼ ounce each)
1 cup sugar
1 cup sambuca (licorice-flavored liqueur)
1 small ripe papaya, peeled and seeded
1 mango, pitted and peeled
1 pint strawberries, rinsed and hulled
1 cantaloupe, halved and seeded
1 two-pound wedge seedless watermelon
1 half-pint fresh raspberries

1 In a small bowl, sprinkle gelatin over 1 cup water. Let stand 5 minutes to soften. Bring 2 cups water and sugar to a boil in a small saucepan over medium-high heat, stirring to dissolve sugar. Stir gelatin mixture into pan, and cook until dissolved, about 30 seconds. Set aside to cool, then stir in sambuca.

2 Cut papaya into ½-inch dice. Cut mango into ¼-inch-thick slices. Cut strawberries into thin wedges. Use two different-size melon ballers to scoop out cantaloupe and watermelon.

3 On a rimmed baking sheet, line up 24 molds (3 ounces each). Place a few pieces of assorted fruit (including whole raspberries) in each mold, and pour 1 to 2 teaspoons gelatin mixture over the fruit. Refrigerate 15 minutes.

4 Fill molds three-quarters full with remaining fruit. Add enough gelatin mixture to cover fruit, leaving ¼ inch at the top. Refrigerate another 15 minutes. Fill molds with remaining gelatin mixture, covering any fruit that has floated to the top. Cover with plastic wrap, and refrigerate until completely set, at least overnight and up to 2 days.

5 When ready to serve, remove molds from refrigerator; dip bottoms of molds in hot water for 5 seconds. Tap sides against countertop to loosen gelatin; invert onto a serving tray.

from A Mexican Feast

meringue cups

SERVES 8 | PHOTO ON PAGE 78

- 6 large egg whites, room temperature
- 1 teaspoon freshly squeezed lemon juice
- ½ teaspoon pure vanilla extract
- 1 cup superfine sugar
- 1½ tablespoons cornstarch
  - Lemon Curd (recipe follows)
  - Caramelized Pineapple (recipe follows)

1 Preheat oven to 200°F. In the bowl of an electric mixer fitted with the whisk attachment, combine whites, lemon juice, and vanilla. Beat on low speed, gradually increasing to high, until soft peaks form, about 1½ minutes.

2 Sprinkle sugar over the egg-white mixture; beat on high speed until glossy peaks form, about 3 minutes. Sift cornstarch over mixture, and fold to combine.

3 Using two soup spoons, drop balls of meringue onto a parchment-lined baking sheet. Press down on center of each ball with back of one spoon to form a small cup.

4 Bake 1 hour. Reduce oven heat to 175°F; continue baking cups until outsides are dry and crisp and insides are chewy, about 1 hour more (test by cutting into one). Remove from oven; let cool completely. Store in an airtight container at room temperature up to 1 day. Before serving, let come to room temperature; fill cups with lemon curd. Serve with pineapple on the side.

from Dessert Party

lemon curd

MAKES 2¾ CUPS | PHOTO ON PAGE 78

Lemon curd can be refrigerated for up to two days. Serve it chilled, or reheat over a pan of simmering water.

- 14 large egg yolks
  - Grated zest of 2 lemons (about 2 tablespoons)
- 1¼ cups freshly squeezed lemon juice (about 6 lemons)
- 1¾ cups sugar
- 4½ tablespoons chilled unsalted butter, cut into small pieces

1 In a medium saucepan, whisk together egg yolks, lemon zest and juice, and sugar. Cook over medium heat, stirring with a wooden spoon, until mixture is thick enough to coat back of spoon, about 8 minutes. Remove from heat. Add butter, one piece at a time, stirring until smooth.

2 Pass mixture through a fine sieve into a small bowl. Cover with plastic wrap, pressing plastic directly on surface to prevent a skin from forming. Refrigerate until firm and thoroughly chilled, at least 1 hour.

caramelized pineapple

SERVES 8 | PHOTOS ON PAGES 78 AND 79

This dish can be made up to eight hours ahead and kept at room temperature; reheat in a 450 degree oven.

- 4 tablespoons unsalted butter
- 4 tablespoons sugar
- 1 pineapple (about 3½ pounds), peeled, cored, and cut into 1-inch chunks
- 2 whole star anise

In a 10-inch skillet over medium-high heat, cook 2 tablespoons each butter and sugar, stirring constantly, until melted and golden, 2 to 3 minutes. Add half the pineapple in a single layer with 1 star anise. Sauté, shaking pan occasionally, until the fruit is browned, 3 to 4 minutes. Turn; cook until other side is browned. Transfer to a gratin dish. Repeat process with remaining ingredients. Discard star anise.

pain perdu

MAKES 8 THREE-INCH ROUNDS | **PHOTO ON PAGE 78**

We like to serve these custard-soaked bread rounds with scoops of ice cream.

1 pound day-old brioche loaf
  Unsalted butter, for pan
2 cups milk
2 cups heavy cream
1 cup sugar
1 vanilla bean, split lengthwise and scraped
¼ cup hazelnut liqueur, such as Frangelico
4 large whole eggs
4 large egg yolks
  Warm Chocolate Sauce (recipe follows)

1 Preheat oven to 350°F. Trim side and bottom crusts from brioche, leaving top crust intact. Slice brioche ¼ to ⅓ inch thick. Butter a 9-by-13-inch baking pan; lay bread pieces in pan so they overlap slightly, with top crusts visible.

2 Make custard: In a medium saucepan over medium heat, whisk together milk, cream, sugar, vanilla scrapings, and liqueur. Cook until hot but not simmering.

3 In a large bowl, whisk together eggs and yolks. Whisking constantly, pour 1 cup of the hot milk mixture into eggs; slowly add remaining milk mixture.

4 Pour custard over bread, making sure to soak completely. Bake until firm to the touch, about 1 hour; if needed, press down bread with a spatula to keep it moist during cooking.

5 Remove pan from oven. Let cool slightly before cutting bread mixture into rounds with a 3-inch biscuit cutter. Serve warm, drizzled with chocolate sauce.

from Dessert Party

warm chocolate sauce

MAKES 3 CUPS | **PHOTO ON PAGE 78**

8 ounces bittersweet chocolate, finely chopped
1 cup heavy cream
3 tablespoons amaretto or Frangelico (optional)

Place chocolate in a large heatproof bowl. Bring cream and liqueur, if using, to a simmer over medium-high heat; pour over chocolate. Let stand 10 minutes, then stir to combine with a rubber spatula. If not serving immediately, let cool, then transfer to an airtight container. Sauce can be refrigerated up to 3 days; warm by setting container in a bowl of hot water.

poached pears with ginger

SERVES 4

These pears may be made through step three a day ahead and refrigerated in their cooking liquid.

1 cup dry white wine
2 tablespoons port or another full-bodied red wine
¼ cup honey
1 piece (¾ inch) fresh ginger, peeled and cut crosswise into 6 slices
1 vanilla bean, split lengthwise and scraped
4 ripe but firm Bartlett or Comice pears

1 In a large saucepan, combine all ingredients except pears. Add 3 cups water, and bring to a simmer over medium-high heat. Reduce heat to medium-low, and cook 5 minutes.

2 Meanwhile, peel pears and cut in half lengthwise. Leaving stems intact, use a small spoon or melon baller to scoop out core and seeds from each half. Trim fibrous strip from center with a paring knife. Gently lower pears into pan. If they're not completely covered by liquid, lay a piece of parchment paper directly on pears to keep them submerged.

3 Cook until a paring knife slides easily into pears, meeting only slight resistance, 15 to 20 minutes. Remove from heat; let cool in liquid 30 minutes.

4 Use a slotted spoon to transfer pears to a large bowl; cover with parchment paper. Cook liquid over medium heat until syrupy, about 15 minutes; discard vanilla pod and ginger. Let syrup cool. Place two pear halves in each of four bowls; spoon syrup over pears. Serve warm or at room temperature.

PER SERVING: 235 CALORIES, 1 G FAT, 0 MG CHOLESTEROL, 50 G CARBOHYDRATE, 10 MG SODIUM, 1 G PROTEIN, 5 G FIBER

from Fit to Eat: Ginger

prune tart

SERVES 4 | **PHOTO ON PAGE 88**

Serve with crème fraîche or whipped cream.

2 cups dry red wine

⅔ cup freshly squeezed orange juice (2 oranges)

½ cup plus 2 tablespoons sugar

1 whole cinnamon stick

3 cups pitted prunes (1 pound), halved

1 sheet frozen puff pastry (from a 17.3-ounce package), thawed

Finely grated zest of 1 orange

1 large egg

1 tablespoon heavy cream

1 Preheat oven to 375°F. In a medium saucepan, bring wine, orange juice, ½ cup sugar, and cinnamon to a boil over high heat. Remove from heat; add prunes, and let steep 10 minutes. Use a slotted spoon to transfer prunes to a bowl. Return liquid to a boil; cook until slightly reduced and thickened, 10 to 12 minutes. Remove from heat; discard cinnamon.

2 Meanwhile, roll out puff pastry into a 12-by-18-inch rectangle. Place on a baking sheet. In a small bowl, combine remaining 2 tablespoons sugar and the orange zest; sprinkle evenly over pastry. Arrange prunes in rows over pastry, leaving a 1-inch border on all sides. In a small bowl, whisk together egg and cream; brush mixture over edges of pastry.

3 Bake until crust is golden, rotating sheet and brushing tart with reserved cooking liquid halfway through, about 20 minutes. Remove from oven; let cool slightly. Serve warm.

from What's for Dinner?

torrejas en miel de azafran

SERVES 12 | **PHOTO ON PAGE 87**

This dessert is prepared similarly to French toast, except it is soaked in a saffron (*azafran* in Spanish) syrup.

½ cup sliced almonds

4 cups sugar

½ teaspoon saffron threads

1 cup heavy cream

1 cup milk

24 slices (¾ inch thick) French baguette

2 large eggs

Pinch of salt

4 tablespoons unsalted butter

Mint sprigs, for garnish

1 Preheat oven to 350°F. Spread almonds in a single layer in a rimmed baking sheet; toast in oven until golden and fragrant, tossing occasionally, about 7 minutes. Remove from oven, and set aside.

2 Bring sugar and 4 cups water to a boil in a medium saucepan over medium-high heat, stirring to dissolve. Stir in saffron, and cook 5 minutes. Set aside.

3 Combine cream and milk in a large bowl; add bread. Stir to coat, and let stand 5 minutes. Combine eggs and salt in a small bowl; beat lightly with a fork.

4 Melt butter in a large sauté pan over medium heat. Working in batches, remove bread from cream mixture, letting excess drip off. Dip both sides in egg, and cook in pan until golden on both sides, about 4 minutes total. Transfer to a plate.

5 Return bread to pan in batches; pour enough saffron syrup into pan to cover bread. Turn slices to coat evenly; cook until the syrup is slightly thickened and bread is heated through, about 5 minutes. Transfer to a serving platter. Sprinkle with almonds, and garnish with mint.

from A Mexican Feast

carrot, miso, and ginger salad dressing

SERVES 4

To achieve a uniform consistency, grate the carrot on the small holes of a box grater before puréeing. We like to serve this colorful dressing in its own dish and let each person spoon some over a salad of butter lettuce, sunflower sprouts, sliced radishes, and steamed edamame (soybeans).

1½ tablespoons minced fresh ginger (1½-inch piece)

1 large carrot, finely grated

2 tablespoons plus 1 teaspoon rice-wine vinegar

2 teaspoons white miso paste

3 tablespoons canola or vegetable oil

1 In a food processor, pulse ginger and carrot to a coarse paste. Add vinegar and miso, and pulse to combine.

2 With the machine running, slowly add oil in a thin, steady stream through the feed tube until mixture is emulsified. Add 1 tablespoon water if dressing is too thick. Use immediately, or refrigerate in an airtight container up to 1 week.

PER SERVING: 118 CALORIES, 10 G FAT, 0 MG CHOLESTEROL, 4 G CARBOHYDRATE, 147 MG SODIUM, 1 G PROTEIN, 1 G FIBER

from Fit to Eat: Ginger

spicy lime dipping sauce

MAKES ¾ CUP | **PHOTO ON PAGE 73**

Serve this sauce with grilled coconut shrimp or chicken.

½ cup freshly squeezed lime juice (about 4 limes)

2 teaspoons honey

½ teaspoon coarse salt

2 tablespoons thinly sliced scallion

1 serrano chile, thinly sliced

1 small garlic clove, minced

In a small bowl, whisk together all ingredients with 2 tablespoons water. Let stand at least 30 minutes or up to several hours to allow the flavors to blend.

from Coconut

March

artichoke, fennel, and lemon fritto misto

SERVES 10

Fritto misto "fried mix" is a traditional Italian antipasto.

2 artichokes

1 large bulb fennel, trimmed, cored, and thinly sliced

2 lemons, preferably Meyer, washed and very thinly sliced into rounds

2 cups buttermilk

3 cups all-purpose flour

Coarse salt and freshly ground pepper

5 cups peanut or canola oil

1   To separate artichoke bottoms, slice off upper two-thirds of each bulb, and discard. Snap off tough outer leaves; scoop out choke with a spoon. Using a vegetable peeler or sharp paring knife, remove green skin from around white center; discard. Thinly slice bottoms.

2   In a medium bowl, stir together artichoke bottoms, fennel, lemons, and buttermilk to coat evenly. Place flour in a separate bowl; season with salt and pepper, and whisk to combine.

3   Pour oil into a heavy, deep skillet or deep fryer; place over medium-high heat until it registers 370°F on a deep-fry thermometer. Drain vegetables and lemons; discard liquid.

4   Working with one piece at at time, dredge vegetables and lemons in flour, and carefully place in the hot oil. Cook 6 to 7 pieces at a time until golden brown, about 3 minutes. Using kitchen tongs or a slotted spoon, transfer vegetables and lemons to a paper-towel–lined plate to drain. As soon as each batch is done, sprinkle with salt. Serve immediately.

from Kitchen Party

bruschetta with fontina and asparagus

SERVES 10 | **PHOTO ON PAGE 67**

Truffle oil can be found at most gourmet shops.

1 loaf (about ¾ pound) French bread, sliced into ten ¼-inch-thick slices

1 garlic clove, crushed

2 tablespoons olive oil

Coarse salt

1½ large bunches asparagus (1¼ pounds), tough ends trimmed

8 ounces fontina or Monterey Jack cheese, grated on the large holes of a box grater (about 2 cups)

2 ounces Parmesan cheese, grated on the small holes of a box grater (about ¼ cup)

2 tablespoons truffle oil (optional)

1   Heat grill or broiler. Toast bread slices until golden on both sides. Rub one side with garlic; brush lightly with oil.

2   Preheat oven to 350°F. Bring a large saucepan of water to a boil over high heat; add salt generously. Add asparagus; cook until crisp-tender, about 3 minutes. Drain asparagus.

3   Place toasted bread on a baking sheet, and sprinkle fontina evenly over slices. Arrange 3 to 4 asparagus spears on top of each. Sprinkle Parmesan over asparagus, dividing evenly.

4   Bake until cheese has melted, about 10 minutes. Remove from oven, and drizzle with truffle oil, if using. Serve hot.

from Kitchen Party

carrot and radish bundles

SERVES 4

2 carrots, julienned (about 1 cup)

4 to 6 red radishes, trimmed and julienned (about 1 cup)

½ cup snow-pea shoots

1 cup packed fresh mint leaves

2 tablespoons rice-wine vinegar

Coarse salt and freshly ground pepper

1 small head Bibb lettuce, leaves separated

1 In a medium bowl, combine carrots, radishes, pea shoots, mint, and vinegar; season with salt and pepper. Toss gently.

2 Place a small handful of vegetable filling on a lettuce leaf. Fold sides over filling; roll up to make a bundle. Repeat with remaining ingredients. Serve chilled or at room temperature.

from What's for Dinner?

mixed greens with marinated red onions and sunflower seeds

SERVES 4

2 tablespoons freshly squeezed lime juice

1 tablespoon plus 2 teaspoons low-sodium soy sauce or tamari

2 teaspoons honey

2 small red onions, sliced as thinly as possible into rounds

1 tablespoon plus 1 teaspoon extra-virgin olive oil

6 ounces mixed salad greens, such as arugula, mizuna, and watercress

4 teaspoons raw sunflower seeds

2 teaspoons sesame seeds

1 In a medium bowl, combine 1 tablespoon lime juice, 1 tablespoon soy sauce, and 1 teaspoon honey. Add onions; toss to coat. Cover with plastic wrap, and marinate at room temperature 2 hours or up to 5 days in the refrigerator.

2 When ready to serve, make dressing: In a small bowl, combine remaining tablespoon lime juice with remaining 2 teaspoons soy sauce and 1 teaspoon honey. Add oil in a slow, steady stream, whisking until emulsified.

3 Place greens in a salad bowl. Using tongs or a slotted spoon, transfer onions to bowl, draining off excess marinade. Pour dressing over salad mixture. Add sunflower and sesame seeds; toss to combine. Serve immediately.

PER SERVING: 114 CALORIES, 6 G FAT, 0 MG CHOLESTEROL, 11 G CARBOHYDRATE, 266 MG SODIUM, 3 G PROTEIN, 2 G FIBER

from Fit to Eat: Raw Foods

spring green soup

SERVES 4

This soup can be served straight from the blender, when it is still frothy, or well chilled during warmer months. Sorrel adds a bright, lemony flavor as a garnish. If you are unable to find pencil-thin asparagus, you can trim thicker stalks with a vegetable peeler or paring knife.

1 cucumber, peeled

½ pound pencil-thin asparagus, tough ends trimmed

¼ pound spinach, tough stems removed, washed well

4 scallions, cut into 2-inch lengths

1 ripe avocado, pitted and peeled

¼ cup fresh mint leaves, plus sprigs for garnish

2 tablespoons freshly squeezed lemon juice

¾ teaspoon coarse salt

Freshly ground pepper

4 to 6 fresh sorrel leaves, for garnish (optional)

1 Halve cucumber lengthwise; scoop out and discard seeds. Cut one half into eighths and the other into ¼-inch dice; set aside. Cut asparagus spears into 2-inch lengths. Purée asparagus in a blender with ½ cup cold water until smooth.

2 Add spinach, scallions, cucumber eighths, and another ½ cup cold water. Blend until thoroughly puréed. Add avocado, mint leaves, and lemon juice; purée until smooth, adding up to 1 cup cold water a little at a time until soup is desired consistency. Add salt, and season with pepper. Scrape down sides of blender with a rubber spatula; purée 5 seconds more.

3 Slice sorrel into fine strips, if using. Divide soup among four bowls; garnish each serving with diced cucumber, sorrel, and a mint sprig. Serve immediately.

PER SERVING: 118 CALORIES, 8 G FAT, 0 MG CHOLESTEROL, 11 G CARBOHYDRATE, 389 MG SODIUM, 4 G PROTEIN, 6 G FIBER

from Fit to Eat: Raw Foods

boned leg of lamb stuffed with tapenade

SERVES 8 TO 10 | **PHOTO ON PAGE 72**

¾ cup Niçoise olives, pitted

¾ cup whole almonds

6 anchovy fillets

3 tablespoons capers, rinsed and drained

1 head garlic, cloves separated and peeled

3 tablespoons olive oil

1 butterflied leg of lamb (5 to 6 pounds), trimmed of excess fat

Coarse salt and freshly ground pepper

¾ cup all-purpose flour

2 large eggs, lightly beaten

1 cup plain breadcrumbs, preferably homemade

1 cup dry white wine

1 to 1½ cups Basic Chicken Stock (page 17) or low-sodium canned chicken broth

1 Preheat oven to 400°F. Make tapenade: In a food processor, combine olives, almonds, anchovies, capers, 3 garlic cloves, and 1½ tablespoons oil. Process to a smooth paste, scraping down sides of bowl as needed, about 2 minutes.

2 Season both sides of lamb generously with salt and pepper. Lay meat on a clean work surface, skin side down. Spread tapenade over the top. Starting with one short end, roll up lamb in the shape of a football; secure with twine.

3 Place flour on a plate, and season with salt and pepper. Place eggs and breadcrumbs in two shallow dishes. Dredge lamb first in flour mixture, coating completely, then dip in egg, letting excess drip off. Dredge in breadcrumbs.

4 Place lamb in a small roasting pan, and surround with remaining garlic cloves and ½ cup each white wine and chicken stock. Drizzle remaining 1½ tablespoons oil over lamb.

5 Roast in oven until internal temperature of lamb reaches 130°F on an instant-read thermometer for medium-rare, 1¼ to 1½ hours. If roasting pan becomes dry, add up to ½ cup chicken stock as needed to keep garlic from burning.

6 Transfer lamb to a cutting board, and remove and discard twine; let lamb rest 10 minutes before slicing. Set garlic aside, and pour pan juices from roasting pan into a small bowl, skimming off fat.

7 Make sauce: Place roasting pan over medium heat. Return skimmed cooking juices to pan, and add remaining ½ cup wine and ½ cup chicken stock. Using a wooden spoon, scrape up any browned bits from bottom of pan as sauce gently boils. Pass sauce and garlic through a fine sieve into a small saucepan, pressing with spoon to extract as much liquid and garlic as possible.

8 Bring sauce to a boil over medium-high heat; reduce heat, and simmer gently, 1 minute. Season with salt and pepper, and serve hot with sliced lamb.

from Kitchen Party

hoisin-roasted game hens

SERVES 4 | **PHOTO ON PAGE 71**

Hoisin, a blend of soybeans, garlic, chiles, and spices, is available in the Asian section of most supermarkets.

4 Cornish game hens (each about 2 pounds), rinsed and patted dry

3 garlic cloves, minced

2 tablespoons minced fresh ginger (2-inch piece)

2 fresh red chiles, seeded and minced (about 2 tablespoons)

1 bunch cilantro, rinsed well and drained

½ cup hoisin, plus more for basting

1 Preheat oven to 375°F. Place hens in a roasting pan. Mix together garlic, ginger, and chiles in a small bowl. Rub garlic mixture over hens and under skin; stuff cavities with cilantro sprigs. Tie legs of each hen together with kitchen twine. Refrigerate hens 20 minutes.

2 Remove hens from refrigerator; brush with ½ cup hoisin. Roast 35 to 40 minutes, basting occasionally with additional hoisin. Remove from oven; let rest 10 minutes before serving.

from What's for Dinner?

asparagus and shiitake stir-fry

SERVES 4 | **PHOTO ON PAGE 75**

To clean the mushrooms, simply wipe the caps with a damp paper towel; do not rinse, as they will become soggy. Toast the sesame seeds in a dry skillet over medium heat until golden.

1 tablespoon dark sesame oil

1 bunch medium or thick asparagus, tough ends trimmed, stalks sliced into 1½-inch lengths

8 ounces fresh shiitake mushrooms, trimmed and sliced into ½-inch-thick pieces

1 tablespoon sesame seeds, toasted
  Coarse salt and freshly ground pepper

Heat oil in a large skillet or wok over medium-high heat. Add asparagus and mushrooms, and sauté until just tender, about 5 minutes. Remove from heat. Sprinkle with toasted sesame seeds, and season with salt and pepper. Serve hot.

from What's for Dinner?

beet, cabbage, and carrot slaw with caraway seeds

SERVES 6

1 teaspoon caraway seeds

2 tablespoons freshly squeezed lemon juice

1 tablespoon white or yellow miso paste

1 small shallot, halved lengthwise and thinly sliced into half-moons

2 tablespoons extra-virgin olive oil
  Freshly ground pepper

2½ cups grated beets (about 2)

2 cups finely shredded red cabbage (¼ head)

1½ cups grated carrots (about 3)

1 Make dressing: In a small bowl, combine caraway, lemon juice, miso, and shallot. Whisk in oil in a slow, steady stream until emulsified. Season with pepper. Set aside.

2 In a large bowl, combine beets, cabbage, and carrots. Drizzle dressing over vegetables, and toss to combine. Serve chilled or at room temperature.

PER SERVING: 79 CALORIES, 5 G FAT, 0 MG CHOLESTEROL, 8 G CARBOHYDRATE, 172 MG SODIUM, 2 G PROTEIN, 3 G FIBER

from Fit to Eat: Raw Foods

colcannon

SERVES 4 | **PHOTO ON PAGE 75**

This traditional Irish potato dish can be assembled up to two hours ahead and browned just before serving.

1½ pounds russet potatoes

1 savoy cabbage, trimmed, pale-green leaves finely shredded (4 cups)

1 leek, white and pale-green parts only, cut into ½-inch dice

1 cup milk

4 tablespoons unsalted butter

¼ teaspoon freshly grated nutmeg
  Coarse salt

1 Preheat broiler. Peel and quarter potatoes, and place in a medium saucepan; add enough cold water to cover. Bring to a boil over high heat; reduce heat to a simmer, and cook until tender when pierced with a fork, about 15 minutes. Drain potatoes, and return to saucepan. Mash with a potato masher or pass through a ricer; cover pan to keep warm.

2 Meanwhile, in another saucepan, combine cabbage, leek, milk, 2 tablespoons butter, and nutmeg; season with salt. Cover, and cook over medium heat, stirring occasionally, until cabbage and leek are soft but not browned, about 15 minutes. Stir mixture into potatoes.

3 Spread mixture in an 8-inch square baking dish. Make a small well in the center, and place under the broiler until lightly browned on top, about 5 minutes.

4 Remove from broiler. Place remaining 2 tablespoons butter in well. Serve immediately, spooning melted butter from well onto each serving, if desired.

from Classic Potato Dishes

gratin Dauphinoise

SERVES 4 TO 6

2 tablespoons unsalted butter, room temperature, plus more for baking dish

3 pounds Yukon gold potatoes (8 to 10 small)

1 large garlic clove, minced

1¼ cups milk

1 cup heavy cream

1½ teaspoons coarse salt

¼ teaspoon freshly grated nutmeg

1 dried bay leaf

Freshly ground pepper

3 ounces Gruyère cheese, finely grated (about 1 cup)

1 Preheat oven to 400°F, with rack in center. Generously butter a 9-by-12-inch glass baking dish. Peel potatoes, and slice into ⅛-inch-thick rounds; place slices in a bowl of cold water as you work to prevent discoloration.

2 In a medium saucepan, combine garlic, milk, heavy cream, salt, nutmeg, and bay leaf. Bring just to a simmer over medium heat, and pour into prepared baking dish. Discard bay leaf.

3 Drain potatoes in a colander, and transfer to baking dish. Using a large spoon, toss potatoes with milk mixture, pressing down gently to distribute the potato slices evenly. Season with pepper. Dot with butter, distributing evenly over entire surface; sprinkle evenly with cheese.

4 Place in oven, and bake until potatoes are tender when pierced with the tip of a paring knife and top is brown, 45 to 50 minutes. Serve immediately.

from Classic Potato Dishes

grilled ratatouille Niçoise

SERVES 8 TO 10

6 medium tomatoes, halved and cored

Coarse salt

2 eggplants, trimmed and sliced lengthwise into ¼-inch-thick slices

2 tablespoons olive oil, plus more for brushing

Freshly ground black pepper

4 zucchini, trimmed and sliced lengthwise into ¼-inch-thick slices

2 small red onions, halved through the root and thinly sliced

1 red bell pepper, ribs and seeds removed, thinly sliced

1 yellow bell pepper, ribs and seeds removed, thinly sliced

2 garlic cloves, minced

¼ cup chopped fresh flat-leaf parsley

3 tablespoons sherry vinegar

1 Preheat oven to 350°F. Place tomatoes skin sides down in a roasting pan, and sprinkle with salt. Roast until tomatoes are very soft and lightly browned around edges, about 1 hour. Remove from oven, and set aside.

2 Meanwhile, heat a grill to medium. Brush both sides of eggplant slices with oil; season with salt and pepper. Grill until softened, about 3 minutes per side. Transfer to a large plate. Brush zucchini slices with oil; grill until tender, 2 to 3 minutes per side; set aside. Transfer to plate.

3 In a large sauté pan, heat 2 tablespoons oil over medium-high heat. Add onions, peppers, and garlic. Cook, stirring, until onions are soft and translucent, about 5 minutes.

4 Remove pan from heat. Stir in reserved tomatoes, eggplant, and zucchini. Season with salt and pepper; fold in parsley. Serve warm, drizzled with vinegar.

from Kitchen Party

parsleyed potatoes

SERVES 4 | **PHOTO ON PAGE 74**

For a decorative touch, use a vegetable peeler or paring knife to peel a strip from the middle of each potato before cooking.

2 **pounds small red potatoes**
2 **teaspoons coarse salt**
2 **tablespoons unsalted butter**
2 **tablespoons coarsely chopped fresh flat-leaf parsley**
Freshly ground pepper

1 Place potatoes in a large saucepan, and cover with cold water. Bring to a boil over high heat; add salt, and reduce heat to medium-low. Cook until a fork inserted into center of potatoes meets only slight resistance, about 20 minutes.

2 Drain potatoes in a colander; return to warm saucepan. Toss with butter and parsley, and season with pepper. Transfer to a serving dish, and serve immediately.

from Classic Potato Dishes

potato galettes

MAKES 6

Galettes are perfect as a side dish or as an hors d'oeuvre, topped with crème fraîche and caviar. Each one requires about ten minutes to cook. Make two at a time to minimize time at the stove. Once you have started the first galette, heat a second pan and begin making another. The finished galettes will stay warm in the oven while you work.

1½ **pounds russet potatoes (about 3), peeled**
6 **tablespoons Clarified Butter (recipe follows)**
Coarse salt and freshly ground pepper

1 Preheat oven to 200°F. Line a baking sheet with parchment paper. Using a mandoline or sharp knife, slice potatoes into paper-thin rounds. Place a 7-inch nonstick sauté pan over medium-low heat. Add 1 tablespoon butter; swirl to coat pan.

2 Working quickly, arrange potato slices in pan, slightly overlapping in a circle, beginning at outer edge of pan. Place a smaller ring of potato slices (about 4) inside outer ring; finish with a slice in the center. Season lightly with salt and pepper. Repeat, arranging a second layer of potatoes on top of first.

3 Place a small heatproof plate inside pan to weight down potatoes. Cook until edges and bottom of galette begin to turn golden, 5 to 7 minutes. Use a rubber spatula to loosen plate, and remove it; flip galette. Press down lightly with spatula, and cook until galette is golden and edges are crisp, 2 to 4 minutes.

4 Transfer galette to prepared baking sheet; keep warm in oven up to 45 minutes. Repeat with remaining butter and potatoes. Before serving, pat galettes gently with paper towels.

from Classic Potato Dishes

clarified butter

MAKES ⅔ CUP

We use clarified butter to make Potato Galettes (above) and Rösti Potatoes (page 61). Because it has no milk solids, it can withstand higher cooking temperatures without burning.

1 **cup (2 sticks) unsalted butter**

1 Melt butter in a small saucepan over low heat until foamy and milk solids have fallen to bottom of pan, about 15 minutes. Remove from heat, and let cool.

2 Carefully skim foam from top; discard. Slowly pour liquid butter into a storage container, leaving the solids behind. Use immediately, or keep covered in refrigerator up to 1 month.

roasted new potatoes

SERVES 8 TO 10

3 **pounds small new potatoes**
3 **tablespoons olive oil**
Coarse salt and freshly ground pepper
Assorted fresh herbs, such as rosemary, thyme, and marjoram

1 Preheat oven to 400°F. In a roasting pan, toss potatoes with oil; season with salt and pepper. Roast in oven, stirring occasionally, until potatoes are tender when pierced with a fork, about 50 minutes.

2 Line a serving bowl or platter with the herbs. Transfer hot potatoes to bowl on top of herbs, and serve.

from Kitchen Party

rösti potatoes

SERVES 6

3½ pounds Yukon gold potatoes (about 10)
Coarse salt and freshly ground pepper
¼ cup Clarified Butter (page 60)

1 Preheat oven to 400°F. Peel potatoes, placing them in a bowl of cold water as you work to prevent discoloration. Shred potatoes on the large holes of a box grater. Wrap potatoes in a clean kitchen towel; squeeze out liquid. Place in a medium bowl; season with salt and pepper.

2 Melt half the butter in a 9- or 10-inch ovenproof nonstick sauté pan over medium-low heat. Spread potatoes in pan evenly; press down with a spatula to flatten cake. Cook until bottom is golden and turning crisp, about 18 minutes.

3 Remove pan from heat. Invert cake onto a plate; slide back into pan. Return to heat, and spoon remaining butter around edge of pan. Cook until other side begins to get crisp, about 10 minutes, shaking pan several times to loosen.

4 Transfer pan to oven and bake until cake is cooked through and tender in the center, about 12 minutes. Serve cake cut into wedges.

from Classic Potato Dishes

sautéed potatoes

SERVES 4

For crisp, browned potatoes, avoid crowding the pan.

1½ pounds russet potatoes (about 4)
2 tablespoons olive oil
Coarse salt and freshly ground pepper
1 tablespoon unsalted butter
2 tablespoons chopped fresh chives

1 Peel potatoes, placing them in a bowl of cold water as you work to prevent discoloration. Cut into ¾-inch cubes.

2 Heat half the oil in a large sauté pan over medium heat. Pat potatoes dry; add half to pan. Season with salt and pepper. Cook, tossing frequently, until potatoes are golden, 12 to 15 minutes. Add half the butter; as it melts, toss to coat potatoes.

3 Transfer potatoes to a serving plate; keep in a warm place while repeating process with remaining oil, potatoes, and butter. Toss potatoes with chives. Serve immediately.

from Classic Potato Dishes

shaved fennel salad with almonds

SERVES 6

Look for fennel bulbs with delicate green fronds still attached to stalks. Most bulbs also have small wisps inside.

2 large bulbs fennel
½ cup whole almonds (2 ounces), coarsely chopped
2 tablespoons freshly squeezed lemon juice
2 tablespoons extra-virgin olive oil
½ teaspoon coarse salt
Freshly ground pepper

1 Trim outer layer of fennel bulbs; cut stalks from tops. Roughly chop enough green fronds to yield about 2 tablespoons; set aside. Using a mandoline or sharp knife, slice bulbs crosswise as thinly as possible. Discard tough core. Place sliced fennel bulbs and reserved chopped fronds in a salad bowl. Add almonds to bowl.

2 Make dressing: In a small bowl, whisk together lemon juice, oil, and salt; season with pepper. Pour dressing over fennel mixture, and toss well to combine. Serve immediately.

PER SERVING: 106 CALORIES, 9 G FAT, 0 MG CHOLESTEROL, 5 G CARBOHYDRATE, 177 MG SODIUM, 2 G PROTEIN, 2 G FIBER

from Fit to Eat: Raw Foods

almond-orange financier

SERVES 6 | **PHOTO ON PAGE 81**

4½ ounces whole almonds (1 cup)

¾ cup (1½ sticks) unsalted butter, melted, plus more for pan

1⅔ cups confectioners' sugar, plus more for dusting

½ cup all-purpose flour

¼ teaspoon salt

Finely grated zest of 1 orange

6 large egg whites, lightly beaten

Candied Orange Peel (recipe follows), for garnish

1 Preheat oven to 350°F. Spread almonds in a single layer on a rimmed baking sheet; toast in oven until fragrant and lightly toasted, tossing occasionally, about 7 minutes. Remove from oven; set aside to cool.

2 Raise oven temperature to 450°F. Butter a 13½-by-4-inch tart pan without a removable bottom; transfer to freezer.

3 In a food processor, pulse almonds until finely ground. In a large bowl, combine ground almonds, confectioners' sugar, flour, salt, and orange zest. Add egg whites, and whisk to combine. Slowly stir in melted butter.

4 Remove tart pan from freezer. Pour batter into pan; place on a baking sheet. Bake until dough just begins to rise, about 10 minutes. Reduce oven heat to 400°F, and continue baking until financier begins to brown, 7 to 8 minutes more. Turn off oven, and let cake stand in oven until firm, about 10 minutes. Transfer pan to a wire rack to cool completely.

5 Invert financier onto a serving platter; reinvert, and slice into six pieces. Garnish with candied peel; dust with sugar.

from Dessert of the Month

candied orange peel

MAKES ½ CUP

Candied peel can be made up to three weeks ahead; store it with the syrup in an airtight container in the refrigerator.

3 oranges

1 cup sugar

1 Using a citrus zester or vegetable peeler, shred long strips of orange peel. Place strips in a medium saucepan. Cover with cold water, and bring to a boil over medium heat. Drain; repeat two more times with fresh water.

2 Place sugar in a clean saucepan with 1½ cups water. Bring to a boil over medium heat, stirring occasionally, until sugar has dissolved, about 3 minutes. Add the citrus strips to the boiling syrup; reduce heat, and simmer until strips are trans-lucent, about 12 minutes. Remove from heat; let strips cool in syrup at least 1 hour. Remove from syrup when ready to use.

banana and coconut cashew-cream tart

MAKES 1 NINE-INCH TART | **PHOTO ON PAGE 81**

FOR TART SHELL:

6 ounces whole pecans (1½ cups)

Pinch of coarse salt

1½ cups pitted dates

2 teaspoons pure maple syrup

FOR FILLING:

5 ounces raw cashews (1 cup), soaked overnight and thoroughly drained

2 tablespoons plus 2 teaspoons pure maple syrup

1 vanilla bean, split lengthwise and scraped

¾ cup desiccated coconut

3 or 4 ripe but firm bananas

1 Make tart shell: Coarsely chop pecans with salt in a food processor. Add dates, and pulse until thoroughly combined, 15 to 20 seconds. Add syrup; pulse until just combined and mixture sticks together. Press nut mixture firmly and evenly into bottom and up sides of a 9-inch pie plate, wetting your fingers as needed. Set tart shell aside.

2 Make filling: Grind cashews to a coarse paste in a blender. Add ½ cup water, syrup, and vanilla scrapings; blend until smooth, about 5 minutes, scraping down sides as needed with a rubber spatula. Mixture should be the consistency of thick pancake batter. Set aside 2 tablespoons coconut; add

remainder to blender, and process to combine. Pour into prepared shell, spreading evenly.

3 Thinly slice bananas on the bias; arrange in slightly overlapping rings, beginning at edge of tart. Sprinkle with reserved coconut, and serve immediately.

PER SERVING: 309 CALORIES, 19 G FAT, 0 MG CHOLESTEROL, 37 G CARBOHYDRATE, 67 MG SODIUM, 4 G PROTEIN, 5 G FIBER

from Fit to Eat: Raw Foods

fresh pear and berry compote in red wine

SERVES 8 TO 10

We like to serve this compote in wine goblets with the tuiles draped over the rims.

1 pint fresh strawberries, hulled and halved
½ pint fresh raspberries
3 small ripe but firm pears, such as Seckel or Bosc, cored and thinly sliced
½ cup sugar
2 to 3 large, sweet geranium leaves (pesticide-free) or 1 sprig mint
½ 750-ml bottle (1⅔ cups) Gamay Beaujolais or other light-bodied fruity red wine
Almond Tuiles, for serving (recipe follows)

1 In a medium bowl, combine strawberries, raspberries, and pears; set aside. In a medium saucepan, heat sugar and 1 cup water over medium-high heat until sugar has completely dissolved. Add geranium leaves, and remove from heat. Cover; let steep 10 minutes.

2 Stir wine into mixture in pan; pour over fruit. Cover bowl with plastic wrap; refrigerate until well chilled, at least 1½ hours. Remove from refrigerator 30 minutes before serving.

from Kitchen Party

almond tuiles

MAKES 2 DOZEN

For best results, make these cookies the same day you plan to serve them—they are quite fragile.

5 tablespoons unsalted butter, cut into small pieces
½ cup sugar
2 teaspoons freshly squeezed orange juice
¼ cup all-purpose flour
⅔ cup sliced blanched almonds (2 ounces)
Finely grated zest of ½ orange

1 Preheat oven to 375°F. Line two baking sheets with parchment paper or Silpat baking mats; set aside.

2 In a small saucepan over medium heat, combine butter, sugar, and orange juice, stirring until butter has completely melted. Remove from heat, and add flour, almonds, and orange zest, whisking to combine.

3 Place a heaping teaspoon of batter on a prepared baking sheet; flatten with the back of a spoon. Repeat to make about 6 cookies on each sheet, placing them about 4 inches apart.

4 Bake one sheet at a time until cookies are golden, 8 to 10 minutes, rotating sheet once cookies have fully flattened.

5 Transfer baking sheet to a wire rack; let cool 20 seconds. Using a thin spatula, carefully lift tuiles; quickly drape over a rolling pin. Let stand until completely cooled and hardened.

ginger rice pudding

SERVES 4

We dipped pieces of crystallized ginger in melted chocolate to use as a garnish. Serve pudding with steaming cups of tea.

1¼ cups jasmine rice, rinsed and drained

1 quart milk

¼ cup sugar

2 tablespoons grated fresh ginger (2-inch piece)

1 teaspoon ground ginger

Pinch of salt

½ cup heavy cream

Combine rice, milk, sugar, fresh and ground ginger, and salt in a medium saucepan; bring to a simmer over medium heat. Cook, stirring occasionally, until rice is tender and has absorbed most but not all of the liquid, about 20 minutes. Remove from heat; stir in cream until combined. Serve warm.

from What's for Dinner?

no-cook mint ice cream

MAKES 1 PINT

This recipe doesn't call for a conventional cooked-custard base, making it very easy.

1 cup fresh mint, preferably peppermint, leaves washed and dried, stems discarded

½ cup sugar

1 cup milk

1 cup heavy cream

Using the back of a wooden spoon, crush mint leaves with sugar in a medium bowl until sugar resembles wet sand. Stir in milk and cream until sugar dissolves. Cover with plastic wrap, and refrigerate at least 2 hours. Strain mixture; discard solids. Freeze liquid in an ice-cream maker according to manufacturer's instructions. Transfer to an airtight container, and freeze until set, at least 30 minutes. Ice cream can be stored in an airtight container in the freezer up to 1 week.

from Good Things

MISCELLANEOUS

fresh-herb tisane

SERVES 8

Tisanes are herbal infusions made by steeping fresh herbs in boiling water, a process similar to brewing hot tea. Be sure to buy only pesticide-free herbs from a reliable source.

1 sprig lemon balm

4 sprigs fresh mint

1 sweet geranium leaf (optional)

1 sprig rosemary, thyme, or lavender

Bring 4 cups water to a boil. Place herbs in a warmed teapot; cover with the boiling water. Let steep 5 minutes, then strain liquid into serving cups. Serve immediately.

from Kitchen Party

HEARTY BEEF STEW | **PAGE 18**

SPICED RED LENTIL SOUP WITH
CRISPY FRIED GINGER | **PAGE 35**

BRUSCHETTA WITH
FONTINA AND ASPARAGUS | **PAGE 55**

CHICKEN AND KALE SOUP WITH
WHITE BEANS | **PAGE 16**

ROASTED EGGPLANT DIP | **PAGE 15**

UDON NOODLES WITH SHIITAKE MUSHROOMS
IN GINGER BROTH | **PAGE 35**

COCONUT FISH CHOWDER | **PAGE 34**

BOEUF BOURGUIGNON | **PAGE 36**

TURKEY MEATBALL SOUP | **PAGE 20**

SHREDDED CHICKEN AND
SOBA NOODLE SOUP | **PAGE 19**

SAUTEED SHRIMP | **PAGE 21**

PANCETTA-WRAPPED PORK ROAST | **PAGE 38**

PESCADO TIKIN XIK | **PAGE 38**

MOLE DE ZARZAMORAS | **PAGE 37**

CHILES ANCHOS RELLENOS | **PAGE 41**

HOISIN-ROASTED GAME HENS | **PAGE 57**

CHILI WITH CHICKEN AND BEANS | **PAGE 20**

MAKE-YOUR-OWN-SANDWICH BUFFET | **PAGE 21**

TURKEY MEATLOAF | **PAGE 22**

GARLIC MASHED POTATOES | **PAGE 22**

BONED LEG OF LAMB STUFFED
WITH TAPENADE | **PAGE 57**

COCONUT ALMOND RICE | **PAGE 42**

SPICY LIME DIPPING SAUCE | **PAGE 52**

MERINGUE CUPS WITH LEMON CURD
AND CARAMELIZED PINEAPPLE | **PAGE 49**

ALMOND-POLENTA POUND CAKE
WITH SAUTEED APPLES AND
CARAMEL SAUCE | **PAGES 43 AND 44**

PAIN PERDU WITH WARM
CHOCOLATE SAUCE | **PAGE 50**

SAUTEED APPLES | **PAGE 44**

MACERATED CITRUS | **PAGE 44**

CARAMELIZED PINEAPPLE | **PAGE 49**

HOT HONEY LEMONADE WITH GINGER | **PAGE 28**

SPICY HOT-CHOCOLATE WITH CINNAMON | **PAGE 28**

ALMOND-ORANGE FINANCIER | **PAGE 62**

BANANA AND COCONUT CASHEW-CREAM TART | **PAGE 62**

COFFEE WITH COGNAC AND CARDAMOM | **PAGE 27**

A FEW TIPS FOR MAKING THE MERINGUE CAKE

When folding the egg-white mixture into the chocolate batter, use the largest spatula you own and as few strokes as possible to maintain a light, airy consistency.

Hazelnut skins will come right off when you toast the nuts; rub them vigorously inside a folded kitchen towel while they're still warm.

An offset spatula lets you reach easily into the springform pan to gently coax the meringue over the half-baked cake.

CHOCOLATE AND HAZELNUT MERINGUE CAKE | **PAGE 44**

PRUNE TART | **PAGE 51**

Spring

AS SPRING APPROACHES, OUR THOUGHTS TURN to picnic menus, main-course salads, and desserts that are a bit more ethereal than the dense, rich delights of the colder months. Classic lighter-than-air angel food cake, a low-fat favorite, is entirely appropriate, arriving just as we begin to throw off the accoutrements of winter and make way for a new kind of warmth.

April

baba ghanoush
MAKES 2¼ CUPS

If you're making this dip ahead of time, store it in an airtight container in the refrigerator for up to one week. Garnish with parsley just before serving with toasted pita bread.

2 eggplants (about 2½ pounds)
1 garlic clove, coarsely chopped
¼ cup tahini (sesame-seed paste)
3 tablespoons freshly squeezed lemon juice (1 lemon)
1 teaspoon coarse salt
  Pinch of freshly ground pepper
2 tablespoons olive oil
  Chopped fresh flat-leaf parsley, for garnish

1 Heat broiler. Place eggplants on a rimmed baking sheet lined with aluminum foil. Broil until skin is charred, turning as each side blackens, about 12 minutes.

2 Reduce oven heat to 425°F. Continue cooking eggplants until flesh is very soft, 12 to 15 minutes. Remove from oven, and let stand until cool enough to handle. Halve eggplants. Scrape out seeds with a spoon (some seeds may remain), and discard. Slice off stems, and remove skins; discard.

3 Place flesh in a food processor, and pulse until smooth. Add remaining ingredients except parsley; pulse a few more times to combine. Transfer to a serving bowl, and garnish with parsley. Serve immediately.

from Easy Entertaining: A Mezze Menu

couscous salad
SERVES 6 TO 8 | PHOTO ON PAGE 143

½ cup whole blanched almonds
1½ cups Israeli couscous
2¼ cups water or chicken stock
2½ tablespoons extra-virgin olive oil
1 onion, finely chopped
1 garlic clove, minced
1 tablespoon Spice Mixture (recipe follows)
½ cup dried apricots, cut into ⅓-inch dice
½ cup Kalamata olives, pitted and quartered
  Coarse salt and freshly ground pepper
1½ cups packed julienned arugula, plus leaves for garnish

1 Preheat oven to 375°F. Spread almonds in a single layer on a rimmed baking sheet; toast in oven until light brown and fragrant, stirring occasionally, about 10 minutes. Remove from oven, and let cool.

2 Place a medium saucepan over medium-high heat. Add couscous, stirring occasionally until deep golden brown and fragrant, 3 to 4 minutes. Reduce heat to medium-low; add 1¾ cups water all at once. Cover, and let grains steam until tender, about 5 minutes. Remove from heat; keep covered.

3 In a medium skillet, heat 1 tablespoon oil over medium-high heat. Add onion and garlic; cook, stirring occasionally, until soft, about 4 minutes. Stir in spice mixture, apricots, and the remaining ½ cup water. Reduce heat to a simmer; continue cooking until most of the liquid has evaporated, about 3 minutes. Stir in olives and toasted almonds; remove from heat.

4 Fluff couscous with a fork, and add onion mixture. Season with salt and pepper. Add julienned arugula, and drizzle with remaining 1½ tablespoons oil; toss well to combine. Transfer to a serving bowl. Serve warm or at room temperature, garnished with arugula leaves.

from Easy Entertaining: A Mezze Menu

spice mixture
MAKES ¼ CUP

This recipe can easily be multiplied to make larger quantities that you can store for later use.

4½ teaspoons ground coriander
4 teaspoons ground cumin
1½ teaspoons ground nutmeg
1 teaspoon ground cinnamon
½ teaspoon ground cloves
½ teaspoon cayenne pepper

Mix spices together in a small bowl or container. Store, tightly sealed, at room temperature up to 6 months.

crisped Haloumi cheese

SERVES 6 TO 8

Haloumi is a semihard cheese made from sheep's milk; look for it at Middle Eastern markets.

5 teaspoons nonpareil capers, drained and chopped
Grated zest and juice of 1 lemon
1 pound (2 packages) Haloumi cheese

1 In a small bowl, mix capers with lemon zest and juice; set aside. Using a sharp knife, slice each block of cheese crosswise into ¼-inch-thick slices.

2 Heat a nonstick skillet over medium heat. Working in batches, arrange cheese slices in a single layer in skillet. Cook until golden brown, about 3 minutes per side. Transfer to a serving dish; spoon caper mixture over cheese. Serve warm.

from Easy Entertaining: A Mezze Menu

dressed feta cheese

SERVES 6 TO 8

We particularly like the flavor and firm texture of Bulgarian feta cheese, but other types of feta can also be used.

1 pound feta cheese, drained well
5 large sprigs dill
5 sprigs flat-leaf parsley
1 scallion, including green parts, thinly sliced
1 teaspoon whole pink peppercorns
1 teaspoon crushed red-pepper flakes
2 tablespoons extra-virgin olive oil

1 Using a sharp knife, cut block of feta crosswise into ½-inch-thick slices, wiping knife each time to keep cheese from crumbling. Arrange on a serving dish.

2 Pick leaves from herbs, and chop finely. Combine herbs and scallion in a small bowl; stir in peppercorns, red-pepper flakes, and 1 tablespoon oil. Spoon herb mixture over feta. Drizzle with remaining tablespoon oil, and serve.

from Easy Entertaining: A Mezze Menu

hummus dip

MAKES 1¾ CUPS

1 can (15½ ounces) chickpeas, drained and rinsed
1 small garlic clove, coarsely chopped
Pinch of ground cumin
Pinch of ground nutmeg
¼ cup tahini (sesame-seed paste)
½ teaspoon coarse salt

Purée all ingredients with 1 tablespoon water in a food processor until smooth and creamy, adding more water as needed to reach desired consistency. Store in an airtight container in the refrigerator until ready to serve, up to 2 days.

from Easy Entertaining: A Mezze Menu

lamb köfte

SERVES 6 TO 8 | PHOTO ON PAGE 143

Köfte can be prepared up to thirty minutes before serving; place patties on a baking sheet, cover with aluminum foil, and keep warm in a 250 degree oven. Toast pine nuts in a dry skillet over medium heat, shaking frequently to color evenly.

1 pound ground lamb
4 teaspoons Spice Mixture (page 93)
1 teaspoon paprika
¼ teaspoon ground cinnamon
1 large egg
½ onion, grated on the large holes of a box grater (½ cup)
1 garlic clove, minced
⅓ cup pine nuts, toasted and chopped
⅓ cup finely chopped fresh flat-leaf parsley
1 teaspoon coarse salt
1 tablespoon olive oil
Yogurt Mint Sauce, for serving (recipe follows)

1 In a large bowl, combine all ingredients except oil and yogurt sauce. Mix thoroughly with your hands or a wooden spoon. Form mixture into 1½-inch balls, and flatten into ovals or football shapes, about ¼ inch thick.

2 In a large nonstick skillet, heat ½ tablespoon oil over medium-high heat. Add half the lamb patties. Cook until undersides are golden brown, about 3 minutes; flip patties, and cook 2 minutes more. Transfer to a paper-towel–lined plate.

3 Wipe skillet with a paper towel; heat remaining ½ tablespoon oil. Repeat process with remaining lamb patties. Serve warm or at room temperature with yogurt sauce.

from Easy Entertaining: A Mezze Menu

yogurt mint sauce

MAKES 1 CUP

8 ounces plain whole-milk yogurt, preferably Greek-style

3 tablespoons finely chopped fresh mint

1½ teaspoons freshly squeezed lemon juice

1 small garlic clove, minced

Combine all ingredients in a small bowl; stir well. Sauce can be made up to 1 day ahead; store in an airtight container in the refrigerator. Serve chilled or at room temperature.

tomatoes à la grecque

SERVES 6 TO 8

This dish can be prepared through step three up to several hours in advance; serve chilled or at room temperature.

2 pounds small ripe tomatoes

Coarse salt and freshly ground pepper

¼ cup olive oil

1 garlic clove, minced

¼ cup white-wine vinegar

1 tablespoon freshly squeezed lemon juice

½ teaspoon ground coriander

2 cucumbers

3 teaspoons dried oregano, for garnish

1 Slice tomatoes into quarters lengthwise, through the stem. Place in a medium bowl; season with salt and pepper.

2 Heat oil in a small saucepan over medium heat. Add garlic; cook, stirring, until soft but not browned, about 1 minute. Stir in vinegar, lemon juice, and coriander; simmer 1 minute.

3 Immediately pour hot vinaigrette over tomatoes; let marinate at room temperature until completely cooled.

4 Peel cucumbers, leaving on stripes of skin for decoration, if desired. Halve cucumbers lengthwise; scrape out seeds with a spoon. Cut cucumber into ½-inch-thick semicircles. Garnish tomatoes with oregano; serve cucumbers in a separate bowl.

from Easy Entertaining: A Mezze Menu

SOUPS

puréed spinach-potato soup

SERVES 4

2 tablespoons unsalted butter

1 onion, coarsely chopped

3 garlic cloves, minced

1½ pounds Yukon gold potatoes (about 5 small), peeled and cut into ½-inch pieces

¼ cup dry sherry or white wine

1 quart Basic Chicken Stock (page 17) or low-sodium canned chicken broth

2 bunches spinach (about 1¼ pounds), tough stems removed, leaves washed well

Coarse salt and freshly ground pepper

1 Melt butter in a large saucepan over medium heat. Add onion, garlic, and potatoes; cook, stirring, 2 minutes.

2 Pour sherry, chicken stock, and 2 cups water into pan; stir to combine. Bring to a boil. Reduce heat to medium-low; cover, and simmer until potatoes are very tender when pierced with a fork, about 15 minutes.

3 Stir spinach into mixture in pan, and cook until wilted and bright green, about 3 minutes. Remove from heat. Purée soup with an immersion blender until smooth. (Alternatively, use a regular blender, working in batches so as not to fill jar more than halfway. Return mixture to saucepan.) Season with salt and pepper, and serve.

from What's for Dinner?

stracciatella

SERVES 4 TO 6

In this traditional Italian soup, you whirl beaten eggs into the stock, creating "ragged" (*stracciata* in Italian) pieces.

1½ quarts Basic Chicken Stock (page 17) or low-sodium canned chicken broth

4 large eggs, lightly beaten

2 tablespoons fresh flat-leaf parsley, coarsely chopped, plus more for garnish

2 tablespoons freshly grated Parmesan cheese, plus more for garnish

Coarse salt and freshly ground pepper

1 In a large saucepan, bring stock to a boil over medium-high heat. Reduce heat to low; keep at a gentle simmer.

2 In a medium bowl, whisk together eggs and parsley. Using a fork, stir stock in a quick circular motion, creating a whirlpool;

pour egg mixture into center in a steady stream. Sprinkle in cheese, and season with salt and pepper. Ladle into bowls, and garnish with parsley and cheese.

from Egg Suppers

MAIN COURSES

broiled flank-steak sandwiches

SERVES 4

You can use store-bought roasted bell peppers for these open-face sandwiches, if you prefer.

¼ cup sour cream

¼ cup mayonnaise

2 tablespoons prepared horseradish

1 tablespoon grainy mustard

 Coarse salt and freshly ground black pepper

1½ pounds flank steak

3 tablespoons extra-virgin olive oil

1 bunch watercress, tough stems trimmed

1 tablespoon freshly squeezed lemon juice

4 thick slices rustic bread, toasted

 Roasted Peppers with Garlic and Basil (recipe follows)

1 Make horseradish sauce: In a small bowl, whisk together sour cream, mayonnaise, horseradish, and mustard. Season with salt and pepper. Cover with plastic wrap, and refrigerate until ready to serve, up to several days.

2 Heat broiler, with rack 6 inches from heat. Season steak well on both sides with salt and pepper; rub with 2 table-spoons oil. Place in a roasting pan fitted with a rack. Broil 6 minutes on each side for medium-rare. Remove from broiler; let rest 5 minutes before slicing ¼-inch-thick pieces.

3 Place watercress in a bowl; toss with remaining table-spoon oil and the lemon juice. Season with salt and pepper. Spread toasted bread with horseradish sauce, and top with watercress, steak, and roasted peppers.

from What's for Dinner?

roasted peppers with garlic and basil

SERVES 4

These colorful peppers are great on sandwiches, in pasta dishes, or as part of an antipasto platter. The recipe can easily be doubled, and the peppers can be stored in an airtight container in the refrigerator for up to one week.

4 bell peppers (red, yellow, or orange)

¼ cup extra-virgin olive oil

1 tablespoon white-wine vinegar

2 garlic cloves, halved lengthwise

 Few sprigs of basil

 Coarse salt and freshly ground black pepper

1 Heat broiler. Cut peppers in half through the stem; discard stems, ribs, and seeds. Place peppers cut side down on a rimmed baking sheet.

2 Roast peppers under the broiler until skins are charred, rotating baking sheet occasionally, about 10 minutes. Transfer peppers to a bowl, and cover with plastic wrap. Let steam until cool enough to handle, about 10 minutes.

3 Using a paper towel, rub peppers to remove charred skin. Cut peppers into strips; place in bowl with any accumulated juice. Add oil, vinegar, garlic, and basil; season with salt and pepper. Toss to combine. Serve warm or at room temperature.

curried eggs

SERVES 5 | **PHOTO ON PAGE 139**

We like to serve this dish with slices of thick, crusty bread.

4 teaspoons vegetable oil

1 shallot, minced

1 garlic clove, crushed

2 tablespoons grated fresh ginger

1 can (28 ounces) chopped tomatoes with juice

2 small green chiles, such as jalapeño or serrano, finely chopped, plus more for garnish

2 teaspoons ground turmeric

½ teaspoon ground cumin

3 sprigs cilantro, finely chopped, plus more sprigs for garnish

 Coarse salt and freshly ground pepper

5 large eggs

1 Heat oil in a large skillet over medium heat. Add shallot, garlic, and ginger; cook, stirring occasionally, until soft, 5 to 7 minutes. Add tomatoes and their juice, chiles, turmeric,

cumin, and chopped cilantro. Season with salt and pepper. Cook, stirring occasionally, until tomatoes are soft and sauce has thickened, about 15 minutes.

2 Break 1 egg into a small bowl; slide onto tomato sauce. Repeat with remaining eggs, arranging them around skillet. Cover, and cook until egg whites are just set, 4 to 5 minutes. Remove from heat. Season with salt and pepper, and garnish with chiles and cilantro. Serve immediately.

from Egg Suppers

egg, prosciutto, and asparagus pizza

SERVES 4 | PHOTO ON PAGE 138

9 ounces asparagus (about ½ bunch), trimmed and cut into 2-inch lengths

2 pounds frozen pizza dough, thawed
   All-purpose flour, for work surface

8 ounces ricotta cheese

8 ounces fresh mozzarella cheese, sliced

2 large tomatoes, sliced

4 ounces oil-cured black olives, pitted and halved
   Coarse salt and freshly ground pepper

4 large eggs

4 ounces prosciutto, thinly sliced
   Fresh basil, thinly sliced, for garnish

1 Preheat oven to 400°F, with pizza stone on lower rack, if using. Prepare an ice bath; set aside. Bring a pot of water to a boil. Add asparagus; cook until bright green and just tender, about 2 minutes. Transfer to ice bath to stop the cooking. Drain, and set aside.

2 Divide pizza dough into four equal pieces. On a lightly floured work surface, roll each piece into a 7-inch round. Top rounds with ricotta, mozzarella, asparagus, tomatoes, and olives. Season with salt and pepper.

3 Place rounds on pizza stone, if using, or a baking sheet. Bake until crust is golden and cheese has melted, 10 to 12 minutes. Break an egg into a bowl, and slide onto a pizza; repeat with remaining eggs. Continue baking until egg whites are just set, 4 to 5 minutes. Arrange prosciutto and basil on top, and serve immediately.

from Egg Suppers

fried-egg–topped sandwiches

SERVES 4 | PHOTO ON PAGE 139

8 slices good-quality white bread

4 ounces fontina, Gruyère, or mozzarella cheese, thinly sliced

2 tablespoons fresh oregano, coarsely chopped, plus more for garnish
   Coarse salt and freshly ground pepper

2 tablespoons milk

6 large eggs

4 tablespoons extra-virgin olive oil

1 Cut bread slices into 8 rounds with a 3¾-inch cookie cutter. Top half of the slices with cheese, dividing evenly; sprinkle with oregano, salt, and pepper. Place remaining bread rounds on top; press gently to adhere.

2 In a small bowl, whisk together milk and 2 eggs. Heat 2 tablespoons oil in a large nonstick skillet over medium heat. Dip sandwiches, one at a time, into egg mixture, letting excess drip back into bowl; transfer to skillet. Cook until golden and cheese has melted, about 2 minutes per side. Transfer to serving plates.

3 Wipe skillet with a paper towel. Heat remaining 2 tablespoons oil. Crack remaining 4 eggs into skillet, one at a time. Fry until egg whites are just set, about 2 minutes. Carefully place an egg on each sandwich. Season with salt and pepper; garnish with oregano, and serve.

from Egg Suppers

grilled tuna with cherry-tomato salad and herbed bulghur

SERVES 4

1   cup bulghur wheat

1½ teaspoons coarse salt

¼   cup loosely packed inner celery leaves, coarsely chopped

¼   cup loosely packed fresh mint leaves, coarsely chopped

¼   cup loosely packed fresh cilantro leaves, coarsely chopped

¼   teaspoon ground coriander

½   pint cherry tomatoes, halved

2   scallions, thinly sliced

2   teaspoons extra-virgin olive oil, plus more for grill

3   tablespoons freshly squeezed lemon juice (1 lemon)
    Freshly ground pepper

4   tuna steaks (each 6 ounces and about 1 inch thick)

1 Bring 2 cups water to a boil. Place bulghur in a large heat-proof bowl; cover with the boiling water. Add ¼ teaspoon salt; stir just to combine, and cover tightly with plastic wrap. Let

steam until tender but still slightly chewy, 22 to 25 minutes. If all water has not been absorbed, drain bulghur in a sieve, then return to dried bowl. Let cool. Using a fork, stir in celery leaves, mint, cilantro, and coriander.

2   Make cherry-tomato salad: In a medium bowl, toss the tomatoes and scallions with the oil, lemon juice, and ¼ teaspoon salt. Season with pepper. Set aside.

3   Heat a lightly oiled grill or grill pan over medium-high heat. Sprinkle both sides of each tuna steak with about ¼ teaspoon salt; season evenly with pepper. Cook until undersides are seared with grill marks, 3 to 4 minutes. Flip tuna, and cook 3 minutes more for medium-rare. Serve with herbed bulghur on the side and cherry-tomato salad spooned on top.

PER SERVING: 340 CALORIES, 5 G FAT, 77 MG CHOLESTEROL,
31 G CARBOHYDRATE, 781 MG SODIUM, 45 G PROTEIN, 7 G FIBER

from Fit to Eat: Heart-Healthy Fish

pasta with fennel, sardines, and pine nuts

SERVES 4 | PHOTO ON PAGE 146

1   pound penne, trenette, or other short tubular pasta
2   tablespoons extra-virgin olive oil
¼   cup pine nuts
1   onion, finely chopped
2   bulbs fennel, trimmed and thinly sliced, plus ¼ cup green fronds
4   garlic cloves, finely chopped
1   teaspoon coarse salt
    Freshly ground pepper
2   cans (3.75 ounces each) sardines packed in olive oil
    Grated zest and juice of 1 lemon, plus 1 lemon for serving

1   Bring a large pot of water to a boil. Cook pasta until al dente according to package instructions, about 8 minutes.

2   Meanwhile, cook oil and pine nuts in a large sauté pan over medium heat until nuts are lightly toasted, 3 to 4 minutes.

3   Add onion, sliced fennel, garlic, and salt to pan; season with pepper. Cook, stirring occasionally, until onion is soft and light golden, 9 to 10 minutes. Add sardines; stir in lemon zest and juice. Chop reserved fennel fronds; stir into mixture.

4   Drain pasta, reserving about ¼ cup cooking liquid. Add pasta to mixture in pan along with enough cooking water to coat; toss to combine. Divide among four serving plates; grate lemon zest over each. Serve immediately.

PER SERVING: 571 CALORIES, 17 G FAT, 20 MG CHOLESTEROL,
73 G CARBOHYDRATE, 548 MG SODIUM, 28 G PROTEIN, 13 G FIBER

from Fit to Eat: Heart-Healthy Fish

slow-roasted salmon with caper-and-herb relish

SERVES 4 | PHOTO ON PAGE 145

4   skinless salmon fillets (6 ounces each)
1¼   teaspoons coarse salt
    Freshly ground pepper
1   small shallot, finely chopped
2   tablespoons capers, drained
    Grated zest and juice of 1 lemon
1   tablespoon extra-virgin olive oil
1   cup loosely packed fresh flat-leaf parsley, coarsely chopped
⅔   cup coarsely chopped mixed fresh herbs, such as tarragon, chervil, dill, and mint
1   bunch pencil-thin asparagus, tough ends snapped off

1   Preheat oven to 250°F, with rack in upper third. Place salmon on a parchment-lined baking sheet. Sprinkle both sides of each fillet with ¼ teaspoon salt; season evenly with pepper. Roast until opaque but still bright pink in the middle, 25 to 30 minutes. Remove from oven.

2   Meanwhile, make relish: In a small bowl, stir together shallot, capers, lemon zest and juice, and remaining ¼ teaspoon salt; season with pepper. Add oil, parsley, and mixed herbs, and toss gently to combine.

3   Place asparagus in a steamer basket or colander set over a pot of simmering water; steam until spears are crisp-tender and bright green, 3 to 4 minutes. Divide asparagus among serving plates. Place a salmon fillet on each plate next to asparagus, and spoon relish on top of fish.

PER SERVING: 360 CALORIES, 22 G FAT, 112 MG CHOLESTEROL,
5 G CARBOHYDRATE, 206 MG SODIUM, 36 G PROTEIN, 2 G FIBER

from Fit to Eat: Heart-Healthy Fish

smoked mackerel, cucumber, and potato salad with mustard dressing

SERVES 4 | **PHOTO ON PAGE 143**

Although fresh mackerel can be hard to find, smoked mackerel is often sold next to smoked salmon in the refrigerated section of supermarkets; it is also available from mail-order sources. We used the peppered variety, but any type will do.

¾ pound small waxy potatoes, such as fingerling or new potatoes

1 small shallot, very thinly sliced

4 teaspoons white-wine vinegar

2 teaspoons Dijon mustard

4 teaspoons olive oil

2 tablespoons coarsely chopped fresh dill

½ cucumber, peeled, halved lengthwise, seeded, and sliced into ½-inch-thick semicircles

Freshly ground pepper

12 ounces smoked mackerel, broken into bite-size pieces

Handful of tender salad greens, such as arugula, watercress, or tatsoi, for garnish

1 Place potatoes in a small saucepan, and cover with cold water. Bring to a boil; reduce heat, and simmer until tender when pierced with the tip of a paring knife, about 12 minutes. Drain in a colander; let cool slightly. Slip off skins, and discard. Cut potatoes into halves or quarters, if desired.

2 Meanwhile, make dressing: In a medium bowl, combine shallot, vinegar, and mustard. Whisk in oil in a slow, steady stream until emulsified. Sprinkle dill into bowl.

3 Add cucumber and cooked potatoes to the dressing; season with pepper. Toss to coat evenly. Divide salad among four plates, and arrange mackerel on top of each. Serve, garnished with greens.

PER SERVING: 234 CALORIES, 15 G FAT, 15 MG CHOLESTEROL, 7 G CARBOHYDRATE, 800 MG SODIUM, 20 G PROTEIN, 3 G FIBER

from Fit to Eat: Heart-Healthy Fish

warm spring salad with poached eggs

SERVES 4

Small young peas are tender and can be eaten raw; blanch larger ones before adding to the salad.

4 slices smoked bacon (4 ounces)

4 thick slices country bread, cut into 2-inch cubes

Coarse salt and freshly ground pepper

4 teaspoons red-wine vinegar

1 tablespoon freshly squeezed lemon juice

8 ounces baby spinach (1 bunch), washed well

3 ounces fresh young garden peas

2 ounces feta cheese, crumbled

2 tablespoons chopped fresh chives

4 large eggs

1 Preheat oven to 375°F. Cook bacon in a large skillet over medium heat until crisp, flipping slices as needed, about 7 minutes. Transfer to a paper-towel–lined plate to drain. Set aside ¼ cup rendered bacon fat, leaving the rest in the skillet.

2 Make croutons: Toss bread cubes in bacon fat remaining in skillet, coating evenly; season with salt and pepper. Arrange cubes in a single layer on a rimmed baking sheet. Bake until crisp, about 10 minutes. Set aside.

3 Make vinaigrette: In a small bowl, whisk together vinegar and lemon juice; season with salt and pepper. Whisk in reserved ¼ cup bacon fat until emulsified.

4 In a large bowl, combine spinach, peas, feta, chives, and croutons. Pour vinaigrette over spinach mixture, and toss to coat. Divide among four serving plates.

5 Fill a deep skillet or wide saucepan with 3 inches of water. Bring to a boil over high heat; reduce to a full simmer. Break 1 egg into a small bowl. Lower the bowl over the simmering water, and quickly slide egg into it. Use a large spoon to keep egg white together, if needed. Simmer until yolk is just set, about 2½ minutes. Using a slotted spoon, transfer egg to a paper-towel–lined plate to drain. Repeat with remaining eggs.

6 Arrange a poached egg and one of the reserved bacon slices on top of each spinach salad. Season with salt and pepper. Serve immediately.

from Egg Suppers

basic chocolate cookies

MAKES ABOUT 40

We cut the cookie dough into assorted egg and bunny shapes using two- to four-inch cookie cutters.

   3 cups sifted all-purpose flour, plus more for work surface
1¼ cups unsweetened cocoa powder
   ½ teaspoon ground cinnamon
   ¼ teaspoon salt
1½ cups (3 sticks) unsalted butter, room temperature
2½ cups sifted confectioners' sugar
   2 large eggs, lightly beaten
   2 teaspoons pure vanilla extract
      Royal Icing, for decorating (optional; recipe follows)

1 Preheat oven to 350°F. Into a large bowl, sift together flour, cocoa, cinnamon, and salt; set aside. In the bowl of an electric mixer fitted with the paddle attachment, cream butter and sugar until light and fluffy. Beat in eggs and vanilla. Add flour mixture all at once, and beat on low speed until just combined. Divide dough in half, and flatten into disks. Wrap each in plastic, and chill at least 1 hour.

2 On a lightly floured surface, roll out one disk to ⅛ inch thick, dusting with flour as needed. Cut into shapes as desired. Transfer to baking sheets; chill until firm, about 15 minutes.

3 Bake until cookies are just firm to the touch, 10 to 12 minutes, rotating sheets halfway through. Transfer cookies to wire racks to cool completely. Repeat with remaining dough. Decorate cookies with icing, if desired.

from Marbleizing Eggs

royal icing

MAKES ABOUT 2½ CUPS

Meringue powder and gel-paste food coloring can be found at most baking-supply stores.

5 tablespoons meringue powder
1 pound confectioners' sugar (4 cups)
  Gel-paste food coloring

1 Combine meringue powder, sugar, and ⅓ cup water in the bowl of an electric mixer; whisk on low speed until smooth, about 1 minute. Add more water, 1 tablespoon at a time, until mixture is the consistency of honey.

2 Pour icing into a separate bowl for each color, and tint as desired. Use immediately.

Elke Wood's lemon squares

MAKES 1 DOZEN THREE-INCH SQUARES

This recipe comes from an aunt of Heidi Johannsen, senior associate food editor at Martha Stewart Living.

   ⅓ cup whole almonds
1¾ cups sifted all-purpose flour
   ⅓ cup sifted confectioners' sugar
   ¼ teaspoon salt
   ¾ cup (1½ sticks) chilled unsalted butter, cut into small pieces, plus more for baking dish
   1 teaspoon plus 1 tablespoon finely grated lemon zest
   2 cups granulated sugar
   4 large eggs, lightly beaten
   ½ cup freshly squeezed lemon juice (2 to 3 lemons)
   ½ teaspoon baking powder

1 Preheat oven to 350°F. Spread almonds in a single layer in a rimmed baking sheet; toast in oven until fragrant, stirring occasionally, about 10 minutes. Let cool, then coarsely chop.

2 Into a medium bowl, sift together 1½ cups flour, the confectioners' sugar, and salt. Cut in butter, 1 teaspoon zest, and almonds until mixture just clings together.

3 Press mixture into a lightly buttered 9-by-13-inch baking dish. Bake until just firm and lightly golden, about 20 minutes. Let cool slightly before filling.

4 In a large nonreactive bowl, stir together granulated sugar, eggs, lemon juice, baking powder, and remaining ¼ cup flour and tablespoon zest until combined. Pour into crust.

5 Bake until filling is set and lightly browned, 25 to 30 minutes. Transfer to a wire rack to cool. Cut into squares.

from Lemon Desserts

lemon, blackberry, and meringue parfait

SERVES 6 | **PHOTO ON PAGE 149**

      Swiss Meringue (recipe follows)
   1 cup crème fraîche
1½ cups Lemon Curd (page 49)
   1 cup ripe blackberries
   1 cup chilled heavy cream, whipped

1 Preheat oven to 200°F, with racks in upper and lower thirds. Line two large rimmed baking sheets with parchment paper. Fit a pastry bag with a star tip (Ateco #22), and fill with meringue. Pipe 12 to 18 long swirly shapes onto one of

the prepared sheets. Using a rubber spatula, gently spread remaining meringue ¾ inch thick onto the other.

2 Bake both sheets 20 minutes. Reduce oven temperature to 175°F; continue baking until meringue is dry but still white, 35 minutes more, rotating baking sheets halfway through. Transfer to a wire rack to cool completely. Set aside swirls; crumble meringue sheet.

3 Meanwhile, in a small bowl, combine crème fraîche and 1 cup lemon curd; refrigerate until ready to use, up to 1 day.

4 To assemble, layer crème-fraîche mixture, crumbled meringue, and blackberries in parfait glasses. Spoon some of the remaining ½ cup lemon curd into each glass. Top with whipped cream; garnish with meringue swirls.

from Lemon Desserts

Swiss meringue

MAKES 4 CUPS

4 large egg whites, room temperature
1 cup sugar
   Pinch cream of tartar
½ teaspoon pure vanilla extract

1 Whisk egg whites, sugar, and cream of tartar in the heat-proof bowl of an electric mixer set over a pan of simmering water until sugar has dissolved and whites are hot to the touch, 3 to 3½ minutes.

2 Remove from heat. Using paddle attachment, beat on low speed, gradually increasing to high, until stiff, glossy peaks form, about 10 minutes. Beat in vanilla. Use immediately.

lemon-blueberry petits fours

MAKES 15 | **PHOTO ON PAGE 149**

We baked these treats in mini brioche pans; small fluted tartlet pans with removable bottoms work just as well.

1¼ cups all-purpose flour
1½ tablespoons sugar, plus more for blueberries
½ cup (1 stick) chilled unsalted butter, cut into small pieces
1 large egg yolk
¼ cup ice water
15 fresh blueberries, rinsed
2 teaspoons meringue powder dissolved in 2 tablespoons warm water
1½ cups Lemon Curd (page 49)

1 Pulse flour and sugar in a food processor to combine. Add butter, and pulse until mixture resembles coarse meal. In a small bowl, lightly beat egg yolk and ice water. With the motor running, slowly pour egg mixture through the feed tube, and process until dough just comes together. Place on a piece of plastic wrap; flatten into a disk. Wrap; chill at least 1 hour.

2 Preheat oven to 350°F. On a clean work surface, roll out dough to ⅛ inch thick. Using a 3½-inch biscuit cutter, cut out 15 rounds. Fit rounds into mini brioche pans, pressing dough into bottom and up sides. Chill 30 minutes.

3 Remove tart shells from refrigerator. Line with parchment paper; fill with pie weights or dried beans. Bake 15 minutes; remove paper and weights. Continue baking until golden, about 10 minutes. Transfer pans to a wire rack to cool completely.

4 Using a toothpick, dip each blueberry in the meringue-powder mixture, and roll in sugar. Transfer to a parchment-lined baking sheet; let dry 30 minutes.

5 Remove tart shells from pans. Fill each shell with about 2 teaspoons lemon curd, and top with a sugared blueberry. Serve chilled or at room temperature.

from Lemon Desserts

lemon jellies

MAKES ABOUT 3 DOZEN

2½ tablespoons unflavored gelatin (2½ envelopes)
2 cups sugar, plus more for rolling
¾ cup freshly squeezed lemon juice (4 lemons)

1 In a small bowl, sprinkle gelatin over ¼ cup cold water, and stir to combine; let soften 5 minutes.

2 In a medium saucepan, combine sugar and ½ cup water. Place over medium heat, stirring until sugar has dissolved. Raise heat; without stirring, bring to a boil, washing down sides of pan with a wet pastry brush to prevent crystals from forming. Continue boiling until a candy thermometer registers 255°F. Remove from heat.

3 Whisk gelatin mixture and lemon juice into syrup in sauce-pan. Pour the mixture into an 8-inch square baking pan. Cover with plastic wrap, and let stand at room temperature until firm, at least 4 hours or overnight.

4 Invert pan onto a clean cutting board. Using a hot, wet knife, cut into squares. Dip gently in sugar, turning to coat.

from Lemon Desserts

lemon madeleines

MAKES 2 DOZEN | **PHOTO ON PAGE 149**

¾ cup (1½ sticks) unsalted butter, melted, plus more for pan

1½ cups sifted cake flour (not self-rising)

½ teaspoon baking powder

¼ teaspoon salt

3 large whole eggs

2 large egg yolks

¾ cup granulated sugar

1 teaspoon pure vanilla extract

2 tablespoons freshly squeezed lemon juice

2 tablespoons finely grated lemon zest (2 lemons)

Confectioners' sugar, for dusting (optional)

1 Preheat oven to 400°F. Lightly butter madeleine pans (you will need 24 molds), and set aside. Into a medium bowl, sift together the flour, baking powder, and salt. Set aside.

2 In the bowl of an electric mixer fitted with the paddle attachment, beat eggs, yolks, granulated sugar, vanilla, and lemon juice and zest on medium speed until thick and pale, about 5 minutes. Beat in melted butter. Using a rubber spatula, gently fold flour mixture into egg mixture; let rest 30 minutes at room temperature.

3 Pour batter into prepared pans, filling molds three-quarters full. Bake until cookies are golden and crisp around the edges, 7 to 8 minutes. Transfer pans to a wire rack to cool slightly before inverting cookies onto a serving platter. Dust with confectioners' sugar, if desired.

from Lemon Desserts

lemon pine-nut tart

MAKES 1 TEN-INCH TART | **PHOTO ON PAGE 151**

If you don't have Meyer lemons, you can use regular, thin-skinned lemons: Before you begin, blanch the slices for one minute. Increase the amount of granulated sugar to one cup, and let lemon slices macerate overnight.

5 Meyer lemons, sliced paper-thin

¾ cup granulated sugar

4 large egg yolks

¼ teaspoon salt

All-purpose flour, for work surface

Cornmeal Tart Dough (recipe follows)

2 tablespoons unsalted butter, cut into small pieces

1 large whole egg

1 tablespoon heavy cream

2 tablespoons pine nuts

Confectioners' sugar, for dusting

1 In a shallow nonreactive bowl, combine lemon slices and granulated sugar. Cover with plastic wrap; let macerate in refrigerator at least 4 hours or overnight.

2 In a medium bowl, lightly beat egg yolks and salt. Add lemon slices, and gently toss to coat.

3 On a lightly floured work surface, roll out one disk of cornmeal dough to a 12-inch round. Fit dough into a 10-inch fluted round tart pan with a removable bottom, pressing gently into edges and sides. Trim edges with a sharp paring knife.

4 Pour lemon filling into tart shell, distributing lemon slices evenly. Dot with butter pieces. Roll out remaining disk of dough to a 10-inch round. Carefully place dough on tart, pressing edges gently to adhere.

5 Preheat oven to 350°F. Whisk together egg and heavy cream in a small bowl; brush mixture evenly over top of dough. Sprinkle tart with pine nuts, and chill 30 minutes.

6 Place tart on a baking sheet, and bake until golden, about 40 minutes. Transfer to a wire rack to cool completely. Serve sprinkled with confectioners' sugar.

from Lemon Desserts

cornmeal tart dough

MAKES ENOUGH FOR 1 DOUBLE-CRUST TEN-INCH TART

This dough can be made ahead and refrigerated for up to
three days, or frozen for up to one month.

1¾ cups all-purpose flour
1 cup coarse yellow cornmeal
½ cup sugar
1 teaspoon baking powder
¼ teaspoon salt
½ cup (1 stick) chilled unsalted butter, cut into small pieces
2 large egg yolks
2 tablespoons ice water, plus more as needed

1 Place flour, cornmeal, sugar, baking powder, and salt in a
food processor; pulse to combine. Add butter, and process
until mixture resembles coarse meal. In a small bowl, lightly
beat egg yolks with 2 tablespoons ice water.

2 With machine running, pour egg mixture in a slow, steady
stream through the feed tube. Process until dough just holds
together, about 20 seconds. If dough feels dry, add more ice
water, 1 tablespoon at a time.

3 Divide dough in half, and flatten into disks. Wrap each in
plastic; chill at least 1 hour.

lemon poppy-seed lady cake

MAKES 1 EIGHT-INCH FOUR-LAYER CAKE | **PHOTO ON PAGE 150**

1 cup (2 sticks) unsalted butter, room temperature,
   plus more for pans
3 cups sifted cake flour (not self-rising), plus more for pans
1½ tablespoons baking powder
¼ teaspoon salt
1¾ cups sugar
1¼ teaspoons pure vanilla extract
2 tablespoons poppy seeds, plus more for garnish
1 tablespoon finely grated lemon zest
1 cup milk
8 large egg whites, room temperature
   Pinch cream of tartar
1 cup chilled heavy cream
1½ cups Lemon Curd (page 49)
   Seven-Minute Frosting (page 104)

1 Preheat oven to 350°F. Butter two 8-by-2-inch round cake
pans, and line bottoms with parchment paper. Butter parchment, and dust bottoms and sides with flour, tapping out

excess; set aside. Into a medium bowl, sift together flour,
baking powder, and salt twice; set aside.

2 In the bowl of an electric mixer fitted with the paddle attachment, cream butter until smooth. Gradually add 1½ cups
sugar; beat until light and fluffy, about 3 minutes. Beat in
vanilla, poppy seeds, and lemon zest. With mixer on low
speed, add flour mixture in two batches, alternating with the
milk; beat until thoroughly combined after each addition.
Scrape down sides of bowl with a rubber spatula, and beat
10 seconds more. Set aside.

3 In another mixer bowl, whisk egg whites and cream of tartar on low speed until foamy. Increase speed to medium-high;
gradually add remaining ¼ cup sugar, beating until peaks are
just stiff. Gently fold whites into batter; do not overmix.

4 Divide batter between prepared pans; bake until golden
and a cake tester inserted in centers comes out clean, about
40 minutes. Transfer pans to a wire rack to cool completely.
To remove cakes, invert onto plates; peel off parchment paper,
and reinvert so top sides are up.

5 Meanwhile, make filling: In a small bowl, whip heavy cream
to soft peaks. Fold in lemon curd; cover with plastic wrap, and
refrigerate until chilled and firm, at least 2 hours.

6 To assemble cake, use a serrated knife to trim tops of both
cakes to make level, if desired. Slice each in half horizontally
to make a total of four layers. Brush away crumbs from tops
of layers with a pastry brush.

7 Place one of the bottom layers on a serving platter; spread
with 1 cup lemon filling. Top with another cake layer, and
spread with 1 cup filling. Repeat with another cake layer and
filling; top with remaining cake layer. Cover entire cake with
plastic wrap, and carefully transfer to the refrigerator, steady-
ing it with your hands to keep the layers from sliding. Chill
until the filling is firm, at least 2 hours.

8 When ready to serve, spread frosting over top and sides of
cake with an offset spatula. Garnish with poppy seeds.

from Lemon Desserts

seven-minute frosting

MAKES ENOUGH FOR 1 EIGHT-INCH FOUR-LAYER CAKE

1¾ cups sugar
2 tablespoons light corn syrup
6 large egg whites

1   In a small saucepan, combine 1½ cups sugar with corn syrup and ¼ cup water. Place over medium heat, stirring until sugar has dissolved. Raise heat, and bring to a boil, washing down sides of pan with a wet pastry brush to prevent crystals from forming. Continue boiling until a candy thermometer registers 230°F, 5 to 7 minutes.

2   Meanwhile, in the bowl of an electric mixer, whisk egg whites on medium speed until soft peaks form. Gradually beat in remaining ¼ cup sugar. As soon as syrup reaches 230°F, reduce mixer speed to medium-low. Carefully pour syrup in a stream down side of mixing bowl. Beat until frosting is cool, thick, and glossy, 5 to 10 minutes. Use immediately.

lemon sponge pudding

SERVES 6 | PHOTO ON PAGE 149

For individual servings, bake the pudding in six six-ounce ramekins; reduce cooking time to twenty-five minutes.

3 tablespoons unsalted butter, room temperature, plus more for baking dish
⅔ cup granulated sugar
¼ teaspoon salt
3 large eggs, separated
3 tablespoons all-purpose flour
1 cup milk
6 tablespoons freshly squeezed lemon juice (2 lemons)
2 tablespoons finely grated lemon zest (2 lemons)
Confectioners' sugar, for dusting

1   Preheat oven to 325°F. Butter a shallow 9-inch round glass or ceramic baking dish; set aside. In a large bowl, stir together butter, granulated sugar, and salt. Stir in yolks. Add flour, milk, and lemon juice and zest; mix until incorporated.

2   In the bowl of an electric mixer, whisk egg whites until stiff but not dry peaks form. Using a rubber spatula, gently fold egg whites into butter mixture.

3   Ladle batter into prepared dish. Set dish in a roasting pan; pour boiling water into pan to reach halfway up sides of dish. Bake until just set and lightly golden, 30 to 35 minutes. Carefully remove baking dish from roasting pan; let cool slightly. Dust with confectioners' sugar, and serve warm.

from Lemon Desserts

mango-pineapple buckle

SERVES 4 | PHOTO ON PAGE 157

½ cup (1 stick) unsalted butter, room temperature, plus more for baking dish
1 small or ½ medium pineapple (about 1¾ pounds), peeled, cored, and cut into ½-inch pieces
2 ripe mangoes, peeled, pitted, and cut into ½-inch pieces
2 tablespoons dark-brown sugar
¾ cup plus 2 tablespoons all-purpose flour
1 teaspoon ground cinnamon
½ teaspoon salt
¼ teaspoon baking soda
½ cup granulated sugar
1 teaspoon pure vanilla extract
2 large eggs

1   Preheat oven to 350°F. Butter a 2-quart baking dish. Toss pineapple, mangoes, and brown sugar together in a bowl; set aside. In a separate bowl, whisk together flour, cinnamon, salt, and baking soda. Set aside.

2   In the bowl of an electric mixer fitted with the paddle attachment, beat butter and granulated sugar until light and fluffy, about 2 minutes. Beat in vanilla. Add eggs one at a time, beating well after each. Add flour mixture; beat until just combined. Measure out 1 cup fruit mixture; fold the rest into batter.

3   Spread batter evenly in prepared baking dish; sprinkle reserved fruit mixture over the top. Bake until golden on top and a cake tester inserted in the center comes out clean, 45 to 50 minutes. Serve warm.

from What's for Dinner?

Meyer lemon gelato

MAKES ABOUT 1 QUART | PHOTO ON PAGE 148

This tangy gelato is delicious on its own, but we like to cradle scoops in store-bought brioche. You can make this gelato with regular lemons; look for ones with thin skins.

¾ cup freshly squeezed Meyer lemon juice (5 or 6 medium lemons)

2 cups milk

Grated zest of 1 Meyer lemon

5 large egg yolks

1 cup sugar

1 cup heavy cream

1 In a small saucepan, cook lemon juice over medium-low heat until reduced by three-quarters, about 30 minutes. Remove from heat; let cool completely.

2 In a medium heavy-bottom saucepan, bring milk and lemon zest just to a simmer over medium heat. Remove from heat; cover, and steep 30 minutes.

3 In the bowl of an electric mixer fitted with the paddle attachment, beat yolks and sugar on medium-high speed until very thick and pale, about 5 minutes.

4 Prepare an ice bath; set aside. Return milk mixture to a simmer; whisk half into egg-yolk mixture. Return mixture to saucepan with remaining milk mixture. Cook over low heat, stirring constantly with a wooden spoon, until thick enough to coat the back of the spoon.

5 Remove pan from heat, and immediately stir in cream. Pass mixture through a fine sieve into a medium bowl set in the ice bath; let stand, stirring frequently, until thoroughly chilled. Stir in reduced lemon juice.

6 Freeze mixture in an ice-cream maker according to manufacturer's instructions. Store in an airtight container in the freezer until ready to serve, up to 1 week.

from Lemon Desserts

pastiera with strawberry sauce

SERVES 8 | PHOTO ON PAGE 152

Pastiera is a traditional Italian Easter cake.

1 quart milk

¾ cup Arborio rice

1 teaspoon ground cinnamon

½ teaspoon coarse salt

1 vanilla bean, split lengthwise and scraped

1¼ cups granulated sugar

Unsalted butter, for pan

All-purpose flour, for pan

3 pounds fresh ricotta cheese, drained overnight or at least 3 hours

3 whole large eggs plus 3 large yolks, lightly beaten

Confectioners' sugar, for dusting

Strawberry Sauce (recipe follows)

1 Bring milk to a boil in a large saucepan over medium-high heat. Stir in rice, cinnamon, salt, and vanilla bean and scrapings. Reduce heat to medium-low; cook, stirring occasionally with a wooden spoon, until rice is very tender and has absorbed all liquid, about 30 minutes.

2 Remove pan from heat. Stir in ¾ cup granulated sugar until dissolved. Cover; let cool completely, stirring occasionally. Discard vanilla pod.

3 Preheat oven to 350°F. Butter and flour an 8-inch springform pan. In a large bowl, combine the rice mixture, ricotta, beaten eggs, and remaining ½ cup sugar; gently stir with a rubber spatula. Pour into prepared pan.

4 Bake until golden on top and almost set in the center, 65 to 70 minutes; cover with foil if starting to brown too much. Transfer pan to a wire rack to cool completely.

5 To serve, run a knife around edge of cake to loosen. Remove ring; transfer cake to a platter. Dust with confectioners' sugar, and serve with sauce.

from Dessert of the Month

strawberry sauce

MAKES 1½ CUPS

1 pint strawberries, hulled and halved

2 tablespoons sugar

2 teaspoons freshly squeezed lemon juice

Cook all ingredients in a medium nonreactive saucepan over medium-low heat, stirring occasionally, until strawberries are soft, 5 to 7 minutes. Serve warm or at room temperature.

rose-water sherbet

MAKES 2½ CUPS

If you're using geranium petals, buy them from a reliable source and make sure they are pesticide-free.

¼ cup sugar

2¼ cups buttermilk

½ cup corn syrup

1 teaspoon rose water, plus more for garnish

Roasted pistachios, coarsely chopped, for garnish

Edible geranium petals, for garnish (optional)

1 In a small saucepan over medium heat, dissolve sugar in ¼ cup buttermilk. Pour into a bowl with remaining 2 cups buttermilk. Stir in corn syrup and rose water.

2 Freeze in an ice-cream maker according to manufacturer's instructions. Transfer to a loaf pan; cover with plastic wrap, and freeze at least 1 hour or up to 1 week.

3 To serve, scoop sherbet into bowls; garnish with a few drops of rose water, chopped pistachios, and flower petals.

from Easy Entertaining: A Mezze Menu

sugar cookies

MAKES ABOUT 40

We cut the dough into assorted shapes using two- to four-inch cookie cutters; chilling the cut dough helps the cookies hold their shapes while baking.

4 cups sifted all-purpose flour, plus more for work surface

1 teaspoon baking powder

½ teaspoon salt

1 cup (2 sticks) unsalted butter, room temperature

2 cups sugar

2 large eggs

2 teaspoons pure vanilla extract

Royal Icing, for decorating (optional; page 100)

1 Preheat oven to 325°F. Into a large bowl, sift together flour, baking powder, and salt; set aside. In the bowl of an electric mixer fitted with the paddle attachment, cream butter and sugar until light and fluffy. Beat in eggs and vanilla. Add flour mixture all at once; beat on low speed until just combined. Divide dough in half, and flatten into two disks. Wrap each in plastic; chill at least 30 minutes.

2 On a lightly floured work surface, roll out one disk to ⅛ inch thick. Cut into shapes as desired. Transfer to baking sheets; chill until firm, about 15 minutes.

3 Bake until edges are just starting to brown, 10 to 12 minutes, rotating sheets halfway through. Transfer cookies to wire racks to cool completely. Repeat with remaining dough. Decorate cookies with royal icing, if desired.

from Marbleizing Eggs

MISCELLANEOUS

candied lemon rind

MAKES ABOUT 75 STRIPS

You can use this candied fruit to decorate cakes, tarts, and other pastries; they are also delicious eaten on their own.

Rind of 3 large lemons, plus juice of 1 lemon

2½ cups sugar, plus more for rolling

1 Slice rind into 2-by-¼-inch strips. Blanch in a pot of boiling water three times; start with fresh water each time.

2 In a medium heavy-bottom saucepan, bring sugar and 3 cups water to a boil, stirring to dissolve sugar. Add lemon juice and strips, and return to a boil. Reduce heat to low; cook until strips are translucent, 1 to 1½ hours. Let cool in liquid.

3 Using a slotted spoon, transfer strips to a wire rack; spread out in a single layer. Let stand until completely dry, about 2 hours. Roll in sugar, coating thoroughly.

from Lemon Desserts

phyllo nests

MAKES 1 DOZEN

These edible bird's nests make charming Easter treats when filled with jelly beans. Kataifi, preshredded phyllo dough, is sold frozen at Greek grocers and in large supermarkets.

3 tablespoons unsalted butter, melted, plus more for tin

8 ounces kataifi (½ package), thawed

4 teaspoons sugar

1 teaspoon ground cinnamon (optional)

Jelly beans, for serving

1 Preheat oven to 375°F. Brush a 12-cup standard muffin tin with butter. Pull phyllo into 1-inch-thick bundles; cut bundles into 2-inch lengths. Place in a bowl; separate into a loose pile with fingers. Toss with butter, sugar, and cinnamon, if using.

2 Divide among prepared cups; press into bottom and up sides. Cook until golden and crisp around the edges, 15 to 20 minutes. Let cool; fill with jelly beans.

from Good Things

May

buttermilk vichyssoise with watercress

SERVES 6

We've added the peppery snap of watercress and the tang of buttermilk to this traditional soup.

3 tablespoons unsalted butter

4 leeks, white and pale-green parts only, halved lengthwise then thinly sliced into half-moons, washed well

3 large white potatoes, peeled and cut into 1-inch pieces

4½ cups Basic Chicken Stock (page 17) or low-sodium canned chicken broth, plus more for thinning, if needed

3 cups loosely packed watercress leaves

Coarse salt and freshly ground white pepper

1 cup half-and-half

1 cup buttermilk

1   Melt butter in a medium stockpot over medium-low heat. Add leeks; cook, covered, until tender, about 15 minutes. Add potatoes, stock, and 2 cups water. Bring to a boil; reduce heat, and simmer until potatoes are tender, about 20 minutes. Let cool completely; stir in 2 cups watercress.

2   Working in batches, if necessary, so as not to fill more than halfway, purée soup in a blender until smooth. Transfer puréed soup to a large bowl. Season with salt and white pepper. Stir in half-and-half; cover with plastic wrap, and chill at least 1 hour.

3   When ready to serve, stir in buttermilk; season again with salt and pepper as desired. If necessary, thin the soup with a bit more chicken stock or water to achieve desired consistency. Garnish with remaining cup watercress leaves.

from Backyard Picnic

celery root remoulade

SERVES 4 | **PHOTO ON PAGE 139**

Celery root, also called celeriac, tastes like a cross between celery and parsley; choose a small, firm root.

¼ cup mayonnaise

¼ cup crème fraîche

2 tablespoons freshly squeezed lemon juice

1 teaspoon Dijon mustard

12 cornichons, minced (about ⅓ cup)

1 tablespoon finely chopped fresh flat-leaf parsley

1 teaspoon finely chopped fresh tarragon

1 teaspoon capers, drained and chopped

Coarse salt and freshly ground pepper

1 celery root (about 1 pound), peeled and julienned

1 head Boston lettuce, leaves separated, washed

In a medium bowl, whisk together mayonnaise, crème fraîche, lemon juice, and mustard. Add cornichons, parsley, tarragon, and capers; season with salt and pepper. Whisk to combine. Fold celery root into dressing; serve atop lettuce leaves.

from Bistro Salads

empanadas

MAKES 2 DOZEN | **PHOTO ON PAGE 137**

Our empanadas are fried, but they may also be baked in a 375 degree oven until crisp and browned, about fifteen minutes. Formed but uncooked empanadas can be frozen in an airtight container for up to one month; thaw in the refrigerator before cooking.

- 1 whole chicken breast (1 pound), skin removed
- 1 small white onion, halved
- 1 dried bay leaf
- 1 poblano chile
- 1½ quarts (48 ounces) vegetable oil
- 2 garlic cloves, crushed
- ¾ teaspoon ground cumin
- ¼ teaspoon ground canela (Mexican cinnamon) or regular cinnamon
- 4 canned plum tomatoes, coarsely chopped
- 2 canned chipotle chiles in adobo, coarsely chopped
  Coarse salt and freshly ground pepper
- 2 tablespoons coarsely chopped fresh cilantro
- 1 tablespoon pepitas (pumpkin seeds), toasted and coarsely chopped
  Empanada Dough (recipe follows)
- ½ cup shredded queso blanco or Monterey Jack cheese
  All-purpose flour, for fork
- ¼ cup sugar, for sprinkling
  Crema pura or sour cream, for serving (optional)

1 Make filling: Place chicken breast, half the onion, and the bay leaf in a medium saucepan. Add enough cold water to cover; bring to a boil over medium-high heat. Reduce heat to medium-low; poach chicken until cooked through, about 15 minutes. Transfer chicken to a plate; reserve 1 cup cooking liquid, and discard onion and bay leaf. When chicken is cool enough to handle, shred meat with a fork; set aside.

2 Roast poblano chile directly over a gas flame, turning as each side blackens and blisters. (Alternatively, roast chile on a baking sheet under the broiler.) Transfer to a bowl, and cover with plastic wrap; let steam 10 minutes. Using a paper towel, peel off and discard charred skin. Remove stem, seeds, and ribs, and discard. Slice chile into ¼-inch-thick strips; set aside.

3 Finely chop remaining onion half. Heat 2 teaspoons oil in a medium saucepan over medium heat. Add chopped onion and garlic; cook, stirring occasionally, until soft and translucent, about 3 minutes. Stir in cumin and canela; cook 1 minute. Add shredded chicken, tomatoes, chipotles, poblano, and reserved cooking liquid. Reduce heat to medium-low; cook, stirring occasionally, until liquid has thickened, about 25 minutes. Remove from heat. Season with salt and pepper; stir in cilantro and pepitas. Set aside to cool.

4 Make empanadas: Break off a 1½-inch ball of dough. On a clean work surface, roll out dough to about ⅛ inch thick. Using a 3½-inch cookie cutter or inverted glass, cut out a round of dough. Repeat with remaining dough, rerolling scraps once to cut out more rounds.

5 Place 1 teaspoon filling in the center of each round; sprinkle with cheese. Using a pastry brush, moisten edges of dough with water; fold dough over to seal, pressing gently. Crimp edges with a fork, dipping the tines of the fork periodically in flour to prevent them from sticking to the dough.

6 Pour enough of the remaining oil into a medium saucepan so it is 2 inches deep. Heat over medium heat until oil registers 375°F on a deep-fry thermometer. Working in batches, carefully add a few empanadas to the hot oil; fry until golden, turning once, about 1 minute. Using a slotted spoon, transfer empanadas to a paper-towel–lined baking sheet to drain. While still hot, sprinkle tops with sugar. Serve immediately with crema pura on the side, if desired.

from Celebrating Cinco de Mayo

empanada dough

MAKES ENOUGH FOR 2 DOZEN

- 2 cups all-purpose flour, plus more for work surface
- ¾ cup fine cornmeal or masa harina
- 2 teaspoons sugar
- ½ teaspoon salt
- 3 tablespoons pure vegetable shortening
- 2 large egg yolks

In a food processor, pulse flour, cornmeal, sugar, and salt to combine. Add shortening, and process 5 seconds. Add yolks and ¾ cup water; process until dough is very soft, about 5 minutes. Turn out onto a lightly floured work surface, and knead until smooth. Cover dough with plastic, and let rest 30 minutes before using.

ham-and-cheese tartines

SERVES 6 | PHOTOS ON PAGES 140 AND 141

This recipe works equally well with other cheeses—try a mild fontina or Comté in place of the Gruyère. For the bread, choose a large, oval loaf of sourdough.

½ pound Gruyère cheese, grated on the large holes of a box grater (about 2 cups)

½ pound cream cheese

2 teaspoons fresh thyme leaves

Coarse salt and freshly ground pepper

6 slices (½ inch thick) sourdough bread

4 ounces cooked ham, cut into 12 slices

3 or 4 red radishes, trimmed and very thinly sliced

1 Preheat oven to 400°F, with rack in center. In a food processor, pulse half the Gruyère with all the cream cheese until smooth, about 30 seconds. Transfer to a small bowl. Fold in the thyme; season with salt and pepper. Set aside.

2 Place bread on a baking sheet; toast in oven until golden brown, about 12 minutes, flipping halfway through.

3 Spread reserved cheese mixture on each slice of toast, dividing evenly; sprinkle with remaining Gruyère. Place 2 slices of ham on each toast. Arrange radishes on top, and serve.

from Backyard Picnic

mushroom crostini

SERVES 4

1 small (or ½ large) baguette, cut into 12 slices (about ¼ inch thick)

2 tablespoons extra-virgin olive oil, plus more for brushing

Coarse salt and freshly ground pepper

1 shallot, thinly sliced

8 ounces chanterelles or other wild mushrooms, trimmed and coarsely chopped

6 ounces fresh goat cheese, cut into 12 rounds (about ¼ inch thick)

Snipped fresh chives, for garnish

1 Preheat oven to 375°F, with rack in center. Place bread on a baking sheet. Brush top of rounds with oil; season with salt and pepper. Toast in oven until golden, 8 to 10 minutes. Set aside to cool.

2 Heat oil in a medium skillet over medium heat. Add shallot; cook, stirring, until soft, about 3 minutes. Add mushrooms; cook, stirring occasionally, until tender and released juices have evaporated, 7 to 10 minutes. Season with salt and pepper.

3 Place a round of goat cheese on top of each crostini; top with a tablespoon of mushroom mixture. Serve warm, garnished with chives.

from What's for Dinner?

Niçoise tartines with peperonata

SERVES 6 | PHOTO ON PAGE 140

Traditional peperonata is an Italian mixture of stewed peppers, tomatoes, onions, and garlic. In our version, it is combined with classic Provençal ingredients to make a flavorful topping for toast.

2 tablespoons extra-virgin olive oil

1 large onion, thinly sliced

3 garlic cloves

3 red bell peppers, ribs and seeds removed, julienned

Pinch of hot paprika, plus more to taste

Coarse salt and freshly ground black pepper

6 slices (½ inch thick) sourdough bread, cut from an oval loaf

2 large eggs

1 can (about 6 ounces) tuna packed in oil, drained

Fleur de sel or sea salt (optional)

3 teaspoons capers, drained, for garnish

1 lemon, for garnish

1 Preheat oven to 400°F, with rack in center. Heat oil in a large nonstick sauté pan. Add onion and garlic; sauté over medium heat, stirring frequently, until lightly browned, about 8 minutes. Add bell peppers and paprika; cook until peppers are soft and juicy, about 30 minutes. Season with salt and black pepper.

2 Meanwhile, place bread on a baking sheet; toast in oven until golden brown, about 12 minutes, flipping halfway through.

3 Prepare an ice bath; set aside. Place eggs in a medium saucepan; add enough water to cover by about 1 inch. Bring to a full boil; cook 1 minute. Turn off heat; cover, and let stand 12 minutes. Transfer eggs to ice bath, and let sit until cool. Peel eggs, and slice each about ¼ inch thick.

4 Spread the red-pepper mixture over slices of toast; top with tuna, dividing evenly. Place a few slices of egg on top of the tuna. Season with fleur de sel, if desired, and black pepper. Garnish with capers; zest the lemon over the tops of the tartines just before serving.

from Backyard Picnic

roasted cherry-tomato tartines

SERVES 6 | **PHOTO ON PAGE 140**

If you like, squeeze the roasted garlic from its skin, and spread on the toasted bread before the tapenade. Choose a large, oval loaf of sourdough.

1 pint mixed cherry tomatoes
4 to 6 garlic cloves (unpeeled)
2 tablespoons extra-virgin olive oil
2 or 3 sprigs thyme or rosemary
  Coarse salt and freshly ground pepper
6 slices (½ inch thick) sourdough bread
7 ounces (about ¾ cup) store-bought tapenade
8 ounces mild goat cheese
1 cup loosely packed fresh basil leaves, for garnish

1 Preheat oven to 450°F, with rack in center. In a large cast-iron skillet, toss tomatoes with garlic, oil, and herbs; season with salt and pepper. Spread tomatoes in an even layer.

2 Roast in the oven, stirring occasionally, until tomatoes are soft and slightly blackened, 25 to 30 minutes. Let cool.

3 Reduce oven temperature to 400°F. Place bread on a baking sheet, and toast in oven until golden brown, about 12 minutes, flipping halfway through.

4 Spread 1 to 2 tablespoons tapenade over each toast. Divide the goat cheese evenly among toasts; spoon tomatoes and their juices on top. Garnish with basil leaves, and serve.

from Backyard Picnic

SALADS

endive with pears, walnuts, and Roquefort

SERVES 4 | **PHOTO ON PAGE 139**

½ cup walnut halves
2 tablespoons sherry vinegar
¼ teaspoon coarse salt
¼ teaspoon freshly ground pepper
¼ cup extra-virgin olive oil
2 tablespoons walnut oil
1 ripe but firm pear
2 large heads endive (about 13 ounces), outer leaves reserved, remaining leaves sliced into ½-inch pieces
½ cup crumbled Roquefort cheese

1 Preheat oven to 350°F. Spread walnuts in a single layer in a rimmed baking sheet; toast in oven until fragrant, stirring occasionally, about 10 minutes.

2 Make dressing: In a small bowl, whisk together vinegar, salt, and pepper. Whisk in olive oil and then walnut oil in a slow, steady stream until emulsified; set aside.

3 Core and slice pear ¼ inch thick. Combine in a medium bowl with endive, walnuts, and cheese. Drizzle with dressing; gently toss to coat. Divide evenly among four salad bowls. Serve immediately.

from Bistro Salads

finger salad with anchovy vinaigrette

SERVES 6 | PHOTO ON PAGE 141

1 teaspoon Dijon mustard

6 anchovy fillets, rinsed and mashed

2 tablespoons freshly squeezed lemon juice

⅓ cup extra-virgin olive oil

1 tablespoon finely chopped fresh flat-leaf parsley

Freshly ground pepper

Mixed baby lettuces, for serving

In a food processor, combine mustard, anchovies, and lemon juice; process until smooth. With machine running, add oil in a slow, steady stream through the feed tube until emulsified. Stir in parsley; season with pepper. Serve in small bowls, with lettuces on the side for dipping.

from Backyard Picnic

frisée with lardons and poached eggs

SERVES 4

2 tablespoons white vinegar

4 large eggs

1 large head of frisée (about 5 ounces)

6 ounces (about 4 slices) thick-cut bacon, cut crosswise into ¼-inch-thick lardons

3 tablespoons finely chopped shallot (1 shallot)

¼ cup red-wine vinegar

Coarse salt and freshly ground pepper

1 Bring a large, deep skillet of water to a boil. Reduce to a simmer; add white vinegar. Fill a saucepan with warm water; set aside. Break an egg into a small bowl; holding bowl just over vinegar water, gently slide egg into water. Repeat with remaining eggs. Poach about 2 minutes (longer for firm eggs). Use a slotted spoon to transfer eggs to pan of warm water.

2 Place frisée in a large bowl; set aside. Cook bacon, stirring occasionally, in a medium sauté pan over medium-high heat until golden brown, about 3 minutes. Add shallot; cook 1 minute. Add red-wine vinegar, and bring to a boil, swirling to combine. Pour over frisée. Season with salt and pepper, and toss to coat evenly.

3 Divide salad among four plates. Drain eggs; place one on top of each salad. Season eggs with salt and pepper, and serve.

from Bistro Salads

warm goat-cheese salad

SERVES 4

2½ tablespoons balsamic vinegar

½ teaspoon Dijon mustard

¼ cup extra-virgin olive oil

Coarse salt and freshly ground pepper

6 ounces (about 6 cups) mesclun greens

1 baguette, cut into 12 slices (about ¼ inch thick)

8 ounces fresh goat cheese, cut into 12 rounds (about ¼ inch thick)

1 In a small bowl, whisk vinegar with mustard. Add oil in a slow, steady stream until emulsified. Season with salt and pepper. Place greens in a large bowl; set aside.

2 Meanwhile, heat broiler. Place bread on a baking sheet; top each with a goat-cheese round. Toast until bread is golden brown and cheese has started to melt, 2 to 3 minutes.

3 Drizzle greens with vinaigrette, and toss to coat. Divide among four plates. Place three toasts on each salad; serve.

from Bistro Salads

grilled mushroom burger with white-bean purée

MAKES 4 | PHOTO ON PAGE 143

We topped these burgers with smoked cheddar cheese, but you can use another type of cheese or omit it entirely. To clean the mushroom caps, brush away grit and wipe them with a damp paper towel; do not rinse or soak them because they will remain soggy even after cooking.

2 large garlic cloves, minced

2 tablespoons chopped fresh thyme

1 cup cooked or canned cannellini beans, drained and rinsed

2 tablespoons extra-virgin olive oil

Freshly ground pepper

8 large portobello mushroom caps (about 1 pound), cleaned

4 teaspoons balsamic vinegar

2 large red onions (about 1 pound), cut into thin rings

4 whole-grain hamburger buns

2 ounces smoked cheddar cheese, thinly sliced into 4 equal portions

½ small bunch arugula (about 2½ ounces), rinsed well and dried

Olive-oil cooking spray

1 Heat a grill or grill pan over medium heat. In a food processor, combine about ½ teaspoon garlic, 1 tablespoon thyme, cannellini beans, and 1 teaspoon oil; process to form a smooth, spreadable paste. If mixture is too thick, add 1 teaspoon water. Season with pepper, and pulse to combine. Set aside.

2 Combine remaining garlic, thyme, and oil in a shallow bowl. Place mushroom caps in garlic mixture, and turn to coat. Season with pepper; drizzle with vinegar.

3 Place onion slices on a plate, and lightly coat each side with cooking spray. Grill slices until undersides are lightly charred, about 3 minutes. Flip onions, and continue grilling until tender and charred on the other side, about 3 minutes more. Transfer onions to a clean plate; keep warm.

4 Place mushrooms on the grill, stem side up, working in batches if necessary. Grill until undersides are browned and juices have begun to collect in the centers, about 5 minutes. Flip mushrooms, and continue cooking until the other sides are browned and centers are tender, about 4 minutes more.

5 Place hamburger buns, cut sides down, on the grill; cook until warm and toasted. Transfer to a work surface. Spread ¼ cup bean purée on the bottom half of each bun, and top with two grilled mushroom caps. Top burgers with sliced cheese, grilled onions, and a small handful of arugula; top with roll halves, and serve.

PER SERVING: 327 CALORIES, 14 G FAT, 15 MG CHOLESTEROL, 40 G CARBOHYDRATE, 358 MG SODIUM, 14 G PROTEIN, 7 G FIBER

from Fit to Eat: Meatless Main Dishes

grilled pork paillards

SERVES 4 | PHOTO ON PAGE 142

4 boneless pork chops (6 ounces and about ¾ inch thick each)

¼ cup balsamic vinegar

¼ cup extra-virgin olive oil

Coarse salt and freshly ground pepper

Fresh basil, for garnish

Cherry tomatoes, halved or quartered, for garnish

1 Place a pork chop between two layers of plastic wrap on a work surface. Using a meat pounder, pound to an even ¼-inch thickness. Repeat with remaining chops. Transfer to a large resealable plastic bag or nonmetal container. Add vinegar and oil. Marinate, covered, in refrigerator 15 minutes.

2 Meanwhile, heat a grill or grill pan to medium-high heat. Remove pork from marinade; season with salt and pepper. Grill until cooked through and browned on both sides, about 1 minute per side. Serve hot, garnished with basil and tomatoes.

from What's for Dinner?

ricotta cheese torta

MAKES 1 SEVEN-INCH TORTA; SERVES 4 | **PHOTO ON PAGE 146**

This delicate torta makes a lovely luncheon dish. Served with our Warm Bean, Snap Pea, and Tomato Salad (page 118), it is perfect for a springtime supper. To drain the ricotta cheese, place it in a fine sieve lined with cheesecloth and set over a deep bowl; let stand at least one hour at room temperature or overnight in the refrigerator.

2 to 3 tablespoons fine breadcrumbs, preferably homemade

3 large eggs

¼ cup coarsely chopped fresh flat-leaf parsley

1 tablespoon coarsely chopped fresh marjoram

1 tablespoon coarsely chopped fresh mint

2 teaspoons finely grated lemon zest

2 pounds part-skim ricotta, drained

¾ teaspoon coarse salt

  Freshly ground pepper

  Vegetable-oil cooking spray

1 Preheat oven to 400°F, with rack in center. Lightly coat a 7-inch round springform pan with cooking spray. Sprinkle with breadcrumbs, coating evenly.

2 In a medium bowl, whisk together eggs, parsley, marjoram, mint, and zest. Add ricotta and salt; season with pepper. Stir to combine. Pour into prepared pan. Bake until deep golden brown and firm to the touch, about 1 hour.

3 Remove pan from oven; place pan on a plate to catch juices. Let stand until torta pulls away from sides, about 10 minutes. Remove ring from pan, and serve torta warm or at room temperature.

PER SERVING: 369 CALORIES, 21 G FAT, 211 MG CHOLESTEROL, 14 G CARBOHYDRATE, 697 MG SODIUM, 30 G PROTEIN, 0 G FIBER

from Fit to Eat: Meatless Main Dishes

vegetable biryani

SERVES 6

½ teaspoon saffron threads, crumbled

¼ cup nonfat milk

1½ cups basmati rice, soaked in cold water 10 minutes and drained

3 tablespoons canola oil

2 large onions, thinly sliced

1½ teaspoons whole cumin seeds

¾ teaspoon ground cardamom

1 whole cinnamon stick, broken into 4 pieces

½ teaspoon ground cloves

1 tablespoon minced fresh ginger

2 garlic cloves, minced

3 plum tomatoes (about ½ pound), peeled, seeded, and chopped

6 ounces green beans, cut into thirds (about 1½ cups)

½ head cauliflower, cut into florets (about 2 cups)

2 carrots, cut into ½-inch pieces (about ¾ cup)

1 cup cooked or canned chickpeas, drained and rinsed

1½ teaspoons coarse salt

1 cup fresh or frozen peas

2 ounces (about ½ cup) cashews

1 Preheat oven to 350°F. Combine saffron and milk in a small bowl; set aside. Place rice in a medium saucepan with 1½ cups cold water. Bring to a boil over high heat, stir once, then reduce heat to low. Cover and simmer until rice has absorbed all the water, about 20 minutes.

2 Meanwhile, heat 2 tablespoons oil in a large sauté pan over medium-high heat. Add onions; cook, stirring, until golden brown and slightly crisp, about 10 minutes. Remove half the onions from pan, and reserve. Add remaining tablespoon oil to pan along with the spices, ginger, garlic, and tomatoes. Cook, stirring, until fragrant, about 2 minutes.

3 Pour 1 cup water into pan; bring to a boil over medium-low heat. Add green beans, cauliflower, carrots, chickpeas, and salt; reduce heat to a simmer. Cook, covered, until vegetables are crisp-tender, about 10 minutes. Add peas; cook until bright green, about 2 minutes. Remove from heat.

4 Spread one-third of the rice in a 3½-quart heavy-bottom casserole or baking dish with a tight-fitting lid. Drizzle half the saffron milk over rice. Using a slotted spoon, transfer half the vegetable mixture to the casserole, leaving liquid behind. Spread another one-third of rice on top; drizzle with remaining saffron milk. Repeat with remaining vegetables and rice. Spread reserved onions over the top; sprinkle with cashews.

5 Cover, and bake until rice and vegetables are heated through, about 30 minutes. Remove from oven; let cool slightly before serving.

PER SERVING: 430 CALORIES, 14 G FAT, 0 MG CHOLESTEROL, 67 G CARBOHYDRATE, 516 MG SODIUM, 12 G PROTEIN, 8 G FIBER

from Fit to Eat: Meatless Main Dishes

whole-wheat pasta with lentils, spinach, and leeks

SERVES 4 | **PHOTO ON PAGE 147**

If you like, grate Parmesan cheese over the pasta just before serving, or offer grated cheese on the side.

2 cups (14 ounces) French green lentils, picked over and rinsed

2 garlic cloves

1 dried bay leaf

1 pound small whole-wheat chioccciole or other small tubular pasta

2 tablespoons extra-virgin olive oil

4 leeks (about 1¾ pounds), white and pale-green parts only, sliced into ⅛-inch rounds and washed well

1 teaspoon chopped fresh thyme

1½ teaspoons coarse salt

Freshly ground black pepper

8 ounces baby spinach, washed

1 In a medium saucepan, combine lentils, 1 garlic clove, and the bay leaf. Add enough cold water to cover by 2 inches. Bring to a boil over medium-high heat. Reduce heat to medium-low, and simmer until lentils are tender, 20 to 25 minutes. Drain, and discard garlic clove and bay leaf; set lentils aside.

2 Bring a large pot of water to a boil. Add pasta; cook until al dente according to package instructions, about 7 minutes. Drain pasta, reserving 1 cup cooking liquid.

3 Meanwhile, mince remaining garlic clove. In a large sauté pan, heat oil over medium heat. Add garlic, leeks, and thyme; cook, stirring occasionally, until leeks are soft but not browned, about 5 minutes. Add lentils and salt; season with pepper.

4 Add spinach and reserved cooking liquid to pan; toss to wilt spinach, about 2 minutes. Place pasta in a large bowl. Pour spinach mixture over pasta; toss to combine. Serve.

PER SERVING: 638 CALORIES, 9 G FAT, 0 MG CHOLESTEROL, 120 G CARBOHYDRATE, 793 MG SODIUM, 29 G PROTEIN, 11 G FIBER

from Fit to Eat: Meatless Main Dishes

SIDE DISHES

beet salad

SERVES 4

12 small red beets (about 1½ pounds), trimmed

2 tablespoons plus ¼ cup extra-virgin olive oil

Coarse salt and freshly ground pepper

1½ tablespoons red-wine vinegar

½ bunch fresh chives, snipped into ½-inch pieces (about ¼ cup)

1 Preheat oven to 450°F. Place beets on aluminum foil; toss with 2 tablespoons oil, and season with salt and pepper. Seal foil, and place on a baking sheet. Roast until tender when pierced with a paring knife, about 45 minutes. Let cool slightly, then peel and cut into quarters.

2 Place vinegar in a medium bowl. Whisking constantly, add remaining ¼ cup oil in a slow, steady stream until emulsified. Season with salt and pepper. Add beets and chives; gently toss to combine. Serve chilled or at room temperature.

from Bistro Salads

haricots verts with grainy-mustard vinaigrette

SERVES 6 | **PHOTOS ON PAGES 140 AND 141**

If you can't find haricots verts (slender French green beans), use the thinnest green beans available.

4 teaspoons Dijon mustard

2 teaspoons coarse-grained mustard

2 tablespoons white-wine vinegar

6 tablespoons olive oil

Coarse salt

1½ pounds haricots verts, trimmed

½ small red onion, finely diced

Freshly ground pepper

1 Make vinaigrette: In a small bowl, whisk together mustards and vinegar. Whisking constantly, add oil in a slow, steady stream until emulsified.

2 Prepare an ice bath; set aside. Bring a large pot of water to a boil; add salt. Cook beans until crisp-tender, about 5 minutes; drain. Transfer beans to ice bath to stop cooking; drain.

3 Toss green beans with onion and vinaigrette. Season with salt and pepper. Serve at room temperature.

from Backyard Picnic

leeks with mustard vinaigrette

SERVES 4

6 leeks (about 2½ pounds), roots and all but 1 inch of green tops trimmed, halved lengthwise and washed well

2 tablespoons Dijon mustard

2 tablespoons red-wine vinegar

2 garlic cloves, minced

1 tablespoon minced fresh basil

¼ cup extra-virgin olive oil

Coarse salt and freshly ground pepper

1 Bring a large pot of water to a boil. Using kitchen twine, tie leeks into two bundles, with green tops at the same end. Add bundles to boiling water. Reduce heat, and simmer until leeks are tender, about 15 minutes. Remove leeks; rinse under cold water. Drain well, and gently pat dry with paper towels. Set aside.

2 Make vinaigrette: In a large bowl, whisk together mustard, vinegar, garlic, and basil; season with salt and pepper. Whisk in oil in a slow, steady stream until emulsified.

3 Gently toss leeks in the bowl with the vinaigrette, coating well. Serve chilled or at room temperature.

from Bistro Salads

lentil salad

SERVES 4

12 ounces French green lentils

2 tablespoons red-wine vinegar

6 anchovy fillets, minced

2 garlic cloves, minced

1 teaspoon freshly grated nutmeg

1 teaspoon coarse salt

Freshly ground pepper

¼ cup extra-virgin olive oil

3 scallions, thinly sliced (about ½ cup)

½ cup finely chopped fresh flat-leaf parsley

1 teaspoon finely chopped fresh tarragon

1 Bring a medium saucepan of water to a boil. Add lentils, and reduce heat to medium-low. Gently simmer until lentils are just tender, 20 to 25 minutes. Drain well.

2 Meanwhile, in a large bowl, whisk together vinegar, anchovies, garlic, nutmeg, and salt; season with pepper. Whisk in oil in a slow, steady stream until emulsified. Whisk in scallions, parsley, and tarragon. While lentils are warm, add to dressing; toss to combine, and serve.

from Bistro Salads

pasta verde

SERVES 4 | **PHOTO ON PAGE 142**

2 tablespoons grainy mustard

2 tablespoons white-wine or sherry vinegar

¼ cup plus 2 tablespoons extra-virgin olive oil

Coarse salt and freshly ground pepper

1 pound gemelli or other short pasta

1 sweet onion, halved lengthwise and cut crosswise into ¼-inch-thick pieces

2 small zucchini, halved lengthwise and cut crosswise into ¼-inch-thick pieces

8 ounces snap peas, tough strings removed

3 ounces baby spinach (or 1 bunch regular spinach, stems trimmed and leaves coarsely chopped)

1 small bunch scallions, thinly sliced (about ½ cup)

¼ cup packed fresh basil leaves, cut into very thin strips

1 In a medium bowl, whisk together mustard and vinegar; season with salt and pepper. Whisk in ¼ cup oil in a slow, steady stream until emulsified. Set aside.

2 Bring a large pot of water to a boil; add salt. Cook pasta in boiling water until al dente according to package instructions, about 8 minutes. Drain; return to pot. Set aside.

3 Meanwhile, heat remaining 2 tablespoons oil in a large skillet over medium heat. Add onion; cook, stirring occasionally, until softened, about 4 minutes. Add zucchini; cook, stirring, until tender, about 4 minutes. Add snap peas and spinach; cook, stirring, until bright green, about 2 minutes. Remove from heat; stir in scallions and basil.

4 Add to pasta in pot along with vinaigrette; toss to combine. Serve warm or at room temperature.

from What's for Dinner?

warm bean, snap pea, and tomato salad

SERVES 4 | PHOTO ON PAGE 146

Cannellini are white Italian kidney beans. Try using cranberry, pinto, or other dried beans in this salad instead. To save time, canned beans can be used in place of dried.

- 4 **ounces wax beans, trimmed and cut into 1-inch pieces (about 1 cup)**
- 4 **ounces sugar snap peas, tough strings removed, cut in half (about 1 cup)**
- 1 **tablespoon extra-virgin olive oil**
- 4 **scallions, sliced into ¼-inch rounds**
- 3 **garlic cloves, minced**
- 1½ **cups cooked cannellini beans, drained**
- 2 **beefsteak tomatoes, cut into ½-inch dice, juice and seeds reserved**
- ½ **teaspoon coarse salt**
  Freshly ground pepper
- 1 **cup loosely packed fresh basil leaves**

1 Prepare an ice bath; set aside. Bring a medium pot of water to a boil. Add wax beans, and cook until crisp-tender and bright, about 2½ minutes. Remove beans with a slotted spoon, and immediately plunge into ice bath. Drain; set aside. Repeat with snap peas, blanching them about 1 minute.

2 Heat oil in a large sauté pan over medium heat. Add scallions and garlic; cook, stirring occasionally, until soft but not browned, about 3 minutes. Add cannellini beans, and cook until just heated through, about 2 minutes more.

3 Transfer cannellini mixture to a large bowl. Add wax beans, snap peas, tomatoes and reserved juice and seeds, and salt. Season with pepper. Using a sharp knife, slice basil into very thin strips; add to bean mixture. Toss to combine; serve warm.

PER SERVING: 177 CALORIES, 4 G FAT, 0 MG CHOLESTEROL, 28 G CARBOHYDRATE, 255 MG SODIUM, 9 G PROTEIN, 11 G FIBER

from Fit to Eat: Meatless Main Dishes

DESSERTS

angel food cake

MAKES 1 TEN-INCH CAKE | PHOTO ON PAGE 159

Separate egg whites one at a time into a small bowl, and pour each into a large bowl before breaking the next egg; this will prevent any yolk from getting into whites. Angel-food-cake pans have removable bottoms and legs, but a tube pan works, too. Serve slices topped with a dollop of whipped cream.

- 1 **cup sifted cake flour (not self-rising)**
- 1½ **cups granulated sugar**
- 12 **large egg whites**
- 1 **teaspoon cream of tartar**
- 1 **tablespoon freshly squeezed lemon juice**
- 2 **teaspoons pure vanilla extract**
- ¼ **teaspoon salt**

1 Preheat oven to 325°F, with rack in lower third but not on bottom shelf. Prepare a 10-inch angel-food-cake pan: Using the pan as a guide, cut a ring from a piece of parchment paper; line bottom of pan with it. Sift flour and ½ cup sugar onto another piece of parchment two times.

2 Place egg whites in the bowl of an electric mixer; whisk on medium speed until frothy, about 1 minute. Add cream of tartar, lemon juice, vanilla, and salt; beat until soft peaks form, about 2½ minutes. With mixer running, add remaining cup sugar a little at a time, beating no longer than 1 minute.

3 Raise speed to medium-high; continue beating until firm, but not stiff, peaks form (when beater is lifted, only the tip of the peak should fall over slightly). Gently transfer egg-white mixture to a large, wide bowl. Sprinkle a third of the reserved flour mixture over the whites. Using a whisk, gently combine in a folding motion, allowing batter to fall through the whisk as you fold. Sprinkle remaining flour mixture over whites in two more batches; fold until just combined. Be careful not to overmix because the egg whites will deflate.

4 Using a large rubber spatula, gently transfer batter to prepared pan. Run a knife gently through the center of the batter to remove any large air bubbles. Bake until a cake tester inserted in the middle comes out clean and cake is springy to the touch, 45 to 50 minutes.

5 Remove pan from oven, and invert onto its legs, making sure cake clears the surface of the counter. (If using a tube pan, invert it and hang over the neck of a bottle.) Let cool completely, 1½ to 2 hours. To remove cake, reinvert pan, top side up. Run a knife around the inner and outer edges of the cake before releasing the bottom. Cake will keep up to 2 days at room temperature in an airtight container or wrapped in plastic. To serve, slice with a serrated knife.

from Angel Food Cake 101

cherry ice

SERVES 4 | **PHOTO ON PAGE 160**

½ cup dry white wine

⅓ cup honey

2 tablespoons freshly squeezed lemon juice

2 cups pitted cherries, fresh or frozen, plus whole ones for garnish

1   In a medium bowl, whisk together wine, honey, and lemon juice until combined; set aside. Place cherries in a food processor; pulse until finely chopped. Transfer to bowl with wine mixture; stir until combined.

2   Pour mixture into a shallow metal pan, and place in freezer. Stir with a fork every 10 minutes until mixture is slushy and partially solidified, about 35 minutes. Spoon into serving cups, and garnish with whole cherries.

from What's for Dinner?

Earl grey pots de crème

SERVES 4 | **PHOTO ON PAGE 158**

If you don't have four ovenproof teacups, you can use six-ounce ramekins or custard cups.

1 cup heavy cream

1 cup whole milk

2 tablespoons Earl Grey tea leaves

4 large egg yolks

½ cup sugar

½ teaspoon finely grated lemon zest

⅛ teaspoon salt

Honey Lace Cookies (recipe follows)

1   Preheat oven to 325°F. In a small saucepan, bring cream, milk, and tea leaves just to a boil over medium heat. Turn off heat; cover, and let steep 30 minutes or up to 2 hours.

2   In a medium bowl, whisk together egg yolks, sugar, lemon zest, and salt. Reheat infused cream over medium heat; slowly whisk into yolk mixture. Strain through a fine sieve into a bowl to extract as much liquid as possible without pressing on tea leaves. Discard leaves.

3   Arrange four 6-ounce ovenproof cups in a baking pan large enough to hold the cups without touching. Pour boiling water into pan to reach halfway up sides of the cups.

4   Pour infused liquid into cups, dividing evenly. Cover pan tightly with aluminum foil, poking a few holes to let steam escape. Bake until custards are set but still slightly wobbly in the centers, about 30 minutes.

5   Carefully remove baking pan from oven; remove foil. Transfer cups from the hot water to a wire rack; let cool about 30 minutes. Cover cups with plastic wrap; chill in the refrigerator until custards are firm, at least 2 hours and up to 3 days. Serve with honey cookies on the side.

from Dessert of the Month

honey lace cookies

MAKES 28 | **PHOTO ON PAGE 158**

2 tablespoons unsalted butter

2 tablespoons light-brown sugar

1½ tablespoons honey

2 tablespoons all-purpose flour

Pinch of salt

1   Preheat oven to 375°F. Line two large baking sheets with Silpat baking mats or parchment paper; set aside. In a small saucepan, melt butter, sugar, and honey over medium heat. Transfer to a bowl. Whisk in flour and salt until smooth.

2   Working quickly, drop ½ teaspoons of batter onto prepared baking sheets, at least 3 inches apart. Bake until cookies spread and turn golden brown, about 6 minutes. Transfer sheets to a wire rack; let cool completely. With your fingers, carefully remove cookies from sheets.

strawberry tartlets

MAKES 6 FOUR-INCH TARTLETS | **PHOTO ON PAGE 153**

Dough can be frozen for up to one month; thaw before using.

 1 cup plus 2 tablespoons all-purpose flour

1½ tablespoons plus 3 tablespoons sugar

 ½ teaspoon salt

 ½ cup (1 stick) chilled unsalted butter, cut into small pieces

 1 large egg yolk

 1 tablespoon ice water, plus more as needed

1½ pounds (2 pints) fresh strawberries, hulled, washed, and halved (or quartered if large)

 2 cups crème fraîche

1 Place flour, 1½ tablespoons sugar, and salt in a food processor; pulse to combine. Add butter, and process until mixture resembles coarse meal. In a small bowl, lightly beat egg yolk with the ice water. With machine running, pour egg mixture in a slow, steady stream through the feed tube. Process until dough just holds together, about 20 seconds. If dough feels dry, add more ice water, 1 tablespoon at a time.

2 Preheat oven to 400°F. Divide dough into six equal pieces. Gently press into bottom and up sides of six 4-inch tartlet pans. Prick bottoms all over with a fork. Chill until firm, at least 30 minutes.

3 Line each shell with foil; fill with pie weights or dried beans. Place tartlet pans on a rimmed baking sheet; bake until edges of crusts just begin to brown, about 15 minutes. Remove foil and weights. Continue baking until bottom of crust is golden brown and crisp, about 10 minutes more. Transfer pans to a wire rack; let cool completely. Remove shells from pans.

4 Meanwhile, in a medium bowl, mix strawberries with remaining 3 tablespoons sugar. Cover with plastic wrap, and let macerate at room temperature until juicy, about 1 hour.

5 When ready to serve, fill each tartlet shell with about ⅓ cup crème fraîche; divide strawberries evenly among tartlets.

from Backyard Picnic

June

crostini with salt-cod brandade

SERVES 10

1 pound choice-grade skinless and boneless salt cod
4 garlic cloves, mashed
1 cup heavy cream
½ cup extra-virgin olive oil, plus more for drizzling
1 tablespoon plus 2 teaspoons freshly squeezed lemon juice
Coarse salt and freshly ground pepper
1 baguette, sliced on the bias into ¼-inch-thick pieces

1 Rinse salt cod, and place in a large storage container. Submerge in cold water, and place, covered, in the refrigerator. Let soak overnight. Drain cod, and submerge in fresh cold water. Let soak overnight again.

2 Remove cod from soaking liquid, and place in a large pot. Add enough cold water to cover, and bring to a boil over high heat. Reduce heat to low; simmer 20 minutes. Drain cod; let cool, and break into large pieces. Transfer to a food processor; add garlic, and process until mixture is coarsely chopped.

3 In a small saucepan set over medium heat, warm cream until just steaming; do not boil. With machine running, slowly add cream to cod mixture through the feed tube. Add ½ cup oil and lemon juice in the same manner; process until fluffy. Season with salt and pepper.

4 Heat broiler. Place bread on a baking sheet, and drizzle top of each slice with oil. Season with salt and pepper. Toast bread until lightly browned around edges, about 1 minute. Let cool. Spread brandade on crostini, and serve.

from A Cookout by the Sea

savory apricot luncheon tartlets with cornmeal crust

MAKES 8 FOUR-INCH TARTLETS

For best results, bake these individual pies in tartlet pans with removable bottoms. Serve at room temperature.

Savory Cornmeal Dough (page 124)
1¼ pounds small shallots (about 5 cups)
6 tablespoons unsalted butter
Coarse salt
2½ tablespoons balsamic vinegar
4 teaspoons sugar
1 teaspoon fresh thyme leaves
¾ pound small ripe apricots (about 7), pitted and quartered
½ cup crème fraîche

1 Preheat oven to 375°F, with rack in center. Between two pieces of waxed paper or parchment paper, roll out dough to about ⅛ inch thick. Discard top paper, and cut out eight disks, 5 inches in diameter; fit them into eight 4-inch tartlet pans, pressing into bottoms and up sides. Trim edges, and repair any cracks. Chill 30 minutes.

2 Remove shells from refrigerator; prick bottoms all over with a fork. Bake until crusts are firm and golden around edges, about 25 minutes. Transfer to a wire rack to cool.

3 Meanwhile, thinly slice about two-thirds of the shallots. Melt 4 tablespoons butter in a large nonstick sauté pan over medium-high heat. Add sliced shallots and a pinch of salt. Cook, stirring, until shallots start to brown, about 5 minutes.

4 Add 2 tablespoons vinegar and 1 teaspoon sugar to pan. Reduce heat to medium-low; cook, stirring occasionally, until shallots are completely caramelized, about 15 minutes. Add thyme and ½ cup water. Cook, stirring constantly, until water evaporates and mixture has a jamlike consistency, about 5 minutes. Transfer to a bowl; let cool.

5 In a clean sauté pan, melt remaining 2 tablespoons butter over medium-low heat. Cook remaining whole shallots, stirring occasionally, until soft and browned, about 20 minutes.

6 Raise heat to high. Add a pinch of salt, the remaining ½ tablespoon vinegar and 3 teaspoons sugar, and the apricots. Cook until apricots are lightly browned and glazed, stirring occasionally, 3 to 4 minutes. Let cool.

7 Assemble tartlets: Spread 1 tablespoon crème fraîche in bottom of each shell. Place 2 tablespoons caramelized shallot mixture on top. Divide the apricot mixture evenly among tartlets. Serve immediately.

from Apricots

savory cornmeal dough

MAKES ENOUGH FOR 8 FOUR-INCH TARTLETS

This dough can be made ahead and refrigerated for up to three days, or frozen for up to one month.

2¼ cups all-purpose flour
¾ cup coarse yellow cornmeal
3 tablespoons sugar
1½ teaspoons salt
1 teaspoon dried thyme
¾ cup (1½ sticks) chilled unsalted butter, cut into small pieces
3 large egg yolks
5 tablespoons ice water, plus more as needed

1 In a large bowl, combine flour, cornmeal, sugar, salt, and thyme. Add butter, and toss to coat each piece. Working quickly with your fingertips or a pastry blender, cut in butter until mixture is the consistency of coarse meal.

2 In a small bowl, whisk together egg yolks and the ice water. Using a fork, work egg-yolk mixture into flour mixture. Knead lightly in bowl until dough just holds together. If dough is dry, add up to 1 tablespoon more ice water.

3 Divide dough in half. Place each half on a piece of plastic wrap, and flatten into a disk. Wrap in plastic, and refrigerate until chilled, at least 1 hour.

stuffed quahogs

SERVES 10

Quahogs are found mainly off the eastern coast of the United States; steamer clams may be used instead.

1 baguette, trimmed of crust and cut into ¼-inch cubes (about 4 cups)
¼ pound chorizo, cut into ¼-inch pieces
10 quahogs (about 5 pounds)
⅓ cup olive oil
10 garlic cloves, finely chopped (about ¼ cup)
2 onions, finely chopped (about 3 cups)
½ teaspoon crushed red-pepper flakes
2 large eggs
2 tablespoons finely chopped fresh basil
1 tablespoon finely chopped fresh oregano
2 tablespoons finely chopped fresh flat-leaf parsley
Freshly ground black pepper
2 tablespoons unsalted butter, cut into small pieces

1 Preheat oven to 300°F. Place bread cubes on a rimmed baking sheet. Toast until dry, about 15 minutes. Set aside.

2 In a sauté pan set over medium-high heat, cook chorizo, stirring occasionally, until fat is rendered and chorizo is lightly browned, about 4 minutes. Using a slotted spoon, transfer chorizo to a paper-towel–lined plate. Blot dry, and set aside.

3 Scrub clams under cold running water, then place in a large stockpot. Add ⅔ cup water; cover, and place over high heat. Steam until clams have opened, 10 to 15 minutes. Remove clams from pot, discarding any that do not open; strain broth through a paper-towel–lined fine sieve; set aside.

4 Remove clam meat from shells; chop into ¼-inch pieces, and set aside. Separate shells into halves; clean thoroughly by boiling in a large pot of water for 5 minutes. Transfer shells to paper towels to drain.

5 In a large sauté pan set over medium heat, warm oil. Add garlic, onions, and red-pepper flakes; cook, stirring occasionally, until onions are soft and translucent, about 8 minutes. Let cool to room temperature.

6 In a large mixing bowl, beat 1 cup strained clam broth into eggs. Add onion mixture, clams, chorizo, and herbs; toss well to combine. Add toasted bread. Gently fold until just combined. Season with pepper.

7 Heat grill to medium. Fill each clam shell with stuffing, about ¼ to ⅓ cup filling per shell. Dot top of each filled shell with butter. Place shells, stuffing side up, on grill; cook, covered, 10 minutes. Transfer to a serving plate, and serve warm.

from A Cookout by the Sea

sweet-and-sour cucumber salad

SERVES 10

6 large cucumbers, peeled, halved, seeded, and thinly sliced into half-moons
2 Vidalia or other sweet onions, halved and thinly sliced
¼ cup sugar
2 teaspoons coarse salt
2 teaspoons dry mustard
2 teaspoons celery seeds
½ cup cider vinegar
½ cup corn or canola oil

In a medium bowl, toss together cucumbers and onions. In a small bowl, whisk together sugar, salt, mustard, celery seeds, and vinegar. Whisk in oil in a slow, steady stream until emulsified. Pour vinaigrette over vegetables; toss to coat. Cover with plastic; refrigerate at least 4 hours. Serve chilled.

from A Cookout by the Sea

bluefish with herb stuffing

SERVES 10

2 whole bluefish fillets, preferably from same fish (3½ to 4 pounds total), skin on, rinsed and patted dry

Coarse salt and freshly ground pepper

¾ cup (1½ sticks) unsalted butter

1 cup finely chopped celery (about 2 stalks)

1 cup finely chopped fennel (about 1 small bulb)

½ cup finely chopped shallots (about 2 medium shallots)

2 garlic cloves, minced

1 cup shiitake mushrooms, trimmed and cut into ½-inch pieces

½ cup finely chopped fresh flat-leaf parsley

¼ cup finely chopped fresh basil

2 tablespoons finely chopped fresh sage

½ cup dry white wine

1 loaf Italian bread, trimmed of crust and cut into ½-inch cubes (about 3 cups)

¾ pound sliced pancetta, bacon, or meaty salt pork (about 24 slices)

Lemon wedges, for serving

1 Heat grill to medium. Season fish with salt and pepper; set aside. In a large skillet over medium heat, melt butter. Add celery, fennel, shallots, and garlic. Cook, stirring occasionally, until shallots are translucent, about 5 minutes.

2 Add mushrooms to skillet. Cook, stirring occasionally, until tender, about 4 minutes more. Stir in herbs and wine. Reduce heat, and simmer 2 minutes. Transfer to a large bowl; stir in bread cubes. Season with salt and pepper, and let cool.

3 Lay first fillet, skin side up, on a clean work surface. Cover with half of the pancetta slices, and carefully flip over. Mound stuffing neatly on top of the fillet. Place second fillet on top, skin side up, and cover with remaining pancetta. Tie the stuffed fish securely with kitchen twine at 1-inch intervals. Replace any stuffing that falls out during the process, and make sure that all pancetta is kept in place by the twine.

4 Grill stuffed fish until pancetta is charred, 5 to 10 minutes per side, using two spatulas to carefully turn fish. Cover grill, and continue cooking fish until just opaque throughout, about 15 minutes more. Transfer to a serving platter. Serve warm with lemon wedges.

from A Cookout by the Sea

chicken and apricot stew with couscous

SERVES 4

If sauce has not thickened in step three when chicken is done, transfer chicken to an ovenproof platter and keep warm in a 200 degree oven while sauce continues to reduce.

4 chicken legs and thighs (about 3 pounds)

Coarse salt and freshly ground pepper

¼ cup canola oil

1 yellow onion, halved and thinly sliced

1 large garlic clove, minced

1½ pounds small ripe apricots (12 to 14), quartered and pitted

¾ teaspoon ground cinnamon

¼ teaspoon saffron threads

¼ teaspoon ground ginger

¼ teaspoon ground coriander

4 tablespoons honey, plus more to taste

1½ cups Basic Chicken Stock (page 17) or low-sodium canned chicken broth

1½ cups couscous

1 tablespoon unsalted butter, room temperature

¾ cup whole almonds, coarsely chopped

Sesame seeds, for garnish

1 Season chicken with salt and pepper. Heat oil in a large skillet over medium-high heat until hot but not smoking. Add chicken, and cook until browned, about 4 minutes per side. Transfer to a paper-towel–lined plate to drain. Pour off all but 2 tablespoons oil from skillet.

2 Reduce heat to medium; add onion. Sauté, stirring occasionally, until lightly browned, about 7 minutes. Add garlic; sauté 1 minute. Stir in apricots, cinnamon, saffron, ginger, coriander, ⅔ cup water, and 2 tablespoons honey; season with salt.

3 Return chicken to skillet, and bring mixture to a simmer. Cover, reduce heat to low, and simmer until chicken is cooked through and liquid is thickened, 45 to 50 minutes. Transfer chicken to a serving platter. Stir remaining 2 tablespoons honey into sauce in skillet, and season again with salt. Pour over chicken on platter.

4 Meanwhile, in a medium saucepan, bring stock to a boil. Place couscous and butter in a medium bowl. Pour stock over couscous, and cover with plastic wrap. Let stand until the couscous absorbs all the stock, about 5 minutes. Fluff with a fork, and season with salt. Stir in almonds. Serve couscous with chicken, and garnish with sesame seeds.

from Apricots

grilled chicken tostadas

SERVES 4

4 boneless and skinless chicken breast halves

¼ cup freshly squeezed lime juice (2 limes)

¼ cup extra-virgin olive oil, plus more for brushing

Coarse salt and freshly ground pepper

8 corn tortillas (6 inches each)

2 red onions, sliced into ½-inch-thick rounds

Chopped lettuce, sliced tomatoes and avocados, fresh cilantro, and sour cream, for serving

1 Preheat oven to 375°F, with rack in center. Between two sheets of waxed paper, pound chicken with a meat pounder until about ½ inch thick. Transfer chicken to a shallow bowl or large resealable plastic bag. Add lime juice and oil; season with salt and pepper, and turn to coat thoroughly. Refrigerate chicken until ready to grill.

2 Place tortillas on a baking sheet. Brush tops with oil, and season with salt and pepper. Bake until crisp and golden, 10 to 12 minutes. Remove from oven; set aside to cool.

3 Heat a grill or grill pan to medium-high. Remove chicken from refrigerator; discard marinade. Grill chicken until browned and cooked through, about 5 minutes per side. When cool enough to handle, after about 5 minutes, cut into strips.

4 Brush onions with oil, and grill until browned, about 3 minutes per side. Serve tortillas topped with lettuce, tomato, avocado, chicken, onion, cilantro, and sour cream.

from What's for Dinner?

grilled prosciutto-wrapped cod and onions

SERVES 4 | **PHOTO ON PAGE 144**

Wrapping skinless fish fillets, such as cod or mahimahi, with thin slices of prosciutto—or bacon or pancetta—keeps the fish moist and prevents it from sticking to the grate; the prosciutto also imparts a smoky flavor.

4 skinless cod fillets (6 ounces each)

Coarse salt and freshly ground pepper

6 ounces thinly sliced prosciutto

2 large sweet onions, cut into ½-inch-thick rounds

Extra-virgin olive oil

1 Heat grill or grill pan to medium-high. Place cod fillets on a work surface, and season both sides with salt and pepper. Wrap each fillet with a few slices of prosciutto, making sure only the ends of the fish are visible; set aside.

2 Place onion rounds on a baking sheet, and brush both sides generously with oil. Season with salt and pepper.

3 Place wrapped fillets and onions on the grill (if using a smaller grill, cook the onions first). Grill fish until cooked through, flipping when the lower half of the fish is opaque, about 3 minutes per side. The onions should be well browned, about 3 minutes per side. Season with salt and pepper as desired. Serve immediately.

from Grilling Fish

black beans with poblano

SERVES 4 | PHOTO ON PAGE 146

2 tablespoons extra-virgin olive oil

2 shallots, thinly sliced

1 poblano chile, seeded and chopped

2 cans (15 ounces each) black beans, drained and rinsed

2 tablespoons freshly squeezed lime juice

½ teaspoon ground cumin

Pinch of cayenne pepper

Coarse salt and freshly ground black pepper

Lime wedges, for serving

Heat oil in a medium skillet over medium heat. Add shallots and the chile; cook, stirring frequently, until tender, about 5 minutes. Transfer to a large bowl; add beans, lime juice, cumin, and cayenne pepper. Toss well to combine. Season with salt and black pepper. Serve with lime wedges.

from What's for Dinner?

grilled tomatoes

SERVES 10

3 tablespoons sherry-wine vinegar

2 tablespoons coarsely chopped fresh oregano

Coarse salt and freshly ground pepper

2 tablespoons extra-virgin olive oil

5 large tomatoes (about 3 pounds), cored and cut in half horizontally

1   Heat grill to medium. In a small bowl, whisk together vinegar and oregano; season with salt and pepper. Whisk in oil in a slow, steady stream until emulsified. Pour vinaigrette into a large shallow dish. Place tomatoes, cut side down, in dish. Let marinate at room temperature 30 minutes to 1 hour.

2   Place tomatoes on grill, cut side down, reserving marinade. Grill tomatoes until charred, about 3 minutes per side. Return tomatoes to vinaigrette. Let marinate again at room temperature until ready to serve.

from A Cookout by the Sea

mixed rice salad

SERVES 10

3 teaspoons coarse salt

½ cup wild rice

1 cup long-grain white rice (not converted)

3 large stalks celery, chopped (about 1½ cups)

3 whole scallions, finely chopped

1 cup loosely packed fresh flat-leaf parsley leaves

1½ tablespoons finely chopped fresh sage

1 tablespoon finely chopped fresh thyme

¼ cup extra-virgin olive oil

1 cup whole almonds, coarsely chopped

2 tablespoons white-wine vinegar

1 tablespoon freshly squeezed lemon juice

½ teaspoon freshly ground pepper

1   In a medium saucepan, bring 3 cups cold water to a boil. Add ½ teaspoon salt, and stir in wild rice. Cover, and return to a boil. Reduce heat to low; simmer, uncovered, until rice is just tender, about 45 minutes. Drain rice in a sieve, discarding water, then transfer to a large bowl; set aside.

2   Meanwhile, in another saucepan, bring 1½ cups water to a boil. Add ½ teaspoon salt, and stir in the white rice. Return to a boil; cover, and reduce to a simmer. Cook until rice is just tender, 15 to 20 minutes. Remove from heat; let stand, covered, 5 to 10 minutes, then fluff with a fork. Add white rice to wild rice; stir in celery, scallions, and herbs.

3   In a medium skillet, heat oil over medium heat. Add almonds and remaining 2 teaspoons salt; cook, stirring, until toasted, about 2 minutes. Pour into rice mixture. Stir in vinegar, lemon juice, and pepper. Serve at room temperature.

from A Cookout by the Sea

yellow rice pilaf

SERVES 4 | **PHOTO ON PAGE 146**

  1 teaspoon coarse salt, plus more for seasoning
1½ cups long-grain white rice
  2 tablespoons extra-virgin olive oil
  1 onion, cut into ½-inch dice
  1 carrot, cut into ¼-inch dice
  1 cup frozen peas, thawed
  1 teaspoon ground turmeric
 ½ teaspoon ground cumin
 ¼ teaspoon ground paprika
   Freshly ground pepper

1 Fill a medium saucepan with water, and bring to a boil; add 1 teaspoon salt and rice. Cook until rice is just tender, 15 to 20 minutes. Drain, and transfer rice to a serving bowl.

2 Meanwhile, heat oil in a large skillet over medium-high heat. Add onion, and cook, stirring, until it begins to soften, about 4 minutes. Add carrot; cook, stirring, until vegetables are tender, about 5 minutes. Stir in peas, turmeric, cumin, and paprika; cook until just heated through. Stir mixture into rice. Season with salt and pepper. Serve warm or at room temperature.

from What's for Dinner?

DESSERTS

apricot-and-walnut roll cake

MAKES 1 ELEVEN-INCH LOG | **PHOTO ON PAGE 155**

For best results, roll this cake while it's warm and pliable.

   Unsalted butter, room temperature, for baking sheet
  4 **large eggs, separated**
 ¾ **cup sugar**
  1 **teaspoon pure vanilla extract**
 ¾ **cup sifted cake flour (not self-rising)**
 ¾ **teaspoon baking powder**
 ½ **teaspoon salt**
 ½ **cup walnuts, finely ground**
   Confectioners' sugar for dusting
 ½ **cup Marsala or sweet sherry**
1¾ **cups Apricot Honey-Ginger Jam (recipe follows)**

1 Preheat oven to 375°F. Butter a 12-by-17-inch rimmed baking sheet. Line bottom with parchment paper, allowing it to extend slightly over short sides. Butter paper; set sheet aside.

2 In the bowl of an electric mixer fitted with the paddle attachment, beat egg yolks on medium speed until light, about 4 minutes. Gradually add sugar, and beat until thick and creamy, about 3 minutes more. Stir in vanilla extract.

3 Into a small bowl, sift together flour, baking powder, and salt. With mixer on low speed, gradually add flour mixture to egg-yolk mixture; beat just until smooth.

4 Place egg whites in a clean mixing bowl. Whisk on medium speed until stiff but not dry peaks form, about 3 minutes. Stir one-third of beaten whites into batter to lighten, then gently fold in remaining whites, being careful not to overmix. Gently fold in walnuts.

5 Spread batter evenly in prepared baking sheet, covering all corners. Bake until cake is springy to the touch and browned around the edges, about 10 minutes. Remove from oven; loosen edges of cake with a knife. Invert pan onto a clean kitchen towel that has been liberally dusted with confectioners' sugar. Peel off parchment paper. With a serrated knife, trim off about ½ inch of the cake edges.

6 Using a pastry brush, soak warm cake with Marsala. Spread jam evenly on top. Starting with a short side, gently but firmly roll cake into a log. Place rolled cake on a serving platter, seam side down, and dust with confectioners' sugar. When ready to serve, use a serrated knife to slice roll into 1-inch-thick pieces.

from Apricots

apricot honey-ginger jam

MAKES ABOUT 4 PINTS

This flavorful jam will keep for up to two weeks in the refrigerator; freeze any jam that will not be used within that time. You may need to adjust the amount of sugar you add, depending on the sweetness of the fruit.

- 6 pounds small ripe apricots (about 48), halved, pitted, and cut into eighths
- 3 cups sugar
- 1½ cups honey
- ¼ cup crystallized ginger, minced
- ¼ cup freshly squeezed lemon juice (1 to 2 lemons)

1 In a large bowl, gently toss together all the ingredients until combined. Let stand, covered with plastic wrap, at room temperature 3 hours, or refrigerate overnight.

2 Transfer apricot mixture to a heavy-bottom 5-quart stockpot; bring to a boil over medium-high heat. Reduce heat to medium-low; simmer, skimming foam from surface as needed, until fruit is transparent and falls apart slightly, about 20 minutes (cooking time will vary depending on ripeness of fruit). If mixture seems too watery, strain out fruit; continue cooking syrup about 5 minutes more, then return fruit to pot. Let cool completely, then pour jam into airtight containers.

apricot cherry bake

SERVES 8 TO 10 | PHOTO ON PAGE 155

Unsalted butter, room temperature, for baking dish
- 3 pounds small ripe apricots (about 24), halved, pitted, and sliced into sixths
- ½ pound fresh cherries, pitted (about 1¼ cups)
- ⅓ cup all-purpose flour, plus more for work surface
- 1 cup plus 4 teaspoons sugar
- ½ recipe Pâte Brisée (recipe follows)

1 Preheat oven to 400°F. Butter a 2-quart baking dish, and set aside. In a large bowl, toss apricots and cherries with the flour and 1 cup sugar. Spread evenly in prepared baking dish.

2 On a lightly floured work surface, roll out pâte brisée to a 12-inch round. Cut into four 3-inch-wide strips, then cut strips crosswise into 3- or 4-inch-long pieces. Place over fruit mixture in a patchlike pattern. Refrigerate about 30 minutes.

3 Lightly brush dough with water, and sprinkle with remaining 4 teaspoons sugar. Transfer to oven; bake until crust is golden brown and juices are bubbling, 50 to 60 minutes. Transfer to a wire rack, and let cool before serving.

from Apricots

pâte brisée

MAKES ENOUGH FOR 1 NINE-INCH DOUBLE-CRUST PIE
OR 12 FOUR-INCH HAND PIES

- 2½ cups all-purpose flour
- 1 teaspoon salt
- 1 teaspoon sugar
- 1 cup (2 sticks) chilled unsalted butter, cut into small pieces
- ¼ to ½ cup ice water

1 Place flour, salt, and sugar in a food processor; pulse a few times to combine. Add butter, and process until mixture resembles coarse meal. With machine running, add the ice water a few tablespoons at a time through the feed tube, just until dough holds together, no more than 30 seconds.

2 Divide dough in half, and flatten to form disks. Wrap each in plastic, and refrigerate at least 1 hour or overnight.

apricot sherbet

MAKES 1 QUART

- 1½ pounds small, very ripe apricots (about 12)
- 1 cup sugar
- ¼ cup light corn syrup
- ¼ cup freshly squeezed lemon juice (1 to 2 lemons)
- 1½ cups nonfat buttermilk
- 1 cup milk
- Almond Meringue Wafers (page 130), for serving

1 Quarter apricots, and remove pits. Place apricot quarters in a food processor, and purée until smooth, about 1 minute. Transfer to a medium bowl, and add sugar, corn syrup, and lemon juice. Whisk to combine. Cover bowl with plastic wrap, and let macerate about 1 hour in the refrigerator.

2 Pass apricot mixture through a fine sieve into a medium bowl; discard solids. Whisk in buttermilk and milk. Cover with plastic wrap, and refrigerate until chilled, about 3 hours.

3 Freeze mixture in an ice-cream maker according to manufacturer's instructions. Transfer to an airtight container, and freeze up to 4 days. Serve with almond wafers.

from Apricots

almond meringue wafers

MAKES 2 DOZEN

4¼ ounces sliced almonds (about 1¼ cups)

¾ cup sugar

¼ cup all-purpose flour

3 large egg whites, room temperature

¼ teaspoon salt

1 teaspoon pure vanilla extract

1 Preheat oven to 350°F. Line two baking sheets with parchment paper, and set aside. In a food processor, pulse about 1 cup almonds with ½ cup sugar until almonds are finely ground. Add flour, and pulse until combined. Transfer to a bowl.

2 In the bowl of an electric mixer, whisk egg whites, salt, vanilla, and remaining ¼ cup sugar until soft peaks form. Gently fold egg-white mixture into flour mixture.

3 Drop batter by the tablespoon, about 1½ inches apart, onto prepared baking sheets. Arrange 3 sliced almonds on top of each cookie.

4 Bake cookies until edges are lightly browned, about 15 minutes. Let cool slightly on baking sheets, then transfer to wire racks to cool completely. Cookies can be stored in an airtight container at room temperature up to 1 week.

broiled apricots with stirred custard

SERVES 4 | PHOTO ON PAGE 154

To keep the custard from curdling, make sure to whisk constantly while it cooks, and do not let it boil. The custard can be made up to three days ahead and chilled; broil the apricots just before serving.

FOR CUSTARD:

5 large egg yolks

¼ cup plus 2 tablespoons granulated sugar

2 tablespoons all-purpose flour

1½ cups milk

½ vanilla bean, split lengthwise

FOR BROILED APRICOTS:

6 small ripe apricots

2 tablespoons unsalted butter

2 tablespoons dark-brown sugar

1 Make custard: In the bowl of an electric mixer fitted with the paddle attachment, beat egg yolks and sugar on medium-high speed until pale and thick, 4 to 5 minutes. Reduce speed to low; add flour. Beat just until combined, about 30 seconds.

2 In a medium saucepan, heat milk and vanilla bean over medium heat just until steaming. Discard vanilla bean. With mixer on low speed, pour half the hot milk into egg mixture, and beat until smooth. Return mixture to saucepan; cook over medium heat, whisking constantly, until mixture just begins to bubble, 3 to 4 minutes.

3 Transfer mixture to a large bowl; cover with plastic wrap, placing it directly on surface to prevent a skin from forming. Refrigerate until thoroughly chilled, at least 1 hour.

4 Make apricots: Heat broiler. Halve apricots along their natural line; remove pits. Place halves on a baking sheet, cut side up. Using a melon baller, fill each cavity with ½ teaspoon each butter and brown sugar.

5 Place apricots under the broiler. Cook until butter has melted, sugar has started to bubble and caramelize, and apricots have softened, about 3 minutes, depending on ripeness of fruit. Let cool slightly.

6 Spoon custard into individual serving bowls, dividing evenly; garnish each portion with 3 broiled apricot halves.

from Apricots

buttermilk pie

MAKES 1 TEN-INCH PIE | PHOTO ON PAGE 156

Graham Cracker–Coated Piecrust (recipe follows)

3 cups buttermilk

½ cup (1 stick) unsalted butter, melted and cooled

8 large egg yolks

2 teaspoons pure vanilla extract

2 cups sugar

½ cup all-purpose flour

½ teaspoon salt

1 tablespoon finely grated lemon zest

Blackberry and Blueberry Sauce (recipe follows)

1 Preheat oven to 400°F. Prick bottom of pie shell all over with a fork. Line with foil; fill with pie weights or dried beans. Bake until edges are lightly browned, about 25 minutes. Remove foil and weights; continue baking until bottom of crust is lightly browned, about 10 minutes more. Transfer to a wire rack to cool completely.

2 Reduce oven heat to 350°F. In a medium bowl, whisk together buttermilk, butter, egg yolks, and vanilla. In a large bowl, combine sugar, flour, and salt. Whisk buttermilk mixture into flour mixture. Pass through a fine sieve into a clean bowl. Whisk in lemon zest.

3 Pour mixture into pie shell; bake until center is just set, about 1 hour 10 minutes. Let cool, then refrigerate at least 4 hours. Serve cold with berry sauce.

from A Cookout by the Sea

graham cracker–coated piecrust
MAKES 1 TEN-INCH PIECRUST

1¼ cups all-purpose flour
¾ teaspoon salt
½ cup (1 stick) butter, cut into pieces
¼ cup ice water
4 graham crackers, finely ground (½ cup)

1 Place flour and salt in a food processor; pulse a few times to combine. Add butter, and process until mixture resembles coarse meal. With machine running, add the ice water a tablespoon at a time through the feed tube, and process just until dough holds together, no more than 30 seconds.

2 Turn out dough onto a piece of plastic wrap. Flatten dough into a disk; wrap well. Chill at least 1 hour.

3 Spread ground crackers on a clean work surface. Roll out dough on top of crumbs, coating both sides, into a 14-inch round about ⅛ inch thick. Gently fit dough into a 10-by-2-inch pie plate; crimp edges as desired. Chill at least 30 minutes.

blackberry and blueberry sauce
MAKES 1 QUART | PHOTO ON PAGE 156

½ cup sugar
1 tablespoon freshly squeezed lemon juice
2 pints fresh blueberries, picked over and rinsed
2 containers (6 ounces each) fresh blackberries
1 teaspoon cornstarch

1 In a medium saucepan over medium heat, stir together sugar, lemon juice, and half the blueberries and blackberries. Bring just to a boil. Reduce heat to low, and simmer until blueberries burst and release their juices, about 3 minutes.

2 In a small bowl, dissolve cornstarch in 1 teaspoon cold water; stir into sauce. Simmer, stirring, until sauce thickens slightly, about 1 minute more. Remove from heat; stir in remaining berries. Transfer sauce to a serving bowl. Refrigerate until chilled; stir gently before serving.

cheesecake with poached apricot halves
MAKES 1 EIGHT-INCH SQUARE CAKE | PHOTO ON PAGE 155

Unsalted butter, room temperature, for pan
1½ pounds cream cheese (3 eight-ounce packages), room temperature
¾ cup sugar
½ cup sour cream, room temperature
1 teaspoon pure vanilla extract
3 large eggs
1 tablespoon freshly squeezed lemon juice
16 Poached Apricot Halves (page 132)

1 Preheat oven to 400°F. Butter an 8-inch square cake pan. Line bottom with parchment paper; set pan aside.

2 In the bowl of an electric mixer fitted with the paddle attachment, beat cream cheese until smooth. Add sugar, sour cream, and vanilla; beat until smooth. Add eggs one at a time, beating until each is fully incorporated before adding the next; scrape down sides of bowl as needed. Beat in lemon juice.

3 Fill prepared pan with cream-cheese mixture. Smooth top with a spatula. Place pan in a larger baking pan, and transfer to the oven. Pour enough hot water into baking pan to reach halfway up sides of cake pan. Bake until cake is just set in center and lightly browned on top, about 35 minutes.

4 Carefully transfer cake pan from water bath to a wire rack. Let cool about 30 minutes. While still slightly warm, invert cake onto a platter. Chill, covered, overnight.

5 When ready to serve, arrange poached apricot halves, cut sides down, on top of cheesecake, allowing juices to pool on surface and drizzle over sides.

from Apricots

poached apricot halves

MAKES 2 DOZEN

To prevent apricots from discoloring, keep them submerged in the poaching liquid during cooking and storing. Mix poaching liquid with seltzer water for a refreshing drink.

1½ cups sugar
3 strips (about 2 inches long) fresh lemon peel, pith removed
2 thin slices fresh ginger
7 whole cardamom pods, cracked
1 vanilla bean, split lengthwise and scraped
12 small ripe apricots, halved and pitted

1 In a 4- to 5-quart stockpot over medium heat, combine sugar, lemon peel, ginger, cardamom, and vanilla scrapings with 4 cups water. Bring mixture to a boil. Cook until sugar dissolves, then reduce heat to low. Simmer, uncovered, until liquid has thickened slightly, about 10 minutes.

2 Add apricots to pot. Rinse a double thickness of cheesecloth under cold water, and drape it over apricots so all the fruit is covered by the cloth and submerged in liquid.

3 Continue simmering until apricots soften slightly, 2 to 4 minutes. Remove from heat, and let cool completely. Use immediately, or transfer apricots and poaching liquid to a storage container. Refrigerate until ready to use, up to 4 days.

hummingbird cake

MAKES 1 NINE-INCH LAYER CAKE

Unsalted butter, room temperature, for pans and racks
3 cups all-purpose flour, plus more for pans
1 teaspoon baking soda
1 teaspoon ground cinnamon
½ teaspoon salt
1 cup vegetable oil
2 teaspoons pure vanilla extract
2 cups sugar
3 large eggs
2 cups mashed ripe banana (about 3 large)
1 can (8 ounces) crushed pineapple, drained
1 cup chopped walnuts or pecans
1 cup desiccated coconut
Cream Cheese Frosting (recipe follows)
Dried Pineapple Flowers (optional; recipe follows)

1 Preheat oven to 350°F, with rack in center. Butter two 9-by-2-inch round cake pans. Line bottoms with parchment paper; butter parchment, and dust with flour, tapping out any excess. Set pans aside. Into a medium bowl, sift together flour, baking soda, cinnamon, and salt; set aside.

2 In the bowl of an electric mixer fitted with the paddle attachment, beat oil, vanilla, and sugar until combined, about 2 minutes. Add eggs one at a time, incorporating each before adding the next; scrape down sides of bowl as needed. Continue beating on medium speed until mixture is pale and fluffy, about 3 minutes.

3 In a medium bowl, mix together banana, pineapple, walnuts, and coconut. Add to egg mixture; stir until combined. Add flour mixture, and stir until combined.

4 Divide batter evenly between prepared pans. Bake, rotating pans halfway through, until golden brown and a cake tester inserted in the centers comes out clean, 30 to 40 minutes.

5 Transfer pans to a wire rack; let cool 15 minutes. Run a knife around edges of pans to loosen. Invert cakes onto buttered rack; reinvert, top side up. Let cool completely.

6 With a serrated knife, trim top from one layer. Place layer on a serving platter. Using an offset spatula, spread top with ¼ inch of frosting. Top with untrimmed layer. Frost entire cake with remaining frosting. Decorate with pineapple flowers, if desired. Frosted cake can be refrigerated up to 3 days in a covered container; bring to room temperature before serving.

from Dessert of the Month

cream cheese frosting

MAKES 1½ QUARTS

- 1 **pound cream cheese (2 eight-ounce packages), room temperature**
- 2 **teaspoons pure vanilla extract**
- 1 **cup (2 sticks) unsalted butter, room temperature, cut into small pieces**
- 2 **pounds confectioners' sugar, sifted**

1 In the bowl of an electric mixer fitted with the paddle attachment, beat cream cheese and vanilla until light and creamy, about 2 minutes. With mixer on medium speed, gradually add butter, beating until incorporated.

2 Reduce mixer speed to low. Gradually add sugar, beating until incorporated. Use immediately, or cover and refrigerate up to 3 days. Bring to room temperature before using.

dried pineapple flowers

MAKES ABOUT 2 DOZEN

The thinner you cut the slices of pineapple, the faster they will dry—and the brighter their yellow will be. When the pineapple core dries, it resembles the center of a flower.

- 2 **large or 4 small pineapples**

1 Preheat oven to 225°F. Line two baking sheets with Silpat baking mats or parchment paper.

2 Peel pineapples. Using a small melon baller, remove and discard "eyes." Slice pineapple as thinly as possible; place slices on prepared baking sheets. Cook until tops look dried, about 30 minutes. Flip slices; continue cooking until completely dried, 25 to 30 minutes more. Let cool completely on a wire rack. Refrigerate in an airtight container up to 3 days.

Joey Gallagher's apricot hand pies

MAKES 1 DOZEN | **PHOTO ON PAGE 154**

- **All-purpose flour, for work surface**
- **Pâte Brisée (page 129)**
- 12 **Poached Apricot Halves (page 132)**
- 3 **tablespoons sugar**

1 Line a baking sheet with parchment paper; set aside. On a lightly floured surface, roll out one disk of dough to a large round, about ⅛ inch thick. Using a 3-inch cookie cutter, cut out 12 rounds. Transfer rounds to prepared baking sheet, and chill until firm, about 30 minutes.

2 Repeat process with the remaining dough, using a 4-inch cookie cutter to make 12 more rounds; do not refrigerate. Remove chilled rounds from refrigerator.

3 Using paper towels, blot the poached apricots halves to eliminate excess liquid; place one, cut side down, in center of each chilled round. Brush cold water around edges of dough; cover each with an unchilled round. Gently press edges together to seal. Chill 30 minutes.

4 Preheat oven to 425°F. Remove pies from refrigerator. Using a paring knife, slash the top of each pie in a crosshatch fashion. Brush with water, and sprinkle generously with sugar.

5 Bake 15 minutes. Reduce oven heat to 350°F, and continue baking until crusts are golden brown, 15 to 20 minutes more. Transfer pies to a wire rack to cool slightly before serving. Or let cool completely, and store pies in an airtight container at room temperature up to 4 days.

from Apricots

margarita cheesecake freezes

SERVES 4

You can substitute an equal amount of lime juice for the tequila and triple sec, if you prefer.

- 6 **ounces cream cheese, room temperature**
- ¼ **cup sour cream**
- ⅓ **cup sifted confectioners' sugar**
- 1 **tablespoon finely grated lime zest (2 limes)**
- 2 **tablespoons freshly squeezed lime juice, plus more for glasses**
- 2 **tablespoons tequila**
- 2 **tablespoons triple sec**
- ½ **cup heavy cream**
- 2 **tablespoons granulated sugar**
- 4 **graham crackers**
- 2 **tablespoons unsalted butter, melted**
- **Coarse salt, for glasses**

1 In the bowl of an electric mixer fitted with the paddle attachment, beat cream cheese until smooth. Add sour cream, confectioners' sugar, lime zest, lime juice, tequila, and triple sec; beat until combined. In another bowl, whip heavy cream until stiff peaks form; fold into cream-cheese mixture. Cover with plastic wrap, and freeze until firm, about 30 minutes.

2 Pulse granulated sugar and graham crackers in a food processor until finely chopped; stir in melted butter. To serve, place lime juice on one plate and salt on another. Dip rims of glasses in juice, then salt. Remove mixture from freezer, and scoop into glasses; sprinkle with graham-cracker topping. Let soften slightly before serving.

from What's for Dinner?

vanilla panna cotta with poached apricot halves

SERVES 8 | PHOTO ON PAGE 155

1 envelope (1 scant tablespoon) unflavored gelatin
1 quart heavy cream
1 cup sugar
½ vanilla bean, split lengthwise and scraped
16 Poached Apricot Halves (page 132)

1   Prepare an ice bath; set aside. In a large bowl, sprinkle gelatin over 3 tablespoons cold water. Let soften 5 minutes.

2   Combine cream and sugar in a medium saucepan over medium-high heat. Add vanilla bean and scrapings. Gently simmer until bubbles form around edge, about 5 minutes. Remove from heat; let cool slightly. Discard vanilla pod.

3   Whisk hot cream mixture into gelatin mixture until combined. Set bowl in ice bath. Let cool completely, stirring frequently. Strain mixture through a fine sieve into a medium bowl. Divide among eight custard cups. Cover tightly with plastic wrap; chill until set, at least 4 hours or overnight.

4   To serve, top each custard with two poached apricot halves, placing them cut sides down.

from Apricots

MISCELLANEOUS

cilantro salsa with coconut and lime

MAKES ABOUT ½ CUP; SERVES 4

This salsa makes a wonderful dipping sauce. It can also be spooned over grilled shrimp, fish, chicken, or lamb.

1 teaspoon cumin seeds
6 scallions, coarsely chopped
2 small garlic cloves
1 or 2 serrano chiles (seeded for less heat, if desired)
3 cups loosely packed cilantro leaves
¼ cup freshly squeezed lime juice (about 3 limes)
2 tablespoons shredded sweetened coconut
½ teaspoon coarse salt
1 tablespoon plus 1 teaspoon olive oil

1   In a small skillet, heat cumin seeds over medium heat until toasted and fragrant, about 3 minutes. Let cool slightly, then crush lightly with the side of a knife.

2   In a food processor, combine scallions, garlic, and chiles; process until finely chopped, about 10 seconds. Add cilantro, cumin, lime juice, 2 tablespoons water, coconut, salt, and oil; pulse to form a coarse paste. Serve at room temperature.

PER SERVING: 98 CALORIES, 7 G FAT, 0 MG CHOLESTEROL, 9 G CARBOHYDRATE, 270 MG SODIUM, 2 G PROTEIN, 2 G FIBER

from Fit to Eat: Relishes and Salsas

corn relish

MAKES 2 QUARTS; SERVES 12

This relish is delicious with grilled chicken or shrimp. It also pairs well with piquant quesadillas or crab cakes.

- 6 ears fresh corn, shucked
- 1½ cups cider vinegar
- 3 tablespoons sugar
- ½ teaspoon ground turmeric
- ¾ teaspoon mustard powder
- 1 tablespoon mustard seed
- 1 teaspoon coarse salt
- 1 dried bay leaf
- 4 cups green cabbage (about ½ pound), chopped into ½-inch pieces
- 2 red bell peppers, seeds and ribs removed, finely diced
- 1 large red onion, finely diced

1 Fill a medium stockpot with water, and bring to a boil. Add corn; cook until kernels are tender, about 4 minutes. Using tongs, transfer corn to a platter; let cool. Discard all but 3 cups cooking water. Use a sharp knife to shave kernels from cobs (to yield about 3 cups); set aside.

2 Add vinegar, sugar, turmeric, mustard powder, mustard seed, salt, and bay leaf to pot. Bring to a simmer over medium-high heat. Add cabbage, red peppers, onion, and corn kernels; stir to combine. Bring to a boil; immediately remove from heat, and let stand 5 minutes.

3 Strain mixture, reserving liquid. Let liquid and vegetables cool in separate bowls; discard bay leaf. When cool, strain liquid through a fine sieve into bowl with vegetables.

4 Serve relish chilled or at room temperature, using a slotted spoon to leave liquid behind. Relish can be stored in an airtight container in the refrigerator up to 1 month.

PER SERVING: 86 CALORIES, 1 G FAT, 0 MG CHOLESTEROL, 20 G CARBOHYDRATE, 172 MG SODIUM, 3 G PROTEIN, 3 G FIBER

from Fit to Eat: Relishes and Salsas

Father's Day barbecue sauce

MAKES 1¼ QUARTS

- 3 tablespoons olive oil
- 1 Spanish onion, cut into ¼-inch pieces
- 4 garlic cloves, minced
- 2 cans (28 ounces each) crushed tomatoes
- 2 canned chipotle chiles in adobo sauce, minced, or ¼ teaspoon cayenne pepper
- 3 tablespoons Worcestershire sauce
- 3 tablespoons cider vinegar
- ½ cup unsulfured molasses
- Coarse salt and freshly ground pepper

1 In a medium saucepan, heat oil over medium heat. Add onion and garlic. Cook, stirring occasionally, until onion is soft and translucent, about 5 minutes.

2 Stir tomatoes, chiles, Worcestershire, vinegar, and molasses into onion mixture. Simmer until reduced by one-third, stirring occasionally, about 45 minutes. Let cool slightly.

3 Working in batches so as not to fill more than halfway, purée sauce in a blender. Season with salt and pepper. Refrigerate in a tightly covered jar up to 2 weeks.

from Good Things

fennel, roasted tomato, and basil relish

MAKES ABOUT 3 CUPS; SERVES 6

Serve with grilled shrimp, fish, or pork.

1 pound ripe plum tomatoes (about 6)

4 garlic cloves

1 bulb fennel (about 1 pound), trimmed and cut into ¼-inch dice

¼ cup red-wine vinegar

1 tablespoon capers, drained

¼ teaspoon crushed red-pepper flakes or finely chopped fresh red chile

2 tablespoons extra-virgin olive oil

1 cup loosely packed fresh basil leaves

1 cup loosely packed fresh flat-leaf parsley leaves, coarsely chopped

Olive-oil cooking spray

1 Preheat oven to 400°F. Coat a baking sheet with cooking spray. Slice tomatoes in half lengthwise; arrange them, cut side down, in a single layer on prepared baking sheet. Place garlic cloves on baking sheet next to tomatoes. Roast in oven until tomatoes are soft and wrinkled and garlic is aromatic and tender, about 35 minutes. Remove from oven; let cool.

2 In a medium bowl, combine fennel with vinegar, capers, red-pepper flakes, and oil. Stir to combine. Finely chop garlic, and roughly chop tomatoes; add to bowl. Slice basil into fine strips; add to bowl along with parsley. Stir to combine; serve chilled or at room temperature.

PER SERVING: 78 CALORIES, 5 G FAT, 0 MG CHOLESTEROL, 9 G CARBOHYDRATE, 56 MG SODIUM, 2 G PROTEIN, 3 G FIBER

from Fit to Eat: Relishes and Salsas

spicy pineapple and mint salsa

MAKES ABOUT 3 CUPS; SERVES 6

Serve this fruity salsa with grilled pork; the bright flavors also pair well with fish, such as red snapper or striped bass.

½ red onion, thinly sliced

1 or 2 serrano chiles (seeded for less heat, if desired), very thinly sliced

1 small garlic clove, minced

½ cup freshly squeezed orange juice (about 2 oranges)

1 tablespoon freshly squeezed lime juice (about 1 lime)

1 pineapple, peeled, cored and chopped into ½-inch pieces

1½ teaspoons extra-virgin olive oil

1 cup loosely packed fresh mint leaves

In a medium bowl, combine onion, chiles, garlic, orange and lime juices, and pineapple. Add oil; stir to combine. Let stand at room temperature at least 15 minutes or up to 1 hour. Just before serving, add mint; toss to combine.

PER SERVING: 176 CALORIES, 3 G FAT, 0 MG CHOLESTEROL, 42 G CARBOHYDRATE, 5 MG SODIUM, 2 G PROTEIN, 4 G FIBER

from Fit to Eat: Relishes and Salsas

strawberry jam

MAKES 48 OUNCES

Use slightly underripe strawberries for best results.

4 pounds strawberries, rinsed, hulled, and cut into 1-inch pieces

5 cups sugar (2¼ pounds)

1 Put a small plate in the freezer. Place berries in a nonreactive 10-quart stockpot set over medium-high heat. Using a wooden spoon, stir ¼ cup sugar into berries. Cook, stirring, until berries are juicy, 5 to 6 minutes. Stir in one-third of remaining sugar until dissolved. Repeat until all the sugar has been added and dissolved, about 7 minutes total.

2 Bring mixture to a full boil; cook, stirring, 10 minutes. Continue boiling, using a stainless-steel spoon to skim foam from surface, until most of the liquid has evaporated, mixture thickens, and temperature registers 220°F on a candy thermometer, about 30 minutes.

3 Perform a gel test: Place a spoonful of jam on chilled plate, and return to freezer 1 to 2 minutes; remove plate, and gently press jam with fingertip; it should wrinkle slightly.

4 After jam passes the gel test, remove from heat. Pour warm jam into jars; cover, and refrigerate up to 4 months.

from Clip-Art Craft

...DIVE WITH PEARS, WALNUTS, AND ROQUEFORT | **PAGE 112**

FRIED-EGG–TOPPED SANDWICHES | **PAGE 97**

...RRIED EGGS | **PAGE 96**

CELERY ROOT REMOULADE | **PAGE 109**

GRILLED PORK PAILLARDS | **PAGE 114**

PASTA VERDE | **PAGE 117**

COUSCOUS SALAD | **PAGE 93**

GRILLED MUSHROOM BURGER
WITH WHITE-BEAN PUREE | **PAGE 114**

SMOKED MACKEREL, CUCUMBER, AND POTATO
SALAD WITH MUSTARD DRESSING | **PAGE 99**

LAMB KOFTE | **PAGE 94**

GRILLED PROSCIUTTO-WRAPPED
COD AND ONIONS | **PAGE** 126

SLOW-ROASTED SALMON WITH
CAPER-AND-HERB RELISH | **PAGE 98**

PASTA WITH FENNEL, SARDINES, AND PINE NUTS | **PAGE 98**

YELLOW RICE PILAF | **PAGE 128**

BLACK BEANS WITH POBLANO | **PAGE 127**

RICOTTA CHEESE TORTA | **PAGE 115**

WARM BEAN, SNAP PEA, AND TOMATO SALAD | **PAGE 118**

WHOLE-WHEAT PASTA WITH LENTILS, SPINACH, AND LEEKS | **PAGE 116**

MEYER LEMON GELATO | **PAGE 105**

LEMON, BLACKBERRY, AND MERINGUE PARFAIT | **PAGE 100**

LEMON-BLUEBERRY PETITS FOURS | **PAGE 101**

LEMON MADELEINES | **PAGE 102**

LEMON SPONGE PUDDING | **PAGE 104**

LEMON POPPY-SEED LADY CAKE | **PAGE 103**

LEMON PINE-NUT TART | **PAGE 102**

PASTIERA WITH STRAWBERRY SAUCE | **PAGE 105**

STRAWBERRY TARTLETS | **PAGE 120**

JOEY GALLAGHER'S APRICOT
HAND PIES | **PAGE 133**

BROILED APRICOTS WITH
STIRRED CUSTARD | **PAGE 130**

VANILLA PANNA COTTA WITH POACHED
APRICOT HALVES | PAGE 134

APRICOT CHERRY BAKE | PAGE 129

APRICOT-AND-WALNUT ROLL CAKE | PAGE 128

CHEESECAKE WITH POACHED
APRICOT HALVES | PAGE 131

BUTTERMILK PIE | **PAGE 130**

BLACKBERRY AND BLUEBERRY SAUCE | **PAGE 131**

MANGO-PINEAPPLE BUCKLE | **PAGE 104**

ANGEL FOOD CAKE | **PAGE 118**

CHERRY ICE | **PAGE 119**

Summer

IF SPRING HINTS AT THE PROMISE OF NATURE'S BOUNTY, summer delivers in spades. Markets overflow with vegetables and fruit, their various colors and textures prompting us to experiment in the kitchen and on the grill. Mostly, however, we yearn for the familiar flavors of the season: burgers, fresh corn on the cob, and lattice-topped cherry pie with homemade vanilla ice cream.

July

(continued on next page)

avocado with lemon and olive oil

SERVES 4 | **PHOTO ON PAGE 235**

Because this recipe is so simple, using the finest ingredients is important. Choose ripe avocados that give slightly when pressed. Use smooth, richly flavored extra-virgin olive oil, and splurge on good sea salt; we recommend fleur de sel. Serve with toasted rustic bread, and let guests spread the avocado on it as they would butter.

2 ripe avocados

2 tablespoons extra-virgin olive oil

2 tablespoons freshly squeezed lemon juice (about 1 lemon)

   Sea salt and freshly ground pepper

Halve avocados lengthwise. Twist halves to separate them, and remove pits. Run a large spoon between the flesh and skin, scooping out the flesh in one piece; discard skins. Slice avocados into wedges, and place on a serving platter. Drizzle with oil and lemon juice, and season with salt and pepper. Serve at room temperature.

from What's For Dinner?

Bûcheron with cucumbers, basil, and figs

SERVES 6

Bûcheron is a mild goat cheese. We like to serve it drizzled with a deep, intensely flavored extra-virgin olive oil.

1 baguette, halved lengthwise and cut into 3-inch-long slices

8 ounces Bûcheron or other soft goat cheese, sliced, room temperature

6 fresh figs, halved

3 tablespoons extra-virgin olive oil

2 cucumbers

   Fresh basil leaves, for garnish

1   Preheat oven to 300°F. Arrange bread slices on a baking sheet. Toast in oven, turning once, until golden, about 5 minutes per side. Remove from oven; set aside on a platter.

2   Arrange cheese with figs on six plates, dividing evenly. Drizzle oil over cheese. Slice cucumbers into spears, peeling the skins if waxy; arrange around cheese. Garnish with basil. Serve with toast on the side.

from Summer Lunch on Shelter Island

chicken pasta salad

SERVES 6

½ cup whole almonds

   Chicken Salad (page 166)

½ pound penne, cooked

1 cucumber, peeled and thinly sliced crosswise

1 pint cherry tomatoes, halved

   Romaine or other lettuce, for serving

1   Preheat oven to 350°F. Spread almonds in a single layer on a rimmed baking sheet; toast in oven until crisp and fragrant, tossing occasionally, about 10 minutes. Let cool.

2   In a bowl, toss chicken salad with pasta, cucumber, tomatoes, and nuts. Divide lettuce evenly among six plates; scoop pasta salad on top. Serve chilled or at room temperature.

from Impromptu Entertaining

chicken salad

SERVES 4

In addition to using this salad to make Chicken Pasta Salad, you can also serve it tucked into whole-wheat flour tortillas.

- 1 rotisserie chicken (3 to 4 pounds), meat removed and shredded
- 3 stalks celery, thinly sliced
- ½ cup chopped dill pickles or cornichons
- 1 shallot, thinly sliced
- 2 tablespoons chopped fresh tarragon
  Mustard Vinaigrette (recipe follows)
- 2 tablespoons mayonnaise (optional)
  Coarse salt and freshly ground pepper

In a medium bowl, mix together shredded chicken, celery, pickles, shallot, and tarragon. Toss with vinaigrette and mayonnaise, if desired. Season with salt and pepper. Serve immediately, or refrigerate in an airtight container up to 2 days.

mustard vinaigrette

MAKES ¾ CUP

- 1 tablespoon grainy mustard
- 2 tablespoons honey
- 2 tablespoons white-wine vinegar
- ½ cup extra-virgin olive oil

Place all ingredients in a glass jar; seal tightly. Shake until emulsified. Use immediately, or keep refrigerated in jar up to 1 week. Before using, let come to room temperature, and shake to emulsify.

chickpea fritters

MAKES ABOUT 20 | **PHOTO ON PAGE 228**

- 7 tablespoons extra-virgin olive oil
- 1 onion, finely diced
- 2 tablespoons sesame seeds
- 1 tablespoon ground cumin
  Pinch of cayenne pepper
- 1 can (15½ ounces) chickpeas, drained and rinsed
- 2 tablespoons freshly squeezed lemon juice
- 1 large egg white
- 1 teaspoon coarse salt, plus more for seasoning
- 5 tablespoons all-purpose flour
  Tzatziki, for serving (recipe follows)

1 In a medium sauté pan, heat 3 tablespoons oil over medium heat. Add onion; cook, stirring, until soft and translucent, about 3 minutes. Add sesame seeds, cumin, and cayenne; cook, stirring, until sesame seeds have begun to brown lightly and spices are very fragrant, about 2 minutes; set aside.

2 In a food processor, combine chickpeas, lemon juice, egg white, salt, and 1 tablespoon oil. Pulse several times to form a semismooth paste. Transfer to a large bowl; stir in onion mixture. Fold in flour until just combined. Using your hands, form batter into 1¼-inch patties, each about ⅓ inch thick.

3 In a 12-inch sauté pan, heat 2 tablespoons oil over medium-low heat. Cook half the patties, without flattening, until golden brown, about 3 minutes per side. Using a slotted spoon, transfer to a paper-towel–lined plate; season with salt. Repeat with remaining patties and tablespoon oil. Serve immediately with tzatziki.

from The Flavors of Greece

tzatziki

MAKES 2 CUPS | **PHOTO ON PAGE 228**

This garlicky yogurt sauce is a traditional Greek mezze, or appetizer; it's often served with warm pita bread. If you can't find Greek-style yogurt, which is thicker than other types, you can make your own version; drain thirty-two ounces plain whole-milk yogurt in a cheesecloth-lined sieve set over a bowl. Cover sieve with plastic; refrigerate at least four hours. Discard liquid.

1 **English cucumber, cut into 1½-by-⅛-inch matchsticks**
1½ **teaspoons coarse salt, plus more for seasoning**
1¼ **cups Greek-style yogurt**
1 **large garlic clove, minced**
2 **tablespoons white-wine vinegar**
2 **tablespoons extra-virgin olive oil**
¼ **cup chopped fresh dill**
Freshly ground pepper

1 In a colander, sprinkle cucumber with salt; toss to combine. Let stand at room temperature 30 minutes.

2 In a medium bowl, combine cucumber, yogurt, garlic, vinegar, oil, and dill. Season with salt and pepper. Serve immediately, or refrigerate, covered, up to 2 hours.

classic panini

SERVES 4 TO 6

If you have a sandwich press, you can use it to grill the panini. Serve along with olives, pickled onions, and cold beer.

1 **loaf ciabatta, halved horizontally and then crosswise**
1 **small jar pesto**
4 **ounces thinly sliced prosciutto**
6 **ounces mozzarella and fontina cheeses, sliced**
1 **small jar tapenade**
1 **medium jar roasted red and yellow peppers**
Extra-virgin olive oil, for brushing

1 Preheat oven to 200°F. Spread a ciabatta quarter with some pesto, and layer with prosciutto and mozzarella; cover with matching quarter. Spread some tapenade on other quarter; layer with peppers and fontina; cover with remaining bread.

2 Heat a griddle or cast-iron skillet over medium-low heat. Brush bread with oil. Place a sandwich on griddle; weigh down with another skillet. Cook until golden brown on first side, 3 to 4 minutes; flip, and cook until other side is golden and cheese has melted, 3 to 4 minutes more.

3 Transfer to a baking sheet; keep warm in oven while grilling other sandwich. Cut each half into slices; serve.

from Impromptu Entertaining

cucumber and smoked-salmon sandwiches

SERVES 8 TO 10 | **PHOTO ON PAGE 227**

¼ **pound smoked salmon, finely chopped**
2 **tablespoons finely chopped red onion**
2 **teaspoons finely chopped fresh cilantro**
1 **jalapeño chile, seeded and finely chopped**
Finely grated zest of 1 lime
Coarse salt and freshly ground pepper
1 **English cucumber**
¼ **cup crème fraîche, chilled**
1 **lime, peeled and segmented, each segment cut into 4 pieces**

1 Make tartare: In a small bowl, combine salmon, onion, cilantro, jalapeño, and zest. Season with salt and pepper.

2 Using a paring knife or vegetable peeler, remove skin on two opposite sides of cucumber. Trim ends; slice cucumber crosswise ¼ inch thick. Place slices on paper towels to dry.

3 Using a butter knife or a small offset spatula, spread about ½ teaspoon crème fraîche on half the cucumber slices, then top with a teaspoon of tartare. Place remaining cucumber slices on top, followed by a small dollop of crème fraîche and then a piece of lime. Serve immediately, or chill up to 1 hour.

from Cutting-Edge Cocktails

deviled eggs

SERVES 8

Use medium-size eggs so these will be small enough to serve as hors d'oeuvres.

    8 medium eggs
    1 tablespoon Dijon mustard
    ¼ cup mayonnaise
       Coarse salt and freshly ground pepper
       Finely chopped fresh flat-leaf parsley, for garnish
       Smoked paprika, for garnish
       Poppy seeds, for garnish

1 Place eggs in a large saucepan; add enough cold water to cover by 1 inch. Bring to a boil; cook 1 minute. Remove from heat, and cover; let stand 13 minutes. Drain, and place in cold water until cool. Peel eggs, and slice in half lengthwise; separate yolks from whites. Trim bottoms of whites so they won't wobble. Set aside on a platter.

2 Place yolks in a sieve set over a medium bowl, and press through with a wooden spoon. Mix in mustard and mayonnaise, and season with salt and pepper. Fill egg-white halves with yolk mixture. Refrigerate eggs, covered, up to 4 hours. Before serving, garnish each deviled egg with either parsley, paprika, or poppy seeds.

from Fourth of July Barbecue

Parmesan-dusted meatballs

SERVES 8 TO 10 | **PHOTO ON PAGE 226**

    ⅓ cup plus 3 tablespoons sliced almonds
    1½ teaspoons sugar
    ¾ cup plain breadcrumbs, preferably homemade
    ¼ cup milk
    ½ pound ground chuck
    ½ pound ground pork
    1 large egg, lightly beaten
    ½ cup finely grated Parmesan cheese, plus more for garnish
    ⅓ cup finely chopped fresh flat-leaf parsley
    3 tablespoons dried currants
    2 teaspoons coarse salt
    ⅛ teaspoon ground allspice
    3 tablespoons olive oil

1 Preheat oven to 350°F. Spread almonds in a single layer on a rimmed baking sheet; toast in oven until golden and fragrant, tossing occasionally, about 7 minutes. Let cool. In a food processor, pulse ⅓ cup almonds with sugar until finely ground. Coarsely chop remaining 3 tablespoons almonds.

2 In a medium bowl, mix together breadcrumbs and milk. Add almonds and remaining ingredients, except oil. Mix until combined. Form into 1-inch balls.

3 Heat 1½ tablespoons oil in a 12-inch heavy skillet over medium heat. Add half the meatballs; sauté until cooked through, about 7 minutes. Transfer to a platter. Repeat with remaining oil and meatballs. Garnish with Parmesan; serve.

from Cutting-Edge Cocktails

pickled vegetables

MAKES 2 QUARTS

Vegetables can be stored for up to one week in the refrigerator.

3 tablespoons coarse salt, plus more for cooking water

1 small head cauliflower (about 1 pound),
 cut into 1½-inch florets

½ pound baby carrots

4 stalks celery, cut diagonally into ⅓-inch-thick pieces

2 cups white-wine vinegar

1 teaspoon whole black peppercorns

4 dried bay leaves

4 garlic cloves, lightly crushed

¼ cup sugar

1 jar (12 ounces) pepperoncini, drained

1 Bring a large saucepan of water to a boil over high heat; add a generous amount of salt. Add cauliflower, and cook until crisp-tender, about 3½ minutes. Using a slotted spoon, transfer to a large heatproof bowl. Repeat with carrots, cooking about 2½ minutes, and then with celery, cooking about 2 minutes; combine with the cauliflower.

2 In a medium saucepan over high heat, combine 2 cups water with the vinegar, peppercorns, bay leaves, garlic, sugar, and 3 tablespoons salt. Boil until sugar and salt have completely dissolved, about 2 minutes. Immediately pour over vegetables; gently stir in pepperoncini. Let cool completely.

3 Transfer mixture to an airtight container; chill at least 1 hour. Discard bay leaves. Serve chilled or at room temperature.

from The Flavors of Greece

savory pain perdu

SERVES 4

Unlike traditional *pain perdu*, or French toast, which is sweet, this version is a savory brunch dish. Baking it in the oven eliminates the need for making multiple batches in a skillet.

2 large eggs

1½ cups milk

1 teaspoon coarse salt

¼ teaspoon freshly ground pepper

¼ cup grated Parmesan cheese (optional)

1 day-old baguette or other white bread,
 cut into 1-inch-thick slices

Ricotta cheese, for serving

Tomato-Cucumber Salad, for serving (recipe follows)

1 Preheat oven to 350°F. In a medium bowl, whisk together eggs, milk, salt, pepper, and cheese, if desired. Place bread in an 8-inch square glass baking dish. Pour batter over bread. Let stand until both sides of bread are soaked through, about 10 minutes, turning slices once after 5 minutes.

2 Transfer baking dish to oven. Bake until bread is golden brown, about 25 minutes. Serve hot, topped with ricotta and tomato salad.

from Impromptu Entertaining

tomato-cucumber salad

SERVES 4

1 small red onion, thinly sliced

½ English cucumber, thinly sliced

2 beefsteak tomatoes, thinly sliced

½ cup pitted black olives

Sherry or balsamic vinegar

Extra-virgin olive oil

Coarse salt and freshly ground pepper

In a medium bowl, combine onion, cucumber, tomatoes, and olives. Drizzle with vinegar and oil, as desired. Season with salt and pepper, and let marinate 30 minutes at room temperature or in the refrigerator.

shrimp and avocado seviche

SERVES 8 TO 10 | **PHOTO ON PAGE 227**

4 limes, plus ¼ cup freshly squeezed lime juice (about 3 limes)

2 pounds medium shrimp

6 scallions, finely chopped

2 to 4 serrano chiles, finely chopped

¼ cup cider vinegar

2 teaspoons finely chopped fresh thyme

1 teaspoon dried oregano, preferably Mexican

2 large ripe avocados

¼ cup finely chopped fresh cilantro

2 teaspoons coarse salt

Tortilla chips, for serving

1   Fill a large pot with 1 quart water. Cut 4 limes in half, and squeeze their juice into pot; add squeezed lime halves. Bring to a boil. Turn off heat; let steep 10 minutes. Return to a boil.

2   Add shrimp to boiling water in pot. As soon as water returns to a rolling boil, pour shrimp into a colander; discard cooking liquid and limes. Return shrimp to pot; cover, and let stand 15 minutes. Spread shrimp on a baking sheet; let stand until cool enough to handle.

3   Peel and devein shrimp, and cut into thirds. Transfer to a medium bowl; add lime juice, scallions, chiles, vinegar, thyme, and oregano, stirring to coat. Let stand 1 hour at room temperature, stirring occasionally.

4   When ready to serve, pit, peel, and dice avocados. Gently stir avocados, cilantro, and salt into shrimp mixture. Serve with tortilla chips.

from Cutting-Edge Cocktails

watermelon skewers

SERVES 8 TO 10 | **PHOTO ON PAGE 225**

¼ large seedless watermelon, cut into ¾-inch cubes

2 bunches fresh mint, leaves separated

10 ounces ricotta salata, cut into ½-inch cubes

Freshly ground pepper (optional)

Arrange melon cubes on a serving platter. Lay a mint leaf on top of each, then add a cheese cube. Insert skewers through stack; sprinkle with pepper, if desired. Chill, covered, until ready to serve, up to 3 hours.

from Cutting-Edge Cocktails

white bean, yogurt, and feta dip

MAKES 2 CUPS

This dip can be stored, covered, in the refrigerator for up to one week. Serve it with your favorite olives.

1 can (15½ ounces) cannellini or navy beans, drained and rinsed

4 ounces feta cheese

1 container (7 ounces) Greek-style yogurt

1 tablespoon freshly squeezed lemon juice

¼ cup finely chopped fresh dill

Coarse salt and freshly ground pepper

Toasted Pita Chips, for serving (recipe follows)

In a food processor, purée beans, feta, yogurt, and lemon juice until smooth. Transfer to a bowl; stir in dill. Season with salt and pepper. Serve immediately with pita chips.

from Impromptu Entertaining

toasted pita chips

SERVES 8

Chips will keep for up to a week in an airtight container.

8 pita rounds (6 to 7 inches each)

Extra-virgin olive oil

Dried oregano or parsley

Coarse salt and freshly ground pepper

Preheat oven to 350°F. Using kitchen scissors, halve each pita horizontally. Cut each piece in half. Place, rough side up, on a baking sheet. Brush with oil; season with oregano, salt, and pepper. Bake until golden, 12 to 15 minutes. Serve warm or at room temperature.

zucchini fritters

MAKES ABOUT 28 | PHOTO ON PAGE 228

1 pound (about 2 medium) zucchini, grated on the large holes of a box grater

2½ teaspoons coarse salt, plus more for seasoning

3 large scallions, thinly sliced

½ cup finely chopped fresh mint

¼ cup finely chopped fresh dill

3 large eggs, lightly beaten

½ cup grated Kefalotyri cheese or Pecorino Romano cheese

5 tablespoons all-purpose flour

3 tablespoons extra-virgin olive oil

Tzatziki, for serving (page 167)

1 In a colander, sprinkle zucchini with 1¼ teaspoons salt; toss to combine, and let stand at room temperature 45 minutes. Transfer zucchini to a clean kitchen towel; squeeze to remove any remaining liquid.

2 In a large bowl, place zucchini, 1¼ teaspoons salt, scallions, mint, dill, eggs, and cheese; stir gently to combine. Fold in flour until just combined.

3 In a large sauté pan, heat 2 tablespoons oil over medium-low heat. Using half the batter, drop heaping teaspoons directly into pan to create about fourteen 1½-inch patties, each about ¼ inch thick. Cook patties, without flattening, until golden brown, about 2 minutes per side. Using a slotted spatula, transfer to a paper-towel–lined platter; season with salt. Repeat with remaining batter and tablespoon oil. Serve immediately with tzatziki.

from The Flavors of Greece

MAIN COURSES

barbecued chicken

SERVES 8 | PHOTO ON PAGE 234

If using a gas grill, cook chickens over medium heat.

4 whole fryer chickens (about 3 pounds each)

1¼ quarts Barbecue Sauce (recipe follows)

1 Rinse the chickens inside and out under cold water, and pat dry. Truss legs with kitchen twine, and set aside.

2 Heat a charcoal grill. Arrange hot coals in a circle inside edge of grill. Arrange chickens, breast sides up, in a row across the center. Cook until brown on all sides, rotating every 5 to 7 minutes; cover grill as needed to maintain heat.

3 Baste chickens with barbecue sauce. Continue cooking, basting frequently, until an instant-read thermometer registers 170°F in breast and 180°F in thickest part of the thigh (avoiding bone), about 1 hour. If chickens begin to brown too quickly before they are cooked through, transfer to baking pans and finish in a 350°F oven.

from Fourth of July Barbecue

barbecue sauce

MAKES 2½ QUARTS

This recipe makes enough sauce for eight chickens; refrigerate any leftover sauce in an airtight container for up to two weeks.

3 tablespoons canola oil

2 large onions, finely chopped

6 garlic cloves, minced

2 cans (28 ounces each) crushed tomatoes

2½ cups cider vinegar

2 cups firmly packed dark-brown sugar

1 cup honey

3 tablespoons chili powder

2 tablespoons soy sauce

2 tablespoons hot dry mustard

2 tablespoons paprika

1 tablespoon coarse salt

Heat oil in a large heavy-bottom saucepan over medium heat. Add onions and garlic; cook, stirring, until golden brown, about 15 minutes. Add remaining ingredients, and bring to a boil. Reduce heat; simmer uncovered, stirring occasionally, until sauce thickens, about 2 hours.

chicken, potato, and butter lettuce with lemon-garlic dressing

SERVES 4

Using part-skim ricotta cheese instead of sour cream or mayonnaise makes this dressing lower in fat and calories without sacrificing texture or flavor.

5 garlic cloves
1 dried bay leaf
4 boneless and skinless chicken breasts (about 1¾ pounds)
3 tablespoons freshly squeezed lemon juice (about 1 lemon)
½ teaspoon coarse salt
6 tablespoons part-skim ricotta cheese
2 tablespoons extra-virgin olive oil
½ cup loosely packed small dill sprigs, coarsely chopped
Freshly ground pepper
¾ pound small boiling potatoes, such as golden creamers
1 head butter lettuce, leaves torn in half
½ pint cherry tomatoes, halved

1 Fill a large saucepan with enough water to cover chicken breasts. Add garlic and bay leaf; bring to a boil. Place chicken in pan, and gently simmer until cooked through, 15 to 20 minutes. Use a slotted spoon to transfer chicken and garlic to a plate; let cool. Reserve poaching liquid; discard bay leaf.

2 Make dressing: Pulse garlic in a food processor to form a coarse paste. Add 2 tablespoons reserved poaching liquid and the lemon juice, salt, and ricotta; pulse to combine. With machine running, add oil in a slow, steady stream until emulsified. Stir in dill; season with pepper. Set aside.

3 In a medium saucepan, cover potatoes with cold water. Bring to a boil; cook potatoes until easily pierced with the tip of a paring knife, about 20 minutes. Drain, and let cool. Peel if desired, and cut into quarters.

4 Slice each chicken breast crosswise into about six strips. Divide lettuce, potatoes, tomatoes, and chicken among serving plates. Drizzle with some of the dressing, and serve immediately with remaining dressing on the side.

PER SERVING: 483 CALORIES, 27 G FAT, 134 MG CHOLESTEROL, 12 G CARBOHYDRATE, 334 MG SODIUM, 47 G PROTEIN, 4 G FIBER

from Fit to Eat: Main Course Salads

Greek salad with feta in grape leaves and grilled swordfish kebabs

SERVES 6 | PHOTO ON PAGE 239

You'll need nine-inch bamboo or metal skewers. If using bamboo skewers, soak them in water at least thirty minutes to keep them from burning on the grill.

24 grape leaves packed in brine
1 cup freshly squeezed lemon juice (about 8 lemons)
2 cups extra-virgin olive oil
1½ teaspoons crushed red-pepper flakes
⅓ cup coarsely chopped fresh oregano leaves, plus small sprigs for garnish
3 tablespoons fresh thyme leaves, plus small sprigs for garnish
8 garlic cloves, crushed
1¼ pounds feta cheese, cut crosswise into twelve ½-inch-thick slices
Freshly ground black pepper
2¼ pounds swordfish steaks (1¼ inches thick), cut into 1¼-inch cubes
4 small red onions, cut into 1-inch wedges, roots intact
1 pound cherry tomatoes
Coarse salt
2 hearts of romaine, washed and cut into bite-size pieces (about 5 cups)
1 large bunch arugula, tough stems discarded, washed well (about 4 cups)
1 green bell pepper, ribs and seeds removed, cut into 1-by-¼-inch strips
1 English cucumber, halved lengthwise and cut into ¼-inch-thick half-moons
Zest of 1 lemon, cut into thin strips (about ½ cup loosely packed)
1 cup Kalamata olives, pitted if desired
Grilled Pita Bread, for serving (optional; recipe follows)
Parsley Sauce (optional; recipe follows)

1 Fill a large saucepan with water; bring to a boil. Rinse the grape leaves several times under cold water, and place in saucepan. Reduce heat to a simmer; cook, uncovered, 45 minutes. Drain leaves in a colander, and set aside.

2 In a medium bowl, combine lemon juice, oil, red-pepper flakes, oregano, thyme, and garlic. Measure out ⅓ cup to use as a dressing; reserve remaining mixture for a marinade.

3 On a large, clean work surface, lay out pairs of grape leaves so that they are slightly overlapping, making twelve sets. Lay a slice of feta in center of each pair. Whisk the marinade so it

is well combined, and spoon 1 teaspoon of it over each slice of feta. Season with black pepper, and top each with an oregano and thyme sprig. Fold leaves to completely enclose the cheese; secure with kitchen twine. Place feta bundles in a large, shallow baking dish; cover with ½ cup of marinade. Set aside.

4   Heat grill to medium. In a large bowl, combine cubed swordfish, onions, tomatoes, and remaining marinade; gently toss to coat well. Let marinate 20 minutes at room temperature, gently stirring occasionally.

5   Thread skewers, alternating between the fish and vegetables; discard remaining marinade. Season each skewer generously with salt and black pepper, and set aside.

6   Using a slotted spatula, transfer feta bundles to grill, letting excess marinade drip off into dish. Grill until leaves are browned and crisp but not falling apart, about 2½ minutes on each side. Transfer to a plate. Grill skewers, turning occasionally with tongs, until fish is just cooked through and opaque, about 10 minutes total. Transfer to a plate.

7   In a large bowl, combine romaine, arugula, green pepper, cucumber, lemon zest, and olives. Toss salad with just enough dressing to coat lettuce. Season with salt and black pepper. Serve salad, kebabs, and feta bundles with pita bread and parsley sauce, if desired.

from The Flavors of Greece

grilled pita bread
SERVES 6

6 pita rounds (6 to 7 inches each)
2 tablespoons extra-virgin olive oil
   Coarse salt and freshly ground pepper

Heat grill to medium. Lightly brush each pita with oil; season with salt and pepper. Grill bread on each side until lightly browned, about 2 minutes. Transfer to a serving platter.

parsley sauce
MAKES 1¾ CUPS

You can omit the egg from this recipe; the sauce will be less creamy but equally delicious. Sauce can be made four hours ahead, and stored in an airtight container in the refrigerator.

2 slices (½ inch thick) hearty white bread, torn into small pieces
4 cups loosely packed flat-leaf parsley sprigs
½ shallot, sliced
1 large egg
3 tablespoons white-wine vinegar
¾ cup extra-virgin olive oil
   Coarse salt and freshly ground pepper

1   Place bread in a small bowl, and cover with cold water. Let stand until moistened, about 3 minutes. Drain the bread, squeezing with your hands to remove excess moisture.

2   In a food processor, pulse bread, parsley, shallot, egg, and vinegar until mixture is finely chopped. With machine running, pour oil into feed tube in a slow, steady stream until emulsified. Season with salt and pepper.

Note: Raw eggs should not be used in food prepared for pregnant women, babies, young children, the elderly, or anyone whose health is compromised.

grilled hamburgers with goat cheese

SERVES 6

If your grill is large enough, you can cook the hamburgers and grill the vegetables at the same time. Give the burgers about a two-minute head start so that everything is ready to come off the grill at the same time.

3 pounds lean ground chuck

1 tablespoon each finely chopped fresh thyme, oregano, rosemary, and flat-leaf parsley

  Coarse salt and freshly ground pepper

3 large tomatoes, thickly sliced

2 large onions, thickly sliced

2 tablespoons extra-virgin olive oil

1 log (5 ounces) fresh goat cheese, sliced into 6 equal portions

1 head romaine lettuce, coarsely chopped

1 head red or white endive, thinly sliced crosswise

1 Heat grill to medium. In a large bowl, place ground chuck and herbs; season with salt and pepper. Using your hands, gently mix ingredients until just combined. Form into six patties, and set aside.

2 Brush tomato and onion slices with oil, and season with salt and pepper. Grill tomato and onion slices until slightly charred on both sides (onion should be tender), 4 to 6 minutes for tomatoes and 6 to 8 minutes for onions. Remove from the grill, and keep warm.

3 Grill hamburger patties, 3 to 5 minutes per side for medium-rare. When they have reached desired doneness, place cheese on top of each patty. Grill until cheese is melted.

4 To serve, stack slices of onion and tomato on a serving platter with greens and hamburgers.

from A Lazy Weekend in the Country

grilled squid with fried capers and skordalia sauce

SERVES 6 | PHOTO ON PAGE 229

Be careful not to overcook squid because it will toughen.

1 pound fingerling or small new potatoes

  Coarse salt

4 tablespoons plus ⅓ cup extra-virgin olive oil

¼ cup capers, rinsed

1 pound small squid, cleaned, cartilage discarded

  Freshly ground pepper

¼ cup freshly squeezed lemon juice (about 2 lemons)

1 small bulb fennel, thinly sliced

⅓ cup packed fresh flat-leaf parsley leaves

  Skordalia Sauce (recipe follows)

1 Place potatoes in a medium saucepan, and fill with enough cold water to cover by 1 inch. Bring to a boil, and add salt. Reduce heat to a simmer, and cook until potatoes are just tender when pierced with a fork, about 15 minutes. Drain in a colander, and let potatoes cool completely. Slice into 1-inch pieces; set aside.

2 In a small sauté pan, heat 2 tablespoons oil over medium-high heat until hot but not smoking. Add capers; cook, stirring occasionally, until crisp, about 3 minutes. Using a slotted spoon, transfer to a paper-towel–lined plate.

3 Heat grill to medium. Cut squid bodies open to make flat pieces: Holding a sharp knife at a 30-degree angle, score the inner side of each squid in a crosshatch pattern, being careful not to cut all the way through. Toss squid with 2 tablespoons oil; season with salt and pepper. Grill squid, turning once, until just cooked through and charred (squid will curl up as it cooks), 2 to 3 minutes. Cut into 2-inch pieces.

4 In a small bowl, whisk together lemon juice and remaining ⅓ cup oil. In a medium bowl, combine reserved potatoes, fennel, and parsley. Coat with half the lemon mixture, and season with salt and pepper. In another bowl, toss squid with remaining lemon mixture; season with salt and pepper.

5 To serve, place about 2 tablespoons skordalia sauce on each of six plates. Top with a mound of potato salad. Arrange squid on top, and garnish with the capers.

from The Flavors of Greece

skordalia sauce

MAKES 1 CUP

This sauce is traditionally made with puréed potatoes as well as bread. We took out the potatoes for lighter results.

2½ ounces blanched almonds (½ cup)

3 garlic cloves

1 slice hearty white bread, trimmed of crust and torn into small pieces

6 tablespoons extra-virgin olive oil

3 tablespoons freshly squeezed lemon juice (about 1 lemon)

Coarse salt and freshly ground pepper

In a food processor, pulse together almonds, garlic, and bread until the almonds are finely ground. With machine running, pour in oil, then lemon juice and 6 tablespoons water; mix until smooth. Season with salt and pepper. Refrigerate in an airtight container up to 2 days. Serve at room temperature.

grilled top-round of lamb

SERVES 6 | PHOTO ON PAGE 234

The top round comes from the inside of a leg of lamb and is very tender. Because of its size, it does not take long to cook and is perfect for grilling.

2 top rounds of lamb (about 1½ pounds each)

¼ cup extra-virgin olive oil

¼ cup Dijon mustard

1 cup loosely packed fresh mint leaves, coarsely chopped, plus sprigs for garnish

Coarse salt and freshly ground pepper

Yellow and red grape tomatoes, for garnish (optional)

1 Heat grill to medium-high. Rinse lamb, and pat dry with paper towels. In a shallow dish, whisk together oil and mustard. Stir in mint, and season with salt and pepper. Place lamb in dish, and rub mixture evenly over meat.

2 Place lamb on grill, and cover grill (to help the inside of the lamb cook before the outside begins to char). Grill, turning lamb as it cooks, until dark brown on the outside and pink inside, about 12 minutes per side for medium-rare, depending on heat of grill. The meat should register 123°F on an instant-read thermometer for medium-rare.

3 Transfer lamb to a carving board, and let rest 15 minutes before thinly slicing. Serve lamb on a large platter; garnish with mint sprigs and grape tomatoes, if desired.

from Summer Lunch on Shelter Island

salmon and golden beet salad with crisp bacon

SERVES 4

8 small golden beets (about 10 ounces)

3 tablespoons extra-virgin olive oil

¼ teaspoon coarse salt

4 slices turkey bacon (about 2¼ ounces), sliced crosswise into thin strips

½ lemon, sliced into 4 rounds

4 salmon fillets (6 ounces each)

1 shallot, finely chopped

1½ tablespoons white-wine vinegar

1 pound baby spinach

Freshly ground pepper

1 Preheat oven to 350°F. On a large piece of aluminum foil, toss beets with 1 tablespoon oil and the salt; wrap beets in foil to make a packet. Cook until beets are easily pierced with the tip of a paring knife, about 35 minutes. Let cool, then peel beets, and slice into ¼-inch-thick rounds.

2 Cook bacon on a baking sheet until crisp, about 10 minutes. Transfer to a paper-towel–lined plate; let drain.

3 Place lemon slices and 1½ quarts water in a large, wide saucepan; bring to a boil. Reduce heat to a bare simmer; add salmon, and gently cook until flaky, about 12 minutes. Transfer fish to a plate, and let cool.

4 Make dressing: In a small bowl, whisk together shallot, vinegar, and remaining 2 tablespoons oil until emulsified.

5 Place spinach and beets in a large bowl. Add dressing and some of the bacon; season with pepper. Toss to combine. Divide salad among four plates; top each with a salmon fillet. Garnish with remaining bacon.

PER SERVING: 465 CALORIES, 26 G FAT, 122 MG CHOLESTEROL, 12 G CARBOHYDRATE, 537 MG SODIUM, 46 G PROTEIN, 5 G FIBER

from Fit to Eat: Main Course Salads

seared tuna with tomatoes and basil

SERVES 4 | **PHOTO ON PAGE 235**

  5 tablespoons olive oil
1½ pounds tuna (1 inch thick), cut into 1-inch chunks
    Coarse salt and freshly ground pepper
  1 onion, coarsely chopped (about 1 cup)
  2 cups (about 12 ounces) small cherry tomatoes,
    stemmed and cut in half
  ½ cup dry white wine or water
  3 sprigs basil, leaves coarsely chopped

1 In a 12-inch skillet, heat 1½ tablespoons oil over medium-high heat. Season tuna generously with salt and pepper. Arrange half the tuna in skillet in a single layer. Cook, turning halfway through, until golden brown on top and bottom, about 1½ minutes per side. Tuna should be slightly pink in the middle. Transfer to a platter, and cover to keep warm. Add another 1½ tablespoons oil, and repeat with second batch.

2 Wipe skillet clean. Add remaining 2 tablespoons oil and the onion. Cook over medium heat, stirring, until onion is golden brown and soft, 4 to 6 minutes. Add tomatoes and wine; simmer, stirring often, until the tomatoes' skins just begin to wrinkle, about 2 minutes. Continue cooking at a bare simmer until sauce thickens slightly, about 5 minutes more. Add basil; cook, stirring, until just wilted. Season with salt and pepper. Spoon sauce over tuna just before serving.

from What's For Dinner?

soba noodles with tofu, avocado, and snow peas

SERVES 4 | **PHOTO ON PAGE 240**

  1 two-inch piece fresh ginger, peeled and sliced
    into very thin strips
  1 serrano or jalapeño chile, seeded and sliced
    into very thin strips
  ¼ cup sugar
  3 tablespoons freshly squeezed lime juice (about 3 limes)
  2 tablespoons low-sodium soy sauce
  1 package (14 ounces) extra-firm tofu, cut into ¾-inch cubes
    and patted dry
  1 package (about 8 ounces) soba noodles
  4 ounces snow peas, thinly sliced
  1 teaspoon vegetable oil
  1 English cucumber, peeled, halved crosswise, and sliced
    lengthwise into thin strips
 10 to 12 chives, cut into 1-inch pieces
  1 ripe avocado, pitted, peeled, and thinly sliced
  2 tablespoons sesame seeds

1 In a small saucepan, bring ginger, chile, sugar, and ⅓ cup water to a boil. Reduce heat to low; cook until ginger and chile are soft, about 5 minutes. Use a slotted spoon to transfer ginger and chile to a bowl; set aside. Reserve syrup.

2 Make dressing: In a shallow bowl, whisk together lime juice, soy sauce, and 2 teaspoons reserved syrup. Add tofu, and toss gently to coat. Set aside.

3 In a large pot of boiling water, cook soba noodles according to package instructions. Drain; transfer to a large bowl. Add snow peas; drizzle with oil and 1 tablespoon dressing. Toss to coat, and let cool.

4 To serve, add cucumber and chives to bowl with noodles along with the tofu and dressing; toss to combine. Divide among four plates; top with avocado and reserved ginger and chile. Sprinkle with sesame seeds, and serve.

PER SERVING: 547 CALORIES, 20 G FAT, 0 MG CHOLESTEROL, 75 G CARBOHYDRATE, 822 MG SODIUM, 28 G PROTEIN, 7 G FIBER

from Fit to Eat: Main Course Salads

Thai beef salad

SERVES 4

2 tablespoons unsalted peanuts

1 one-inch piece fresh ginger, peeled and minced
(1 tablespoon)

Grated zest and juice of 2 limes

1 jalapeño chile, halved lengthwise, or 2 Thai chiles

4 shallots, finely chopped (about 4 tablespoons)

2½ teaspoons sugar

2 tablespoons Thai fish sauce (nam pla)

2 tablespoons plus 1 teaspoon canola oil

1½ pounds sirloin steak

6 ounces green beans, trimmed

1 head red cabbage, halved and thinly sliced (about 3 cups)

½ head napa cabbage, halved and thinly sliced (about 3 cups),
plus a few whole outer leaves

2 carrots, thinly sliced diagonally

2 scallions, cut into 2-inch lengths and sliced
into thin strips

1 Heat grill to medium-high. In a small skillet over medium
heat, toast peanuts, tossing occasionally, until fragrant and
lightly browned, 2 to 3 minutes. Remove from heat. Let cool,
then coarsely chop; set aside.

2 Make marinade: In a food processor, process ginger, lime
zest, chile, half the chopped shallots, and 2 teaspoons sugar
to form a coarse paste, about 1 minute. Add 1 tablespoon fish
sauce and 1 teaspoon oil; pulse to combine. Place steak on a
large plate, and coat both sides with marinade.

3 Make dressing: In a small bowl, combine lime juice with
the remaining shallots, ½ teaspoon sugar, and tablespoon
fish sauce. Whisking constantly, add the remaining 2 tablespoons oil in a slow, steady stream until emulsified.

4 Prepare an ice bath; set aside. Bring a medium pot of water
to a boil; add beans, and cook until crisp-tender and bright
green, about 2 minutes. Using a slotted spoon, plunge beans
into ice bath to stop the cooking. When cool, drain and pat dry.

5 Grill steak 6 minutes on first side. Turn steak, and continue cooking 4 minutes more for medium-rare. Transfer to
a cutting board to rest at least 5 minutes before slicing.

6 Arrange green beans, cabbages, and carrot slices around
perimeter of a large serving platter. Drizzle dressing over
vegetables. Thinly slice steak on the bias, and fan out slices in
middle of platter. Sprinkle with peanuts, and scatter scallions
on top of steak. Serve immediately.

PER SERVING: 516 CALORIES, 31 G FAT, 112 MG CHOLESTEROL,
22 G CARBOHYDRATE, 827 MG SODIUM, 39 G PROTEIN, 8 G FIBER

from Fit to Eat: Main Course Salads

SIDE DISHES

beets and asparagus with lemon mayonnaise

SERVES 6

Since the mayonnaise contains raw eggs, it should be used
the day it is made. Keep chilled until ready to serve.

2 bunches small beets (about 1½ pounds),
scrubbed and trimmed of all but 1 inch of stems

Coarse salt

2 bunches asparagus (about 1 pound), tough ends trimmed

1 large egg yolk, room temperature

2 teaspoons Dijon mustard

2 to 3 tablespoons freshly squeezed lemon juice
(about 2 lemons)

¾ cup olive oil

¼ cup canola oil

Freshly ground pepper

1 Place beets in a large saucepan, and fill with enough cold
water to cover by 2 inches. Add salt, and bring to a boil. Reduce heat; simmer until beets are tender when pierced with
the tip of a paring knife, about 20 minutes. Drain; let stand
until cool enough to handle. Using paper towels, rub off beet
skins; set beets aside.

2 Prepare an ice bath; set aside. Fill same saucepan halfway
with water, and bring to a boil. Add salt and asparagus; cook
until asparagus are bright green and tender enough to bend
without breaking, about 4 minutes. Using a slotted spoon or
tongs, carefully transfer asparagus to ice bath to stop cooking. Drain immediately; pat dry. Set aside.

3 In a blender, combine egg yolk, mustard, and lemon juice.
With machine running, add olive oil and then canola oil in
a slow, steady stream until mixture is emulsified and forms a
thick mayonnaise. Season with salt and pepper. Transfer to
an airtight container, and refrigerate at least 1 hour. Mayonnaise will thicken when refrigerated. Serve chilled with beets
and asparagus, for dipping.

Note: Raw eggs should not be used in food prepared for pregnant women, babies, young children, the elderly, or anyone
whose health is compromised.

from Summer Lunch on Shelter Island

crunchy jícama, apple, and carrot slaw with creamy orange dressing

SERVES 8

- 1 cup mayonnaise
- ½ cup sour cream
- ¼ cup freshly squeezed orange juice
- 2 tablespoons cider vinegar
- 1 tablespoon minced fresh basil
- Coarse salt and freshly ground pepper
- 2 Granny Smith apples
- 1 jícama (about 1 pound), peeled
- 2 carrots
- ½ head small green cabbage, finely shredded

1 In a small bowl, whisk together mayonnaise, sour cream, orange juice, vinegar, and basil; season with salt and pepper. Refrigerate, covered, until ready to use.

2 Slice the apples, jícama, and carrots on the thinnest setting of a mandoline or with a sharp knife, then cut slices into fine julienne, about 2 inches long.

3 In a large bowl, toss apples, jícama, carrots, and cabbage with the mayonnaise mixture. Cover with plastic wrap; refrigerate until ready to serve, up to 2 hours.

from Fourth of July Barbecue

farm-stand raw vegetable salad

SERVES 6 | **PHOTO ON PAGE 241**

Chioggia beets are pink on the outside and striped on the inside. Because they are not cooked in this recipe, choose tender baby beets. You can use red or golden beets if Chioggia beets are unavailable. If desired, grill the lemon halves, cut side down, until lightly charred. Let cool slightly before squeezing their warm juice over the vegetables.

- 6 ounces sugar-snap peas, sliced diagonally into 1-inch lengths
- 2 Kirby cucumbers, sliced
- 2 ears fresh corn, kernels cut off cobs
- 12 baby Chioggia beets, scrubbed and halved lengthwise
- 1 lemon, halved
- 2 tablespoons extra-virgin olive oil
- Coarse salt and freshly ground pepper

In a large bowl, combine peas, cucumbers, corn, and beets. Squeeze lemon juice over vegetables, and drizzle with oil. Season with salt and pepper. Toss to combine, and serve at room temperature.

from A Lazy Weekend in the Country

green beans with lemon butter

SERVES 4 | **PHOTOS ON PAGES 235 AND 241**

Try substituting green beans with haricots verts or wax beans in this recipe, depending on what's available at the market.

- Coarse salt
- 1 pound green beans, trimmed
- 2 tablespoons unsalted butter, cut into small pieces
- 1 tablespoon finely grated lemon zest (about 1 lemon)
- Freshly ground pepper

1 Bring a medium pot of water to a boil. Add salt and beans. Cook until beans are crisp-tender and bright green, 4 to 5 minutes. Remove from heat, and drain.

2 Immediately return beans to saucepan; add butter and zest. Toss to combine, and season with salt and pepper. Transfer to a serving bowl; serve warm.

from What's For Dinner?

grilled corn with cayenne and cheese

SERVES 8

1 cup sour cream or crème fraîche

⅛ teaspoon cayenne pepper

2 cups dry, aged cheese, such as Jack or Asiago

8 ears fresh corn

1 Heat grill to medium-high. Place sour cream in a small bowl, and sprinkle with cayenne; set aside. Grate cheese into a separate bowl; set aside. Grill corn, turning frequently, until kernels are tender, about 15 minutes.

2 Remove corn from grill; when cool enough to handle, pull back husks and remove silk. Let guests brush corn with the seasoned sour cream, then roll in cheese.

from Fourth of July Barbecue

grilled herbed potatoes and shallots

SERVES 6

When placed directly on the grill, potatoes will burn before they are cooked through. Parboil potatoes and then wrap them in a foil packet with seasonings for perfect results.

2½ pounds small new potatoes

Coarse salt

4 tablespoons extra-virgin olive oil

8 shallots, halved

12 sprigs oregano

Freshly ground pepper

1 Place potatoes in a large saucepan, and fill with enough cold water to cover by 2 inches. Bring to a boil over high heat, and add salt. Reduce heat; simmer until potatoes are slightly tender when pierced with the tip of a paring knife (but not cooked through), about 10 minutes. Drain; let stand until cool enough to handle, then cut each potato in half.

2 Heat grill to high. Overlap two pieces of foil, each about 3 feet long, to form a cross. Place potatoes in one layer in center of cross. Drizzle potatoes with 2 tablespoons oil; add shallots and oregano, and season with salt and pepper. Fold foil, enclosing potatoes, and seal edges by crimping.

3 Place foil packet on grill. Cook, shaking packet occasionally with tongs, until potatoes are cooked through and golden brown, about 20 minutes, depending on heat of grill. Carefully remove packet from grill, watching for any steam and hot oil that might escape. Transfer potatoes to a serving bowl. Drizzle with remaining 2 tablespoons oil, and season with additional salt and pepper, as desired.

from Summer Lunch on Shelter Island

DESSERTS

Carolynn's chocolate-chip cookies

MAKES 30

These cookies are just as delicious without nuts.

1 cup walnuts

2 cups plus 2 tablespoons all-purpose flour

½ teaspoon salt

½ teaspoon baking soda

1 cup (2 sticks) unsalted butter

1 cup plus 2 tablespoons firmly packed dark-brown sugar

½ cup granulated sugar

1 large whole egg

1 large egg yolk

½ tablespoon pure vanilla extract

1½ cups semisweet chocolate chips

1 Preheat oven to 350°F. Spread walnuts in a single layer on a rimmed baking sheet; toast in oven until crisped and fragrant, tossing occasionally, about 10 minutes. Remove from oven; let cool, then break into large pieces. Set aside.

2 In a large bowl, whisk together flour, salt, and baking soda; set aside. In a medium saucepan over medium heat, melt butter. Turn off heat, and add both sugars; whisk until smooth and combined. Transfer butter mixture to a medium bowl, and let cool to room temperature.

3 Whisk egg, egg yolk, and vanilla into butter mixture. Fold in flour mixture until just combined. Fold in chocolate chips and walnuts. Cover dough with plastic wrap; refrigerate until firm, about 30 minutes.

4 Preheat oven to 325°F. Using two large spoons, place golf-ball–size mounds of dough 3 inches apart on baking sheets. Bake until cookies are golden brown and the tops no longer look wet, 12 to 14 minutes. Let cool on baking sheet 5 minutes, then transfer to a wire rack to cool completely. Store in an airtight container at room temperature up to 3 days.

from Fourth of July Barbecue

cherry spoon sweets

MAKES ABOUT 2 CUPS | PHOTO ON PAGE 242

1½ pounds sweet fresh cherries, pitted, or 20 ounces frozen

1 cup sugar

½ vanilla bean, split lengthwise

2 tablespoons freshly squeezed lemon juice

Ice cream or Greek-style yogurt, for serving

1   In a medium saucepan, combine cherries, sugar, vanilla bean, and 2 tablespoons water. Bring to a simmer; cook, stirring frequently, until cherries are very soft, 5 to 7 minutes. Using a slotted spoon, transfer cherries to a heatproof jar.

2   Bring juice to a boil over medium-high heat; continue cooking until reduced to ¾ cup, 9 to 11 minutes. Discard vanilla bean; stir lemon juice into syrup.

3   Pour syrup over cherries. Let cool completely, uncovered at room temperature, about 45 minutes. Cover jar with lid; refrigerate until cold, about 35 minutes, or store up to 2 weeks. Serve with ice cream or yogurt.

from The Flavors of Greece

chocolate brownie spoon bread

SERVES 8

If you prefer a molten center that oozes chocolate when served, reduce the cooking time slightly.

½ cup (1 stick) unsalted butter, plus more for skillet

4 ounces semisweet chocolate, coarsely chopped

½ cup all-purpose flour

½ cup unsweetened cocoa powder

½ teaspoon baking powder

Pinch of salt

4 large eggs, room temperature

1 teaspoon pure vanilla extract

1 cup sugar

1   Preheat oven to 350°F. Butter an 8-inch cast-iron skillet; set aside. Place chocolate and butter in a medium heatproof bowl set over a pan of simmering water; stir until melted and smooth. Remove from heat; let cool, stirring occasionally.

2   Into a medium bowl, sift together flour, cocoa, baking powder, and salt two times; set aside. In the bowl of an electric mixer fitted with the paddle attachment, beat eggs and vanilla until thick and pale, about 6 minutes. Beat in sugar until light and fluffy. Stir in chocolate mixture. Fold in dry ingredients until just combined.

3   Pour batter into prepared skillet. Bake until spoon bread is just set but still soft in the center, about 40 minutes. Let cool 10 minutes; serve warm.

from Skillet Desserts

crêpe gâteau with strawberry preserves and crème fraîche

SERVES 6 TO 8

Crêpe batter can be made through step one up to one day in advance; store, covered, in the refrigerator. When assembling the gâteau, which resembles a many-layered cake, do not spread cream and jam to the edges of the bottom layers, because the weight of the top will push out the filling. Assemble gâteau no more than two hours before serving.

¾ cup all-purpose flour
4 tablespoons confectioners' sugar
Pinch of salt
2 large whole eggs, room temperature
2 large egg yolks, room temperature
1¼ cups milk, room temperature
4 tablespoons unsalted butter
1½ cups crème fraîche
½ teaspoon pure vanilla extract
1 cup strawberry or other fruit preserves

1 Into a medium bowl, sift together flour, 1 tablespoon confectioners' sugar, and salt. Make a well in the center, and fill it with eggs, egg yolks, and a few tablespoons milk; whisk ingredients in the well to combine, then gradually incorporate flour mixture, whisking until a thick, smooth paste forms. Add the remaining milk, and whisk until no lumps remain.

2 Melt butter in an 8-inch nonstick skillet (the bottom should be 6 inches in diameter). Pour butter into batter, leaving a coating of butter in skillet. Set skillet with butter aside. Let batter rest at room temperature 1 hour.

3 Warm skillet thoroughly over medium heat, melting layer of butter. Remove from heat; stir batter, and carefully ladle 3 tablespoons into skillet. Immediately rotate skillet to evenly spread batter in a thin layer. Return skillet to heat; cook crêpe until edges are golden brown and lacy, about 1 minute. Using a heatproof rubber spatula, carefully flip crêpe; cook other side until golden brown, about 30 seconds. Slide crêpe out of skillet onto a plate. Repeat with remaining batter, stacking cooked crêpes on top of one another. Let crêpes cool completely.

4 Prepare an ice bath. Place crème fraîche in a medium bowl set in ice bath. Add vanilla and remaining 3 tablespoons confectioners' sugar to crème fraîche; whip until mixture is thick enough to hold a line drawn by the whisk.

5 To assemble: Place a crêpe on a serving platter. Spoon 1 heaping tablespoon preserves on top; using an offset spatula, spread in a thin layer over crêpe, leaving a ½-inch border

around the edge. Cover with another crêpe, stacking neatly. Spread 2 heaping tablespoons crème-fraîche mixture evenly over crêpe, again leaving a ½-inch border around the edges. Continue alternating fillings with crêpes, finishing with a crêpe on top. If necessary, insert two long toothpicks through the layers to hold gâteau together. Refrigerate at least 15 minutes. Remove toothpicks; cut into wedges before serving.

from Skillet Desserts

homemade vanilla ice cream

MAKES 1½ QUARTS; SERVES 8

Ice cream will be soft after churning in the ice-cream maker. For hard-packed consistency, transfer ice cream to an airtight container, and freeze until set.

2 cups milk
2 vanilla beans, split lengthwise and scraped
6 large egg yolks
¾ cup plus 2 tablespoons sugar
2 cups heavy cream, chilled
1 teaspoon pure vanilla extract

1 In a medium saucepan over medium heat, combine milk with vanilla beans and scrapings. Bring to a gentle boil. Remove from heat; let steep, covered, 30 minutes. Discard vanilla pods.

2 In the bowl of an electric mixer fitted with the paddle attachment, beat egg yolks and sugar on medium-high speed until thick and pale, about 4 minutes.

3 Place milk mixture over medium-high heat, and bring just to a simmer. With mixer on low speed, slowly pour about ¼ cup hot milk mixture into egg-yolk mixture; beat until blended. Continue adding milk, about ½ cup at a time, beating until incorporated after each addition.

4 Prepare an ice bath; set aside. Return mixture to saucepan; stir with a wooden spoon over low heat until mixture is thick enough to coat back of spoon, 3 to 5 minutes. Custard should retain a line drawn across the back of the spoon with your fingertip.

5 Remove pan from heat; immediately stir in chilled cream to stop the cooking. Pour custard through a fine sieve into a medium bowl set in ice bath; let stand, stirring occasionally, until chilled. Stir in vanilla extract. Freeze in an ice-cream maker according to manufacturer's instructions.

from Fourth of July Barbecue

fig flambé with port and gelato

SERVES 4

- 3 tablespoons unsalted butter
- ¼ cup sugar
- ½ pound ripe but firm fresh Black Mission figs (about 10), halved lengthwise
- Freshly ground pepper
- ½ cup port
- 1 pint hazelnut gelato or vanilla ice cream, for serving

1   Heat broiler. In a large, heavy, ovenproof skillet, melt butter over medium-high heat; sprinkle with sugar. Add figs to skillet, and stir gently to combine. Season with pepper. Turn figs cut side up, and place skillet under broiler until figs are browned around the edges, about 4 minutes.

2   Remove from broiler, and carefully pour port over figs. Ignite with a match. When flame subsides, use a slotted spoon to transfer figs to a plate. Set aside.

3   Return skillet to medium-high heat, and reduce liquid by about one-half, until thick and syrupy. Remove from heat, and return figs to skillet. Spoon syrup over figs to coat. Place one quarter of the gelato on each of four dishes; top with warm figs and syrup, and serve.

from Skillet Desserts

fresh cherry pie

MAKES 1 NINE-INCH PIE

- All-purpose flour, for work surface
- Pâte Brisée (page 129)
- 2¼ pounds fresh yellow and red sweet cherries, pitted and halved
- ¼ cup sugar
- 2 tablespoons instant tapioca powder
- Vanilla ice cream, for serving (optional)

1   Preheat oven to 400°F. On a lightly floured work surface, roll out one disk of dough to a ⅛-inch-thick round, about 13 inches in diameter. Fit dough into a 9-inch pie plate. Using a sharp paring knife, trim edge flush with rim.

2   In a large bowl, combine cherries, sugar, and tapioca; toss to coat evenly. Pour filling into prepared pie plate; set aside.

3   Roll out remaining disk of dough as in step 1. Using a pastry wheel or a sharp pairing knife, cut dough into 1-inch-wide strips. Lightly brush rim of dough in pie plate with water, and weave strips of dough on top of filling to form a lattice. Using kitchen scissors, trim strips to create 1-inch overhang. Tuck strips under rim of shell, and crimp to seal. Chill pie in refrigerator at least 30 minutes.

4   Bake pie 20 minutes. Reduce oven heat to 350°F, and continue baking until crust is deep golden brown and juices begin to bubble, 40 to 50 minutes more. Transfer pie to a wire rack, and let stand until just warm or at room temperature. Serve with ice cream, if desired.

from A Lazy Weekend in the Country

orange spoon sweets with peel

MAKES ABOUT 4 CUPS | **PHOTO ON PAGE 242**

- 4 navel oranges
- 1 cup sugar
- 1 cup honey
- ¼ teaspoon orange-blossom water (optional)
- Pinch of salt
- ⅓ cup whole blanched almonds, lightly toasted
- Ice cream or Greek-style yogurt, for serving

1   Using a sharp paring knife, cut each orange into quarters; remove flesh from peels, and reserve for another use. Halve each peel lengthwise; place in a large saucepan. Cover with cold water, and bring to a boil over high heat. Drain peels in a sieve. Place peels back in saucepan; repeat blanching process.

2   Thread a needle with a 3-foot piece of thin kitchen twine or sewing thread; tie a large knot at the end. Roll a piece of peel

lengthwise into a tight spiral. Push the needle through the spiral to string. Repeat with all the strips of peel. Tie a knot after the last peel to secure.

3   In a large saucepan, combine 4 cups water with sugar and honey; bring to a boil. Add the string of peels. Reduce heat to a simmer, then cover peels with a lid slightly smaller than saucepan to keep them submerged. Cook 45 minutes. Transfer peels to a plate, and set aside.

4   Simmer remaining liquid in pan until reduced to 1¾ cups, about 18 minutes. Stir in orange-blossom water, if using, salt, and almonds. Cut string to release orange peel curls; place in a heatproof glass jar. Pour mixture over the peels. Let cool completely, uncovered, at room temperature, about 45 minutes. Cover with a lid; refrigerate until cold, about 35 minutes, or store up to 2 weeks. Serve with ice cream or yogurt.

from The Flavors of Greece

peaches with honey syrup

SERVES 4

Adding the peach skins to the poaching liquid helps to infuse the liquid with flavor and creates a pretty rose-colored sauce. Serve the peaches with your favorite chocolate bar.

4   ripe peaches
½   cup honey

1   Prepare an ice bath; set aside. Using a sharp knife, lightly score bottom (not stem end) of each peach with hatch marks.

2   Fill a large (4-quart) saucepan with enough cold water to cover peaches. Bring water to a boil over high heat; add peaches, and blanch about 1 minute (more if skin is not pulling away from peach). Using a slotted spoon, quickly plunge peaches in ice bath to stop the cooking. When cool enough to handle, peel peaches, reserving skins.

3   Pour off all but 4 cups poaching liquid in pan; add reserved skins and the honey. Bring to a boil; cook until reduced to 1½ cups. Pour liquid through a fine sieve set over a bowl; discard skins. Immediately spoon syrup over peaches, and serve.

from What's For Dinner?

plum tarte Tatin

MAKES 1 TEN-INCH TART │ **PHOTO ON PAGE 242**

This dessert can be served warm or at room temperature. Either way, serve it immediately after inverting. If serving at room temperature, gently reheat the pan on the stove so it releases more easily. If you can't find Italian plums, you can use eight regular plums; remove the pits and slice thinly.

3   tablespoons unsalted butter
¾   cup sugar
2⅓   pounds Italian plums (about 35), pitted and halved
All-purpose flour, for work surface
½   recipe Pâte Sucrée (page 184)

1   Melt butter in a 10-inch ovenproof skillet over medium-low heat. Remove from heat, and sprinkle sugar evenly over bottom of skillet. Starting at outside edge, arrange plum halves in overlapping concentric circles.

2   Return skillet to medium-low heat; cook until juices are bubbling and sugar is beginning to caramelize, 15 to 20 minutes. Holding fruit in place with a wide spatula, tilt skillet and drain syrup into a bowl; set syrup aside. Slide any dislodged plums back into place. Let cool slightly, about 10 minutes.

3   Preheat oven to 400°F. On a lightly floured work surface, roll out disk of dough to a 10-inch square. Using an inverted 10-inch round cake pan as a guide, cut dough into a round. Place dough over plums, and prick dough all over with a fork.

4   Bake in oven until crust is golden brown and juices are bubbling, 30 to 35 minutes. If top begins to brown too much before fruit is cooked through, drape with aluminum foil.

5   Remove skillet from oven. Let cool 1 hour. When ready to serve, quickly invert tart onto a serving plate. If desired, reduce reserved syrup in a small saucepan over medium heat until thickened, about 5 minutes. Serve tart with warm sauce.

from Skillet Desserts

pâte sucrée

MAKES ENOUGH FOR 2 TEN-INCH TARTS

Dough can be refrigerated for up to one week or frozen for up to one month; thaw overnight in refrigerator before using.

2½ cups all-purpose flour
¼ cup sugar
1 teaspoon salt
1 cup (2 sticks) chilled unsalted butter, cut into small pieces
2 large egg yolks
¼ cup ice water

1   In a food processor, pulse flour, sugar, and salt until combined. Add butter, and process until mixture resembles coarse meal, 8 to 10 seconds.

2   In a small bowl, beat together egg yolks and ice water. With machine running, pour egg-yolk mixture in a steady stream through the feed tube; process until dough just holds together when pinched, 10 to 15 seconds.

3   Divide dough in half. Flatten each half into a disk, and wrap in plastic. Refrigerate dough at least 1 hour.

red-currant and raspberry pie

MAKES 1 TEN-INCH PIE | PHOTO ON PAGE 245

All-purpose flour, for work surface
Pâte Brisée (page 129)
1 large egg
1 tablespoon milk
2 cups fresh red currants (about 10 ounces), stemmed
2 cups fresh raspberries (about 8 ounces)
¼ cup instant tapioca
Grated zest and juice of 1 lemon
1 cup granulated sugar
2 tablespoons unsalted butter, cut into small pieces
Coarse sanding sugar, for sprinkling (optional)

1   On a lightly floured work surface, roll out one disk of dough into a ⅛-inch-thick round about 12 inches in diameter. Drape dough over a 10-inch pie plate; chill 30 minutes.

2   In a small bowl, whisk together egg and milk; set egg wash aside. In a medium bowl, toss together currants, raspberries, tapioca, lemon zest and juice, and granulated sugar. Transfer mixture to chilled pie dough. Dot top with butter.

3   Preheat oven to 425°F. Roll out remaining disk of dough as in step 1. Brush rim of chilled dough with egg wash; place other round of dough on top, and trim to a ½-inch overhang. Crimp edges as desired; chill until firm, about 20 minutes in the freezer or 40 minutes in the refrigerator.

4   Remove pie plate from freezer. Cut a few slits in top of dough. Brush with egg wash, and sprinkle with sanding sugar, if desired. Bake 20 minutes. Reduce oven heat to 350°F. Continue baking until crust is golden brown and juices are bubbling, about 40 minutes more. Let cool completely before cutting and serving.

from Currants

red-currant fool

SERVES 4 TO 6

4 tablespoons unsalted butter
3½ cups fresh red currants (about 18 ounces), stemmed
¾ cup sugar
1½ cups heavy cream

1   Melt butter in a large skillet set over medium heat, and stir in currants and sugar. Cover, and reduce heat to low. Cook, stirring occasionally, until sugar has dissolved and currants have softened, about 5 minutes.

2   Remove skillet from heat, and lightly crush fruit with the back of a wooden spoon. Don't mash to a purée; some texture should remain. Transfer mixture to a bowl, and refrigerate until completely cool.

3   In a small bowl, whisk cream until it holds soft peaks. Set aside ½ cup of chilled fruit mixture. Gently fold whipped cream into the remaining fruit mixture, leaving it marbled. Serve immediately in individual bowls; garnish each portion with a spoonful of reserved fruit mixture.

from Currants

rolled baklava

MAKES 16 PIECES | **PHOTO ON PAGE 242**

When finishing baklava, pour the cooled syrup over the hot pastry to preserve its crispness.

¾ cup (1½ sticks) unsalted butter, melted, plus more for baking pan

½ cup (2 ounces) shelled pistachios, finely chopped, plus more for garnish

½ cup (2 ounces) walnuts, finely chopped

¼ cup (2 ounces) dried apricots, finely chopped

¼ cup (1 ounce) dried currants

⅓ cup sugar

¼ teaspoon ground ginger

¼ teaspoon ground cinnamon

Pinch of ground nutmeg

¼ teaspoon salt

8 sheets frozen phyllo dough, thawed

½ cup honey, plus more for garnish

1 tablespoon freshly squeezed lemon juice

1 Preheat oven to 350°F, with rack in center. Butter an 8-inch square baking pan; set aside. In a small bowl, whisk together pistachios, walnuts, apricots, currants, sugar, ginger, cinnamon, nutmeg, and salt; set aside.

2 On a large, clean work surface, stack phyllo sheets; trim long side to measure 15½ inches. Lay out 1 sheet of phyllo with long side toward you. Keep remaining phyllo covered with a damp kitchen towel, and then plastic wrap. Brush sheet generously with butter. Top with a second sheet of phyllo; brush with butter. Sprinkle one-quarter of nut mixture horizontally 1 inch from the bottom edge of phyllo.

3 Gently roll up phyllo, brushing dough occasionally with butter as you roll, to create a long, thin cylinder. Cut cylinder in half, and place the two halves next to each other in prepared pan. Repeat with remaining dough and nut mixture to make three more cylinders, and arrange in same manner in pan. Using a sharp knife, halve logs again, being careful not to disturb them, making 16 cigar-shaped pieces. Bake until golden brown, 40 to 45 minutes.

4 Meanwhile, make syrup: In a small saucepan, combine honey with ½ cup water. Boil until reduced by one-quarter, about 4 minutes. Remove from heat; stir in lemon juice. Pour into a small bowl; refrigerate until completely cool.

5 Remove baklava from oven; pour cooled syrup over it to cover evenly. Let baklava cool completely. Drizzle with more honey and garnish with pistachios just before serving.

from The Flavors of Greece

Southern-style individual peach cobblers

MAKES 4 SIX-INCH COBBLERS | **PHOTO ON PAGE 242**

You will need four six-inch ovenproof skillets for this recipe. To make a larger dessert, melt two teaspoons butter in a ten-inch skillet before adding batter; bake for thirty-five minutes.

2 pounds ripe but firm peaches (about 4), each pitted and cut into 8 wedges

1 cup sugar

1 teaspoon ground cinnamon

1½ cups all-purpose flour

2 teaspoons baking powder

½ teaspoon salt

4 tablespoons unsalted butter, melted, plus 4 teaspoons for skillets

½ cup milk

1 large egg

1 Preheat oven to 400°F. In a large bowl, toss peaches with ¼ cup sugar and ½ teaspoon cinnamon; set aside. In a medium bowl, whisk together flour, baking powder, salt, remaining ¾ cup sugar, and remaining ½ teaspoon cinnamon. In another bowl, whisk 4 tablespoons melted butter with milk and egg. Whisk butter mixture into flour mixture.

2 Melt 1 teaspoon butter in a 6-inch ovenproof skillet over medium heat. Once skillet is hot, remove from heat. Pour one-quarter of batter into skillet. Spread batter evenly over bottom. Spoon one-quarter of peach mixture over batter. Repeat with remaining three skillets.

3 Transfer skillets to oven, and bake until cobblers are set, 25 to 30 minutes. Remove from oven, and let cool slightly. Serve cobblers warm in skillets.

from Skillet Desserts

sticky buckwheat cake

MAKES 1 TEN-INCH CAKE

Buckwheat flour adds heartiness to this dessert.

FOR TOPPING:

½ cup raisins

½ cup brandy

1 tablespoon unsalted butter

½ cup firmly packed dark-brown sugar

1½ teaspoons ground cinnamon

⅔ cup light corn syrup

½ cup coarsely chopped pecans (1¾ ounces)

1 apple, cored, peeled, and cut into ½-inch cubes

FOR CAKE:

¾ cup (1½ sticks) unsalted butter, room temperature

1¼ cups packed light-brown sugar

3 large eggs

1¾ cups all-purpose flour

1 cup buckwheat flour

1½ teaspoons ground ginger

1 tablespoon baking powder

½ teaspoon salt

1 cup milk

1 tablespoon peeled and grated fresh ginger

1 Make topping: In a small bowl, combine raisins and brandy; let stand until raisins are plump, about 20 minutes. Drain raisins, discarding liquid.

2 In a 10-inch cast-iron skillet, melt butter over medium heat. Sprinkle with brown sugar and cinnamon, and remove from heat. Drizzle with corn syrup. Strew pecans, apple, and raisins over corn syrup; set aside.

3 Preheat oven to 350°F. Make cake: In the bowl of an electric mixer fitted with the paddle attachment, cream butter until smooth. Add sugar; beat until light and fluffy. Add eggs one at a time, beating until combined after each addition.

4 Into a large bowl, sift together flours, ground ginger, baking powder, and salt. In another bowl, combine milk and fresh ginger. With mixer on low, add the flour mixture to butter mixture in three batches, alternating with the milk mixture. Beat until just combined after each addition.

5 Pour batter into prepared skillet; smooth top with an offset spatula. Bake until golden brown and a cake tester inserted in center comes out clean, about 50 minutes. Transfer skillet to a wire rack; let stand 5 minutes before inverting cake onto a serving platter. Serve warm or at room temperature.

from Skillet Desserts

strawberry shortcakes

MAKES NINE 2½-INCH OR TWENTY-FIVE
1½-INCH SHORTCAKES | PHOTO ON PAGE 244

For a deeper flavor, try substituting one-third cup firmly packed dark-brown sugar for one-third cup granulated sugar in the shortcake dough.

4 pints fresh strawberries, hulled and halved

¼ cup freshly squeezed lemon juice (1 to 2 lemons)

½ cup plus ⅓ cup granulated sugar

4 cups all-purpose flour, plus more for work surface

4½ teaspoons baking powder

1½ teaspoons salt

¾ cup (1½ sticks) unsalted butter, chilled and cut into small pieces

2 cups plus 4 tablespoons heavy cream

1 large egg yolk

2 tablespoons turbinado sugar, for sprinkling (optional)
Vanilla Whipped Cream (recipe follows)

1 Place strawberries in a bowl; add lemon juice and ½ cup granulated sugar, and toss to combine. Let stand until berries are very juicy, about 1 hour.

2 Meanwhile, in a large bowl, whisk together remaining ⅓ cup granulated sugar, flour, baking powder, and salt. Using a fork or pastry blender, cut in butter until mixture resembles coarse meal. Add 2 cups plus 2 tablespoons cream; mix just until dough comes together.

3 Transfer dough to a lightly floured work surface; pat into a 1-inch-thick square. Using a 2½-inch or 1½-inch round cookie cutter, cut out 9 large or 25 small rounds; transfer to a parchment-lined baking sheet. Cover with plastic wrap, and refrigerate 20 minutes or overnight.

4 Preheat oven to 400°F. Remove rounds from refrigerator. Whisk together remaining 2 tablespoons cream with egg yolk. Brush tops of rounds with egg wash. Sprinkle with turbinado sugar, if desired. Bake until golden brown, 12 to 15 minutes for small shortcakes and 15 to 18 for large. Let cool slightly on wire racks, about 15 minutes.

5 To serve, slice shortcakes in half horizontally with a serrated knife; place bottom halves on serving plates. Add a dollop of whipped cream and the strawberries with their juice, and top off with remaining shortcake halves.

from Summer Lunch on Shelter Island

vanilla whipped cream

MAKES ABOUT 3½ CUPS

Look for organic heavy cream. It whips, holds its shape, and tastes better than regular heavy cream does. Chill whisk and mixing bowl well before you begin, and whip mixture just before serving.

2 cups high-quality heavy cream

2 tablespoons pure vanilla extract or kirsch

2 tablespoons confectioners' sugar

Combine heavy cream, vanilla, and sugar in chilled bowl. Using a chilled whisk, beat until stiff but not dry peaks form.

sweet pain perdu

SERVES 4

This French toast is a great way to use leftover bread.

2 large eggs

1½ cups milk

2 tablespoons sugar

1 day-old baguette or other white bread, cut into 1-inch-thick slices

Fresh fruit, such as bananas, oranges, and pineapples, cut into bite-size pieces, for serving

Maple syrup, for serving

1 Preheat oven to 350°F. In a medium bowl, whisk together eggs, milk, and sugar. Place bread in an 8-inch square glass baking dish. Pour batter over bread. Let stand until both sides of bread are soaked through, about 10 minutes, turning slices once after 5 minutes.

2 Transfer dish to oven. Bake until bread is golden brown, about 25 minutes. Serve hot, topped with fruit and maple syrup.

from Impromptu Entertaining

ultimate malted brownie sundae

SERVES 8

2 pints vanilla ice cream, softened

¾ cup (about 3 ounces) malted-milk powder

½ cup malt balls, coarsely crushed, plus more for garnish

Malted Brownies (recipe follows)

Chocolate Sauce (page 188)

1 In the bowl of an electric mixer fitted with the paddle attachment, beat ice cream, malted-milk powder, and crushed malt balls until blended, about 1 minute. Transfer to an air-tight container; freeze until firm, at least 4 hours or overnight.

2 Just before serving, cut brownies into 24 rectangles, making four even columns and six even rows.

3 Assemble sundaes: Divide half the ice cream evenly among eight serving dishes. Top each with a brownie, then another layer of ice cream. Garnish each with 2 more brownies. Drizzle with chocolate sauce; sprinkle with crushed malt balls.

from Dessert of the Month

malted brownies

MAKES ABOUT 2 DOZEN

1 cup (2 sticks) unsalted butter, cut into small pieces, plus more for pan

1 cup all-purpose flour, plus more for pan

10 ounces semisweet chocolate, coarsely chopped

1 cup (about 4½ ounces) malted-milk powder

1 cup (about 4 ounces) malt balls, coarsely crushed

1½ cups firmly packed light-brown sugar

3 large eggs

1 tablespoon pure vanilla extract

1 Preheat oven to 350°F. Butter and lightly flour a 9-by-13-inch baking pan; set aside. Combine chocolate and butter in a heatproof bowl set over a pan of simmering water; stir until melted and smooth. Let cool slightly, about 5 minutes.

2 In a medium bowl, whisk together flour, malt powder, and malt balls; set aside. In the bowl of an electric mixer fitted with the paddle attachment, beat sugar and eggs until thick and fluffy, about 2 minutes. Add melted chocolate mixture and vanilla; mix to combine, about 30 seconds. Using a rubber spatula, fold in flour mixture until just combined.

3 Pour batter into prepared pan, spreading it evenly with the spatula. Bake until a cake tester inserted in center comes out with just a few crumbs attached, 30 to 35 minutes. Transfer pan to a wire rack to cool completely.

chocolate sauce

MAKES 2 CUPS

Extra sauce may be refrigerated in an airtight container for up to two weeks; reheat gently before serving.

- 1 can (14 ounces) sweetened condensed milk
- 2 ounces unsweetened chocolate, coarsely chopped
- 2 ounces semisweet chocolate, coarsely chopped
- ¾ cup heavy cream

In a small saucepan, warm all ingredients gently over medium heat, stirring constantly, until chocolate is completely melted and sauce is smooth. Let cool slightly before serving.

warm nectarine turnovers

MAKES ABOUT 1½ DOZEN | **PHOTO ON PAGE 243**

If at any point the dough gets too soft to work with or begins to shrink, refrigerate for fifteen minutes before proceeding.

- 2 cups all-purpose flour, plus more for work surface and fork
- 1 teaspoon baking powder
- ½ teaspoon salt
- ½ cup (1 stick) chilled unsalted butter, cut into small pieces
- ½ cup ice water
- 1¾ pounds large ripe nectarines (about 4)
- ¼ cup granulated sugar
- ¼ cup honey
- 2 to 3 cups vegetable oil, for frying
  Confectioners' sugar, for dusting

1 Sift flour, baking powder, and salt into a large bowl. Using your fingertips, work butter into flour mixture until it resembles coarse meal. Pour in ice water; toss lightly, gathering the dough into a ball. Turn out onto a clean work surface. Dust dough with a little flour; flatten into a disk. Wrap in plastic; refrigerate at least 1 hour or overnight.

2 Halve nectarines lengthwise; discard pits. Leaving skins on (to give filling a rose color), chop fruit into ½-inch chunks.

3 In a large heavy skillet, fold together nectarines, granulated sugar, and honey. Bring to a boil over high heat; reduce heat to medium-low. Simmer, stirring, until mixture is thick enough to hold its shape in a spoon, about 25 minutes. Transfer filling to a bowl, and let cool.

4 On a lightly floured work surface, roll out dough as thinly as possible (about 1/16 inch thick). With a 4-inch fluted cutter, cut out as many rounds as possible. Gather scraps into a ball; roll out dough as before, and cut out more rounds.

5 Place about 1 tablespoon filling on the lower third of each round. Moisten edges of rounds lightly with cold water. Fold rounds in half over filling; press edges together tightly. Seal edges with fork tines that have been dipped in flour.

6 Preheat oven to lowest setting. Line a shallow baking dish with paper towels, and place in oven. Fill a large heavy skillet with 1 inch of oil. Place over medium-high heat until oil registers 350°F on a deep-fry thermometer. Working in batches to avoid crowding skillet, cook turnovers, turning them occasionally with tongs or a slotted spoon, until crisp and golden, about 4 minutes. Transfer turnovers to lined dish in oven to drain. Keep warm until all the turnovers are cooked. Dust warm turnovers with confectioners' sugar just before serving.

from Skillet Desserts

DRINKS

caipirinhas

SERVES 6

Cachaça is a potent sugarcane liquor used in Brazil's national drink. You can use light rum instead.

- 3 limes, halved
- 12 teaspoons sugar
- 1½ cups cachaça

Place a lime half in each of six tumblers, and sprinkle each with 2 teaspoons sugar. Using a wooden reamer or spoon, crush the flesh of the limes. Fill glasses with crushed ice, and divide cachaça evenly among them. Stir well, and serve.

from A Lazy Weekend in the Country

coconut margaritas

SERVES 2 | **PHOTO ON PAGE 227**

- 1 cup sweetened shredded coconut
- ½ teaspoon salt
- ½ cup freshly squeezed lime juice, plus 2 tablespoons for glasses (about 5 limes)
- ¾ cup cream of coconut such as Coco Lopez
- ½ cup plus 2 tablespoons tequila
- ¼ cup Cointreau or other orange liqueur

1 Preheat oven to 350°F. On a rimmed baking sheet, toss coconut with salt. Spread out on sheet; toast in oven, stirring frequently, until golden brown, 8 to 10 minutes. Let cool, then crush with your hands until crumbly.

2 Pour 2 tablespoons lime juice into a shallow dish. Place coconut mixture in another dish. Dip rims of two cocktail glasses in lime juice, then in coconut mixture, coating well.

3 Combine remaining ingredients with 1 cup ice in a blender; purée until smooth. Divide mixture evenly between prepared glasses, and serve immediately.

from Cutting-Edge Cocktails

grapefruit sparklers

SERVES 8 | **PHOTO ON PAGE 225**

1 cup sugar

8 whole star anise

6 cups ruby-red grapefruit juice, chilled

⅓ cup Campari

2 cups Champagne or sparkling wine, chilled

1 In a small saucepan, combine 1 cup water with the sugar and star anise; bring to a boil, stirring occasionally until sugar has dissolved. Remove from heat; let cool completely.

2 Pour syrup through a fine sieve into a glass measuring cup (to yield 1 cup); discard star anise. Cover with plastic wrap; refrigerate until well chilled.

3 In a large pitcher, combine grapefruit juice, Campari, and chilled syrup. Divide mixture among eight glasses, and top off with Champagne. Serve immediately.

from Cutting-Edge Cocktails

homemade cassis

MAKES 1 QUART

This recipe must be started at least two weeks in advance to allow the flavors to develop fully.

2 cups (10 ounces) fresh black currants, stemmed

1 cup sugar

2 cups brandy or Cognac

1 Using a potato masher or the back of a wooden spoon, mash currants in a medium saucepan. Add sugar and 1 cup water; bring to a simmer over medium-high heat. Cook until sugar has dissolved and fruit has released all juices, stirring occasionally, about 5 minutes.

2 Remove pan from heat; stir in brandy. Transfer mixture to a glass jar. Seal tightly, and refrigerate 1 week.

3 Pour mixture through a fine sieve into a medium bowl, then pour again through sieve lined with cheesecloth into a clean jar. Refrigerate at least 1 week before using.

from Currants

honeydew fizz

SERVES 2

½ large honeydew melon (about 3 pounds)

½ cup Midori or other melon liqueur

1 cup seltzer water, chilled

1 With a large spoon, scrape out and discard honeydew seeds. Using a ¾-inch melon baller, scoop out 10 balls; place in a large airtight container. Pour Midori over melon balls; transfer to freezer, and let macerate about 1 hour.

2 Meanwhile, scrape remaining honeydew into a blender, and purée until smooth. Let stand until juice settles to the bottom of blender and foam rises to the top. Skim off foam, and measure out ½ cup juice.

3 Remove Midori mixture from freezer, and stir in melon juice and seltzer. Divide mixture evenly between two cocktail glasses, and serve immediately.

from Cutting-Edge Cocktails

lime apricot rum coolers

SERVES 4 | **PHOTO ON PAGE 227**

2 tablespoons freshly grated lime zest (about 6 limes)

6 tablespoons sugar

¼ cup plus 2 tablespoons freshly squeezed lime juice (about 3 limes)

2 cups apricot nectar, chilled

1¼ cups white rum

1 In a food processor, finely grind lime zest with sugar. Measure out ¼ cup mixture; transfer the rest to a shallow dish. Pour 2 tablespoons lime juice into another dish. Dip rims of four glasses in juice, then in sugar mixture, coating well.

2 In a blender, purée apricot nectar, rum, remaining ¼ cup lime juice, reserved zest mixture, and 2 cups ice. Divide mixture among prepared glasses, and serve immediately.

from Cutting-Edge Cocktails

lychee martinis

SERVES 2 | **PHOTO ON PAGE 227**

Lychees are small fruits native to Southeast Asia; they have a slightly sweet, delicate flavor and creamy white flesh. For even more Asian flavor, substitute sake for the gin in this recipe to make a "saketini."

2 **whole canned lychees, plus ½ cup drained syrup**

½ **cup gin**

Place 1 lychee in each of two martini glasses. Fill a cocktail shaker with ice. Pour in gin and lychee syrup. Shake well; strain into glasses. Serve immediately.

from Cutting-Edge Cocktails

pineapple gin "kirs"

SERVES 2 | **PHOTO ON PAGE 227**

¾ **cup pineapple juice**

½ **cup gin**

2 **tablespoons freshly squeezed lemon juice**

2 **teaspoons crème de cassis**

In a pitcher, mix together pineapple juice, gin, and lemon juice. Divide mixture between two highball glasses. Pour 1 teaspoon cassis into center of each glass; do not stir. Carefully fill glasses with ice; serve immediately.

from Cutting-Edge Cocktails

strawberry ginger caipiroscas

SERVES 2

10 **fresh strawberries, hulled and quartered**

30 **fresh mint leaves**

¼ **lime, cut into 4 pieces**

1 **teaspoon freshly grated ginger**

2 **tablespoons sugar**

½ **cup vodka**

Place berries, mint, lime, and ginger in a cocktail shaker. Sprinkle sugar over mixture; muddle with a long spoon until almost puréed. Add 2 cups cracked ice and vodka, and shake well. Divide mixture between two glasses; serve immediately.

from Cutting-Edge Cocktails

vodka thyme lemonade

SERVES 8 | **PHOTO ON PAGE 226**

2 **cups sugar**

12 **sprigs thyme, plus more for garnish**

4 **cups freshly squeezed lemon juice (about 24 lemons)**

2 **cups vodka**

1   In a small saucepan, combine 2 cups water with the sugar and thyme; bring to a boil over high heat, stirring occasionally until sugar has dissolved. Remove from heat; let cool.

2   Pour mixture through a fine sieve into a large glass measuring cup (to yield 2 cups); discard thyme. Cover with plastic wrap; refrigerate until well chilled.

3   In a large serving pitcher, stir together lemon juice, vodka, and chilled syrup; garnish with thyme. Divide mixture evenly among eight tumblers filled with ice; serve immediately.

from Cutting-Edge Cocktails

angel biscuits

MAKES 2 DOZEN

The dough will keep in the refrigerator, wrapped in plastic, for up to three days. Once formed into balls, it can be refrigerated overnight, covered with plastic wrap.

4 teaspoons active dry yeast (about 1⅓ envelopes)

5 cups all-purpose flour

2 tablespoons sugar

2½ teaspoons coarse salt

1 tablespoon baking powder

1 teaspoon baking soda

1 cup (2 sticks) unsalted butter, melted and cooled

2 cups buttermilk

1   In a small bowl, sprinkle yeast over ½ cup warm water; let stand until foamy, about 5 minutes. Into a large bowl, sift together flour, sugar, salt, baking powder, and baking soda.

2   Transfer 1 cup flour mixture to another bowl. Add butter, yeast mixture, and 1 cup buttermilk; stir to combine. Add remaining flour mixture in three batches, alternating with remaining cup buttermilk and stirring well between additions, until dough is sticky and just holds together. Cover bowl with plastic wrap; refrigerate at least 2 hours.

3   Preheat oven to 450°F. Pinch off 24 equal pieces of dough, and roll into 2-inch balls; place them, just touching one another, on a baking sheet. Bake until biscuits are golden brown on top, 20 to 25 minutes. Serve warm.

from Fourth of July Barbecue

blueberry topping

MAKES 1⅓ CUPS | **PHOTO ON PAGE 245**

This topping pairs wonderfully with vanilla ice cream. Garnish with more blueberries, if desired.

2 teaspoons unsalted butter

1 pint fresh blueberries, picked over and rinsed

¼ cup sugar

Melt butter in a medium saucepan over medium heat; add blueberries and sugar. Cook, stirring, until blueberries release their juices, about 2 minutes. Cool slightly before serving.

from Good Things

currant jelly

MAKES 1 QUART

3 pounds fresh red, black, or white currants, stemmed and washed well

3 cups sugar

1   In a large saucepan, combine currants with ⅓ cup water. Cook over medium-high heat, stirring frequently, until fruit has broken down and released its juices, about 8 minutes. Mash the fruit mixture with a potato masher or the back of a wooden spoon. Strain through a fine sieve into a large measuring cup, pressing on solids to extract as much juice as possible. You should have about 4 cups juice. Discard solids.

2   Place a small plate in the freezer. Return juice to clean saucepan; add sugar. Bring to a boil over medium-high heat. Reduce heat to a simmer; cook, stirring occasionally, about 20 minutes. When a teaspoon of jelly placed on chilled plate ripples if pushed with your finger, it is ready.

3   Remove pan from heat, and skim off any foam from surface. Ladle jelly into sterilized canning jars; wipe rims with a dishtowel. Seal tightly.

4   Meanwhile, bring a stockpot of water to a boil over high heat. Using tongs, carefully place filled jars in boiling water, letting them sit 10 minutes. Remove, and let cool. If center of jar lids give when pushed with your finger, jars have not sealed properly. Jelly in sealed jars will keep up to 1 year. After opening, jelly will keep up to 2 months in the refrigerator.

from Currants

fluffy pancakes

SERVES 6

We cooked these pancakes outdoor on a grill; you can also cook them on the stove over medium-high heat.

2 cups all-purpose flour

6 tablespoons nonfat dry milk

¼ cup sugar

4 teaspoons baking powder

1 teaspoon salt

4 tablespoons unsalted butter, melted, plus more for griddle

2 large eggs, lightly beaten

Maple syrup, for serving

Fresh berries, for serving (optional)

1 Heat grill to medium. Place a cast-iron griddle on grill. In a medium bowl, mix together flour, nonfat dry milk, sugar, baking powder, and salt. Add butter, eggs, and 1¼ cup plus 2 tablespoons cold water. Stir until just combined; batter will be slightly lumpy.

2 Test griddle heat by sprinkling a few drops of water on it: If water bounces and spatters, it is ready. Add about ½ table-spoon butter to griddle. Pour a scant ¼ cup batter per pan-cake onto griddle, and cook until surface bubbles and edges are slightly dry, about 2 minutes. Flip pancakes, and cook until undersides are golden brown. Repeat with remaining batter, adding butter before each batch. Serve pancakes immediately with syrup and berries, if desired.

from A Lazy Weekend in the Country

fresh herb and garlic marinade

MAKES ¾ CUP

This basic marinade, especially good with chicken, imparts a bright flavor and keeps meats moist. It's perfect for grilling and also enhances the flavors of fresh vegetables, tofu, and soft cheeses (marinate thirty minutes). The marinade doesn't work well as a sauce; discard it before cooking.

½ cup extra-virgin olive oil

½ cup coarsely chopped mixed fresh herbs, such as oregano, thyme, savory, flat-leaf parsley, and rosemary, plus more for garnish

6 garlic cloves, coarsely chopped

Zest of 1 lemon

¾ teaspoon coarse salt, plus more for seasoning

½ teaspoon freshly ground pepper, plus more for seasoning

2½ pounds meat or fish

Lemon wedges, for serving

1 Whisk together oil, herbs, garlic, lemon zest, salt, and pepper in a nonreactive dish. Arrange meat or fish in dish, and rub with marinade. Cover; refrigerate 30 minutes for thin, flaky fish, 1 hour for thick and fatty fish, and 6 to 24 hours for meat, turning occasionally.

2 Before cooking, let meat or fish come to a cool room tem-perature. Remove from marinade; discard marinade. Using a paper towel, wipe off any large pieces of herbs or garlic from meat or fish. Season with salt and pepper.

3 Cook meat or fish as desired. Garnish with herbs, and serve with lemon wedges.

from Marinades

garlic-scape toasts

SERVES 6 TO 8

Scapes are garlic shoots often found at farmers' markets in midsummer. Thin young scallions can be used as well. If you prefer, you can toast the rolls under the broiler.

4 French-bread rolls (about 4 inches long), halved horizontally
3 tablespoons unsalted butter, room temperature
2 garlic scapes, thinly sliced diagonally
2 tablespoons coarsely chopped fresh chives
  Coarse salt and freshly ground pepper

Heat grill to medium-high. Place rolls, cut sides down, on grill; toast until golden brown. Remove from grill; spread cut sides with butter. Scatter scapes and chives on top of bread; season with salt and pepper. Serve warm.

from A Lazy Weekend in the Country

olive-oil biscuits

MAKES 26 | PHOTO ON PAGE 242

½ cup extra-virgin olive oil
½ cup sugar
¼ teaspoon baking soda
1½ teaspoons freshly squeezed lemon juice
¼ cup dry white wine
¼ cup sesame seeds, plus more for sprinkling
2 teaspoons freshly grated lemon zest
1 teaspoon fennel seeds, crushed, plus more for sprinkling
½ teaspoon salt
  Pinch of freshly ground white pepper
1¾ cups plus 2 tablespoons all-purpose flour
1 large egg

1 Preheat oven to 350°F, with racks in upper and lower thirds. In the bowl of an electric mixer fitted with the paddle attachment, beat oil and sugar on medium speed until smooth, about 2 minutes. In a small bowl, dissolve baking soda in the lemon juice; add to oil mixture along with wine, sesame seeds, zest, fennel seeds, salt, and white pepper. Beat until combined. Add flour, and beat until just combined.

2 Line two baking sheets with parchment paper; set aside. In a small bowl, beat egg with 2 teaspoons water; set aside.

Form biscuits by rolling tablespoons of dough into 5-inch logs and joining the ends to make circles. Brush tops with egg wash; sprinkle with sesame seeds and fennel. Arrange on prepared baking sheets, 1 inch apart. Bake biscuits until lightly browned, about 20 minutes, rotating sheets halfway through. Serve warm or at room temperature.

from The Flavors of Greece

red wine, juniper, and bay leaf marinade

MAKES 1 CUP

This marinade works well with gamy meats, such as Cornish hens, duck, quail, and venison.

½ cup dry red wine
2 shallots, coarsely chopped
3 dried bay leaves
2 tablespoons dried juniper berries, crushed
2 tablespoons extra-virgin olive oil
1 teaspoon whole black peppercorns, crushed
2 pounds meat
  Coarse salt and freshly ground pepper

1 Whisk together red wine, shallots, bay leaves, juniper berries, oil, and peppercorns. Arrange meat in a shallow non-reactive dish or resealable plastic bag. Pour marinade over meat; rub gently to coat evenly. Cover; refrigerate at least 6 hours and up to 24 hours, turning meat occasionally.

2 Before cooking, let meat come to a cool room temperature. Discard marinade. Season meat with salt and pepper, and cook as desired.

from Marinades

rosemary balsamic marinade

MAKES ¾ CUP

This marinade goes well with beef, lamb, and pork.

- ½ cup balsamic vinegar
- 2 tablespoons extra-virgin olive oil
- 6 garlic cloves, coarsely chopped
- ½ teaspoon freshly ground pepper, plus more for seasoning
- 6 rosemary sprigs, coarsely chopped
- 2 pounds meat
  Coarse salt

1 Whisk together vinegar, oil, garlic, and pepper in a non-reactive bowl. Scatter half the rosemary in a shallow nonreactive dish; arrange meat on top. Cover with marinade; rub gently into meat. Sprinkle with remaining rosemary. Cover; refrigerate 6 to 24 hours, turning meat occasionally.

2 Before cooking, let meat come to a cool room temperature. Wipe off bits of garlic or rosemary; discard marinade. Season meat with salt and pepper, and cook as desired.

from Marinades

soy-scallion dipping sauce

MAKES 1 CUP

Serve with store-bought steamed dumplings or edamame.

- ½ cup soy sauce
- 3 scallions, thinly sliced
  Pinch of crushed red-pepper flakes (optional)

In a small bowl, mix together ingredients with ¼ cup plus 2 tablespoons water. Refrigerate sauce in an airtight container up to 4 days.

from Impromptu Entertaining

spicy hoisin marinade

MAKES ¾ CUP | **PHOTO ON PAGE 234**

This Asian-inspired marinade pairs perfectly with pork—turning into a sticky, spicy, sweet glaze when cooked. We like to serve the meat thinly sliced as part of a salad made of mung-bean sprouts, cilantro, mint, toasted peanuts, and julienned carrots and red peppers.

- ¼ cup soy sauce
- ¼ cup firmly packed dark-brown sugar
- 2 tablespoons sherry
- 2 tablespoons freshly squeezed orange juice
- 2 tablespoons hoisin sauce
- 2 tablespoons freshly grated ginger
- 2 garlic cloves, minced
- 2 scallions, thinly sliced into rounds, plus more for garnish
- 1 tablespoon dry mustard
- 1 teaspoon crumbled dried chile or crushed red-pepper flakes
  Grated zest of 1 orange
- 2½ pounds pork

1 Whisk together all ingredients except pork in a nonreactive bowl. Arrange pork in a shallow nonreactive dish or resealable plastic bag. Pour marinade over pork; rub gently to coat evenly. Cover; refrigerate at least 6 hours and up to 24 hours, turning pork occasionally.

2 Before cooking, let pork come to a cool room temperature. Cook as desired, basting with marinade during the first half of cooking to create a glaze (discard any remaining marinade). Garnish with more scallions.

from Marinades

sweet and spicy dipping sauce

MAKES 1 CUP

Serve with store-bought steamed dumplings or edamame.

- ½ cup plus 2 tablespoons seasoned rice-wine vinegar
- ¼ cup honey
- 2 tablespoons toasted sesame oil
- 1 teaspoon chili sauce
- 1 piece (about 1 inch) fresh ginger, finely julienned

In a small bowl, mix together ingredients. Refrigerate sauce in an airtight container up to 4 days.

from Impromptu Entertaining

tandoori marinade

MAKES 2 CUPS

Besides adding tangy flavor, the yogurt in this traditional Indian mixture tenderizes what you're marinating. It goes well with chicken, pork, fish, and shrimp.

1 cup plain yogurt

1 onion, coarsely chopped

¼ cup loosely packed fresh cilantro, coarsely chopped

Grated zest of 1 lime

4 garlic cloves, coarsely chopped

2 to 3 tablespoons freshly grated ginger

2 tablespoons coarsely chopped fresh mint

1 teaspoon ground cumin

1 teaspoon garam masala

1 teaspoon ground turmeric

¼ teaspoon ground nutmeg

¼ teaspoon ground cinnamon

¼ teaspoon cayenne pepper

3 tablespoons olive oil

1 teaspoon coarse salt

¼ teaspoon freshly ground black pepper

2 to 2½ pounds meat or fish

1   Whisk together all ingredients except meat or fish in a nonreactive bowl. Arrange meat or fish in a shallow nonreactive dish or resealable plastic bag. Pour marinade over meat or fish; rub gently to coat evenly. Cover; refrigerate 30 minutes for thin, flaky fish; 1 hour for thick and fatty fish; and 6 to 24 hours for meat, turning occasionally.

2   Before cooking, remove meat or fish from the refrigerator; let come to a cool room temperature. Cook as desired, basting occasionally with marinade during the first half of cooking (discard any remaining marinade).

from Marinades

Thai marinade

MAKES 1 CUP

This beautiful bright-green marinade is piquant and creamy. Its distinctive flavors are enhanced when grilled.

½ cup unsweetened coconut milk

½ cup loosely packed fresh cilantro

¼ cup Asian fish sauce

4 garlic cloves, coarsely chopped

2 tablespoons freshly grated ginger

Juice of 1 lime

1 tablespoon sugar

1 small red chile, coarsely chopped

2 pounds chicken, fish, or shellfish

1   In a blender or food processor, purée all ingredients except chicken or fish until smooth, about 30 seconds. Arrange chicken or fish in a shallow nonreactive dish or resealable plastic bag. Pour marinade over; rub gently to coat evenly. Cover; refrigerate 20 minutes for shellfish; 30 minutes for thin, flaky fish; 1 hour for thick and fatty fish; and 6 to 24 hours for chicken, turning occasionally.

2   Before cooking, let chicken or fish come to a cool room temperature. Cook as desired, basting occasionally with marinade during first half of cooking (discard remaining marinade).

from Marinades

thyme, shallot, and lemon marinade

MAKES ⅔ CUP

This classic marinade pairs particularly well with shellfish and fish fillets. Don't marinate shellfish for longer than twenty minutes; the acid in the lemon juice will cook the flesh.

3 tablespoons freshly squeezed lemon juice (1 lemon)
3 tablespoons dry white wine
2 tablespoons extra-virgin olive oil
1 bunch thyme (12 to 15 sprigs)
2 shallots, thinly sliced
1 lemon, sliced into ¼-inch rounds
   Coarse salt and freshly ground pepper
2 pounds fish, shellfish, or meat

1   Whisk together juice, wine, and oil in a shallow nonreactive dish. Arrange meat or fish in a single layer in dish; turn to coat. Evenly scatter thyme, shallots, and lemon slices over meat or fish. Cover; refrigerate 20 minutes for shellfish; 30 minutes for thin, flaky fish; 1 hour for thick and fatty fish; and 6 to 24 hours for meat, turning occasionally.

2   Before cooking, let meat or fish come to a cool room temperature; discard marinade. Season with salt and pepper. Cook as desired.

from Marinades

August

creamy tomato soup

SERVES 6

This soup can be made without any half-and-half. Or, if you prefer, double the amount for extra creaminess.

- 2 tablespoons unsalted butter
- 1 onion, finely chopped
- 3 garlic cloves, minced
- ½ cup gin or dry white wine
- 2 cans (28 ounces each) crushed tomatoes
- 1 quart Basic Chicken Stock (page 17) or low-sodium canned chicken broth
- 3 sprigs oregano or marjoram
- ½ cup half-and-half
  Coarse salt and freshly ground pepper
  Baked Cheese Croutons (recipe follows)

1   In a medium saucepan, melt butter over medium-low heat. Add onion and garlic; cook, stirring occasionally, until onion is soft and translucent, about 6 minutes.

2   Pour gin into pan; cook until most of the liquid has evaporated, about 1 minute. Add tomatoes, stock, and oregano; bring to a boil. Reduce heat; simmer gently until thickened, about 45 minutes. Remove from heat. Using a slotted spoon, remove herbs. (For a smooth consistency, purée soup in a blender, working in batches so as not to fill more than halfway.)

3   Slowly pour half-and-half into soup, stirring constantly. Season with salt and pepper. Serve immediately with cheese-topped croutons on the side.

from Croutons

baked cheese croutons

MAKES 6

- 6 slices (each about ½ inch wide and 5 inches long) focaccia or other wide bread
- ½ cup grated Gruyère, fontina, or Swiss cheese
- 2 tablespoons freshly grated Parmesan cheese

1   Preheat oven to 350°F. Place bread slices on a baking sheet, and bake until slightly golden and dry, 10 to 15 minutes.

2   In a small bowl, combine cheeses, and sprinkle over bread slices. Continue baking until cheese is melted and bubbling, about 8 minutes. Serve immediately.

fresh green tart

MAKES ONE 13½-BY-4-INCH TART

You can substitute any variety of ripe tomato for the heirlooms called for in this recipe.

- Whole almonds, for garnish
- Almond Tart Dough (page 200)
- 2 teaspoons sherry vinegar
- 1 teaspoon extra-virgin olive oil
- 1 green bell pepper, ribs and seeds removed, diced
- 1 English cucumber, peeled, halved lengthwise and cut into ¼-inch-thick half-moons
- 2 small green heirloom tomatoes, quartered
- 2 scallions, white and pale-green parts only, cut diagonally into ⅛-inch-wide pieces
  Coarse salt and freshly ground black pepper
  Almond-Arugula Pesto (page 200)
- ¼ cup fresh chervil, for garnish

1   Preheat oven to 350°F. Spread almonds in a single layer on a rimmed baking sheet; toast in oven until crisp and fragrant, tossing occasionally, about 10 minutes. Set aside to cool. Raise oven heat to 375°F.

2   Press tart dough into a 13½-by-4-inch rectangular tart pan with a removable bottom. Using a fork, lightly prick all over bottom of dough. Refrigerate 20 minutes.

3   Remove tart shell from refrigerator. Line with parchment paper; fill with pie weights or dried beans. Bake until edges start to brown, about 15 minutes. Remove weights and parchment; continue baking until crust is golden, 8 to 10 minutes more. Transfer to a wire rack, and let cool completely.

4   In a medium bowl, whisk together vinegar and oil. Add bell pepper, cucumber, tomatoes, and scallions; toss to combine. Season with salt and black pepper.

5   Spread pesto evenly over bottom of tart shell. Arrange vegetable mixture on top. Garnish with chervil and almonds. Serve at room temperature.

from Vegetable Tarts

almond tart dough

MAKES ENOUGH FOR ONE 13½-BY-4-INCH TART

Toast sesame seeds in a dry skillet over medium heat, shaking pan, until golden and starting to pop, about two minutes.

- 1 cup all-purpose flour
- 3 tablespoons whole almonds, toasted
- 2 tablespoons sesame seeds, toasted
- 1¼ teaspoons salt
- ¼ teaspoon ground coriander
- ¼ teaspoon ground cumin
- 6 tablespoons chilled unsalted butter, cut into small pieces
- 1 large egg yolk
- 2 tablespoons ice water

1 In a food processor, pulse flour, almonds, sesame seeds, salt, coriander, and cumin until nuts are finely ground. Add butter, and process until mixture resembles coarse meal. In a small bowl, whisk together egg yolk and ice water. With machine running, add egg mixture through the feed tube in a slow, steady stream. Process until dough just comes together.

2 Turn out dough onto a piece of plastic wrap. Flatten into a disk. Wrap in plastic; chill at least 1 hour or overnight.

almond-arugula pesto

MAKES ENOUGH FOR ONE 13½-BY-4-INCH TART

- ¼ cup whole almonds, toasted
- ¾ cup arugula, rinsed well
- ¼ cup fresh flat-leaf parsley leaves
- 1 tablespoon crème fraîche
- 3 tablespoons extra-virgin olive oil
- 2 teaspoons freshly squeezed lemon juice
- 1 garlic clove
  Coarse salt and freshly ground pepper

In a food processor, pulse almonds, arugula, parsley, crème fraîche, oil, lemon juice, and garlic until smooth. Season with salt and pepper. Refrigerate in an airtight container up to 2 days; before using, let come to room temperature.

roasted-pepper saffron tart

MAKES 1 NINE-INCH TART

- 1¼ pounds (2 to 3) red bell peppers
  All-purpose flour, for work surface
- ½ recipe Pâte Brisée (page 129)
- 1 cup heavy cream
- 1 teaspoon saffron threads
- 1 large whole egg plus 2 large egg yolks
  Coarse salt
- 1 tablespoon unsalted butter
- 1 shallot, minced
- 3 tablespoons sherry vinegar
  Freshly ground black pepper

1 Roast bell peppers directly over a gas burner until charred, turning as each side blackens. (Alternatively, roast peppers on a baking sheet under the broiler.) Transfer peppers to a large bowl, and cover with plastic wrap; let steam about 15 minutes. Using paper towels, rub off charred skins. Remove seeds and ribs. Finely chop peppers, and set aside.

2 Preheat oven to 375°F. On a lightly floured work surface, roll out pâte brisée to a ⅛-inch-thick round about 12 inches in diameter. Fit into a 9-inch round fluted tart pan; press into sides and bottom. Trim dough flush with edge. Using a fork, lightly prick all over bottom of dough. Freeze 20 minutes.

3 Remove tart shell from freezer. Line with parchment paper; fill with pie weights or dried beans. Bake until edge begins to brown, about 20 minutes. Remove weights and parchment; continue baking until bottom of crust is golden, about 7 minutes more. Transfer to a wire rack; let cool completely.

4 Reduce oven temperature to 350°F. In a small saucepan, heat cream over medium-low heat until just warm; remove from heat. Add saffron, and let steep, covered, 15 minutes. In a small bowl, whisk together the saffron cream, egg, and yolks; season with salt. Set aside.

5 In a medium skillet, melt butter over medium heat. Add shallot, and cook, stirring, until fragrant and soft, 1 to 2 minutes. Stir in vinegar and reserved peppers. Season with salt and pepper, and set aside.

6 To assemble tart, spread red-pepper mixture evenly over bottom of tart shell. Carefully pour cream mixture over red-pepper mixture. Bake until custard is set, 20 to 25 minutes. Transfer tart to a wire rack; let cool slightly before serving.

from Vegetable Tarts

salad-quiche tartlets

MAKES 6 FOUR-INCH TARTLETS | **PHOTO ON PAGE 230**

Try substituting any deli-style smoked ham for the French ham in this recipe.

All-purpose flour, for work surface
Herbed Dough (recipe follows)
1½ ounces Brie cheese, sliced into 6 pieces (½ inch thick)
¾ ounce French ham, sliced into ½-inch strips
½ cup whole milk
2 large eggs
Coarse salt and freshly ground pepper
1 small bulb fennel, thinly sliced
1 green apple, cored and sliced into matchsticks
½ small red onion, very thinly sliced
½ cup watercress, trimmed
1 teaspoon walnut oil
1 teaspoon freshly squeezed lemon juice

1 Preheat oven to 375°F. On a lightly floured surface, roll out dough ⅛ inch thick. Using a 5½-inch inverted bowl as a guide, cut out 6 rounds. Transfer rounds to 4-inch tartlet pans with removable bottoms, and gently press into sides and bottoms. Trim dough flush with edges of pans. Using a fork, lightly prick all over bottom of dough. Refrigerate 20 minutes.

2 Remove tartlet shells from refrigerator. Line with parchment paper, and fill with pie weights or dried beans. Bake until edges begin to turn golden brown, about 12 minutes. Transfer pans to a wire rack, and remove weights and parchment. Let cool completely.

3 Place 1 slice of Brie and 4 or 5 strips of ham in the bottom of each shell. In a small bowl, whisk together milk and eggs; season with salt and pepper. Pour mixture into tartlet shells; bake until custard is set, 12 to 14 minutes. Transfer tartlets to a wire rack, and let cool completely.

4 Meanwhile, in a medium bowl, toss together fennel, apple, onion, watercress, oil, and lemon juice. Season with salt and pepper. Divide mixture evenly among tartlets, and serve.

from Vegetable Tarts

herbed dough

MAKES ENOUGH FOR 6 FOUR-INCH TARTLETS

1¼ cups all-purpose flour
½ teaspoon salt
½ cup (1 stick) chilled unsalted butter, cut into small pieces
1 tablespoon fresh thyme leaves
3 tablespoons ice water

1 In a food processor, pulse flour and salt to combine. Add butter, and process until mixture resembles coarse meal. Add thyme, and pulse a few more times. With machine running, add ice water through the feed tube in a slow, steady stream until dough just holds together. Do not overmix.

2 Turn out dough onto a piece of plastic wrap. Flatten into a disk. Wrap; chill at least 30 minutes or overnight.

tomato aspic

SERVES 10 TO 12

Aspic can be made up to two days ahead and stored, covered, in the refrigerator.

5 pounds ripe but firm beefsteak tomatoes
3¼ tablespoons unflavored gelatin (3¼ envelopes)
2 teaspoons coarse salt
Basil sprigs or chive blossoms, for garnish
Chiffonade Dressing, for serving (page 202)

1 Core tomatoes; coarsely chop. Working in batches, transfer to a food processor or food mill. Process to a rough purée.

2 Rinse two 24-inch square pieces of cheesecloth. Wring out excess water from cheesecloth; layer pieces in a large glass bowl. Pour purée into cheesecloth; gather up ends, and cinch with kitchen twine. Tie ends of cloth together to make a loop. Hang sack from a cupboard door, placing bowl underneath to collect juices.

3 Let drain at least 1 hour; liquid will be pale. Transfer liquid to a large glass measuring cup, and set aside.

4 Squeeze bundle over emptied bowl to extract remaining liquid; pour into another measuring cup. You should have about 4 cups dark-red tomato juice; if needed, add enough reserved pale liquid to make 4 cups (discard remaining pale liquid). Pass juice through a fine sieve into a bowl.

5 Place 1 cup tomato juice in a small bowl. Sprinkle gelatin over liquid; let soften, about 5 minutes. Transfer mixture to a medium saucepan; stir over very low heat until gelatin dissolves. Stir in some of the juice to lower the temperature of the gelatin mixture, then add remaining juice and salt.

6 Pour mixture into a 9-by-4¾-by-2½-inch loaf pan. Cover with plastic wrap, and refrigerate until set, at least 1 hour.

7 To unmold: Slide a knife around inside edge of pan. Wrap loaf pan in a hot towel, and invert onto a serving platter. Garnish with basil sprigs. To serve, cut aspic into thick slices, and top each slice with dressing.

from Tomato Aspic

chiffonade dressing

MAKES 1 CUP

Hard-boiled eggs can be made a day ahead and refrigerated; peel just before proceeding.

2 beets, trimmed and scrubbed
1 teaspoon coarse salt, plus more for seasoning
3 large eggs
¼ cup white-wine vinegar
¾ cup extra-virgin olive oil
Freshly ground pepper
4 fresh chives, finely chopped

1 Fill a medium saucepan three-quarters full of water. Add beets and salt; bring to a boil. Simmer beets until tender, about 30 minutes. Drain; set aside until cool enough to handle.

2 Meanwhile, place eggs in a small saucepan, and add enough water to cover by 1 inch. Bring to a boil; continue boiling 1 minute. Turn off heat; let stand 13 minutes. Drain, and run under cold water until cool (to chill faster, plunge into an ice bath).

3 Using a paper towel, rub off beet skins. Cut beets into ¼-inch pieces. Peel eggs, and separate yolks from whites. Cut whites into ¼-inch pieces; press yolks through a fine sieve into a small bowl.

4 In a small bowl, whisk together vinegar and oil until emulsified. Season with salt and pepper.

5 To serve, drizzle vinaigrette over each aspic serving. Spoon reserved beets, egg whites, and egg yolks over top, and sprinkle with chives.

Asian pear salad

SERVES 4 | **PHOTO ON PAGE 231**

4 cups mixed frisée, baby arugula, and other small greens (about 11 ounces)
8 dates, pitted and quartered lengthwise
8 paper-thin slices prosciutto (about 4 ounces), cut into ¼-inch-wide strips
1 cup loosely packed mint leaves (about 8 sprigs)
1 Asian pear, cored and sliced into ½-inch-thick wedges
2 tablespoons freshly squeezed lemon juice
2 tablespoons extra-virgin olive oil
Coarse salt and freshly ground pepper

In a large bowl, toss together greens, dates, prosciutto, mint, and pear. In a small bowl, whisk together lemon juice and oil; season with salt and pepper. Pour dressing over salad. Toss to coat well, and serve immediately.

from Asian Pears

grilled peppers and goat cheese salad

SERVES 4 | **PHOTO ON PAGE 231**

2 large red bell peppers
2 tablespoons extra-virgin olive oil
Coarse salt and freshly ground black pepper
6 ounces aged goat cheese
1 small head lettuce, such as red leaf or Bibb

1 Heat grill to high. Roast bell peppers on grill until charred, turning as each side blackens. Transfer to a large bowl, and cover with plastic wrap. Let steam about 15 minutes. Using paper towels, rub off charred skin. Remove seeds and ribs, and slice peppers into ½-inch-wide strips. Drizzle with 1 tablespoon oil; season with salt and black pepper. Set aside.

2 Slice goat cheese into four pieces; place directly on grill. Heat, covered, until cheese starts to soften and melt.

3 Place one piece of goat cheese on each serving plate. Arrange lettuce leaves next to cheese on each plate. Drizzle greens and cheese with remaining tablespoon oil; season lightly with salt and black pepper. Divide reserved peppers among plates, and serve immediately.

from What's For Dinner?

summer salad with blueberries

SERVES 6 | **PHOTO ON PAGE 231**

2 teaspoons minced or grated fresh ginger

1 tablespoon rice-wine vinegar

2 teaspoons freshly squeezed lemon juice

¼ teaspoon coarse salt

3 scallions, cut diagonally into ¼-inch pieces

½ small jícama (about 4 ounces), peeled and cut into ¼-inch-thick matchsticks

½ honeydew melon, peeled, seeded, and cut into ½-inch cubes (about 2 cups)

1 orange bell pepper, seeds and ribs removed, cut into ¼-inch-thick strips

1½ cups fresh blueberries (about ½ pound), picked over and rinsed

4 ounces baby arugula

2 teaspoons canola oil

Freshly ground black pepper

1   In a small bowl, whisk together ginger, vinegar, lemon juice, and salt; set dressing aside.

2   In a serving bowl, combine scallions, jícama, honeydew, bell pepper, and blueberries. Pour ginger mixture over salad, and toss to coat (salad can be made up to this point 30 minutes ahead of time, and refrigerated, covered).

3   Just before serving, add arugula to salad mixture; drizzle with oil. Season with black pepper. Toss to combine.

PER SERVING: 76 CALORIES, 2 G FAT, 0 MG CHOLESTEROL, 15 G CARBOHYDRATE, 96 MG SODIUM, 1 G PROTEIN, 3 G FIBER

from Fit to Eat: Blueberries

buttermilk-leek galette

MAKES 1 NINE-INCH TART

All-purpose flour, for work surface

1 sheet frozen puff pastry from standard package (17.3 ounces), thawed

2 tablespoons unsalted butter

5 leeks, white and pale-green parts only, cut crosswise into ½-inch-thick pieces, washed well

¼ cup nonfat buttermilk

2 teaspoons Dijon mustard

Coarse salt and freshly ground pepper

5 ounces fresh goat cheese, crumbled

1 large egg yolk

1 tablespoon heavy cream or water

1   Line a baking sheet with parchment paper, and set a 9-inch tart ring (about 2 inches deep) on top; set aside. On a lightly floured work surface, roll out puff pastry to about ⅛ inch thick. Using a sharp paring knife, trim the dough to a 13-inch round, and lay over tart ring. Fit dough into ring, and fold in edges against the inside of the ring, pressing gently to seal. Refrigerate dough 20 minutes.

2   Preheat oven to 400°F. In a large nonstick skillet, melt butter over medium heat. Add leeks; cook, stirring, until soft, about 7 minutes. Add buttermilk and mustard, and cook until slightly thickened, about 2 minutes. Season with salt and pepper. Remove from heat; set aside.

3   To assemble tart, layer goat cheese and leek mixture on chilled pastry, ending with goat cheese, and leaving a 1-inch border around edge. In a small bowl, beat together egg yolk and cream. Brush exposed dough with egg wash, and bake until golden, about 35 minutes. Serve warm.

from Vegetable Tarts

grilled chicken with blueberry-basil salsa

SERVES 6

½ tablespoon olive oil, plus more for grill

2 jalapeño chiles (ribs and seeds removed for less heat)

24 scallions

3 cups blueberries (about 1 pound), picked over and rinsed

½ small red onion, finely chopped

¼ cup freshly squeezed lime juice (2 limes)

½ teaspoon coarse salt

½ cup loosely packed basil leaves, very thinly sliced, plus whole leaves for garnish

½ cup loosely packed cilantro leaves, coarsely chopped, plus whole leaves for garnish

2 pounds chicken cutlets

Pinch of cayenne pepper

1   Heat grill to medium-high; lightly brush with oil. Grill jalapeños until slightly charred and blistered, turning frequently, about 15 minutes. Using a paper towel, rub off charred skins. Roughly chop flesh and seeds; set aside. Meanwhile, grill scallions, turning often, until soft and charred in spots, 3 to 4 minutes; set aside.

2   Place 2 cups blueberries in a food processor; pulse until coarsely chopped, about five times. Transfer to a medium bowl, and stir in onion, jalapeños, lime juice, and ¼ teaspoon salt until combined. Add basil, cilantro, remaining cup blueberries, and oil; stir to combine.

3   Sprinkle chicken with remaining ¼ teaspoon salt and the cayenne. Grill chicken until cooked through, 3 to 4 minutes per side. Place 4 grilled scallions on each plate; top with chicken. Serve immediately, topped with a generous spoonful of blueberry salsa. Garnish with basil and cilantro leaves.

PER SERVING:, 237 CALORIES, 3 G FAT, 88 MG CHOLESTEROL, 16 G CARBOHYDRATE, 266 MG SODIUM, 36 G PROTEIN, 3 G FIBER

from Fit to Eat: Blueberries

grilled sea scallops and fennel

SERVES 4 | PHOTO ON PAGE 234

If using wooden skewers, soak them for thirty minutes before grilling to prevent them from scorching. We serve the scallops and fennel with Mixed Fresh Herb Pasta (page 205); slide the scallops off the skewers, then toss everything together.

2½ tablespoons olive oil

¼ cup freshly squeezed lemon juice (2 lemons)

1 tablespoon Pernod (anise-flavored liqueur; optional)

24 sea scallops (about 1¼ pounds), tough muscles removed

Coarse salt and freshly ground pepper

1 bulb fennel, trimmed, fronds reserved for pasta sauce

1   Heat grill to medium-high. In a large bowl, combine 2 tablespoons oil with the lemon juice and liqueur, if using. Add scallops, and toss to coat. Thread scallops horizontally onto small skewers (about 6 on each). Season with salt and pepper.

2   Grill, rotating, until scallops are golden outside and just cooked through, 2 to 3 minutes. Remove from grill.

3   Halve fennel bulb lengthwise, then slice again lengthwise into ¼-inch-thick pieces. Toss with remaining ½ tablespoon oil; grill, turning, until fennel just wilts and starts to brown, about 5 minutes. Slide scallops off skewers; serve with fennel.

from What's For Dinner?

mixed fresh herb pasta

SERVES 4 | **PHOTO ON PAGE 234**

Vary the sauce with any tender herbs you have on hand.

Coarse salt

¾ pound spaghetti or other long pasta

3 shallots, minced (about ¼ cup)

6 tablespoons extra-virgin olive oil

1 tablespoon freshly squeezed lemon juice

2 cups packed mixed fresh herbs, such as mint, flat-leaf parsley, tarragon, and basil, finely chopped

¼ cup snipped fresh fennel fronds, finely chopped

Freshly ground pepper

1 Bring a large pot of water to a boil over high heat. Add salt and pasta. Cook until pasta is al dente according to package directions. Drain, and return pasta to pot.

2 Meanwhile, place shallots on a cutting board; sprinkle lightly with salt. Using the side of a chef's knife, crush into a paste. Transfer to a medium bowl; add oil and lemon juice. Whisk to combine. Add herbs and fennel fronds; mix well. Season with salt and pepper. Stir sauce into pasta; serve warm.

from What's For Dinner?

rustic market tarts

MAKES 6 TARTS | **PHOTOS ON PAGES 236 AND 237**

This crust, spread with ricotta, makes a good base for any combination of fresh vegetables. In addition to the grilled eggplant topping, we like tomatoes with fontina cheese and basil, as well as sliced yellow squash and zucchini paired with grated Parmesan cheese, oregano, and squash blossoms. The dough may be frozen, wrapped in plastic, for up to one month; thaw overnight in the refrigerator before using.

1¼ cups warm water (about 110°F)

1 teaspoon active dry yeast

Pinch of sugar

3 to 4 cups all-purpose flour

2 teaspoons coarse salt

3 tablespoons unsalted butter, room temperature, cut into small pieces

Extra-virgin olive oil, for bowl and wrap, plus more for drizzling (optional)

3 cups fresh ricotta cheese (24 ounces), drained in a fine-mesh sieve lined with cheesecloth 3 hours or overnight

Grilled Eggplant with Rosemary and Feta (page 206) or other assorted vegetable toppings

Coarse salt and freshly ground pepper

1 In the bowl of an electric mixer, combine the warm water, yeast, and sugar. Let stand until foamy, about 10 minutes.

2 Using the dough-hook attachment, slowly beat in the flour, ½ cup at a time, until dough is tacky, but not sticky. Add salt; mix until combined. Add butter a few pieces at a time, beating on low speed until incorporated. Continue beating until smooth, 7 to 10 minutes. Transfer to a large oiled bowl. Cover with oiled plastic wrap; let dough rise in a warm place until doubled in bulk, about 2 hours.

3 Preheat oven to 500°F. If using, heat a pizza stone on lower rack. Punch down dough. Divide into six equal pieces. Place one piece on a clean work surface; cover others with a clean kitchen towel. Gently stretch dough into an 11-by-5-inch rectangle. Spread with ½ cup ricotta. Add toppings; season with salt and pepper. Repeat with remaining dough and toppings.

4 Place tarts directly on stone or on a baking sheet. Bake until crust is golden brown, 10 to 12 minutes. Drizzle tarts with oil, if desired. Serve warm or at room temperature.

from Vegetable Tarts

grilled eggplant with rosemary and feta

MAKES ENOUGH FOR 6 RUSTIC TARTS

1½ pounds small eggplants, trimmed and sliced lengthwise into 1-inch-thick strips

Coarse salt

3 tablespoons extra-virgin olive oil

1 garlic clove, minced

1 tablespoon fresh rosemary, finely chopped

Freshly ground black pepper

6 ounces feta cheese

1 Heat grill to medium. Place eggplant in a colander in a single layer, and sprinkle generously with salt. Let stand 20 minutes; rinse eggplant, and pat dry.

2 In a medium bowl, combine eggplant, oil, garlic, and rosemary. Season with salt and pepper, and toss to combine. Grill eggplant until tender and golden, 2 to 3 minutes per side. Crumble feta over the top, and toss to combine.

Swiss chard and goat cheese galette

MAKES 1 TEN-INCH TART | PHOTO ON PAGE 238

Toast pine nuts in a dry skillet over medium heat, shaking skillet, until golden and starting to pop, about five minutes.

12 ounces Swiss chard, washed, stems removed and reserved

2 tablespoons extra-virgin olive oil

1 large onion, sliced into ¼-inch-thick rounds

3 tablespoons balsamic vinegar

Coarse salt and freshly ground pepper

3 anchovy fillets, coarsely chopped (optional)

2 tablespoons fresh thyme leaves

6 ounces fresh goat cheese, room temperature

3 tablespoons heavy cream

½ teaspoon freshly grated nutmeg

Oatmeal Tart Dough (recipe follows)

2 tablespoons pine nuts, toasted

2 tablespoons golden raisins

1 large egg yolk

1 Slice chard stems into ¼-inch pieces. In a large skillet, heat 1 tablespoon oil over medium heat. Add stems and onion; cook, stirring, until lightly browned, 8 to 10 minutes.

2 Cover skillet, and reduce heat to low. Cook, stirring occasionally, until stems are very soft, about 15 minutes. Add vinegar, and cook, stirring, until liquid is reduced by half, about 2 min-

utes. Season with salt and pepper. Remove from heat, and transfer onion mixture to a nonreactive bowl; set aside.

3 Heat remaining tablespoon oil in the same skillet over medium-high heat. Add anchovies, if using; sauté, stirring frequently, 1 minute. Add chard leaves, and sauté until slightly wilted, about 1 minute. Stir in thyme; season with salt and pepper, and set aside.

4 In the bowl of an electric mixer fitted with the paddle attachment, beat goat cheese and 2 tablespoons cream until smooth, about 1 minute. Stir in nutmeg; season with salt and pepper, and set aside.

5 Preheat oven to 375°F. On a large piece of parchment paper, roll out dough to a ¼-inch-thick round, about 12 inches in diameter. Arrange onion mixture evenly over the dough, leaving a 3-inch border around edge. Spread goat-cheese mixture over onion mixture, and top with the chard mixture. Sprinkle with pine nuts and golden raisins. Fold edges of dough over, and press down gently to seal. Transfer tart, on parchment paper, to a baking sheet, and refrigerate 15 minutes.

6 In a small bowl, beat egg yolk with remaining tablespoon cream. Brush dough with egg wash; bake until crust is golden, 40 to 45 minutes. Serve warm or at room temperature.

from Vegetable Tarts

oatmeal tart dough

MAKES ENOUGH FOR 1 TEN-INCH TART

½ cup all-purpose flour

½ cup whole-wheat flour

½ cup old-fashioned rolled oats

1 teaspoon salt

½ cup (1 stick) chilled unsalted butter, cut into small pieces

3 ounces cream cheese

1 large egg yolk

1 In a food processor, pulse the flours, oats, and salt to combine. Add butter, cream cheese, and egg yolk, and process until dough just holds together, 15 to 20 seconds. If dough is too crumbly, add 1 to 2 tablespoons ice water through the food processor's feed tube. Pulse until just combined.

2 Turn out dough onto a piece of plastic wrap. Flatten into a disk. Wrap; chill at least 1 hour or overnight.

Asian pear sorbet

MAKES 1 QUART | **PHOTO ON PAGE 248**

2¼ pounds Asian pears (about 3), peeled, cored, and cut into eighths

1½ cups sake

½ cup sugar

2 tablespoons freshly squeezed lemon juice

1 In a large saucepan, combine pears and 1 cup sake. Bring to a simmer over medium heat; cook, covered, until tender when pierced with the tip of a paring knife, 30 to 35 minutes.

2 Transfer pears and cooking liquid to a food processor. Add sugar; process until smooth. Add lemon juice and remaining ½ cup sake; pulse to combine. Transfer mixture to an airtight container; refrigerate until chilled, at least 2½ hours.

3 Pour mixture into an ice-cream maker, and freeze according to manufacturer's instructions. Transfer sorbet to an airtight container; freeze at least 2 hours before serving.

from Asian Pears

berry brown betty

SERVES 4 | **PHOTO ON PAGE 245**

To make breadcrumbs, process day-old brioche in a food processor until coarsely ground; you will need about one-half pound of bread.

3 cups fresh raspberries (red and golden, if available)

1½ teaspoons freshly squeezed lemon juice

5 tablespoons unsalted butter, melted

1 tablespoon granulated sugar

2 cups fresh brioche breadcrumbs

⅓ cup packed light-brown sugar

2 tablespoons all-purpose flour

Pinch of freshly grated nutmeg

Sweetened whipped cream, for serving

1 Preheat oven to 375°F. In a medium bowl, mix all but ¼ cup berries with lemon juice, and set aside to macerate. Brush four 6-ounce ramekins with 1 tablespoon butter; coat inside of each with granulated sugar, and set aside.

2 In a small bowl, combine breadcrumbs with remaining 4 tablespoons butter, and set aside. Sprinkle brown sugar, flour, and nutmeg over raspberries, and gently toss to combine. Divide one-third of breadcrumbs evenly among ramekins. Top with half the berries, and then with another third of breadcrumbs. Repeat with remaining berries and breadcrumbs. Gently press down on layers.

3 Place ramekins on a baking sheet. Bake until crumbs are golden and juices are bubbling, about 20 minutes. Remove from oven; let cool 5 minutes.

4 Invert desserts onto serving plates, and top each with whipped cream; garnish with reserved berries.

from What's For Dinner?

blackberry-peach trifle

SERVES 6 TO 8 | **PHOTO ON PAGE 245**

Unsalted butter, room temperature, for baking dish

1 cup all-purpose flour, plus more for baking dish

1 pound ripe but firm yellow peaches (about 3)

1 pound ripe but firm white peaches (about 3)

1 pound fresh blackberries (about 3 heaping cups)

¾ cup plus 2 tablespoons sugar

3 cups heavy cream

2 large eggs

1 teaspoon pure vanilla extract

1¼ teaspoons baking powder

¼ teaspoon salt

1 Preheat oven to 350°F, with rack in center. Butter and flour a 9-by-13-inch baking dish; set aside. Prepare a large ice bath; set aside. Fill a large saucepan two-thirds full with water; bring to a simmer over medium-high heat. Score the bottom of each peach. Gently place peaches in simmering water. Using a slotted spoon, remove peaches from water when skin easily peels away from the flesh, 1 to 2 minutes. Plunge into ice bath until cool enough to handle; peel immediately.

2 Halve peaches; remove and discard pits. Cut each peach into 8 slices. Cut one-third of the slices in half crosswise, and set aside. Reserve the remaining slices for topping. In a medium bowl, combine blackberries and 2 tablespoons sugar. Set aside to macerate, stirring occasionally.

3 In a small bowl, whip 1 cup cream until stiff peaks form; set aside for batter. Whip remaining 2 cups cream in a medium bowl; cover with plastic wrap, and refrigerate.

4 In the bowl of an electric mixer fitted with the paddle attachment, lightly beat eggs. Add remaining ¾ cup sugar, and beat until mixture is pale and thick, about 3 minutes. Stir in vanilla. Into a small bowl, sift together flour, baking powder, and salt. Gradually stir flour mixture into egg mixture. Gently fold the reserved whipped cream into the batter in three additions. Pour batter into prepared dish; spread evenly.

5 Scatter reserved peach pieces and a third of the blackberries over batter. Bake until cake is golden and a cake tester inserted in the center comes out clean, about 35 minutes. Transfer to a wire rack, and let cool completely.

6 To assemble: Cut cake into six pieces. Place three pieces in the bottom of a straight-sided glass serving dish or compote. Spoon half of the reserved peach slices, blackberries, and juice over cake. Spoon half of the refrigerated whipped cream over fruit. Repeat with remaining cake, fruit, and cream. Drizzle remaining berry juice over trifle.

from Dessert of the Month

chilled blueberry soup

SERVES 6

Adding extra lemon juice in step two will give the soup more tartness. Serve it thoroughly chilled, accompanied by tuiles, biscotti, or other crisp cookies.

½ cup sugar

4¾ cups fresh blueberries (about 1½ pounds), picked over and rinsed

¾ cup sweet white wine, such as Sauternes, Riesling, or Gewürztraminer

2 teaspoons grated lemon zest

1½ teaspoons freshly squeezed lemon juice

¾ cup low-fat buttermilk

1 In a medium saucepan, combine sugar with 2 cups water; bring to a boil over high heat. Add blueberries, wine, and lemon zest; return to a simmer. Cook, stirring, until blueberries begin to burst, about 3 minutes.

2 Pass mixture through a food mill or a fine sieve into a large bowl, discarding solids. Stir lemon juice into strained liquid. Cover with plastic wrap, and refrigerate until completely chilled, about 1½ hours.

3 Divide soup among six bowls. Swirl about 2 tablespoons buttermilk into each bowl, and serve immediately.

PER SERVING: 174 CALORIES, 1 G FAT 2 MG CHOLESTEROL, 36 G CARBOHYDRATE, 76 MG SODIUM, 3 G PROTEIN, 3 G FIBER

from Fit to Eat: Blueberries

plum and pineapple sangria

MAKES ABOUT 2¼ QUARTS | PHOTO ON PAGE 247

We used a variety of plums for a colorful sangria.

1 pineapple, peeled, halved lengthwise, and cored

4 ripe but firm plums, pitted and cut into wedges

1 tablespoon superfine sugar, or more as desired

3 ounces Cointreau

3 ounces brandy

1 750-ml bottle chilled fruity red wine

1⅓ cups pineapple juice

1 cup sparkling water or seltzer

Cut half of the pineapple into ¾-inch-thick spears and the other half into 1-inch chunks. Transfer all pineapple to a pitcher, and add plums. Sprinkle with sugar, and stir to combine. Add Cointreau and brandy; let sit at least 1 hour at room temperature. Stir in wine, pineapple juice, and sparkling water. Sweeten with more sugar, if desired, and serve chilled.

from Sangrias

Prosecco sangria

MAKES ABOUT 2 QUARTS | PHOTO ON PAGE 247

1 ripe but firm peach, pitted and cut into wedges

1 ripe but firm nectarine, pitted and cut into wedges

3 ripe but firm apricots, pitted and cut into wedges

5 ounces peach brandy

1 750-ml bottle chilled Prosecco (Italian sparkling wine)

1 cup peach nectar

Superfine sugar (optional)

In a pitcher, combine peach, nectarine, and apricots. Stir in brandy, and let sit at least 1 hour at room temperature. Stir in Prosecco and peach nectar. Sweeten with superfine sugar, if desired. Serve chilled.

from Sangrias

red-wine sangria

MAKES ABOUT 2 QUARTS | PHOTO ON PAGE 247

1 cup seedless red or black grapes

1 lemon, sliced and seeded

1 orange, sliced and seeded

2 apples, red and green, cored and cut into ½-inch wedges

1 tablespoon superfine sugar, or more as desired

3 tablespoons Grand Marnier

3 tablespoons brandy

2 whole cinnamon sticks

1 750-ml bottled chilled dry red wine

1 cup orange juice

In a pitcher, combine grapes, lemon, orange, and apples. Sprinkle with sugar, and stir to combine. Add Grand Marnier, brandy, and cinnamon; let sit at least 1 hour at room temperature. Stir in wine and orange juice. Sweeten with more sugar, if desired. Discard cinnamon sticks, and serve chilled.

from Sangrias

rosé sangria

MAKES ABOUT 2 QUARTS | PHOTO ON PAGE 246

2 cups fresh blueberries, picked over and rinsed

2 cups fresh blackberries, picked over and rinsed

2 cups fresh strawberries, hulled and rinsed

2 cups mixed fresh red and golden raspberries, picked over and rinsed

1 tablespoon superfine sugar, or more as desired

5 ounces framboise (raspberry liqueur)

1 750-ml bottle chilled rosé wine

1⅓ cups white cranberry juice

In a pitcher, combine blueberries, blackberries, strawberries, and raspberries. Stir in sugar. Add framboise; let sit at least 1 hour at room temperature. Stir in rosé and cranberry juice. Sweeten with more sugar, if desired, and serve chilled.

from Sangrias

watermelon nectar

MAKES ABOUT 5½ QUARTS

This pink juice tastes as sweet and refreshing as a slice of the fruit—with less mess.

1 seedless watermelon (about 12 pounds)

Halve watermelon lengthwise, and cut the flesh into chunks. Purée melon in batches in a blender or food processor. Strain through a fine sieve; chill before serving. Store juice in an air-tight container in the refrigerator up to 1 week.

from Good Things

white-wine sangria

MAKES ABOUT 2 QUARTS | PHOTO ON PAGE 247

1 cup seedless green grapes

1 kiwi, peeled and sliced

1 wedge (about 1 pound) seedless watermelon, scooped into 1-inch balls

¼ honeydew melon, seeded and cut into 1-inch cubes

1 lime, sliced and seeded

1 star fruit, sliced and seeded

1 pink grapefruit, seeded, sliced, and quartered

1 tablespoon superfine sugar, or more as desired

3 ounces Cointreau or Grand Marnier

3 ounces brandy

1 750-ml bottle chilled fruity white wine

1 cup white cranberry juice

In a pitcher, combine grapes, kiwi, watermelon, honeydew, lime, star fruit, and grapefruit. Sprinkle with sugar, and stir to combine. Add Cointreau and brandy; let sit at least 1 hour at room temperature. Stir in wine and cranberry juice. Sweeten with more sugar, if desired. Serve chilled.

from Sangrias

blueberry cornmeal muffins

MAKES 1 DOZEN

These muffins can be made up to one day ahead and stored in an airtight container at room temperature.

1½ cups all-purpose flour

¾ cup cornmeal

½ cup granulated sugar

1½ teaspoons baking powder

½ teaspoon baking soda

½ teaspoon ground cinnamon

¼ teaspoon salt

2 teaspoons finely grated orange zest (optional)

1¼ cups low-fat buttermilk, plus about 2 tablespoons for tops

2 large eggs, separated

2 tablespoons unsalted butter, melted

1½ cups fresh blueberries (about ½ pound), picked over and rinsed

2½ teaspoons coarse sanding sugar (optional)

Nonstick cooking spray

1 Preheat oven to 400°F, with rack in center. Lightly coat a standard muffin tin with cooking spray. In a medium bowl, whisk together flour, cornmeal, granulated sugar, baking powder, baking soda, cinnamon, salt, and orange zest, if using.

2 In a small bowl, whisk together buttermilk, egg yolks, and butter. Stir buttermilk mixture into flour mixture until just blended. In a mixing bowl, whisk the egg whites until just stiff. Gently fold whites and blueberries into the batter.

3 Spoon batter into prepared muffin tin, filling each cup three-quarters full. Bake 12 minutes. Remove from oven; gently brush tops with buttermilk, and sprinkle with sanding sugar, if desired. Continue baking until golden and a cake tester inserted in centers comes out clean, 6 to 8 minutes more. Let cool slightly before turning out of tin.

PER MUFFIN: 167 CALORIES, 3 G FAT, 42 MG CHOLESTEROL, 30 G CARBOHYDRATE, 497 MG SODIUM, 4 G PROTEIN, 2 G FIBER

from Fit to Eat: Blueberries

classic croutons

MAKES ABOUT 60

These classic croutons can be used in salads and soups—plain or covered with melted cheese—or as appetizers topped with spreads and vegetables.

6 tablespoons unsalted butter, melted, plus more
   for baking sheet
1 baguette (16 ounces), sliced into ¼-inch rounds

Preheat oven to 350°F. Lightly brush a baking sheet with butter. Place bread slices on sheet. Brush top of each slice with butter. Toast until crisp and golden, 15 to 20 minutes. Transfer croutons to a wire rack. Let cool completely.

from Croutons

grilled croutons

MAKES 8 LARGE CROUTONS

For added flavor, rub the warm croutons with the cut side of a halved garlic clove.

8 slices (about ½ inch thick) crusty Italian bread,
   such as ciabatta
2 tablespoons extra-virgin olive oil, plus more
   for drizzling (optional)

1 Heat grill to medium. Brush each side of bread with oil, and grill until lightly charred on both sides, about 4 minutes.

2 Remove from grill; drizzle croutons with a little more oil if desired. Serve warm or at room temperature.

from Croutons

panfried croutons

MAKES ABOUT 2½ CUPS

Croutons will keep for one to two days in an airtight container after they've cooled, but they taste best right out of the pan. For extra flavor, add minced fresh herbs to the melted butter, and toss with the bread cubes.

6 to 8 slices day-old white sandwich bread,
   trimmed of crusts
4 tablespoons unsalted butter
   Coarse salt and freshly ground pepper

1 Cut bread into ½-inch cubes, yielding about 4 cups. Heat a large nonstick sauté pan over medium heat. Add 1½ tablespoons butter; cook until bubbling. Add half the bread cubes; cook, tossing occasionally, until crisp and golden, about 2 minutes. Add ½ tablespoon butter to pan, swirl to melt, and cook croutons 5 minutes more. Set aside on a plate.

2 Repeat process with remaining butter and bread cubes. Season croutons with salt and pepper, and serve.

from Croutons

spiced pita triangles

MAKES 4 DOZEN

Triangles will keep for up to one week in an airtight container at room temperature.

2 tablespoons plus 2 teaspoons ground cumin
5 tablespoons sesame oil
   Coarse salt and freshly ground pepper
2 tablespoons finely chopped fresh thyme (optional)
4 pita breads (8 inches each)

1 Preheat oven to 350°F, with rack in center. In a small saucepan, heat cumin and sesame oil over medium-low heat, stirring frequently, until fragrant, 5 to 6 minutes. Season with salt and pepper, and add thyme, if desired.

2 Brush both sides of each pita bread with spice mixture. Cut each bread in half into semicircles, then cut each half into six triangles, each about 1 inch wide.

3 Place triangles in a single layer on a baking sheet, and bake until crisp and golden brown, 20 to 30 minutes. Transfer to a wire rack; let cool before serving.

from Croutons

sweet brioche croutons

MAKES ABOUT 2 CUPS

Brioche is a sweet, rich bread. Cinnamon and sugar make these croutons even sweeter, but they can be made with just butter, too.

4 slices brioche (¾ inch thick) trimmed of crusts
1½ teaspoons ground cinnamon
2 teaspoons sugar
3 tablespoons unsalted butter, melted

Preheat oven to 350°F. Cut bread slices into ¾-inch cubes; place in a medium bowl. Sprinkle cinnamon and sugar over bread cubes. Pour in butter; toss until bread cubes are evenly coated. Spread on a baking sheet in a single layer. Bake until golden brown and beginning to crisp, 10 to 12 minutes.

from Croutons

torn croutons

MAKES ABOUT 3 CUPS

These croutons have a rustic shape. They are especially crunchy because they are made from a dense bread and are cooked slowly. They will keep for up to one week stored in an airtight container at room temperature.

½ large loaf sourdough, miche, or levain bread (about ¾ pound), trimmed of crust
1 tablespoon extra-virgin olive oil
   Coarse salt and freshly ground pepper

Preheat oven to 325°F, with rack in center. Pull bread into rough pieces, each about ½ to 1 inch long. Place pieces in a medium bowl, and toss with oil. Season with salt and pepper, and spread on a baking sheet in a single layer. Bake until golden brown and crisp, stirring once as edges begin to brown, about 25 minutes. Let cool before serving.

from Croutons

September

clam and corn chowder

SERVES 8 TO 10 | PHOTOS ON PAGES 232 AND 233

The corn stock in step one can be made up to one week
ahead; let cool, then refrigerate in an airtight container.

6 ears fresh corn, shucked
2 Spanish onions (unpeeled)
1 large carrot, cut into large pieces
3 stalks celery, cut into large pieces
1 teaspoon whole black peppercorns
1 dried bay leaf
4 sprigs thyme
  Coarse salt and freshly ground pepper
1 cup dry white wine
4 pounds littleneck clams, scrubbed
2 tablespoons unsalted butter
1¼ pounds small red potatoes, cut into chunks
¾ cup heavy cream
2 tablespoons chopped fresh chives
1 jalapeño chile, chopped (remove ribs and seeds
  for less heat)

1 Make stock: Cut kernels from cobs, and set kernels aside.
Slice 1 unpeeled onion into 8 wedges. In a stockpot, combine
corn cobs, onion wedges, carrot, celery, peppercorns, bay
leaf, and thyme. Add 2 quarts water; bring to a boil. Reduce
heat to a simmer; cook 1 hour. Season with salt and pepper.
Strain; discard solids.

2 In a large, wide saucepan, bring wine to a simmer. Add
clams. Cover; steam until clams open, 5 to 7 minutes. Discard
any unopened clams. Drain in a sieve set over a bowl; reserve
and chill liquid. Shuck clams; halve large ones. Refrigerate in
a separate bowl, submerged in a bit of reserved liquid.

3 Finely dice remaining onion. In a large stockpot set over
medium heat, melt butter. Add onion; cook, stirring occasionally, until translucent, about 6 minutes. Add potatoes and
reserved corn kernels; cook 3 to 4 minutes.

4 Add 3½ cups reserved stock and 1 cup reserved clam
liquid to pot, leaving behind sediment. Bring to a boil, then
reduce to a simmer. Cook until potatoes are fork-tender,
about 25 minutes. Stir in cream, and remove from heat.
Purée 2 cups chowder; stir purée back into chowder in pot.
(Cooled chowder can be refrigerated, covered, overnight.)

5 Add chives, jalapeño, and reserved clams to pot. Season
with additional salt and pepper, if desired; serve.

from Three Great Soups

herbed cheese with pears, pine nuts, and honey

SERVES 4

8 ounces part-skim ricotta cheese
3 tablespoons pine nuts
6 ounces fresh goat cheese, room temperature
1 teaspoon fresh thyme leaves, finely chopped
2 teaspoons fresh flat-leaf parsley, finely chopped
½ teaspoon finely grated lemon zest
2 ripe but firm Bartlett pears
2 tablespoons plus 2 teaspoons flavorful honey,
  such as buckwheat, chestnut, or leatherwood

1 Preheat oven to 350°F. Place ricotta in a fine sieve set over
a bowl; let excess liquid drain, about 30 minutes (discard
liquid). Meanwhile, spread nuts in a single layer on a rimmed
baking sheet. Toast in oven until lightly browned, tossing
occasionally, about 7 minutes. Transfer to a plate; let cool.

2 In a food processor or medium bowl, mix together goat
cheese and drained ricotta until creamy and thoroughly combined. Stir in thyme, parsley, and lemon zest; set aside.

3 Slice each pear into six wedges. Divide herbed cheese
among four serving plates, spooning it into mounds. Arrange
three pear wedges next to cheese on each plate. Sprinkle
with nuts; drizzle about 2 teaspoons honey over each portion
of cheese and pears. Serve immediately.

PER SERVING: 320 CALORIES, 17 G FAT, 37 MG CHOLESTEROL,
28 G CARBOHYDRATE, 229 MG SODIUM, 16 G PROTEIN, 2 G FIBER

from Fit to Eat: Honey

mushroom and wild-rice soup

SERVES 8 TO 10 | PHOTOS ON PAGES 232 AND 233

- ½ teaspoon coarse salt, plus more for seasoning
- ½ cup wild rice
- 3 teaspoons olive oil
- 1¼ pounds assorted fresh mushrooms, such as button, cremini, shiitake (stems removed), and chanterelle, sliced into bite-size pieces

  Freshly ground pepper
- 1 tablespoon unsalted butter
- 3 leeks, white and pale-green parts only, quartered lengthwise and thinly sliced, washed well
- 1 tablespoon Porcini Powder (recipe follows)
- ½ cup sherry or Madeira
- 3 tablespoons soy sauce
- 6 cups Basic Chicken Stock (page 17) or low-sodium canned chicken broth
- 2 tablespoons heavy cream
- 1 tablespoon finely chopped fresh flat-leaf parsley

1 In a small saucepan, bring 1 cup water to a boil. Add ½ teaspoon salt and wild rice. Cover; reduce heat to medium-low. Cook until tender, 45 to 50 minutes. Drain; set aside.

2 In a large saucepan, heat half the oil over medium-high heat. Add half the mushrooms; season with salt and pepper. Cook, stirring, until browned and tender, about 7 minutes; transfer to a bowl. Repeat with remaining oil and mushrooms.

3 Reduce heat to medium-low. Melt butter, and add leeks. Cook, stirring occasionally, until softened, about 5 minutes. Stir in mushroom powder; cook 1 minute. Add sherry and soy sauce, and cook 1 minute more.

4 Add stock to pot; bring to a boil over medium-high heat. Add mushrooms, and return to a boil. Reduce heat to medium; cook 20 minutes. Stir in wild rice, cream, and parsley; season with additional salt and pepper, if desired, and serve.

from Three Great Soups

porcini powder

MAKES ⅓ CUP

- 1 ounce dried porcini mushrooms

In a spice mill or coffee grinder, pulse porcini to a fine powder. Store in an airtight container at room temperature.

roasted vegetable soup

SERVES 8 TO 10 | PHOTOS ON PAGES 232 AND 233

Soup can be made the day before and then refrigerated in an airtight container; let cool completely before storing.

- 2 medium eggplants (about 2 pounds)
- 2 red onions, each cut into 8 wedges
- 2 tablespoons olive oil

  Coarse salt and freshly ground black pepper
- 2½ pounds ripe plum tomatoes
- 6 large garlic cloves
- 3 large red bell peppers (about 2 pounds)
- 1 quart Basic Chicken Stock (page 17) or low-sodium canned chicken broth
- 2 cups lightly packed fresh basil leaves (about 1 large bunch), plus more for garnish
- 1 sprig marjoram
- 1 large piece (3 by 4 inches) Parmesan rind (from a 3-ounce piece), plus grated Parmesan for garnish
- 1 can (15 ounces) chickpeas, drained and rinsed

1 Preheat oven to 425°F, with racks in upper and lower thirds. Prick eggplants, and place in a baking pan with onions; toss with oil. Season with salt and pepper. Roast in upper third of oven, turning once, until eggplants are soft and onions are browned, about 1¼ hours. Let cool.

2 Meanwhile, place tomatoes in another baking pan with garlic; season with salt and pepper. Roast on lower rack of oven until tomatoes are soft and juicy, about 30 minutes. Let cool.

3 Roast peppers directly over a gas burner until charred, turning as each side blackens. (Alternatively, roast on a baking sheet under the broiler.) Transfer peppers to a large bowl, and cover with plastic wrap; let steam about 15 minutes. Using paper towels, rub off charred skins; remove seeds and ribs.

4 Remove stems and skins from eggplants. Coarsely chop flesh; place in a stockpot. Add roasted vegetables and any accumulated juices from baking pans. Add stock, 1½ cups basil, marjoram, cheese rind, and chickpeas; bring to a boil over medium-high heat. Reduce heat; simmer, partially covered, until vegetables are very tender, about 1½ hours.

5 Discard cheese rind; pass soup through a food mill, discarding solids. Thin with water if necessary. Finely chop remaining ½ cup basil, and stir into soup. Season with salt and pepper. Garnish soup with cheese and more basil leaves.

from Three Great Soups

grilled fish

SERVES 4

We serve this dish with Green-Tomato Salsa (page 223).

¼ cup extra-virgin olive oil

2 tablespoons freshly squeezed lemon juice

4 halibut or cod fillets (each 8 ounces and about 1 inch thick)

Coarse salt and freshly ground pepper

1 In a large resealable plastic bag or airtight container, combine oil and lemon juice. Shake well. Add fillets, and toss gently until coated with marinade. Refrigerate 30 minutes.

2 Meanwhile, heat grill or grill pan to medium-high. Remove fish from marinade, letting excess marinade drip off. Season fish with salt and pepper; grill until browned and cooked through, 2 to 3 minutes per side. Serve immediately.

from Green Tomatoes

grilled lamb chops with garam masala

SERVES 4

Garam masala is an Indian spice blend available in specialty stores and some supermarkets. To make your own, mix together one-half teaspoon each of ground pepper, cinnamon, cardamom, cumin, and coriander, along with a pinch of cloves.

2 teaspoons garam masala

2 teaspoons coarse salt

1 teaspoon freshly ground pepper

4 lamb shoulder chops (each 6 to 7 ounces and ¾ inch thick)

2 tablespoons extra-virgin olive oil

Cilantro sprigs, for garnish

1 Heat grill or grill pan to medium-high heat. In a small bowl, combine garam masala, salt, and pepper. Place lamb chops on a baking sheet or platter, and drizzle with oil; rub chops to coat evenly all over. Sprinkle both sides of chops with spice mixture, gently rubbing it onto meat.

2 Grill lamb chops until they reach desired doneness, about 3 minutes per side for medium-rare. Serve immediately, garnished with cilantro.

from What's For Dinner?

honey-glazed pork with wilted greens

SERVES 4

2 teaspoons Dijon mustard

3½ tablespoons red-wine vinegar

4 tablespoons raw honey

1 large garlic clove, finely chopped

1 teaspoon coarsely chopped fresh rosemary

1 tablespoon plus 4 teaspoons olive oil

1¾ pounds pork tenderloin (about 2)

¾ teaspoon coarse salt

Freshly ground pepper

1 large bulb fennel, trimmed and sliced lengthwise into thin strips

½ head escarole, cut into 2-inch strips

½ pound spinach, washed well

1 Preheat oven to 375°F. Make glaze: In a small bowl, whisk together 1 teaspoon mustard, 2 tablespoons vinegar, 2 tablespoons honey, garlic, rosemary, and 2 teaspoons oil.

2 Place pork tenderloin in a shallow baking dish; pour glaze over pork, turning to coat evenly. Sprinkle with ½ teaspoon salt; season with pepper.

3 Roast in oven, spooning glaze over pork occasionally, until thickest part of pork registers 155°F on an instant-read thermometer, 30 to 35 minutes. Remove from oven; let rest until pork reaches 160°F, about 10 minutes.

4 Meanwhile, make vinaigrette: In a small bowl, whisk together remaining teaspoon mustard, 1½ tablespoons vinegar, and 2 tablespoons honey until honey has dissolved. Whisk in 1 tablespoon oil until emulsified. If desired, whisk in any accumulated cooking juices from baking dish.

5 Heat remaining 2 teaspoons oil in a 12-inch sauté pan over medium-high heat. Add fennel, escarole, spinach, and a splash of water; cook, tossing occasionally, until greens are slightly wilted, about 1½ minutes.

6 Add vinaigrette and remaining ¼ teaspoon salt to pan, stirring just to coat greens, about 30 seconds. Remove from heat; divide among four serving plates. Slice pork about ½ inch thick; arrange alongside greens. Serve immediately.

PER SERVING: 417 CALORIES, 15 G FAT, 129 MG CHOLESTEROL, 26 G CARBOHYDRATE, 578 MG SODIUM, 45 G PROTEIN, 5 G FIBER

from Fit to Eat: Honey

orecchiette with green tomatoes, caramelized onions, and corn

SERVES 6 TO 8

2 tablespoons unsalted butter

1 large Vidalia or other sweet onion, cut into ¼-inch-thick slices

2 pounds green tomatoes (about 6), coarsely chopped

3 tablespoons sugar

1 cup fresh corn kernels (about 2 ears)

Coarse salt and freshly ground pepper

1 tablespoon chopped fresh thyme

1 pound orecchiette or other short pasta, cooked according to package instructions

1   In a large skillet over medium heat, melt butter. Add onion; cook, stirring, until it begins to soften, about 6 minutes. Add tomatoes; sprinkle sugar over mixture. Cook, stirring, until tomatoes are tender and golden brown, about 20 minutes.

2   Add corn to skillet; season mixture with salt and pepper. Cook, stirring, until corn is tender and just starting to brown, about 4 minutes. Stir in thyme.

3   Place cooked pasta in a serving dish; add vegetable mixture, and stir until combined. Serve immediately.

from Green Tomatoes

....

SIDE DISHES

....

broccoli and white-bean salad

SERVES 4

1 large bunch broccoli (about 1 pound)

Coarse salt

1 can (15½ ounces) cannellini beans, drained and rinsed

½ small red onion, halved and thinly sliced into half-moons

1 tablespoon freshly squeezed lemon juice, plus 1 tablespoon finely grated lemon zest (about 1 lemon)

2 tablespoons extra-virgin olive oil

¼ teaspoon crushed red-pepper flakes

Freshly ground black pepper

¾ cup shaved Pecorino Romano or Parmesan cheese (about 2 ounces)

1   Cut the tops off each head of broccoli, and trim into 1-inch florets; set aside. Peel each stem to remove tough outer layer. Slice peeled stems on the bias into ¼-inch pieces; set aside.

2   Prepare an ice bath; set aside. Bring a large pot of water to a boil. Add a generous amount of salt and the broccoli florets. Cook until florets are tender when pierced with the tip of a

paring knife, about 4 minutes. Using a slotted spoon, transfer florets to ice bath to stop cooking. Repeat with stems, cooking them 3 minutes. Transfer to ice bath. Let broccoli cool completely, then drain.

3   In a large mixing bowl, combine broccoli, beans, onion, lemon juice and zest, oil, and red-pepper flakes. Stir to combine; season with salt and pepper. Top with cheese.

from Good Things

corn and couscous salad

SERVES 4 | PHOTO ON PAGE 241

1 teaspoon curry powder

2 teaspoons grainy mustard

1 tablespoon white-wine or sherry vinegar

Coarse salt and freshly ground pepper

4 tablespoons extra-virgin olive oil

¾ cup couscous

1 cup boiling water

1 Vidalia or other sweet onion, diced

3 garlic cloves, minced

1 red chile, minced (optional)

3 cups fresh corn kernels (about 4 cobs)

¼ cup finely chopped fresh cilantro

1   In a medium bowl, whisk together curry powder, mustard, and vinegar. Season with salt and pepper. Whisk in 3 tablespoons oil in a slow, steady stream until emulsified. Set aside.

2   Place couscous in a large bowl. Pour boiling water over couscous; stir to combine. Cover with a plate; let steam until water is absorbed, about 5 minutes. Fluff with a fork; set aside.

3   Heat remaining tablespoon oil in a large skillet over medium heat. Add onion, and cook, stirring, until softened, about 4 minutes. Stir in garlic and chile; cook, stirring, until softened, about 2 minutes. Add corn, and cook until bright yellow and just tender, about 2 minutes. Stir corn mixture into couscous. Add curry vinaigrette and cilantro, and toss to combine. Serve warm or at room temperature.

from What's For Dinner?

fried green tomato wedges

SERVES 4 TO 6 | PHOTO ON PAGE 231

2 cups yellow cornmeal

4 teaspoons coarse salt, plus more for seasoning

1 teaspoon freshly ground black pepper

½ teaspoon ground cayenne pepper

2 cups buttermilk

2 large eggs

2 tablespoons freshly squeezed lime juice (about 2 limes)

Canola oil, for frying

3 large green tomatoes, cut into 1-inch-thick wedges

Basil-Lime Mayonnaise (recipe follows)

1 In a medium shallow bowl, combine cornmeal, salt, black pepper, and cayenne; set aside. In another shallow bowl, whisk together buttermilk, eggs, and lime juice (the mixture may appear curdled); set aside.

2 In a large cast-iron or heavy skillet, pour oil to a depth of ½ inch; heat until a deep-fry thermometer registers 375°F. Meanwhile, dip tomatoes in buttermilk mixture, then in cornmeal mixture. Set aside on a large plate.

3 Working in batches, fry tomatoes until golden brown, about 1 minute on each side. Drain on a paper-towel–lined plate. Season with salt while hot. Serve with mayonnaise.

from Green Tomatoes

basil-lime mayonnaise

MAKES 1¼ CUPS

This mayonnaise can be refrigerated in an airtight container for up to five days.

1 large egg

½ teaspoon coarse salt

¼ teaspoon freshly ground pepper

1 cup canola oil

2 teaspoons freshly squeezed lime juice

¼ cup finely sliced fresh basil leaves

1 In a food processor, pulse egg with salt and pepper until foamy and pale, about 1½ minutes. With the machine running, add oil through the feed tube, a drop at a time, until the mixture starts to thicken (do not stop the machine at this point or the mayonnaise may not come together). Add the remaining oil in a slow, steady stream.

2 When all the oil has been incorporated, slowly add lime juice, mixing until combined. Add basil; pulse until combined. Refrigerate before serving.

Note: Raw eggs should not be used in food prepared for pregnant women, babies, young children, the elderly, or anyone whose health is compromised.

sautéed okra and tomatoes

SERVES 4 | PHOTO ON PAGE 241

The secret to cooking crisp-tender okra is a hot skillet.

1 tablespoon mustard seeds

½ teaspoon cumin seeds

½ teaspoon ground coriander

2 tablespoons extra-virgin olive oil

1 small red onion, cut into ½-inch-thick wedges

1 pound fresh okra, stems trimmed

3 tomatoes, seeded and cut into ½-inch-thick wedges

Coarse salt and freshly ground pepper

1 In a small bowl, combine mustard seeds, cumin seeds, and coriander; set aside. Heat oil in a large skillet over medium heat. Add onion; cook, stirring, until soft, about 3 minutes.

2 Raise heat to medium-high, and add spice mixture, okra, and ½ cup water. Cook, stirring occasionally, until okra is bright green and just tender, about 6 minutes, adding more water if the skillet becomes too dry.

3 Add tomato wedges; cook until just heated through, about 1 minute. Season with salt and pepper. Serve immediately.

from What's For Dinner?

ice cream sandwiches

MAKES 1 DOZEN

2 pints coffee or dulce de leche ice cream

Molasses-Ginger Cookies or Chocolate Cookies
(recipes follow)

Using a ¼-cup ice-cream scoop, place a ball of ice cream
on an upside-down cookie. Top with a second cookie, right
side up. Press cookies together until ice cream reaches
edges. Repeat with remaining cookies and ice cream. Freeze
until firm, at least 30 minutes. To store, wrap in plastic.

from Three Great Soups

molasses-ginger cookies

MAKES 2 DOZEN

Cookies can be stored in airtight containers at room
temperature for up to three days.

1½ cups all-purpose flour

1 teaspoon baking soda

¼ teaspoon baking powder

2 teaspoons ground ginger

½ teaspoon ground cinnamon

¼ teaspoon ground cloves

¼ teaspoon salt

Pinch of freshly ground white pepper

½ cup (1 stick) unsalted butter, room temperature

¾ cup firmly packed light-brown sugar

¼ cup plus 1 tablespoon molasses

1 large egg, room temperature

½ cup granulated sugar, for rolling

1　Into a medium bowl, sift together flour, baking soda, baking powder, ginger, cinnamon, cloves, salt, and pepper.

2　In the bowl of an electric mixer fitted with the paddle
attachment, cream butter, brown sugar, and molasses until
light and fluffy. Beat in egg until smooth. Gradually add
flour mixture; beat until combined. Turn out dough onto a
piece of plastic wrap; flatten into a disk. Wrap; refrigerate
until firm, about 1 hour or overnight.

3　Preheat oven to 375°F, with racks in upper and lower
thirds. Line two baking sheets with parchment paper. Remove
dough from refrigerator. Pour sugar for rolling cookies into a
small, shallow dish. Form dough into 1½-inch balls; roll each

in sugar to coat completely. Place balls 2 inches apart on prepared baking sheets. Refrigerate 20 minutes.

4　Transfer baking sheets to oven. Bake cookies, rotating
baking sheets halfway through, until firm around the edges
but still slightly soft in the center, 12 to 14 minutes. Transfer
to a wire rack to cool completely.

chocolate cookies

MAKES 2 DOZEN

Cookies can be stored in airtight containers at room
temperature for up to three days.

1 cup plus 2 tablespoons all-purpose flour

⅔ cup unsweetened cocoa powder

1 teaspoon baking soda

¼ teaspoon baking powder

¼ teaspoon salt

¾ cup (1½ sticks) unsalted butter, room temperature

1¼ cups sugar, plus more for rolling

2 tablespoons corn syrup

1 large egg, room temperature

1　Line two baking sheets with parchment paper; set aside.
Into a medium bowl, sift together flour, cocoa, baking soda,
baking powder, and salt; set aside.

2　In the bowl of an electric mixer fitted with the paddle
attachment, cream butter, sugar, and corn syrup until light
and fluffy. Beat in egg until smooth. Gradually add flour
mixture; beat until combined.

3　Preheat oven to 375°F, with racks in upper and lower
thirds. Pour sugar for rolling cookies into a small, shallow
dish. Form dough into 1½-inch balls, and roll each in sugar
to coat completely. Place balls 2 inches apart on prepared
baking sheets. Refrigerate 20 minutes.

4　Transfer baking sheets to oven. Bake cookies, rotating baking sheets halfway through, until firm around the edges but
still slightly soft in the center, 12 to 14 minutes. Transfer to a
wire rack to cool completely.

orange-almond cake

MAKES 1 NINE-INCH CAKE

Boiling the oranges beforehand mellows any bitterness from peel and pith. The cake can be baked up to two days in advance; store, covered, in the refrigerator, and add topping just before serving.

6 navel or other sweet oranges
   Unsalted butter, room temperature, for pan
½ cup all-purpose flour, plus more for pan
1¾ cups finely ground blanched almonds (about 6 ounces)
1½ teaspoons baking powder
½ teaspoon salt
6 large eggs
2 cups sugar

1 Place whole unpeeled oranges in a large saucepan or pot, and add enough cold water to cover by 2 inches. Bring to a boil over high heat. Reduce heat, and simmer gently 2 hours. Drain, and set oranges aside to cool.

2 Preheat oven to 350°F. Butter and flour a 9-inch spring-form pan; set aside. Slice cooked oranges into halves, and remove any seeds (do not peel). Place 7 halves in a food processor, and pulse until puréed but still chunky. This should yield about 3 cups.

3 In a small bowl, whisk together ground almonds, flour, baking powder, and salt. In the bowl of an electric mixer, whisk eggs with 1 cup sugar on medium speed until light and fluffy. Stir in orange purée until just combined. Stir in flour mixture; pour into prepared pan.

4 Bake cake until golden brown and a cake tester inserted in the center comes out clean, about 1 hour. Transfer pan to a wire rack to cool 15 minutes. Run a small spatula or paring knife around edge to loosen cake; let cool completely.

5 Meanwhile, make orange topping: Chop remaining 5 orange halves into ½-inch pieces, and set aside. In a medium sauce-pan, combine remaining cup sugar with ¾ cup water. Bring mixture to a boil, stirring until sugar has dissolved.

6 Add chopped oranges to saucepan, and reduce heat to medium. Simmer gently until most of the liquid has evap-orated and thickened into a syrup, about 15 minutes. Remove from heat, and set aside to cool completely.

7 To assemble, place cooled cake on a serving platter. Arrange chopped oranges and any remaining syrup over top of cake. Cut into wedges, and serve.

from Dessert of the Month

papaya with coconut-lime yogurt

SERVES 4

Papayas are native to Central America. Choose fruit with almost completely reddish-orange skin that yields slightly to the touch. Avoid green papayas, which have been picked too early and will not ripen.

¼ cup shredded sweetened coconut
1 container (about 7 ounces) Greek-style yogurt
1 tablespoon honey
1 tablespoon freshly squeezed lime juice
1 large or 3 small ripe papayas, peeled, halved lengthwise, and seeded
   Lime wedges, for serving

1 Spread coconut evenly over the bottom of a small skillet, and toast over medium heat, tossing occasionally, until just golden, about 2 minutes. Let cool completely.

2 In a medium bowl, whisk together coconut, yogurt, honey, and lime juice. Slice papaya into 1-inch-thick wedges. Serve papaya with yogurt and lime wedges on the side.

from What's For Dinner?

walnut honey cake

SERVES 10

    3   ounces walnut halves (about ¾ cup)
        Unsalted butter, room temperature, for pan
 1½   cups all-purpose flour, plus more for pan
    1   cup raw honey, plus 2 to 3 tablespoons more for glaze
    1   cup unsweetened applesauce
    3   large eggs, room temperature
  ¾   teaspoon baking soda
  ¼   teaspoon salt
  ¼   teaspoon ground ginger

1   Preheat oven to 350°F, with rack in center. Spread walnut halves in a single layer on a rimmed baking sheet. Toast in oven until fragrant, tossing occasionally, 5 to 7 minutes. Transfer nuts to a plate; let cool. Pulse nuts in a food processor until finely chopped, about 10 times. Set aside.

2   Butter and flour an 8½-inch springform pan; set aside. In a large bowl, combine honey and applesauce; whisk until honey is mostly dissolved. Add eggs; whisk until combined.

3   Into a medium bowl, sift together flour, baking soda, salt, and ginger. Stir into honey mixture. Using a rubber spatula, fold in walnuts. Pour batter into prepared pan.

4   Bake cake until golden brown and a cake tester inserted in the center comes out clean, about 55 minutes. Transfer pan to a wire rack; let cool until sides of cake begin to pull away from pan, about 15 minutes.

5   Place cake on a serving platter. While cake is still warm, use an offset spatula to gently spread remaining honey on top as a thin glaze. Serve warm.

PER SERVING: 278 CALORIES, 8 G FAT, 58 MG CHOLESTEROL, 51 G CARBOHYDRATE, 178 MG SODIUM, 5 G PROTEIN, 1 G FIBER

from Fit to Eat: Honey

---

golden nectar smoothie

SERVES 4

This energizing drink can be served at breakfast, or over ice as a pick-me-up at any other time of day.

    2   cups freshly squeezed orange juice (about 6 oranges)
  ¼   cup plus 1 tablespoon raw honey
    1   tablespoon freshly squeezed lemon juice
    2   teaspoons finely grated fresh ginger
    2   ripe bananas, broken into large pieces

Combine all ingredients in a blender, and purée until smooth and thick. Serve immediately.

PER SERVING: 192 CALORIES, 1 G FAT, 0 MG CHOLESTEROL, 49 G CARBOHYDRATE, 3 MG SODIUM, 2 G PROTEIN, 2 G FIBER

from Fit to Eat: Honey

green-tomato chutney

MAKES 1½ QUARTS

Use firm green tomatoes that have not yet begun to turn red. If you do not plan to can the chutney, let it cool completely before storing in an airtight container in the refrigerator for up to two weeks.

    4   pounds green tomatoes (about 12 medium), diced
    2   yellow bell peppers, ribs and seeds removed, finely diced
    2   small Vidalia or other sweet onions, finely diced
    1   cup golden raisins
    1   tablespoon mustard seeds
  ¼   teaspoon ground cayenne pepper
    2   cups packed light-brown sugar
        Finely grated zest of 1 lemon
    2   whole cinnamon sticks
  ½   cup cider vinegar

1   Place all ingredients in a large saucepan. Bring to a boil over high heat, stirring until sugar dissolves. Reduce heat to medium-high, and simmer until mixture has thickened and most of the liquid has evaporated, about 1 hour.

2   Using a slotted spoon, remove cinnamon sticks. Ladle chutney into sterilized canning jars, and wipe excess from rims; screw on lids.

3   Bring a large pot of water to a boil over high heat. Using canning tongs, gently place jars in boiling water, making sure the water covers the jars (if not, pour in additional water to cover). Let jars sit in gently simmering water 10 minutes.

Remove; let cool slightly. Check seal by pressing in center of lid. If it doesn't pop back, it is properly sealed; if it does, return jars to water for another 10 minutes. Let sealed jars cool completely.

4 Store sealed jars in a cool, dark place up to 6 months. Once opened, jars will keep in the refrigerator up to 3 weeks.

from Green Tomatoes

green-tomato salsa

MAKES 4 CUPS

Salsa can be refrigerated in an airtight container for up to three days. Serve it over grilled fish, chicken, or pork.

1 poblano chile
2 pounds (about 6 medium) green tomatoes, seeded and finely chopped
1 small Vidalia or other sweet onion, finely chopped
1 medium cucumber, peeled, seeded, and finely chopped
4 scallions, sliced thinly crosswise
2 tablespoons freshly squeezed lime juice (about 2 limes)
1 tablespoon extra-virgin olive oil
½ cup finely chopped fresh cilantro
   Coarse salt and freshly ground pepper

1 Roast chile directly over a gas burner until charred, turning as each side blackens. (Alternatively, roast chile on a baking sheet under the broiler.) Transfer to a bowl, and cover with plastic wrap; let steam about 10 minutes. Using paper towels, rub off charred skin; remove stem and seeds. Finely chop chile, and place in a medium bowl.

2 Stir in tomatoes, onion, cucumber, scallions, lime juice, oil, and cilantro. Season with salt and pepper; let stand 30 minutes before serving to allow flavors to blend.

from Green Tomatoes

pickled green tomatoes

MAKES 3 QUARTS OR 6 PINTS

If you do not plan to can the tomatoes, let the mixture cool completely before storing in an airtight container in the refrigerator for up to two weeks.

1 onion, thinly sliced
1 red bell pepper, ribs and seeds removed, thinly sliced
3 pounds green tomatoes (about 9 medium), cut into 1-inch wedges, or left whole if small
3 to 6 garlic cloves
3 to 6 small red chiles
3 cups sugar
2 tablespoons coarse salt
4 teaspoons mustard seeds
2 teaspoons whole cloves
2 teaspoons celery seeds
2 teaspoons whole allspice
4 cups cider vinegar

1 In a large bowl, combine onion, bell pepper, and tomatoes. Pack mixture into 3 one-quart or 6 one-pint sterilized canning jars. Place a garlic clove and a red chile in each jar; set aside.

2 In a large saucepan, combine sugar, salt, mustard seeds, cloves, celery seeds, allspice, and vinegar. Bring to a boil over medium-high heat; stir until sugar dissolves. Pour mixture over tomato mixture in jars, leaving a ½-inch space at the top of each jar. Wipe excess from rims; screw on lids.

3 Bring a large pot of water to a boil over high heat. Using canning tongs, gently place jars in boiling water, making sure the water covers the jars (if not, pour in additional water to cover). Let jars sit in gently simmering water 10 minutes. Remove; let cool slightly. Check seal by pressing in center of lid. If it doesn't pop back, it is properly sealed; if it does, return jars to water for another 10 minutes. Let sealed jars cool completely.

4 Store pickled tomatoes at least 2 weeks to allow flavors to blend. Store sealed jars in a cool, dark place up to 6 months. Once opened, jars will keep in the refrigerator up to 1 month.

from Green Tomatoes

whole-grain oat bread

MAKES 1 NINE-INCH LOAF | **PHOTOS ON PAGES 232 AND 233**

- 1 cup steel-cut oats
- 2 cups boiling water
- ⅓ cup bulghur wheat
- 3 tablespoons honey
- ½ cup warm water (about 110°F)
- 1 envelope active dry yeast (1 scant tablespoon)
- 1½ cups whole-wheat flour
- 1 tablespoon plus 1 teaspoon coarse salt
- 2 to 3 cups all-purpose flour
- Unsalted butter, room temperature, for bowl, plastic wrap, and pan
- ½ cup old-fashioned rolled oats

1 In a medium bowl, cover steel-cut oats with the boiling water. Let stand until mixture has cooled to room temperature. Stir in bulghur wheat and honey; set aside.

2 Place the warm water in a small bowl. Sprinkle yeast over water. Let stand until foamy, about 5 minutes.

3 In the bowl of an electric mixer fitted with the dough-hook attachment, combine the reserved oat mixture with the yeast mixture, whole-wheat flour, salt, and 2 cups all-purpose flour; beat until smooth. With mixer on low speed, add up to 1 cup more all-purpose flour until dough is tacky, but not sticky. Continue kneading about 5 minutes more.

4 Place dough in a buttered bowl, and cover with buttered plastic wrap, pressing it directly on the surface. Let rise in a warm place until dough is doubled in bulk, about 90 minutes, or refrigerate overnight.

5 Turn out dough onto a clean work surface; form into a loaf about 9 inches long. Lightly mist with water; sprinkle with rolled oats. Place in a well-buttered 9-by-5-by-2½-inch loaf pan; let stand until doubled in bulk, about 1 hour.

6 Preheat oven to 375°F. Using a serrated knife, slash top of loaf lengthwise down center. Place immediately in oven. Bake until evenly browned and cooked through, about 1 hour. Remove from oven; let cool slightly, then invert onto a wire rack. Reinvert, and let cool, top side up.

from Three Great Soups

VODKA THYME LEMONADE | **PAGE 190**

PARMESAN-DUSTED MEATBALLS | **PAGE 168**

GRILLED SQUID WITH FRIED CAPERS AND SKORDALIA SAUCE | **PAGE 174**

ASIAN PEAR SALAD | **PAGE 202**

FRIED GREEN TOMATO WEDGES | **PAGE 219**

GRILLED PEPPERS AND GOAT CHEESE SALAD | **PAGE 202**

SUMMER SALAD WITH BLUEBERRIES | **PAGE 203**

OASTED VEGETABLE SOUP | **PAGE 216**

MUSHROOM AND WILD-RICE SOUP | **PAGE 216**

LAM AND CORN CHOWDER | **PAGE 215**

WHOLE-GRAIN OAT BREAD | **PAGE 224**

SPICY HOISIN MARINADE WITH PORK SALAD | PAGE 194

BARBECUED CHICKEN | PAGE 171

GRILLED TOP-ROUND OF LAMB | PAGE 175

GRILLED SEA SCALLOPS AND FENNEL | PAGE 204

MIXED FRESH HERB PASTA | PAGE 205

ASSORTED RUSTIC MARKET TARTS | PAGE 205

SWISS CHARD AND GOAT CHEESE
GALETTE | **PAGE 206**

GREEK SALAD WITH FETA IN GRAPE LEAVES AND GRILLED SWORDFISH KEBABS | **PAGE 172**

SOBA NOODLES WITH TOFU, AVOCADO, AND SNOW PEAS | **PAGE 176**

GREEN BEANS WITH LEMON BUTTER | **PAGE 178**

FARM-STAND RAW VEGETABLE SALAD | **PAGE 178**

SAUTEED OKRA AND TOMATOES | **PAGE 219**

CORN AND COUSCOUS SALAD | **PAGE 218**

ORANGE SPOON SWEETS WITH PEEL | **PAGE 182**

CHERRY SPOON SWEETS | **PAGE 180**

SOUTHERN-STYLE INDIVIDUAL
PEACH COBBLERS | **PAGE 185**

PLUM TARTE TATIN | **PAGE 183**

ROLLED BAKLAVA | **PAGE 185**

OLIVE-OIL BISCUITS | **PAGE 193**

WARM NECTARINE TURNOVERS | **PAGE 188**

STRAWBERRY SHORTCAKES | **PAGE 186**

LACKBERRY-PEACH TRIFLE | **PAGE 208**

RED-CURRANT AND RASPBERRY PIE | **PAGE 184**

ERRY BROWN BETTY | **PAGE 207**

BLUEBERRY TOPPING | **PAGE 191**

RED-WINE SANGRIA │ **PAGE 209**

PROSECCO SANGRIA │ **PAGE 209**

WHITE-WINE SANGRIA │ **PAGE 210**

PLUM AND PINEAPPLE SANGRIA │ **PAGE 209**

ASIAN PEAR SORBET | **PAGE 207**

Autumn

HOME COOKING BECOMES MORE DELIBERATE in the autumn months, with family feasts to host and holiday treats to prepare and package. So to keep the year-end schedule more manageable, we offer a gift of our own: one basic recipe for sugar-cookie dough, with four delicious variations. It will help make easy work of giving out boxes or tins of assorted cookies this season.

October

fig, ricotta, and honey open-face sandwiches

SERVES 6

This recipe makes enough for some second helpings.

1¼ cups fresh ricotta cheese
10 slices (⅓ inch thick) rustic bread
4 teaspoons fresh thyme leaves
Coarse salt and freshly ground pepper
10 fresh green or red figs, cut into ¼-inch-thick wedges
Honey, for drizzling

Spread ricotta over each bread slice; sprinkle with thyme, and season with salt and pepper. Arrange figs on top, dividing evenly among slices. Drizzle honey over figs; serve.

from A Packable Feast

Mediterranean crostini

SERVES 4

In this recipe, toast rounds are topped twice, first with a garlicky chickpea spread, then with an olive relish.

1 can (15½ ounces) chickpeas, drained and rinsed
¼ cup plus 2 tablespoons extra-virgin olive oil
1 tablespoon freshly squeezed lemon juice
1 small garlic clove, minced
Coarse salt and freshly ground pepper
8 large pitted green olives, cut into ⅛-inch slivers
2 tablespoons finely diced celery, plus inner leaves for garnish
12 slices (⅓ inch thick) baguette, toasted

1 Make spread: In a food processor, combine chickpeas, ¼ cup oil, lemon juice, and garlic. Pulse to form a smooth paste. Season with salt and pepper, and set aside.

2 Make relish: In a small bowl, combine 1 tablespoon oil, olives, and celery. Season with salt and pepper, and set aside.

3 Divide chickpea spread evenly among toasts, and top with olive relish. Drizzle with remaining tablespoon oil; season with pepper. Serve garnished with celery leaves.

from What's for Dinner?

savory pumpkin puffs

MAKES 18 TO 24

All-purpose flour, for parchment
1 standard package (17.3 ounces) frozen puff pastry, thawed
1½ teaspoons paprika
4 tablespoons unsalted butter, melted
2½ tablespoons Dijon mustard
1½ cups finely grated Gruyère cheese
1 cup finely grated Parmesan cheese
Freshly ground pepper

1 Generously flour two pieces of parchment paper; on each, roll out a pastry sheet to form a 15-by-13-inch rectangle, about 1/16 inch thick. Chill until firm, about 15 minutes. Meanwhile, stir paprika into melted butter.

2 Remove pastry from the refrigerator; brush off excess flour. Spread one pastry sheet with mustard; sprinkle with both cheeses. Season with pepper. Lay second pastry sheet on top.

3 Preheat oven to 375°F. Place a sheet of parchment on top of the stacked pastry; roll until smooth and pastry layers are sealed together. Remove parchment, and brush top of pastry with butter mixture. Chill until firm, about 30 minutes.

4 With a pumpkin-shaped cookie cutter, cut out shapes. Immediately place shapes on a parchment-lined baking sheet. Using a sharp paring knife, score each shape four or five times to make pumpkin ridges. Bake until golden, 15 to 20 minutes. Transfer puffs to a wire rack; let cool slightly.

from Good Things

tamari and maple roasted almonds

MAKES 2 CUPS

These tangy glazed nuts go perfectly with a glass of sherry.

- 10 ounces whole shelled almonds (2 cups)
- ¼ cup reduced-sodium tamari
- 3 tablespoons pure maple syrup

  Nonstick cooking spray

1 Preheat oven to 350°F. Spread almonds in a single layer on a rimmed baking sheet; toast in oven until fragrant, stirring occasionally, about 10 minutes.

2 In a medium bowl, combine tamari and maple syrup. Add almonds; toss until thoroughly coated. Lightly coat baking sheet with cooking spray; spread almonds evenly on sheet.

3 Roast in oven until nuts are deep brown, stirring halfway through, 15 to 17 minutes. Immediately transfer to a clean baking sheet; spread out almonds, separating them. Serve warm or at room temperature.

PER SERVING: 306 CALORIES, 24 G FAT, 0 MG CHOLESTEROL, 17 G CARBOHYDRATE, 401 MG SODIUM, 11 G PROTEIN, 6 G FIBER

from Fit to Eat: Almonds

SOUPS

butternut squash soup

SERVES 6

- 1 orange
- 3 thin slices fresh ginger
- 10 whole black peppercorns
- 2 teaspoons coriander seeds
- 2 tablespoons unsalted butter
- 1 Spanish onion, cut into ½-inch pieces

  Pinch of cayenne pepper
- 6 cups Basic Chicken Stock (page 17) or low-sodium canned chicken broth
- 1 sweet potato, peeled and cut into 1-inch pieces
- 2 small butternut squash (about 1¾ pounds each), peeled, halved, seeded, and cut into 1-inch pieces

  Orange Spiced Cashews, for garnish (optional; recipe follows)

1 Using a vegetable peeler, remove zest from orange in long strips; reserve flesh for another use. Make a bouquet garni by wrapping zest, ginger, peppercorns, and coriander in a piece of cheesecloth; secure bundle with kitchen twine.

2 In a medium stockpot, melt butter over medium heat. Add onion and cayenne; cook, stirring occasionally, until onion is soft and starts to brown, 4 to 5 minutes. Add bouquet garni; cook 2 minutes more. Add stock, and bring to a boil over medium-high heat.

3 Add sweet potato and squash to pot; return just to a boil, then reduce heat to a gentle simmer. Cook, partially covered, until vegetables are just beginning to fall apart, about 25 minutes. Remove from heat, and let cool slightly.

4 In a blender, purée soup in batches, being careful not to fill more than halfway. Return soup to pot; warm over medium heat. Serve garnished with spiced nuts, if desired.

from Cooking with Winter Squash

orange spiced cashews

MAKES ABOUT 2½ CUPS

- ¾ pound whole cashews (2½ cups)
- ¼ cup light corn syrup
- 1½ teaspoons finely grated orange zest
- ¾ teaspoon ground ginger
- ½ teaspoon ground coriander
- ½ teaspoon ground cumin
- ½ teaspoon coarse salt

  Pinch of cayenne pepper

1 Preheat oven to 350°F. Line two baking sheets with parchment paper; set aside. In a medium bowl, mix cashews with corn syrup until evenly coated. Set aside.

2 In a small bowl, combine zest, ginger, coriander, cumin, salt, and cayenne. Sprinkle mixture over nuts, and stir until nuts are evenly coated. Transfer to one of the prepared baking sheets; spread in a single layer, separating nuts.

3 Bake until nuts are golden and syrup is bubbling, about 15 minutes. Immediately transfer nuts to the other baking sheet. Spread out cashews, separating them. Serve warm or at room temperature.

fresh tomato soup

SERVES 6 | PHOTO ON PAGE 318

We used orange tomatoes for their beautiful color, but red tomatoes make a soup that's just as delicious.

- 6 tablespoons extra-virgin olive oil
- 1 large yellow onion, finely chopped
- 9 garlic cloves, crushed
- 7 pounds ripe orange tomatoes (about 14), coarsely chopped
- 6 sprigs marjoram, plus more for garnish
- 1 teaspoon sugar

Coarse salt and freshly ground pepper

1 In a large stockpot, heat oil over medium-low heat. Add onion and garlic; cook, stirring occasionally, until onion is translucent and very soft, about 15 minutes. Stir in tomatoes, marjoram, and sugar; season with salt and pepper.

2 Raise heat to medium-high; bring to a boil. Reduce heat to medium; simmer until liquid is reduced by one-quarter and has thickened slightly, 15 to 20 minutes. Remove from heat. Remove marjoram. Let soup cool 10 minutes.

3 Pass soup through a food mill into a bowl; discard solids. Season again with salt and pepper, as desired. Serve garnished with marjoram sprigs.

from A Packable Feast

SALADS

iceberg lettuce with blue-cheese dressing and toasted almonds

SERVES 4

- 2 ounces whole shelled almonds (about ½ cup)
- 4½ ounces blue cheese, crumbled
- 1½ tablespoons freshly squeezed lemon juice
- ⅓ cup buttermilk
- 1½ tablespoons olive oil

Freshly ground pepper

- 1 head iceberg lettuce, cut into 4 wedges
- 1 Granny Smith apple, cored and cut into ½-inch cubes

1 Preheat oven to 350°F. Spread almonds in a single layer on a rimmed baking sheet; toast in oven until fragrant, stirring occasionally, about 10 minutes. Let cool, then coarsely chop.

2 In a medium bowl, whisk together cheese, lemon juice, buttermilk, and oil until smooth; season with pepper.

3 Break each lettuce wedge in half. Divide among four plates; top with apple. Spoon dressing over each serving. Garnish with almonds, and serve immediately.

PER SERVING: 290 CALORIES, 22 G FAT, 25 MG CHOLESTEROL, 14 G CARBOHYDRATE, 478 MG SODIUM, 12 G PROTEIN, 5 G FIBER

from Fit to Eat: Almonds

MAIN COURSES

butternut-squash ravioli with fried sage leaves

MAKES ABOUT 2 DOZEN; SERVES 4 | PHOTO ON PAGE 321

- 1¾ cups Roasted Squash Purée made with butternut squash (page 256)
- 6 tablespoons unsalted butter
- ½ cup chopped shallots (about 3)
- 1½ tablespoons chopped fresh sage, plus 24 whole sage leaves for garnish

Coarse salt and freshly ground pepper

Pinch of ground nutmeg

- ½ cup semolina or all-purpose flour, for dusting

Fresh Pasta Dough (page 256)

All-purpose flour, for dusting

- ¼ cup olive oil
- ¼ cup freshly grated Parmesan cheese, for garnish (2 ounces)

1 In a small saucepan, cook squash purée over medium heat, stirring frequently, until it is reduced to 1¼ cups, 10 to 12 minutes. Transfer to a small bowl to cool.

2 In a small saucepan, melt 2 tablespoons butter over medium heat. Add shallots; cook, stirring, until soft and beginning to brown, 3 to 5 minutes. Add chopped sage; cook, stirring, 1 minute more. Remove from heat; combine with squash. Season with salt and pepper; stir in nutmeg. Let cool completely.

3 Generously flour two baking sheets with semolina; set aside. Divide pasta dough into four equal pieces; dust one piece lightly with flour, keeping others covered with plastic wrap while you work.

4 Using a pasta maker, roll dough through the widest opening. Fold dough into thirds, and pass through machine again, layered side first. Repeat process three or four more times, until dough is smooth. Continue running the dough through the remaining settings, using additional flour sparingly, until the pasta sheet is very thin. The dough should be at least 5 inches wide.

5 Place dough on a lightly floured surface; halve crosswise. Cover half with plastic wrap. On the other half, place scant tablespoons of squash filling 1 inch apart in 2 rows. Using a pastry brush dipped in water, lightly moisten pasta around each mound of filling. Top with the remaining half sheet of pasta; press around mounds to eliminate air pockets and to seal. Using a pastry wheel or a sharp paring knife, cut pasta into 2½-inch squares. Brush away excess flour. Place ravioli on a prepared baking sheet; cover with plastic wrap. Repeat with remaining dough and filling.

6 For fried sage leaves: In a small saucepan, heat oil over medium-high heat. Drop a few sage leaves at a time into the hot oil, and fry until oil around leaves stops bubbling but leaves are not yet brown, about 5 seconds. Using a slotted spoon, transfer to a paper-towel–lined plate; set aside.

7 Bring a large stockpot of water to a boil. Add salt and ravioli. Gently stir once, and cook at a gentle boil until the ravioli have floated to the top and are just tender, 3 to 5 minutes. Using a slotted spoon, transfer to four plates, dividing evenly.

8 In a small saucepan, melt the remaining 4 tablespoons butter over medium heat, and cook until lightly browned and fragrant, 6 to 8 minutes. Drizzle over ravioli, and garnish with cheese and fried sage leaves. Serve immediately.

from Cooking with Winter Squash

roasted squash purée

MAKES ABOUT 2¼ CUPS

3 **pounds squash, such as butternut, orange Hokkaido, or buttercup, halved and seeded**
   Canola oil, for baking sheet

1 Preheat oven to 400°F. Place squash halves, skin sides up, on an oiled rimmed baking sheet. Bake until tender when pierced with a fork, about 1¼ hours. Remove from oven. Turn halves skin side down; let stand until cool enough to handle.

2 Scoop the flesh into a food processor, and discard skin. Purée until smooth. Refrigerate squash purée in an airtight container up to 4 days or freeze up to 1 month.

fresh pasta dough

MAKES 1 POUND

2 **cups all-purpose flour, plus more for work surface**
4 **large eggs**

1 Mound flour on a clean work surface, and make a well in the center. Crack eggs into well; beat lightly with a fork. Gradually beat small amounts of flour into the eggs using the fork. When most of the flour has been incorporated, use a bench scraper to quickly fold in the remaining flour.

2 Lightly dust work surface with flour; knead dough until smooth and elastic, about 10 minutes. Wrap in plastic; let rest 1½ hours at room temperature or refrigerate overnight.

chicken cacciatore

SERVES 4 TO 6

This fragrant stew is even better when made in advance, so the flavors have time to meld. It can be refrigerated for up to three days or frozen for up to one month in an airtight container. Cool completely before storing. In addition to our Creamy Polenta, which soaks up the stew's sauce, buttered pasta, mashed potatoes, and crusty bread are also good partners for this hearty dish.

1   **cup plus 1½ tablespoons all-purpose flour**
3   **pounds (about 8 pieces) chicken parts (we used legs and thighs), skin removed and reserved**
     Coarse salt and freshly ground pepper
2   **tablespoons extra-virgin olive oil (optional)**
1   **large onion, cut into 1-inch dice**
4   **garlic cloves, finely chopped**
12   **ounces button mushrooms, cleaned and halved (or quartered if large)**
1   **cup dry white wine**
1   **cup Basic Chicken Stock (page 17) or low-sodium canned chicken broth**
2   **cans (28 ounces each) whole tomatoes, coarsely chopped, juice reserved**
1   **dried bay leaf**
2   **tablespoons finely chopped fresh oregano**
1   **tablespoon finely chopped fresh rosemary**
1   **tablespoon unsalted butter, room temperature**
     Creamy Polenta (optional; recipe follows)

1 Place 1 cup flour in a large shallow dish. Season chicken with salt and pepper, and dredge in flour, turning to coat evenly. Transfer chicken to a platter, and set aside.

2 Heat a large Dutch oven over medium heat. Add the reserved chicken skin; cook, turning occasionally, until fat has been rendered and skin is golden brown and crisp. Using a slotted spoon, remove skin, and discard. Remove all but 2 tablespoons rendered fat from pot. (Alternatively, use olive oil, heating until it is hot but not smoking.)

3 Add half the chicken to pot, being careful not to overcrowd; cook over medium heat, turning occasionally with tongs, until well browned on all sides, about 5 minutes. Transfer to a platter; set aside. Repeat with remaining chicken.

4 Add onion to pot; cook, stirring occasionally, until onion is translucent, about 4 minutes. Add garlic and mushrooms; cook, stirring, until vegetables are soft, about 5 minutes more. Raise heat to medium-high. Pour in the wine; deglaze pot, scraping up any browned bits from the bottom with a wooden spoon. Cook until most of the liquid has evaporated.

5 Add stock, tomatoes with reserved juice, bay leaf, oregano, and rosemary to pot; stir to combine. Return chicken to pot along with any accumulated juices. Submerge chicken in sauce. Bring to a gentle simmer; cover, and cook until chicken is cooked through and very tender, about 30 minutes.

6 In a small bowl, mix together butter and remaining 1½ tablespoons flour to form a smooth paste. Stir half the paste into the simmering stew, and cook about 3 minutes. If the stew is still not as thick as desired, stir in the remaining paste, and cook 3 minutes more. Remove and discard bay leaf; serve stew hot over warm polenta, if desired.

from Chicken Cacciatore 101

creamy polenta
SERVES 4 TO 6

Traditional polenta (coarse-ground cornmeal) can be substituted for the instant variety, but plan for it to take longer to cook—at least thirty minutes.

3 **cups milk**
Coarse salt
1½ **cups instant polenta**
Freshly ground pepper

1 In a large saucepan, combine milk and 3 cups water; bring to a boil. Season with salt. Slowly sprinkle polenta into the liquid, whisking constantly, until all the polenta is incorporated and the mixture just begins to thicken.

2 Reduce heat to medium. Cook, stirring constantly, until mixture has completely thickened, about 5 minutes. Continue cooking, stirring, 5 minutes more. Season with salt and pepper. Serve immediately.

panfried potato and fontina frittata
SERVES 6

1 **tablespoon extra-virgin olive oil**
1 **tablespoon unsalted butter**
¾ **pound fingerling or other small potatoes, cut into ½-inch-thick pieces**
Coarse salt and freshly ground pepper
¼ **cup chopped mixed fresh herbs, such as parsley, rosemary, thyme, and sage, plus more for garnish**
10 **large eggs**
8 **ounces fontina cheese, coarsely grated (2 cups)**

1 Preheat oven to 375°F. Heat oil and butter in a 10-inch ovenproof nonstick skillet over medium heat. Add potatoes, spreading evenly, and season with salt and pepper. Cook, stirring occasionally, until potatoes are tender and golden brown, 12 to 15 minutes. Stir in chopped herbs.

2 Meanwhile, whisk eggs in a medium bowl; season with salt and pepper. Stir in cheese, and pour mixture over potatoes. Stir until eggs begin to set slightly, about 30 seconds. Without stirring, continue cooking until eggs are set on the sides and bottom, about 2 minutes. Transfer skillet to oven; bake until just set, 12 to 15 minutes.

3 Slide frittata onto a serving platter, and serve garnished with chopped herbs.

from A Packable Feast

panfried trout with almonds and parsley
SERVES 4

4 **trout fillets (6 to 8 ounces each)**
¾ **teaspoon coarse salt**
Freshly ground pepper
1 **tablespoon plus 1 teaspoon olive oil**
3 **ounces whole shelled almonds, coarsely chopped**
1 **cup loosely packed fresh flat-leaf parsley leaves, coarsely chopped**
Finely grated zest plus juice of 2 lemons
Nonstick cooking spray

1 Lightly coat a large skillet with cooking spray. Place over medium-high heat. Sprinkle trout with salt, and season with pepper. Gently place 2 fillets in skillet, skin sides up. Reduce heat to medium, and cook until undersides are golden brown, 4 to 5 minutes. Carefully turn fish, using two spatulas if necessary. Cook until fish is slightly flaky in center when poked

with a fork, about 2 minutes more. Transfer fish to a platter; keep warm. Wipe out skillet; repeat with remaining 2 fillets.

2 Wipe out skillet; add oil and almonds. Cook, stirring, over medium heat until almonds start to turn golden, about 1 minute. Remove from heat. Immediately add parsley and lemon zest; stir to combine. Stir in lemon juice; as soon as it starts to bubble, pour sauce over fish. Serve immediately.

PER SERVING: 347 CALORIES, 20 G FAT, 84 MG CHOLESTEROL, 9 G CARBOHYDRATE, 413 MG SODIUM, 34 G PROTEIN, 4 G FIBER

from Fit to Eat: Almonds

roasted chicken salad

SERVES 6

Use a store-bought roasted chicken to save time. Salad can be made up to several hours ahead and refrigerated.

3 ounces pecan halves (about 1 cup), broken in half lengthwise
1 whole roasted chicken (about 3 pounds), skin removed
8 scallions, trimmed and thinly sliced
2 stalks celery, strings removed and thinly sliced
8 ounces lady apples (about 4), or Fuji apples (about 2 medium), cored and sliced into bite-size pieces
5 tablespoons golden or dark raisins
1 tablespoon coarsely chopped fresh oregano
   Coarse salt and freshly ground pepper
   Sour Cream Dressing (recipe follows)

1 Preheat oven to 350°F. Spread pecans in a single layer on a rimmed baking sheet; toast in oven until crisp and fragrant, stirring occasionally, about 10 minutes. Remove from oven; let cool completely.

2 Pull chicken meat from the bone, and cut into ¾-inch pieces. Transfer to a medium bowl; add scallions, celery, apples, raisins, and oregano. Season with salt and pepper. Add dressing; toss to combine. Chill, covered, until ready to serve.

from A Packable Feast

sour cream dressing

MAKES ABOUT 1 CUP

½ cup mayonnaise
2 tablespoons sour cream
¼ cup cider vinegar
   Coarse salt and freshly ground pepper

In a small bowl, whisk together mayonnaise, sour cream, and vinegar; season with salt and pepper. Refrigerate, covered, until ready to use, up to 4 days.

savory squash soufflés

SERVES 4

We like to make these soufflés with orange Hokkaido squash, which are a sweet and dry Japanese variety; they're also delicious with butternut squash.

4 tablespoons unsalted butter, plus more for ramekins
4 tablespoons all-purpose flour, plus more for ramekins
1¼ cups half-and-half
3 sprigs thyme
1 dried bay leaf
2 shallots, coarsely chopped
1 cup Roasted Squash Purée made with orange Hokkaido squash (page 256)
4 large egg yolks
¾ teaspoon finely chopped fresh marjoram
   Coarse salt and freshly ground pepper
4 ounces Gruyère cheese, grated on the large holes of a box grater (1 cup)
6 large egg whites

1 Preheat oven to 375°F. Butter four 12-ounce ramekins, and line bottoms and sides with parchment paper. Dust with flour; tap out excess. Set aside.

2 In a small saucepan, bring half-and-half, thyme, and bay leaf to a simmer. Remove from heat; let stand, covered, 10 minutes. Strain mixture through a fine sieve into a small bowl; discard solids. Cover, and keep warm.

3 In a medium saucepan, melt butter over medium heat. Add shallots; cook, stirring, until soft, about 3 minutes. Add flour, and cook, stirring, 3 minutes. Whisking constantly, slowly add hot half-and-half; continue cooking, whisking, until mixture has thickened, about 2 minutes more.

4 Pour mixture into the bowl of an electric mixer fitted with the paddle attachment. Beat in squash purée, followed by egg yolks and marjoram, until smooth and combined. Season with salt and pepper, and fold in cheese; set aside.

5 In the clean bowl of an electric mixer, whisk egg whites with a pinch of salt just until stiff peaks form. Gently fold into squash mixture in three additions.

6 Spoon batter into ramekins. Bake until soufflés stop rising and a cake tester inserted gently in the centers comes out clean, 30 to 35 minutes. Serve immediately.

from Cooking with Winter Squash

squash panada with wild mushrooms and chard
SERVES 6 | **PHOTO ON PAGE 321**

This dish is a variation of a classic panada, which is a soup thickened with breadcrumbs.

½ ounce dried porcini mushrooms

6 tablespoons unsalted butter

3 leeks, white and pale-green parts only, halved lengthwise, sliced into half-moons, and washed well

1 cup dry white wine

1 small bunch Swiss chard, trimmed, washed, and cut into 2-inch pieces

6 cups Basic Chicken Stock (page 17) or low-sodium canned chicken broth

1 pound assorted fresh mushrooms, such as chanterelle, oyster, and cremini, cleaned and very thinly sliced

Coarse salt and freshly ground pepper

2 tablespoons fresh thyme leaves, coarsely chopped

1 loaf (about 12 ounces) hearty Italian bread, cut into ¾-inch-thick slices and toasted

2 pounds butternut squash, halved, seeded, peeled, and flesh cut crosswise into ½-inch-thick slices

1 In a small bowl, cover porcini with 1 cup warm water. Let soak, stirring occasionally, 20 minutes. Using a slotted spoon, remove mushrooms; reserve soaking liquid. Gently squeeze porcini in paper towels to remove excess moisture, then coarsely chop. Set aside.

2 Preheat oven to 375°F. In a stockpot over medium heat, melt 2 tablespoons butter. Add leeks; cook, stirring occasionally, until very soft and translucent, about 7 minutes. Add wine, and cook until evaporated. Add chard; cook, stirring, until chard is wilted and bright green, about 2 minutes. Add stock and ½ cup reserved soaking liquid, leaving behind any sediment. Bring to a simmer.

3 Meanwhile, in a large sauté pan, melt 2 tablespoons butter over medium-high heat. Add half the mushrooms (including reserved porcini); season with salt and pepper. Cook, stirring occasionally, until mushrooms are golden brown. Transfer to

pot with the stock and vegetables. Repeat with remaining butter and mushrooms. Stir in thyme.

4 To assemble, cover bottom of a 5-quart Dutch oven with toasted bread. Pour half the stock and vegetables over bread. Top with a single layer of squash slices, followed by more of the stock and vegetables, then another layer of squash. Pour any remaining stock over entire dish.

5 Cover pot, and bake until squash is tender when pierced with the tip of a paring knife, about 1 hour. Remove from oven, and let cool slightly before serving.

from Cooking with Winter Squash

steak with caramelized onions
SERVES 4

2 boneless sirloin steaks (each about 1 pound and ½ inch thick)

1 large garlic clove, minced and mashed into a paste

5½ tablespoons extra-virgin olive oil

Coarse salt and freshly ground pepper

1¾ pounds small red onions, halved lengthwise and cut into ⅓-inch-thick wedges (keeping root ends intact)

½ teaspoon sugar

3 tablespoons balsamic vinegar

1 Place steaks on a large platter; rub with garlic paste and 2 tablespoons oil, coating completely. Season with salt and pepper. Let marinate 15 minutes at room temperature.

2 Meanwhile, in a large skillet, heat 2 tablespoons oil over medium-high heat until hot and just starting to smoke. Reduce heat to medium. Add onions; cook, stirring occasionally, until soft and golden brown, about 7 minutes. Add sugar, vinegar, and 2 tablespoons water; simmer, stirring occasionally, until onions are caramelized, about 3 minutes. Transfer onions to a bowl; season with salt and pepper. Set aside.

3 Wipe skillet clean. Heat remaining 1½ tablespoons oil in skillet over high heat until hot but not smoking. Cook steaks until golden brown, about 2 minutes per side for medium-rare. Transfer to a cutting board, and let rest 5 minutes before slicing. Serve hot with caramelized onions.

from What's for Dinner?

sweet dumpling squash with Moroccan vegetable stew

SERVES 6

Sweet dumpling squash are a small, single-serving variety with a skin tender enough to eat.

7 sweet dumpling squash

2 tablespoons unsalted butter, melted

Coarse salt

6 sprigs thyme

3 carrots, cut into ¾-inch pieces

3 parsnips, peeled and cut into ¾-inch pieces

1 turnip, peeled and cut into ¾-inch pieces

1 russet potato, peeled and cut into ¾-inch pieces

3 tablespoons olive oil

1 Spanish onion, cut into ½-inch pieces

2 garlic cloves, finely chopped

1 tablespoon Ras El Hanout (recipe follows)

4 plum tomatoes, cut into ¾-inch pieces

1 can chickpeas (15½ ounces), drained and rinsed

½ cup dried apricots (about 3 ounces), quartered

2 cups Basic Chicken Stock (page 17) or low-sodium canned vegetable or chicken broth

¼ cup chopped fresh flat-leaf parsley, plus more for garnish

1 Preheat oven to 375°F. Using a large knife or cleaver, slice off and reserve the top inch of each of 6 squash. Scoop out and discard seeds and stringy fibers. Arrange squash and their tops, skin sides down, in a small roasting pan. Brush insides of squash and tops with butter; sprinkle with salt. Place a thyme sprig in each squash. Bake until squash are very tender when pierced with a fork, about 1¼ hours.

2 Meanwhile, peel and halve remaining squash; remove and discard seeds and stringy fibers. Cut flesh into ¾-inch pieces; combine with carrots, parsnips, turnip, and potato. In a 5-quart Dutch oven, heat 2 tablespoons oil over medium heat. Add half the vegetables; season with salt. Sear on one side until lightly browned, about 3 minutes. Using a slotted spoon, transfer to a medium bowl. Add remaining tablespoon oil to pot. Cook remaining vegetables.

3 Reduce heat to medium-low, and add onion and garlic to pot. Cook, stirring occasionally, until onion is soft, about 15 minutes. Add Ras El Hanout; cook, stirring, 1 minute more. Add tomatoes; cook, stirring occasionally, until they have broken down and formed a thick sauce, about 15 minutes.

4 Return reserved vegetables to pot; stir in chickpeas, apricots, and stock. Bring to a simmer. Cover; continue simmering until vegetables are tender, about 12 minutes. Stir in parsley. Fill baked squash with stew. Serve immediately, or place in oven until heated through, if desired. Garnish with more parsley.

from Cooking with Winter Squash

ras el hanout

MAKES ABOUT ¼ CUP

1 tablespoon ground ginger

2 teaspoons ground turmeric

2 teaspoons ground nutmeg

1½ teaspoons ground cardamom

1½ teaspoons ground allspice

1 teaspoon ground cinnamon

1 teaspoon freshly ground black pepper

¼ teaspoon cayenne pepper

Place all ingredients in a jar. Cover tightly, and shake to combine. Store in a cool, dry place up to 6 months.

SIDE DISHES

delicata squash with caramelized seeds

SERVES 6 | **PHOTO ON PAGE 328**

The succulent delicata most closely resembles butternut squash, which would make a worthy substitute.

2 delicata squash

2 tablespoons unsalted butter

1 tablespoon dark-brown sugar

Coarse salt and freshly ground pepper

1 tablespoon olive oil

1 Halve squash. Scoop out seeds and stringy fibers; reserve seeds. Halve each squash half; slice into 1½-inch-thick half-moons. Place in a large saucepan; set aside.

2 In a small saucepan, melt butter over medium heat. Add seeds; cook, stirring, 2 to 3 minutes. Stir in sugar; cook, stirring occasionally, until seeds are browned and caramelized, 5 to 7 minutes. Transfer to a plate; let cool.

3 Season squash with salt and pepper, and drizzle with oil. Pour 1 cup water into pan, and bring to a simmer over medium-high heat. Cover, and simmer until squash is fork-tender, 20 to 25 minutes. Drain; transfer to a serving platter. Serve immediately, garnished with seeds.

from Cooking with Winter Squash

lemon and caper mashed potatoes

SERVES 4

To keep mashed potatoes warm for up to two hours, place them in a heatproof bowl set over a pot of barely simmering water; cover with foil to seal in the steam.

2 pounds Yukon gold potatoes, peeled and quartered
   Coarse salt
6 tablespoons unsalted butter
¾ cup milk
2 teaspoons freshly squeezed lemon juice,
   plus 2 teaspoons finely grated lemon zest
3 tablespoons capers, drained and coarsely chopped
¼ cup coarsely chopped fresh flat-leaf parsley
   Freshly ground pepper

1 Place potatoes in a large saucepan; fill pan with enough water to cover potatoes by 1 inch. Bring to a boil over high heat. Add a generous amount of salt; reduce heat to a simmer. Cook until potatoes are tender when pierced with a fork, about 15 minutes. Drain; using a potato masher or potato ricer, mash potatoes.

2 Meanwhile, in a medium saucepan over medium heat, combine 5 tablespoons butter with the milk, lemon juice and zest, and capers. Cook, stirring, until butter is melted and mixture is warm to the touch.

3 Fold milk mixture and parsley into mashed potatoes; season with salt and pepper. Dot potatoes with remaining tablespoon butter just before serving.

from What's for Dinner?

roasted acorn squash with pomegranate glaze

SERVES 6

Use a citrus reamer, juicer, or press to extract the pomegranate juice from the seeds.

2 cups fresh pomegranate juice (about 7 pomegranates),
   plus seeds from ½ pomegranate for garnish
¼ cup sugar
5 whole allspice
5 whole black peppercorns
1 dried bay leaf
1 whole cinnamon stick
   Unsalted butter, melted, for parchment and brushing,
   plus more at room temperature for pan
3 acorn squash, seeded and sliced into 1-inch-thick rings
   Coarse salt

1 Preheat oven to 450°F. In a small saucepan, combine juice, sugar, allspice, peppercorns, bay leaf, and cinnamon stick. Bring to a boil; reduce heat, and simmer until reduced to a syrup. Strain through a fine sieve into a small bowl, and discard spices. Set glaze aside.

2 Line a baking sheet with parchment paper; butter parchment. Lay squash rings on top of parchment; brush tops of rings with melted butter, and season with salt.

3 Roast squash until tender when pierced with the tip of a paring knife and undersides are well browned, about 30 minutes. Turn squash, and brush tops with pomegranate glaze. Continue cooking 5 minutes more.

4 Remove squash from oven; brush tops again with glaze. Transfer to a serving platter; serve immediately, garnished with pomegranate seeds.

from Cooking with Winter Squash

roasted baby potatoes with romesco sauce

SERVES 4 | **PHOTO ON PAGE 329**

Romesco sauce, from the Catalonian region of Spain, is traditionally served with shellfish. We serve our version with roasted potatoes. It's even better the next day, when the flavors have had a chance to blend: Refrigerate, covered, overnight; bring to room temperature before serving.

3 ounces blanched whole almonds (about ⅓ cup)
2 red bell peppers
1 small garlic clove
1 teaspoon coarse salt
⅛ teaspoon smoked hot paprika
¼ cup loosely packed mint leaves
1 teaspoon sherry vinegar or red-wine vinegar
1½ tablespoons extra-virgin olive oil
1 pound mixed small red and yellow potatoes

1 Preheat oven to 350°F. Spread almonds in a single layer on a rimmed baking sheet; toast in oven until light brown and fragrant, stirring occasionally, about 10 minutes. Remove from oven, and let cool.

2 Meanwhile, roast peppers directly over a gas burner until charred, turning as each section blackens. (Alternatively, roast on a baking sheet under the broiler.) Transfer to a large bowl, and cover with plastic wrap; let steam about 15 minutes. Using paper towels, rub off charred skins. Remove and discard seeds and ribs.

3 Raise oven heat to 375°F. In a food processor, combine toasted almonds, roasted red peppers, garlic, ¾ teaspoon

salt, paprika, mint, and vinegar. Process to a coarse paste, about 1 minute. With machine running, add 1 tablespoon oil in a slow, steady stream through the feed tube until sauce is smooth. Transfer sauce to a small bowl, and set aside.

4 On a rimmed baking sheet, toss potatoes with remaining ½ tablespoon oil and ¼ teaspoon salt. Spread out potatoes evenly, and roast until skins are slightly crisp and potatoes are tender when pierced with the tip of a paring knife, shaking pan once to turn potatoes, 20 to 30 minutes. Serve hot with romesco sauce on the side.

PER SERVING: 218 CALORIES, 16 G FAT, 0 MG CHOLESTEROL, 15 G CARBOHYDRATE, 488 MG SODIUM, 7 G PROTEIN, 7 G FIBER

from Fit to Eat: Almonds

DESSERTS

apple Napoleons

SERVES 4 | PHOTO ON PAGE 331

½ teaspoon ground cinnamon
6 tablespoons plus 1 teaspoon sugar
1 sheet frozen puff pastry (from a 17.3-ounce package), thawed
   All-purpose flour, for work surface
2 tablespoons unsalted butter
4 Granny Smith apples, peeled, cored, and cut lengthwise into ⅓-inch-thick wedges
½ cup heavy cream
¼ teaspoon pure vanilla extract

1 Preheat oven to 400°F. In a small bowl, combine cinnamon and 6 tablespoons sugar. Place pastry on a lightly floured work surface. Sprinkle evenly with 2 tablespoons cinnamon mixture. Carefully roll out to ⅛ inch thick. Cut out eight 3-inch squares, and place on a parchment-lined baking sheet. Cover with more parchment and another baking sheet. Chill in freezer until firm, about 15 minutes.

2 Transfer pastry, still between baking sheets, to oven. Bake until crisp and lightly browned, about 30 minutes. Remove top parchment and baking sheet. Transfer pastry on bottom parchment to a wire rack to cool.

3 Meanwhile, in a medium saucepan, melt butter over medium-high heat until foam subsides. Add apples; cook, stirring occasionally, until golden brown, about 7 minutes. Add remaining cinnamon mixture. Cook until apples are tender when pierced with the tip of a paring knife, but not falling apart. Let cool completely.

4 When ready to assemble, whisk cream, vanilla, and remaining teaspoon sugar in a bowl until soft peaks form. Layer four pastry squares with half the whipped cream and then half the apples; top with another pastry square, and then another layer of whipped cream and apples. Serve immediately.

from What's for Dinner?

Halloween petits fours

MAKES ABOUT 40

This recipe makes petits fours that resemble ghosts. For witch hats, make petits fours through step two. Then create a brim using a dab of icing: Affix each petit four to a two- to two-and-a-half-inch chocolate wafer. Proceed to step three, coating with Chocolate Glaze (recipe follows) instead of Butter Glaze. In lieu of step four, wrap one or two pieces of licorice lace around the base of the hat immediately after glazing.

   White Sheet Cake (recipe follows)
   Confectioners' Sugar Icing (recipe follows)
   Butter Glaze (recipe follows)
8 ounces semisweet chocolate, for eyes and mouth (optional)

1 Using a 1½-inch cookie cutter, cut out rounds from cake. Brush off any crumbs with a pastry brush.

2 Using a pastry bag fitted with a plastic coupler, pipe icing on top of cake rounds, forming a 1-inch-tall cone shape.

3 Place a wire rack over a rimmed baking sheet; set aside. Set an iced cake round on the tines of a fork; hold over bowl of glaze. Using a large spoon, drizzle glaze evenly over cake and icing until completely covered. Transfer to wire rack. Repeat with remaining rounds. Let set, about 5 minutes.

4 Place chocolate in a heatproof bowl set over a pan of barely simmering water; stir chocolate until melted. Transfer to a disposable pastry bag or resealable plastic bag; snip off tip with scissors. Pipe eyes and a mouth onto ghosts.

from Dessert of the Month

white sheet cake

MAKES 1 TWELVE-BY-SEVENTEEN-INCH CAKE

- 1 cup (2 sticks) plus 2 tablespoons unsalted butter, room temperature, plus more for baking sheet and wire rack
- 4½ cups sifted cake flour (not self-rising), plus more for baking sheet
- 2 tablespoons baking powder
- ¾ teaspoon salt
- 1½ cups milk
- 1½ tablespoons pure vanilla extract
- 2¼ cups sugar
- 7 large egg whites

1   Preheat oven to 350°F. Butter a 12-by-17-inch rimmed baking sheet. Line bottom with parchment paper. Butter parchment, and dust with flour, tapping out any excess.

2   Into a medium bowl, sift together flour, baking powder, and salt; set aside. In a liquid measuring cup, combine milk and vanilla; set aside. In the bowl of an electric mixer fitted with the paddle attachment, cream butter until very smooth. With mixer on medium speed, add sugar in a slow, steady stream; beat until mixture is light and fluffy, about 3 minutes.

3   Reduce mixer speed to low. Add reserved flour mixture in three batches, alternating with milk mixture and starting and ending with flour. Mix until just combined; set aside.

4   In a clean bowl, beat egg whites until stiff but not dry peaks form. Fold one-third of the egg whites into batter to lighten, then gently fold in remaining whites in two batches.

5   Scrape batter onto prepared sheet, and smooth top with an offset spatula. Bake in oven until cake is springy to the touch and a cake tester inserted in the center comes out clean, about 30 minutes.

6   Transfer sheet to a wire rack; let cool 15 minutes. Loosen sides of cake with an offset metal spatula or paring knife; invert onto a buttered wire rack. Peel off parchment. To prevent splitting, reinvert cake top side up. Let cool completely.

confectioners' sugar icing

MAKES ABOUT 7 CUPS

- 1½ cups (3 sticks) unsalted butter, room temperature
- 3 pounds confectioners' sugar
- 3 tablespoons pure vanilla extract
- ¾ cup milk, plus more if needed
- ¾ teaspoon salt

In the bowl of an electric mixer fitted with the paddle attachment, beat butter and sugar until well combined. Add vanilla, milk, and salt; beat until icing is smooth, creamy, and thick enough to hold its shape. If icing seems too thick to pipe, add milk 1 tablespoon at a time until proper consistency is reached. Use immediately, or refrigerate in an airtight container up to 2 days; before using, bring icing to room temperature and lightly beat until creamy, if necessary.

butter glaze

MAKES ABOUT 1½ CUPS

- 2½ cups sifted confectioners' sugar
- ½ cup (1 stick) unsalted butter
- 5 tablespoons milk

Place sugar in a medium bowl, and set aside. In a small saucepan, melt butter over medium heat. Immediately pour melted butter over sugar. Whisk in milk until mixture is smooth. Cover bowl with plastic wrap, and store at room temperature until ready to use.

chocolate glaze

MAKES ABOUT 1½ CUPS

- 6 ounces best-quality bittersweet or semisweet chocolate, finely chopped
- 1 cup heavy cream

Place chocolate in a medium heatproof bowl. In a small saucepan, heat cream over medium-high heat until just steaming; pour cream over chocolate. Let stand 5 minutes, then stir until smooth. Let cool about 10 minutes before using.

Indian puddings

SERVES 6

4 tablespoons unsalted butter, room temperature, plus more for ramekins

1½ cups Roasted Squash Purée made with butternut squash (page 256)

6 large eggs

½ teaspoon ground ginger

½ teaspoon ground cinnamon

½ teaspoon ground nutmeg

½ teaspoon salt

1 quart milk

½ cup pure maple syrup

¼ cup unsulfured molasses

½ cup yellow cornmeal

1 pint vanilla ice cream

1 Preheat oven to 325°F. Butter six 12-ounce ramekins. In a large mixing bowl, whisk together squash purée, eggs, spices, and salt; set aside.

2 In a medium saucepan, bring milk, syrup, molasses, and butter to a simmer. While whisking, slowly add cornmeal in a steady stream. Cook, whisking constantly, until mixture thickens, 5 to 7 minutes.

3 While whisking, pour the hot milk mixture into reserved squash mixture; whisk until combined. Divide among ramekins; place in a roasting pan. Transfer to oven; pour boiling water into pan to reach halfway up sides of ramekins.

4 Bake until puddings are firm to the touch, about 1 hour. Carefully remove ramekins from pan; serve puddings warm with a scoop of ice cream.

from Cooking with Winter Squash

mini pear and blueberry spice cakes

SERVES 6

These individual upside-down cakes are baked in a muffin tin.

7 tablespoons unsalted butter, room temperature, plus more for tin

6 tablespoons light corn syrup

¼ cup packed light-brown sugar

¾ cup fresh blueberries, picked over and rinsed

1 ripe but firm Bartlett pear, halved lengthwise, cored, and cut into thin slices

1 cup all-purpose flour

¾ teaspoon baking powder

¼ teaspoon baking soda

⅛ teaspoon salt

½ teaspoon ground cinnamon

¼ teaspoon ground nutmeg

¼ teaspoon ground allspice

¼ teaspoon ground ginger

⅔ cup granulated sugar

1 large whole egg plus 1 large egg yolk

¾ cup buttermilk

½ teaspoon pure vanilla extract

1 Preheat oven to 350°F. Generously butter the cups and top of a muffin tin with six 8-ounce cups. Place 1 teaspoon butter in each muffin cup. Top each with 1 tablespoon corn syrup; sprinkle with 2 teaspoons light-brown sugar. Arrange 7 or 8 blueberries in each cup. Cut pear slices to fit into muffin cups; arrange 4 or 5 pieces on top of berries, covering berries. Sprinkle remaining berries over the pears, and set tin aside.

2 Into a small bowl, sift flour, baking powder, baking soda, salt, cinnamon, nutmeg, allspice, and ginger; set aside. In the bowl of an electric mixer fitted with the paddle attachment, cream granulated sugar and remaining 5 tablespoons butter on medium speed until light and fluffy. Add egg and egg yolk, and beat until smooth.

3 With mixer on low speed, add flour mixture to butter mixture in two batches, alternating with the buttermilk, and beginning and ending with the flour. Stir in the vanilla.

4 Pour ⅓ cup batter over the fruit in each muffin cup. Gently tap bottom of tin against countertop several times to evenly distribute the batter.

5 Bake cakes until golden around the edges and a cake tester inserted in the centers comes out clean, about 25 minutes. Remove from oven; let cakes cool in tin.

from A Packable Feast

soft and chewy chocolate chip cookies

MAKES ABOUT 3 DOZEN | **PHOTO ON PAGE 336**

This recipe makes cookies that are soft and chewy. For other types, follow the variations below. You can use one, two, or several of the following add-ins: 1 cup coarsely chopped nuts; 2 tablespoons instant espresso powder (add to dry ingredients); 1 cup unsweetened cocoa powder (omit 1 cup flour from recipe); 1½ cups shredded sweetened coconut; 1 cup chopped dried fruit; ½ cup finely chopped candied ginger or up to 1 teaspoon ground ginger or cinnamon (add to dry ingredients); 1 cup chopped chocolate candies, such as malt balls (omit 1 cup chips); 1½ cups old-fashioned rolled oats; ½ cup smooth peanut butter (mix in with butter and sugar, and reduce butter to ¾ cup). If desired, use a small ice-cream scoop for uniform-size cookies.

2¼ cups all-purpose flour
½ teaspoon baking soda
1 cup (2 sticks) unsalted butter, room temperature
½ cup granulated sugar
1 cup firmly packed light-brown sugar
1 teaspoon salt
2 teaspoons pure vanilla extract
2 large eggs
2 cups semisweet or milk chocolate chips (about 12 ounces)

1   Preheat oven to 350°F. In a small bowl, whisk together flour and baking soda; set aside. In the bowl of an electric mixer fitted with the paddle attachment, cream butter and both sugars on medium speed until light and fluffy. Reduce speed to low; add salt, vanilla, and eggs. Beat until well combined, about 1 minute. Add flour mixture; mix until just combined. Stir in chocolate chips.

2   Drop heaping tablespoons of dough about 2 inches apart on parchment-paper–lined baking sheets. Bake until cookies are golden around the edges but still soft in the centers, 8 to 10 minutes. Remove from oven, and let cool on baking sheets 1 to 2 minutes. Transfer cookies to wire racks, and let cool completely. Store cookies in an airtight container at room temperature up to 1 week.

from Chocolate Chip Cookies

cakey chocolate chip cookies variation:

MAKES ABOUT 3 DOZEN

Follow the recipe for Soft and Chewy Chocolate Chip Cookies, decreasing the amount of unsalted butter to 14 tablespoons (1¾ sticks); increase granulated sugar to ¾ cup, and use only ¼ cup light-brown sugar. Bake at 350°F until cookies are golden around edges and just set in centers, 10 to 12 minutes.

thin and crisp chocolate chip cookies variation:

MAKES ABOUT 3 DOZEN

Follow the recipe for Soft and Chewy Chocolate Chip Cookies, increasing the amount of butter to 1¼ cups (2½ sticks) and the granulated sugar to 1¼ cups, and decreasing the amount of light-brown sugar to ¾ cup. Add ¼ cup water to the recipe with the other wet ingredients. Bake at 350°F until cookies are golden brown, 12 to 15 minutes.

cookie tart variation:

MAKES 1 NINE-INCH TART

Press 3 cups of dough into a buttered and sugared 9-inch round tart pan with a removable bottom or a 9-inch pie plate lined with buttered and sugared parchment. Bake at 325°F until edges are golden and center is almost set, 40 to 45 minutes. Let cool at least 20 minutes, then remove from pan. (If desired, bake remaining dough as cookies at 350°F 8 to 10 minutes.)

....

DRINKS

....

berry scary martini

SERVES 1

1 ounce black vodka
2 ounces cherry juice
Fresh raspberries and blueberries, for garnish

Combine vodka, cherry juice, and 1 cup ice in a cocktail shaker; shake vigorously. Pour into a martini glass. Thread berries onto a cocktail skewer, and place in drink. Serve immediately.

from Bad Things

ghost in the graveyard
SERVES 1

2 ounces black vodka

2 ounces crème de cacao or other coffee-flavored liqueur

1 scoop vanilla ice cream

Pinch of finely grated nutmeg, for garnish

In a glass, combine vodka and liqueur. Place ice cream in a highball glass, and slowly pour vodka mixture over top. Garnish with nutmeg; serve immediately.

from Bad Things

hot mint lemonade
MAKE 3 QUARTS

If you're packing this lemonade for a picnic, pour it into a large thermos while it's still hot.

1½ cups sugar

2 bunches fresh mint, plus more sprigs for garnish

3 cups freshly squeezed lemon juice (about 15 lemons)

1 Combine sugar and mint in a large bowl. Using a wooden spoon, press the mint and sugar against the side of the bowl until the sugar is moistened and the mint is bruised. Stir in 2 quarts water.

2 Transfer mixture to a medium pot; heat over high heat until almost at a boil. Turn off heat, and stir in lemon juice. Pass mixture through a fine sieve; discard mint. Serve hot, garnished with a sprig of mint.

from A Packable Feast

screwed-up screwdriver
SERVES 1

½ cup freshly squeezed tangerine juice

1½ ounces black vodka

1 black licorice twist, for serving

Place ¼ cup ice in a tall glass. Pour juice into glass. Pour vodka over the back of a cocktail spoon into glass so it sits on top of juice in a separate layer. Slice off each end of licorice, and use as a straw. Serve immediately.

from Bad Things

buttercup squash tea bread
MAKES 1 NINE-BY-FIVE-INCH LOAF

This tea bread can be frozen, wrapped well in plastic, for up to one month.

½ cup (1 stick) unsalted butter, melted, plus more at room temperature for pan

1½ cups all-purpose flour, plus more for pan

1 teaspoon baking soda

¼ teaspoon salt

½ teaspoon ground cinnamon

½ teaspoon ground nutmeg

½ teaspoon ground ginger

⅛ teaspoon ground clove

1 cup firmly packed light-brown sugar

2 large eggs

1 cup Roasted Squash Purée made with buttercup squash (page 256)

½ cup coarsely chopped pecans (about 2 ounces)

1 Preheat oven to 350°F. Butter and flour a 9-by-5-by-3-inch loaf pan, and set aside. Into a large bowl, sift together flour, baking soda, salt, and spices; set aside.

2 In a medium bowl, whisk together sugar, eggs, squash purée, melted butter, and ¼ cup water. Fold squash mixture into flour mixture. Stir in pecans.

3 Pour batter into prepared loaf pan, and bake until a cake tester inserted in the center comes out clean, about 1 hour. Turn bread out onto a wire rack, and let cool completely.

from Cooking with Winter Squash

November

broccoli soup with cheddar toasts

SERVES 8

This soup derives its body and rich flavor from puréed broccoli stems and florets.

1½ tablespoons extra-virgin olive oil

1 onion, coarsely chopped

2 garlic cloves, coarsely chopped

2 bunches broccoli (about 3¼ pounds), stems and florets chopped separately into ½-inch pieces

7 cups Basic Chicken Stock (page 17) or low-sodium canned chicken broth

1 teaspoon coarse salt

1 cup skim milk

⅛ teaspoon cayenne pepper

2 ounces extra sharp cheddar cheese, grated or crumbled (about ½ cup)

8 thin slices crusty baguette

1 Heat oil in a large pot over medium heat until hot but not smoking. Add onion, garlic, and broccoli stems; cover, and cook, stirring occasionally, until vegetables are soft, about 15 minutes. Add stock and salt; cover, raise heat to medium-high, and bring to a boil. Add florets; reduce heat, and simmer, uncovered, until florets are just tender, about 10 minutes.

2 Remove soup from heat, and let cool, about 10 minutes. Working in batches so as not to fill more than halfway, purée soup in a blender until smooth. Return soup to pot; stir in milk and cayenne. Cook over medium heat until heated through (do not boil).

3 Meanwhile, heat broiler. Divide cheese among bread slices; toast under broiler until melted and golden brown, 45 to 60 seconds. Divide soup among eight bowls. Top each bowl with a cheese toast, and serve.

PER SERVING: 161 CALORIES, 6 G FAT, 9 MG CHOLESTEROL, 16 G CARBOHYDRATE, 812 MG SODIUM, 10 G PROTEIN, 5 G FIBER

from Fit to Eat: Cruciferous Vegetables

California-style devils on horseback

MAKES 2 DOZEN │ **PHOTOS ON PAGES 322 AND 323**

12 very soft, plump dried Black Mission figs, stemmed and halved lengthwise

12 strips bacon (about 12 ounces), halved crosswise

24 fresh sage leaves

1 Preheat oven to 400°F. Wrap each fig half with a bacon slice, tucking 1 sage leaf under bacon as you go; secure with a toothpick. Arrange bundles, 1 inch apart, on a rimmed baking sheet fitted with a rack.

2 Bake until tops are browned and crisp, about 25 minutes. Turn bundles; continue baking until other sides are browned and crisp, 10 to 15 minutes more. Let cool on rack 5 minutes; remove toothpicks before serving.

from Thanksgiving in Wine Country

cauliflower soup with toasted pumpkin seeds

SERVES 8 TO 10 │ **PHOTO ON PAGE 319**

We like to season this pale soup with white pepper because it can't be seen, but black pepper would work as well.

1 fresh or dried bay leaf

4 whole cloves

1¾ cups Basic Chicken Stock (page 17) or low-sodium canned chicken broth

1 head cauliflower, trimmed and cut into 1-inch florets

1 russet potato, peeled and quartered

1 bulb fennel, trimmed and chopped into 2-inch pieces

1 large white onion, coarsely chopped

½ cup milk

Pinch of freshly grated nutmeg

Coarse salt and freshly ground white pepper

Toasted Pumpkin Seeds (page 270)

¼ cup pumpkin-seed oil (optional)

1 Wrap bay leaf and cloves in a piece of cheesecloth; tie with kitchen twine. Place bundle in a large saucepan; add stock, cauliflower, potato, fennel, onion, and 5½ cups water. Bring to a boil; reduce heat, and simmer until vegetables are very tender, about 25 minutes. Discard clove bundle.

2 Working in batches so as not to fill more than halfway, purée soup in a blender until smooth. Return soup to sauce-pan, and stir in milk; place over medium heat until just heated through (do not boil). Add nutmeg, and season with salt and pepper.

3 Sprinkle soup with pumpkin seeds, and drizzle with pump-kin-seed oil, if desired. Serve hot or at room temperature.

from Thanksgiving in Wine Country

toasted pumpkin seeds

MAKES 1 CUP

1 cup pumpkin seeds
1 tablespoon olive oil
Coarse salt

Preheat oven to 375°F. Combine seeds and oil on a parchment-lined rimmed baking sheet. Season with salt; toss to combine. Spread out seeds in a single layer. Bake until crisp, stirring occasionally, about 10 minutes.

four-onion and ginger soup with goat-cheese toasts

SERVES 6 | **PHOTO ON PAGE 320**

You will need to make the stock at least one day before you plan to make the soup. Just before serving, warm the reserved bacon in a 300 degree oven.

12 thin slices bacon (about ½ pound)
1½ pounds each white, yellow, and red onions, thinly sliced lengthwise
1 piece fresh ginger (1 ounce), cut into fine julienne (⅓ cup)
1½ pounds shallots, thinly sliced lengthwise
2 tablespoons very thinly sliced fresh sage leaves
2 quarts Dark Chicken Stock (recipe follows)
Coarse salt and freshly ground pepper
½ baguette, halved lengthwise
Olive oil, for brushing
1 log fresh goat cheese (3 ounces)

1 In a large, deep skillet over medium heat, cook bacon, turning occasionally, until crisp, about 10 minutes. Transfer bacon to a paper-towel–lined plate to drain. Pour off all but 1½ tablespoons rendered fat.

2 Add onions and ginger to skillet; cook over medium heat, stirring occasionally, for 30 minutes. Add shallots and sage. Continue cooking, stirring more frequently as onions cook down, until onions are very soft and caramelized, about 1 hour more. (Add a few tablespoons stock or water if onions start to stick to skillet.)

3 Preheat oven to 350°F. Pour stock into skillet; bring to a boil. Reduce heat to a simmer, and cook 15 minutes more. Season with salt and pepper.

4 Slice each baguette half diagonally into six ½-inch-thick pieces. Brush with oil, and season with salt and pepper. Arrange slices on a rimmed baking sheet; toast in oven until golden, about 20 minutes.

5 Spread toasts with goat cheese, and top each with a bacon slice. Divide soup among six bowls; serve toasts on the side.

from Onions Unearthed

dark chicken stock

MAKES 2 QUARTS

Refrigerate stock in airtight containers for up to three days, or freeze for up to six months.

3 pounds chicken thighs
3 pounds chicken wings
2 large Spanish onions, quartered
1 bunch carrots, trimmed and cut into 2-inch pieces
7 stalks celery, cut into 2-inch pieces
1 garlic head, halved crosswise
2 fresh or dried bay leaves
1 tablespoon whole black peppercorns
½ bunch fresh flat-leaf parsley

1 Preheat oven to 450°F. Arrange chicken in a single layer in a large roasting pan. Roast until skin is golden brown and crisp, about 1½ hours. Add onions, carrots, celery, and garlic; continue roasting 30 minutes more. Transfer mixture to a large stockpot, and set aside.

2 Pour 1 cup water into roasting pan, and bring to a boil over high heat. Deglaze pan, scraping up any browned bits from the bottom with a wooden spoon; pour liquid into pot. Add bay leaves, peppercorns, parsley, and 3½ quarts water; bring to a boil over high heat, skimming foam from surface as needed. Reduce heat to a simmer, and cook 3 hours.

3 Using a large slotted spoon, remove solids from stock, and discard. Strain stock through a fine-mesh sieve into a large bowl. Let cool completely. Transfer stock to airtight containers; refrigerate at least 6 hours or overnight. Skim off and discard layer of fat on surface. If storing, leave layer of fat intact (it helps to seal in flavor).

scallion tartlets

MAKES 8 FOUR-INCH SQUARE TARTLETS | PHOTO ON PAGE 326

You can use this recipe to make two larger tarts: Cut pastry into two eight-inch squares, and place each on a lined baking sheet. Bake for about thirty minutes. Once baked, tartlets can be frozen for up to three weeks. Without defrosting, reheat them in a 350 degree oven for about ten minutes.

All-purpose flour, for work surface

1 **standard package frozen puff pastry (17.3 ounces), thawed**

8 **bunches scallions (about 2¼ pounds), trimmed and cut into matchsticks**

1 **garlic clove, minced**

1 **red Thai chile, ribs and seeds removed, minced**

½ **cup walnuts (2 ounces), finely chopped**

½ **cup Kalamata olives, pitted and coarsely chopped**

2 **tablespoons extra-virgin olive oil**

Coarse salt and freshly ground pepper

1 **large egg yolk**

½ **cup freshly grated Parmesan cheese (2 ounces)**

1 Preheat oven to 400°F. Line a baking sheet with parchment paper, and set aside. On a lightly floured work surface, roll out pastry sheets just to smooth creases. Trim edges slightly to make them even. Cut each pastry sheet into four squares; transfer to prepared baking sheet, placing squares 2 inches apart. Chill 20 minutes in the freezer.

2 Place scallions, garlic, chile, nuts, olives, and oil in a medium bowl. Season with salt and pepper, and toss. Set aside.

3 In a small bowl, whisk together egg yolk and 1 teaspoon water. Brush a ½-inch border around edges of dough squares with egg wash. Divide scallion mixture evenly among squares, leaving a ¼-inch border; sprinkle cheese over filling.

4 Bake until crust is golden brown, about 20 minutes. Transfer to a wire rack. Serve warm or at room temperature.

from Onions Unearthed

shallot-and-date empanadas

MAKES 1 DOZEN | PHOTO ON PAGE 317

Try using the same quantity of Roasted Shallots (page 278) in place of the raw shallots in this recipe; gently press roasted shallots to remove skins, and slice into thirds. Unbaked empanadas can be frozen for up to three weeks in resealable storage bags; bake frozen empanadas in a 375 degree oven for about thirty minutes. Once baked, they can be refrigerated for up to one day or frozen for up to two weeks; reheat in a 350 degree oven for fifteen to twenty minutes.

1¾ **cups all-purpose flour, plus more for work surface**

1½ **teaspoons caraway seeds, coarsely crushed**

1 **teaspoon sugar**

1 **teaspoon table salt**

¾ **cup (1½ sticks) chilled unsalted butter, cut into small pieces**

8 **ounces cream cheese, well chilled**

2 **tablespoons olive oil**

1 **pound shallots, cut lengthwise into sixths**

Coarse salt and freshly ground pepper

6 **dried dates, pitted and quartered**

2 **teaspoons fresh thyme leaves**

1 **large egg yolk**

1 **tablespoon heavy cream**

1 In a food processor, pulse flour, caraway seeds, sugar, and table salt several times to combine. Add butter and cream cheese; pulse until mixture just begins to come together. (Squeeze dough gently; if it doesn't hold together, add 1 tablespoon cold water.) Turn out dough onto a piece of plastic wrap, and flatten into a disk. Wrap in plastic, and refrigerate 1 hour.

2 Preheat oven to 400°F. Line a baking sheet with parchment paper; set aside. Heat oil in a medium skillet over medium heat. Add shallots; cook, stirring, until golden, about 10 minutes. Season with coarse salt and pepper; remove from heat.

3 On a generously floured work surface, roll out dough to ⅛ inch thick. Using a 4-inch cookie cutter, cut out 12 rounds from dough. Brush border of 1 round with water. Place 2 date quarters in center of round, then top with the shallots, dividing evenly. Add a pinch of thyme, and season with coarse salt and pepper. Bring sides together in the center to form a pyramid, enclosing the filling. Pinch edges to seal. Place on prepared baking sheet. Repeat with remaining dough and filling. Chill 15 minutes in the freezer.

4 In a bowl, beat egg yolk and cream; brush over tops of empanadas. Bake until golden brown, about 30 minutes. Transfer to a wire rack. Serve warm or at room temperature.

from Onions Unearthed

spinach and goat-cheese salad

SERVES 8 TO 10 | **PHOTO ON PAGE 322**

¾ cup walnut halves (3 ounces)

1 tablespoon Dijon mustard

2 tablespoons balsamic vinegar

Coarse salt and freshly ground pepper

5 tablespoons extra-virgin olive oil

8 to 10 ounces baby spinach

4 ounces fresh goat cheese, crumbled

8 to 10 fresh figs, halved

1 Preheat oven to 350°F. Spread walnuts in a single layer on a rimmed baking sheet; toast in oven until fragrant, stirring occasionally, about 10 minutes. Let cool, then coarsely chop.

2 In a small bowl, whisk together mustard and vinegar; season with salt and pepper. Add oil in a slow, steady stream, whisking constantly, until emulsified.

3 Place nuts and spinach in a serving bowl. Sprinkle with cheese, and add figs; gently toss with vinaigrette to combine.

from Thanksgiving in Wine Country

chicken salad with mango and Jerusalem artichokes

SERVES 6

1 whole bone-in chicken breast (about 1½ pounds), skinned and halved

½ cup rice-wine vinegar (unseasoned)

1 tablespoon grated fresh ginger

1 teaspoon sugar

Coarse salt and freshly ground pepper

3 tablespoons canola oil

1 tablespoon dark sesame oil

1 mango, pitted, peeled, and thinly sliced lengthwise

¾ pound (7 or 8 small) Jerusalem artichokes, peeled and cut into ¼-inch-thick wedges

2 heads watercress, stems trimmed

¼ cup lightly packed fresh mint leaves, torn if large

1 Place chicken in a large saucepan; cover with cold water. Bring to a boil; reduce heat, and simmer until chicken is cooked through, about 25 minutes. Drain; when cool enough to handle, pull meat from bones. Shred meat into large pieces.

2 In a large bowl, whisk together vinegar, ginger, and sugar; season with salt and pepper. Whisking constantly, add canola and then sesame oil in a slow, steady stream until emulsified.

3 Add shredded chicken, mango, and artichokes to vinaigrette; toss to combine. Gently fold in watercress and mint, and serve immediately.

from Jerusalem Artichokes

Jerusalem artichoke soufflé

SERVES 4 TO 6 | **PHOTO ON PAGE 329**

⅓ cup plus 2 tablespoons hazelnuts

4 tablespoons unsalted butter, plus 1 tablespoon melted for dish

¼ cup plus 2 tablespoons freshly grated Parmesan cheese

3 cups milk

1 pound Jerusalem artichokes (about 10 small), peeled, cut into 1-inch chunks, and reserved in cold water (drain and pat dry before using)

¼ cup all-purpose flour

4 large egg yolks

2 teaspoons coarse salt

1 teaspoon finely chopped fresh rosemary

1 teaspoon finely chopped fresh thyme

½ teaspoon finely chopped fresh sage

5 large egg whites, room temperature

1 Preheat oven to 350°F. Spread hazelnuts in a single layer on a rimmed baking sheet. Toast in oven until fragrant and skins start to crack, 10 to 15 minutes, tossing halfway through. Remove from oven; while still hot, rub vigorously with a clean kitchen towel to remove skins. Let nuts cool, then coarsely chop. Raise oven temperature to 400°F.

2 Brush the inside of a 1½-quart soufflé dish with melted butter. Add 2 tablespoons each hazelnuts and cheese to dish; toss to coat. Set aside.

3 Combine milk and artichokes in a medium saucepan; bring just to a boil over medium heat. Reduce heat to medium-low; simmer, uncovered, until tender when pierced with the tip of a paring knife, about 30 minutes. Drain in a colander set over a heatproof bowl, reserving 1¼ cups milk.

4 In a food processor, purée artichokes until smooth. Pass purée through a fine sieve into a bowl; discard solids.

5 Melt remaining 4 tablespoons butter in a medium saucepan over medium heat. Whisk in flour; cook, stirring, 2 minutes. While whisking, slowly add reserved milk; whisk until smooth, then whisk in artichoke purée. Remove from heat.

6 Whisk in egg yolks, one at a time, until smooth. Whisk in salt, herbs, and remaining ⅓ cup hazelnuts and ¼ cup cheese.

7 In the bowl of an electric mixer, whisk egg whites until stiff peaks form; gently fold into artichoke mixture, then spoon mixture into prepared dish. Bake until puffed and golden brown, about 40 minutes. Serve immediately.

from Jerusalem Artichokes

lamb stew with Jerusalem artichokes

SERVES 6 | PHOTO ON PAGE 321

3 tablespoons extra-virgin olive oil

1½ pounds boneless lamb shoulder, cut into 1½-inch cubes

   Coarse salt and freshly ground black pepper

1½ pounds Jerusalem artichokes (about 15 small), peeled, cut into ¾-inch cubes, and reserved in cold water (drain and pat dry before using)

2 cups coarsely chopped onion (about 1 large)

2 garlic cloves, minced (about 1 tablespoon)

1 tablespoon freshly grated ginger (1-inch piece)

1 whole cinnamon stick

2 whole cloves

2 green cardamom pods, lightly crushed

½ teaspoon crushed red-pepper flakes

1 can (35 ounces) whole peeled plum tomatoes with juice

1 cup Basic Chicken Stock (page 17) or low-sodium canned chicken broth

⅛ teaspoon crumbled saffron threads

1 jar (10 ounces) small caperberries, drained

¼ cup finely chopped fresh cilantro

1 Heat 2 tablespoons oil in a large, heavy pot over medium-high heat. Season lamb with salt and black pepper; brown the meat (in batches, if necessary) on all sides, about 8 minutes. Transfer to a large bowl.

2 Cook artichokes in remaining tablespoon oil in same pot over medium-high heat, stirring occasionally, until well browned on all sides, about 7 minutes. Using a slotted spoon, transfer artichokes to a separate bowl.

3 Add onion, garlic, and ginger to remaining oil in pot; sauté over medium-high heat, stirring occasionally, until onion is translucent, about 4 minutes. Add cinnamon, cloves, cardamom, and red-pepper flakes; cook, stirring constantly, 2 minutes.

4 Stir in tomatoes and juice, stock, saffron, and 1 teaspoon salt. Using the side of a wooden spoon, break up tomatoes.

Add reserved lamb; bring mixture to a boil. Reduce heat to low; cover, and simmer until meat is tender, about 1 hour.

5 Return reserved artichokes to pot. Continue to simmer until artichokes are tender, about 25 minutes; add caperberries during final 5 minutes of cooking. Season with salt and black pepper, and stir in cilantro. Discard cinnamon, cloves, and cardamom before serving.

from Jerusalem Artichokes

pasta with sausage and escarole

SERVES 4 | PHOTO ON PAGE 321

   Coarse salt

1 pound rigatoni or other tubular pasta

2 tablespoons extra-virgin olive oil

2 garlic cloves, minced (about 1 tablespoon)

1 pound hot Italian sausage, removed from casing and crumbled

1 cup dry white wine

1 cup heavy cream

¼ cup finely chopped fresh flat-leaf parsley

2 teaspoons finely chopped fresh rosemary

½ teaspoon crushed red-pepper flakes

   Freshly ground black pepper

1 large head escarole, cut horizontally into thirds and stemmed

   Parmesan cheese, for garnish

1 Bring a large pot of water to a boil. Add salt and pasta; cook 2 to 3 minutes less than package instructions. Drain.

2 Meanwhile, in a Dutch oven, heat oil over medium heat. Add garlic; cook, stirring, until fragrant, about 1 minute. Add sausage; cook, stirring, until cooked through, about 6 minutes. Pour in wine; deglaze pan, scraping up any browned bits from the bottom with a wooden spoon. Add cream, parsley, rosemary, and red-pepper flakes; season with salt and pepper. Bring to a simmer. Add escarole; cook, stirring occasionally, until just wilted, 8 to 10 minutes.

3 Stir pasta into skillet; cook until cream has started to thicken and pasta is al dente, about 3 minutes. Garnish with Parmesan, and serve.

from What's for Dinner?

roasted turkey
with garlic-herb butter

SERVES 8 TO 10

If you have extra herbs, stuff sprigs into the turkey cavity before roasting, or use them as a garnish when serving.

1 head garlic

Olive oil, for drizzling

3 tablespoons each chopped fresh thyme, rosemary, sage, and flat-leaf parsley

1 cup (2 sticks) unsalted butter, room temperature, plus more for basting

Coarse salt and freshly ground pepper

1 fresh turkey (12 to 14 pounds)

Sautéed Cipollini Onions (recipe follows)

1   Preheat oven to 350°F, with rack in center. Place garlic head on a square of aluminum foil, and drizzle with oil. Loosely wrap garlic in foil, and roast until fragrant and very soft, about 1 hour. Remove from oven; let cool.

2   In a small bowl, combine herbs and butter. Slice off tip of roasted garlic head with a serrated knife; discard. Squeeze garlic head firmly over bowl to release softened cloves. Season with salt and pepper, and mix until smooth.

3   Raise oven heat to 400°F. Rinse turkey with cool water; pat dry. Tuck wing tips under body. Place turkey on a roasting rack in a heavy roasting pan; pour ½ cup water into pan.

4   Using your hands, gently separate skin from turkey breast at both ends; smear about one-fourth of herb butter between skin and meat. Smear exterior and cavity with remaining herb butter.

5   Roast until skin begins to brown, 50 to 55 minutes (tent with foil if herbs begin to burn). Reduce oven temperature to 350°F. Continue roasting turkey, basting with additional butter, until a leg rotates easily in the joint and an instant-read thermometer inserted into thickest part of thigh (avoiding bone) registers 180°F, 70 to 90 minutes more (depending on size of turkey). Let turkey rest, loosely covered with foil, at least 30 minutes before carving. Arrange turkey on a platter with onions, and serve.

from Potluck Thanksgiving

sautéed cipollini onions

SERVES 8 TO 10

Coarse salt

1½ pounds cipollini onions or small shallots, peeled

1 tablespoon unsalted butter

1 tablespoon extra-virgin olive oil

½ teaspoon finely chopped fresh thyme

1   Bring 6 cups water to a boil in a medium saucepan; add salt. Add onions to water, and boil until softened, about 4 minutes. Drain, and pat dry. Set aside.

2   Heat butter and oil in a large sauté pan over high heat, stirring to combine, until butter is melted. Add onions, and cook, stirring occasionally, until browned, about 4 minutes. Reduce heat to medium-low; add thyme, and season with salt. Cover, and cook until onions are tender, 4 to 5 minutes. Serve warm.

spaghetti with baked
onions and cockles

SERVES 4

1 pound cockles or small littleneck clams, scrubbed well

2 yellow onions (1½ pounds), thinly sliced

2 small tomatoes, halved

12 cherry tomatoes, halved

¼ cup oil-cured black olives, pitted and coarsely chopped

¼ cup dry white wine

3 tablespoons extra-virgin olive oil

2 teaspoons chopped fresh thyme

1 tablespoon chopped fresh oregano

Coarse salt and freshly ground pepper

1 pound spaghetti

1 tablespoon unsalted butter, room temperature

¼ cup coarsely chopped fresh flat-leaf parsley

1   Preheat oven to 375°F. Bring a large pot of water to a boil. Place an 18-by-30-inch piece of aluminum foil on a rimmed baking sheet. Place cockles and onions in center of foil.

2   Squeeze seeds and juice from tomatoes (not cherry) and discard. Cut flesh into 1-inch chunks; add to foil packet along with cherry tomatoes. Add olives, wine, oil, thyme, and oregano; season with salt and pepper. Toss to combine. Fold foil into a tight packet, enclosing contents; seal ends well.

3   Bake until onions are tender and cockles have opened, 25 to 30 minutes (check packet carefully; steam will escape). Discard any cockles that have failed to open.

4 About 10 minutes before packet is done, add salt and pasta to boiling water. Cook until pasta is al dente according to package instructions. Drain pasta in a colander; transfer to a serving dish. Dot with butter; toss to coat evenly.

5 Carefully open packet to allow the steam to escape; turn out contents onto pasta. Toss to combine. Sprinkle with parsley, and serve immediately.

from Onions Unearthed

Thanksgiving-leftovers shepherd's pie

SERVES 4 TO 6

To bake individual pies, use six ten-ounce ramekins, and reduce the cooking time to twenty-five to thirty minutes.

3 cups cooked stuffing

1 cup cranberry sauce, plus more for topping (optional)

1 pound sliced cooked turkey

10 ounces glazed carrots (or another leftover vegetable)

4 to 6 tablespoons gravy

3 to 4 cups mashed potatoes

1 Preheat oven to 350°F. In a 9- to 10-inch pie plate, mound stuffing across bottom; layer with cranberry sauce, turkey, and carrots. Drizzle with gravy; spread potatoes over surface, reaching all the way to the edge of the dish. Top with more cranberry sauce, if desired.

2 Place pie on a baking sheet; bake until heated through and potatoes are golden, 35 to 40 minutes. Let cool slightly.

from Good Things

wild turkey with lavender masala

SERVES 8 TO 10 | PHOTO ON PAGE 322

If you are unable to find wild turkey, you can use a regular bird for equally flavorful results. To spit-roast the turkey, follow this recipe up to the roasting step, then cook according to the manufacturer's instructions for your roaster.

½ cup garam masala

2 teaspoons dried lavender

1 wild turkey (12 to 14 pounds), neck and giblets removed
   Coarse salt and freshly ground pepper

½ cup bacon fat or unsalted butter, plus more
   for basting, if needed

1 Combine garam masala and lavender in a small bowl; stir to combine. Set aside.

2 Rinse front and back cavities of turkey under cold running water; pat dry. Season turkey inside and out with salt and pepper. Rub with bacon fat, then sprinkle with spice mixture; rub to coat evenly. Place turkey in a large metal bowl. Cover with plastic wrap; refrigerate 24 hours, or at least overnight.

3 Preheat oven to 425°F. Tuck wings under turkey, and tie legs together with kitchen twine. Place turkey in a large, heavy roasting pan fitted with a roasting rack. Roast turkey 30 minutes, then reduce oven temperature to 375°F.

4 Continue roasting, basting turkey with pan juices every 30 minutes and tenting with foil after 1 hour, until juices run clear when thigh is pierced, 2½ to 3 hours more, depending on size of turkey. If pan becomes dry during cooking, add bacon fat or butter. Let turkey rest 30 minutes before carving.

from Thanksgiving in Wine Country

....

SIDE DISHES

....

the best onion rings

SERVES 4 TO 6 | PHOTO ON PAGE 327

Keep each batch of cooked onion rings warm in a 200 degree oven while you finish making the rest.

1 cup plus 2 tablespoons all-purpose flour

1 teaspoon ground cumin
   Pinch of cayenne pepper

1 teaspoon coarse salt, plus more for seasoning

¾ cup buttermilk

¾ cup beer

1 large egg

4 cups peanut oil

2 large white onions (about 2 pounds), sliced crosswise
   ½ inch thick and separated into rings

1 Combine flour, cumin, cayenne, and salt in a medium bowl. Slowly whisk in the buttermilk, beer, and egg. Let batter stand 15 minutes.

2 In a large saucepan (preferably cast iron), heat oil over medium-high heat until it registers 375°F on a deep-fry thermometer. Working in batches, dip onion slices in batter, turning to coat. Gently drop into hot oil. Cook, turning rings once, until golden brown, about 2 minutes. (Adjust heat between batches as necessary to keep oil at a steady temperature.)

3 Using a slotted spoon, transfer onion rings to a paper-towel–lined baking sheet to drain. While still hot, season with salt, and serve immediately.

from Onions Unearthed

braised endive
in mustard vinaigrette
SERVES 4

We like to serve endive family-style as a side dish for Pasta with Sausage and Escarole (page 273).

- 1 tablespoon unsalted butter
- 1½ pounds Belgian endive (about 6 heads)
- 3 cups Basic Chicken Stock (page 17) or low-sodium canned chicken broth
- 1½ tablespoons grainy mustard
- 2 tablespoons red-wine vinegar
- Coarse salt and freshly ground pepper
- ¼ cup extra-virgin olive oil
- 1 tablespoon finely chopped fresh flat-leaf parsley, for garnish

1 In a large skillet, melt butter over medium heat. Add endive, and cook, turning occasionally, until browned on all sides, about 5 minutes. Pour stock into skillet; bring to a boil, and cover. Reduce heat to medium-low, and simmer, turning endive occasionally, until just tender, about 20 minutes.

2 Using a slotted spoon, transfer endive to a paper-towel–lined plate; discard stock. Pat endive dry; set aside.

3 In a bowl, whisk together mustard and vinegar. Season with salt and pepper. Add oil in a slow, steady stream, whisking constantly, until emulsified. Gently toss each endive in dressing, coating well. Garnish with parsley, and serve at room temperature; serve any extra dressing set on the side.

from What's for Dinner?

cranberry sauce with dried figs
MAKES 2¾ CUPS; SERVES 8 TO 10

This cranberry sauce has dried Calimyrna figs and a chutneylike texture. Chopped dried apricots, prunes, or cranberries could be used in place of the figs.

- 1 bag fresh or frozen (thawed) cranberries (12 ounces)
- 5 ounces dried Calimyrna figs, halved (about 1 cup)
- ½ cup sugar
- ¼ cup dry red wine or cranberry juice

1 In a small saucepan, combine ingredients; cook over low heat until most cranberries have burst, about 15 minutes.

2 Transfer cranberry sauce to a small bowl. Let cool; cover, and refrigerate up to 3 days. Let stand at room temperature 30 minutes before serving.

from Potluck Thanksgiving

grilled winter squash
SERVES 8 TO 10 | **PHOTOS ON PAGES 322 AND 323**

- 4½ to 5 pounds winter squash, such as pumpkin, kabocha, or calabaza, halved, seeded, and cut into 1-inch wedges
- ¼ cup extra-virgin olive oil, plus more for grill
- Coarse salt and freshly ground pepper

1 Heat grill to medium. Preheat oven to 350°F, with rack in center. Place squash in a large baking pan; drizzle with oil. Season with salt and pepper, and toss to coat. Arrange wedges, flesh sides down, in a single layer. Roast squash 15 minutes; turn slices, and continue roasting until tender when pierced with a fork, 15 to 20 minutes more.

2 Lightly oil grill, and transfer roasted squash, flesh sides down, to grill. Cook, turning once, until browned and heated through, 7 to 8 minutes. Serve warm.

from Thanksgiving in Wine Country

Jerusalem artichoke
and chestnut gratin
SERVES 6 TO 8

- 1 pound Jerusalem artichokes (about 10 small), peeled, sliced ¼ inch thick, and reserved in cold water (drain and pat dry before using)
- 3 cups milk
- 8 ounces crème fraîche
- 2 tablespoons freshly squeezed lemon juice
- 1 cup grated Gruyère cheese (4 ounces)
- 1 tablespoon minced fresh thyme
- 1½ teaspoons coarse salt
- ¼ teaspoon freshly ground pepper
- ½ pound Yukon gold potatoes, peeled and sliced ¼ inch thick
- 5 ounces shallots, thinly sliced
- 5 ounces jarred or vacuum-packed peeled chestnuts, halved lengthwise
- 4 slices white bread, trimmed of crusts, toasted and torn into small pieces

1 Preheat oven to 450°F. In a large saucepan, bring artichokes and milk to a boil. Reduce heat; simmer 10 minutes. Drain artichokes in a colander set over a bowl, reserving ¾ cup milk.

2 In a large bowl, whisk together reserved milk, crème fraîche, lemon juice, ¼ cup cheese, thyme, salt, and pepper. Add artichokes, potatoes, shallots, and chestnuts; stir to combine.

3 Pour mixture into a 1½-quart gratin dish; cover tightly with foil. Bake on a baking sheet until artichokes are tender when pierced with the tip of a paring knife, about 1 hour. Remove foil;

sprinkle top of gratin with breadcrumbs and remaining ¾ cup cheese. Continue baking, uncovered, until golden brown, 8 to 10 minutes more. Serve warm.

from Jerusalem Artichokes

onion-and-potato cakes

MAKES 6

2 tablespoons unsalted butter, room temperature, plus more for tin
Coarse salt and freshly ground pepper
3 teaspoons dark-brown sugar
3 teaspoons balsamic vinegar
3 teaspoons red-wine vinegar
1½ teaspoons finely chopped fresh rosemary, plus tops of 6 sprigs
1 small red onion, sliced into 6 rounds
2 Yukon gold potatoes (about 1 pound), scrubbed
1 large egg yolk, lightly beaten

1 Preheat oven to 400°F. Generously butter a 6-cup large muffin tin. Lightly sprinkle cups with salt and pepper; sprinkle each with ½ teaspoon brown sugar, and drizzle with ½ teaspoon each balsamic and red-wine vinegar. Add 1 rosemary top to each cup; cover with an onion slice. Set aside.

2 Using a mandoline, slice potatoes into matchsticks. In a medium bowl, toss potatoes with chopped rosemary and egg yolk; season with salt and pepper. Divide mixture among cups. Dot each with butter.

3 Bake until potatoes are tender and browned around the edges, about 30 minutes. Run a thin knife around edge of cups to loosen; turn cakes out onto a platter, and serve.

from Onions Unearthed

red-wine cranberry sauce

MAKES 3 CUPS | PHOTO ON PAGE 322

1 cup dry red wine, such as Syrah or Cabernet Sauvignon
1½ cups sugar
1 pound fresh or frozen (thawed) cranberries

Combine wine, sugar, and 1 cup water in a medium saucepan. Bring to a boil, and continue to boil 1½ minutes. Add cranberries, and reduce heat to medium-low. Cook, stirring frequently, until berries burst and mixture is reduced to 3 cups, about 15 minutes. Let cool completely, then transfer to an airtight container; refrigerate until ready to serve, up to 1 week.

from Thanksgiving in Wine Country

roasted brussels sprouts with almonds and honey

SERVES 8 TO 10 | PHOTOS ON PAGES 322 AND 323

3 pounds brussels sprouts, trimmed and halved
½ cup (1 stick) unsalted butter, melted
1 cup slivered almonds (4 ounces)
Coarse salt and freshly ground pepper
3 tablespoons honey
3 tablespoons freshly squeezed lemon juice (1 lemon)

1 Preheat oven to 400°F. Place sprouts, butter, and almonds on a rimmed baking sheet. Season with salt and pepper; toss to combine. Roast sprouts, stirring occasionally, until golden brown and tender, 35 to 40 minutes.

2 Transfer to a serving bowl; immediately dress with honey and lemon juice, and season with salt and pepper. Serve warm or at room temperature.

from Thanksgiving in Wine Country

roasted curried cauliflower

SERVES 4

An Indian-inspired spice blend gives this dish exotic flavor.

1½ tablespoons extra-virgin olive oil
1 teaspoon mustard seeds
1 teaspoon cumin seeds
¾ teaspoon curry powder
¾ teaspoon coarse salt
1 large head cauliflower (about 2 pounds), cut into large florets
Olive-oil cooking spray

1 Preheat oven to 375°F. Coat a rimmed baking sheet with cooking spray. In a large bowl, stir together oil, mustard seeds, cumin seeds, curry powder, and salt. Add cauliflower, tossing to coat thoroughly with spice mixture.

2 Arrange cauliflower in a single layer on prepared sheet. Roast until florets are browned on bottom and tender when pierced with the tip of a paring knife, about 35 minutes.

PER SERVING: 88 CALORIES, 6 G FAT, 0 MG CHOLESTEROL, 8 G CARBOHYDRATE, 404 MG SODIUM, 3 G PROTEIN, 4 G FIBER

from Fit to Eat: Cruciferous Vegetables

roasted shallots

MAKES ABOUT 2 DOZEN

Serve these with grilled or roasted meat or poultry.

1½ pounds shallots, root ends trimmed

3 tablespoons unsalted butter, melted

2 tablespoons sugar

1 teaspoon coarse salt

Freshly ground pepper

Preheat oven to 350°F. Place ingredients in a baking dish just large enough to hold shallots in a single layer; toss to combine. Cover with foil; bake, stirring every 20 minutes, until shallots are very tender and caramelized, 1½ to 1¾ hours.

from Onions Unearthed

simple stuffing

SERVES 8 TO 10

Unbaked stuffing can be stored, covered, in the baking dish for up to two days in the refrigerator. If refrigerated, you may need to increase the baking time slightly.

4 tablespoons unsalted butter, plus more for dish

4 onions, coarsely chopped (about 4 cups)

5 stalks celery, coarsely chopped (about 2½ cups)

1 tablespoon finely chopped fresh rosemary

1 tablespoon finely chopped fresh sage

1 large bulb fennel, coarsely chopped (about 2 cups), optional

Coarse salt and freshly ground pepper

1 pound sweet fennel sausage, casings removed, cut into 1-inch pieces

6 ounces jarred or vacuum-packed whole, peeled chestnuts (about 1 heaping cup)

2 day-old Italian bread loaves (about 8 ounces each), cut into ½-inch cubes

2 to 3 cups Brown Turkey Stock (recipe follows) or low-sodium canned chicken broth

¾ cup chopped fresh flat-leaf parsley

1 Preheat oven to 350°F. In a large sauté pan, melt butter over medium heat. Add onions, celery, rosemary, sage, and fennel, if desired; season with salt and pepper. Cook, stirring occasionally, until vegetables are soft and golden, about 10 minutes. Transfer to a large bowl.

2 Meanwhile, cook sausage in a medium nonstick skillet over medium heat, stirring occasionally, until browned and cooked through, about 8 minutes. Add to bowl with vegetables.

3 Using your fingers, break chestnuts into large pieces; add to bowl. Add bread cubes, and toss well to combine.

4 Drizzle 2 cups stock over mixture, tossing to moisten evenly. Add remaining stock, a little at a time, just until mixture feels moist when squeezed. Season with salt and pepper. Stir in parsley. Place stuffing in a buttered 2½- to 3-quart shallow baking dish or in an ovenproof gratin dish.

5 Bake stuffing until heated through and top is browned and crusty, 35 to 45 minutes. Serve hot.

from Potluck Thanksgiving

brown turkey stock

MAKES ABOUT 11 CUPS

We like to make turkey stock a day or two (or even several weeks) before Thanksgiving. That way, we can prepare the gravy a day early and have stock on hand for other dishes. Refrigerate stock in airtight containers for up to three days or freeze for up to six months.

6 to 7 pounds turkey parts, such as necks, wings, and legs

1 teaspoon coarse salt

½ cup Madeira or sherry

1 stalk celery, cut into 3-inch pieces

2 carrots, cut into 3-inch pieces

1 onion (unpeeled), quartered

A few sprigs each flat-leaf parsley, thyme, and rosemary

A few dried porcini mushrooms

A few whole black peppercorns

1 dried bay leaf

1 Preheat oven to 425°F. Place turkey parts in a large, heavy roasting pan (do not crowd); season with salt. Roast, stirring occasionally (pour off accumulated fat after about an hour), until very well-browned, about 2 hours total.

2 Transfer turkey parts to an 8- to 10-quart stockpot. Pour off fat from roasting pan; discard. Place roasting pan over medium-high heat. Add wine, and bring to a boil. Deglaze pan, scraping up browned bits from bottom with a wooden spoon.

3 Transfer deglazing liquid to pot, and add remaining ingredients. Add enough water to cover ingredients by 2 inches (about 4 quarts). Simmer 3 hours over low heat, skimming surface as needed. Let cool slightly. Pour stock through a large sieve set over a heatproof bowl; discard solids. Let cool completely. Transfer stock to airtight containers; refrigerate at least 6 hours or overnight. With a large metal spoon, skim off and discard layer of fat that has collected on surface. If storing, leave layer of fat intact (it helps to seal in flavor).

skillet sweet potatoes with wild mushrooms

SERVES 8 TO 10 | PHOTOS ON PAGES 322 AND 323

- 1 ounce dried wild mushrooms, such as porcini
- 1 cup boiling water
- 2 tablespoons brandy
- 6 tablespoons unsalted butter, melted
- Olive oil, for skillet
- 6 sweet potatoes (about 5 pounds), peeled and cut into ⅛-inch-thick rounds
- Coarse salt and freshly ground pepper

1 Place dried mushrooms in a small bowl, and cover with boiling water. Let soak, stirring occasionally, until mushrooms are soft, about 30 minutes. Remove mushrooms; reserve ⅓ cup soaking liquid. Using paper towels, squeeze out excess water from mushrooms; roughly chop, and set aside.

2 Preheat oven to 400°F, with rack in center. In a small bowl, whisk together brandy, 5 tablespoons butter, and reserved mushroom liquid. Rub a 9-inch cast-iron skillet lightly with oil. Arrange one-quarter of the potatoes in a single layer in bottom of skillet, overlapping slightly. Scatter one-third of mushrooms over potatoes, then drizzle with one-quarter of brandy mixture. Season with salt and pepper. Repeat layering three times, ending with potatoes and liquid; season with salt.

3 Cover skillet with foil. Bake until potatoes are just fork-tender, about 35 minutes. Remove foil; brush top with remaining tablespoon butter. Continue baking until golden brown and tender, 25 to 30 minutes. Let stand 10 minutes before serving.

from Thanksgiving in Wine Country

turnip hash with broccoli rabe

SERVES 4

- ½ pound plum tomatoes
- ½ pound turnips, peeled and cut into ½-inch dice
- ½ pound parsnips, peeled and cut into ½-inch dice
- ½ pound Yukon gold potatoes, peeled and cut into ½-inch dice
- 1 bunch broccoli rabe, trimmed and cut into ½-inch pieces (about 6½ cups)
- 1½ tablespoons extra-virgin olive oil
- 1 medium onion, coarsely chopped
- 4 garlic cloves, smashed
- ¾ teaspoon coarse salt
- ¼ teaspoon crushed red-pepper flakes
- 1 teaspoon coarsely chopped fresh thyme

1 Bring a large pot of water to a boil. Prepare an ice bath; set aside. Score an X on the bottom of each tomato with a paring knife. Boil tomatoes in water until skins are loosened, about 30 seconds; remove tomatoes with a slotted spoon, and immediately plunge them into the ice bath. Drain, peel, and seed tomatoes; coarsely chop flesh.

2 Add turnips to pot; boil until just tender when pierced with a fork, 3 to 5 minutes. Using a slotted spoon, transfer turnips to a colander to drain. Repeat process with parsnips, then potatoes. Add broccoli rabe to pot, and boil until bright green and crisp-tender, about 1 minute. Drain in a separate colander.

3 Heat oil in a large, heavy skillet over medium heat until hot but not smoking. Add onion, garlic, salt, red-pepper flakes, thyme, and reserved turnips, parsnips, and potatoes; spread evenly to cover bottom of skillet. Cook, without stirring, until vegetables begin to brown on bottom, about 15 minutes.

4 Add reserved tomatoes and broccoli rabe to skillet. Stir once; cook until vegetables are very tender and browned, about 25 minutes. Serve hot.

PER SERVING: 189 CALORIES, 6 G FAT, 0 MG CHOLESTEROL, 32 G CARBOHYDRATE, 489 MG SODIUM, 7 G PROTEIN, 7 G FIBER

from Fit to Eat: Cruciferous Vegetables

Tuscan kale with caramelized onions and red-wine vinegar

SERVES 4 | PHOTO ON PAGE 329

- 1 tablespoon extra-virgin olive oil
- 1 large red onion, halved and thinly sliced into half-moons
- 1 large garlic clove, thinly sliced
- ¾ teaspoon coarse salt
- 2 tablespoons red-wine vinegar
- 1 pound Tuscan kale, tough stems removed, leaves cut into 1½-inch pieces

1 Combine oil, onion, garlic, and ¼ teaspoon salt in a large sauté pan; cook over medium heat, stirring occasionally, until onion is lightly browned, about 5 minutes. Reduce heat to medium-low; cook until onion is soft, about 10 minutes.

2 Add vinegar to pan, and raise heat to medium-high. Add kale, ¼ cup water, and remaining ½ teaspoon salt; cook, stirring, until kale begins to soften, about 3 minutes. As the pan becomes dry, add another ¼ cup water, and cook until kale is tender, about 3 minutes more. Serve immediately.

PER SERVING: 105 CALORIES, 4 G FAT, 0 MG CHOLESTEROL, 15 G CARBOHYDRATE, 410 MG SODIUM, 4 G PROTEIN, 3 G FIBER

from Fit to Eat: Cruciferous Vegetables

caramel-walnut pie

MAKES 1 NINE-INCH PIE | PHOTO ON PAGE 330

- 3 cups walnut halves (12 ounces)
- All-purpose flour, for work surface
- ½ recipe Pâte Brisée (page 129)
- 4 large eggs
- 2 tablespoons heavy cream
- 1¾ cups sugar
- 1½ cups crème fraîche

1 Preheat oven to 350°F. Spread walnuts in a single layer on a rimmed baking sheet; toast in oven until crisp and fragrant, stirring occasionally, about 10 minutes. Let cool, then coarsely chop. Raise oven temperature to 400°F.

2 On a lightly floured work surface, roll out dough to a 13-inch round, about ⅛ inch thick. Brush off excess flour; fit dough into a 9-inch pie plate, pressing into bottom and up sides. Trim to a ½-inch overhang. Tuck dough under, forming a rim; crimp as desired. Chill 30 minutes.

3 In a small bowl, whisk together 1 egg and cream. Prick bottom of dough all over with a fork. Line with parchment paper; fill with pie weights or dried beans. Bake until edges begin to turn golden, about 10 minutes. Remove weights and parchment. Brush pie shell with egg wash, leaving rim uncoated. Continue baking until center is golden, 5 minutes more. Let cool on a wire rack.

4 Reduce oven temperature to 350°F. Bring sugar and ½ cup water to a boil in a medium saucepan, stirring until sugar dissolves. Without stirring, cook until caramel is light amber, about 7 minutes, washing down sides of pan with a wet pastry brush to prevent crystals from forming. Remove from heat, and carefully stir in crème fraîche (it will spatter). Let cool 5 to 10 minutes. If caramel starts to harden, place pan briefly over low heat, stirring constantly.

5 In a small bowl, whisk together remaining 3 eggs; slowly whisk in 1 cup caramel until combined. Whisk mixture back into caramel in saucepan. Stir in nuts.

6 Pour filling into pie shell; bake until slightly puffy and set, 30 to 40 minutes. Let cool on a wire rack. Store at room temperature up to 2 days.

from Thanksgiving in Wine Country

chai-spice apple pie

MAKES 1 NINE-INCH DOUBLE-CRUST PIE | PHOTO ON PAGE 330

If desired, dough scraps can be rolled out and cut into grape and stem shapes; attach to pie in clusters with a beaten egg white. Brush top with an egg wash made of one egg yolk and two tablespoons heavy cream.

- ¼ cup all-purpose flour, plus more for work surface
- Pâte Brisée (page 129)
- 3 pounds assorted apples, such as Macoun, Granny Smith, and Cortland
- 2 tablespoons freshly squeezed lemon juice
- ¼ cup packed light-brown sugar
- ½ teaspoon salt
- ½ teaspoon fennel seeds
- ½ teaspoon ground cinnamon
- ⅛ teaspoon ground cloves
- ⅛ teaspoon ground cardamom
- 1 tablespoon unsalted butter, cut into small pieces
- 1 large egg white, lightly beaten
- 2 tablespoons sanding sugar

1 On a lightly floured work surface, roll out one disk of dough to a 13-inch round, about ⅛ inch thick. Brush off excess flour. Fit dough into a 9-inch pie plate, pressing into bottom and up sides; trim to a ¼-inch overhang. Chill 30 minutes.

2 Peel, core, and cut apples into ½-inch slices. In a large bowl, gently toss apples with lemon juice, brown sugar, flour, salt, fennel, cinnamon, cloves, and cardamom.

3 Preheat oven to 400°F, with a baking sheet on center rack. Arrange apple mixture in chilled dough; dot with butter. Roll out remaining dough disk as above; drape over pie plate. Trim to a ½-inch overhang; fold edge under bottom crust, and crimp with a fork. Cut a ¼-inch hole in center and make four slits for steam vents. Chill at least 15 minutes.

4 Brush dough with egg white; sprinkle with sanding sugar. Bake on heated sheet until crust is golden brown, about 20 minutes. Reduce oven heat to 350°F; continue baking until juices are bubbling, 30 to 35 minutes more. Let cool on a wire rack. Store at room temperature up to 2 days.

from Thanksgiving in Wine Country

individual strawberry-jam cakes

MAKES 6 | PHOTO ON PAGE 331

½ cup (1 stick) unsalted butter, room temperature, plus more for tin

¾ cup granulated sugar

1 teaspoon finely grated orange zest

2 large eggs, separated

1½ cups all-purpose flour

½ teaspoon baking powder

¼ teaspoon salt

¼ cup milk

6 tablespoons strawberry jam or preserves

1½ cups confectioners' sugar

¼ cup freshly squeezed orange juice

1 Preheat oven to 350°F. Butter a standard 6-cup muffin tin; set aside. In a medium bowl, beat butter, granulated sugar, and zest until light and fluffy. Beat in egg yolks one at a time until creamy; set aside. Into a small bowl, sift together flour, baking powder, and salt. Add flour mixture to butter mixture in two batches, alternating with milk; set aside.

2 In a clean bowl, whisk egg whites until soft peaks form; fold into batter. Divide half of the batter among muffin cups. Using your thumb, make an indentation in the center of each; fill with 1 tablespoon jam. Top with remaining batter.

3 Bake until a cake tester inserted in top cake layer comes out clean, about 30 minutes. Unmold cakes; transfer to a wire rack to cool. In a small bowl, whisk together confectioners' sugar and juice. Place rack over a piece of parchment paper, and drizzle cakes with glaze.

from What's for Dinner?

lavender-grape tart

MAKES 1 EIGHT-INCH TART | PHOTO ON PAGE 330

3 tablespoons all-purpose flour, plus more for work surface

½ recipe Pâte Brisée (page 129)

4 cups assorted seedless grapes, halved

1 cup sugar, plus more for sprinkling

Grated zest and juice of 1 large lemon

½ teaspoon dried or 1 teaspoon chopped fresh lavender leaves

2 tablespoons unsalted butter, cut into small pieces

1 large egg white, lightly beaten

1 Preheat oven to 425°F, with rack in center; line bottom rack with foil. On a lightly floured work surface, roll out dough to a 13-inch round, about ⅛ inch thick. Transfer to a parchment-lined baking sheet, and chill 30 minutes.

2 Meanwhile, in a bowl, toss together grapes, sugar, lemon zest and juice, lavender, and flour. Transfer mixture to a sieve set over a bowl; drain 30 minutes.

3 Mound grape mixture in center of chilled dough, leaving a 2½-inch border. Dot with butter. Fold edge of dough over filling, leaving center open. Brush dough with egg white, and sprinkle with sugar.

4 Bake until pastry is golden brown, about 20 minutes. Reduce oven heat to 350°F, and loosely cover center of tart with foil. Continue baking until juices are bubbling, 15 to 20 minutes more. Let cool on a wire rack. Serve at room temperature.

from Thanksgiving in Wine Country

pomegranate-cardamom ice

SERVES 8 TO 10

To make your own juice, use a citrus reamer, juicer, or press to extract juice from about fifteen halved large pomegranates. Strain through a fine sieve set over a bowl, discarding solids.

1 cup sugar

4 whole cardamom pods, crushed

3 cups pomegranate juice

1 Prepare an ice bath; set aside. Bring sugar and 1 cup water to a boil in a small saucepan, stirring until sugar dissolves. Add cardamom; reduce heat, and simmer 5 minutes. Transfer to a heatproof bowl set in ice bath; chill, stirring frequently.

2 In a large bowl, stir together juice and chilled syrup. Pour through a fine sieve into a 1½- to 2-quart shallow pan; discard solids. Cover with plastic wrap; freeze at least 5 hours or up to overnight. Stir ice to soften slightly before serving. Store in an airtight container up to 1 week.

from Thanksgiving in Wine Country

pumpkin-chocolate tart

MAKES 1 TEN-INCH TART

This tart is drizzled with chocolate to create stripes. To make them neat and even, let the first drops of chocolate fall back into the bowl before moving the spoon quickly over the tart.

1   can (15 ounces) pumpkin purée
¾   cup firmly packed light-brown sugar
8   ounces crème fraîche
3   large eggs
1   teaspoon ground cinnamon
1   teaspoon ground ginger
¼   teaspoon ground nutmeg
¼   teaspoon salt
⅛   teaspoon ground cloves
    Chocolate Crust (recipe follows)
2   ounces best-quality semisweet chocolate

1   Preheat oven to 350°F, with rack in center. In a medium bowl, whisk together pumpkin purée, brown sugar, crème fraîche, eggs, cinnamon, ginger, nutmeg, salt, and cloves until smooth. Pass mixture through a fine sieve set over a clean bowl; discard solids. Pour filling into prepared crust.

2   Bake until filling is set, about 40 minutes. Transfer to a wire rack, and let cool at least 30 minutes.

3   Set a heatproof bowl over a pan of barely simmering water. Melt chocolate in bowl, stirring occasionally; remove from heat. Dip a spoon in melted chocolate, then drizzle chocolate over tart, forming decorative stripes. Refrigerate until well set, at least 1 hour and up to 1 day.

from Dessert of the Month

chocolate crust

MAKES 1 TEN-INCH TART SHELL

1   cup all-purpose flour, plus more for work surface
¼   cup plus 1 tablespoon sugar
¼   cup unsweetened cocoa powder
½   teaspoon salt
½   teaspoon ground cinnamon
¼   teaspoon ground cloves
½   cup (1 stick) chilled unsalted butter, cut into small pieces
1   large egg
4   ounces best-quality semisweet chocolate, finely chopped

1   In the bowl of an electric mixer fitted with the paddle attachment, combine flour, sugar, cocoa, salt, cinnamon, and cloves. Add butter; mix on low speed until butter is the size of small peas, about 5 minutes. Add egg; mix just until ingredients come together to form a dough.

2   Preheat oven to 350°F. On a lightly floured work surface, roll out dough to a 13-inch round, about ⅛ inch thick. Brush off excess flour; transfer dough to a 10-inch tart pan with a removable bottom. Press dough into bottom and up sides of pan; trim excess flush with edge. Lightly prick bottom of dough all over with a fork. Chill until firm, about 30 minutes.

3   Bake shell until firm, about 15 minutes. Immediately sprinkle chocolate over bottom of shell; smooth with a spatula.

DRINKS

---

apple-pie spiced cider

SERVES 6

1¼ quarts apple cider
3   tablespoons firmly packed light-brown sugar
1   whole cinnamon stick, plus 6 sticks for garnish
1   teaspoon ground allspice
½   teaspoon ground ginger
    Pinch of ground cloves
    Pinch of freshly grated nutmeg
    Pinch of salt
½   cup Calvados or another brandy (optional)

In a medium saucepan, whisk together cider, brown sugar, spices, and salt. Bring to a simmer over medium-low heat. Remove from heat, and pour in brandy, if desired. Strain mixture through a fine sieve into a pitcher; discard solids. Serve cider hot in mugs, garnished with cinnamon sticks.

from Good Things

cornbread muffins

MAKES 1 DOZEN | PHOTO ON PAGE 319

5 tablespoons unsalted butter, melted, plus more for muffin tin

1 cup coarse yellow cornmeal

1 cup all-purpose flour

¼ cup confectioners' sugar

¼ cup granulated sugar

½ teaspoon baking powder

1 teaspoon baking soda

1 teaspoon salt

2 large eggs

1½ cups buttermilk

½ vanilla bean, split lengthwise and scraped

1 Preheat oven to 375°F. Brush a 12-cup standard muffin tin with melted butter; set aside. In a large bowl, whisk together cornmeal, flour, sugars, baking powder, baking soda, and salt.

2 In another bowl, whisk together eggs, buttermilk, and vanilla seeds. Pour over flour mixture. Add butter; stir until blended, using as few strokes as possible.

3 Spoon batter into prepared tin, filling each cup about three-quarters full. Bake until golden and firm to the touch, 17 to 20 minutes. Serve warm.

from Thanksgiving in Wine Country

garlic-rosemary flatbread

MAKES 4

Premade pizza dough, either refrigerated or frozen, can be purchased at your local pizza parlor or grocery store.

1 tablespoon unsalted butter

1 tablespoon extra-virgin olive oil, plus more for drizzling

1 garlic clove, minced

1 teaspoon coarse salt, plus more for seasoning

Cornmeal, for sprinkling

1 pound premade pizza dough, room temperature

½ teaspoon finely chopped fresh rosemary, plus a handful of small sprigs

1 Preheat oven to 425°F. In a small saucepan, heat butter and oil over medium heat. Add garlic and salt; cook, stirring, until garlic is fragrant but not browned, about 1 minute. Remove from heat; set aside.

2 Sprinkle the bottom of two rimmed baking sheets with cornmeal. Divide dough into four equal pieces. Roll out each piece into a ¼-inch-thick round. Arrange two rounds on each sheet. Brush with butter mixture, leaving most of the garlic behind. Sprinkle rounds with chopped rosemary, and arrange a few small sprigs on top of each.

3 Bake flatbreads until golden brown, about 15 minutes. Transfer to wire racks to cool slightly. Drizzle with oil, and season with salt. Serve warm or at room temperature.

from What's for Dinner?

mole sauce

MAKES 3 CUPS | PHOTO ON PAGE 322

We served this sauce with ready-made tamales. Mole can be made up to one week ahead and refrigerated in an airtight container.

1 slice white bread or 2 slices baguette

1 garlic clove (unpeeled)

⅓ cup whole almonds (2 ounces)

1 ancho chile

1 tablespoon vegetable oil or lard

½ white onion, finely chopped

1 pint grape tomatoes

½ small canned chipotle pepper in adobo sauce, plus 1 teaspoon adobo sauce

½ large ripe banana, cut into pieces

2 tablespoons plus 1 teaspoon unsweetened cocoa powder

1½ teaspoons light-brown sugar

¼ teaspoon ground cinnamon

¼ teaspoon dried oregano

⅛ teaspoon ground cloves

1½ cups Basic Chicken Stock (page 17) or low-sodium canned chicken broth

Coarse salt and freshly ground pepper

1 In a 9-inch cast-iron skillet, toast bread over medium-high heat, turning once, until golden. Tear toast into large pieces; pulse in a blender or food processor until fine crumbs form. Transfer breadcrumbs to a large bowl.

2 In the same skillet, cook garlic over medium-high heat, turning occasionally, until soft and charred, about 5 minutes. When cool enough to handle, squeeze clove from skin, and add to bowl with breadcrumbs. Toast almonds in skillet over medium heat, tossing occasionally, until golden brown, about 3 minutes. Transfer to bowl.

3 Wipe ancho chile with a damp paper towel. Slit chile lengthwise; remove stem, ribs, and seeds, reserving seeds. Cook chile in skillet over medium-low heat, turning once, until it begins to blister, 10 to 30 seconds. Transfer to bowl.

4 Pour oil into skillet, and add onion. Cook over medium heat, stirring occasionally, until soft and translucent, about 3 minutes. Transfer to bowl. Add tomatoes to skillet, and cook, tossing occasionally, until skins are slightly charred, about 5 minutes. Transfer tomatoes to bowl.

5 Add chipotle, adobo sauce, reserved ancho seeds, banana, cocoa, brown sugar, cinnamon, oregano, and cloves to bowl; stir to combine. Working in batches, if necessary, purée mixture in a blender until smooth, adding stock a little at a time.

6 Transfer purée to a medium saucepan. Cook over medium-low heat, stirring with a rubber spatula, about 20 minutes. Pass mole through a sieve into a serving bowl, discarding solids. Serve warm.

from Thanksgiving in Wine Country

mushroom gravy

MAKES 3 CUPS

The chopped fresh mushrooms in this gravy provide the texture of giblets, making it an ideal substitute for traditional Thanksgiving gravy. This recipe can be prepared up to one day ahead, then reheated over low heat.

6 cups Brown Turkey Stock (page 278)
½ ounce dried porcini mushrooms (about ½ cup)
1 cup boiling water
2 tablespoons unsalted butter
10 ounces white mushrooms, trimmed and cut into ¼-inch dice
Coarse salt and freshly ground pepper
3 tablespoons all-purpose flour
½ cup Madeira or sherry

1 In a large saucepan, bring stock to a gentle boil over medium heat; cook until reduced by half, about 30 minutes.

2 Meanwhile, place porcini in a small bowl, and cover with boiling water. Let soak until porcini are soft, about 10 minutes. Remove porcini, and gently squeeze out excess water; finely chop. Set aside.

3 Heat butter in a medium saucepan over medium-high heat until foamy. Add white mushrooms, and season with salt and pepper. Add reserved porcini. Cook, stirring, until white mushrooms are soft, about 10 minutes.

4 Sprinkle flour over mushroom mixture, and cook until flour starts to brown, 2 to 3 minutes more. Add wine; deglaze pan, scraping up browned bits from bottom with a wooden spoon.

5 Stir stock into mushroom mixture. Bring to a gentle simmer over very low heat, and cook until thickened slightly, about 30 minutes. If gravy thickens too much, thin with a little water or stock. Season with salt and pepper; serve hot.

from Potluck Thanksgiving

sticky buns

MAKES 3 BATCHES OF NINE | **PHOTO ON PAGE 314**

Make pull-apart buns in a square baking pan or round ones in a large-muffin tin. If you aren't baking them all at once, chill the remaining dough in resealable plastic bags for up to three days, or freeze it for up to one month (let dough come to room temperature before proceeding). Refrigerate extra topping for up to one week. Buns are best the day they are baked.

FOR DOUGH:

2 tablespoons active dry yeast
⅓ cup warm water (110°F)
1 cup milk, room temperature
1 cup (2 sticks) unsalted butter, room temperature, cut into small pieces, plus more for bowl
3 large eggs
⅓ cup granulated sugar
2 teaspoons salt
1 teaspoon pure vanilla extract
4 to 6 cups all-purpose flour, plus more for work surface

FOR TOPPING:

1 cup (2 sticks) unsalted butter
¼ cup granulated sugar
1¼ cups firmly packed light-brown sugar
1 cup light corn syrup

FOR ASSEMBLING EACH BATCH:

1 tablespoon unsalted butter, melted
1 recipe Sticky-Bun Filling (recipe follows)

1 Make dough: Stir together yeast and warm water in a small bowl; let stand until foamy, about 5 minutes.

2 In the bowl of an electric mixer, whisk together milk, butter, eggs, sugar, salt, and vanilla on low speed until combined, about 2 minutes. Add yeast mixture; mix 1 minute. Add 4 cups flour, and mix until smooth.

3 Switch to the dough-hook attachment; continue mixing, adding up to 2 cups more flour, ½ cup at a time, just until dough no longer sticks to bowl. Beat dough on medium-high speed for 10 minutes.

4 On a lightly floured work surface, knead dough until very smooth, about 2 minutes; transfer to a large buttered bowl. Cover dough with a clean kitchen towel, and let rise until doubled in bulk, about 1 hour.

5 Make topping: Melt butter in a medium saucepan; stir in sugars and corn syrup. Cook, stirring, over low heat, until sugars dissolve, about 5 minutes. Set aside.

6 Punch down dough, then turn out onto a lightly floured work surface. Divide dough into three equal pieces; roll each into a ball. (Work with one ball at a time; refrigerate or freeze any not being used.)

7 Assemble buns: Roll out dough ball into a 10-by-13-inch rectangle. If it springs back, let it rest a few minutes, then continue rolling. Brush dough with melted butter. Top with filling, leaving a ½-inch border. Starting on one long side, roll dough into a log. To seal, pinch dough edge to log; turn roll seam side down. With a sharp knife and a sawing motion, cut log into nine slices approximately 1⅓ inches thick; avoid pressing down.

8 For each batch, divide 1 cup topping among nine cups of a large (1-cup capacity) muffin tin, or cover bottom of an 8-inch square baking pan. Transfer buns to tin or pan, making sure end pieces are cut side up.

9 Preheat oven to 375°F, with rack on lower level. Place a wire rack over a baking sheet; set aside. Let buns rise in a warm place until doubled in bulk, about 30 minutes. Bake buns, rotating pan halfway through, until golden brown and bubbling, 30 to 35 minutes. Immediately invert onto rack. Serve warm.

from Sticky Buns

mini sticky buns variation:

MAKES 3 BATCHES OF FOUR DOZEN | **PHOTO ON PAGE 315**

Follow steps 1 through 6 of Sticky Buns recipe. Follow step 7, but roll dough into a 7-by-19-inch rectangle; halve lengthwise. After dough is filled and rolled, cut each log into 24 slices (¾ inch thick). Follow step 8, dividing 1 cup topping among four (12-cup) mini-muffin tins. Follow step 9, but bake the mini buns 15 to 20 minutes.

sticky-bun filling

EACH FILLING OPTION MAKES ENOUGH FOR 9 REGULAR OR 48 MINI STICKY BUNS

FOR CLASSIC PECAN FILLING:

⅓ **cup packed light-brown sugar**

⅓ **cup pecans (about 1¼ ounces), toasted and finely chopped**

1 **teaspoon grated orange zest**

FOR MACADAMIA NUT AND WHITE CHOCOLATE FILLING:

½ **cup macadamia nuts, coarsely chopped (about 2 ounces)**

1 **ounce white chocolate, finely chopped**

2 **tablespoons light-brown sugar**

FOR MEXICAN CHOCOLATE FILLING:

2 **ounces semisweet chocolate, finely chopped**

2 **tablespoons light-brown sugar**

½ **teaspoon ground cinnamon**

FOR BANANA, MAPLE, AND WALNUT FILLING:

2 **tablespoons light-brown sugar**

2 **tablespoons pure maple syrup**

½ **cup walnuts (about 2 ounces), toasted and finely chopped**

1 **banana, thinly sliced**

FOR RASPBERRY AND CREAM FILLING:

½ **pint fresh raspberries**

⅓ **cup crème fraîche**

⅓ **cup mascarpone cheese**

For first three filling options, toss ingredients together in a small bowl. For the Banana, Maple, and Walnut Filling, whisk brown sugar and maple syrup in a small bowl until combined, then gently fold in walnuts and banana slices. For the Raspberry and Cream Filling, lightly crush raspberries in a small bowl with a rubber spatula. Add crème fraîche and mascarpone, and stir until smooth. Refrigerate until ready to use, up to 2 hours.

turkey gravy

MAKES 2 CUPS

The secret to delicious gravy is a homemade stock, which you can prepare while the turkey roasts in the oven.

Giblets and neck reserved from turkey (liver discarded)
3 **sprigs thyme**
3 **sprigs flat-leaf parsley**
1 **sprig rosemary**
3 **tablespoons unsalted butter**
2 **stalks celery, coarsely chopped**
1 **small carrot, coarsely chopped**
1 **leek, white and pale-green parts only, coarsely chopped and washed well**
1 **onion, coarsely chopped**
5 **whole black peppercorns**
1 **fresh or dried bay leaf**
¾ **cup dry white wine or water**
3 **tablespoons all-purpose flour**
Coarse salt and freshly ground black pepper

1   Make stock while turkey roasts: Trim fat and membrane from giblets. Rinse giblets and neck; pat dry. Add to roasting pan with turkey, and roast until browned, about 30 minutes. Remove giblets and neck from pan; set aside.

2   Bundle together thyme, parsley, and rosemary, and tie with kitchen twine to make a bouquet garni; set aside.

3   Melt butter over medium-high heat in a large (4-quart) saucepan. Add celery, carrot, leek, and onion; cook, stirring occasionally, until just browned, 5 to 10 minutes. Reduce heat to medium; add giblets, neck, bouquet garni, peppercorns, bay leaf, and 4 cups water. Cover; bring to a boil. Uncover, and reduce heat to medium-low. Cook until liquid reduces to about 3 cups, skimming foam from surface, 50 to 60 minutes.

4   Pour stock through a fine sieve set over a large clean saucepan. Reserve giblets and neck; discard vegetables. Keep stock warm over medium-low heat. Coarsely chop giblets, and shred neck meat off the bone with a fork.

5   Make gravy when turkey comes out of the oven: Pour juices from roasting pan into a fat separator; reserve pan. Let the juices separate, about 10 minutes.

6   Set pan on top of stove across two burners; add wine. Bring to a boil over medium-high heat, scraping up browned bits on bottom with a wooden spoon. Reserve deglazing liquid.

7   Add 3 tablespoons reserved pan fat (from top of separator) to a large, clean saucepan, and place over medium-low heat. Add flour to make a roux, whisking vigorously to combine. Cook, whisking, until flour is deep golden brown and fragrant, about 7 minutes. Whisking vigorously, add stock in a steady stream to roux. Bring mixture to a boil, then reduce heat to a simmer.

8   Add reserved deglazing liquid, pan juice (from bottom of separator), giblets, and neck meat to mixture. Return to a simmer; cook, stirring occasionally, until mixture is thickened, about 20 minutes.

9   Pour gravy through a fine sieve set over a large saucepan; discard giblets and neck meat, if desired. Keep gravy warm over low heat until ready to serve (up to 30 minutes); season with salt and pepper.

from Perfect Gravy

December

(continued on next page)

(continued from previous page)

Christmas crostini with smoked trout

SERVES 20

The crostini is made with a wreath-shaped loaf of peasant bread, found in artisanal bakeries and gourmet food shops. You can also use a round loaf; cut out the center.

1 pound boneless smoked trout fillets, skins removed

4 ounces cream cheese, room temperature

4 ounces crème fraîche

¼ cup prepared horseradish

¼ cup freshly squeezed lemon juice (about 2 lemons)

Freshly ground pepper

1 loaf peasant bread (1 to 1½ pounds)

Extra-virgin olive oil, for brushing

1 bunch watercress, tough stems removed

6 ounces cherry tomatoes, halved

1 kirby cucumber, halved lengthwise and thinly sliced crosswise into half moons

1 Preheat oven to 375°F. In a food processor, pulse trout fillets several times until broken up into small pieces. In a medium bowl, whisk together cream cheese, crème fraîche, horseradish, and lemon juice. Fold in trout; season with pepper. Cover with plastic wrap; refrigerate until ready to use, up to 2 days.

2 Using a long serrated knife, trim top of loaf to make level. Cut bread into ¾-inch-thick slices, keeping shape of loaf intact. Brush top with oil. Arrange loaf, oiled side up, on a baking sheet; toast until golden brown, about 12 minutes. Let cool.

3 Transfer loaf to a serving platter. Spread trout mixture on bread. Arrange watercress, tomatoes, and cucumber on top. Serve immediately.

from New England Open House

deviled eggs with lobster

SERVES ABOUT 30

Deviled eggs can be prepared up to six hours ahead; cover, and refrigerate. Garnish with tarragon just before serving.

18 large eggs

2 fresh lobsters (1½ pounds each)

2 tablespoons olive oil

1 large shallot, finely chopped

½ red bell pepper, ribs and seeds removed, finely chopped

⅓ cup mayonnaise

3 tablespoons cider vinegar

1½ teaspoons coarsely chopped fresh tarragon, plus leaves for garnish

½ teaspoon coarse salt

Pinch of cayenne pepper

1 Bring a large pot of water to a boil. Prepare an ice bath, and set aside. Gently drop eggs into boiling water, and cook 9 minutes. Using a slotted spoon, transfer eggs to ice bath to cool, about 5 minutes.

2 Fill a large stockpot halfway with water; bring to a boil over medium-high heat. Add lobsters; cover, and cook until shells are bright red, about 12 minutes. Drain; let stand until cool enough to handle. Remove lobster meat from shells, and finely chop. Transfer to a medium bowl; set aside.

3 Heat oil in a medium skillet over medium heat. Add shallot and bell pepper, and cook, stirring occasionally, until softened, 5 to 7 minutes. Transfer mixture to bowl with lobster.

4 Peel eggs; slice in half lengthwise. Remove yolks, and add to lobster meat along with mayonnaise, vinegar, tarragon, salt, and cayenne. Mix until well combined. Spoon lobster mixture into each halved egg white; garnish with tarragon.

from New England Open House

ham-and-Gruyère thumbprints

MAKES 3 DOZEN | PHOTO ON PAGE 316

If baking these savory cheese puffs immediately, skip step four (baking time may be slightly shorter).

½ cup (1 stick) unsalted butter, cut into large pieces
½ teaspoon coarse salt
1 cup all-purpose flour
4 large eggs
½ teaspoon freshly ground pepper
½ cup finely chopped or ground Black Forest ham (2 ounces)
1 cup finely shredded Gruyère cheese, plus 36 half-inch cubes for centers (8 ounces total)

1 Preheat oven to 400°F. Bring butter, salt, and 1 cup water to a boil in a large (4-quart) heavy saucepan over medium-high heat, stirring occasionally, until butter is melted. Stir in flour; cook, stirring frequently, until flour is incorporated and mixture pulls away from sides of pan. Continue cooking, stirring, until a thin film forms on bottom of pan, 1 to 2 minutes more. Remove from heat; let cool 5 minutes.

2 Transfer dough to a large bowl; add eggs, and beat with a wooden spoon until well incorporated, about 2 minutes. Stir in pepper, ham, and 1 cup shredded cheese.

3 Spoon dough into a pastry bag fitted with a ½-inch star tip. Onto a baking sheet lined with a Silpat baking mat or parchment paper, pipe 1½-inch-wide rosettes, spacing them 1 inch apart. Make a deep indentation in center of each rosette with your thumb (dampen thumb with water to keep it from sticking to dough). Bake until crisp and golden, 25 to 30 minutes. Remove from oven; transfer to a wire rack to cool completely. Press a cheese cube into indentation in each puff.

4 Arrange puffs in a single layer on clean baking sheets, and freeze (uncovered) until firm, about 1 hour. Transfer to a large resealable plastic bag or airtight container, and freeze until ready to use, up to 6 weeks.

5 To serve, preheat oven to 425°F. Place thumbprints on baking sheets, and bake until heated through and cheese is melted, 10 to 14 minutes. Serve immediately.

from Freezer Hors D'oeuvres

mini Asian crab cakes

MAKES ABOUT 2 DOZEN | PHOTO ON PAGE 317

If baking these crab cakes immediately, skip step five (baking time may be slightly shorter).

8 ounces jumbo lump crabmeat, picked over and rinsed
¼ cup mayonnaise, plus 3 tablespoons for garnish
2 scallions, trimmed and finely chopped
2 tablespoons soy sauce
2 teaspoons wasabi paste
1 teaspoon finely grated lime zest
½ cup plus 2 tablespoons plain breadcrumbs
½ cup all-purpose flour
½ teaspoon coarse salt
½ teaspoon freshly ground pepper
2 large eggs
¼ cup sesame seeds
⅔ cup vegetable oil, plus more if needed
1 English cucumber, for garnish
½ cup drained pickled ginger, for garnish

1 Using a fork, flake crabmeat in a medium bowl, then stir in ¼ cup mayonnaise, scallions, soy sauce, ½ teaspoon wasabi paste, and lime zest. Add 2 tablespoons breadcrumbs, and stir until combined. Cover with plastic wrap; chill 1 hour.

2 In a medium bowl, whisk together flour, salt, and pepper; set aside. In a small bowl, beat eggs with 1 tablespoon water. Set aside. In a shallow bowl, stir together sesame seeds and remaining ½ cup breadcrumbs.

3 Form one scant tablespoon crab mixture into a ball, then dip in seasoned flour. Flatten ball into a ¾-inch-high cake, about 1¼ inches in diameter; transfer to a large plate. Repeat with remaining crab mixture. Dip cakes in egg mixture, then roll in breadcrumb mixture, coating completely.

4 Heat oil in a large, heavy skillet over medium heat until hot but not smoking. Add half the crab cakes, and cook, turning once, until golden and crisp on both sides, about 1½ minutes. Using a slotted spatula, transfer cakes to paper-towel–lined plates to drain. Repeat with remaining cakes, adding more oil if needed. Let crab cakes cool completely.

5 Transfer crab cakes to a parchment-lined baking sheet. Freeze (uncovered) until firm, about 1 hour. Transfer to a large resealable plastic bag or airtight container, and freeze until ready to use, up to 6 weeks.

6 To serve, preheat oven to 425°F. Place crab cakes on a baking sheet, and bake until heated through, 10 to 14 minutes.

7 Meanwhile, stir together remaining 3 tablespoons mayonnaise and 1½ teaspoons wasabi paste. Using a vegetable peeler, make 24 (2-by-¾-inch) ribbons from cucumber; fold each ribbon into thirds.

8 Dot each crab cake with about ½ teaspoon wasabi mayonnaise, then top with a cucumber ribbon and a slice of pickled ginger. Serve immediately.

from Freezer Hors D'oeuvres

mini chicken b'steeyas

MAKES 54

These hors d'oeuvres are miniature versions of a classic Moroccan savory pie. If baking them immediately, skip step seven (baking time may be slightly shorter).

4 tablespoons vegetable oil
1 large whole boneless and skinless chicken breast (about 10 ounces), halved
   Coarse salt and freshly ground pepper
1 onion, minced
½ teaspoon ground ginger
¼ teaspoon ground turmeric
1½ teaspoons ground cinnamon, plus more for dusting
¾ cup confectioners' sugar, plus more for dusting
2 large eggs, lightly beaten
¼ cup golden raisins, finely chopped (optional)
½ cup whole blanched almonds (2 ounces)
12 sheets frozen phyllo dough, thawed
½ cup (1 stick) unsalted butter, melted, for brushing

1 Heat 1 tablespoon oil in a medium nonstick skillet over medium heat. Season chicken on both sides with salt and pepper; cook until just cooked through, turning once, about 10 minutes. Transfer chicken to a plate; let cool, then finely chop. Transfer chicken and any accumulated juices from plate to a large bowl. Set aside.

2 Heat remaining 3 tablespoons oil in skillet over medium heat. Add onion; cook, stirring occasionally, until softened, about 4 minutes. Add ginger, turmeric, and ½ teaspoon cinnamon; cook, stirring, until fragrant, about 1 minute.

3 Stir ¼ cup sugar into onion mixture. Add eggs, and cook, stirring, until scrambled but still moist. Transfer egg mixture to bowl with chicken. Stir in raisins, if desired. Season with salt and pepper, and let cool.

4 In a food processor, pulse almonds until finely ground. Transfer to a small bowl, and add remaining ½ cup sugar and 1 teaspoon cinnamon; stir to combine.

5 On a clean work surface, unfold a sheet of phyllo with a short side facing you; keep remaining sheets covered with a damp kitchen towel while you work. Lightly brush phyllo with some melted butter; sprinkle with about one-sixth of almond mixture. Lay another phyllo sheet on top, and lightly brush with butter. Using a sharp knife, cut stack lengthwise and then crosswise into thirds to make nine equal rectangles.

6 Working with one rectangle at a time, place 1 tablespoon chicken mixture 1 inch from the end of a short side, leaving a ½-inch border on long sides. Fold ½ inch of long sides over filling. Starting from end with filling, roll phyllo into a log. Repeat process with remaining phyllo, butter, and almond mixture to make 54 logs. Brush logs with melted butter; arrange seam sides down on parchment-lined baking sheets.

7 Freeze (uncovered) until firm, about 1 hour. Transfer to large resealable plastic bags or airtight containers, and freeze until ready to use, up to 6 weeks.

8 To serve, preheat oven to 425°F. Arrange logs on parchment-lined baking sheets, and bake until golden brown and crisp, rotating sheets halfway through, 12 to 15 minutes. Let cool slightly. Serve dusted with sugar and cinnamon.

from Freezer Hors D'oeuvres

mushroom-polenta diamonds

MAKES ABOUT 5 DOZEN | PHOTO ON PAGE 317

You can use store-bought roasted red peppers for the garnish, if you like, or make your own: Place peppers directly over a gas burner or under the broiler until charred, turning as each side blackens. Transfer peppers to a bowl, and cover with plastic wrap; let steam about fifteen minutes. Using paper towels, rub off charred skins; remove seeds and ribs.

6 ounces shiitake mushrooms, stemmed and wiped clean
1 tablespoon unsalted butter, plus more for baking sheet
1 small onion, minced
2 tablespoons port or dry white wine
6 tablespoons heavy cream
1 teaspoon coarse salt, plus more for seasoning
   Freshly ground pepper
1 cup instant polenta
½ cup freshly grated Parmesan cheese (2 ounces)
2 roasted red bell peppers, cut into thin slivers, for garnish (optional)
   Mascarpone cheese, for garnish (optional)

1 In a food processor, pulse mushrooms until finely chopped. Melt butter in a medium skillet over medium heat. Add onion; cook, stirring occasionally, until softened, about 4 minutes.

Add mushrooms; cook, stirring, until softened, about 3 minutes. Add port, and stir until evaporated. Stir in cream, and simmer until mixture is thick, about 3 minutes. Season with salt and pepper. Remove from heat, and let cool.

2 Butter a 10-by-15-inch rimmed baking sheet. Bring 1 quart of water to a boil in a large saucepan; add 1 teaspoon salt. Whisking constantly, gradually add polenta in a steady stream. Reduce heat to a simmer; cook, whisking constantly, until polenta is soft and has absorbed all water, about 5 minutes. Stir in Parmesan. Transfer polenta to prepared baking sheet, spreading evenly with a small offset spatula. Let cool completely. Polenta can be made up to 1 day ahead; cover with plastic, and refrigerate until ready to proceed.

3 Halve polenta sheet crosswise. Transfer one half, smooth side down, to a clean work surface; spread mushroom mixture on top. Place remaining polenta half, smooth side up, on top of filling; trim edges with a sharp knife.

4 Cut sandwiched polenta lengthwise into ¾-inch-wide rows; cut rows at an angle to form 1-inch-long diamonds. Arrange diamonds on parchment-lined baking sheets. If not baking immediately, wrap tightly in plastic, and freeze until ready to use, up to 6 weeks.

5 To serve, preheat oven to 425°F. Transfer sheets to oven. Bake until diamonds are heated through, rotating sheets halfway through, 12 to 15 minutes. Garnish each diamond with a sliver of bell pepper and a dab of mascarpone, if desired. Serve immediately.

from Freezer Hors D'oeuvres

....

SALADS

....

arugula and bresaola salad with pumpernickel croutons

SERVES 4

  2 slices (½ inch thick) pumpernickel bread, torn into 1-inch pieces (2½ cups)
  2 tablespoons extra-virgin olive oil, plus more for drizzling
     Coarse salt and freshly ground pepper
  4 cups baby arugula, washed well (about 5 ounces)
1½ ounces Pecorino Romano cheese, thinly shaved
  8 thin slices bresaola or salami, torn into 1½-inch pieces
  2 tablespoons freshly squeezed lemon juice

1 Preheat oven to 325°F. In a small bowl, drizzle bread pieces with oil; season with salt and pepper. Toss to coat; spread out in a single layer on a rimmed baking sheet. Bake until slightly crisp, tossing once, about 7 minutes. Let cool.

2 Toss together arugula, cheese, and bresaola in a medium bowl. Drizzle with lemon juice and 2 tablespoons oil. Season with salt and pepper. Toss in croutons, and serve.

from What's for Dinner?

mixed green salad with date-walnut vinaigrette

SERVES 6 TO 8 | PHOTO ON PAGE 325

  1 cup walnut halves (4 ounces)
  5 ounces dates, pitted
  1 teaspoon Dijon mustard
  ½ cup cider vinegar
  ½ cup extra-virgin olive oil
     Coarse salt and freshly ground pepper
  1 head green-leaf lettuce (about 10 ounces)
  3 heads Belgian endive (about 12 ounces)
  1 bunch baby spinach, stemmed (about 4 ounces)
  1 head red Bibb lettuce

1 Preheat oven to 350°F. Spread walnuts in a single layer on a rimmed baking sheet; toast in oven until golden and fragrant, tossing occasionally, 10 to 12 minutes. Let cool.

2 In a food processor, pulse 5 dates, mustard, and vinegar until puréed. With machine running, slowly pour oil through the feed tube. Season with salt and pepper.

3 Quarter remaining dates lengthwise. In a large bowl, combine greens, quartered dates, and walnuts; drizzle with dressing, and toss to combine. Serve immediately.

from New England Open House

red-and-green salad with cranberry vinaigrette

SERVES 8

  1 head frisée (about 5 ounces)
  1 head red-leaf lettuce (about 10 ounces)
  1 bunch baby spinach, stemmed (4 ounces)
  ½ cup fresh or frozen (thawed) cranberries
  1 tablespoon raspberry vinegar
  2 teaspoons freshly squeezed lime juice
  1 teaspoon sugar
  ½ teaspoon coarse salt
  ¼ cup extra-virgin olive oil
  ¾ cup dried cranberries
1½ ounces manchego cheese

1 Tear frisée and red-leaf lettuce into bite-size pieces; combine with spinach in a large bowl. Set aside.

2 In a blender, combine cranberries, vinegar, lime juice, sugar, salt, and oil; purée until mixture becomes slightly thick.

3 Sprinkle dried cranberries over greens in bowl. Drizzle with cranberry dressing, and toss to combine. Divide salad among serving plates. Using a vegetable peeler, shave some cheese over the top of each salad, and serve.

PER SERVING: 140 CALORIES, 9 G FAT, 5 MG CHOLESTEROL, 15 G CARBOHYDRATE, 192 MG SODIUM, 3 G PROTEIN, 2 G FIBER

from Fit to Eat: Cranberries

....

MAIN COURSES

....

apricot pork tenderloin with cranberry black-pepper sauce

SERVES 4

1 tablespoon extra-virgin olive oil
1 pork tenderloin (1 to 1¼ pounds)
16 whole shallots, halved lengthwise with root intact, plus ⅓ cup coarsely chopped shallots for sauce (about 2)
1 jar (10 ounces) all-fruit apricot jam
½ cup low-sodium canned chicken broth
½ teaspoon coarse salt
1 cup fresh or frozen (thawed) cranberries
1½ tablespoons red-wine vinegar
½ teaspoon freshly ground pepper
1 teaspoon chopped fresh thyme, plus more for garnish

1 Preheat oven to 425°F. Heat oil in a large ovenproof skillet over medium-high heat until hot but not smoking. Add pork and halved shallots. Brown pork on all sides, turning occasionally, 6 to 8 minutes. Remove skillet from heat.

2 Brush pork with half the jam, then drizzle 2 tablespoons stock over shallots. Transfer to oven. Roast, turning shallots occasionally, until an instant-read thermometer inserted into center of pork registers 155°F, 30 to 35 minutes.

3 Remove skillet from oven. Using tongs, transfer pork and shallots to a plate; let pork rest until ready to slice (pork will continue to cook slightly; temperature should reach 160°F).

4 Place skillet over medium-high heat, and stir in remaining chopped shallots. Immediately sprinkle with salt; add remaining jam and 6 tablespoons stock. Deglaze pan, stirring up browned bits from bottom with a wooden spoon; add cranberries, vinegar, and pepper. Cook until berries are soft and juicy, about 5 minutes. Stir in thyme.

5 Slice pork into rounds, and divide among plates; garnish with thyme. Serve with cranberry sauce and roasted shallots.

PER SERVING: 415 CALORIES, 8 G FAT, 83 MG CHOLESTEROL, 59 G CARBOHYDRATE, 397 MG SODIUM, 29 G PROTEIN, 3 G FIBER

from Fit to Eat: Cranberries

cranberry-stuffed cornish hens with port sauce

SERVES 6

8 ounces rye bread (about ½ loaf), trimmed of crust
½ tablespoon extra-virgin olive oil
1 small leek, white and pale-green parts only, halved lengthwise and thinly sliced into half-moons, washed well
3 ounces shiitake mushrooms, stemmed, wiped clean, and coarsely chopped
1 garlic clove, finely chopped
1 teaspoon coarse salt
1 tablespoon chopped fresh sage, plus more for garnish
1 tablespoon chopped fresh flat-leaf parsley
½ teaspoon dry mustard
½ teaspoon dried thyme
¾ cup dried cranberries
¾ cup reduced-fat, low-sodium canned chicken broth
6 Cornish game hens (about 1½ pounds each)
1 tablespoon unsalted butter, room temperature
¼ teaspoon freshly ground pepper
½ cup port

1 Preheat oven to 350°F. Cut bread into ¼-inch dice. Spread out in a single layer on a rimmed baking sheet; toast in oven until lightly browned and dry, tossing occasionally, 10 to 12 minutes. Remove from oven; set aside.

2 Raise oven heat to 450°F. In a large nonstick skillet, heat oil over medium-high heat until hot but not smoking. Add leek, mushrooms, garlic, and ½ teaspoon salt. Cook, stirring occasionally, until leek and mushrooms have softened, about 2 minutes. Transfer to a large bowl; stir in bread, sage, parsley, mustard, thyme, ½ cup dried cranberries, and ½ cup stock.

3 Spoon stuffing into bird cavities; tie legs together with kitchen twine. Rub birds with butter, then sprinkle with pepper and remaining ½ teaspoon salt.

4 Arrange birds on a roasting rack in a large roasting pan. Roast until golden brown, about 30 minutes. Reduce oven heat to 350°F; continue roasting until an instant-read thermometer inserted into thighs (avoiding bone) registers 170°F, 15 to 20 minutes more. Transfer rack with birds to a rimmed baking sheet, and let rest until ready to serve.

5 Set roasting pan on top of stove across two burners, and place over medium-high heat. Pour port and remaining ¼ cup stock into pan; deglaze pan, scraping up any browned bits from bottom with a wooden spoon. Add remaining ¼ cup dried cranberries; continue cooking until sauce reduces slightly, 2 to 3 minutes. Transfer sauce to a bowl.

6 Place birds on a serving platter, and garnish with more sage, if desired. Drizzle sauce over birds, and serve.

PER SERVING: 487 CALORIES, 13 G FAT, 223 MG CHOLESTEROL, 36 G CARBOHYDRATE, 759 MG SODIUM, 53 G PROTEIN, 3 G FIBER

from Fit to Eat: Cranberries

Juki's short ribs

SERVES 8

Beef short ribs, also known as flanken, become very tender when braised. Each rib should be about five inches long and about one and a half inches thick, with three short bones. You can serve the meat with the bones (it should be falling from them anyway) or remove the bones for a neater presentation. This dish is best made one or two days ahead of time, which makes it convenient for entertaining.

- ¾ cup all-purpose flour
- 8 beef short ribs (about 6 pounds)
- Coarse salt and freshly ground pepper
- 2 tablespoons chicken fat or olive oil
- 3½ tablespoons finely chopped fresh rosemary, plus more for garnish
- 2 large onions, cut into ½-inch pieces
- 2 large carrots, cut into ½-inch pieces
- 2 stalks celery, cut into ½-inch pieces
- 1½ cups dry red wine
- 2 cups Basic Beef Stock (page 18) or low-sodium canned beef stock or water
- 1 teaspoon Worcestershire sauce
- Freshly grated or prepared horseradish, for serving (optional)

1 Place flour in a shallow bowl. Season ribs with salt and pepper, then dredge in flour, shaking off excess. Heat 1 tablespoon fat in a large Dutch oven over medium-high heat until hot but not smoking. Add half the ribs, being careful not to crowd pot; sprinkle with half the rosemary. Brown ribs very well on all sides, 5 to 7 minutes total. Transfer ribs to a plate. Repeat with remaining ribs, tablespoon fat, and rosemary.

2 Add onions, carrots, and celery to pot; season with salt and pepper. Cook over medium heat, stirring frequently, until vegetables are golden brown, about 15 minutes.

3 Add wine, and bring to a boil; deglaze pan, scraping up browned bits from bottom with a wooden spoon. Add stock and Worcestershire sauce; return to a boil. Return ribs to pot; add just enough water to cover ribs, if necessary. Cover; simmer over very low heat until meat is very tender and falling off the bone, about 2 hours. Let cool completely, then refrigerate, covered, until ready to proceed.

4 About 1 hour before serving, skim fat from surface of mixture. If desired, remove meat from bones; return meat to pot. Bring to a simmer; cook until meat is heated through, about 20 minutes. Using a slotted spoon, transfer meat to a plate.

5 Raise heat to medium-high; reduce liquid, stirring occasionally, until slightly thickened, 20 to 25 minutes. Return meat to pot; cook until just heated through. Garnish with rosemary; serve with some horseradish on the side, if desired.

from Hanukkah

roasted turkey breast with fennel-herb stuffing

SERVES 6 TO 8 | **PHOTOS ON PAGES 324 AND 325**

This recipe can be doubled or tripled to serve larger groups.

- 4 tablespoons unsalted butter
- 1 yellow onion, finely chopped
- 2 garlic cloves, minced
- 1 small bulb fennel, trimmed and finely chopped
- 11 slices (½ inch thick) country bread, trimmed of crusts and cut into ½-inch cubes (about 5 cups)
- 1 tablespoon fresh thyme leaves
- 2 tablespoons coarsely chopped fresh rosemary, plus sprigs for garnish
- ½ cup coarsely chopped fresh flat-leaf parsley
- 2¼ to 3¼ cups Basic Chicken Stock (page 17) or low-sodium canned chicken broth
- Coarse salt and freshly ground pepper
- 1 whole boneless turkey breast (6 pounds)
- 2 tablespoons extra-virgin olive oil
- 1 blood orange, thinly sliced, for garnish (optional)

1 Melt butter in a large skillet over medium heat. Add onion and garlic; cook, stirring occasionally, until onion is soft and translucent, about 4 minutes. Add fennel, and cook, stirring, until tender, about 4 minutes. Transfer mixture to a large bowl. Stir in bread, thyme, rosemary, parsley, and 1¼ cups stock. Season with salt and pepper. Set stuffing aside.

2 Preheat oven to 375°F. Place turkey, skin side down, on a clean work surface. Using a sharp knife, remove tenderloins. To butterfly turkey, slice vertically through right side of breast, starting at thickest part and slicing almost to edge without cutting through (it should resemble a book, with a flap in the center). Spread open; gently press down to flatten. Repeat on left side. Cover with plastic wrap. Using a meat mallet or heavy skillet, pound meat until uniform in thickness.

3 Season turkey with salt and pepper, then spread stuffing down center lengthwise. Fold both sides of turkey over stuffing. Using kitchen twine, tie turkey at 1-inch intervals to completely encase stuffing and form a long cylinder.

4 Transfer turkey to a roasting rack in a roasting pan. Pour 1 cup stock into bottom of pan. Brush turkey with oil, and season with salt and pepper. Roast, basting with pan juices every 30 minutes (add remaining cup stock if pan gets too dry), until well browned and an instant-read thermometer inserted into thickest part of turkey registers 165°F, about 1¾ hours. If skin begins to get too dark, tent pan with foil. Transfer turkey to a carving board, and let rest 20 minutes before slicing. Garnish with orange slices, if desired.

from New England Open House

roasted wild striped bass

SERVES 4

This recipe calls for the stalks and fronds of two bulbs of fennel. If desired, reserve the bulbs to make Orange-Braised Fennel (page 297); substitute one-half cup of the cooking juices remaining in the roasting pan for the white wine called for below.

2 **bulbs fennel**

1 **cup dry white wine**

1¾ **pounds wild striped bass fillets (each about 1 to 1½ inches thick)**

1 **tablespoon extra-virgin olive oil**

Coarse salt and freshly ground pepper

1 Preheat oven to 450°F. Remove stalks from fennel bulbs; reserve bulbs for another use. Remove feathery fronds from stalks; chop, and reserve for garnish. Using a sharp knife, halve stalks lengthwise. Arrange stalks in the bottom of a 9-by-13-inch roasting pan; pour wine over stalks. Lay fish fillets on top; drizzle with oil, and season with salt and pepper.

2 Cover pan tightly with foil. Bake until fish is just cooked through and opaque throughout, 20 to 25 minutes. Transfer fish fillets to serving plates, discarding fennel stalks. Garnish with reserved fennel fronds.

from What's for Dinner?

smoked Vermont-maple-glazed ham

SERVES 15 TO 20 | **PHOTOS ON PAGES 324 AND 325**

Remove the ham from the refrigerator one to two hours before baking to let it come fully to room temperature.

1 **smoked bone-in ham (10 to 12 pounds), room temperature**

½ **cup apricot jam**

2 **tablespoons Dijon mustard**

¾ **cup pure maple syrup**

2 **tablespoons dark rum**

1 **garlic clove, minced**

Fresh bay leaves, for garnish (optional)

Kumquats, for garnish (optional)

1 Preheat oven to 350°F. Place ham on a roasting rack in a large roasting pan. Cover tightly with foil. Bake 4 hours, rotating pan halfway through.

2 Meanwhile, make glaze: In a small saucepan, heat jam until liquefied. Strain through a fine sieve into a small bowl; discard solids. Stir in mustard, maple syrup, rum, and garlic.

3 After 4 hours, remove ham from oven, and brush with glaze. Continue baking, glazing every 15 minutes, until an instant-read thermometer inserted into thickest part of ham (avoiding bone) registers 140°F, about 1 hour more. Remove ham from oven; transfer to a carving board or platter. Garnish with bay leaves and kumquats, if desired. Slice thinly around bone, and serve hot or at room temperature.

from New England Open House

barley pilaf with pearl onions

SERVES 8

This pilaf is perfect for soaking up the rich juices from Juki's Short Ribs (page 294). You can substitute frozen pearl onions for fresh, if you like, and skip step one.

10 ounces white pearl onions (about 2 cups)
 1 tablespoon chicken fat, margarine, or unsalted butter
 2 cups pearl barley
 1 quart Basic Chicken Stock (page 17) or low-sodium canned chicken broth, plus more if needed
    Coarse salt and freshly ground pepper

1 Bring a large saucepan of water to a boil. Add onions, and blanch until skins loosen, about 1 minute. Drain in a colander, and rinse with cold water. Peel onions, and set aside.

2 Heat fat in a large saucepan over medium-low heat until hot but not smoking. Add barley, and cook, stirring frequently, until browned and fragrant, 15 to 20 minutes.

3 Add stock and reserved onions to saucepan. Bring to a boil, then reduce heat to a simmer. Season with salt and pepper. Cover pan, and cook until barley is tender but chewy, and has absorbed all the liquid, about 40 minutes; if all liquid is absorbed and barley is not done, add a few tablespoons stock or water, and continue cooking. Serve hot.

from Hanukkah

butternut-squash crumble

SERVES 8 | **PHOTOS ON PAGES 324 AND 325**

You can make this recipe through step two up to one day in advance; refrigerate, covered with plastic wrap. The crumb topping can also be made one day in advance; store in an airtight container in the refrigerator.

¾ cup (1½ sticks) chilled unsalted butter, cut into ½-inch pieces, plus more for dish
 3 tablespoons extra-virgin olive oil
 3 small butternut squash (about 4 pounds), peeled and cut into ¾-inch chunks
    Coarse salt and freshly ground pepper
 2 large shallots, thinly sliced
 ¼ cup coarsely chopped fresh flat-leaf parsley
 ½ cup Basic Chicken Stock (page 17) or low-sodium canned chicken broth
1½ cups all-purpose flour
 ¾ teaspoon sugar
 2 tablespoons fresh thyme leaves
 1 teaspoon table salt
 2 large egg yolks
 3 or 4 tablespoons ice water

1 Preheat oven to 375°F. Generously butter a 9-by-2-inch square baking dish; set aside. Heat 1 tablespoon oil in a large skillet over medium-high heat. Add half the squash, and season with coarse salt and pepper. Cook, stirring occasionally, until well browned, 8 to 10 minutes. Transfer to prepared dish. Repeat with another tablespoon oil and remaining squash.

2 Reduce heat to medium; add remaining tablespoon oil and the shallots to skillet. Cook, stirring frequently, until shallots are lightly browned, 3 to 5 minutes. Transfer shallots to baking dish along with parsley and stock; stir well to combine. Cover dish tightly with foil; bake, stirring occasionally, until squash is just tender, about 30 minutes.

3 Meanwhile, place flour, sugar, thyme, and table salt in a food processor; pulse to combine. Add butter, and process until mixture resembles coarse meal. Whisk together yolks and 3 tablespoons ice water in a small bowl; add to flour mixture. Pulse until mixture forms pea-size crumbs. If dough is too dry, add remaining tablespoon ice water.

4 Remove squash from oven. Arrange crumb mixture on top. Return to oven, and bake until topping is golden brown and squash is very tender, about 30 minutes. Transfer to a wire rack to cool slightly. Serve warm or at room temperature.

from New England Open House

green beans with panfried shiitake mushrooms

SERVES 6 TO 8 | PHOTOS ON PAGES 324 AND 325

Coarse salt

1½ pounds green beans, stem ends trimmed

½ cup extra-virgin olive oil, plus more as needed

¾ pound shiitake mushrooms, stemmed, wiped clean, and thinly sliced

Freshly ground pepper

1 Bring a large saucepan of water to a boil; add salt. Prepare an ice bath; set aside. Working in two batches, cook green beans in boiling water until crisp-tender, 3 to 5 minutes. Using a slotted spoon, plunge beans into ice bath to stop the cooking. Drain, and pat dry; set aside.

2 Heat oil in a large skillet over high heat until hot but not smoking. Working in batches so as not to crowd skillet, add mushrooms; season with salt and pepper. Cook, stirring frequently, until golden and crisp, 2 to 3 minutes. Using a slotted spoon, transfer mushrooms to paper towels to drain. Add more oil as needed for subsequent batches.

3 Reduce heat to medium. Add beans; season with salt and pepper. Cook, tossing, until beans are heated through, about 3 minutes. Transfer to a large serving dish. Add mushrooms; toss to combine. Serve warm or at room temperature.

from New England Open House

orange-braised fennel

SERVES 4 | PHOTO ON PAGE 329

2 bulbs fennel, trimmed

1 tablespoon unsalted butter

1 tablespoon extra-virgin olive oil

1½ cups freshly squeezed orange juice (about 3 oranges)

Coarse salt and freshly ground pepper

½ cup dry white wine

1 With a large knife, cut fennel bulbs lengthwise into eight slices. In a large skillet over medium heat, heat butter and oil until sizzling. Lay fennel slices in pan, and cook until browned, about 6 minutes. Turn slices; cook until other sides are browned, about 5 minutes more.

2 Pour orange juice over fennel; season with salt and pepper. Bring mixture to a boil, then reduce heat to a simmer. Cook until fennel is tender, about 15 minutes. Add wine, and continue cooking until fennel is very tender and sauce has thickened, about 10 minutes more. Season with salt and pepper.

from What's for Dinner?

pickled red-cabbage slaw

SERVES 8

We like to serve this slaw with Juki's Short Ribs (page 294).

1 small head red cabbage (about 2¼ pounds)

½ cup red-wine vinegar

1 tablespoon sugar

Coarse salt and freshly ground pepper

3 tablespoons olive oil

2 tablespoons poppy seeds

1 Quarter cabbage, and discard core. Shred cabbage as finely as possible with a sharp knife. Transfer to a large bowl.

2 In a small bowl, stir together vinegar and sugar until sugar has dissolved. Season with salt and pepper. Whisking constantly, add oil in a slow, steady stream. Drizzle vinaigrette over cabbage; toss to combine. Let stand loosely covered, tossing occasionally, 1 to 2 hours at room temperature. Just before serving, sprinkle with poppy seeds.

from Hanukkah

Talia's favorite latkes

SERVES 8; MAKES 2 DOZEN | PHOTO ON PAGE 317

This recipe can easily be doubled or tripled.

2 tablespoons all-purpose flour

3 tablespoons plain breadcrumbs

¾ teaspoon coarse salt, plus more for seasoning

¼ teaspoon freshly ground pepper

2 large eggs, lightly beaten

3 pounds russet potatoes

1 onion, grated on the large holes of a box grater

Peanut oil, for frying

Chunky Applesauce, for serving (optional; page 298)

Sour cream, for serving (optional)

1 In a medium bowl, combine flour, breadcrumbs, salt, pepper, and eggs. Mix well with a fork, and set aside.

2 Fill a large bowl with cold water. Peel half the potatoes, and grate on the small holes of a box grater, transferring potatoes to cold water as you work to prevent discoloration. Repeat process with remaining potatoes, grating on the large holes.

3 Line a colander with a clean kitchen towel, and set in sink. Using a slotted spoon, transfer potatoes to colander; add onion. Fold towel over mixture, then press down to squeeze out most of the liquid. Wring potatoes and onion in towel until they are as dry as possible; transfer to a large bowl.

4 Add reserved egg mixture to potatoes and onions, and mix well. Using your hands, form into 3- to 4-inch patties (some additional liquid may seep out).

5 In a medium nonstick skillet, heat ¼ inch oil over medium-high heat until a drop of potato mixture added to the skillet sizzles upon contact. Reduce heat to medium. Working in batches so as not to crowd skillet, carefully add latkes to hot oil. Fry latkes, turning once, until deep golden brown on both sides, 2 to 3 minutes per side. Transfer cooked latkes to paper towels to drain, then season with salt. Serve warm with applesauce and sour cream, as desired.

from Hanukkah

chunky applesauce
MAKES 2 CUPS

Using a combination of McIntosh and Granny Smith apples will ensure the right texture—the McIntosh will break down and become saucy, while the Grannies will stay chunky.

2 Granny Smith apples (about ¾ pound)
3 McIntosh apples (about 1 pound)
1 tablespoon margarine or unsalted butter
½ teaspoon ground cinnamon
3 tablespoons sugar

Peel, core, and cut apples into ¾-inch chunks. Melt margarine in a medium saucepan over medium-low heat. Add apples, cinnamon, sugar, and 2 tablespoons water. Cook, stirring occasionally, until apples are tender, about 10 minutes. Serve warm or chilled. Sauce can be refrigerated in an airtight container up to 2 days.

banana-pecan cake
MAKES 1 SIX-INCH CAKE | **PHOTO ON PAGE 331**

4 tablespoons unsalted butter, room temperature, plus more for pan
1 cup sifted cake flour (not self-rising), plus more for pan
½ teaspoon baking soda
¼ teaspoon baking powder
¼ teaspoon salt
¼ teaspoon ground cinnamon
Pinch of ground cloves
1 very ripe large banana, mashed (about ½ cup)
¼ cup buttermilk
½ teaspoon pure vanilla extract
½ cup packed dark-brown sugar
1 large egg
⅓ cup chopped toasted pecans
Confectioners' sugar, for dusting

1 Preheat oven to 350°F. Butter a 6-by-2-inch professional round cake pan. Line bottom with parchment paper; butter parchment, and dust with flour, tapping out excess. Set aside. Into a medium bowl, sift together flour, baking soda, baking powder, salt, cinnamon, and cloves. Set aside. In a small bowl, whisk together banana, buttermilk, and vanilla.

2 In the bowl of an electric mixer fitted with the paddle attachment, cream butter and brown sugar on medium speed until light and fluffy. Beat in egg. With mixer on low speed, add flour mixture in two batches, alternating with two batches of the banana mixture, scraping down sides of bowl with a rubber spatula after each batch. Mix until well combined. Beat in pecans.

3 Pour batter into pan; smooth top with an offset spatula. Bake until golden brown and a cake tester inserted in the center comes out clean, about 45 minutes. Transfer pan to a wire rack; let cool 10 minutes. Run a small knife around edge of cake to loosen; invert cake onto rack, and peel off parchment. Reinvert cake, top side up, and let cool completely. Just before serving, dust with confectioners' sugar.

from What's for Dinner?

chocolate-raspberry thumbprints

MAKES ABOUT 4½ DOZEN

¼ recipe Basic Sugar-Cookie Dough (recipe follows)
3½ ounces bittersweet chocolate, melted
4 ounces walnuts, finely chopped (1 cup)
⅓ cup seedless raspberry jam, warmed

1 Preheat oven to 350°F. Place dough in the bowl of an electric mixer fitted with the paddle attachment. Drizzle dough with chocolate; mix until just combined.

2 Place walnuts in a shallow dish. Form dough into 1-inch balls; roll balls in nuts, coating completely. Place balls on parchment-lined baking sheets. Use your thumb to make an indentation in center of each ball. Chill 20 minutes.

3 Bake cookies until firm to the touch, rotating sheets halfway through, 12 to 16 minutes. Remove from oven. Using the handle of a wooden spoon, press indentation of each cookie to redefine shape; fill each with about ¼ teaspoon jam. Transfer to a wire rack; let cool completely. Store cookies in an airtight container at room temperature up to 5 days.

from Holiday Cookies

basic sugar-cookie dough

MAKES ENOUGH FOR 4 BATCHES OF SUGAR COOKIES

2 cups (4 sticks) unsalted butter, room temperature
2 cups sugar
2 large eggs
2 tablespoons pure vanilla extract
2 teaspoons salt
5 cups all-purpose flour

1 In the bowl of an electric mixer fitted with the paddle attachment, cream butter and sugar on medium speed until light and fluffy. Add eggs, vanilla, and salt; beat until combined. Add flour, 1 cup at a time, mixing on low speed until incorporated before adding more.

2 Divide dough into four equal pieces. Place each on a piece of plastic wrap; flatten into disks. Wrap in plastic; refrigerate until firm, at least 2 hours or up to 1 week.

coconut-cranberry cookies

MAKES 3 DOZEN | **PHOTO ON PAGE 332**

3 cups all-purpose flour
1 teaspoon baking powder
¼ teaspoon salt
1½ cups (3 sticks) unsalted butter, room temperature
1¾ cups sugar
2 teaspoons pure vanilla extract
Grated zest of 1 navel orange
1½ cups dried cranberries
1½ cups sweetened shredded coconut

1 Preheat oven to 350°F. Line two baking sheets with parchment paper; set aside. In a medium bowl, whisk together flour, baking powder, and salt; set aside.

2 In the bowl of an electric mixer fitted with the paddle attachment, beat butter, sugar, vanilla, and orange zest on medium speed until creamy and light. Add flour mixture, and beat on medium-low speed until mixture comes together to form a dough. Beat in cranberries and coconut.

3 Shape dough into 1¼-inch balls; place 2 inches apart on prepared baking sheets. Flatten each ball slightly. Bake until edges begin to brown, rotating baking sheets halfway through, 15 to 17 minutes. Let cool on baking sheets 5 minutes, then transfer to wire racks to cool completely.

from New England Open House

cranberry-vanilla compote with orange ice

SERVES 6

2 cups freshly squeezed orange juice (3 to 4 oranges)
¼ cup freshly squeezed lemon juice (2 to 3 lemons)
2 tablespoons orange-flavored liqueur
½ cup plus 1 tablespoon sugar
3 navel oranges
1 vanilla bean, split lengthwise and scraped
1 whole cinnamon stick
2 cups fresh or frozen (thawed) cranberries

1 Make orange ice: In a large bowl, combine orange juice, lemon juice, liqueur, and 1 tablespoon sugar. Stir until sugar is dissolved. Pour mixture into a 9-by-13-inch baking dish or pan. Cover with plastic wrap; freeze until firm, about 3 hours.

2 Using a vegetable peeler, remove zest from 1 orange, leaving white pith behind; slice into long thin strips, and set

aside. Use a paring knife to peel pith from orange; discard pith, and set flesh aside.

3 Make candied zest: Heat ½ cup water and remaining ½ cup sugar in a medium saucepan over medium-high heat, stirring until sugar dissolves. Add reserved orange zest; bring to a simmer. Cook 2 minutes. Using a slotted spoon, transfer zest to a bowl; set aside.

4 Reduce heat to medium; add vanilla bean and scrapings and the cinnamon stick. Bring to a simmer; add cranberries. Cook until cranberries burst and mixture thickens to a sauce, 6 to 8 minutes. Remove from heat; let cool. Remove and discard vanilla pod and cinnamon stick.

5 Working over a bowl to catch the juices, peel remaining 2 oranges with a paring knife, following the curve of the fruit. Cut between sections of these oranges and reserved orange to remove segments. Squeeze juice from membranes into bowl; roughly chop segments. Add oranges and juice to cranberry mixture. Transfer to a bowl; cover with plastic wrap, and chill until ready to serve, up to 2 days.

6 Using a fork, scrape orange ice to create a slush. Spoon into serving dishes; top with cranberry compote. Garnish with candied orange zest, and serve immediately.

PER SERVING: 167 CALORIES, 0 G FAT, 0 MG CHOLESTEROL, 39 G CARBOHYDRATE, 3 MG SODIUM, 1 G PROTEIN, 3 G FIBER

from Fit to Eat: Cranberries

eggnog mousse

SERVES 8 TO 10 | **PHOTO ON PAGE 333**

We like to serve this mousse with assorted toppings, such as whipped cream, chopped toasted nuts, and crushed peppermint candies, in addition to the caramel. You can also dust each serving with cocoa powder, cinnamon, or nutmeg.

3 **tablespoons dark rum**
3 **tablespoons brandy**
1 **envelope unflavored gelatin (1 scant tablespoon)**
3 **large eggs, separated**
1 **cup sugar**
2 **cups heavy cream**
1 **teaspoon ground cinnamon**
½ **teaspoon freshly grated nutmeg**
⅛ **teaspoon ground cloves**
2 **teaspoons pure vanilla extract**
   Coffee Caramel, for serving (recipe follows)

1 Combine rum and brandy in a small bowl. Sprinkle with gelatin, and let soften, about 5 minutes.

2 Meanwhile, combine egg yolks and ½ cup sugar in a medium heatproof bowl set over a pan of simmering water; whisk constantly until mixture is pale and fluffy, about 2 minutes. Remove bowl from heat; whisk in gelatin mixture.

3 Return bowl to pan; cook, whisking constantly, until gelatin has dissolved, about 3 minutes. Remove from heat; scrape down sides of bowl, and refrigerate, stirring frequently, until cooled slightly, 2 to 3 minutes.

4 In the bowl of an electric mixer, combine remaining ½ cup sugar with the cream, cinnamon, nutmeg, cloves, and vanilla. Whisk until stiff peaks form. Fold one-third of cream mixture into gelatin mixture, then gently fold mixture into remaining cream mixture. Refrigerate while preparing egg whites (no more than 5 minutes).

5 In a clean mixing bowl, whisk egg whites until stiff peaks form. Gently fold into cream mixture. Transfer to a serving dish; cover, and chill until firm, at least 30 minutes or overnight. Serve chilled, sprinkled with caramel.

Note: Raw eggs should not be used in food prepared for pregnant women, babies, young children, the elderly, or anyone whose health is compromised.

from Dessert of the Month

coffee caramel

MAKES 1 CUP

1½ **cups sugar**
2 **teaspoons pure coffee extract**
   Vegetable-oil cooking spray

1 Coat a rimmed baking sheet with cooking spray, wiping off any excess with a paper towel; set aside. Coat a metal spatula with cooking spray; set aside.

2 Combine sugar and ¼ cup water in a medium, heavy-bottom saucepan. Cover, and bring to a boil over high heat; cook until sugar has dissolved. Remove lid; reduce heat to medium. Continue cooking, swirling pan occasionally, until mixture registers 300°F on a candy thermometer. Remove pan from heat, and stir in extract (it will spatter). Pour mixture onto prepared baking sheet. Working quickly, spread mixture into a thin layer with oiled spatula. Let cool completely, at least 15 minutes.

3 Break brittle into pieces, and place in a food processor. Process until finely chopped. Store caramel in an airtight container at room temperature up to 1 week.

frosted fruitcake with meringue mushrooms

MAKES 1 TEN-INCH CAKE | **PHOTO ON PAGE 334**

8 ounces dried apricots, chopped into small pieces (1⅓ cups)

8 ounces dried figs, chopped into small pieces (1½ cups)

8 ounces dates, pitted and chopped into small pieces (1¼ cups)

¼ cup Frangelico or other nut-flavored liqueur

¾ cup all-purpose flour

1½ teaspoons baking powder

½ teaspoon salt

4 tablespoons unsalted butter, room temperature

½ cup packed light-brown sugar

¼ cup granulated sugar

3 large eggs

2 tablespoons honey

1½ teaspoons pure vanilla extract

½ pound hazelnuts (about 2 cups), toasted, skinned, and coarsely chopped

½ recipe Seven-Minute Frosting (page 104)

Meringue Mushrooms (recipe follows)

Vegetable-oil cooking spray

1   Preheat oven to 300°F. Coat a 10-inch springform pan with cooking spray. Line bottom with parchment paper; spray parchment, and set aside. In a medium bowl, toss apricots, figs, and dates with liqueur; set aside. In another bowl, whisk together flour, baking powder, and salt; set aside.

2   In the bowl of an electric mixer fitted with the paddle attachment, cream butter and sugars on medium speed until light and fluffy. Add eggs one at a time, beating until incorporated after each. Beat in honey and vanilla. Add flour mixture; beat until just combined. Stir in dried-fruit mixture and nuts.

3   Spread batter in prepared pan, and bake until a cake tester inserted in center comes out clean, about 1¼ hours; if cake starts to brown too quickly, cover loosely with foil. Transfer to a wire rack; let cool in pan 30 minutes, then remove ring, and let cool completely.

4   Spread frosting over cake, smoothing top and creating swirls on sides. Decorate top with mushrooms.

from Woodland Sweets

meringue mushrooms

MAKES ABOUT 3 DOZEN

For a crop of "mushrooms" in realistic hues, we tinted some of the meringue with varying amounts of cocoa powder.

Swiss Meringue (page 101)

3 tablespoons unsweetened cocoa powder, sifted

2 ounces bittersweet chocolate, finely chopped

3 ounces white chocolate, finely chopped

1   Preheat oven to 200°F. Line two rimmed baking sheets with parchment paper; set aside. Divide meringue among three small bowls. Set one aside. Fold 1 tablespoon cocoa into second portion; fold remaining 2 tablespoons cocoa into third. Place each portion in an 18-inch pastry bag fitted with a large round tip. Pipe domes, ½ to 2 inches in diameter, onto prepared baking sheets; flatten tips with a damp finger. Pipe stems onto baking sheets, making one for each cap.

2   Bake 1 hour, then reduce oven temperature to 175°F. Continue baking until meringues are completely dry to the touch but not browned, 45 to 60 minutes.

3   Melt bittersweet chocolate in a small heatproof bowl over a pan of simmering water, stirring occasionally. Using a small offset spatula, spread bottoms of caps with a thin layer of dark chocolate; let set. Melt white chocolate in another bowl. Let cool until thickened; spread over dark chocolate. Use a toothpick to draw lines from center to edge of caps. Let set.

4   Using a paring knife, make a small hole in center of each coated cap. Dip one end of stems in remaining white chocolate; insert into holes. Let set. Store in an airtight container in a cool, dry place up to 1 week.

ginger cheesecake bars

MAKES ABOUT 4 DOZEN | **PHOTO ON PAGE 332**

12 ounces gingersnaps (about 47 cookies)

4 tablespoons unsalted butter, melted

12 ounces cream cheese, room temperature

¾ cup sugar

1 large whole egg

1 large egg yolk

3 tablespoons sour cream

¾ teaspoon pure vanilla extract

2 tablespoons finely chopped crystallized ginger

Vegetable-oil cooking spray

1   Preheat oven to 350°F. Coat a 9-by-13-inch rimmed baking sheet with cooking spray; set aside. Place gingersnaps in a food processor; pulse to a powder. Transfer to a small bowl,

and stir in butter until well combined. Press gingersnap mixture evenly into bottom of prepared baking sheet. Bake until firm, about 12 minutes. Let cool completely.

2   Meanwhile, in the bowl of an electric mixer fitted with the paddle attachment, beat cream cheese until smooth and softened. Beat in sugar, egg, egg yolk, sour cream, and vanilla until well combined. Beat in crystallized ginger.

3   Pour cream-cheese mixture onto crust, and spread evenly to edges. Bake, rotating baking sheet halfway through, until filling has puffed and feels slightly firm to the touch (don't let it brown), about 25 minutes. Transfer to a wire rack to cool completely. Refrigerate, covered with plastic wrap, until chilled and set, at least 1 hour and up to 2 days. To serve, cut into bars with a serrated knife.

from New England Open House

Hawaiian snowballs

MAKES ABOUT 4 DOZEN

 1 cup roasted, salted macadamia nuts, finely chopped
⅔ cup finely chopped dried pineapple
¼ recipe Basic Sugar-Cookie Dough (page 299)
    Confectioners' sugar, for dusting

1   Preheat oven to 350°F. Line baking sheets with parchment paper; set aside. On a clean work surface, toss nuts with dried fruit. Sprinkle over dough, and knead until just blended.

2   Form dough into 1-inch balls; place 2 inches apart on prepared baking sheets. Bake, rotating sheets halfway through, until barely golden around edges, about 15 minutes. Transfer cookies to a wire rack to cool completely. Dust with sugar. Store in airtight containers at room temperature up to 5 days.

from Holiday Cookies

maple-pecan shortbread

MAKES ABOUT 2 DOZEN | **PHOTO ON PAGE 332**

Turbinado sugar, which has a golden color, can be found in many supermarkets; sanding sugar is a fine substitute.

2¼ cups all-purpose flour, plus more for work surface
 ½ cup cake flour (not self-rising)
 ½ teaspoon salt
 ¾ cup pecan halves, finely chopped
  1 cup (2 sticks) unsalted butter, room temperature
 ¾ cup granulated sugar
 ¼ cup pure maple syrup
  1 large egg yolk
 ¼ teaspoon pure maple extract
  1 large whole egg, lightly beaten
     Turbinado sugar, for sprinkling

1   Preheat oven to 350°F. Line a baking sheet with parchment paper; set aside. Into a medium bowl, sift together flours and salt. Whisk in ½ cup chopped pecans; set aside.

2   In the bowl of an electric mixer fitted with the paddle attachment, cream butter and sugar on medium speed until smooth and light, about 1 minute. Add maple syrup, egg yolk, and extract; beat until well combined. With mixer on low, gradually add flour mixture, beating until just combined. Dough should be smooth and pliable. Flatten dough into a disk. Wrap in plastic; chill until firm, 1½ hours or overnight.

3   On a lightly floured work surface, roll out dough to ¼ inch thick. Cut out rounds using a 2-inch cookie cutter; place rounds 1 inch apart on prepared baking sheet. Brush tops with beaten egg; sprinkle centers with remaining ¼ cup pecans. Sprinkle entire surface with turbinado sugar.

4   Bake cookies until golden around the edges, rotating baking sheet halfway through, 10 to 12 minutes. Transfer cookies to a wire rack to cool completely. Store in an airtight container at room temperature up to 4 days.

from New England Open House

marshmallow snowflakes

MAKES ABOUT 100

Float these snowflakes in hot chocolate.

  2 envelopes unflavored gelatin (each 1 scant tablespoon)
1½ cups sugar
 ⅔ cup light corn syrup
 ⅛ teaspoon salt
  1 teaspoon pure vanilla extract
     Vegetable-oil cooking spray

1 Coat a 12-by-17-inch rimmed baking sheet with cooking spray; line with parchment paper. Spray parchment; set aside. Pour ⅓ cup cold water into the bowl of an electric mixer. Sprinkle with gelatin; let soften, about 5 minutes.

2 Place sugar, corn syrup, salt, and ⅓ cup water in a medium saucepan. Cover; bring to a boil over high heat. Remove lid; cook, swirling pan occasionally, until syrup reaches 238°F (soft-ball stage) on a candy thermometer, about 5 minutes.

3 Attach bowl with gelatin mixture to mixer fitted with the paddle attachment. With mixer on low speed, slowly pour syrup in a steady stream down side of bowl. Gradually raise speed to high; beat until mixture is thick, white, and has almost tripled in volume, about 12 minutes. Add vanilla; beat 30 seconds to incorporate.

4 Pour mixture onto prepared baking sheet; smooth with an offset spatula. Let stand at room temperature, uncovered, until firm, at least 3 hours or overnight.

5 Lightly coat a 2-inch snowflake-shaped cookie cutter with cooking spray, and cut out marshmallows, coating with more spray as needed. Serve immediately or store in an airtight container at room temperature up to 1 week.

from Woodland Sweets

orange spritz

MAKES ABOUT 2 DOZEN

¼ recipe Basic Sugar-Cookie Dough (page 299)
1 tablespoon finely grated orange zest
2 ounces bittersweet chocolate, melted

1 Preheat oven to 350°F. On a piece of parchment paper, pat out dough to ½ inch thick. Sprinkle zest evenly over top; knead to incorporate. Transfer to a cookie press; pipe shapes, about 1 inch apart, onto baking sheets.

2 Bake until cookies are lightly golden around the edges, rotating baking sheets halfway through, about 15 minutes. Transfer cookies to a wire rack to cool completely.

3 Place rack over a baking sheet. Using a small spoon, drizzle chocolate in a zigzag pattern over tops of cookies. Let stand until chocolate has set. Store in an airtight container at room temperature up to 5 days.

from Holiday Cookies

orange-walnut bûche de noël

MAKES 1 TWELVE-INCH LOG | PHOTO ON PAGE 334

2 tablespoons all-purpose flour, plus more for pan
1½ cups walnuts, toasted
6 large eggs, separated, room temperature
10 tablespoons granulated sugar
½ teaspoon pure vanilla extract
¼ teaspoon salt
   Confectioners' sugar, for dusting
   Orange Mascarpone Filling (page 304)
   Chocolate Bark (page 304)
   Fig-and-Marzipan Acorns, for garnish (optional; page 304)
   Tuile leaves, for garnish (optional; page 304)
   Vegetable-oil cooking spray

1 Preheat oven to 300°F. Coat a 12-by-17-inch rimmed baking sheet with cooking spray. Line with parchment paper; spray and flour parchment, tapping out excess. In a food processor, pulse walnuts and flour until coarsely ground.

2 In the bowl of an electric mixer, whisk egg yolks with 5 tablespoons granulated sugar until thick and pale. Beat in vanilla. In a clean mixing bowl and using a clean whisk, beat egg whites and salt until soft peaks form. Slowly add remaining 5 tablespoons sugar; beat until stiff but not dry peaks form. Fold egg whites into yolk mixture in three batches, adding walnut mixture with last batch.

3 Spread batter evenly on prepared baking sheet. Bake until a cake tester inserted in center comes out clean, about 30 minutes. Run a small sharp knife around edges of cake to loosen, and invert onto a clean kitchen towel dusted with confectioners' sugar. Peel off parchment paper. Starting at a short side, gently roll cake into a log, incorporating towel. Transfer cake to a wire rack to cool completely, about 1 hour.

4 Reserve 1½ cups filling. Unroll cake, and spread remaining filling on top, leaving a ½-inch border on all sides. Carefully reroll cake. Arrange seam side down on a parchment-lined baking sheet. Using a serrated knife, trim ends of log diagonally. Spread reserved filling over log. Working quickly, arrange chocolate bark all over cake, overlapping pieces slightly. Refrigerate until firm, at least 1 hour. Garnish with acorns and leaves, if desired; dust with confectioners' sugar.

from Woodland Sweets

orange mascarpone filling

MAKES ENOUGH FOR 1 TWELVE-INCH LOG

- 8 ounces mascarpone cheese, room temperature
- 8 ounces cream cheese, room temperature
- ½ cup sugar
- 1 tablespoon finely grated orange zest
- 1 tablespoon Cointreau or other orange-flavored liqueur
- 1 teaspoon pure vanilla extract
- 1 cup heavy cream, whipped to soft peaks

In the bowl of an electric mixer fitted with the paddle attachment, blend all ingredients except cream until smooth. Gently fold in whipped cream. Use immediately, or refrigerate, covered, up to 3 days. Before using, bring to room temperature and beat until smooth with the paddle attachment.

chocolate bark

MAKES ENOUGH TO COVER 1 TWELVE-INCH LOG

- 5 ounces semisweet chocolate, finely chopped

Line a baking sheet with parchment paper; set aside. Place chocolate in a small heatproof bowl set over a pan of simmering water, stirring with a rubber spatula until melted. Remove bowl from heat; let cool, stirring occasionally, until chocolate registers 88°F on a candy thermometer. Pour chocolate onto prepared baking sheet; spread evenly over entire surface with an offset spatula. Refrigerate until firm but still pliable, 8 to 10 minutes. Tear chocolate into jagged pieces, no larger than 1½ inches. Return to refrigerator until firm, about 15 minutes.

fig-and-marzipan acorns

MAKES 30 | PHOTO ON PAGE 334

- 7 ounces marzipan
- Brown food coloring
- 30 dried Calimyrna figs

1 Place marzipan in the bowl of an electric mixer fitted with the paddle attachment. Add food coloring a drop at a time, beating until desired shade is reached. Keep marzipan covered well in plastic while you proceed.

2 Roll a teaspoon of tinted marzipan into a small ball. Flatten ball in your hand; using a toothpick, make a hole in center. Insert stem of a fig into hole; mold marzipan around top of fig. Roll marzipan cap firmly against small holes of a box grater to make dimples. Repeat with remaining marzipan and figs. Refrigerate in an airtight container up to 1 week.

tuile leaves

MAKES SIXTEEN 4¼-INCH TUILES | PHOTO ON PAGE 334

The batter can be made ahead and kept in the refrigerator for up to two days before spreading and baking.

- 1 large egg white
- ¼ cup superfine sugar
- ¼ cup all-purpose flour, sifted
- Pinch of salt
- 4 teaspoons unsalted butter, melted
- 2 teaspoons heavy cream
- ¼ teaspoon pure almond extract

1 Preheat oven to 350°F. Line a rimmed baking sheet with a Silpat baking mat. In the bowl of an electric mixer, whisk together egg white and sugar on medium speed until combined, about 30 seconds. Reduce speed to low; add flour and salt. Beat until combined. Add butter, cream, and extract; beat until combined, about 30 seconds.

2 Place a leaf stencil in corner of prepared baking sheet. Using a small offset spatula, spread batter in a thin layer over stencil. Carefully lift stencil. Repeat, filling baking sheet with leaves. Bake until tuiles are golden, 6 to 8 minutes. Remove from oven. Using a small offset spatula, lift cookies, and quickly drape over a rolling pin to cool.

3 Repeat process until all batter is used. Store leaves in an airtight container at room temperature up to 2 days.

pear tart

MAKES 1 FOUR-BY-THIRTEEN-INCH TART

- ¾ cup whole blanched almonds (4 ounces)
- ½ cup (1 stick) unsalted butter, room temperature
- ½ cup sugar, plus more for sprinkling
- 1 large egg
- 2 tablespoons heavy cream
- ¼ teaspoon pure almond extract
- Almond Tart Shell (recipe follows)
- 1 ripe but firm red Bartlett or Comice pear, cored and cut into ¼-inch-thick slices
- Vanilla-Bean Crème Anglaise, for serving (recipe follows)

1 Preheat oven to 350°F. Spread almonds in a single layer on a rimmed baking sheet; toast in oven until lightly golden and fragrant, tossing occasionally, 7 to 10 minutes. Let cool completely, then finely grind in a food processor. Set aside.

2 In the bowl of an electric mixer fitted with the paddle attachment, cream butter and sugar on medium speed until

smooth and light, about 1 minute. Add almonds, egg, cream, and extract; beat until well combined, about 2 minutes.

3 Using a small offset spatula, spread filling in cooled tart shell. Arrange pear slices on top of filling down length of tart, slightly overlapping. Generously sprinkle sugar over top, and place tart on a baking sheet. Bake until filling is slightly puffed and golden brown, about 35 minutes. Transfer to a wire rack to cool. Serve warm or at room temperature with crème anglaise on the side.

from New England Open House

almond tart shell

MAKES 1 FOUR-BY-THIRTEEN-INCH SHELL

¼ **cup whole blanched almonds (1 ounce)**

1 **cup plus 2 teaspoons all-purpose flour, plus more for work surface**

¼ **teaspoon baking soda**

⅛ **teaspoon salt**

½ **cup (1 stick) unsalted butter, room temperature**

½ **cup sugar**

1 **large egg yolk**

¼ **teaspoon pure vanilla extract**

1 Preheat oven to 350°F. Spread almonds in a single layer on a rimmed baking sheet; toast in oven until lightly golden and fragrant, tossing occasionally, 7 to 10 minutes. Let cool completely, then finely grind in a food processor. Set aside.

2 In a small bowl, whisk together flour, baking soda, and salt; set aside. In the bowl of an electric mixer fitted with the paddle attachment, cream butter and sugar on medium speed until smooth and light, about 1 minute. Add almonds, egg yolk, and extract; beat until well combined. With mixer on low speed, gradually add flour mixture, beating until just combined. Turn out dough onto a piece of plastic wrap; pat into a flattened rectangle. Wrap in plastic; refrigerate until firm, at least 1 hour or overnight.

3 Reheat oven to 350°F. On a lightly floured work surface, roll out dough to a 6-by-16-inch rectangle, about ⅜ inch thick. Fit dough into a 4-by-13-inch rectangular tart pan with a removable bottom, pressing dough into bottom and up sides. Trim dough flush with edge of pan. Prick bottom of dough all over with a fork. Freeze or refrigerate until firm, about 15 minutes.

4 Place tart pan on a baking sheet; bake until crust starts to brown around the edges, 13 to 14 minutes. (Dough will be slightly puffed in spots.) Transfer to a wire rack. Using a metal spatula, gently press on dough until it is smooth and flat. Let cool completely.

vanilla-bean crème anglaise

MAKES ABOUT 2 CUPS

4 **large egg yolks**

¼ **cup sugar**

Pinch of salt

1 **cup milk**

¾ **cup heavy cream**

1 **vanilla bean, split lengthwise and scraped**

1 Prepare an ice bath; set aside. In the bowl of an electric mixer, whisk egg yolks, sugar, and salt on high speed until pale yellow and very thick. Meanwhile, in a small saucepan, bring milk, cream, and vanilla bean and scrapings just to a boil. Remove from heat.

2 With mixer on low speed, gradually pour half the hot milk mixture into yolk mixture. Return mixture to saucepan. Cook over medium-low heat, stirring constantly with a wooden spoon, until mixture is thick enough to coat back of spoon and hold a line drawn by your finger, about 5 minutes. Pass mixture through a fine sieve into a bowl. Place in the ice bath, stirring occasionally, until chilled. Use immediately, or refrigerate, covered, up to 3 days. Whisk gently before using.

peppermint sticks

MAKES ABOUT 45

The candy will be very hot to handle initially; wear protective plastic gloves and work quickly. For best results, split the work with another person as you begin to pull the candy. To temper chocolate, heat two-thirds of chocolate in a heatproof bowl set over a pan of barely simmering water until it registers 118°F on a candy thermometer. Off heat, add remaining chocolate, and stir with a rubber spatula (do not use a wooden spoon) until chocolate cools to 84°F. Remove any unmelted pieces, and return bowl to pan; stir until chocolate reaches 88°F to 90°F. Use immediately.

2 **cups sugar**

½ **cup light corn syrup**

2 **teaspoons freshly squeezed lemon juice**

1 **teaspoon pure peppermint extract**

4 **drops red food coloring**

6 **ounces bittersweet chocolate, finely chopped and tempered**

Vegetable-oil cooking spray

1 Coat a 12-by-17-inch rimmed baking sheet with cooking spray; set aside. Place sugar, corn syrup, and ½ cup water in a medium saucepan. Cover; bring to a boil over high heat. Remove lid; cook, swirling pan occasionally, until syrup reaches 305°F (hard-crack stage) on a candy thermometer,

about 10 minutes. Remove from heat, and carefully stir in lemon juice, extract, and food coloring.

2   Pour hot syrup onto prepared baking sheet, being careful not to touch it. Using a metal spatula coated with cooking spray, fold edges toward the center (this will help cool syrup). When cool enough to handle, using plastic gloves, stretch and pull the candy, folding it over onto itself before pulling again, about 10 minutes.

3   When candy is opaque and just starting to firm up, pull off pieces to form long pencil-thin ropes. Working quickly, cut into 7-inch lengths with a pair of kitchen scissors. Continue pulling until all candy is used or is no longer pliable.

4   Dip top 3 inches of each peppermint stick in chocolate. Allow excess chocolate to drip off, and set stick on a parchment-lined baking sheet to harden. Store in an airtight container at room temperature up to 1 week.

from Woodland Sweets

pinecone cakes

MAKES EIGHT 3½-INCH CAKES | **PHOTO ON PAGE 335**

We dusted the cakes with confectioners' sugar for a snowy effect; chocolate shavings stand in for pinecone needles.

 10 tablespoons (1¼ sticks) unsalted butter, plus more for pan
  1 cup whole blanched almonds (4 ounces)
 1½ cups sugar
  1 cup all-purpose flour
  2 tablespoons dark rum
  2 teaspoons pure vanilla extract
  8 large egg whites, room temperature
     Pinch of salt
     Chocolate Frosting (recipe follows)
  6 cups sliced almonds (1½ pounds)
     Confectioners' sugar, for dusting (optional)
     Chocolate shavings, for garnish (optional)

1   Preheat oven to 350°F. Butter a 10-inch round cake pan. Line bottom with parchment paper; butter parchment, and set pan aside. Spread whole almonds in a single layer on a rimmed baking sheet; toast in oven until lightly golden and fragrant, tossing occasionally, 7 to 10 minutes. Let cool.

2   Place toasted almonds and ¾ cup sugar in a food processor; pulse until finely ground. Transfer to a bowl, and stir in flour; set aside. Melt butter in a small saucepan; remove from heat, and stir in rum and vanilla. Let cool slightly.

3   In the bowl of an electric mixer, whisk egg whites and salt until soft peaks form. Gradually beat in remaining ¾ cup sugar, and continue beating until stiff peaks form.

4   Fold flour mixture into egg-white mixture in three batches, alternating with the butter mixture. Pour batter into prepared pan, smoothing top with an offset spatula. Bake until golden brown and firm to the touch, about 40 minutes. Transfer to a wire rack to cool 20 minutes. Invert cake onto rack; reinvert, and let cool completely, top side up.

5   Using a 3-inch oval cookie cutter, cut out eight ovals from cake. Discard scraps. Trim each oval to resemble a pinecone, with rounded edges and a pointed tip. Spread about ⅓ cup frosting over each cake, smoothing and rounding tops and sides so that surface is completely covered.

6   Starting at the broader end of one cake, arrange sliced almonds in a row, overlapping slightly, to make the base. Continue arranging almonds in closely set rows to cover the entire surface. Transfer finished cake to a baking sheet in the refrigerator to set while repeating with remaining cakes. Just before serving, dust with confectioners' sugar and garnish with chocolate shavings, if desired.

from Woodland Sweets

chocolate frosting

MAKES ABOUT 3 CUPS

 3½ cups confectioners' sugar
  1 cup unsweetened cocoa powder
  ¾ cup (1½ sticks) unsalted butter, room temperature
  ½ cup milk, room temperature
  2 teaspoons pure vanilla extract

Into a medium bowl, sift together sugar and cocoa. Beat in butter, milk, and vanilla until smooth. Use immediately, or refrigerate, covered, up to 3 days. Use at room temperature.

pistachio-chocolate bûche de noël

MAKES 1 TWELVE-INCH LOG | **PHOTO ON PAGE 334**

Begin preparing Chocolate Wood-Grain at the end of step four.

5 tablespoons all-purpose flour

5 tablespoons unsweetened cocoa powder, plus more for dusting

1 teaspoon baking powder

¼ teaspoon salt

5 large eggs, separated, room temperature

¾ cup sugar

1 teaspoon pure vanilla extract

3 pints pistachio ice cream, beaten until spreadable

Chocolate Wood-Grain (recipe follows)

Chocolate leaves, for garnish (optional)

Vegetable-oil cooking spray

1 Preheat oven to 350°F. Coat a 12-by-17-inch rimmed baking sheet with cooking spray. Line with parchment paper; spray paper, and set aside. Into a small bowl, sift together flour, cocoa, baking powder, and salt. Set aside.

2 In the bowl of an electric mixer, whisk yolks and half the sugar until thick and pale. Beat in vanilla. In a clean mixing bowl and using a clean whisk, beat whites until soft peaks form. Slowly add remaining sugar; beat until stiff but not dry peaks form. Fold whites into yolk mixture in three batches, adding flour mixture with last batch.

3 Spread batter evenly on prepared baking sheet. Bake until a cake tester inserted in center comes out clean, about 30 minutes. Run a small sharp knife around edges of cake to loosen, and invert onto a clean kitchen towel dusted with cocoa powder. Peel off parchment paper. Starting at a short side, gently roll cake into a log, incorporating towel. Transfer cake to a wire rack to cool completely, about 1 hour.

4 Unroll cake, and spread ice cream evenly over top. Carefully reroll cake. Arrange seam side down on a parchment-lined baking sheet; freeze until ice cream is firm, at least 1 hour. Using a hot serrated knife, trim ends of log diagonally.

5 Wrap log in chocolate wood-grain: Tuck one end of chocolate-coated acetate under cake while lifting other end up and over cake, being careful not to let chocolate touch cake until sheet is completely surrounding cake and ready to be tucked under at other end. Place cake, seam side down, on inverted baking sheet; return to freezer until chocolate has hardened, about 10 minutes.

6 When ready to serve, remove cake from freezer. Carefully peel acetate from cake, and gently break off ends of chocolate wood-grain to line up with ends of cake.

from Woodland Sweets

chocolate wood-grain

MAKES ENOUGH TO COVER 1 TWELVE-INCH LOG

You will need a tool called a graining rocker used in making faux bois to give the chocolate the appearance of grained wood. You will also need a thin sheet of acetate. Both items are available at most hardware and paint-supply stores.

3 ounces white chocolate, melted

6 ounces bittersweet chocolate, finely chopped

1 Cut a thin piece of acetate into a 13½-by-16-inch rectangle. Place on a clean work surface, with a long side facing you. Coat surface of faux-bois tool well with a thick layer of white chocolate. Starting at the left side and working from top to bottom of acetate sheet, rock coated tool back and forth while dragging it in one swift motion to make a vertical striation. Continue until entire sheet is covered in vertical striations. Transfer acetate, chocolate side up, to an inverted rimmed baking sheet; refrigerate until set, about 6 minutes.

2 Meanwhile, temper bittersweet chocolate: Melt two-thirds of chocolate in a heatproof bowl set over a pan of barely simmering water until it registers 118°F on a candy thermometer. Remove pan from heat; add remaining chocolate. Stir with a rubber spatula (do not use a wooden spoon) until chocolate cools to 84°F. Remove any unmelted pieces, and return bowl to pan; stir until chocolate reaches 88°F to 90°F.

3 Immediately transfer coated acetate to work surface, and pour bittersweet chocolate over the top. Working quickly, spread it evenly over entire surface with a small offset spatula. Try not to spread too much or the white chocolate will smear. Use immediately.

rum balls

MAKES 4 DOZEN | **PHOTO ON PAGE 332**

Refrigerate balls in an airtight container for up to two days.

- ¾ cup (1½ sticks) unsalted butter
- 6 ounces semisweet chocolate, finely chopped
- 3 large eggs
- ½ cup packed light-brown sugar
- 1 teaspoon pure vanilla extract
- ½ teaspoon salt
- ¾ cup all-purpose flour
- ¼ cup plus 2 tablespoons dark rum
- Red sanding sugar, for rolling
- Vegetable-oil cooking spray

1 Preheat oven to 350°F. Coat a 12-by-17-inch rimmed baking sheet with cooking spray; set aside. Combine butter and chocolate in a small heatproof bowl set over a pan of simmering water, stirring occasionally, until chocolate is melted and mixture is smooth and combined.

2 In a large bowl, whisk together eggs, brown sugar, vanilla, and salt. Stir in chocolate mixture, then fold in flour. Pour batter into prepared baking sheet; spread evenly with an offset spatula. Bake until top is shiny, rotating sheet halfway through, about 10 minutes. Do not overbake; a cake tester should come out with some crumbs attached. Let cool completely.

3 Break up brownie into small pieces, and place in the bowl of an electric mixer fitted with the paddle attachment. With mixer on low speed, slowly pour rum into bowl; mix until crumbs start to come together to form a ball.

4 Shape mixture into 1-inch balls. Roll in sanding sugar, coating completely. Place on a baking sheet; refrigerate, uncovered, until chilled, about 2 hours.

from New England Open House

Saint Lucia's Day coffee cake

MAKES 1 BRAIDED WREATH | **PHOTO ON PAGE 313**

Saint Lucia's Day marks the beginning of the Swedish Christmas season. Traditionally, the eldest daughter plays the role of Saint Lucia and serves coffee and saffron-laced coffeecake wreaths or buns to family members.

- ¼ cup warm water (about 110°F)
- 1 envelope active dry yeast (1 scant tablespoon)
- ½ cup granulated sugar, plus a pinch for yeast
- ¾ cup plus 2 tablespoons whole milk
- ½ teaspoon saffron threads, crushed
- ½ cup (1 stick) unsalted butter, melted
- 2 large whole eggs, lightly beaten
- 1 teaspoon salt
- 4 to 5 cups all-purpose flour, plus more for work surface
- ⅓ cup golden raisins
- ⅓ cup dried tart cherries
- Grated zest of 1 orange
- Canola oil, for bowl and plastic wrap
- 1 large egg yolk, room temperature
- 1 tablespoon heavy cream
- 1 cup confectioners' sugar

1 In the bowl of an electric mixer, stir together warm water, yeast, and pinch of granulated sugar. Let stand until foamy, about 5 minutes. Meanwhile, heat ¾ cup milk in a small saucepan until just steaming. Remove pan from heat. Add saffron; cover, and let steep 5 minutes.

2 In a medium bowl, whisk together saffron milk, butter, whole eggs, remaining ½ cup granulated sugar, and salt. Add to yeast mixture. Using the dough-hook attachment, beat until combined, about 1 minute. With mixer on low speed, gradually add flour, 1 cup at a time, until dough pulls away from sides of bowl but is still sticky. Add raisins, cherries, and zest. Mix until dough is elastic and smooth, 7 to 8 minutes.

3 Place dough in a large, lightly oiled bowl; cover loosely with oiled plastic wrap. Let rise in a warm place until doubled in bulk, about 1 hour, or refrigerate overnight.

4 Preheat oven to 375°F, with rack in center. Punch down dough, and divide into three equal pieces. Gently roll each piece into a rope, 18 to 20 inches long and about 1½ inches thick. On a lightly floured work surface, lay ropes vertically in front of you. Starting at top and working down, braid ropes together, then form into a circle. Pinch ends together to seal. Transfer to a parchment-lined baking sheet; cover loosely with plastic wrap, and let rise 20 minutes.

5 In a small bowl, whisk together egg yolk and heavy cream. Brush dough with egg wash. Bake 15 minutes; reduce oven heat to 350°F. Continue baking until golden brown, about 15 minutes more. Transfer to a wire rack to cool completely.

6 When ready to serve, make icing: In a small bowl, stir together confectioners' sugar and remaining 2 tablespoons milk until smooth. Drizzle icing generously over cake.

from Saint Lucia's Day

Santa's snowflakes

MAKES ABOUT 2 DOZEN | **PHOTO ON PAGE 334**

¼ recipe Basic Sugar-Cookie Dough (page 299)
  Sanding sugar or colored sprinkles, for decorating

1 Divide dough in half. Roll out each half between two pieces of parchment paper to about ⅛ inch thick. Transfer each half to a baking sheet; cover tightly with plastic wrap. Refrigerate until firm, about 2 hours or overnight.

2 Preheat oven to 350°F. Remove one sheet of dough from refrigerator, and let stand 1 minute. Using a 3-inch snowflake-shaped cookie cutter, cut out shapes. Place shapes 2 inches apart on parchment-lined baking sheets. Gather together scraps, and reroll as above; chill 10 to 15 minutes. Cut out more shapes. Repeat with second sheet of dough. Decorate with sanding sugar or sprinkles, as desired.

3 Bake cookies until golden around the edges and slightly firm to the touch, rotating baking sheets halfway through, about 15 minutes. Let cool on baking sheets 1 minute, then transfer to wire racks to cool completely. Store in an airtight container at room temperature up to 5 days.

from Holiday Cookies

sufganiyot

MAKES ABOUT 20

These doughnuts are surprisingly easy and fun to make, and children love to get involved in forming them.

¾ cup warm water (about 110°F)
1 envelope active dry yeast (1 scant tablespoon)
2½ cups all-purpose flour, plus more for work surface
¼ cup sugar, plus ½ cup for coating
  Pinch of salt
2 large eggs, separated
2 tablespoons margarine or unsalted butter, room temperature
  Peanut oil, for frying, plus more for bowl
¼ cup raspberry or strawberry jam

1 In a large metal bowl, stir together warm water and yeast. Let stand until foamy, about 5 minutes. Add ¾ cup flour, ¼ cup sugar, and salt; mix until well combined. Add egg yolks and remaining 1¾ cups flour. Mix until combined, then knead dough in bowl until all flour is incorporated. Turn out dough onto a lightly floured work surface; knead a few minutes until smooth. Knead in margarine until incorporated.

2 Transfer dough to a well-oiled bowl; turn dough several times to coat entirely with oil. Cover tightly with plastic wrap, and refrigerate overnight.

3 About 30 minutes before you're ready to form doughnuts, let dough come to room temperature. On a lightly floured work surface, roll out dough to an 11-inch square, about ⅛ inch thick. Using a 2-inch cookie cutter, cut out about 24 rounds from dough, dipping cutter in flour as needed to prevent sticking. Reroll scraps; cut out about 16 more rounds.

4 Line a baking sheet with a clean kitchen towel. In a small bowl, lightly beat egg whites. Brush edge of a dough round with egg white, then mound ½ teaspoon jam in center. Top with another round, and press edges to seal. Repeat process with remaining rounds. Transfer to prepared baking sheet; let rise until puffy, 20 to 30 minutes.

5 Heat a few inches of oil in a large (4- to 5-quart) heavy pot until it registers 360°F on a deep-fry thermometer. Working in batches of 4 or 5, carefully slip doughnuts into hot oil. Fry until golden brown, turning once, about 1 minute (doughnuts will fry very quickly and puff up). Using a slotted spoon, transfer doughnuts to paper towels to drain.

6 Place remaining ½ cup sugar in a medium bowl. While still hot, dip doughnuts in sugar, turning to coat. Serve.

from Hanukkah

twig taffy

MAKES 40

This recipe requires fast work; for best results, split the work with another person as you begin to pull the taffy. Liquid glycerin is sold at baking-supply stores.

2½ cups sugar
1 cup light corn syrup
2 tablespoons cornstarch
2 teaspoons liquid glycerin
1½ teaspoons salt
3 tablespoons unsalted butter, plus more for fingers
½ teaspoon pure vanilla extract
1 teaspoon pure coffee extract
  Vegetable-oil cooking spray

1   Coat a rimmed baking sheet with cooking spray; set aside. In a medium nonstick saucepan, combine sugar, 1 cup water, corn syrup, cornstarch, glycerin, and salt. Bring to a boil over medium heat, stirring with a wooden spoon to dissolve sugar. Without stirring, cook until mixture registers 275°F (soft-crack stage) on a candy thermometer, about 8 minutes. Remove pan from heat; carefully stir in butter and extracts.

2   Pour hot mixture onto prepared baking sheet. Allow edges to cool and set slightly. Using a metal spatula coated with cooking spray, fold edges toward the center (this will help to cool taffy). When cool enough to handle, stretch and pull taffy with lightly buttered fingers, folding it over onto itself before pulling again, about 20 minutes.

3   Before taffy cools and hardens too much, pull off ropelike pieces; using kitchen scissors, make snips along the sides. Gently stretch and pull snipped taffy on either end, forming thorny twigs. Snip into 7-inch lengths. Transfer twigs to a parchment-lined baking sheet to cool completely.

from Woodland Sweets

DRINKS

cranberry, tangerine, and pomegranate punch

SERVES ABOUT 20

You will need sixty cranberries to make twenty swizzle sticks.

1   bag (12 ounces) fresh whole cranberries, for swizzle sticks
1   bunch mint leaves, for swizzle sticks
2   cups freshly squeezed pomegranate juice (about 5 pomegranates)
3   cups freshly squeezed tangerine juice (about 7 tangerines)
5   cups cranberry-juice cocktail
2   750-ml bottles sparkling wine

1   Spear 3 cranberries alternately with 2 mint leaves on each of twenty wooden skewers. Place skewers on a baking sheet; cover with damp paper towels. Refrigerate up to 1 hour.

2   In a large punch bowl, stir together fruit juices. Fill glasses with ice. Ladle about ½ cup punch into each glass, then top with sparkling wine. Garnish each with a swizzle stick.

from New England Open House

MISCELLANEOUS

cheddar cheese and sage biscuits

MAKES ABOUT 16 | PHOTOS ON PAGES 324 AND 325

4   cups all-purpose flour, plus more for work surface
4   teaspoons baking powder
1   teaspoon baking soda
1   teaspoon salt
1   teaspoon sugar
½   teaspoon paprika
1   cup (2 sticks) chilled unsalted butter, cut into small pieces
3   cups grated cheddar cheese (9 ounces)
⅔   cup thinly sliced fresh sage leaves
2   cups buttermilk
1   large egg, lightly beaten
1   tablespoon heavy cream

1   Preheat oven to 375°F. In a medium bowl, whisk together flour, baking powder, baking soda, salt, sugar, and paprika. Using a pastry blender or two knives, cut in butter until mixture resembles coarse crumbs. Stir in cheese and sage. Add buttermilk; stir with a fork until mixture just comes together to form a sticky dough. On a lightly floured work surface, with floured hands, pat dough into a 1-inch-thick round.

2   Using a 2½-inch biscuit or cookie cutter, cut out biscuits as close together as possible, dipping cutter into flour each time to prevent sticking. Transfer biscuits to a baking sheet.

3   In a small bowl, stir together egg and cream. Lightly brush top of each biscuit with egg wash. Bake until golden brown, rotating baking sheet halfway through, 20 to 30 minutes. Transfer to a wire rack. Serve warm or at room temperature.

from New England Open House

cranberry, sour cherry, and grapefruit chutney

MAKES ABOUT 3 CUPS | PHOTOS ON PAGES 324 AND 325

12   ounces fresh or frozen (thawed) cranberries
¾   cup sugar
2   tablespoons cider vinegar
¼   teaspoon ground cardamom
     Pinch of ground cloves
     Pinch of salt
½   cup dried sour cherries
2   ruby-red grapefruits, pith and peel removed, separated into sections

In a small saucepan, combine cranberries, sugar, vinegar, cardamom, cloves, and salt. Stir well to combine. Place over medium heat; cook, stirring constantly, until cranberries just begin to burst and soften, about 5 minutes. Turn off heat; stir in cherries, and transfer to a medium bowl. Let cool completely, then gently mix in grapefruit. Cover with plastic wrap; refrigerate until ready to serve, up to 5 days.

from New England Open House

crunchy vanilla hazelnuts

MAKES ABOUT 6 CUPS

To give these an espresso flavor, fold one-half cup plus two tablespoons freshly ground espresso into the egg white mixture just before adding the hazelnuts.

6 cups hazelnuts (about 1¾ pounds)
1 vanilla bean, split lengthwise and scraped
2 cups sugar
4 large egg whites
½ teaspoon salt
2 tablespoons coffee-flavored liqueur

1 Preheat oven to 250°F with racks in upper and lower thirds. Spread hazelnuts in a single layer on two rimmed baking sheets. Toast in oven until fragrant and skins begin to crack, tossing halfway through, about 20 minutes. Remove from oven; while still hot, rub vigorously with a clean kitchen towel to remove skins. Let nuts cool completely.

2 In a small bowl, add vanilla scrapings to sugar; mix well, and set aside. In the bowl of an electric mixer, whisk egg whites and salt until frothy. Slowly pour in sugar mixture, whisking until mixture is thick and foamy. Whisk in liqueur, and fold in hazelnuts. Spread mixture evenly on two baking sheets lined with Silpat baking mats.

3 Bake, stirring gently every 10 minutes, until nuts are golden, about 50 minutes. Let cool on baking sheets 10 minutes, then carefully transfer coated nuts to another baking sheet, and let cool completely, 6 hours or overnight. Store in an airtight container at room temperature up to 5 days.

from Seasoned Nuts

gingered peanuts and pumpkin seeds with dried cranberries

MAKES ABOUT 8 CUPS

4 cups raw pumpkin seeds
¾ cup sanding sugar
2 tablespoons coarse salt
2½ teaspoons ground ginger
⅓ teaspoon ground cinnamon
1 tablespoon plus 2 teaspoons pure vanilla extract
⅓ cup granulated sugar
3 tablespoons grated fresh ginger
2 cups roasted, salted peanuts (about ½ pound)
1 cup dried cranberries

1 Preheat oven to 300°F. Spread pumpkin seeds in a single layer on a rimmed baking sheet; toast in oven until lightly browned, stirring occasionally, about 12 minutes. Remove from oven; let cool completely.

2 Meanwhile, whisk together sanding sugar, 1 tablespoon coarse salt, 1½ teaspoons ground ginger, and the cinnamon in a large bowl. Set aside.

3 In a large saucepan, combine vanilla, granulated sugar, 3 tablespoons water, and remaining tablespoon salt and teaspoon ground ginger. Bring to a boil over medium-high heat; cook, stirring, 2 minutes. Stir in fresh ginger. Add peanuts and toasted seeds; cook, stirring constantly, until liquid has almost evaporated (do not let mixture burn), about 4 minutes.

4 Immediately toss hot nut mixture in reserved sanding-sugar mixture until well coated. Spread coated nuts on a baking sheet lined with parchment paper, and let cool completely, 6 hours or overnight. Stir in dried cranberries. Store in airtight containers at room temperature up to 2 weeks.

from Seasoned Nuts

maple-sugared walnuts

MAKES ABOUT 8 CUPS

6 cups walnut halves (about 1¼ pounds)
½ cup maple sugar
1 tablespoon plus 1½ teaspoons coarse salt
½ teaspoon ground cinnamon
¼ cup brandy
2 tablespoons pure vanilla extract
1⅓ cups pure maple syrup
2 tablespoons unsalted butter

1   Preheat oven to 350°F. Spread walnuts in a single layer on a rimmed baking sheet; toast in oven until fragrant, stirring occasionally, about 10 minutes. Let cool completely.

2   Meanwhile, combine maple sugar, salt, and cinnamon in a medium bowl; set aside. In a large deep skillet, combine brandy, vanilla, maple syrup, and butter. Bring to a boil over medium heat. Cook until liquid has reduced by half, about 5 minutes. Stir in walnuts; continue cooking, stirring, until skillet is almost dry, about 3 minutes more.

3   Immediately toss nuts in reserved sugar mixture until well coated. Spread nuts on a baking sheet lined with parchment paper; let cool completely, 6 hours or overnight. Store nuts in airtight containers at room temperature up to 2 weeks.

from Seasoned Nuts

olive-oil-roasted almonds

MAKES ABOUT 2 CUPS

2 cups whole blanched almonds (12 ounces)
1½ tablespoons extra-virgin olive oil
1 teaspoon coarse sea salt

Preheat oven to 350°F. Spread almonds in a single layer on a rimmed baking sheet; toast in oven until golden, tossing occasionally, about 15 minutes. Let cool completely. Transfer to a bowl. Add oil and salt, and toss to combine. Store in an airtight container at room temperature up to 2 days.

from New England Open House

peppered mixed nuts with lemon and capers

MAKES ABOUT 9 CUPS

3 cups capers
1 quart canola oil
6 cups assorted roasted, unsalted nuts (about 1½ pounds)
2 tablespoons freshly squeezed lemon juice
2 teaspoons freshly ground pepper
2 tablespoons finely grated lemon zest

1   Preheat oven to 300°F. Rinse and drain capers; transfer to a paper-towel–lined baking sheet, and gently dab with more paper towels. Set aside to dry 1 hour.

2   Heat oil in a medium saucepan until it registers 350°F on a deep-fry thermometer. Carefully add ¼ cup capers, and fry until golden brown, about 3 minutes. Using a long-handled slotted spoon, transfer capers to a paper-towel–lined baking sheet. Continue adding capers in ¼-cup batches until all

capers have been fried; adjust heat as necessary to maintain oil at 350°F. Reserve 2 tablespoons cooking oil; let cool.

3   In a bowl, toss nuts with reserved oil, lemon juice, and pepper. Spread mixture evenly on a rimmed baking sheet. Toast in oven until golden brown, stirring occasionally, about 25 minutes. Remove from oven; let cool, about 20 minutes. Sprinkle nuts with lemon zest, and toss with fried capers. Store in airtight containers at room temperature up to 2 weeks.

from Seasoned Nuts

sesame-soy cashews with wasabi peas and nori

MAKES ABOUT 6 CUPS

Nori, which are thin sheets of dried seaweed, can be found in Japanese markets and many grocery stores.

¼ cup reduced-sodium soy sauce
2 tablespoons sugar
1½ tablespoons sake
1 teaspoon sesame oil
1 teaspoon grated fresh ginger
¾ teaspoon ground ginger
4 cups roasted, unsalted cashews (about 1¼ pounds)
¼ cup sesame seeds
1 sheet nori, toasted
2 cups wasabi peas (about ½ pound)

1   Preheat oven to 250°F. In a medium bowl, combine soy sauce, sugar, sake, sesame oil, and fresh and ground ginger. Add cashews and sesame seeds; toss until well coated.

2   Spread nut mixture on two baking sheets lined with Silpat baking mats. Bake, stirring every 10 minutes, until glaze turns golden brown and is almost completely dried, about 40 minutes. Remove from oven; let cool about 20 minutes.

3   Break nut mixture into clusters, and place in a bowl. Using kitchen scissors, cut toasted nori into ¾-inch-wide strips; add to bowl along with wasabi peas. Store in airtight containers at room temperature up to 1 week.

from Seasoned Nuts

SAINT LUCIA'S DAY
COFFEE CAKE | **PAGE 308**

MAKING STICKY BUNS

Roll out dough into a rectangle. Brush dough with melted butter, and top with filling, leaving a ½-inch border. Starting on one long side, roll dough into a log.

To seal, pinch dough edge to log, then turn roll seam side down. With a sharp knife and a sawing motion, cut log into equal slices. Avoid pressing down.

Divide topping among muffin cups. Place buns in pan, making sure end pieces are cut side up.

STICKY BUNS | **PAGE 284**

MINI STICKY BUNS | **PAGE 285**

INI ASIAN CRAB CAKES | **PAGE 290**

MUSHROOM-POLENTA DIAMONDS | **PAGE 291**

ALIA'S FAVORITE LATKES | **PAGE 297**

SHALLOT-AND-DATE EMPANADAS | **PAGE 271**

FRESH TOMATO SOUP | **PAGE 255**

BUTTERNUT-SQUASH RAVIOLI WITH
FRIED SAGE LEAVES | **PAGE 255**

SQUASH PANADA WITH WILD MUSHROOMS
AND CHARD | **PAGE 259**

PASTA WITH SAUSAGE AND ESCAROLE | **PAGE 273**

LAMB STEW WITH JERUSALEM ARTICHOKES | **PAGE 273**

ROASTED BRUSSELS SPROUTS WITH
ALMONDS AND HONEY | **PAGE 277**

GRILLED WINTER SQUASH | **PAGE 276**

SKILLET SWEET POTATOES WITH
WILD MUSHROOMS | **PAGE 279**

CALIFORNIA-STYLE DEVILS ON HORSEBACK | **PAGE 269**

THE BEST ONION RINGS | **PAGE 275**

RANGE-BRAISED FENNEL | **PAGE 297**

TUSCAN KALE WITH CARAMELIZED ONIONS AND RED-WINE VINEGAR | **PAGE 279**

OASTED BABY POTATOES WITH ROMESCO AUCE | **PAGE 261**

JERUSALEM ARTICHOKE SOUFFLE | **PAGE 272**

INDIVIDUAL STRAWBERRY-JAM CAKES | **PAGE 281**

BANANA-PECAN CAKE | **PAGE 298**

APPLE NAPOLEONS | **PAGE 262**

PUMPKIN-CHOCOLATE TART | **PAGE 282**

EGGNOG MOUSSE WITH
ASSORTED TOPPINGS | PAGE 300

ORANGE-WALNUT BUCHE DE NOEL | **PAGE 303**

FROSTED FRUITCAKE WITH MERINGUE MUSHROOMS | **PAGE 3**

SANTA'S SNOWFLAKES | **PAGE 309**

PISTACHIO-CHOCOLATE
BUCHE DE NOEL | **PAGE 307**

PINECONE CAKES | **PAGE 306**

CHOCOLATE CHIP COOKIES WITH ASSORTED ADD-INS | **PAGE 262**

Menus

Sources

ACHIOTE PASTE *Kitchen / Market*

ALLSPICE *Kitchen / Market*

ANCHO CHILES *Kitchen / Market*

ANDOUILLE SAUSAGE *Igourmet.com*

ANGEL FOOD PAN *Bridge Kitchenware*

BABA AU RHUM, 3 OZ. MOLD
Bridge Kitchenware

BAKING MAT, SILPAT *Martha Stewart:
The Catalog for Living*

BAKING SHEETS *Martha Stewart:
The Catalog for Living*

BAKING SHEETS, RIMMED
Broadway Panhandler

BLACK VODKA *Black Vodka Co.*

BRESAOLA *Igourmet.com*

BROCCOLI RABE *Indian Rock Produce*

BUCHERON CHEESE *Murray's Cheese*

BULGHUR WHEAT *Whole Foods Market*

CAKE PAN, 6-INCH ROUND
Sweet Celebrations

CAKE PAN, 8-BY-2-INCH ROUND
Bridge Kitchenware

CAKE PAN, 8-INCH SQUARE
Bridge Kitchenware

CAKE STAND *Martha Stewart:
The Catalog for Living*

CANDY THERMOMETER
Sweet Celebrations

CANELA, GROUND *Kitchen / Market*

CARAWAY SEEDS *Adriana's Caravan*

CARDAMOM PODS *Adriana's Caravan*

CAST-IRON SKILLETS
Lodge Manufacturing

CHILE DE ARBOL *Kitchen / Market*

CHIOGGIA BEETS *Indian Rock Produce*

CHIPOTLE IN ADOBO *Kitchen / Market*

CINNAMON STICKS, MEXICAN
Kitchen / Market

COCKTAIL SHAKER, CRYSTAL
Martha Stewart: The Catalog for Living

COCONUT, CREAMED *Foods of India*

COCONUT FLAVORING *Garden of Eden*

COCONUT MILK *Foods of India*

COCONUT-MILK POWDER *Foods of India*

COOKIE CUTTERS, 3-INCH OVAL
Sweet Celebrations

COOKIE CUTTERS, ALPHABET SET
Bridge Kitchenware

COOKIE CUTTERS, ROUND
Bridge Kitchenware, Sweet Celebrations

COOKIE PRESS *Martha Stewart:
The Catalog for Living*

COOLING RACKS *Martha Stewart:
The Catalog for Living*

COUPLER *Sweet Celebrations*

CREMA MEXICANA (MEXICAN
SOUR CREAM) *Kitchen / Market*

CRYSTAL SUGAR *Sweet Celebrations*

CRYSTALLIZED GINGER *Adriana's Caravan*

DESICCATED COCONUT *Foods of India*

EPAZOTE, DRIED *Kitchen / Market*

FETA CHEESE, BULGARIAN
Whole Foods Market

FIGS, DRIED *Kalustyan's*

FISH SAUCE *ImportFood.com*
Thai Supermarket

FLEUR DE SEL *Whole Foods Market*

FONDANT, ROLLED *Sweet Celebrations*

GARAM MASALA *Adriana's Caravan*

GEL PASTE, ASSORTED COLORS
Sweet Celebrations

GERANIUMS, EDIBLE *The Herb Lady*

GINGERBREAD COOKIE MIX
Martha Stewart: The Catalog for Living

GLYCERIN *Sweet Celebrations*

GRAINING ROCKER, STANDARD
O-Gee Paint Co.

GREEN CHILES *Whole Foods Market*

GREEN LENTILS *Whole Foods Market*

GREEN TOMATOES *Indian Rock Produce*

HALOUMI CHEESE *Whole Foods Market*

HAND MIXER, KITCHENAID
Martha Stewart: The Catalog for Living

HEART-SHAPED PAN, 9-INCH
Bridge Kitchenware

HOISIN SAUCE *Whole Foods Market*

HONEY DROP HARD CANDIES
The Sweet Life

ICE CREAM MAKER, WHITE MOUNTAIN,
MANUAL *Williams-Sonoma*

ISRAELI COUSCOUS *Kalustyan's*

JERUSALEM ARTICHOKES
Indian Rock Produce

JUNIPER BERRIES, DRIED
Adriana's Caravan

KAFFIR LIME LEAVES *Kalustyan's*

KEFALOTYRI CHEESE *Igourmet.com*

LACINATO KALE *Indian Rock Produce*

LAVASH, WHITE AND WHOLE-WHEAT *Kalustyan's*

LAVENDER, DRIED *World Spice Merchants*

LEAF STENCIL *Candyland Crafts*

LEMON BALM *Indian Rock Produce*

LITTLENECK CLAMS *Wild Edibles*

LOAF PAN *Bridge Kitchenware*

LOBSTER *Wild Edibles*

LYCHEE FRUITS *ImportFood.com Thai Supermarket*

MADELEINE PAN *Bridge Kitchenware*

MAPLE SUGAR *New Hampshire Gold*

MARZIPAN *Sweet Celebrations*

MASA HARINA, YELLOW COARSE *Kitchen / Market*

MEASURING SPOONS, STAINLESS STEEL *Martha Stewart: The Catalog for Living*

MEDJOOL DATES *Kalustyan's*

MERINGUE POWDER, DELUXE *Sweet Celebrations*

MISO PASTE *Whole Foods Market*

MUFFIN PAN, JUMBO *Bridge Kitchenware*

MUFFIN PAN, MINI *Bridge Kitchenware*

MULATO CHILES *Kitchen / Market*

MUSCOVY DUCK *D'Artagnan*

NORI SHEETS *Pacific Rim Gourmet*

NOUGAT WITH PISTACHIOS *Kalustyan's*

OIL-CURED BLACK OLIVES *EthnicGrocer.com*

OLIVE TAPENADE *Dean & DeLuca*

OREGANO, MEXICAN *Kitchen / Market*

PASILLA CHILES *Kitchen / Market*

PASTRY BAGS *Sweet Celebrations*

PASTRY RING *Bridge Kitchenware*

PASTRY TIPS *Sweet Celebrations*

PICKLED GINGER *Pacific Rim Gourmet*

PILONCILLO *Adriana's Caravan*

PISTACHIOS, ROASTED *Kalustyan's*

PITA, WHITE AND WHOLE-WHEAT *Kalustyan's*

PIZZA STONE *Bridge Kitchenware*

POBLANO CHILES *Kitchen / Market*

POMEGRANATES *Indian Rock Produce*

PORCINI MUSHROOMS *Whole Foods Market*

PUMPKIN SEEDS (PEPITAS) *Kitchen / Market*

QUARTER SHEET PAN, 9-BY-12-INCH PROFESSIONAL NONSTICK *Williams-Sonoma*

QUESO BLANCO (MEXICAN CHEESE) *Kitchen / Market*

RAMEKINS *Bridge Kitchenware, Williams-Sonoma*

RAW HONEY *Really Raw Honey*

RED SNAPPER *Wild Edibles*

RED THAI CHILES *Kitchen / Market*

ROLLING PINS, PROFESSIONAL *Martha Stewart: The Catalog for Living*

ROSE ESSENCE *Kalustyan's*

SAFFLOWER OIL *Whole Foods Market*

SAFFRON THREADS *Kitchen / Market, Whole Foods Market*

SERRANO CHILES *Kitchen / Market*

SMOKED HAM *Harrington's of Vermont*

SMOKED MACKEREL *Ducktrap River Fish Farm*

SMOKED RAINBOW TROUT *Petrossian Paris*

SNOWFLAKE COOKIE CUTTER *Sweet Celebrations*

SOBA NOODLES *Whole Foods Market*

SORREL LEAVES *Indian Rock Produce*

SOUFFLE DISH, 1½-QUART *Bridge Kitchenware*

SPRINGFORM PAN, 8½-INCH *Dorothy McNett's Place*

TAMALES *Tamale Lady, Tamara's Tamales*

TAMARI, REDUCED SODIUM *Whole Foods Market*

TART DISH, 12-INCH, FLUTED *Bridge Kitchenware*

TART PANS *Bridge Kitchenware, Wilton Industries*

TRUFFLE OIL *Whole Foods Market*

TURBINADO SUGAR *Whole Foods Market*

TURKISH DELIGHT *Kalustyan's*

UNSWEETENED COCONUT, SHREDDED *Foods of India*

WASABI PASTE *Pacific Rim Gourmet*

WHITEFISH *Wild Edibles*

WILD STRIPED BASS *Wild Edibles*

WINTER SQUASH *Indian Rock Produce*

Directory

Addresses and telephone numbers of sources may change prior to or following publication of this book, as may availability of any item.

ADRIANA'S CARAVAN
321 Grand Central Terminal
New York, NY 10017
800-316-0820
www.adrianascaravan.com

BLACK VODKA CO.
415-239-9415
www.blackvodka.com

BRIDGE KITCHENWARE
214 East 52nd Street
New York, NY 10022
800-274-3435
www.bridgekitchenware.com

BROADWAY PANHANDLER
477 Broome Street
New York, NY 10013
212-966-3434
866-266-5927
www.broadwaypanhandler.com

CANDYLAND CRAFTS
201 West Main Street
Somerville, NJ 08876
908-685-0410
www.candylandcrafts.com

D'ARTAGNAN
800-327-8246
www.dartagnan.com

DEAN & DELUCA
877-826-9246
www.deananddeluca.com

DOROTHY MCNETT'S PLACE
800 San Benito Street
Hollister, CA 95023
831-637-6444
www.happycookers.com

DUCKTRAP RIVER FISH FARM
57 Little River Drive
Belfast, ME 04915
800-828-3825
www.ducktrap.com

ETHNICGROCER.COM
866-438-4642
www.ethnicgrocer.com

FOODS OF INDIA
SINHA TRADING COMPANY
121 Lexington Avenue
New York, NY 10016
212-683-4419

GARDEN OF EDEN
162 West 23rd Street
New York, NY 10011
212-675-6300

HARRINGTON'S OF VERMONT
210 East Main Street
Richmond, VT 05477
802-434-4444
www.harringtonham.com

THE HERB LADY
52792 42nd Avenue
Lawrence, MI 49064
269-674-3879

IGOURMET.COM
877-446-8763
www.igourmet.com

IMPORTFOOD.COM
THAI SUPERMARKET
2117 West Berwyn Avenue
Chicago, IL 60625
888-618-8424
www.importfood.com

INDIAN ROCK PRODUCE
530 California Road
Quakertown, PA 18951
800-882-0512
www.indianrockproduce.com

KALUSTYAN'S
123 Lexington Avenue
New York, NY 10016
800-352-3451
www.kalustyans.com

KITCHEN/MARKET
218 Eighth Avenue
New York, NY 10011
888-468-4433
www.kitchenmarket.com

LODGE MANUFACTURING
P.O. Box 380
South Pittsburg, TN 37380
423-837-7181
www.lodgemfg.com

MARTHA STEWART:
THE CATALOG FOR LIVING
800-950-7130
www.marthastewart.com

MURRAY'S CHEESE
257 Bleecker Street
New York, NY 10014
888-692-4339
www.murrayscheese.com

NEW HAMPSHIRE GOLD
P.O. Box 291
Huckleberry Road
New Hampton, NH 03256
888-819-4255
www.nhgold.com

O-GEE PAINT CO.
6995 Bird Road
Miami, FL 33155
866-666-1935
www.o-geepaint.com

PACIFIC RIM GOURMET
4905 Morena Boulevard
Suite 1313
San Diego, CA 92117
800-910-9657
www.pacificrim-gourmet.com

PETROSSIAN PARIS
911 Seventh Avenue
New York, NY 10019
212-245-2217
www.petrossian.com

REALLY RAW HONEY
3500 Boston Street
Baltimore, MD 21224
800-732-5729
www.reallyrawhoney.com

SWEET CELEBRATIONS
P.O. Box 39426
Edina, MN 55439
800-328-6722
www.sweetc.com

THE SWEET LIFE
63 Hester Street
New York, NY 10002
212-598-0092

TAMALE LADY
Judy Lowery
8033 Krim Drive NE
Albuquerque, NM 87109
505-822-0482
www.tamalelady.com

TAMARA'S TAMALES
Marina Plaza
13352 West Washington Blvd.
Los Angeles, CA 90066
310-305-7714

WHOLE FOODS MARKET
250 Seventh Avenue
New York, NY 10001
212-924-5969
www.wholefoods.com

WILD EDIBLES
318 Grand Central Terminal
New York, NY 10017
212-687-4255

WILLIAMS-SONOMA
800-541-2233
www.williams-sonoma.com

WILTON INDUSTRIES
800-794-5866
www.wilton.com

WORLD SPICE MERCHANTS
206-682-7274
www.worldspice.com

Index

*Page numbers in italics indicate
color photographs

Photography Credits

WILLIAM ABRANOWICZ *page 72 (top right)*

ANTONIS ACHILLEOS *pages 137, 231 (bottom right), 241 (bottom two), 246, 247, 336*

SANG AN *pages 68 (top left), 72 (top left, bottom left), 73, 75 (top left), 76, 77, 80, 81 (top left, bottom two), 82, 85, 86, 234 (top left), 240, 329 (top right), 334, 335*

JAMES BAIGRIE *pages 143 (bottom left), 145, 146 (top left)*

CHRISTOPHER BAKER *pages 148-151, 156*

STEVE BAXTER *pages 158, 331 (bottom right)*

EARL CARTER *pages 70, 71 (bottom right), 75 (top right, bottom right), 78, 79, 88, 329 (bottom left), 331 (bottom left)*

BEATRIZ DA COSTA *pages 314, 315*

ROB FIOCCA *page 159*

DANA GALLAGHER *pages 154, 155, 228, 229, 239, 242 (top left, bottom right), 245 (top right, bottom right), 318, 321 (bottom left), 331 (top left)*

MATTHEW HRANEK *page 241 (top right)*

LISA HUBBARD *page 83 (top three)*

FRANCES JANISCH *page 313*

DEBORAH JONES *pages 67 (top left), 72 (bottom right)*

RICHARD GERHARD JUNG *pages 66, 67 (bottom two), 69, 84*

JOHN KERNICK *pages 71 (top two, bottom left), 87, 143 (top left, bottom right), 232, 233, 317 (bottom left)*

STEPHEN LEWIS *pages 225-227*

DAVID LOFTUS *pages 234 (bottom left), 242 (top right, bottom left), 243, 244, 245 (top left)*

MAURA MCEVOY *page 234 (top right)*

WILLIAM MEPPEM *pages 68 (top right), 74, 75 (bottom left), 142, 144, 146 (top right, bottom left), 157, 160, 231 (bottom left), 234 (bottom right), 235, 241 (top left), 245 (bottom left), 316, 317 (top two), 321 (bottom right), 329 (bottom right)*

VICTORIA PEARSON *pages 319, 321 (top two), 322, 323, 328, 330*

MARIA ROBLEDO *pages 65, 67 (top right), 68 (bottom), 230, 231 (top right), 236-238*

CHARLES SCHILLER *pages 81 (top right), 138, 139 (top right, bottom left), 143 (top right), 146 (bottom right), 147, 152*

SHIMON + TAMMAR *pages 329 (top left), 331 (top right)*

ANNA WILLIAMS *pages 83 (bottom), 139 (top left, bottom right), 140, 141, 153, 231 (top left), 248, 317 (bottom right), 320, 324-327, 332, 333*

FRONT COVER AND FRONT FLAP:
ALAN BENSON

BACK COVER *(clockwise from top left):*
MARIA ROBLEDO, ANNA WILLIAMS, DANA GALLAGHER, EARL CARTER
BACK FLAP: **WILLIAM WALDRON**

CONVERSION CHART *Equivalent Imperial and Metric Measurements*

American cooks use standard containers, the 8-ounce cup and a tablespoon that takes exactly 16 level fillings to fill that cup level. Measuring by cup makes it very difficult to give weight equivalents, as a cup of densely packed butter will weigh considerably more than a cup of flour. The easiest way, therefore, to deal with cup measurements in recipes is to take the amount by volume rather than by weight. Thus the equation reads: 1 cup = 225 ml = 8 fl. oz.; ½ cup = 110 ml = 4 fl. oz. It is possible to buy a set of American cup measures in major stores around the world. In the States, butter is often measured in sticks. One stick is the equivalent of 8 tablespoons. One tablespoon of butter is therefore the equivalent to ½ ounce/15 grams.

SOLID MEASURES

U.S./IMPERIAL MEASURES		METRIC MEASURES	
ounces	pounds	grams	kilos
1		28	
2		56	
3½		100	
4	¼	112	
5		140	
6		168	
8	½	225	
9		150	¼
12	¾	340	
16	1	450	
18		500	½
20	1¼	560	
24	1½	675	
27		750	¾
28	1¾	780	
32	2	900	
36	2¼	1000	1
40	2½	1100	
48	3	1350	
54		1500	1½
64	4	1800	
72	4½	2000	2

LIQUID MEASURES

FLUID OUNCES	U.S.	IMPERIAL	MILLILITERS
	1 teaspoon	1 teaspoon	5
¼	2 teaspoons	1 dessert spoon	7
½	1 tablespoon	1 tablespoon	15
1	2 tablespoons	2 tablespoons	28
2	¼ cup	4 tablespoons	56
4	½ cup or ¼ pint		110
5		¼ pint or 1 gill	140
6	¾ cup		170
8	1 cup or ½ pint		225
9			250, ¼ liter
10	1¼ cups	½ pint	280
12	1½ cups	¾ pint	340
15		¾ pint	420
16	2 cups or 1 pint		450
18	2¼ cups		500, ½ liter
20	2½ cups	1 pint	560
24	3 cups or 1½ pints		675
25		1¼ pints	700
27	3½ cups		750, ¾ liter
30	3¾ cups	1½ pints	840
32	4 cups or 2 pints or 1 quart		900

OVEN TEMPERATURE EQUIVALENTS

FAHRENHEIT	CELSIUS	GAS MARK	DESCRIPTION
225	110	¼	cool
250	130	½	
275	140	1	very slow
300	150	2	
325	170	3	slow
350	180	4	moderate
375	190	5	
400	200	6	moderately hot
425	220	7	fairly hot
450	230	8	hot
475	240	9	very hot
500	250	10	extremely hot

EQUIVALENTS FOR INGREDIENTS

all-purpose flour	plain flour
arugula	rocket
buttermilk	ordinary milk
confectioners' sugar	icing sugar
cornstarch	cornflour
eggplant	aubergine
granulated sugar	caster sugar
half-and-half	12% fat milk
heavy cream	double cream
light cream	single cream
lima beans	broad beans
scallion	spring onion
squash	courgettes or marrow
unbleached flour	strong, white flour
zest	rind
zucchini	courgettes

LINEAR AND AREA MEASURES

1 inch	2.54 centimeters

chickpea fritters, PARMESAN-DUSTED MEATBALLS, CUCUMBER AND SMOKED-SALMON SANDWICHES, ZUCCHINI FRITTERS, WHITE BEAN, YOGURT, AND FETA DIP, CHICKEN, POTATO, AND BUTTER LETTUCE WITH LEMON-GARLIC DRESSING, salmon and golden beet salad WITH CRISP BACON, GREEK SALAD WITH FETA IN GRAPE LEAVES AND GRILLED SWORDFISH KEBABS, GRILLED TOP-ROUND OF LAMB, SEARED TUNA WITH TOMATOES AND BASIL, grilled hamburgers with goat cheese, SOBA NOODLES WITH TOFU, AVOCADO, AND SNOW PEAS, THAI BEEF SALAD, BEETS AND ASPARAGUS WITH LEMON MAYONNAISE, FARM-STAND RAW VEGETABLE SALAD, GREEN BEANS WITH LEMON BUTTER, GRILLED CORN WITH CAYENNE AND CHEESE, fresh cherry pie, CHOCOLATE BROWNIE SPOON BREAD, HOMEMADE VANILLA ICE CREAM, PEACHES WITH HONEY SYRUP, PLUM TARTE TATIN, RED-CURRANT AND RASPBERRY PIE, rolled baklava, STRAWBERRY SHORTCAKES, FIG FLAMBE WITH PORT AND GELATO, SWEET PAIN PERDU, SOUTHERN-STYLE INDIVIDUAL PEACH COBBLERS, RED-CURRANT FOOL, coconut margaritas, GRAPEFRUIT SPARKLERS, HONEYDEW FIZZ, LYCHEE MARTINIS, LIME APRICOT RUM COOLERS, VODKA THYME LEMONADE, ANGEL BISCUITS, FLUFFY PANCAKES, OLIVE-OIL BISCUITS, ROSEMARY BALSAMIC MARINADE, SPICY HOISIN MARINADE, TANDOORI MARINADE, THYME, SHALLOT, AND LEMON MARINADE, creamy tomato soup, ROASTED-PEPPER SAFFRON TART, SALAD-QUICHE TARTLETS, GRILLED PEPPERS AND GOAT CHEESE SALAD, TOMATO ASPIC, ASIAN PEAR SALAD, SUMMER SALAD WITH BLUEBERRIES *rustic market tarts,* GRILLED SEA SCALLOPS AND FENNEL

BERRY BROWN BETTY, BLACKBERRY-PEACH TRIFLE, PROSECCO SANGRIA, RED

WINE SANGRIA, WATERMELON NECTAR, *white-wine sangria*

BLUEBERRY CORNMEAL MUFFINS, CLAM AND CORN CHOWDER, MUSHROOM AN

WILD-RICE SOUP, ROASTED VEGETABLE SOUP, GRILLED LAMB CHOPS WIT

GARAM MASALA, *honey-glazed pork* WITH WILTED GREENS

ORECCHIETTE WITH GREEN TOMATOES, CARAMELIZED ONIONS, AND CORN

BROCCOLI AND WHITE-BEAN SALAD, CORN AND COUSCOUS SALAD, SAUTEE

OKRA AND TOMATOES, *fried green tomato wedges*

ORANGE-ALMOND CAKE, PAPAYA WITH COCONUT-LIME YOGURT, WALNUT HONE

CAKE, GOLDEN NECTAR SMOOTHIE, GREEN-TOMATO CHUTNEY, PICKLED GREE

TOMATOES, *savory pumpkin puffs,* TAMARI AND MAPL

ROASTED ALMONDS, FIG, RICOTTA, AND HONEY OPEN-FACE SANDWICHES, FRES

TOMATO SOUP, ICEBERG LETTUCE WITH BLUE-CHEESE DRESSING AND TOASTE

ALMONDS, *chicken cacciatore,* BUTTERNUT-SQUASH RAVIOL

WITH FRIED SAGE LEAVES, PANFRIED POTATO AND FONTINA FRITTATA, PAN

FRIED TROUT WITH ALMONDS AND PARSLEY, SWEET DUMPLING SQUASH WIT

MOROCCAN VEGETABLE STEW, SQUASH PANADA WITH WILD MUSHROOMS AN

CHARD, *lemon and caper mashed potatoes*

ROASTED BABY POTATOES WITH ROMESCO SAUCE, STEAK WITH CARAMELIZE

ONIONS, APPLE NAPOLEONS, MINI PEAR AND BLUEBERRY SPICE CAKES, SOF

AND CHEWY *chocolate chip cookies,* HOT MINT LEMONAD